Examination Guide for *The Human 1*

In *The Human Experience,* special attention has been given to blending content, skill development, and visual presentation. The text helps students to understand the causes and effects of events in world history through the variety of elements outlined below.

pp. 1-3	A special **Prehistory** section introduces the text with a discussion of the contribution of prehistoric cultures to the rise of civilization.
pp. 4-5, 108-109	**Unit Openers** contain a full-color panoramic photograph, an introduction that familiarizes students with unit content, a time line that illustrates important events, and a table of contents by chapter.
pp. 276, 304, 482, 744	**Chapter Openers** include a colorful photograph, a quotation from a contemporary source to stimulate student interest, and an introductory paragraph on the facing page that previews chapter content.
pp. 38, 91	**Chapter Organization** consists of numbered sections and two levels of subheads to provide a formal outline of content, and review questions at the end of each section to reinforce learning.
pp. 18, 231	Brief **Excerpts** from primary and secondary sources enrich the chapter narrative.
pp. 57, 231	**Footnotes** add important information without disrupting the narrative flow.
pp. 125, 164, 747	Unfamiliar **Terms** and **Concepts** appear in boldface type when first introduced and are defined in context.
pp. 124, 338, 693	**Photographs,** most in full color, include captions with a question that relates the illustration to the text.
pp. 45, 366, 650	**Maps,** all in full color, contain scales and, when appropriate, latitude/longitude indicators, with color used functionally to highlight key subject matter.
pp. 334, 669, 757, 608	Full-color **Graphics** include charts, graphs, tables, and diagrams that correspond directly to the narrative and visually reinforce or extend concepts.
pp. 344-345, 434-435	**Chapter Reviews** provide a point summary, vocabulary list, review questions, discussion questions, and an exercise on using graphics.
pp. 386-387, 660-661	**Unit Reviews** provide a point summary of generalizations from the unit, cross-chapter review questions, a skill-developing exercise, suggested activities for individuals and groups, and suggested readings for student research and enjoyment.
pp. 15, 444	**History and People** features are profiles of historical figures.
pp. 323, 725	**History and Cities** features focus on the history and distinctive features of a city that was important during the time period of the chapter.
pp. 167, 219	**History and the Arts** features present an artistic theme related to the chapter.
pp. 332, 764-765	**Science and Technology** features highlight important inventions and discoveries relevant to the chapter.
p. 789	The **Appendix** consists of an Atlas, Glossary, and Index.
pp. 790-791 792-793	The **Atlas** provides full-color reference maps of the world and on special topics such as the distribution of climates, natural resources, populations, and languages.
p. 801	The **Glossary** contains all important terms and concepts.
p. 812	The **Index** provides easy reference to all important topics in the text.

THE
HUMAN
EXPERIENCE

A WORLD HISTORY
TEACHER'S ANNOTATED EDITION

Mounir Farah
Andrea Berens Karls
Carl Max Kortepeter

Charles E. Merrill Publishing Co.
A BELL & HOWELL COMPANY
Columbus, Ohio
Toronto London Sydney

ISBN 0-675-02271-1

Published by
Charles E. Merrill Publishing Co.
A BELL & HOWELL COMPANY
Columbus, Ohio 43216

ii

TABLE OF CONTENTS

INTRODUCTION

Program Rationale

The experience of every individual is unique. Every people, every city, every nation has its own distinct history of politics and war, religion and art, triumph and tragedy. The study of world history reveals this rich diversity and complexity, yet it also reveals the unifying elements of the human experience. For thousands of years people have engaged in an arduous struggle to survive, to conquer the forces of nature, to organize societies and governments, and to create beauty and meaning in their lives. Although progress has been made, it has often failed to endure. *The Human Experience* is a record of the struggle and the progress, showing both continuity and change in the history of the world.

Program Objectives

The Human Experience is designed to achieve the following objectives:
1. Present a comprehensive treatment of world history in a clear, concise, and meaningful manner.
2. Inform students about the origin and development of the world's major civilizations, both eastern and western.
3. Give students the critical-thinking skills they need to make objective judgments of historical and contemporary issues.
4. Provide a global perspective on the forces and movements that have made the past continuous with and relevant to the present.

Program Components
Student Text

The Human Experience is a basal high school world history text that presents a chronological, topical history of the world for average and above-average students. The balanced treatment of eastern and western civilizations provides a global perspective on human history. Colorful photos, graphs, charts, tables, maps, and diagrams complement the text narrative and aid student understanding.

The text provides comprehensive coverage of world history, from the origins of ancient civilization to the challenges of the future. It explores social and cultural history as well as political and military history. Interactions among the world's various cultures are emphasized.

Teacher's Annotated Edition

The Teacher's Annotated Edition of *The Human Experience* is designed to reduce teacher preparation time and to facilitate both teaching and learning. It includes both the Teacher's Guide bound into the front of the student text and the Teacher's Annotations printed throughout the book.

The Teacher's Guide consists of the following major sections: Introduction, How to Use the Teacher's Annotated Edition, Instructional Approaches, Text Implementation, and Suggested Resources. The Introduction contains the program rationale and objectives; program components; information on the organization of the text, including sample pages; and a special note about evaluating the program.

The How to Use the Teacher's Annotated Edition section familiarizes the teacher with the guide and explains how to use it effectively. The Instructional Approaches section presents basic techniques for teaching world history.

The Text Implementation section, the cornerstone of the guide, contains teaching strategies on a unit-chapter-section basis. In addition, it provides answers to the questions that appear in the text. The Suggested Resources section lists books and audiovisual materials that can be used to supplement the text.

The annotations, appearing in blue at the top of the student text pages, are of three kinds. Content annotations offer additional or clarifying information that the teacher may wish to share with the students. Pedagogical annotations offer additional topics of discussion and other teaching suggestions. Cross-referencing annotations point out relationships between the subject under discussion and material in other parts of the text.

Student Activity Book

The Student Activity Book is organized on a unit-chapter basis with three activities per chapter and two per unit. The chapter activities vary, but focus on skill-building activities, vocabulary exercises, and primary-source studies. The unit activities summarize the unit.

Student Activity Book, Teacher's Edition

The Teacher's Edition of the Student Activity Book contains the student material plus answers for the student activities.

Teacher's Resource Book

The Teacher's Resource Book is a timesaving teacher aid that provides effective tools and materials for teaching content, reinforcing skills, enriching lessons, and evaluating student performance. It includes lecture notes, consisting of in-depth outlines of content and section-by-section commentaries that highlight important understandings; special geography skills activities; documents, speeches, and other primary source materials important in world history; and numerous outline maps. The Teacher's Resource Book contains the Evaluation Program.

Evaluation Program

The Evaluation Program is organized on a unit-chapter basis with two one-page quizzes for each chapter and one multipage test for each unit. Quiz A consists of matching questions and true-false questions. Quiz B consists of completion questions and true-false questions. Each unit test contains 40 multiple choice questions, chronology or primary-source exercises, essay questions, and social studies skill exercises.

Key Features of the Text
Content Organization

The student text of *The Human Experience* is organized into 8 units with 33 chapters. It begins with a special section on prehistory that deals with the origins of human civilization. The last chapter considers the issues that challenge the world today and in the future. In keeping with the need to emphasize more recent developments, over 60 percent of the text is devoted to modern history. In addition, the text includes a full-color atlas, a detailed glossary, and a comprehensive index.

Each unit opens with a two-page, full-color presentation that is designed to motivate students and to familiarize them with the content of the unit. A colorful, panoramic two-page photograph representing a scene or event related to the unit is used to convey to students a significant concept that is developed in the unit. A time line, spanning both pages, highlights important events from the unit, helping students to see at a glance the entire unit's major chronological relationships. The unit opening also contains an introduction that presents the main themes discussed in the narrative of the text. Finally, a table of contents is provided that lists the chapters in the unit.

Each chapter begins on a left-hand page with a colorful photograph reflecting the theme of the chapter. Included on the opening page is a brief quotation from a contemporary source. The quotation is related to the theme of the chapter and is designed to create student interest and motivate further inquiry. On the right-hand page is the chapter title and a brief introduction. The introduction, usually a few paragraphs in length, previews the content of the chapter.

The reading level is controlled throughout the text. The Dale-Chall readability formula was applied to the entire narrative, including special features, not just to random samples. Other reading aids are also built into the program. Throughout the book, key concept terms appear in boldface type. They are defined or explained in context when first introduced. These terms are found again in the vocabulary section of chapter reviews and in the glossary at the end of the text.

In their internal structure, chapters follow the format of a standard outline, consisting of sections and subsections with tertiary divisions where necessary. Students can use this outline to preview and review content. Each major section of the chapter concludes with recall questions that help reinforce student understanding.

Chapter narratives are enriched by the use of short excerpts from primary and secondary sources. These excerpts help to humanize history as well as to reinforce major points in the chapters. Occasionally, footnotes have been used to provide information that would otherwise break the reading flow of the narrative.

The Human Experience has four types of special features that further enrich chapter presentations. Each type is color coded for easy identification. There are 42 special features in the text, one or two for each chapter. All are accompanied by photographs or original art.

One type of special feature is "History and People." These features focus on the lives of individuals who have contributed to the development of world civilization. The leading purpose of this feature is to help humanize history for students. Altogether, there are 16 of these biographical profiles in the text. Another type of special feature in the text is "History and Cities." Each of these 11 features describes the distinctive characteristics of a city that was of major importance during the time period covered by the chapter. The third type of special feature—"History and the Arts"—looks at the role of the arts in history. There are seven of these features, each introducing students to an art form associated with a particular historical period or civilization. The final type of special feature is "Science and Technology." These features discuss specific scientific and technological developments and their impact on history. There are eight of these features in the text. The last three types of special features provide questions at the end of the narratives for reviewing content and checking student comprehension.

Numerous photographs and several cartoons, most in full color, reinforce and expand chapter material. Many photographs are reproductions of paintings that are contemporary to the historical period under study. Each photograph and cartoon accompanying the chapter narrative has an informative caption and one or two questions that relate it to the narrative. Unit- and chapter-opening photographs also carry brief descriptive captions.

The Human Experience contains many graphics, most rendered in full color. Graphs, charts, tables, diagrams, and maps supply valuable supplemental data and/or clarify important historical, cultural, economic, political, and social relationships mentioned in the narrative. There are 94 full-color maps in the text in addition to the full-color atlas appearing on pages 790-800. The maps and other graphics have been designed as integral components of the text. Students should be encouraged to practice the skills of "reading" and interpreting them.

At the end of each chapter is a comprehensive review that begins with a point summary of the key understandings developed in the chapter. The Summary can be used for quick review. It is followed by a vocabulary section, Building Vocabulary, that lists all the boldface concept terms in the chapter, in the order that they first appear. Next is a series of questions, Reviewing the Main Ideas, that help students review the chapter and test their ability to remember the facts. In Discussing Important Ideas, students are presented with discussion questions that help them gain further insight into chapter concepts through critical-thinking skills of analysis, synthesis, and evaluation. The last section in the chapter review, Using Maps (Graphs, Diagrams, Illustrations), focuses on the interpretation of graphics and map-reading. Questions provide opportunities for use of these skills.

Each unit review begins with a point summary that contains the major generalizations of the unit and serves to reinforce the themes developed in the chapters of the unit. The Summary is followed by Developing Understandings, a series of questions that help students review the unit and tie together the main points presented in the different chapters of the unit. The next section of the unit review—Developing Skills—helps students develop such social studies skills as evaluating primary sources, analyzing historical points of view, and synthesizing information. Following this is the Suggested Activities section. Ideas are presented for individual and group projects that permit students to examine in greater depth the concepts presented in the unit. The Suggested Readings section provides an annotated list of books suitable for students.

Sample Pages

Many of the features discussed above are highlighted in the sample pages that follow starting on page 5. These pages may serve as examples to familiarize students with the text design.

Evaluating the Program

Perhaps one of the best ways to ensure that effective learning-teaching materials are produced is to let authors and publishers know how the classroom teacher feels about the ones currently in use. Please help in the planning of revisions and new programs by completing and mailing the form found on the last two pages of the Teacher's Guide. After removing *The Human Experience* survey form from the book, fold and staple it so that the Charles E. Merrill Publishing Company label shows. The authors and publisher appreciate hearing from you.

Prehistory

A special section on prehistory introduces *The Human Experience* with a discussion of the key cultural features of prehistoric peoples and the origins of civilization.

PREHISTORY

HISTORY is the story of humanity. It is also the record of that story. Historians get most of their information from written records. For this reason, history is said to begin with the development of writing about 5,000 years ago. However, the human story is much, much older. People have lived on earth for about 2,000,000 years. This long period of human existence before writing is often called prehistory.

Culture Early in prehistory, people developed ways of living known as culture. Although conditions have changed today, culture is still basic to human life. It includes an economy, or the ways people use their environment to meet their basic material needs. It also includes technology, or the combination of skills and tools that makes economic activity possible. But culture is more than an economy and its technology. It contains all of the ideas, customs, and objects that people have developed for living in social groups. Thus, a group's political and religious beliefs, its arts and sciences, and its leisure activities are aspects of culture.

Culture is not biologically determined; it must be learned. Each new generation builds upon knowledge that already exists. It then goes on to make its own contributions. Today the world is made up of many cultures. But all have their roots in the prehistoric past.

Archeology To understand prehistory, historians rely on archeologists, or scientists who search for sites that contain the remains of past cultures. Once sites are discovered, archeologists carefully dig to find plant and animal remains. They also search for artifacts, or objects made by humans. By studying these materials, archeologists are able to learn about past environments and cultures. Their work has broadened our understanding about the economy and technology of prehistoric peoples. However, much has yet to be learned about other aspects of prehistoric cultures.

THE WORLD OF EARLY PEOPLES

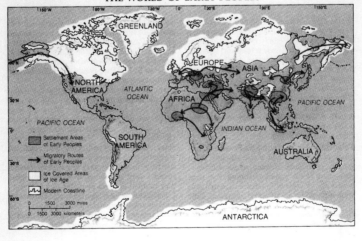

Unit Openers

Time line highlights the chronology of major events and eras covered in the unit.

Unit introduction familiarizes students with unit content.

Unit title

Unit number

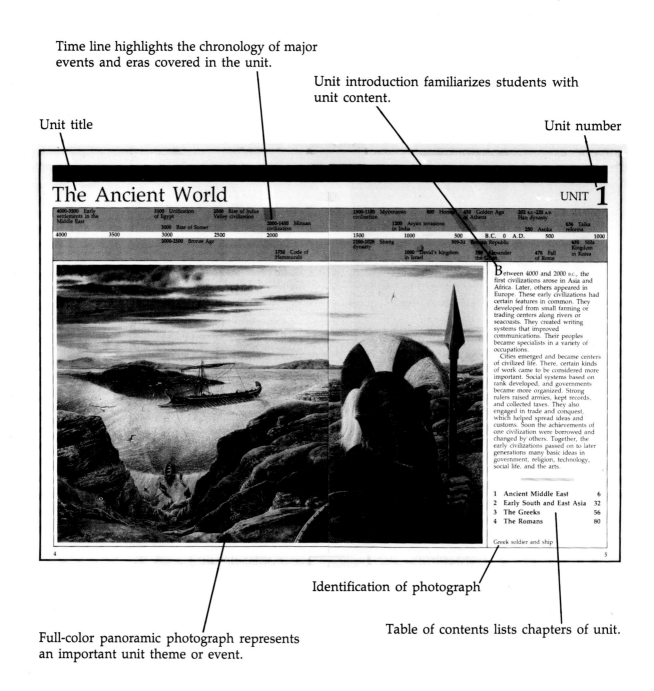

The Ancient World

UNIT 1

| 4000 | 3500 | 3000 | 2500 | 2000 | 1500 | 1000 | 500 | B.C. 0 A.D. | 500 | 1000 |

4000-3500 Early settlements in the Middle East
3100 Unification of Egypt
2800 Rise of Indus Valley civilization
2000-1400 Minoan civilization
1500-1100 Mycenaean civilization
800 Homer
450 Golden Age of Athens
202 B.C.-220 A.D. Han dynasty
636 Taika reforms
3000 Rise of Sumer
1200 Aryan invasions in India
250 Asoka
3000-2500 Bronze Age
1500-1028 Shang dynasty
509-31 Roman Republic
650 Silla Kingdom in Korea
1750 Code of Hammurabi
1000 David's kingdom in Israel
330 Alexander the Great
475 Fall of Rome

Between 4000 and 2000 B.C., the first civilizations arose in Asia and Africa. Later, others appeared in Europe. These early civilizations had certain features in common. They developed from small farming or trading centers along rivers or seacoasts. They created writing systems that improved communications. Their peoples became specialists in a variety of occupations.

Cities emerged and became centers of civilized life. There, certain kinds of work came to be considered more important. Social systems based on rank developed, and governments became more organized. Strong rulers raised armies, kept records, and collected taxes. They also engaged in trade and conquest, which helped spread ideas and customs. Soon the achievements of one civilization were borrowed and changed by others. Together, the early civilizations passed on to later generations many basic ideas in government, religion, technology, social life, and the arts.

Greek soldier and ship

4

5

Identification of photograph

Full-color panoramic photograph represents an important unit theme or event.

Table of contents lists chapters of unit.

T6

Chapter Openers

Full-color photograph visually portrays a significant chapter theme or event.

Chapter number

Chapter title

CHAPTER 23

Japanese Rural Scene

Today the alien barbarians of the West . . . are dashing about across the sea, trampling other countries underfoot, and daring . . . to override the noble nations.

Aizawa Seishisai, Japanese nationalist (1782-1863)

524

East
Asia

In the 1600's and 1700's, imperial China and Japan largely concentrated on domestic affairs. In China, the Ming dynasty was overthrown by invaders from the north, and a new dynasty was established. In Japan, the feudal domains were united under a strong central government.

Both countries deliberately isolated themselves from the world as much as possible, trying to protect their civilizations from foreign influences. In the 1800's, however, both were forced to bow to pressures from western powers to increase their foreign contacts. China was weakened by these contacts, but Japan used them to strengthen itself until it was able to meet the western powers on equal terms.

1 Imperial China

By the early 1600's, the Ming dynasty in China was in serious decline. Corruption and incompetence had sapped the strength of the government. The last Ming emperor, Ch'ung-chen, tried to reverse the decline, but it was too late. Soon after he came to the throne in 1628, a terrible famine struck in Shangxi province. Starved peasants ravaged the countryside. At the same time, soldiers mutinied because they had not been paid for a long time. The rebellion grew. Meanwhile, the Manchus, invaders from Manchuria, moved southward to attack Beijing. They stopped only when they reached the Great Wall.

In 1644 Chinese rebels entered Beijing. The desperate Ming commander asked the Manchus for help and opened the narrow pass that controlled access from Manchuria. The Manchus swept in and defeated the rebels. Once in Beijing, however, the Manchus refused to leave.

Qing Dynasty

After several years of struggle, the Manchus defeated the Ming and set up a new dynasty, known as the Qing (Ch'ing) dynasty. They successfully maintained control for almost 300 years, during which time they extended their empire to the north and west, to include Manchuria, Mongolia, Sinkiang, and Tibet. They also conquered neighboring countries, such as Korea, Burma, and Vietnam. The island of Taiwan was added to the empire in 1683.

Qing Emperors The Qing were fortunate in having a series of able emperors in its first two centuries of rule. The period of their reign brought prosperity to China. Qing emperors tried to improve the lives of the Chinese. They worked to lighten taxes and undertook public works projects, such as flood control on the Huang He River. They also supported the arts. Some of the emperors were scholars, poets, and painters.

Qing rulers imposed new regulations on the Chinese. A Chinese man was required to wear Manchu clothing and shave his head, leaving a pigtail. A Chinese woman was not allowed to follow the traditional practice of binding her feet. However, this rule could not be enforced.

Otherwise, Qing rulers did not try to alter the basic elements of Chinese culture. They used Chinese institutions and traditions to govern the country. They also took steps to win Chinese support, such as lowering taxes. These policies worked well, and most Chinese came to accept Qing rule. Eventually Chinese culture was adopted by the Manchus, who came to think of themselves as Chinese.

Economic Life The Manchus made few basic changes in China's economy. The Qing policy of internal peace and government-spon-

525

Identification of photograph

Brief introductory paragraphs preview chapter content.

Quotation from contemporary source characterizes chapter theme and creates student interest.

Narrative Organization

Chapter title appears on each left-hand page for easy reference.

Type is readable and two-column format is uncluttered.

Major section heads are numbered for easy identification.

Excerpts from primary sources enrich chapter material.

Unit title is found on each right-hand page for easy reference.

Footnotes add important information that does not fit into the narrative flow.

Three-level heading structure provides a formal outline of content.

Key terms are printed in boldface type and immediately defined or explained in context.

Review questions following each major section reinforce student understanding of content.

American corporation to search for oil in his country. A major discovery was made in 1936. After World War II, Saudi Arabia began to develop into a major oil-producing country.

1. Identify: Treaty of Sèvres, Mustapha Kemal, Treaty of Lausanne, Ankara, Reza Khan, Majles, Balfour Declaration, Zionists, Peel Commission, Ibn Saud, Wahabis.
2. What changes did Atatürk introduce in Turkey?
3. How did Reza Shah Pahlavi become ruler of Iran?
4. What two national groups claimed the right to live in Palestine? On what basis did each make its claim?

3 Africa

After World War I, the first stirrings of nationalism occurred in Africa. Many African leaders hoped that their continent would receive greater political freedom. Their hopes turned to disappointment when the peace settlements enlarged rather than reduced the size of European empires. During the 1920's and 1930's, groups of European-educated Africans emerged in support of nationalism.

North Africa

After World War I, nationalist movements arose in British and French territories in North Africa. Egypt wanted to break its ties with Britain and become an independent kingdom. In French North Africa—Morocco, Algeria, and Tunisia—the Arab majority began to demand freedom.

Egypt After World War I, nationalism became a powerful force in Egypt. The strongest nationalist party, the Wafd, had grown tremendously after the war. It particularly attracted the support of the emerging middle class. To counter the Wafd, the British exiled the party's leader, Saad Zaghlul, to the Mediterranean island of Malta in 1919. In doing so, they hoped to prevent Zaghlul from presenting Egypt's case for complete independence at the Paris peace conference.[1] The exile of Zaghlul was followed by strikes and riots in Egypt.

[1] Saad Zaghlul eventually was allowed to attend the Paris peace conference, but he failed to win support for Egypt's cause among the delegates.

Early in 1920, the British Parliament sent a commission headed by Lord Alfred Milner to Egypt to investigate the disorders. The Milner Commission's report recommended Egyptian independence. It proposed the establishment of a constitutional monarchy and a parliament. Independence, however, was to be limited by an alliance with Britain. The alliance was to guarantee British interests, permitting the British army to stay in Egypt to defend the Suez Canal.

In 1921 Zaghlul returned to Egypt to direct the cause for complete independence. In London, British and Egyptian leaders met and conducted negotiations toward this goal. The discussions collapsed over the question of keeping British forces in Egypt. Following the conference, the Wafd party proclaimed a policy of nonviolent resistance to the British.

In 1922 Britain declared Egypt independent. This decision was made without consulting the Egyptians. In acting on its own, the British government was able to set its own terms. British troops were to remain in Egypt in spite of Egyptian opposition.

In the same year, Egypt held its first elections, which resulted in a strongly nationalist government headed by the Wafd. Tensions continued over the next decade between Egypt and Britain. However, the growing threat of Mussolini's Italy to the eastern Mediterranean eventually brought the two countries closer together. In 1936 Egypt and Britain signed a defens... drew all British troops from ... those in the Suez Canal ... Egyptians into Sudan, which ... to Egyptian settlement since t... of the area in 1896. The Brit... was a step toward Egypt's f...

French North Africa Du... 1930's, Tunisia and Morocco v... torates. Algeria was a French... ism became a major force amo... population in all three areas. ... with its strongly pro-French l... became the major center o... colonial officials and the nat...

Various organizations pro... in North Africa. They dre...

---

penalty. Another important collection, *Basilica*, was completed in the 900's A.D. It made the law easier to understand.

Judges appointed by the emperor administered justice in the civil courts. These courts applied the law to ordinary citizens. Judges presented their decisions in writing and were required to sign them.

Art and Architecture

Byzantine art was based on classical and early Christian artistic styles. The art of ancient Greece and Rome stressed the reality of the material world. Some Byzantine art showed this influence with fully formed, lifelike figures. However, the major influence was the early Christian tradition. It reflected the viewpoint of the east, which stressed spiritual values. Most Byzantine art, therefore, was devoted to religious subjects. Flat, two-dimensional figures were drawn according to set patterns that emphasized their holiness.

Byzantine artists served the needs of the emperor's court and the Orthodox Church. Many were monks, whose works were required to be anonymous, or without the artist's name. This was done so that praise for a work of art would go to God, not to the individual artist.

Icons were the most popular art form. They were made on wood for display in churches, shrines, and homes. In Orthodox churches, the **sanctuary**, or altar area, was separated from the rest of the church by an **iconostasis**, a high thin wall covered with icons. Icons were also placed in other areas of the churches. **Iconography**, or the making of icons, suffered a setback during the iconoclastic controversy. At that time, many icons were destroyed. Few new ones were made because many Byzantine artists had fled from Constantinople to Italy. When icons were once again permitted, iconography again became a flourishing art form.

The Byzantines also developed an art form known as **mosaic**. Mosaics were made by fitting small flat pieces of stone or colored glass in mortar to form a picture or design. Mosaic artists used vivid colors to add brilliance to the images that they created. They also used a special technique in arranging the colored pieces. A

visitor to Hagia Sophia described the church's mosaics in the following way:

> As you move, the figures seem to move too. You could swear that their eyes are turning and shining and that their garments are rustling . . . the Byzantine mosaicist [artist] has succeeded in creating the illusion that his jig-saw puzzle has come to life. . . .*

Byzantine artists also excelled in making luxury crafts. They produced beautiful products in embroidery, enamel, ivory, silver, and gold. They also **illuminated**, or decorated, manuscript pages with elaborate designs and miniature pictures in brilliant colors.

The Byzantines were also noted for their architecture. Their most important accomplishment in this field was the construction of domed churches with richly decorated interiors. Hagia Sophia in Constantinople is considered the most magnificent of the Byzantine churches. Rectangular in shape, the church has a huge circular dome over its central part.

Erecting domes over rectangular or square buildings was a major architectural advance. Before the Byzantines, domes could only be built on circular walls. The Byzantine innovation gave designers more flexibility in the use of space. The Byzantines later built cross-shaped, multidomed churches. A fine example of this style is St. Mark's Cathedral in Venice, Italy.

Like the empire itself, Byzantine art and architecture went through periods of advance and decline. But their influence lasted long after the fall of Constantinople and spread beyond the borders of the empire. Byzantine styles in art and architecture later affected Russian, Balkan, and Turkish cultures. Byzantine art forms are still used today in Eastern Orthodox church buildings throughout the world.

1. Identify: Blues and Greens, Basil, Cyrillic.
2. What was the role of women in Byzantine society?
3. How did Byzantine missionaries influence the culture of eastern Europe?
4. What contributions did the Byzantines make in art and architecture?

*Constantine Porphyrogenitus and His World, Arnold Toynbee, © 1973 by Oxford University Press, p. 545.

Chapter Reviews

Discussing Important Ideas provides discussion questions to help students acquire further insight into chapter concepts through analysis, synthesis, and evaluation.

Using Maps (Graphs, Illustrations, and Diagrams) gives students practice in map-reading and graphics interpretation skills.

5. What were the goals of Vasco da Gama's voyage that began in 1497? What did he discover and why was it important?
6. By what means did the Portuguese establish dominance in the spice trade?
7. How did Ferdinand Magellan's expedition alter the geographic knowledge of his time?
8. What was the status of conquered Indians under Spanish rule? under British and French rule?
9. Why did slavery become important to the plantation economies of the English colonies in North America and the West Indies?
10. What did the voyages in search of a Northwest Passage accomplish?
11. Why did Dutch power begin to decline by the 1700's?
12. Why did the French and Indian War begin? What contributed to the English victory at Quebec in 1759?

Discussing Important Ideas

1. In your opinion, what was Prince Henry the Navigator's most important contribution to the voyages of discovery?
2. Which voyage of discovery do you think was most important? Why?
3. How were European nations' goals for trade and settlement similar and how were they different? Did geography, population size, religion, and timing affect their goals? In what ways?
4. Some observers think that space exploration today is motivated by factors similar to those that motivated European overseas explorations. Do you agree or disagree? Why?
5. To what extent did naval superiority determine the progress and outcome of European expansion by 1763?
6. How might history have been changed if the French had held on to its territories in North America?
7. Who benefited the most from the period of discovery and expansion? Who suffered the most?
8. What remnants of European discovery and expansion are still visible today in the Americas? Which European nation has left the most enduring legacy in the New World? Give examples.

Using Maps

on page 286 to answer the

pe of Good Hope? the Strait e Isthmus of Panama? Hud-ississippi River? Mexico? ngitude and latitude of the the East Indies?

3. How would you describe the route of Francis Drake's voyage?
4. About how far is it from England to the West Indies?
5. Which country made the most voyages of discovery to the Americas?
6. Which country made voyages to India?

CHAPTER 12 REVIEW

Summary

1. During the late 1400's and early 1500's, European nations led by Portugal undertook voyages of discovery that rounded the tip of Africa, found a sea route to the East Indies, discovered the Americas, and circumnavigated the globe.
2. Portugal dominated trade with the East Indies throughout the 1500's. By the 1530's, it had trading settlements in Africa and Asia, and a colony in South America. The Portuguese settlers brought black Africans to Brazil as slaves to work their plantations, a practice used later by other countries.
3. In 1580 Portugal was defeated by Spain. Many of its possessions were seized by the Dutch and the English.
4. In 1492 Christopher Columbus made his first voyage across the Atlantic for Spain. He discovered islands that he believed to be off the coast of India but were actually in the New World.
5. In 1493 the Pope divided the lands of the New World between Spain and Portugal.
6. Between 1519 and 1532, Spanish conquistadores destroyed the Indian empires of Mexico and Peru and established a vast colonial empire in their place. Although

Indians were considered subjects of Spain, abuses to them were widespread.
7. Between 1497 and 1609, the English, Dutch, and French sent explorers to search for a Northwest Passage to Asia.
8. In the mid-1500's, the English and the Dutch challenged the Spanish and the Portuguese domination in trade.
9. In the early 1600's, the English established trading settlements in India, Malaya, the East and West Indies, and North America. The first successful English settlement in the Americas was at Jamestown, Virginia, in 1607.
10. By 1625 the Dutch had taken over the East Indies trade, and in the same year they tried to gain commercial control in North America by establishing New Amsterdam.
11. The first permanent French settlement in the New World was founded at Quebec in 1608. They established trading settlements in North America, India, and the West Indies.
12. In the mid-1700's, conflicting claims in North America and India led to wars that paralleled wars on the European continent. As a result of the Treaty of Paris in 1763, the French lost its colonial empire to England and Spain.

The Summary reinforces chapter content by listing key understandings in a concise, straightforward format.

Building Vocabulary

lateen sail	entrepreneurs	line of demarcation	creoles
rudder	mercantilism	scurvy	mestizos
compass	bullion	conquistadores	mulattos
astrolabe	balance of trade	viceroy	zambos
joint stock companies	mutiny	peninsulares	sea dogs

Building Vocabulary displays important concept terms in the order of presentation in the chapter.

Reviewing the Main Ideas

1. What technological improvements were made in European ships in the late 1400's?
2. How did joint stock companies serve expanded commercial needs?
3. What were some weaknesses of the mercantilist system?
4. What events contributed to Portugal's rise to supremacy in the 1500's?

Questions in Reviewing the Main Ideas stimulate learning and help students review chapter content.

Unit Reviews

The point Summary highlights the major generalizations developed in the unit.

Developing Understanding questions tie together major points presented in the unit and help students review.

Developing Skills gives students the opportunity to practice high-level, critical-thinking skills.

Suggested Activities provide individual and group projects that allow students to examine unit concepts in greater depth.

Suggested Readings lists works suitable for in-depth study and student enjoyment.

UNIT 7 REVIEW

Summary

1. In the late 1800's and early 1900's, the industrialized nations of Europe came into conflict as they extended their empires. The rise of nationalism and militarism increased their rivalries. By 1907, Europe had divided into two opposing military alliances.
2. In 1914 the assassination of the heir to the Austrian throne triggered World War I. The Central Powers—Germany, Austria-Hungary, Bulgaria, and the Ottoman Empire—fought against the Allies—Britain, France, Russia, Serbia, Belgium, and later, Japan, Montenegro, and the United States.
3. During most of the war, each side suffered heavy casualities, but won no decisive victories. In 1918 World War I finally ended. The peace settlements punished and weakened Germany and the other Central Powers. National boundaries were altered, and the League of Nations was established.
4. Following the war, totalitarian dictatorships arose in Russia, Italy, and Germany, alarming the western democracies. In Asia, Africa, and Latin America, nationalist movements demanded independence from foreign influence or control.
5. World War II began in 1939 when Hitler invaded Poland. During the war, the major world powers were once again divided into two opposing alliances: the Axis (Germany, Italy, and Japan) and the Allies (Britain, France, the United States, and the Soviet Union).
6. Eleven months after the invasion of Normandy in 1944, the Germans surrendered. The war with Japan did not end until the United States dropped atomic bombs on Japan.
7. As the Allies liberated Europe, the truth about the Holocaust was revealed. More than 12 million people, half of whom were Jews, had been slaughtered by the Nazis.
8. In 1945 the United Nations was established as an international organization for peace.

Developing Understanding

1. What conditions in Europe led to World War I? What was the turning point in the war?
2. How did totalitarian governments come to power in Russia, Italy, and Germany?
3. What were the causes and impact of the depression of the 1930's?
4. What did nationalist movements in Asia, Africa, and Latin Ame[...]
5. How did the World W[...] contribute to the outbr[...]
6. Why do you think the [...] in World War II?

Developing Skills

Primary sources—firsthand accounts or evidence such as letters, business contracts, government documents, photographs, and diaries—provide valuable information about historical events and developments. Historians and students of history must learn how to analyze a primary source.

The following reading [...] primary source. It was [...] Benito Mussolini for the [...] (1932). Mussolini was aided [...] the editor of the encyclope[...] as the "philosopher of Fasc[...] source, answer the questi[...]

Fascism . . . believes neither in the possibility nor the utility of perpetual peace. . . . War alone brings up to its highest tension all human energy and puts the stamp of nobility upon the peoples who have the courage to meet it. . . .

. . . . Fascism combats the whole complex system of democratic ideology. . . . [It] denies that the majority, by the simple fact that it is a majority, can direct human society; it denies that numbers alone can govern by means of a periodical consultation, and it affirms the immutable, beneficial, and fruitful inequality of mankind. . . . The foundation of Fascism is the conception of the State, its character, its duty, and its aim. Fascism conceives of the State as an absolute, in comparison with which all individuals or groups are relative. . . .

For Fascism, the growth of empire . . . is an essential manifestation of vitality. . . . Fascism is the doctrine best adapted to represent the tendencies and aspirations of a people, like the people of Italy, who are rising again after many centuries of abasement and foreign servitude. But empire demands discipline, the coordination of all forces, and a deeply felt sense of duty and sacrifice: This fact explains many aspects of the practical working of the regime, the character of many forces in the State, and the necessarily severe measures which must be taken. . . .*

1. What qualifications did the author have to write on this subject?
2. When, where, and for what purpose was the article written?
3. What information does the article give you about fascism? What are its main points?
4. How could this information be verified by other sources?

*"The Political and Social Doctrine of Fascism," by Benito Mussolini, quoted in *International Conciliation*, January 1935, No. 306, pp. 7-9, 13-16.

Suggested Activities

1. Which of Wilson's Fourteen Points should have been included in the Treaty of Versailles? Participate in a dramatization of the conference negotiations to arrive at an answer.
2. For one week, record the activities you do outside your home. Then, consider how each might be affected if you lived in a totalitarian state.
3. Read several poems or stories by twentieth-century African writers. Discuss how the authors view the relationship between traditional lifestyles and modern ones.
4. If you had been a military adviser for the Allies in World War II, which recommendation would you have given for ending the war with Japan? Would you have proposed an invasion of Japan or dropping the bomb?

Suggested Readings

Appel, Benjamin. *The Age of Dictators*. Crown, 1968. Looks at the rise of totalitarianism in Europe during the twentieth century.

Feis, Herbert. *Churchill, Roosevelt, and Stalin*. Princeton, 1966. Studies the careers of the three main Allied leaders from 1941 to 1945.

Paradis, Adrian A. *The Hungry Years: The Story of the American Great Depression*, Chilton, 1967. Discusses the causes of the depression and its impact on the American people.

Remarque, Erich Maria. *All Quiet on the Western Front*. Fawcett, 1979. Novel about a young German soldier in World War I.

Schnabel, Ernst. *Anne Frank: A Portrait of Courage*. Harcourt, 1958. Story about a young Jewish girl living in Nazi-controlled Europe.

Special Features

"History and the Arts" presents an artistic or cultural theme related to the chapter.

Full-color illustrations reinforce the narrative.

"History and Cities" focuses on the history and distinctive features of a city that was important during the time period covered by the chapter.

HISTORY AND THE ARTS
Chinese Landscape Painting

During the T'ang and Song dynasties, Chinese artists developed a unique form of landscape painting. They painted scenes of nature on silk and paper scrolls. These paintings were done with fine-pointed brushes dipped in black ink. An artist was able to form many kinds of lines on each painting. This was done by adjusting the angle of the brush and the pressure on it.

In their works, Chinese artists did not try to copy nature. Instead, they wanted to express a mood or feeling. Chinese landscape painting stresses the harmony of nature and the human spirit. Most works show towering mountains and vast expanses of water and forest. Human figures, on the other hand, are small in appearance. In this way, it is suggested that human life is only part of a greater whole.

Chinese painting was closely linked with poetry and calligraphy. Poems were often added to landscape paintings as part of the overall design. The painting shown here is called *Spring over the Elixir Terrace*. It celebrates the reunion of two friends, who had been separated during a war. To express joy at meeting his friend, the painter included the following poem:

> For ten years, I wandered, homeless and away
> from worldly entanglements:
> Now, returning home by the river, I see
> ...things differently from most others.
> ...ating in the sky, it is
> ...rain,
> ...d from a well turn to
> ...vind I lean on my dragon
> ...d hearing your mouth-organ
> ...light.
> ...with the venerable
> ...the military strategists;
> ...paintings and talk about

...se artists paint their works?
...cape painting express the
...ween humanity and nature?

HISTORY AND CITIES
Manchester, England

Manchester is located in northern England. It developed where three easily bridged rivers, the Irk, Medlock, and Irwell, come together. Early records show that Manchester was a Roman fort in the first century A.D. During the Middle Ages, it became an important trade and religious center in northern England.

In the sixteenth century, Manchester became a leading textile center. Merchants living in the city passed out raw materials to peasant weavers and collected their finished cloth products for shipment to Liverpool, London, and foreign ports.

Although the city grew rapidly during the eighteenth century, it still had a quiet atmosphere. People enjoyed sailing on the Irwell. Cattle grazed close to the center of town, and orchards dotted the banks of the Irk. Pigs roamed the unpaved, narrow, barely lit streets. Leading merchants had their homes in the center of town close to their businesses. There were no great commercial or industrial buildings.

By the early 1800's, the impact of the Industrial Revolution on Manchester was apparent. Between the late 1780's and 1800, the population rose from 40,000 to over 70,000. A boom in the newly mechanized cotton industry created a small class of wealthy industrialists. It also resulted in a new working class made up, in large

part, of immigrant workers from surrounding English counties and from Ireland.

During this period, the appearance of Manchester changed. Mills and warehouses, the city's new architectural landmarks, replaced private homes and shops in certain areas. With the coming of the railways, industrialists built large mansions on the outskirts of the city, leaving the city center to working-class slums. The Irwell became so badly polluted that it was described as "a flood of liquid manure."

In 1835 Alexis de Tocqueville, a French writer and political philosopher, visited Manchester and gave his impressions of it.

> . . . .Thirty or forty factories rise on the tops of the hills. . . . The wretched dwellings of the poor are scattered haphazard around them. . . . The roads which connect the still-disjointed limbs of the great city show, like the rest, every sign of hurried and unfinished work; the incidental activity of a population bent on gain. . . . Here humanity attains its most complete development and its most brutish; here civilization works its miracles, a civilized [person] is turned back almost into a savage.*

Others, however, were more optimistic about Manchester. *The Edinburgh Journal*, a leading British magazine, stated in 1858 that

> Manchester streets may be irregular, its smoke may be dense, and its mud ultra-muddy, but not any or all of these things can prevent the image of a great city rising before us as the very symbol of civilization, foremost in the march of improvement, a grand incarnation [embodiment] of progress.

1. What were the causes of Manchester's transformation from a small trading town to a large industrial city?
2. Do you think that what happened to Manchester can be called "progress"? Why, or why not?

*Journeys to England and Ireland, Alexis de Tocqueville, tr. by G. Lawrence and K. P. Mayer, © 1958 by Arno, pp. 105-106.

Excerpts from primary sources enrich many special features.

Questions reinforce learning.

Special Features

HISTORY AND PEOPLE

Jean Baptiste Colbert

Jean Baptiste Colbert, the son of a wool merchant in Rheims, France, had a strong interest in economics and a talent for organization and detail. From 1662 to 1683, he was Louis XIV's minister of finance. Some historians think he was the most remarkable government minister France ever had.

As a young man, Colbert worked for a banking firm that had business with Cardinal Mazarin. Colbert straightened out the cardinal's financial affairs and impressed Mazarin with his abilities. Colbert remained in Mazarin's service for many years. It was reported that Mazarin, on his deathbed, said that he was leaving his king a gift more valuable than money or jewels. That gift was Colbert.

After Mazarin died in 1661, Louis XIV depended on Colbert. The finance minister taught the king how to keep accounts. Within two years, Colbert had improved France's financial standing. During the next decade, he doubled the national revenue by reforming the tax system and raising taxes.

Colbert ran every government department except the department of war. He created the French navy, built roads and canals, and worked tirelessly to develop commerce and manufacturing. To develop trade, Colbert also encouraged settlement of France's empire in the New World.

Colbert wanted France to have more exports and he taxed imports heavily. He set up factories to make linen, glass, lace, and other luxury items. To advertise French goods, sample products were sent to foreign visitors at Versailles. Worried that France did not have enough workers, Colbert prohibited artisans from leaving France. He also gave tax exemptions to large families and raised the age at which young people could enter religious orders. Although a Catholic, Colbert opposed government restrictions on Protestants. He realized the importance of their merchants to France's economy.

Colbert was not a likeable man. He seldom smiled and seldom talked. He worked 15 hours a day and never took a vacation. His only passion, he said, was for work. However, he was interested in science and the arts, since they could be used to promote tr[...] observatory and a scientifi[...] was responsible for choo[...] artwork for Versailles.

Colbert hated war, but [...] humane. He disliked it beca[...] money and deprived France [...] He also hated Louvois, the w[...] men were archrivals. It amus[...] against the other.

Louvois influenced Louis[...] wars that made it impossible [...] France on a sound financia[...] brilliant Colbert could not rai[...] pay for constant war. When [...] France was deeply in debt d[...]

SCIENCE AND TECHNOLOGY

Telegraph

During the nineteenth century, the invention of the telegraph revolutionized long-distance communication. Until its invention, messengers served as the chief means of transmitting information over a distance. In the 1790's, the French inventor Claude Chappe had set up a system of semaphores, or visual signals, that relayed messages throughout France. However it was too inefficient to be used for any but the most urgent messages. Only with discoveries in electricity were inventors able to develop successful telegraphs. These devices were able to change coded messages into electrical impulses and send them over wires.

The development of the telegraph as a practical device for transmitting messages over great distances is particularly associated with the names William Cooke and Charles Wheatstone. Although a variety of forms of telegraphs had been designed and demonstrated before theirs, these two British scientists were the first to prove the value of the invention.

By 1845, the partners had installed a demonstration line between Paddington and Slough in England for the Great Western Railway. The line and its possibilities for expanding communication attracted enormous publicity when a suspected murderer was seen boarding a London-bound train at Slough. The news was quickly telegraphed to police in Paddington where he was arrested on arrival.

The 1840's were a period of rapid expansion of telegraph service. This resulted in Britain from the success of the Paddington to Slough line. In the United States, Samuel Morse, who invented the universal telegraph code of dots and dashes, completed the first American telegraph line, linking Baltimore, Maryland, with Washington, D.C., in 1844. The line was in service one day before it carried to Washington the results of the Democratic presidential convention meeting in Baltimore. Four years later, Florida was the only state east of the Mississippi River not to be part of the American telegraph network. In addition to Britain and the United States, telegraph systems were also expanding across the European continent.

In 1846 Wheatstone proposed a submarine cable to link Britain with the European network. This was completed in 1851 after numerous failures in laying cable across the English Channel. Seven years later, Europe and North America were first joined by telegraph. The first submarine cable across the Atlantic, however, broke down shortly after it was put into service. Not until 1866 were the two continents linked with regular service.

By the late 1860's, the world's telegraph system covered almost 150,000 miles (240,000 kilometers), including 95,000 miles (152,000 kilometers) in Europe and 48,000 miles (76,800 kilometers) in the United States. In 1872 the first telegrams were exchanged between the mayors of London, England, and Adelaide, Australia. The countries of the world grew closer together by way of a web of telegraph lines, the first step in a worldwide communication network.

1. Who demonstrated the first practical use of the telegraph in Britain? in the United States?
2. What technological achievement allowed telegraph communication between Britain and continental Europe and between North America and Europe?

"History and People" profiles individuals who have contributed significantly to world events.

"Science and Technology" highlights important inventions and discoveries relevant to the chapter.

Photographs and Illustrations

Numerous photographs and illustrations, most in full color, promote visual perception of ideas.

through negotiation, and to work to prevent nuclear war. At the same time, the Strategic Arms Limitation Talks agreement, SALT I, was approved. It limited the number of nuclear warheads and missiles each country could maintain.

Détente For the next several years, the United States and the Soviet Union continued to cooperate in many areas. In August 1975, the heads of government of the United States, Canada, and all the countries of Europe except Albania met in Helsinki, Finland, to sign the final act of the Conference on Security and Cooperation in Europe. There, they officially recognized Eastern Europe as a Soviet sphere of influence. They pledged to work for peaceful cooperation in Europe, to give the United Nations their support, and to respect human rights. In the view of many, the conference marked the high point of East-West relations during the decade. It was followed in 1979 by the signing of a SALT II agreement.

Détente did not put an end to the rivalry between the two countries. Nor did it stop the Soviet Union and the United States from stockpiling conventional weapons, building up their armed forces, or placing their military in other countries.

Global Intervention Throughout the 1970's, despite détente, the United States and the Soviet Union competed against each other in world. In 1973, during the example, the United States lis while the Soviets backed

ally, the two superpowers financial and technical aid. ates and the Soviet Union Cuban troops and advisers bique, Namibia, and Angola with pro-Soviet groups ll Marxist governments in by one, the groups achieved

ca, made up of the countries Ethiopia, and Somalia, the uccessful and unsuccessful.

In 1974 the Ethiopian emperor Haile Selassie was overthrown, and a socialist government came to power. A pro-Soviet government was already in power in Somalia. The Soviet Union provided both countries with military aid and advisers. In 1977 Ethiopia and Somalia clashed over Ogaden, a region ruled by Ethiopia but whose people wanted independence. When the Soviet Union sided with Ethiopia, Somalia expelled Soviet advisers from the country. The Somalis accepted aid from the United States and gave it access to naval bases that had been used by the Soviets. Meanwhile, the Soviets strengthened their ties to Ethiopia.

With the aid of Soviet advisers and Cuban troops, Ethiopia in early 1978 staged a major offensive in the Ogaden. This led to the withdrawal of Somali troops from the region. By the early 1980's, the fighting had significantly declined.

As Cold War tensions eased in the early 1970's, friendlier relations developed between the United States and the Soviet Union. What was the high point of East-West relations during the 1970's?

THE ODD COUPLE

Long winters and dry summers on the treeless steppes in central Asia forced many clans to move with the seasons in search of pasture for their herds. What were the principal foods of these nomadic clans?

Mongol Conquests The Mongol armies under Genghis Khan first conquered the other steppe peoples, most of whom were Turks. These victories brought tribute money to the Mongol state as well as new recruits for the Mongol armies. By 1211 the Mongols were strong enough to attack major civilizations. In that year, 100,000 Mongol horsemen invaded China. While fighting the Chinese, the Mongols learned Chinese techniques of siege warfare. Using gunpowder, storming ladders, and battering rams, they won significant victories against their opponents. In spite of Genghis Khan's death in 1227, the Mongols continued their advance. By 1270 all of China was in their hands, and a Mongol dynasty ruled the country.

Under Ogadai Khan, the other Mongol forces moved westward. During the 1230's and 1240's, a Mongol army led by the commander Batu conquered Russia and then crossed the Carpathian Mountains into eastern and central Europe. Upon hearing of Ogadai's death, Batu's army returned to Russia. There they awaited the selection of a new khan. Meanwhile, Ogadai's widow ruled the Mongols.

During the same period, another group of Mongols invaded the Middle East. Using terror to subdue the region, the Mongols destroyed cities and killed large numbers of people. In 1258 the commander Helagu captured Baghdad, the old Abbasid capital, and enslaved its inhabitants. The destruction of the city represented a major setback to Islamic civilization. However, the Mongol advance was finally halted by the Mamluks, a Muslim military group that ruled Egypt.

Mongol Empire The Mongols created the largest land empire in history. Their territories extended from China to the frontiers of western Europe. Many of the great trade routes between Europe and Asia passed through Mongol lands. During the 1200's, Mongol rule brought peace to the region. This advanced the growth of trade and encouraged closer cultural contacts between East and West.

The Mongols respected the highly advanced cultures of conquered groups and learned from them. In China, the Mongol rulers gradually

were expert fighters on horseback, using bow and arrow. About 1200 a Mongol leader named Temuchin organized the scattered clans under one government. He brought together Mongol laws in a new code known as the **yasa**. Under Temuchin's guidance, an assembly of tribal chiefs met for the first time to plan military campaigns and to appoint future leaders.

Temuchin's greatest achievement was in military affairs. He organized the Mongol armies into disciplined cavalry units. These units were then placed under the command of officers chosen for their abilities and not for their family ties. These changes made the Mongols the most skilled fighting force in the world at that time. As a result of his efforts, Temuchin was recognized as **khan**, or absolute ruler. Now called Genghis Khan, he set out to create a large empire.

Captions identify photographs and illustrations. Caption questions relate illustrations to the narrative.

Graphics

A variety of full-color illustrations, including maps, tables, charts, graphs, and diagrams, supply valuable data and visually reinforce the narrative.

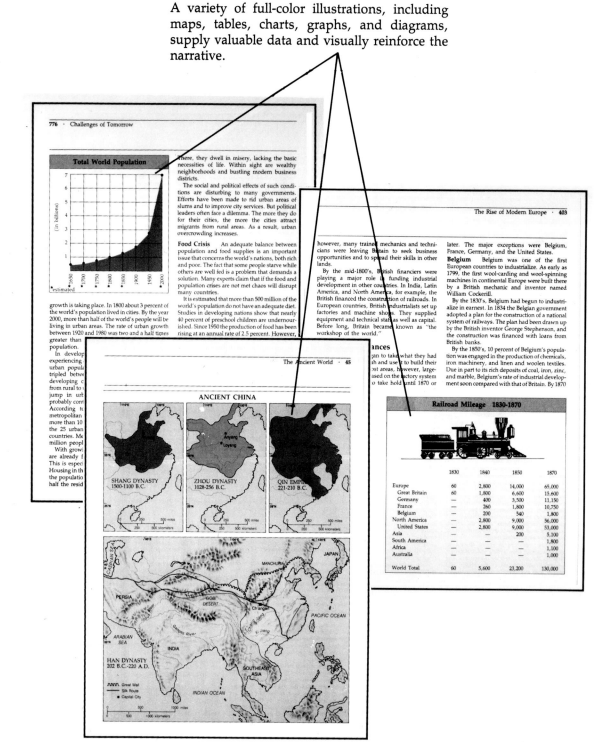

Appendix

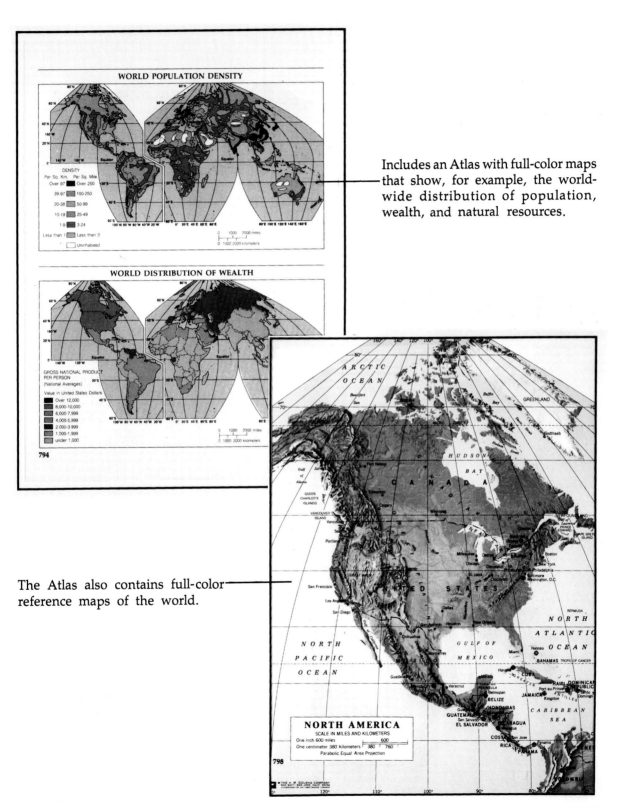

Includes an Atlas with full-color maps that show, for example, the world-wide distribution of population, wealth, and natural resources.

The Atlas also contains full-color reference maps of the world.

Appendix

The Glossary contains the definitions of all important concept terms. A pronunciation aid follows many terms.

Terms and key words are in boldface to permit fast location.

The Index provides easy reference to important historical topics.

HOW TO USE
THE TEACHER'S
ANNOTATED EDITION

The Teacher's Guide in the Teacher's Annotated Edition is divided into five major sections—Introduction, How to Use the Teacher's Annotated Edition, Instructional Approaches, Text Implementation, and Suggested Resources. To help assure the most efficient use of the guide, its four substantive sections are described below.

Introduction

The Introduction serves to acquaint teachers with the program rationale, objectives, and components. Because the student text is the most important component, its key features are explained and illustrated with sample pages.

Instructional Approaches

This is a "how to" section, providing general guidelines for several strategies that are particularly effective in teaching world history. For example, it may be of value to have students debate historically significant issues. This section gives guidelines for conducting debates. In addition, the section explains how to use reading guides to help students who may have difficulty with comprehension.

Text Implementation

This section offers specific strategies for implementing the student text in the classroom. It begins with a Text Timetables section that suggests how the text may be divided when taught for different lengths of time. Following this is an Introducing the Text section that shows how to introduce the text by means of the special prehistory section that precedes Chapter 1.

The remainder of the Text Implementation section is organized on a unit-chapter basis to correspond with the 8 units and 33 chapters of the text. Each unit begins with a statement of unit objectives, followed by an overview of unit themes and a strategy for introducing the unit. Each chapter begins with a statement of chapter objectives, followed by an overview of chapter themes and concepts, a Teaching Strategies section, and an Answers section.

The Teaching Strategies section is designed to make full use of the various aspects of the text. For each numbered section of the chapter, introductory and developmental ideas are suggested. In general, the introductory idea "sets up" the section, directing the student's reading. The developmental idea is a more substantive exercise, allowing students to pursue themes or concepts. Following the last section, a conclusion for the chapter is suggested.

The Answers section gives answers to section review questions; special feature questions; photo caption questions; and chapter review questions, including discussion questions and Using Maps (Graphs, Illustrations, Charts, Diagrams) skill exercises at the end of each chapter. Following the last chapter of a unit, answers to the unit review questions are provided. The unit material ends with suggestions for implementing the Developing Skills activity in the unit review.

Suggested Resources

The last section of the Teacher's Guide contains a bibliography of resources that can be used to enrich and supplement the study of world history. Materials are listed according to the unit for which they are most appropriate.

INSTRUCTIONAL
APPROACHES

The following strategies are designed to reinforce or supplement the teaching strategies provided in the Text Implementation section. They are especially suitable for enhancing more active student participation in the study of history.

Brainstorming

The suggestions in the Text Implementation section of this Teacher's Guide frequently ask teachers to have students speculate over the meaning or outcome of an issue and then read to see if their speculations are correct. The teaching technique upon which this recommendation is based is brainstorming. Brainstorming involves students in a free and open exchange of ideas. Besides generating ideas about a particular topic or problem, brainstorming fosters student creativity and thinking. When brainstorming is used prior to a reading activity, it gives students ideas to look for in their reading and thus enhances reading comprehension. It is an activity in which all students can participate, regardless of academic ability.

To conduct a brainstorming session, follow these suggestions:

1. Set aside a limited amount of time and keep up the pace.
2. Allow students to say anything that comes to mind and jot it on the chalkboard.
3. Do not criticize ideas. Be receptive.
4. Try to lead students to build upon the ideas of others.

Audiovisual Materials

Audiovisual materials include films, filmstrips, tapes, records, cassette recordings, picture files, cartoon files, and maps. Literally thousands of materials are available commercially, and many can be created by teachers and students. These materials may provide an overview of major historical eras and events as well as in-depth study of an important concept or theme. They are especially suitable for students who have difficulty reading. At the same time, they reinforce concepts and information for others.

When teachers use films and filmstrips, it is useful to keep some suggestions of audiovisual educational experts in mind:

1. Always preview the material. Look for major ideas and ways to tie in these ideas with previously covered topics.
2. Place on the chalkboard or in a handout the major ideas or facts of which you want students to be aware. Tell the students to watch for this information. Most audiovisual specialists advise students *not* to take notes during the presentation of the film or filmstrip.
3. Debrief the class using your list of facts and ideas. This is the point at which students should take notes. Here the whole class can participate, with the teacher addressing questions with simple or more obvious answers to slower students. In this manner, all of the students are reinforced for paying attention.

Visual materials (tables, maps, graphs, cartoons, etc.) are also an important part of modern textbooks. They break up the print and reduce the reading level, but they also supplement the narrative. The teaching ideas in this manual frequently focus the teacher's attention on these valuable resources. Often students will be asked to analyze a visual. The teacher may aid the students in their analyses by directing them through the following steps:

1. Note details.
2. Look for relationships between details.
3. Draw inferences or generalizations from these relationships.
4. Make a statement summarizing these inferences or generalizations.

Reading Guides

Although *The Human Experience* has a closely controlled reading level, some students may have difficulty with comprehension. To help these students, the teacher may use reading guides. Reading guides are designed to lead students through the various levels of reading comprehension. Rather than assuming that students read and understand the material, reading guides are based on the assumption that students have difficulty comprehending written material. They serve, in effect, as an important ''crutch'' to readers having difficulty.

A reading guide is a series of statements each of which either accurately or inaccurately repeats an idea presented in the text. In this example, the guide fosters two levels of reading comprehension, the "literal" and the "interpretive." On the literal level of the guide, students are asked to read a statement from the guide, then read the text to determine if the statement in the guide accurately restates what the authors say in the text. On the interpretive level, students are asked to determine whether or not a more general statement in the guide is a valid inference or generalization from the text. The example below is a two-level reading guide for Chapter 15, Section 3, "The French Revolution," pages 357-364.

Literal Level: Read the following statements. Then as you read the selection, refer back to the statements in the guide and indicate those that you believe say what the authors *said* in the selection (not what you believe they *meant* by what they said). To indicate that a statement is an accurate restatement of what the author said, place the page, column, and paragraph numbers in the blank to the left of the statement. If a statement is not an accurate restatement, leave the blank empty. Be prepared to explain each statement that you found to be inaccurate.

357-2-1   **1.** The American Revolution increased the desire of many French people for change in their form of government.

357-2-4   **2.** The Third Estate was the least
to   privileged of the three orders of
385-2-2   society.

     3. The nobles were not interested in reforming the government.

360-2-1   **4.** The Declaration of the Rights of Man and Citizen followed certain ideas of the Enlightenment.

     5. The Catholic Church was in favor of the Revolution.

363-1-4   **6.** Most of the victims of the Reign of Terror were members of the Third Estate.

     7. After the Reign of Terror, Jacobin ideas became more popular.

Interpretive Level: You have read the selection and are familiar with its content. Immediately below is a guide for responding to the selection at the interpretive level. Place an X in the blank to the left of each statement you believe represents what the authors meant by what they said. Refer back to the text to find bits of information that, when considered together, would form a relationship represented by that statement.

  X   **1.** One cause of the French Revolution was the inequality of social classes.

  X   **2.** The government of other European countries were alarmed by the French Revolution.

     3. The French Revolution resulted in equality for every person in France.

To develop a reading guide, first read a section and determine the most important points and generalizations. (The section review questions will help in this effort because they can be turned into statements.) Then, for the literal level, develop a list of statements that either accurately or inaccurately restate the points made in the text. For very slow readers, these statements could be taken verbatim from the text, with gross errors included to develop inaccuracies. For better readers, wording can be turned around and synonyms used, or for inaccuracies, statements taken out of context can be used. To develop a guide for the interpretive level, list accurate and inaccurate generalizations.

Reading guides can be used as homework or seatwork, and students can be grouped to compare responses and arrive at consensus within the group. In this manner, group-interaction skills are fostered. Reading guides lend themselves readily to differentiation or individualization. They are effective tools and are highly recommended by the authors.

Games and Simulations

Games and simulations are techniques that require active student participation. For this reason, advocates declare that better learning takes place. Gaming and simulation are actually separate dimensions of the same student-oriented technique. They may be combined in simulation games.

Games: The most simple game is the learning game. In the case of the learning game, a student plays a game to win—there are specific rules and procedures—but no prior knowledge is needed. The student learns by playing the game.

A little more sophisticated is the instructional game. This type of game combines competition and rules with drill and practice. The students must know a certain amount of information, and the game drills them on this knowledge. Any number of popular games or sports have been adapted to the classroom for instructional gaming. The title of the old "Who, What, and Where" game suggests its suitability for history drill. In each adaptation, the class is divided into teams. The team with the most correct answers wins.

Simulations: The most basic component of simulations is role-playing. In role-playing, students assume the role of another person in the reenactment of a historical event or problem. Make sure students playing roles have enough background information to portray their individual's opinions accurately. Do not let the role-playing drag on. Stop it when you feel the crucial points have been covered or when students "run out of gas." Have the whole class review the major points made.

A more sophisticated form of simulation is the "social simulation." The social simulation combines role-playing with a forum for social interaction and decision making. In designing a social simulation, the teacher should take the following steps:[1]

1. Select a problem or issue with alternative solutions.
2. Determine simulation groups, their positions, and how the class decision will be made.
3. Provide students with background information or allow them time for its development.
4. Provide some forum in which the various groups will present their cases. Have the class (or decision-making group) make its decision based upon these presentations.
5. Establish limits for behavior, time, research activities, etc.

Simulation Games: Simulation games combine all features of the previously mentioned activities. As such, they are time-consuming to produce. A great number, however, are available commercially.

Debate

Debating involves students in orally defending and/or attacking viewpoints on a specific topic, theory, or principle. The goal of each debater is to convince others that his or her position is either correct or the most persuasive. The process helps students gain skill in using structured oral communication to persuade others to change their positions or points of view. Debating may be a one-on-one or a group activity. Either way, the whole class can be involved because students who do not take part directly in the debate are still involved in the learning process as they listen to new information, consider the arguments, make judgments about the quality of the presentations, and come to decisions about a conclusion.

To initiate the debate, select a topic or issue about which there is a diversity of opinion. Have students indicate their positions on the issue, and then divide them into groups according to position or viewpoint. Explain that each group will have a certain amount of time in which to present its views and the justification for those views to the rest of the class. Allow each group time to analyze and solidify its position and prepare the most valid arguments possible. This will probably require additional reading or research.

Give each group (or a spokesperson for each group) an opportunity to present its argument, allowing for rebuttal. As arguments can get heated, it is best to set a specific time frame within which all argument and discussion must be contained. After each viewpoint has been debated, survey the class to determine if the debate has led any students to change their positions on the issue.

Case Studies

A case study is used to supplement material in the text by focusing on a particular problem, topic, or issue for which alternative solutions or courses of action existed. Students should take the following steps:

1. Identify the problem or conflict situation.
2. Review (analyze and evaluate) alternative positions or courses of action. Here the teacher may want to use a range of materials, including primary and secondary sources. Anthologies of documents are readily available, and many documents are included in the Teacher's Resource Book.
3. Choose a course of action or position and develop a defense for it.
4. Present their positions orally or in writing.

Case studies are especially useful if teachers want their students to practice inquiry and higher-level thinking skills. This strategy may be implemented any time there is an issue or conflict to be considered.

---

[1]Adapted from Jo Michalski, "Developing A Social Simulation, 'The Land Use Simulation'" in *Handbook of Simulation Gaming in Social Education* (Institute of Higher Education Research and Services, The University of Alabama, 1974).

TEXT IMPLEMENTATION

Text Timetables

One of the major problems in teaching world history is finding enough time to cover the material adequately. Because a school year generally ranges from 170 to 180 days, *The Human Experience* has been designed to be taught within that time. With 33 chapters, 144 sections within chapters, plus a special section on prehistory, the text provides a full and comprehensive course. One practical plan is to cover approximately one numbered section in each daily class meeting. However, the sections vary in length, importance, and difficulty, and teachers are encouraged to adjust their lesson plans to meet student needs. In order to allow extra time for review, testing, and activities, teachers may want to use the text selectively.

The text is also suitable for short, limited-content courses of one semester or less. Selection of material for courses on special topics is facilitated by the Table of Contents, which lists not only chapter titles but also section titles, special features, graphics, and maps.

Introducing the Text

Prehistory Section

At the conclusion of this special introductory section, students should be able to:
1. explain the concept of culture and the role it played in the development of civilization.
2. describe how the work of historians and archeologists is related.
3. discuss the key cultural features that characterize the three divisions of the Stone Age.

Overview

This special section on prehistory traces the human experience from its inception to the rise of civilization. It emphasizes that the historical period constitutes only the last 5,000 years of human existence. Much of our cultural heritage developed many centuries earlier in the prehistoric period. Cultural features of the Stone Age are outlined, followed by a discussion of the transition from food-gathering to food-producing economies—a development that led to permanent settlements and, eventually, to civilizations. Important concepts to be discussed are prehistory, culture, economy, technology, adaptation, domestication, and civilization.

Teaching Strategy

Refer students to the map on page 1. Point out the inhabited regions of the world that were affected by the Ice Age. Explain that the Ice Age we speak of is only the latest in a series of such phenomena. It began about 1 million years ago and ended around 10,000 B.C. As students read the section, ask them to note (1) the ways that early peoples adapted to their environments and (2) the key developments in the rise of civilization.

Answers
Section Review Questions
page 3
1. The recorded story of humanity; it began with the development of writing. Long period of human existence before writing. From written records and archeological findings of past cultures.
2. Human ways of living—all the ideas, customs, and objects used by people in social groups. Economic activity, technology, political and religious beliefs, arts, sciences, and leisure activities, among other things. One generation teaches the next.
3. It tells us about past environments and cultures, particularly, technology.
4. Paleolithic, or Old Stone Age: People hunted and gathered food. They adapted to their environment, developed spoken languages, learned the use of fire, and made tools. Late in the period, some people painted figures on cave walls. Mesolithic, or Middle Stone Age: Large ice-age animals became extinct, causing people to depend on smaller game, fish, and the gathering of grains, fruits, nuts, and berries. Some Middle Eastern people learned to harvest wild grains, which permitted the development of permanent villages. Neolithic, or New Stone Age: People learned to irrigate the land, domesticate animals, and make pottery. The plow was invented; the resultant larger harvests led to larger villages.

Photo Question
page 3
Stone, bone, horn, ivory, wood.

UNIT 1
The Ancient World

At the conclusion of this unit, students should be able to:
1. identify the major turning points and personalities of ancient times.
2. discuss the important achievements of ancient civilizations.
3. explain the impact of geography on developments in the ancient world.

Overview

This unit describes the emergence and development of civilization from its inception in various parts of the world to the fall of Rome. Chapter 1 deals with the Fertile Crescent and the Nile Valley to the end of the Persian Empire in the fourth century B.C. Chapter 2 describes the rise of civilizations in South and East Asia, from their beginnings through the flourishing of their empires and philosophies. Chapter 3 covers Greek history and achievements through Alexander the Great and his successors. Chapter 4 surveys the Roman world from the rise of Rome as an important city in the fifth century B.C. to its fall in the fifth century A.D.

Introducing the Unit

Ask students to recall what they remember about the ancient world. Their information may come from sources such as historical fiction, movies, the Bible, mythology, and travel advertisements showing ancient monuments. Then, give them an overview of the topics that will be covered in this unit, using available colorful pictures of famous structures such as the pyramids and the Roman Colosseum.

CHAPTER 1
Ancient Middle East

At the conclusion of this chapter, students should be able to:
1. outline the Fertile Crescent on a map of the Middle East and locate the centers of ancient civilizations.

2. describe important features of ancient civilizations of the Middle East.
3. discuss the reasons for the rise and fall of the major kingdoms and empires in the region.

Overview

Chapter 1 surveys the rise and fall of the important kingdoms and empires of the ancient Middle East. The chapter emphasizes the cultural features and the achievements of each of these states. It describes the way of life in some of the ancient communities and explains their political organization. Trade and other contacts between and among these states should be related to the process of cultural diffusion. The fact that most ancient urban centers in the Middle East grew along or near major bodies of water should be discussed. Other important concepts are civilization, monarchy, theocracy, dynasty, bureaucracy, monotheism, and social class.

Teaching Strategies
Section 1

Introduction: Ask students where most food for city dwellers comes from. Can they conceive of city living and nonagricultural employment without developed agriculture? Farmers and peasants, people who work the land and live in villages, must be able to produce a surplus above the level of their subsistence in order to provide cities and armies with adequate food supplies. From this introduction, lead students to the importance of the discovery of agriculture in the ancient world.

Development: Have students examine the maps on pages 7 and 11 to discuss the importance of the twin rivers to agriculture. Review the definition of civilization on page 3. Have students list the features of Sumer that qualify it as a civilization. Discuss Sumer's influence on subsequent kingdoms in the Fertile Crescent.

Section 2

Introduction: Have students study the picture and caption on page 12. Use this as a springboard to discuss the relationship between geography and history. Ask students to give examples of ways in which their local community's history has been affected by geography.

Development: There are many interesting and familiar aspects of ancient Egyptian history that may be used to motivate students. Most students know something about the pyramids, King Tutenkhamon, mummification, and hieroglyphics. Students may discuss and compare ancient Egyptian achievements vs. military conquests. Which of the two has had a more lasting impact?

Section 3

Introduction: Begin this section by discussing the archeological discoveries at Ebla. Comment on how such discoveries may alter our perception and understanding of the ancient history of the Middle East and how history is "updated" by archeology.

Development: Discuss the lasting contributions of the Phoenicians and the Hebrews. Have students compare the provisions of the Code of Hammurabi with the Law of the Hebrews on page 23. How do these compare with today's laws?

Section 4

Introduction: Use the maps on pages 26 and 29 to have students compare the geographical extent of the Assyrian, the Chaldean, and the Persian empires. Ask students to answer the questions in the Using Maps activity on page 31.

Development: Ask about the advantages of large empires over small but belligerent kingdoms in the areas of trade, road building, and cultural and technological transfer of knowledge. What caused the downfall of each of the empires discussed in this section?

Conclusion: Review the concept of cultural diffusion (p. 14). Ask students to give examples from the chapter.

Answers

Section Review Questions

page 11
1. Fertile Crescent—strip of fertile land that curves from the Mediterranean Sea to the Persian Gulf.

   Mesopotamia—eastern part of the Fertile Crescent between the Tigris and Euphrates Rivers.

   Tigris and Euphrates Rivers—rivers of Mesopotamia that flow into the Persian Gulf.

   Sumer—one of the world's first civilizations.

   Ur—prosperous city-state of Sumer.

   Semites—people from the Arabian Peninsula who settled in the Fertile Crescent.

   Akkad—Semitic kingdom in northern Mesopotamia.

   Sargon I—Akkadian king who united the city-states of Mesopotamia into an empire.

   Gilgamesh—hero in Sumerian tale, which is the oldest written story in the world.

   Hammurabi—ruler of Mesopotamia who established a written code of law.

   Amorites—Semitic people who conquered Mesopotamia.

2. People developed ways to control flood waters and improve farming; surplus of food allowed people to build cities and develop a civilization.

3. Dams and canals, temple architecture, arch, potter's wheel, wagon wheel, bronze, sundial, metal tools, writing system, literature, written code of law, calendar, and number system; also, systems of government, trade, and religion.

4. Established a single code of justice for all.

page 19
1. Narmer (Menes)—king of Upper Egypt.

   Thebes—capital of Egypt during the Middle Kingdom.

   Hyksos—people from western Asia who defeated Egypt.

   Ahmose—Egyptian prince who drove the Hyksos out of Egypt.

   Thutmose III—pharaoh who conquered Syria and Mesopotamia; he made Egypt an empire.

   Akhenaton—pharaoh Amenhotep IV; he tried to establish monotheism in Egypt.

   Ramses II—last powerful pharaoh of Egypt; he ruled for 67 years.

   Hatshepsut—Egyptian queen who pursued peaceful policies, expanded trade, and brought new wealth to Egypt.

   Nefertiti—wife of Akhenaton; she encouraged religious reforms.

   Rosetta Stone—slab of stone on which were carved two forms of Egyptian writing and a Greek translation.

   Ptahhotep—vizier during the early Middle Kingdom.

2. Old Kingdom, Middle Kingdom, New Kingdom.

3. Absolute authority.

4. Many gods were worshiped; each region also worshiped a local god; it emphasized life after death.

1. Ebla—early kingdom in northern Syria.

   Arameans—Semitic people who settled in central Syria around 1200 B.C.

   Damascus—capital of Aramean kingdom.

   Aramaic—language of Arameans.

   Asia Minor—peninsula between the Black Sea and the Mediterranean Sea.

   Anatolia—large plateau in Asia Minor.

   Hittites—people known for their army and iron weapons; they established an empire covering Asia Minor, Syria, and part of Mesopotamia.

   Hattusus—capital of Hittite empire.

   Canaan—land between ancient Egypt and Syria.

   Phoenicians—Canaanites of western Syria who traded and settled throughout the Mediterranean.

   Tyre—Phoenician city-state.

   Carthage—Phoenician colony in northern Africa.

   Hebrews—Semitic people of Canaan who had a monotheistic religion.

   Judaism—Hebrew religion.

   Yahweh—god of the Hebrews.

   Abraham—person to whom the Hebrews trace their origins.

   Moses—Hebrew leader who led the Hebrews out of slavery in Egypt.

   Saul—first king of the Hebrews.

   David—second king of the Hebrews; he formed a strong central government in the capital of Jerusalem.

   Torah—book of Hebrew laws.

   Diaspora—communities of Jews who lived outside their homeland.

2. Through conquest.

3. It promoted the exchange of customs and ideas, such as the alphabet.

4. Ethical monotheism; it laid the foundation of Judaism, Christianity, and Islam.

page 30

1. Persia—mountainous area between Mesopotamia and India.

   Assyrians—Semitic people who established an empire in Mesopotamia about 750 B.C.

   Nineveh—capital of Assyria.

   Medes—group that joined with Persians to defeat the Assyrians.

   Chaldeans—established an empire in Mesopotamia around 600 B.C.

   Nebuchadnezzar—Chaldean king who extended the empire and rebuilt Babylon.

   Aryans—Indo-European peoples.

   Persians—Aryan people who established an empire in Persia.

   Cyrus II—Persian king who established the largest empire in the world at that time.

   Darius I—Persian king; he set up the administration of provinces.

   "Eyes and Ears of the King"—special inspectors of the Persian government who reported on the activities of local officials.

   Royal Road—major road from Susa in Persia, to Sardis in Asia Minor.

   Zoroaster—religious leader who urged reform of the Persian religion.

   Ahura-Mazda—Persian god of the forces of good.

   Ahriman—Persian god of the forces of evil.

   Persepolis—most magnificent city in the Persian Empire.

2. Cruelly; they burned cities and tortured, killed, and deported thousands of people.

3. To learn the plans of the gods and goddesses.

4. By dividing it into satrapies, each headed by a satrap.

Special Feature Questions

page 28

1. Glazed brick gates, beautiful palaces and temples, "Hanging Gardens," streets and markets, and a great wall.

2. Mostly by barter, but some used silver and gold.

Photo Questions

page 9

By keeping business, government, and religious records; they also wrote literary works.

page 10

Architecture, number system, calendar, wagon wheel, arch, sundial, potter's wheel, bronze, metal tools, plows.

page 12

They built dams and ditches to drain the land; reservoirs and canals for irrigation.

page 18

Wealthy women enjoyed an active social life and could own property.

Internal rebellions, external disputes, invasion by Chaldeans and their allies.

Chapter Review

page 31, Reviewing the Main Ideas

1. At first, by a council of nobles and a general assembly of citizens; later, by a monarch. Warfare among its city-states caused it to become weak and vulnerable to invaders.
2. It provided a sense of security.
3. They introduced bronze weapons and tools, and horse-drawn chariots.
4. It became an empire; established a dynasty of pharaohs; absorbed ideas and customs from the Fertile Crescent; and for a time had a monotheistic religion.
5. Royalty and rich people had their bodies embalmed and placed in tombs with the possessions they needed for journeying to the afterlife. Poor people had messages, prayers, and magic spells placed in their coffins that asked the god Osiris to help them in the afterlife.
6. By kings chosen by the people.
7. It facilitated the growth of civilization through the exchange of ideas and customs.
8. They saw it as a movement of events from a beginning to an end.
9. The Persians were fair and tolerant; the Assyrians were cruel.
10. From worship of many gods to Zoroaster's teaching that the world was divided by a struggle between two gods, one representing good, and the other, evil.
11. Written language, water control structures, the arch, architecture and engineering feats, sundials, wagon wheel, potter's wheel, metal vessels and statues, bronze and iron tools, shadoof, chariots, number systems, calendar, astronomy, geometry, navigation, weights and measures, bills of sale and contracts, alphabet, embalming, medical treatment.
12. Generally subservient to men, though some had property rights. In Egypt, wealthy women had an active social life, and succession to the throne was through the female line.

page 31, Discussing Important Ideas

1. Answers may vary, but mention should be made of each generation having access to the learning of the past and not having to redo everything; they build on previous accomplishments.
2. Answers may vary, but exchange of knowledge should be mentioned.
3. The Middle East was the site of the beginnings of western civilization.
4. Answers may vary. Mention should be made of the unifying effects of religion.
5. Answers may vary.
6. It was more severe. Answers may vary.
7. Answers may vary.
8. Tales of heroes and deities; prayers; religious books; hymns; magic formulas; secular adventure stories, fairy tales, love stories and songs, poems, quotes, proverbs. Answers may vary.

page 31, Using Maps

1. Cyprus.
2. Memphis.
3. Byblos, Sidon, Tyre.
4. Between 800 and 900 miles; between 1,280 and 1,440 kilometers.
5. Caspian Sea.
6. Euphrates River.

CHAPTER 2
Early South and East Asia

At the conclusion of this chapter, students should be able to:

1. list and locate the areas where major ancient civilizations developed in South and East Asia.
2. compare the major religions of South and East Asian civilizations.
3. describe the important contributions of each of these civilizations.

Overview

Chapter 2 covers the ancient civilizations of India, China, Korea, and Japan. First, it examines the impact of the environment on the development of each of these civilizations. It then proceeds to cover their cultures and history. Special emphasis is placed on the relationship between religious beliefs and social structure. Note that neither the Indians nor the Chinese occupied the other's land in ancient times, although their influence on each other was evident through the spread of Buddhism. Likewise, the Chinese culture affected the Japanese culture through the peaceful means of trade and Buddhist missionary work. Important concepts in the chapter include polytheism, the caste system, reincarnation, karma, nirvana, ethics, yin and yang.

Teaching Strategies

Section 1

Introduction: Begin this section by asking students to state briefly what comes to their minds when they think of India. Remind students that in this chapter India refers to the territory occupied today by the states of India, Pakistan, and Bangladesh.

Development: Give students the following quote from the *Bhagavad Gita:* "The truly wise mourns neither for the living nor for the dead. There never was a time when I did not exist, nor you . . . nor is there any future in which we shall cease to be. . . ." Ask students what Hindu belief this quote refers to. Discuss how this belief contrasts with what they know of Christianity and Judaism.

Section 2

Introduction: Before having students read the section, tell them that they will be expected to compare Indian society in the Magadha, Mauryan, and Gupta states in terms of government, religious influence, contacts with non-Indian cultures, and achievements. Suggest that students outline these topics as they read. Have students discuss their comparisons of the Magadha, Mauryan, and Gupta empires and identify reasons for the collapse of each.

Development: Have students read the feature "Ajanta Caves" on page 41. Ask them to discuss the following question: In your opinion, what motivated the monks who carved the caves to commit the better years of their lives to such a project?

Section 3

Introduction: Begin this section with a general discussion on what students recall about China. Their answers may range from politics to Chinese food. Next bring up the size and population of China. Nearly one of every five people in the world lives in China. Using a physical map, describe the important features of China's environment.

China has had a long history. Although much of its history is known, some of the details are still shrouded with questions. Have students read the caption to the picture on page 43. State that, as in the case of Ebla, archeologists continue to extend our knowledge of ancient history.

Development: Use the maps on page 45 to reinforce the study of early Chinese history. Have students read pages 46 and 47, then write short paragraphs describing fictitious situations or anecdotes about Chinese family and village life during the Zhou period. Ask them to read "Sayings of Confucius" on page 46 and discuss whether these sayings have any relevance today.

Section 4

Introduction: Lao-tzu once described rulers as follows:

> Of the best rulers, the people
> only know that they exist;
> The next best they love and
> praise;
> The next they fear;
> And the next they revile.*

Have students comment on the preceding quote. Tell them to keep it in mind as they begin to read about the rise of Chinese empires.

Development: Have students read the caption for the photo on page 49. Ask if the human and material sacrifices that the Chinese made to build the Great Wall were justified. Have students relate the Pax Sinica, with its long periods of peace and stability, to cultural achievements.

Section 5

Introduction: Begin this section exploring students' knowledge about Japan and Korea. Use the map on page 51 as well as a physical map to point out the major geographic features of the Japanese and the Korean environments.

Development: Emphasize that although the Chinese, Korean, and Japanese civilizations are strongly related to one another, each is still distinct. Have students discuss the similarities and differences among these three civilizations.

---

*Lao-tsu as quoted in *A Source Book in Chinese Philosophy,* tr. and compiled by Wing-tsit Chan, © 1963, Princeton University Press, p. 148.

Conclusion: Ask students to make a list of the lasting accomplishments of early South and East Asian civilizations. Then have them make a diagram to show how these civilizations influenced one another. Also, discuss which major religion had the greatest impact in South and East Asia.

Answers
Section Review Questions

page 38

1. Himalayas—tall mountain chain in northern India.

 Ganges—river in northern India.

 Harappa—one of two cities that were the center of the first Indian civilization.

 Aryans—Indo-European peoples who invaded the Indus Valley around 1200 B.C.

 Dravidians—people of the Ganges Plain who were displaced or enslaved by the Aryans; present-day people of southern India.

 Vedas—ancient Indian holy scriptures.

 Bhagavad Gita—most important text in the Hindu religion.

 Mahavira—guru who founded Jainism.

 Jainism—early Hindu religious movement.

 Siddharta Gautama—Buddha, founder of Buddhism.

 Four Noble Truths—main ideas of Buddha's religious philosophy.

 Theravada—branch of Buddhism closest to the ideals of Buddha.

 Mahayana—branch of Buddhism that worshiped Buddha as divine.

2. According to a plan; each city was a citadel surrounded by government and residential districts.

3. Into four varnas: brahmans, kshatriyas, vaishyas, and shudras.

4. Oneness of the universe. Non-violence. Practice of the Eightfold Path.

page 43

1. Magadha—most important northern Indian kingdom in the 500's B.C.

 Bimbisara—Magadha king; he brought the kingdom to its height.

 Chandragupta Maurya—founder of the Mauryan dynasty.

 Pataliputra—Mauryan capital.

 Asoka—most famous Mauryan ruler; after expanding his kingdom through warfare, he became a Buddhist and sought peace.

 Gandhara—northern Indian kingdom noted for its statues that reflect Greek influence.

 Gupta—northern Indian empire between 320 and 600 A.D.

 Chandragupta I—ruler of Magadha; he founded the Gupta dynasty.

 Chandragupta II—ruler who brought the Gupta Empire to its height.

 Panchatantra—collection of tales written in the Gupta period.

 Kalidasa—most famous playwright of the Gupta period.

2. He was horrified by it.

3. Though taxes were eased and some people gained more freedom, the pariahs received little help, and the position of women declined.

4. Greek, Mesopotamian, Chinese.

page 48

1. Chung-kuo—early name for China.

 Huang He—Yellow River of eastern China.

 P'an-ku—giant who created the universe, according to Chinese legend.

 Mandate of Heaven—early Chinese principle that a just ruler would receive from heaven the right to rule.

 Shang—first Chinese dynasty.

 Anyang—capital city of the Shang dynasty.

 Zhou—western Chinese people who overthrew the Shang dynasty.

 Loyang—town to which the Zhou royal family fled and from which they ruled between 771 and 256 B.C.

 Confucius—founder of the earliest and most important Chinese philosophy.

 Lao-tzu—founder of Taoist philosophy.

2. Cities, silk cloth, fine pottery and bronze vessels, writing system, literary works, record keeping, mathematics, eclipse predictions, calendar.

3. By kings at first; later, by independent nobles.

4. He believed that each person should set a good example for others, who in turn would do the same—then peace would come to the world.

page 50

1. Qin—first Chinese empire.

 Shih Huang Ti—first emperor of China.

 Han—dynasty that ruled China from 202 B.C. to 220 A.D.

Wu Ti—greatest of the Han emperors.

Ch'angan—capital of the Han Empire.

Pax Sinica—long period of peace during the Han dynasty.

Silk Route—overland route through central Asia that carried trade between East and West.

2. It established a strong central government, a common currency, standard weights and measures, a law code, and a tax system; it crushed internal opposition and outlawed Confucianism.

3. To select government officials on their merits in accordance with Confucian teachings.

4. Paper production, new methods of making silk cloth and ceramics, sundials, water clocks, a new calendar, astronomy, observations of sunspots, acupuncture.

page 54
1. Choson—kingdom in northern Korea around 300 B.C.

Silla—kingdom in Korea around 100 A.D.

Honshu—largest island of Japan.

Shinto—Japanese religious beliefs.

Yamato—dynasty that has ruled Japan since about 500 A.D.

Taika—name used for a pro-Chinese reform movement in Japan during the 600's A.D.

Nara—capital city of Japan; was built by Taika reformers.

2. United most of Japan into a single state.

3. Korea: writing system, ideas in science and the arts, Buddhism and arts associated with it, Confucianism, government administrative system.

Japan: same as Korea plus ideas in medicine, astronomy, and philosophy; civil service exams; systems of landownership and taxation.

4. Reforms instituted in Japan to establish a strong central government patterned after that of China.

Special Feature Questions

page 41
1. By carving into cliffs.
2. Lives of Buddha and his followers; Buddhist legends.

Photo Questions

page 34
That the Harappans worshiped spirits that lived in animals.

page 37
To follow dharma so the soul will enter a higher state in the next life.

page 39
China, Korea, Japan.

page 43
3,500 years.

page 49
Qin.

page 50
Work in bronze.

page 52
Because they were clan leaders, they linked religion with government.

Chapter Review

page 55, Reviewing the Main Ideas
1. They were isolated by mountains, jungles, deserts, and oceans.
2. Bad weather, poor water and soil, earthquakes, floods, diseases, and invasions.
3. To maintain control and a separate identity; they thought they were superior people.
4. Jainism denounced Hindu sacrifices, the killing of any living thing, and the caste system. Buddhism rejected the ceremonies, polytheism, and the caste system.
5. Missionary work. Split into two branches.
6. Literature, drama, architecture; concepts of infinity and zero; numbers 1 to 9; knowledge that earth is a sphere; principle of gravity; medical practices and instruments.
7. They believed China was the center of the world and civilization.
8. That harmony depended on a balance between yin and yang.
9. Civil service system was instituted.
10. Carried trade between East and West.
11. By clans grouped by occupation.
12. Shinto priests were also clan leaders.

page 55, Discussing Important Ideas
1. Answers may vary.
2. Answers may vary.
3. Answers may vary, but mention should be made of its later consequences.
4. Answers may vary; examples should be given.

5. Answers may vary. The division of the Indian castes, contrasted with the sense of unity in a common culture of China, could be one point of comparison.
6. Heaven "approved" a just ruler's rule; if a dynasty was overthrown the Mandate of Heaven justified the rebel seizure of power. Answers may vary.
7. Answers may vary.
8. Answers may vary. This could be a springboard for a discussion on censorship.
9. Answers may vary.
10. Answers may vary.

page 55, Using Maps
1. Because it is a vast subdivision of the Asian continent.
2. North. North.
3. Between 700 and 750 miles.
4. Ganges, Indus, Huang He.
5. About 1,250 miles (2,000 kilometers).

CHAPTER 3
The Greeks

At the conclusion of this chapter, students should be able to:
1. discuss the extent of Greek influence on world civilization in the areas of art, architecture, philosophy, literature, science, and government.
2. describe the major features of ancient Athenian society and how it differed from that of Sparta.
3. explain the distinction between Hellenic and Hellenistic cultures.
4. list important persons in ancient Greek history and their specific contributions.

Overview

Chapter 3 provides students with a historical chronology of the ancient Greeks, from the rise of the early Aegean settlements to the end of Alexander the Great's empire. Emphasis is on explaining the major cultural contributions of the Greeks and on describing the various social settings and lifestyles. Major concepts in the chapter are city-state, democracy, tragedy, Socratic method, logical reasoning, Epicureanism, and Stoicism.

Teaching Strategies
Section 1

Introduction: Have students study the map on page 59 and the photos on pages 58 and 60. Ask them to speculate on what influence geography might have had on early Greek history. When they read the section they will discover if their speculations are correct.

Some students may have become acquainted with the *Iliad* and the *Odyssey* in their English classes. Some may have read or seen in movies the story of the Trojan War. Arouse their interest by exploring their familiarity with these subjects.

Development: Have students compare the Minoan and Mycenaean civilizations in terms of their economies and cultures. What were the major accomplishments of each?

Section 2

Introduction: The suffix in the word "metropolis" and in the names of several cities in the United States is "-polis." Point out the meaning of the suffix and its origin (Greek city-states). You may also want to explain the origin of the word "anarchy." Due to conflicts and chaotic conditions in Athens between 590 and 585 B.C., the people were unable to elect archons. They called this period *"anarchia."*

Development: Once students finish reading the section, divide them into two groups representing Sparta and Athens and have each group defend its values and lifestyle.

Be sure students understand the causes and effects of the Greek economic expansion that began around 800 B.C. This period is sometimes called Greek *colonial* expansion. Also, have students compare and evaluate the reforms of Draco, Solon, and Peisistratus (pp. 63-64).

Section 3

Introduction: Most students are familiar with marathon races. Ask them if they know the origin of the word (p. 66) and use that to introduce them to the Persian Wars. The wars had important effects on the Greek city-states, including the rise of Athens to eminence.

Development: Generate a discussion by asking students to identify the most impressive feature of Athens during its "golden age." Apparently, not all Athenians were in favor of democracy as practiced under Pericles. Ask students to explain the reasons for opposition to Pericles. Have them read the quote from the oration on page 68, then ask them to compare the stated principles with their own conception of good government.

Section 4

Introduction: Greek-style architecture has frequently been used in public buildings in the United States, particularly in Washington, D.C. Ask students if they can identify some of these buildings. Have them read the section for other cultural contributions of the Greeks.

Development: Have students list Hellenic and Hellenistic achievements in two separate columns, then ask them to contrast these achievements in a quest to determine the most outstanding accomplishments of each. Emphasize the more universal perspective of the Hellenistic world and its Greek and non-Greek cultural influences.

Conclusion: Ask students to debate the question of what was the most important Greek achievement that has influenced the western world. The students may be divided into advocates of art, drama, architecture, politics, and philosophy.

Answers
Section Review Questions

page 61
1. Heinrich Schliemann—German archeologist who discovered "lost" Aegean cities.
   Sir Arthur Evans—British archeologist who excavated ruins of ancient Crete.
   Crete—first Aegean civilization.
   Minoan—name for Cretan civilization.
   Linear A—earliest Minoan writing.
   Knossos—largest city in ancient Crete.
   Theseus—Greek legendary hero who killed the Minotaur.
   Achaeans—early name of the Mycenaeans.
   Mycenae—principal city of the Mycenaeans.
   Troy—city in Asia Minor.
   Iliad—Greek epic poem.
   Odyssey—Greek epic poem.
   Homer—poet who composed the *Iliad* and the *Odyssey*.
   Hesiod—Greek poet of the "dark age."
2. It had reached the height of its power, wealth, and artistic achievements.

3. Fortified by thick walls, inside were palaces and administrative buildings, outside were estates and villages.
4. It entered a "dark age" that lasted more than 300 years.

page 65
1. Hellenic era—beginning of Greek civilization and city-states.
   Attica—peninsula of central Greece; location of Athens.
   Draco—Athenian tyrant known for harsh laws.
   Solon—Athenian tyrant known for political reforms.
   Peisistratus—Athenian tyrant known for civil reforms.
   Peloponnesus—peninsula of southern Greece; location of Sparta.
2. Acropolis, palace, temple, agora, homes, shops, gardens, villages, fields, orchards.
3. Reduced the power of the nobles and made government more open to the people.
4. Rulers were Spartans; next were the perioeci; lowest were the helots.

page 71
1. Miletus—Greek city in Ionia.
   Marathon—plain in Attica; site of Athenian victory over the Persians.
   Salamis—site of a naval battle in which the Greeks defeated the Persians.
   Xerxes—Persian king who invaded Greece.
   Thermopylae—mountain pass; site of Persian victory over the Greeks, which led to the capture of Athens.
   Delian League—alliance of Greek city-states against Persia.
   Pericles—Athenian leader known for democratic reforms.
   Peloponnesian League—alliance formed by Sparta against the Delian League.
   Macedonia—kingdom north of the Greek city-states.
   Philip II—king of Macedonia; he conquered the city-states on the Greek mainland.
   Alexander the Great—son of Philip II; he conquered nearly all of the civilized world.
   Hellespont—narrow body of water separating Asia Minor and Europe.
   Darius III—Persian king; defeated by Alexander the Great.
   Issus—site in Syria where Alexander defeated Darius III.

T33

Alexandria—city in Egypt founded by Alexander the Great.

Seleucus—general in Alexander's army; he became ruler of the Asian domain of Alexander's empire.

Antioch—capital of the Seleucid dynasty.

Ptolemy—general in Alexander's army; he became ruler of Egypt.

Cleopatra—ruler of Egypt; she later lost Egypt to the Romans.

Antigonus—general in Alexander's army; he became ruler of Macedonia and Greece.

page 72

2. Public works program of beautification; extended democracy so all male citizens could take part in the government.

3. Athens' transformation of the Delian League into an Athenian empire; the struggle for power between Sparta and Athens. Brought disaster to all the Greek city-states.

4. 11,000 miles (17,600 kilometers) across, from western Greece to northern India. To unite Europe and Asia and to combine the best from both cultures into one civilization.

page 78

1. Parthenon—temple of the goddess Athena.

Aeschylus—Greek dramatist; recognized as first great tragedian.

Sophocles—next great Greek tragedian after Aeschylus.

Euripides—last of the great Greek tragedians.

Aristophanes—important Greek playwright of comedies.

Socrates—first great Greek philosopher.

Plato—Greek philosopher; student of Socrates.

Aristotle—last great Greek philosopher; student of Plato and teacher of Alexander the Great.

Herodotus—Father of History, first Greek historian.

Thucydides—Greek historian; first to use scientific methods.

Thales of Miletus—first important Greek scientist.

Hippocrates—Father of Medicine, Greek physician known for Hippocratic Oath.

Aspasia—Greek woman who set up a school for women in Athens; she worked to improve the status of women.

Hellenistic—period of Greek culture influenced by the civilizations conquered by Alexander.

Euclid—mathematician who wrote a summary of geometry.

Archimedes—scientist who studied mass and motion of objects.

Menander—writer of the Hellenistic era.

Epicurean—belief that people should seek happiness and peace of mind.

Stoic—belief that happiness is attained by ignoring emotions and following reason.

2. Sculptures, including the human body; pottery and painted vases; architecture using marble columns.

3. Tragedy and comedy.

4. Boys were taught reading, writing, and poetry; poor boys were sent to learn a trade, while those from wealthy families were tutored in geometry, astronomy, rhetoric, ethics, philosophy, and politics.

Special Feature Questions

page 73

1. Originally it was part of religious festivals in which a chorus chanted a story and danced to flute music; later, actors were added who recited poems that explained the songs and dances of the chorus; eventually the actors became more important than the chorus. In outdoor theaters.

2. It provided entertainment, news, commentary, and moral instruction.

Photo Questions

page 58
Those in the Middle East and throughout the eastern Mediterranean.

page 60
Isolated by mountain ranges but favored with short, swift rivers and many fine harbors, many self-governing communities could exist, nourished by sea trade.

page 65
To maintain a strong army that could quell rebellion by conquered peoples.

page 66
They united against their common enemy; a naval battle turned the tide for the Greeks.

page 72
For defensive purposes.

page 74
They believed in "a sound mind is in a sound body."

page 76
Socrates taught his students to defend their answers so they would learn to think for themselves. Plato organized the ideas of Socrates into the first system of philosophical thought and wrote on several political systems. Aristotle made important contributions in the fields of logic, biology, political science, and physics.

Chapter Review

page 76, Reviewing the Main Ideas
1. By providing chronologies and suggesting the ways in which people lived.
2. They enjoyed it. Their art work was beautiful and brightly colored; sports were incorporated into their religion and social life.
3. It fostered cultural exchange that provided new ideas and practices.
4. The relationship between humanity and the gods; justice and punishment of wrongdoing; preordained fate of the individual.
5. Merchants, artisans, peasants. Aristocrats. By edicts of tyrants who seized power and set up their own rule.
6. At first, Athens was governed by a king who was elected by an assembly and advised by a council of nobles; later, by an assembly composed of wealthy citizens. Sparta had two kings who served jointly, but an assembly really ruled. The assembly elected ephors to manage public affairs. The ephors were assisted by a senate that proposed laws and served as a supreme court.
7. Spartan women had more freedom than women of other city-states; they mixed freely in society. In Hellenic society, lower-class women were helpmates to their husbands; they mixed socially; upper-class women were restricted to performing household duties. In Hellenistic times, women moved more freely about the cities and could attend schools of higher learning.
8. It gained self-confidence and security, which contributed to the development of its civilization.

9. To free the Ionian city-states and to ward off any future Persian invasion.
10. Through conquest. It was split into three regions, each ruled by a general from Alexander's army.
11. Hellenic culture emphasized art, literature, and philosophy; Hellenistic culture stressed science and mathematics.
12. He disliked it. One composed of intelligent, well-educated citizens dedicated to service to the state above interest in personal goals.

page 79, Discussing Important Ideas
1. Mountainous terrain with short, swift rivers and excellent harbors. Answers may vary.
2. Answers may vary.
3. Answers may vary, but students should give specific examples of different lifestyles.
4. Answers may vary.
5. Answers may vary, but mention should be made of the lack of rights for slaves, women, and landless men.
6. Answers may vary, but should include that the Delian League was formed against the Persians. The Peloponnesian League was formed against Athens.
7. Answers may vary.
8. Answers may vary.
9. Answers may vary.
10. Answers may vary, but should include a description of Plato's theory.

page 79, Using Maps
1. About 2,400 miles (3,840 kilometers).
2. Between 55°E and 60°E latitude and about 30°N longitude.
3. Danube, Tigris, Euphrates, Oxus, Indus, Nile. Answers may vary.
4. Yugoslavia, Romania, Bulgaria, Albania, Greece, Egypt, Libya, Turkey, Syria, Lebanon, Israel, Jordan, Cyprus, Iraq, Iran, Saudi Arabia, U.S.S.R., Afghanistan, Pakistan, northern India.

CHAPTER 4
The Romans

At the conclusion of this chapter, students should be able to:
1. discuss the circumstances that led Rome to world supremacy.

2. identify the causes for the decline of the Roman Republic.
3. describe the Roman world and its achievements during the height of the empire.
4. analyze the impact of Roman civilization on western history.
5. outline the development of Christianity.
6. explain the factors and conditions that led to Rome's decline.

Overview

Chapter 4 covers nearly 1,000 years of Roman history. It begins with a description of the geography of the Italian peninsula, which was the home of the Roman Empire. As the chapter explains the rise of Rome from a small city-state to a powerful republic with vast landholdings, it describes the social and economic conditions that influenced the policies and the organization of Rome's government.

After defeating Carthage, its major competitor and adversary in the west, Rome extended its domain in the eastern Mediterranean. Following the change in government from a republic to a monarchy in 27 B.C., the Roman world experienced a long period of peace and prosperity. In teaching this period emphasis should be placed on the achievements and contributions of Roman civilization. It was also during this time that Christianity rose from its status as a religion of a persecuted minority to become established throughout the Roman Empire. The last section deals with the decline and fall of Rome. Important concepts include republic, executive and legislative powers, indemnity, inflation, and classical.

Teaching Strategies
Section 1

Introduction: No doubt most students have had some exposure to the Roman world through films and other media. Introduce the chapter with a discussion outlining the students' perceptions of this world. Next, use a physical map of the Mediterranean region, or the maps on pages 83 and 86, to explain the geographic features of the Italian peninsula and Rome's special geographic advantages in the region. Ask students to take a few minutes to make a sketch of the map on page 83. As they read the section, they should mark up their sketches with arrows

and other symbols to help them visualize and understand the movements of people and the cultural influences that resulted in the settlement and growth of Rome.

Development: Have students use the description in the subsection "Government" on page 83 to construct an organizational chart, similar to the one below, that shows the structure of the executive and legislative bodies of the Roman Republic. Ask them to modify the chart in light of the discussion in "Plebians Against Patricians" on pages 83 and 84. When they finish, draw their attention to the extraordinary power (veto over legislative body) wielded by tribunes.

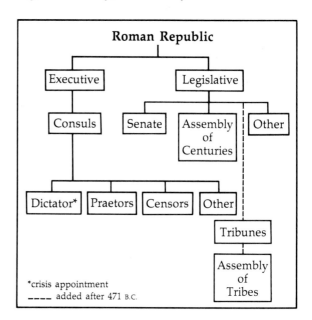

Ask students to differentiate between the republican form of government in Rome and the democratic form practiced in ancient Athens.

Section 2

Introduction: Cato, an influential Roman senator, prior to the Third Punic War used to end every speech with "Carthage must be destroyed." Why did Cato urge the destruction of Carthage? As students read the section, have them jot down the causes of each of the Punic Wars and their ideas about why Rome wanted Carthage destroyed at this time.

Development: Based on their notes, ask students whether they think Rome was justified in entering the first Punic conflict, the second, and the third. What about Carthage? Refer students to the picture on page 85. Ask them to answer the caption question and discuss whether they would have invaded Rome if they had been Hannibal.

Section 3

Introduction: This section covers a critical period in Roman history—the decline of the republic and the rise of military rule and influence. As students read the section, ask them to look for the factors that weakened the republic. Which of these do they believe were the most destructive to the republic?

Development: Have students make a chronological list of important events that occurred between 133 and 31 B.C. and have them explain, step by step, how the structure of Roman government changed during this time. Ask students to turn to the illustration on page 88, read the caption, and answer the question. Do students agree with Cicero that the triumvirate was a threat to the republic?

Section 4

Introduction: Using the map on page 91, ask students to compare the boundaries of the Roman world at the time of Caesar's death with the boundaries of the Roman Empire in 130 A.D. In which regions did Rome expand? As students read the selection, have them note which emperors were responsible for expansion in these regions. Just before students begin the subsection "Roman Civilization" on page 94, have them read the feature "Zenobia" on page 93. Zenobia, as ruler of Palmyra, also pursued a policy of expansion. Ask students to compare her rule with that of the Roman emperors discussed in this section. Have students read the rest of the section.

Development: Ask students to comment on the significance of the reforms instituted by Roman emperors during the Pax Romana. Have them compare the accomplishments of Rome during this period with the accomplishments of China during the Pax Sinica (pp. 49-50). Students should conclude that long periods of peace and stability create conditions that are conducive to great achievements.

Section 5

Introduction: This section covers significant periods of history for both Judaism and Christianity. To help students understand more clearly the Jewish origins of Christianity, have them do the following time line exercise. Draw a long horizontal line on the chalkboard. Label the left end *167* B.C. and the right end *500* B.C. Above the line and to the left of the first date, write the word *Judaism;* below the line, the word *Christianity.* Ask students to copy the time line. As they read the section, have them write dates and events at appropriate places on their time lines to illustrate (1) the struggle by Jews to preserve Judaism and (2) the development and spread of Christianity. When students finish reading the section, ask volunteers to complete the time line on the board. Use the time line as a springboard for further discussion. Ask the class questions such as: When did the Jews of Palestine come under Roman rule? At this time, how was Rome dealing with the Christians? When and why were Jews forced to leave Palestine? When and why was Jesus crucified? When was Christianity outlawed by the Romans? How had Jews and Christians preserved their faiths in the few centuries before 500 A.D.?

Development: What allowed Christianity to survive in the face of intense persecution by the Romans? Ask students to study the illustration and caption on page 99. Discuss their answers to the caption question about Roman opposition to Christianity. Divide the class into three groups to represent Roman soldiers, wealthy landowners, and poor farming families who lived in the eastern Mediterranean region during the first century A.D. Ask each group to discuss the following question and present their answers to the class: What do you think about the spread of Christianity?

Section 6

Introduction: Have students read through the chart "Famous Roman Emperors" on page 101. Point out that during Diocletian's rule the empire was divided into eastern and western regions. Ask students to turn to the map on page 103. Have them study the limits of these regions. Tell students that the Germanic invasions only affected the western part of the Roman Empire; the eastern part continued on. Emphasize that the invasions were only one of several factors responsible for the decline of the empire. As students read the section, have them list the external and internal conditions that undermined the Roman state. Does our country have similar problems? What lessons could we learn from the decline and fall of Rome?

Development: Ask students to evaluate Diocletian's decision to divide the empire. Had the division of the empire been a wise move, saving the eastern region from destruction? Or an unwise move, leading to the fall of Rome and the disintegration of the western region?

Conclusion: Have students do a research report on one or two of the many personalities in the 1,000 years of Roman history. Some may wish to depict their impressions of the Roman world in dioramas of scenes from Roman life in the second century A.D.

Answers
Section Review Questions

page 84

1. Apennines—mountain chain that runs the length of the Italian Peninsula.

   Latins—Indo-Europeans who settled on the plain of Latium in central Italy.

   Etruscans—people from Asia Minor who settled on the Italian plain of Etruria.

   Tarquins—Etruscan family that ruled Rome and made it into a large and rich city-state.

   Assembly of Centuries—represented concerns of the Roman army; it elected officials and decided issues of war and peace.

   Assembly of Tribes—plebian assembly that became the legislative body of Rome.

   Twelve Tables—bronze tablets carved with Roman laws.

2. Italy's central location helped Romans control the Mediterranean; its lack of harbors and short rivers were conducive to overland trade, resulting in the development of close economic ties and political unity among its regions.

3. Executive power was shared by two consuls; later, ten tribunes were added. Other governing power rested with the Senate and the Assembly of Centuries; later, the Assembly of Tribes was added.

4. They resented patrician control of the government and wanted to share political power. Plebians could elect tribunes and form the Assembly of Tribes; later, they were successful in getting Roman laws into written form.

page 87

1. Pyrrhus—king of Epirus who was defeated by the Romans in southern Italy.

   Carthage—capital of an empire on the North African coast.

   Sicily—island at the toe of Italy; object of the First Punic War.

   Hamilcar Barca—general who tried to unify Carthage's Spanish territories.

   Hannibal—Carthaginian governor of Spain; he defeated the Romans at Cannae but was defeated at Zama.

   Publius Scipio—Roman general who defeated Hannibal at Zama.

   Zama—site near Carthage where Scipio defeated Hannibal.

   Philip V—king of Macedonia who formed an alliance with Hannibal during the Second Punic War.

   Antiochus III—Seleucid king who failed twice to drive the Romans from Greece.

   Corinth—Greek city-state that was burned to the ground when it rebelled against Rome.

   Pergamum—kingdom in Asia Minor that came under Roman rule in 133 B.C.

2. By division into legions, strict discipline and training, and the construction of roads for faster deployment of troops and supplies.

3. Rome gained complete control of the western Mediterranean; Carthage was destroyed and its people were killed or enslaved.

4. Rome expanded into Greece as the Greeks, incited by Rome's "divide and conquer" policy, quarreled among themselves.

page 91

1. Tiberius Gracchus—Roman tribune who began land reform.

   Gaius Gracchus—Roman tribune who backed land reform and provided low-priced grain to poor city dwellers.

   Marius—Roman general and consul who created a professional army that owed its loyalty to its commanders, not to the republic.

   Sulla—Roman general who used his army to control the government and become dictator for life; he made the army the most powerful institution in the republic.

   Pompey—Roman general and member of the first triumvirate; was defeated by Caesar in a power struggle.

T38

Julius Caesar—Roman aristocrat and member of the first triumvirate; he defeated Pompey and became dictator for life.

Gaul—name for the area that is now France.

Octavian—member of the second Roman triumvirate; became sole ruler of the Roman world.

Antony—member of the second Roman triumvirate; he ruled the eastern Roman world and shared the Egyptian throne with Cleopatra; was defeated by Octavian.

Cleopatra—queen of Egypt.

Actium—Grecian site of the naval battle in which Antony and Cleopatra were defeated.

2. By proconsuls who were appointed by the Senate to one-year terms.

3. Latifundias replaced small independent farms.

4. Government jobs for unemployed persons; public land for the poor; citizenship to more people; provinces represented in the Senate. It was feared that he would replace the republic with a monarchy.

page 98

1. Caesar Augustus—Rome's first emperor.

Julian Emperors—Roman emperors who belonged to the family of Julius Caesar.

Hadrian's Wall—built to protect Roman-occupied Britain from the Picts.

Marcus Aurelius—last of the Good Emperors; he brought the empire to its economic height.

Pax Romana—Roman Peace, period of peace and prosperity that lasted from 27 B.C. to 180 A.D.

Circus Maximus—Roman arena where festivals and chariot races were staged.

Virgil—important Roman poet; he wrote the *Aeneid*.

Germania—work by Tacitus that contrasted the robust life of the Germans with the pleasure-seeking life of the Romans.

Galen—Roman physician who assembled the medical knowledge of the ancient world into several volumes.

2. By strengthening the central government, improving the provincial government, and securing nearly all the empire's borders.

3. It gave the peoples of the Mediterranean area a common culture and it spread the ideas and customs of many cultures.

4. They built roads, aqueducts, water, and sewage systems; probably the first to use concrete; combined architectural features of Greek columns with Etruscan domes and arches.

page 100

1. Pontifex Maximus—chief priest of the Roman religion; position held by Roman emperors starting with Augustus.

Judas Maccabeus—leader of successful Jewish revolt in Palestine against the Seleucids in 167 B.C.

Talmud—book of interpretations and teachings of the Torah.

Jesus—founder of Christianity.

Paul—Christian convert who wrote on behalf of the new religion.

Church Fathers—scholars who, between 100 and 500 A.D., wrote works that explained Christian teachings.

City of God—Bishop Augustine's history of humanity from a Christian standpoint.

2. Worship of gods and goddesses; divination.

3. To keep their religion from being influenced by others and to have the freedom to practice monotheism.

4. Through the travels and teachings of Jesus, his disciples, and apostles.

page 104

1. Sassanids—group of Persian warrior-kings in the Middle East; Rome's greatest Asian rivals.

Praetorian Guard—personal soldiers of Roman emperors.

Severi—dynasty of incompetent Roman rulers.

Diocletian—Roman emperor who divided the empire into two administrative regions.

Constantine—successor to Diocletian; he supported Christianity.

Edict of Milan—order that granted religious freedom to all; it made Christianity legal in the Roman Empire.

Visigoths—Germanic group in the western part of the Roman Empire that defeated a Roman army in 378 A.D. and sacked Rome in 410 A.D.

Attila—chief of the Huns; he led his forces into Europe and Italy.

Odoacer—Roman general who overthrew the emperor in 476 A.D.

2. Economic decay, civil war, plague, political instability, outside attacks.
3. Going into battle, he saw a flaming cross and the inscription "By this sign you will conquer." He attributed the vision to the Christian god.
4. Some were looking for a better climate and new grazing lands; some wanted a share of Rome's wealth and culture; many were pushed by the Huns. Contributed to its collapse.

Special Feature Questions

page 97
1. To bring water to growing urban centers.
2. It was unsurpassed for hundreds of years.

Photo Questions

page 82
Murals.

page 85
He hoped for a negotiated settlement.

page 88
Caesar was ambitious; his growing power was feared by Pompey. After Crassus was killed, Caesar defeated Pompey in battle.

page 90
Members of the second triumvirate worked for their personal power and not toward a republican government.

page 92
To protect Roman-occupied Britain from raids by the Scottish Picts.

page 96
They united the empire by linking the provinces to Rome.

page 99
Romans felt Christians were treasonous because they did not honor the emperor as a god, rejected military service, and criticized Roman festivals and games.

Chapter Review

page 105, Reviewing the Main Ideas
1. They drained the marshes around Rome and gave the Romans building skills, religious rituals, and social customs.

2. In the early republic, its laws were unwritten; later, they were carved on bronze tablets known as the Twelve Tables; it was these written laws that became the basis of future Roman law.
3. Threats from neighboring communities and fighting among Greek city-states.
4. Many were permitted to keep their own government, laws, and social customs. They exacted tribute and demanded supreme allegiance to Rome.
5. Its rulers failed to find long-term solutions to its social, political, and economic problems.
6. It strengthened the central bureaucracy, united the empire into a single state, and brought better government to the provinces.
7. Wealthy Romans lived in luxurious homes that had running water and baths. Poor Romans suffered from frequent unemployment, low wages, and fire-prone housing. Both groups were provided by the government with free entertainment—circuses, chariot races, gladiatorial combats, and festivals.
8. Women had social freedom, but no legal rights; some owned shops; wealthy women had slaves for domestic chores.
9. They left Palestine and resettled in other parts of the Mediterranean and the Middle East.
10. Each church parish had a priest, several parishes were combined into a diocese headed by a bishop; important bishops were known as archbishops and governed the churches of the larger cities. In the 400's A.D., the archbishop of Rome became known as Pope.
11. Absolute rule of emperor; division of the empire; currency reform; maximum prices for wages and goods; religious freedom; legality of Christianity; workers and sons in the same jobs; increased farm production; more government service from wealthy citizens; increased taxes from the general population. Temporary stability that delayed the fall of Rome by about 200 years.
12. Overthrow of the emperor in 476 A.D.

page 105, Discussing Important Ideas
1. Answers may vary.
2. Answers may vary, but students should mention the military versus commercial aspects of the antagonists.

3. Among possible answers—Strengths: republican form of government, strong army, good relations with conquered peoples of Italy. Weaknesses: large empire strained institutions and resources, migration to cities caused crowding, use of slaves left migrants unemployed, civil wars. Possibly, but answers may vary.
4. Answers may vary.
5. Answers may vary.
6. Answers may vary, but students should mention that Christianity gave unity of purpose to converts.
7. Answers may vary.
8. Answers may vary.

page 105, Using Maps
1. Those of the Visigoths, Angles/Saxons, and Vandals.
2. Vandals.
3. From 400 to 450 miles.
4. In Gaul.
5. Egypt and Asia Minor.

Unit Review

page 106, Developing Understanding
1. Early civilizations developed in fertile river valleys, where food production emerged. Later, the Greeks settled the coastal plains and developed a seagoing civilization; the Romans had a central Mediterranean location that helped unify their empire.
2. Sumer and Babylonia: rulers, priests, nobles; artisans, merchants, scribes, farmers; slaves. Egypt: same as above, but put farmers in the last group. India: priests (brahmans); warriors (kshatriyas); merchants, artisans, farmers (vaishyas); unskilled laborers; servants (shudras). Zhou China: nobles, merchants, peasants. Early Japan: clans subdivided into groups by occupation, warriors were highest. Minoan: nobles; merchants and artisans; farmers; slaves. Athens: aristocrats; merchants and artisans; peasants and slaves. Sparta: Spartans; merchants, artisans, farmers (perioeci); slaves (helots). Rome: patricians; plebians; slaves.

3. Very influential because in most early civilizations religious and political leadership were held by the same person.
4. It made improvements possible in building and farming. Weapons of bronze and iron made conquest and defense easier.
5. Theocracy, monarchy, democracy, republicanism, tyranny.
6. Allowed the exchange of ideas and cultures that was vital to the growth of knowledge and progress of all peoples.

pages 106-107, Developing Skills
Conclude the unit with the Developing Skills activity. In this activity, which is suitable for individuals or groups, students are given practice in evaluating the reliability of sources. Instructions are given in five steps, and students are asked to choose the most reliable of two sources for five historical topics.

You may want to have students go explicitly through each step before making their choices. The answers are not black and white. Students will receive the most benefit from discussing various aspects of reliability. Following is an analysis of the sources:
1. *Troy and Its Remains.* Although it is a secondhand account written after the fact, it is a scholarly work and thus more likely to be reliable than a work in which facts may be obscured by literary requirements and the need to entertain.
2. *Life of Antony.* Same analysis as 1.
3. The archeological findings are more objective, being based on physical evidence, but the writings of Berosus are more contemporary and have value.
4. Caesar's account has the advantage of firsthand knowledge, although it may be "contaminated" by self-glorification or purposes other than recording the facts. Emphasize to students that, when possible, sources should always be verified by comparison to other sources.
5. The British historian's analysis. The poems, which tell about the Hindu deity Rama, are excellent sources for understanding Hindu mythology, but cannot be taken literally.

UNIT 2
The Middle Ages

At the conclusion of this unit, students should be able to:
1. explain the significance of Byzantine contributions to western civilization.
2. trace the development of early Russia from the founding of Kiev to the rise of Moscow.
3. describe the emergence of Islam and the achievements of the Islamic Empire.
4. define the "Middle Ages" and describe its major developments.
5. profile the important centers of civilization in Africa and the Americas prior to European contact.
6. identify the political, economic, and religious factors that significantly influenced world civilizations from about 500 to 1500 A.D.

Overview

This unit covers the civilizations in four large regions of the world from about the fall of Rome to the discovery of the New World. Chapter 5 deals with the Byzantine and Russian states. It focuses on the culture of the Byzantine Empire and its importance to the heritage of Russia and the western world. Islam and the Islamic Empire are the primary subjects of Chapter 6. Special attention is paid to Islamic achievements in science and the arts. In Chapter 7, the civilization of medieval Europe is traced from its decline after the fall of Rome through its recovery and renewal in the late Middle Ages. Chapter 8 describes the civilizations of Sub-Saharan Africa and the Americas from their emergence in ancient times through European contact.

Introducing the Unit

Write a few medieval terms and names on the chalkboard, such as, *knights, Arabian Nights, Aztecs, crusades, Robin Hood,* and *Timbuktu.* Ask students if they know what each stands for. Have them speculate on what these words have in common. (They all came from the time of the Middle Ages.) Proceed to define this historical period. Emphasize that the change from ancient times to the Middle Ages did not occur overnight or in one year. It was a process that took many years, phasing out one mode of living and introducing another. Point out that the term "Middle Ages" and the chronological breakdown of the period were determined largely by western historians who were looking at historical events in Europe. The histories of Asia, Africa, and the Americas do not fit into the same framework.

CHAPTER 5
Byzantines and Russians

At the conclusion of this chapter, students should be able to:
1. explain the features that distinguished the Byzantine Empire from its predecessor, the Roman Empire.
2. describe the role that the Byzantine Empire, relative to its geographic location, played during the Middle Ages.
3. list major Byzantine achievements in the areas of art and architecture.
4. identify the problems that arose between the eastern and western Christian Church.
5. describe the development of the Russian principalities and city-states, and their external relations before the 1400's A.D.
6. explain how Eastern Orthodoxy gained acceptance in Russia.

Overview

Chapter 5 introduces students to major developments in the eastern region of the Roman Empire long before the fall of Rome. It explains the circumstances that led to the rise of the Byzantine Empire as a powerful and distinct state, and it describes the empire's political structure and cultural achievements. Special emphasis is placed on the role of religion in government and daily affairs. The last section traces the rise of the Russians from their early settlements to the fifteenth century A.D. It points out the unique relationship that the Russians had with the Byzantine Empire and the influence of the latter on the development of Russian culture. Concepts to emphasize are Byzantine, ethnic group, clergy and laity, hierarchy, chronicles, and veche.

Teaching Strategies

Section 1

Introduction: Ask students if they know a city whose name was changed more than once. Tell them that one such city is Constantinople. Have students locate it on the map on page 116. Ask if anyone recognizes the location from their earlier reading (Byzantium). In modern times, the city's name was changed to Istanbul. Have students speculate on the value of Constantinople's location, then have them check their answers by reading this section and the lefthand column on page 120 of the feature "Constantinople."

Development: After students have read the section, divide them into two groups. One is to be critical and the other supportive of Justinian's rule. Have them take turns presenting a point and rebutting it. Ask students also to include an evaluation of Theodora's role during Justinian's reign. Following this activity, have each student write one or two sentences identifying what they would have done differently and why, if they had been in Justinian's position. Compare and discuss their answers.

Section 2

Introduction: Introduce this section with a discussion of the impact of wars on powerful states. Students may cite examples from various historical periods. Ask them to read the section introduction and the subsection "Invasions" on pages 114 and 115. Follow this by asking students to compare the impact of these invasions on the Byzantine Empire with the impact of the Germanic invasions on the Roman Empire. Have students read the rest of the section.

Development: Ask students if they think the religious controversies within the Byzantine Empire were responsible in part for some of the empire's weaknesses. In what ways? Debate the advantages and disadvantages of having church and state so closely associated and interdependent.

Section 3

Introduction: Read to the class the quotation by Pope Innocent III that is found on pages 117 and 118. Tell students that the quote is in reference to the Fourth Crusade. Who was the Pope criticizing? ("Crusaders" is an acceptable answer. As students read, they will discover that Venetians were also involved.) What actions did the Pope condemn? Tell students to refer to the map on page 120 as they read the last subsection, "End of the Byzantines."

Development: Ask students to make a chronological list of the religious controversies that troubled the Byzantine world between the fourth and eleventh centuries A.D. In a sentence or two, have them explain each and describe its impact.

Section 4

Introduction: Have students finish reading the feature "Constantinople" (pp. 120-121) and answer its review questions. Ask them to name some of the likely occupations and kinds of people who would have lived in Constantinople, for example, a soldier, a middle-class man or woman, a child, an artisan, and so forth. Write their responses on the chalkboard; they will be used below. Instruct students to read the section. As they read, they may get other ideas, which they can write on the board.

Development: Have each student assume the role of one of the persons on the board. Ask students to write a fictitious description of a day in the life of the persons they selected. For an alternate project, through class discussion develop a list of what students feel is the most impressive of the Byzantine contributions to western civilization. Students must justify their suggestions.

Section 5

Introduction: Using a physical map of Russia and the map on page 126, point out the Russian steppe and other basic geographic features. Ask students if the country's rivers might have had a role in drawing the Russian people closer to the Byzantines rather than to western Europeans. Have them develop an answer as they read the section.

Development: Have students read the proverbs on page 127 and comment on their wisdom. They may compare them with the Sayings of Confucius on page 46. Make sure students understand the difference between writing chronicles and writing history. What features of Byzantine civilization do students feel had the greatest effect on the Russians?

Conclusion: There are more than 1,500 Eastern Orthodox churches of various ethnic affiliation in the United States. All retain some evidence of Byzantine influence. If you have one of these churches nearby, arrange for a field trip to it.

Priests are usually well informed about the Church's Byzantine heritage.

Another way to conclude the chapter would be to have students write an outline of the major events in Byzantine history. The outline would be accompanied by a map showing the greatest territorial extent of the empire and its extent after the Islamic conquest in the seventh century A.D.

Answers

Section Review Questions

page 114

1. Constantinople—capital of the Byzantine Empire.
   Eastern Orthodoxy—Byzantine form of Christianity.
   Nicaea—site of the first important church council in the Byzantine Empire.
   Justinian—Byzantine emperor under whose rule the empire reached its greatest extent.
   Theodora—Justinian's wife; she assisted him in ruling and worked to improve the position of women.
   Sassanian—Persian empire that was defeated by Justinian.
   Belisarius—Byzantine general who reorganized the armies.
   Tribonian—codified the Byzantine Empire's Roman laws.
   Corpus of Civil Law—Justinian Code; written by Tribonian.
   Hagia Sophia—"Holy Wisdom," largest church in the Byzantine Empire.

2. Its location at the crossroads of important land and water trade routes; it could also be easily defended.

3. Greeks, Syrians, Egyptians, Armenians, Jews, Persians, Slavs, Arabs, Turks. The Greeks.

4. He preserved the Roman legal heritage; strengthened ties between church and state; and built public works, including the Hagia Sophia.

page 116

1. Heraclius—Byzantine emperor who saved the empire through government and military reforms that lasted over 500 years.
   Arabs—people from the Middle East who invaded the Byzantine Empire in 634 A.D.
   Islam—Muslim religion.

Leo III—Byzantine emperor who banned all images and paintings in churches.
   Irene—first Byzantine empress who held the throne in her own right; the iconoclastic controversy was resolved during her reign.
   Basil II—first emperor of a Macedonian dynasty that ruled the Byzantine Empire.
   Seljuks—Turks, Muslim people from central Asia who defeated the Byzantines and gained control of Asia Minor, Syria, and Palestine.
   Manzikert—Asia Minor battle site where the Seljuks defeated the Byzantines.
   Alexius I—first Byzantine emperor of the Comneni dynasty; he requested that Pope Urban II begin the crusades.

2. It was weakened by invasions, religious conflicts, and political rivalries. He defeated the Persian invaders.

page 117

3. Leo III suppressed church leaders who favored images; emperors after Leo also supported iconoclasm, but Empress Irene allowed images as long as they did not receive the worship due to God.

4. Recovery of some lost territories, control of eastern Mediterranean trade, revival of Constantinople as a port and craftmaking center, period of peace, new artistic and intellectual achievements, the growth of religious institutions.

page 118

1. Franks—people of France.
   Venice—it joined forces with the French during the Fourth Crusade and attacked the Byzantine Empire, capturing Constantinople.
   Michael VIII—Greek noble who took Constantinople back from the Latin Empire, reestablished the Byzantine Empire and the Eastern Orthodox Church, and made himself emperor.
   Palaeologi—dynasty founded by Michael VIII; it ruled the Byzantine Empire for nearly 200 years.
   Ottoman Turks—Muslims from central Asia who defeated the Byzantines and established a new empire.
   Mehmet II—Ottoman sultan who captured Constantinople and established the new Ottoman Empire.

2. The crusades; disputes over religious authority, doctrine, and control of the new churches; Byzantine failure to aid the Pope during the Lombard invasion of Italy; and political differences.
3. It was burned and looted by Venetians and French crusaders.
4. The empire was weak after being reestablished by Michael VIII. Under Michael's successors, the empire was divided by conflict between rich and poor and factional differences in the Church. The empire was also being invaded and losing territory.

page 125
1. Blues and Greens—groups composed of Constantinople's citizens; they competed in athletic contests and chariot races.
   Basil—Eastern Orthodox bishop who developed a list of rules for monasteries and convents, which became the model for religious life.
   Cyrillic—Slavic alphabet devised by Byzantine missionaries Cyril and Methodius.
2. They generally performed household tasks and had separate quarters at home and in churches. They had certain guardianship and property rights under the law. Some women overcame social restrictions and were well educated, operated businesses, managed estates, and even became regents and empresses.
3. They transmitted Byzantine culture to eastern Europe as well as an alphabet and Orthodox Christianity.
4. Flat, two-dimensional art of religious subjects, illuminated manuscripts, iconography, domes over rectangular or square buildings, and mosaics.

page 131
1. West Slavs—ancestors of the peoples of Poland and Czechoslovakia.
   South Slavs—ancestors of the Yugoslavians.
   East Slavs—ancestors of the Russians, Ukrainians, and Belorussians.
   Varangians—group of Scandinavian warriors and traders who set up the first Russian state.
   Russian Chronicles—collection of Russian history, tales, and legends written in the 1100's A.D.
   Kiev—first capital of Russian territories.

Olga—princess of Kiev who was the first member of Russian nobility to accept Eastern Orthodoxy.
Vladimir—prince of Kiev who established Eastern Orthodox Christianity as the official religion of Russia.
Yaroslav—prince of Kiev who created a code of law that provided more just punishments.
Mongols—people from central Asia who destroyed Kiev and conquered most of the Russian territories.
Alexander Nevsky—Russian prince who successfully defended Eastern Orthodoxy against the Catholic Swedes and the Teutonic Knights; he also negotiated more freedom from Mongol rule.
Moscow—small Russian town first ruled by Nevsky's son David; it became the most powerful Russian city.
2. The steppe of Russia allowed invaders from Europe and Asia to easily move in; the rivers were used by the Russian people for trade and transportation, uniting the country. However, during a good portion of the year the rivers were frozen and impassable; the harsh climate also made agriculture very difficult.
3. Prince Vladimir I of Kiev ordered his people to convert.
4. They caused many Russians to move northward and become united.

Special Feature Questions
page 121
1. It was bounded on three sides by water; it was at the crossroads between Europe and Asia Minor.
2. It blended Roman, Greek, and eastern architecture. It had magnificent churches (e.g., Hagia Sophia), palaces, and monuments; protective walls; aqueducts; open-air markets; stone mansions and simpler wooden residences; public baths; forums; basilicas; central squares; and an arena, the Hippodrome.

Photo Questions
page 113
Invaders attacked from all sides; religious conflicts; political rivalries for the throne.

page 114
Roads, fortresses, aqueducts, monasteries, and churches.

page 117
To acquire its prosperous trade in the Middle East.

page 119
Empress Theodora.

page 122
It meant more land was controlled by the aristocrats who did not pay their taxes.

page 124
Mosaics.

page 128
Prosperous trade and political power.

page 129
Onion-shaped domes.

page 130
The organization of Russian laws.

page 131
He was declared a saint by the Russian Orthodox Church.

Chapter Review
page 132, Reviewing the Main Ideas
1. It had more people and was richer in economic resources, making it able to withstand invasions.
2. It became the center of Christianity in the east as well as a prosperous city; it became the foundation for a separate empire.
3. The Byzantines stressed the Greek heritage and used Greek ideas in the development of Christianity; it was open to cultural influences from eastern civilizations.
4. Co-ruler.
5. They extended Byzantine rule in the west.

page 133
6. Tensions were increased, causing a rift that lasted hundreds of years.
7. The Fourth Crusade had sapped Constantinople of its trade and wealth; Greeks captured the city and brought the empire to an end.

8. Classical literature, law, and philosophy; manuscript illumination; iconography; mosaics; architecture.
9. West Slavs in east-central Europe; South Slavs in the Balkan Peninsula; East Slavs near the Black Sea.
10. It dominated the north-south water trade route and became the chief political and commercial center of early Russia.
11. Confederation of self-governed principalities that paid tribute to the grand prince of Kiev. Princes were assisted in governing by boyars and veches. In a few northern towns and cities, the veches came close to representational government.
12. He successfully defended Eastern Orthodox Christianity against the Roman Catholic Swedes and Teutonic Knights.

page 133, Discussing Important Ideas
1. Answers may vary, but comparison should be made with the Empire of the West.
2. Answers may vary.
3. Answers may vary, but mention should be made of the role of typical women in the society.
4. Answers may vary depending on the interpretation of power and strength.
5. Answers may vary.
6. Answers may vary.
7. Answers may vary, but there should be reference to the unity of one religion.
8. Answers may vary.

page 133, Using Maps
1. Nine
2. Nine
3. Forums, Hippodrome, aqueduct, roads.
4. Harbor to the southwest; harbor to the southeast; Golden Horn to the north.
5. Walls protected the city and harbors; a chain protected the Golden Horn.

CHAPTER 6
Islam

At the conclusion of this chapter, students should be able to:
1. describe the development and the spread of Islam.
2. explain the Five Pillars of Islam.

3. list the distinguishing characteristics of the Rightly Guided Caliphs, the Umayyads, and the Abbasids.
4. discuss the significant cultural achievements of the Islamic Empire.

Overview

Chapter 6 describes the social and economic conditions that prevailed in Arabia before the rise of Islam. A biographical sketch of Mohammed follows, which explains the role that Mohammed played in the emergence and the spread of Islam. His leadership and political administration in Medina provided the foundation for future Islamic states. The chapter introduces students to Islam by explaining its basic tenets and practices. Covered next are the major accomplishments of the Rightly Guided Caliphs, the Umayyads, and the Abbasids and the territorial expansion that occurred under their rule. The special role of the Arabs in the early period of expansion is identified. The cultural achievements and the organization of Islamic society are detailed in the last section. Important concepts covered in this chapter include blood feuds, the Five Pillars, jihad, caliph, and chronicles.

Teaching Strategies

Section 1

Introduction: Ask students to review the subsection "Invasions" (pp. 114-115) in Chapter 5. Point out that the religion of Islam was in its infancy when Muslims attacked the Byzantine Empire in 634 A.D. to spread their faith and gain new lands. After the Arab conquests in the 670's A.D., the Byzantine Empire was greatly reduced in size. Ask students to use the maps on pages 116 and 143 to identify the Byzantine territories taken over by the Arabs by 750 A.D. Have students read the chapter introduction and section 1.

Development: Have students look at the picture on page 138. Tell them that Muslims generally refrain from depicting the image of Mohammed, although some Muslim artists in Persia and South Asia did incorporate likenesses of the prophet's face in their art work. Today, this practice is still considered objectionable by most Muslims. Review with students the teachings of Mohammed and the important events in his life that led to the establishment of Islam.

Section 2

Introduction: Give students the following quote from the Koran:

> *Say O Mohammed: We believe in God and that which is revealed unto us and that which was revealed unto Abraham, Ishmael, Isaac, Jacob, and the tribes, and that which was vouchsafed [given] unto Moses and Jesus and the Prophets from their Lord. We make no distinction between them and unto Him we have surrendered. (Sura 3:84)*

Ask students what they think the quote reveals about the relationship among Judaism, Christianity, and Islam. (Islam considers the prophets of all three religions to be important, therefore, Muslims should respect the messages from God's prophets, regardless of religious affiliation; it is implied that the three religions worship the same god.) Muslims believe that the three religions represent a series of divine revelations that began in the Old Testament and were completed in the Koran. As students read the section, have them make a list of beliefs that Muslims share with Jews and Christians.

Development: Have students discuss the list of shared beliefs they drew up as they read the section. They may gain more from the discussion if they revise their lists by reviewing Chapter 1, subsection "Hebrews" (pp. 22-25); and Chapter 4, section 5, "Rise of Christianity" (pp. 98-100). Ask students to look at the illustration on page 141 and answer the question regarding the pillars of faith.

Section 3

Introduction: Have students look at the maps on pages 143 and 146 to compare the territorial extent of the three lines of rulers who succeeded Mohammed. Note that in the case of the Abbasid Empire, North Africa and Spain continued to be part of the Muslim world although they remained outside the domain of the Abbasids.

Refer students to the list of English words of Arabic origin on page 142. Point out that these are only a few of the many English words of Arabic origin. Spanish has several hundred.

Development: After reading about the three lines of caliphs, ask students to list the main characteristics of each one and discuss their differences and similarities. Points to consider in the discussion are the ways the lines of caliphs were chosen, the concerns and accomplishments of each, how and why each ended, and the relationship each maintained between Arabs and non-Arabs.

Section 4

Introduction: Have students read the subsection "Islamic Family" on page 147, then express their views regarding the role of women in Arabia before and after the coming of Islam. State that the position of women within their families, in general, reflected the cultural attitudes and values of the people at the time. Women were relegated to an inferior position among Muslims and non-Muslims alike. When Islam emerged, it advanced the status of women and gave them rights that they had not enjoyed before.

Direct students to read the feature "Islamic Medicine" on page 149 and answer the two review questions. As students read the section, they should note the many achievements of the Islamic civilization.

Development: After reading this section, ask students to comment on the role of non-Muslims in furthering literary and scientific achievements in Islamic civilization and on the intellectual freedom and cooperation that these scholars enjoyed throughout most of Islamic rule. The feature "Maimonides" on page 152 is especially relevant. Give special attention to the achievements of Islamic Spain. The nearly 700 years of Islamic rule in the Iberian Peninsula is often treated as a peripheral topic in both Middle Eastern and European histories.

Conclusion: Schools and public libraries usually have numerous sources that contain colorful pictures and informative captions about Islamic accomplishments, particularly in art and architecture. Ask some students to bring a few of these sources to class to be viewed and discussed. Students may also enjoy reading to the class excerpts from Islamic literary works such as the *Rubaiyyat* and *The 1,001 Nights.*

Answers

Section Review Questions

page 139
1. Islam—religion of the Middle East.
   Mecca—religious center; site of the Ka'bah.
   Ka'bah—building containing a black stone; holy to Muslims.
   Mohammed—founder of Islam.
   Allah—god of the Muslims.

Medina—city that became the center of Islam after the Hegira.
   Medina Compact—document written by Mohammed that defined the principles of Islamic life.
2. Unity of language; military and commercial contacts gave Arabs knowledge of the monotheistic religions of Judaism and Christianity.
3. Worship and obey only Allah; prepare for the Day of Judgment. Wealthy merchants and religious leaders rejected it.
4. It marks the beginning of the Muslim era.

page 141
1. Koran—book containing the divine messages received by Mohammed.
   Hadith—book containing the sayings of Mohammed.
   Five Pillars—five essential duties that Muslims should fulfill.
   Ramadan—season of fasting for Muslims.
2. As the final authority of faith and practice for Muslims.
3. It lays down specific rules.
4. At sunrise, noon, afternoon, sunset, and evening.

page 147
1. Abu Bakr—Mohammed's father-in-law, first caliph.
   Rightly Guided Caliphs—first four caliphs of the Islamic state.
   Ali—leader of the Shiites.
   Shiites—Muslim group that believes only members of Mohammed's family can become caliphs.
   Mu'awiya—military leader opposed to Ali.
   Sunnis—Muslim group opposed to the Shiites.
   Umayyad—dynasty founded by Mu'awiya.
   Damascus—capital of Umayyad dynasty.
   Tours—limit of Islamic expansion in the west.
   Abbasids—branch of Mohammed's family; it overthrew the Umayyad dynasty.
   Baghdad—capital of Abbasid dynasty.
2. They viewed their conquests as a holy war, since the Koran taught that to struggle for the faith was a religious duty and that Muslims who died in war gained immediate entry into paradise; Arabs had well-developed warfare skills. Those who surrendered

had to pay taxes; those who resisted lost their land and had to work for the Arabs.

3. Reorganization of government; stressed political rather than religious importance of the caliphate; minted first Arabic currency.
4. Fostered intermingling of cultures between the Arabs and people with whom they had contact.

page 154
1. House of Wisdom—Islamic institute of science under the Abbasids.
   Kalila and Dimna—Arabic collection of animal fables with moral lessons.
   Rubaiyyat—poem by Persian poet Omar Khayyam.
   The 1,001 Nights—collection of stories from Arab, Persian, and Indian life.
   Ibn Khaldun—first Muslim to examine history scientifically.
   Cordoba—capital of Islamic Spain.
   Granada—Muslim territory in Spain.
2. Translated scientific works into Arabic; increased knowledge in mathematics, astronomy, medicine, and chemistry; made practical use of theories; developed algebra, trigonometry, and geography; and established the place-value system of numbers.
3. It was forbidden for artists to make images of living creatures so they developed abstract and geometric designs, such as arabesque.
4. Its poetry, music, and literature were adopted by European Christians.

Special Feature Questions
page 149
1. They based medical treatments on observation; had skills in diagnosing diseases; performed surgery; and founded the science of optics.
2. It formed the basis of European medical practice.

Photo Questions
page 136
Honor, generosity, loyalty, bravery.

page 137
Answers may vary.

page 138
Mecca.

page 139
The Koran.

page 141
Faith, prayer, alms, fasting.

page 148
Conversation, games, music.

page 151
Arab, Persian, Indian.

page 153
Christian, Jewish, Arab.

Chapter Review
page 155, Reviewing the Main Ideas
1. They had a warrior society.
2. Business ties replaced some tribal ties; loyalty to the Islamic community was placed above tribal loyalty; blood feuds were outlawed; centralized political and religious authority.
3. Monotheism, opposition to the worship of idols, social justice, moral values.
4. He was accepted as the messenger of Allah, Islam's lawgiver, and commander in chief.
5. They followed Mohammed's example, were close to the people, and took the advice of other Muslim leaders.
6. Because of the large numbers of converts, the government had less income from taxes with which to pay their increasingly large armies; growing friction between Arab and non-Arab Muslims.
7. Sunnis believed in an elective caliphate; Shiites believed the caliph should be a family member of Mohammed.
8. Under the Rightly Guided Caliphs, the caliph was close to the people; the Umayyad caliphs ruled through a large bureaucracy of non-Muslims; the Abbasid caliphs lived like Persian kings and let the vizier run the empire.
9. Islamic science was based on Greek and Indian traditions; its art was developed from a blend of Persian, Egyptian, and Syrian styles.

page 155, Discussing Important Ideas
1. Answers may vary, but mention should be made of the contact through these trading centers.

2. Answers may vary.
3. Answers may vary.
4. Answers may vary, but mention should be made of the jihad against unbelievers.
5. Answers may vary.
6. Answers may vary.
7. Answers may vary.
8. Answers may vary.
9. Answers may vary, but students should mention that the Koran specifies "men are in charge of women."
10. Answers may vary, but current affairs in the Middle East should be discussed.

page 155, Using Maps
1. It followed the eastern coast of the Red Sea.
2. Umayyad caliphs.
3. Mediterranean, Black, and Caspian Seas.
4. Libya, Egypt, Saudi Arabia, Jordan, Israel, Lebanon, Syria, Iraq, Iran, Afghanistan, Kuwait, Qatar, United Arab Emirates, Oman, Yemen (Aden), Yemen (Sana).

CHAPTER 7
Medieval Europe

At the conclusion of this chapter, students should be able to:
1. describe the social and political structures of European medieval society.
2. identify the impact of the crusades on European economic and cultural developments.
3. explain the role of the Roman Catholic Church in European medieval history.
4. discuss the factors involved in the economic and cultural revival of western Europe during the High Middle Ages.

Overview

Chapter 7 covers nearly seven centuries of medieval European history beginning with the aftermath of the fall of Rome. It explains how the Germanic peoples settled in western and central Europe and the process of their conversion to Roman Catholicism. By the eighth century, a new set of political relationships had emerged called feudalism. Feudalism existed side by side with the manorial system, a socioeconomic system based on the economic self-sufficiency of rural communities.

The chapter describes the role of the Roman Catholic Church in medieval European society and the part it played in the revival of European culture after the tenth century. In the last section, the rise of monarchies in France, England, and central Europe is explained. Other important concepts are the Middle Ages, vassals, guilds, universities, scholasticism, and common law.

Teaching Strategies
Section 1

Introduction: The Middles Ages in Europe is known as the medieval period, from the Latin for "middle" and "age." Write on the chalkboard:

Early Middle Ages ("Dark Ages")	High Middle Ages	Late Middle Ages
500-1000 A.D.	1000-1300 A.D.	1300-1500 A.D.

Explain that this chapter deals with the early and High Middle Ages. The late Middle Ages is covered in Chapter 10. Point out that "Dark Ages" is being discarded by historians as an appropriate label for the early Middle Ages. Instead, it is important for students to recognize that despite the decline of the Roman Empire of the West and the Germanic invasions, western Europe combined Greco-Roman culture, Christianity, and Germanic culture into a new, progressive civilization that prepared the way for modern western civilization. Ask students to keep these three elements in mind as they read the section.

After reading the subsection "Conversion of Europe" on pages 157 and 158, ask students to evaluate and discuss the work of missionaries in Europe during the sixth and seventh centuries A.D. What types of persons were they? What motivated them? How did their work affect medieval society?

Development: Point out that the coronation of Charlemagne as Roman emperor by the Pope angered the Byzantine emperor and heightened tension between Constantinople and Rome. Also, Charlemagne exchanged missions and gifts with the Abbasid caliph Harun al-Rashid (p. 145), who fought intermittent wars against the Byzantines. If students were in the place of Charlemagne's descendants, would they have opted for the division of the Frankish empire among themselves or for keeping it unified under one of them? Refer to the maps on page 160 in the text.

Ask students to study the map on page 161 until they can trace the invasion routes on another map of the region. Have students look at the illustration on page 162 and answer the caption question.

Section 2

Introduction: Bring a chess game to the class and display its pieces. Tell students that after reading the section, they will be able to identify the relationship between the game and medieval society in terms of roles, duties, and power.

Development: Use colorful pictures or slides of medieval castles to discuss their purposes in feudal life. Have students refer to the illustration on page 165 and explain how manorialism worked. Divide the class into one or more sets of medieval peasants, priests, artisans, knights, nobles, bishops, a king and a queen, and others. Have the students within each set develop a short play that would involve all the roles represented in their set.

Section 3

Introduction: To introduce this section, ask students to read the section introduction on pages 166 and 168 and the feature "Cathedral Architecture" on page 167.

Development: This section covers a period during which the power of the Roman Catholic Church reached a new height. Point out that the ultimate authority of the Church was its administration of the sacraments. Withholding the sacraments meant a person was cut off from society. Marriage, ownership of land, bearing arms, and communication with friends became impossible. For a king, as in the case of Henry IV (p. 168), his subjects would be free to refuse payment of taxes, serve in his army, and defy his orders. Being cut off from the Church meant eternal damnation. Popes used their power to extend their authority over European rulers and to stamp out resistance. Ask students to discuss the impact of papal power on the political developments of medieval Europe.

When discussing the crusades review with students the actions of the Fourth Crusade, described in Chapter 5 (pp. 117-118). Stress the significance of the crusades in promoting changes in medieval Europe.

Section 4

Introduction: Read to students selections from *The Canterbury Tales, Beowulf,* or other medieval works. Ask them to describe medieval life as they perceive it through this literature. Divide them into two groups, one advocating literature in vernacular languages and the other favoring writing in a universal language such as Latin. As they read the section, have them develop arguments to defend their group's position.

Development: Ask students if they are familiar with unions in their state. Have them find out the requirements of becoming a practicing plumber or electrician. Draw an analogy between this process and the medieval guilds. In fact, most craft unions today use the same terms of apprentice, journeyman, and master that were used by the medieval guilds.

Section 5

Introduction: Have students read the feature "Eleanor of Aquitaine" on page 176. Point out that the duchy of Aquitaine was the size of a small kingdom. Eleanor governed her domain with great political skill.

Development: After reading the section have students make a list comparing the important accomplishments, the political institutions, and the relationships among nobles, clergy, and townspeople of the French and English monarchs and the Holy Roman Emperors between the tenth and early fourteenth centuries. It was once said that the Holy Roman Empire was neither Roman nor holy. Have students speculate on the reasons for such a statement.

Conclusion: Write on the chalkboard: *Greco-Roman culture, Christianity, Germanic culture.* Out of these traditions grew a new western European civilization. Have students list the new ideas, institutions, social groups, and other features that developed in medieval Europe. Ask them to assign these to the appropriate traditions on the board. Do students agree with modern historians that the "Dark Ages" is an inappropriate term for the Middle Ages? Discuss.

Answers
Section Review Questions

page 161

1. Benedict—Roman official who established a monastery in Italy and wrote a set of rules for monks.

    Gregory I—Pope; he sent missionaries to northern and eastern Europe; organized churches of the Franks.

Clovis—Frankish king; first Germanic ruler to accept Roman Catholicism.

Charles Martel—led the Franks to victory against the Muslims in the Battle of Tours.

Battle of Tours—blocked Muslim expansion in Europe.

Pepin—son of Charles Martel, king of the Franks; he created close ties with the papacy.

Charlemagne—son of Pepin, king of the Franks; was the first important western monarch.

Treaty of Verdun—divided Charlemagne's empire among his three grandsons.

Alfred the Great—English king; he defeated the Danes and united England.

Holy Roman Empire—consisted of Germany and northern Italy.

Hugh Capet—noble who seized the throne of France from the Carolingians.

2. They ensured the survival of western learning; became centers of Christian living; spread Christianity throughout Europe by means of missionary work.

3. He relied on counts for local administration; royal envoys annually checked the counts' performance.

4. It was divided among three grandsons.

page 166
1. Ties of loyalty and duty among nobles, landholding, and local rule.
2. They provided military service, gave advice at the lord's court, and contributed money.
3. They supplied food and other services that enabled the nobles to fight wars.
4. New farming methods that increased the productivity of the land.

page 172
1. Cluny—site of Benedictine monastery.

Gregory VII—Pope; he attacked the practice of lay investiture of church officials.

Henry IV—Holy Roman Emperor; had conflict with Gregory VII.

Canossa—site where Henry IV and Gregory VII met.

Innocent III—Pope; declared that the Pope was the final authority in the Christian world.

Albigensians—group of heretics in southern France.

Inquisition—court of the Church; established to punish heretics.

Francis of Assisi—founder of the Franciscan order of friars.

Urban II—Pope; pronounced the First Crusade.

"Crusade of Kings"—Third Crusade.

Acre—last Christian stronghold in Palestine.

2. To give the Pope complete jurisdiction over all church officials.
3. Two orders of friars.
4. To free Christian shrines from Turkish rule; an opportunity to escape problems, seek adventure, or gain wealth.

page 175
1. Flanders—region on northwestern coast of Europe; area of leading centers of trade.

Champagne—site of most famous trade fair; served as the crossroads of Europe.

Bologna—site in Italy of model school of law.

Peter Abelard—writer and teacher of theology; he had students use logical thinking.

Thomas Aquinas—most important writer and thinker of the 1400's A.D.

Song of Roland—most famous French epic poem; written about 1110 A.D.

Dante Alighieri—Italian writer of narrative poetry in the vernacular; he wrote *Divine Comedy*.

Geoffrey Chaucer—English writer of *Canterbury Tales*.

2. Walled, had crowded wooden buildings that extended over narrow, unpaved streets.
3. They represented members of a trade or business; set standards, prices, and wages.
4. It sought to reconcile classical philosophy with church teachings.

page 179
1. Philip Augustus—Philip II of France; he increased the size and power of the monarchy.

Louis IX—king of France; he established the monarchy as the source of national unity.

Philip IV—Philip the Fair; he laid the foundations for national unity in France.

Battle of Hastings—battle in which English king Harold was defeated by William of Normandy.

William I—William "the Conqueror" of England.

Domesday Book—1086 A.D. census figures of the people of England.

Henry I—king of England; he established a court system and bureaucracy.

Exchequer—department set up to handle royal finances in England.

Henry II—king of England; reformed English judiciary system.

Magna Charta—it placed limits on royal power in England.

Model Parliament—set up a system of representation for all classes in England.

Frederick Barbarossa—Holy Roman Emperor; he tried to restore the emperors' authority and the empire's unity.

2. They established a central government, a court system, and the Estates-General.
3. There was a system of circuit courts, an established common law, and trial by jury.
4. A power struggle with the papacy; each domain was ruled as an independent state.

Photo Questions

page 158
Operated schools; cared for the poor; introduced new farming methods; ensured the survival of western learning.

page 159
Encouraged formation of schools; promoted use of a common language; created a Christian Roman Empire.

page 162
They caused suffering, lost population, economic collapse, which led to the development of the social organization of feudalism.

page 169
They helped break down feudalism; many serfs were able to buy their freedom; brought Europe out of isolation; opened new trade routes; improved living standards.

page 173
People recognized the importance of working together to better their lives.

page 175
It was written in the vernacular about typical people of the period.

page 178
A king could no longer collect taxes without representation; the right to trial and to a jury of peers; the king was also bound to the law.

page 179
He forced the nobles to swear allegiance to him; he tried to regain control of northern Italy. No.

Chapter Review

page 180, Reviewing the Main Ideas
1. It established schools, hospitals, and farms. Spread ideas and improved tools through its missionaries. Use of a common language helped preserve and spread a common set of ideas.
2. Encouraged the formation of schools; gathered scholars from every part of Europe to preserve and consolidate learning.

page 181
3. Protection from internal feuding and invasions from the north and east.
4. They had few rights and were only expected to raise children and care for the household.
5. To free Christian shrines from the Seljuks and remove their threat to the Byzantine Empire.
6. Many serfs gained their freedom; kings increased their authority; they opened new trade routes; improved European standards of living because of new knowledge.
7. New farming techniques opened up new land; towns grew in size and number; trade fairs made luxury goods available; rise of a money economy led to a banking system.
8. To establish standards of production; set prices, wages, and employment practices.
9. City dwellers resented paying taxes and services to lords who did nothing for the towns.
10. Students and teachers started meeting apart from the monastery and cathedral schools to teach secular subjects. They acquired new knowledge of the physical world that led to the rise of western science.
11. Epic poems that celebrated the heroes of the past, romances, political satires, and tales of everyday people written in the vernacular.
12. In France: a central government, the royal right to mint coins, new court of justice system, formation of the Estates-General. In England: formation of a parliamentary advisory body, trial by jury, and a court system of justice. Throughout Europe a system of government bureaucracy.

page 181, Discussing Important Ideas
1. Answers may vary.
2. Answers may vary; mention should be made that the means of paying for knights in medieval times was from loot gathered

during battles versus paying for soldiers from taxes in modern times.
3. Answers may vary.
4. Answers may vary.
5. Answers may vary.
6. Answers may vary.
7. Answers may vary.
8. Answers may vary; mention should be made of the limitation of local goods compared with the variety of goods available from distant trade.
9. Answers may vary.
10. Answers may vary.

page 181, Using Maps
1. First, second, third, fourth.
2. One. The first.
3. Third. Began in England and France, ended in Tyre.
4. Europe, Africa, Asia. Europe, Asia.
5. About 1,125 miles. About 1,800 kilometers.

CHAPTER 8
Africa and the Americas

At the conclusion of this chapter, students should be able to:
1. explain the influence of the environment on the histories of early Africa and pre-Columbian America.
2. describe the outstanding features and accomplishments of the African states of Kush, Axum, Ghana, Mali, and Songhai.
3. describe the cultural diversity and lifestyles of native North Americans before the coming of the Europeans.
4. list the major achievements of the Maya, the Toltecs, the Aztecs, and the Inca.

Overview

Sections 1 and 2 of Chapter 8 describe the rise of early Sub-Saharan African civilizations through medieval times. African kingdoms and empires developed in the eastern part of the continent in ancient times and in the western part during the Middle Ages. Both regions maintained trade relations with neighboring states. Sections 3 and 4 cover historical and cultural developments in the Americas before the coming of the Europeans. Emphasis is on the cultures of North America and on the history and achievements in Central and South America. Concepts covered in the chapter include oral tradition, "Dark Continent," Bantu, culture area, and potlatch.

Teaching Strategies
Section 1
Introduction: Explain to students why Africa was known as the "Dark Continent" as late as the early twentieth century. Refer students to the map on page 184. Tell them to use the map as they read about the geographic and environmental factors that limited African contact with other parts of the world.

Development: Ask students if they think Herodotus had ever been in the interior of Africa. Explain that he was conveying misconceptions, just as the old Tarzan movies did. Were students surprised to learn about the accomplishments of early African civilizations? Point out that one modern archeologist has described the ancient city of Meroë as having been the Birmingham of Africa. Mention also that East Africa and southwestern Arabia had a long history of extensive interactions.

Have students discuss common reasons for human migrations and compare their statements with reasons for the Bantu migrations described on page 186.

Section 2
Introduction: Ask students to study the map on page 190 and to point out the geographic extent of the empires of Ghana, Mali, and Songhai. In what part of Africa were these civilizations located (West Africa)? As students read the section, ask them to list the major features of these empires and compare the reasons for their decline. Before students go on to the subsection "East and South Africa" (p. 190), have them read the feature "Timbuktu" on page 191 and answer its review questions.

Development: Refer students to the photo on page 192 and have them answer the caption question about Karanga's decline. This would be a good time to ask students to do the Using Maps skill on page 203.

Section 3
Introduction: Have students examine the map on page 199. Ask them how they think the Americas were originally populated. Discuss

their ideas and then explain the land bridge migration described on page 193. Most scholars agree that the Bering Strait was the major, if not the only, entry point. However, trans-Pacific migrations have not been ruled out. Tell students to look for the diversity of Indian life as they read the section. A common misconception about American Indians is that they speak the same languages and have the same customs and lifestyles.

Development: Divide students into six groups corresponding to the culture areas described in the text. Assign each group a tribe in its culture area to research. Group members will research different aspects of the tribe's culture, such as food-gathering activities, housing, social customs, and government organization. These categories should be decided on at the beginning so that each group will research the same ones, thus permitting comparison. Each group will make a presentation, to be followed by a discussion focusing on the similarities and differences among the tribes. (Note that culture area is a term geared more to geographic similarity than to cultural similarity. For example, Pueblo tribes had a quite different lifestyle from most Apache groups, yet, because they resided in the same general geographic area, they were assigned to the same culture area.)

Section 4

Introduction: Have students discuss the geography of Central and South America and compare it to that of North America. They may use the map on page 199 to aid their discussion.

Development: Ask students to make a bulletin board display depicting the cultural achievements of the Maya, the Aztecs, and the Inca. The display should include a comparison of their religions and societies.

Conclusion: Organize a panel discussion on the meaning of culture and the diversity of cultural patterns that one finds when studying the early cultures and civilizations of Africa and the Americas. Have students speculate on the reasons for such diversity (history, external contacts and influence, the environment, etc.).

Answers
Section Review Questions

page 187
1. Sahara—desert in North Africa.

Sub-Saharan Africa—region south of the Sahara Desert.
Kush—territory in the southern part of the Nile River.
Napata—old capital of Kush.
Meroë—new capital of Kush.
Axum—territory in northeastern Africa.
Ezana—king of Axum.
Ethiopia—mountainous area in the interior of East Africa.
Nok—earliest culture in Sub-Saharan Africa.
Bantu—peoples of Sub-Saharan Africa; their language.
2. It was cut off from outsiders by natural barriers; there were few written records of early cultures.
3. Kushites developed iron tools and weapons. Axum's control of trade routes linked European and Asian cultures to Africa.
4. Bantu villages comprised of several families. The family included all descendants from one set of grandparents. The village was ruled by a chief and a council of elders.

page 192
1. Mandingo—people of Mali.
Sundiata Keita—king of Mali.
Mansa Musa—Mali's greatest ruler.
Timbuktu—capital of Mali.
Sunni Ali—king of Songhai.
Mohammed Askia—Songhai king; he extended kingdom to greatest extent.
Kilwa—East African city-state.
Swahili—language of East Africans.
Karanga—Bantu kingdom; its people built the Great Zimbabwe.
2. Because of their location at the center of trade routes between North and West Africa.
3. Merchants preached Islam and won converts; developed a civilization that blended Islamic and African traditions; language contained many Persian and Arabic words.
4. Because of the Indian Ocean trade routes and rich mineral resources.

page 196
1. Native Americans—American Indians.
Bering Strait—covers the original land bridge between Asia and the Americas.
Pueblo Indians—group of Southwest Indian tribes.
Apache—nomadic hunters and gatherers of the Southwest.

Navajo—nomadic hunters and gatherers of the Southwest.

Mound Builders—groups of Indians of the Ohio and Mississippi River Valleys.

League of the Iroquois—league of five Indian tribes formed around 1400 A.D.; its purpose was to maintain peace.

2. They adapted to the environment of the area in which they settled and developed a variety of cultures and civilizations.

3. They raised crops of maize, beans, cotton, sweet potatoes, and pumpkins; settled permanent villages.

4. Arctic and Far North: consisted of small nomadic bands without official leaders; Northwest: settled in villages and based their rank on wealth and prestige; California-Great Basin: settled in small villages along the coast, or became nomadic groups in the inland desert; Southwest: developed multistoried buildings in large villages, or became nomadic hunters; Great Plains: built villages along the rivers and raised crops; men were warriors and hunted the buffalo; Eastern Woodlands: farmed the land and fished. In many ways, including languages, social organization, religion, government.

page 202

1. Olmecs—earliest civilization in Mexico.
La Venta—site of Olmec ceremonial center.
Maya—civilization in southern Mexico and Central America.
Tikal—largest Mayan city.
Toltecs—earliest civilization in Central America.
Teotihuacán—Indian city in central Mexico.
Tula—Toltec capital.
Aztecs—people of northern and central Mexico.
Tenochtitlán—Aztec city.
Lake Texcoco—site of Tenochtitlán.
Montezuma I—Aztec emperor.
Sun Stone—Aztec calendar stone.
Inca—civilization in the Andes.
Pachacuti—first great Inca emperor.
Cuzco—Inca capital.

2. Skilled in mathematics and astronomy; developed a writing system.

3. Polytheism; gods and goddesses related to farming, nature, and war.

4. By an emperor and his officials; nobles were appointed to administer the provinces.

Special Feature Questions

page 191

1. It was ideal for communications and trade.
2. Overthrown by Moroccans; a series of Berber invasions; famine and epidemics.

Photo Questions

page 185
That the Sahara was once a well-watered grassland.

page 186
Muslim expansion in surrounding territories weakened the kingdom. King Ezana.

page 187
A chief and a council of elders.

page 188
Metalwork, cloth, salt, dried fruits, tools.

page 189
Gold, iron, copper.

page 192
Civil wars, arrival of Europeans.

page 194
Severe climate prevented raising of crops.

page 195
Irrigation, pottery, cloth, adobe houses.

page 195
Snowshoes.

page 198
They were centers of religious ceremonies.

page 201
They cut terraces in hillsides; used irrigation; built fertile artificial islands.

Chapter Review

page 203, Reviewing the Main Ideas

1. Metalworking, iron production, farming skills.
2. Adopted skills and customs from contact with Egypt, Rome, early Christianity, Islam.
3. Carried knowledge of iron tools, agricultural skills, and domestic animals with them; developed a common language.
4. Used myths and legends to explain and interpret the meaning of life, recognized a supreme god and a number of lesser deities.

5. Trade, gold, control of trade routes.
6. Across a land bridge between Siberia and Alaska.
7. Mexican Indians planted and improved the quality of maize. Many others settled in villages and grew crops of beans, squash, pumpkins, cotton, sweet potatoes. Farming spread to other areas.
8. Pueblos lived in cities, farmed, made pottery, and wove cloth. Plains Indians planted crops; then, in summer left to hunt the buffalo. In fall they returned to harvest crops and prepare the buffalo meat and hides.
9. A league composed of representatives from five tribes. To resolve problems and maintain peace.
10. Religion was the center of Indian life; it affected all aspects of farming, war, art, and architecture.
11. Extensive trade routes were established; goods were carried over land and water.
12. They promoted unity, allowed food distribution, trade, and communication.

page 203, Discussing Important Ideas
1. Answers may vary; mention should be made of geography of the specific area.
2. Answers may vary; mention should be made of immigration and conquests.
3. Answers may vary; mention should be made of cultural exchange.
4. Answers may vary.
5. Answers may vary; contrast should be made between specific cultural groups.
6. Answers may vary.
7. Answers may vary.

page 203, Using Maps
1. About 3,000 miles. About 4,800 kilometers.
2. About 10°S, 40°E.
3. Coastal lowlands, savanna.
4. Because the major area of the continent lies within the tropic zone.
5. On a major river, easy access to the Sudan on the west, and the Red Sea on the east.

Unit Review

page 204, Developing Understanding
1. Byzantine art, ideas, and practices spread to neighboring countries and helped shape their development by preserving Greek philosophy and literature, Roman political and legal ideas, and Christian theology.

2. The Roman Catholic Church was the center of life for western Europeans, as Islam was for the Islamic Empire. Unlike the popes, Islamic religious leaders also held the political power in the empire. Therefore, while the politics of western European kingdoms was sometimes affected by the political wishes of the Pope, politics in Muslim countries was always affected by religious leaders.
3. They embittered relations with the Byzantine and Muslim worlds.
4. Economy: Byzantine Empire: depended on trade. Western Europe: based on agriculture; later was stimulated by trade. Islamic Empire: urban society based on trade of goods and scientific advances. Sub-Saharan Africa: depended primarily on the gold trade, but iron, copper, and wooden carved figures were also in demand by traders. The Americas: farming, hunting, and gathering were prevalent. Technology: Byzantine Empire: based on city life to accommodate trading interests in the Mediterranean Sea and the east. Western Europe: new plow that had a mould-board; three-field system of crop rotation. Islamic Empire: built roads to expand trade routes and communication; developed the arts, science, and medicine in the cities. Sub-Saharan Africa: metalworking skills. The Americas: basket weaving, irrigation systems, pottery, snowshoes, terraces cut into the hills, built artificial islands of fertile land.

pages 204-205, Developing Skills
Conclude the unit with the Developing Skills activity. This activity is best suited to individuals, followed by group discussion. The exercise is designed to help students understand and become sensitive to cultural bias.

Analysis of the reading is aided by several questions. It may be useful to go over the questions with the class before assigning the written exercise. Answers to the questions are as follows:
1. One of the crusaders sat in the chair reserved for the Basileus. According to custom, vassals did not sit in the same chairs as lords.
2. From the crusader's point of view, it was rude for the Basileus to sit while others had to stand.
3. Each side felt that the other showed lack of respect.

UNIT 3
Early Modern Times

At the conclusion of this unit, students should be able to:
1. outline the early history of the Ottoman, Mongol, Mogul, and Chinese empires.
2. explain the origins of modern Japan.
3. list the main developments in the history of Renaissance Europe from 1300 to 1600.
4. discuss the principal leaders and ideas that led to the Reformation.
5. identify the major discoveries of the Portuguese, Spanish, Italian, French, English and Dutch explorers and explain how they promoted European expansion into Asia, the New World, and Africa.

Overview

Unit 3 surveys early modern times in Europe and Asia from about 1000 to the mid-1700's. Chapter 9 introduces students to the history of the leading empires of Asia. Chapter 10 describes the European Renaissance. Chapter 11 covers the Reformation, the term applied to the movement for church reform in the 1500's that resulted in the birth of Protestantism. Chapter 12 discusses the principal voyages of discovery of the late 1400's and early 1500's, and the subsequent rivalry among European nations to colonize the newly discovered lands.

Introducing the Unit

Emphasize to students that the cultural achievements of the early empires of Asia rivaled, if not surpassed, those of medieval Europe. Ask students what elements of the Renaissance and Reformation still affect our daily lives, such as styles of architecture and important works of literature. Perhaps the most obvious result of the Reformation was the development of many church denominations out of the original Catholic and Greek Orthodox churches of medieval times. Ask students to name some explorers of the 1400's-1600's and the lands they discovered. Have them speculate on why this unit signals modern times.

CHAPTER 9
Asian Empires

At the conclusion of this chapter, students should be able to:
1. describe how the peoples and cultures of eastern Europe, the Middle East, and eastern Asia were transformed by the invasions of the Seljuk Turks, the Mongols, and the Ottoman Turks.
2. describe the rise of the Islamic Mogul Empire in India and its culture.
3. review the major features of Chinese civilization under the T'ang, Song, Mongol, and Ming dynasties.
4. discuss the changes in political organization that occurred in Japan during the Heian, Kamakura, and Ashikaga periods.

Overview

This chapter introduces students to the important central Asian tribes and rulers whose conquests influenced the course of European history. Students will learn how Turkish Muslim invaders from central Asia seized control of India and formed the Mogul Empire. Finally, students will be introduced to the rich cultures of China, Japan, and Korea. Some important concepts in the chapter include millet, isolationism, abdication, shogunate, Zen, and bushido.

Teaching Strategies
Section 1

Introduction: Explain to students that one of the most important differences between our style of life and the lifestyle of Asian peoples in medieval and early modern times was the presence of large numbers of nomads. Point out that in an environment where rainfall is scarce, nomadism is one of the most efficient means of raising animal herds.

Development: Historians are not in full agreement about why nomads from the steppes of Asia periodically moved into the settled farming regions of Persia, Mesopotamia, southern Russia, and Asia Minor, but students should be asked to consider the importance of overpopulation on the steppe and the effect on the flocks of years of drought. Prominent leaders united the tribes periodically and attacked the settled lands, for reasons of trade or encroachment on their territories by farmers. These events have parallels in the settling of the American West.

The Ottoman Turks appear in Asia Minor as a settled group after much of this region had become Turkish-speaking and Muslim under the Seljuks. It is important to emphasize that they built a strong bureaucratic empire based on cities and farming communities and that they discouraged nomadism.

Have students review the chart on page 211 before they study the map on page 214. Ask volunteers to outline the major steps that resulted in the territorial expansion indicated on the map.

Section 2

Introduction: Give students an outline map of India to mark up as they read the section. They should indicate the areas under Turkish or Mogul rule from the early 700's to 1707 (see map p. 215). Point out the efforts of Mogul rulers to establish a united empire and culture.

Development: Have each student make a chronological list of the religions that were practiced in India between about 800 B.C. and the 1600's A.D. Students should base their lists on the information in this section and on pages 36-42 in Chapter 2. Ask them to discuss the differences among Indian ruling groups regarding toleration for other religions. Who was the most lenient? the most repressive?

Section 3

Introduction: Agriculture in China was based on two large rivers and their accompanying irrigation systems. In his book *Oriental Despotism*, Karl Wittfogel connects autocratic government in China to the necessity of maintaining food production by keeping dikes and canals in repair. Another important element contributing to rule by one person was the practice of selecting, through a stiff examination system, a bureaucracy to aid the emperor or empress. A third element was China's constant exposure to invasions from the steppe. The Great Wall was built to keep out such nomads as the Turks and Mongols. Ask students to discuss these ideas after they read the section.

The feature "Chinese Landscape Painting" on page 219 may be read after the subsection "The Song" (pp. 220-221). The feature "Ibn Battuta" on page 212 may be read earlier in conjunction with sections 1 or 2, or following the discussion of Marco Polo on page 222.

Development: Tell students that before Genghis Khan and his sons conquered China, the Khitay (hence the word Cathay), also of Mongol origin, took control of northern China from the 900's to the 1100's. Mongol rule was a direct result of the superior military strength and organization of the Mongols. Ask students to point out the benefits to China of the Mongol period of rule. Stress the continuity of Chinese society despite dynastic changes. The Using Maps exercise (p. 229) is based on the map of Asian empires on page 223. It may be assigned at this time.

Section 4

Introduction: Have students examine a physical map of Japan. Ask how Japan's geography affected its history. (The islands of Japan made it possible for the Japanese to avoid nomad incursions, but political unity was hampered greatly by the mountainous terrain. For this reason, much of the political history of early Japan is dominated by feudal warfare.)

Development: Have students compare Japanese feudalism to European feudalism. They should consider the codes of honor, the loyalty oaths, and the roles of peasants, landowners, warriors, and rulers.

Have students observe the location of Korea on a map of Asia. Why was Korea often the object of conquest for both China and Japan? Students will need to skim sections 3 and 4 to answer this question.

Conclusion: Have students develop a chart or bulletin board display comparing and contrasting the political, economic, social, and cultural life of China under the T'ang, Song, Mongol, and Ming dynasties. This activity can be adapted for use with the other major civilizations covered in this section.

Answers
Section Review Questions
page 215
1. Seljuk Turks—steppe people who moved into Persia and the Middle East.
    Manzikert—battle site where Seljuks defeated the Byzantines.
    Mongols—people native to the Asian steppe north of the Gobi desert.

Genghis Khan—founder of the Mongol Empire.

Batu—grandson of Genghis Khan; founder of the Golden Horde, the Mongol dominion in Russia.

Helagu—grandson of Genghis Khan; founder of the Ilkhan Mongol dominion in Persia.

Ottoman Turks—Turkish clans who settled in Asia Minor; founders of the Ottoman Empire.

Kossovo—battle site where the Ottomans defeated Serbia.

Janissaries—Balkan Christian youths selected to serve Ottoman rulers, usually as soldiers.

Tamerlane—Turkish-Mongol chief; extended Mongol rule over much of the Middle East.

Lepanto—naval victory of western Europeans over the Ottomans.

Suleiman I—ruler of the Ottoman Empire during its most powerful phase.

Ulema—Islamic law administrators.

Istanbul—previous Byzantine city of Constantinople.

2. By gaining control over main trade routes; invasion.

3. Local rulers became increasingly independent and developed separate domains.

4. The sultan had absolute power, he was assisted by a grand vizier who headed the bureaucracy.

page 217

1. Delhi—capital of Turkish sultanate in India.

Mogul—Muslim nomadic warriors who overthrew Delhi sultanate.

Babur—founder of Mogul dynasty in India.

Akbar—grandson of Babur; noted for his wise rule and tolerance of other religious beliefs.

Taj Mahal—mausoleum built by Shah Jahan as a memorial to his wife.

Urdu—new language in India developed under the Moguls; included many Persian and Arabic words.

Sikhs—followers of a religion that believed in one god like the Muslims, and reincarnation like the Hindus.

Gura Nanak—founder of the Sikhs.

Aurangzeb—Mogul ruler who oppressed Hindus.

2. As a false religion because of its many gods.

3. He extended the Mogul's rule over all of India; reformed the government; tried to unite Hindus and Muslims.

4. Brought a cultural awakening in science, art, architecture, and literature by introducing Persian and Arabic styles.

page 224

1. Sui—dynasty that reunited China.

T'ang—dynasty that reestablished the Chinese Empire.

Wu—T'ang empress who sought to reduce the size of mandarin estates.

Li Po—famous poet of the T'ang era.

Tu Fu—famous poet of the T'ang era.

Song—dynasty noted for its peace and public works.

Wang An-Shih—reformer who wished to change the state examinations from the knowledge of classical writings to practical problems.

Jurchen—nomadic people who conquered northern China.

Kublai Khan—grandson of Genghis Khan, ruler of Mongol China.

Cambuluc—Mongol capital.

Marco Polo—member of an Italian merchant family; traveled to China in the 1270's.

Hung-wu—Buddhist monk who overthrew the Mongols; he established the Ming dynasty.

Ming—Chinese dynasty that lasted from 1368 to 1644.

Beijing—Chinese name for Cambuluc.

Forbidden City—imperial court, a complex of palaces in the center of Beijing.

Manchus—group who invaded China from the north.

2. They reestablished the examination system to select officials; organized bureaucrats into ranks.

3. T'ang: block printing, scholarly works, poetry, fine porcelain, landscape printing, calligraphy. Song: irrigation ditches and canals, compass, gunpowder, landscape painting.

4. Under the Mongols foreign contacts were increased. The Ming established a strong navy and sponsored sea explorations.

page 228

1. Heian—first capital of Japan.

Fujiwara—family of Japanese nobles who controlled the emperor and usurped his power.

The Tale of Genji—by Lady Murasaki; probably the world's first novel.

Kamakura—town in eastern Japan that became the seat of the first shogunate.

Taira—one of the court families hoping to succeed to the power of the Fujiwara.

Minamoto Yoritomo—founder of the shogunate in Kamakura.

Dannoura—sea battle in which the Minamoto defeated Taira.

Hojo—family that succeeded Yoritomo in Kamakura.

Zen—form of Buddhism that stressed harmony with nature.

Ashikaga Takauji—he established a new military government in Kyoto.

Noh—form of drama used to teach Buddhist ideas.

Choson—dynasty that came to power in Korea in 1392.

2. He established the shogunate, a form of military government peculiar to Japan.
3. It developed a feudal economy; the Ashikaga promoted regional specialization; introduced copper coins instead of barter.
4. The Choson centralized the government; introduced a new alphabet, civil service examinations, and Confucian teachings.

Special Feature Questions

page 219
1. Ink and brush.
2. By making human figures small.

Photo Questions

page 210
Meat and mare's milk.

page 216
Miniature paintings.

page 217
By Shah Jahan to honor his wife.

page 218
Empress Wu.

page 222
Glass, hides, honey, slaves, clothes, silver, cotton, carpets.

page 227
Ikebana, landscape gardening.

Chapter Review

page 229, Reviewing the Main Ideas
1. They gained control of the main trade routes and used its wealth to build an empire.
2. As nomadic herders.
3. They allowed non-Muslims to practice their faith in return for payment of a tax.
4. Inflation, increased population, war on two fronts, civil war.
5. To combine the best from all religions and unify the religious communities.
6. Brief moments of intense feelings caused by the sight of natural beauty.
7. Many believed the government and society were too rigid.
8. It broke with past traditions and developed new styles.
9. It provided Europeans with their first real information about the Far East.
10. Political corruption, internal disorder, invasions.
11. By marrying their daughters into the royal family, guiding court affairs through child emperors.
12. Through the shogun; military government.

page 229, Discussing Important Ideas
1. Answers may vary; mention should be made of the growing population.
2. Answers may vary.
3. Answers may vary; mention should be made of the power of the grand vizier.
4. Answers may vary.
5. Answers may vary.
6. Answers may vary; mention should be made of the rigidity of traditional practices.
7. Answers will vary; mention should be made of the advanced civilization of China compared with that of Europe.
8. Answers may vary.
9. Answers may vary.
10. Because it closed off all contact with foreign lands.

page 229, Using Maps
1. West. Northwest.
2. Northern. Eastern.
3. Southeastern.
4. Caspian.
5. About 2,750 miles. About 4,400 kilometers.

CHAPTER 10
Decline and Renaissance

At the conclusion of this chapter, students should be able to:

1. explain why European civilization declined in late medieval times.
2. analyze the revival of monarchies in France, England, Spain, Germany, eastern Europe, and Scandinavia.
3. discuss the causes and accomplishments of the Italian Renaissance.
4. trace the spread of the Renaissance spirit and its ideas into France, Germany, the Netherlands, and England.

Overview

This chapter introduces students to three major developments in the history of western Europe during the time span of 1300 to 1600: the social and political problems in late medieval times, the decline of feudalism and the emergence of strong royal governments in major states of Europe, and finally, the powerful impact of the Renaissance. Important concepts include humanism, balance of power, the humanities, and perspective.

Teaching Strategies
Section 1

Introduction: Remind students of the relative orderliness of feudal society—the nobility and landowners served the king; the peasants, merchants, and artisans performed their tasks; and the Church administered the sacraments. The purpose of this section is to explain why this system proved inadequate. Tell students to read the section to find reasons why the system broke down. However, be sure to point out that as the old system was crumbling, new forces were emerging to create a new Europe.

Development: Ask students what happens to a family living in a small house or apartment when the family grows larger or when relatives move in. Contrast this overcrowded dwelling situation with an overcrowded town in terms of law and order, public health, and food supplies.

Students should be asked to explain how each division of society broke down in the Late Middle Ages. (Among the reasons: the peasantry because of poor soil and farming techniques, and large families; the townspeople because of overcrowding, diseases, and lack of regional specialization; the monarchs, the nobility, and the clergy because of the poverty of their subjects and abuse of them, and a constant desire for wealth resulting in continual warfare. Squabbles over the authority of monarchs and clergy confused the loyalties of the common people.)

Ask students to explain the significance of the Babylonian Captivity and the Great Schism. Have them look at the photo on page 235 and answer the question about Pope Urban VI.

Section 2

Introduction: This section examines the resurgence of monarchy in the Late Middle Ages. Under the feudal system, monarchs were quite weak because provincial dukes and bishops possessed their own armies and collected their own taxes. Ask students to consider how difficult it would be for the government in Washington, D.C., if all the state governors and church leaders collected their own taxes and possessed their own armies. Assign the section.

Development: In this section, it is important for students to learn how the monarchs of Europe increased their power over nobles and church leaders. Provide students with a chart similar to the following, and have them fill in the blanks:

Country	Methods Used to Increase Royal Power
France	taxes imposed and standing army created during Hundred Years' War quarrels encouraged between Burgundy and Swiss treaties and marriages
England	
Spain	
Austria	
Poland	
Hungary	
Scandinavia	

Section 3

Introduction: At first the concept of Renaissance, or "rebirth," may seem obscure to students. Tell them that the Renaissance was a period of transition between medieval and modern times. Ask them to read the section and compare life during the Renaissance to feudalism, a social system in which everyone stayed in his or her place as a member of a collective group. (By contrast, the Italian Renaissance encouraged individual mobility and creativity.) Since Venice was the last major center of the Italian Renaissance, have students save the feature "Venice" (pp. 244-245) to read at the end of the section.

Development: Tell students that the style of life in Italy from 1300 to 1550 was determined largely by the prosperous merchants who sprang up in every major city. These leading families were fiercely loyal to their own cities; consequently, they used their wealth to beautify their home communities and their own palaces. City vied against city and family against family, leading to feuds and new styles of warfare and government. The competition was a great boon to creative artists, writers, and musicians. Ask students if they know of wealthy families who helped to beautify their own home cities or towns. What is the role of the art patron, then and now? Do cities still compete?

Section 4

Introduction: This section deals with the spread of Renaissance lifestyles, humanism, literature, music, and art to other parts of Europe. Ask students for examples of clothing styles or fads in music that have moved from country to country in recent years. Have students read to find out by what methods the ideas of the Renaissance spread. (By the development of a rich middle class in the Netherlands and Germany; through the patronage of monarchs—Francis I of France, Henry VII and Henry VIII of England; by the movement of artists to and from Italy; and by the publication of books.)

Development: Students should be encouraged to distinguish among the various Renaissance styles in northern Europe, particularly the Flemish, English, and Italian.

Conclusion: Ask students if they think that the effects of the Renaissance are still noticeable today. Do we live in a society that values individuality and intellectual inquiry?

Answers
Section Review Questions

page 236

1. Black Death—name given to bubonic plague.

   Edward III—king of England; declared himself King of France; caused the Hundred Years' War.

   Hundred Years' War—fought between France and England from 1339 to 1453.

   Joan of Arc—young peasant woman who led the forces of France against the English.

   Calais—last English stronghold in France at the end of the Hundred Years' War.

   Avignon—town in southern France where a Pope resided from 1309 to 1377.

   Great Schism—controversy in the Church during which there were two popes.

2. Decline of population due to plague; decreased production due to natural disasters; corruption in government; peasant rebellions; war.

3. English monarchs held lands in southern France as vassals of the French monarchs. The French monarchs wanted to rid France of these English "landlords." In turn, the English monarchs wanted to take over all of France. Victory gave the French a feeling of unity; defeat led to bitterness among English nobles who lost their French lands.

page 242

1. Louis XI—king of France; united most of the country under rule of the monarchy.

   Wars of the Roses—civil wars in England between the followers of the House of Lancaster and the House of York over who would inherit the English crown.

   Isabella—princess of Castile who married Ferdinand of Aragon.

   Hapsburg—most powerful European royal family.

   Margrethe I—Queen of Denmark, brought Sweden and Norway under her rule.

   Johann Gutenberg—German craftsman who perfected the movable type printing press.

2. Monarchy in France grew stronger with the acquisition of all feudal lands by King Louis IX. In England, consolidation took place under the Tudors. In Spain, monarchy was strengthened by the union of the Houses of Castile and Aragon.

3. The emperors could not control the German princes. In Poland and Hungary, strong monarchies emerged who resisted German expansion. Norway, Sweden, and Denmark grew closer together under Danish leadership formed by the Union of Kalmar.
4. Trade flourished; new methods were applied to the mining, smelting, and shaping of metals; change from barter to the use of coins.

page 250
1. Petrarch—Father of Humanism; promoted the revival of classical studies.

   Boccaccio—Italian Humanist; he wrote *Decameron*.

   Lorenzo dé Medici—ruler of Florence; he promoted learning and the arts.

   Girolamo Savonarola—overthrew the Medicis, imposed strict regulations on public behavior in Florence.

   Alexander VI—Borgia Pope; used wealth of the Church for political reasons.

   Saint Peter's Basilica—largest church in the Christian world.

   Niccolò Machiavelli—Florentine diplomat; he wrote *The Prince*.

   Isabella d' Este—ruled Mantua; she promoted learning and the arts.

   Masaccio—Florentine artist who used light and shade to gain perspective in painting.

   Leonardo da Vinci—artist whose paintings were able to reflect personality; a capable scientist and inventor.

   Michelangelo Buonarroti—outstanding artist and sculptor.
2. Economic prosperity; close contact with Byzantine Empire; attachment to classical traditions.
3. Accuracy and legibility in writing. They introduced schools based on the humanities so they would develop well-rounded citizens; began to replace the clergy as leaders of education.
4. Forms and techniques based on classical ideals of beauty; simplicity, elegance, and balance.

page 252
1. Francis I—King of France; promoted Renaissance architecture and painting in France.

   François Rabelais—physician-monk; wrote comical and satirical tales such as *Gargantua* and *Pantagruel*.

Praise of Folly—book written by Erasmus that questioned the need for monasticism, worship of saints, and the maintenance of many church rituals.

Peter Brueghel—Dutch artist; noted for his realistic scenes of peasant life.

Thomas More—leading English humanist; he wrote *Utopia*.

William Shakespeare—famous Engish Renaissance playwright.
2. It led writers to adopt new writing styles using classical and Italian words to enrich their language.
3. They wanted reforms to eliminate abuses in the Church and restore the simple piety of early Christianity.
4. Artists and scholars studied under Italian masters and took the new ideas home.

Special Feature Questions
page 245
1. By a doge and the Council of Ten, representing the leading merchants.
2. Venice was unique because it was situated on a number of islands and its streets were canals. Its proximity to the eastern Mediterranean facilitated its colonizing, and its trade in the Orient.
3. Initially, Venice came under the influence of Byzantine culture. Later, Gothic, Romanesque, and Renaissance styles dominated.
4. With the discovery of the New World, trade shifted to centers along Europe's western coastline: Portugal, Spain, England, and the Netherlands. Meanwhile the eastern Mediterranean trade dried up as the Ottoman Empire expanded into Europe, Asia, and North Africa.

Photo Questions
page 232
Carried by fleas from infected rats.

page 233
Cannon, long bow.

page 235
Roman mobs forced his election; he refused to resign.

page 237
He married Elizabeth of York; was careful to gain the approval of Parliament in making laws.

page 238
Set up the Spanish Inquisition to strengthen the power of the monarchy and unite Spain under Catholicism.

page 241
Firearms, machine parts, housewares, clocks, coins, printing press with movable type.

page 246
Lorenzo dé Medici.

page 250
Florence.

Chapter Review Questions

page 253, Reviewing the Main Ideas
1. It lowered the population and put increased economic burdens on the people; peasants and workers rebelled; they gained more social freedom.
2. Improved firearms, tools, and housewares. More accurate measuring devices, mechanical clock, use of water power, printing press. More ordered lives, learning no longer restricted to the clergy and wealthy.
3. People realized that stronger rulers were needed to keep law and order and to promote economic stability.
4. The Great Schism; pressures on the papacy to accept limits on their political authority.
5. He set out to unite all the French feudal territories under the crown.
6. Henry Tudor defeated Richard III, became Henry VII and founded the Tudor dynasty.
7. The reconquest of most of Spain from the Moors by Christian kingdoms. They united to force the Moors from Granada.
8. The electors avoided giving the throne to a strong prince and elected politically weak nobles.
9. It halted German expansion into Poland.
10. They turned political power over to the signori who often set up dictatorships.
11. Grace, harmony, beauty.
12. It had a more religious tone in the north.

page 253, Discussing Important Ideas
1. Answers may vary.
2. Answers may vary; mention should be made of peoples' belief that popes had abandoned Rome, the center of the Church.
3. Answers may vary; mention should be made of England's monarchy being limited by the Parliament. England more stable because middle and lower classes could achieve power without overthrowing the monarchy.
4. Answers may vary.
5. Answers may vary; mention should be made of availability of learning that led to rise of middle class, and loss of clerical monopoly on education.
6. Answers may vary; mention should be made of humanistic values.
7. Answers may vary.
8. Answers may vary; mention should be made of modern women still being expected to meet some of the same duties as Renaissance women, such as household tasks and child-raising.
9. Answers may vary.

page 253, Using Maps
1. To show areas of political unity. They are part of the same alliance.
2. Eastern.
3. Lowland countries, Germany, Austria, Switzerland.
4. Denmark, Norway, Sweden.
5. About 700 miles (1,120 kilometers). About 300 miles (480 kilometers).

CHAPTER 11
Reformation

At the conclusion of this chapter, students should be able to:
1. trace the origins of the religious reform movement prior to the sixteenth century.
2. describe Martin Luther's education, his struggle, and his beliefs about Christianity.
3. compare the ideas of other Protestant reformers.
4. discuss how the Catholic Church devised methods for halting conversions and modernizing traditional beliefs.
5. explain why Europe became involved in a series of religious wars.

Overview

Every large organization develops flaws in its structure as time goes on. The 1,000-year-old Church of the Middle Ages was no exception. There had been other reforms in structure and ideology, such as those of St. Augustine, St. Bernard, and St. Francis of Assisi. But the Renaissance emphasis on individual perfection, in conjunction with the rise and mobility of the new middle class, led to a questioning of medieval practices based on communal rather than individual interests. After the invention of the printing press, religious questions could be widely debated.

Reformers such as Luther and Calvin challenged papal authority and brought about a split in the Church. One result was a number of religious wars. Key concepts discussed in this chapter include reformation, salvation, purgatory, Protestantism, predestination, separation of church and state, and Counter Reformation.

Teaching Strategies
Section 1

Introduction: Remind students that Europe in 1300 was still a religious community. All of life was oriented to the Church. The Church was a very successful institution—wealthy and powerful. Ask students what dangers might go along with too much success, and have them read the section to see if their speculations are correct.

Development: Discuss with students the fact that during the time of the Protestant Reformation many people were willing to fight and die for their interpretation of religious doctrine. Would this be likely to happen in the United States today? In other parts of the world?

Western European society was the first to go through the process of secularization, in which religion ceases to be the central force and becomes instead one of many forces that motivate human beings. Even during the Reformation period, there were other factors that influenced religious decisions. Note the Czech nationalism of the Hussites and tell students to look for other factors as they read the next section.

Section 2

Introduction: Explain the meaning of indulgences and purgatory (p. 258). Then, have students study the picture and caption on page 258. Why did the issue of indulgences illustrate many of the grievances against the Church? (Many of the grievances were related to money.) As students read the section, they should keep in mind that the Reformation was a political and social movement as well as a religious one.

Development: Have students list the teachings stressed by Luther and explain how they were different from Catholicism. Emphasize Luther's views on vocations and making profits. How did his views suit Europe's changing economy?

Section 3

Introduction: Once people started to break away from the established Church, the process snowballed. Ask students why they might expect this to have happened. Have them read the section to see if their speculations are correct.

Development: Ask students how a belief in predestination would be likely to affect behavior. They might say that it would cause people to give up trying to control their own destinies. Explain that the Calvinists believed they could tell if they were among the saved if they persisted in leading a moral life despite temptations. Thus, the effect of Calvinism was to motivate people to live lives of strict discipline.

Section 4

Introduction: Have students examine the picture on page 269 and discuss the use of force as a means to decide religious questions. Is force effective in controlling religious beliefs? In controlling outward behavior? Why or why not?

Development: Ask students to list the reforms undertaken by the Catholic Church versus the reforms it refused to make. Was the Counter Reformation successful?

Section 5

Introduction: Have students examine the map on page 272 and answer the questions in the "Using Maps" exercise on page 275. What overall picture do they get of the results of the Reformation? (Northern Europe predominately Protestant; southern Europe predominately Catholic.)

Development: Prior to the Reformation the papacy and Catholic rulers had been able to crush religious revolt, except in Bohemia, by sending armies to destroy "heretics." Have students discuss why conditions were different in the sixteenth century. (Dissenters were too widespread, money problems, political complications.) Have students summarize the results of religious wars in Germany, Spain, and France.

Conclusion: Have students read the feature "Mary Queen of Scots" on page 267. How does her story exemplify the interaction between religion and politics during the Reformation period? Be sure students do not confuse her with Mary I.

Answers
Section Review Questions

page 257

1. **Martin V**—Pope who restored papal authority.
   John Wycliffe—called for reform in the church, translated the Bible into English.
   Lollards—followers of Wycliffe.
   Bohemia—birthplace of Queen Anne.
   Jan Hus—leader of Czech reform movement.

2. Money-raising devices that hurt spiritual life; practice of simony; higher clergy living in luxury.

3. Removal of immoral or corrupt church officials, removal of images of saints in the churches, an end to ceremonies not mentioned in the Bible. They spread to influence later, more radical, reformers.

page 261

1. **Martin Luther**—former monk; he began the Protestant Reformation.
   95 theses—Luther's written criticisms of some church practices.
   Pope Leo X—excommunicated Luther.
   Diet of Worms—council of German princes who met in Worms.
   Frederick of Saxony—Luther's protector.

2. To stimulate debate in the Church. A full-scale revolution that destroyed Europe's religious unity.

3. Salvation came from faith and trust in God's mercy, not through good works; truth was to be found only in the Bible; church services should be in the vernacular.

4. Religious conviction; some used it for political gain; to protest against Catholic ruling class.

page 268

1. **Huldreich Zwingli**—leader of Reform church in Switzerland.
   John Calvin—leader of Reform group in Geneva.

   Geneva—site of most powerful reform group.
   Anabaptists—collective name for numerous Protestant sects that believed in the practice of baptizing only adult members; deeply involved in social unrest.
   Henry VIII—king of England; separated the Church of England from Rome; became head of English Church.
   Mary I—queen of England; tried to restore Roman Catholicism in England.
   Elizabeth I—Protestant queen of England; ended Pope's authority in England.
   Anglicanism—blend of Protestant belief and Catholic practice in English church.
   Puritans—Protestants opposed to Church of England's Catholic ways.

2. Luther's challenge made it easier to carry out reform goals. Printing press and vernacular translations of the Bible allowed more people to interpret scripture on their own.

page 269

3. To divorce his first wife.

4. It was supported by strong monarchs; blended Protestantism and Catholicism.

page 271

1. **Pope Paul III**—he called for reform in the Catholic Church.
   Index of Prohibited Books—list of written works banned by the Church.
   Ignatius of Loyola—Catholic reformer; founder of the Jesuits.
   Jesuits—order of the Society of Jesus; founded by Ignatius of Loyola.

2. To define official doctrine of the Church; restore the power and influence of the Pope. Never realized because it took a hard line against Protestantism.

3. Worked to strengthen Catholicism; worked in missionaries, schools, universities; helped the poor and preached to the people; served as advisors in royal courts.

page 274

1. **Schmalkaldic League**—Lutheran defensive alliance in Germany.
   Peace of Augsburg—religious compromise between Catholics and Lutherans in Germany.
   William of Orange—Dutch leader against the Spanish.

Sea Beggars—Dutch fighting groups that opened the dikes to flood the Spanish armies.

Huguenots—French Protestants.

Henry IV—he became a Catholic in order to inherit the French crown.

2. Heavy taxes to pay for Spain's religious wars; acts of the Inquisition in the attempt to remove all Protestants.

3. Both sides submitted to a strong monarchy to ensure stability and peace.

Photo Questions

page 257
They combined new firearms technology with ancient Bohemian fighting tactics.

page 258
It raised money.

page 259
He needed the Pope's support against the French.

page 261
Marches; articles and letters to newspapers; cartoons.

page 262
Purgatory, monasteries, celibacy, music, images of saints in the churches.

page 266
Catherine was the aunt of the Hapsburg Emperor; he pressured the Pope to reject Henry's request.

page 268
Her persecution of Protestants turned many people away from her policies.

page 269
It was banned.

page 270
Southern Germany, Bohemia, Poland, Hungary.

page 273
Over 30 years.

Chapter Review Questions

page 275, Reviewing the Main Ideas
1. Councils were traditionally called by popes who were reluctant to limit their own authority; it was difficult to agree on a site for the council; if the Pope could be deposed by a council, who was the real head of the Church?

2. Hussites and the Church. A compromise was reached.

3. He feared for the peace and unity of Germany.

4. They stressed that salvation came from faith alone; that all humanity is sinful in God's eyes.

5. They both supported a religious reformation based entirely on the Bible. Zwingli placed more value on the achievements of classical civilizations, was more optimistic about human nature.

6. The church government was distributed among many people, harder for enemies to eliminate a few leaders to destroy the movement.

7. The common practice of baptizing only adult members. They denied the right of civil governments to direct their lives.

8. Her persecution of Protestants. Tudor.

9. England became the leading defender of Protestantism. Protestants opposed a strong monarchy and helped extend the rights of Parliament in England.

10. He called a council of bishops at Trent to define official doctrine.

11. Other German princes feared his power if he should end Lutheranism; the size of the Empire made it difficult to move effectively against them; he had two foreign enemies who forced him to defend his borders.

12. They reached a compromise with the Catholics to ensure political stability in France.

page 275, Discussing Important Ideas
1. Answers may vary; mention should be made of the desire of many leaders to reduce the power of the Hapsburgs; and those who felt the Church had become too wealthy from tithes and owned too much property.

2. Answers may vary; mention should be made of Calvin's logical approach to religious issues unclouded by Luther's self-doubts.

3. Answers may vary.

4. Answers may vary.

5. Answers may vary.

6. Answers may vary; mention should be made of the desire to restore Christian unity and define Catholic doctrine.

7. Answers may vary; mention should be made of the resistance to the emperor.
8. Answers may vary.
9. Answers may vary; mention should be made of the political and economical consequences of internal discord.

page 272, Using Maps
1. Roman Catholic.
2. Jewish, Hussite.
3. France, Austria, Poland, Hungary.
4. Lutheran, Calvinism, Roman Catholic, Jewish. Church of England, Roman Catholic.
5. Worms.
6. France, Germany, Bohemia, Poland, Hungary, Ottoman Empire.

CHAPTER 12
Discovery and Expansion

At the conclusion of this chapter, students should be able to:
1. outline the underlying causes that made the voyages of discovery possible during the late 1400's and early 1500's.
2. discuss how Portugal and Spain became major sea powers and list the factors that led to their decline.
3. explain the motives for Spain's overseas involvement and the changes that its colonization brought to Latin America.
4. compare and contrast the explorations and colonizing efforts of England, the Netherlands, and France.

Overview

This chapter describes major changes in the attitude of western European monarchies between the late fifteenth and mid-seventeenth centuries regarding discovery and expansion as means to gain greater financial resources. Monarchs grew more and more interested in the tales of fabulous wealth in distant lands. They consequently risked thir treasuries to support systematic exploration. This drive to explore corresponded with a great wave of missionary activity on the part of the Catholic Church and Catholic states, and to a lesser extent on the part of the new Protestant states of England and the Netherlands. The latecomers—France, the Netherlands, and England—concerned about the financial and military power of Spain, gradually overcame their disadvantages. In the end, these states fought among themselves until the Treaty of Paris was signed in 1763, marking the ascendancy of England. Important concepts include the Commercial Revolution, mercantilism, balance of trade, colonial empire, and mestizos.

Teaching Strategies
Section 1
Introduction: Ask students to consider the first time they traveled some distance from their home towns alone. Maybe some can recall the fear and, perhaps, the thrill of the experience. The early explorers no doubt felt these same emotions. Have students study the maps on page 279. Note how little of the world was known to Europeans in 1400, and how much that changed by 1600.

Development: This section deals with the "push and pull" of history. Did European states push into unknown areas because they needed financial resources to fund larger state bureaucracies and armies? Or, were Europeans pulled into new areas by daring explorers; fear of being overwhelmed by Muslim warriors; or by navigational improvements, better maps, and more seaworthy ships? Have students discuss these ideas.

Section 2
Introduction: Ask students to note the location of Portugal on a map and its close proximity to Africa. Remind them that Spain became a united state and a great power in the fifteenth century. Tell them to remember these points as they read the section, and to determine their relevance to Portugal's early supremacy in sea exploration. (These points are two major reasons why Portugal became the first nation to explore the coastlines of Africa and Asia. The Portuguese dared not challenge their powerful neighbor, hence, they turned to exploration by sea.)

Development: Ask students to explain how the goals of Prince Henry were fulfilled in the late 1400's by explorers such as Dias and da Gama. Have students look at the map on page 286 and study the routes of Portuguese explorations. Ask them to locate on another map the bases set up by the Portuguese to control the spice trade:

Hormuz, Goa, Malacca, and Macao. Did the size of its colonial population affect Portugal's settlement of Brazil? What caused the decline of Portugal's trading empire?

Section 3

Introduction: Refer students to the picture and caption on page 285 that depicts Columbus seeking support from Spain's monarchs for his voyage westward to the Indies. As they read the section, have them answer the caption question. Have students read the feature "Mexico City" (p. 291) after they read about Cortés and the Aztecs on page 288.

Development: Ask students to explain how Spain's conquistadores differed from the earlier European explorers. Apart from the conquistadores came the colonists and the issue of how to deal with native populations. Have students discuss the differences between Las Casas and de Sepulveda regarding treatment of the Indians in the empire. Each student could be assigned to write a short essay suggesting how he or she would have changed the policy of the Spanish Crown toward Indians or how abuse of the laws protecting Indians could have been corrected.

Section 4

Introduction: Have students study the map on page 293 and refer to it as they read the section. Ask them to record on a comparison chart the explorations and settlements of England, Holland, and France; and the reasons for each country's exploration and colonizing efforts.

Development: Have students discuss the information on their comparison charts. Why did England and France fight the French and Indian War? What enabled the English to be victorious?

Conclusion: It is important for students to understand the different types of naval power; colonization objectives; and national goals of Spain, France, the Netherlands, and England that allowed England to come out on top by the mid-eighteenth century. Also consider the role that mercantilism played in that outcome.

Answers
Section Review Questions

page 282
1. East Indies—archipelago of Southeast Asia.
   Prester John—legendary king of a Christian kingdom in Africa.

Commercial Revolution—changes in the arrangements for investing money; the flow of wealth; reduced risks in commercial ventures.
   Fuggers—banking family in Augsburg.
   Bank of Amsterdam—offered complete banking services including minting of coins.
2. Limited knowledge of geography; navigational tools; superstitions of the unknown.
3. Technological improvements, economics, religion.
4. To make a profit. Acquisition of gold and silver through trade or from colonies.

page 284
1. Prince Henry the Navigator—prince of Portugal, he established a school for navigators.
   Nicholas V—Pope who issued a bull that allowed Portugal to occupy certain islands, ports and seas.
   Bartholomeu Dias—Portuguese traveller; he showed that the Far East could be reached by sailing around Africa.
   Vasco da Gama—Portuguese leader of an expedition to India.
   Alphonso de Albuquerque—set up a string of fortified bases for Portugal's control of shipping in and out of the Indian Ocean.
   Pedro Álvares Cabral—discovered Brazil.
2. Knowledge of previous voyages was made available to the expeditions that followed.
3. Their policies created many enemies in Europe and Asia; lack of personnel.

page 292
1. Christopher Columbus—sought a new route to India for Spain by traveling west.
   Amerigo Vespucci—contended that the West Indies was not part of Asia but a "New World."
   Treaty of Tordesillas—line of demarcation to protect the claims of Spain and Portugal.
   Vasco Núñez de Balboa—first European to cross the Isthmus of Panama and sight the Pacific Ocean.
   Juan Ponce de León—discovered and explored Florida.
   Ferdinand Magellan—proved the world was round.
   Hernán Cortés—conquered the Aztecs.
   Francisco Pizarro—conquered the Incas.

Hernando de Soto—found the Mississippi River mouth.

Francisco Vásquez de Coronado—discovered the Grand Canyon.

Bartolomé de Las Casas—Catholic missionary; tried to protect the Indians from exploitation.

2. The Spanish had horses and guns.
3. Finding gold. Seized control of much of Central and South America.
4. Inflation, war.

page 297
1. John Cabot—explored the coasts of Newfoundland, Nova Scotia, New England.

Martin Frobisher—explored the coast of Greenland.

Francis Drake—first Englishman to sail around the world.

Barbados—island in the West Indies.

Jamestown—first successful English settlement in the Americas.

Pilgrims—group of Puritans who founded a colony in Massachusetts.

Henry Hudson—English navigator and explorer.

New Amsterdam—Dutch settlement on Manhattan Island.

Boers—Dutch peasants.

Giovanni da Verrazano—sought the Northwest Passage for the French.

Jacques Cartier—explored the St. Lawrence River.

Samuel de Champlain—founder of Quebec.

Jacques Marquette—explored the Mississippi Valley.

Louis Joliet—explored the Mississippi Valley with Marquette.

Robert Cavelier—sailed down the Mississippi River to the Gulf of Mexico.
2. They both needed raw materials, trade, and colonies. The English wanted more colonies; the Dutch wanted commercial control.
3. They both encouraged settlements by the granting of royal charters. France was more concerned with struggles in Europe than with establishing new colonies.
4. Spain held most of South America; the Dutch maintained their position in the East Indies; England controlled North America and India; France lost its territories in India and much of North America.

Special Feature Questions
page 291
1. By building on the site of the old Aztec capital; rebuilding of principal Aztec roads and canals.
2. According to strict regulations set by the Spanish crown; at its center was a plaza with cathedral and palace on opposite sides; surrounding the plaza was a grid of streets.

Photo Questions
page 278
Economic needs, religious zeal.

page 280
Making of loans, transfer of funds, coining, bank notes.

page 282
To find gold, and to discover a new route to the Far East.

page 285
The Pope had banned interference in Portugal's eastern sea route.

page 287
Mutiny; bad weather; strong winds and currents; ships separated; scurvy; massacre by islanders.

page 288
The massacre of Aztec leaders.

page 290
Spanish, religion.

page 295
Spain, Portugal, France, England.

page 296
Granted royal charters.

Chapter Review
page 298, Reviewing the Main Ideas
1. Lateen sail, multiple masts, rudder, improved navigational tools.
2. Investors no longer risked their money on the fate of one ship.
3. Silver and gold could not be held as royal stockpiles, monopolies.
4. Official sustained support for exploration, for example, Prince Henry's school.

5. To determine the costs and benefits of direct trade with India. Proved that the Indian Ocean could be reached by sea; direct trade with India and the Far East.
6. Set up a string of fortified bases along the Indian coast to the Persian Gulf; colonized the East Indies.
7. It proved that the earth was round and larger than was thought.
8. They were enslaved by the Spanish; pushed out by the English; converted by the French.
9. It was cheaper than hiring servants.
10. They gave France a claim in North America.
11. Wars; shipping restrictions among other European countries.
12. Over rival claims in the Ohio Valley. English superiority on the seas.

page 299, Discussing Important Ideas
1. Answers may vary.
2. Answers may vary.
3. Answers may vary; mention should be made of specific countries and their goals.
4. Answers may vary.
5. Answers may vary; mention should be made of the superiority of Spain, and later, England.
6. Answers may vary.
7. Answers may vary; mention should be made of the exploitation of American Indians.
8. Answers may vary.

page 299, Using Maps
1. Southern point of Africa. Between South America and Tierra del Fuego. Between North and South America. Northeast Canada. Central United States. South of North American continent.
2. About 25°N, 80°W. About 5°N, 120°E.
3. From east to west.
4. About 6,000 miles (9,600 kilometers).
5. England.
6. Portugal.

Unit Review

page 300, Developing Understanding
1. Answers may vary; mention should be made of the rise of the Mongol dynasties in Asia, and the increasing power of monarchs in Europe.
2. The Renaissance laid the foundations of modern western thought and brought in new forms of art and literature.
3. It prompted an interest in classical writings, encouraged the development of study and interpretation of the Bible, which led to the rise of Protestantism and a reformed Catholic Church.
4. They led to a new understanding of the world, old cultures and traditions were shattered by a borrowing and blending of ideas from different civilizations.
5. Answers may vary.
6. Answers may vary.
7. Europe became the center of world power.

page 300-301, Developing Skills
Conclude the unit with the Developing Skills activity. In this activity, which may be used as an individual or group exercise, students are introduced to the concept of historical schools and given practice in recognizing them.

An example of a historical school is given in Max Weber's thesis that the Protestant ethic had a decisive influence on the development of modern capitalism. The student then reads three quotations from other historians and determines whether or not they belong to the Weber school.

It may be helpful to have students find the main idea and look for unstated assumptions before making their determinations. The answers are as follows:
1. Does not support the Weber school. The main idea is that the business abilities of Puritans did *not* come from their religious ethics.
2. Does not support the Weber school. The main idea is that capitalism existed before the Reformation. The assumption is that since capitalism predated the Reformation, it was not caused by the Reformation.
3. Supports the Weber school. The main idea is that Calvin approved of trade and making profits. One assumption is that what Calvin approved became part of the general values of Protestants.

UNIT 4
From Monarchy to Revolution

At the conclusion of this unit, students should be able to:

1. compare and contrast the monarchies of Spain, England, France, Austria, Prussia, and Russia during the Age of Monarchs.
2. describe the developments that led to the Age of Reason.
3. explain the basic ideas of the Enlightenment and describe their effects on society, art, and literature.
4. compare and contrast the causes and the results of the English Glorious Revolution, the American Revolution, and the French Revolution.
5. discuss the attempts by early nineteenth-century conservative leaders to return Europe to the strong royal governments that existed before the French Revolution.

Overview

Unit 4 traces European history from the 1500's to the mid-1800's. It focuses on how the strong monarchies of Europe were affected by the Enlightenment and the revolutions it inspired. Chapter 13 describes Europe's monarchies at the height of their power. Chapter 14 outlines the relationship between the scientific revolution of the 1600's and the Enlightenment movement of the 1700's. It shows how Enlightenment ideas were applied by thinkers to the institutions and values of European society. Chapter 15 describes the revolutions in England, North America, and France, which brought an end to the age of absolute monarchy. Chapter 16 indicates how conservative leaders in Europe tried to reestablish the old order after the defeat of Napoleon.

Introducing the Unit

Ask students to recall the crises of the Late Middle Ages in Europe (economic decline, religious uncertainty, disease, famine, rebellion, and war) that weakened feudalism and led to the emergence of strong monarchies. Write the definition of absolutism (p. 305) on the chalkboard. Read the quote by Jacques Bossuet on page 312. Explain that Bossuet's seventeenth-century book containing the quote became a famous justification of absolute rule. As students study the unit, they should consider the following questions: Why would people put up with absolute rule? What were their options? What was the relationship between the Enlightenment and revolution?

CHAPTER 13
Age of Monarchs

At the conclusion of this chapter, students should be able to:

1. list the economic and social problems that weakened the Spanish Hapsburgs.
2. analyze the strengths and weaknesses of the English Tudors.
3. review how the balance of power principle was employed in Europe during Elizabeth I's reign.
4. outline France's rise to prominence in the seventeenth century.
5. identify the causes and outcome of the Thirty Years' War.
6. describe how Peter the Great opened Russia to western ideas and how the lives of Russian serfs changed under Catherine the Great.

Overview

The chapter is divided into five sections that describe the monarchies of Spain, England, France, the German states (particularly, Austria and Prussia), and Russia at their height. The focus is on the shaping of modern Europe and the excesses of absolute rule and ambition. Important concepts include absolutism, balance of power, wars of succession, oprichnina, and dvorianie.

Teaching Strategies
Section 1

Introduction: As learned in the previous unit, Spain gained great wealth from the New World. In the latter half of the sixteenth century, during Philip II's reign, Spain was the leading power in Europe, but by 1588, with the defeat of the

Spanish Armada, it began a decline that continued under Philip's successors. As students read the section, have them note the economic and social problems that weakened the Spanish Hapsburgs. (Costly wars, foreign loans, inflation, deterioration of industry and agriculture, raids on Spain's treasure ships; revolts by groups within Spain and in the Netherlands, famine, and plague.)

Development: In Spain, Christianity had played a secondary role to Islam and Judaism since the eighth century. For nearly 800 years, Islamic Spain had been regarded as the most advanced civilization in Europe and the Middle East. It is possible that part of Philip II's concern about the loyalty of the Marranos and Moriscos was due to a type of cultural inferiority complex or jealousy. How did Philip attempt to eliminate these groups, as well as Protestants, from his domain? (Through the use of military force and the Inquisition.) How was Protestant rebellion in the Netherlands related to the Spanish Armada? (Philip was angry at Elizabeth I for aiding the rebels.)

Section 2

Introduction: Ask students to turn to the photo of William Shakespeare on page 308 and read the caption. Do students know that Elizabeth I had been educated in the Renaissance tradition? (For example, she spoke English, French, and Latin; she was skilled at translating Latin and Greek.) Be sure that students understand the term "Elizabethan period." Ask them to prepare a written or oral report on a poet or writer from the Elizabethan period.

Development: Divide the class in two. Have one group make a list of the strengths of the Tudor monarchs, and the other make a list of their weaknesses. Ask students to indicate on their lists whether an item is related to foreign or domestic policy. Have them debate whether Elizabeth I made a greater contribution to the unity of England through her foreign or domestic policies.

Section 3

Introduction: Ask students to look at the picture on page 312 and read the caption. The lavish court of Louis XIV became the model for other European monarchies.

Louis, a Catholic, believed completely in absolute monarchy and saw the Protestant

Huguenots as a threat to his rule. Louis persecuted them, forcing many to leave France. The political and economic talents of these people were lost to France to the benefit of England, the Netherlands, and later to the United States. Have students look at the picture and read the caption on page 315. But the political and economic problems of eighteenth-century France did not stem only from misguided religious zeal. Louis involved France in a number of unnecessary wars that contributed greatly to the near financial collapse of the state—despite the efforts of conscientious ministers like Jean Baptiste Colbert.

Have students read the feature on Colbert (p. 314) just before they begin the subsection "Religious Policy" on page 315. Also, ask students to consider the following question as they read: Is there any similarity between the impoverishment of France in the eighteenth century and the impoverishment of Spain in the seventeenth century?

Development: Ask students to compare the religious tolerance exhibited by Elizabeth I of England (p. 268) with that of Henry IV (p. 310). (Both rulers effectively neutralized religious strife. Elizabeth forged a compromise that resulted in Anglicanism; Henry issued the Edict of Nantes.) How did religious tolerance help these rulers strengthen their states? (Talented minorities were not driven out; internal order allowed monarchs to centralize their power and concentrate on other problems, such as outside threats.)

Section 4

Introduction: This section discusses the effects of the Thirty Years' War and the Treaty of Westphalia on Germany and other parts of Europe. It also presents the rise of Austria and Prussia as the leading German states and their subsequent rivalry for control of central Germany. Have students compare the maps on pages 317 and 319. Ask them to focus on the German states and to suggest the territorial changes that took place between 1560 and after the Treaty of Westphalia in 1648. Responses might include: "The Holy Roman Empire looks smaller." "The Spanish Hapsburgs lost most of the Netherlands." "Brandenburg-Prussia appears." Ask students to find reasons for these changes as they read the section.

Development: Compare and contrast the reigns of Maria Theresa and Frederick II. What major contributions did they make to their respective states? (Maria Theresa strengthened the central government, provided public services, and built a strong economy; Frederick II expanded Prussian territory and made Prussia into an important power in Europe.) It is important to note that the seizure of Silesia doubled the population of Prussia and gave it important industries. This was a significant factor in Prussia's emergence as a European power.

Section 5

Introduction: Russia did not become independent of Mongol rule until 1480, during the reign of Ivan III. From this time to the beginning of Peter the Great's reign in 1689 is known as the Muscovite Period. During the eighteenth century, Russia turned to western models to improve its state and society. Thus, the section covers three broad phases of Russian history: the Mongol phase, characterized by the rise of Moscow at the expense of other Russian territories (p. 320); the Muscovite period, during which the tsars united Russian territories under their increasing absolute rule (pp. 320-322); and the Romanov period, in which absolute rule and serfdom become complete (pp. 322-326). Have students read the feature "Saint Petersburg" (p. 323) just before the subsection "Foreign Policy" on page 322.

Development: One Russian historian has called autocracy, Orthodoxy, and serfdom the "three pillars" of the traditional Russian state. Lead students in a discussion on this observation. Also, ask students if they think Russia's development would have been closer to the West had Russia become Roman Catholic instead of Orthodox.

Conclusion: The balance of power principle was important in foreign policy during the Age of Monarchs. Have each student make a visual display that illustrates and explains one of the situations cited in the chapter in which this principle was employed.

Answers
Section Review Questions

page 307
1. El Escorial—palace built by Philip II.
   Madrid—site of El Escorial, capital of Spain.

Marranos—Jews who had converted to Christianity.
Moriscos—Muslims who had converted to Christianity.
Spanish Armada—Spanish fleet built to invade England.
Charles II—last of the Spanish Hapsburgs.
2. Separate regional forms of government; unrest among large religious minorities.
3. England's aid to Protestant rebels in the Netherlands, Elizabeth allowed English sailors to attack Spanish fleets from the Americas. The Armada was defeated by the English and the weather.
4. Mismanagement, corruption, and a series of conflicts caused its breakdown as a powerful empire.

page 310
1. Henry VII—first Tudor monarch.
   Henry VIII—most powerful Tudor monarch.
   Calais—England's final foothold on European continent.
   Elizabeth I—last Tudor monarch.
   Poor Laws—made local areas responsible for their homeless and unemployed.
   James I—founded Stuart dynasty, united England and Scotland.
2. They worked within the framework of Parliament and courts of law.
3. She worked for a balance of power in Europe.

page 316
1. Henry IV—founded the Bourbon dynasty.
   Edict of Nantes—allowed Protestant worship in areas of Protestant majority.
   Richelieu—cardinal who built a strong monarchy in France.
   Fronde—series of Protestant uprisings in France.
   Louvois—minister of war under Louis XIV.
   Treaty of Utrecht—ended the War of the Spanish Succession.
2. He issued the Edict of Nantes.
3. To build a strong absolute monarchy in France. He destroyed their fortified castles and stripped them of their administrative authority. He took away their right to independent, fortified towns.
4. He strengthened the power of the monarchy and the state. He failed to reform the tax system; repealed the Edict of Nantes, which caused further Protestant uprisings.

1. Ferdinand of Syria—King of Bohemia and Hapsburg heir to the Holy Roman Empire.

   Peace of Westphalia—ended the Thirty Years' War.

   Pragmatic Sanction—agreement by Europe's rulers to accept Maria Theresa as monarch, and not to divide the Hapsburg lands.

   Hohenzollerns—rulers of Brandenburg-Prussia.

   Junkers—nobles of Brandenburg-Prussia.

   Royal Drill Sergeant—Frederick William I, made the Prussian army the most efficient fighting force in Europe.

   Silesia—Austrian province.
2. Ferdinand's curtailment of the freedoms of Bohemian Protestants.
3. By having the central government accept responsibility for public health, prisons, and roads; to deal with the national economy and encourage exports.
4. The signing of the Treaty of Aix-la-Chapelle; it recognized Prussia as a rising nation.

page 326

1. Ivan III—"the Great," drove the Mongols out of Russia and extended its territory.

   Third Rome—Moscow, as the successor to Constantinople.

   Ivan IV—"the Terrible," most powerful of the early tsars.

   Oprichniki—Ivan IV's secret police.

   Livonia—territory between Russia and the Baltic Sea.

   Time of Troubles—time of famine, epidemics, revolts, invasions, and succession to the throne was contested.

   Boris Godunov—elected tsar by the Zemski Sobor.

   Zemski Sobor—representative assembly in Russia.

   Cossacks—groups of pioneers in the Ukraine.

   "Window to the West"—Saint Petersburg.

   Table of Ranks—hierarchy of positions in civilian and military service.

   Holy Synod—council of bishops responsible to a secular official appointed by the tsar.
2. The head of the Church moved to Moscow. Claimed Moscow was the Third Rome; made the Byzantine two-headed eagle Russia's symbol.

3. To increase its trade and contacts with western Europe. Ivan tried to gain control of Livonia. Peter fought the Swedes for control of the Baltic coastline, and the Turks for a port on the Black Sea.
4. More peasants were forced into serfdom, their conditions worsened. To put down peasant rebellions.

Special Feature Questions

page 323

1. It seemed to be suspended between the water and the sky.
2. Answers may vary; mention should be made of Peter's absolute power.

Photo Questions

page 306

England.

page 308

Poetry; language was transformed.

page 309

Sold lands, offices, licenses, monopolies, rights to collect customs.

page 311

Strengthened the army; built up the economy; strengthened national unity.

page 312

He surrounded himself with ceremony.

page 313

To feel secure from Parisian mobs.

page 315

In the Netherlands and England.

page 321

To make a more direct link to the Byzantine Empire.

page 325

Because of her successful foreign policy.

Chapter Review

page 327, Reviewing the Main Ideas

1. To increase their power; monarchs supported absolutism; nobles resisted restrictions of their power. Strengthened government bu-

reaucracy to bring many areas of national life under royal control.
2. They wanted peace and stability to further trade.
3. No uniform system of government; dissent among religious factions; inflation.
4. The monarchs worked within the structure of Parliament and the law.
5. She worked for a balance of power among European nations.
6. French monarchs worked to maintain an absolute monarchy that was imitated throughout Europe.
7. Because he had power and style.
8. France and Austria had claims to the throne, the rest of Europe was afraid the balance of power would become upset. France fought against the Grand Alliance; lost territory in Europe and Americas.
9. Provisions of the Treaty of Westphalia; to preserve the balance of power principle.
10. Louis XIV of France accepted the provisions of Charles II, and Philip of Anjou became king of Spain. Spain lost the Spanish Netherlands; France lost Nova Scotia and Newfoundland; increased opposition to Louis' rule.
11. The location of Moscow gave it good strategic access to Siberia and the Baltic and Black Seas; leaders of the Church added its support to Moscow.
12. Ordered court members to wear western clothing; men had to shave their beards; women had to attend social gatherings; sent Russians abroad to study; invited foreign experts to Russia; established schools; built Saint Petersburg as the "Window to the West."

page 327, Discussing Important Ideas
1. Answers may vary; mention should be made of strong central government versus independence of cities. They encouraged national peace and furthered trade. They denied economic, political, or religious freedom to some people.
2. Answers may vary; mention should be made of specific monarchs.
3. Answers may vary; mention should be made of individual freedoms under each monarch.
4. Answers may vary; mention should be made of the theory helping monarchs overcome potential rivals.

5. Answers may vary.
6. Answers may vary; mention should be made of the possibility of a division of power between church and state.
7. Answers may vary.
8. Answers may vary; mention should be made of a standard national language adding to national unity.
9. Answers may vary; mention should be made of the relaxation of serfdom in most European countries, but strengthened in Russia.

page 327, Using Maps
1. Ivan III.
2. Areas from the Barents Sea in the north to the Caspian and Black Seas in the south, and the Baltic Sea in the west.
3. Southeast.
4. Saint Petersburg, Novgorod.
5. Black and Caspian Seas and mountains.

CHAPTER 14
Age of Reason

At the conclusion of this chapter, students should be able to:
1. explain how the scientific movement of the 1600's stimulated the Enlightenment movement of the 1700's.
2. name some of the ways that law, history, and religion were affected by a scientific world view.
3. outline the attitudes that Enlightenment thinkers shared.
4. compare and contrast the views of Hobbes, Locke, Montesquieu, and Rousseau on ideal systems of government.
5. identify and describe the styles and themes of European art and literature during the 1600's and 1700's.

Overview

The chapter begins with a discussion of the scientific revolution that began in Europe in the 1500's and flourished in the 1600's. It describes how the scientific tools of observation and reason were applied to the institutions and values of society, resulting in the Enlightenment movement. The thoughts and attitudes of the most important Enlightenment thinkers are reviewed, as well as the arguments of the movement's critics. The final section presents the major styles and themes of seventeenth- and eighteenth-century European art and literature. Other important concepts in the chapter include the Copernican theory, the law of inertia, natural law, deism, salon society, laissez faire, skepticism, enlightened despotism, social contract, sovereignty, and categorical imperative.

Teaching Strategies
Section 1

Introduction: Lead a discussion about the chapter opening picture (p. 328) to introduce this section. Questions from the "Using Illustrations" exercise on page 345 may be helpful. Have students read the feature "Telescopes and Microscopes" (p. 332) before they begin the subsection "Bacon and Descartes" on page 330.

Development: Have students review the section, pulling out the contributions each thinker made to the development of the Age of Reason tools of reason and observation. (For example, Bacon held that precise words should be used in observation to avoid vague thinking.)

Section 2

Introduction: The central idea of this section is the analogy between the physical universe and society. As students read the section, ask them to jot down ideas about how natural law was used to justify *both* constitutional and absolutist governments.

Development: Ask students to discuss other areas of society that were influenced by the scientific view of the world. Then have them share their thoughts on how natural law was used to justify constitutional and absolutist governments.

Section 3

Introduction: Have students look again at the picture on page 328 and at the picture and caption on page 335. Explain how salons stimulated Enlightenment thought. Have students study the illustrations and captions on page 334 in conjunction with the subsection "Enlightenment Thought" on page 336.

Development: Enlightenment thought may be viewed as the end result of a process that began in the Renaissance—liberation of the mind. Steps in the process were: (1) an interest in humanism; (2) desire for personal perfection; (3) greater freedom to speculate about the nature and expectations of God; (4) discoveries about the physical laws of the universe; and (5) the quest for secular laws governing human behavior. After students have read the section, have them skim the present material and earlier parts of the text to determine when and where in history these steps first appeared.

Section 4

Introduction: Ask students to assess the importance of reason and emotion in their daily living. Do they have a more serious, rational attitude about doing homework than they do about dealing with classmates, attending football games, or talking with their parents about house rules? It is important for students to realize that both rationality and emotion are desirable personality traits that have particular roles to play in everyone's life. The feature on John Wesley (p. 340) is best read at the end of the section.

Development: Some thinkers began to take a broader view of the role of reason. Rousseau almost went so far as to say that the emotional needs of people were the most important building block of society. He was the first to emphasize popular sovereignty, in which leaders would be elected by the people based on their feelings and perceptions of the leaders' abilities and talents. Kant wondered what sort of moral climate society would have if it were based on pure reason. He concluded that one's sense of right action depended on feelings as well as reason. What was the religious reaction to the Enlightenment?

Section 5

Introduction: Just as freedom of thought was an important theme of the Age of Reason, so also was freedom of expression important to artists, writers, musicians, and architects. However, feelings of the artist were only part of what was expressed by a work of art. It was still necessary for most artists to find patrons to support their work. Hence, the various artistic products of the Age of Reason reflected the ideas and feelings of *both* artists and patrons. As students read the section, they should notice to what degree patrons influenced the arts of the time.

Development: Ask students to explain how the styles and themes of the arts of the 1600's and 1700's were related to the political, social, and intellectual developments of the times. For example, the baroque style was an expression of the power and glory of the great monarchs as well as a way to inspire religious feelings.

Conclusion: Refer students to the quote by Voltaire on page 328. Have them analyze its meaning in a brief paragraph or two. Ask them to do the same thing with all or some of the thoughts that appear on page 334.

Answers
Section Review Questions

page 331

1. Nicholas Copernicus—Polish astronomer and mathematician; held that the sun was center of the solar system.

    Johannes Kepler—German mathematician; showed that planets move in ellipses.

    Francis Bacon—English philosopher; taught people to rely on observation and experimentation.

    René Descartes—French mathematician; believed truth was reached through reason.

    Principia—Newton's book, *Mathematical Principles of Natural Philosophy*.

    Royal Society of London—scientific academy founded by Charles I.

2. It believed that the earth was the center of the universe according to gospel.

3. His theory of gravity reconciled Galileo's law of inertia with Kepler's idea of planetary ellipses.

4. Brought scientists together; provided scientific information; translated and published scientific works; coordinated scientific efforts.

page 333

1. *Leviathan*—Thomas Hobbes' book stating the idea that natural law justified absolute monarchy.

    John Locke—English philosopher; advocated that people have natural rights to life, liberty, and property.

    Hugo Grotius—Dutch jurist; called for a universal code based on natural law.

2. Hobbes said human beings are violent and disorderly and need strong government to maintain order. Locke said human beings are reasonable and moral, and people have the right to overturn a government that fails to uphold their natural rights.

3. People began to look for evidence that met scientific standards; placed less value on hearsay.

4. People became less certain that their religion was the only truth.

page 337

1. Voltaire—François Marie Arouet; French writer and philosophe.

    The Spirit of the Laws—Montesquieu's book that classified governments.

    Denis Diderot—French philosophe, conceived and published a 17-volume encyclopedia.

    Joseph II—co-ruler of Austria; promoted Enlightenment reforms.

2. It brought writers, artists, and intellectuals together to discuss and support Enlightenment ideas.

3. It involved too much government interference in the economy; they believed in laissez faire.

4. That society needed them to increase prosperity and make government more effective.

page 339

1. Jean Jacques Rousseau—French philosophe; he criticized Enlightenment philosophy for its excessive reliance on reason.

    David Hume—Scottish philosopher; he questioned the value of human reason.

    Immanuel Kant—German philosopher; he said human feelings were based upon reality, though science and reason could not explain them.

    Count Von Zinzendorf—he established the Moravian Brethren, a sect that emphasized the emotional and mystical side of religion.

2. He attacked science and the arts for corrupting morals; that human beings were naturally good, civilization was evil.

3. The categorical imperative; that people's actions should be such that they would be willing to have them as universal laws.

4. They rejected reason in favor of an enthusiastic faith.

page 343

1. El Greco—Domenikos Theotokopoulos, "The Greek," mannerist painter.

    Peter Paul Rubens—Flemish master of baroque style.

Diego Velázquez—Spanish master; painted portraits at court.

Alessandro Scarlatti—Italian composer of baroque music.

Don Quixote—baroque novel by Miguel de Cervantes Saavedra, said by some to be the greatest novel ever written.

Jan Vermeer—Dutch realist artist; portrayed scenes of everyday life.

Rembrandt van Rijn—Dutch realist painter; often chose religious subject matter.

Daniel Defoe—English novelist; wrote *Robinson Crusoe*.

Jacques Louis David—French artist; leader of neoclassical movement.

2. They rejected Renaissance principles of balance and perspective, and portrayed what they saw subjectively.
3. It was less grand, lighter, more delicate, daintier.
4. Neoclassicism.

Special Feature Questions

page 332
1. The invention of printing led to a need for spectacles.
2. He studied the life cycles of weevils and fleas; showed they hatched from eggs.

Photo Questions

page 329
They brought Galileo before the Inquisition and forced him to denounce his theory.

page 330
Kepler.

page 335
Paris.

page 336
Reformed the judicial system; urged religious tolerance; gave aid to peasants.

page 338
Rousseau.

page 341
To advertise their power and glory; to inspire patriotism.

page 341
Elaborate, light, delicate.

page 342
Defoe, Richardson, Fielding.

page 343
It began to stress balance, contrast; became a refined expression of emotion.

Chapter Review

page 344, Reviewing the Main Ideas
1. One based on reason and observation.
2. It seemed to prove that science was the hope of the human race; that people would understand and master nature.
3. It was argued that absolute monarchy was the best form of government because only an absolute monarch could maintain order and allow natural law to prevail.
4. Scholars looked for evidence to support accounts of the past; examined manuscripts; studied old coins; analyzed historical inscriptions; developed an interest in chronology to relate to the dating systems of different peoples.
5. Traditional beliefs were questioned; religious tolerance spread; people were less certain that their religion was the only truth.
6. Skepticism; freedom of all kinds; faith in progress.
7. Urged religious tolerance; protection of human rights; education for all. It was limited by vested interests of the aristocracy and the churches.
8. Locke thought that there was an agreement between people and the ruler. Rousseau thought that sovereignty belonged to the people, and people had the right to change governments.
9. It was encouraged by the Church as a way to inspire religious feelings; by the monarchs to advertise their power, and to inspire patriotism.
10. Realism; scenes of everyday life, still life.
11. Greek and Roman classicism reflected order and reason.

page 345, Discussing Important Ideas
1. Answers may vary.
2. Answers may vary; mention should be made of at least one example of society and government.
3. Answers may vary; mention should be made of the theory of a contract between the people and the government.

4. Answers may vary.
5. Answers may vary.
6. Answers may vary; mention should be made of vested interest of the Church.
7. Answers may vary.
8. Answers may vary.

page 328, Using Illustrations
1. Lady at table. Answers may vary.
2. Globe, atlases.
3. A geography lesson.
4. Answers may vary.
5. No. They are obviously servants.
6. Its popularity.

CHAPTER 15
Age of Revolution

At the conclusion of this chapter, students should be able to:
1. discuss the development of Britain's parliamentary government from the time of Charles I.
2. list the key events and Enlightenment ideas that produced the American Revolution.
3. describe the makeup of the three estates of French society and their roles in the outbreak of the French Revolution.
4. identify the factors that enabled Napoleon to replace a revolutionary republic with a dictatorship.
5. describe Napoleon's important domestic reforms.

Overview

In the cases of the three major revolutions presented in this chapter, there was never a complete breakdown of law and order. However, in each revolution, the power of the monarchy was greatly reduced. As a result of England's Glorious Revolution, Parliament assured that it would remain the dominant force in all matters pertaining to political power. The American Revolution, which took place nearly a century after the English Revolution, came about because the colonists felt that the English Parliament and king no longer represented their interests. The French Revolution, the most violent of the three, was a reaction to the wealth and the tyranny of the privileged classes. It was carried out by the middle class with the help of reform-minded nobles and the underprivileged

classes of Paris. The final section on Napoleon describes what can happen when a revolutionary body loses control of the government and order is restored by a military dictator. Important concepts include the divine right of kings, universal manhood suffrage, constitutional monarchy, parliamentary government, federal system, bourgeoisie, "right" and "left," and the Continental System.

Teaching Strategies
Section 1

Introduction: Have students consider revolution in government as partly due to a breakdown in communication between the leadership and the people. In medieval times, communications were difficult. It was easy for a ruling elite to hide its shortcomings from the people. Ask students what changed about this relationship during the Renaissance, the reformation period, and the Age of Reason. They should realize that a middle class had taken root. At first it spent energy acquiring wealth or position through commerce or serving monarchs. But, by the late 1600's, portions of the middle class had become as wealthy as the nobility. By the 1700's, the middle class had begun to control armies and parliaments. In England, this process had taken place in the early 1600's.

Ask students what happens in a student organization when its officers and members fail to communicate. As they read the section, they should recognize the role that poor communication played in fostering revolution in England.

Development: Have students prepare a written assignment that describes the English governmental structure at each major juncture from absolute monarchy to parliamentary government.

Section 2

Introduction: To orient students to the section, ask them to recall what they know about the causes of the American Revolution. Have them check their recollections as they read the section.

Development: Ask students to turn to the picture on page 355 and answer the caption question. Have a class reading of the entire Declaration of Independence, then elicit more responses about how it reflects Enlightenment thought. Were there other aspects of the new nation's government that showed Enlightenment influence? (Political power was divided according to Montesquieu's recommendations; the Constitution was a social contract.)

Section 3

Introduction: The chapter opening picture on page 346 captures some of the violence of the French Revolution. The date historians usually assign to the French Revolution is 1789, however, it should be understood that the revolution did not actually end until Napoleon Bonaparte gained control of the state in 1799. To further set the mood for this section, have students read the feature "Revolutionary Music" (p. 362). Ask students to look for four phases of the revolution as they read the section.

Development: Ask students to discuss the phases of the revolution that they discerned in their reading. The four most often cited are: (1) 1789-1792, establishment of a constitutional monarchy; (2) 1792-1793, Jacobin revolt and establishment of a republic (actually lasted until 1795, but the Reign of Terror constitutes a third phase); (3) 1793-1795, Reign of Terror; and (4) 1795-1799, establishment of the conservative Directory.

Section 4

Introduction: Although France was given a new constitution after Napoleon's takeover in 1799, its government actually became a dictatorship. Napoleon promised that he would safeguard the revolution's reforms. Have students evaluate how well he kept his promise.

Development: Napoleon's retreat from Russia proved to be the beginning of the end. Have students illustrate on an outline map (with arrows and other symbols) the invasion of Russia and how it was crushed by allied European forces.

Conclusion: Ask students to make a chart that shows the causes and outcomes of the Glorious Revolution, the American War of Independence, and the French Revolution. This may be an individual or group project.

Answers
Section Review Questions

page 353
1. James I—inherited English throne after Elizabeth I's death.

William Laud—Archbishop of Canterbury under Charles I.

Petition of Right—prevented the monarch from collecting taxes; no imprisonment without just cause; no billeting; no declaration of martial law in peace time.

Long Parliament—it continued to meet for 20 years.

Oliver Cromwell—Puritan leader of the Roundheads; executed Charles I.

Levelers—group of radicals; called for religious freedom and universal male suffrage.

"Nonconformists"—Protestants who did not conform to the Church of England.

Whigs—those who wanted to exclude James from the throne.

Act of Settlement—stated that the throne of England could not be held by a Catholic.

William of Orange—became William III.

Robert Walpole—Whig leader, first prime minister of England.

2. Appointed a hated enemy as Archbishop; levied "forced loans"; billeted troops; persecuted the Puritans.

3. Puritan rules were abandoned; dancing, sports, and the theater were restored.

4. Bill of Rights was passed; Parliament's power could not then be challenged.

page 357
1. Navigation Acts—forbad manufacture of certain goods in the colonies; listed colonial products that could be sold only to Britain.

George Grenville—first Lord of the Treasury.

Quebec Act—annexed to Quebec all territory north of the Ohio River.

Thomas Paine—radical publisher.

Saratoga—site of British defeat by Americans.

Yorktown—site of British surrender to Americans.

Articles of Confederation—agreement for league of independent American states.

Bill of Rights—amendments added to the American constitution to protect states' rights and individual liberties.

2. To force colonists to help pay the cost of their own defense.

3. A skillful general; help from the French; did not have to fight a long-distance war.

4. A federal system with power divided between a central and regional governments.

page 364
1. Third Estate—all people of France except clergy and nobility.
   Robert Turgot—finance minister under Louis XVI.
   Abbe Sieyès—writer of a pamphlet presenting the case of the Third Estate.
   Tennis Court Oath—made by members of the National Assembly to remain in session until a constitution for France was completed.
   Bastille—Parisian prison.
   Jacobins—extreme left radicals.
   Maximilien Robespierre—head of the Committee of Public Safety.
   The Directory—members of France's legislative assembly.
2. To solve the financial crisis.
3. Feudal dues and tithes were abolished; freedom under law of speech, religion, and press.
4. To stop the counter-revolutionaries.

page 367
1. Concordat of 1801—freedom of religion given to French Catholics.
   Napoleonic Code—made law clear and consistent.
   Treaty of Amiens—France's peace treaty with Britain.
   William Pitt—British prime minister.
   Confederation of the Rhine—organization of German states under Napoleon.
   Alexander I—ruler of Russia.
   Horatio Nelson—defeated the French navy in the Battle of Trafalgar.
   Continental System—Napoleon's plan to destroy Britain's trade.
   Elba—island in the Mediterranean, site of Napoleon's first exile.
   Waterloo—site of Napoleon's final defeat.
2. The power of the British navy prevented his invasion.
3. The Russians burned everything as they retreated; French army left without supplies or shelter for the winter.

Special Feature Questions
page 362
1. It can stir people to action.

2. "The Liberty Song," "Yankee Doodle," "The Marseillaise," "The Internationale."

Photo Questions
page 348
He dissolved it.

page 350
People were forced to accept a strict Puritan moral code.

page 353
Head of a cabinet that makes up the executive branch of government.

page 354
That all documents, newspapers, ship's papers, and advertisements had to be stamped and taxes paid.

page 355
It reflected the ideas of natural law and the social contract.

page 358
Feudal dues, fees, fines, church tithe, taille, fees for mills and presses.

page 359
Nobles wanted three chambers; one noble, one clergy, one Third Estate, each to have an equal vote. Third Estate wanted representation based on number of people.

page 360
Forced the king and queen to return to Paris.

page 364
He defeated the Austrian and Sardinian armies.

Chapter Review
page 368, Reviewing the Main Ideas
1. James's belief in the divine right of kings; his extravagance; foreign policy; rejection of Puritan cause.
2. Charles was beheaded; England declared a commonwealth.

page 369
3. The king could not raise taxes, maintain an army, or suspend laws.
4. It left Britain in debt with more land to protect; began taxing colonists for their defense.

5. Duties placed on glass, lead, paper, and tea.
6. They were familiar with Locke and other Enlightenment thinkers.
7. The United States was formed and recognized as an independent nation.
8. It inspired those who wanted a republican government in France.
9. They were the most outspoken for freedom and social justice.
10. It was unable to control inflation or put down unrest.
11. He imposed his code of law, allowed freedom of religion in countries he controlled.

page 369, Discussing Important Ideas
1. Answers may vary.
2. Answers may vary; mention should be made of the English fear of Spanish dominance.
3. Answers may vary; mention should be made of the idea of natural law and social contract.
4. Answers may vary.
5. Answers may vary.
6. Answers may vary; mention should be made of specific classes in each country.
7. Answers may vary; mention should be made of protest, voting.
8. Answers may vary; specific aspects should be contrasted and compared, reasons, results.

page 369, Using Maps
1. European claims in North America in 1763 and 1783.
2. The addition of the United States.
3. Gained: United States; lost: Russia, Britain, Spain, France.
4. Britain, Russia, Spain.

CHAPTER 16
Reform and Reaction

At the conclusion of this chapter, students should be able to:
1. discuss the peace arrangements in Europe after the era of Napoleon and explain the rationale underlying them.
2. outline the grievances that led to (1) the French revolutions of 1830 and 1848 and (2) the wave of revolutions in 1848 in Austria, Italy, and Prussia.
3. analyze the roles that liberalism and nationalism played in the political events in Europe between 1815 and 1848.
4. review the reasons for the breakdown of the Concert of Europe, focusing on the Crimean War.

Overview
The chapter begins with the Congress of Vienna. It explains why the Congress was convened and how the European powers sought to restore absolute monarchy in Europe and to suppress the liberal ideas of the French Revolution and the Napoleonic era. The next section in the chapter discusses the revolutionary upheavals in Europe during the first half of the nineteenth century. In most cases these revolutions had inconclusive outcomes. The final section covers the Crimean War and its negative effect on European cooperation. This chapter has many important concepts. They include: nationalism, liberalism, territorial compensation, legitimate rule, balance of power, status quo, socialism, realpolitik, and autonomy.

Teaching Strategies
Section 1
Introduction: A few months after Napoleon's defeat in 1815, a peace conference was convened in Vienna. Besides wanting to restore peace and stability to the European continent, the conservative, aristocratic leaders of the five great powers wanted something more—restoration of the "good old days" of absolute monarchy when royalty, nobility, and high-ranking clergy could once again wield absolute power.

Although a dictator, Napoleon had challenged several aspects of the old order, such as the large landholdings and the collection of tithes by the Catholic Church, a legal system that favored the nobility and wealthy classes, a university system that admitted mostly the upper classes, a requirement for lifelong military service, and a policy that denied the right of assembly and freedom of religion. (Students should be able to come up with a few of these.) Behind the facade of high-sounding names such as the Concert of Europe, the Holy Alliance, and the Quadruple Alliance, were the goals of reestablishing traditional royal governments and maintaining the status quo (defined on p. 374). As students read the section, have them make a list of the measures taken by the leading powers of Europe to reestablish the old order. How successful were these measures between 1814 and 1830?

Development: Have students compare the map on page 373 with the map of Europe at the height of Napoleon's power on page 366. Ask students to evaluate how each of the five major European powers fared in terms of territorial compensation accomplished at the Congress of Vienna.

Section 2

Introduction: Draw a long horizontal line on the chalkboard, labeling the left end *Liberalism* and the right end *Conservatism*. Ask students: Which forms of government experienced by France between 1800 and 1850 were linked to liberalism (republic and constitutional monarchy) and which to conservatism (dictatorship and absolute monarchy)? Have them discuss and determine where along the line, or continuum, on the board they would place each of these. Note that this exercise implies that the liberal-conservative continuum is for governments. In the United States today, such a continuum would make little sense—except, perhaps, to compare different administrations. But a liberal-conservative continuum for political groups or individuals would be a reasonable comparison. Sketching a continuum is a fast, easy way for students to visually compare data when dealing with relatively opposite concepts that have a more or less continuous range of possible positions between them. To provide more practice in this technique, students could do a liberal-conservative continuum for the different social and political groups involved in the French revolutions of 1830 and 1848.

Development: Have students compare and contrast the revolutions of 1848 in Austria, Italy, and Prussia in terms of their causes and results. What roles did nationalism and liberalism play in each?

Section 3

Introduction: Many historians believe that the tragedy of the Crimean War was that its purpose could have been accomplished by diplomacy rather than by force. Ask students to read the section and jot down statements in the text that they feel would support this conclusion. What *was* the war's purpose? Have students read the feature on Florence Nightingale (p. 381) before going to page 383.

Development: By the second half of the nineteenth century, it had become clear that the liberal, parliamentary government of Britain was beginning to dominate world politics, thus departing from the ideals of the Concert of Europe. Ask students how other nations were departing from the Concert and the balance of power established at the Congress of Vienna. What role did realpolitik play in these developments?

Conclusion: It seems surprising that between 1815 and 1848 tiny power elites in many European countries were able to suppress the liberal and nationalist desires of the vast majority of Europeans. Have students discuss the reasons for this (for example, elites controlled the "legitimate" force of courts and armies).

Answers
Section Review Questions
page 375

1. Clemens Prince von Metternich—chief delegate at Congress of Vienna; Austrian minister of foreign affairs.
   German Confederation—thirty-nine German states headed by Austria.
   Concert of Europe—advisory congress, the Metternich system.
   Carlsbad Decrees—imposed censorship on publications, suppressed freedom of speech in Prussia.
   Troppau Protocol—statement to never recognize the right of the people to revolt against their leader.
2. Britain: Viscount Castlereagh. Prussia: Frederick William III. Russia: Alexander I. France: Tallyrand. Austria: Metternich.
3. It reestablished a balance of power in Europe.
4. To establish international order on principles of "Justice, Christian Charity, and Peace." To maintain the settlements of Vienna.

page 379

1. Charter of Liberties—guarantee of equal law and individual liberties.
   July Ordinances—dissolved the legislature; restricted voting rights; censored the press.
   Citizen-King—Louis-Philippe of France.
   Louis Blanc—French socialist reformer.

T85

François Guizot—Prime Minister under Louis-Philippe.

Louis Kossuth—leader of Magyar nationalists.

Francis Joseph—Austrian emperor.

2. Issuance of the July Ordinances.
3. Republicans, socialists. Neither wanted a monarchy.
4. Austria: revolutionists were given concessions that were later rescinded. Italy: revolts were crushed. Prussia: the status quo was restored.

page 384

1. Felix Schwarzenberg—Austrian diplomat; advanced the practice of realpolitik.

Lord Aberdeen—British prime minister.

Lord Clarendon—British foreign secretary.

Lord Palmerston—former foreign secretary of Britain.

Crimean Peninsula—Russian peninsula in the Black Sea.

Florence Nightingale—set up hospitals during the Crimean War.

Battle of Balaklava—site of British cavalry defeat by Russian artillery.

Wallachia and Moldavia—two territories of Russia; later became Romania.

2. It introduced realpolitik based on practical goals to promote the interests of a group or nation.
3. He regarded himself as defender and protector of all Eastern Orthodox people.
4. Lord Palmerston, public opinion, the press.

Photo Questions

page 372
Britain: Castlereagh. Prussia: Frederick William III. Russia: Alexander I. France: Talleyrand. Austria: Metternich.

page 374
Britain, Austria, Prussia, Russia; to maintain the status quo in Europe.

page 376
The returning, extremely conservative, émigrés.

page 377
Republicans, socials, liberal monarchists.

page 379
France, Austria, Italy, Prussia.

page 382
Nicholas I's efforts to extend his power over Ottoman territory; British and French fear of Russian expansion; British public opinion.

Chapter Review

page 384, Reviewing the Main Ideas

1. Compensation; legitimacy; balance of power.
2. Reduced to the borders of 1790; buffer states established around France; the Bourbon monarchy restored.
3. Pius VII; the papacy needed no new interpretation of Christian truth. Prince regent of Britain; did not have approval of Parliament.
4. A revolt against the Spanish government.
5. They objected to the return of the old order.
6. It established a constitutional monarchy.
7. They demanded an extension of voting rights.
8. Louis Kossuth; their own constitution and separate parliament.
9. To draw up a constitution for a united Germany.
10. Russia's territorial expansion; France and Britain's fears for their Middle East trade; no well-defined British foreign policy.
11. It was permanently destroyed.
12. Guaranteed independence of the Ottoman Empire; self government to Wallachia and Moldavia; established international sea trade rules during war. It gave them independence from Russia.

page 385, Discussing Important Ideas

1. Answers may vary; mention should be made of status quo and realpolitik.
2. Answers may vary; mention should be made of vested interests.
3. Answers may vary.
4. Answers may vary.
5. Answers may vary.
6. Answers may vary.
7. Answers may vary.
8. Answers may vary; mention could be made of the power of the press and public opinion.

page 385, Using Maps

1. German States, Prussia, part of the Austrian Empire, part of Belgium.
2. Italian States, German States, Switzerland, Belgium.
3. Austria, Prussia.

4. Ottoman Empire, Russian Empire.
5. East-southeast.

Unit Review

page 386, Developing Understanding
1. The major powers worked together to support absolutism and the divine right of monarchs.
2. The difficulties of ruling a scattered empire periodically torn by political and religious revolts. The French Bourbons unified and strengthened France.
3. Institutions and values were reexamined with reason and observation.
4. They emphasized subjective mannerism, baroque, rococo, realism, and neoclassicism. These reflected the influence of Enlightenment and other major movements.
5. It helped prevent any major takeover of one country by another.
6. In Britain it limited the powers of the monarchs. In America and France they eliminated monarchy entirely.
7. They created alliances to protect the agreements of Congress of Vienna.

pages 386-387, Developing Skills
Conclude the unit with the Developing Skills activity. This activity is most suitable for individuals, although class discussion is recommended. The exercise gives students an opportunity to see how a historical account may be biased by the selection or stressing of certain facts.

The exercise provides two topic sentences, each of which gives a different slant to the subject of Napoleon Bonaparte's reforms. It also provides a list of ten facts, some of which support one topic sentence and some of which support the other—but all of which are true. Students are asked to write a paragraph, choosing one of the sentences and four or five facts to support it.

You may want to begin by discussing the difference between the two topic sentences. After the exercise is completed, have several students read their paragraphs aloud. Topic sentence "a" may be supported by facts 2, 4, 5, 6, and 10. Topic sentence "b" may be supported by facts 1, 3, 7, 8, and 9.

UNIT 5
The Rise of Modern Europe

At the conclusion of this unit, students should be able to:
1. explain how the Industrial Revolution profoundly altered economic, social, demographic, and political traditions.
2. describe the responses to industrialism of economic and political theorists and of writers and artists.
3. analyze the process of governmental change in western and central Europe.

Overview

This unit covers the economic, social, political and intellectual changes in Europe that were triggered by the Industrial Revolution. Chapter 17 focuses on the Industrial Revolution itself, set against a background of existing social and demographic conditions. Chapter 18 looks at the range of responses to the changes brought about by industrialization, including capitalism, utopian and Marxian socialism, and a variety of literary and artistic movements. Chapter 19 considers the development of democratic forms of government in western Europe with emphasis on the contrasts between Britain and France. Chapter 20 treats the unification of Italy and Germany and their forms of government.

Introducing the Unit

To remind students of what daily life was like before the Industrial Revolution, ask them to list the items in their homes that were made by machines and factories, or brought to their homes by cars or trucks. Small groups could work on lists for particular categories of items: shelter and clothing; kitchen and food; information and entertainment; and transportation. Write their reported lists on the chalkboard and ask students what their lives would be like without those items. Would they live in the same place? Be as well informed or know as many people? Live as long? Participate in government? Conclude with an essay assignment, "My Life if I Lived in 1700."

CHAPTER 17
The Industrial Revolution

At the conclusion of this chapter, students should be able to:
1. describe the social, economic, and demographic conditions in pre-industrial Europe.
2. identify the causes of the Industrial Revolution, significant early breakthroughs, and key inventions.
3. describe important changes that took place as a result of the Industrial Revolution.

Overview

Chapter 17 places the Industrial Revolution in social and demographic context so that students can judge the tremendous upheavals brought by the Industrial Revolution. The chapter details the reasons for Britain's early lead, the key developments in energy, textiles, iron and steel, transportation and communication. It describes the spread of the Industrial Revolution to the European continent and North America. It concludes with a look at some of the social and demographic changes that followed. Important concepts are self-sufficiency, subsistence living, mass production, division of labor, and urban development.

Teaching Strategies
Section 1

Introduction: Have some students read aloud their essays on "My Life if I Lived in 1700." Then tell students to read the introduction to the chapter and the first section. They should watch for surprising or additional pieces of information about pre-industrial life.

Development: Pre-industrial life was extremely stable and predictable. A circle diagram can help

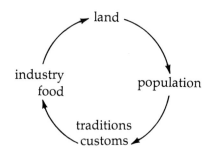

students analyze and review the components that kept the small rural systems functioning the way they always had. The families and the village they belonged to made up a closed system that was fairly isolated from most other changes.

Section 2

Introduction: Discuss what types of events or developments could break the stable system that existed. Have students read the section to find out what in fact did happen.

Development: Gradual changes resulting in declining death rates and increasing birthrates led to rapid population growth across Europe. Point out that this was a precondition of the Industrial Revolution, not a direct cause. Emigration, famine, or war could have reduced the population pressures. Industrialization occurred first in Britain due to the coincidence of conditions described.

Section 3

Introduction: Use the image of a logjam or a bottleneck to describe conditions in basic industries around 1700. Output in each industry was limited because of a number of technical problems. Once the problems were solved—which took place over the first 100 years of the Industrial Revolution—other changes came rapidly. Have students watch for the bottlenecks or the problems causing the logjam as they read this section.

Development: A chart can help students keep track of the important early developments. Draw a chart on the chalkboard with five columns and the following headings: *Industry, Bottlenecks, How Solved, By Whom,* and *When.* Ask students to copy and fill in the chart as they review the section. Which breakthrough do students think was the most important for the advance of the Industrial Revolution? Have them explain why.

Section 4

Introduction: The Industrial Revolution spread to other countries with differing rates of industrialization. Ask students what factors might be behind these differing rates. Have students read the section to confirm or revise their answers. Students should note differences in available resources, government policies, economic conditions, and attitudes toward change.

Development: During the second phase of the Industrial Revolution, from the 1870's on, advances in science and technology greatly accelerated the pace of industrialization. Have students add additional information from this section to their charts above. The attitude toward change and the linkage between science, technology, and industrial growth were important factors in the change of industrial leadership from Britain to the United States and Germany after the 1870's.

Section 5

Introduction: Compare the changes caused by the Industrial Revolution to a stone thrown into a pond. The Industrial Revolution produced a ripple effect that was far-reaching and in many ways unexpected. Tell students that the changes they read about in this section are only a few of the changes. They should try to identify others. Political consequences will be discussed in the following chapters.

Development: The changes discussed in the section are generally negative early changes. Discuss and/or have students research positive changes, such as improvements in medicine, better standards of living, more leisure time, and broader access to books, education, and entertainment.

Conclusion: Remind students of the statement of the historian in the chapter introduction (p. 391), that the Industrial Revolution has been so vast that it is comparable only to the Neolithic Revolution. Do students agree or disagree with his conclusion based on what they have learned during the course of this chapter? In answering the question, they may also compare the Industrial Revolution to other revolutions they have studied earlier, such as the Renaissance, Reformation, or French Revolution.

Answers
Section Review Questions

page 394
1. Rural villages or in the countryside.
2. Land was the source of livelihood and well-being. Marriage and inheritance.
3. Farming was the main occupation. Tradition was central; it determined farming practices.

page 398
1. Increased demand for food and rising prices led to increased production, beginning of an agricultural revolution.

2. Increased food supplies; better sanitation and hygiene.
3. Enclosed fields to increase efficiency and productivity; introduced new methods and crops; conducted scientific experiments to increase yields.

page 402
1. Thomas Newcomen—invented a practical steam pump.
   Abraham Darby—developed a process for turning coal into coke for smelting iron.
   Henry Bessemer—developed a process of producing cheap steel in a blast furnace.
   Sir William Siemens—developed the open hearth process of steel production.
   Emile and Pierre Martin—improved the open hearth process with Siemens.
   John Kay—invented the flying shuttle.
   James Hargreaves—invented the spinning jenny.
   Richard Arkwright—developed the water frame, which used water power to do spinning.
   Edmund Cartwright—invented a power loom.
   Samuel Crompton—invented a spinning machine named the mule.
   Eli Whitney—invented the cotton gin.
   James Watt—developed the steam engine.
   Robert Fulton—developed the first practical steamboat, the *Clermont*.
   Robert Trevithick—developed the first rail locomotive.
   George Stephenson—developed the first railroad.
2. With increased coal production, there was more fuel to smelt iron ore.
3. The new machines became too large, too heavy, and too costly to be used in workers' homes.
4. Railroads, river steamboats, and later, oceanic steamships provided faster, cheaper transportation.

page 408
1. William Cockerill—built the first wool-carding and wool-spinning machines in Belgium.
   Eli Whitney—developed the idea of mass production and standardized interchangeable parts.
   Cyrus McCormick—invented the mechanical reaper.

Zénobe Théophile Gramme—developed the first commercially successful electric dynamo.
Morse Code—system of dots and dashes representing letters of the alphabet; used internationally to send telegraph messages.
Alexander Graham Bell—invented the telephone.
Thomas Edison—invented the incandescent electric light bulb.
Guglielmo Marconi—invented the radio.
Sir Charles Parsons—developed a steam turbine for use with steam, air, or water.
Gottlieb Daimler—developed a small portable internal-combustion engine.
Rudolf Diesel—patented the first oil-burning internal-combustion engine.
Henry Ford—developed the assembly-line process for production of cars.
Ferdinand von Zeppelin—designed and built motor-powered, gas-filled dirigibles.
Alberto Santos-Dumont—designed and built dirigibles.
Orville and Wilbur Wright—early inventors of airplanes.
2. Internal tolls made it costly to distribute goods; Napoleonic Wars had hurt the economy; French produced mostly luxury and hand-crafted goods.
3. Discovered that science and technology could be useful in developing new industrial ideas, applications, and methods of production. It greatly speeded the pace and scope of industrialization.

page 411
1. People moved from rural areas to towns and cities.
2. Inadequate housing and poor sanitation.
3. Hours were long—12 to 19 hours a day, six days a week; conditions were often dangerous; child labor; and low wages.
4. Separation broke the family as a cooperative unit; men centered on jobs outside of the home; women became restricted to homes and child rearing.

Photo Questions
page 392
A son expected to inherit enough land to support a family. A daughter was not allowed rights of ownership.

page 393
Industry served local needs; the workers joined the farmers in harvest, performed industrial trades in the winter months.

page 396
They used fertilizer, began breeding livestock for desired quality.

page 399
Water was pumped out; safety lamps; dust control.

page 400
A method that brought workers and machines together under control of management.

page 402
Coal and steel; transportation of goods and people.

page 407
France.

page 410
Dumping of industrial refuse polluted waterways with chemical waste and the air with smoke and poisonous gases.

page 411
Could be paid less and were easier to train than adults.

Special Feature Questions
page 409
1. Population increase; mechanization of textile industry.
2. Answers may vary.

Chapter Review
page 412, Reviewing the Main Ideas
1. The textile industry was related to raising sheep. Coal was mined on farm property by workers who often became farm laborers during the harvest.
2. Most people lived in rural villages, and work was done in nearby fields or in family cottages and workshops. All members of the family had to work to survive.
3. Marriages were arranged to protect property and economic status. Marriages were often postponed until property was inherited to insure being able to support a family.
4. Population growth was caused by a drop in the death rate due to increased food supply, improved sanitation; by a growth in the birthrate due to earlier marriages. Population growth led to increased demand for land, food, and other goods; increased tensions within families; the possibility of large-scale disaster in case of widespread crop failure; increased migration and emigration.
5. The enclosure movement increased agricultural productivity but displaced many small farmers.
6. Britain had the advantages of agricultural prosperity, a large labor force, plentiful capital, important natural resources, and talented inventors and entrepreneurs. Many mechanics and technicians took their skills to other lands, and British financiers invested in other countries.
7. The price of steel dropped. Its use was expanded to the construction of bridges, ships, buildings.
8. Developments such as the water frame and power loom led to the decline of the domestic system and the rise of the factory system.
9. Steam power was cheap, reliable, and allowed more flexibility in locating factories. It led to the development of railroads and steamships.

page 413
10. One invention led to another through improvement and innovation.
11. The dramatic shift in centers of population. It broke down family life and established new roles for men and women.

page 413, Discussing Important Ideas
1. Answers may vary.
2. No, because the Industrial Revolution required a large labor force and high demand for goods.
3. Some people think population growth should be limited to avoid mass starvation.
4. Answers may vary. One example is the demand for cars leading to development of the petroleum and rubber industries.
5. Answers may vary.
6. Answers may vary.
7. Answers may vary.
8. The chief advantage was the increased standard of living over the long run.

Disadvantages included the decline of traditional values, hardships for workers, pollution, effects on family life.

page 413, Using Charts
1. The immediate effect of one area of impact on the next.
2. They are interrelated.
3. Increased leisure and travel, decline in transportation costs, coordination of time zones, breakdown of regional barriers, access to frontiers, increased military mobility, spread of products, new jobs, growth of suburbs, increased cultural exchange.
4. They are affected by two areas of impact.
5. Answers may vary; building of railroads, manufacture of rails, locomotives, should be mentioned.

CHAPTER 18
Response to the Industrial Revolution

At the conclusion of this chapter, students should be able to:
1. explain the economic theories developed by Smith, Ricardo, Bentham, and Mill.
2. compare and contrast utopian socialism with scientific socialism.
3. identify major literary and artistic movements that developed in response to the Industrial Revolution.

Overview

Chapter 18 surveys the intellectual and artistic response to the Industrial Revolution. It is divided into three broad sections. The first looks at the attempts of classical economic theorists to explain the economic forces underlying capitalism. Natural laws, such as supply and demand, are used to justify laissez-faire policies. These views become those of the mainstream in the nineteenth century. The second section considers socialist alternatives to capitalism offered by utopian socialists and by Marx and Engels. The final section describes the major literary and artistic responses that evolved through apparent avoidance of change, and later acceptance of change. Major concepts include capitalism, laissez faire, supply and demand, utilitarianism, utopian socialism, scientific socialism, communism, romanticism, evolution, realism, naturalism, and impressionism.

Teaching Strategies
Section 1

Introduction: Tell students about the Luddites, the angry mobs of workers who, in the earliest days of the Industrial Revolution, attempted to halt the spread of industrialization by smashing machines. Ask students what might have motivated their actions. Explain that the early years of industrialization produced pride, fears, uncertainties, and many questions. Was this progress? Could the workers' lot be improved? How? What should be the role of governments? Tell students that they will encounter a variety of answers during their reading.

Development: Make sure that students understand Smith's explanation of the workings of capitalism, the role of competition, supply and demand, and "the invisible hand." Ask how laissez faire follows from his thinking. Have students analyze Ricardo, Bentham, and Mill to see where these later thinkers agree and disagree with Smith. How does Mill hold out a more optimistic vision of the future?

Section 2

Introduction: Have students read this section. Make sure they understand utopian socialism by asking these questions: What were the aims of the utopian socialists? Why did they reject capitalism? What were their programs for achieving their goals? Why did they fail? Could they have succeeded? Does the desire to create ideal communities still exist? Some students may be interested in discussing the efforts to establish communes in the 1970's.

Development: After students have seen that utopian socialists were well-intentioned, but impractical in their approach, have them consider how Marx and Engels altered socialist theory with their concepts of scientific socialism, the economic foundations of history, and change through class struggle. What appeal does the term "scientific" hold out to workers?

Marxism should be presented so that students understand the power of Marx's insights and the flaws in his conclusions. Most notably, class solidarity has proved erroneous. Ideas about liberty, equality, nationalism, self-determination, democracy, and human rights have proven to be more important than the struggle between labor and capitalists.

Section 3

Introduction: Compare and contrast three of the paintings provided in the text, one romantic, one realist, and one impressionist. Students should consider the subject matter, technique, composition, and emotional messages of the paintings. Have them read the section to learn more about the different movements that encompassed literature, art, and music.

Development: To reinforce and extend student understanding of the movements described in the section, provide additional samples organized thematically. Poems, prose extracts, paintings, drawings, and synopses of operas could be compared for their treatment of nature, industry, machines, cities, the worker, and average people.

Conclusion: In review, have students try to categorize the movements and individuals described in the chapter according to their attitudes toward industrial change. Propose three categories: positive (approving of change), negative (rejecting change), and neutral (neither approving nor rejecting). Did attitudes change as the Industrial Revolution developed? How? Where do twentieth-century feelings about industrialization fit?

Answers
Section Review Questions

page 418

1. *The Wealth of Nations*—published in 1776 by Adam Smith; argued that individual welfare, wealth, self-interest, and competition should be the basis of national wealth.

   Adam Smith—Scottish professor; developed the theory of capitalism as a free market system that operated best without government interference.

   David Ricardo—British economist; had a gloomy view of the prospects for improving the lot of the poor.

   Principles of Political Economy and Taxation—published in 1819 by Ricardo.

   Iron Law of Wages—Ricardo's theory that wages could not rise above subsistence level because of the forces of supply and demand.

Jeremy Bentham—British thinker; developed the concept of utilitarianism as the criterion for determining and judging government policy.

   John Stuart Mill—British thinker; made contributions in logic, ethics, philosophy, politics, and economics.

   Principles of Political Economy—published in 1848 by John Stuart Mill; he argued that wealth of individuals was determined not by natural law, but by custom and government policy.

2. Smith believed that nations should be concerned with individual welfare and wealth rather than amassing national bullion. He opposed government interference in such areas as tariffs and other trade restrictions.

3. Ricardo thought that wages would never rise above subsistence because wages were linked to population, and the labor pool would rise and fall based on the laws of supply and demand.

4. Since the distribution of wealth was determined by custom and government policy, Mill believed government policies could be changed to protect against monopolies, preserve competition, and safeguard individual rights.

page 422

1. Comte de Saint-Simon—early French utopian socialist; believed workers, not aristocrats, should receive the highest income.

   Charles Fourier—early French utopian socialist; developed the idea of regrouping society into phalansteries, model communities.

   Robert Owen—Scottish manufacturer and utopian socialist; created the model cooperative communities of New Lanark and New Harmony.

   Karl Marx—German originator of the ideas of scientific socialism.

   Friedrich Engels—German businessman and intellectual collaborator with Marx.

   Georg Wilhelm Friedrich Hegel—German philosopher; believed that history advanced through the clash of ideas.

   The Communist Manifesto—published by Marx and Engels in 1848; it became the platform of the Communist League, urged workers to unite in the struggle against capitalists.

Das Kapital—three-volume theoretical foundation of scientific socialism written by Marx with help from Engels.

2. Utopian socialism sought the development of ideal societies in which there would be no poverty and all would benefit fairly from their labors.

3. The idea that history is the result of struggle between classes.

4. Ruling classes would give up their control of production only through revolution.

page 433

1. Jean-Jacques Rousseau—French philosopher; emphasized the senses and emotions over reason and intellect.

Johann Wolfgang von Goethe—important German romantic; had a mystical feeling for nature and a love of Germany's medieval past.

George Sand—pseudonym of female writer Aurore Dupin; French aristocrat and romantic novelist.

Victor Hugo—French romantic novelist, author of *The Hunchback of Notre Dame* and *Les Miserables*.

William Wordsworth—British poet; revered nature and had a strong influence on the development of British romantic literature.

Madame Bovary—controversial realist novel by Gustave Flaubert.

Charles Dickens—British novelist and social critic.

Ivan Turgenev—Russian naturalist writer; portrayed peasants in a sensitive, positive way.

Émile Zola—French naturalist writer.

Stephen Crane—American naturalist, author of *The Red Badge of Courage*.

Henrik Ibsen—Norwegian naturalist, playwright best remembered for his portrayals of women trapped by social conventions in *A Doll's House* and *Hedda Gabler*.

Claude Monet—French impressionist painter; he was fascinated with the differences made by variations of light and atmosphere on a given scene.

2. As a source of protection and solace. They loved its beauty, energy, and power.

3. The realistic portrayal of the world and of the efforts of all classes to live and adapt to the changes brought by industrialization. The need for social reform.

4. Impressionist paintings aimed to catch a fleeting moment rather than to be timeless. They violated accepted rules of line, perspective, and studio lighting. The observer had to fill in details.

Special Feature Questions

page 425

1. Developments included discovery of basic elements; atomic theory; discovery of X rays and radium; theory of relativity.

2. Medical advances led to longer and easier life; but the theories of Freud and Darwin were disturbing.

Photo Questions

page 417

A better code of law, universal education, public health service.

page 419

A person's character was formed in part by environment; change the environment to develop the character.

page 420

Marx edited a newspaper; Engels, a successful businessman.

page 421

Once people could produce a surplus.

page 423

That it contributed to the world being cold, overly rational, machinelike.

page 428

Conditions of the poor, prisons, hospitals, poorhouses, law courts.

page 429

Heredity and environment.

page 431

Monet, Manet, Degas, Renoir, Pisarro, Sisley.

page 432

His paintings were composed of small dots of color; pointillism.

Chapter Review

page 434, Reviewing the Main Ideas
1. Population growth, improved health care, increased production of goods, lower prices, higher wages, extended education, rise of unions.
2. Revolutionized and introduced science into the field.

page 435
3. Belief that rightness was based on usefulness.
4. Efficient administration of the state and freedom of the individual from governmental restrictions.
5. The laws and customs of society.
6. Saint-Simon thought workers, not the idle class, should get the highest income. So did Fourier, who wanted to destroy the artificial restraints of society. Owen thought that competition should be replaced by cooperation.
7. Took over textile mill, improved working and living conditions for workers.
8. Because workers were not paid the full value of their labor.
9. Workers' wages increased, they gained the right to vote, reforms were made.
10. Romanticism, realism, naturalism, symbolism.
11. Wrote about social ills.
12. Art that did not concern moral problems or social ills, but was pleasant and sentimental.

page 435, Discussing Important Ideas
1. Answers may vary.
2. Smith believed that the government should not interfere with economics. Mill believed that the government had to preserve competition and protect individual rights. Both believed in free trade. Most people today, even those who believe that government's role in the economy should be decreased, agree that the government should protect individual rights and perform other minimal functions in the economy. Answers may vary.
3. Answers may vary.
4. Answers may vary; mention should be made that Marx assumed that goods would become abundant and would be distributed according to need. But communist economies have not been that successful. Are

governments needed to organize the allocation of resources? Do most people want to live in a classless society?
5. Unlike the utopian socialists, Marx thought that government would eventually be abolished and that family and religious values would disappear. Saint-Simon wanted a government run by an elite group of scientists and engineers, and did not envision classlessness. Owen did not abolish capitalism from his utopia, although he treated the workers well.
6. Romantic writers wrote sympathetically of workers and made them into heroes. Realists and naturalists also portrayed the suffering of exploited workers.
7. Answers may vary.

page 435, Using Illustrations
1. At the bottom are the workers and farmers; next level are business people; the army; the Church; the rulers.
2. Bottom. Answers may vary.
3. That the worker and farmer supplies all labor and food.
4. They receive few benefits.
5. It would not be a pyramid, all people would receive equal benefits.

CHAPTER 19
Democracy in Western Europe

At the conclusion of this chapter, students should be able to:
1. describe the British constitutional structure in 1800 and the key developments in its reform during the nineteenth century.
2. explain how France achieved a lasting transformation from monarchy to republic.
3. compare and contrast the reform efforts of other western European nations with the British and French experiences.

Overview

Chapter 19 describes the conditions and processes that led to the development and extension of democracy in western Europe. The process of gradual parliamentary reform in Britain is compared with the violent zigzags of

France and its experimentation with different forms of government. The final section provides details on political developments in other western European nations.

The chapter gives students a good opportunity to consider the basic elements of democracy and how democracy can develop in countries with age-old traditions supporting other forms of government. Students should see that democracy can exist in a number of different constitutional arrangements that may combine monarchy with different levels of popular representation. The importance of consensus on political goals, and the influence of the Industrial Revolution in creating vocal, politically active constituencies should also be stressed. Major concepts are parliamentary government, liberalism, conservatism, women's rights, home rule, coalition government, and direct democracy.

Teaching Strategies
Section 1

Introduction: Ask students to define democracy. Can democracy exist in a monarchy? What distinguishes democracy from other forms of government? Tell students that democratic elements were gradually added to the British constitution. Have them read Section 1 to learn how this was achieved.

Development: Review with students the basic constitutional arrangements in Britain in 1800. Make sure students understand how the aristocracy dominated both houses of Parliament through such means as the limited franchise, "rotten boroughs," public voting, and unsalaried representation. Stress the importance of consensus between the Liberal and the Conservative parties in achieving peaceful reform.

Section 2

Introduction: This section considers the efforts of groups who were still dissatisfied—the working class, women, and the Irish—to reach their goals. Ask students whether they think it is possible for such groups to be fully represented by persons who are not members of these groups. To what extent must the experiences and natural interests of the representative and the represented coincide?

Development: Explore with students the alternatives open to disfranchised groups who seek change. The changes can be political, economic,

legal, or social. What advantages are there to working within the political system, as did the Fabians and later the Labor party? What are the disadvantages? Is violence justified? Would the same answers apply in non-democratic systems?

Section 3

Introduction: Ask students whether they can imagine the United States President being overthrown in a coup d'etat. Discuss why it is hard to imagine such an occurrence. Remind students that coups and experimentation with different forms of government occurred several times in France. Have them read the section to learn why this was so.

Development: Contrast the situation in France with developments in Britain. Why was France less stable? Why were there so many factions? What goals and fears prevented the development of a consensus on the form of government? Do students think it was wise or unwise to have universal male suffrage in mid-century France? What are the benefits and the drawbacks to a form of government such as the Second Empire?

Section 4

Introduction: The series of forms of French government provide a good platform for considering what is good or effective government. Analyzing the structure of government takes on greater meaning when the practical ramifications are also explored. Ask students to make a three-column chart with the following headings: *Name of Government, Executive Powers,* and *Legislative Powers.* As they read the section, have them fill in the chart with details about the Second Republic and the Second Empire.

Development: After students have completed the chart above, they should be able to explain where the real power was located in each of the French governments analyzed. Develop criteria for judging good and effective governments. How would students grade each of the governments based on the actions and developments described in the chapter?

Section 5

Introduction: Assign the section, telling students to watch for the factors that influenced the timing and the level of popular participation in the countries described.

Development: Compare the developments in northern Europe with those on the Iberian Peninsula. Why did democracy spread more easily in the more northern countries? Is gradual extension of popular participation better or worse than rapid change?

Conclusion: In small groups, have students try to develop a description of conditions that might result in the lasting extension of democratic elements in a nation's government. Encourage them to be as detailed in their descriptions as possible. Have them test their descriptions against the countries described in the chapter. If they were to choose one country from among the ones they have studied as a model for democratic change in other countries, which one would they choose, and why?

Answers
Section Review Questions

page 442

1. Reform Act of 1832—gave more representation to urban areas; gave vote to middle-class men.

   People's Charter—platform of the Chartists; demanded the extension of democracy through universal male suffrage; the secret ballot; abolition of property requirements for seats in Parliament; pay for representatives; the creation of equal electoral districts.

   Anti-Corn Law League—political group formed to repeal the Corn Law that placed a duty on all imported grains.

   Reform Act of 1867—extended the right to vote to more men.

   William Gladstone—leader of the Liberal party for 50 years; prime minister of Britain four times.

   "Great Ministry"—name given to Gladstone's first term as prime minister, from 1868-1874, because of its many social reforms.

   Redistribution Act of 1885—divided Britain into approximately equal electoral districts.

   Benjamin Disraeli—Gladstone's great rival; leader of the Conservative party and prime minister twice, in 1868 and from 1874-1880.

2. The House of Commons of the British Parliament represented the people in theory. Members were elected by only six percent of British males.

3. Parliament did not reflect the economic, social, and demographic changes that were taking place as a result of the Industrial Revolution.

4. Liberals had their base among the new industrial and commercial classes and members of the old Whig party. Conservative party members were typically landed aristocracy and old Tory party members.

page 447

1. Fabian Society—group of middle class socialists who favored improving the condition of workers through the parliamentary process.

   Labor party—new party in Britain formed by the workers.

   Emmeline Pankhurst—founder, along with her two daughters, of the Women's Social and Political Union, a militant women's suffrage organization.

   The Irish Question—concerned the nature of Ireland's political relationship with Britain.

   Act of Union of 1800—joined Ireland and Britain.

   Charles Stewart Parnell—Irish nationalist leader for home rule.

   David Lloyd George—minister of the treasury who sought to shift some of the tax burden from workers and the middle class to wealthy landowners.

   1911 Parliament Act—removed money bills from control of the House of Lords.

2. An old-age pension bill, health and unemployment insurance, a minimum wage, and workers' accident and illness insurance.

3. Limited control over their own lives, the right to vote in local elections.

4. The Irish resented the economic, political, and religious subordination of Ireland to Britain. Parliament resisted home rule in order to protect the Irish Protestant minority. The British government freed Catholics from payment of church taxes and restored land to displaced tenants.

page 450

1. Louis Napoleon—nephew of Napoleon Bonaparte; elected president of France in 1848.

   Corps Législatif—legislative body in France under Louis Napoleon.

Napoleon III—title taken by Louis Napoleon when he was made king.

Crédit Mobilier—investment bank that sold shares to raise capital for industrial projects.

Adolphe Thiers—Orleanist opposition leader against Napoleon III, and later leader of the National Assembly that defeated the Commune of Paris.

Sedan—site of German victory over the French; Napoleon III taken captive.

Commune of Paris—socialist government established by workers.

Communards—supporters of the Commune of Paris, largely working class Parisians.

2. Legislative authority rested with a unicameral legislature; executive authority with a president. Louis Napoleon—first president.

3. The economy expanded vigorously under Napoleon III with his encouragement of public and private investment.

4. Worsening economic conditions and the embarrassment of the execution of Archduke Maximilian in Mexico were followed by the rapid defeat of France in the Franco-Prussian War.

page 454

1. Count of Chambord—Bourbon heir who refused the offer of the crown after the Franco-Prussian War because of the constitutional restrictions placed upon the crown.

Marshal MacMahon—first president of the Third Republic.

George Boulanger—popular French war hero and minister of war who threatened to overthrow the Third Republic.

Ferdinand de Lesseps—builder of the Suez Canal and president of Panama Company.

Alfred Dreyfus—Jewish officer in the French army accused and wrongly convicted of selling military secrets to the Germans.

''J'accuse''—headline of Zola's letter to newspapers about Dreyfus case.

2. The multiparty system made coalition governments necessary. Cabinets fell when they failed to win legislative support.

3. It protected the rights of people to hold public meetings, lifted press restrictions, and permitted the formation of trade unions. Free compulsory primary education was established and secondary education opened to women. Control of education was taken from the Church.

4. Boulanger, with backing from diverse groups, threatened to overthrow the Third Republic, but failed to carry through. The Panama Company scandal, which involved the corruption of politicians, discredited the government. The Dreyfus affair divided France for more than 10 years over the miscarriage of justice concerning Alfred Dreyfus.

page 456

1. Leopold I—first constitutional monarch of Belgium.

Cuba—Spanish colony that revolted in 1898.

Philippines—Spanish colony in the Pacific that revolted in 1898.

Carlos I—Portuguese king; assassinated in 1908.

2. The strength of tradition in various countries; differences in the rate of industrialization and the development of a large literate, politically active population; and other individual circumstances.

3. Lack of large middle class; influence of Catholic Church; revolts in colonies.

Special Feature Questions

page 452

1. It is the seat of the national government and also the cultural capital.

2. Wide boulevards and big squares replaced narrow streets. Central markets and modern water and sewer systems were built.

Photo Questions

page 438

People of densely populated industrial cities.

page 440

Public rallies; the press.

page 441

Gladstone directed reform in civil administration, education, elections. Disraeli often supported popular conservative legislative efforts, for example, the Reform Act of 1867.

page 442

Increased membership, demonstrations, and strikes. Distressful economic conditions.

page 443
In 1918 for women over 30, 1928 for women over 21.

page 445
Encouraged science and the arts.

page 446
Gladstone, Parnell.

page 448
Economic growth in France.

page 450
They were arrested or killed.

page 453
Royalists, Catholics, anti-Semites, critics of the republic.

Chapter Review

page 457, Reviewing the Main Ideas

1. Redistribution of election districts to reflect greater population of cities; expansion of franchise.
2. Toward democracy. Aristocracy. Democracy.
3. Middle and working class.
4. Parties organized as Conservatives and Liberals and competed for votes.
5. Demonstrations and strikes. At first, working through established parties and then through their own Labor party.
6. House of Lords agreed to higher taxes on wealthy landowners; Lords lost control of money bills.
7. Moderate republicans: supported Second Republic Leftists, called for swift changes in the direction of more democracy. Legitimists: supported Bourbon monarchy. Orleanists: supported Louis Philippe.
8. Through censorship and political repression.
9. The government intervened directly in the economy.
10. A bicameral legislature; executive presidency.
11. Boulanger case: threatened to overthrow the government. Panama scandal: caused distrust of the government. Dreyfus affair: proved that a republican form of government could work in France.
12. Belgium: moved gradually from constitutional monarchy toward democracy with electoral reforms in the 1890's. The Netherlands: executive power shifted away from the monarch and toward a prime minister and cabinet; universal manhood suffrage came about in 1917. Switzerland: had a tradition of democracy in the canton system; a central government was established in 1848; later its powers were expanded, and citizens were given referendum and initiative rights. Denmark: electoral reforms and social legislation passed in 1915. Norway: became independent constitutional monarchy in 1905, with real authority in legislature; votes for women in 1907. Sweden: constitutional monarchy; universal manhood suffrage in 1909 and shortly after, votes for women. Spain: little progress. Portugal: by 1914 had unstable republic as a result of revolution.

page 457, Discussing Important Ideas

1. Fear of change, fear of mob rule, and fear of what the lower classes might do to property rights.
2. May be ceremonial only, or with limited powers.
3. Set a precedent for peaceful, evolutionary change rather than revolution.
4. Name association.
5. Answers may vary; in Crimean War, won greater recognition for himself and France. Maximilian affair and Franco-Prussian War were mistakes.
6. His rule rested on illegal seizure of authority. At first, less secure because of this.
7. Answers may vary.
8. Denmark: old-age and health insurance. France: secondary education opened to women, labor unions and strikes allowed. Britain: gains for women, old-age and unemployment insurance, minimum wage and workers' compensation. Probably not; answers may vary.

page 457, Using Maps

1. Date of independence.
2. They were independent nations before 1800.
3. Ireland, Great Britain.
4. Denmark, part of Norway, Sweden.
5. New nations formed in the 1800's.
6. It shows political borders. No.

CHAPTER 20
Unification of Italy and Germany

At the conclusion of this chapter, students should be able to:

1. describe the three options for the unification of Italy and explain how one of the three was achieved.
2. explain how Bismarck used war to unite Germans into the German Empire.
3. explain why effective democracy did not develop in Germany.

Overview

Chapter 20 focuses on the process of unification in Italy and Germany and the developments in Germany following unification. In both cases, internal apathy or opposition to unity, and foreign opposition had to be overcome. After years of frustration, unity was achieved quickly. National identity and loyalty had to develop as the new governments established themselves.

The chapter provides an excellent context for discussing such matters as loyalties, nationalism, and means as ends—realpolitik as practiced by Cavour and Bismarck. Other important concepts include armistice, guerrilla war, papal infallibility, and Kulturkampf.

Teaching Strategies
Section 1

Introduction: Tell students to imagine they have met someone from another country. The person asks, "What are you? Where are you from?" How would they answer the questions? Tell them that an Italian in 1850 would not have answered "I'm an Italian," but rather "I'm a Roman" or "I'm a Venetian." Explain that for most Italians a sense of "Italianness" did not exist. Ask students if a nation can be formed if the people do not have a sense of national loyalty. Assign the section reading.

Development: Make sure students understand both the internal and external reasons that Italy failed to become united before 1860. Why were more people willing to risk their lives in a popular uprising after the defeat of Austria in 1859? Were Cavour's methods justified?

Section 2

Introduction: Tell students that the situation in Germany was similar to that in Italy. There were again internal and external reasons for Germany's long political fragmentation. There were two options for unification—one under Prussia's leadership, the other under Austria's. Assign the section, having students watch to see how the Prussian option prevailed.

Development: Refer students to the excerpt of Bismarck's "Blood and Iron" speech on page 468. To what did Bismarck attribute Germany's failures? What did he propose as an alternative? Analyze with students the three wars Bismarck undertook. What were the objectives and the specific results of each? Were Bismarck's methods justified? How did the wars affect unification?

Section 3

Introduction: Germans were euphoric after the defeat of France in 1871. At the time, Heinrich von Sybel, a historian, wrote:

> Tears run down my cheeks. By what have we deserved the grace of God, that we are allowed to live to see such great and mighty deeds. What for twenty years was the substance of all our wishes and efforts, is now fulfilled in such an immeasurably magnificent way.

With such feelings endorsing Bismarck's actions, he was given great latitude in the way he structured the German constitution and ran the government. Assign the section, having students watch how Bismarck used his power as chancellor.

Development: Bismarck is an extremely controversial figure. While honored for uniting Germany, he is condemned by others for his destructive attacks on Catholics, socialists, and liberals, and for his failure to encourage the development of democratic institutions. How do students assess Bismarck? Do they think Germany's history under William II would have been different if stronger restraints on autocratic rule had been developed earlier?

Conclusion: What lessons do students think nationalists in other parts of Europe drew from the experiences of Italy and Germany? Do students believe that realpolitik has become accepted or discredited in international affairs today? Have other political methods replaced it?

Answers

Section Review Questions

page 466

1. Carbonari—Society of Charcoal Burners; early secret organization formed to unite Italy.

   Giuseppe Mazzini—Italian nationalist revolutionary and intellectual who founded Young Italy.

   Young Italy—revolutionary group dedicated to the creation of a united and free Italian republic.

   Risorgimento—Italian word for the movement for Italian unity.

   Vincenzo Gioberti—advocated the formation of an Italian federation under the leadership of the Pope.

   Pius IX—Pope whose early liberal reforms led people to hope he would support the Risorgimento.

   Charles Albert—king of Piedmont who abdicated to his son Victor Emmanuel II after being defeated by the Austrians in 1848.

   Guiseppe Garibaldi—Italian revolutionary guerrilla leader.

   Victor Emmanuel II—king of Piedmont who completed the unification of Italy.

   Count Camillo di Cavour—prime minister for Victor Emmanuel and political mastermind of Italian unification.

   "Red Shirts"—name given to Garibaldi's guerrilla fighters because of the red shirts they wore.

2. Cultural, economic, and political divisions within Italy and the opposition of outside powers, most notably Austria.

3. A united and free Italian republic. A broad-based revolutionary uprising.

4. A united Italy under a constitutional monarchy. Slow, orderly reform, the building of Piedmont's economic and political strength in ways that would win the support of outside powers for Italian unification.

page 472

1. Zollverein—economic union formed by Prussia including most German states, but excluding Austria.

   William I—succeeded Frederick William IV as king of Prussia; became head of German empire in 1871.

   Otto von Bismarck—Junker and prime minister of Prussia from 1862 and later the first chancellor of Germany. His shrewd use of *realpolitik* led to the unification of Germany.

   Convention of Gastein—agreement between Austria and Prussia after the Danish War, placing Schleswig under Prussian control, Holstein under Austrian control.

   North German Confederation—government of all German states north of the Main River; formed after Austro-Prussian War.

   Prince Leopold—Hohenzollern prince to whom the Spanish throne was offered.

   Ems Telegram—demanded promise that Hohenzollern would never sit on Spanish throne; altered by Bismarck.

2. It provided experience for the Prussian army, aroused Prussian patriotic support for the army, and made the rest of Europe recognize Prussia's growing military strength and leadership in Germany.

3. It ended the possibility that Germany might be united under Austria.

4. It overcame the opposition of southern German states opposed to unification under Prussia.

page 476

1. *Syllabus of Errors*—document published by Pope Pius IX in 1864 condemning liberalism, socialism, nationalism, and other progressive views.

   First Vatican Council—met in 1870 and endorsed the idea of Papal infallibility.

   Center party—party formed to represent Catholic interests in Germany.

   National Liberal party—majority party, made up of Protestants.

   Conservative party—dominated by Junkers; it was forced by the Kulturkampf to oppose Bismarck. It also supported organized religion.

   Pope Leo XIII—succeeded Pius IX in 1878; made peace with Bismarck in the church-state struggle in Germany.

   Social Democratic party—party of socialists favoring gradual reform.

   Frederick III—son of William I; kaiser for 91 days; a liberal; father of William II.

   Kaiser William II—grandson of William I who became kaiser in 1888.

2. The publication of *Syllabus of Errors;* the Pope's efforts to strengthen his authority over Catholics; the growing strength of the Center party in Germany.
3. The destruction of Catholic influence in Germany.
4. William II strengthened the army and Germany industrialized rapidly, becoming a major industrial power. The population shifted from being primarily rural to being primarily urban.

Special Feature Questions
page 469
1. Britain: William Cooke and Charles Wheatstone. United States: Samuel Morse.
2. Submarine cable.

Photo Questions
page 460
The expulsion of Austria from Italian peninsula.

page 461
Young Italy.

page 462
Naples, Spain, France.

page 463
He displayed political shrewdness by sending an army to the Crimea, which established a claim of equality with other nations.

page 464
Genoa. 1860.

page 467
By making prices lower and more uniform; improved transportation; common system of weights and measures.

page 468
He was convinced that Prussia could establish a position of leadership in Europe if it had a strong army.

page 470
The Danish War.

page 474
He believed that any form of socialism posed a serious threat to the empire.

page 475
Answers may vary; mention should be made of William II's belief in absolute authority.

Chapter Review
page 477, Reviewing the Main Ideas
1. Mazzini provided inspiration that helped build the Italian identity.
   Garibaldi: military leadership for the uprising in the south that linked southern Italy with the north.
   Cavour: the strategy and diplomacy to gain the military support of France and the acquiescence of the powers other than Austria.
2. France provided essential military aid to overcome Austria, which controlled Lombardy and Venetia and opposed Italian unification.
3. The Pope opposed unification.
4. Venetia was given to Italy as part of a deal between Italy and Prussia in which Italy supported Prussia in the Austro-Prussian War. Italians occupied Rome after French troops withdrew to fight the Franco-Prussian War.
5. The German confederation provided for a diplomatic meeting ground for delegates of German governments. The Zollverein facilitated the economic unification and development of Germany by lowering trade barriers among the German states.
6. The Danish War, the Austro-Prussian War, and the Franco-Prussian War. To test and strengthen the Prussian army; to eliminate Austria as a possible leader of German unity; to overcome the opposition of southern Germans and French to the unification of Germans under Prussian leadership.
7. The North German Confederation. It excluded Austria from a union of all German states north of the Main River.
8. The Prussian king was the emperor of German empire. He made appointments, commanded the military and determined foreign policy. As the most populous state in the empire, Prussia controlled the legislature.
9. Austria and Prussia.
10. He passed the May laws, which put the education of the clergy under the state, ended the Church's right of self-govern-

ment, dissolved religious orders, and required civil marriages.

11. By banning socialist activities and publications and by passing social welfare legislation to win workers' loyalties.

12. Both men wanted to rule Germany. Bismarck tried to exert pressure on William II by threatening to resign and William accepted his resignation.

page 477, Discussing Important Ideas

1. Answers should include mention of internal political, economic, and cultural divisions within Italy, and external interference from other powers.

2. Italians were not sufficiently strong or united to defeat Austria by themselves. The help of France was essential. The neutrality of Prussia, Britain, and Russia enabled Piedmont with the French to defeat Austria.

3. No. Mazzini sought a united republic for Italy. Cavour created a monarchy in which Piedmont dominated the rest of Italy.

4. Answers may vary. Idealistic approaches strive to reach broad ideas such as democratic values, or civil and human rights, by means that are in accord with the ideals. A policy of realpolitik is willingness to use any means to reach desired goals.

5. Answers may vary.

6. An expanded, greatly strengthened Germany upset the balance of power.

7. Possible answers include the dominant role of Bismarck, the creation of the empire by force under Prussia's leadership, the creation of a constitution that enabled Prussia to continue to dominate, and the discrediting of the liberals before unification and after.

page 477, Using Maps

1. Lombardy, Piedmont, Venetia, Tuscany, the Papal States, Naples.

2. Piedmont, Lombardy, Parma, Modena, Venetia, the Papal States, Lucca, Tuscany, Naples, Sardinia.

3. Lombardy, Venetia. Tyrol.

4. San Marino remained independent, Sardinia became part of unified Italy.

5. A peninsula bounded by the Adriatic, Mediterranean, and Tyrrhenian Seas; the Alps (Switzerland), France, Austria, Hungary; two major islands lie to the west and south of the boot.

6. It was independent.

Unit Review Questions

page 478, Developing Understanding

1. Answers may vary; mention should be made of the rapid progress of industrialization when all three were present.

2. Answers may vary; mention should be made of population shifts, changes in family life and class structure, emergence of social problems of urban society.

3. Answers may vary; mention should be made of specific people's responses.

4. Answers may vary; mention should be made of suffrage, social reforms.

5. Answers may vary; mention should be made of republicanism and suffrage.

6. Answers may vary; mention should be made of the role of Catholic Church, territorial interests of other nations.

pages 478-479, Developing Skills

Conclude the unit with the Developing Skills activity. This activity, which may be used as either an individual or a group exercise, gives the student practice in analyzing and interpreting statistical data. Students are asked to determine which of 10 statements are true, based on the data in two tables.

This exercise requires the skills of analyzing relationships and drawing inferences. Students will benefit from discussion. Answers are as follows:

1. True
2. False
3. False (Russia was not industrialized.)
4. True
5. False (unwarranted inference)
6. True
7. True (reasonable inference)
8. True
9. False (South America did not have great railroad mileage.)
10. False (unwarranted inference)

UNIT 6
Imperialism and Modernization

At the conclusion of this unit, students should be able to:

1. profile the ways in which the multinational Austrian, Russian, and Ottoman empires coped with the liberal and nationalist movements within their borders.
2. describe the nineteenth-century independence movement in Latin America.
3. explain the problems Latin Americans faced after independence, including relations with the United States.
4. trace the development of China and Japan from the sixteenth to the early twentieth centuries as they came in closer contact with the West.
5. define imperialism and describe the types of control exercised by imperialist nations over other states.
6. name the continents and areas of the world most affected by nineteenth-century imperialism.

Overview

Among the important themes in this unit is the desire of traditional ruling elites to maintain the status quo against challenges from new middle and urban worker classes, and from abused minority and ethnic groups. More and more challengers pushed with revolutions for national rights, liberal reforms, and social justice.

Chapter 21 covers the struggle of the Austrian, Russian, and Ottoman empires to deal with the desires of their subjects for nationalism and liberalism. The nineteenth-century Latin American independence movement is described in Chapter 22, as are the problems faced by Latin Americans after independence and the growing involvement of the United States in Latin American affairs. Chapter 23 profiles China and Japan between the 1500's and the early 1900's. The focus is on their different responses to western contacts in the 1800's. Imperialism is the subject of Chapter 24. Imperialist activities of the nineteenth century are reviewed for Africa, Asia,

Oceania, and British North America. The unit ends just before the outbreak of World War I.

Introducing the Unit

Students should have fresh in their minds the important social, cultural, scientific, and ideological changes that took place during the Industrial Revolution and were studied in the previous unit. By and large these changes occurred in western Europe or the United States, where a great deal of social and political turmoil had existed prior to the nineteenth century. How did these changes reach other parts of the world and what was their effect? Ask students to list some of the more important of these changes and note as they read the following chapters the different ways that western ideas and technology affected other world communities.

CHAPTER 21
Multinational Empires

At the conclusion of this chapter, students should be able to:

1. outline how the Austrian monarchy was affected by nationalism between 1848 and 1914.
2. trace the conflict in Russia between the Romanov dynasty and the reformers and revolutionaries of the nineteenth and early twentieth centuries.
3. discuss the social and economic changes that led to the rise of Marxism in Russia.
4. describe the reform movement that resulted in the Young Turk Revolution and why it failed to hold the Ottoman Empire together.

Overview

This chapter describes the effects of liberalism and nationalism on the Austrian, Russian, and Ottoman empires of the nineteenth and early twentieth centuries. It discusses the changing social order within these empires—notably the rise of an urban working class. Revolutionary forces were so strong in Russia that the old order was replaced by a new social and political structure. Some important concepts in the chapter include multinational empires, urbanization, assimilation, emancipation. anarchy, autocracy, and jingoism.

Teaching Strategies

Section 1

Introduction: Before assigning this section, have students review the discussion of the 1848 Austrian revolutions on pages 377 and 378 in Chapter 16. The present section discusses what happened after the Hungarian revolution had been crushed. As students read the section, have them list the measures taken by the Austrian government to maintain control over its non-German nationalities. (Centralized bureaucracy, secret police, church control of schools, "Germanization," etc.)

Development: Lead students in a discussion regarding the weaknesses of the Austrian Empire (fragmented national populations, foreign policy, lack of internal administrative unity). What factors finally led Francis Joseph into a compromise with the Magyars? What was the result? Why did nationalist problems persist after the Ausgleich of 1867?

Section 2

Introduction: Russian literature of the mid-1800's reflects the concern of the nobility for genuine reform. Young army officers who had helped defeat Napoleon in Europe had accepted many western liberal ideas. An unsuccessful military revolt in 1825 startled Tsar Nicholas I, but he went on to oppose liberal ideas in Europe as well as in Russia. He did not realize that many of the nobility and the growing middle class would no longer support absolute rule. Ask students to note the reforms enacted by Alexander II and to what degree they satisfied the empire's various social groups. Have students also pay attention to the rise of Marxism.

Development: Ask students to compare the "Russification" policy of Alexander III with Hungary's "Magyarization" policy and Austria's "Germanization" policy. What were their purposes, how were they implemented, and how successful were they? Have students debate the idea of an "Americanization" policy. Does such a concept exist in the United States today?

Section 3

Introduction: Use the map on page 499 to prepare students for this section. Point out the extent of the Ottoman Empire in 1699 (all areas except those colored tan). Compare this to its extent in 1914. Ask students to point out the locations of the following geographic features: Asia Minor, the Balkan Peninsula, Tripoli, Crete, and Cyprus. When students finish reading about the Russo-Turkish War (pp. 499-500), have them turn back to page 482. Can they now explain the meaning of the cartoon? (From left to right: Austria-Hungary's Francis Joseph is taking the Ottoman provinces of Bosnia and Herzegovina; Russia's Alexander II is trying to take Bulgaria from the Ottoman Empire; and Abdul-Hamid II is trying to hold on to these pieces of his empire.)

Development: Have students use the map on page 499 to draw a time line illustrating the Ottoman decline. Also, ask students to discuss the Young Turk Revolution, its successes and its failures.

Conclusion: The goals of most revolutionaries were quite similar almost everywhere in Europe during the nineteenth and early twentieth centuries (constitutional government; abolition of feudal dues; and freedom of religion, press, and assembly.) Ask students to make a chart, individually or as a group project, that indicates the liberal reforms that were in place in Austria-Hungary, Russia, and the Ottoman Empire as of 1914.

Answers
Section Review Questions

page 488

1. Francis Joseph—emperor of Austria.
   Bach system—strong bureaucracy to enforce government decisions.
   "Germanization"—making and enforcing German language and culture on non-Germans within the Austrian Empire.
   Francis Deak—Magyar nationalist leader.
   Ausgleich—compromise between Austria and Hungary.
2. They felt they should retain their historical rights and cultural differences.
3. Austria needed peace to keep the empire together; to Hungary it seemed to be the only way to preserve its national existence.

page 497

1. Decembrist Uprising—uprising against Nicholas I.
   Tsar Liberator—Alexander II; so named because of his many reforms.
   Westerners—reform group that wished to establish a limited monarchy in Russia.

Slavophiles—group that wanted to base reform on Slavic traditions.

Michael Bakunin—radical reformer; he advocated anarchy.

"Russification"—attempt to make Russia's various nationalities into one people.

Pale—southwestern part of the empire; Jews forced to live there.

Marxism—teachings of Karl Marx.

page 498

Social Democratic Labor party—formed by Marxists.

Lenin—leader of socialist group.

Bloody Sunday—day of march on the Winter Palace.

Leon Trotsky—leader of Saint Petersburg soviet.

Duma—national legislature.

Freedom Manifesto—granted individual rights and allowed the Duma to make laws.

2. Emancipation of serfs, created local councils, eased restrictions on the press, introduced jury system, expanded education system.

3. Bolsheviks believed that a socialist society should come immediately by force; Mensheviks believed that Russia needed to develop an industrial state before a revolution could occur.

4. They revolted and seized control of some cities.

page 502

1. Hatt-I Humayun—far-reaching reform decree that removed civil authority from religious leaders.

Young Ottomans—group of reformers.

Young Turks—group formed to overthrow the government of the sultan.

Abdul-Hamid II—sultan; forced into exile by the Young Turks.

Pan Slavism—Slavic movement opposed to Russian autocracy.

San Stefano—site of treaty ending Russo-Turkish War.

Congress of Berlin—meeting to revise the previous treaty.

Balkan League—Balkan states formed to free themselves from Ottoman rule.

Treaty of Bucharest—end of second Balkan War.

2. They lost civil authority in their own communities.

3. By becoming leaders of the Pan-Slavic movement. The Treaty of San Stefano which gave Russia control of much of the Balkans.

4. They feared Russian territorial expansion.

Special Feature Questions

page 492

1. Composers who help create a national identity through their work.

2. Borodin, Rimsky-Korsakov, Mussorgsky.

Photo Questions

page 484
Prince Felix Schwarzenberg.

page 487
Francis Deak.

page 488
Absolute rule by the tsars; manual labor by the serfs.

page 489
The system of serf labor.

page 493
To strengthen Alexander's hold on the empire.

page 494
The preservation of the status quo.

page 495
Russia could not easily send supplies or troops; it reduced Russia's prestige.

page 496
The Bolsheviks.

page 497
To grant individual rights and a representative legislature.

page 501
The overthrow of the sultan.

Chapter Review

page 503, Reviewing the Main Ideas

1. To enforce government decisions.

2. Its role in the Crimean War; the Schleswig-Holstein war; the Seven Weeks' War; the Compromise with Hungary.

3. The Magyars assumed absolute control over the Slavs in Hungary.

4. Though technically free, in reality the majority were bound to mirs where they had trouble growing enough food to eat.

5. Upper- and middle-class groups that ranged from reformers who demanded peaceful, democratic changes, to revolutionaries who wanted the destruction of all authority.

6. Organizers worked to coordinate labor activity against the government; formed the soviets to voice workers' grievances.

7. In the long run it had no effect.

8. Harsh and uncompromising.

9. They lost control of territory in the Balkan Peninsula and Cyprus.

10. The overthrow of the sultan's government.

11. It forced the Ottoman Empire to give up its last territory in North Africa.

12. Land distribution. Bulgarians attacked Serbian and Greek forces in the disputed area. Serbia and Greece.

page 503, Discussing Important Ideas

1. Answers may vary; mention should be made of secret police and "Germanization."

2. Answers may vary.

3. Answers may vary; mention should be made of the serfs being kept illiterate and unskilled.

4. Answers may vary; mention should be made of the revolutionary groups.

5. Answers may vary; mention should be made of the "Russification" policies of Alexander, and Nicholas III's lack of understanding of Russia's plight.

6. Answers may vary; mention should be made of the fear of punishment.

7. Answers may vary.

8. Answers may vary.

page 503, Using Maps

1. 1867-1913.

2. Vladivostok, St. Petersburg.

3. Moscow, Vladivostok.

4. About 1,500 miles (2,400 kilometers).

5. Sweden. Arctic Ocean.

CHAPTER 22
The Americas

At the conclusion of this chapter, students should be able to:

1. name the major leaders of the independence movements in Latin America in the nine-teenth century and describe their accomplishments.

2. list and explain the common problems that Latin Americans faced in building stable nations.

3. discuss the reasons for the rapid growth of the United States and its involvement in Latin America during the nineteenth and early twentieth centuries.

Overview

Chapter 22 describes the independence movements in Latin America in the nineteenth century. Inspired by the American and French revolutions, Spanish Americans threw off colonial rule. The Portuguese colony of Brazil had a more peaceful transition to independence. Independence often resulted in chaos as political systems continued to be autocratic and repressive in the face of problems that hindered national unity. The chapter also reviews the growth of the United States and its involvement in Latin American affairs. Important concepts include social revolution, caudillos, collective bargaining, and arbitration.

Teaching Strategies
Section 1

Introduction: To introduce this section, have students read the feature on François Dominique Toussaint L'Ouverture on page 506. Tell them that Haiti became the second republic in the Western Hemisphere—the United States being the first. Advise students to note the influence the French and American struggles for liberty and independence had on Spanish America.

Development: Ask students to make a visual display for each of the viceroyalties of Spanish America. They should indicate, for example, what independence events took place in New Spain, their dates, their leaders, and descriptions of the events. Also, note the social and economic goals of the independence leaders, for example, in New Spain—independence, distribution of wealth, and an end to slavery. A similar display can be made for Brazil and Haiti. Ask students how different this exercise would be for the American and the French Revolutions.

Section 2

Introduction: Students need to understand the real challenges that geography posed to building stable nations in Central and South America. Let students examine a large physical map of these regions before they begin reading the section introduction and the subsection "Common Problems" (pp. 511-512). Follow this part of the reading with a discussion of the various obstacles to nation building in Central and South America. Have students list the "common problems" nations faced in this part of the world.

Development: Have students compare and contrast the rise of caudillos in Mexico and Argentina. How was the experience of Brazil different?

Section 3

Introduction: Read to students the statement made in 1823 that became known as the Monroe Doctrine (p. 519). Some of the problems of United States policy in Latin America today stem from this statement to European powers to leave the Western Hemisphere alone. The Roosevelt Corollary of 1904 involved the United States even further in Latin American affairs. As students read the section, they should note why the United States became so involved in Latin America.

Development: Ask students to discuss the rapid territorial growth of the United States. The "Using Maps" exercise (p. 523) on United States territorial expansion on page 519 can be assigned at this time.

Conclusion: Students should have enough information from this chapter and previous chapters to compare the development of the United States after independence with the development of Latin America after independence. It might be more fruitful to select one Latin American country, such as Mexico, for the comparison. Why did caudillos emerge in Latin America (Mexico) after independence, and not in the United States? What were the political, social, and economic issues facing these countries? How were they equipped to handle their problems?

Answers
Section Review Questions

page 511
1. Saint-Domingue—French colony; later renamed Haiti.
   Jean Jacques Dessalines—took over leadership of revolution in Haiti.

Miguel Hidalgo—parish priest; leader of revolutionists in Mexico.
Guadalajara—site of revolutionary attack against Spanish in Mexico.
José María Morelos—priest leader of revolutionists after Hidalgo's death.
Agustín de Iturbide—leader of upper-class royalists in Mexico; declared Mexico's independence from Spain.
Francisco de Miranda—began struggle for independence in New Granada.
Gran Colombia—name of independent nation; extended over present-day Colombia, Venezuela, Panama, Ecuador.
United Provinces of La Plata—name of independent nation; later Argentina.
Bernardo O'Higgins—leader of army in fight for Chile's independence.
Pedro I—first emperor of independent Brazil.
2. It was a social revolution.
3. San Martín hoped to get military help from Bolívar. San Martín withdrew to France; Bolívar continued to fight for independence of Bolivia.
4. Liberals took over the Portuguese government; recognized Brazil's independence in 1825.

page 518
1. Antonio Lopez de Santa Anna—had himself elected president of Mexico.
   Alamo—mission in San Antonio; site of battle against Texans.
   Gadsden Purchase—strip of land sold to the United States by Santa Anna.
   Benito Pablo Juárez—liberal reform leader who ousted Santa Anna.
   Maximilian—prince of Austria; crowned emperor of Mexico.
   Porfirio Díaz—mestizo who became president of Mexico in 1877.
   PRI—Partido Revolucionario Institucional; Mexican political party.
   Juan Manuel Rosas—leader of Argentine federalists.
   Domingo Faustino Sarmiento—Argentine president who helped develop modern institutions.
   Pedro II—emperor of Brazil during period of growth and prosperity.
   Joaquim Nabuco—leader of abolitionists in Brazil.

2. They suspected that the United States wanted to acquire Texas.
3. They favored a strong central government administered from Buenos Aires.
4. A compromise with the Law of Free Birth; later abolition.

page 521
1. Monroe Doctrine—a warning to European powers not to interfere in Western Hemisphere countries.
   James Blaine—United States secretary of state.
   Maine—United States battleship; sunk in Havana harbor.
   Roosevelt Corollary—extension of Monroe Doctrine by Theodore Roosevelt.
   Anastasio Somoza—United States-backed dictator of Nicaragua.
2. Economic differences; slavery issue.
3. The United States did not want a strong European power close to its borders; Britain felt that its commercial interests would not be served by the return of Spanish control to the region.
4. They signed a lease with the new Panamanian government.

Photo Questions
page 509
23 years.

page 510
His father, João.

page 512
The governments had little political experience; disorder and instability of the caudillo regimes.

page 514
He signed a treaty recognizing the independence of Texas.

page 515
He placed restrictions on individual freedoms.

page 516
Gauchos wanted a federal system; porteños favored a central government.

page 520
By a sanitation program to control mosquitos.

Chapter Review
page 522, Reviewing the Main Ideas
1. They were encouraged by the successes of the American and French revolutions.
2. It ended Spanish rule in New Granada.
3. Mexico: Hidalgo, Morelos; declaration of independence by upper-class royalists. Central America: representatives declared independence and established the United Provinces of Central America. New Granada: Miranda, Bolívar; defeat of Spanish at Battle of Boyacá. La Plata and Chile: San Martín, O'Higgins; defeat of Spanish near Santiago. Peru and Bolivia: San Martín; Bolívar; defeat of Spanish in Peru, and one year later in northern La Plata or Bolivia.
4. They lacked experience in self-government, weak judicial system, rigid class structure.
5. Mexico passed a law forbidding Americans to settle in Texas; provided for military occupation. President Jackson acted as negotiator between Texas and Mexico.
6. They lost Texas, southern Arizona, California territory.
7. Civilian control of government; limit the power of the Church; break up large estates and return land to the Indians.

page 523
8. The gauchos wanted a federal form of government; the porteños wanted a strong central government centered in Buenos Aires.
9. There had been no violent revolution; administrators who helped the change to independent nation.
10. It presided over the first Pan-American Conference; urged arbitration over payment of debts; involved in the Spanish-American War; invoked the Monroe Doctrine.
11. New territories in the Pacific and Caribbean for the United States.

page 523, Discussing Important Ideas
1. Answers may vary.
2. Answers may vary.
3. Answers may vary.
4. Answers may vary.
5. Santa Anna was from a wealthy creole family; he was a trained soldier. Juárez was a Mexican-Indian who wanted a liberal reform government. Díaz, a mestizo, relied heavily

on his army and stifled individual freedoms. Answers may vary.

6. Answers may vary; mention should be made of the rigid class systems brought into Latin America by the Spanish, and immigration to the United States from the more industrialized European countries, the breaking down of class distinctions within the United States.

7. Answers may vary; mention should be made of the Law of Free Birth and later bill of abolition in Brazil; and the Civil War and Emancipation Proclamation in the United States.

8. Answers may vary.

page 523, Using Maps
1. 1819. 1848.
2. Britain, Spain, France, Russia. None.
3. 1803, from France. 1848, from Mexico.
4. 1783 and 1842.
5. California, New Mexico, Texas, Arizona.

CHAPTER 23
East Asia

At the conclusion of this chapter, students should be able to:
1. describe the traditional lifestyle of the Chinese under the Qing dynasty.
2. outline the attempts by China to meet the western demands for contact.
3. trace the failure by conservatives and moderates to reform China and the ultimate success of Sun Yat-sen's revolution.
4. describe the unification of Japan under the Tokugawa shogunate.
5. review the industrialization and modernization of Japan during the Meiji era.
6. compare and contrast the Chinese and Japanese responses to western demands in the 1800's.

Overview

This chapter describes the social and economic conditions of China and Japan before and after their forced contact with westerners. China was weakened, its centuries-old Qing dynasty overturned by revolution, and a republic established in its place by the early twentieth century. Japan used western contacts to industrialize and modernize, until by 1914, it had become a power

equal to those of the West. Some important concepts in this chapter are hegemony, extraterritoriality, most-favored-nation status, and san-kin-kotai.

Teaching Strategies
Section 1

Introduction: Use the quote by Qing emperor Ch'ien Lung (p. 527) to introduce this section. It is important to emphasize to students that imperial China at its height under the Qing dynasty had the same characteristics as other successful, self-contained systems. For one, the Chinese did not feel a need for contact with other countries because they had confidence that their own system was best. This smugness and, to some extent, complacency has been witnessed in the Ottoman Empire, the British Empire, and even in the United States. (It is partly for this reason that Americans, until recently, have not fully understood the resentment Latin Americans and Canadians have felt about United States interference in their internal affairs.) Another reason for cultural isolation is that a society may fear losing control over the education of its youth, thus "perverting" the system to which the elders are accustomed. Yet, as students will learn from this chapter, a society generally decays from within before it is subject to attack from outside.

Development: Ask students to explain how western trade was handled in China between the late 1600's and the mid-1800's. What role did monopoly play? Why did Chinese commercial activity not lead to an industrial revolution?

Section 2

Introduction: With all the apparent prosperity of China in the eighteenth century, what went wrong in the 1800's to lead it into a decline? Ask students to look for answers as they read this section. (Less able emperors; strain on resources from growing population; famine, floods, and drought hurt the economy; widespread banditry, uprisings, and rebellions; inability to halt the opium trade.)

Development: While the declining Chinese imperial government was still strong enough to ban the production of large quantities of opium on its own farmland, it could not halt the influx of opium from abroad. Not only were its people becoming addicted to the drug, but the economy was suffering as well. European traders could always find Chinese merchants who were willing to trade silver and valuable Chinese products for opium that the merchants would, in turn, sell to the Chinese population. The empire was losing its material wealth as well as the productive labor of many Chinese, a devastating economic problem that was compounded by the Opium War, the "unequal treaties," and other internal problems.

Section 3

Introduction: As explained in the previous section (p. 529), despite dissatisfaction with the Qing dynasty, following the Taiping Rebellion many Chinese supported the government, viewing foreigners as a greater threat. Introduce this section by assigning students the feature "Tz'u-hsi" on page 532. The feature highlights China's struggle over modernization.

Development: Ask students if they see a pattern in the response of non-western governments to contact with Europeans. In this section, three typical types of responses are evident. The non-western government (1) attempts to isolate its subjects from western influence and to strengthen its traditional institutions, (2) it persuades lower classes in its society to resist all foreigners, and (3) a small group within its society learns about western society and subsequently tries to enact reforms. Have students identify in this section how these responses were demonstrated by China in the latter half of the nineteenth century. (Isolation and "self strengthening," the Boxer Rebellion, successful revolution.)

Section 4

Introduction: Have students review the discussion in Chapter 9 (pp. 226-227) of the Ashikaga shogunate, particularly the part on Japanese feudalism, before they read this section. Ask students to compare the Tokugawa social and political structure with that of France under Louis XIV (pp. 312-316).

Development: Ask students to outline the Japanese response to western contacts in the sixteenth and seventeenth centuries. Have them describe the economic and social changes that took place in the eighteenth and nineteenth centuries. Have students speculate on why the Japanese could not resist the demands of the United States to end their isolation. Students

might mention "threat of war" or "lack of support for shogun." This could be a research assignment.

Section 5

Introduction: It is important for students to realize that the Japanese leaders who assumed power after the fall of the Tokugawa had observed the fate of China when it had failed to modernize after being forced to open its doors to the West. As students read the section, have them write down the steps that the Meiji leaders took to modernize Japan. Be sure students read the important photo captions on pages 539 and 540.

Development: Have students imagine what would happen to the United States if the government were suddenly confronted with overwhelmingly powerful invaders from another planet who demanded diplomatic missions and trade relations. Would American leaders put their heads in the sand? Allow fanatics to try to fight off the invaders? Send scholars and scientists to study the culture of the invaders?

Conclusion: Have students trace the course of social reforms in China and Japan from the mid-1800's to the early 1900's.

Answers
Section Review Questions

page 528
1. Ch'ung-chen—last Ming emperor.
   Manchus—invaders of China from Manchuria.
   Qing—dynasty set up by the Manchus.
   Lord George Macartney—leader of British trade mission to China.
2. Brought prosperity, lightened taxes, undertook public works programs, supported the arts, outlawed feet-binding of females, introduced agricultural improvements.
3. They established their hegemony over much of Southeast Asia.

page 530
1. Opium War—clash when China sought to end Britain's opium imports.
   Treaty of Nanjing—ended the Opium War, abolished Chinese foreign trade monopolies, first of the "unequal treaties."
   Taiping Rebellion—uprising that climaxed many internal disorders.

Hung Hsiu-ch'uan—leader of the Taiping Rebellion.

"Heavenly Kingdom of Great Peace"—ideal society based on equality and shared property of the Taiping rebels.

2. To stop the flow of silver to China for tea, silk, and porcelain.

3. The rebels sought to end both and replace them with a new society.

4. Leaders killed in a coup d'etat; opposition became stronger; foreign powers aided the Qing.

page 534

1. Hundred Days Reform—period in which a series of decrees calling for drastic changes were issued by the emperor.

Tz'u-hsi—Dowager Empress, ruled for nearly half a century.

Boxers—Society of Righteous and Harmonious Fists; organization to expel all foreigners from China.

Boxer Protocol—agreement that ended the Boxer Rebellion.

Liang Ch'i-ch'ao—leader of a revolutionary group.

Sun Yat-sen—rival of Liang Ch'i-ch'ao.

2. A program of reform started by the government to revive the Confucian values and to borrow ideas and practices from the West. Conservatives who believed that technical subjects were not as important as the classics and should not be part of the civil service examination system; they would corrupt traditional culture.

3. Japan wished to detach Korea from Chinese influence; China did not want Japanese foothold on the Asian mainland. It was forced to recognize Korea's independence; lost territories to Japan.

4. They planned to upset the existing social order and establish a new society.

page 538

1. Oda Nobunaga—began the process of Japan's unification.

Toyotomi Hideyoshi—replaced Nobunaga; placed nearly all of Japan under his rule.

Tokugawa Ieyasu—after Hideyoshi's death seized power; completed unification under his rule.

Battle of Sekigahara—last battle of challenge to Ieyasu's rule.

Council of Elders—Tokugawa family and a select group of daimyo that controlled the government.

Francis Xavier—earliest of Jesuit missionaries in Japan.

Matthew Perry—American admiral who forced Japan to end its isolation.

Mutsuhito—emperor of Japan.

2. Asked the emperor to name him shogun; took measures to ensure the power stayed in his family.

3. Perry threatened war if trading privileges and refueling stations were not granted.

page 541

1. Meiji Emperor—"Enlightened Emperor," Mutsahito, ruled from 1867 to 1912.

Mitsubishi—large business enterprise that controlled an entire industry.

Diet—Japanese bicameral legislature.

Russo-Japanese War—war with Russia over control of Korea and Manchuria.

2. The samurai.

3. Privileges were abolished, samurai were not to wear their swords; all people were declared equal; class restrictions ended.

4. Revised tax structure to raise investment money; sent students abroad to study western methods; supported industrial companies.

Photo Questions

page 526
They did not try to alter the basic elements of Chinese culture.

page 527
All western trade was funneled through Guangzhou; foreigners were restricted to a small area of the port city and placed under Chinese law.

page 528
Britain's trade in opium to China.

page 531
Was forced to recognize Korea's independence; lost Taiwan and the Liaotung Peninsula.

page 533
Foreign powers were given the right to station troops at their legation sites; $333 million indemnity to be paid.

page 534
Sun Yat-sen opposed traditional Chinese ways; Liang favored gradual reform and argued for a constitutional monarchy.

page 535
People were divided into classes; only samurai were permitted to wear swords; marriage was forbidden among classes; reinforced the feudal system.

page 537
Singing, dancing, conversation.

page 538
He has been given the face of a kabuki villain. Answers may vary.

page 539
They were persuaded to turn their lands over to the emperor; the government paid them for their losses.

page 540
They feared foreign takeovers if the loans could not be repaid.

Chapter Review

page 542, Reviewing the Main Ideas
1. Traditions and institutions of the past.
2. It was believed that merchants produced nothing of value so there was little investment in trade or production.
3. Through a system of tribute; foreign visitors were required to pay homage and were treated as inferiors.
4. As the most prosperous and advanced civilization in the world. As barbarians.
5. It abolished Chinese monopolies of foreign trade; gave Britain extraterritoriality and most-favored-nation status. Other nations demanded treaties with the same, or better, trade conditions.
6. China was forced to recognize independence of Korea; lost territories to Japan.
7. The Boxer Rebellion was to remove all foreigners from China; the Taiping Rebellion was to topple the Qing dynasty.
8. Anti-Qing revolts throughout the country.
9. Four classes; at the top were the samurai, and three lower classes; peasants, artisans, merchants.
10. Loyalty to the shogun, duty, honor, and self-discipline.
11. The emperor at the head; a bicameral legislature; later, a system of cabinet rule led by a prime minister.
12. It achieved equality with the West and recognized as a world power.

page 543, Discussing Important Ideas
1. Answers may vary.
2. Answers may vary; mention should be made of Chinese traditions and their belief in their superiority.
3. Answers may vary.
4. Answers may vary.
5. Answers may vary.
6. Answers may vary.
7. Answers may vary.
8. Answers may vary.

page 543, Using Maps
1. On Russian territory.
2. East. North.
3. Manchuria and Siberia.
4. About 750 miles; 1,200 kilometers.
5. Seoul, Tokyo.
6. North America.

CHAPTER 24
Empire Building

At the conclusion of this chapter, students should be able to:
1. explain the concept of imperialism.
2. review the reasons why European powers built empires in Africa.
3. discuss the conflicts between European and Asian cultures and their consequences.
4. outline the rivalry among European powers for spheres of influence in central, eastern, and Southeast Asia.
5. describe the European settlement of the region of Oceania.
6. list the important steps that led to self-government for Canada.

Overview

The nineteenth century witnessed several of the world's most powerful nations vying for the territories of militarily weaker and less modernized states in Africa, Asia, and Oceania. The imperialist nations built empires for political, military, economic, and even social reasons. Most became deeply involved in the states they controlled. There was much opposition, and a rising tide of desire for self-government arose as the century drew to a close. Ironically, Britain led the retreat from empire, granting self-government to Canada in the mid-1800's. Important concepts include imperialism, sphere of influence, westernization, self-government, dominion, and devolution.

Teaching Strategies

Section 1

Introduction: Until the advent of the gunboat around 1840 and quinine as a treatment for malaria in the 1840's, Africa was known as the "white man's grave." Reliable repeating rifles and the telegraph became available in the 1860's and 1870's. With this technology, explorers, missionaries, and imperialists had little trouble with Africans armed with spears. Ask students to study the maps of Africa on page 547. Note how little of the continent had been claimed by other nations in 1800 compared to its virtual complete partition by 1914. Have students note the two exceptions (Liberia and Ethiopia). Ask them to read the feature "The Mahdi and Gordon" (p. 549) just before they begin the subsection "Sudan" on page 546.

Development: Ask students to develop a chart that shows the following information for each of the imperialist powers involved in Africa and discussed in this section: territories claimed or controlled, type of control, African groups subjected to imperialism, reasons for imperialist action, and resistance efforts by local populations.

Section 2

Introduction: As the resistance of local populations to foreign penetration increased, imperialist governments began to take over local control from the private individuals, companies, and church organizations that had originally set up trading posts, colonies, and missions. They became deeply involved in the internal affairs of Asian and African states. Have students add information on imperialism in Asia from this section to the chart they developed for Africa.

Students may refer to the map on page 560 as they read about the Dutch East Indies (p. 553),

the map on page 556 for India (pp. 553-556), the map on page 541 for Russian expansion (pp. 556-557), and the maps on pages 560 and 698 for Indochina and Siam (p. 557).

Development: Have students trace the growth of British rule in India and the spheres of influence that were developed in China by 1900. Ask students to note the Russian move into Afghanistan in 1874. Can students recall a similar occurrence in recent years?

Section 3

Introduction: Many students are unfamiliar with the term Oceania. Use the map on page 560 to point out the three major divisions of the Pacific Islands: Melanesia, Micronesia, and Polynesia. Have students note the relative locations of the United States and its possessions to Russia, China, Korea, Japan, India, Indochina, Australia, New Zealand, and the Philippines. Ask students to turn back to the unit opening photo on pages 206 and 207. This picture depicts Captain James Cook's expedition to the Pacific in 1776. His ships the *Resolution* and the *Adventure* are shown anchored in a Tahitian harbor.

Development: Ask students to add information from this section to the chart they developed on Africa. Have them describe the European settlement of Australia and New Zealand.

Section 4

Introduction: This section describes how British rule in Canada changed from the mid-1700's to the end of the 1800's. Self-government for Canada signaled a retreat from empire building. Have students draw a time line showing the important events in Canadian history that are described in this section.

Development: Many Americans remain quite ignorant of our neighbor to the north. Point out major geographic features of Canada on a large physical map. Of particular note is the extensive Canadian Shield that blocks both large-scale farming and settlements. The United Empire Loyalists mentioned in the text settled in the fertile regions of Ontario.

Ask students to prepare a sketch map of Canada indicating its provinces and territories. Then have each of them profile a province or territory. They should cover areas such as manufacturing and production, ethnic composition, geographic features, housing, education, and government. One or more students may wish to do a report on Canada-United States relations, for example, the issue of acid rain.

Conclusion: Have students go through the chapter and list the major issues that arose between imperialist powers and their controlled foreign populations. Through class discussion develop a master list from which to make assignments. Divide students into small groups and assign each group an issue. Groups can take turns researching their issues and presenting them to the class. Alternatively, students within a single group can assume the roles of the imperialist nation and its controlled population. The group could role play a meeting in which both sides present their opinions on the issue.

Answers
Section Review Questions

page 553
1. Barbary Coast—North African lands.
   Ahmed Arabi—Egyptian nationalist leader.
   David Livingstone—Scottish medical missionary.
   Henry Morton Stanley—explorer and newspaperman.
   Congo Association—formed to explore and gain trading rights in the Congo River Basin.
   Leopold II—king of Belgium; formed the Congo Association.
   Battle of Adowa—battle where Ethiopians defeated invading Italians.
   Menelik II—Ethiopian emperor.
   Cecil Rhodes—British prime minister of the Cape Colony.
   Boers—Afrikaners.
   Leander Jameson—British administrator; sent into the Transvaal by Rhodes.
   Zulu War—confrontation when Zulus defeated the British.
2. They viewed it as an important lifeline to their colonies in Asia and the Pacific.
3. Britain: South Africa, Rhodesia, Uganda, Sudan, Egypt, Nigeria, Gold Coast, Sierra Leone. France: French West Africa, French Congo. Germany: Togo, Cameroon, German South-West Africa, German East Africa.
4. Afrikaners resisted British rule and migrated north; when diamonds and gold were discovered in the new area, British people pushed into Afrikaner territory to strike it rich. Afrikaners accepted British sovereignty in exchange for right to maintain certain institutions and practices.

page 558
1. Java—center of Dutch colonial economy in the East Indies.
   Pan-Islamism—political and cultural movement emphasizing common bonds of all Muslims.
   Robert Clive—leader of British forces in India.
   Lord Wellesley—Governor General of India.
   Sikhs—people of the Punjab region of India.
   Ranjit Singh—leader of the Sikhs.
   James Andrew Dalhousie—Governor General of India; had little regard for Indian civilization.
   India Councils Act of 1909—gave Indians an active voice in the councils.
   Vladivostok—"lord of the east"; Russian seaport on the Pacific coast.
   Turkestan—Muslim territory east of the Caspian Sea; overtaken by Russia.
   Indochina—various areas of Southeast Asia; claimed by France were Tonkin, Laos, Annam, Cambodia, Cochin-China.
   Open Door Notes—United States' proposal concerning trading rights in China.
2. It had varied natural resources; was consistently profitable for the Dutch.
3. British disruption of many aspects of Indian culture that offended Muslims and Hindus. The introduction of cartridges supposedly lubricated with cow and pig fats.
4. Political.

page 561
1. Oceania—region in the Pacific; Australia, New Zealand, and Pacific Islands.
   James Cook—explorer of the Pacific and its land areas.
   New South Wales—Australian penal colony.
   Arthur Phillip—founder of first Australian settlement in Sydney.
   Commonwealth of Australia—united the former colonies and the Northern Territory.
   Treaty of Waitangi—provided for protection of Maori rights under British sovereignty of New Zealand.
   Wellington—one of the first permanent British settlements in New Zealand.

Maori Wars—conflict between Maoris and newcomers who violated the Treaty of Waitangi.

2. Cook's explorations of the areas.
3. Discovery of gold.
4. As a coaling station for American ships.

page 563

1. United Empire Loyalists—people from former American colonies who remained loyal to Britain during the American Revolution.

   Lower Canada—French-speaking area of Quebec.

   Upper Canada—English area of Quebec.

   Lord Durham—sent by British Parliament to investigate situation in Canada.

   British North America Act—joined Upper and Lower Canada, Nova Scotia, New Brunswick into Dominion of Canada.

   John A. Macdonald—first Canadian prime minister; Scottish lawyer.

   Canadian Pacific Railway—rail link between eastern and western provinces.

2. They felt threatened by the growing English-speaking minority.
3. Quebec was divided into two provinces.

Photo Questions

page 546
They first bought shares of stock; later intervened militarily and made Egypt a British protectorate.

page 548
International Association for the Exploration and Civilization of Central Africa formed by Leopold II of Belgium.

page 550
Liberia.

page 551
Transvaal; Orange Free State.

page 552
They captured the Zulu chief, Cetywayo.

page 555
Muslims considered the pig unclean; Hindus regarded the cow as sacred.

page 559
The discovery of gold.

page 563
The Canadian Pacific Railway; the grain-producing prairies of the west.

Chapter Review

page 564, Reviewing the Main Ideas

1. France invaded Algiers; present-day Algeria.
2. It defeated the Egyptian army.
3. The agreement between France and Britain angered Germany; the crisis was settled by an international conference.
4. The British, French, Germans, and Portuguese took exception to the Belgian claim to the Congo River Basin. It drafted a code governing the ways to proceed in acquiring African territory; set up the Congo Association and the Congo Free State.
5. Ethiopia, Liberia.
6. British invasion of the Transvaal caused the Anglo-Boer War; expansion into southern Africa brought Britain into conflict with the Zulus.

page 565

7. British victories on land and sea over the French; treaties with Indian princes; war and annexation.
8. The British became involved to prevent Russian expansion.
9. Indochina, Malay Peninsula, China. By settlements and agreements between the conflicting European powers.
10. The Opium War; treaties; leases; later the Open Door policy of the United States.
11. Britain claimed Australia and New Zealand based on Cook's explorations; annexed the Fijis. France made Tahiti a colony; occupied the Society, Marquesas, and Tuamotu Archipelago. Germany took a share of New Guinea, Bismarck Archipelago, annexed the Marshalls, purchased the Carolines and Marianas. United States secured the Philippines and Guam in the Spanish-American War; annexed Hawaii.
12. A recommendation by Lord Durham to give self-government to Canada. It set a precedent adopted for other British territories.

page 565, Discussing Important Ideas

1. Answers may vary.
2. Answers may vary.
3. Answers may vary.

4. Answers may vary; mention should be made of the effects of apartheid on international relations of today.

5. Answers may vary; mention should be made of the better understanding of similar cultural traditions of European colonies versus misunderstanding of non-European cultures and traditions.

6. Answers may vary.

7. Answers may vary.

8. Answers may vary.

page 565, Using Maps

1. Britain: part of Borneo, part of New Guinea, New Zealand, Solomons, Fijis, Cook, Gilbert. Germany: Marianas, Carolines, part of New Guinea.

2. The Dutch. United States. Portugal.

3. Fijis, Midway, Aleutians, Hawaii, Cook, Samoa, Marquesas, Tahiti.

4. Indochina, India, Korea.

5. Britain.

Unit Review

page 566, Developing Understanding

1. Liberalism and nationalism threatened the unity of the Austrian and Ottoman empires and challenged the rule of the tsars in Russia. Industrialization brought challenges to the empires that were not met successfully because of internal dissent and fragmented authority.

2. They were inspired by the revolutions in the United States and France and threw off colonial rule. They had to create political systems to meet their own needs; for several decades most of the new nations were ruled by military dictatorships.

3. To promote prosperous trade. China was weakened by foreign contacts; Japan used them to strengthen itself until it was able to meet the western powers on equal terms.

4. The reasons were political, economic, and social. Each worked to secure new markets and new supplies of raw materials, some groups wanted also to introduce their ways of doing things to other cultures.

pages 566-567, Developing Skills

Conclude the unit with the Developing Skills activity on pages 566-567. This activity, which is suitable for either individuals or groups, gives students practice in synthesizing evidence from multiple sources. The exercise provides four primary-source readings on the subject of imperialism. Students are asked to analyze them for clues as to the causes of imperialism. Additional clues may be found in the textbook illustrations.

You may want to have students list the causes of imperialism suggested by each separate source, then check to see which causes were suggested by more than one source. Finally, have the students write a brief paragraph explaining the rise of imperialism. Following are some of the causes of imperialism suggested by the readings:

1. Need for markets, outlet for excess population, economic return.

2. Need for markets, need for new places to invest capital, need to create jobs.

3. Need for world power.

4. Desire to spread western civilization and Christianity.

UNIT 7
World in Conflict

At the conclusion of this unit, students should be able to:
1. describe the developments leading to World War I, the significant aspects of the war, and its impact on the rest of the century.
2. explain why totalitarian governments came to power in Russia, Italy, and Germany, and how their response to problems following the war differed from the responses of Britain, France, and the United States.
3. describe major nationalist developments in Asia, Africa, and Latin America in the 1920's and 1930's.
4. analyze the causes, the major events, and the legacy of World War II.

Overview

Unit 7 covers the tumultuous years from World War I through World War II. Chapter 25 treats the underlying and immediate causes of World War I, the progress of the war, and the peace settlements. Chapter 26 focuses on the rise of totalitarian governments in Russia, Italy, and Germany as those nations struggled to recover from the war and from a severe worldwide depression. Their actions are contrasted with those of the democracies of Britain, France, and the United States. Chapter 27 looks at the growth of nationalism and other developments in Asia, Africa, and Latin America between the two world wars. Chapter 28 deals with the events leading to World War II; the major campaigns in Europe, North Africa, and Asia; and the formation of the United Nations.

Introducing the Unit

Ask students for the major developments of the twentieth century. They may mention events such as the two world wars, the Russian Revolution, the rise of Hitler, the Holocaust, Pearl Harbor, and the dropping of the atomic bomb on Hiroshima. Record their responses on the chalkboard. Compare the relative stability of the nineteenth century with the turmoil of the twentieth century. Why do students think the

present century has been more troubled by conflict? As the unit is studied, have students analyze how many of this century's developments have had their roots in World War I, and how many in World War II.

CHAPTER 25
World War I

At the conclusion of this chapter, students should be able to:
1. explain the underlying and immediate causes of World War I.
2. list and describe the major events of the war.
3. explain ways in which World War I was the transition between traditional and modern warfare.
4. outline the major provisions of the peace settlements.

Overview

Chapter 25 surveys the conditions contributing to the outbreak of World War I, the immediate spark of the assassination in the Balkans, the events of the war, and the peace settlements that brought the war to a close. Major emphasis should be put on explaining why the war happened, not only the forces that made the great powers willing—even eager—to risk war, but also those that made it impossible to stop the war until total exhaustion was reached. Care should be taken in considering the failure of the peace treaties. Important concepts in the chapter include imperialism, nationalism, militarism, alliance systems, and propaganda.

Teaching Strategies
Section 1

Introduction: Tell students that when the first world war began, most Europeans were happy and excited. Bands played patriotic anthems; young women gave flowers to departing soldiers. One soldier wrote that he expected a "brisk, merry war." Why did it turn out so differently? Ask how the war could happen? Assign the section.

Development: Help students to see how the three "isms" described in the section—imperialism, nationalism, and militarism—affected the major European powers. Have students prepare a chart to identify the central economic, political, and military interests of these nations. Go over the chart with students, having them note where nations' interests intersected or clashed. Try to judge how these rivalries and conflicts affected relations between and among these countries. Do students think alliances were made out of a sense of strength or of weakness? If out of weakness, how important was it to maintain an alliance?

Section 2

Introduction: Have students read the account of the assassination. Tell them that Archduke Francis Ferdinand and his wife visited Sarajevo on St. Vitus's Day, a holiday when Serbian patriotism was at a peak. Practically no security arrangements had been made. Francis Ferdinand was not particularly loved in Austria, and he was buried quickly and unceremoniously after the assassination. Ask students what options were open to Austria-Hungary? How could it respond? How did other nations respond to Austrian actions? Assign the rest of the section. Ask students to watch for the motivations of each European power.

Development: Consider the element of timing in the outbreak of wars. Why did the assassination become the spark for war rather than an earlier crisis or some later event? Analyze with students how national unity, national security, and national prestige influenced each nation's decision to go to war. Does it seem that nations welcomed the war? How might they have behaved if they had wanted to avoid it? Was it inevitable that the alliance system would drag nations into war? How do students assess each nation's responsibility for the war?

Section 3

Introduction: Ask students to read the opening portion of this section, which describes the decisive first six weeks of the war. Remind students that when most Europeans thought of war, they envisioned the brief Franco-Prussian War, not the lengthy, bloody American Civil War. Use the map of the western front on page 578 to help students understand the Schlieffen Plan and why it failed. How evenly matched were the two sides after the opening month of the war? What were their options?

Development: Review the war with students by constructing a time line on the chalkboard showing parallel activities on the different fronts. Explain that after the western front became deadlocked, generals unimaginably continued to order new offensives, hoping for a breakthrough even though advance heavy bombardment eliminated any possible surprise; those attacked easily regained the advantage. To break the stalemate, nations sought other options—new weapons, new fronts, and new allies. Discuss the conditions that took Russia out of the war and brought the United States into it. Why did the war end when it did?

Section 4

Introduction: Tell students that the peace treaty with Germany caused great and lasting controversy. Wilson raised expectations high, but results fell far from the mark. Unlike earlier peace conferences, heads of state led their delegations, thus increasing the political pressures on the outcome. Have students read the section.

Development: Review the major features of the Treaty of Versailles, listing the key territorial, economic, and military features. Why were these provisions agreed upon by the "Big Four"? How did they meet the needs of France, Britain, and the United States? Do students think the treaty was the best that could be achieved? Have them explain their answers.

Conclusion: Do students think that World War I was worth fighting? How do the experiences of World War I shed light on the generalization that wars are easier to start than to stop?

Answers
Section Review Questions
page 573
1. Albania—territory along Adriatic; area of dispute between Serbia and Austria-Hungary.
   Triple Alliance—alliance of Austria, Germany, Italy in 1882.
   Entente Cordiale—agreement between France and Britain.
   Triple Entente—joined Russia to the Entente Cordiale.
2. Economics, imperialism, nationalism.
3. Serbian desires to set up a Slavic state threatened the stability of the Austro-Hungarian Empire.
4. The rise of militarism among European powers.

1. Sarajevo—capital of Bosnia; site of assassination of Francis Ferdinand.

   Francis Ferdinand—Archduke of Austria.

   Gavrilo Princip—Bosnian student who assassinated Francis Ferdinand and his wife, Sophie.

   Black Hand—Union of Death; secret society of Serbian nationalist-terrorists.

   Leopold Berchtold—Austro-Hungarian foreign minister.

2. Austria-Hungary gave Serbia an ultimatum; it would declare war if the ultimatum was not accepted by Serbia.

3. It had lost face by not supporting Serbia in the past. Germany gave Russia and France ultimatums to stay out of the situation; Germany declared war on Russia; two days later declared war on France.

page 585

1. Central Powers—Germany, Austria-Hungary, Ottoman Empire, Bulgaria.

   Allied Powers—Britain, France, Russia, Serbia, Belgium; later Japan and Montenegro.

   Schlieffen Plan—a war strategy drawn up by Schlieffen, chief German general.

   Helmuth von Moltke—German commander; he weakened the Schlieffen Plan.

   Joseph Jacques Joffre—French chief of command.

   Joseph Simon Gallieni—French general; evacuated Paris.

   Henri Pétain—French general; headed the longest, bloodiest battle of the war.

   Winston Churchill—First Lord of the Admiralty in Britain.

   Lusitania—British luxury liner; sunk by German submarine.

   Sussex—French steamer; torpedoed by German submarine.

   Treaty of Brest-Litovsk—site of treaty between new Bolshevik government of Russia and the Central Powers.

   Zimmermann Note—telegram sent to Mexican government by German foreign minister Zimmermann.

   Sykes-Picot Agreement—British agreement with France and Russia; provided for the division of Ottoman Empire.

   Ferdinand Foch—French general; commanded first unified Allied command in the west.

2. Forced Germany to regroup, alter its leadership, get reinforcements.

3. It was inconclusive.

4. Russia's withdrawal from the war, entrance of the United States.

page 590

1. Fourteen Points—Wilson's peace plan.

   Peace of Paris—five separate peace treaties.

   Woodrow Wilson—President of United States; representative at Paris peace talks.

   Georges Clemenceau—Prime Minister of France; representative at Paris peace talks.

   David Lloyd George—Prime Minister of Great Britain; representative at Paris peace talks.

   Vittorio Orlando—Prime Minister of Italy; representative at Paris peace talks.

   League of Nations—international assembly of nations.

   Treaty of Versailles—military, territorial, economic provisions agreed upon.

   Polish Corridor—strip of land separating East Prussia and Germany.

2. International recognition of freedom of the seas and trade, limitation of arms, end to secret alliances, settlement of colonial claims, self-determination for all nations, general assembly of nations to settle future problems peacefully.

3. Wilson: no annexations, no contributions, no damages. Clemenceau: demand for reparations. George: no open seas policy.

4. The settlement was harsh; freedom of the seas was not assured; economic barriers were not lowered; little disarmament secured; failed to settle old wounds, and opened new ones.

Photo Questions

page 573
Issued an ultimatum to Serbia.

page 575
They were unprepared for what lay ahead.

page 577
It forced Germany to pull reinforcements from the western front.

page 580
They instituted submarine warfare.

page 581
The North Atlantic Ocean.

page 584
Used to bomb enemy positions.

page 585
By relaying information about important Turkish locations.

page 587
By using the acceptance of his League of Nations as a bargaining point.

Chapter Review

page 591, Reviewing the Main Ideas
1. They each contributed to the intensification of rivalries among European nations.
2. In the interest of Slavic nationalism.
3. Britain declared war on Germany.
4. That Russia would be slow to mobilize. Von Moltke weakened the right wing of the offense; then decided not to send the army through Holland but through a Belgian area that was heavily fortified.
5. That neither side was capable of a quick or easy victory.
6. Entire populations were thrown into the war effort; the smallest victories were given big headlines; propaganda presented the enemy in the worst light.
7. Soldiers lived in the trenches for weeks; they endured the cold, mud, rats, dysentery; forced to move through barbed wire, heavy artillery and machine gun emplacements; later, poison gas was carried into the trenches.
8. The existing naval code stated that enemy ships were to give warning before attacking a non-military target. That submarines would become easy targets if they surfaced to give warning.
9. Russia's army was poorly equipped; food shortages; inadequate transport; food riots; mutinies; strikes; socialists campaigned for peace. It allowed Germany to shift troops to the western front.
10. Sinking of American ships; Zimmermann telegram.
11. It became the guiding framework for the peace settlement.
12. The German army was reduced and conscription prohibited; navy limited to a few ships and no submarines; air force and major weapons of aggression forbidden; Alsace-Lorraine returned to France as well as control of the Saar Basin; the Rhineland occupied; lost the Polish Corridor, the city of Danzig, and all colonies; forced to pay for damages caused by the war.

page 591, Discussing Important Ideas
1. Answers may vary; mention should be made of the reaction caused by other nations' fears of alliances.
2. Answers may vary.
3. Answers may vary; mention should be made of needed resources as well as Allied morale.
4. Answers may vary; mention should be made of new weapons and new methods.
5. Answers may vary; mention should be made of different expectations of United States and European countries.
6. Answers may vary.
7. Answers may vary; mention should be made of the resentment of the harsh provisions against Germany, and the loss of life in all countries involved.

page 591, Using Maps
1. Southern front.
2. A Central Powers offensive into Poland and Russia.
3. 1918.
4. As a blue line labeled "stabilized front."
5. Middle Eastern front.
6. Allied Powers.

CHAPTER 26
Totalitarianism and Democracy

At the conclusion of this chapter, students should be able to:
1. describe the conditions in Russia under which the Bolsheviks seized power and the new structure of their government.
2. compare and contrast the social, economic, and political policies of Russia under Lenin and Stalin.
3. explain the factors that led to the creation of totalitarian dictatorships in the countries of Italy and Germany.

4. list major steps taken by Britain, France, and the United States to recover from World War I and the depression.

Overview

Chapter 26 focuses on internal political developments in Europe and the United States in the period between the wars. Because of their significance for the rest of the century, the Russian Revolution and the creation of the Communist state in Russia are explained in some detail. The political and economic instability in Italy and Germany that contributed to the rise of totalitarian governments is described. Democracies in Britain, France, and the United States were shaken, but managed to survive the demands placed on them by the war and the depression.

The chapter provides an excellent opportunity to study the origins and characteristics of totalitarian systems of government and to contrast them with earlier forms of government, such as monarchies, dictatorships, and democracies. Other important concepts include communism, fascism, nazism, and economic depression. Some additional concepts to be developed during the study of the chapter are extremism, propaganda, scapegoating, state ownership of property, human rights, and legitimate government action.

Teaching Strategies
Section 1

Introduction: Have students read the introduction to the chapter. Ask them how a dictatorship differs from a totalitarian dictatorship. Point out the importance of ideology in totalitarian government and the great extent of control such a government exerts over individuals. Tell students to find examples of these features as they read the chapter. Students should also try to figure out why people would be willing to adopt a totalitarian form of government.

Development: Personalize the conditions that existed in Russia in 1917: war weariness, desperate food shortages, feeble and inept leaders. Ask students how they would have felt, what they might have done, where they would have turned for improvement. Then consider what the various factions offered. Would revolution have occurred without the extreme pressures posed by the war? How did the decision of the provisional government to stay in

the war play into the hands of the Bolsheviks? In the November Revolution and the civil war, why did the more radical groups have an advantage over the moderates?

Section 2

Introduction: While the war set the conditions for revolution, success and the shape of the new Russian government were largely set by three individuals: Lenin, Trotsky, and Stalin. They were deeply indebted to Marx. Lenin had the organizational genius and vision to see that Marxist revolution was possible in Russia; Trotsky devised the strategy and tactics for the successful November Revolution; Stalin shaped the new society. Have students watch for Lenin's flexibility and Stalin's influence as they read the section.

Development: Analyze the political and economic structure in the U.S.S.R. Who held the real political power? Compare and contrast the NEP with the organization of the economy under the Five-Year Plans. The success of collectivization, the power of the secret police, and the purges are examples of the totalitarian control that Stalin instituted in Russia.

Section 3

Introduction: Explain how totalitarian governments can have strikingly different political ideologies, though their control over individuals and economies may be similar. Fascism in Italy and Germany were right-wing reactions to communism. They succeeded in part because of peoples' fear that communism would spread to their countries. Assign the section.

Development: Review the conditions in Italy following the war. What did Mussolini offer that was appealing to the Italian people? How did the Black Shirts destroy the legitimate government? What measures did Mussolini take against basic civil rights once he became dictator?

Section 4

Introduction: Have students read to the subsection "Rise of Nazism" (p. 603). Discuss conditions under the Weimar Republic. Why did the Weimar government lack wide political support? Did it seem able to weather the economic difficulties it faced after World War I? Tell students that despite its weaknesses the Weimar Republic would probably have survived longer had it not been for the depression. That, on top of other trials, made Germans vulnerable to the brilliant, insane demagoguery of Hitler. Assign the remainder of the section.

Development: Refer students to the quotation by Adolf Hitler that opens the chapter (p. 592). Have students identify examples from Hitler's domestic and foreign policies that support his claim. Why did people inside and outside of Germany believe his lies? What were the consequences of disbelief? of belief? Could the statement have equally been made by Mussolini or Stalin?

Section 5

Introduction: Review with students the traditions of democratic government that existed in Britain, France, and the United States. Before World War I, which was the most stable? Which was the least stable? Though they were victors in the war, these nations still faced serious difficulties afterward. Ask students to note as they read the section, how these different democratic traditions provided strength to their peoples and governments in the 1920's and 1930's.

Development: Ask students which of the three countries were the most and least stable after the war. Why did extremists fail to win power in these countries? Were postwar economic and social conditions significantly better? How did each country handle their major crises? Encourage students to ask older people about conditions they remember in the 1920's and 1930's to add further details to their understanding of the period.

Conclusion: Have students compare and contrast totalitarian dictatorships with democracies in terms of their respective positions on human rights. Have them support their statements with specific examples from the chapter.

Answers

Section Review Questions

page 596

1. Nicholas II—tsar of Russia.
   Rasputin—monk; influenced government policies.
   Petrograd Soviet—made up of workers and peasants belonging to socialist and revolutionary groups.
   Bolshevik Revolution—coup d'etat staged by the Bolsheviks against the provisional government of Petrograd.

Whites—groups of Russians opposed to the Bolsheviks.
Communist party—Bolsheviks and their supporters.
Reds—Communist party members.
Cheka—Lenin's secret police force.

page 597

2. The provisional government was under pressure from the Allies.
3. "Peace, Land, and Bread." Russia was to leave the war, peasants were to gain land, and people would receive adequate food.
4. The Whites.

page 600

1. New Economic Policy—some private businesses, small manufacturers, and farmers were permitted to own their own businesses in order to stimulate the economy.
   Leon Trotsky—rival to succeed Lenin.
   Joseph Stalin—rival to succeed Lenin.
   Comintern—international organization of Communist parties.
   Five-Year Plans—Stalin's plans to strengthen the economy.
   Old Bolsheviks—associates of the old revolutionary colleagues who had sided with Trotsky.
2. It was a socialist country; the Communist party would rule through a federal system of republics with a central government in Moscow.
3. As secretary general, Stalin made sure his own followers were placed in positions so they would back him.
4. Increased the powers of the secret police; encouraged workers and family members to tell on each other; purges of any group that had disagreed with his policies.

page 602

1. Benito Mussolini—Italian political leader.
   Black Shirts—members of Fascist party.
   Victor Emmanuel III—king of Italy.
   Il Duce—"The Leader"; Mussolini's name for himself as dictator.
2. Massive war debts; economic depression; unemployment; social unrest; political instability.
3. Beat up political opponents; broke up rallies and strikes; elected officials who opposed them were driven from office.

4. He played upon fears of communism; vowed to end social unrest; protect private property and restore Italy's greatness; promised full employment and workers' benefits.

page 605
1. Weimar Republic—German democratic republic from 1919 to 1933.
   Ruhr Valley—industrial area taken over by France in 1923.
   Locarno—site in Switzerland of treaty signed with France and Belgium.
   Nazi party—National Socialist Workers' party.
   Adolf Hitler—became leader of Nazi party.
   Brown Shirts—Hitler's private army.
   Beer Hall Putsch—attempt by Hitler to seize power in Munich.
   Mein Kampf—*My Struggle*; Hitler's autobiography.
   Reichstag—German parliament.
   Third Reich—Hitler's government.
   Der Führer—"The Leader"; title Hitler took for himself.
   Nuremberg Laws—against all Jews' civil rights.
   Gestapo—Hitler's secret police.
2. It was a condition of the Versailles Treaty.
3. To control Germany's coal mines and steel mills in lieu of reparations owed.
4. Savings became worthless; confidence in democracy was shaken.

page 613
1. Trade Disputes Act—made strikes illegal in Britain.
   Ramsay MacDonald—prime minister; Scottish labor leader.
   Easter Rebellion—Irish rebellion against British rule.
   Irish Free State—southern part of Ireland; commonwealth status.
   Ulster—Northern Ireland; remained part of Britain.
   Popular Front—socialistic and communistic political movement in France.
   Leon Blum—Popular Front prime minister.
   Maginot Line—series of fortifications built on the French-German border.
   Franklin D. Roosevelt—President of the United States; originated New Deal.
   New Deal—Roosevelt's plan for economic recovery.

Kellogg-Briand Pact—agreement making war illegal.
2. To put pressure on the government to solve the economic problems of unemployment and export trade.
3. As an insurance against any future German invasion. The Belgian border was undefended.
4. To avoid becoming involved in alliances with other nations. Supported the policy of isolationism.

Special Feature Questions
page 610
1. It became the major source of family entertainment.
2. To take government policies directly to the people.

Photo Questions
page 594
"Peace, Land, and Bread." To pull out of the war; give land to peasants; provide adequate food supplies.

page 596
He dissolved the elected assembly and seized control.

page 598
He believed that the Soviet Union should concentrate on growing strong before trying to spread revolution around the world.

page 601
That the power of ancient Rome stood behind Mussolini; that Italy would again attain the power of that past.

page 603
Four trillion marks (4,000,000,000,000.)

page 605
By stripping the Jews of citizenship and all civil rights and liberties.

page 606
It outlawed strikes and restricted political activities of unions.

page 609
Cars, telephones, radios, appliances.

1932.

page 612
It helped restore the confidence of the nation and lessened human suffering.

Chapter Review

page 614, Reviewing the Main Ideas

1. He organized the Bolsheviks; gained control of the Petrograd Soviet; ousted the elected constituent assembly.
2. They had improved the military and gained the loyalty of Russian soldiers; Whites weakened by internal divisions.

page 615

3. Each major nationality was given its own republic, each with its own soviet, bureaucracy, language, cultural traditions.
4. Trotsky felt that socialism should be spread all over the world before it could be built in U.S.S.R. Stalin believed that the Soviet Union should grow strong first, before it tried to spread socialism throughout the world.
5. The government took over all aspects of industrial production; demanded great sacrifices of the people; concentrated on building heavy industry; began the Five-Year Plans.
6. It gave the state absolute authority and the right to rule by force.
7. They were used as a threat by Mussolini and Hitler.
8. It became a debtor instead of creditor in world trade; lost its position as a leading trade nation.
9. Irish demands for independence.
10. Many political parties, none of which could gain a majority; cabinets and prime ministers changed frequently.
11. Prosperity of the 1920's was an illusion; workers' wages lagged behind rising prices; buying power was based on credit; low farm prices; United States economic isolation; high tariffs; buying stocks on margin.
12. It expanded the role of the Federal Government in business and society.

page 615, Discussing Important Ideas

1. Answers may vary.
2. Answers may vary.
3. Answers may vary.
4. Answers may vary; mention should be made of the economic depression; peoples' inexperience with self-government.
5. Answers may vary; mention should be made of economic stability versus the suspension of individual rights.
6. Answers may vary.
7. Answers may vary.
8. Answers may vary; mention should be made of the lack of confidence in unstable, weak government policies.

page 615, Using Graphs

1. Percentage of unemployed industrial workers from 1932 to 1933.
2. Percentage of unemployed industrial workers.
3. It was the peak year of the depression.
4. Denmark. Czechoslovakia.
5. More than 30%; more than 24%; about 22.5%; more than 25%.
6. Industrial manufacturing was down by about 25%.

CHAPTER 27
Nationalism Between the Wars

At the conclusion of this chapter, students should be able to:

1. describe how World War I affected nations in Asia, Africa, and Latin America.
2. compare independence efforts in India with those in the Middle East and Africa.
3. explain the origins of the Arab-Israeli conflict.

Overview

Chapter 27 surveys the changes that took place in South and East Asia, the Middle East, Africa, and Latin America between World Wars I and II. World War I is shown to have left widespread bitterness among nonwestern nations after having inspired broad hope for independence and improved conditions in the world.

Details are provided on the development of independence movements in India, the Middle East, and Africa. Internal developments in China, Japan, and Latin America are also described. Nationalism is the conceptual focus of the chapter. Other concepts developed include self-determination, cultural conflict, civil disobedience, modernization, and self-worth.

Teaching Strategies
Section 1

Introduction: Read the following quotation by Sun Yat-sen:

> The Chinese people have only family and clan solidarity; they do not have national spirit . . . they are just a heap of loose sand . . . . Other men are the carving knife and serving dish; we are the fish and the meat.

Have students explain what they think Sun's statement means. (Carving knife and serving dish represent countries that seized Chinese territories and/or handed them to others; fish and meat represent Chinese territories and resources.) Ask students whether Sun is suggesting that the Chinese are powerful or powerless (powerless). Tell students that in the early twentieth century, nonwestern peoples sought to become the carving knife—to develop national pride and to gain independent control over their own lives and territories. As students read the section, have them note instances where western nations acted as "carving knives" or "serving dishes."

Development: Have students complete a chart that will allow them to compare and contrast the three nations described in this section. Identify the postwar foreign and domestic barriers that stood in the way of these nations becoming united, powerful countries. What actions were undertaken to remove the barriers? Which country faced the most difficult task?

Section 2

Introduction: As students read the subsections on Turkey and Iran (pp. 622-624), have them make a list of conditions that were altered by World War I. How did Turkey and Persia (Iran) respond to the changed conditions? What conflicts did they face as they attempted to modernize? Do students think it is possible to modernize without becoming westernized? Ask them to read the rest of the section.

Development: Review how Britain became involved in Palestine during World War II. (By

making promises to both Arabs and Jews in order to gain their support during the war.) Refer students to the excerpt of the Balfour Declaration on page 624. How do they interpret it? Does it promise the creation of a separate Jewish state? Have students weigh the options that were open to Britain in the 1930's. How did the Peel Commission suggest that its recommendations be implemented? Britain would retain a mandate only over Jerusalem, Bethlehem, and a corridor to the sea. Remind students that Britain was also concerned with India and worsening conditions in Europe.

Section 3

Introduction: Tell students that Africans, like other nonwestern peoples, believed that Wilson's idea of self-determination, contained in the Fourteen Points, also applied to them. They were bitter to discover that self-determination was "for whites only." Educated Africans began to lay the groundwork for independence. As students read the section, have them note the various efforts made by African nationalists to move their countries toward self-determination.

Development: Refer students to the quotation by Kenyatta on page 629. What does he say about the differences in perceptions and values between Europeans and Africans? What were European goals for Africans? What were African goals? Ask students to rank the relative importance of the following as instruments to win independence: literature such as Kenyatta's, violence, negotiation, and nonviolent resistance.

Section 4

Introduction: Explain that although Latin American nations were independent, they were not free of foreign influence. Because of their geographical location, they were less involved in World War I and more closely involved with the United States, than other regions. Nationalistic feelings in Latin America were more anti-American than anti-European. Tell students to be prepared to answer the following questions after they read the section: What was the source of United States involvement in Latin America? How was this similar or different to European involvement in Asia or Africa?

Development: Have students prepare a chart to compare the governments and policies of the three countries described in the section. Include the role of the military and the reforms undertaken. Remind students of what they learned about the social structure of Latin America in earlier chapters. How does that help them understand the extremism that developed as Latin American countries sought to strengthen themselves? Do they think American intervention was justified to protect American economic interests? Why might Latin Americans have continued to mistrust the United States despite its Good Neighbor policy?

Conclusion: Have students review the major nationalist leaders described in the chapter. Whose vision for national independence or national growth do they find most appealing? Which one of these leaders do they think has had the greatest impact between the years after World War I and the mid-1980's? Have students note their answers so they can refer back to them as they read the later chapters of the text.

Answers
Section Review Questions

page 622

1. Amritsar Massacre—British troops killed 379 unarmed Indians.

   Mohandas K. Gandhi—leading Indian nationalist; pacifist.

   Salt Act—made possession of salt not bought from the government illegal.

   Government of India Act—placed agriculture, education, public health, public works under control of provincial councils.

   Mohammed Ali Jinnah—leader of Muslim League.

   Jawaharlal Nehru—Hindu leader; follower of Gandhi.

   Kuomintang—Chinese Nationalist party.

   Chiang Kai-shek—head of army; successor to Sun Yat-sen.

   Mao Tse-tung—Communist leader.

   Long March—Communist retreat over 5,000 miles (8,000 kilometers).

   Twenty-one Demands—would make China a Japanese protectorate.

2. Nonviolent protest and civil disobedience.
3. Through a series of military campaigns against local warlords; set up a national government.
4. Its industry grew rapidly; working class increased in importance; democracy grew; universal male suffrage granted.

page 626

1. Treaty of Sévres—formally ended the Ottoman Empire.

   Mustapha Kemal—first president of Republic of Turkey.

   Treaty of Lausanne—allowed the Turks all Asia Minor; withdrawal of Allied troops from the area.

   Ankara—new Turk capital.

   Reza Khan—ruler of Persia (Iran).

   Majles—Persian parliament.

   Balfour Declaration—established a national homeland for Jews.

   Zionists—Jewish nationalists.

   Peel Commission—concluded that Palestine should be divided into separate Arab and Jewish states.

   Ibn Saud—independent Arab ruler of much of the Arabian Peninsula; head of the Wahabis.

   Wahabis—strict sect of Sunni Muslims.

2. Economic reforms; adopted western calendar, Latin alphabet, metric system; reduced the influence of Islam; limited authority of religious leaders; did away with wearing of the veil and fez; outlawed polygamy.
3. Attacked the monarchy and established a new government as dictator; later became shah.
4. Arabs, Jews. On vague promises the British had made to each group.

page 629

1. French North Africa—Morocco, Algeria, Tunisia.

   Wafd—nationalist party in Egypt.

   Saad Zaghlul—leader of the Wafd.

   Milner Commission—recommended Egypt's independence.

   North African Star—nationalist party in Algeria.

   Harry Thuku—nationalist leader in Kenya.

   B. N. Azikiwe—nationalist leader in Nigeria.

   Leopold Senghor—nationalist and ethnic writer from Senegal; lived in France.

   Jomo Kenyatta—writer of his traditional culture in Kenya.

2. Britain declared its independence in 1922, without consulting the Egyptians.
3. Democracy and the self-determination of people; some African thinkers hoped to unite their people by giving them an appreciation of their rich cultural heritage.

page 631
1. Lázaro Cárdenas—president of Mexico.
   Hipólito Irigoyen—president of Argentina.
   Getúlio Vargas—president of Brazil.
   Juan Vicente Gómez—president of Venezuela.
   Augusto César Sandino—leader of rebel forces in Nicaragua.
   Good Neighbor Policy—Roosevelt's renunciation of military intervention in Latin America.
2. Mexico: redistribution of land to peasants; cooperative farms established; nationalization of foreign-controlled railroads and oil companies. Argentina: adoption of universal male suffrage; improved factory conditions, boosted workers' wages, regulated working hours. Brazil: increased workers' wages, shortened working hours; legalized unions.
3. Renounced military intervention; ended restrictions on Cuba's sovereignty; withdrew American troops from Haiti and Nicaragua.

Special Feature Questions

page 627
1. European art was concerned with the outward appearance, while African art gave shape and form to a spiritual reality or abstract idea.
2. Paintings reflected the lines, angles, and shapes of African sculpture; led to a movement of "primitivism."

Photo Questions

page 618
The British Parliament passed the Government of India Act that gave many bureaucratic responsibilities to Indian provincial councils.

page 619
Three years.

page 620
They were closer to Soviet supply lines and farther removed from Chiang's army.

page 621
1925.

page 622
The Treaty of Lausanne, which allowed the Turks all of Asia Minor, and the withdrawal of Allied troops.

page 623
To gain higher revenues and assert greater control over foreign companies.

page 628
Educated Africans living in urban areas.

page 630
Recognition of unions; better wages; shorter hours; better working conditions in factories.

page 631
Renounced past military intervention; recognized Cuba's sovereignty; withdrew troops from Haiti and Nicaragua.

Chapter Review

page 632, Reviewing the Main Ideas
1. Independence from British rule.
2. National government had no real power; local warlords.
3. To escape Chiang's army.
4. It felt that the West did not accept it as an equal; refusal of the League of Nations to approve a statement of racial equality in the League's charter; United States ban on Japanese immigration.

page 633
5. It became a democracy with universal suffrage; raised tariffs; began a five-year plan to increase industrial production; did away with wearing of the veil and fez, outlawed polygamy; limited the authority of Muslim religious leaders.
6. Improved the military; built railroads, paved roads, renegotiated oil contracts.
7. He conquered more territory; proclaimed himself king.
8. Oil.
9. Milner was sent to investigate disorders in Egypt; recommended its independence. Britain declared independence in 1922.
10. To protect the Suez Canal.
11. Many Africans accepted western ideas but opposed European rule of their lands and developed an appreciation of their local cultures.
12. Leadership based on the support of urban workers rather than wealthy landowners.

page 633, Discussing Important Ideas
1. Answers may vary; mention should be made of the declining influence of Europe, and the

idea that self-determination should apply to all people.

2. Answers may vary; mention should be made of each area's cultural expectations.
3. Answers may vary.
4. Answers may vary; the discovery of oil should be mentioned.
5. Answers may vary; mention should be made of pride in cultural heritage; foundation of nationalist organizations.
6. Answers may vary.

page 633, Using Maps
1. Egypt, part of Saudi Arabia, Iraq, Transjordan, Palestine, Lebanon, Syria, Turkey.
2. Turkey, Syria, Lebanon, Palestine, Egypt. Egypt, Transjordan, Syria, Lebanon.
3. Turkey. Saudi Arabia.
4. Britain, France.
5. Iran.

CHAPTER 28
World War II

At the conclusion of this chapter, students should be able to:

1. identify and explain the significance of the major events leading to the outbreak of World War II.
2. describe the successful tactics used by Germany and Japan in the early years of the war, the strategy of the Allies, and the contributions of Britain, the Soviet Union, and the United States in achieving victory over the Axis powers.
3. discuss measures taken by the Nazis to achieve lebensraum and to implement Hitler's racist goals.
4. explain how relations between the Soviet Union and the West were affected by World War II.

Overview

Chapter 28 focuses on the prelude and major campaigns of World War II. It discusses the aggressive moves of Japan, Italy, and Germany in the 1930's and why the western democracies were acquiescent. The Nazi-Soviet Non-aggression Pact is shown to remove the last obstacle to war. The events of World War II are presented chronologically by theaters of war. The chapter

concludes with the Nuremberg Trials and the creation of the United Nations.

Appeasement and the questions of how peace can be maintained or war avoided should be the focus of the first section of the chapter. The influence of World War I on World War II is also significant. Students should understand how domestic politics and conditions are related to international politics. Other important concepts include collective security, nonbelligerency, and propaganda.

Teaching Strategies
Section 1

Introduction: Tell students that World War II began only 21 years after the end of World War I. Ask them why they think peace was so short-lived. Have them jot down their answers for reference as they read the first section.

Development: No single event triggered World War II, as was the case in World War I. Analyze with students the events described in the section. What options were open to the western democracies in each case? Why was the League of Nations ineffective? How were the feeble responses of the western democracies interpreted by Japan, Mussolini, Hitler, and Stalin? Did fear of war make war inevitable? Some historians believe that firm actions short of war in the early 1930's would have deterred Hitler; by 1938 it was too late.

Section 2

Introduction: In World War I the defensive position had held the advantage for most of the war. In World War II, the opposite was true. Tanks, planes, and mobile troop transports first used in World War I were fully developed in World War II, as the Germans stunningly demonstrated in their blitzkrieg attacks. Have students read the feature "Warsaw" (p. 641) before they go to the subsection "Western Front" on page 640.

Development: From 1939 to the summer of 1941, Germany appeared invincible. Only Britain and the Soviet Union remained to resist the Nazis in Europe. As students discuss this section, consider with them the possible factors that enabled Britain and the U.S.S.R. to stand fast, while France and the others collapsed. Geography and the quality of political leadership should be raised. Tell students of news commentator

Edward R. Murrow's description of Winston Churchill: "He mobilized the English language and sent it into battle."

Section 3

Introduction: The involvement of the European colonial powers in war in Europe left East and Southeast Asia vulnerable to Japanese takeover. Only the United States posed a serious obstacle. Have students read the section to see how Japan's attack on Pearl Harbor altered the nature of the war.

Development: Discuss the progression of American involvement in the war from neutrality to full belligerency. Because President Roosevelt had been trying unsuccessfully to overcome isolationist opposition to participation in the war for several years, some controversy still focuses on how much the United States government knew about the planned Japanese attack on Pearl Harbor. This might be a topic for students to research.

Section 4

Introduction: To help students follow the events taking place simultaneously around the globe, have them prepare a time line of events as they read this section. Get them started in class with a review of events beginning with the attack on Poland in September 1939. Different lines should be included for each of the major theaters. The time line should note significant events and battles, countries occupied, and allied conferences.

Development: The war years were unmatched years of suffering, which brought out the best and worst in people. The vast war literature is filled with accounts of personal heroism, tragedy, endurance, courage, sacrifice, cowardice, and evil. Ask students to research a single event or a person—combatant, civilian, or war correspondent—and present their findings to the class in an imaginative way, such as a news account of the event, an interview with the individual, or a fictionalized diary excerpt.

Section 5

Introduction: As the end of the war neared, the Allies began to address postwar arrangements. The Allied wartime solidarity began to crumble. Political matters replaced strategy in the discussions of Churchill, Roosevelt, and Stalin. Have students read the section, watching for significant decisions or events that shaped the postwar political structure.

Development: The end of the war saw the destruction of the cities of Hiroshima and Nagasaki by atomic bombs and revealed the mass murder of Jews, Slavs, and political enemies of the Nazis. Discuss why both of these holocausts occurred. How was personal responsibility involved in each situation? Jews believe that what happened in Germany was not due to some deep flaw in the German character, but that it was due to conditions that could occur in any country. What might these conditions be? Do students agree with this conclusion?

Conclusion: What generalizations can be made about war and the maintenance of peace based on the experiences of World War II?

Answers
Section Review Questions

page 639

1. Axis—Germany, Italy, Japan, seven supporting countries.
   Allies—Britain, France, the Soviet Union, the United States.
   Manchukuo—new name for Manchuria.
   Haile Selassie—king of Ethiopia.
   Rome-Berlin Axis—political and military pact between Hitler and Mussolini.
   Anschluss—the annexation of Austria to Germany.
   Neville Chamberlain—British Prime Minister.
   Édouard Daladier—French Premier.
   Munich Crisis—meeting to discuss Germany's aggression in Europe.
   Francisco Franco—leader of Spanish Nationalists.
   International Brigades—sympathizers from Britain, France, and United States to the Spanish Loyalists.
   Hermann Göring—head of the German Luftwaffe.
   Luftwaffe—German air force.
   Nazi-Soviet Non-aggression Pact—agreement between Hitler and Stalin to remain neutral if either were attacked by some other country.
2. They were bitter about the war treaties, and willing to risk war to revise the treaties and improve their positions.

3. Right-wing groups in Spain wished to restore the old order. Franco established a right-wing dictatorship.
4. It would buy time to prepare and improve the Soviet's strategic position. Western leaders were outraged as it destroyed the last barrier to war.

page 644
1. Panzers—armored tank divisions.
   Wehrmacht—Hitler's army.
   Ardennes—area on the Belgian-French border.
   Charles de Gaulle—French tank commander and military leader.
   Vichy—site of French puppet government.
   Battle of Britain—German air offensive against Britain.
   Atlantic Charter—program between the United States and Britain.
   Battle of the Atlantic—convoy system in the Atlantic used to counter German submarines.
2. The Battle of Britain. Poland, Belgium, Netherlands, France.
3. Provided destroyers, food, and armaments to Britain.

page 647
1. Greater East Asia Co-prosperity Sphere—Japan's plan to a "new order in Greater East Asia."
   Tripartite Pact—agreement between Japan, Italy, and Germany.
   Pearl Harbor—Hawaiian site of American Pacific fleet; bombed by the Japanese.
   Isoroku Yamamoto—Japanese admiral.
   Neutrality Acts—forbad American involvement in foreign wars.
2. To control East and Southeast Asia in order to have access to their resources.
3. To make the United States see how powerful they were and that it would be wise to allow them to proceed with their expansionist plans.
4. Germany posed a more direct threat to the Western Hemisphere.

page 653
1. Erwin Rommel—leader of Germany's Afrika Korps.
   Battle of Midway—American victory over Japanese navy.

Stalingrad—major industrial center on the Volga River, site of battle.
   Casablanca—city in Morocco; site of Allied leaders' conference.
   Normandy—region of northwestern France.
   Tehran—site of meeting between Stalin, Churchill, Roosevelt.
   Warsaw—capital of Poland.
   El Alamein—site of British last line of defense in North Africa.
   Bernard Montgomery—commander of British forces in North Africa.
   Dwight D. Eisenhower—Allied commander.
   François Darlan—Vichy official.
   Pietro Badoglio—new prime minister of Italy.
   Anzio—site of Allied landing in Italy.
   Operation Overload—Allied invasion of France.
   D-Day—June 6, 1944; date of Operation Overlord.
   George Patton—American tank commander.
   Douglas MacArthur—American general in the Pacific theater.
   Chester W. Nimitz—American admiral in the Pacific theater.
2. They encircled the Germans, cut off supplies, and tightened the trap.
3. They used a "pincers movement" from Egypt in the east, and Morocco and Algiers in the west.
4. A British-American invasion of western Europe, and a Soviet offensive on the eastern front at the same time.
5. To capture some islands, those bypassed would be cut off from supplies and would "wither on the vine."

page 657
1. Yalta—site in the Crimea of Stalin, Roosevelt, Churchill meeting.
   United Nations—permanent international organization to preserve peace.
   Dumbarton Oaks—near Washington, D.C., site of conference on United Nations charter.
   Battle of the Bulge—critical battle between Allies and Germans.
   V-E Day—Victory in Europe Day; May 8, 1945.
   Battle of Leyte Gulf—last naval engagement of the war.

Iwo Jima—island site of one of the two fiercest battles of the Pacific theater.

Okinawa—island site of one of the two fiercest battles of the Pacific theater.

Harry Truman—President of the United States; succeeded Roosevelt.

Potsdam—site of conference in Germany.

Hiroshima—site in Japan of first atomic bomb attack.

Nagasaki—site in Japan of second atomic bomb attack.

V-J Day—Victory over Japan Day; August 14, 1945.

Missouri—battleship; location of formal surrender of Japan.

Holocaust—mass murder of European Jews by the Nazis.

Nuremberg—site of trials of Nazi criminals.

2. Stalin agreed to hold elections in Soviet-occupied countries; Germany to be occupied by the four Allied powers; United Nations agreements to include France and China as sponsors.

3. They broke though the Allied lines causing a "bulge" in them. The Allies finally checked the German drive at Bastogne, France, in the Battle of the Bulge.

4. By the dropping of two atomic bombs on Japanese cities.

Special Feature Questions

page 641
1. Much of the city was in ruins.
2. They defied the storm of war and rebuilt their city.

Photo Questions

page 636
It had to gain new territory to provide the materials and markets it needed.

page 636
Members were allowed to sell Italy the materials needed to make war.

page 638
Hitler put an end to the Versailles treaty and began to rearm Germany.

page 642
Germany was to occupy all of northern France and the Atlantic coastline; southern France was to be governed by a puppet government.

page 644
They were without winter clothing; lack of medical supplies.

page 645
To counter a United States embargo on scrap metals to Japan; and aid to China.

page 645
Nineteen ships disabled or sunk; 188 planes destroyed.

page 646
They prohibited shipments to belligerents.

page 647
To open a second front in Europe.

page 648
It was the only remaining overland supply route to the Chinese.

page 651
Eleven weeks; from June 6 to August 5.

page 655
About 200,000.

page 656
Many governments disbelieved the rumors.

page 657
For pursuing "aggressive war" and "crimes against humanity."

Chapter Review

page 658, Reviewing the Main Ideas
1. They felt they had been treated unfairly in the peace settlements.
2. Hitler sent armies into the western part of Czechoslovakia, and the eastern part became a German puppet state.

page 659
3. He claimed that he was promoting political stability by uniting German-speaking peoples. They refused to act.
4. He doubted that the West would come to the aid of his country if threatened by Germany. The Soviets would also gain spheres of influence.
5. They depended upon the strength of the Maginot Line.

6. He thought they would be easily defeated; he wanted the wheat of the Ukraine and oil supplies of the Caucasus. The Russians were not prepared to surrender; the winter set in and Germans were forced to wait for spring and warmer weather.
7. It was decided to secure the Mediterranean.
8. In a month and a half almost all of France had been liberated.
9. He feared that Stalin intended to establish Communist governments in eastern Europe.
10. Most people still remained loyal.
11. More than 6 million Jews had been slaughtered.
12. Security Council: primarily responsible for maintaining peace and security. The General Assembly: has the right to make recommendations on all matters within the scope of the charter. The Economic and Social Council: initiates activities related to development, world trade, natural resources, human rights, population, social welfare, science and technology, and other economic and social questions. Trusteeship Council: to deal with nonindependent territories. International Court of Justice: give opinions on cases of states and international organizations. Secretariat: international working staff at UN headquarters, carries out day-to-day work of the UN.

page 659, Discussing Important Ideas
1. Answers may vary.
2. Answers may vary.
3. Answers may vary.
4. Answers may vary; mention should be made of Göring using Spain as a testing ground for his Luftwaffe.
5. Answers may vary.
6. Answers may vary.
7. Answers may vary.
8. Answers may vary.

page 659, Using Illustrations
1. The major powers playing with the world.
2. That Tojo is supporting Hitler; Stalin is waiting for Roosevelt and Churchill to win; Mussolini is sweating it out alone. Answers may vary.
3. Churchill's.
4. Answers may vary.
5. Churchill and Roosevelt.
6. Answers may vary.

Unit Review
page 660, Developing Understanding
1. The rise of nationalism and militarism and its resulting rivalries. Russia's withdrawal and the United States' entry into the war.
2. To fight such a total war, governments had temporarily assumed extraordinary powers to mobilize their resources. After the war totalitarian dictatorships adopted such powers and extended them to all areas of life. They used their authority to remodel society, transform the economy, and conquer other lands. Totalitarian governments were established in Germany, Italy, and Russia.
3. American prosperity was mostly an illusion; buying power was based on credit; farm prices low; isolationism of the United States. It expanded the role of the government and made government and business responsible for the economy.
4. In Asia, organized independence movements resisted and disrupted colonial rulers. European-educated Africans emerged to support nationalist movements that wanted to break their ties with European ruling countries. Strong nationalist leaders in Latin America established a new type of government based on the support of urban workers, rather than that of wealthy landowners; they acted to restrict foreign influences in their countries.
5. Dissatisfaction and bitterness about the peace treaties became a primary factor; the settlements were harsh and punitive, and the resulting poor economy, unstable governments, and rise of totalitarian dictators set the stage for future war.
6. Answers may vary; mention should be made of the resources of the Allies, and the fact that resources in Europe were being depleted by the activities of the war being fought there.

pages 660-661, Developing Skills
Conclude the unit with the Developing Skills activity. This activity, which is suitable for individuals or groups, will give students practice in analyzing a primary source. After reading a selection from an article on fascism by Benito Mussolini, students are given a series of questions to guide them in their analysis. Variation in their answers is to be expected.

You may want to go over the definition of a primary source (given in the exercise) and make sure students are able to distinguish between primary and secondary sources (secondhand sources include history texts and encyclopedias). One set of possible answers to the questions is as follows:

1. As one of the founders and leaders of fascism, Mussolini is certainly qualified to write about its philosophy. Of course, the question of bias can be raised.

2. As explained in the exercise, the article was written in Italy in 1932 for an encyclopedia, presumably with the purpose of providing information as well as persuasive argument.

3. Fascism is pro-war, anti-socialist, anti-democratic, imperialistic. The central definition of fascism is in the third paragraph: "Fascism conceives of the State as an absolute, in comparison with which all individuals or groups are relative. . . ."

4. By checking against other writings and speeches about the philosophy of fascism; also by checking the historical record of actions taken by fascist leaders and the governments they created.

UNIT 8
The Contemporary World

At the conclusion of this unit, students should be able to:
1. discuss East-West relations after World War II and explain the issues that have divided the two superpowers.
2. explain the rise of the Third World and the challenges that face it.
3. outline the major postwar developments in Japan, China, India, Southeast Asia, the Middle East, Africa, and Latin America.
4. describe the achievements of contemporary culture.
5. describe the problems and issues that face humanity and the efforts currently being made to deal with them successfully.

Overview

This unit treats the postwar developments from a global perspective. It explains the polarization of the world powers into eastern and western blocs and the escalation of confrontations into a cold war, which flared into actual fighting in several areas. The unit describes the independence movements that have led to the liberation of many Asian and African countries. The rise of the Third World is discussed in the context of the Asian, African, and Latin American nations that have chosen the road of nonalignment in international conflicts. The unit also presents our contemporary culture and explores the challenges of the future.

Introducing the Unit

Ask students to list the world problems and the post-World War II wars that they can recall from their own background before they read the unit. They might have seen some movies or read about the Korean and the Vietnam wars. They may suggest issues such as situations in the Middle East or the status of nuclear arms. On a world map point out the troubled areas that students identify in their statements. As the unit is studied, emphasize the growing interdependence among the nations of the world.

CHAPTER 29
East-West Relations

At the conclusion of this chapter, students should be able to:
1. explain Soviet and United States foreign policy goals after World War II.
2. describe the steps taken by the United States to face Soviet expansion in the late 1940's.
3. identify the Soviet satellites and discuss how the Soviet Union has been able to dominate them.
4. describe major foreign and domestic developments in the West between 1945 and 1961.

Overview

Chapter 29 covers East-West relations in the post-World War II period. It examines the goals of American and Soviet policies, the escalation of political confrontations into a "cold war," and the rise of alliances. The European scene is described as the continent became polarized between the eastern and western blocs. Next the chapter pursues domestic developments within each bloc until the early 1960's. Change from the Stalinist to the post-Stalinist eras in the Soviet world is described, together with the process of de-Stalinization. Within the western world, events in each major country are explained. Lastly, the chapter explains how the new policy of peaceful coexistence evolved in the late 1950's. Important concepts include bipolarism, "iron curtain," arms race, containment, racial segregation, pluralism, and terrorism.

Teaching Strategies
Section 1

Introduction: Read the quote on page 666 from Churchill's address and ask students if they know what the term "iron curtain" has come to mean. Have volunteers try to point it out on a map.

Development: Ask students to list the goals of American and Soviet foreign policies after World War II. Compare these goals and have a discussion on whether they can be accommodated without confrontation between the two powers. Students may also look at the goals in terms of ideological differences. Ask them to make a list of the issues in 1945 that had to be resolved by the Allies. (These should include the future of Germany and Eastern Europe.)

Section 2

Introduction: Introduce this section with a discussion of the meaning of "containment" as used by George Kennan (p. 668). Ask students if they think containment implied acceptance of the Soviet Union's domination of its satellites.

Development: Hold a discussion on foreign aid as an instrument of foreign policy. Ask if the United States should base its aid strictly on the need of the recipients, or if it should consider the attitude of the recipients in world affairs before it extends the aid. Another consideration may be the types of government the recipients maintain in their countries. Discuss the Marshall Plan as an example of a unique, massive program of foreign aid. Ask students if the United States gained anything through the plan.

Section 3

Introduction: Ask students if they know anyone who came to the United States from Eastern Europe after the 1940's. Tens of thousands of immigrants, mainly Hungarians, came from their countries as political refugees. If the students know anyone, ask them to see if the person would permit an interview. Although there may be only one or two interviewers, other students should submit questions to be asked at the interview.

Development: After reading this section, ask students to write a few sentences that describe Stalinism. Have them list the de-Stalinization measures that were carried out after the death of Stalin.

Ask students to list the Eastern European countries and to write two sentences describing Communist rule in each. Regarding Hungary, point out that the 1956 revolt coincided with an Israeli-British-French attack on Egypt (p. 703) that distracted world opinion from focusing on the events in Hungary.

Section 4

Introduction: Ask students to make a list of the western countries. As they read the section, have them list the postwar problems that each of these countries faced in the late 1940's and during the decades of the 1950's and 1960's. At the end of their reading, discuss how each of these problems was resolved or handled. Emphasize how

the democratic systems and cooperation within the Western bloc, with the exception of Spain and Portugal, enhanced their power, helped them rebuild after the war, and raised their standards of living.

Development: Ask students to pretend they were French citizens living during the late 1950's and 1960's. How would they view de Gaulle's policy regarding the French colonies, particularly Algeria? Have them discuss these views and explain their reasons.

Section 5

Introduction: Explain the meaning of "peaceful coexistence." Should students expect peaceful coexistence to resolve all East-West problems to the satisfaction of both sides? Ask them if they can think of an alternative to peaceful coexistence.

Development: Point out, with regard to the U-2 incident, that today the two superpowers monitor each other constantly through their satellites. Organize a panel discussion on the Bay of Pigs and one on the Cuban missile crisis. Ask students to pretend that they were members of the National Security Council that was advising President Kennedy. What advice would they have given him in each case? Debate the question.

Conclusion: Organize a mock United Nations Security Council meeting to debate a number of issues that were discussed in this chapter. Two or three students may represent each member and cooperate in gathering information and making presentations. The five permanent members should be represented. Note that China was represented by the Republic of China in Taiwan at the time.

Answers
Section Review Questions
page 667

1. "iron curtain"—Soviet-made barrier across Europe dividing east from west.
   Azerbaijan—a northern province of Iran; held by Iranian Communists.
   Bernard Baruch—United States Atomic Energy Commissioner.
2. Stalin devoted his attention to territorial expansion and economic reconstruction; the United States expected an era of tranquility

in foreign affairs, friendly relations with the Soviet Union, and the United Nations to solve international disputes.

3. They recognized that Europe was divided into two parts; urged western democracies to cooperate in stemming Soviet expansion.

4. That the United Nations supervise all nuclear energy production; after controls had been set up, the United States would destroy its stockpile of atomic weapons. The Soviets rejected the plan, demanded that America destroy its bombs at once; the United States refused to agree; both countries became involved in an arms race.

page 671

1. George Kennan—State Department expert on the Soviet Union.

   Truman Doctrine—new statement of United States foreign policy.

   George Marshall—Secretary of State; he proposed a European aid program.

   COMECON—Council of Mutual Economic Assistance; Soviet rival plan to the Marshall Plan.

   West Berlin—American, British, and French zones of Berlin.

   NATO—North Atlantic Treaty Organization; treaty formed by Belgium, Britain, Canada, Denmark, France, Iceland, Italy, Luxemburg, the Netherlands, and the United States.

   Warsaw Pact—military alliance of Soviet Union and Eastern European satellites.

2. To restore the confidence of European people in the economic future of their countries.

3. To prevent the setting up of a West German state by the American, French, and British zones combining.

page 676

1. Nikita Khrushchev—Soviet Communist party secretary; he succeeded Stalin.

   Leonid Brezhnev—Soviet Communist party secretary; he succeeded Khrushchev.

   Aleksei Kosygin—Soviet prime minister; shared leadership with Brezhnev.

   Berlin Wall—concrete wall that separated east and west Berlin to shut off the flow of refugees from the East.

   Wladyslaw Gomulka—popular Communist leader in Poland.

Imre Nagy—Hungarian prime minister; he supported withdrawal from Soviet bloc.

Nicholae Ceausescu—Communist leader; as president, he preserved Romania's independence.

Josip Broz Tito—he led the resistance against the Nazis; Yugoslav nationalist and Communist; resisted Soviet pressures and kept Yugoslavia neutral.

Titoism—tendency to place nationalism over Soviet communism.

2. End of certain restrictions; intellectuals gained more freedom; reduced terror of secret police; release of many political prisoners; promise of better wages and more consumer goods.

3. Romania, Yugoslavia.

4. To guard against the West.

page 684

1. Martin Luther King, Jr.—civil rights leader.

   "Great Society"—Johnson's reforms in education and social welfare.

   EEC—European Economic Community; the Common Market.

   EFTA—European Free Trade Association; looser organization than the EEC to allow Britain to keep trade agreements.

   Clement Attlee—British prime minister; Labor party leader; replaced Churchill.

   Konrad Adenauer—formed the first West German government.

   Willy Brandt—mayor of West Berlin.

   Alcide de Gasperi—Italian prime minister.

   Benelux—economic union of Belgium, Luxemburg, the Netherlands.

   Antonio de Oliveira Salazar—dictator of Portugal.

   George Papandreou—liberal opposition leader; became prime minister of Greece.

2. United States: discrimination against blacks and other minorities; anti-Communist charges by conservatives. Canada: "Americanized" economy; French Canadians' protest movement in Quebec.

3. Nationalization of coal, steel, transportation industries; national health service; greater freedoms to unions.

4. The existence of many political parties undermined government stability. Voters approved de Gaulle's creation of a strong presidency and establishment of Fifth French Republic.

1. Anthony Eden—Britain's prime minister.
   "Spirit of Geneva"—reduction of tensions between West and Soviet leaders at summit meeting in Geneva.
   Bandung—site of conference of 29 Asian and African leaders.
   John F. Kennedy—United States President; succeeded Eisenhower.
   Alliance for Progress—Kennedy's plan to aid economic development in Latin American countries.
   Peace Corps—sent Americans as teachers, farmers, technicians, to other countries to promote economic development.
   Fidel Castro—dictator of Cuba.
2. Soviet shooting of an American spy plane over their territory.
3. A loss of prestige to the United States; closer alliance between Cuba and the Soviet Union.
4. An American blockade of Cuban shipping; demand that weapons be removed.

Special Feature Questions

page 677
1. Development of liquid-fueled rockets.
2. The superpowers carried out a space race.

Photo Questions

page 666
Stalin's refusal to accept the western interpretation of the Yalta agreements.

page 668
That Britain was unable to continue its commitment to check the Communist advance.

page 671
To prevent the western powers setting up a West German state by joining their zones of occupation.

page 673
Artists and intellectuals given more freedom; reduced terror of the secret police; freed many political prisoners; citizens promised better wages and more consumer goods.

page 675
Farmers forced to combine into collective farms; lower workers' living standards; restrictions on religion.

page 676
Tito's independent policies that stressed nationalism over communism.

page 678
Through nonviolent protests against discrimination.

page 679
They feared that their culture would be engulfed.

page 681
His strongly nationalistic policies angered France's allies.

page 683
After difficult negotiations, Britain, Greece, and Turkey agreed to independence for Crete in 1960.

Chapter Review

page 687, Reviewing the Main Ideas
1. The major powers split into two opposing camps; the western bloc led by the United States; and the eastern bloc led by the Soviet Union.
2. Stalin's territorial expansion in Eastern Europe.
3. By using the presence of its armies to establish Communist regimes.
4. Provided economic and military aid to non-Communist countries.
5. The Republic of Germany was proclaimed; Soviets then set up the German Democratic Republic.
6. There was more personal freedom; less fear of secret police.
7. Economic incentives for farmers; ownership of small farm plots; investments in farm equipment and agricultural training; reversal of de-Stalinization program; tightened controls over artists and intellectuals; arrest and imprisonment of dissidents.
8. East Germany: workers' uprisings; many fled to West Berlin. Poland: workers' riots. Hungary: full-scale revolution. Czechoslovakia: bloody purges crushed all opposition. Romania: retained its independence. Yugoslavia: resisted Soviet domination under Tito.
9. To abolish all tariffs and form a single economic market.

10. West Germany: became Europe's leading industrial nation. Spain: enjoyed one of the highest rates of economic growth in the world. Italy: the gap between the industrial north and agricultural south caused many problems.
11. The threat of nuclear war.
12. They sought influence in the emerging nations of Asia, Africa, and Latin America.
13. They opened contacts through diplomatic channels and summit conferences.

page 687, Discussing Important Ideas
1. Answers may vary.
2. Answers may vary.
3. Answers may vary.
4. Answers may vary.
5. Answers may vary; mention should be made of the fear of nuclear war.
6. Answers may vary.
7. Answers may vary.
8. Answers may vary.

page 687, Using Graphs
1. United States' economic aid to European countries.
2. To show the proportion of money each country received.
3. That the money came from the United States.
4. 18.
5. $1,390,000,000. Four years.

CHAPTER 30
Postwar Asia, Africa, and Latin America

At the conclusion of this chapter, students should be able to:
1. discuss the impact of the American occupation of Japan after World War II.
2. describe the rise of communism in East Asia with particular emphasis on China, Korea, and Indochina.
3. explain the reasons and the circumstances that led the Indian subcontinent from colonial rule to partition.
4. understand the reasons behind Middle East tension and wars, and the conflicting views that are associated with them.
5. discuss the political and economic issues that faced Africa and Latin America after World War II.

Overview

Chapter 30 provides students with basic information about the important developments in postwar Asia, Africa, and Latin America. The chapter begins with the description of Japan's evolution within one generation from a defeated and occupied nation into a thriving industrial democracy. It continues with a description of the transformation of China into a Communist state and the upheavals that followed. After dealing with the Korean conflict, the chapter turns to the developments that led the Indian subcontinent from a British colony to independence and partition. Events in Indochina and in other parts of South and Southeast Asia are then discussed. The chapter proceeds to the changes that took place in the Middle East and the conflicts and wars that have plagued the region. Following explanations of the retreat of colonial powers from Africa and the rise of independent states in that continent, the chapter analyzes the major developments in Latin America to the 1960's. Important concepts include Third World, "Great Leap Forward," Cultural Revolution, and Pan-Arabism.

Teaching Strategies
Section 1

Introduction: Ask students if they know the term "Third World." After this is clarified explain the meanings of "First World" and "Second World" (see annotation top of p. 689).

Development: Have students list two or three decisions that they might have made if they had been in General MacArthur's position in postwar Japan. Use their views to discuss the measures that he carried out and the United States policies toward Japan after the war.

With a large map of Asia or the world displayed before the class, ask students to assess China's strategic importance to the rest of Asia. From that point proceed to discuss options that the non-Communist Chinese and the United States could have taken to prevent the Communist victory. Point out that the Sino-Soviet split proves that the adoption of Marxian socialism does not remove national, political, and economic friction between nations, as the Communists claim. Regarding the Korean conflict, ask students to speculate on what would have happened if the United Nations, with strong American support, had not intervened in Korea.

Section 2

Introduction: The roots of the Vietnam War extend into the period of French control. Mention that the Communists in Indochina were instrumental in leading the struggle against the Japanese during World War II and the fight for independence from France after the war. Many Indochinese, particularly in Vietnam, accepted the Communists as leaders for liberation rather than for ideological reasons.

Development: Divide students into two groups and assume they were Indians living in India at about the time of its independence. One group is to advocate a separate country for the Muslims and another is to insist on keeping India unified. Have them debate the issue and devise a plan for partition.

Section 3

Introduction: On May 14, 1948, the British withdrew from Palestine. As students read the section, have them determine the role of Great Britain in the development of the conflict between the Palestinian Arabs and the Jews before 1947. What option did the British, the Jews, and the Arabs have besides an open conflict? Note that Britain did not hold an election to establish a legal government before its withdrawal from Palestine. Have students read the feature on Golda Meir (p. 701) before they begin the discussion of Arab states on page 702.

Development: Point out that historically Lebanon was a province within Syria and that France decided to partition the country in two. The apportionment of government positions in Lebanon has been based on the 1932 census, which was arranged by the French. The census gave the Christians a slight majority.

Tell students that the territorial concessions demanded by the Soviet Union from Turkey (Kars and Ardahan in northern Turkey) after the war were instrumental in shifting Turkish public opinion from neutrality to anti-Soviet.

Section 4

Introduction: Explain to students that in France's view, Algeria was different from its other colonies in Africa. It was regarded a part of France, not as a colony. The Algerians, who are part of the Arab world, received strong support from other Arabs in North Africa and the Middle East.

Point out that most Africans believed that independence would bring prosperity and a higher standard of living. Read to students the quote by Kenyatta on page 688. Once Africans attained their goal, they faced problems associated with economic development, shortage of capital, and inadequate administrative structures. The resulting frustration aggravated the ethnic tension within numerous countries.

Development: Divide students into several small groups, each to prepare a presentation on the problems of one of the major African countries.

Section 5

Introduction: Ask if any students have seen the play or the movie *Evita*. Relate the story of Juan and Eva Perón of Argentina. Although the play is a dramatization of Eva's story, it should serve to arouse student interest in Latin America.

Development: Ask students to list the countries of Latin America and to place them on an outline map. Have them select the four or five important countries and list the challenges or the problems that each is facing.

Conclusion: Ask students to make a flow chart of world events between 1945 and 1960. It should be large enough to fill a bulletin board. Students may divide themselves into five groups to share the responsibility. Each group should concentrate on collecting materials, including pictures, on one of the world regions.

Answers
Section Review Questions
page 695

1. Third World—newly independent countries that officially refuse to support either the United States or Soviet Union.

   Shigeru Yoshida—first elected prime minister of Japan.

   Taipei—capital of Taiwan.

   People's Republic of China—mainland China.

   Chou En-lai—prime minister of People's Republic of China.

Liu Shao-ch'i—Mao's closest adviser and heir apparent.

"Great Leap Forward"—Mao's second five-year plan.

Teng Hsiao-p'ing—leading pragmatist in China.

Cultural Revolution—time of civil disorder and confusion throughout China.

Red Guards—Communist faction loyal to Mao.

Syngman Rhee—president of South Korea.

Inchon—site of United Nations landing behind North Korean lines.

2. It ended the political powers of the emperor; safe-guarded individual rights; renounced militarism; introduced a greater measure of local self-government.

3. It united China in a common dislike of the Soviets.

4. A stalemate was reached; a truce signed that once again divided Korea near the 38th parallel.

page 699

1. New Delhi—site of proclamation of the Dominion of India.

Karachi—site of proclamation of the Dominion of Pakistan.

Lal Bahadur Shastri—prime minister of India; succeeded Nehru.

Indira Gandhi—Nehru's daughter; succeeded Shastri.

Mohammed Ayub Khan—ruler of Pakistan.

Vietminh—Vietnamese nationalists.

Ho Chi Minh—leader of Vietminh.

Dien Bien Phu—fortress site of French defeat.

Ngo Dinh Diem—South Vietnam president.

Vietcong—South Vietnamese Communists.

Achmed Sukarno—nationalist leader in Indonesia.

T. N. J. Suharto—leader of coup in Indonesia; elected president.

Burma—became independent of Britain.

Malaysia—became independent of Britain.

Luzon—one of larger Philippine islands.

Thailand—formally Siam.

SEATO—Southeast Asia Treaty Organization; formed to block Communist expansion in Southeast Asia.

2. To unite the diverse groups; establish equality of all people; universal suffrage; Hindu the official language.

3. Burma, Laos, Thailand, Kampuchea, Malaysia, Indonesia, Brunei, Vietnam, Philippines.

page 706

1. David Ben-Gurion—first Israeli prime minister.

Knesset—Israeli legislative body.

PLO—Palestinian Liberation Organization; group of Palestinian Arab terrorists.

Pan-Arabism—political and cultural movement emphasizing ties among all Arabs.

Gamel Abdel Nasser—leader of military takeover in Egypt.

Baghdad Pact—alliance of Britain, Turkey, Iraq, Pakistan, Iran.

United Arab Republic—union between Egypt and Syria.

Ba'ath party—leftist party in Syria.

Faisal II—king of Iraq; assassinated.

Hussein—king of Jordan.

Kuwait—independent state on the Arabian Peninsula.

Ismet Inönü—prime minister of Turkey.

Adnan Menderes—prime minister of Turkey; succeeded Inönü.

Mohammed Mossadegh—prime minister of Iran; nationalist; anti-shah.

2. Into a Jewish and an Arab state.

3. Egypt, Syria, Lebanon, Iraq refused to recognize Israel and invaded it in 1949. Egypt's nationalization of the Suez Canal in 1956.

4. It caused the overthrow of pro-western governments.

page 710

1. Ahmed Ben Bella—first president of Algeria.

Sékou Touré—leader of Guinea; he turned to the Soviets for economic support.

Djibouti—last French colony in Africa to become independent.

Ghana—first British colony to gain independence.

Kwame Nkrumah—dictator of Ghana.

Mau Mau—African movement; attacked Europeans and their supporters.

Tanzania—Tanganyika and Zanzibar union.

Julius Nyerere—leader of Tanzania.

Rhodesia Front—political party of Europeans in Rhodesia.

Patrice Lumumba—prime minister of the Republic of Congo.

Moise Tshombe—leader of Congo province of Katanga.

2. It forced France to offer the Sub-Saharan colonies complete independence, or to become self-governing in a French-sponsored community of nations.

3. There were many experienced African leaders and few European settlers.

4. In Nigeria tension grew between the Muslim north, and Christian south and east; the Ibo establishment of Biafra and its resulting war with the Hausa-controlled central government. The declaration of independence by the province of Katanga resulted in civil war that became an East-West conflict.

page 713
1. OAS—Organization of American States; founded to encourage closer political and economic ties among Western Hemisphere nations.
   CIA—Central Intelligence Agency; United States agency to gather information.
   Jacobo Arbenz Guzman—head of leftist government of Guatemala.
   Juan Perón—dictator of Argentina between 1946 and 1955.
   Eva Perón—popular wife of Juan Perón.
   Getulio Vargas—president of Brazil.
   João Goulart—president of Brazil; he instituted land and wage reforms.
   Fidel Castro—dictator of Cuba.
2. Political upheaval.
3. He failed to establish a democracy; seized American property in Cuba; persecuted his opponents.

Photo Questions
page 690
That the emperor renounce the divinity attributed to him.

page 692
The growth of the economy could not keep pace with the expanding population.

page 693
It promoted the idea that Mao embodied the ideals of Chinese communism.

page 695
17 years.

page 696
They accepted a UN-sponsored cease fire; eventually divided between the two nations.

page 699
Nazi persecution of Europe's Jews.

page 703
Tried to promote Arab unity under Egypt's leadership.

page 705
A reform program and strong army support.

page 707
Seven and a half years.

page 708
Its first president.

page 709
It broke its ties and declared itself a republic outside the Commonwealth of Nations.

page 711
Concern over the spread of communism.

page 712
The army.

page 713
The promise of Soviet protection.

Chapter Review
page 714, Reviewing the Main Ideas
1. Introduced democratic reforms; universal suffrage; liberalized education; local government and labor unions strengthened; reorganization of industry and agriculture.
2. Increases in the GNP and foreign trade.
3. The government received wide support; public sanitation and health improved; illiteracy reduced; women given full equality; communal farming replaced traditional farm structure; industrial output placed China among the top ten nations in the world.
4. A feud of Communist ideology and for leadership among Communist countries.
5. Before they were able to introduce reforms the pragmatist leaders were attacked by Mao's followers; civil disorder and confusion resulted.

6. Thousands of widows, orphans, unemployed; governments unable to handle problems; North Korea developed along Communist lines; South Korea developed a capitalist industrial economy.

7. To try to prevent a civil war between Hindus and Muslims. The migration of nearly 10 million people; religious riots; decisions made over which country to join.

8. Vietnam, Laos, and Cambodia were battlegrounds for independence; elsewhere in the region the transition to nationhood progressed peacefully.

9. An agreement in Geneva provided for a division; it created a Communist state in North Vietnam and a pro-western government in South Vietnam; the division was reinforced by civil war between the two states.

page 715
10. The first Arab-Israeli war resulted in an easy victory for the Israeli forces; the second war resulted in a UN emergency force sent to patrol the Egyptian-Israeli border.

11. Both nations experienced nationalistic upheavals and the issues of modernization and democratic reform.

12. Once African states achieved independence they turned to unity and economic development; many Latin American nations struggled with political and economic instability. Answers may vary.

page 715, Discussing Important Ideas
1. Answers may vary; mention should be made of the development of a stable democracy and strong economy of Japan under western influences.
2. Answers may vary.
3. Answers may vary; mention should be made of the cultural and physical separation of East and West Pakistan.
4. Answers may vary.
5. Answers may vary.
6. Answers may vary; mention should be made of the United States support of unpopular or military governments.
7. Answers may vary.
8. Answers may vary.

page 715, Using Maps
1. Egypt, Jordan, Lebanon, Syria.

2. Arab-Israeli War, 1948. Greek-Turkish conflict.
3. Soviet-Iranian conflict. 1946; on the Soviet-Iranian border.
4. Beirut, Lebanon.
5. Iraq, Iran, Saudi Arabia.

CHAPTER 31
Global Dimensions

At the conclusion of this chapter, students should be able to:
1. discuss the extent of world interdependence.
2. explain the fatal consequences of a total war.
3. list the significant changes that occurred in each world region since the 1960's.
4. explain the role of the superpowers in maintaining world peace and in promoting stability.

Overview

Chapter 31 follows world developments from the 1960's to the present. It includes coverage of the several areas of conflict in the Middle East and the major changes taking place in Africa, South America, and Central America. It considers changes in the Indian subcontinent, China, and Southeast Asia, including a discussion of the Vietnam War. The last two sections shift the focus to Europe and the superpowers. Important concepts include shuttle diplomacy, amnesty, "democratize," détente, and stagflation.

Teaching Strategies
Section 1

Introduction: Have students review the summaries of Chapters 24 (p. 564), 27 (p. 632), and 30 (p. 714) to prepare for this chapter and section.

Development: Point out that the vast majority of Lebanese, Muslims, and Christians now favor some revision in the structure of their government that would give greater representation to non-Christians. Also, make students aware of the fact that the Khomeini government in Iran is strongly anti-Communist as well as anti-American.

Organize a panel discussion on the Arab-Israeli conflict. Have students make a list of the issues involved such as the future of the refugees, Jerusalem, the occupied territories (the West Bank, Gaza, and the Golan Heights), the welfare and the security of the Israeli people. Each student or group should research one of these topics and present various solutions that have been proposed for it. Students should keep in mind that within Israel and among the Palestinians there may be conflicting opinions as to how to deal with each issue. Students should not take sides.

Section 2

Introduction: Point out that ethnic rivalry continued to play an important role, although a diminishing one, in the domestic affairs of many newly independent African countries. However, the frustration with the lack of rapid economic progress promoted conditions of instability. Some army officers took advantage of these circumstances, overthrew the legitimate governments, and established military dictatorships. However, make sure that students are aware that countries like Senegal, Ivory Coast, and Kenya have relative political stability and prosperous economies.

Development: After reading the verses on page 723, ask students to relate them to the aspiration of black Africans. Have them comment on the white supremacists' attitude in Zimbabwe and in the Republic of South Africa. Then have students speculate on the future of South Africa if whites continue apartheid.

Section 3

Introduction: Point out that the people of Latin America have been anxious for improvement in their standard of living, as have other Third World peoples. Military officers took advantage of troubled economies to stage coups in Chile, Argentina, Brazil, and other countries. Refer students to the map on page 726. Have them note the forms of government in Latin America as of 1984.

Development: Organize a discussion on the war in the Falkland Islands. Have students research and analyze the causes of the war in terms of the domestic conditions that prevailed in Argentina prior to the invasion. Ask them to comment on the consequences of the military confrontation.

Section 4

Introduction: Ask students if democracy is possible in a developing country where the majority of the people are poor with a sizeable number of illiterate peasants. Then point to India. Emphasize the fact that India is the largest democracy in the world and that it is a developing country with a large population of poor and illiterate peasants.

Development: Mention that the East and West Pakistanis, prior to the partition of their country, were ethnically different despite their common religion. The language in the East is Bengali and its historical and cultural links tie the region to South and Southeast Asia. In what was West Pakistan, the language is Urdu and its historical and cultural links tie the area more closely to the Middle East.

Ask students to make a chronological chart of events in Southeast Asia and China since 1970. Have them evaluate and compare United States relations with the People's Republic of China before and after the Shanghai Communique.

Section 5

Introduction: As students read this survey of Europe, they should note the problems shared by some of the nations.

Development: Assign each country in Western and Eastern Europe to a student to report on its domestic affairs since 1970. Next, hold a discussion on common problems that these countries have recently had and on their relationships with each other and with the rest of the world. Have students consult news articles for recent data.

Section 6

Introduction: Have students turn to page 741 and name the world leaders in the photo. Can students think of the names of the leaders' current counterparts?

Development: Divide the class into two groups to research and to make presentations representing the views and the interests of either the Soviet Union or the United States. Focus the work of the two groups on specific issues such as détente, the Soviet invasion of Afghanistan, trade, and arms control.

Conclusion: After reading the chapter and doing further research, ask each student to submit a list of the ten most influential leaders in the world since 1970, regardless of whether or not their influence has been favorable. Have students compare and explain their selections. This may be done in writing or in a class discussion.

Answers
Section Review Questions

page 721
1. Six-Day War—third Arab-Israeli war.
   Golan Heights—area in Syria taken by Israel during the Six-Day War.
   West Bank—west of the Jordan River.
   October War—fourth Arab-Israeli war.
   Henry Kissinger—United States Secretary of State who used shuttle diplomacy.
   Arab League—group of states to promote Arab unity.
   Anwar el-Sadat—succeeded Nasser; president of Egypt.
   Jimmy Carter—president of the United States.
   Menachem Begin—Israeli prime minister.
   Camp David—site of conference between Begin and Sadat.
   Hosni Mubarak—vice president of Egypt; succeeded Sadat.
   East Jerusalem—area of contention between Arabs and Israelis.
   Phalangists—group of Christian Palestinians.
   Ayatollah Ruhollah Khomeini—Iranian Shiite Muslim leader.
   Strait of Hormuz—route necessary to Iraq's exportation of oil.
2. In the Six-Day War, Israel occupied areas of Jordan, Syria, and Egypt; after the October War, Egypt made a separate peace with Israel.
3. Demands for reform of the parliamentary system of elections; presence of Palestinians and PLO; religious conflict.
4. He often disregarded religious and traditional values. The shah was deposed; Khomeini became ruler.

page 724
1. Zaire—formerly Republic of Congo.
   Mobutu Sese Soko—dictator of Zaire.
   Idi Amin—dictator of Uganda.
   Milton Obote—elected president of Uganda.
   Alhaji Shehu Shagari—deposed as president of Nigeria.
   Abel Muzorewa—first black prime minister of Rhodesia.
   Robert Mugabe—elected prime minister of Zimbabwe.
   Zimbabwe—new name of Rhodesia.

2. A dictatorship in the Congo, renamed Zaire; an unstable democracy in Uganda.
3. Economic, civil, and religious problems accelerated.
4. A black nationalist leader was voted prime minister by an absolute majority; Britain declared its independence; it was renamed Zimbabwe.

page 727
1. Salvador Allende—Socialist president of Chile.
   Augusto Pinochet—military dictator of Chile.
   Isabel Perón—first woman president of Argentina; widow of Juan Perón.
   Leopold Galtieri—military leader who ousted Perón.
   Falkland Islands—Malvinas; British island group off the Argentine coast.
   Raul Alfonsin—voted president of Argentina.
   Carlos Umberto Romero—president of El Salvador.
   Álvaro Magaña Borjo—president of El Salvador after Romero overthrown.
   José Napoleon Duarte—president of El Salvador; succeeded Borjo.
   Sandinista National Liberation Front—leftist guerrilla group in Nicaragua.
   Anastasio Somoza Debayle—dictator of Nicaragua; overthrown by the Sandinistas.
2. He was a Marxist who angered Americans with his socialist policies.
3. Because they were opposed to the government and refused to take part in it.
4. They placed the country under a state of emergency status; handed out harsh penalties for acts such as strikes, unauthorized occupation of land, or obstruction of production; postponed free elections.

page 732
1. Khalistan—autonomous state desired by Sikhs.
   Zia-ul-Haq—military dictator of Pakistan.
   Hussein Mohammed Ershad—military leader of Bangladesh.
   Gulf of Tonkin Resolution—gave the United States president broad war-making powers.
   Ho Chi Minh Trail—system of supply routes used by the North Vietnamese.

"Vietnamization"—program that would replace American troops with Vietnamese.

Paris Accords—led to end of American involvement in Vietnam War.

"boat people"—ethnic Chinese and Vietnam refugees who fled Vietnam.

Khmer Rouge—Cambodian Communists.

Lon Nol—American-backed ruler of Cambodia; overthrown by Khmer Rouge.

Pol Pot—Communist Cambodian ruler who replaced Lon Nol.

Ferdinand E. Marcos—president of the Philippines; declared himself dictator under martial law.

Shanghai Communique—pledge to improve relations between China and U. S.

Four Modernizations—plan to completely modernize China by year 2000.

2. She sent troops into Assam; a new chief minister was sworn in; she offered to officially recognize Sikhism as a separate religion; put into effect a law that allows imprisonment for two years without trial.

3. Government dominated by West Pakistanis, when East Pakistan won a majority in the government, West Pakistanis refused to convene, sent troops to quell protest riots in East Pakistan; Indian troops sent to help East Pakistanis in civil war.

4. North Vietnamese and Vietcong helped overthrow American-backed government in Cambodia, and established a reign of terror under Communist Pol Pot government; Vietnam invaded Cambodia and overthrew Pol Pot; changed the country's name to Kampuchea. Laos was used by North Vietnamese to move their supplies; became a Communist country; anti-Communists started hostilities; government asked Vietnam for help.

page 736

1. Harold Wilson—Labor party prime minister of Britain.

Margaret Thatcher—Conservative party prime minister of Britain.

Muammar al-Qaddafi—Libyan leader.

Northern Ireland—area of confrontations between Protestants and Catholics.

Georges Pompidou—succeeded de Gaulle as president of France.

Valéry Giscard d'Estaing—succeeded Pompidou as president of France.

François Mitterand—Socialist leader; defeated Giscard in 1981 elections.

Willy Brandt—chancellor of West Germany.

Ostpolitik—Eastern Policy; Brandt's policy to improve relations with Eastern Europe.

Helmut Schmidt—succeeded Brandt.

Helmut Kohl—leader of Christian Democrats; succeeded Schmidt.

"the Colonels"—right-wing army officers; took over Greek government.

Andreas Papandreou—Socialist prime minister of Greece.

Juan Carlos I—restored monarch of Spain.

Felipe González—Socialist prime minister of Spain.

Alexander Dubček—Communist party leader in Czechoslovakia.

Solidarity—Polish independent labor union.

Lech Walesa—Solidarity leader.

Wojciech Jaruzelski—prime minister of Poland.

2. Libyan and anti-Libyan terrorist activities; terrorist bombing by both sides on the status of Northern Ireland.

3. Dubček began to "democratize" the country; intellectuals demanded more freedoms; Soviets viewed liberal policies as a threat to their security. Dubček was replaced as party leader; Soviets maintain tight controls on Czechoslovakia.

4. Debt, high prices, shortages of food and raw materials.

page 741

1. Brezhnev Doctrine—policy that stated that any threat to communism in one Warsaw Pact country would be militarily opposed by others.

Yuri Andropov—succeeded Brezhnev as leader of Soviet Union.

Konstantin Chernenko—elected to replace Andropov.

Politburo—policymaking bureau of Soviet Union.

ERA—Equal Rights Amendment; proposal that rights could not be denied or abridged on account of sex.

SALT I—Strategic Arms Limitation Talks, agreement between Nixon and Brezhnev to work to prevent nuclear war.

Helsinki—site of meeting of heads of the governments of Europe and the United States to work for peaceful cooperation.

Mujahidin—Muslim fighters in Afghanistan.

Grenada—Caribbean island; site of American intervention to overthrow leftist regime.

2. Reforms in agriculture; attempt to introduce market forces in the economy.
3. It forced Nixon to resign from office.
4. Nixon visited the Soviet Union; SALT I was approved.
5. The United States and the Soviets competed against each other in various parts of the world.

Special Feature Questions

page 725
1. In a hope to develop the economically backward interior.
2. Represents Brazil's determination to develop its resources and become a leading world power.

Photo Question

page 718
Sinai Peninsula to the Suez Canal; Gaza Strip.

page 720
United States, France.

page 721
They had supported the shah for years; refused to allow him to be returned for trial.

page 722
As part of his plan to "Africanize" the country.

page 728
By sending in troops; offering to recognize Sikhism as a separate religion. Religious differences.

page 729
Bombing raids; sending military personnel.

page 731
It has brought China into closer contact with Japan and industrial western nations.

page 733
Sent in troops to restore order; suspended Northern Ireland's government and took control of the area.

page 735
Political parties were allowed; first free elections held; a democratic constitution approved.

page 736
Solidarity members held strikes and demonstrations; called for free elections.

page 737
Meat and other food supplies.

page 739
The signing of the final act of the Conference on Security and Cooperation in Europe.

page 740
It refused to ratify the SALT II agreements; sale of grain and high technology to the Soviets was halted; boycott of the Summer Olympic Games in Moscow.

page 741
The Soviets walked out of the talks.

Chapter Review

page 742, Reviewing the Main Ideas
1. Hostilities between Israelis and Arabs; oil; conflict between the modern and traditional.
2. For the first time an Arab country recognized the legal existence of Israel.
3. They became subject to military rule.
4. Nigeria was reorganized into many small states, the country was run by the military. Zimbabwe was forced to hold free elections.

page 743
5. The government submitted a plan that gave Asians and people of mixed blood a limited voice in government; blacks were still excluded.
6. They both came under military rule.
7. To win popular support and unite the country.
8. Gandhi sent in troops; offered to give official recognition to Sikhism.
9. A rift between China and the Soviet Union; fear that the two superpowers might work together against China.
10. Most countries have suffered from rapid inflation, slow economic growth, and rising unemployment.
11. The Soviet invasion of Afghanistan.

page 743, *Discussing Important Ideas*
1. Answers may vary, but mention should be made of superpower involvement.
2. Answers may vary.
3. Answers may vary.
4. Answers may vary.
5. Answers may vary.
6. Answers may vary.
7. Answers may vary.

page 743, *Using Maps*
1. Sinai Peninsula, Gaza Strip, West Bank, Golan Heights. Egypt, Jordan, Syria.
2. Egypt, Syria. Lebanon.
3. 1983.
4. The West Bank and the Gaza Strip.
5. Answers may vary.
6. About 40 miles (64 kilometers).

CHAPTER 32
Twentieth-Century Culture

At the conclusion of this chapter, students should be able to:
1. explain the relationship between contemporary culture and ongoing political and economic developments in the world.
2. describe the impact of recent advances in transportation and communication on world events.
3. review the world's outstanding intellectual accomplishments in the twentieth century.
4. describe the major social and cultural changes in the world that have occurred in this century.

Overview

Chapter 32 provides students with a survey of global cultural developments in the twentieth century. It lists important changes in technology and explains their impact on society. The chapter explores new ideas and theories in the social and natural sciences. The impact of the two world wars on social and intellectual trends is assessed as these trends are described and examined. Important concepts include avant-garde, psychoanalysis, cubism, theory of relativity, relativism, socialist realism, existentialism, feminism, and automation.

Teaching Strategies
Section 1

Introduction: Write on the chalkboard: *television, jet plane, Freud, Picasso, The Great Gatsby,* and *Einstein.* Ask students what relationship do all these "unrelated" words have in common. After they read the section, they should realize that the common thread is the twentieth century. Discuss each one and elicit comments. To dramatize the change in this century, compare the status of transcontinental transportation 50 years ago and today.

Development: Have groups of students choose areas of interest such as music, dance, and science. Ask them to prepare presentations describing change in the chosen areas over the past several decades. Emphasize the fact that changes in human understanding of nature and in the creative fields have been taking place throughout history. However, the pace of change has accelerated as we move closer to the present.

Section 2

Introduction: Ask students if they have seen any movies from the golden age of motion pictures, the 1930's. Name some famous actors and actresses from that period. (A few are listed on page 750.) Point out that the ability of people to spend time for leisure, such as going to the theater, is associated with the rise of their productivity. At the beginning of the century, a workweek consisted of at least 60 hours. By the late 1930's, the average workweek in industry had dropped to 48 hours, but output per worker had risen substantially.

Development: Refer students to page 131 in Chapter 5 to refresh their memories about Alexander Nevsky. Point out that the Soviet government encouraged the production and the distribution of the film *Alexander Nevsky* at the time when Stalin was trying to arouse Russian patriotism against the German Nazis. Ask students to speculate on the reason for this. (Note that Nevsky defeated the German Teutonic Knights decisively.)

Section 3

Introduction: Have students discuss the consequences of war, particularly the two world wars, in terms of human and emotional suffering. The tragic events may lead people to disillusionment, frustration, and sometimes to "withdrawal" from society.

Development: Have students make a book report. They may choose a work by a leader of the women's movement or by a recognized Third World writer.

Mention that shortly after this text was printed, the men of Liechtenstein voted in favor of granting women the right to vote (table on p. 757).

Sections 4 and 5

Introduction: Ask students to name technological devices that improve communications and tend to make the world "smaller." Included should be the radio, which through short-wave broadcasting can reach anyplace anywhere in the world. Maybe a student knows someone who would bring a portable short-wave radio to class. From your classroom you can tune in London, Moscow, Cairo, and other capital cities. There are more than a hundred capitals whose radio stations broadcast in English.

If your school has computers, ask some students to interview the computer programming teacher. They should inquire about the uses and advantages of computers in business, science, and education. Also have them ask about the pace of change in computer technology.

Development: After looking at the map of Ford's multinational network (pp. 760-761), have students identify the continents in which Ford has a subsidiary or a branch. Then have students do the "Using Diagrams" exercise on page 767. Ask them to name other multinational companies.

Explore with the students new timesaving inventions and discuss their impact. The microwave oven may be used as an example. Other topics in Section 5 would lend themselves well to research assignments.

Conclusion: The names of numerous authors, artists, and scientists appear in this chapter. Reference is also made to inventions and devices. Have each student make a selection and write a short report on it.

Answers
Section Review Questions

page 750

1. Bloomsbury Group—group of British intellectuals.

   Harlem Renaissance—black American movement in literature.

   Salvador Dali—Spanish surrealist painter.

   Bauhaus—most influential school of architecture and interior design.

   Isadora Duncan—revolutionized dance.

   Sergei Diaghilev—impresario of the Ballet Russes.

   Igor Stravinsky—Russian composer; his music was a turning point for ballet.

   Louis Armstrong—trumpet player and band leader of jazz musicians.

   Lise Meitner—Austrian physicist; her work focused on the splitting of atoms.

2. He brought new methods in psychology, education, and sociology.

3. Joyce studied Freud's theories and brought them into his work with the style of "stream of consciousness." Picasso reduced figures to their simplest planes; cubism. Schönberg composed new musical arrangements. All worked with the interpretation of feelings and thoughts and moved away from the realism of the 1800's.

4. It seemed to reinforce the idea that there were no absolutes in any field of knowledge or in moral values.

page 753

1. John Maynard Keynes—British economist.

   Maxim Gorky—Soviet writer who promoted socialist realism.

   Mikhail Sholokhov—Soviet author of *And Quietly Flows the Don.*

   Sergei Eisenstein—Soviet filmmaker of films based on Russian history.

   Leni Riefenstahl—German filmmaker; her work was brilliant and controversial.

   The Grapes of Wrath—John Steinbeck's novel of the poor, oppressed Oklahoma farmers who settled in California.

   Guernica—Picasso's powerful cubist painting of the bombing of Guernica.

   George Orwell—British author and novelist.

2. Dramas, musicals, and historical epics. They were escapist, designed to let viewers briefly forget the strains of the depression.

3. The United States government created a variety of projects for artists and writers; the Soviet Union directed all artists to help in building the new Communist society; Nazi Germany tightly controlled artistic activity and directed it to propaganda purposes.

page 758
1. Jean Paul Sartre—France's leading philosopher and writer who developed existentialism.

   Samuel Beckett—playwright influenced by existentialism; his plays were labeled the Theater of the Absurd.

   Boris Pasternak—Soviet winner of the Nobel prize for literature.

   Rudolf Nureyev—Soviet ballet dancer who defected to the West.

   James Watson—co-discoverer of the structure of DNA.

   Francis Crick—co-discoverer of DNA.

   Betty Friedan—feminist leader and author.

   Wole Soyinka—Nigerian playwright.

   Gabriel García Márquez—Colombian winner of the Nobel prize for literature.
2. Both eras were times of rebuilding and social change.
3. It set up programs in politics, education and training, housing, health and nutrition, families, and mass communications.
4. They have become smaller; more children are raised by single parents; child care centers, nursery schools, and after-school programs have taken over some of the traditional family relationships; mothers are increasingly working outside the home.

page 762
1. Satellites have enabled people around the world to watch the same television programs; jet travel has increased contacts between foreigners; cities are being built in an international style, as are international airports around the world.
2. They have brought technology and employment to local people; some countries feel such companies exploit their resources.
3. Jazz and rock have become international favorites. Caribbean, Oriental, and western rhythms and instruments have been adapted to other musical traditions. Religion reflects the impact of global changes as many people no longer accept traditional religious teachings.
4. Advantage has been taken of new technologies of communication and jet travel to publicize the cause of groups or countries to a worldwide audience; the use of protest demonstrations and terrorism can spread across national barriers quickly and easily.

page 763
1. Some companies have introduced new ways to increase worker participation and responsibility by forming teams to complete assignments. Their tasks are reorganized and enlarged to help prevent boredom.
2. Such areas as the rights of the patient, the rights of the family, the obligations of society and government in extreme medical situations.
3. Experiments that combine lights, drama, and electronic music have been tried. Artists and engineers collaborate in mixing sounds, lasers, and video tapes. Others have experimented with computer art or music.

Special Feature Questions
page 765
1. They have become the heart of today's technology.
2. It is capable of welding miniature metal parts, removing diseased tissue from the eye, and transmitting audio and visual signals over long distances.
3. Answers may vary.

Photo Questions
page 746
His method involved listening to patients discuss whatever thoughts came into their minds. By analyzing memories, dreams, and random statements, he could help patients determine the reasons for their actions.

page 747
It used dreamlike images and unnatural combinations of objects to explore the unconscious mind.

page 748
To develop art forms appropriate to modern technology and materials.

page 749
It seems to reinforce the belief that there were no absolutes in any field of knowledge or in moral values.

page 750
They were designed to make viewers forget the strains of depression and the political tensions of the times.

page 752
To draw attention to injustice, corruption, and human suffering.

page 754
American prosperity and material values.

page 755
Some writers secretly sent their work abroad to be published, others resisted the government.

page 756
It poses unknown potentials and dangers.

page 759
Their lifestyles and music have a strong influence on their young international fans.

page 759
The Roman Catholic Church has become a leading source of opposition to the Communist government.

page 763
At times it confuses and angers audiences.

Chapter Review

page 766, Reviewing the Main Ideas
1. Assembly lines for mass production of cars and radios; the movie film.
2. Traditions in art and music were discarded for experimentation with new styles, media, and subject matter. In all areas of the arts, realism was abandoned for the more personal, subjective view of the artist.
3. Einstein's theory of relativity was published; the atom was split, research on radium.
4. They were designed to help viewers forget the strains of the depression and growing political turmoil.
5. It was a means to rescue the capitalist system.
6. Artists turned from personal interests and became committed to social and political causes.

page 767
7. There were signs of stress and uncertainty, some people rejected the emphasis on material goods and turned away from science and reason, which had created the weapons of war. Many felt alienated by material values and tried not to set goals for their lives.
8. The increased population; twenty-five percent of all human beings are living now, and ninety percent of all scientists; research is carried on by well-financed teams; computers increase the speed and complexity of analyses that can be performed.
9. Barriers to equal rights; more activity in politics, education, housing, health and nutrition, families, and mass communication.
10. They relied less on western models and drew from their own cultural heritage and its conflicts with western culture.
11. Instant global communication by satellites; radio; jet travel; dance and music companies sell tapes and records in all continents; international sports competitions; introduction of foods, clothing, arts, and books to all areas of the world.
12. Television, video tape, and computers have increased educational and entertainment programming to the home. The sophisticated office and manufacturing machines are reducing the number of workers needed; this forces the need for retraining and learning of new skills upon the work force. All these factors affect the quality of life at home and in the work place.

page 767, Discussing Important Ideas
1. Relativity is a scientific theory; relativism is an idea that there are no absolutes in knowledge or moral values.
2. Answers may vary; mention should be made of the rejection of materialism, and individual choice.
3. Answers may vary.
4. Answers may vary.
5. Answers may vary.
6. Answers may vary.
7. Answers may vary.

page 767, Using Diagrams
1. To show the global dimension of a multinational company.
2. North America, Europe.
3. No.
4. Eastern Hemisphere.
5. Finance companies, communications, insurance, land development, tractor manufacture, stamping company.

CHAPTER 33
Challenges of Tomorrow

At the conclusion of this chapter, students should be able to:

1. discuss the dangers and the escalating cost of an unchecked arms race.
2. explain the problems associated with urban population growth in the developing Third World.
3. describe the great potential for human use of the available natural resources on this planet.
4. profile the struggle for human rights and the self-determination of many peoples throughout the world.

Overview

Chapter 33 describes the important challenges that the world faces near the close of the twentieth century. The first, and perhaps the gravest issue that is presented in this chapter, is the question of war and peace. Emphasis is placed on the current status of nuclear arms control and on the very costly expenditures that nations of the world are making to arm themselves.

The next set of challenges examines the world's wealth and its distribution among and within these nations as well as the prevailing conditions in the developing countries of the Third World. Lastly, the chapter explores the status of human rights around the world with emphasis on the maintenance of international order and security, conditions of displaced persons and refugees, and social justice and self-determination. Other important concepts include deterrence, parity, nuclear freeze, developed and developing nations, revolution of rising expectations, and the "technological revolution."

Teaching Strategies
Section 1

Introduction: Introduce this section by asking students to read page 769, then figure the world expenditures on armaments per day and per hour (about $1,644 million per day and $69 million per hour). Relative to claims that military production creates and maintains jobs, point out that the last 20-25 percent of military expenditures in the United States created and sustained about 10,000 jobs for every $1 billion spent. In civilian areas such as education and construction the spending of each additional $1 billion creates and sustains more than 30,000 jobs.

Development: Have students research back issues of weekly newsmagazines over the last six or seven years to find out and compare the various arms control and arms reduction proposals. Ask them also to list the countries that possess or have the potential to develop nuclear arms, then check those who did or did not sign the Nuclear Nonproliferation Treaty.

Section 2

Introduction: Mention that in some sources students may encounter different names for what the term "developing" nations stands for in this chapter. Originally, these nations were called "undeveloped," then the depiction changed to "underdeveloped," then "less developed countries" or "LDC's," and lately the "developing" countries.

Development: The British playwright George Bernard Shaw, who was bald and had a long thick beard, once likened the world's wealth to his hair. He said that he had a lot of production, but bad distribution. After reading the section, ask students if they agree with Shaw's view and to comment on it.

Note one of the unique features of the growing cities of the Third World. Rural migrants from each village tend to congregate in the same area within the cities, thus creating pockets of rural-urban ("rurban") communities that become culturally distinct from both the village of their origin and the city in which they live.

Section 3

Introduction: Read to students the annotations at the top of page 779. Then have them look at the photo on the same page, read the caption, and try to answer the question.

Development: You may organize two panel discussions or debates on this section. In the first, students explore the current energy situation in the world. They should include in their research the safety, the technology, and the future of nuclear energy as well as other sources such as hydrocarbons (oil and coal).

The second group of students can research and discuss the conflicting views about the Law of the Sea. Back issues of weekly newsmagazines, newspapers on microfilm, and United Nations publications will provide information about this subject. The main theme of the debate should be on how to strike a balance between a fair return on investment for companies who develop the technology and fair treatment for the developing countries who insist that the high sea is a treasure for all humanity to share. Note that many of these countries would rather not have the wealth of the oceans exploited, than to allow companies in developed countries to reap all the benefits. They feel that sooner or later their own technological advances will permit them to do the work.

Section 4

Introduction: Introduce this section with a discussion on the value of education in the development of a country's economy. Students are accustomed to evaluating education in terms of their personal benefits. If time permits, they may also include in the discussion how education helped the United States develop and preserve its institutions.

Development: Ask students to define the word "terrorism." Point out that not every violent act against a state is termed terrorism by everyone. Some "terrorists" may be regarded as "freedom fighters" by their own supporters. Note that Jomo Kenyatta, Menachem Begin, and others have been considered terrorists in the past and were convicted for acts of violence by their governments. There should be a distinction between fighting for independence, justice, or freedom and the senseless killing of innocent victims.

Conclusion: Have students write or make oral presentations to the class on some of the important issues that were mentioned in this chapter. Another project can be to have students write a composition on an aspect of life in the year 2000. The composition should express their own outlook and expectations.

Answers
Section Review Questions

page 772
1. A nuclear war could mean the destruction of the planet and extinction of the human race.

2. Proposals have been made to encourage more nations to sign the Nuclear Nonproliferation Treaty; that nuclear nations set an example by reducing their existing stockpiles.
3. Many nations profit from the arms trade. In an attempt to solve local and international conflicts.

page 777
1. Developed countries are highly industrialized and have well-developed economies; developing countries are economically poor and primarily agricultural.
2. Higher birthrates and lower death rates.
3. Because of the unequal distribution of wealth and technology between the developed and developing countries.

page 781
1. A major concern is whether the amount of the world's natural resources is decreasing; the global demand for energy has increased due to the spread of industrialization.
2. Nuclear, solar, wind, and water power.
3. Accumulation of salts and minerals in the soil; overgrazing; use of chemicals; acid rain; and other forms of pollution.

page 784
1. Innocent citizens are often harmed or killed by terrorist activities.
2. Some give in to terrorist demands in order to save lives; others tend to follow a hard-line policy and have special police and army units to deal with the problem.
3. Wars and other upheavals have uprooted millions of people. Some have spent years in refugee camps.

Special Feature Questions
page 773
1. It began as an important trading center; during the 1800's it developed a growing textile industry; today it is still a leading textile manufacturing city, but its economy is more varied, producing chemicals, machinery, and food products; it is also the center of India's banking and motion picture industry.
2. Immigration of rural peoples who bring their own lifestyles and maintain many rural ways in the urban center.

Photo Questions

page 771
On the willingness of the superpowers to improve their relations and trust each other.

page 777
Development of new types of grain, programs to improve farming methods.

page 778
Some minerals such as cobalt, manganese, and nickel, but at present in small quantities.

page 779
Nuclear, solid waste, wind, and water power.

page 780
Building of dams and canals, chemical wastes, pesticides.

page 782
Political differences among nations and their attitudes toward terrorists make a single agreement all but impossible.

page 783
Because of the possible burden on their economies.

Chapter Review

page 785, Reviewing the Main Ideas
1. Because of increased tensions between the two nations.
2. The superpowers compete with each other by backing and arming opposing sides in the disputes among Third World nations.
3. In the developing countries of Asia, Africa, and Latin America. Religious objections; agricultural areas need many children to help work the land.
4. They want fairer terms of trade with the developed countries.
5. Because of the spread of industrialization, and higher standards of living.
6. The amount of proven reserves will rise.
7. They claim that their private companies have been spending a great deal of money on research and development, and it would not be profitable for them to share the proceeds with others.
8. Canada urges the United States to impose stricter controls on American industry; the United States says the Canadians are exaggerating, and views it as Canada's problem.
9. Some people are injured or killed; even if not affected directly, air travelers have their clothing and luggage searched, others may be restricted in work and travel; in some countries people live in constant danger of terrorist activities.
10. Growing numbers claim that their nations can no longer afford to accept a flood of people; other people argue that democratic societies have an obligation to help those seeking freedom from political oppression.

page 785, Discussing Important Ideas
1. Answers may vary.
2. Answers may vary.
3. Answers may vary; mention should be made of balance of trade between nations.
4. Answers may vary.
5. Answers may vary; mention should be made of those European countries in which nuclear power is the major source of electricity versus the problems of nuclear waste disposal.
6. Answers may vary.
7. Answers may vary.
8. Answers may vary.

page 785, Using Graphs
1. Population in millions of people. To show real figures against projected figures.
2. 1,500,000,000 (1,500 million); 325,000,000 (325 million).
3. East Asia.
4. Africa.
5. Europe.

Unit Review

page 786, Developing Understanding
1. Each superpower sought world influence by the use of force, propaganda, and the sending of military and economic aid to weaker nations.
2. The United States helped rebuild Western Europe; those countries became allies in seeking to contain communism. In Southeast Asia, newly formed governments did not have the support of the people.
3. Answers may vary.
4. The economic reorganization enabled Japan to become the leading economic power of Asia.

5. Because they broke with tradition and experimented with new styles, media, and subject matter.

6. The United Nations adoption of the Declaration of Human Rights that requests nations to strive to attain equal rights and better standards of life for all people. Gains have been made, especially in the area of education.

pages 786-787, Developing Skills

Conclude the unit with the Developing Skills activity. This activity, which is appropriate for either individuals or groups, introduces the concepts of frame of reference and revisionism, and gives students practice in analyzing frame of reference. Students are given a series of questions to help them understand two readings that are examples of widely different frames of reference on the subject of the cold war. The answers to the questions are as follows:

1. Very strong—this was the McCarthy era. People were shocked by Soviet actions in Eastern Europe and elsewhere.

2. By 1970 it had become clear that communism was not a monolithic force. Americans had become more critical of United States actions, especially in relation to the war in Vietnam.

3. Reading 1 presents the view that the Soviet Union was the aggressor in the cold war, that its intentions were bad from the beginning (even before the end of World War II), and that Great Britain and the United States were innocent. This reflected the 1950's view of the cold war as a "good guys vs. bad guys" conflict. The second reading reflects the later viewpoint that the United States should bear part of the responsibility, the view of those disillusioned by the Vietnam War. (Note that Vietnam is mentioned at the end of the first paragraph.)

SUGGESTED RESOURCES

UNIT 1

BOOKS

Asimov, Isaac. *The Land of Canaan*. Boston: Houghton Mifflin, 1971. Depicts the Hebrews, Phoenicians, Assyrians, Babylonians, and others who lived in Canaan.

Auboyer, Jeanne. *Daily Life in Ancient India*. New York: Macmillan, 1965. Describes social and economic conditions in ancient India.

Baines, John and Jaromir Malek. *Atlas of Ancient Egypt*. New York: Facts on File, 1980. A colorful, informative reference on ancient Egypt.

Collins, Robert. *The Medes and Persians: Conquerors and Diplomats*. New York: McGraw-Hill, 1975. Recounts the daily lives, beliefs, and government of the ancient Persians.

Cottrell, Leonard. *The Mystery of Minoan Civilization*. New York: World Publishing, 1971. Discusses the development and accomplishments of the Minoan civilization.

Dillon, Ellis. *Rome under the Emperors*. New York: Thomas Nelson, Inc., 1974. Describes the daily lives of several families who represent a cross section of the population.

Evslin, Bernard. *Greeks Bearing Gifts: The Epics of Achilles and Ulysses*. New York: Four Winds Press, 1976. A retelling of the *Iliad* and the *Odyssey*.

Fagg, Christopher. *Ancient Greece*. New York: Warwick Press, 1978. Tells about the ancient Greek civilization, emphasizing political, social, and historical aspects.

Fagg, Christopher. *Ancient Rome*. New York: Warwick Press, 1978. Describes the Roman Empire from its inception through its decline.

Knox, Robert. *Ancient China*. New York: Warwick Press, 1979. Presents the important features of Chinese civilization from 1500 B.C. to 900 A.D.

Macaulay, David. *Pyramid*. Boston: Houghton Mifflin, 1982. Paperback. A glimpse of Egyptian society through an illustrated account of the building of a pyramid.

Macnamara, Ellen. *Everyday Life of the Etruscans*. New York: G. P. Putnams' Sons, 1973. Details the art and artifacts found in Etruria.

National Geographic Society. *Splendors of the Past: Lost Cities of the Ancient World*. Washington, D.C.: National Geographic Society, 1981. Illustrated description of seven cities in the ancient Middle East, Africa, Asia, and Europe.

MEDIA

The Ancient Egyptian. International Film Foundation. Film, color, 27 minutes. Shows ancient Egyptians, their culture, and their achievements.

Ancient Mesopotamia. Coronet Films. Film, color, 11 minutes. Presents the accomplishments of the Sumerians, Babylonians, and Assyrians.

Athens: The Golden Age. Encyclopaedia Britannica Educational Corp. Film, color, 30 minutes. Describes Athens in the fifth century B.C.

China in Perspective: Roots of Civilization. Guidance Associates. Sound filmstrips (3), color. Explore the achievements of ancient Chinese civilization.

India: Early Civilization. Coronet Films. Film, color, 11 minutes. Shows the main features of ancient Indian civilization.

Roman World. International Film Bureau. Film, color, 23 minutes. Depicts life in the Roman Empire and highlights Roman contributions to western civilization.

The Romans: Life, Laughter, and Law. Learning Corporation of America. Film, color, 27 minutes. Portrays the everyday lives of Roman generals, legislators, peasants, and city dwellers.

Xian [Ch'angan], City in China. National Endowment for the Humanities. Film, color, 58 minutes. Compares and contrasts the Chinese urban experience in Ch'angan in the present with the urban experience during the Han and T'ang dynasties. Contains footage of the tomb that contains 6,000 life-size clay horses and soldiers.

UNIT 2

BOOKS

Bishop, Morris, ed. *Middle Ages*. New York: McGraw-Hill, 1970. A well-illustrated volume on the customs, history, and art of the Middle Ages.

Browning, Robert. *The Byzantine Empire*. New York: Charles Scribner's Sons, 1980. Portrays the Byzantine world from about 500 A.D. to the fall of

Constantinople in 1453. Discusses in some detail its impact on the ancient world.

Cherniavsky, Michael, ed. *Structure of Russian History*. New York: Random House, 1970. A collection of essays describing the various periods of Russian history.

Culbert, T. Patrick. *The Lost Civilization: The Story of the Classic Maya*. New York: Harper and Row, 1974. Describes the lifeways and the achievements of Mayan civilization.

Gies, Frances and Joseph Gies. *Women in the Middle Ages: The Lives of Real Women in a Vibrant Age of Transition*. New York: Barnes and Noble, 1978. A well-documented, lively account of women's lives in the Middle Ages.

Josephy, Alvin M. *Indian Heritage of America*. New York: Knopf, 1968. Examines the prehistory, history, and culture of Indians of North and South America.

Lewis, Bernard, ed. *Islam and the Arab World*. New York: Knopf and American Heritage, 1976. Colorful and authoritative reference that describes the faith, the people, the culture, and the achievements of Islamic civilization.

Lyons, Malcolm and David Jackson. *Saladin: The Politics of the Holy War*. New York: Cambridge University Press, 1982. A study of the famous Muslim leader during the crusades.

Murray, Jocelyn, ed. *Cultural Atlas of Africa*. New York: Facts on File, 1981. A richly illustrated account describing the diversity of African cultures and their ancient roots.

Oliver, Roland, ed. *The Middle Age of African History*. London: Oxford University Press, 1967. A collection of 14 essays covering the civilizations of Africa during the Middle Ages.

Zenkovsky, Serge A., ed.; tr. by Serge A. and Betty J. Zenkovsky. *The Nikonian Chronicle, Vol. 1*. Princeton, New Jersey: Kingston Press, 1984. This is the first English translation of one volume of what is commonly known as the *Russian Chronicles*.

MEDIA

The Ancient Africans. International Film Foundation. Film, color, 27 minutes. Provides information about the history of Africa as it examines art, trade, architecture, and religion.

The Ancient New World. Churchill Films. Film, color, 16 minutes. Describes the early cultures of Mesoamerica emphasizing the rise and decline of the Maya and the Aztecs.

The Ancient Peruvians. International Film Foundation. Film, color, 26 minutes. Begins with the collapse of the Inca Empire, then moves backward through time to cover the Inca and pre-Inca civilizations.

The Byzantine Empire. Coronet Films. Film, color, 14 minutes. Features the major events and achievements of Byzantine civilization.

The Crusades. Educational Audio Visual. Sound filmstrips (2), color. Cover the crusades and their impact on Europe and the Middle East.

Early Russia. Educational Record Sales. Sound filmstrips (2), color. Describe the early Russian history and the influence of Byzantine civilization on Russian culture.

The Genius of Arab Civilization. Eye Gate Media. Sound filmstrips (4), color. The first three cover the rise of Islam through its empires.

Indians of North America. National Geographic Society. Sound filmstrips (5), color, 13-14 minutes each. Cover the peopling of North America, the cultures of the Eastern Woodlands, Plains, and western groups, and the challenges Native Americans faced in the early 1970's.

The Middle Ages. National Geographic Society. Sound filmstrips (3), color, 14-16 minutes each. Emphasize feudal life and the development of towns.

The Story of the Aztecs. Encyclopaedia Britannica Educational Corp. Film, color, 19 minutes. Shows the glory of Tenochtitlán and the influence of Aztec civilization on modern Mexico.

When People Lived in Castles. Multi-Media Productions. Sound filmstrips (2), color. Stress the design elements needed for defense.

UNIT 3
BOOKS

Bainton, Roland H. *The Age of the Reformation*. New York: Van Nostrand Reinhold, 1956. The story of the Reformation told by a recognized authority.

Goodenough, Simon. *The Renaissance.* New York: Arco, 1979. Discusses life during the Renaissance.

Grant, Neil. *The Renaissance.* New York: Franklin Watts, 1971. Describes events and people important in the development of the Renaissance.

Grousset, René. *The Empire of the Steppes.* New Brunswick, N. J.: Rutgers University, 1970. Standard work on the steppe empires by a leading French historian.

Hershberger, Guy F., ed. *The Recovery of the Anabaptist Vision.* Scotland, Pa.: Herald Press, 1957. Discusses the contributions of the Anabaptists to the democratic and religious freedoms associated with democracy.

Kristeller, Paul O. *Renaissance Thought.* New York: Harper Torchbook, 1961. Presents the leading ideas of the Renaissance.

Morison, Samuel E. *The European Discovery of America: The Northern Voyages.* New York: Oxford University Press, 1971. A well-illustrated review of the discoveries of North America.

Munro, Eleanor S. *Through the Vermilion Gates.* New York: Pantheon, 1971. An account of the events and cultural achievements of China's T'ang dynasty.

Reischauer, Edwin O. *Japan: The Story of a Nation.* New York: Knopf, 1974. Excellent short history of Japan.

Sanderlin, George. *Eastward to India: Vasco Da Gama's Voyages.* Oxford, N.Y.: Harper and Row, 1965. Recounts the early voyages of the Portuguese explorers.

Wilber, Donald N. *Iran, Past and Present: From Monarchy to Islamic Republic.* Princeton: Princeton University Press, 1981. Up-to-date introduction to Iranian history.

Yapp, Malcolm. *Ghengis Khan and the Mongol Empire.* St. Paul, Minn.: Greenhaven, 1980. Covers the exploits of Genghis and the creation of the empire.

MEDIA

Chinese History. Indiana University. Films (16), color. In-depth series that examines China's history from its beginnings to 1911.

The Glory That Remains: The Great Mogul Empire. BBC TV and Time-Life. Film, color, 30 minutes. Dramatizes history and culture through the remains of past civilizations in India.

Great Explorers. National Geographic Society. Sound filmstrips (4), color, 13-15 minutes each. Cover the explorations of Columbus, Magellan, Drake, and Cook.

Japan: A Historical Overview. Coronet Films. Film, color, 17 minutes. Traces the major events in Japan's history from 800 B.C. to the early 1960's.

Joan of Arc. Fleetwood Films. Film, color, 10 minutes. Recounts the life of the heroic patron saint of France.

The Reformation: The Age of Revolt. Encyclopaedia Britannica Educational Corp. Film, color, 24 minutes. Introduces the political, social, and religious climate that existed in Europe during the sixteenth century.

The Renaissance. National Geographic Society. Sound filmstrips (3), color, 14-16 minutes each. Describe the events and ideas that led to the Renaissance, portray its famous artists, and show examples of their work.

UNIT 4
BOOKS

Anderson, M. S. *The Eastern Question, 1774-1923.* New York: St. Martin's Press, 1966. Contains an excellent description of nineteenth-century diplomacy as applied to eastern Europe and the Ottoman Empire.

Andrews, Allen. *The King Who Lost America: George III and Independence.* London: Jupiter Books, 1976. Discusses how the king and his ministers misjudged the American colonies.

Anticaglia, Elizabeth. *Heroines of '76.* New York: Walker and Company, 1976. Presents the lives of 14 women who played important roles in the American Revolution.

Berlin, Isaiah. *The Age of Enlightenment.* New York: Oxford University Press, 1979. Details the philosophical thought of the movement.

Boardman, Fon W., Jr. *Around the World in 1776.* New York: Henry Z. Walck, Inc., 1975. Recounts major worldwide events that took place in 1776.

Brinton, Clarence Crane, ed. *The Portable Age of Reason Reader*. New York: Penguin Books, 1979. Paperback. Provides selections from the period.

Davis, Burke. *Black Heroes of the American Revolution*. New York: Harcourt Brace Jovanovich, 1976. Describes the role of Blacks in the struggle for American independence.

Dickens, Charles. *A Tale of Two Cities*. New York: Macmillan, 1962. Paperback. A classic novel about the French Revolution during the Reign of Terror.

Fraser, Antonia, ed. *Kings and Queens of England*. New York: Knopf, 1975. Tells about the lives of the men and women who have ruled England for nearly 1,000 years.

Hibbert, Christopher. *The Days of the French Revolution*. New York: Morrow, 1980. Paperback. Describes the major events of the revolution, focusing on firsthand accounts.

Hill, Christopher. *The Century of Revolution, 1603-1714*. New York: Norton, 1966. Focuses on the political and social structure of England during this turbulent era.

Reinerman, Alan J. *Austria and the Papacy in the Age of Metternich: Between Conflict and Cooperation, 1809-1830, Vol. 1*. Washington, D.C.: Catholic University Press, 1979. Discusses the era of Metternich in Austria.

Sylvester, David. *Napoleon and the French Empire*. New York: Longman, 1978. Paperback. Short, informative account with illustrations. Part of *Then and There* series.

MEDIA

The American Revolution—1770-1783—A Conversation with Lord North. BFA Educational Media. Film, color, 33 minutes. Presents Eric Sevareid "interviewing" Lord North. It explores political events prior to the revolution.

Catherine the Great: A Profile of Power. Learning Corporation of America. Film, color, 26 minutes. Portrays an "interview" with the Russian empress revealing her life and times.

The England of Elizabeth. International Film Bureau. Film, color, 26 minutes. Presents the art, literature, architecture, and famous personalities of Elizabethan England.

England: The Puritan Revolution and Cromwell. Learning Corporation of America. Film, color, 30 minutes. Describes the revolution and the 12 years of Puritan rule under Cromwell.

The Enlightenment and the Age of Louis XIV. New York Times. Sound filmstrips (2), color. Describe the revolutionary ideas of the time and the reign of the Sun King.

French Revolution. Encyclopaedia Britannica Educational Corp. Films (2), color, 17 and 21 minutes. The first explains the nature of the old regime; the second deals with challenges of the new republic.

French Revolution: The Terror. Learning Corporation of America. Film, color, 17 minutes. Shows the transformation of France from the idealism of the revolution to the Reign of Terror.

The Metternich Era. Encyclopaedia Britannica Educational Corp. Sound filmstrip, color. Examines the influence of Metternich in Europe following the defeat of Napoleon.

Napoleon: The Making of a Dictator. Learning Corporation of America. Sound filmstrips (2), color. Explore the nature and causes of dictatorship, using the example of Napoleon.

The Revolutions of 1848. Multi-Media Productions. Sound filmstrips (2), color. Describe the revolutions in France, Italy, Austria, and Germany and the reactions of each nation's people after the revolts.

UNIT 5
BOOKS

Briggs, Asa. *A Social History of England*. New York: Viking Press, 1983. Offers the human side of change, drawing on art and literature as well as economic and political developments. Well illustrated.

Cobban, Alfred. *A History of Modern France, Vol. 2: 1799-1945*. Baltimore: Penguin Books, 1966. Paperback. Presents a balanced view of the political and institutional changes of nineteenth-century France.

Crankshaw, Edward. *Bismarck*. New York: Viking Press, 1981. Lively biography of this controversial figure, stressing his impact on Germany.

Heilbroner, Robert L. *The Worldly Philosophers.* New York: Simon and Schuster, 1980. Paperback. Makes clear the main contributions of Adam Smith, Ricardo, Malthus, the utopian socialists, and Marx.

Holland, Ruth. *Mill Child.* New York: Crowell-Collier Press, 1970. Describes what life was like in America for children who were forced to work in the mills.

Holt, Edgar. *The Making of Italy: 1815-1870.* New York: Atheneum, 1971. Explains why Italy failed to become united for so long and then succeeded in a short period of time.

Mackenzie, Midge. *Shoulder to Shoulder: A Documentary.* New York: Knopf, 1975. Oversize paperback. Photographs, extracts from speeches, diaries, memoirs, and newspaper articles document the WSPU's fight for women's suffrage in Britain.

Mirsky, Jeanette and Allan Nevins. *The World of Eli Whitney.* New York: Macmillan, 1962. Paperback. Details the importance of Whitney's inventions to American industrialization.

Montgomery, Elizabeth R. *The Story Behind Great Inventions.* New York: Dodd, Mead, 1953. Provides biographical sketches of inventors and descriptions of their inventions.

Schneider, Pierre and the Editors of Time-Life Books. *The World of Manet.* New York: Time-Life Books, 1971. Describes the artistic changes wrought by Manet and his contemporaries. Set against the political events of the period.

Strandh, Sigvard. *A History of the Machine.* New York: A and W Publishers, 1979. From prehistoric times to the computer. Excellent reference with many clear technical drawings and a readable text.

Thomson, David. *England in the Nineteenth Century (1815-1914).* Baltimore: Penguin Books, 1963. Paperback. Explains the gradual changes in the British political structure resulting from economic, social, and international developments and policies.

MEDIA

The Age of the Individual. Time-Life Video. Film, color. Treats the musical giants of the romantic period. From *The Music of Man* series.

T162

The Industrial Revolution in England. Britannica Films Video. Film, color. Shows the devices that led to the shift from the domestic system to the factory system.

Man and the Industrial Revolution. CRM/McGraw-Hill Films. Film, color. Describes the factors that led to the Industrial Revolution and the economic, social, and political consequences.

Marxism: The Theory that Split a World. Learning Corporation of America. Sound filmstrips (2), color. Use "interviews" with Marx's wife, Engels, and others to examine Marx's theories and their continuing influence in the world. Also cover the evolution of capitalism in western Europe, the revolutions of 1848, revolution in Russia, and the appeal of Marxism in the Third World today.

The Premodern Era. Prentice-Hall Media. Sound filmstrips (3), color. Examine art and culture of the late nineteenth century and the period immediately before World War I.

The Spirit of Romanticism. Britannica Films Video. Film, color. Dramatizes key events and literary, artistic, and musical figures in the romantic movement (1789-1838).

Years of Revolt and Revolution. New York Times. Sound filmstrips (2), color. Show the political, social, and artistic changes across Europe from 1830 to 1872, encompassing the election of Louis Philippe and the unification of Italy and Germany.

UNIT 6
BOOKS

Clark, Leon, ed. *Through African Eyes, Vol. III: The African Past and the Coming of the Europeans.* New York: Praeger, 1971. Paperback. Includes explanation of how oral tradition and archeology help reconstruct the past. Stops at about 1850.

Clavell, James. *Tai-Pan.* New York: Delacorte Press, 1983. A historical novel about the founding of Hong Kong.

Davison, Rodric H. *Reform in the Ottoman Empire, 1856-1876.* New York: Gordian Press, 1973. Examines the empire's most serious reform movement in the nineteenth century.

Gordon, Donald C. *The Moment of Power: Britain's Imperial Epoch.* Englewood Cliffs, N.J.: Prentice-Hall, 1970. Popular study of the rise and fall of the British Empire.

Hibbert, Christopher. *The Great Mutiny: India, 1857.* New York: Penguin Books, 1980. Relates the story of the Indian Mutiny.

Loewe, Michael. *Imperial China: The Historical Background to the Modern Age.* London: Allen and Unwin, 1966. Describes the imperial system and its deterioration in the modern era.

Markun, Patricia M. *The Panama Canal.* New York: Franklin Watts, 1979. Traces the Panama Canal from planning through construction.

Minear, Richard H., ed. *Through Japanese Eyes, Vol. I: The Past—The Road from Isolation.* New York: Center for International Training and Education, 1981. Paperback. Describes Japanese society from the opening of the country by American naval power to the American occupation following World War II.

Mosse, Werner E. *Alexander II and the Modernization of Russia.* New York: Macmillan, 1962. Paperback. Provides a highly readable account of Russia from 1855 to 1881.

Roberts, John G. *Black Ships and Rising Sun.* New York: Julian Messner, 1971. Tells how Japan was opened by Commodore Perry and how it industrialized and modernized.

Syme, Ronald. *Juárez, the Founder of Modern Mexico.* New York: Morrow, 1972. A biography of the Mexican statesman.

Webb, Robert M. *Simón Bolívar: The Liberator.* New York: Franklin Watts, 1966. A biography.

Werstein, Irving. *The Boxer Rebellion.* New York: Franklin Watts, 1971. Explains how and why Chinese revolutionaries tried to drive out foreigners.

MEDIA

The Boer War. Multi-Media Productions. Sound filmstrip, color. Describes the conduct of the war and its impact on blacks and Asians in South Africa.

Bolívar: South American Liberator. Coronet Films. Film, color, 11 minutes. Explains his role in the liberation of Latin America.

The Boxer Rebellion. Multi-Media Productions. Sound filmstrip, color. Looks at the causes and effects of the rebellion. Uses rarely seen archival photographs.

Imperialism. Educational Audio Visual. Sound filmstrips (2), color. Describe imperialism in India and Africa, motives and consequences.

Introduction to Japan. Harvard University Press. Sound filmstrips (8), color. Trace history from earliest times, through Tokugawa and Meiji rule, the arrival of Commodore Perry, and World War II—to the present.

The Maharajas: Imperialism by Conspiracy. Centron Educational Films. Film, color, 25 minutes. Describes the rise and fall of the maharajas during the period of British imperialism in India.

Latin America, Part 2: Its History, Economy and Politics. McGraw-Hill. Film, b/w, 33 minutes. Surveys Latin American history from pre-European conquest until recent times. Emphasizes struggles for independence and subsequent problems.

The Sinking of the Maine. Prentice-Hall Media. Sound filmstrip, color. Examines factors that led to the Spanish-American War. Describes the war and explores its ramifications.

UNIT 7

BOOKS

Bullock, Alan. *Hitler, A Study in Tyranny.* New York: Harper and Row, 1964. Shows the life of Hitler, the elements in his rise to power, and his demise.

Deutscher, Isaac. *Stalin: A Political Biography.* New York: Oxford University Press, 1978. Reviews Stalin's career and impact on Russia through the end of World War II.

Fischer, Louis. *The Life of Mahatma Gandhi.* New York: Harper and Row, 1983. Describes the evolution of Gandhi's philosophy and political beliefs.

Hadawi, Sami. *Bitter Harvest: Palestine Between 1914-1967.* Los Angeles: Caravan Press, 1967. A Palestinian's perspective on the plight of Palestinians vis-à-vis the emerging Israeli state.

Keegan, John. *Six Armies in Normandy: From D-Day to the Liberation of Paris, June 6–August 25, 1944.* New York: Viking Press, 1982. Describes the D-Day invasion from early planning to execution by American, Canadian, British, German, French, and Polish armies.

Kinross, Lord. *Attaturk: A Biography of Mustafa Kemal, Father of Modern Turkey.* New York: Morrow, 1973. A scholarly biography.

Petrova, M. *Stalin's Doctor, Stalin's Nurse.* Princeton, N.J.: Kingston Press, 1983. Account of Stalin's rise to power and the turmoil of the 1930's. Written from the perspective of Stalin's doctor, who headed the Kremlin hospital, and the nurse who recorded the recollections.

Poppino, Rollie. *Brazil: The Land and People.* New York: Oxford University Press, 1973. Covers immigration, economic development, and political problems.

Prange, Gordon W. *At Dawn We Slept: The Untold Story of Pearl Harbor.* New York: Penguin Books, 1982. Paperback. Best-selling, exhaustive study of the attack on Pearl Harbor.

Schurmann, Herbert Franz and Schell, Orville, eds. *The China Reader: Vol. 2, Republican China: Nationalism, War, and the Rise of Communism, 1911-1949.* New York: Random House, 1967. Contains documents and articles by Chinese and foreign participants and observers, prefaced by helpful background by the editors.

Shirer, William L. *The Rise and Fall of the Third Reich.* New York: Simon and Schuster, 1981. Classic study of Nazi Germany.

Smith, Denis Mack. *Mussolini.* New York: Knopf, 1982. Political biography of Mussolini showing his rise to power and his important influence on Hitler.

Stokesbury, James L. *A Short History of World War I.* New York: Quill, 1981. Paperback. Presents a readable account of the war and the broad issues raised by it.

Toland, John. *Rising Sun.* New York: Bantam, 1971. Describes World War II from the perspective of the Japanese.

Tuchman, Barbara W. *The Guns of August.* New York: Macmillan, 1962. Paperback. Vivid account of the crucial first six weeks of World War I.

MEDIA

China in Revolution: A Sleeping Giant Awakes. New York Times. Sound filmstrip, color. Depicts revolutionary efforts in China from the late 1800's to the defeat of the Nationalists in 1949.

Czarist Russia: The Russian Revolution. New York Times. Sound filmstrips (2), color. Cover the early twentieth-century events contributing to the economic and social unrest in Russia and to the fall of the tsar.

The End of Colonialism: 20th Century Upheaval. New York Times. Sound filmstrips (2), color. Show the relationship between the two world wars and the development of nationalism and independence movements in India, Southeast Asia, and Africa.

Europe: The Mighty Continent. BBC and Time-Life Films. Films (10), color. Films from this series cover topics from 1900 through World War II.

From Kaiser to Feuhrer. Association Films. Film, b/w, 26 minutes. Shows the creation and the destruction of the Weimar Republic.

The Great War. Multi-Media Productions. Sound filmstrips (3), color. Examine World War I from its inception to the failure of the peace of 1919.

India—The Brightest Jewel. Films Incorporated. Film, color. Describes India on the verge of independence, its leaders, their strategies, and the divisive Hindu-Muslim conflict.

The Known and the Unknown. Time-Life Video. Film, color. Focuses on the change in music between the two world wars. From *The Music of Man* series.

The Wasted Years: The Depression. New York Times. Sound filmstrips (2), color. Show the worldwide impact of the 1929 crash. Include special coverage of Germany and the economic proposals of Keynes, Hitler, and Roosevelt.

UNIT 8

BOOKS

Abadi, Jacob. *Britain's Withdrawal From the Middle East: The Economic and Strategic Imperatives (1947-1971).* Princeton, N.J.: Kingston Press, 1984. Examines the factors that led to Britain's withdrawal east of the Suez.

Asimov, Isaac. *Change! 71 Glimpses of the Future.* Boston: Houghton Mifflin, 1981. A noted writer offers short, readable essays on future-related topics.

Carr, E. H. *The Russian Revolution: From Lenin to Stalin (1917-1929).* London: Macmillan, 1979. A reliable, recent survey by a well-known British scholar.

Cracraft, James, ed. *The Soviet Union Today: An Interpretive Guide.* Chicago: University of Chicago Press, 1983. A collection of essays on Soviet life, economy, government, technology, and armed forces.

Fitzgerald, Frances. *Fire in the Lake: The Vietnamese and the Americans in Vietnam.* Boston: Little-Brown, 1972. Describes and analyzes the American experience in Vietnam.

Goode, Stephen. *The End of Detente? U.S.-Soviet Relations.* New York: Franklin Watts, 1981. Covers Soviet-American relations from the Russian Revolution to 1981. Focuses on the role of détente.

Graham, Shirley. *Julius K. Nyerere: Teacher of Africa.* New York: Messner, 1975. Describes the famous African leader who became president of Tanzania.

The Harvard Nuclear Study Group. *Living with Nuclear Weapons.* Cambridge: Harvard University Press, 1983. A balanced study of nuclear weapons and their uses in the modern world.

Hauser, Philip M., et al. *Population and the Urban Future.* Albany: State University of New York Press, 1982. Describes the present urban conditions in the world and projects trends and alternatives for the future. Has useful and extensive tables.

Hensen, Roger D., et al. *U. S. Foreign Policy and the Third World: Agenda 1982.* New York: Praeger, 1982. Describes the social, political, and economic conditions in the Third World and the role of United States foreign policy in Third World countries. Emphasis is on trade and aid relations.

Independent Commission on International Development Issues. *North-South: A Program for Survival* (The Brandt Report). Cambridge: MIT Press, 1980. Outlines the economic relations between the world's rich and poor countries. An extensive report by an international commission headed by former West German chancellor Willy Brandt.

Lambert, Rosemary. *Cambridge Introduction to the History of Art: The Twentieth Century.* New York: Cambridge University Press, 1981. Outlines the characteristics of the period's visual arts. Includes notes on the artists' lives and reproductions of their work.

Lewis, Bernard. *The Emergence of Modern Turkey.* New York: Oxford University Press, 1968. Covers the Ottoman Empire (later Turkey) from the early nineteenth century to the mid-twentieth century.

Treadgold, Donald W. *Twentieth Century Russia.* Chicago: Rand McNally, 1972. Excellent study of twentieth-century Russia.

MEDIA

The Aftermath of World War II: Prologue to the Cold War. McGraw-Hill. Film, b/w, 25 minutes. Describes the settlements after the war, the breakup of the war alliance, and the emergence of the United States and the Soviet Union as superpowers.

The Changing Middle East. International Film Foundation. Film, color, 25 minutes. Describes the culture of the Middle East with emphasis on changes in the early 1970's and their impact.

China's Changing Face. National Geographic Society. Film, color, 25 minutes. Describes life today in the People's Republic of China. Shows an agricultural commune and a steel factory. Also provides information on China before the republic and on Chinese education and medicine.

The Cold War. Educational Record Sales. Sound filmstrips (2), color. Describe international relations and political attitudes between the end of World War II and the early 1960's.

Crescent of Crisis. Educational Audio Visual. Sound filmstrips (8), color. Provide background on recent developments in Central America and United States relations with that region.

Cry, The Beloved Country. Media Basics. Sound filmstrips (3), color. Filmstrip version of the motion picture starring Sidney Poitier. Deals with apartheid in South Africa.

The Holocaust. Audio Visual Narrative Arts. Sound filmstrips (2), color. Examine the Holocaust from the experience of the victims and the historical background of European anti-Semitism and Hitler's regime.

The Human Condition in the Nuclear Age. Educational Audio Visual. Sound filmstrips (2), color. Using an interdisciplinary approach, these filmstrips examine the impact of political developments on artistic, literary, and philosophical movements since World War II.

The Human Face of Japan. Learning Corporation of America. Films (6), color, 28 minutes each. Films are up-to-date, introducing students to individuals from diverse socioeconomic backgrounds. Themes include education and job competition; lifetime employment; rural and seafaring life; changing role of women; modern technology and ancient culture; and urban family life.

Inside the U.S.S.R. New York Times. Sound filmstrips (8), color. Present a wide-ranging view of the Soviet Union today, emphasizing the great variety of cultures and peoples.

Japan: Of Tradition and Change. National Geographic Society. Film, color, 23 minutes. Focuses on the life of a young woman who works in a Tokyo department store. Her life demonstrates the resolution of conflict between tradition and change.

Leaders of the 20th Century. Educational Record Sales. Sound filmstrips (6), color. Include Gandhi, Nasser, Nkrumah, Kenyatta, Sukarno, and Mao.

Revolt in Hungary. McGraw-Hill. Film, b/w, 26 minutes. Uses documentary footage covering the Hungarian revolt of 1956 and the brutal suppression by the Red Army.

Southeast Asian Studies: Emerging Nations of Indochina. New York Times. Sound filmstrips (4), color. Recent profile of the land and peoples of Laos, Cambodia, Thailand, and Vietnam.

The United Nations: Organization for Peace. Journal Films. Film, b/w, 21 minutes. Explains the organization of the UN and traces its accomplishments and work to 1963.

NOTES

NOTES

NOTES

NOTES

THE HUMAN EXPERIENCE

Circle the number that corresponds most nearly to your opinion of each of the following items of *The Human Experience*. Please also star (★) three factors that most influence your choice of a text.

Student Text	Excel-lent	Very Good	Satis-factory	Fair	Poor	Comments
1. Appendix Materials	1	2	3	4	5	_____
2. Approach	1	2	3	4	5	_____
3. Boldfaced Terms	1	2	3	4	5	_____
4. Chapter Openers	1	2	3	4	5	_____
5. Chapter Reviews	1	2	3	4	5	_____
6. Using Skills	1	2	3	4	5	_____
7. Concept Development	1	2	3	4	5	_____
8. Content	1	2	3	4	5	_____
9. Section Questions	1	2	3	4	5	_____
10. Factual Accuracy	1	2	3	4	5	_____
11. Special Features	1	2	3	4	5	_____
12. Graphics	1	2	3	4	5	_____
13. Organization	1	2	3	4	5	_____
14. Photographs	1	2	3	4	5	_____
15. Readability	1	2	3	4	5	_____
16. Unit Openers	1	2	3	4	5	_____
17. Unit Reviews	1	2	3	4	5	_____
18. Visual Impact	1	2	3	4	5	_____

Teacher's Annotated Edition

	Excel-lent	Very Good	Satis-factory	Fair	Poor	Comments
1. Teachability	1	2	3	4	5	_____
2. Introduction	1	2	3	4	5	_____
3. How to Use the Teacher's Annotated Edition	1	2	3	4	5	_____
4. Instructional Approaches	1	2	3	4	5	_____
5. Text Implementation	1	2	3	4	5	_____
6. Suggested Resources	1	2	3	4	5	_____
7. Annotations	1	2	3	4	5	_____

Supplements

	Excel-lent	Very Good	Satis-factory	Fair	Poor	Comments
1. Student Activity Book	1	2	3	4	5	_____
2. Student Activity Book—T.E.	1	2	3	4	5	_____
3. Evaluation Program	1	2	3	4	5	_____
4. Teacher's Resource Book	1	2	3	4	5	_____

Circle the appropriate information.

1.	Grade level of students	9	10	11	12
2.	Enrollment of that grade	1-50	51-100	101-200	201+
3.	Total school enrollment	1-200	201-500	501-1000	1001+
4.	Locale of school	rural	small town	suburban	large city
5.	Ability level of class	below average	average		above average
6.	Appropriateness of text for your class	easy	about right		difficult
7.	Number of years text used	1	2	3	4 5
8.	May we quote you?	Yes No			

Name_____ Position_____

School_____City_____ State_____ Zip_____

Date_____

Fold

BUSINESS REPLY MAIL
FIRST CLASS   PERMIT NO. 284   COLUMBUS, OHIO

Postage will be paid by:

CHARLES E. MERRILL PUBLISHING CO.
A Bell & Howell Company
Managing Editor, Elhi Social Studies
1300 Alum Creek Drive
Columbus, Ohio 43216

NO POSTAGE
NECESSARY
IF MAILED
IN THE
UNITED STATES

 BELL & HOWELL

THE
HUMAN
EXPERIENCE
A WORLD HISTORY

Mounir Farah
Andrea Berens Karls
Carl Max Kortepeter

Charles E. Merrill Publishing Co.
A BELL & HOWELL COMPANY
Columbus, Ohio
Toronto London Sydney

AUTHORS

Mounir Farah is Department Chairperson of Social Studies in the Monroe, Connecticut, public schools and an adjunct lecturer of Social Science at Western Connecticut State University, Danbury. He is a past president of the Connecticut Council for Social Studies and the Connecticut Liaison of the Social Studies Supervisors Association. Farah has lived and traveled in the Middle East for twenty years. He has coauthored *Global Insights* by Merrill.

Andrea Berens Karls is a free lance writer having coauthored *Global Insights* by Merrill. Educated at Wellesley College and Harvard University, she has taught at the elementary and secondary levels. Karls was formerly Program Associate at Global Perspectives in Education, Inc., where she edited and wrote curriculum materials and worked with teachers. She is a member of the National Council of Social Studies and the American Historical Association.

Carl Max Kortepeter is Professor of Modern Middle Eastern History at New York University. A graduate of Harvard University, he obtained his PhD degree in the School of Oriental and African Studies at London University. Kortepeter has formerly taught at the University of Toronto, Princeton University, and Roberts College in Istanbul, Turkey.

Contributing Writers

John C. Butler
Social Studies Teacher
University High School
Urbana, Illinois

Daniel Rosen
Free Lance Writer
New York City

ISBN 0-675-2270-3

Published by
Charles E. Merrill Publishing Co.
A BELL & HOWELL COMPANY
Columbus, Ohio 43216

Printed in the United States of America.

PREFACE

The historical sense involves a perception, not only of the pastness of the past, but of its presence.

T. S. Eliot

The Human Experience is a chronological topical history of the world. It takes a global approach to world history by providing a balanced treatment of both eastern and western civilizations. It provides comprehensive treatment of ancient and medieval history and gives in-depth coverage of modern history, centering on such key concepts as monarchy, revolution, democracy, totalitarianism, and industrialization.

The Human Experience explores key developments of the past from a human perspective. Human ideas and actions are shown to be vital elements in the making of history. The text takes an interdisciplinary approach to world history. It recognizes the importance of the contributions of sociology, philosophy, and anthropology to an understanding of the human past and incorporates the findings of these and other disciplines in the text. *The Human Experience* also stresses that history concerns itself with all areas of human life. It explores developments in the arts and sciences as well as in government and social life.

The text is divided into 8 units which are further divided into 33 chapters. It begins with an introduction dealing with the origins of human civilizations. The final chapter discusses the challenges of today's world that will affect the future.

Each unit opens with a colorful two-page photograph, a listing of the chapters in the unit, and a time line highlighting important historical events. Each chapter begins with a photograph and a quote from a contemporary source. The quotation serves as a thought-provoking introduction to the theme of the chapter.

Within the text, facts and concepts are presented in a readable narrative with excerpts from primary and secondary sources. Chapters are divided into sections and sub-sections that contribute to easier reading and understanding. Concept terms appear in boldface type and are defined or explained in context immediately after being introduced. These same terms appear in the vocabulary lists at the end of the chapter and in the glossary at the end of the book.

Four kinds of special features appear in the text. They are: "History and People," "History and the Arts," "Science and Technology," and "History and Cities." These present the human side of history by focusing on interesting topics relevant to text content.

Photographs are used extensively to reinforce and expand chapter material. Precisely executed maps, graphs, and charts, all in full color, provide supportive data and clarify important historical, economic, political, or social relationships.

The Human Experience also contains numerous study aids. Review questions at the end of each main section serve as a check on students' understanding of important facts. Comprehensive chapter reviews include a summary of key points, a vocabulary list, questions of varying difficulty, and an exercise on using graphics. Unit reviews include a list of major generalizations, analytical questions, a skill-developing exercise, suggested activities, and an annotated bibliography.

An appendix at the end of the text includes a number of special items. A full-color atlas contains both general reference maps and a graphics section that provides data on such topics as world population, natural resources, and economic development. A glossary provides definitions of key terms, and a complete index provides easy reference to important historical topics.

REVIEWERS

Henry Guse
Director of Curriculum
Albert Lea Public Schools
Albert Lea, Minnesota

Beverley C. Lacy
Social Studies Chairperson
Chesterfield County Public Schools
Richmond, Virginia

Barbara Moll
Social Studies Teacher
Detroit Public Schools
Detroit, Michigan

Charlene S. Ragsdale
Academic Dean
Episcopal High School
Bellaire, Texas

Darlene Sherrick
Social Studies Teacher
Shoreline High School
Seattle, Washington

James K. Tillotson
Social Studies Supervisor
Springfield Public Schools
Springfield, Massachusetts

STAFF

Project Editor: **Robert A. Kohan;** Editors: **Donna Roxey, Jacquelyn Whitney, Carol Bloom, Myra Immell, Donald Lankiewicz, Mary Nye;** Production Editor: **Kimberly Munsie;** Designer: **Joan Shaull;** Project Artist: **Barbara White;** Artist: **Jeff Clark;** Map Artists: **Intergraphics;** Illustrators: **Intergraphics;** Photo Editor: **Barbara Buchholz.**

TABLE OF CONTENTS

UNIT 4
From Monarchy to Revolution

UNIT 5
The Rise of Modern Europe

UNIT **8**
The Contemporary
World 662

Special Features

Charts, Graphs, and Tables

ACKNOWLEDGMENTS

Thanks are due to the following authors and publishers for the material quoted on the pages indicated: **p. 15;** Carter, Howard and Mace A. C. *The Tomb of Tut-ankh-Amen.* Vol. 1. Cassell, 1923, pp. 95-96. **p. 18:** Kelly, William (ed.). *The Literature of Ancient Egypt: An Anthology of Stories, Instructions, and Poetry.* Yale University Press, 1972, pp. 168, 300. Reprinted by permission. **p. 29:** Herodotus. *Histories.* Rawlinson, H. J. (tr.). Nonesuch Press, 1935, p. 737. **p. 42:** James Legge (tr.) *Fa-hsien's Journal* as quoted in Durant, Will. *Our Oriental Heritage.* Simon and Schuster, 1935, p. 452. **p. 68:** Thucydides. *The Peloponnesian Wars.* Harmondsworth, R. W. (tr.). Penguin Books, 1954, pp. 116-121. **p. 94:** Tertullian. *Concerning the Soul* as quoted in Katz, S. *The Decline and Rise of Medieval Europe.* Cornell University Press, 1955, p. 7. **p. 95:** Ulpian. *Digest* as quoted in Strayer, Gatzke, and Harbison. *The Mainstream of Civilization.* Harcourt Brace Jovanovich, Inc., 1974, p. 97. **p. 118:** Bury, J. B. *Cambridge Medieval History.* Vol. 4. Macmillan, 1923, p. 420. **p. 120:** Fulk of Chartres as quoted in Sherrard, Philip. *Byzantium.* Time-Life Books, 1966, p. 36. **p. 125:** Toynbee, Arnold. *Constantine Porphyrogenitus and His World.* Oxford University Press, 1973, p. 545. **p. 152:** Letter of Maimonides as quoted in *Encyclopedia Judaica.* Vol. 11, col. 757. **p. 170.** Fulcher of Chartres. *History of Jerusalem.* McGinty, M. E. (tr.). University of Pennsylvania Press, 1941, p. 16. **p. 183:** Herodotus. *Histories.* Vol. I, Book 4. Rawlinson, George (tr.). New York: E. P. Dutton, Inc., 1910, p. 362. **p. 220:** Poetry of Tu Fu as quoted in Grousset, Rene. *The Rise and Splendour of the Chinese Empire.* University of California Press, 1953, p. 155. Reprinted by permission. **p. 231:** *Short Chronicle of an Anonymous Cleric,* as quoted in Gasquet, Francis Aidan. *The Black Death of 1348 and 1349,* 1908, p. 46. **p. 249:** Vasari, Giorgio. *Lives of the Artists.* Bull, George (tr.). Penguin Books, 1965, pp. 360-361. **p. 259:** Durant, Will. *The Reformation.* Simon and Schuster, 1957, p. 361. **p. 281:** Braudel, Fernand. *The Mediterranean and the Mediterranean World in the Age of Philip II.* Vol. 1. Harper and Row, 1972, p. 462. **p. 285:** Iglesia, Ramon. *Columbus, Cortes, and Other Essays.* Simpson, Lesley Bird (tr.). University of California Press, 1969, p. 13. **p. 312:** Jacques Bossuet as quoted in Robinson, James H. (ed.). *Readings in European History.* Ginn, 1906, pp. 275-276. **p. 330:** Galileo Galilei, as quoted in Ergang, Robert (ed.) *Europe from the Renaissance to Waterloo.* Heath, 1954, p. 364. **p. 337:** Frederick the Great as quoted in Ergang, Robert (ed.). *Europe from the Renaissance to Waterloo.* Heath, 1954, p. 502. **p. 350:** Charles I as quoted in Willson, David Harris. *A History of England.* Holt, Rinehart, and Winston, 1967, pp. 410-411. **p. 359:** Sieyes, Abbe. "What Is To Be Done?" as quoted in *Translations and Reprints from the Original Sources of European History,* Vol. VI. University of Pennsylvania Press, pp. 33-35. **p. 362:** Ewen, David. *All the Years of American Popular Music.* Prentice Hall, Inc., 1977, p. 12. Reprinted by permission. **p. 379:** Craig, Gordon A. *Europe Since 1815.* Holt, Rinehart, and Winston, 1961, p. 163. **p. 382:** Thomas Carlyle as quoted in Craig, Gordon A. *Europe Since 1815.* Holt, Rinehart, and Winston, 1961, p. 1169. **p. 394:** Langer, William. "The Population Explosion" as quoted in Stearns, Peter N. (ed.) *The Other Side of Western Civilization: Readings in Everyday Life.* Vol. II. Harcourt Brace Jovanovich, Inc., 1979, p. 97. **p. 422:** Marx, Karl and Engels, Friedrich. *The Communist Manifesto* as quoted in Tucker, Robert C. (tr.). *The Marx-Engels Reader.* Norton, 1972, p. 362. **p. 426:** Blake, William. "Complete Writings," Keynes, Geoffrey (ed.). Oxford University Press, 1966, p. 19. Reprinted by permission. **p. 428:** Dickens, Charles. *Hard Times.* Dent, 1907, p. 19. **p. 443:** Tennyson, Lord Alfred. "The Princess" as quoted in *Modern Classics.* Houghton Mifflin, n.d., pp. 112-113. **p. 448:** Napoleon III as quoted in Anderson Frank Maloy (ed.). *Select Documents of the History of France.* Russell and Russell, 1904, pp. 559-560. **p. 461:** Mazzini, Guiseppe. *The Duties of Man and Other Essays.* Dutton, 1907, pp. 54-55. **p. 468:** Kohl, Horst (ed.). *The Political Speeches of Prince Bismarck.* Vol. II. Berlin, 1892, p. 30. **p. 478:** Blum, J.; Cameron, R.; and Barnes, T. G. *The European World.* Little Brown and Co., 1966, p. 563. **p. 487:** Francis Deak as quoted in Ergang, Robert. *Europe Since Waterloo.* Heath, 1967, p. 292. **p. 500:** Palmer, R. R. and Colton, Joel. *A History of the Modern World.* Knopf, 1950, p. 632. **p. 510:** Masur, Gerhard. *Simon Bolivar.* University of New Mexico Press, 1948, p. 482. **p. 527:** Ch'ien Lung as quoted in MacNain, Harley Farnsworth. *Modern Chinese History, Selected Readings.* Commercial Press, Ltd., 1923, pp. 2-9. **p. 549:** Ohrwalder, Joseph. *Ten Years' Captivity in the Mahdi's Camp.* Wingate, 1892, p. 37. **p. 555:** Stearns, R. P. (ed.). *Pageant of Europe.* Harcourt Brace Jovanovich, Inc., 1961, p. 641. **p. 561:** Craig, Gordon A. *Europe Since 1815.* Holt, Rinehart, and Winston, Inc., 1961, p. 450. **p. 570:** Hausrath, Adolf. *Treitschke.* G. P. Putnam, 1914, pp. 197, 205-207; Beveridge, Albert J. as quoted in *The Library of Oratory,* 1902, pp. 438-440.; Cosgrave, J. J. and Kreiss, J. K. *Two Centuries,* Sydney, Whitcombe and Tombs Pty. Ltd., p. 239. **p. 629:** Kenyatta, Jomo. *Facing Mount Kenya.* Random House, Inc., 1938, p. 305. **p. 642:** Churchill, Winston S. *Their Finest Hour.* Houghton Mifflin, 1949, pp. 25-26. **p. 644:** Arnold Foster-Mark. *The World At War.* Thames Television Ltd. (Stein and Day, U.S. Publishers), 1973, p. 132. **p. 659:** Mussolini, Benito. "The Political and Social Doctrine of Fascism" as quoted in *International Conciliation,* January 1935, pp. 7-9, 13-16. **p. 666:** Donnelly, Desmond. *Struggle for the World.* St. Martin's Press, 1965, p. 211. **p. 723:** Osadebay, Dennis. "Young Africa's Plea" as quoted in Bassir, Olumbe (ed.). *An Anthology of West African Verse.* Ibadan University Press, 1957, p. 57. **p. 753:** Reader's Digest (ed.). *Great Events of the Twentieth Century.* Reader's Digest Association, 1977, p. 264. **p. 754:** Jean-Paul Sartre as quoted in Kauffman, Walter (ed.). *Existentialism from Dostoevsky to Sartre.* Meridian Books, pp. 292, 310, 311. **p. 769:** *The Global Report to the President of the United States.* Vol. 1. Pergamon Press, 1980, p. 1. **p.p. 787-88:** Alperovitz, Gar. *Cold War Essays.* Anchor Books, Doubleday, Inc., 1970, pp. 101-102.

PHOTO CREDITS

Cover

First row: (l) (c) The Photo File, (r) Larry Hamill.
Second row: (l) Robert Lee, II, (c) The Photo File, (r) Larry Hamill.

Prehistory

3, French Government Tourist Office.

Unit 1

4-5, (c) Grisewood & Dempsey Ltd., London, published in USA by Warwick Press; 6, Farrell Grehan/FPG; 9, Smithsonian Institution; 10, Lee Boltin; 12, Farrell Grehan/FPG; 15, Lee Boltin; 18, The Granger Collection; 23(l) Smithsonian Institution, (r) The Granger Collection; 25, Far Eastern Museum, Berlin; 28, The Bettmann Archive, Inc.; 32, D. J. Forbert/Shostal Associates; 34, Smithsonian Institution; 37, Joseph F. Viesti/Alpha; 39, Borromeo/Art Resource; 41, Jules Zalon/FPG; 43, Earl Dibble/FPG; 49, Eugene Gilliom; 50, File Photo; 52, International Society for Educational Information, Tokyo; 56, Scala/Art Resource; 58, The Granger Collection; 60, Don C. Nieman; 65, The Bettmann Archive, Inc.; 66, Historical Pictures Service, Cgo.; 72, Royal Ontario Museum; 73, Don C. Nieman; 74 (l) Scala/Art Resource, (r) Dan Helm/duomo; 76(l) Historical Pictures Service, Cgo., (c) The Granger Collection, (r) Scala/Art Resource; 80, Don C. Nieman; 82, Scala/Art Resource; 85, American Stock Photos/Tom Stack & Assoc.; 88, File Photo; 90, The Granger Collection; 92, British Tourist Authority; 93, 94, The Bettmann Archive, Inc.; 96, SEF/Art Resource; 97, Rapelye/Art Resource; 99, National Gallery of Art.

Unit 2

108-9, 110, 113, The Granger Collection; 114, Don C. Nieman; 117, File Photo; 119, 121, 122, 124, 128, The Granger Collection; 129, 130, John Kohan; 131, Historical Pictures Service, Cgo.; 134, N. Faridani/Globe Photos; 136, Vivienne Silver/Art Resource; 137, Historical Pictures Service, Cgo.; 138, Edinburgh University Library; 139, SEF/Art Resource; 141, 148, Historical Pictures Service, Cgo.; 149, SEF/Art Resource; 151, The Bettmann Archive, Inc.; 152, Historical Pictures Service, Cgo.; 153, Robert Kohan; 156, 158, The Granger Collection; 159, Giraudon/Art Resource; 162, Historical Pictures Service, Cgo.; 167, Josse/Art Resource; 169, The Granger Collection; 173, Historical Pictures Service, Cgo.; 175, The Granger Collection; 176, 178, Historical Pictures Service, Cgo.; 179, SEF/Art Resource; 182, Eliot Elisofon National Museum of African Art, Eliot Eliosfon Archives, Smithsonian Institution; 185, Erich Lessing/Magnum; 186, George Gerster/Photo Researchers; 187, Mary M. Thacher/Photo Researchers; 188, Victor Englebert; 189, Larry Burrows, LIFE Magazine © 1966, Time, Inc.; 191, Eliot Elisofon National Museum of African Art, Eliot Elisofon Archives, Smithsonian Institution; 192, Historical Pictures Service, Cgo.; 194, Fred Bruemmer; 195(t) Courtesy of the School of American Research, (b) The Granger Collection; 197, Rich Brommer; 201, Victor Englebert.

Unit 3

206-7, The Granger Collection; 208, Art Resource; 210, R. & S. Michaud/Woodfin Camp & Assoc.; 216, The Granger Collection; 217, Colour Library International; 218, The Granger Collection; 219, Metropolitan Museum of Art; 222, The Granger Collection; 227, Kroop Miyanoshita/FPG; 230, Scala/Art Resource; 232, The Bettmann Archive, Inc.; 233, 235, Historical Pictures Service, Cgo.; 237, The Granger Collection; 238, Historical Pictures Service, Cgo.; 241, The Granger Collection; 244, Historical Pictures Service, Cgo.; 246, Robert Kohan; 250, Scala/Art Resource; 254, Fred Peer, Vienna; 257, 258, Historical Pictures Service, Cgo.; 259, German Information Center; 261, Historical Pictures Service, Cgo.; 262, The Granger Collection; 266, Historical Pictures Service, Cgo.; 267, The Granger Collection; 268, Historical Pictures Service, Cgo.; 269, The Granger Collection; 270, 273, Historical Pictures Service, Cgo.; 276, City Art Gallery, Bristol; 278, Scala/Art Resource; 280, 282, 285, 287, The Granger Collection; 288, Historical Pictures Service, Cgo.; 290, Columbus Memorial Library, OAS; 291, Historical Pictures Service, Cgo.; 295, The Granger Collection; 296, New York Public Library.

Unit 4

302-3, 304, Scala/Art Resource; 306, 308, The Granger Collection; 309, 311, Historical Pictures Service, Cgo.; 312, 313, The Granger Collection; 314, Alinari/Art Resource; 315, BBC Hulton Picture Library/Bettmann Archive, Inc.; 321, File Photo; 325, The Granger Collection; 328, Scala/Art Resource; 329, The Granger Collection; 330, Ann Ronan Picture Library; 332, 335, The Granger Collection; 336, Historical Pictures Service, Cgo.; 338, 340, The Granger Collection; 341 (l) Lee Boltin, (r) The Bettmann Archive, Inc.; 342, The Granger Collection; 343, Scala/Art Resource; 346, Giraudon/Art Resource; 348, Scala/Art Resource; 350, Giraudon/Art Resource; 353, Historical Pictures Service, Cgo.; 354, 355, The Granger Collection; 358, Historical Pictures Service, Cgo.; 359, The Granger Collection; 360, 362, Historical Pictures Service, Cgo.; 364, Scala/Art Resource; 370, The Phillips Collection, Detail; 372, Historisches Museum der Stadt Wien; 374, Historical Pictures Service, Cgo.; 376, 377, Giraudon/Art Resource; 379, Historical Pictures Service, Cgo.; 381, The Granger Collection; 382, Historical Pictures Service, Cgo.

Unit 5

338-9, 390, The Granger Collection; 392, Historical Pictures Service, Cgo.; 393, The Granger Collection; 396, Photri; 399, The Granger Collection; 400(l) Historical Pictures Service, Cgo., (r) The Granger Collection; 402, The Granger Collection; 406, Manchester Public Libraries; 407(l) The Granger Collection; (r) Goodyear Tire and Rubber Company; 409, The Bettmann Archive, Inc.; 410, The Granger Collection; 411, Brown Brothers; 414, Winterthur Kunstmuseum; 417, By Courtesy of the National Portrait Gallery; 419, 420, Historical Pictures Service, Cgo.; 421, The Granger Collection; 423, Photri; 425, The Royal Institution; 428, Robert E. Kellar Collection; 429, 431, Scala/Art Resource; 432, The Granger Collection; 433, Scala/Art Resource; 436, By Courtesy of Birmingham Museums and Art Gallery; 438, By Courtesy of the National Portrait Gallery; 440, 441, The Granger Collection; 442, 443, Historical Pictures Service, Cgo.; 444, Giraudon/Art Resource; 445, 446, Historical Pictures Service, Cgo.; 448, Scala/Art Resource; 450, Historical Pictures Service, Cgo.; 452, Kunstmuseum Dusseldorf; 453, 458, SEF/Art Resource; 460, The Bettmann Archive, Inc.; 461, Historical Pictures Service, Cgo.; 462, Scala/Art Resource; 463, Historical Pictures Service, Cgo.; 464, SEF/Art Resource; 467, ADN/Zentralbild; 468, Ullstein-Bilderdienst; 469, SEF/Art Resource; 470, Historical Pictures Service, Cgo.; 474, German Information Center; 475, Historical Pictures Service, Cgo.

Unit 6

480-1, British Museum; 482, Snark International; 484, Historical Pictures Service, Cgo.; 487, Suddeutscher Verlag; 488, Tass from Sovfoto; 489, Historical Pictures Service, Cgo.; 492, Tass from Sovfoto; 493, Historical Pictures Service, Cgo.; 494, Brown Brothers; 495, SEF/Art Resource; 496, Tass from Sovfoto; 497, Sovfoto; 501, Brown Brothers; 504, Carl Frank/Photo Researchers; 506, Historical Pictures Service, Cgo.; 509, Museum of Modern Art of Latin America; 510, The Granger Collection; 512, Historical Pictures Service, Cgo.; 514, Texas Highway Department, Austin; 515, 516, Historical Pictures Service, Cgo.; 520, Columbus Memorial Library, OAS; 524, Orion/Art Resource; 526, The British Library; 527, 528, The Granger Collection; 531, The Library of Congress; 532, The Granger Collection; 533, Historical Pictures Service, Cgo.; 534, Eastfoto; 535, The Granger Collection; 537, Brown Brothers; 538, 539, Sekai Bunka Photo; 540, Orion/Art Resource; 544, India Office/The British Library; 546, The Granger Collection; 548, 549, Historical Pictures Service, Cgo.; 550, The Mansell Collection; 551, Historical Pictures Service, Cgo.; 552, 555, National Army Museum; 559, Art Gallery, New South Wales; 563, Historical Pictures Service, Cgo.

Unit 7

568-9, Imperial War Museum; 570, Historical Pictures Service, Cgo.; 575, 576, The Granger Collection; 577, Sovfoto; 580, The Bettmann Archive, Inc.; 581, Historical Pictures Service, Cgo.; 583, 584, 585, The Granger Collection; 587, Historical Pictures Service, Cgo.; 592, File Photo; 594, Historical Pictures Service, Cgo.; 596, The Granger Collection; 598, Sovfoto; 601, SEF/Art Resource; 603, Historical Pictures Service, Cgo.; 605, The Bettmann Archive, Inc.; 606, Historical Pictures Service, Cgo.; 609, Courtesy of Treasures of Westport, Inc., Selectman's Office, Westport, CT.; 610, Kansas State Historical Society; 611(l) Herbert Hoover Presidential Library, (r) The Bettmann Archive, Inc.; 612, © 1935 (renewed 1963) by the Condé Nast Publications, Inc.;

616, FPG; 618, File Photo; 619, J. P. Laffont/Sygma; 620, Rene Burri/Magnum; 621, Historical Pictures Service, Cgo.; 622, The Granger Collection; 623, NYT Pictures; 627(t) Sassoonian/Art Resource; (b) Art Resource; 628, Eliot Elisofon National Museum of African Art, Eliot Elisofon Archives, Smithsonian Institution; 630, File Photo; 631, Historical Pictures Service, Cgo.; 634, Naval Photographic Center/DAVA; 636(t) Wide World Photos, (b) FPG; 638, Hugo Jaeger/Life Magazine © 1964, Time, Inc.; 641, Eastfoto; 642, Mariruis/Black Star; 644, Ullstein Bilderdienst; 645(t) U. S. Air Force/DAVA, (b) National Archives; 646, Library of Congress; 647, Art Resource; 648 U. S. Army; 651, U. S. Coast Guard; 655, AP/Wide World Photos; 656, Osnabruck Museum, Germany; 657, National Archives.

Unit 8

662-3, Fred Ward/Black Star; 664, AP/Wide World Photos; 666, FDR Library; 668, AP/Wide World Photos; 671, Fenno Jacobs/Black Star; 673, Sovfoto; 675, Black Star; 676, Lessing/Magnum; 677, NASA; 678, UPI/Bettmann Archive; 679, Owen Franken/Stock Boston; 681, AP/Wide World Photos; 683, Keystone; 688, Sovfoto/Eastfoto; 690, U. S. Army Signal Corps; 692, Henri Cartier-Bresson/Magnum; 693, Harry Redl/Black Star; 695, AP/Wide World Photos; 696, Popperfoto; 699, AP/Wide World Photos; 701, Dennis Brack/Black Star; 703, UPI/Bettmann Archive; 705, Marilyn Silverstone/Magnum; 707, D. McCullin/Magnum; 708, Wide World Photos; 709, Historical Pictures Service, Cgo.; 711, Caterpillar Tractor Co.; 712, UPI/Bettmann Archive; 713, Wide World Photos; 716, United Nations; 718, D. Rubinger/Black Star; 720, Azar/Gamma-Liaison; 721, C. Spengler/Sygma; 722, Eliot Elisofon Museum of African Art, Eliot Elisofon Archive, Smithsonian Institution; 725, Messerschmidt/FPG; 728, AP/Wide World Photos; 729, File Photo; 731, The Granger Collection; 733, M. Philippot/Sygma; 735, Jean Gaumy/Magnum; 736, Chris Niedenthal/Black Star; 737, AP/Wide World Photos; 739, By permission of Bill Mauldin and Will-Jo Associates, Inc.; 740, AP/Wide World Photos; 741, Alex Webb/Magnum Photos; 744, T. Carroll/FPG; 746, 747, The Granger Collection; 748, AP/Wide World Photos; 749, S. Byk/Black Star; 750, From the MGM release "Gone With the Wind" © 1939 Selznick International Pictures, Inc. Renewed 1967 Metro-Goldwyn-Mayer, Inc.; 752, Courtesy, The Saint Louis Art Museum; 754, Burt Glinn/Magnum; 755, Wide World Photos; 756, John Marmaras/Woodfin Camp & Assoc.; 759(l) Zimmerman/FPG; (r) Wide World Photos; 763, Scala/Art Resource; 764, J. P. Laffont/Sygma; 765, Eiji Miyuzawa/Black Star; 768, Wide World Photos; 771, Blair Seitz/FPG; 773, J. P. Laffont/Sygma; 777, Chris Steele-Perkins/Magnum; 778, Dennis Brack/Black Star; 779, Wide World Photos; 780, James Westwater; 782, AP/Wide World Photos; 783, Dirck Halstead/Gamma-Liaison.

PREHISTORY

HISTORY is the story of humanity. It is also the record of that story. Historians get most of their information from written records. For this reason, history is said to begin with the development of writing about 5,000 years ago. However, the human story is much, much older. People have lived on earth for about 2,000,000 years. This long period of human existence before writing is often called prehistory.

Culture   Early in prehistory, people developed ways of living known as culture. Although conditions have changed today, culture is still basic to human life. It includes an economy, or the ways people use their environment to meet their basic material needs. It also includes technology, or the combination of skills and tools that makes economic activity possible. But culture is more than an economy and its technology. It contains all of the ideas, customs, and objects that people have developed for living in social groups. Thus, a group's political and religious beliefs, its arts and sciences, and its leisure activities are aspects of culture.

Culture is not biologically determined; it must be learned. Each new generation builds upon knowledge that already exists. It then goes on to make its own contributions. Today the world is made up of many cultures. But all have their roots in the prehistoric past.

Archeology   To understand prehistory, historians rely on archeologists, or scientists who search for sites that contain the remains of past cultures. Once sites are discovered, archeologists carefully dig to find plant and animal remains. They also search for artifacts, or objects made by humans. By studying these materials, archeologists are able to learn about past environments and cultures. Their work has broadened our understanding about the economy and technology of prehistoric peoples. However, much has yet to be learned about other aspects of prehistoric cultures.

THE WORLD OF EARLY PEOPLES

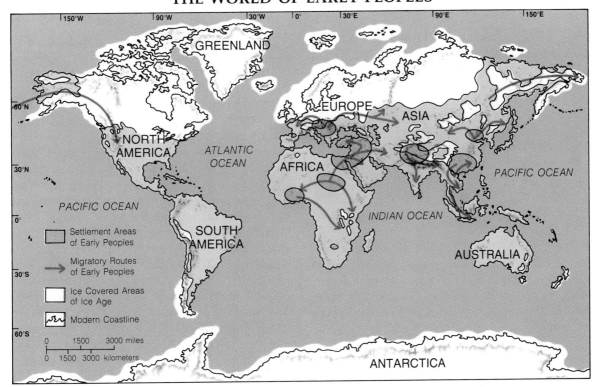

Have students refer to the map on p. 1 to locate the migratory routes of early peoples.

Fossilized bones and crude tools that date back over 2.6 million years were discovered in East Africa by the Leakey family. Scientists believe that the first humans lived in Africa.

Prehistoric People

	Date	Location	Elements of Culture
Java man Peking man	2,000,000 to 500,000 years ago	East Indies Central Europe Northern China North and East Africa	Used simple stone tools Built primitive shelters Hunted animals Gathered nuts, fruits, roots, and grains
Neanderthal	70,000 to 40,000 years ago	East Indies Middle East Eastern Africa Central Asia Europe	Improved stone and bone tools Made fish hooks of bone Discovered fire for cooking Tamed dogs for hunting Sewed skins for clothing Used bows and arrows Buried their dead Painted hunting scenes
Cro-Magnon	300,000 to 2,500 years ago	Southern Europe Northern Africa Middle East Central Asia	Started farming Invented pottery making Made wood and ivory carvings Built small villages Tamed sheep, goats, and cattle Developed irrigation Learned to weave baskets Wove and used fishing nets

Stone Age Since most of the artifacts found in prehistoric sites are made of stone, the period of prehistory is commonly known as the Stone Age. In their studies, experts have noted gradual changes in prehistoric cultures. As a result, they have often divided the Stone Age into three stages: the Paleolithic (Old Stone) Age, the Mesolithic (Middle Stone) Age, and the Neolithic (New Stone) Age.[1] The Paleolithic Age was very long; it lasted from about 2,000,000 to about 10,000 B.C. The Mesolithic Age may be dated from 10,000 to about 8000 B.C. The Neolithic Age lasted from about 8000 to 5000 B.C.

Paleolithic Age During the Paleolithic Age, much of the world had a cold climate. Huge glaciers periodically covered areas of Europe, Asia, and North America. During the same period, the ice fields of Antarctica stretched over wide regions in the Southern Hemisphere. Only the middle portion of the earth remained warm enough to support human life. Toward the end of the Paleolithic Age, the climate became warmer. During this time, people gradually adapted to thousands of new environments and climates. By 10,000 B.C. groups had expanded into almost every area of the world.

The early Paleolithic economy involved hunting wild animals and gathering plants for food. People lived in small groups. When the food supply was used up in one place, a group moved on. Paleolithic peoples had a simple, but effective technology. They made tools from stone, bone, and wood. They also produced weapons, such as spears and clubs. For protection from the weather, they dug shallow pits and covered them with brush or hides. Sometimes they camped in caves or under rock ledges.

Paleolithic peoples adapted to cold climates by wearing animal furs and hides. They also learned how to make fire. This discovery allowed them to keep their shelters warm, cook their food, and

[1]The ending "-lithic" comes from the Greek word *lithikos*, meaning "made of stone."

The results of the change from food gathering to food producing were so great that experts call the origins of farming the Neolithic Revolution.

The earliest known villages are in the Middle East. Jericho in Israel dates back to 8000 B.C.

scare away wild animals. Spoken languages were another significant development. The use of language allowed people to work more closely together and to share their cultural knowledge.

Later during the Paleolithic Age, people made new types of artifacts and tools for a variety of purposes. They made beads, ornaments, needles, traps, fishing hooks, and bows and arrows. Depending on what they found in their environments, people made these items from stone, bone, horn, ivory, and wood.

The late Paleolithic period is known for its cave paintings, some of which may be over 30,000 years old. Paleolithic artists used brilliant colors to paint cave walls with pictures of animals such as bison, horses, reindeer, and mammoth. Many experts believe that the paintings were linked to religious ceremonies that were performed to ensure success in hunting.

Mesolithic Age   Around 10,000 B.C. the prehistoric ice age came to a close. Glaciers shrank toward the Arctic and Antarctic regions, and new environments developed. In some areas, forests replaced the ice sheets. In others, large stretches of grasslands and desert appeared. Many large animals of the ice age became extinct. As a result, Mesolithic peoples hunted smaller animals such as wild pigs and deer. They also fished in lakes and rivers. Mesolithic tools were improved, and new ones were made for special tasks.

In the late Mesolithic period, groups learned to harvest wild barley and wheat. Stone sickles and grinding stones were used to prepare the grain for meals. Soon gathering activities no longer required long-distance travel. Some groups settled down and built permanent homes.

Neolithic Age   During the Neolithic Age, people began to produce their own food. Most scholars believe that Middle Eastern peoples were the first to discover that seed from wild grains could be planted. During this same period, animals such as dogs, cattle, pigs, sheep, and goats were domesticated, or tamed. By raising these animals, people had another ready source of food.

A food-producing economy made it possible for larger groups of people to live together in one place. Villages and permanent settlements began to develop. With a fairly steady food supply, Neolithic villagers could spend more time at activities other than farming. They began to make pottery and baskets and to weave cloth on looms. Jewelry, eating utensils, weapons, and other goods were made by hammering copper, lead, and gold. Later, a harder metal called bronze was developed by mixing tin with copper. Transportation and trade improved with the invention of the wheel and the sail.

Farmers made their work easier by inventing the plow and by training oxen to pull it. More land was farmed, and larger harvests were possible. This led to larger populations. To maintain order in growing villages, leaders emerged who made rules and settled disputes. By 5000 B.C. these developments had contributed to the rise of civilizations, or highly organized societies with a developed knowledge of farming, trade, government, art, and science.

1. What is history? What is prehistory? How do experts obtain their knowledge of each?
2. What is culture? What does it include? How is it passed on?
3. How has archeology contributed to our understanding of the past?
4. What were the periods of the Stone Age? What were the main cultural features of each period?

Archeologists found paintings of early peoples deep within caves, a primary source of shelter. In addition to caves, Paleolithic hunters usually had separate work sites for butchering and toolmaking. From what materials were their tools made?

The Ancient World

4000-3500 Early settlements in the Middle East		3100 Unification of Egypt	2500 Rise of Indus Valley civilization	
		3000 Rise of Sumer		2000-1400 Minoan civilization
4000	**3500**	**3000**	**2500**	**2000**
		3000-2500 Bronze Age		
				1750 Code of Hammurabi

1500	1000	500	B.C. 0 A.D.	500	1000
1500-1100 Mycenaean civilization		**800** Homer	**450** Golden Age of Athens	**202 B.C.-220 A.D.** Han dynasty	**636** Taika reforms
	1200 Aryan invasions in India			**250** Asoka	
1500-1028 Shang dynasty		**509-31** Roman Republic			**650** Silla Kingdom in Korea
	1000 David's kingdom in Israel		**330** Alexander the Great	**476** Fall of Rome	

Between 4000 and 2000 B.C., the first civilizations arose in Asia and Africa. Later, others appeared in Europe. These early civilizations had certain features in common. They developed from small farming or trading centers along rivers or seacoasts. They created writing systems that improved communications. Their peoples became specialists in a variety of occupations.

Cities emerged and became centers of civilized life. There, certain kinds of work came to be considered more important. Social systems based on rank developed, and governments became more organized. Strong rulers raised armies, kept records, and collected taxes. They also engaged in trade and conquest, which helped spread ideas and customs. Soon the achievements of one civilization were borrowed and changed by others. Together, the early civilizations passed on to later generations many basic ideas in government, religion, technology, social life, and the arts.

Greek soldier and ship

CHAPTER 1

Egyptian Monument

66 *To every thing there is a season,
and a time to every purpose under heaven:
A time to be born, and a time to die;
a time to plant, and a time to uproot
that which is planted. . .* **99**

from Ecclesiastes, a book of the Bible

Ancient Middle East

Vocabulary terms appear in bold type within the narrative. These terms also are listed in the Chapter Review for students to identify.

Point out that the term "Near East" is also used to describe southwest Asia and the Nile Valley.

About 4000 B.C. early civilizations developed in the Middle East.[1] In this region, an improved food supply and better protection led to an increase in population. Small farming settlements developed into urban societies. New techniques changed human life and promoted improvements in agriculture and crafts. Trade increased between different regions and resulted in the exchange of ideas and inventions. Systems of writing were created to record daily activities and to pass on information. Also, governments were set up to maintain order and to organize social life.

By 3000 B.C. urban communities in various parts of the Middle East had united into kingdoms. Powerful rulers raised armies and conquered neighboring lands. These military conquests led to the rise of **empires,** or groups of territories under one government. These Middle Eastern empires developed new ways of ruling, increased trade, and spread their ideas and customs among many peoples.

The heritage of the ancient Middle East was passed on to the civilizations of East and West. Western civilization, beginning with the Greeks and Romans, was built in part on Middle Eastern achievements in religion, law, and government. As a result, historians of the West have referred to the Middle East as "the cradle of civilization."

1 Mesopotamia

Early Middle Eastern civilizations developed in the Fertile Crescent. This crescent-shaped strip of fertile land begins near the southeastern end of the Mediterranean Sea, curves around

[1]The term "Middle East" describes the region stretching from Egypt to Pakistan.

northern Syria, and ends at the Persian Gulf. Modern scholars consider the ancient Fertile Crescent as two separate areas: Syria in the west and Mesopotamia in the east.[2]

About 5000 B.C. groups of herders moved north into Mesopotamia from the Arabian Peninsula. At that time, the lakes and grasslands of the peninsula were drying up as a result of declining rainfall. During the same period, other peoples were migrating south into the region from the grassy highlands near present-day Turkey. They were forced to move as a result of wars, overpopulation, and poor weather. Both groups found that they could produce a larger and more regular food supply by farming the fertile soil of Mesopotamia. They also fished and traded along the Persian Gulf.

[2]The Fertile Crescent included portions of the present-day nations of Turkey, Iraq, Syria, Lebanon, Israel, and Jordan.

THE FERTILE CRESCENT

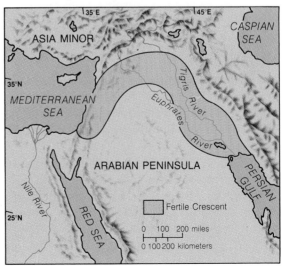

Note that the Tigris and Euphrates rivers in ancient times did not meet before reaching the Persian Gulf as they do today. Ask students to explain what they think happened to the course of the rivers over the centuries.

Twin Rivers

Most of the new arrivals settled in a low-lying plain between the Tigris and Euphrates, the two great rivers of Mesopotamia that flowed into the Persian Gulf.[3] There, the newcomers drained the swamps, built mud-brick villages, and grew dates and grain. They also raised cattle, goats, and sheep.

The early peoples of the Mesopotamian plain depended on the Tigris and Euphrates Rivers for water. In the summer, Mesopotamia received no rainfall. As a result, there often was a shortage of water during the fall planting season. Thus, farmers had to use the rivers to irrigate their fields. During the spring harvest season, the rivers flooded, with unpredictable results. Often, floods were strong enough to sweep away whole villages and fields. In addition, the water level could vary from year to year.

To meet this challenge, the early Mesopotamians organized into larger communities and learned to work together. With greater cooperation, they were able to develop methods for controlling and using the flood waters. They built dams and escape channels to keep the floods away from the fields. They also constructed canals and ditches to hold the water that they needed.

As a result of these technological achievements, Mesopotamian farming had gradually improved. By 4000 B.C. it was sufficiently developed to produce a food surplus. With more food available, people could live in cities and engage in crafts and trade.

Sumer

About 3000 B.C. a people known as the Sumerians established one of the world's first-known civilizations in the lower part of the Tigris-Euphrates River Valley. Their land became known as Sumer.

City-States   Sumer was made up of several city-states united in a loose league. The most prosperous of them were Ur, Eridu, and Uruk. The people of the city-states shared a common culture, spoke the same language, and wor-

shiped the same gods and goddesses. A typical Sumerian city-state consisted of the city itself and the farmland around it. The population of each of the city-states ranged from 20,000 to 250,000 persons.

Sumerian city-states had certain common features. Each was built around a **ziggurat,** or temple, made of sun-dried brick and decorated with colored tile. Ziggurats looked like tall artificial mountains or raised platforms. They consisted of a series of square terraces. Each terrace was smaller than the one below. A stairway led to a shrine at the top of the ziggurat. Only priests were allowed to enter the shrine, which was dedicated to the city-state's chief god or goddess.

Near the base of the ziggurat were other buildings. They included temples to the other deities, living quarters for the priests, workshops, storehouses, and the city **archives,** or public records. Not far from the temple grounds were the residential areas of the upper and middle social groups. Farther away were the living quarters of the poor.

Government   Each Sumerian city-state was self-governing. At first, a council of nobles and a general assembly of citizens controlled political affairs. But around 2700 B.C., this type of representative government was limited by the rise of **monarchy,** or rule by a king or queen. At first, monarchs were elected by the assembly. Later, their office became **hereditary,** or passed down from parent to child.

Sumerian governments were also **theocracies,** or governments in which religious and political leadership is held by the same person. The king served as the **patesi,** or ruler-high priest, who represented the god or goddess of the city-state. The Sumerians believed that the land was the property of the city-state's god or goddess. As a result, the patesi supervised farming and collected taxes for the temple treasury. He also enforced the law and set punishments for lawbreakers. Most punishments consisted of fines and did not involve bodily injury or loss of life.

Sumerian city-states fought each other over land and water rights. A powerful city-state

---

[3]Mesopotamia comes from a Greek word meaning "between the rivers."

The term "Semitic" comes from Shem, the son of Noah. Semites are supposed to be descendants of Shem.

Some historians believe that writing developed in response to the need for keeping trade records.

would often conquer its weaker neighbors and establish a larger state. However, the political situation in Sumer was so unstable that such unions did not last very long. Growing warfare weakened the city-states and soon made them prey to outside invaders.

Akkadians By about 2500 B.C., groups of nomads called Semites[4] moved into the Fertile Crescent from the Arabian Peninsula. They were attracted by Sumerian culture and built cities on the Sumerian model. One of these groups, known as the Akkadians, established a kingdom called Akkad in northern Mesopotamia.

Around 2300 B.C. an Akkadian king named Sargon I expanded south and conquered Sumer. He became the first ruler to unite all of the city-states of Mesopotamia into a single empire. Under Sargon's rule, the Akkadians adopted Sumerian religious and agricultural practices. At the same time, they brought their own language and culture to the Sumerians. Sargon's **dynasty,** or a line of rulers from one family, governed Mesopotamia until 2200 B.C.

Sumerian Culture

The Sumerians created one of the first Middle Eastern civilizations. Their ideas and customs were copied and improved by later groups who settled in the Fertile Crescent. Through trade, the Sumerians also influenced and were influenced by developing communities in the Arabian Peninsula and India.

Religion Sumerians regarded religion as the center of their lives. They believed that the world was controlled by numerous gods and goddesses, each one fulfilling a special function. Each city-state had its own god or goddess to whom it prayed and offered sacrifices.

Sumerians believed that their gods and goddesses were unpredictable, selfish beings, who had little regard for humans. To please the deities, priests performed a variety of religious ceremonies and rituals. Otherwise, the gods and goddesses would be angry and bring misfortunes such as floods or famine. With such

___
[4]The Semites included a number of groups in the Middle East that spoke a common language. Today's Jews and Arabs are Semites.

Sumerian students attending eddubas memorized hundreds of word signs by writing on clay tablets about the size of a postcard. After becoming scribes, how did they serve the Sumerian people?

powerful deities, the Sumerians believed that humans had little control over their lives and could not expect a happy life after death. They pictured their afterlife as a grim underworld, empty of light and air, where the dead existed as pale shadows.

Writing Scholars believe that the world's oldest writing system developed in Sumer about 3100 B.C. Special schools called **eddubas** taught writing and prepared **scribes,** or writers, for service in business, government, and religion. Scribes produced business records, lists of historical dates, and literary works. One of their tales is the oldest written story in the world. It is about Gilgamesh, a god-like man who performs heroic deeds.

The Sumerian system of writing, called **cuneiform,** consisted of hundreds of wedge-shaped markings that represented syllables. The Sumerians made these markings by pressing the end of a sharp reed on wet clay tablets. The tablets were then dried or baked until they were hard. Sumerian cuneiform became the model for the writing systems of other civilizations in the Fertile Crescent.

Daily Life Sumerian affairs were largely run by men. Males had control of property rights and were heads of households. They had great authority over their wives and children. A Sumerian man could easily divorce his wife. He could even sell his children as slaves if he needed the money. He could also arrange the marriages of his children and dependents. Sumerian women, however, did enjoy certain rights. They could buy and sell property and could operate their own businesses. They were also allowed to own and sell slaves.

Arts and Inventions   The Sumerians excelled in architecture, an example of which is the ziggurat. They also produced many crafts. The variety of Sumerian work included gold and silver vessels, pottery figurines, ceramic jewelry, and statues of lapis lazuli, a precious blue stone imported from India.

The Sumerians also developed many inventions, some of which are still in use today. They developed a number system based on 60. From this system came the 360-degree circle, the

Artisans of Ur were known for their metalwork. This golden goat is decorated with lapis lazuli. In addition to artistic achievement, for what other contributions to civilization is Sumer noted?

60-second minute, and the 60-minute hour. They also invented a 12-month calendar based on cycles of the moon. Other notable inventions were the wagon wheel to transport people and goods, the arch to make sturdier buildings, the sundial to keep time, and the potter's wheel to shape pottery. The Sumerians also made bronze out of copper and tin, and developed the first metal plows.

Babylonia

Around 1800 B.C., the Amorites, a Semitic people from western Syria, rose to power and conquered Mesopotamia. Settling in the Mesopotamian cities, they absorbed Mesopotamian religion, culture, and writing. Around 1750 B.C., Hammurabi, an Amorite king, established his capital at Babylon and became supreme throughout Mesopotamia. He organized a strong government and worked to increase the economic prosperity of his people. The tax system was reorganized, and local officials were ordered to build and repair the irrigation canals. Hammurabi also improved roads and furthered trade. Under Hammurabi's rule, Babylon became an important trade center. Merchants came to it from as far away as India and China. These traders paid gold and silver for the grain and cloth that the Babylonians produced.

Hammurabi's Code   Hammurabi's greatest achievement, however, was in the field of justice. He collected the laws of the various Mesopotamian city-states and created a single law code for the entire region. When completed, Hammurabi's code consisted of 282 sections dealing with most aspects of daily life. It clearly stated what actions were considered violations and assigned a specific punishment for each violation. Hammurabi's code, however, was more severe than the old Sumerian laws. Instead of punishing violators by fines, it based punishment on the legal concept of "an eye for an eye, and a tooth for a tooth." That is, a person who injured or killed someone suffered a similar fate.

The development of written law in Mesopotamia was a major advance toward justice and order. Before this achievement, people who had been offended or cheated often acted on their

The first known Mesopotamian law code was that of Ur-Nammu, a Sumerian King ruling about 2100 B.C. It established standard weights and measures for trade and set down penalties for theft.

KINGDOMS OF THE FERTILE CRESCENT

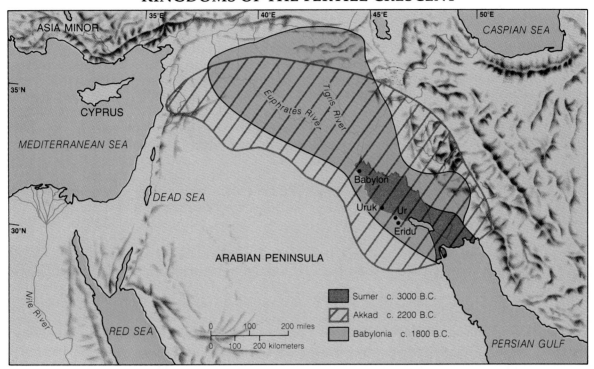

own and used violence against their opponents. Now, crimes against people or property became the concern of the whole community. Government assumed the responsibility of protecting its citizens in return for their loyalty and service.

Babylonian Literature The Babylonians borrowed heavily from Sumerian culture. They used the cuneiform script for their Semitic language and wrote on clay tablets. Babylonian literature was similar to that of Sumer. Scribes in Babylonia further developed the Gilgamesh story and told of a great flood that covered the entire world. Their account of the flood is similar to the biblical story of Noah and the ark.

Babylonian Society Babylonian society was divided into three groups. At the top were the kings, priests, and nobles. Next were the artisans, or craftspeople, small merchants, scribes, and farmers. Slaves made up the lowest group. Most slaves were people who had been captured in war or who had failed to pay their debts.

After Hammurabi's death, Babylonia declined, and Mesopotamia was again divided into a number of small states. During the 1600's B.C., the region was overrun by invaders. Little is known about this period. Babylon, however, resumed an important role in the development of Mesopotamian civilization in the 700's B.C.

1. Identify: Fertile Crescent, Mesopotamia, Tigris and Euphrates Rivers, Sumer, Ur, Semites, Akkad, Sargon I, Gilgamesh, Hammurabi, Amorites.
2. How did civilization develop in Mesopotamia?
3. What were the major cultural achievements of the Mesopotamian civilizations?
4. Why was Hammurabi's code important?

2 Egypt

While city-states and empires rose and fell in Mesopotamia, the Egyptians were building a great civilization 900 miles (1,440 kilometers) farther west in northeastern Africa. The lifeline

In the 400's B.C., the Greek historian Herodotus referred to Egypt as "the gift of the Nile."

According to an ancient Egyptian legend, a god sneezed and the world was created. Then a goddess in heaven cried. Her tears splashed down to earth and formed the Nile.

of their civilization was the Nile River. The Nile begins in the mountains of eastern Africa and flows north 4,000 miles (6,400 kilometers) to the Mediterranean Sea. The last 650 miles (1,040 kilometers) of the Nile's journey are in Egypt, where it cuts a lush green valley through vast areas of desert. The fertile area varies between 10 miles (16 kilometers) and 40 miles (64 kilometers) in width. Shortly before entering the Mediterranean, the Nile splits into many branches and forms a **delta,** a fan-shaped area of swampy land. Aside from oases, the Nile Valley and its delta are the only productive areas in Egypt.

Egypt's physical environment gave the people a sense of security. For a long time, Egyptians were protected from foreign invasions by the desert, sea, and cataracts, or waterfalls, of the Nile River. As a result, they were able to create a stable society that lasted for nearly 3,000 years.

Beginnings

About 5000 B.C. small agricultural communities appeared along the banks of the Nile. They were made up of a variety of people who sought protection there from the surrounding desert. Because of the dry climate and scarce rainfall, these early Egyptians relied on the Nile River. The river had an abundance of plant and animal life. Also, it overflowed its banks every summer and flooded the nearby land. Nile floodings generally rose to nearly the same level every year. By late fall, the flood waters receded. They deposited a rich black soil that was useful in growing cereal crops like barley and wheat.

The early Egyptians adjusted their lives to the rhythmic regularity of the river. They formed small kingdoms along the Nile and organized efforts to control the flood waters. They built dams and ditches to drain the extra water from the land. They also constructed reservoirs, or artificial lakes, to hold and store the water. Canals were built to bring water to the fields during the dry season.

The Egyptians became skillful farmers. They developed new farming equipment such as the **shadoof,** a machine that lifted water from the river for irrigation. With better technology, enough food was raised to support people in occupations besides farming. Egyptians became priests, government officials, scribes, carpenters, and potters. They lived in urban centers, developed writing systems, and promoted trade.

A growing economy and a more complex society brought conflicts among the small Egyptian kingdoms. To end the disorder, the kingdoms gradually merged into larger political

Egyptian life depended on the Nile River. When the river flooded, it brought prosperity. When it was shallow, there was often famine. The Egyptians used the water level of the Nile to divide the year into three seasons. How did the Egyptians control the flooding to their advantage?

To distinguish the two regions of Egypt, the king had the titles "Lord of Two Lands" and "Wearer of Both Crowns."

The Great Pyramid contains over 2 million stone blocks. Each is about 5,500 pounds (2,475 kilograms).

units. By 4000 B.C. Egypt consisted of two large kingdoms: Lower Egypt in the north and Upper Egypt in the south.

Around 3000 B.C., Narmer, also known as Menes, a king of Upper Egypt, invaded Lower Egypt and established the first government that ruled all of the country. To unify his people, he built a national capital at Memphis in the delta. Narmer's reign marked the beginning of the first Egyptian dynasty. From 3000 to 332 B.C., a series of 30 dynasties ruled Egypt.

During the first centuries of the Egyptian kingdom, Upper and Lower Egypt kept their separate identities. However, Egyptians eventually accepted their unity and viewed themselves as subjects of one kingdom.

Old Kingdom

Modern scholars refer to the first great period in Egyptian history as the Old Kingdom. The Old Kingdom lasted from about 2700 to 2200 B.C. During this time, Egypt built a strong national government under its kings. It also developed the basic features of its civilization.

Egyptian Monarchy   Egyptians believed that the strength and unity of their nation depended on a strong king. As a result, Egyptian kings acquired absolute power. Their authority was unquestioned. They were regarded as rulers, priests, and gods. Egyptian rulers set up a **bureaucracy,** or branch of government that administers public policy. A large number of **bureaucrats,** or government officials, carried out the commands of the kings. These commands were regarded as the law of the land. The most important bureaucrat was the **vizier,** or prime minister, who served as the king's assistant. Under the vizier were the governors of the **nomes,** or provinces.

As a god, the Egyptian king owned all of Egypt's land. In order to use the land, farmers paid rent—usually one-fifth of their crop—to the king. Trade was also controlled by the ruler, who issued permits to merchants and collected taxes on goods. The king also supervised the building of dams, canals, and granaries, or storehouses for grain.

Egyptian kings were at the center of national life. They enjoyed great respect and lived in splendor apart from ordinary Egyptians. During their rare public appearances, they performed many ritual actions, such as cutting the first ripe grain or driving a sacred bull around the capital. Egyptians believed that these actions ensured the prosperity of the kingdom.

Pyramids   During the Old Kingdom, the Egyptians built their most notable and lasting achievement: the pyramids. Many of them are located on the west bank of the Nile near the town of Gizeh. The largest, which covers 13 acres (5.2 hectares), is the Great Pyramid. It was built around the year 2500 B.C. for King Khufu. The Great Pyramid measures 481 feet (144 meters) high and 775 feet (233 meters) long at each of its four bases. Its length is equal to that of two football fields.

Inside the pyramids are small chambers and a grand gallery connected by narrow passages. The size, design, and structure of the pyramids reveal the skill of ancient Egyptian engineers and builders. Farmers built the pyramids during the three months each year when the fields were flooded by the Nile.

The pyramids were great monuments and tombs for the kings. Egyptians believed that a king's soul continued to guide the affairs of the kingdom after death. Therefore, they tried to preserve the king's body. The Egyptians used a process called **embalming** to keep the king's body intact. First, the body was washed and all the organs removed. Then the body was covered with pine resin and filled with a substance called natron. Natron dried up the water in the body, causing it to shrink. After the shrunken body had dried, it was wrapped with long strips of linen. Finally, the wrapped body, called a **mummy,** was placed in an elaborate coffin and taken to the pyramid. Along with the coffin, the kings' clothing, weapons, furniture, and jewelry were placed in the burial chamber. Egyptians believed that the king could enjoy these personal possessions in the afterlife.

Collapse   Around 2200 B.C. the power of Egyptian kings weakened. As a result, ambitious nobles fought each other for control of Egypt. At the same time, the governors of the nomes demanded independence for their territories and led successful rebellions against the king's government. The political chaos soon damaged the economy and caused trade to decline.

Middle Kingdom

Around 2050 B.C. a new dynasty of kings reunited Egypt and moved the capital south to Thebes, a city of Upper Egypt. These rulers began a new period of Egyptian history called the Middle Kingdom. The new kingdom lasted until 1800 B.C.

After a weak beginning, the Theban kings became as powerful as the Egyptian rulers of the Old Kingdom. They controlled local government and collected taxes. They built fortresses, irrigation canals, and reservoirs along the Nile River. They also dug an important canal between the Nile and the Red Sea. Instead of building pyramids, they carved out tombs for themselves in the cliffs of southern Egypt.

During the Middle Kingdom, Egyptian kings became strong enough to expand Egypt's borders. They moved south into Nubia (part of modern Sudan) and northeast into Syria. They also increased trade with surrounding countries. During the Middle Kingdom, Egyptian trading ships traveled along the coasts of the Arabian Peninsula and East Africa.

Around 1800 B.C. Egypt once again suffered from weak rulers and internal conflicts. At the same time, the country faced its first serious invasion. The Hyksos, a people from western Asia, swept into Egypt with new tools of war—bronze weapons and horse-drawn chariots. The Egyptians had always fought on foot with weapons made of copper and stone. As a result, they were quickly defeated by the Hyksos. A Hyksos leader took over the throne of Egypt and established a dynasty that ruled for over 150 years.

New Kingdom

Although the Hyksos adopted Egyptian culture, the Egyptians hated Hyksos rule and worked to gain their freedom. They learned to use the weapons and fighting style of the Hyksos. About 1600 B.C., Ahmose, an Egyptian prince, formed an army that drove out the Hyksos and regained control of the land. This Egyptian victory brought in a period known as the New Kingdom, which lasted from 1570 to 1090 B.C.

Empire Ahmose founded a new dynasty of kings that established a firm control over Egypt. These powerful rulers assumed the title **pharaoh,** an Egyptian word meaning "great house of the king." They concentrated on strengthening Egypt's army and fighting wars of conquest.

The first great warrior-pharaoh was Thutmose III, who ruled about 1500 B.C. Thutmose conquered Syria and expanded Egyptian control into Mesopotamia. During his reign, Egypt abandoned its centuries-old tradition of isolation and became an empire. For the next 500 years, Egypt was the dominant power on land and sea in the Middle East.

Under Thutmose's successor, Amenhotep III, the Egyptian Empire reached the height of its strength and splendor. It grew wealthy from both commerce and **tribute,** or taxes, from conquered territories. The pharaoh, priests, and nobles spent large sums of money on homes, tombs, and monuments. The capital of Thebes, with its palaces and temples, became the most magnificent city in the world.

The wars of conquest and the creation of an empire transformed Egypt and the regions that it ruled. Egyptian culture spread throughout the Middle East. In turn, Egypt absorbed new ideas and customs from the Fertile Crescent. This **cultural diffusion,** or exchange of ideas and customs among different regions, shook the stability of Egyptian society. It led to a great period of change in Egyptian history.

Akhenaton Around 1363 B.C. Amenhotep IV became pharaoh of Egypt. He wanted to create a new Egypt based on **monotheism,** or the worship of one god. Amenhotep declared that the one true god was Aton, the sun god. He claimed equality with the god and changed his royal name to Akhenaton, which means "spirit of Aton." To stress the break with the past, Akhenaton moved the capital from Thebes to a new city in central Egypt dedicated to Aton.

HISTORY AND PEOPLE

Tutenkhamon

In the middle of the 1300's B.C., Egypt was ruled by a pharaoh named Tutenkhamon. Tutenkhamon ruled for only nine years and died before he reached the age of 20. He is often referred to as the Boy-King or as King Tut.

Tutenkhamon married a daughter of Akhenaton and later succeeded Akhenaton to the throne of Egypt. However, he disagreed with his father-in-law's religious policies. Under the influence of the powerful priesthood, Tutenkhamon ended the worship of Aton and returned the country to the old religion of many gods. When Tutenkhamon died, the priests and nobles honored him with an elaborate burial.

Tutenkhamon's burial place was veiled in mystery and remained unknown for thousands of years. Then in 1922, Howard Carter, an English archeologist, accidentally discovered it while on a dig in the Valley of the Kings, the traditional burial site of Egyptian pharaohs. Carter later wrote about the suspense that he and his team had experienced:

> Slowly . . . the remains of passage debris that encumbered [blocked] the lower part of the doorway were removed, until at last we had the whole door clear before us. The decisive moment had arrived. With trembling hands I made a tiny breach in the upper left-hand corner. Darkness and blank space, as far as an iron testing-rod could reach, showed that whatever lay beyond was empty, and not filled like the passage we had just cleared. Candle tests were applied as a precaution against possible foul gases, and then, widening the hole a little, I inserted the candle and peered in . . . At first I could see nothing, . . . but presently, as my eyes grew accustomed to the light, details of the room within emerged slowly from the mist, strange animals, statues, and gold . . .*

Carter eventually uncovered four rooms filled with magnificent objects that had belonged to the Boy-King. These treasures included animal-shaped couches, clothing, statues, jewels, chairs, and a gold throne. All of them had been virtually untouched since ancient times.

In the final chamber, Carter found the mummy of "Tut" enclosed in three coffins. The innermost coffin was made of solid gold. The two other ones were made of gold hammered over wooden frames. On the king's head was a beautiful, golden portrait mask inlaid with enamel. Numerous pieces of jewelry, amulets, and charms lay upon the mummy and in its wrappings.

Tutenkhamon's burial chamber and its priceless objects gave scholars a better understanding of ancient Egyptian culture. They also had a sensational impact on the general public. Except for his tomb, Tutenkhamon has little claim to fame. But as a result of Carter's discovery, he is perhaps better known than any of the other ancient Egyptian rulers.

*The Tomb of Tut-ankh-Amen, Howard Carter and A. C. Mace, © 1923 by Cassell, Vol. 1, pp. 95-96.

Archeologists have uncovered the remains of Akhenaton's capital near the present-day town of Amarna.

The peace treaty between the Egyptians and the Hittites was the first of its kind in history. Terms provided for the marriage of Ramses II to the daughter of the Hittite king.

Akhenaton's policies had an unsettling effect on the country. The worship of Aton was not popular among the common people. Many of them still continued to believe in many gods. Also, the priests of the old religion were upset about their loss of power. They actively opposed Akhenaton. At the same time, Akhenaton showed little interest in government activities. As a result, Egypt lost some of its foreign territories and declined as a military power.

After Akhenaton's death, the priests restored the old religion. They had Akhenaton's successor, Tutenkhamon, return the capital to Thebes.

ANCIENT EGYPT

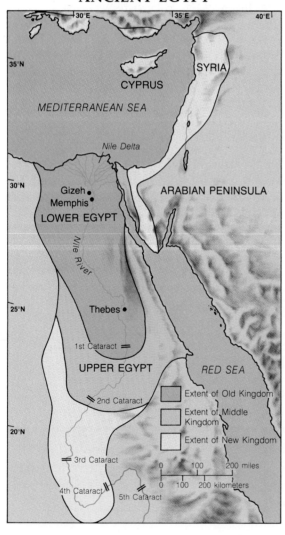

Soon the army, dissatisfied with Egypt's decline, overthrew the dynasty and created a new one.

Recovery and Decline   During the 1200's B.C., powerful pharaohs regained some of the territory and prestige that Egypt had lost. One of the most important of these rulers was Ramses II, who ruled for 67 years. Ramses was the last of the great pharaohs to hold absolute sway over the empire. He built many temples and erected large statues of himself throughout the country.

Ramses, however, led Egypt into a long and costly war with the Hittites, a people from Asia Minor. In this war, the Egyptians and Hittites fought for control of Syria. By 1278 B.C. the conflict had exhausted both powers, and they signed a peace treaty.

Following the war with the Hittites, Egypt began a long period of decline. Its empire was lost to invaders. At home, rival groups of nobles struggled for power. Eventually, the country was divided into two kingdoms. Beginning in 945 B.C., Egypt came under control of foreigners.

Egyptian Life

According to modern historians, about 8 million persons lived in ancient Egypt at its height. Most Egyptians resided in the Nile River Valley and the delta region. Their society was divided into different groups. In spite of these divisions, social barriers were not rigid. An ambitious person from the lowest group could rise to the highest offices in the land.

Social Groups   At the top of Egyptian society were royalty, nobles, and priests. These wealthy Egyptians controlled the country's religious and political affairs. They lived in the cities or on large estates along the Nile River. There, they built large homes of brick and wood, with magnificent gardens, pools, and orchards. Inside, the large rooms had colorful wall paintings and were filled with elaborate furniture, rugs, ebony chests, and objects of copper and gold. A wealthy household consisted of the family, its slaves, and the artisans who worked on the estate.

A middle group of artisans, scribes, and merchants carried out the business activities of Egypt. Most of them lived and worked in the cities. Their homes were comfortable, but not as elegant as those of the upper group. During the New Kingdom, this middle group benefited from the prosperity of the empire and grew in numbers. Some of its members became very wealthy and moved into the upper group.

The majority of Egyptians, however, were poor. They farmed the land and provided labor service to the king, priests, and nobles. Poor people lived in small villages on or near the large estates along the Nile. Their homes were small huts of mud bricks, covered with straw or palm leaves. These huts were built on high ground for protection from yearly floods. Each hut had only one or two rooms, which were simply furnished with a stool, some boxes, and a few pottery jars.

Women   Women enjoyed a favorable position in ancient Egypt. They had the right to own property and to pass it on to female, instead of male, relatives. For example, if a wife died before her husband, her possessions could go to her daughter rather than to the surviving husband.

Women from lower social groups worked long hours on their daily chores. Among other things, they prepared food, raised children, and tended animals. They had little leisure time. Wealthy women, however, enjoyed an active social life. They often accompanied their husbands to parties, hunts, and other festivities.

Within the royal family, women held an honored place. The right of succession to the throne passed through the female line. Since the king was considered divine, he had to marry someone of similar standing. Therefore, his choice of a queen was limited to a member of his own family, sometimes a sister. The queen was treated with a respect almost equal to that of the king.

Queen Hatshepsut ruled Egypt jointly with her stepson Thutmose III from 1504 to 1482 B.C. She, however, had an upper hand in the government and pursued a peaceful policy that strengthened Egypt's economy. During her reign, Egyptian traders sailed to East Africa and brought new wealth to Egypt. Hatshepsut also built many temples and palaces.

Another famous queen was Nefertiti, wife of the pharaoh Akhenaton. Nefertiti supported her husband's religious reforms. Due to her influence, the Egyptian royal family lived a more informal lifestyle and appeared freely in public.

Religion   Every aspect of Egyptian life was guided by religion. The Egyptians honored many gods, but each region worshiped a local god. Often, the gods were represented as part human and part animal. Later, rulers and priests promoted the worship of certain gods over all of Egypt. These gods included Re,[5] the sun god; Horus, the sky god; and Osiris, the harvest god.

Osiris became a very popular god among the poor people. He was responsible for the life, death, and rebirth of all living things. He and his wife, the goddess Isis, were honored as the rulers of the realm of the dead. Egyptians believed that Osiris determined a person's fate after death.

Egyptian religion stressed the importance of an afterlife. As a result, Egyptians devoted much of their time and wealth to assure survival in the next world. At first, they believed that only kings and rich people could enjoy eternal life. The bodies of these privileged people were embalmed and placed in elaborate tombs. In this way, their souls would survive and have a home in the realm of the dead. By the time of the New Kingdom, however, poorer people could also hope for eternal life through the help of Osiris.

Egyptians believed that the souls of the dead went on a long and dangerous voyage to the afterlife. To aid the dead on their journey, they placed written messages, prayers, and magic spells in coffins and carved them on the walls of tombs. A written message in one of the coffins advised the dead person to tell Osiris that "I gave bread to the hungry . . . I ferried him who had no boat . . . I never oppressed anyone . . . never did I take the property of any man by violence."

Writing   Ancient Egyptian writing was based on a system of picture symbols known as **hieroglyphics**. The Egyptians believed that these symbols came from the gods. But for everyday purposes, they used a cursive, or flowing, script known as **hieratic**. It simplified and connected the pictures. Egyptians wrote the hieratic script

---

[5]Re later was known as Amon-Re and became the chief god of the New Kingdom. His center of worship was at Thebes.

The Rosetta Stone was found by French soldiers during Napoleon's campaign in Egypt in 1799.

Ask students what they think of Ptahotep's advice, and if his remarks hold true today.

In early Egypt, peasant women worked along with their husbands in the fields, harvesting wheat and barley. How were the lives of wealthy women different from those of peasant women?

on a type of paper called **papyrus.** Papyrus was made from the papyrus reed that grew along the Nile River.

After the decline of ancient Egypt, the hieroglyphic system was forgotten. For nearly 2,000 years, it remained a mystery to the world's scholars. Then in 1799 A.D., French soldiers found the Rosetta Stone in Egypt. This slab of stone dated to the 200's B.C. On it were carved Greek and two forms of Egyptian writing. In 1822 A.D., Jean Francois Champollion, a French archeologist, discovered that the Greek was a translation of the Egyptian. In this way, he was able to **decipher,** or decode, the long-forgotten Egyptian language. As a result of Champollion's work, scholars were able to learn more about ancient Egypt's history.

Literature   Religion was often the subject of Egyptian literature. Scribes wrote many prayers and hymns in praise of the gods. Some of the oldest religious writings from the Old Kingdom were carved on the inside walls of the pyramids. Over 200 prayers and magic formulas were included in a series of texts called the Book of the Dead. Egyptians studied the Book of the Dead to learn how to reach a happy afterlife.

The ancient Egyptians also wrote **secular,** or non-religious, adventure stories, fairy tales, love stories, and poems. The following selection is a love song written by a young Egyptian:

> *Now I'll lie down inside*
> *and act as if I'm sick.*
> *My neighbors will come in to visit,*
> *and with them my girl.*

> *She'll put the doctors out,*
> *for she's the one to know my hurt.**

Collections of quotes and proverbs, or wise sayings, were popular among Egyptians. Many proverbs were written by kings and government officials. Ptahhotep, a vizier during the early Middle Kingdom, wrote the following advice:

> *. . . Do not repeat slander; you should not hear it, for it is the result of hot temper. Repeat a matter seen, not what is heard. . . .†*

Arts and Sciences   The Egyptians excelled in the arts. Their outstanding achievements were in architecture: the pyramids, temples, and other monuments. Paintings of gods, people, animals, and plants covered the walls of homes, palaces, and temples. Artists painted these images according to fixed rules. For example, the human figure always appeared in a serene, formal position. The head, waist, and legs were shown sideways and the chest faced the front.

The Egyptians also made contributions in the sciences and mathematics. They developed a number system that was used to calculate area and volume. They used geometry to survey flooded land and replace boundary markers. They also developed a calendar. It consisted of

*A love poem from *The Literature of Ancient Egypt: An Anthology of Stories, Instructions, and Poetry,* ed. William Kelly, © 1972 by Yale University Press, p. 300. Reprinted by permission.

†Maxims of Ptahhotep from *Ibid.,* p. 168. Reprinted by permission.

Note that Syria's location, which gave it a commercial advantage, also exposed it to invasions.

Some archeologists believe that Ebla was as powerful as Egypt or Mesopotamia in the Middle East.

365¼ days and was divided into three seasons: flood, seedtime, and harvest.

Egyptian doctors made important contributions to medicine. Through the practice of embalming, they learned about the anatomy of the human body. They also were the first to use splints, bandages, and compresses. On papyrus scrolls, they recorded directions for the treatment of wounds, fractures, and diseases. As dentists, eye doctors, veterinarians, and surgeons, Egyptians were the world's first medical specialists. Their contributions advanced the knowledge of medicine in the ancient Middle East.

1. Identify: Narmer (Menes), Thebes, Hyksos, Ahmose, Thutmose III, Akhenaton, Ramses II, Hatshepsut, Nefertiti, Rosetta Stone, Ptahhotep.
2. What are the three periods of ancient Egypt?
3. What powers did Egyptian kings have?
4. What was the nature of Egyptian religion?

3 Age of Kingdoms

While Egyptian civilization flourished, civilizations arose in the regions between Egypt and Mesopotamia. One of these regions was called Syria and formed the western half of the Fertile Crescent. Its geography included fertile river valleys, mountains, rolling plains, and a desert. By 3000 B.C. kingdoms developed in Syria along the major trade routes that linked Egypt and the Fertile Crescent.

Ebla

During the 2000's B.C., the kingdom of Ebla controlled northern Syria. It was unknown to scholars until the twentieth century. In the late 1960's and early 1970's archeologists unearthed the remains of the city of Ebla. They discovered a palace and 15,000 clay tablets that contained information about Ebla's law, government, and religion. The archeological work at Ebla has convinced scholars that highly developed civilizations prospered in Syria earlier than previously believed.

Society   The people of Ebla were called Eblaites. They spoke a Semitic language but wrote in Sumerian cuneiform. The Eblaites earned their living by making metal and wool products, textiles, and pottery. Most Eblaites were urban dwellers. Their city was surrounded by walls with four gates. Temples and the king's palace stood in the center. Inside the palace were a large archives and an audience court. The palace did not have walls. This may indicate that a close relationship existed between the king and the people.

The kings of Ebla were chosen by the people. They served seven-year terms and were responsible for political and military affairs. In addition, kings had to look after the welfare of the poor, widows, and orphans. If the kings failed their duties, they could be removed from office by a council of elders.

Kings employed about 11,000 government officials. Most of these officials were scribes. They recorded royal decrees, wrote peace treaties and trade agreements, and collected prayers and hymns to the gods.

Trading Center   Between 2400 and 2300 B.C., Ebla was a wealthy and powerful city-state. Its prosperity was based on the overland trade that passed between Egypt and Mesopotamia. Ebla grew so powerful that it controlled a number of neighboring towns. These towns paid tribute to Ebla in grain and livestock. At their height, Ebla and the nearby towns had 260,000 persons.

After 2300 B.C. Ebla began to decline. About that time, it unsuccessfully fought a war against Sargon I of Akkad for control of the Euphrates River trade. Sargon captured the city, destroyed it, and burned the royal archives. Ebla, however, recovered and enjoyed a brief period of prosperity. Around 2000 B.C. it was destroyed by the Amorites, who rebuilt the city. After 1800 B.C., Ebla declined once again. Within two hundred years, it disappeared.

Arameans

Around 1200 B.C. a Semitic people known as the Arameans settled in central Syria. They were ruled by kings, who established a capital at Damascus. The authority of Aramean kings was weak, while the provinces continued to retain much power. Consequently, the country was soon divided into a loose grouping of small states. Weakened by internal feuding, the Arameans were easily overrun by powerful invaders from Mesopotamia.

In spite of their political and military weaknesses, the Arameans gained control of the overland trade between Egypt and Mesopotamia. Aramean merchants were known for their trading skills and traveled thoughout the Middle East. They brought with them the Aramaic language, which soon became the international language of the Middle East. Until the 800's A.D., most of the people of the region spoke Aramaic. Some parts of the Bible were also written in the language.

Hittites

North of Syria is Asia Minor, a large, mountainous peninsula between the Black Sea and the Mediterranean Sea. Today it is part of the nation of Turkey. In the center of Asia Minor is a large plateau called Anatolia. There, small city-states developed as early as 2000 B.C. These city-states traded with Mesopotamia, exchanging such metals as copper, silver, and gold for cloth and tin. In the process, they borrowed writing and other cultural practices from the Mesopotamians and developed a civilization.

Empire   Around 1700 B.C. a people called the Hittites established the first well-organized territory in Asia Minor. Until the early 1900's, scholars knew very little about the Hittites. Then archeologists discovered the ruins of Hattusas, the Hittite capital. They uncovered several thousand clay tablets that made up the archives of the Hittite rulers. Soon scholars were able to decipher the language and study the history of the Hittites.

The Hittites were ruled by kings. At first, Hittite kings shared their power with a council of nobles. Later, the kings became absolute rulers. However, they were never considered gods as in Egypt. Hittite kings developed a powerful army, which was the first in the Middle East to use iron weapons. Hittite soldiers went into battle in three-person chariots and easily overcame their enemies. By 1200 B.C. the Hittites had established an empire that covered all of Asia Minor, Syria, and part of Mesopotamia. After 1000 B.C. the

Hittite empire slowly fell apart. It was weakened as a result of wars with Egypt and other neighboring countries. In place of the Hittites, several small states flourished in Anatolia until the 800's B.C.

Law   Hittite culture was largely borrowed from Mesopotamia and Egypt. However, the Hittites made their own important contribution to Middle Eastern civilization. They developed a legal system that was considered less harsh than Hammurabi's code. Hittite law emphasized payments for damages rather than "an eye for an eye, and a tooth for a tooth."

Phoenicians

Between ancient Egypt and Syria was the land of Canaan. Today Canaan is made up of the countries of Lebanon, Israel, and Jordan. Because of its location, Canaan was often invaded by neighboring peoples.

About 3000 B.C. Semitic groups migrated from the Arabian Peninsula into Canaan. Known as Canaanites, they lived there along with the Philistines, a people from the eastern Mediterranean. The Canaanites who settled in the northern part of Canaan were called the Phoenicians. Their land, known as Phoenicia, consisted of a narrow strip of fertile land between the mountains of western Syria and the Mediterranean Sea. Because of the lack of space for farming, many Phoenicians turned to the sea to earn a living. They used timber from the cedar forests on nearby mountains to build strong, fast ships. Soon, they became skilled sailors, fishing and trading along the Phoenician coastline.

City-States   By 1200 B.C. the Phoenicians had built cities and towns along the coast. Many of them became independent city-states. The principal ones were Tyre, Byblos, and Sidon. In spite of a common language and religion, the Phoenicians remained divided into city-states throughout their history. In order to maintain their freedom, the Phoenician city-states signed peace treaties with their large, powerful neighbors.

Trade   From these coastal cities, Phoenicians sailed throughout the Mediterranean. They learned to plot their voyages by the sun and the stars. Some experts believe that Phoenician ships

The name "Phoenician" means "the purple people." It is a Greek word that refers to an expensive purple dye made in Canaan.

Two letters in the Phoenician language, "alef" and "beth," form the word "alphabet."

MIDDLE EAST 1350 B.C.

actually sailed around the west coast of Africa to India. They may even have sailed across the Atlantic to the Americas 2,000 years before Columbus.

Using their navigational skills, the Phoenicians became astute traders and business people. They soon controlled the shipping and trade of the Mediterranean world. At ports of call, they exchanged cedar logs, textiles, pottery, and perfume for gold and other precious metals. They also brought the business practices of the Middle East to developing areas in other parts of the Mediterranean region. For example, they passed on the Babylonian system of weights and measures. They also spread the use of such business methods as bills of sale and contracts.

Alphabet   The most important contribution of the Phoenicians was the idea of an **alphabet,** a series of symbols that represent sounds. The alphabet proved to be the best system of writing for keeping records.

The Phoenicians obtained their basic alphabet from southern Canaan. It consisted of 22 consonant symbols. They developed this alphabet and later carried it to Europe. The Greeks borrowed the Phoenician alphabet and made changes, including the addition of vowel symbols. The Romans finally obtained it in this form from the Greeks. Most western alphabets, including English, are based on the Roman alphabet.

Colonies   The Phoenicians never developed an empire. However, their sailors and traders set up temporary trading posts and established **colonies,** or permanent settlements, along the coasts of the Mediterranean. The most famous of the colonies was Carthage, founded in 814 B.C. in what is now Tunisia. About 200 years later,

Carthage became a great trading city. Merchants traded with lands as far away as Britain.

Note that the land of Canaan was later known as Palestine and then Israel.

Ancient and Modern Alphabet				
Phoenician Letter	Greek Letter	Greek Name	Hebrew Name	English Letter
∀	∧	Alpha	Aleph	A
9	⅃	Beta	Beth	B
△	△	Delta	Daleth	D
⇛	⇛	Epsilon	He	E
⊞	⊟	Eta	Heth	H
ㅋ	Ӿ	Kappa	Kaph	C–K
ㄴ	Ψ	Lamoda	Lamedh	L
ฯ	M	Mu	Mem	M
५	५	Nu	Nun	N
า	า	Pi	Pe	P
የ	የ	Rho	Resh	R
ო	Ƨ	Xsi	Shin	S
ฯ	4	Tau	Tau	T

Carthage developed its own civilization. It had a population of nearly 750,000 and was the most prosperous and powerful city in the western Mediterranean.

While Carthage was growing, the Phoenician homeland grew weak. During the 700's B.C., the city-states were conquered by a warrior people from Mesopotamia called the Assyrians.

Hebrews

Another Semitic group in Canaan was the Hebrews. Like the Phoenicians, the Hebrews were not known for their military or political achievements. Instead, they gave to the world a religious idea known as **ethical monotheism.** In its final form, the Hebrew religion taught the worship of one god, who was both good and all-powerful. It stressed that its god expected people to deal justly with each other and to accept moral responsibility for their actions.

The religious experience of the Hebrews made them aware of their history. They saw it as a purposeful movement of events from a beginning to an end. The Hebrews were the first people to record and interpret their history in a collection of books. These writings are recorded in the Old Testament of the Bible.

The Hebrew religion still exists today and is known as Judaism. Many of the religious teachings of Judaism have been passed on to other religions. From Judaism have come the two largest monotheistic religions of the modern world: Christianity and Islam.

Abraham   The Hebrews traced their origins to Abraham, a wealthy herder and trader, who lived in the Mesopotamian city of Ur around 1900 B.C. According to the Bible, Abraham and his household left Ur and settled in Canaan at the command of the god Yahweh. The Hebrews believed that Yahweh had made a **covenant,** or agreement, with Abraham. This covenant stated that Abraham and his descendants were to worship and obey Yahweh as their only god. In return, Yahweh promised that Canaan would belong to them forever.

Moses   While in Canaan, the Hebrews divided into **tribes,** or groups having a common language and culture, and farmed the land. A drought later forced them to move to Egypt. A few generations later, the Hebrews became slaves under the Egyptians. A Hebrew leader, Moses, rallied his people and, in the name of Yahweh, led them out of Egypt. The Egyptian pharaoh failed to recapture them. The Hebrews believed Yahweh had helped them in their **exodus,** or escape.[6] To commemorate the event, they began an annual festival called Passover.

The Hebrews fled Egypt into the deserts of the Sinai Peninsula. According to the Bible, Yahweh and Moses made a covenant during the desert journey. In this covenant, the Hebrews pledged to reject other gods and to follow only Yahweh. They also began to observe certain laws, the most

[6]Some historians believe that the exodus occurred during the reign of the pharaoh Ramses II during the 1200's B.C.

Hebrew writers called Canaan "a land flowing with milk and honey." Much of Canaan, however, had a dry climate and little water. The Hebrews had many problems farming the land.

Have students compare and contrast the Code of Hammurabi and the Law of the Hebrews.

important of which became known as the Ten Commandments. The Ten Commandments forbade the making and worship of idols, since Yahweh was invisible in form. They also linked the worship of Yahweh to good moral behavior. In return for their loyalty, Yahweh promised to protect the Hebrews and lead them back to Canaan.

Land   After the death of Moses, the Hebrews entered Canaan and gradually regained the land. Once they had settled there, the tribes chose leaders called judges. The judges settled dis-

putes and led troops into battle. They helped the Hebrews fight the Canaanites, the Philistines, and other peoples of the area.

The Hebrews, however, wanted stronger leadership to unite them against their enemies. They finally replaced the system of judges with a monarchy. In 1015 B.C. the farmer-warrior Saul became the first Hebrew king. After a brief period of popularity, Saul lost support. The people then turned to Saul's rival, David, and made him king. David set up a capital at Jerusalem and formed a central government.

The Code of Hammurabi	Law of the Hebrews
1. A son who strikes his father will have his hands cut off.	1. He who strikes his mother or father will be put to death.
2. If a man strikes and wounds another, then he will pay the physician. But, if the man puts out the eye of another, his own eye will be put out; and if he breaks another's bones, his bones will be broken.	2. If men fight, but no lasting harm is done, they will pay as the judge determines. But, if there is lasting harm, then the punishment will be a life for a life, an eye for an eye, a tooth for a tooth, a hand for a hand, and a foot for a foot.
	3. If an ox gores anyone to death, then the ox will be stoned, and the owner will be acquitted. But, if it is known that the ox has gored before and the owner has not kept it confined, then the owner will be put to death.
	4. If a man lets loose an animal and it feeds in another man's field, the animal's owner will make restitution from the best of his own field.
3. If a man's ox is a gorer and he knows of it and has not blunted the ox's horns, or shut it up, and the ox kills anyone, the man will pay in silver.	5. If a man hires an animal and it is injured or dies, he will replace it. If the animal is stolen from him, he will replace it. But, if it is torn to pieces by a wild beast, then the animal will not be replaced.
4. If a shepherd lets the sheep into a field to graze without permission, then the shepherd will pay to the owner of the field, twenty bushels of wheat for every ten yards grazed.	6. If a thief is found trying to steal and he is killed, there will be no guilt for his death.
5. If anyone hires an ox and a lion kills it, the loss is on the owner. But, if the ox is killed by bad treatment, the one who hired it will replace it with another.	
6. A thief will be put to death and he that has received the stolen property will also be put to death.	
7. If a witness testifies falsely, he will receive the penalty of the crime of the accused.	7. If a witness testifies falsely, he will be sentenced for the crime he testified against.
8. If anyone is too lazy to keep his dam in good condition and it breaks so fields are flooded, he will be sold into slavery, and the price will pay for the damage caused.	8. A merchant will not have different weights, a heavy and a light; or different measures, a large and a small. He will give perfect and just weights and measures.

A fine musician, David wrote many of the psalms found in the Bible.

During David's reign, the Hebrew kingdom enlarged its borders and enjoyed a period of economic prosperity.

David's son and successor, Solomon, brought peace, security, and cultural growth to the internal development of the country. Solomon founded new cities and rebuilt old ones. He also spent money on building projects. His most memorable achievement was the construction of a huge temple to Yahweh in Jerusalem.

High taxes and forced labor, however, caused unrest among the people. Opposition to the king was especially strong among citizens in the northern half of the kingdom. After Solomon's death, the Hebrews in the north revolted and set up their own separate kingdom called Israel. Those in the south formed the kingdom of Judah, with the capital at Jerusalem. For the next two hundred years, the two kingdoms fought each other. At the same time, they faced threats from Assyrians, who wanted to add the Hebrews' lands to their empire.

Exile and Return During this difficult period, **prophets,** or religious reformers, claiming to be Yahweh's messengers, arose and began to preach to the people. They condemned abuses in Hebrew society and reminded the Hebrews of their duties to Yahweh and to one another. They warned that Yahweh would punish them if they did not obey his laws.

Meanwhile, the Hebrews headed toward a political downfall. Powerful neighbors soon took over both Hebrew kingdoms. In 722 B.C. the Assyrians of Mesopotamia conquered the kingdom of Israel. The people of Israel were scattered among other peoples and gradually disappeared as a separate group. In 586 B.C., the Chaldeans, another Mesopotamian people, took over the kingdom of Judah. After a Hebrew revolt, the Chaldeans destroyed the temple of Jerusalem. They made captives of the city's inhabitants and carried them to Babylon, their capital city.

The Hebrews' loss of their land and temple promoted the growth of their religion. While in Babylon, the people of Judah, now known as Jews, had no place to worship. They soon came to believe that Yahweh was the god of the universe, who resided in the heart and conscience, not in a building or place. Groups of Jews began to meet on the **sabbath,** the holy day of rest, for prayer and discussion. From these gatherings came the rise of the **synagogue,** or a local community of Jews who meet to study and practice their religion.

Many Jews, however, continued to hope for their return to Jerusalem. Finally, in 538 B.C. the Persians conquered Babylon and granted freedom to the Jews. Some Jews returned to their homeland and rebuilt Jerusalem and the temple. There, they created a close-knit community based on a stricter observance of their laws. These laws were recorded in five books called the

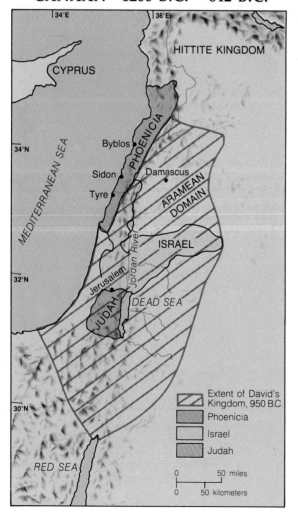

CANAAN 1200 B.C. – 842 B.C.

34°E

36°E

HITTITE KINGDOM

CYPRUS

MEDITERRANEAN SEA

34°N

Byblos

PHOENICIA

Sidon

Damascus

Tyre

ARAMEAN DOMAIN

Jordan River

ISRAEL

32°N

Jerusalem

DEAD SEA

JUDAH

30°N

RED SEA

Extent of David's Kingdom, 950 B.C.

Phoenicia

Israel

Judah

0   50 miles

0   50 kilometers

Torah, or "the law." Other writings—history, songs, proverbs, and messages of the prophets —were added later to the Old Testament.

While a Jewish community flourished in Jerusalem, the majority of Jews remained in Babylon or moved to other areas of the Middle East. These communities of Jews living outside of their homeland were known as the *Diaspora*, a Greek word meaning "scattered." However, they still looked to Jerusalem as the center of their religion.

1. Identify: Ebla, Arameans, Damascus, Aramaic, Asia Minor, Anatolia, Hittites, Hattusus, Canaan, Phoenicians, Tyre, Carthage, Hebrews, Judaism, Yahweh, Abraham, Moses, Saul, David, Torah, Diaspora.
2. How did the Hittites acquire their empire?
3. How did Phoenician trade affect the growth of civilization?
4. What was the major contribution of the Hebrews to later civilizations?

4   Age of Empires

After the 700's B.C., a series of large empires again developed in the Middle East. These empires were created by the Assyrians, Chaldeans, and Persians. The Assyrians and Chaldeans based their empires in Mesopotamia. The center of the Persian Empire was Persia, a mountainous area between Mesopotamia and India. For the next 400 years, the empires improved techniques of warfare, developed government administrations, and promoted trade throughout the region. They created favorable conditions for the exchange of ideas and practices among different peoples.

Assyrians

The first of the new empires was created by the Assyrians. The Assyrians were a Semitic people who lived in the hilly country of northern Mesopotamia. There they faced constant invasions from Asia Minor. About 900 B.C. the Assyrians halted these northern invasions and began to conquer their Mesopotamian neighbors. By about 750 B.C., they had established an empire over all of Mesopotamia. Then, they moved westward and conquered Syria, the

The Ishtar Gate was the most impressive of eight gateways to Babylon, the world's largest city during the 500's B.C. The word "Babylon" means "gate of God." What factors led to the decline of the Chaldean Empire?

Phoenician cities, the kingdom of Israel, and Egypt.

Army   Assyria's rise to power was due to its strong army. After 900 B.C., the Assyrian army was the most efficient and powerful military force in the Middle East. It was made up of long-service professional soldiers. These soldiers were formed into well-organized units of charioteers, cavalry, and infantry. They were also well equipped with iron weapons and chariots. Written records of the time described them as warriors "whose arrows were sharp and all their bows bent, the horses' hooves were like flint, and their [chariot] wheels like a whirlwind." Assyrian military engineers also developed new techniques of warfare. They tunneled under enemy cities and used battering rams against their walls.

The map below is the subject of the "Using Maps" section of the Chapter 1 Review.

Ashurbanipal, an Assyrian monarch, established one of the world's first libraries in Nineveh. It contained about 22,000 tablets of hymns, stories, and biographies.

EMPIRES OF THE MIDDLE EAST

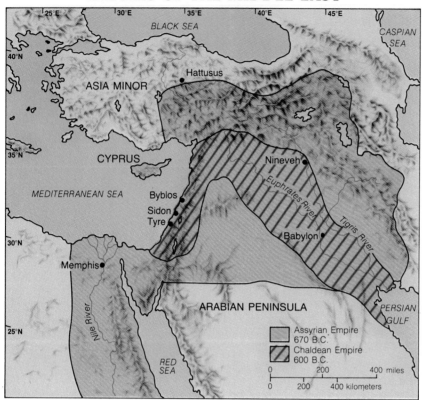

The Assyrians treated their conquered peoples cruelly. They burned cities and tortured and killed thousands of captives. Whole peoples were deported, or removed from their homelands, and sent to new areas. The land was then resettled with people from other parts of the empire. These settlers were forced to pay heavy taxes. If they refused, they were punished.

Empire   To control their empire, Assyrian kings developed a well-organized government. They divided the empire into provinces. Each province was headed by a governor directly responsible to the king. Government officials collected taxes from the conquered people and made certain that the king's laws were obeyed. Most of the taxes were used to strengthen the army and support building projects in Nineveh, the Assyrian capital.

The Assyrians borrowed much of their architecture, art, literature, and religion from the Babylonians. They, however, excelled in monumental wall sculpture. Palace walls were decorated with carved stone slabs showing scenes of war, hunting, and religious ceremonies.

The Assyrian Empire led to increased trade and the growth of wealth in the Middle East. To improve transportation and communication, a system of roads connecting the provinces was built. Government messengers and Aramean merchants made the most use of the roads. Soldiers were stationed at points along the roads to protect these travelers from bandits.

By the 600's B.C., the Assyrians were having difficulty holding their large empire together. Cruel treatment of the conquered peoples and heavy taxes led to rebellions. Disputes with neighboring countries also weakened the empire. In 612 B.C., the Chaldeans, who lived in the ancient city of Babylon, formed an alliance with the Medes and Persians against the Assyrians. This alliance captured Nineveh and brought down the Assyrian Empire.

During the reign of Nebuchadnezzar, the temple at Jerusalem was destroyed and the Kingdom of Judah fell.

Lydia was the first country to mint metal coins. Persia later began the practice.

Chaldeans

The Chaldeans succeeded the Assyrians as the dominant empire in the Fertile Crescent. Sometimes called the New Babylonians, the majority of the Chaldeans were descendants of the people who had made up Hammurabi's empire during the 1700's B.C. The ruling group, however, was Aramean in origin.

One of the greatest Chaldean rulers was King Nebuchadnezzar. During his reign (604-561 B.C.), the Chaldeans reached the height of their power. They extended their boundaries as far west as Syria and Canaan. They also acquired great wealth and rebuilt Babylon as one of the largest and most beautiful cities in the ancient world.

The Chaldeans were especially noted for their interest in astrology. They believed that changes in the heavens revealed the plans of the gods and goddesses. The Chaldeans recorded their observations of the stars and made maps that showed the positions of the planets and the phases of the moon. Their studies laid the foundation for the science of astronomy. These early astronomers measured the length of a year to within 26 minutes of the correct time. They also developed a calendar based on a seven-day week.

In spite of its splendor, the Chaldean Empire was short-lived. After Nebuchadnezzar's death, a series of weak kings held the throne. At the same time, poor harvests and slow trade sapped the empire's strength. Then, in 539 B.C., the Persians, who lived in the mountains to the northeast, captured Babylon. They brought all of the Chaldean territory into the new Persian empire.

Persians

The Persians originated in central Asia as part of a larger group of people known as Aryans, or Indo-Europeans. During their early history, the Persians were primarily cattle herders and warriors in constant search of new grasslands. About 2000 B.C., they and the Medes, another Indo-European group, moved south and conquered the Elamites, a people who lived on a plateau between the Persian Gulf and the Caspian Sea. The two groups intermarried with the Elamites and made the region their permanent home.[7] At first, the Medes were the more powerful group and ruled the Persians. But in the 500's B.C., Cyrus, a Persian warrior, became King Cyrus II and conquered the Medes.

Conquests Cyrus II organized a powerful army and began to expand into neighboring lands. During the 540's B.C., he took over the kingdom of Lydia and the Greek city-states of Asia Minor. As a result of his conquest of the Chaldeans in 539 B.C., he added Mesopotamia, Syria, Palestine, and the Phoenician cities to his empire. Finally, in 525 B.C., Cyrus's son conquered Egypt. This last conquest brought all of the Middle East under Persian rule.

At that time, the Persian Empire was the largest empire the world had known. It stretched from the Nile River to the Indus River, a distance of 3,000 miles (4,800 kilometers) and an area of about 2 million square miles (5.2 million square kilometers). The empire had a population of more than 50 million.

Empire Darius I (521-486 B.C.) was the great organizer among the Persian kings. After the period of conquests, he set up the administration of the Persian Empire. Darius divided the empire into provinces called **satrapies.** Each was assigned a governor known as a **satrap.** In carrying out the king's decrees, the satrap was assisted by local military officials and tax inspectors appointed by the king. Special inspectors called the "Eyes and Ears of the King" made unannounced tours of the satrapies and reported directly to the king on the activities of officials. In this way, the king's court was able to keep close watch on local government.

In contrast to the Assyrians, the Persians were tolerant rulers who allowed each of the conquered peoples to keep their own language, religion, and laws. They believed that loyalty could be won more easily with fairness than with fear or force. When faced with rebellion, however, the Persians did not hesitate to take extreme military measures.

The Persians themselves did not engage in trade, which they considered an indecent occupation. But they did encourage it among the

---

[7]This area came to be known as Persia. Today, it is called Iran, meaning "land of the Aryans."

HISTORY AND CITIES

Babylon

For nearly 2,000 years, Babylon was one of the ancient world's most important cities. Under Nebuchadnezzar, in the 500's B.C., Babylon became a wealthy city of 500,000 persons. It was the capital of the Chaldean Empire and an important commercial hub in the Middle East.

Babylon was located on the plain of southern Mesopotamia. The Euphrates River flowed through the city, dividing it into two sections. Originally in the form of a square, Babylon was enclosed by two huge brick walls. The outer wall, 13 miles (21 kilometers) long, was so thick that a four-horse chariot could drive on top of it. People entered or left the city through several gates. The most famous of these gates was dedicated to the goddess, Ishtar. Its front was made of glazed baked brick with colorful wall tiles.

In the center of the city stood magnificent palaces and temples linked by wide avenues. The most prominent building was a large ziggurat that reached more than 300 feet (90 meters), the height of a modern 35-story skyscraper. It gleamed with a gold roof and brightly colored enameled walls. Some scholars today believe that the ziggurat was the Tower of Babel mentioned in the Bible.

South of the ziggurat was the temple of the god Marduk. Every spring, thousands of pilgrims gathered near the temple to watch a gold statue of Marduk being wheeled along the Processional Way, a special street paved with limestone and marble.

Also in the center of Babylon was the palace of Nebuchadnezzar. The palace walls were adorned with glazed tiles and reliefs, or raised sculptures, of wild animals. A short distance from the palace were the famous "Hanging Gardens," later described as one of the Seven Wonders of the Ancient World. The "Hanging Gardens" were actually a series of terraces planted with trees, flowers, and shrubs that seemed to hang in midair. Slaves were employed to care for the gardens. They helped pump water to the terraces from the Euphrates River. Nebuchadnezzar is said to have built the "Hanging Gardens" for his Median wife, who missed the lush greenery of her native land.

Outside the center of the city were the residential areas. There, streets were narrow and the houses were crowded together. At nearby shops, craftspeople made pottery, cloth, and baskets. These items were taken to city markets. They were put on sale for local customers and for traveling merchants from as far away as India and Egypt. At the markets, coins were not used as a medium of exchange. Instead, trading was carried on through barter, or the exchange of one commodity for another. Pieces of silver or gold were also used for trade. Business was even carried out in the temples. There, the priests, who received gifts of money from kings and nobles, granted loans to poor people.

After Nebuchadnezzar's death, Babylon was weakened by political disputes. In 539 B.C. the Persians captured the city. Later, when the Babylonians revolted, the Persians destroyed much of Babylon. By 200 A.D. Babylon was totally neglected. Crumbled ruins and mounds are all that remain of the once proud city.

1. What were some of the features of Nebuchadnezzar's Babylon?
2. How did Babylonians of the 500's B.C. carry out their business affairs?

Zoroaster is also known as Zarathustra. Today, there are about 500,000 followers of Zoroaster's teaching living in India. They are called "Parsis."

PERSIAN EMPIRE

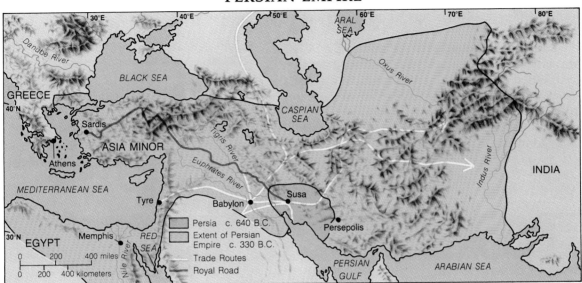

peoples of their empire. Persian engineers improved and expanded the great network of roads begun by the Assyrians. These roads aided travel, commerce, and the movement of soldiers. Royal messengers journeyed on the roads, allowing "neither snow, nor rain, nor heat, nor the darkness of night to hinder them in the prompt completion of their . . . tasks."

The most important thoroughfare was the Royal Road. It ran more than 1,500 miles (2,400 kilometers) from Susa in Persia to Sardis in Asia Minor. Along the Royal Road, stations were built every 14 miles (22.4 kilometers) to provide travelers with food, water, and horses. A journey that took three months before the Royal Road was built took only seven days after it was built.

Religion and Culture   The Persians followed a strict moral code that stressed bravery and honesty. They taught their sons "to ride horses, to draw a bow, and to speak the truth." Before the 500's B.C., the Persians worshiped many gods associated with the sky, sun, and fire. Then about 570 B.C., Zoroaster, a religious leader, called for the reform of the old Persian religion. He taught that the world was divided by a struggle between good and evil. The forces of good, Zoroaster declared, were led by the god

Ahura-Mazda. The forces of evil were directed by another god named Ahriman. At the end of time, Ahura-Mazda would eventually triumph over Ahriman.

Zoroaster also taught that humans were caught up in this struggle and had to choose between good and evil. Those who chose good and followed Ahura-Mazda would be rewarded with eternal life in paradise, or heaven. Those who followed evil and Ahriman would be condemned to eternal darkness and misery.[8]

Persian rulers believed that they ruled by the divine power of Ahura-Mazda and were responsible to him alone. Darius I had the following statement carved on the Behistun cliff:

> On this account Ahura-Mazda brought me health . . .
> Because I was not wicked, nor was I a liar, nor was I a tyrant, neither I nor any of my line.
> We had ruled according to righteousness.*

---

[8]Some scholars believe that Judaism, Christianity, and Islam may have been influenced by Zoroaster's teachings about paradise, hell, and the Last Judgment, or the separation of good and evil at the end of time.

*Behistun inscription modified from *Histories* by Herodotus, tr. H. J. Rawlinson, © 1935 by Nonesuch Press, p. 737. Reprinted by permission.

One of the oldest in the world, the Persian monarchy lasted nearly 3,000 years. It was overthrown in a revolution in 1979 A.D.

Because the monarchy was viewed as a sacred institution, Persian kings commanded great respect and were always surrounded by formal ceremony.

Under Persian kings, the cultures of Egypt, Mesopotamia, Syria, and Persia blended and contributed to each other. The Persians themselves learned much in the areas of art, architecture, and literature from their conquered peoples. Darius I brought craftspeople from many lands to build Persepolis, the most magnificent city in the Persian Empire. After building a strong civilization in the Middle East, the Persians were ready to extend their influence into Europe.

1. Identify: Persia, Assyrians, Nineveh, Medes, Chaldeans, Nebuchadnezzar, Aryans, Persians, Cyrus II, Darius I, "Eyes and Ears of the King," Royal Road, Zoroaster, Ahura-Mazda, Ahriman, Persepolis.
2. How did the Assyrians treat their conquered peoples?
3. Why did Chaldeans study the heavens?
4. How did Darius I organize the Persian Empire?

CHAPTER 1 REVIEW

Summary

1. Around 4000 B.C. early civilizations developed in the Middle East. They appeared in the Tigris-Euphrates River Valley of Mesopotamia and the Nile River Valley of Egypt.
2. Between 3500 and 1600 B.C., city-states and empires rose and fell in Mesopotamia. In spite of disunity and war, Mesopotamian contributions in writing, mathematics, trade, and government spread and became the basis of civilization in the Fertile Crescent.
3. About 3000 B.C. Egypt became one nation. Under powerful kings, the Egyptians developed a relatively stable civilization that lasted for nearly 3,000 years.
4. Egyptian civilization reached its height during the 1400's B.C. At this time, wars of conquest led to the rise of an empire. The spread of new ideas and customs within the empire transformed Egyptian society.
5. From 3000 to 750 B.C., civilizations also developed in Asia Minor and Syria. The Hittites of Asia Minor built a powerful army and acquired an empire. In Syria, the Eblaites, and later the Arameans, profited from trade between Egypt and Mesopotamia.
6. The Phoenicians along the coast of Syria engaged in trade and spread new ideas, such as the alphabet, throughout the Mediterranean world.
7. The Hebrews survived exiles and the destruction of their kingdoms. Their major contributions were the belief in one god and the Ten Commandments.
8. From 800 B.C. to 300 B.C., the Assyrians, Chaldeans, and Persians built powerful empires that united most of the Middle East. They expanded trade and developed new methods of war and government.

Building Vocabulary

empires	hereditary	eddubas	shadoof
ziggurat	theocracies	scribes	bureaucracy
archives	patesi	cuneiform	bureaucrats
monarchy	dynasty	delta	vizier

nomes	monotheism	alphabet	prophets
embalming	hieroglyphics	colonies	sabbath
mummy	hieratic	ethical monotheism	synagogue
pharaoh	papyrus	covenant	satrapies
tribute	decipher	tribes	satrap
cultural diffusion	secular	exodus	

Reviewing the Main Ideas

1. How was Sumer governed? What caused its decline?
2. How did the physical environment of Egypt affect the development of its civilization?
3. How did the Hyksos influence Egypt?
4. How was Egypt changed during the New Kingdom?
5. How did Egyptians try to assure their survival in the afterlife?
6. How was Ebla governed?
7. Why was Phoenician trade important in the Mediterranean area?
8. How did the Hebrews regard their history?
9. How did the Persians and the Assyrians treat their conquered peoples?
10. What change occurred in Persian religion?
11. What were some of the technological accomplishments of the ancient Middle East?
12. What social position did women hold in the ancient Middle East?

Discussing Important Ideas

1. A well-known historian once stated that "the invention of writing and of a convenient system of records on paper has had a greater influence in uplifting the human race than any other achievement." Do you agree or disagree with this statement? Explain.
2. How did trade influence the growth of civilization in the Middle East? What role does trade play in the modern world?
3. The Middle East is often called "the cradle of civilization." Explain.
4. Why were religious rituals and ceremonies important in the ancient Middle East?
5. Compare and contrast life in the Nile Valley with life in the Tigris-Euphrates Valley. In which place was life easier? Explain.
6. How did Hammurabi's code differ from earlier Sumerian laws? If you had lived in ancient Mesopotamia, which legal system would you have preferred?
7. Do you think that Akhenaton's monotheistic religion was an improvement over the old Egyptian religion? Why or why not?
8. What kinds of literature were produced in the ancient Middle East? Can these writings have meaning for us today? Explain.

Using Maps

Refer to the map on page 26 to answer the following questions:

1. What island is south of Asia Minor?
2. Which city is located on the Nile River?
3. What ports lie between 32°E longitude and 35°E longitude?
4. How far is it from Memphis to Babylon in miles? in kilometers?
5. What large body of water lies northeast of Nineveh?
6. What river valley was the heartland of the Chaldean Empire?

CHAPTER 2

Chinese Rice Field

❝ *Discipline of speech means speaking the truth.* ❞
from the Bhagavad Gita, *a Hindu text*

Early South and East Asia

Have students locate on a map the major rivers and mountain ranges of South and East Asia. Discuss how geographical features have affected the development of civilizations in these regions.

While some civilizations developed in the Middle East, others arose in South and East Asia.[1] About 2500 B.C. cities emerged in the Indus River Valley of India. About 1,000 years later, communities appeared in the Huang He (Yellow River) Valley of China. The people of early India and China were more isolated than the people of the Middle East. They were cut off from the outside world by mountains, jungles, grasslands, and large bodies of water. Thus, during their early history, they became relatively self-sufficient and borrowed little from foreign sources.

After 500 B.C. geographic barriers were slowly overcome. Warriors, missionaries, and merchants brought the peoples of South and East Asia closer together. India and China established economic and cultural ties. They also made their first contacts with western peoples, such as the Greeks and the Romans.

During this time, India and China often suffered from invasions and civil wars. But, in spite of these upheavals, the Indians and the Chinese were able to develop their civilizations. They made important technological and scientific contributions, many of which were later passed on to the western world.

The ideas and practices of India and China also spread to neighboring Asian lands. Buddhism began as an Indian religion. It influenced the people of China, and became the dominant faith of Southeast Asia, the region east of India and south of China. Chinese philosophy, religion, art, and architecture spread northward through Korea and into Japan. The Koreans and Japanese developed distinctive civilizations by blending their own traditions with those of the Chinese.

1 Early India

The civilization of India is one of the oldest in the world. It began about 4,500 years ago. Three modern nations—India, Pakistan, and Bangladesh—trace many of their cultural roots to early Indian civilization.

Environment of India

Like other civilizations, India's was shaped by geography and climate. The area of South Asia that comprises India is called a **subcontinent**—a large land mass like a continent, only smaller.[2] Shaped like an upside-down triangle, the Indian subcontinent covers about 1.7 million square miles (4.4 million square kilometers), making it greater in size than western Europe.

India is separated from the rest of Asia by natural barriers. Water surrounds the subcontinent on its eastern and western sides. To the north are two tall mountain ranges—the Himalayas and the Hindu Kush. Throughout India's history, invaders have used the high mountain passes of the Hindu Kush to cross into the subcontinent. The most famous of these passes is the Khyber Pass.

South of the mountains, are deserts in the west and jungles in the east. Most of northern India, however, is made up of plains which are crossed by three rivers: the Indus, the Ganges, and the Brahmaputra. Because of its fertility, the plains became the most populous region of the country and the leading center of Indian civilization. South of the plains, most of India is a plateau called the Deccan. A range of hills—the Vindhya—separates the Deccan Plateau from the plains. To the east and west of the Deccan are the

---

[1]South Asia refers to India; East Asia includes China, Korea, and Japan.

[2]Before India and Pakistan became independent in 1947, the entire subcontinent was known as India.

Monsoons bringing the right amount of rain at the right time are often celebrated with parties.

During the 2000's B.C., the Indus Valley had a rainy climate. Forests grew where dry desert areas are now located. Over the centuries, the river also shifted course from east to west.

Ghats, low mountain ranges that descend to the coastlines. There, settlements emerged that developed extensive trade with the Middle East and Southeast Asia.

Most places in India are warm or hot most of the year. The northern mountains block the cold air of central Asia from entering the subcontinent. India's climate is also affected by the **monsoon,** or seasonal winds. During fall and winter, northeast winds from the cool mountains bring dry air. In spring and summer, southwest winds from the ocean bring rain. If the monsoon is late, or if rainfall is light, crops are lost and there is famine. If the rains are heavy, floods destroy property and cause many deaths.

Indus River Valley

Unlike ancient Middle Eastern peoples, the early people of India left few written records. However, archeologists working in the Indus River Valley have uncovered the ruins of what they believe to be the first Indian civilization. This civilization, called Harappan, was centered in the cities of Harappa and Mohenjo-Daro. It lasted from 2500 to 1700 B.C.

This small Harappan seal has an inscription above a carved animal figure. Experts feel that such seals were used as labels for merchandise or as good luck charms. What do the seals reveal about Harappan religion?

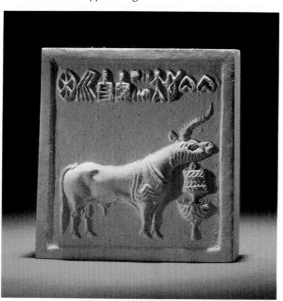

Planned Cities   Harappa and Mohenjo-Daro were built according to a particular plan. Overlooking each city was a **citadel,** or fortress, built on a platform of bricks. The urban area surrounding the citadel was divided into two districts. One district included government buildings, public baths, granaries, and workshops. The other consisted of homes.

The districts of Harappa and Mohenjo-Daro were laid out on a street **grid,** or uniform network. The streets were straight and crossed each other at almost perfect right angles. The buildings that lined the streets were arranged in blocks of about equal size. They were made of bricks and had flat roofs. Many had several stories, and some had courtyards and staircases. Drains from the buildings ran into a central brick-lined sewer system.

Harappan Life   The Harappans, or the people of the Indus River Valley, grew grain and vegetables in the fields surrounding the cities. They dug ditches and canals to irrigate their farmlands. While most Harappans worked the land, urban dwellers engaged in commerce. They made bronze articles, clay pottery, and cotton cloth.[3] Due to craft production, the Indus River Valley eventually became an important trading center. The Harappans traded with the people of Mesopotamia as early as 2300 B.C.

Language and Religion   The Harappans developed a written language based on **pictograms,** or picture symbols. **Linguists,** or scientists who study languages, have yet to decipher the Harappan language. Some, however, believe that the Harappans learned the idea of writing from the Mesopotamians and then developed their own characters.

Although Harappan religious writings have not been found, archeologists have discovered clues about Harappan religion. From animal and human-like figurines found in ruins, archeologists conclude that the Harappans worshiped spirits. These spirits were associated with natural forces that represented power and life, and were believed to live in water, trees, animals, and humans. A mother goddess, honored as the

[3]The use of cotton for clothing is one of India's major contributions to world civilization.

What is known about the early Aryan invaders of India comes from the Rig-Veda, a collection of religious literature.

ANCIENT INDIA

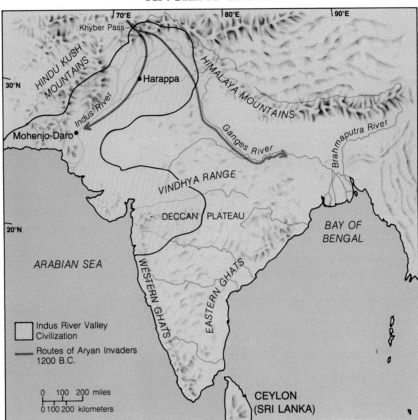

source of growing things, may have played an important role in Harappan worship. Aspects of Harappan religion later became a part of Indian religion, especially in far away villages.

Decline   About 2000 B.C. the Harappan civilization began to decline. By 1500 B.C., it had ended. Historians are still not sure about the reasons for this collapse. Some believe that bad weather, as well as poor water and soil conditions, destroyed agriculture. Others think that natural disasters, such as earthquakes, floods, and diseases, reduced the population. Many, however, feel that destructive invasions were responsible for the end of the Indus River Valley civilization.

Aryans

About 1200 B.C. Aryan peoples from central Asia crossed through the passes of the Hindu Kush and invaded the Indus River Valley. The Aryans were warrior-shepherds who herded cattle and sheep. They spoke Sanskrit, an Indo-European language, and were loosely organized into tribes. Each tribe was ruled by a **rajah,** or chief, assisted by a council of leading warriors.

Aryan Life   The Aryans settled in villages and lived in grass cottages. They farmed the land and tended their herds. For pleasure, men fought, gambled with dice, and drank a powerful brew called **soma.** Fathers had absolute authority in Aryan households, which included the wives and children of married sons. Women worked in the home and in the fields. They were not allowed to own property or take part in village government.

Religion   Aryans were **polytheists.** That is, they worshiped many gods and goddesses.

Shudras and Vaishyas may also be spelled as Sudras and Vaisyas.

Note the two different meanings for the term brahman. One refers to the Hindu idea of eternal spirit; the other to the highest level of caste.

Aryan deities were believed to have power over the forces of nature. For example, Agni was the god of fire; Indra, the god of thunder; and Ushas, the goddess of dawn. Aryan men offered animal sacrifices to these deities. Later, sacrifices were carried out only by priests, who followed a complex set of rules for performing religious ceremonies.

Conquest   After conquering the people of the Indus River Valley, the Aryans moved southeast into the Ganges Plain. There, they subdued the region's darker-skinned inhabitants. To escape Aryan rule, many of these people fled south. They later became Dravidians, the present-day people of southern India. Most of those who remained in the north became slaves of the Aryans, and were known as **dasyus.**

The Aryans believed that they were culturally superior to the dasyus. However, the dasyus out-numbered them. To maintain control, and a separate identity, the Aryans did not allow personal contact between the two groups. For example, it was ruled that no member of the dasyus' could marry an Aryan.

Social Groups   The Aryans were divided into four main social groups known as **varnas.** In time, the varnas were ranked according to social prestige. The most honored varna was the **brahmans,** or priests. They alone offered sacrifices to the gods and carried out other religious duties. Their acts were believed necessary to win the favor of the gods and to ensure the well-being of the people. Warriors, or **kshatriyas,** made up the second most important varna. They were in charge of political affairs and defense. The third varna, known as the **vaishyas,** was made up of merchants, artisans, and farmers. Unskilled laborers and servants formed the lowest varna, known as the **shudras.**

By 500 B.C. the division among the four varnas had become more rigid. Varnas were divided into smaller groups known as **jati.** Jati had separate activities and occupations. Each of these subdivisions followed its own rules for diet, marriage, and other social practices. People born into a particular jati could not leave it. To maintain social standing, they had to perform all of the duties of their jati. Men carried out the same kind of work as their fathers. Women sometimes helped their husbands at their jobs, but most women managed households and raised children. Members of a jati lived together in the same neighborhood. They were not allowed to mix socially with those outside their group.

Pariahs   Many non-Aryans belonged to a group known as **pariahs.** They never became a part of the varna system. They worked at the dirtiest jobs, such as handling dead animals and sweeping the streets. Because they worked with dirt and blood, pariahs were viewed as inferior and impure beings by the Aryans. Aryans carefully avoided all forms of contact with pariahs. Centuries later, the varna system became known as the caste system. Pariahs were called "outcasts" or "untouchables."

Hinduism

Over time, the Aryan religion slowly changed into Hinduism and became the national religion of India. Hinduism was not founded on the teachings of one person. Instead, it was based on a number of different beliefs and practices.

Vedas   Indian history from 1200 to 500 B.C. is called the Vedic Age. The term "Vedic" comes from the Vedas, the ancient Indian holy scriptures. The Vedas were repeated for hundreds of years before they were written down. They were later divided into four parts: hymns, poems, legends, and religious rituals. The part known as the Rig-Veda dates from 1000 B.C. and is the world's oldest religious text still in use.

Upanishads   Between 800 and 400 B.C., educated Indians began to look for a single religious truth behind the many Hindu deities and rituals. Their search was reflected in religious writings known as the Upanishads.

The central teaching of the Upanishads is the oneness of the universe. All living things, including gods, humans, and animals, have souls. Souls are part of Brahman, the one eternal spirit. Their bodies, however, tie them to the material world, which lasts only a short time. To know true freedom, a soul must be separated from the material world and gain complete unity with Brahman.

In the *Ramayana*, King Rama searches for his kidnapped wife, Sita. He finally rescues Sita, kills her captor, and returns in triumph to his homeland. For centuries, the Indian people have regarded Rama and Sita as the model of a devoted married couple.

Hindus worship many gods. This Hindu manuscript shows a scene from the court of Ganesa, the elephant god. Hindus pray to Ganesa to bring success to their lives. What is the primary religious goal of each Hindu?

Before such unity is realized, however, the soul must be purified through a process known as **reincarnation.** That is, the soul has to live in many bodies in many lifetimes. This cycle of rebirth is determined by a principle called **karma.** Karma states that every action of a person in one life influences how he or she will be born in the next life. In each existence, a person must follow **dharma,** or a set of rules that determines moral conduct.[4] If dharma is fulfilled, a person's soul will enter a higher or purer state. For example, a kshatriya might be reborn as a brahman. If a person does not obey his or her dharma, the soul will be born into a lower state, perhaps as a lowly animal. The cycle of reincarnation continues until a person reaches spiritual perfection. Then, the soul enters **moksha,** or a state of complete oneness with Brahman. Many Hindus were taught that the way to moksha could be advanced through prayer, religious rituals, strict self-denial, and rejection of all worldly possessions.

Epics   About 500 B.C. Indian writers began composing epics, or tales about gods and heroes. The *Mahabharata,* the oldest epic, consists of about 200,000 lines. It is considered the world's longest poem. It tells about a series of battles between two warrior families, fought with the help of the gods. Contained in the *Mahabharata* is the *Bhagavad Gita,* the most important text of Hinduism. The *Bhagavad Gita* teaches that people should always carry out the duties of their varna. Another popular epic was the *Ramayana.* It relates the adventures of the heroic king, Rama.

Jainism

During the 500's B.C., changes occurred in Indian religious life. Many devout Hindus became dissatisfied with external rituals and wanted a more spiritual faith. They left the towns and villages and looked for solitude in the forests. Through meditation, many of these religious seekers developed new insights and became **gurus,** or religious teachers. Their ideas and practices often led to the rise of new religions.

One of these gurus was Mahavira, a noble from northern India. He gave up his rich lifestyle and traveled for many years throughout the country. Mahavira's teaching placed special emphasis on the Hindu idea of **ahimsa,** or non-violence. Hindus had traditionally regarded animals, such as cows and monkeys, as sacred and forbade their killing. Mahavira, however, extended the ban on killing to include all living

---

[4]To certain Hindu thinkers, a person's dharma meant performing the duties of his or her jati. In this way, the concept of reincarnation was used to explain and to justify the caste system.

The name "Jainism" comes from word *jina*, meaning "conqueror."

Theravada Buddhism is sometimes called Hinayana. Today, it is the principal religion of Sri Lanka (formerly Ceylon), Burma, Thailand, Kampuchea (formerly Cambodia), and Laos.

things, even insects. In addition, he spoke against sacrifices and rejected the caste system.

Mahavira's teachings became known as Jainism and his followers were called Jains. The Jains would not farm for fear of plowing under living things. Instead, they turned to commerce and gained great wealth and influence.

Buddhism

Another new religion, which emerged in India during the 500's B.C., was Buddhism. Siddharta Gautama, the founder of Buddhism, was born a prince in northern India. He was brought up in luxury, but at an early age, he became dissatisfied with his life. Tradition states that one day Gautama left his palace to see how ordinary people lived. On his journey, he was shocked at scenes of misery and poverty. He then decided to find out why people suffered, and how suffering could be ended. At the age of 29, he left his family and wandered throughout India.

For seven years, Gautama lived as a hermit, seeking the truth through fasting, study, and self-denial. However, he had no success. Then one day, while meditating under a tree, he gained a flash of insight that he felt gave him an answer to the problem of suffering. He began to share with others the meaning of his "enlightenment." Dressed in a yellow robe, he preached his message to people and began to gather followers. His closest friends began calling him Buddha, or Enlightened One.

Buddha's Teaching   Buddha developed a new religious philosophy. He outlined his main ideas in the Four Noble Truths. These were: 1) suffering is a basic condition of life and results in the cycle of rebirths; 2) desires and attachments are the causes of suffering; 3) suffering can cease, and peace of mind can be achieved; and 4) the way to end suffering is through the Eightfold Path.

Buddha defined the Eightfold Path as knowing the truth, resisting evil, saying nothing to hurt others, respecting life, working for the good of others, freeing the mind of evil, controlling thoughts, and practicing meditation.

Sangha   According to Buddha's teaching, anyone, regardless of caste, could gain enlight-

enment and reach **nirvana.** In nirvana a person would be in a state of oneness with the universe. Buddha's beliefs caused discord in Indian society. Brahmans and kshatriyas did not like Buddha's attitude toward the castes. Because of such opposition, Buddhism gradually separated from Hinduism. Small groups of Buddhists formed a **sangha,** or community of monks and nuns. Living apart from the world, they meditated, studied, and practiced non-violence.

Spread of Buddhism   Because of the zeal, or strong desire, of Buddha's followers, Buddhism became the world's first missionary religion. After Buddha's death, the religion lost support in India. However, Buddhist missionaries traveled far beyond India's borders. They won many converts in China and Southeast Asia. In the end, Buddhism became the dominant faith of East Asia. It is now one of the world's major religions.

Divisions   As Buddhism spread, disagreements developed among Buddha's followers. Two branches of Buddhism soon arose. One branch known as Theravada was established in Southeast Asia. It remained fairly close to the original teachings of Buddha.

The other branch of Buddhism was known as Mahayana. It became dominant in China, Korea, and Japan. Mahayana encouraged the worship of Buddha as both a divine being and the savior of humanity.

1. Identify: Himalayas, Ganges, Harappa, Aryans, Dravidians, Vedas, *Bhagavad Gita*, Mahavira, Jainism, Siddharta Gautama, Four Noble Truths, Theravada, Mahayana.
2. How were the cities of the Indus River Valley built?
3. How did the Aryans organize their society?
4. What are the central teachings of the Upanishads? of Mahavira? of Buddha?

2   Indian Kingdoms and Empires

During the 500's B.C., northern India was made up of a number of feuding kingdoms. The most important of these states was Magadha, located in the eastern Ganges Valley. Magadha reached its greatest height under King Bimbisara. Bimbisara, who ruled from 542 to 495 B.C., expanded Magadha's territory through wars and marriages. He appointed loyal and skilled officials, built roads and bridges, improved tax collection, and sent ambassadors to other Indian kingdoms.

Persians and Greeks

During the period of Magadha's greatness, India made its first contacts with the West. In the 500's B.C., Persian kings Cyrus and Darius I conquered territories in the Indus River Valley. They collected tribute from local Indian rulers, but allowed them to retain control of their territories.

About 200 years later, Alexander the Great, a powerful ruler of Greece, established an empire that covered most of the eastern Mediterranean and Middle East. His forces invaded the Indus River Valley. Alexander planned to advance into the Ganges Plain, but his weary soldiers refused. The Greek leader then withdrew from Indian territory, leaving a Greek governor to rule in his place.

Mauryan Empire

While Alexander was occupying the Indus River Valley, a new leader arose in Magadha. Chandragupta Maurya, a military officer, overthrew the Magadhan king and proclaimed himself ruler. He founded the Mauryan dynasty, which ruled from 322 to 184 B.C. After strengthening his hold on the throne, Chandragupta Maurya conquered most of northern and central India.[5] Historians think of his kingdom as the first Indian empire.

Mauryan Life Chandragupta Maurya developed a strong bureaucracy and economic system. His government encouraged the growth of cities, supported building projects, and maintained a postal service that linked the provinces. The rise of a money economy benefited artisans and merchants. Mauryans traded with places as far away as Persia and China.

[5]Southern India remained under the rule of separate Hindu kingdoms. These kingdoms traded overseas and later built commercial empires in Southeast Asia.

Pataliputra, the Mauryan capital, became India's greatest city. It was surrounded by a wooden wall with 64 gates and 570 towers. The well-planned streets of Pataliputra were lined with markets, inns, shops, gambling houses, and theaters. The imperial palace was located in the center of the city in an enclosed park.

Asoka Chandragupta Maurya's grandson, Asoka, became the most famous Mauryan ruler. Shortly after becoming emperor in 270 B.C., he engaged in wars of conquest that enlarged the empire. However, he was horrified by the killing and suffering on both sides. Upon his return to Pataliputra, he spoke against war and devoted himself to the welfare of his people.

Asoka soon became a Buddhist and followed a policy of non-violence. In keeping with his beliefs, Asoka discouraged the slaughter of animals and ate no meat himself. He issued new laws stressing compassion, and had them carved

Gandhara artists were the first to show Buddha as a person. Buddha's robed body and youthful face were modeled after the sculptures of Greek and Roman gods. In what countries was Buddha regarded as divine?

Chandragupta I was not related to the Mauryan ruler, Chandragupta Maurya.

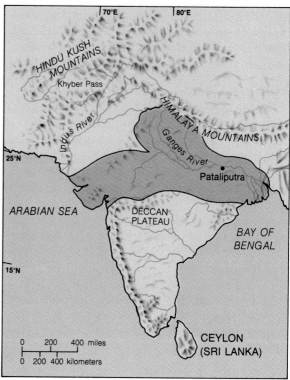

MAURYA EMPIRE 250 B.C.

GUPTA EMPIRE 400 A.D.

on stone pillars throughout the empire. These laws softened the harsh penalties set up by earlier rulers and extended government protection to the poor.

Asoka encouraged the peaceful spread of Buddhism in India and other parts of Asia. He also supported the use of Buddhist ideas in art and architecture. **Stupas,** or large stone mounds, were built over the bones of Buddhist saints. Stupas were known for their elaborately carved stone railings and gateways. Colorful paintings and carvings of Buddha and other figures lined the walls of cave temples. Although he supported the advance of Buddhism, Asoka was careful to allow his non-Buddhist subjects to practice their religions freely. As a result, the Hindu caste system was maintained.

Collapse After the death of Asoka in 232 B.C., the Mauryan Empire began to decline. Mauryan rulers still enjoyed absolute power, but they were often either weak or ruthless. They placed heavy taxes on the goods of merchants and seized large shares of produce from the peasants. Because of these harsh policies, the people turned against the Mauryan dynasty. With the murder of the last Mauryan ruler in 185 B.C., India once again split into a number of small kingdoms.

In spite of political decline, India, between 200 B.C. and 200 A.D., increased its ties with the outside world. Trade was stepped up with China and the Greek kingdoms of the Middle East. Greek ideas and practices came into India and had a profound influence on Indian philosophy, art, and science. Gandhara, a northern Indian kingdom, became known for its statues of Buddha, which reflected the realism of Greek sculpture.

Gupta Empire

About 320 A.D. Chandragupta I became the ruler of Magadha and worked to extend his authority throughout northern India. He founded the Gupta dynasty, which lasted from 320 to

HISTORY AND THE ARTS

Ajanta Caves

One of the wonders of Indian art and architecture is the Ajanta caves. Located in the Deccan region, the caves reveal the religious devotion and artistic splendor of early India. They are primarily known for their elegant sculpture, colorful wall paintings, and detailed carvings.

From 300 to 600 A.D., Buddhist monks carved 29 caves out of a 70-foot (21-meter) granite cliff. The cliff overlooks the rapid Waghora River near the village of Ajanta. Within the caves, the monks constructed temples, monasteries, and shelters for travelers. Construction work reached its height at the time of the Guptas in the 400's A.D. The decline of Indian Buddhism, 200 years later, led to the breakup of the community. The caves were forgotten and abandoned. Then in 1819, several British soldiers on a tiger hunt accidentally discovered the caves. Their find gave the world its first look at the artistic skills of early Indians.

The construction of the Ajanta caves was an enormous undertaking. Builders first carved out the ceilings. Then they worked their way downward, cutting out the walls and floors. This process eliminated the need for scaffolding, or temporary ladder structures used in building. Finally, sculptors decorated the entrances and the interiors of the caves with statues and finely-carved pillars. Most of this art deals with episodes in Buddhist history.

Among the more elaborate examples of Ajanta construction is a prayer hall, 68 feet (20 meters) long. At the heart of this chamber is a round stupa, which symbolizes the dome of the heavens. On festivals, Buddhist monks walked around the stupa chanting Buddhist holy scriptures. Other caves were used as shrines. They contained large stone images and wall carvings of Buddha.

The most outstanding feature of the caves, however, is the vast number of paintings on chamber walls and ceilings. Artists followed a special process in preparing the stone for the paintings. They plastered the rock walls with a coating made from clay, cow manure, animal hair, and crushed rice husks. A smooth coat of lime was then placed over the coating. Next, the artists drew the outlines of figures with a stick of cinnabar, a red mineral. Faces and bodies were skillfully modeled so that each resembled a distinct personality. After the sketches were completed, the painters applied a variety of rich colors made from plants and minerals. Once an entire wall was colored, brown or black lines were drawn around the figures. These flowing lines gave the figures shape and a sense of movement.

The subjects of most Ajanta paintings were the lives of Buddha and some of his followers, as well as Buddhist legends. In spite of the general religious emphasis, some of the paintings showed scenes of everyday life in early India. Some paintings show kings, queens, and their courts accompanied by large numbers of musicians and dancers. Others portray ships, architecture, and such animals as elephants, bulls, and tigers. The subjects and styles of the Ajanta cave paintings spread to other parts of India. They influenced later Buddhist art throughout Asia.

1. How were the Ajanta caves built?
2. What are the major subjects of Ajanta cave paintings?

about 600 A.D. Gupta rulers governed a prosperous empire; however, their domain never became as large as the Mauryan Empire.

Religion   The Guptas made Hinduism the official religion of India. During their rule, Hinduism reached the height of its development. Hindu intellectuals formed schools of thought based on the teaching of the Upanishads. To discipline both mind and body, some Hindus practiced a form of physical exercise known as **yoga.** Most Indians, however, still followed a religion of ceremonies in which they worshiped many deities. The three most important gods at this time were Brahma, the Creator; Vishnu, the Preserver; and Shiva, the Destroyer.

Although they preferred Hinduism, the Guptas were tolerant of other faiths. However, Buddhism became so weak that it nearly disappeared from India. Even so, many Buddhist ideas and practices later became part of Hinduism.

Gupta Life   The Gupta Empire reached its height under Chandragupta II, who ruled from 375 to 415 A.D. During this time, the government eased tax burdens and allowed the people a greater degree of freedom. Fa-hsien, a Buddhist monk from China, traveled in India and wrote about Indian life under the Guptas:

> In the Gupta Empire, people are numerous and happy; only those who cultivate the royal land have to pay [in] grain. . . . If they want to go, they go; if they want to stay, they stay. The king governs without decapitation [cutting off heads] or corporal [bodily] punishment. . . . The leaders of vaishya families have houses in the cities for dispensing charity and medicine.*

Although Fa-hsien exaggerated the benefits of Gupta rule, life improved for many Indians at this time. However, the rigidity of the caste system allowed little help for the pariahs. It also led to lower social status for women. During the Gupta period, wealthy men had many wives, a practice that was rare in earlier times. **Suttee** also became common. This was the practice of widows burning themselves to death at their husbands' funerals.

Science and Art   While building an empire, Gupta rulers supported learning and the arts. Poets, philosophers, and scientists were honored at the imperial court.

Important advances took place in the sciences. Gupta mathematicians explained the concept of infinity and used algebra for working on difficult problems. Their most important inventions were the concept of zero and the number symbols 0 through 9. These symbols became known as Arabic numerals. Later, by way of the Middle East, this system came to the West. Work in mathematics helped Gupta astronomers to develop their understanding of heavenly bodies. They knew that the world was round, and they had some knowledge of the principle of gravity. In medicine, Gupta doctors set bones, performed operations, and invented hundreds of medical instruments.

Indian literature flourished under the Guptas. Many short stories, fables, and fairy tales were written. The most popular was a collection of tales known as the *Panchatantra*. Written in Sanskrit, it presented moral lessons through animals who acted like humans. Many of these stories eventually spread to the Middle East and the West, where they were retold by other authors. Drama was also important during Gupta times. The most famous writer of plays was Kalidasa. His work *Shakuntala* dealt with romantic love between a king and a forest maiden.

During the Gupta era, the Hindu temple emerged as India's most celebrated kind of architecture. Each temple was considered the home of a specific deity, where worshipers went to pray and offer gifts. It had a sanctuary, which housed a statue or **relic,** or holy object, of the deity, and a large, square hall, where the worshipers gathered. Outside was a porch, often decorated with **reliefs,** or raised carvings. Roofs had great towers, which were usually covered with images of gods and goddesses in various forms.

Decline   After the death of Chandragupta II in 415 A.D., the Gupta Empire began to fail. Later

---

*Fa-hsien's Journal, tr. James Legge, from *Our Oriental Heritage*, Will Durant, © 1935 by Simon and Schuster, p. 452.

Chinese names for places and dynasties in this textbook are spelled using the Pinyin system. Whenever a Pinyin name is introduced, the traditional Wade-Giles spelling will usually follow in a clause or in parentheses. For the names of people, only the Wade-Giles system is used.

Gupta rulers gave away much government land. They used private individuals, instead of government officials, to collect taxes. This system led to corruption and inefficiency. As the central government grew weaker, the governors of the provinces became more independent. Peasants, who now owned their own lands, paid less in taxes to the government and often ignored its decrees. Meanwhile, the Guptas faced invasions along India's northwestern border.

All of these factors steadily undermined Gupta control. By 600 A.D., the Gupta Empire had dissolved into a collection of small states. For the next 500 years, India was torn apart by conflict.

1. Identify: Magadha, Bimbisara, Chandragupta Maurya, Pataliputra, Asoka, Gandhara, Gupta, Chandragupta I, Chandragupta II, *Panchatantra*, Kalidasa.
2. What was Asoka's attitude toward war?
3. What was Indian society like under the Guptas?
4. What foreign influences came to India under the Mauryas and Guptas?

3 Early China

China has an ancient civilization, with more than 3,500 years of recorded history. For many centuries, the Chinese lived in relative isolation from the rest of the world. The lack of outside contacts aided in the formation of a common culture thoughout China. The Chinese were able to develop a strong sense of national identity. They called their country *Chung-kuo*, or the "Middle Kingdom." To them, it was the center of the world and of civilization.

Environment of China

The varied geography of China explains much of its early isolation. The western two-thirds of the country is covered with mountains and deserts. These natural barriers hindered contacts with lands farther west. The eastern one-third of China borders on the Pacific Ocean. The coastline is nearly 7,000 miles (11,200 kilometers) long. Yet the Chinese never became a strong seafaring people. Instead, they concentrated on developing the eastern region's fertile river valleys, plains, and hills. Throughout most of China's history, four out of five Chinese have lived in this area.

Three major rivers are located in eastern China. They are the Huang He, or Yellow River; the Chang Jiang, also known as the Yangtze; and the Xi Jiang, also known as the West River. The Huang He was the first of these rivers to play an important role in Chinese history. It flows over 2,900 miles (4,640 kilometers) through northern China. The river at times floods, destroying villages and fields. Because of this, the Huang He is called the "Great Sorrow." However, its silt has provided China with rich farmland.

China has a varied climate. The northern part of the country has cold winters, hot summers, and irregular rainfall. The southeastern part has mild winters, hot summers, and abundant rainfall. In the west, desert areas are hot all year round; although at the higher elevations, they are always cool or cold.

In 1975 construction workers uncovered a life-size army of 6,000 clay soldiers and horses guarding a Chinese ruler's tomb. Excavations like this reveal much about Chinese civilization. How old is China's history?

In some sources, the Shang dynasty is called the Yin dynasty.

Point out that the reference to "heaven" or "gods" as the source of political authority was common in most parts of the pre-modern world.

Origins of China

About 2000 B.C., the first Chinese settlements appeared along the Huang He. The people lived in round clay houses with thatched roofs. They farmed the land, which was covered with a thick layer of rich yellow soil called **loess.** They also dug canals for irrigation and flood control. The early Chinese produced clay pottery as well as polished stone axes, hoes, and knives.

Very little is known about the origins of Chinese civilization. The Chinese have developed many legends to explain their remote past. One legend tells how the universe was created from the body of a giant named P'an-ku. Others describe a line of heroic kings who founded the basic institutions of Chinese society.

Early Dynasties

From the beginning of its recorded history until the present century, China was ruled by a series of dynasties. The Chinese have divided their history into periods based on the reigns of these ruling families. Western historians have also followed this practice when writing about China's past.

The early Chinese believed that their rulers governed according to a principle known as the Mandate of Heaven. If rulers were just, they received a mandate, or the right to rule, from heaven. If they did not govern properly, they lost this mandate to someone else who then started a new dynasty. Throughout Chinese history, rebels who succeeded in overthrowing an unpopular dynasty appealed to the Mandate of Heaven to justify their seizure of power.

Shang   About 1500 B.C., a family known as the Shang established the first dynasty in recorded Chinese history. Shang kings were political leaders, but they were also high priests. The Shang people worshiped spirits of nature and honored their departed ancestors. It was believed that Shang kings had special powers to communicate with their royal ancestors and with spirits on behalf of the people. For this reason, religion and government were closely linked in early China.

Shang Achievements   Under the Shang kings, the Chinese made important achievements. They built their first cities, the most important of which was the Shang capital Anyang. At the center of Anyang stood the king's palace and temple. Public buildings and the homes of government officials were built around the royal sanctuary. An outer district of homes, burial grounds, and workshops surrounded the city's center.

Chinese artists developed several skills and crafts during the Shang dynasty. They made cloth from silk, carved ivory and jade figurines, and used **kaolin,** a fine white clay, to make pottery. Skilled in casting metal, they produced works of bronze. These included sculpture, cups, vases, and large ceremonial vessels. Art experts consider these objects the finest works of bronze ever made.

The Chinese of the Shang period developed a writing system of many characters written in vertical columns. The characters represented objects, ideas, or sounds. Each character had to be memorized. Because there were so many characters, reading and writing were limited at first to a small percentage of the population. Later, the Chinese writing system spread to other parts of East Asia.

Under Shang kings, the Chinese produced their first literary works and began to keep records. They made mathematical calculations and learned to predict eclipses. They also developed a calendar based on the position of the moon. It was used to determine the times of planting and harvest.

Shang Expansion   At first, Shang kings governed a small area that included Anyang and nearby territories in northern China. Later, they developed a powerful army by using chariots, and weapons made of bronze. With this military force, Shang rulers conquered more distant territories and controlled most of the Huang He Valley.

In spite of military victories, the Shang domain eventually weakened as a result of poor leadership. The remote areas of Shang China came under the control of local nobles, who fought each other for land. Soon after 1100 B.C., a western Chinese people called the Zhou overthrew the Shang and set up a new dynasty.

The maps below are the subject of the "Using Maps" section of the Chapter 2 Review.

ANCIENT CHINA

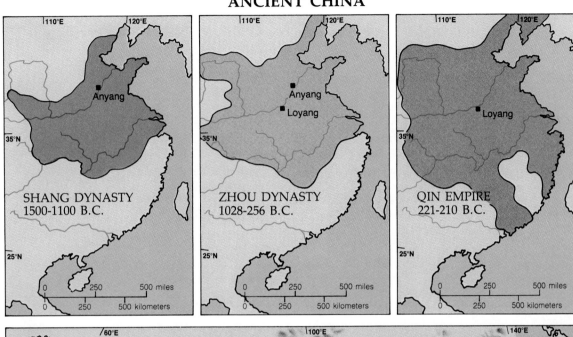

SHANG DYNASTY
1500-1100 B.C.

ZHOU DYNASTY
1028-256 B.C.

QIN EMPIRE
221-210 B.C.

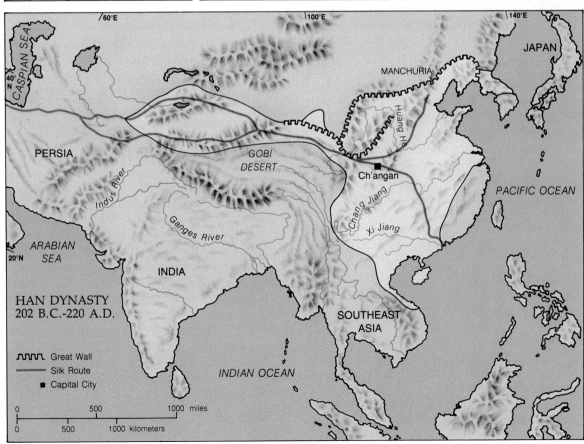

HAN DYNASTY
202 B.C.-220 A.D.

〰〰 Great Wall
—— Silk Route
■ Capital City

Ask students to explain the "Sayings of Confucius" that are listed below. Discuss their responses.

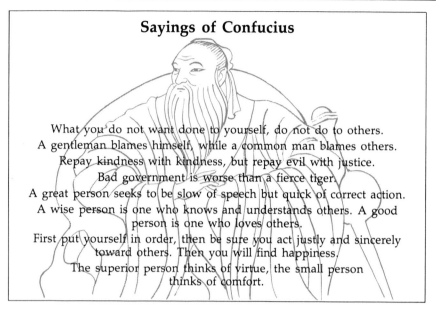

Sayings of Confucius

What you do not want done to yourself, do not do to others.
A gentleman blames himself, while a common man blames others.
Repay kindness with kindness, but repay evil with justice.
Bad government is worse than a fierce tiger.
A great person seeks to be slow of speech but quick of correct action.
A wise person is one who knows and understands others. A good person is one who loves others.
First put yourself in order, then be sure you act justly and sincerely toward others. Then you will find happiness.
The superior person thinks of virtue, the small person thinks of comfort.

Zhou The Zhou (Chou) established the longest reigning dynasty in Chinese history. Their rule lasted from 1028 to 256 B.C. However, the Zhou were continually troubled by political turmoil.

The Zhou came to power with the help of other groups from western China. To reward these allies, Zhou kings made their warriors and nobles give them land throughout the country. In return, the new landowners were to be loyal and to provide soldiers in time of war. They also paid tribute to the king and promised not to fight against his forces.

This policy of land distribution, however, soon undermined royal authority. Landowners defied the king and became independent rulers in their own regions. They fought each other for territory and plunged China into civil war. By the 400's B.C., Zhou kings had no real power outside of their own estates.

Confusion increased when the Zhou kingdom was attacked by armies from central Asia. In 771 B.C., some Chinese nobles took control of the capital and killed the Zhou king. However, members of the royal family fled east and re-established the dynasty in the town of Loyang. There, the Zhou ruled until 256 B.C. During the next decade, China was in much disorder until a new dynasty came to power.

Early Chinese Society

Under the Zhou dynasty, Chinese society consisted of three groups: nobles, merchants, and peasants. The nobles were wealthy landowners. They lived in town in large mansions with tiled roofs, courtyards, and gardens. A small group of merchants lived in the towns and provided luxury goods for the royal court and the nobles. Homes of the wealthy had fine furniture and carpets. Their occupants feasted on a variety of seasoned foods, and wore silk tunics and jackets.

The peasants made up the vast majority of Chinese. They were poor and lived in rural villages surrounded by mud walls. They grew grains and raised farm animals. They worked long hours in the fields and faced the constant threats of famine and flood. A part of their produce went as rent to the local landlord. Some of it was also used to pay taxes. Peasants also served in the landlord's army and performed labor services, such as building roads and canals. They wore straw sandals and clothes made from a plant fiber called hemp. Millet, rice, beans, turnips, and fish made up the diet of peasant families.

Family The family was very important in early China. Each family consisted of a father, a

Note that four of the five important relationships according to Confucius involved obedience of one person to another. The fifth, "friend to friend," was to be conducted along a principle similar to that of the Golden Rule.

mother, sons with their families, and unmarried daughters. Under the Shang dynasty, descent and inheritance rights had come through the mother's side of the family. But during the Zhou period, the father became the dominant figure upon whom other family members depended. Another change in family life was the respect given to elderly people. Old age was considered a sign of wisdom, and younger family members were expected to honor and obey older ones.

Economy   Under Zhou rulers, China's economy underwent many changes. Under the supervision of landowners, peasants drained swamps and built irrigation canals on a large scale. The amount of arable, or farmable, land expanded, and fertilizers were used to increase crop yields. While agriculture prospered, production and trade increased. Copper and gold coins replaced shells and rolls of silk as money. Iron was substituted for bronze in the making of tools and weapons. Greater economic security soon led to a rise in population. By 700 B.C., China was the most populated country in the world.

Chinese Thought

During the Zhou period, the Chinese became more concerned with life in this world than with the supernatural. They sought to explain the underlying principles of nature. They also became interested in **ethics,** or the study of moral principles. To the Chinese, humans should adapt to nature rather than change it. In this way, a harmonious balance would be achieved in human affairs that would bring together opposing views. During the late Zhou period, two philosophies developed that emphasized these themes.

Confucianism   The earliest and most important Chinese ethical philosophy was Confucianism. It was based on the teachings of Kung-fu-tzu, or Confucius.[6] Confucius was born in 551 B.C. He began his career as a government official. Later he became a traveling teacher and attracted a large number of students. His major concern was the creation of a just society that would end China's political disorder.

Confucius believed that people should obey certain moral principles in their relations with each other. He stated that there were five important relationships—ruler and ruled, father and son, husband and wife, older brother and younger brother, and friend and friend. Each person, Confucius believed, owed respect and obedience to those above him or her. Those above were expected to set a good example for those below. Confucius believed that if these principles were carried out, a just society would result. He stated: "With harmony at home there will be order in the nation. With order in the nation, there will be peace in the world."

Confucius hoped to reform the government of China. He advised rulers to put aside military conquests and to work for the good of their people. He also criticized the appointment of government officials on the basis of family ties rather than on ability. Only well-educated officials, Confucius believed, should serve in the government.

Within a century, the ideas of Confucius were widely accepted and greatly affected Chinese life. They became the basis of Chinese society and government, and remained so until the early twentieth century.

Taoism   Another ethical philosophy was Taoism. It was based on the teachings of Lao-tzu, who lived in the 600's B.C. However, Taoism did not emerge as a system of thought until 100 years later. Its followers believed in the existence of *Tao,* or "The Way," a mysterious force that governs the universe and all of nature. People, according to Taoists, should not strive for education, wealth, and power. Instead, they should leave society and learn directly from nature. Then they would understand Tao and bring themselves into harmony with it.

Taoism adopted old Chinese beliefs about the workings of the universe. It taught that harmony depended on a balance between the forces of **yin** and **yang.** Yin represented peace, darkness, and coldness. Yang stood for the opposite—fury, light, and heat. Both existed in a delicate balance and were not in direct conflict with each other. The Taoists believed that all evil—famines, floods, disease, and war—was caused by lack of

---

[6]Confucius is the western name for Kung-fu-tzu.

Ask students to compare, in terms of value and labor, the building of the Great Wall with that of other monuments in the ancient world.

balance between the two. All people, therefore, should seek a balance in their lives between yin and yang.

Many Chinese followed Taoism. It won support among the peasants, who lived and worked close to the soil. It also influenced poets and artists, who sought inspiration in natural beauty. The Taoist emphasis on nature led to studies of plants, animals, and minerals. However, Taoism also had a negative influence on Chinese life. Many Taoists added rituals, superstition, and legends to the basic teachings. In time, Taoism came to mean that people should not try to improve their lives if their actions interfered with nature.

1. Identify: Chung-kuo, Huang He, P'an-ku, Mandate of Heaven, Shang, Anyang, Zhou, Loyang, Confucius, Lao-tzu.
2. What were the main achievements of the Shang period?
3. How was China governed under the Zhou dynasty?
4. Why did Confucius stress the importance of human relationships?

4   Chinese Empires

In 247 B.C., China was still divided into a number of territories. One of these regions was controlled by a group called the Qin (Ch'in). The Qin had the most disciplined army in China. Their cavalry was armed with bows and arrows, weapons that were new to other Chinese armies.

Shih Huang Ti

The Qin ruler at this time was a young warrior named Chi'ng. He strengthened the government of the Qin state and expanded its borders. By 221 B.C., Chi'ng had conquered all of the other Chinese states. Naming himself Shih Huang Ti, or First Emperor, he became an absolute ruler. His dynasty, the Qin, created the first true Chinese empire.

Strong Government   Shih Huang Ti established a strong central government that united China into one state. He provided a common currency and a standard system of weights and measures. He set up a single law code and tax

system for the entire country. For more effective local government, he had China divided into provinces. These local units were run by governors appointed by and directly responsible to the emperor.

Shih Huang Ti ruthlessly put down any opposition to his rule. He tried to keep China's scholars from discussing and writing freely about the country's problems. When scholars began to criticize the government, Shih Huang Ti burned their books and outlawed Confucianism. Confucian teachers were removed from their posts. Those who refused to obey the emperor were either killed or forced to work on government building projects.

Expansion   Shih Huang Ti expanded China's borders. He sent his armies north into Mongolia and south into Southeast Asia. As a result of these conquests, the Qin dynasty ruled a larger area than any previous dynasty.

Shih Huang Ti, however, constantly had to defend the northern and western frontiers against attack by nomadic groups. Earlier rulers had attempted to seal off China's northern borders by building a number of separate walls. To end the attacks, Shih Huang Ti and his successor ordered the joining of these walls to form a large structure known as the Great Wall of China. About 300,000 laborers were forced to work long hours each day on the project. When completed, the wall stretched 1,350 miles (2,160 kilometers) across northern China. It was 25 feet (7.5 meters) in height and 15 feet (4.5 meters) wide. A road ran along the top of the wall, enabling soldiers to travel quickly to any section of the frontier. Parts of the Great Wall still stand today.

In spite of its strength, the Qin dynasty lasted only a short time. Harsh laws, forced labor, and wars of conquest aroused discontent among the Chinese people. After the death of Shih Huang Ti in 210 B.C., his successor was quickly overthrown in a military revolt. In 202 B.C., a general named Lui Pang founded the Han dynasty.

Han Dynasty

The Han dynasty continued the Qin tradition of strong government and military power. Han

While the *Pax Sinica* reigned in China, the Mediterranean world enjoyed a period of peace known as the *Pax Romana* under the Roman Empire.

The Great Wall of China winds from the sea over mountains, rivers, and valleys. Many Chinese workers lost their lives building the wall and were buried beneath it. The wall provided little defense against a major invasion, but it kept out nomadic groups who attacked China from the north and west. During what Chinese empire was the Great Wall built?

emperors governed from 202 B.C. to 220 A.D. They made China the greatest power in all of Asia.

Wu Ti The greatest of the Han emperors was Wu Ti, who ruled from 140 to 87 B.C. As an absolute ruler, Wu Ti put down rebellions and built up the central government. A national capital was established at Ch'angan. Governors were named to run the provinces. They and lesser officials handled such matters as religious ceremonies, historical records, public building, and tax collection.

Wu Ti also engaged in wars of conquest. He fought battles against the peoples along China's northern and western borders. He extended Chinese control northward into Manchuria, southward into Southeast Asia, and westward into central Asia. To support his wars, Wu Ti gained government control of the profitable salt and iron production centers.

Civil Service Wu Ti and his successors made important changes in government administration. They created a **civil service**, or bureaucracy in which officials are hired on the basis of examinations. Wu Ti admired scholarship and made Confucianism the official philosophy of the state. Confucius taught that government service should be based on ability rather than birth. Civil service examinations were intro-

duced to select government officials. Candidates were tested on their knowledge of Confucian teachings. Successful candidates were appointed to government posts.[7]

At first only members of the nobility were allowed to take the tests. Later, the system grew to include people from other groups. This new group of scholarly civil servants was known as **mandarins.** Mandarins controlled the government administration of China until the present century.

Pax Sinica The strength of the Han state brought a long period of peace and order to China. Historians call this period the *Pax Sinica,* or "Chinese Peace."

During the Pax Sinica, China made important contributions in science, technology, and literature. Chinese inventors produced paper, which was made from tree bark and rags. They developed new methods for making such products as silk and ceramics. They invented sundials, water clocks, and a new calendar based on approximately 365 days. Astronomers measured the moon's orbit, mapped stars, and observed sunspots. Doctors used **acupuncture,** a way of treating pain by piercing the skin with needles at

---

[7]In 124 B.C., Wu Ti started a school to help candidates prepare for civil service examinations.

Have students compare the size of Japan and/or Korea to that of the United States. Then have them compare population.

vital points. Writers created new styles and forms of literature. They wrote histories, short poems, hymns, and diaries of court life. Scholars studied the meaning of words and compiled the world's first dictionary.

Under Han rulers, stability led to trade and other contacts in foreign lands. During the Pax Sinica, an overland road through central Asia, known as the Silk Route, carried trade between East and West. Camel caravans brought silk, jade, and other Chinese goods to the markets of India, the Middle East, Greece, and Rome. The traders returned to China with foreign goods, such as glass, tin, asbestos, wool, and linen textiles.

Religion   During the Han period, Confucianism became a religion as well as a philosophy. This was supported by the emperors, who encouraged the offering of sacrifices to the spirit of Confucius. At the same time, Indian missionaries brought Mahayana Buddhism to China. They explained the faith to the Chinese people and translated Buddhist writings into the Chinese language. The Han emperors allowed the new religion to win converts. To the Chinese, it was possible to accept Buddhism and also remain loyal to their Confucian and Taoist beliefs. Buddhism brought new artistic ideas to China. For example, the Chinese **pagoda,** a tower-like temple, was modeled on Indian Buddhist shrines.

Korea prospered after the Silla rulers united the country. A "golden age" in Korean art lasted for two centuries. These gold vessels were found in a Silla tomb. What other type of metalworking was done by the Koreans?

Collapse   During the 200's A.D., a series of weak and incompetent Han emperors governed China. The peasants were heavily taxed and faced constant drought and famine. They joined with nobles in supporting rebellions against the Han government. In 220 A.D., the Han Empire ended and was replaced by several rival kingdoms. During the next 350 years, northern China was plagued by weak government, wars, and invasions. To escape the disorder, many Chinese fled to southern China. There, they adopted new practices like drinking tea and growing rice. At this time, Mahayana Buddhism, with its promise of future happiness, became popular among the common people. It was not until the late 500's A.D. that China was once again united under one government.

1. Identify: Qin, Shih Huang Ti, Han, Wu Ti, Ch'angan, Pax Sinica, Silk Route.
2. How did the Qin dynasty change Chinese government and society?
3. Why did Han rulers introduce civil service examinations?
4. What scientific and technological advances occurred during the Pax Sinica?

5   Korea and Japan

While China was emerging in East Asia, other civilizations were developing in Korea and Japan. Under Chinese influence, Korea produced one of the oldest civilizations in East Asia. Japan later came into contact with mainland Asia and created its own civilization.

Environment

Geography played an important role in the rise of Korea and Japan. Korea forms a peninsula on the east coast of Asia. It extends southward from Manchuria toward the western tip of Japan. Only a few hundred miles of ocean separate Korea from Japan. As a result of its location, Korea has served as a land bridge between Japan and the Asian mainland.

Japan consists of a long narrow **archipelago,** or chain of islands. There are four main islands and thousands of smaller ones. The four main islands are Hokkaido, Honshu, Shikoku, and Kyushu. Honshu is the largest and most populous. It

EARLY KOREA AND JAPAN

became the leading center of Japanese civilization and culture.

Korea and Japan have many mountains, valleys, and forests. In both countries, less than one-fifth of the land is suitable for farming. The Koreans and the Japanese, however, have made good use of the soil that is available. Rice is a major crop. Barley, millet, tea, vegetables, and fruits are also grown.

The climates of Korea and Japan are generally well balanced, with mild winters and warm summers. Both countries receive abundant rainfall. However, nature has often brought trying times to Japan. The Japanese islands have suffered much from volcanoes, earthquakes, floods, and **typhoons,** or hurricanes.

Korean Kingdoms

Around 5,000 to 10,000 years ago, the ancestors of the Koreans left central Asia and settled in the Korean peninsula. There, they lived in villages, grew rice, and made bronze articles. As they developed, the early Koreans formed **clans,** or groups based on family ties.

Around 300 B.C., a kingdom called Choson emerged in northern Korea. Choson rulers soon came under Chinese influence. In 108 B.C., China's Han dynasty conquered Choson and set up four colonies in Korea. Through contacts with the Chinese, the Koreans developed a writing system. They also borrowed Chinese ideas in government, science, and the arts.

During the 100's A.D., Korea broke away from Chinese control. For the next 500 years, the country was divided into three independent states: Koguryo, Paekche, and Silla. Historians call this period of Korean history the Age of the Three Kingdoms. The three kingdoms adopted Buddhism from China. They also successfully fought back invaders from Japan.

In the 600's A.D., Silla conquered the other two kingdoms and gained control of the entire

Point out that at the beginning of the 200's B.C. an alliance of some 30 regions in Japan was headed by a woman.

peninsula. The kings of Silla were powerful rulers. They set up a strong central government and divided Korea into provinces. They supported the arts and built many palaces and temples. Trade was begun with lands as distant as India and Persia. Silla, however, developed its closest ties with China. Confucianism was introduced and became a strong influence on Korean life. After 700 A.D., Silla began to decline. As a result, Korea entered a 100-year period of civil war.

Early Japan

Japan was settled as early as 3000 B.C., but very little is known about its earliest inhabitants. During the 300's B.C. and 200's B.C., invaders from Korea and other parts of northeastern Asia entered Japan. These groups gradually settled the main islands. They introduced agriculture and the use of bronze and iron. They mixed with the earlier peoples and formed the first known Japanese culture.

Clans Early Japan was divided into a number of separate regions controlled by clans. The clans grew wealthy and powerful. Each was subdivided into groups based on occupation. Warrior groups were given special honors above the others. From their families came the chiefs who governed each clan. Women were highly esteemed in early Japanese society, and many of them served as clan chiefs.

Clan life was very simple. There were no cities or towns. People lived in villages of wooden homes and wore clothing made of bark or hemp. They made their living by farming, fishing, or hunting. Money was not used so the Japanese bartered for the goods they needed. Also, there was no system of writing. To explain their beginnings, the Japanese developed legends and passed them by word of mouth from the old to the young.

Shinto The early Japanese people had their own religious beliefs. These beliefs were later called *Shinto*, or "the way of the gods." At the heart of Shinto was the worship of a sun goddess and other clan deities and ancestors. Shinto also included the worship of the wonders of nature. Trees, mountains, waterfalls, animals, and per-

A masked Shinto priest performs a traditional dance known as bugaku. Each dance tells a particular story, such as human courage in war, an animal hunt, or the delight of the gods in the Japanese people. What role did Shinto priests play in early Japanese society?

Note that although Shinto was the official religion of Japan, Buddhism eventually became the religion of the majority of the Japanese people.

Empress Suiko, aunt of Prince Shokotu, played an important role in bringing Chinese culture to Japan.

sons were honored and worshiped as **kami,** or sacred objects.

Early Shinto had no clearly defined rules of moral conduct. Instead, people were expected to take part in rituals. Many shrines were built throughout the country in places that were thought to be sacred. At these shrines, festivals and rituals were held to honor ancestors and the forces of nature. Clan leaders served as Shinto priests, closely linking religion and government.

Political Unity   Around 500 A.D., a clan known as Yamato became powerful in central Japan. Its rule soon extended over most of the country. The defeated clans kept control of their lands but had to give their loyalty to the Yamato chief.[8] The Yamato clan then invaded the Asian mainland. For a brief period, it ruled the southern part of Korea. By way of Korea, Chinese ideas slowly spread to Japan.

Chinese Influences

From 400 to 700 A.D., the Japanese developed close ties with China. During this period, the Chinese had one of the most advanced civilizations in the world. The Japanese were impressed with Chinese achievements and began to model their society on Chinese principles.

Writing   Around 400 A.D. the Japanese became familiar with Chinese writing. The Japanese and Chinese languages have little in common. Yet, the Japanese were able to develop a writing system based on Chinese characters. Learning the new system was difficult because the numerous characters had to be memorized. Most Japanese writers used Chinese.

Buddhism   During the 500's A.D., Chinese and Korean missionaries brought Mahayana Buddhism to Japan. They won converts among Japanese scholars and nobles. These educated Japanese saw Buddhism as a more advanced religion than Shinto. They were attracted to its complex ideas and elaborate ceremonies.

Soon the court of the Yamato rulers was divided. One group of officials favored Bud-

dhism, while the other group opposed it. About 587 A.D., Prince Shokotu, the most powerful court official, gave his support to Buddhism, thus ensuring its survival. Shokotu was also interested in Confucianism and began applying its principles to Japanese government.

Shokotu's acceptance of Buddhism increased the flow of Chinese culture into Japan. Libraries of Buddhist and Chinese writings were set up. Japanese scholars studied Chinese medicine, astronomy, and philosophy. Buddhist temples and shrines were built by the government. Inside the shrines were bronze, wooden, and **lacquer,** or varnished, statues of Buddha, religious paintings, and other works of art. Buddhist monasteries were founded in many parts of the country. Chinese priests, scholars, and artists visited Japan and taught new skills to the Japanese. Sometimes, Japanese Buddhists crossed to the mainland to study their religion.

Taika Reforms   In 645 A.D., pro-Chinese nobles seized power in the name of the Yamato ruler and began a series of reforms. They proclaimed a new age, which they named *Taika,* or "Great Change." The purpose of their reforms was to establish a strong central government patterned after that of China.

To make the throne more important, the reformers proclaimed the Yamato ruler emperor of all Japan. They then set up a bureaucracy made up of several bureaus and agencies. Government officials were chosen by a system of civil service examinations, which tested a person's understanding of Chinese philosophy. The reformers also set up local governments on the Chinese model. That is, they divided the land into several provinces and appointed officials to run them.

The Japanese systems of land ownership and taxation were also borrowed from the Chinese. The reformers said that, in theory, all land belonged to the emperor. In practice, however, the land was to be divided equally among its former owners, who would then become tenants, or renters. Every six years, the land would be divided again. In this way, all tenants would continue to have equal shares. Everyone would pay the government the same amount in taxes,

---

[8]Yamato chiefs later became emperors of Japan. Their dynasty has ruled without interruption into modern times. It is the oldest ruling royal family in the world.

partly in produce and partly in military service. These land and tax measures did not succeed because of the opposition of the powerful landed nobles. However, the administrative reforms made a lasting change in the organization of Japan's government.

Nara To provide a setting for the new government, in 710 A.D., the Taika reformers built a capital city called Nara. Nara had broad streets, large squares, and rows of homes, palaces, and Buddhist temples. Most of Nara's buildings were made of wood, and some still stand today. Located in central Japan, Nara soon became a political and religious center. Its construction symbolized Japan's emergence as an important Asian civilization.

1. Identify: Choson, Silla, Honshu, Shinto, Yamato, Shokotu, Taika, Nara.
2. Why were the Yamato chiefs important?
3. What aspects of Chinese civilization were borrowed by Korea? by Japan?
4. What were the Taika reforms?

CHAPTER 2 REVIEW

Summary

1. Between 2500 and 1700 B.C., the Harappans developed the first Indian civilization in the Indus River Valley.
2. About 1200 B.C. Aryan invaders conquered northern India, enslaved its people, and established a new society based on the varna system.
3. Hinduism, India's national religion, developed a variety of ideas and practices, such as a belief in the oneness of the universe, the worship of many deities, reincarnation, and a duty to social obligations.
4. During the 500's B.C., Siddharta Gautama founded Buddhism, which spread from India to East Asia and became one of the world's major religions.
5. The Mauryas (322-184 B.C.) and the Guptas (320-600 A.D.) founded Indian empires that made important achievements in the arts, sciences, and government organization.
6. About 2000 B.C., Chinese civilization appeared in the Huang He Valley.
7. Under the Shang and Zhou dynasties, the Chinese made important achievements in the arts and sciences and set up a basic government administration. Poor leadership and civil war weakened early Chinese government.
8. During the 500's B.C., Confucius developed an ethical philosophy that served as the basis of Chinese society and government until modern times.
9. The Qin and Han dynasties united China under powerful central governments that enacted strict laws, expanded China's borders, and increased Chinese contacts with the outside world.
10. The early Koreans and Japanese combined Chinese ways with their own traditions and created civilizations.

Building Vocabulary

subcontinent	pictograms	polytheists	kshatriyas
monsoon	linguists	dasyus	vaishyas
citadel	rajah	varnas	shudras
grid	soma	brahmans	jati

pariahs	nirvana	loess	acupuncture
reincarnation	sangha	kaolin	pagoda
karma	stupas	ethics	archipelago
dharma	yoga	yin	typhoons
moksha	suttee	yang	clans
gurus	relic	civil service	kami
ahimsa	reliefs	mandarins	lacquer

Reviewing the Main Ideas

1. Why did early Indian and Chinese civilizations develop in relative isolation from the rest of the world?
2. What factors might have caused the fall of the Harappan civilization?
3. Why did the Aryans avoid contact with the dasyus and later, the pariahs?
4. What aspects of Hinduism were criticized by Jainism and Buddhism?
5. What factors contributed to the spread of Buddhism? How did the spread of Buddhism affect the unity of the religion?
6. What contributions did the early Indians make in the arts and sciences?
7. Why did the Chinese call their land the "Middle Kingdom"?
8. What did Taoist scholars teach about the workings of the universe?
9. How did Confucian principles affect the later organization of Chinese government?
10. Why was the Silk Route important?
11. How was early Korea governed?
12. How were religion and government linked in early Japan?

Discussing Important Ideas

1. Did the caste system hold back India's social and economic development?
2. Do you accept the concept of reincarnation? Why or why not?
3. Was Asoka's renunciation of war a wise policy? Explain.
4. Why was the Gupta period a "golden age" for the arts and sciences?
5. In what ways did the peoples of India and China differ in their general attitudes toward life?
6. Explain the concept of the Mandate of Heaven. Did it work to serve the wishes of the Chinese people?
7. Did the teachings of Confucius encourage inquiry and change? Why or why not?
8. Do you agree with Shih Huang Ti's policy toward scholars? Why or why not?
9. If you had been a Yamato court official, would you have supported Buddhism?
10. Could Korea and Japan have developed civilizations without borrowing from China?

Using Maps

Refer to the map on page 45 to answer the following questions:
1. Why is India called a subcontinent?
2. In terms of north and south, what is the relative location of China to Southeast Asia? of the Gobi Desert to the Indian Ocean?
3. One inch equals about how many miles on the map of Han China?
4. Which rivers in South and East Asia have deltas?
5. About how many miles long is the Japanese archipelago? how many kilometers?

CHAPTER 3

Greek Scholars

" *Reason is the gods' crowning gift to humanity.* "

from Antigone, *a play by Sophocles*

The Greeks

Point out that the Greek civilization influenced people in the Middle East and South Asia as well as people in Europe.

While important civilizations emerged in the East, the Greeks developed the first great civilization in the West. They influenced western civilization more than any other people of the ancient world. Greek philosophers gave the West such basic ideas as democracy and the worth of the individual. Greek thinkers also developed the scientific method, the basic rules of geometry, and the principles of **logic,** or the science of reasoning. The Greek language shaped every major language in the western world. Other important contributions of ancient Greece were drama, athletic competition, and various styles of architecture. In fact, much of what has been accomplished in the West since ancient times is based on Greek thought and culture.

Like other peoples, the Greeks were influenced by the geography of their homeland. Ancient Greece included the southern part of Europe's Balkan Peninsula and an archipelago in the Aegean Sea. The Greek mainland is divided by mountain ranges and water inlets. Short, swift rivers flow from the interior to the sea. This type of terrain was not favorable for the development of a land-based civilization. However, the long, indented coastline of Greece provided many fine harbors. Most Greeks therefore settled on the coastal plains and the islands. Isolated from each other, they formed many small self-governing communities dependent on sea trade.

1 Early Aegean Civilizations

Greek civilization grew out of earlier civilizations that flourished in the Aegean area between 3100 and 1100 B.C. These Aegean societies were eventually destroyed by natural disasters and foreign invasions.

For nearly 3,000 years, the Aegean past was shrouded in mystery and legend. Then during the 1870's, Heinrich Schliemann, a German archeologist, uncovered many of the "lost" cities of the Aegean world. Schliemann's discoveries soon led to more excavations by other archeologists. In 1900, Sir Arthur Evans, a British archeologist, unearthed the remains of a great civilization on the island of Crete.[1] Further discoveries in this century have helped historians piece together the puzzle of early Aegean civilizations.

Minoans

The first Aegean civilization arose on Crete around 3100 B.C. Sir Arthur Evans named this Cretan civilization "Minoan" after King Minos, its legendary founder. He also divided Minoan history into three periods: Early Minoan (3100-2100 B.C.), Middle Minoan (2100-1600 B.C.), and Late Minoan (1600-1100 B.C.). Evans was able to determine these dates as a result of his discovery of both Egyptian and Minoan pottery in the same archeological layers. Knowing the age of the Egyptian pottery, he was able to figure the age of the Minoan pottery. Evans then worked out the Minoan periods of history so that they roughly matched the Egyptian periods of the Old Kingdom, Middle Kingdom, and New Kingdom.

Early Crete   During the Early Minoan period, the people of Crete settled in small communities ruled by chiefs. They lived in brick houses, made bronze goods, and became expert sailors. By about 2000 B.C. the Minoans had developed a thriving trade throughout the eastern Mediterranean. As a result, Minoan culture was influenced by the cultures of Egypt and the Fertile Crescent. For example, Linear A, the earliest style of Minoan writing, is related to the Semitic languages. Scholars, however, have yet to decipher it completely.

---

[1]Crete is the largest Greek island and stretches over 150 miles (240 kilometers) from east to west. It is located at the southern end of the Aegean archipelago where the Aegean and Mediterranean Seas meet.

Egypt was a journey of two days by boat from Crete.
The Fertile Crescent was three days away.

Knossos   During the Middle Minoan period,
the city of Knossos rose to power and controlled
all of Crete. Around 1800 B.C. the ruler of Knossos
completed the building of a large palace, the
ruins of which still stand today. The palace
covered about 5 acres (2 hectares). It consisted of
several stone houses that surrounded a central
courtyard. Passageways and rooms twisted and
turned in all directions to form a **labyrinth,** or
maze. The palace had a drainage system, hot and
cold running water, and portable fireboxes to
heat the rooms. In its warehouses were stored
large jars containing grain, wine, and olive oil.
About 1400 B.C. the palace was either destroyed
by invaders or a natural disaster.

Crete's Golden Age   During the Late Minoan period, Crete reached the height of its
power. Minoans grew wealthy from their control
of trade between the Middle East and the Aegean
area. Their rulers rebuilt the palace at Knossos
and constructed three new palaces elsewhere on
the island. These residences, as well as the cities
surrounding them, had no fortifications or walls
to protect them. To guard against outside attack,
the Minoans relied on their strong navy.

More than 90 cities and towns developed
throughout Crete. Knossos was the largest city,
with a population of about 100,000. Cobblestone
roads connected the important cities on the
island. The most famous road ran from Knossos
to Phaestus. It was 40 miles (64 kilometers) long
and had an inn where travelers could rest their
animals and eat in a beautifully decorated dining
hall.

Society and Culture   The Minoans were
divided into four main social groups: nobles,
merchants and artisans, farmers, and slaves.
Minoan women enjoyed a higher status than
women in other civilizations. In addition to
household duties, they were permitted to attend
sporting events. Minoan religion had more
goddesses than gods. The chief deity was the
Great Goddess, or Mother Earth, whom the
Minoans believed caused the growth of all living
things.

The Minoans enjoyed life and delighted in
beautiful objects. Minoan artisans designed
delicate jewelry and made decorative cups and
vases with paintings of flowers and animals.
They also produced a type of pottery that was as
thin as an eggshell. The walls of Minoan homes
were painted with brightly colored murals
showing scenes from daily life.

The Minoans loved sports. They probably built
the world's first arena, where boxing matches
were held. Another favorite sport was bull
leaping, a combination of acrobatic skill and
bullfighting. Men and women "fought" the bull
together. A man would grab the bull's horns and
do a somersault, landing on the bull's back. Then
he would do a back flip. Standing behind the
bull, a woman would catch her partner as he
landed. Many experts believe bull leaping was a
religious ritual as well as a sport.

Minoan civilization lasted until about 1400 B.C.
At that time, unknown invaders attacked Knossos and left it in ruins. Other Minoan cities soon
declined, and eventually disappeared. Around
1100 B.C. new invaders called the Mycenaeans
arrived in Crete from the Greek mainland.

The Mycenaeans linked Crete to the emerging
civilization of Greece. Minoan words entered the
Greek language, and Minoan styles influenced
Greek art. The Greeks also borrowed Minoan
legends, and added to them. The most famous is
the story of the warrior Theseus and his killing of

*This Minoan fresco, a painting done on plaster, from the
fifteenth century B.C. depicts the importance of trade to the
Minoan civilization of the island of Crete. What peoples
traded with the Minoans?*

Have students compare the cities of Knossos and Mycenae. Have them make generalizations about life and government in these two ancient cities.

Homer referred to the Mycenaeans as Achaeans.

the Minotaur, a mythological Cretan monster that was half-man and half-animal. The Greeks also believed that Zeus, their chief god, was born in the mountains of Crete.

Mycenaeans

Before their invasion of Crete, the Mycenaeans had built a major civilization in southern Greece. They originally entered Greece from the north around 2000 B.C. At that time, the Mycenaeans were known as Achaeans. By 1600 B.C. they had intermarried with the local population and were settled in farming towns and villages.

Mycenae   The principal center of Mycenaean civilization was Mycenae, a city on the mainland about ten miles (16 kilometers) inland from the Aegean Sea. In 1876, Heinrich Schliemann discovered six tombs in Mycenae that revealed the wealth of the Mycenaeans. The most impressive finds were several golden masks, which had been placed over the faces of deceased warrior-kings.

Cities   Unlike the Minoan cities, Mycenaean cities were highly fortified. For example, the walls of Mycenae were 23 feet (6.9 meters) thick. Outside the walls were the estates of warrior-nobles. Slaves and tenants lived in villages on the estates. They farmed the nobles' land and brought produce to city markets. Mycenaean cities were connected by good roads and bridges. In times of danger, the cities provided protection to people from the rural areas.

The dominant buildings in many Mycenaean cities were palaces. They served as centers of production as well as government administration. Within the palaces, artisans tanned leather, sewed clothes, fashioned jars for storing wine and olive oil, and made bronze weapons. Government officials kept detailed accounts of production and trade. To help in collecting taxes, they also kept records of the wealth of every person in the city. Taxes were collected in kind, or in the form of grain and other produce. These items were stored in the palace and used to pay government employees.

Heroic Age   By the 1400's B.C., the Mycenaeans had developed into powerful seafarers and had begun raiding nearby lands. Once they

AEGEAN CIVILIZATION 1400 B.C.

conquered Crete, the Mycenaeans dominated the Aegean area. They remained powerful until the 900's B.C. This period of Mycenaean strength is called the Heroic Age of Greece.

The Mycenaeans left no written history. Instead, they passed on stories about their kings and heroes by word of mouth. Some of these stories were based on actual people and events. With constant retelling, they became legends and were used to explain the relationships between humans and gods. In this form, the Mycenaean stories became the basis of Greek mythology.

Trojan War   The most famous episode of the Heroic Age was the Trojan War. This conflict was fought in the mid-1200's B.C. between the Mycenaeans and the people of Troy, a major trading city of Asia Minor. According to later Greek accounts, Paris, a prince of Troy, fell in love with Helen, the wife of a Mycenaean king. Paris kidnapped Helen and took her to Troy. To avenge this deed, the Mycenaeans laid siege for several years to Troy, but were unable to capture the city. Finally, they tricked the Trojans by building a huge wooden horse. The best Mycenaean soldiers hid inside the horse, while the rest boarded their ships and pretended to sail away. Thinking that the Mycenaeans had gone, the Trojans brought the horse into the city. The

In addition to the caption question below, ask students, "How did geography hinder political, social, and economic unity among the Greeks?"

The Greeks were great seafarers. This view shows a harbor on one of the Greek islands in the Aegean Sea. In this area, the Ionians built the early Greek civilization. How did geography affect the growth of Greek civilization?

Mycenaeans later crept out and attacked and burned Troy.

Although the details of the Trojan War are legendary, Heinrich Schliemann in 1870 proved that the city of Troy had actually existed. Since then, archeologists have uncovered the remains of nine cities on the site. Each successive city was built on the ruins of the one before it. Experts now believe that the seventh city was the legendary Troy of the 1200's B.C.

Dark Age About 1100 B.C., invaders known as Dorians entered Greece from the north. Because of their superior iron weapons, they were able to conquer the Mycenaeans. The Ionians, a people related to the Mycenaeans, fled from southern Greece to a region of Asia Minor bordering the Aegean Sea. They set up a group of self-governing communities and called their new homeland Ionia.

Due to these disruptive events, the Aegean world entered a "dark age" that lasted for more than 300 years. Contacts with the highly devel-

oped civilizations of the Middle East were cut off. Overseas trade stopped, and the urban population declined. The Aegean people soon lost their skills in record-keeping, painting, and crafts.

In spite of these setbacks, a new civilization slowly emerged in Ionia and spread to the Greek mainland. Small, separate communities appeared along the coast of Greece and in the interior. The people of Ionia and Greece called themselves *Hellenes*, or "Greeks." This early Greek population was made up of two classes: landowning **aristocrats,** or nobles, and poor peasants. The peasants served the nobles by tilling the land and fighting in local wars.

By 800 B.C. the Greeks began to produce their first literary works. Storytellers known as **bards** glorified the Mycenaean period and made it into an age of heroes. The greatest of these performers was the blind poet Homer. He composed two great epic poems about the Trojan War and its results: the *Iliad* and the *Odyssey*. The ancient Greeks memorized these epics and

Have students list some cities in the United States with the suffix *polis*, which means "city."

Using Greek expansion as an example, emphasize the relationship between trade and cultural diffusion.

repeated them orally until they were written down during the 500's B.C. Today, the *Iliad* and the *Odyssey* are considered the first masterpieces of Greek literature.

Another early literary figure was Hesiod, a small landowner from southern Greece. Instead of praising war heroes of the past, he reflected on the injustices of the "dark age" in which he was living. In his poem "Works and Days," he described the hard life of the landless peasants, who worked the fields of their ruthless landlords. He also predicted the decline of the world through five stages. The first was the Age of Gold; the last, which spanned Hesiod's lifetime, was the Age of Iron. Hesiod characterized the Age of Iron as a time when "might made right" and when people turned against their neighbors. In spite of his pessimism, Hesiod praised the values of rural life, such as hard work, thrift, and simplicity. These values would later contribute to the rise of a new Greek civilization.

1. Identify: Heinrich Schliemann, Sir Arthur Evans, Crete, Minoan, Linear A, Knossos, Theseus, Achaeans, Mycenae, Troy, *Iliad, Odyssey,* Homer, Hesiod.
2. Why do some historians view the Late Minoan period as a "golden age"?
3. What were the physical features of Mycenaean cities?
4. How did the Dorian invasions affect Greece?

2   Rise of Hellenic Civilization

By 800 B.C. the Greeks had emerged from the "dark age" with a great deal of cultural unity. They spoke a common language, shared the same customs, and worshiped the same deities. However, they did not unite under a single government. Instead, farming communities in Ionia and Greece joined together and formed separate city-states. This period of Greek history is known as the Hellenic era.

Polis

Each city-state, known as a **polis,** was independent and developed its own pattern of life. The typical Greek polis grew around a fortified hill called an **acropolis.** At the top of the acropolis was the royal palace and the temple of the local god or goddess. At its foot was the **agora,** or public square. The agora became the political and business center of the polis. Citizens gathered there to discuss politics and public affairs. The agora also served as a marketplace where artisans and merchants conducted business. Near the agora were many homes, shops, and gardens. The villages, fields, and orchards outside this built-up area were also part of the city-state.

The polis was the geographical and political center of Greek life. It gave its citizens a sense of belonging and received from them the highest loyalty. Citizens had certain rights that non-citizens living in the polis did not have. They could vote, own property, hold public office, and speak for themselves in court. In return, they were expected to participate in government and to defend the polis in time of war.

Economic Expansion   From 800 to 700 B.C., the Greek city-states began to play an important role in the Mediterranean world. Economic prosperity returned after the "dark age," and trade increased. The population rose, and the city-states became overcrowded. As a result, many Greeks migrated to coastal areas around the Mediterranean and Black Seas. There, they established colonies. By 500 B.C. Greek colonies flourished from Spain in the west to the Black Sea in the east.

The colonists maintained a strong attachment to their homeland. Each colony tended to come from the same city-state. Colonists called the city-state of their origin *metropolis,* or "mother city." Greek colonies were fully independent, but each kept close religious and cultural ties with its metropolis. Colonies provided grain, wool, dried and salted fish, and slaves to the homeland. In return, they received olive oil, wine, pottery, and clothing. As a result of this trade, the Greek world prospered.

Trade greatly influenced the development of Greek civilization. Greek merchants and traders traveled throughout the Mediterranean and came into contact with other civilizations. As a result, they borrowed new ideas and techniques.

Using the map below, have students estimate the distance from Greece to its farthest trading posts.

GREEK COLONIES   600 B.C.

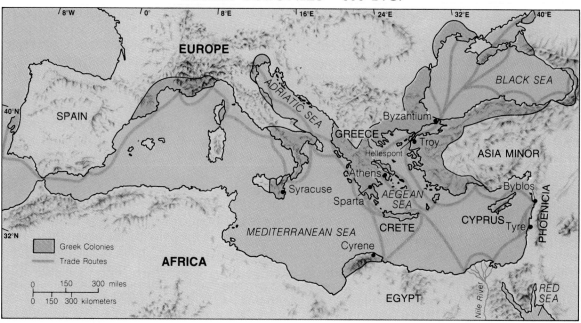

From the Phoenicians, the Greeks obtained an alphabet and adapted it to their language. They also used Phoenician skills to build longer and faster ships. Other foreign contributions to Greece were the Sumerian system of weights and measures, and the Lydian practice of coining money.

Political Change   Increased trade and commerce changed Greek political life. During the "dark age," each Greek community had been governed by a king with the assistance of a council of elders. Around the 700's B.C. the city-states emerged, and the kings gradually lost power to the landholding aristocrats. Many aristocrats profited from the increase in trade. With their new economic power, they took control of city-state governments.

During the mid-600's B.C., the city-states were divided by political conflicts. The aristocrats fought among themselves, and their hold on the city-states weakened. At the same time, new fighting techniques made their military role obsolete, or outdated. Greek armies traditionally had consisted of a small number of aristocratic warriors equipped with horses and chariots. Later, economic prosperity enabled a larger number of Greeks to buy arms. As a result, the aristocratic army was replaced by a citizen army composed mainly of prosperous farmers. This new army was based on the **phalanx,** an infantry unit armed with spears and swords that fought in close formation, 16 rows deep.

The aristocrats were soon challenged by a rising middle class of wealthy merchants and artisans. The merchants and artisans wanted to protect and expand trade routes, while many of the aristocrats sought to protect and expand their lands. To advance their interests, the merchants and artisans opposed the power of the aristocrats and demanded a greater role in government.

As the rich grew richer, the poor fell further into debt. Many peasants lost their land to the aristocrats and had to join part-time workers in the cities. Other poor people were sold into slavery. At the same time, some landowners began to shift large areas of land from grain production to more profitable orchards and vineyards. As a result, many agricultural workers lost full-time employment and became seasonal laborers. In protest, the lower class backed the wealthy merchants and artisans against the aristocrats.

Compare the religious role of Athenian monarchs with that of ancient Near Eastern monarchs.

The word *draconian* is derived from Draco. It refers to an extremely harsh or cruel code of laws.

Tyrants　To advance their cause, the discontented groups backed the rise of leaders known as **tyrants.**[2] Tyrants were champions of the common people and promised better government. Each tyrant seized power from the aristocrats and set up one-person rule. Once in power, tyrants weakened the landed aristocracy and supported the merchants and artisans. Most were good administrators and reformers. They promoted trade, carried out many public works projects, and treated the people justly. However, a few were harsh and gave the word "tyrant" its present meaning—a cruel and unjust ruler.

Tyrants ruled in the various Greek city-states until the end of the 500's B.C. They especially helped shape the early development of the greatest Greek city-states, Athens and Sparta.

Athens

Before the 600's B.C. Athens was a small town in Attica, a peninsula of central Greece. The region around Athens had poor, rocky soil, which made farming difficult. As a result, many Athenians worked in the silver mines or made ceramics. They also became skilled traders and seafarers. Athens, however, did not establish overseas colonies as had other city-states. Instead, it extended its territory on the Greek mainland. By the 600's B.C. it had brought all of the villages of Attica under its leadership.

Government　Athens was at first ruled by kings. Athenian monarchs were primarily religious and ceremonial leaders. They were elected by an assembly of citizens and advised by a council of nobles. Other executives included a **polemarch,** who led the armed forces, and an **archon,** who supervised government administration. All important government officials served one-year terms. When their terms ended, they joined a council of past officeholders.

In the 600's B.C. the final authority in Athens was the Assembly, made up of all wealthy citizens. Athenian citizens were males born of Athenian parents. Women, slaves, and **metics,** or resident aliens, were not considered citizens and could not participate in political life.

Many inequalities existed in Athenian life. Government was largely controlled by aristocrats. The laws were not written down, and hardships were imposed on the debt-ridden peasants and artisans. Soon the merchants became discontented and demanded reforms.

Draco　The first reforms in Athens were introduced by tyrants, who had the support of most of the people. In 621 B.C. a tyrant named Draco issued a written code of laws that applied to rich and poor alike. Draco's code made many improvements, such as distinguishing between intentional and unintentional killing. However, it became better known for its severe penalties. For example, the death sentence was ordered for many offenses. In making the code so harsh, Draco hoped to end violent quarreling among Athenian families.

Draco's code helped peasants and artisans in many ways; however, it showed preferences for certain groups of people. The murderers of citizens were treated more severely than the murderers of slaves and non-Athenians. The code also favored the interests of wealthy merchants and aristocrats over the interests of artisans and farmers, who were unable to pay their debts. In fact, debtors became slaves of their creditors, or those to whom a debt was owed.

Solon　The next series of reforms took place under the tyrant Solon in 594 B.C. Solon was born an aristocrat but made his living from trade. When he became an archon, he issued new regulations and revised the law. His reforms favored the merchants at the expense of the aristocrats. For example, wealth, rather than birth, became the major requirement for high public office. Solon also set up the Council of 400, which was open to wealthy merchants as well as aristocrats. The Council drafted measures that went to the Assembly for approval.

Solon also introduced reforms that were popular among the common people. He canceled all debts and freed debtors from slavery. He placed limits on landownership and gave small landowners the right to vote in the Assembly. Finally, citizenship was extended to merchants and artisans who were not born Athenians.

---

[2]The Greeks borrowed a Lydian word, *tyrannos,* which means "a ruler."

Have students list the contributions of Draco, Solon, and Peisistratus to Athenian government.

Free Spartan citizens were called "equals."

After Solon left office, Athens was plunged into turmoil. During this time, the aristocrats, farmers, merchants, and artisans quarreled over Solon's reforms. The aristocrats thought that Solon had gone too far, while the farmers thought he had not gone far enough. The merchants and artisans, however, believed that Solon had wisely followed a moderate course.

Peisistratus About 560 B.C. the government of Athens was taken over by the tyrant Peisistratus. Although a wealthy man, Peisistratus won the support of the farmers and the other lower classes. He pushed reforms in a more radical direction. Large estates were divided among the landless peasants. The poor were given loans, and jobs on large public works projects. Peisistratus also promoted trade, craft production, and colonial expansion. At the same time, he maintained peace with Athens's Greek neighbors.

Reformers after Peisistratus continued to reduce the powers of the nobles and expand the participation of the common people in the government. They introduced the practice of **ostracism,** by which the people voted to exile undesirable politicians for ten years. They also enlarged the membership of the Council to 500. Representation on the Council was determined by residence in geographic districts, rather than by wealth or birth. The Athenian army was reorganized, and its generals were elected by the people. By 500 B.C. Athens had taken major steps toward democracy.

Sparta

The development of Sparta contrasted greatly with that of Athens. Sparta was the most important city-state in the Peloponnesus, a peninsula of southern Greece. It was located in a fertile valley with a mild climate, adequate water, and rich soil. As a result, Sparta's economy was based on agriculture. Although the Spartans sought new wealth, they avoided trade and did not establish overseas colonies. Instead they invaded neighboring areas, added to their farmlands, and enslaved the local people.

Population The population of Sparta was divided into three groups. The first group was the Spartans themselves. Descended from the Dorians, the Spartans made up only ten percent of the population. In spite of their small numbers, they were the ruling class. Male Spartans had full equality among themselves and were the only ones who could be citizens. The second group was the **perioeci,** made up of merchants, artisans, and farmers from the conquered communities. Although they were free, the perioeci had few political rights. The third group was the **helots,** or slaves, who worked the land for the Spartans. The helots made up about 60 percent of the population of Sparta.

Government Sparta was officially governed by two kings who ruled jointly. The kings, however, had little power. Their only tasks were to lead the army and conduct religious services. An assembly, made up of all citizens over the age of 30, passed laws and decided questions of war and peace. Each year the Assembly chose five overseers, known as **ephors,** to manage public affairs. A senate assisted the ephors. It was made up of men over 60, who were chosen to serve for life. The Senate proposed laws to the Assembly and served as a supreme court.

Social Life The Spartans feared rebellion by the conquered peoples. After an unsuccessful revolt in the 600's B.C., they placed secret agents among the helots and perioeci to report on any plots against the polis. To maintain order, male Spartans were organized into a permanent army and soon became known as the toughest soldiers in the Greek world. Since the helots did all the work on the land, the Spartans were free to devote themselves to full-time military training.

Life in Sparta revolved around the army and military values. Ephors examined all newborn infants to see if they were healthy. If they were, they were allowed to live. If they were not, they were left on a hillside to die. At the age of seven, boys were taken from their homes and trained for military service. They lived in military camps under strict discipline. The goals of their training were physical strength, endurance, fighting skills, and loyalty. At 20, young men became citizen-soldiers and were sent to frontier areas. At 30, they were expected to marry but they

Discuss with students what they think life as a free citizen in Sparta would have been like.

The education of Spartan males stressed physical conditioning with many gymnastic and athletic exercises. Spartan men held brutal tests of endurance, competing sometimes to the death. Even today one definition of the word "Spartan" is "not afraid of pain or danger." Why did Spartans emphasize military training?

could not have a household of their own. They had to live and eat in military barracks, where they shared expenses with other soldiers. They could retire from the army when they reached age 60.

Spartan women had more freedom than the women of other Greek city-states. They mixed freely with their husbands' friends and enjoyed sports like wrestling, boxing, and racing. They were trained to run their own households and to raise healthy and strong children. When Spartan women sent their men into battle, they told them to return either as victors carrying their shields or as dead men on their shields.

As Sparta became more militaristic, its people became known for their extreme simplicity and distaste for luxury. Spartans shunned the arts and intellectual activities. They were suspicious of any new ideas or practices that would bring changes to their society. For example, they used heavy iron bars instead of coins as currency. In this way, Spartans hoped to discourage trade and to maintain their traditional self-reliance. While other Greek city-states improved their production, trade, and standards of living, Sparta remained a poor agricultural society that depended on the labor of slaves.

1. Identify: Hellenic era, Attica, Draco, Solon, Peisistratus, Peloponnesus.

2. What were the physical features of a typical Greek polis?
3. How did political reforms change the government of Athens?
4. How was Spartan society organized?

3 Wars and Expansion

The developing Greek city-states faced a growing threat from the Persian Empire. At this time, the Persians were the strongest military power in the world. In 546 B.C. Persian armies conquered the Greek city-states in Ionia. The Ionians disliked their conquerors and were restless under Persian rule.

Persian Wars

In 499 B.C. the Ionians revolted against the Persians. They were supported in their rebellion by Athens and other cities on the Greek mainland. The Athenian fleet arrived in Asia Minor, and the Athenian army burned Sardis, the Persian headquarters in the area. Four years later, the Persians counterattacked and burned the Ionian city of Miletus. The men of Miletus were killed, and the women and children were taken to Persia as slaves.

Marathon   After putting down the Ionian rebellion, King Darius I of Persia realized that his

Some teachers might wish to discuss the naval strategy involved in the Battle of Salamis.

Spartan military discipline can best be illustrated by the Battle of Thermopylae. A small force of Greeks led by Spartan king Leonidas resisted attacks by the huge Persian army for three days before they were annihilated. Even when they faced certain defeat, the 300 Spartans among the Greek soldiers chose to fight to the end rather than retreat. What did the Greeks do to win the Persian Wars?

victory would not be complete as long as Athens and the other Greek city-states continued to aid the Ionians. In 490 B.C. he sent an army and a fleet across the Aegean Sea to attack the Greek city-states. The Athenians hurriedly prepared for defense. They sent Philippides, a long-distance runner, to Sparta to ask for that city's help. Philippides covered the 140 miles (224 kilometers) in less than 48 hours. The Spartans, who were celebrating a religious festival, did not help immediately. Except for the aid of several small towns, Athens had to face the Persians alone.

The Athenians and the Persians met at Marathon, a seaside plain 26 miles (41.6 kilometers) north of Athens. There, the smaller Athenian force decisively defeated the larger Persian army. According to legend, the Athenians sent a runner to carry news of the victory to Athens. The runner reached the agora of the city and cried out "*Nike!*," the Greek word for victory. Then, he fell to the ground, dead of exhaustion.[3]

The Athenian triumph at Marathon gave the Greeks more time to organize their forces. Athens gained enormous prestige from this victory, and was soon recognized as a rival to Sparta.

Salamis After Marathon, the Persians left Greece, but they did not stay away for long.

[3]Today the term "marathon" refers to a 26-mile (41.6-kilometer) race. The marathon is one of the important events in the modern Olympic Games.

Xerxes, Darius I's son and successor, was determined to avenge the defeat and punish the Greeks. The Greeks were aware of the Persian threat and worked to increase their military strength. Athens built a new fleet and became the strongest sea power among the city-states. Sparta developed the strongest army.

In 480 B.C. Xerxes assembled an army of 100,000 Persian soldiers. The soldiers moved along the northern Aegean shore while the fleet, numbering about 3,000 ships, sailed along the coast. When the Persians entered Greece, Xerxes sent messengers to demand the surrender of the Greek city-states. Many of the weaker city-states were frightened by the Persian invasion and declared their neutrality. But Athens and Sparta, along with their allies, banded together to defend their territories.

At first the Greeks suffered many setbacks. As the Persian forces moved steadily southward toward Athens, a Spartan-led Greek force tried to delay them by holding a narrow mountain pass at Thermopylae. After a heroic defense, all the Greeks at Thermopylae were killed and the Persians broke through. Xerxes and his forces captured Athens, now a deserted city, and burned its acropolis.

Although Athens was destroyed, the Greeks continued to fight the war. A Greek fleet, mostly Athenian, met the Persian fleet at the Bay of Salamis. There, the Persians were defeated in one of the great naval battles of history.

Have students explain the phrase "Golden Age."

After the battle at Salamis, the fighting turned in favor of the Greeks. Greek armies defeated the Persians in several important battles, and the Persian forces retreated from the Greek mainland. As a result of their triumph, the Greeks gained security and a new pride and self-confidence, which enabled them to advance their civilization.

Golden Age of Athens

After the departure of the Persians, the people of Athens quickly rebuilt the city and reorganized its government. They further reduced the power of the aristocrats. At the same time, a new officer called a **strategos,** or general, emerged. The strategos, elected by male citizens, became the most important Athenian official.

Athens organized a defensive alliance with the other Greek city-states. The alliance aimed to free the Ionian city-states that were still under Persian rule, and to ward off any future Persian invasions. Athens provided most of the land and naval forces. The other city-states had to furnish money and ships. The treasury of the alliance was kept at the Aegean island of Delos. Because of the important role of Delos, the alliance became known as the Delian League. As head of the the Delian League, Athens became strong and influential.

Pericles   In 461 B.C. a young aristocrat named Pericles was elected strategos. With the exception of the year 444 B.C., he was reelected annually until his death in 429 B.C. While in power, Pericles carried out a large public works program to make Athens the most beautiful city-state in Greece.

The government of Athens did not have planned budgets, and the Assembly approved building expenditures without providing funds. As a result, Pericles had to tap private sources of wealth. First, he forced the rich to make generous "donations" to the city. Later, he moved the treasury of the Delian League to Athens. The money contributed to the treasury by Athens' allies was then used to improve the city. Pericles justified this policy on the grounds that the allies were paying Athens for protection.

PERSIAN WARS

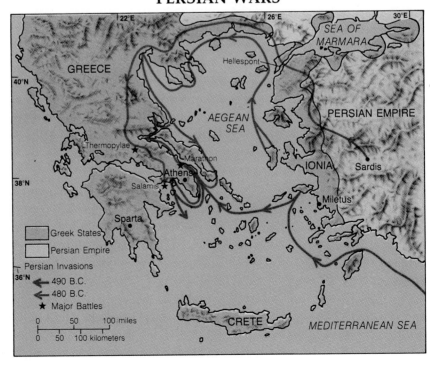

The term *pantheon* describes the group of all officially recognized Greek gods and goddesses.

Compare Pericles's view of democracy with that of the students' views.

Greek Gods and Goddesses

The ancient Greeks believed the universe began as a great emptiness known as *Chaos*. From *Chaos* there arose gods and goddesses who lived on Mount Olympus in northern Greece. There were many gods and goddesses, each with different personalities and responsibilities.

Zeus	chief god
Hera	wife of Zeus
Poseidon	god of the sea
Apollo	god of the sun
Ares	god of war
Athena	goddess of wisdom and art
Aphrodite	goddess of love and beauty
Dionysus	god of hospitality and joy
Artemis	goddess of the hunt
Hermes	messenger of the gods
Hephaestus	god of fire
Hades	god of the Underworld
Demeter	goddess of agriculture
Hestia	goddess of home and family

Although the allies complained, the people of Athens supported Pericles, who was able to provide them with jobs and money.

Athenian Democracy   Pericles favored the extension of democracy in Athens. He increased the number of government officials and provided pay for their services. This reform made it possible for even the poorest citizen to hold public office. Soon about one-third of Athenian citizens were involved in government work. Many wealthy Athenians saw democracy as a threat and attacked Pericles' reform. They claimed that it would bankrupt the city and encourage laziness. In a famous address, recorded by the historian Thucydides, Pericles defended the ideals of Athenian democracy:

> Our constitution is called a democracy because power is in the hands not of a minority but of the whole people. When it is a question of settling private disputes, everyone is equal before the law; when it is a question of putting one man before another in positions of public responsibility, what counts is not membership of a particular class, but the actual ability which the man possesses. No one, so long as he has it in him to be of service to the state is kept in political obscurity because of poverty. . . .*

There were still limits, however, to Athenian democracy. All male citizens could take part in the government, and many of them exercised this right. Yet other Athenians could not participate in political life. Women were acknowledged as citizens, but still could not vote or hold office. Metics and slaves continued to be refused citizenship, and could not participate in government. Nonetheless, politics at this time was more advanced in Athens than anywhere else in the world. In spite of its limitations, ancient Athens contributed much to the western concept of democratic government.

Peloponnesian Wars

In foreign relations, Pericles favored peace with Persia and with Athens's Greek neighbors. As Athens gained more power and prestige, he

*The Peloponnesian Wars, Thucydides, tr. by R.W. Harmondsworth, © 1954 by Penguin Books, pp. 116-121.

Have students comment on the consequences of the Peloponnesian Wars for the Greeks.

also worked to extend trade and shipping. As a result of Pericles' policies, the Delian League was gradually transformed into an Athenian empire.

Many member city-states, however, became dissatisfied with Athenian control of the League. Some tried to leave it, but they were treated as rebels and punished. Sparta, Corinth, and other city-states outside the League grew alarmed at the rise of Athens. Led by Sparta, they formed an alliance known as the Peloponnesian League.

A struggle for power soon developed between Athens and Sparta. In 431 B.C. tensions led to a series of conflicts known as the Peloponnesian Wars. At the beginning of the fighting, Pericles planned Athenian strategy. To avoid a direct battle with the well-trained Spartan troops, he moved the rural population of Athens behind the city walls. In addition, he ordered the Athenian navy to attack the Spartan coast and to keep the sea-lanes open for supplies.

The first year of war passed without a clear outcome. Since Sparta had no navy, the Athenians expected to hold out indefinitely. But in the second year, a plague broke out in Athens. It killed about one-third of the population. One of those who died was Pericles. Following his death, Athens was governed by weak leaders. They made peace with Sparta in 424 B.C., but war broke out five years later. In 405 B.C., during this second phase of the Peloponnesian Wars, Athens was defeated by Sparta.

The Peloponnesian Wars brought disaster to all the Greeks, both victors and vanquished. Many city-states declined in population, unemployment became widespread, and prices rose sharply. Sparta fell from its top position, and there was no powerful city-state to take its place. As a result, fighting broke out once more among the city-states. This warfare wasted their resources and endangered their freedom.

Rise of Macedonia

While the Greek city-states were fighting each other, people known as the Macedonians were building a strong kingdom north of Greece. The Macedonians, like the Greeks, were a mixture of

PELOPONNESIAN WARS

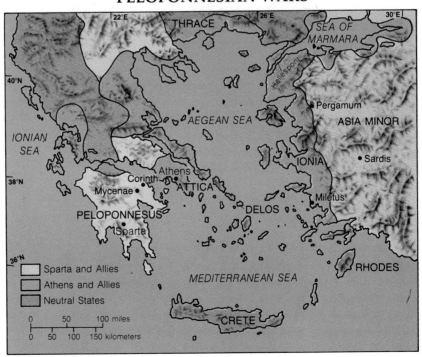

Philip II of Macedonia and his son Alexander considered themselves Greeks.

Indo-European groups. The Macedonian language contained many Greek words and expressions. The Greeks, however, thought of the Macedonians as "backward," and refused to accept them as true Greeks.

Philip II, the Macedonian king, admired Greek culture and wanted to make Macedonia the leading power in Greece. During his youth, he had been a hostage in Thebes, a Greek city-state. While imprisoned, he had learned a great deal about Greek political affairs and war tactics. As king, he used this knowledge to organize his troops and train an excellent cavalry. In a short time, Philip unified Macedonia and conquered the northern Greek city-states.

The Greek city-states farther south relied on Philip's support to fight each other. By prolonging their battles, Philip weakened his Greek opponents. In 339 B.C. he defeated them at the Battle of Chaeronea. After this victory, Philip, as ruler of Greece, announced that he would lead the Greeks in a war against Persia. However, before he could carry out his plans, Philip was murdered. His son Alexander became king.

Alexander the Great

Alexander was only 20 when he became the ruler of Macedonia and Greece. He was handsome, strong, intelligent, and very ambitious. A commander of the Macedonian army since he was 16, Alexander was highly respected by both his Macedonian and Greek soldiers. By 334 B.C. Alexander's troops were ready to invade the Persian Empire. With 35,000 soldiers, Alexander crossed the Hellespont, a narrow body of water separating Asia and Europe. This act was the first step in the creation of a new empire.

Early Conquests   Alexander had his first major encounter with the Persians at the Granicus River in western Asia Minor. He led his cavalry through the shallow water and up the riverbank to the enemy's ranks. Foot soldiers followed to win a decisive victory. After this triumph, Alexander sent 300 coats of Persian armor to Athens as a thanksgiving offering to the goddess Athena.

Alexander then marched along the coast of Asia Minor, freeing Greek city-states from Persian rule. Meanwhile, Darius III, the Persian king, gathered a large army to stop Alexander's advance. The Greeks and Persians finally met at Issus in Syria. Alexander's superb tactics once again resulted in a Greek victory. Darius III fled to Persia, but his mother, wife, and daughters were captured by Alexander, who treated them with respect.

Instead of pursuing Darius, Alexander and his troops moved south along the Mediterranean coast. They captured the seaports of Phoenicia and cut off the Persian fleet from its main supply bases. After a long siege, the port city of Tyre was captured, and the entire Persian fleet surrendered to Alexander.

Late in 332 B.C., Alexander reached Egypt. The Egyptians, discontented under Persian rule, welcomed Alexander and declared him a pharaoh. In Egypt, Alexander established a new city and named it Alexandria after himself. Alexandria soon became the leading port on the Mediterranean and a major center of civilization in the ancient world.

Final Campaigns   In 331 B.C. Alexander entered Mesopotamia. He met Darius and a large Persian army east of the Tigris River near Arbela. The Persian army included infantry, elephants, and chariots with knives extending from the wheels. It was no match for Alexander's forces, however, who won a great victory. Alexander then captured the key cities of the Persian Empire: Babylon, Susa, and Persepolis. His soldiers destroyed the royal palaces and seized the great treasures of gold and silver in these cities. When it was learned that Darius had been killed by one of his generals, Alexander declared himself king of Persia.

After the defeat of Persia, many Greek soldiers were tired of fighting and wanted no more conquests. Alexander allowed them to return home. But the Macedonian troops remained with him. In 327 B.C. Alexander led them east to India. During three years of fighting, he conquered lands in central Asia and the Indus River Valley. Alexander hoped to go farther into India, but his army refused. He finally returned to Babylon, which he planned to make the capital of his empire.

Have students speculate about the goals of Alexander and what might have happened had he lived longer.

The map below is the subject of the "Using Maps" section of the Chapter 3 Review.

ALEXANDER'S EMPIRE 336–323 B.C.

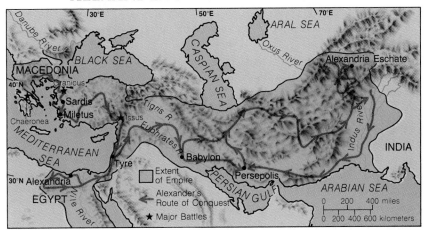

Alexander's Empire

In his conquests, Alexander acquired much of the civilized world. His empire stretched from western Greece to northern India. It covered more than 11,000 miles (17,600 kilometers).

Goals Alexander hoped to create a strong government for the empire that would permanently unite Europe and Asia. He wanted to combine the best of eastern and western cultures into one civilization. Alexander personally tried to promote these goals. He wore eastern dress and imitated the court life of Persian kings. He married a Persian woman and also ordered thousands of his soldiers to marry Persian women.

Alexander spread Greek culture throughout the Middle East. He brought botanists, geographers, historians, surveyors, and architects with him on his conquests. Soon Greek settlements were founded throughout the Asian parts of the empire.

Alexander, however, did not live long enough to fully realize his goals. In 323 B.C., he died of fever in Babylon at the age of 33. In spite of his short life, Alexander had become a legendary figure and was known as "the Great." His military accomplishments were remembered and admired by succeeding generations.

Divided Empire Following Alexander's death, his generals divided his vast empire into three domains. Seleucus, a cavalry officer, ruled the Asian provinces and founded the Seleucid dynasty. The Seleucids built many cities, the most famous of which was the capital Antioch in Syria. By the 100's B.C. the Seleucids had lost most of their provinces. Syria, however, remained their stronghold until the coming of the Romans in the next century.

Another general, Ptolemy, ruled Egypt and made Alexandria his capital. He and his successors governed with the absolute power of the ancient pharaohs. They claimed divinity and owned all the land. They fought frequent wars with the Seleucids. The most famous Ptolemaic ruler was Queen Cleopatra, who lost her kingdom to the Romans in 30 B.C.

Macedonia and Greece made up the third domain of Alexander's empire. At first, the entire region was ruled by the general, Antigonus. But within a short time, the Greek city-states declared their independence and began fighting with each other. The successors of Antigonus continued to rule Macedonia. They sometimes intervened in Greek affairs to settle disputes among the city-states. Finally, in the 100's B.C. Macedonia and Greece were defeated by Rome and absorbed into the Roman Empire.

1. Identify: Miletus, Marathon, Salamis, Xerxes, Thermopylae, Delian League, Pericles, Peloponnesian League, Macedonia, Philip II, Alexander the Great, Hellespont, Darius III, Issus, Alexandria, Seleucus, Antioch, Ptolemy, Cleopatra, Antigonus.

2. What reforms did Pericles bring to Athens?
3. What were the causes and consequences of the Peloponnesian Wars?
4. How large was Alexander's empire? What were his goals?

4 Greek Civilization

During the 400's B.C. Athens became the chief center of Greek civilization. Its thinkers, writers, artists, and builders set standards that were admired and copied by other Greek city-states.

Art and Architecture

After the Persian Wars, the people of Athens rebuilt their city. Under the rule of Pericles, they turned their acropolis into an architectural treasure. On the summit of the acropolis, builders erected magnificent temples and palaces. These buildings were known for their rows of marble columns, beautiful statues, and harmonious geometric designs. Some of them still stand today. They include the Propylaea, or the gateway to the Acropolis, and the Erectheum, a temple to two noted Athenian goddesses. But the most splendid piece of architecture that has survived is the Parthenon, the temple of the goddess Athena.[4] Built in 14 years, the Parthenon measures 230 feet (69 meters) by 100 feet (30 meters) and is 65 feet (19.5 meters) tall.

The Athenians also excelled in sculpture and painting. Sculptors showed an interest in the beauty of the human body. They carved monumental figures with amazing skill and simplicity. Beautiful pottery was also produced. On elegantly-shaped vases, painters made graceful designs and portrayed scenes of daily life.

Drama

The Greeks were the first to write and perform plays. Most of their dramatic productions appeared in poetic form during the 400's B.C. The earliest ones were **tragedies,** or stories about human suffering that often had unhappy endings. Based on ancient legends, they presented various moral and philosophical issues.

---

[4]Athena was regarded as the patroness, or protector, of Athens.

This model shows the Acropolis of Athens. Each Greek city built a temple on its acropolis to house the patron deity. Why was the acropolis of each city built on a hill?

Aeschylus The first great **tragedian,** or writer of tragedies, was Aeschylus (525-456 B.C.). He wrote more than 70 plays, of which only seven have survived. In his tragedies, Aeschylus looked at the relationships of gods and people as well as the conflicts that emerge in human society. His most famous work is a **trilogy,** or set of three plays, called the *Oresteia.* The *Oresteia* traces a series of violent and tragic events in the family of the legendary king Agamemnon. In the end, the plays show that punishment for wrongdoing should be decided by the law of the community rather than by personal revenge.

Sophocles Sophocles (496-406 B.C.) was the next great tragedian. He served as a general in the Athenian army and lived through the tragic years of the Peloponnesian Wars. In his works, Sophocles examined human pride and guilt. His most famous play, *Oedipus Rex,* deals with the plight of Oedipus, a king who unknowingly kills his father and marries his mother. Oedipus uses all his powers to solve the crime, only to discover that he is the murderer. Another play, *Antigone,* relates the story of a young woman who chooses to obey her conscience and accept suffering rather than follow the orders of her uncle. Although Sophocles showed the limitations of human nature in his works, he also revealed human compassion and courage.

Euripides Euripides (484-406 B.C.) was the last of the great Greek tragedians. In his works, he supported Athenian democracy and criticized

HISTORY AND THE ARTS

Greek Drama

Western drama began in ancient Greece during the 600's B.C. The earliest performances were part of religious festivals that honored Dionysus, the god of nature. The audiences sharing in these celebrations sat in rows on the slope of a hill. Below, a chorus performed on a flat, circular area called the orchestra. It chanted a story about Dionysus and danced in geometric patterns to the music of a flute.

Over the years, the settings for the festivals changed greatly. They became known as theaters. In a theater, the hillside was carved into the shape of a semicircle, stone seats were added, and the orchestra was paved. A low building called a skene was erected behind the orchestra. The skene was used as a dressing room by the performers. Greek theaters were known for their remarkable acoustics, or sound effects. A person could speak softly from the orchestra and be heard in the highest seats about 200 feet (60 meters) away.

The performances themselves also underwent changes. Around 550 B.C. the dramatist Thespis introduced an actor to recite poems that explained the songs and dances of the chorus. Later, two more actors were added, and a painted canvas was installed as a backdrop. Soon actors became more important in the performance than the chorus. In this way, the earliest play was born.

All of the performers in a Greek play were men. Women were allowed to watch the performances but could not act in them. Actors played more than one role. They wore large masks that showed the sex, age, and mood of a particular character. The mouth of the mask was shaped like a funnel. This helped carry the actor's voice to the entire audience. Actors also wore heavy padding under their robes and boots with thick soles. This enabled them to be more easily seen by the audience.

Greek plays were performed only at community festivals. Performances began at sunrise and continued all day. Tragedies were presented in the morning and comedies in the afternoon. Anyone who could not afford to buy a ticket was admitted free.

Greek drama was a means to provide entertainment, news, commentary, and moral instruction. The Greeks considered support of the theater to be a public responsibility. A public official decided which plays were to be performed and selected a prominent citizen to stage them. At each festival, a panel of citizens judged the plays. The author of the winning play was awarded an ivy crown.

1. How did Greek drama develop over the years? Where were plays performed?
2. What role did the theater play in the lives of the ancient Greeks?

Greek plays were based on events from tales about gods and legendary heroes. Playwrights often showed the complex relationship between gods and humans. In these works, humans often struggled against impossible odds. Those who challenged the gods often met disaster; those who obeyed them were rewarded.

long-standing beliefs and practices. He was also sensitive to the plight of women. In his play *The Alcestis*, a husband allows his wife to die in order to save his own life. After her death, he suffers remorse for his foolish decision. Another play, *The Trojan Women*, describes the horrors of the Trojan War. It portrays the cruelty of Greek soldiers toward the women of Troy whom they have captured. Because of their frank treatment of issues, the plays of Euripides shocked many Athenians. As a result, Euripides was an unpopular figure during his lifetime.

Comedy   The Greeks also developed a second type of play known as a **comedy,** or a play with a humorous theme and a happy ending. Comedies reflected everyday life and were popular among the common people. The most famous **comedian,** or writer of comedies, was Aristophanes (448-380 B.C.). In his works, Aristophanes made witty comments about the leading figures and issues of his day. For example, in the comedy *The Clouds*, Socrates is shown as a lofty thinker who appears in a basket floating in midair.

Education and Sports

The Greeks believed that people should strive for excellence in developing their minds and bodies. They emphasized the importance of a well-rounded education.

Learning   Beginning in the 400's B.C., the sons of citizens were able to receive some form of schooling. At the age of seven, they began their education at private schools. There they learned such subjects as music, reading, writing, and poetry. After four years, boys from poorer families left school and learned a trade. Those from wealthy backgrounds continued their education under tutors called **sophists.** They learned geometry, astronomy, and **rhetoric,** or public speaking. Tutors and the more advanced students also discussed ethical, political, and philosophical questions.

Sports   The Greeks believed that "a sound mind is in a sound body." Thus, they gave an important place to gymnastics and sporting activities. Because of their interest in physical fitness, the Greeks were the first people to develop organized athletic competitions.

The most famous sporting events in ancient Greece were the Olympic Games. Begun in 776 B.C., they were held every four years at Olympia in honor of the god Zeus. All trading and fighting stopped during the Olympics. The Olympics were so important that the Greeks measured time by the four-year intervals between the games. Each interval was called an **olympiad.**

Athletes from all over the Greek world came to compete in the games. Only male athletes, however, were allowed to take part. Women

Wrestling was one of the most popular Greek sports. Modern wrestlers, like world champion Lee Kemp (in red uniform), use the same style of wrestling as the ancient Greeks. Only today's rules differ. Why were sports important to the Greeks?

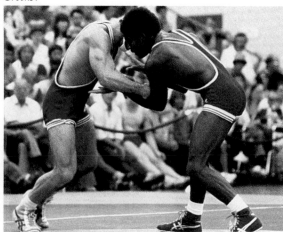

Socrates was regarded as a great teacher as well as a great philosopher. Demonstrate the Socratic method of teaching.

One of Plato's important goals was to explain the fall of Athens.

could not compete in, or even watch, the games. About 40,000 spectators sat on grassy slopes overlooking the field area. Olympic competition at first consisted of only a footrace. Later it grew into several athletic events.

Olympic winners were regarded as heroes. At the games, they received crowns made from olive leaves. They were held in high esteem by their city-states. Statues were built in their honor, and parades were held. Some city-states even excused great athletes from paying taxes.

Greek Thought

The 400's and 300's B.C. saw the flowering of Greek thought in Athens. During this period, a number of important thinkers developed and organized ideas that have since formed the intellectual heritage of western civilization.

Socrates   Greek philosophers believed that through a process of logical thinking, people could discover wisdom, truth, and the laws of nature. Socrates, an Athenian from a poor family, was the first of the great philosophers. Born in 470 B.C., he gave up his craft as a sculptor and devoted his time to teaching. To instruct his students, Socrates developed a teaching technique later called the **Socratic method.** In using this method, he would ask students pointed questions without giving them answers. Then he would oppose the students' answers with logical arguments. As a result, the students would be forced to defend their statements. In this way Socrates hoped that his students would begin to think for themselves. They would be able to clear away mistaken ideas and discover eternal truths.

Because of his sincerity and sharp intellect, Socrates gained many followers. However, prominent Athenians viewed his teachings as a threat to the city. In 399 B.C. they accused him of corrupting the young people and plotting to overthrow the government. A jury of 500 citizens tried Socrates and sentenced him to death. Declaring his innocence and faithful to his ideas, Socrates carried out the sentence himself. He drank poisonous hemlock juice and died among his grieving followers.

Plato   Socrates' work was carried on by his pupil Plato (427-347 B.C.). Born an Athenian

aristocrat, Plato thought about entering politics. Instead, he became a teacher and opened a school called the Academy. During his teaching, Plato took the ideas of Socrates and organized them into the first system of philosophical thought.

Plato also carried out the earliest studies in political science. In his work *The Republic*, he presented a plan for what he thought would be the ideal society and government. Unlike many Athenians, Plato disliked democracy, claiming that it allowed people too much freedom.[5] He distrusted the lower classes and wanted only the most intelligent and well-educated citizens to participate in government. In addition, Plato gave more importance to the state than to the individual. He believed that each person should place service to the community above strictly personal goals.

Aristotle   The last great philosopher of ancient Greece was Aristotle (384-322 B.C.). A pupil of Plato, and later a tutor of Alexander the Great, Aristotle opened a school in Athens called the Lyceum. At this school, he made important contributions to the field of logic. Aristotle's work in logic gave western thinkers an important intellectual tool for exploring knowledge in any area.

Aristotle also closely observed the natural world and wrote about his findings. He made studies in biology, political science, physics, drama, and other fields. Because of his wide range of knowledge, Aristotle was later called "the master of them that know." His writings became intellectual classics.

Historians   The Greeks used their intellectual skills in the writing of history. Herodotus, known as the Father of History (484-425 B.C.), was the first Greek historian. He wrote about the Persian Wars and arranged his material with great artistry. Although he sometimes failed to separate history from legend, Herodotus passed on important information about the events and customs of his day to later historians.

---

[5]Plato's dislike of democracy probably came from his personal experience. As a young man, he had witnessed much political turmoil in Athens during the Peloponnesian Wars. He had also been shocked by Athenian treatment of Socrates.

Discuss the work of Herodotus and Thucydides.
Explain their importance to modern historians.

The world's first great philosophers were Greek. Among the most noted were Socrates (left), Plato (center), and Aristotle (right). They encouraged learning and logical reasoning. How did each contribute to the development of intellectual inquiry?

Another noted historian of ancient Greece was Thucydides (460-396 B.C.). Thucydides is regarded as the first scientific historian. He wrote a history of the Peloponnesian Wars. To write this work, Thucydides visited battle sites, interviewed eyewitnesses, and carefully examined documents.

Science During the Hellenic period, most Greek achievements were in art, literature, and philosophy. However, at this time, the Greeks did make a few important contributions to science. Lacking scientific equipment, they made most of their discoveries by observation.

The first important Greek scientist was Thales of Miletus, who lived in Ionia during the 600's B.C. Thales worked out a scientific method based on gathering information and developing a **hypothesis,** or possible explanation. His ideas were followed by thinkers such as Aristotle.

Greek scientists also contributed to the field of medicine. Hippocrates, called the Father of Medicine, believed that diseases came from natural, not supernatural, causes. Basing his work on observation, he traveled all over Greece diagnosing illnesses and treating sick people. He drew up an ethical code for doctors known as the Hippocratic Oath. The code, which is still followed today, requires doctors to do their best to help their patients.

Hellenic Society

During the Hellenic period, Greek thinkers and artists gave their primary loyalty to the polis. For its honor and glory, they aimed for excellence in their fields. The benefits of Hellenic culture, however, were enjoyed by only a minority of the population. Wealthy citizens alone had the time and money to spend on art and leisure activities. Slaves, who made up one-third of the Athenian population, did most of the heavy work in craft production and mining. Many of them were household servants and some were artisans in shops.

Women did not share fully in Hellenic society. They were trained to be responsible for their households and the upbringing of children. Lower-class women sometimes assisted their husbands at work, went to the market, and mixed socially with other people. However, upper-class women usually stayed at home and made few public appearances.

In spite of barriers, some Greek women were able to influence culture and public life. One of the most famous women was Aspasia. Born a metic, she set up a school of rhetoric in Athens. Aspasia also worked to improve the social status and education of Athenian women.

Hellenistic Achievements

In the 300's B.C. Alexander's conquests took Greek culture to the Middle East and central Asia. As a result, a new period began known as the Hellenistic era. Hellenistic culture was a mixture of many cultures. Its ideas and practices shaped the civilization of the eastern Mediterranean world for more than three centuries after the death of Alexander.

City Life   Many cities were planned and built during the Hellenistic period. Most of the Hellenistic cities developed in the Middle East or Asia Minor. Alexandria in Egypt, Pergamum in Asia Minor, and Antioch in Syria were the most advanced. They had elegant boulevards with street lighting, water and drainage systems, and large markets and production centers.

Alexandria was the largest and wealthiest of the Hellenistic cities. The lighthouse of its busy Mediterranean port was almost 400 feet (120 meters) high and is considered one of the Seven Wonders of the Ancient World. Alexandria's streets were straight and intersected each other at right angles. This was in contrast to the crooked streets of the ancient world's older cities. Alexandria also had a large stadium, an amphitheater, a **hippodrome,** or racetrack, and a library of nearly a million volumes. Alexandria was a metropolis of many cultures. Its population of over 500,000 consisted of Greeks, Jews, Persians, Syrians, and Egyptians.

The Hellenistic cities of the Middle East soon surpassed the cities of Greece in cultural brilliance. The Hellenistic age also allowed more personal freedom. During this period many of the restrictions placed on women were gradually removed. For example, upper-class women were no longer secluded and could freely move about their cities. Many of them attended schools of higher learning and contributed to scholarship, politics, and the arts.

Science and Mathematics   Many advances in science occurred during the Hellenistic period. Although limited by their simple instruments,

Greek scientists performed many experiments and developed new theories, particularly in astronomy. Anaximander concluded that the earth was a sphere and that its land area was surrounded by water. Eratosthenes made an estimate of the earth's circumference, to within one percent of the correct figure. Aristarchus concluded that the earth revolved around the sun. However, many of these discoveries were not immediately accepted. For example, most Hellenistic scholars insisted that the earth was the center of the universe.

The Hellenistic period also saw important discoveries in mathematics and physics. Euclid of Alexandria wrote *Elements*, a book that collected and organized all existing information about geometry. Archimedes of Syracuse worked out basic problems concerning the mass and motion of objects. He also developed ideas for machines, such as the lever, pulley, and cylinder-screw (used to lift water for irrigation).

Art and Literature   During the Hellenistic era, Greek art departed from the simplicity and idealism of Hellenic times. It became more emotional, detailed, and realistic. Sculptors produced figures in dramatic poses. Artists made mosaics and wall murals that portrayed vivid scenes of daily life.

The Hellenistic period also saw the production of many books and the formation of libraries. Writers carefully followed the literary styles of the Hellenic age. As a result, their work showed little originality. The most creative Hellenistic writer was Menander. His works became models for western writers in later centuries.

Philosophy   Hellenistic philosophy shunned political and social questions. Instead, it centered on personal behavior. Two systems of thought attracted most Hellenistic intellectuals: Epicureanism and Stoicism.

Epicureanism was based on the ideas of the scholar Epicurus. He and his followers, called Epicureans, believed that people should lead quiet lives and seek personal happiness. Their idea of pleasure was peace of mind, not physical enjoyment.

Stoicism was founded by a thinker named Zeno. The Stoics, or the followers of Stoicism, believed that humanity lived under a common moral law. Therefore, all humans were brothers and sisters and should respect one another. According to the Stoics, people would be able to gain happiness if they ignored their emotions and, instead, followed their reason. In this way, they would be able to accept even the most difficult circumstances of life.

After the Roman conquest of the Middle East, Hellenistic philosophy continued to influence the thought of the ancient western world for many years. Stoicism, in particular, affected both Roman intellectuals and early Christian thinkers.

1. Identify: Parthenon, Aeschylus, Sophocles, Euripides, Aristophanes, Socrates, Plato, Aristotle, Herodotus, Thucydides, Thales of Miletus, Hippocrates, Aspasia, Hellenistic, Euclid, Archimedes, Menander, Epicurean, Stoic.
2. What features characterized Athenian art and architecture during the Hellenic period?
3. What kinds of plays were written in Greece?
4. How were young Greeks educated?

CHAPTER 3 REVIEW

Summary

1. Greek civilization began in the area of the Aegean Sea. During the 2000's B.C., the Minoans on the island of Crete developed a seafaring culture. Their achievements eventually reached the Greek mainland.
2. About 1400 B.C. control of the Aegean area passed to the Mycenaeans. Mycenaean warriors ruled Greece and fought a war against Troy in Asia Minor. The Trojan War is described in two epic poems, the *Iliad* and the *Odyssey*, composed by the Greek poet Homer.
3. After 300 years of invasions and chaos, the Greeks fully emerged as a distinct people in the 700's B.C. They built city-states, expanded trade, and established colonies.
4. Athens and Sparta became the dominant Greek city-states. Athens developed a freer society for its citizens, while Sparta used its army to maintain rigid control over most of the population.
5. During the 500's B.C. the Greek city-states, led by Athens, defeated the Persians in a series of wars. Athens then established the Delian League among the victorious city-states. It later transformed the League into an empire.
6. Friction between Athens and Sparta led to the Peloponnesian Wars. The conflicts resulted in the defeat of Athens and the decline of the Greek city-state system.
7. Alexander the Great, ruler of Macedonia, united the Greeks and conquered an area stretching from the Nile to the Indus Rivers. After Alexander's death, his empire was divided among his generals.
8. Greek civilization is divided into the Hellenic and Hellenistic periods. During the Hellenic era, the Greeks excelled in art, literature, and philosophy. During the Hellenistic era, their greatest achievements were in science and mathematics.

Building Vocabulary

logic	polis	tyrants	ostracism
labyrinth	acropolis	polemarch	perioeci
aristocrats	agora	archon	helots
bards	phalanx	metics	ephors

strategos	trilogy	sophists	Socratic method
tragedies	comedy	rhetoric	hypothesis
tragedian	comedian	olympiad	hippodrome

Reviewing the Main Ideas

1. How has archeology advanced our knowledge of Aegean and Greek civilizations?
2. What was the Minoan attitude toward life? How was it reflected in their art, religion, and social life?
3. What role did trade play in the development of early Aegean civilization?
4. What were the major themes of early Greek literature?
5. What social groups supported political change in the Greek city-states? What groups opposed change? How were political reforms achieved?
6. How did Athens differ politically from Sparta?
7. How did women live in ancient Greece?
8. How was Athens affected by the Persian Wars?
9. Why was the Delian League formed?
10. How did Alexander acquire his empire? What happened to the empire after his death?
11. What were the major differences between Hellenic culture and Hellenistic culture?
12. What did Plato think of Athenian democracy? What was his ideal type of government?

Discussing Important Ideas

1. What are some of the geographical features of Greece? Were they important in the development of Greek civilization? Explain.
2. Are legends and folk tales helpful in understanding the past? Why or why not? Support your answer with examples from ancient Greece.
3. Contrast life in Sparta with life in Athens. In which city-state would you have preferred to live? Explain.
4. It has been said that the battles of Marathon and Salamis were important battles in the history of the western world. Do you agree or disagree? Explain.
5. Was Athens, during the 400's B.C., a true democracy? Give reasons for your answer.
6. What role did alliances, such as the Delian League and the Peloponnesian League, play in ancient Greece? Did they help or hinder Greek political unity?
7. If you were an aide of Alexander, would you have advised him to expand his empire as much as he did? Explain.
8. Which of the following Greek accomplishments has had the greatest impact on the modern world: drama, architecture, or government? Give examples.
9. If you were an Athenian, would you have approved or disapproved of the trial of Socrates? Explain.
10. Do you agree with Plato's theory of government? Why or why not?

Using Maps

Refer to the map on page 71 to answer the following questions:
1. What is the approximate distance from Macedonia to the Indus River? Give your answer in miles and kilometers.
2. At what latitude and longitude is Persepolis?
3. What rivers are located in Alexander's empire? Which river do you think was the most important in the empire? Explain.
4. Refer to the map on page 796. List the modern countries whose territories were once part of Alexander's empire.

CHAPTER 4

Roman Temple

❝ *For they conquer who believe they can.* ❞

Virgil, Roman writer (70-19 B.C.*)*

The
Romans

Using a map of the Mediterranean region, point out the central location of Italy. With a relief map of Italy, describe the major geographical features of the peninsula.

Rome began as a small city-state in central Italy. By 200 A.D. its armies had conquered most of the Mediterranean area and had established a large empire. Roman rule brought a period of peace, prosperity, and stability to the conquered territories. As a result, the culture of Rome was diffused, or spread, among many different peoples.

Internal crises and foreign invasions finally brought an end to the Roman Empire in the 400's A.D. Rome, however, passed on a great legacy to the West. Roman engineering contributed many building skills that are still in use today. Latin, the language of the Romans, became the basis of many modern European languages. Roman law, with its ideal of equal justice for all, shaped the legal systems of all western countries. The Roman political system, which strengthened central authority while it protected local government, still affects western societies. Christianity, the leading religion of the West, developed in the Roman Empire. Today, the Roman Catholic Church, the largest Christian body, is still centered in Rome.

1   Early Rome

Geography influenced the rise of Rome. Italy, which was the center of Roman civilization, is a narrow boot-shaped peninsula about 700 miles (1,120 kilometers) long and 150 miles (240 kilometers) wide. It extends south from Europe toward Africa, dividing the Mediterranean Sea into eastern and western halves. Italy's central location helped the Romans to assert their control over the entire Mediterranean world.

Other geographical features also shaped the rise of civilization in Italy. Mountains and foothills cover most of the peninsula. In the north are the Alps Mountains, which separate Italy from the rest of Europe. The Apennines, another chain of mountains, run north and south, forming the backbone of Italy. Nevertheless, these two mountain ranges did not block communication among Italy's regions, nor did they prevent outside invaders from entering Italy.

In spite of its mountainous terrain, Italy has some low areas of land well suited for agriculture. A mild, moist climate enables farmers to grow vegetables, grapes, olives, and citrus fruits. Transporting goods, however, has been difficult. Italy's rivers are short and shallow, and its long coastline has few good harbors. Therefore, the early people of Italy did most of their travel and trade by land rather than by water. As a result, the different regions of the peninsula developed close economic ties, which later made it possible for the Romans to unite them politically.

Settlement of Italy

During the period from 2000 to 1000 B.C., Indo-European peoples related to the Mycenaeans in Greece and the Hittites in Asia Minor invaded Italy. They established villages in various parts of the peninsula and farmed the land. The most important of these invading groups were the Latins, who settled in the central Italian plain of Latium. The Latins were the ancestors of the Romans.

Around 900 B.C., the Etruscans, a people from Asia Minor, settled north of the Latin villages in the plains of Etruria. The Greeks also arrived in Italy about this time. They formed separate farming communities in southern Italy and Sicily, an island at the toe of the Italian peninsula. The Etruscans and Greeks developed close trading ties. In time both peoples passed on their cultures to the Latins.

The Etruscans were strongly influenced by Greek culture. Their language, which has yet to be deciphered, was written with an alphabet based on Greek characters. Etruscan art followed Greek styles; however, the Etruscans showed greater attention to color and line. The most

Some archeologists believe that the site of Rome was settled much earlier than 800 B.C.

The withdrawal of Etruscan merchants from Rome in 509 B.C. resulted in a great economic loss for the city.

Since the remains of Etruscan civilization are few, scholars have learned much about Etruscan culture from rock-carved tombs. Built beneath a mound of earth, an Etruscan tomb was equipped with luxuries for the dead, such as jewelry, garments, and pottery. The body was laid in a bed-shaped stone coffin, complete with pillow. Often, a sculptor shaped a realistic clay figure of the deceased to rest upon the coffin. What other works of art were found in Etruscan tombs?

notable examples of Etruscan art are murals, or wall paintings, of daily life found in large underground tombs.

Etruscan men and women were known for their love of food, music, and sports. Unlike Greek women, Etruscan women enjoyed many freedoms. They were encouraged to take part in public celebrations, and they were allowed to conduct business and own property. According to later Roman tradition, Tanaquil, an Etruscan queen, was skilled in science and politics.

Rise of Rome

About 800 B.C. several Latin villages along the Tiber River in central Italy united into the city of Rome.[1] Built on seven hills, Rome controlled the Tiber, which ran to the sea, as well as the trade routes that ran north and south along the Italian peninsula. This favorable location helped Rome become the most important of the Latin communities.

Etruscan Rule   About 600 B.C. the Etruscans invaded Latium and captured the city of Rome.

There, the Tarquins, a prominent Etruscan family, established a monarchy. Under Etruscan rule Rome became the largest and richest city-state in the Italian peninsula. The Etruscans drained the marshy land around Rome, and in its center built a marketplace called the Forum.[2] The Etruscans gave the Romans building skills, religious rituals, and social customs.

The people of Rome, however, disliked Etruscan rule and wanted their freedom. In 509 B.C. they drove out the Tarquins and established a **republic**, or a form of government in which the people elect their leaders.

Social Groups   After independence, powerful aristocrats called **patricians** took over Rome's government. Although making up only ten percent of the population, they held all important government posts. The vast majority of Romans were known as **plebians**. They included wealthy, non-aristocratic townspeople and landowners as well as merchants, artisans, shopkeepers, small farmers, and laborers. Like patricians, plebians were citizens, paid taxes,

---

[1]Roman legend states that the twin brothers Romulus and Remus founded the city in 753 B.C. As infants, they were abandoned by their mother and raised by a she-wolf.

[2]The Forum later became a vast complex of buildings. It served as the center of Roman government, religion, and commerce.

Censors also acquired the right to pass judgment on the moral fitness and qualifications of Senate nominees and to bar a nominee from membership if he was deemed unfit.

Have students compare the government of Rome with those of Athens and Sparta.

served in the army, and voted. However, they did not enjoy equal rights with patricians. Plebians could not hold public office or marry patricians. Also, if they fell into debt, they could be sold as slaves.

Government   Roman government was made up of executive and legislative bodies. Executive power in the Roman Republic was held by two patrician officials called **consuls**. Consuls were elected for one-year terms. As administrative and military leaders, they held the power of life and death over Rome's people. Each consul could **veto**, or refuse to approve, acts of the other. Both had to agree on policy decisions.

In times of crisis, consuls could appoint a respected official as **dictator**. A dictator held absolute power for a period of six months, or for the duration of an emergency. Other officials under the consuls included **praetors**, or judges, and **censors**, or keepers of tax and population records.

Rome was also governed by legislative assemblies made up of representative groups of citizens. The most important and powerful assembly was the Senate. It was made up of 300 patrician men, called **senators**, who were chosen for life. The Senate handled many tasks. For example, it advised consuls, debated foreign policy, proposed laws, and approved contracts for constructing roads, temples, and government buildings.

Another body was the Assembly of Centuries. It represented the concerns of the army and was divided into **centuries**, or military units of 100 men each. Despite the presence of some plebians, the Assembly of Centuries was largely patrician. Its duties included electing officials and deciding questions of war and peace.

Plebians Against Patricians

During the 400's B.C. the patricians faced mounting opposition from the plebians, who resented their inequality and wanted to share political power. In 471 B.C. the plebians refused to serve in the army. They threatened to withdraw from Rome and set up their own city-state. To prevent economic ruin and civil war, the patricians agreed to some of the plebian de-

mands. As a result, Rome avoided violence and revolution, and its people became more united.

Tribunes   The plebians gained the right to choose ten officials known as **tribunes**. Tribunes were plebians and represented plebian interests in the government. They could veto the actions of a consul or any other official. This veto power defended the plebians against any abuse of power by patricians. In carrying out their duties, tribunes were protected by law. They could not be arrested, and any person who injured them could be put to death.

In addition to tribunes, the plebians gained their own assembly. Known as the Assembly of Tribes, it was composed of plebian representatives, who were divided among 35 groups based

ITALY 500 B.C.

The Twelve Tables constituted one of the most severe law codes in history.

Point out that during the fourth century B.C. Roman soldiers became professionals, being paid for their services.

on geographical area. The Assembly of Tribes elected the tribunes, who presided over its meetings. By 287 B.C. it was the chief legislative body of Rome.

Twelve Tables In the early days of the republic, Roman laws were not written down. As a result, most plebians did not know the laws. They only learned about it from the statements made in court by patrician judges. The plebians resented patrician control of the law. They demanded that the laws be written to protect them against the injustices of patrician officials. Finally, in 451 B.C., Roman laws were inscribed, or carved, on 12 bronze tablets known as the Twelve Tables. The tablets were placed in the Forum so that everyone would see them. The Twelve Tables became the basis for all future Roman law.

Legal changes soon followed that improved the status of plebians. Among these, plebians were allowed to marry patricians, failure to pay debts was no longer penalized by slavery, and all public offices were opened to plebians. In spite of these benefits for the common people, only patricians and rich plebians could afford the expense of holding office. As a result, the republic continued to be dominated by a small group of powerful and wealthy citizens.

1. Identify: Apennines, Latins, Etruscans, Tarquins, Assembly of Centuries, Assembly of Tribes, Twelve Tables.
2. In what ways did geography contribute to the rise of civilization in Italy?
3. How was power distributed in the Roman Republic?
4. Why did the plebians force the patricians to change Rome's government? What changes were made?

2 Roman Expansion

From 500 to 300 B.C., Rome faced threats from neighboring communities in Italy. To protect their territory, the Romans either conquered their opponents or forced alliances on them. At the same time, in southern Italy, several Greek city-states began fighting among themselves. Rome saw this development as an opportunity for further expansion. By 265 B.C. Rome had become the undisputed ruler of most of the Italian peninsula.

The Romans enjoyed good relations with the conquered peoples of Italy. They were known as mild rulers who did not kill or enslave their defeated foes. Many territories were permitted to keep their own governments, laws, and social customs. In turn, they became Roman allies. Rome expected them to provide troops for war and to support its foreign policy. Some of the conquered peoples were even allowed to become citizens of Rome.

Roman Army

Rome's success in war was due to its strong army. In the early days of the republic, every adult male citizen was required to serve in the army when needed. Also, no man could run for public office unless he had been a soldier for at least ten years. Roman soldiers fought without pay and had to supply their own weapons. They were grouped into phalanxes. However, the phalanxes were too large and slow moving for warfare in hilly areas. The Romans eventually ended the phalanx system and reorganized the army into smaller units called **legions**. Each legion consisted of about 6,000 soldiers, who were called **legionaries**. A legion was further divided into smaller units of 60 to 120 soldiers. With legions, the Roman army gained greater flexibility and striking power.

Legionaries were well trained and disciplined. They spent long hours practicing with their convex, or curved, shields and double-edged iron swords. They also went on long marches every day. Any disobedience was severely punished.

During the Italian conquests, Roman ideas and customs spread throughout the peninsula. Roman soldiers built fortified camps known as **colonae**. Some of these later grew into towns and trading centers. Legionaries also built a network of roads, so troops and supplies could move forward more rapidly. These roads increased trade and communication among the different regions of the peninsula. The army also provided thousands of Romans with new lands for settlement. The army's achievements united

The word *Punic* literally means "Phoenician." It was used in reference to Carthage and the Carthaginians because Carthage was founded originally as a Phoenician trading post.

Have students explain how they think the Romans employed land tactics to naval warfare.

Italy, making it a base for further Roman conquests. This expansion, however, took place gradually with no set plan.

By the 200's B.C., Rome's only powerful rival in the Mediterranean was Carthage, a former Phoenician colony on the coast of North Africa. Carthage was the capital of a large commercial empire. It ruled all of North Africa, most of Spain, and the western half of Sicily.

First Punic War   In 264 B.C. Rome and Carthage came into conflict over Sicily. Carthage feared that Rome would take the island. Rome, in turn, believed that Carthage planned to close the Strait of Messina, a narrow passageway between Italy and Sicily. The conflict, which lasted until 241 B.C., was the first of three wars that came to be known as the Punic Wars.

Carthage was wealthier than Rome and had the strongest navy in the Mediterranean. Rome had a better army, and territory that was easier to defend. However, after losing several battles at sea, the Romans built a new fleet and developed a new naval tactic. They used grappling irons and movable bridges to join their ships to Carthaginian ones. Roman soldiers then boarded the Carthaginian vessels and engaged in hand-to-hand combat. With this advantage, Rome defeated Carthage and permanently crippled its naval power. After the war, Rome forced Carthage to surrender Sicily and to pay a huge **indemnity**, or payment for damages.

Second Punic War   Carthage eventually recovered from its defeat. To make up for the loss of Sicily, its army, under General Hamilcar Barca, began to unify Carthaginian territories in Spain. In 221 B.C. Hamilcar's son Hannibal became governor of Spain. Hannibal hoped to use his new position to destroy Rome.

Hannibal, the Carthaginian general, is famous for his tactical skills. When he led his troops across the Alps into Italy, he took the Romans by surprise. Hannibal overcame great handicaps to defeat a Roman army twice the size of his own. He ordered his troops at Cannae to form an arc. Then he deliberately allowed the Romans to advance upon the center, while his cavalry on either side surrounded the thousands of Roman cavalry and foot soldiers. More than 60,000 Romans were killed. Modern military leaders continued to use this tactic successfully. Why did Hannibal refuse to take Rome?

Have students locate the major battle sites on the map below. Ask student volunteers to describe the importance of each battle.

ITALY 218 B.C.

In 218 B.C. Hannibal began a daring attack against Rome. With an army of 40,000 soldiers and 50 elephants, he left Spain, marched through southern Gaul,[3] and crossed the Alps into Italy. Nearly half his troops and all the elephants were lost in the crossing. But Hannibal was still strong enough to challenge the Romans on their own territory.

Although he was outnumbered, Hannibal defeated the Roman armies sent against him. His forces crushed the Romans at Cannae in south-

eastern Italy, and soon he reached the outskirts of Rome. In spite of the urging of his officers, Hannibal refused to take the city. Instead, he hoped for a negotiated settlement. But an agreement was never reached.

The war took a new turn when Roman General Publius Scipio landed an army in North Africa and attacked Carthage. Hannibal was called home to defend the city. In 202 B.C. Scipio met Hannibal and defeated him at Zama, a town near Carthage. Once more the Carthaginians had to accept a harsh peace. They lost Spain to the Romans and had to pay another huge indemnity.

---

[3]Today, Gaul is known as France.

The once-mighty Carthaginian fleet was reduced to ten ships. Carthage remained independent, but its power had finally been broken.

Third Punic War Following the Second Punic War, Rome and Carthage remained at peace for 50 years. Carthage's prosperity once again revived. Although the city was no threat, Rome began the Third Punic War in 149 B.C. in order to end Carthaginian independence. A large Roman army landed in North Africa and laid siege to Carthage for three years. When the Carthaginians finally surrendered, the Romans burned the city and plowed salt in its land so that nothing would ever grow there again. Carthage's people were either killed or sold into slavery. As a result of its victory, Rome gained complete control of the western Mediterranean.

Rome and the Hellenistic East While Rome was fighting the Punic Wars, its forces were drawn into conflicts in the Hellenistic East. In 230 B.C. Roman legions crossed the Adriatic Sea and attacked pirate bases in the region that is now Yugoslavia. Some 20 years later, Rome brought the entire eastern Adriatic coast under its rule.

King Philip V of Macedonia opposed Roman rule in the Adriatic region. To block Roman expansion, he formed an alliance with Hannibal during the Second Punic War. The Romans, however, secured the support of several Greek city-states and defeated Philip in a series of battles. After its victory over Macedonia, Rome pledged to respect the freedom of the Greek city-states. But constant quarreling among the Greeks enabled the Romans to play one territory against another. Through this policy of "divide and conquer," Rome increased its influence in Greece.

Meanwhile, the Seleucids were expanding into Asia Minor and along the Aegean coast. Supported by Hannibal, King Antiochus III of Seleucia decided to drive the Romans from Greece. However, he failed twice to achieve his goal. Following his second defeat in 188 B.C., Antiochus was forced to give the Romans all of the Seleucid territories in Asia Minor.

Two decades later, the Romans fought a war against Macedonia, and subsequently annexed it. The Greek city-states were now under Roman control. In 146 B.C. the Greek city-state of Corinth rebelled against Rome. Roman legions crushed the uprising and burned Corinth to the ground. They killed all the men and sold the women and children as slaves.

In the following decade, Rome made other gains in the eastern Mediterranean. In 133 B.C. the kingdom of Pergamum in Asia Minor came under Roman rule. Syria and Egypt remained independent, but their governments were forced to follow pro-Roman policies. By 130 B.C. Rome was master of the Hellenistic East. With this latest conquest, Rome ruled territories stretching from Spain in the west to Asia Minor in the east. The Romans began to call the Mediterranean *Mare Nostrum,* or "Our Sea."

1. Identify: Pyrrhus, Carthage, Sicily, Hamilcar Barca, Hannibal, Publius Scipio, Zama, Philip V, Antiochus III, Corinth, Pergamum.
2. How was Rome's army improved?
3. What were the effects of the Punic Wars on Rome? on Carthage?
4. Why were the Greeks unable to stop Roman expansion in the east?

3 Republic in Crisis

Rome faced many problems arising from its conquests. The Roman Republic had been created to meet the needs of a small city-state. Now, Rome controlled vast territories with diverse populations.

Political leaders had difficulties adjusting Rome's form of government to this new situation. The political strains were also accompanied by social and economic upheaval. Rome entered a period of profound change that brought much dissatisfaction to both Romans and the newly conquered peoples.

Provinces

Rome organized its non-Italian territories into provinces. Each province was allowed to keep its own language, religion, laws, and customs. However, the people had to pay tribute to Rome and to recognize its supreme authority.

Provincial Government Rome's provinces at first were poorly governed. The leading

Have students imagine that they are living in Rome during the second century B.C. Discuss and evaluate the advantages and disadvantages of Roman political, economic, and social expansion.

officials were governors called **proconsuls**. Appointed by the Senate for one-year terms without salary, proconsuls often accepted bribes, robbed the public treasury, and neglected their official duties. Lesser provincial officials also enriched themselves at public expense.

Corruption was particularly rampant in the collection of taxes. Rome hired officials called **publicans** to bring in taxes from the provinces. The publicans paid Rome the required amount of their collection. Then they were allowed to keep whatever extra money they gathered. Taxes became very heavy as the people were caught between the demands of Rome and the demands of wealth-seeking governors and publicans.

Military Rule   Because of widespread dislike of Roman rule, rebellion was a constant danger in the provinces. Roman legions had to be stationed permanently in most areas. Many military commanders became proconsuls. Strictly enforcing law and order, most used severe discipline that eventually ended the threat of revolts. For the most part, the provinces gradually adjusted to Roman rule.

Cicero, Rome's leading orator, on the floor of the Senate fought to save the republic. He felt the triumvirate was unconstitutional and refused to join his friend Pompey. Why did the first triumvirate fail?

Economic and Social Expansion

Wars of expansion also changed the economic and social life within the Roman Republic. Before these wars, the republic's economic strength had rested upon the small, independent farmer. But as Rome expanded, the importance of this group to the Italian economy declined.

Latifundias   During the period of conquest, the Roman government acquired properties in the conquered territories. It rented these properties to wealthy Romans, who joined individual units into large estates called **latifundias**. Grain was grown on the latifundias for export to Italy. Latifundia owners used slaves acquired from the conquests to work the land.

Since labor costs were cheap, latifundia owners could keep grain prices low. This enabled them to capture the Italian grain market and to bring great wealth to the provinces. At the same time, most Italian latifundias, also using cheap slave labor, switched from grain to fruits, vegetables, and olives. As a result, there were no markets left for the small farmer. Reduced to poverty at home and in the provinces, many farmers sold their land and moved to the cities.

Cities   The large migration from the countryside caused Rome and other Italian cities to increase in size and population. The crowded conditions in the cities showed the sharp gap between rich and poor that had come following Rome's conquests. Meanwhile, many Romans grew wealthy from increased trade with the provinces. These business people made up a new social group called **equites**. The equites struggled for equal political power with the old patrician and wealthy plebian groups. They set new standards for Rome by placing more value on a person's wealth than on his or her background or character.

Most urban dwellers, however, were poor. Those who had recently migrated from the countryside or from the provinces were often unemployed. Small businesses produced most of the goods in ancient Rome. Normally, small businesses would have hired the migrants, but many now used slaves instead. Due to this available, cheap labor source, businesses

Point out that Tiberius's running for reelection as a tribune was unprecedented and traditionally unaccepted in ancient Rome.

Point out that Pompey had conquered Syria and Palestine before joining the first triumvirate.

showed little desire to expand production, invent new technology, or create new jobs.

Reformers

A few wealthy Romans recognized that the condition of the poor had to be improved if Rome was to avoid revolution. They also believed that steps had to be taken to restore the traditional values of discipline, self-sacrifice, and devotion to the republic. One of these reformers was Tiberius Gracchus, a noble and a grandson of Scipio.

Elected tribune in 133 B.C., Tiberius had the Assembly of Tribes pass laws to benefit the poor. These measures limited the amount of public land owned by the rich and gave surplus land to poor urban dwellers. Many senators opposed these reforms and tried to block them. To win public support for his cause, Tiberius decided to run for a second term as tribune. During the election campaign, the opponents of Tiberius organized a riot in which Tiberius and 300 of his followers were killed.

A decade later, Gaius Gracchus, the younger brother of Tiberius, was elected tribune. He backed land reform and tried to increase the number of small farmers. He also provided the urban poor with grain at low prices. Gaius defended his reforms during two terms as tribune.[4] He was killed in 121 B.C. in a riot planned by his enemies. Gaius's death sharply increased tensions between Rome's rich and poor.

Generals

With the failure of the reformers, the common people lost faith in the ability of politicians to solve Rome's problems. A series of civil wars began that further weakened the republic and gave increasing power to military commanders.

Marius In 108 B.C. General Gaius Marius was elected consul. He brought large numbers of landless and unemployed men into the army. In addition to pay and equipment, Marius promised grants of public land to the new recruits

following their military service. Thus, a professional army was created in which soldiers owed their loyalty to their commanders, not to the republic. With obedient soldiers supporting him, Marius was able to force the Senate to pass laws favoring the common people.

Sulla In 88 B.C. the Senate appointed Lucius Cornelius Sulla to lead an army against a Roman opponent in Asia Minor. Marius, however, wanted Sulla's command, and civil war broke out. Sulla drove Marius out of Rome and put his own supporters into power. For the first time, a general was able to use his army to control the government.

While Sulla was fighting in Asia Minor, Marius returned to power. Seven years later, Sulla returned to Rome and defeated Marius' supporters. At Sulla's orders, thousands of citizens were brutally executed.

Sulla then became dictator for life. He limited the powers of the tribunes and the Assembly of Tribes, while increasing the power of the Senate. However, the army was still the most powerful and important institution in the republic.

First Triumvirate After Sulla retired in 79 B.C., a new group of leaders came to power. In 70 B.C. General Gnaeus Pompey and the politician Marcus Licinius Crassus were elected consuls. They gained the support of Julius Caesar, a rising young aristocrat. In 60 B.C. Caesar, Pompey, and Crassus formed a **triumvirate**, a group of three persons with equal power.

The triumvirate soon proved to be an unstable arrangement. Politically ambitious, Caesar was elected a consul in 59 B.C. He also took a military command in Gaul, which was inhabited by a group of Indo-Europeans known as Celts. Caesar conquered the Celts and forced them to accept Roman rule. He also invaded Britain, another Celtic territory. As a result of Caesar's military victories, Rome gained control of much of northwestern Europe.

Crassus was killed in battle in 53 B.C. Pompey meanwhile feared Caesar's growing power and popularity. In 49 B.C. Pompey, with the support of the Senate, ordered Caesar to return to Rome without his army. Caesar refused to yield to Pompey's demand and marched his army

---

[4]The land reforms worked for a number of years. But the sale of grain at cheap prices forced the urban poor to depend on the government for food. This eventually became a drain on the Roman treasury.

Julius Caesar wrote *Commentaries on the Gallic Wars* in which he described his conquest of Gaul. Some teachers might wish to assign parts of this work to students.

The wealthy aristocrats in the Senate objected to the reforms of Julius Caesar. They opposed the idea of a dictator ruling their republic. When the senators saw statues of Caesar and his face on Roman coins, many feared that he planned to make himself king. Sixty conspirators plotted and murdered Caesar. Even though the assassins cried for liberty on the streets of Rome after the stabbing, the same senators were unable to restore the republic. Why were they unsuccessful?

toward Rome. Unable to defend the city, Pompey fled to Greece with most of the Senate.

After securing his position in Rome and the western Mediterranean, Caesar defeated Pompey in Greece. Pompey then fled to Egypt, where he was murdered by the anti-Roman Egyptian king. Caesar later put the king's sister Cleopatra on the throne as an ally of Rome.

Caesar   After his return to Rome, Caesar took control of the government. In 45 B.C. he was named dictator for life. Although the republic was preserved, Caesar ruled like a monarch. He used his power, however, to introduce popular reforms.

Caesar ended the bitter fighting among Rome's political groups. Under his rule, the government gave jobs to the unemployed and provided public land to the poor. Caesar granted citizenship to many people in the provinces. He also added representatives from the provinces to the Senate. Finally, Caesar adopted a new calendar based on the Egyptian year of 365¼ days.[5]

Many Romans believed that Caesar was a wise ruler who had brought order and prosperity to

Rome. Others, however, regarded him as a tyrant who would end the republic and make himself a king. In 44 B.C. a group of senators led by Marcus Brutus and Gaius Cassius plotted Caesar's death. As Caesar entered the Senate on the Ides, or 15th, of March, the conspirators stabbed him to death.

End of the Republic

After Caesar's death, Rome was governed by a second triumvirate. The members of the triumvirate were Octavian, Caesar's grandnephew and heir; Marc Antony, a general and ally of Caesar; and Marcus Lepidus, one of Caesar's top officers. After defeating Caesar's murderers, the three men divided the Roman world among themselves. Octavian took command of the west, while Marc Antony ruled the east. Lepidus had charge of North Africa. All three shared control of the Italian homeland.

Conflict soon broke out among the three leaders. Octavian forced Lepidus to retire from political life and built up his own power in Italy and North Africa. Antony, however, continued to govern the east and became Octavian's rival. He ruled in Egypt with that country's queen, Cleopatra. In 31 B.C. Octavian moved against Antony and Cleopatra, defeating their fleet in a

---

[5]This calendar was called Julian in honor of Caesar. It was used in Western Europe until early modern times, when it was replaced by the Gregorian calendar.

naval battle at Actium in Greece. Antony and Cleopatra returned to Egypt. A year later, they committed suicide. As a result of his victory, Octavian became the sole ruler of the Roman world.

1. Identify: Tiberius Gracchus, Gaius Gracchus, Marius, Sulla, Pompey, Julius Caesar, Gaul, Octavian, Antony, Cleopatra, Actium.
2. How were the Roman provinces governed?
3. How did the wars of expansion affect Italian agriculture?
4. What reforms did Julius Caesar make? Why was he killed?

4 Roman Empire

As a ruler of Rome, Octavian moved carefully to increase his authority. In 27 B.C., the Senate, which was filled with Octavian's supporters, appointed him consul, tribune, and commander in chief for life. To emphasize his dignity and power, Octavian took for himself the title *Augustus*, or "Majestic One." In history, he became known as Caesar Augustus.

The Emperors

Although Augustus declared his support of the republic, he actually laid the foundation of a new state known as the Roman Empire. In practice, he became Rome's first **emperor**, or absolute ruler.

Reforms   Augustus introduced reforms to bring order and security to the empire. He took charge of the army, making all soldiers and officers swear loyalty to him. He strengthened the central bureaucracy in Rome and worked to improve local government in the provinces. Officials were chosen on the basis of ability rather than birth. As part of this reform, civil servants replaced publicans as tax collectors. A

ROMAN EXPANSION

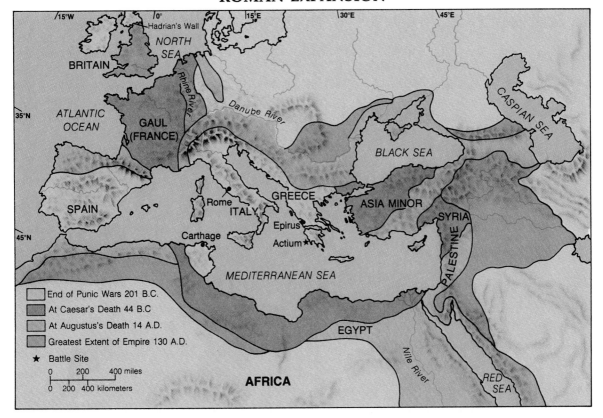

End of Punic Wars 201 B.C.
At Caesar's Death 44 B.C.
At Augustus's Death 14 A.D.
Greatest Extent of Empire 130 A.D.
★ Battle Site

0   200   400 miles
0   200   400 kilometers

Hadrian worked to protect the empire's borders. He oversaw the construction of Hadrian's Wall (73 miles or 117 kilometers) in northern Britain. Why was it built?

census of the population and its wealth was taken on a regular basis so that taxes could be levied fairly. Finally, Augustus supported the construction of many public buildings throughout the empire. It is said of him that "he found Rome a city of brick and left it a city of marble."

Under Augustus, Rome's territory stretched from Spain in the west to Syria in the east, from the Rhine and the Danube Rivers in the north to Egypt and the Sahara Desert in the south. Augustus worked to make the empire's borders more defensible. He established secure boundaries in the Middle East and North Africa. However, he had difficulty defending the frontier in central Europe. There, groups of Indo-Europeans called Germans frequently crossed the Rhine River into Roman territory.[6]

Julian Emperors   Augustus died in 14 A.D. For the next 54 years, the empire was ruled by emperors who belonged to the family of Julius Caesar. Thus, these rulers are known as the Julian Emperors.

---

[6]The Germans originally came from northern and eastern Europe.

Tiberius, the adopted son of Augustus, ruled from 14 to 37 A.D. He was an able ruler who continued his stepfather's policies. However, Caligula, who succeeded Tiberius in 37 A.D., was insane. He offended many Roman senators when he appointed his favorite horse as consul. The palace guards, disgusted at Caligula's unreasonable behavior, killed him in 41 A.D. They then placed the murdered emperor's uncle Claudius on the throne.

Claudius won the support of the Senate and the loyalty of the provinces. He was an able administrator and a noted scholar. During his reign Britain was added to the Roman Empire.

In 54 A.D., Claudius was succeeded by his stepson Nero. Nero was incompetent, and probably insane. Suspecting plots against his life, Nero murdered his wife and his mother. He also executed many senators and seized their lands. In 64 A.D. Rome was swept by a disastrous fire. Public resentment mounted against Nero's rule. Four years later, Roman legions overthrew Nero and forced him to commit suicide.

Good Emperors   For 28 years following Nero's death, Rome was governed by a number of emperors who were backed by the army. Then from 96 to 180 A.D., five rulers known as the Good Emperors ruled the empire. The second of these emperors was the Spanish general, Trajan, who came to power in 98 A.D. During his reign, Trajan fought wars in Mesopotamia and the Balkans. As a result of his conquests, the empire reached its greatest size–about 6.15 million square miles (6.5 million square kilometers).

Hadrian, a cousin of Trajan, became emperor in 117 A.D. He strengthened Rome's fortifications along the frontiers. For example, a wall, known as Hadrian's Wall, was built to protect Roman-occupied Britain from raids by the Picts, a Celtic people in Scotland. Hadrian, however, opposed further wars of conquest and even gave up lands that Trajan had won in Asia.

Hadrian was a good administrator. In the central bureaucracy, he created a regular order of positions as well as a system of promotion. Hadrian was also concerned about better government in the provinces. He made long trips to inspect the work of local government officials.

HISTORY AND PEOPLE

Zenobia

Zenobia was one of the most celebrated women of the Roman world. From 267 to 272 A.D. she was queen of Palmyra, a small Semitic state in central Syria. She was intelligent, and widely known for her beauty and charm. In addition to her native language Aramaic, she spoke Greek and Latin. She is believed to have studied Greek philosophy and literature.

At first Zenobia ruled Palmyra with her husband Odaenthus. Their kingdom was an important center of trade between East and West. It also protected Rome's borders from Persian expansion. Because of its economic and military importance, Palmyra was under Roman control. Thus, Zenobia and Odaenthus governed their kingdom as client rulers. That is, they depended on Rome and followed its policies. The Romans, in turn, respected the royal couple's right to rule. During the 260's A.D., Palmyra's army saved much of the Roman Middle East from Persian conquest. For their services to Rome, Zenobia and Odaenthus were rewarded with the administration of Roman territory in their region.

Zenobia, however, wanted more power. In 267 A.D. she killed Odaenthus and her stepson. She then made herself ruler of Palmyra and governed on behalf of her own young son.

In spite of her treachery in gaining the throne, Zenobia won the support of her people. She was fair and just in treating them. Tolerant of beliefs other than her own, she had good relations with the large Jewish community in Palmyra. Already an experienced ruler, she was praised for selecting competent advisers. Zenobia was also known for her bravery. Skilled in hunting and horseback riding, she sometimes joined her soldiers in battle.

Zenobia wanted to break with Rome and expand Palmyra's territory. In 269 A.D. she seized Egypt, conquered most of Asia Minor, and declared her independence from Rome. From 270 to 272 A.D., Zenobia was the effective ruler of the eastern part of the Roman Empire.

Roman Emperor Aurelian opposed Zenobia's plan and marched two armies east to fight Palmyra. The first army invaded Egypt and the second, led by the emperor himself, attacked Asia Minor. After a long fight, the Romans, in 272 A.D., finally defeated Zenobia's army and destroyed its capital. Zenobia was captured and taken to Rome in gold chains.

Emperor Aurelian and other prominent Romans were so impressed with Zenobia's courage that her life was spared. She influenced Roman writers, who compared her with Queen Cleopatra of Egypt. They wrote stories about Zenobia's beauty, learning, and wealth. Popular in Roman high society, she married a senator and spent the rest of her life in a villa outside the city of Rome.

Remind students of the *Pax Sinica* mentioned on p. 49.

Imperial Rome

1 Circus Maximus
2 Aqueduct of Nero
3 Theater of Marcellus
4 Trajan's Forum
5 Temple of Jupiter
6 Baths of Constantine
7 Royal Palace
8 Temple of Venus
9 Temple of Claudius
10 Colosseum

Marcus Aurelius, who ruled from 161 to 180 A.D., was the last of the Good Emperors. Known as a scholar, he wrote *Meditations*, a work that explained the principles of Stoic philosophy. During the reign of Aurelius, the empire reached the height of its economic prosperity. Commerce and trade spread from one province to another across a network of roads. Traders also went far beyond the empire to trade in luxury goods with India and China.

In spite of economic progress, the empire under Aurelius was repeatedly troubled by invasions. The Germans continued to attack from the north. In the east, the Parthians, a group ruling the old Persian Empire, posed another threat. Aurelius was able to throw back both invaders and to win a temporary peace. After his death in 180 A.D., Rome entered a period of disorder and decline.

Roman Civilization

From 27 B.C. to 180 A.D., the Roman world enjoyed a period of peace and prosperity. This period is known as the *Pax Romana*, or the "Roman Peace". The Roman author Tertullian described the Pax Romana in the following way:

> Everywhere roads are built, every district is known, every country is open to commerce . . . the [fields] are planted; the marshes drained. There are now as many cities as there were once solitary cottages. Reefs and shoals [sandy banks] have lost their terrors. Wherever there is a trace of life, there are houses and human habitations, well-ordered governments, and civilized life.*

During the Pax Romana, the city of Rome had a population of 1 million and was the center of western civilization. Under Rome's leadership, the peoples of the Mediterranean were united for the first time into a single state. Millions of people from different backgrounds shared a common culture. Although this culture was based on Roman principles, it also included many ideas and customs of the conquered peoples. In some cases, they prevailed over Roman ones.

Roman Life

The city of Rome reflected the variety of lifestyles found throughout the empire. Wealthy Romans worked for the government, or were landowners or business people. They had luxurious homes with marble walls, mosaic floors, running water, and baths. Small shopkeepers and artisans led simpler lives, but they

---

*Concerning the Soul, Tertullian, from *The Decline and Rise of Medieval Europe*, S. Katz, © 1955, Cornell University Press, p. 7.

Discuss living conditions for people in ancient Rome.
Compare them to city life today.

benefited from the economic prosperity of the Pax Romana. Many artisans were organized into groups called **collegia**, which provided social and business services to their members. Most Romans were poor and hardworking. Many of them suffered from frequent unemployment and low wages. They lived in six- and seven-story wooden apartment houses. Because of their poor construction, these buildings often caught fire or collapsed.

Amusements   The Roman government provided free amusements for its people. Romans spent much of their time at public events, which included circuses, chariot races, and gladiatorial combats. The combats were often duels to the death between a person, usually a slave, and another person or a wild animal. They were held in a public arena called the Colosseum. Other forms of Roman entertainment were festivals and chariot races. They were held in the Circus Maximus, an oval arena that could seat more than 150,000 people.

Family   The family was the basic unit of Roman society. Roman households were large and close-knit. They included all unmarried children, married sons and their families, all dependent relatives, and household slaves.

As head of a household, a father had absolute authority. He conducted religious rituals in the home, controlled property, and supervised the education of his sons. He also had the power to sell family members into slavery, or even kill them. However, fathers also felt a deep sense of responsibility for the welfare of all family members.

Roman women had no legal rights, but they had more freedom than Greek women. They acted as hostesses for parties, did their marketing, and ran their households with little or no interference. Some women worked in or owned small shops. Wealthy women had slaves to do domestic chores. This gave them leisure time to study the arts, literature, and fashions.

Roman children grew up with firm discipline and had to give complete loyalty to their family. In early Rome, parents taught their children reading, writing, and moral standards. Boys were trained by their fathers to be good farmers

and soldiers. Mothers taught their daughters how to run their households. Later during the empire, the sons of wealthy Romans were educated by tutors, or attended academies. They learned such subjects as oratory, geometry, astronomy, and philosophy. Girls from wealthy families were given private lessons at home. As a result, many Roman women were as well or better educated than Roman men.

Cultural Contributions

The Romans brought together the achievements of the ancient Middle East and Greece. On this foundation, they developed their own unique culture. Unlike the Greeks, who admired beauty, the Romans valued practicality. Their contributions were designed to be used, not looked at.

Law   One of the most significant Roman achievements was in law. After the period of Roman expansion, the Twelve Tables underwent many changes to meet the needs of a large empire. New laws were passed as they were needed, and old laws were adapted to meet new situations. Roman judges and their assistants believed that certain basic legal principles were common to all humans. The Roman judge, Ulpian, summed up the Roman understanding of law when he said:

> Justice is a constant . . . will to give every
> person his due. The principles of law are
> these: to live virtuously, not to harm others,
> to give his due to everyone. Jurisprudence
> [law] is the knowledge of divine and human
> things, the science of the just and the unjust.[*]

As a result of the work of judges like Ulpian, the Romans enacted laws to suit the customs of all peoples throughout the empire.

In their laws, Romans generally stressed the authority of the state over the individual. However, they also recognized that people had definite legal rights. One such right was that a person was considered innocent until proven guilty. In later years, the Roman system of law

---

[*]Ulpian from the *Digest* as quoted in *The Mainstream of Civilization*, Strayer, Gatzke, and Harbison, © 1974, Harcourt Brace Jovanovich, Inc., p. 97.

Roman engineers were ordered to build a road that would last forever. Called the "Queen of Roads," the Appian Way was used for 1,000 years. How did roads serve Rome?

became the basis for the laws of most western nations and of the Christian Church.

Literature   Roman literature was written in Latin, the empire's official language. At first Roman writers were influenced by Greek authors. But during the reign of Augustus, they developed their own style and created a "golden age" of literature. Some of the most important Roman poets appeared during this period. Horace composed odes, satires, and **epistles**, or letters. Ovid wrote love poetry and the *Metamorphoses*, a collection of verses based on Greek mythology. Virgil wrote the *Aeneid*, an epic poem that describes legends about Rome's origins, including the story of Romulus and Remus.

Rome also produced a number of outstanding writers who dealt mainly with history, politics, and philosophy. Cicero, a leading Roman senator and orator, published his speeches, which were written in an elegant Latin style. The philosopher Lucretius, in his work *On the Nature of Things*, presented a view of life that denied the existence of gods. The historian Livy wrote a monumental history of Rome that glorified the patriotism and heroism of early Romans.

During the Pax Romana, some Roman writers were critical of Roman society. The poets Martial and Juvenal wrote about corruption and greed in Roman life. Tacitus, often considered the greatest Roman historian, condemned the tyranny of emperors and the vices of the aristocracy in his *Histories*. In the work *Germania*, he contrasted the robust life of the Germans with what he felt was the weak and pleasure-loving life of the Romans.

Science   Roman science was heavily dependent on Greek sources. Most of the empire's scientists and mathematicians came from the Hellenistic East. Instead of developing new theories, they collected and organized existing information. The physician Galen compiled the medical knowledge of the ancient world in several volumes. The astronomer Ptolemy collected writings on astronomy and later wrote a text called the *Almagest*. Both men were regarded as authorities in their fields until early modern times. However, they often mixed serious errors with useful data. For example, Ptolemy's work made it possible for later astronomers to predict the motions of the planets with accuracy. However, Ptolemy based his understanding on the false idea that the earth was the center of the solar system.

Engineering and Architecture   The Romans excelled in engineering. Roman engineers planned cities, built water and sewage systems, and constructed bridges, aqueducts, and roads. The first major Roman road was the Appian Way. Built in the 300's B.C., it connected Rome and southeastern Italy. During the Pax Romana, a network of roads was built to link Rome with its provinces. Reaching a total length of 50,000 miles (80,000 kilometers), the road network contributed to the empire's unity.

Roman engineers also erected great public buildings—temples, palaces, amphitheaters, triumphal arches, and **basilicas**, or assembly halls. Roman architecture was based on Etruscan and Greek models. From the Etruscans, the Romans adopted the arch and the vaulted dome. From the Greeks, they learned how to use columns. The Romans, however, developed

SCIENCE AND TECHNOLOGY
Roman Aqueducts

An aqueduct is a channel for carrying water from its source to a place of distribution. It sometimes includes a bridge-like structure that brings the water across a valley or through a hill.

About 2500 B.C. people in the Middle East most likely built the first aqueducts. They constructed underground tunnels that carried water from the foot of mountains to nearby fields for crop irrigation. The Romans, however, were the first to use aqueducts to meet the needs of urban populations. For example, the city of Rome used many aqueducts and became one of the few pre-modern urban centers to have an excellent water supply. As a result of this and similar achievements, the Romans are considered the greatest aqueduct builders of the ancient world.

The earliest Roman aqueducts were built entirely underground. They brought water to Rome from mountain springs as far away as 30 miles (48 kilometers). The water descended gradually from a higher to lower level, flowing through a series of stone conduits, or large pipes. At the end of the conduits were cisterns, or storage tanks, where the water was kept for later use. From the tanks, smaller ceramic or stone pipes distributed the water to palaces, water fountains, and public baths throughout the city.

As Rome's population grew, its need for water increased. However, it was difficult to carry the water directly to some of Rome's hilly neighbor-hoods. To solve this problem, Roman engineers built some sections of new aqueducts above the ground. These sections consisted of one- to three-story arches made of cut stone that supported stone pipes. The arches carried water long distances, and crossed steep valleys. Tunnels were dug through hills that were too difficult to skirt.

During the Pax Romana, towns in the Roman provinces followed the lead of Rome and built aqueducts. One of the most famous provincial aqueducts was constructed in Segovia, Spain, between 100 and 110 A.D.. Extending 60 miles (96 kilometers), the Segovia aqueduct brought water to the city from high mountain springs. Its final stretch consisted of an arched section one-half mile (0.8 kilometers) in length.

At the height of the empire, the Romans kept their aqueducts in good repair and in working condition. But with the invasions of the 400's A.D., many were allowed to decay or were damaged or destroyed. However, in the Mediterranean world some aqueducts, like the one at Segovia, remain intact and are still used today. They provide eloquent testimony to Roman engineering skills, many of which were unequaled until the 1800's.

1. Why did the Romans build aqueducts?
2. What do Roman aqueducts reveal about Roman engineering?

Roman engineering talent is seen in the miles of aqueducts built with such simple machinery as wooden hoists and scaffolds lashed together with rope. For each aqueduct, large quantities of stone were brought to the building site in ox carts. One aqueduct required 400 loads a day, taking 14 years to complete.

Have students compile a list of Roman gods and their corresponding names in the Greek religion.

their own style. They were probably the first to use concrete as a building material. Roman structures were large in size and lacked the balance and harmony of Greek architecture. Many buildings were constructed for government functions. Others honored gods, emperors, or military heroes.

1. Identify: Caesar Augustus, Julian Emperors, Hadrian's Wall, Marcus Aurelius, Pax Romana, Circus Maximus, Virgil, *Germania*, Galen.
2. How did Augustus bring order and security to the empire?
3. Why was the Pax Romana important?
4. What contributions did the Romans make in engineering and architecture?

5 Rise of Christianity

A variety of religions flourished in the Roman Empire. Among these faiths was Christianity. It started in the Middle East among the Jews and was later brought to Rome. Most Romans at first ignored or ridiculed the new religion, and some emperors treated Christians cruelly. But despite persecution, Christianity outlasted the empire and shaped the future development of the western world.

Roman Religion

The early Romans worshiped nature spirits. Under Etruscan influence, they came to think of these spirits as gods and goddesses. They also adopted the practice of **divination**, or the foretelling of the future. Priests known as **soothsayers** believed that they could gain knowledge of future events by observing the flight of birds or the intestines of animals.

Later the Romans adopted much of Greek religion and mythology. They identified Greek gods and goddesses with their own deities. Each Roman deity carried out the function of its Greek counterpart, but had a different name. For example, in Roman mythology, the Greek god Zeus became Jupiter and the Greek goddess Aphrodite became Venus.

Romans believed that the observance of religious rituals was a patriotic duty. Important government officials served as priests. Beginning with Augustus, Roman emperors held the position of *Pontifex Maximus*, or chief priest of the Roman religion. In death and, sometimes, in life, they were hailed as gods by the common people. Although all people in the empire were allowed to worship freely, the Roman government expected everyone to honor the emperor and the gods of Rome.

Judaism

Shortly before the Roman conquests, Jews in Israel were ruled by the Seleucids. As monotheists, the Jews refused to acknowledge deities other than Yahweh. Many sought to keep their religion free from Greek cultural influences. Led by Judas Maccabeus, they revolted against the Seleucids and won their freedom in 167 B.C.

About 100 years later, all of the Jewish communities in the eastern Mediterranean came under Roman rule. The Romans called Israel "Palestine." The Jews of Palestine resisted Roman control. Some hoped for divine intervention in the form of a **messiah**, or savior, who would restore the kingdom of David. Others relied on direct human action. In 66 A.D. Jewish freedom fighters rebelled against Roman rule and regained Jerusalem. However, four years later, Roman armies sacked the city, destroyed the temple, and killed thousands of Jews.

After another unsuccessful rebellion in 132 A.D., the Jews were driven out of Palestine. They resettled in other parts of the Mediterranean and the Middle East. In their scattered communities, the Jews continued to follow the Torah. To promote its study, special academies called **yeshivas** were established. Between 200 and 500 A.D., scholars trained in the yeshivas assembled the various interpretations and teachings of the Torah into a book known as the Talmud. The Talmud became the holiest book in Judaism, after the Bible.

Jesus

During the reigns of Augustus and Tiberius, Christianity began in Palestine. Its founder, Jesus of Nazareth, was born a Jew and received a Jewish education. From about 26 to 30 A.D., Jesus traveled throughout Palestine, preaching to the people and winning **disciples**, or followers.

The followers of Jesus were called "Christians" for the first time in the city of Antioch several years after his crucifixion.

Many people believed that he was the long-awaited messiah. Others, however, disputed this claim about Jesus. The controversy troubled the Roman officials of Palestine. They believed that anyone who stirred up strong public feelings might be dangerous to Roman authority. About 30 A.D., Jesus was **crucified**— a Roman form of execution.

Spread of Christianity

After Jesus' death, his disciples claimed that he had risen from the dead and had appeared to them. They began preaching about Jesus as the Son of God and the way of salvation. Small groups of Jews and non-Jews in the Hellenistic cities accepted this message. These people who followed Jesus became known as Christians.[7] They formed communities called **churches** for worship, fellowship, and instruction.

A convert named Paul contributed to the spread of Christianity, especially among non-Jews. He traveled widely and wrote on behalf of the new religion. Paul's epistles to various churches were later combined with the **gospels**, or stories about Jesus, and the writings of other early Christian leaders. Together, these works form the New Testament of the Bible.

Meanwhile, other **apostles**, or Christian missionaries, were spreading Christianity throughout the Roman world. It is believed that Peter, the leader of the group, came to Rome and helped found a church in that city. Other churches were established in Egypt, Asia Minor, Greece, and later in Gaul and Spain.

Persecution

Christians taught that their religion was the only true faith. They refused to honor the emperor as a god, rejected military service, and criticized Roman festivals and games. As a result, many Romans came to dislike the Christians and accused them of treason. In 64 A.D. Christianity was made illegal. Periods of intense persecution lasted until the early 300's A.D.

Christianity also faced a rival in the **mystery religions**. These faiths believed in mythical heroes, elaborate secret rituals, and the promise

[7]Among Greek-speaking believers, Jesus was known as "the Christ," the Greek word for Messiah.

The teachings of Jesus assured his followers that they, as individuals, were responsible only to God and to their fellow humans. Why did many Romans oppose Christianity?

of a blissful life after death. However, they restricted their memberships to certain social groups. For instance, the cult of Mithras excluded women and appealed primarily to soldiers. Christianity, on the other hand, offered salvation to everyone and placed a practical emphasis on doing good for others.

In spite of persecution and competition, Christianity continued to win many converts. It proved to be a dynamic faith at a time when the traditional polytheistic religions no longer satisfied people and were declining. Christian beliefs at first appealed to the poor whose lot in life was difficult. However, when the empire faced collapse in the 200's A.D., Christianity began to draw people from all classes. In a time of confusion, many Romans found Christianity to be a source of strength and hope.

The Church

Christians recognized the importance of having clearly stated teachings and an organized leadership. In this way they were able to face persecution and to handle internal problems.

Church Fathers   Between 100 and 500 A.D. various scholars known as Church Fathers wrote books that explained Christian teachings. They greatly influenced later Christian thinkers. One

Point out that the Pope was considered "first among equals" by the Greek patriarchs of the Eastern Church.

Point out that the Sassanids of Persia maintained an advanced civilization, too.

of the most influential Church Fathers was the North African bishop Augustine. Augustine's writings shaped the future development of Christian ideas in the West. His *City of God* presented the first history of humanity from a Christian standpoint. *Confessions*, another of Augustine's works, is an account of his early life and conversion to Christianity. It is considered one of the first great autobiographies.

Church Structure To bring greater unity to their churches, Christians began to develop a church organization. By 400 A.D. each local church was called a **parish** and had a full-time leader called a **presbyter**, or priest. Several parishes grouped together into a larger unit were called a **diocese**.[8] Each diocese was headed by a **bishop**, who interpreted Christian beliefs, managed church property, and provided aid for the poor and needy. The most important bishops, who were known as **archbishops**, governed churches in the larger cities of the empire. The five leading archbishops were called **patriarchs**. They administered the churches in Rome, Constantinople, Alexandria, Antioch, and Jerusalem.

The bishops met in councils to discuss questions about Christian beliefs. The decisions they reached at these councils came to be accepted as **doctrine**, or official teachings. The points of view the councils did not accept were considered **heresy**, or false doctrine.

During the 400's A.D., the bishop of Rome began to claim authority over the other patriarchs. He was called *Pope*, a Latin word meaning father. Latin-speaking Christians in the west regarded him as the head of all the churches. Greek-speaking Christians in the east, however, would not accept his authority over their churches. In time, the Latin churches as a group became known as the Roman Catholic Church. The Greek churches became known as the Eastern Orthodox Church.

1. Identify: Pontifex, Maximus, Judas Maccabeus, Talmud, Jesus, Paul, Church Fathers, *City of God*.
2. What were the chief features of Roman religion?
3. Why did the Jews resist foreign rule?
4. How did Christianity spread?

---

[8]The term "diocese" orginally referred to a Roman military district.

6 Decline of the Empire

During the 200's A.D., the Germans overran Roman frontiers in central Europe. In the Middle East, the Sassanids, a group of Persian warrior-kings, replaced the Parthians as Rome's greatest Asian rival. Meanwhile, within its borders, the Roman Empire faced economic decay, civil war, and plague. These crises, combined with the outside threats, brought an end to the Pax Romana and led to the decline of the empire.

Political Instability

One of the problems facing the empire during the 200's A.D. was political instability. Since Augustus, there had been no formal rule about succession to the imperial throne. Sometimes the throne was inherited by a son. But usually an emperor adopted an heir to the throne, choosing the most able person that he knew. Between 96 and 180 A.D., all emperors were adopted. Then, the system broke down. Marcus Aurelius died in 180 A.D., and the throne passed to his son Commodus.

The reign of Commodus brought in a period of confusion that undermined respect for the throne. Hated for his cruelty, in 192 A.D. Commodus was murdered by the Praetorian Guard, the personal soldiers of the emperor. A year later, General Septimius Severus defeated several military rivals and became ruler. He founded the Severi dynasty, which held power from 193 to 235 A.D. The Severi rulers, however, were incompetent, and in 235 A.D., the army ended the dynasty.

Between 235 and 284 A.D., there were 23 emperors, most of whom were assassinated. During this time, the army played a leading role in making and deposing emperors. The Senate, weakened by quarreling groups, had to accept the army's decisions. Because of political instability, Rome's leaders could do little to solve the empire's problems.

Economic decline also afflicted the Roman Empire. During the Pax Romana, Rome had received substantial benefits from the provinces. The conquests had opened up new farmlands and mineral resources. In addition, a steady supply of slaves was available for work on the latifundias. Their labor provided the empire with food and raw materials at low prices.

During the 200's A.D. the empire lost these advantages. Its soil and mineral deposits were being exhausted. Roman legions made fewer conquests, and the number of slaves decreased. Frequent plagues and the practice of infanticide, or the killing of unwanted infants, reduced the population. Along with setbacks came a severe economic slump. Large areas of farmland were abandoned, businesses in the cities went bankrupt, and many workers were unemployed.

At the same time, government costs rose sharply and added to public misery. Most funds were spent on the army, since emperors depended on the legions to stay in power and to guard the frontiers. The emperors gave generous rewards to officers and soldiers. Soon the people had to pay higher taxes to meet these and other military expenses. To avoid higher taxes, landowners left the cities and moved to their villas, or country estates. Most estates were like small, independent territories. Each produced enough food and goods to supply the needs of everyone who lived there. As a result, the tax burden increasingly fell on the lower social groups.

The Romans also suffered from **inflation**, or a steady rise in prices. Since there were no new conquests, gold was no longer coming into Rome. However, much gold was going out to pay for imported luxury goods. With the scarcity of gold, emperors began decreasing its use in coins. Money soon declined in value, and prices increased. Many people stopped using money and began to barter to get what they needed.

Famous Roman Emperors

AUGUSTUS

CLAUDIUS

NERO

HADRIAN

DIOCLETIAN

CONSTANTINE

TIBERIUS

CALIGULA

Augustus (27 B.C.-14 A.D.)	Rome's first emperor; his rule of 42 years was called the Golden Age of Rome
Tiberius (14-37 A.D.)	maintained peace and prosperity through tax reforms and good government
Caligula (37-41 A.D.)	began the extensive building of roads and aqueducts throughout the Empire
Claudius (41-54 A.D.)	extended citizenship to many people in the provinces; conquered part of Britain
Nero (54-68 A.D.)	designed and rebuilt Rome after the destructive fire of 64 A.D.
Vespasian (69-79 A.D.)	secured the Empire's frontiers; erected many new buildings, including the Coliseum of Rome
Trajan (98-117 A.D.)	administered public works and welfare programs; brought the Empire to its greatest extent
Hadrian (117-138 A.D.)	admirer of Greek literature and art; built a defensive wall against attackers in Britain
Marcus Aurelius (161-180 A.D.)	gave people of the provinces the right to have representatives in the Roman Senate
Diocletian (284-305 A.D.)	divided the Empire into two administrative areas; proclaimed himself divine
Constantine (307-337 A.D.)	first Christian emperor; made Christianity a legal religion

Diocletian reorganized government as a tetrarchy, or government by four persons ruling jointly.

Constantine's mother, Helen, was a Christian. She influenced his favorable attitude toward Christianity.

Strong Emperors

During the late 200's A.D. and early 300's A.D., two emperors, Diocletian and Constantine, made strong attempts to halt the decline of the empire. Their efforts brought temporary stability and delayed Rome's fall for another 200 years.

Diocletian   Diocletian, a noted general and son of a former slave, was emperor from 284 to 305 A.D. To defend the empire's borders, he enlarged the army and made it more mobile. While commanding his troops, Diocletian left Rome and ruled the empire from towns near the frontier. As a result of this move, the city of Rome became less important as a political center.

Diocletian made important changes in the empire's government. He proclaimed himself divine and made the absolute rule of the emperor official policy. However, he recognized that one person could not govern the entire empire effectively. So he shared power with his generals and divided the empire into two administrative areas. The general Maximian agreed to rule as co-emperor in the western provinces, while Diocletian kept control of the larger and richer eastern provinces. Later, each emperor selected an assistant to help him rule and to be his successor. Although Diocletian shared his authority with others, he himself held supreme power.

Diocletian also tried to strengthen the economy of the empire. To achieve his goal, he set out to bring all economic activities under government control. A new and improved currency was issued. To stop inflation, maximum prices were set for wages and goods. To assure a steady source of tax revenue, workers were required to remain in the same job throughout their lives. Farmers who inherited their land were not allowed to leave it and were encouraged to increase their output. City officials had to stay in office and were held personally responsible for collecting the taxes from their communities. Aside from the currency reform, Diocletian's measures were unpopular and became difficult to enforce.

Constantine   Diocletian retired in 305 A.D. Within a short time, his system of divided rule proved to be unworkable. Civil wars broke out among generals for control of the throne. The general Constantine emerged as the victor and became emperor. As ruler, Constantine increased the emperor's authority and tightened Diocletian's regulations. To keep people from leaving their jobs, he ordered the sons of farmers, workers, and soldiers to follow their fathers' occupations. He also required more government service from wealthy citizens and more taxes from the general population.

Constantine began an important change in the empire's religious policy. In 312 A.D. he threw his support to Christianity, hoping that it would restore the greatness of Rome. Legend states that as he was leading his army into battle, Constantine saw a flaming cross in the sky. Beneath it were the Latin words *In Hoc Signo Vinces*, "by this sign you will conquer." Constantine won the battle and credited the Christian God for his victory. He soon became the leading defender of the Church. In 313 A.D. he issued the Edict of Milan. It granted religious freedom to all, and made Christianity legal.

Constantine aided the growth of Christianity. He had churches built over Christian shrines in Rome and Jerusalem. These buildings were modeled on the Roman basilica with its rectangular hall and long aisles. Constantine also permitted church leaders to enter government service and excused them from paying taxes. Finally, on his deathbed, the emperor converted to Christianity. Other prominent Romans followed his example.

Most of the emperors who succeeded Constantine continued his pro-Christian policies. In 392 A.D. the emperor Theodosius made Christianity the official religion of the empire and outlawed all other religions.

Division   In spite of the changes made by Constantine and his successors, the Roman Empire, particularly in the west, continued to decline. After the death of Theodosius in 395 A.D., the empire was once again divided into eastern and western regions. Although the unity of the empire was still accepted in theory, the division proved to be permanent. Each region, under its own emperor, began to develop a separate civilization.

Germans believed that the souls of people who die in battle go to Valhalla, the place where the gods reside.

The map below is the subject of the "Using Maps" section of the Chapter 4 Review.

GERMANIC INVASIONS 200-500 A.D.

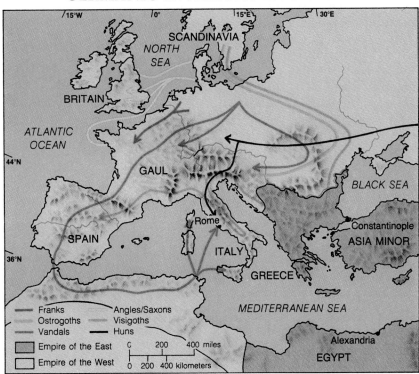

German Invasions

Beginning in the late 300's A.D., large numbers of Germans moved into the Roman Empire and settled in the territory south of the Rhine and Danube Rivers. Many factors were behind this German migration. Some of the Germans moved south, looking for a warmer climate and new grazing land for their cattle. Others wanted a share of Rome's wealth and culture. Many German groups, however, were pushed into the empire by the Huns, fierce invaders from central Asia.

Social Life The Germans were organized into bands made up of warriors and their families. Each band was ruled by a chief and a council of warriors. Chiefs provided warriors with leadership, weapons, and a chance for wealth and adventure. In return, warriors gave their chiefs total loyalty. While the men fought and hunted, the women farmed, herded, and raised children.

Roman Defeats During the late 300's A.D. and the early 400's A.D., a variety of German groups extended their hold over much of the western part of the Roman Empire. They were the Ostrogoths, Visigoths, Vandals, Franks, Angles, and Saxons. The Visigoths, at first, were the most important of these groups. In 378 A.D. they rebelled against Roman rule and defeated a large Roman army at Adrianople in the Balkan Peninsula. The defeat showed the weakness of the once-powerful Roman legions. For a while, Visigothic warriors moved unhindered throughout the empire. In 410 A.D. their leader, Alaric, invaded Italy and sacked Rome.

Huns The next major threat to the empire came from the Huns. Led by their chief, Attila, the Huns advanced into Europe as far as Gaul, where they were stopped by a Roman army. Then Attila and his forces invaded Italy. Their fury and destruction terrified the local population. After 453 A.D. the Huns retreated from the conquered areas and settled in eastern Europe.

Have students evaluate the conditions that led to the fall of Rome.

End of the Empire

After the withdrawal of the Huns, the Germans resumed their move into western Europe. German warriors gained control of Italy, and their chiefs won the right to make or depose Roman emperors. In 476 A.D. the German general Odoacer seized power in Rome, overthrew the emperor, and did not name a replacement. Because of this event, people today refer to 476 A.D. as the year in which the Roman Empire "fell." Actually, no single event brought about the empire's collapse. Instead, its end was caused by the complex interaction of movements and events between 200 and 500 A.D.

By 550 A.D. the Roman Empire in the West had been replaced by many Germanic kingdoms. Although Roman rule had ended in western Europe, the Christian Church remained to shape the culture of the West. It became the chief preserver of **classical**, or Greek and Roman, civilization.

1. Identify: Sassanids, Praetorian Guard, Severi, Diocletian, Constantine, Edict of Milan, Visigoths, Attila, Odoacer.
2. What factors led to the decline of the empire?
3. Why did Constantine support Christianity?
4. Why did the Germans invade Roman territory? What effect did they have on the empire?

CHAPTER 4 REVIEW

Summary

1. In 509 B.C. Rome overthrew its Etruscan monarchy and established a republic that divided power among several institutions and social groups.
2. Through conquests and alliances, Rome expanded its territory until it ruled most of the western world.
3. Rome's expansion brought social, political, and economic problems that led to the decline of the republic and the rise of one-person rule by generals.
4. Roman civilization brought different cultures together, and made lasting contributions in law, literature, science, engineering, and architecture.
5. From 27 B.C. to 180 A.D., Rome enjoyed a period of peace, order, and prosperity known as the Pax Romana.
6. Christianity, based on the life and teachings of Jesus, spread through the Roman world and became the official religion of the empire.
7. During the 200's A.D. the Roman Empire declined due to political instability, economic weakness, and outside invasion.
8. After the failure of efforts to stop its decline, the empire, in 395 A.D., was divided into western and eastern sections.
9. During the 400's A.D., German invaders brought about the downfall of the Roman Empire in the West.

Vocabulary

republic	veto	senators	legionaries
patricians	dictator	centuries	colonae
plebians	praetors	tribunes	indemnity
consuls	censors	legions	proconsuls

publicans	basilicas	churches	bishop
latifundias	divination	gospels	archbishops
equites	soothsayers	apostles	patriarchs
triumvirate	messiah	mystery religions	doctrine
emperor	yeshivas	parish	heresy
collegia	disciples	presbyter	inflation
epistles	crucified	diocese	classical

Reviewing the Main Ideas

1. What contributions did the Etruscans make to Roman civilization?
2. How did Roman law develop over the centuries?
3. What factors led to the territorial expansion of Rome?
4. How did the Romans at first treat conquered peoples? How did their policy later change?
5. Why did the Roman Republic decline?
6. How did the rule of emperors affect the administration of the empire?
7. How did Romans live during the Pax Romana?
8. How were women viewed in Roman society?
9. What happened to the Jews following their unsuccessful rebellion in 132 A.D.?
10. How was the Christian Church organized?
11. What policies did Diocletian and Constantine introduce to save the empire? What effect did their policies have?
12. What event symbolized the fall of the Roman Empire of the West?

Discussing Important Ideas

1. Were the early Romans basically different from the early Greeks in their society and government? Why or why not?
2. Was war between Rome and Carthage inevitable? Why or why not?
3. What were the strengths and weaknesses of the Roman Republic? Could the republic have been saved? Explain.
4. If you had lived in Rome during the 40's B.C., would you have supported Julius Caesar? Why or why not?
5. Which had the greatest impact on the decline of the empire—poor leadership or bad social and economic conditions? Explain.
6. Some historians have believed that Christianity was partially responsible for the fall of Rome. Do you agree or disagree? Explain.
7. Did persecution help or hinder the spread of Christianity?
8. If you were a Roman in 410 A.D., how would you feel about the Germans? Why would you feel this way?

Using Maps

Refer to the map on page 103 to answer the following questions:
1. Which invasions involved travel over water?
2. Which German group covered the most degrees of latitude in its invasion?
3. About how many miles did the Angles and Saxons travel to reach Britain?
4. Where did the Franks settle?
5. What regions of the Roman Empire were not invaded by Germans?

UNIT 1 REVIEW

Summary

1. Beginning about 4000 B.C., a series of kingdoms and empires appeared in the Fertile Crescent. The contributions of the region included an alphabet, law codes, monotheism, and techniques in metalworking.

2. From 3000 to 650 B.C., the Egyptian civilization flourished along the Nile River in northeastern Africa. The Egyptians excelled in architecture, producing massive pyramids and temples.

3. During the 500's B.C., the Persians established a large empire that stretched from Egypt to India. They were known as skilled and tolerant administrators.

4. The first Indian civilization appeared in the Indus River Vally around 2500 B.C. Centuries later, the Aryans settled in the valley and ruled northern India. About 300 B.C. the Mauryan dynasty established the first Indian empire. Hinduism and Buddhism, two important Asian religions, began in early India.

5. About 1500 B.C. Chinese civilization started in the Huang He Valley of northern China. By the 200's A.D., the Chinese state had enlarged its boundaries until it covered most of present-day China. The teachings of Confucius and Lao-tzu, together with Buddhism, influenced Chinese thought and behavior.

Chinese civilization eventually spread to Korea and Japan.

6. Japan was relatively isolated from other parts of the world during its early history. During the 500's A.D., its many clans united into a single, organized state under the Yamato family.

7. Greek civilization reached its height in the city-state of Athens during the 400's B.C. There people participated directly in government and enjoyed many freedoms. The Greeks made notable contributions in philosophy, science, and drama.

8. In the 300's B.C., Alexander of Macedonia united the Greeks and conquered the Middle East and northwestern India. His empire was the basis of the Hellenistic civilization that blended western and eastern ideas and practices.

9. During the 500's B.C., Rome developed as a small Italian city-state. It eventually became the capital of an extensive Mediterranean empire, which lasted until the 400's A.D. A long period of Roman peace and order contributed to increased trade and communication in much of the western world. During this period, Christianity became the major religion of the West.

Developing Understanding

1. How did geography influence the development of early civilizations?

2. What social groups developed in the ancient world?

3. What role did the rulers of ancient civilizations play in the religious life of their peoples?

4. How did advances in the use of metals affect early societies?

5. What forms of government emerged in ancient civilizations?

6. How did commerce and trade influence the growth of civilization in ancient times?

Developing Skills

In studying or writing history, students and historians must be able to evaluate sources of history. That is, they must decide whether a source is reliable. The reliability of a written source, or account, depends on a number of things—who made it, how, and why. In considering the reliability of a historical account, ask yourself the following questions:

1. Is it a firsthand account or a secondhand account? If secondhand, is it based on documents or on hearsay?
2. Is it a contemporary account, or was it written after the event?
3. What were the circumstances under which the account was made?
4. Is the purpose of the account to record history, to entertain, or to persuade?
5. Can the source be verified by other sources?

Below are a number of historical topics. Under each are listed two possible sources of information on the topic. Choose the source that you consider the most reliable. Discuss your answers with the rest of the class.

1. A description of the city of Troy:
   a) *Troy and Its Remains* by archeologist Heinrich Schliemann
   b) Homer's epic poem, the *Iliad*
2. The character of Cleopatra:
   a) Plutarch's *Life of Antony*, based in part on his grandfather's memoirs (about 100 A.D.)
   b) Shakespeare's play, *Antony and Cleopatra* (1623 A.D.)
3. Mesopotamian civilization:
   a) Findings of modern archeological excavations of sites
   b) The writings of Berosus, a Babylonian historian (about 300 B.C.)
4. Julius Caesar's conquest of Gaul:
   a) Caesar's account
   b) An account written by a contemporary of Caesar's after Caesar's death
5. Origins of the Hindu religion:
   a) The *Mahabharata* and *Ramayana*, epic poems that are part of sacred Hindu scriptures
   b) An analysis of Hinduism by a British historian

Suggested Activities

1. Select five important persons from ancient history. Describe how their beliefs or actions affect people's lives today.
2. Develop a visual presentation that shows the different styles of architecture used in ancient civilizations.
3. Take the role of a Roman patrician or plebian. Write a letter to a government official explaining your views on Roman military expansion or government support of the poor.
4. Write a one-week diary of (a) a Carthaginian soldier with Hannibal's army (b) an Egyptian farmer along the Nile River (c) a married woman of Zhou China (d) a Byzantine empress.

Suggested Readings

Cottrell, Leonard. *Five Queens of Egypt*. Indianapolis: Bobbs-Merrill Co., Inc., 1969. Highlights the lives of five outstanding female rulers of ancient Egypt.

Fairservis, Jr., Walter A. *Asia: Traditions and Treasures*. New York: Harry N. Abrams, Inc., 1981. Tells the story of Asian civilizations from ancient to modern times.

Gray, John. *Near Eastern Mythology*. New York: Hamlyn Co., Inc., 1969. Presents various myths and legends of the ancient Middle East.

Liversidge, Joan. *Everyday Life in the Roman Empire*. New York: G. P. Putnam and Sons, Inc., 1976. Emphasizes the social life and customs of the Romans from the period of the Republic to the fall of Rome.

National Geographic Society. *Greece and Rome: Builders of Our World*. Washington, D.C.: National Geographic Society, 1968. Discusses the practical skills of the Greeks and the Romans, especially in constructing roads, bridges, and buildings.

The Middle Ages

500	600	700	800	900	1000

520 Benedictine Rule
550 Justinian
800 Charlemagne
850 Viking invasions

600's Mayan civilization
732 Battle of Tours
900's Kingdom of Ghana
620 Mohammed
750 Rise of the Abbasids

1100	1200	1300	1400	1500

1066 Battle of Hastings

1095 First Crusade

1215 Magna Charta

1240 Mongol conquest of Russia

1400 League of the Iroquois

1100's Toltec Empire

1150 Development of Gothic architecture

1300 Philip IV of France

1300's Mali's "golden age"

1400's Inca and Aztec empires

1453 Fall of Constantinople

The fall of Rome led to a new era in the history of the West. Historians have called this era "the Middle Ages." Lasting from about 500 to 1500 A.D., the Middle Ages was a transition period between ancient and modern times.

During the Middle Ages, the former Roman Empire was divided into three areas: the Byzantine Empire, the Islamic Empire, and western Europe. The Byzantine Empire lasted for 1,000 years and was the leading Christian civilization of the Middle Ages. The Islamic Empire included the Middle East and North Africa. It was based on Islam, a new religion that emerged in the 600's A.D. Western Europe underwent a cultural decline after the fall of Rome. Yet, by 1200 A.D., it had developed a new civilization rooted in Christianity.

From 500 to 1500 A.D., other civilizations flourished beyond the Mediterranean world. In Africa and the Americas, a variety of peoples developed distinctive ways of life. Early African and American achievements, however, were unknown until the 1500's A.D.

Crusaders in battle

CHAPTER 5

Russian Battle

" Art conveys through colors the Soul's prayers. "

Agathias, Byzantine historian (536-582 A.D.)

Byzantines

and

Russians

By 500 A.D. Roman rule in the west had ended. The eastern part of the Roman Empire, however, survived and lasted about 1,000 years longer. It became known as the Byzantine Empire. At its height, the Byzantine Empire consisted of most of the Balkan Peninsula, Asia Minor, Syria, and Egypt. It had more people and was richer in economic resources than the old western empire. As a result, the Byzantine Empire was able to withstand invasions and to develop a flourishing civilization.

After the fall of Rome, the Byzantine Empire considered itself the heir of Roman power and traditions. Its capital, Constantinople, was known as "New Rome." There, Byzantine rulers governed with the authority of Roman emperors. However, the Byzantine Empire was not simply a continuation of the old Roman Empire. Although the Byzantines preserved classical learning, they stressed the Greek, rather than the Latin, heritage. They also used Greek ideas to develop Christian **theology,** or religious teachings. Their form of Christianity, known as Eastern Orthodoxy, played a major role in Byzantine life. At the same time, the Byzantine Empire was open to cultural influences from eastern civilizations, such as Persia.

From a blend of classical, Christian, and eastern cultures, the Byzantine Empire developed a distinct culture of its own. Between 500 and 1200 A.D., it ranked as one of the most advanced civilizations in the world. During this period, it had a higher standard of living than western Europe. Byzantine art, ideas, and practices spread to neighboring lands. They later shaped the development of Russia and other eastern European nations.

1 Foundation of the Empire

During the 300's A.D., the eastern provinces of the Roman Empire grew in wealth and importance. As the Roman Empire in the West declined, Roman leaders began to regard the east as the center of the empire's future greatness.

Beginnings

About 324 A.D., the Roman emperor Constantine decided to move the capital of the Roman Empire to a new location farther east. He selected the Greek town of Byzantium as the site for the new capital.

The most important reason for his choice was Byzantium's favorable location. The Roman Empire depended on trade, and the most prosperous trade centers were in the empire's eastern provinces. Byzantium was situated at the crossroads of important land and water trade routes in this region. The site also could be easily defended against invaders.

It took six years to build the new capital, which was named Constantinople in honor of the emperor. Constantine wanted his capital to resemble Rome. He built government buildings, forums, palaces, and arenas on a lavish scale. Since Constantinople was to be a center of Christianity, many churches and shrines were also constructed.

The establishment of Constantinople laid the basis for Byzantine civilization. A further step in the development of the Byzantine Empire took place in 395 A.D. At that time the Roman Empire split into the Roman Empire of the West and the Roman Empire of the East. The western part was

By 600 A.D. religion became closely linked to the efforts of non-Greek nationalities to resist Greek cultural control. For example, a majority of non-Greek

Christians in Syria, Palestine, and Egypt rejected the Greek form of Christianity and set up their own churches.

ruled from Rome, while the eastern part was governed from Constantinople. The eastern part then evolved into a separate empire.

The Byzantines were not a definite **ethnic group,** or a large group of people having common traits and customs. Instead, they were made up of a variety of nationalities and religions. The major group was Greek in nationality and Eastern Orthodox in religion. The Greeks were located primarily in Greece and western Asia Minor, the central areas of the Byzantine Empire. There were also a variety of non-Greeks living in the surrounding areas of the empire. These people were Syrians, Egyptians, Armenians, Jews, Persians, Slavs, Arabs, and Turks. Many of these groups resented the dominance of Greek culture. They wanted to keep their own languages and cultural traditions.

The Byzantines always considered themselves to be Romans living in the eastern Roman Empire.[1] In the early years of the empire, the Byzantine emperors were Roman and spoke Latin. Many aristocratic Roman families settled in Constantinople after Constantine offered to build them homes and palaces like the ones they had in Rome. However, regardless of their nationality, the majority of Constantinople's people spoke Greek. The emperors and aristocrats eventually did the same. In time, those who were not Greek accepted Greek ways.

Religious Conflict

Religious disputes divided Christianity in the east. As the first Christian emperor, Constantine took the lead in promoting doctrinal unity within Christianity. He called and presided over the first important church council held at Nicaea in 325 A.D. Acting as both a political leader and a protector of the Church, Constantine placed the power of the government behind church decisions. Later Byzantine emperors would follow Constantine's practice of intervening in church affairs.

After Constantine's rule ended, conflicts over church doctrines continued to divide the people

---

[1] The people of the empire did not call themselves "Byzantines." This term is used by modern historians, who want to distinguish Byzantine civilization from the earlier Roman one.

of the Byzantine Empire. Theological arguments were not restricted to the **clergy,** or church officials, only. The **laity,** or church members who are not clergy, talked about theology with great enthusiasm in their homes and shops. Visitors to Constantinople saw shoppers in the marketplaces having heated discussions about such topics as the exact relationship of Jesus the Son, to God the Father. Such arguments often became political issues and led to fights and riots.

Justinian

The Byzantine Empire reached its greatest height under the emperor Justinian, who ruled from 527 to 565 A.D. Justinian was born in Macedonia, a western province of the empire. He was the son of a prosperous peasant family. As a young man at the court of his uncle, Emperor Justin I, Justinian was trained in law, music, theology, and architecture. Later, he served as a commander in the Byzantine army. In 527 A.D. Justin made his nephew the co-ruler. A few months later, the old emperor died, and Justinian became the sole ruler.

Theodora Justinian's wife, Theodora, was beautiful, intelligent, and ambitious. She was an actress when Justinian met her. The people of the empire held actresses in low esteem. In spite of court objections, Justinian married Theodora. She began to assist him in ruling the empire.

As empress, Theodora worked to improve the social standing of women. She had Justinian issue a decree allowing a wife the right to own land equal to her **dowry,** or the wealth she brought with her when she married. Her efforts enabled widows to raise and support their children without government interference. Theodora also promoted charitable work among the poor of Constantinople.

Theodora took an active part in political life. She often was involved in the appointment or dismissal of government officials. In this way, she used her power to reward her friends and punish her enemies. Theodora's political wisdom, at one point, helped save Justinian's throne. In 532 A.D. a revolt in Constantinople threatened the government. Justinian's advisers told the emperor to leave the city. However,

Explain that peasants could rise to high positions, including emperor.

Justinian is surrounded by court officials, soldiers, and priests in this Byzantine mosaic. While Justinian made great contributions in law, political reform, art, and architecture, his efforts to defend the eastern borders and win back the western empire were shortlived. Why did the empire lose on both fronts after Justinian's death?

Theodora persuaded the emperor to stay and fight, rather than flee. Justinian and his troops crushed the uprising, killing 30,000 of the rebels. This victory further strengthened Justinian's power as emperor.

Military Campaigns During Justinian's reign, the Byzantines faced a serious military threat from the East. The Sassanian empire of Persia, under Chosroes I, grew in strength and threatened to conquer the eastern provinces of the Byzantine Empire. The Byzantines rallied their forces and threw back the Persians. Justinian gained a brief period of security for the eastern borders by agreeing to pay tribute in return for peace.

Justinian next turned his attention to the west, where he wanted to restore the Roman Empire. Under the general, Belisarius, the Byzantine armies were strengthened and reorganized. Between 533 and 555 A.D., they fought a series of wars against the Vandals in North Africa, the Ostrogoths in Italy, and the Visigoths in southern Spain. The Byzantines succeeded in conquering these Germanic groups, and in extending Byzantine rule in the west. However, the price of regaining the old Roman Empire was very high. The wars exhausted most of the Byzantine resources. The treasury was bankrupt by the time Justinian died. There were few funds left for a defense of the eastern borders where the Persian threat was renewed. Within a generation of Justinian's death, the Byzantine Empire lost its western territories to new invaders.

Law, Religion, and Art Justinian also shaped the development of Byzantine law, religion, and art. Shortly after becoming emperor, he appointed a commission to codify, or classify, the empire's Roman laws. For centuries, these laws had accumulated without organization or classification.

The commission was made up of ten scholars headed by a legal expert named Tribonian. For more than six years, the commission collected and organized vast numbers of laws. It threw out the ones that were outdated, simplified many, and put the remainder into categories. The commission's work was recorded in a collection of books known as the *Corpus of Civil Law*, or the Justinian Code. This monumental work preserved the Roman legal heritage and passed it on to future generations. Over time, it has had a great impact on the legal systems of many countries.

Justinian further strengthened the ties between church and state. He settled doctrinal disputes and continued a policy of trying to unify the empire under one church organization. Jews and non-Greek Christians were sometimes

Point out that modern-day art historians rank the Hagia Sophia (pictured below) with the Parthenon and with St. Peter's in Rome as one of the most important buildings in European history.

Justinian built churches in all parts of the empire, but he is best remembered for his creation of the Hagia Sophia. It has a vast shallow dome suspended over semidomes set on a great marble rectangle. Hagia Sophia was the largest church in the eastern Mediterranean. What other building projects did Justinian order?

persecuted. To stamp out the last remnants of paganism, Justinian closed the school of philosophy in Athens.

Under Justinian, Byzantine art and architecture thrived and achieved their distinct character. The emperor ordered the construction of new roads, fortresses, aqueducts, monasteries, and other buildings. His most famous project was the church of *Hagia Sophia*, "Holy Wisdom," in Constantinople. The largest and most beautiful church in the empire, Hagia Sophia still stands today as one of the world's great architectural landmarks.

1. Identify: Constantinople, Eastern Orthodoxy, Nicaea, Justinian, Theodora, Sassanian, Belisarius, Tribonian, *Corpus of Civil Law*, Hagia Sophia.
2. Why did Constantine choose Byzantium as the site for a new capital?
3. What groups made up the Byzantine Empire? Which group was dominant?
4. Why is Justinian considered an important Byzantine ruler?

2   Struggle and Survival

After Justinian's death, the Byzantine Empire entered a period of decline. Invaders attacked from all sides, defeated the empire's once-powerful armies, and captured parts of Byzantine territory. At the same time, religious conflicts and political rivalries for the Byzantine throne sapped the empire's strength from within.

Invasions

During the late 500's A.D., the Byzantine Empire faced many invaders. Lombards from Germany occupied Italy. Slavs, Avars, and Bulgars invaded the Balkan Peninsula. Persian attacks in the east also threatened the empire.

Byzantine defeat seemed certain, until 610 A.D., when a new leader emerged. The general Heraclius, son of the Byzantine governor of North Africa, seized the throne and was crowned emperor. Immediately he began political and military reforms to save the empire. He reorganized the countryside into military provinces under the control of generals. With this reform, military governments took the place of civilian governments in an attempt to improve the empire's security. Heraclius counted on small farmers to build a new army. In return for their services, he gave them land. Heraclius's reforms worked so well that they lasted for over 500 years.

While Heraclius was strengthening the empire, Persian armies invaded Syria, Palestine, and Egypt. In 626 A.D. they reached the walls of Constantinople. Heraclius then counterattacked,

Discuss the impact of new weapons upon history. Speculate what might have happened if the Byzantines had not been able to defeat the Arabs by using Greek fire.

The Middle Ages · 115

Point out that John of Damascus defended icons as "silent sermons" and "books for the illiterate."

defeated the Persians, and drove them out of Byzantine territory. The Byzantines, however, did not enjoy peace for very long. A new enemy attacked them in 634 A.D. The Arabs, a group from the Middle East, invaded the outlying areas of the empire. These people were Muslims, or followers of the religion known as Islam. The aims of their military conquest were to spread the teachings of Islam and to acquire new wealth. During the 630's A.D., Arab armies gained victories over Syria and Palestine and continued their expansion into North Africa in the west and Persia in the east.

The Arabs, however, were not strong enough to conquer Constantinople and its surrounding area. They laid siege to the Byzantine capital from 674 to 678 A.D. The Byzantine fleet finally defeated the Arabs and halted the Muslim advance into Europe. In fighting their opponents, the Byantines used **Greek fire,** a chemical mixture that ignited when it came into contact with fire. It burned the skin and was not easily put out. Greek fire was the first secret weapon in history. The Byzantines guarded their secret so carefully that its exact formula is still unknown.

Although the Byzantines stopped the Arabs at Constantinople, they were unable to regain their lost territories in the Middle East and North Africa. The Arabs made these areas part of a new Islamic empire. They promised to establish law and order, as well as religious freedom, in the regions. The Byzantines frequently persecuted Syrian and Egyptian Christians who belonged to non-Orthodox churches. As a result, many of these Christians welcomed the Arabs as their liberators.

After the Arab conquests, the Byzantine Empire was reduced to the territories that were primarily Greek. Byzantine culture lost much of its international character and became even more Greek. Greek also took the place of Latin as the official language of the government.

Religious Controversy

During the 700's and 800's A.D., a major religious crisis divided the empire and drew it into civil war. This crisis was about the use of **icons,** or sacred pictures or images, in church worship. Although Christians had disagreed about this practice since the 200's A.D., they had never allowed it to seriously divide them.

But by the 700's A.D., the use of icons had become a political issue. In 726 A.D., Emperor Leo III issued a decree that all images and paintings should be removed from churches. He believed that the use of icons encouraged superstition and the worship of idols.

Leo's action sparked what is known as the iconoclastic controversy, a dispute that divided the empire into two opposing groups. Leo's supporters were known as **iconoclasts,** or image breakers. They were military leaders, government officials, and many of the people living in Asia Minor. Many iconoclasts used force in carrying out the emperor's decree. However, important church leaders and most of the people in other regions were against the removal of icons. Rioting in favor of having icons broke out in Constantinople and other areas. The emperor saw these disturbances as a challenge to his authority. He acted to put down the demonstrations and to keep church leaders who favored icons from gaining too much political power or influence.

The leading champion of icons was the Byzantine theologian, John of Damascus. Although a resident of the Islamic Empire, he wrote many religious articles defending the use of icons. The supporters of icons also received strong backing from the Pope and the Roman Catholic Church. The Pope's involvement in the controversy strained relations between the eastern and western churches.

A number of emperors after Leo supported iconoclasm, but public opinion backed those who favored icons and helped them to win the struggle. In 787 A.D., a church council at Nicaea approved the use of icons and declared iconoclasm a heresy. Shortly thereafter, Empress Irene[2] permitted the use of icons as long as they did not receive the worship due to God. In 843 A.D., the Eastern Orthodox Church reached a final settlement. It permitted the use of pictures in worship, but not statues.

---

[2] Irene was the first woman to hold the Byzantine throne in her own right.

The expansion of the empire brought new land and revenues under the control of the government.

During his reign, Alexius briefly strengthened the empire and restored some of its glory.

BYZANTINE EMPIRE

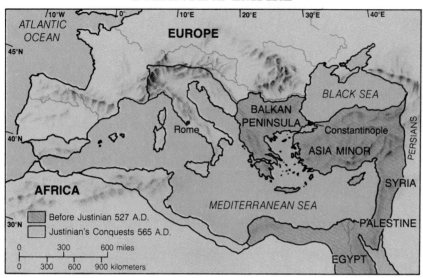

Rise and Decline

During the 800's A.D., the Byzantine Empire entered a period of prosperity and expansion under a new dynasty known as the Macedonians. The most successful emperor during this era was Basil II, who ruled from 976 to 1025 A.D. Under his leadership, the empire regained some of its lost territory in the Middle East, and conquered the Balkan kingdom of Bulgaria. Basil also introduced reforms to slow the rising power of the landed aristocracy, and to improve conditions for poor farmers.

During the late 1000's A.D., the Byzantine Empire entered another period of decline. In 1071 A.D. the Normans, a warrior people from northern Europe, seized Byzantine lands in southern Italy. To fight the Normans, the Byzantines called on Venice, an Italian trading city on the Adriatic Sea.[3] In spite of Venice's assistance, the Byzantines were unable to remove the Normans.

In the same year, the Seljuk Turks, a Muslim people from central Asia, defeated the Byzantines in the Battle of Manzikert. They gained control of Asia Minor, Syria, and Palestine, and threatened to take Constantinople.

While facing these invasions, Byzantines set up a new dynasty under the Comneni family. The most famous Comneni ruler was Alexius I, who ruled from 1081 to 1118 A.D. Shortly after becoming emperor, Alexius asked Pope Urban II and the Christian kingdoms of western Europe to help the Byzantine Empire defend Christianity against the Seljuks. After some delay, the Pope sent the first of a series of military expeditions known as the crusades against the Muslim Seljuks. However, the primary goal of the crusaders was to regain the Holy Land in Palestine for Western Christianity, not to protect the Byzantines. When the First Crusade traveled east in 1096 A.D., Alexius was disappointed and angry that it was not placed under his command. With their own leaders, the crusaders marched into Syria and Palestine, conquered the Seljuks, and set up independent states. However, the success of the First Crusade allowed Alexius to recover territory in Asia Minor.

1. Identify: Heraclius, Arabs, Islam, Leo III, Irene, Basil II, Seljuks, Manzikert, Alexius I.
2. Why did the Byzantine Empire decline shortly after Justinian's death? How did Heraclius save it from collapse?

[3] In return for Venice's aid, the Byzantine emperor allowed Venetian merchants special trading privileges in Constantinople. Eventually this led to Venetian control of Byzantine trade.

3. How did Byzantine rulers influence church affairs during the iconoclastic controversy?
4. What were the major accomplishments of the Macedonian dynasty?

3 East-West Rivalry

The crusades increased tension between Byzantine Christians and western Christians. However, friction between east and west was not a new development. Ever since the time of Constantine, cultural and religious differences had slowly been drawing the two areas apart.

Early Disputes

Since the 300's A.D., the eastern and western churches had disagreed on a number of issues. As centuries passed, these disagreements deepened. The most serious issue concerned the source of religious authority. The Pope in Rome and the Patriarch of Constantinople did not agree on their roles in the Christian Church. The Pope argued that he was the supreme leader of the Church. The Patriarch refused to recognize this claim. In addition, the two church leaders disagreed over points of doctrine. They challenged each other for control of the new churches in the Balkan Peninsula.

At the same time, relations were strained between the Byzantine emperor and the Pope. In the 800's A.D., the Byzantine emperors failed to aid the Pope during the Lombard invasions of Italy. As a result, the Pope broke his ties with the Byzantine emperor and turned to the Franks, a Germanic Catholic group in western Europe, for military protection. In time, the Pope gave the title of emperor to the Frankish king. This action made the Byzantine emperor even more bitter toward the Pope and western Europe. Finally, in 1054 A.D., doctrinal and political differences led to a **schism,** or separation, of the Church into the Roman Catholic Church in the west and the Eastern Orthodox Church in the east.

Economic Rivalry

The crusades led to a rivalry between the Byzantines and western Europeans for control of trade in the eastern Mediterranean. The outcome of this rivalry permanently weakened the By-

zantine Empire and embittered relations between east and west for years to come.

During the 1100's A.D., the economic fortunes of Venice rose. Venetian merchants were eager to capture Constantinople's prosperous trade in the Middle East. In 1204 A.D., Pope Innocent III called the Fourth Crusade against the Muslims. The Venetians agreed to transport the crusaders, mostly French nobles, to the Holy Land. But first, the Venetians required the crusaders to help in an attack on the Byzantine Empire. After a fierce battle, a combined force of crusaders and Venetians captured Constantinople in April 1204 A.D. For three days, the attackers burned and looted the city; many residents were killed. They stole valuable objects from palaces, churches, libraries, homes, and shops. Many priceless manuscripts and works of art were either taken to Venice, lost, or destroyed. The actions of the crusaders and Venetians were so brutal that the Pope publicly condemned them. He wrote:

> *These defenders of Christ, who should have turned their swords only against the infidels [Muslims], have bathed in Christian blood. They have respected neither religion, nor age,*

The Fourth Crusade did little to promote the cause of Christianity. The destruction of Constantinople permanently widened the rift between the eastern and western churches. Why did the crusaders capture Constantinople?

The Latin Empire was made up of several states that stretched from Constantinople to Syria and Palestine.

From the fall of Constantinople until the 1900's, many western historians ignored or discounted the civilization of the Byzantine Empire. Today, most historians write with greater objectivity.

nor sex. . . . It was not enough for them to squander [waste] the treasures of the [Byzantine] Empire and to rob private individuals, whether great or small. . . . They have dared to lay their hands on the wealth of the churches. They have been seen tearing from the altars the silver adornments, breaking them in fragments, over which they quarrelled, violating the sanctuaries, carrying away the icons, crosses, and relics. *

Latin Empire

The western Christians deposed, or removed, the Byzantine emperor and established a Latin empire. From the beginning, the Latin Empire had little chance for survival. The Fourth Crusade had stripped Constantinople of its trade and wealth. The Greek population, aided by the neighboring Bulgarians, actively resisted western rule. During the time the western Christians held Constantinople and the surrounding provinces, Greek nobles, church officials, and soldiers fled to areas that were still free from western control. In these places, they set up rival kingdoms and continued Byzantine culture.

The most important of the Greek kingdoms was located in the Asia Minor city of Nicaea. There the Greeks resumed the struggle against the western Christians. In 1261 A.D., Michael Palaeologus, a Greek noble, formed an army and captured Constantinople. The Byzantine Empire and its Eastern Orthodox Church were reestablished. Palaeologus became Emperor Michael VIII and founded the Palaeologi dynasty, which ruled the empire for nearly 200 years.

End of the Byzantines

The newly restored Byzantine Empire was weak and needed time for its economy to recover. The empire was also invaded, and lost more of its territory. The Serbs and Bulgars moved into Byzantine territory in the Balkans, while Muslim invaders from central Asia, known as Ottoman Turks, began to take over Byzantine lands in the east. By the late 1300's A.D., the empire consisted only of Constan-

tinople and part of mainland Greece. The population of the city dropped to less than 100,000 persons. As its resources became scarce, the Byzantine economy began to decline. Gradually, the empire's trade came under the control of Venice and other Italian city-states.

In 1453 A.D., the Ottoman **sultan,** or ruler, Mehmet II, brought 150,000 soldiers to Constantinople. The Ottomans laid siege to the city, using cannon against its walls. The Ottoman fleet, however, could not enter Constantinople's major harbor, the Golden Horn, because of heavy iron chains that guarded its entrance. The sailors finally pulled small boats overland to enter the harbor. The Ottomans soon had the upper hand, but the Byzantine emperor, Constantine XI, refused to surrender. The Byzantines fought until the emperor himself was slain.

On May 29, 1453 A.D., Mehmet II victoriously entered the city. He made it the capital of the new Ottoman Empire and converted Hagia Sophia into a mosque, or Muslim house of worship. At the same time, Mehmet promised to protect the Greek Christians and to allow them freedom to conduct their own community affairs. He installed a new Greek patriarch to supervise the political and religious life of the Greek Christians. Thus, the 1,000-year-old Byzantine Empire passed into history.

1. Identify: Franks, Venice, Michael VIII, Palaeologi, Ottoman Turks, Mehmet II.
2. What factors caused the split between eastern and western churches?
3. What impact did the Fourth Crusade have on Constantinople?
4. What developments led to the fall of the Byzantine Empire?

4 Byzantine Civilization

From 500 to 800 A.D., the Byzantine Empire remained a center of civilization at a time when most of western Europe was in a period of decline. It preserved Greek philosophy and literature, Roman political and legal ideas, and Christian theology. Later the Byzantine Empire shielded much of Christian Europe from the attacks of Muslim invaders, such as the Arabs and Turks.

---

*Pope Innocent III as quoted in *Cambridge Medieval History*, J. B. Bury, © 1923 by Macmillan, Vol. 4, p. 420.

Social groups in the empire were distinguished from one another by clothing. Farmers and workers wore short linen or wool tunics. The wealthy groups wore longer silk robes with ornate designs.

At the same time, the empire passed Greek philosophy and Byzantine political institutions to these Muslim peoples. Above all, the Byzantines gave a unique art form and Eastern Orthodoxy to Eastern Europe. Byzantine art also shaped cultures in western Europe and the Middle East.

Byzantine Life

Byzantine society was divided into a **hierarchy,** or ranked order, of social groups. However, few barriers existed to prevent a person moving from one group to another. As a result, Byzantine life was characterized by variety and change.

Family Life   The center of social life for most Byzantines was the family. Both church and government laws supported marriage as a sacred institution. Although divorce was not prohibited, it was difficult to obtain. Remarriage was not socially accepted. Repeated remarriage brought severe penalties from the Church.

Women were required, by Byzantine custom, to live partly in seclusion. They often had their own separate rooms at home and in churches. Most women performed household tasks. When they were in public, they sometimes veiled their faces.

Although women did not have equality with men, the law guaranteed them certain rights.

Through the efforts of Empress Theodora, the right to legal guardianship of children in the event of widowhood or remarriage was granted to women. A woman also had the right to control all of her late husband's property.

Some Byzantine women were able to overcome social restrictions. They became well educated and, in some cases, operated businesses and managed estates. A number of women governed the empire as **regents,** or temporary rulers. Some even ruled in their own right as empresses.

High Society   The emperor and the imperial family held the most respected and powerful positions in Byzantine society. They were surrounded by a court of advisers and subordinates. The orders of the emperor were carried out by civilian and military officials who served in various government posts. These officials competed for power and influence. They often plotted to name or depose emperors. Other influential groups were the leaders of the Eastern Orthodox Church, the landowning aristocracy, and wealthy merchants.

Wealthy Byzantines, in both city and country, lived in well-built stone or brick houses. Many homes had two stories and were built in the Roman style with courtyards. The rooms were elaborately decorated and filled with luxurious

The women of Byzantium were taught weaving, embroidery, and other homemaking skills. There were some women who became doctors, however, which suggests that wealthy families provided their daughters with private tutors. Who helped women gain some legal rights?

HISTORY AND CITIES

Constantinople

From the 300's to the 1400's A.D., Constantinople was the political and commercial center of the Byzantine Empire. It successfully fought off invading armies and served as the outpost of Christianity in the East. It was the largest and richest city in the Mediterranean world.

Constantinople's prosperity and security were based on its favorable location. The city was on the waterway between the Black and Aegean Seas. It stood on a small peninsula at the mouth of the Bosporus, a narrow strait between Europe and Asia Minor. To the north of Constantinople was the Golden Horn, a water inlet about four and a half miles (7.2 kilometers) long. Meeting the Bosporus, it provided the city with a safe, excellent harbor. To the south was the Sea of Marmara. It opened into the Aegean Sea through another strait known as the Dardanelles.

Constantinople's location gave it control of the trade routes between Russia and the Mediterranean area. The city also stood at the crossroads of the major trade routes between Europe and Asia. The Golden Horn, named for its shape and the city's wealth, attracted merchants from many parts of Asia, Africa, and Europe. Constantinople made a vivid impression on foreign visitors.

A western European traveler of the 1000's A.D. exclaimed:

> *O what a splendid city . . . how stately, how fair, how many monasteries. . . how many palaces raised by sheer labor in its broadways and streets, how many works of art, marvelous to behold; it would be wearisome to tell of the abundance of all good things. . . Ships are at all times putting in at this port, so that there is nothing that [people] want that is not brought [here].*

As the Byzantine capital and a center of trade, Constantinople had a diverse population of Greeks, Persians, Turks, Armenians, Jews, Slavs, and Italians. About 1100 A.D., nearly 1 million people lived in the city.

Constantinople was surrounded by 13 miles (20.8 kilometers) of walls that protected it from land and sea attacks. Within the walls, the city spread over seven hills and was divided into 14 districts. Its basic design was laid out in the early 300's A.D. by the emperor Constantine. The emperor also had architects build Constantinople's first important buildings. In the 500's A.D., anti-government riots destroyed much of the city. The emperor Justinian rebuilt it on a grand scale, adding more churches and palaces. The construction done under Justinian lasted throughout the rest of Byzantine history.

Builders and engineers modeled Constantinople on ancient Rome. Government buildings, such as the Senate and the emperor's palace, were built in the Roman style. They were adorned with works of classical art taken from other parts of the empire. Public baths, forums, basilicas, arches, and columns lined the major avenues and central squares. The oval-shaped Hippodrome, Constantinople's arena, was a replica, or copy, of Rome's Circus Maximus.

As a Christian city, Constantinople had many monasteries and magnificent churches, such as the Hagia Sophia. Government and church

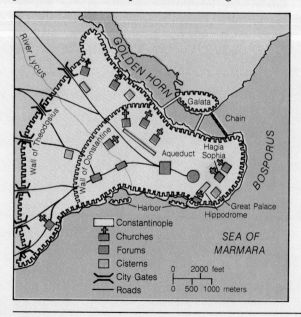

*Fulk of Chartres, as quoted in *Byzantium*, Philip Sherrard, © 1966 by Time-Life Books, p. 36.

leaders gathered relics from all over the Christian world and placed them in monuments, palaces, and churches in the city. The bodies of saints rested in richly decorated shrines. Thousands of people came to the shrines seeking cures for ills.

Most of the city, however, was a complex web of about 3,000 narrow streets. Many of these streets were jammed with caravan traffic, peddlers, and porters. In open-air markets shaded by canopies, a variety of imported and locally produced goods were sold. Commerce was strictly regulated. For example, artisans could set up shops only in places assigned to them by city officials. Rich and poor lived side by side in the residential areas. The great stone mansions of the rich were located next to the modest wooden buildings of the middle classes and the crowded apartment houses of the poor.

Constantinople was a well-governed city. Few of its people starved or were homeless. The Church and the government provided free medical and hospital care. Wealthy citizens formed organizations to care for the poor, aged,

and blind. Free bread was distributed daily to hungry people, and monasteries provided shelter to travelers and homeless persons.

In spite of these benefits, the city had its share of problems. As a result of refuse-filled streets, disease spread rapidly. Living conditions worsened during times when the city was under siege. Plagues took a heavy toll, especially among poor people. During the 500's A.D., a plague killed 300,000 of Constantinople's inhabitants and seriously weakened the empire.

After the Turkish conquest of 1453 A.D., Constantinople became an Islamic city. It became known as Istanbul and became the capital of the Ottoman Empire. By the mid-1500's A.D., Istanbul was a thriving city of almost 500,000 people. When the Ottoman Empire ended in 1921, Istanbul became part of the Republic of Turkey. Today, it is the largest city in that country.

1. How did Constantinople's location contribute to its security and prosperity?
2. What were some of the features of the city of Constantinople?

The diet of most Byzantines consisted of vegetables, bread, and cheese. Some wealthy people ate meat.

furnishings. In their homes, wealthy Byzantines held lavish banquets and parties.

Farmers. Most Byzantines were farmers, shepherds, or laborers. They lived in villages of small one-room huts made of wood or brick. After the reforms of Heraclius in the early 600's A.D., the majority of farmers owned their own land. They raised crops and livestock for themselves as well as for nobles and church officials. The heavy taxes they paid supported the government and the emperor's court. Young farmers served in the army. Village women carried out household chores. They wove cloth on hand looms and worked in the fields.

By the 800's A.D. a powerful group of landed aristocrats had emerged in the countryside. They bought up the properties of small farmers, who were then hired to work the land. The government passed laws to protect the lands of small farmers and to force the aristocrats to pay taxes. But these laws were unsuccessful. Wealthy landowners continued to exploit, or take advantage of, small farmers. As a result, poor people began to lose faith in the government as a defender of their interests. In turn, the government no longer depended on the farmers to serve in the army. Instead, it used mercenaries, or hired soldiers.

Commerce Although the Byzantine economy was basically agricultural, commerce thrived in cities like Constantinople and Thessalonika. There, merchants and artisans were organized into groups based on a particular trade or enterprise. With the help of these groups, the Byzantine government strictly controlled the economy. The government set prices, wages, and hours of business; regulated working conditions; and made rules for trade.

The major Byzantine business was textiles. During the 500's A.D., silkworms were brought to the Byzantine Empire from China. Thus began the production of silk. Silk was used in the making of luxurious clothing and furniture for the Church and the emperor's court. The government controlled the production of silk so that its secrets would not reach the West.

Recreation The Byzantines enjoyed a variety of recreational activities. They held festivals to remember the holy days on the church calendar. Many religious occasions, such as baptism and marriage, were important family celebrations. The government organized public pageants and circuses for the poor.

The people of Constantinople were divided between two competing groups, the Blues and the Greens. These groups held athletic contests

Even in such a city as Constantinople the country was not very far away. Farmers drove their herds and flocks to the city marketplace, and shepherds came into Constantinople to sell their salty, white cheese. Without protection from the law, farmers could not stop aristocrats from taking over their land. How did this takeover affect the economy?

Church organization followed the pattern of the Byzantine government. Like the empire, the Church was divided into provinces. Heading the major provinces were the patriarchs of Constantinople, Alexandria, Antioch, and Jerusalem. The patriarch at Constantinope had first rank among patriarchs.

and chariot races in the Hippodrome, a 40,000-seat arena. Heated rivalries between them took up a great deal of attention and energy. The Blues received the support of the aristocrats, while the Greens were backed by the poor. Even the emperors had to choose sides. Occasionally, when politics became involved in these contests, riots broke out in the arena and spread to the city streets. After the 600's A.D. the political role of the Blues and Greens declined.

Church and State

From its beginnings, the Byzantine Empire was a Christian empire. Eastern Orthodoxy was the official religion, and all Byzantines were required to be Christians. Church and government affairs were closely linked. As a result, theological disputes often became important political issues.

Emperor and Clergy   Regarded as Christ's representatives on earth, Byzantine emperors had a religious as well as a political role. Beginning in the 400's A.D., they were crowned by the Patriarch of Constantinople and took an oath to defend the Eastern Orthodox faith. Emperors appointed top church officials, including the Patriarch of Constantinople. As a result, emperors had extensive control over the Church's leadership. In religious services, the clergy prayed for God to bless the emperor and to give victory to the Byzantine armies.

Monasteries and convents played an important role in Byzantine life. They were first formed in the 300's A.D. by groups of Christians who wanted to lead holy lives apart from the world. In 379 A.D., a leading bishop named Basil made a list of rules for organizing these communities. This list, known as the Basilian Rule, became the model for Eastern Orthodox religious life.

In addition to prayer and worship, monks and nuns helped the poor, provided hospitals, and ran schools for needy children. Monks also preserved classical manuscripts and translated the Bible and other religious writings into several eastern European languages. They believed that more people would accept Christianity if the Bible and church rituals were presented to them in their own language.

Missionaries   The Church began missionary work that spread both Orthodox Christianity and Byzantine culture to neighboring lands. The people who benefited the most from this effort were the Slavs, an Indo-European people who settled in areas of eastern Europe north of the Byzantine Empire.

The most famous Byzantine missionaries were the brothers Cyril and Methodius. They left Constantinople and traveled among the western group of Slavs during the 860's A.D. They developed an alphabet for the Slavic languages based on a modified form of the Greek alphabet. It was called Cyrillic, in honor of Cyril, and is still used today by the Russians, Ukrainians, Bulgarians, and Serbs. Cyril and Methodius took with them translations of the Bible and the worship service of the Eastern Orthodox Church. As a result of Byzantine efforts, Orthodox Christianity became the religion of most Slavs.

Religion and Foreign Affairs   Religion affected the foreign policy of the Byzantine Empire. The long-standing dispute between the eastern and western churches prevented a united resistance to the Muslim invaders. The Fourth Crusade, as well as claims by the Pope, embittered the Byzantine clergy and laity. They developed a hostility toward the west that blocked future attempts to unite Roman Catholicism and Eastern Orthodoxy. After 1261 A.D. most of the Palaeologi emperors favored unification of the churches in order to win western support against the Muslims. However, they failed to reach this goal because of the strong oppositon of Byzantine clergy and laity.

Learning, Literature, and Law

Upper- and middle-income groups in the Byzantine Empire were well educated. Primary instruction was available in cities and in some rural villages. Larger cities had institutions of higher education. The University of Constantinople, established in 425 A.D., was supported by the government. It became an important center of learning during the Middle Ages. In addition to government-supported education, the Church provided religious schools in many areas to train priests and scholars. The leading center of theological studies was the patriarchal academy in Constantinople.

In spite of the central role of the Church in Byzantine society, the content of a Byzantine education was not strictly religious. Secular subjects—medicine, law, philosophy, arithmetic, geometry, astronomy, grammar, and music—were taught in schools and academies. Wealthy people sometimes hired distinguished tutors to instruct their children. Tutors played an especially important role in the education of girls and women, who were usually not admitted to schools and universities. However, some women were trained in professions such as medicine. For example, in the 1100's A.D., a woman doctor is mentioned in a description of a Byzantine hospital.

In literature, the role of the Church was dominant. The salvation of the soul and obedience to God's will were major concerns for Byzantines. As a result, Byzantine literature consisted mainly of hymns, poems, and other writings in praise of Christ and his mother Mary. Stories about the lives of the saints were very popular. They read like novels and told of dramatic events, travel, adventure, and miracles. At the same time, they were intended to teach moral lessons.

As a result of their Roman heritage, the Byzantines were interested in law. The emperor, as absolute ruler, made and issued laws. However, certain limits were placed on the use of this power. For example, the emperor was expected to respect both the teachings of the Church and the principles of the Justinian Code.

The growing influence of religion, as well as changes in Byzantine society, brought modifications in the Justinian Code. In the 700's A.D., a new collection of laws called the *Ekologa* reduced the number of crimes that called for the death

After the austerity of iconoclasm, Byzantine artists excelled in new directions. This church fresco demonstrates the merging of art and architecture that became typical of the later Byzantine period. What other art is associated with Byzantium?

Point out that Byzantine artists paid close attention to naturalistic detail in their mosaics. See p. 56.

penalty. Another important collection, *Basilica,* was completed in the 900's A.D. It made the law easier to understand.

Judges appointed by the emperor administered justice in the civil courts. These courts applied the law to ordinary citizens. Judges presented their decisions in writing and were required to sign them.

Art and Architecture

Byzantine art was based on classical and early Christian artistic styles. The art of ancient Greece and Rome stressed the reality of the material world. Some Byzantine art showed this influence with fully formed, lifelike figures. However, the major influence was the early Christian tradition. It reflected the viewpoint of the east, which stressed spiritual values. Most Byzantine art, therefore, was devoted to religious subjects. Flat, two-dimensional figures were drawn according to set patterns that emphasized their holiness.

Byzantine artists served the needs of the emperor's court and the Orthodox Church. Many were monks, whose works were required to be anonymous, or without the artist's name. This was done so that praise for a work of art would go to God, not to the individual artist.

Icons were the most popular art form. They were made on wood for display in churches, shrines, and homes. In Orthodox churches, the **sanctuary,** or altar area, was separated from the rest of the church by an **iconostasis,** a high thin wall covered with icons. Icons were also placed in other areas of the churches. **Iconography,** or the making of icons, suffered a setback during the iconoclastic controversy. At that time, many icons were destroyed. Few new ones were made because many Byzantine artists had fled from Constantinople to Italy. When icons were once again permitted, iconography again became a flourishing art form.

The Byzantines also developed an art form known as **mosaic.** Mosaics were made by fitting small flat pieces of stone or colored glass in mortar to form a picture or design. Mosaic artists used vivid colors to add brilliance to the images that they created. They also used a special technique in arranging the colored pieces. A visitor to Hagia Sophia described the church's mosaics in the following way:

> *As you move, the figures seem to move too. You could swear that their eyes are turning and shining and that their garments are rustling . . . the Byzantine mosaicist [artist] has succeeded in creating the illusion that his jig-saw puzzle has come to life. . . .**

Byzantine artists also excelled in making luxury crafts. They produced beautiful products in embroidery, enamel, ivory, silver, and gold. They also **illuminated,** or decorated, manuscript pages with elaborate designs and miniature pictures in brilliant colors.

The Byzantines were also noted for their architecture. Their most important accomplishment in this field was the construction of domed churches with richly decorated interiors. Hagia Sophia in Constantinople is considered the most magnificent of the Byzantine churches. Rectangular in shape, the church has a huge circular dome over its central part.

Erecting domes over rectangular or square buildings was a major architectural advance. Before the Byzantines, domes could only be built on circular walls. The Byzantine innovation gave designers more flexibility in the use of space. The Byzantines later built cross-shaped, multidomed churches. A fine example of this style is St. Mark's Cathedral in Venice, Italy.

Like the empire itself, Byzantine art and architecture went through periods of advance and decline. But their influence lasted long after the fall of Constantinople and spread beyond the borders of the empire. Byzantine styles in art and architecture later affected Russian, Balkan, and Turkish cultures. Byzantine art forms are still used today in Eastern Orthodox church buildings throughout the world.

1. Identify: Blues and Greens, Basil, Cyrillic.
2. What was the role of women in Byzantine society?
3. How did Byzantine missionaries influence the culture of eastern Europe?
4. What contributions did the Byzantines make in art and architecture?

**Constantine Porphyrogenitus and His World,* Arnold Toynbee, © 1973 by Oxford University Press, p. 545.

Have students compare Russia's northern location with that of the United States. Use the atlas section of this book to contrast the latitudes of cities such as Moscow and New York.

EARLY RUSSIA

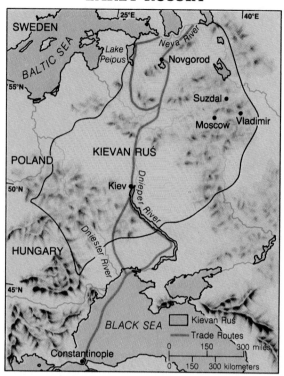

5 Early Russia

After the fall of Constantinople in 1453 A.D., the leadership of the Eastern Orthodox world passed from the Byzantines to the Russians. The Russians were the largest group among the Slavs who lived in eastern Europe. Because of their location, the Russians had been in close contact with the Byzantines since the 900's A.D.

This relationship made a lasting mark on the development of Russian history. The Russians borrowed much from the highly developed Byzantine civilization. On the foundation of Byzantine religion, law, and culture, the Russians built a new civilization. They also borrowed heavily from western European and Asian cultures. As a result of these different influences, Russia never became a completely eastern or western country.

Environment Geography has played an important role in Russian history. Since their earliest days, the Russians have controlled a vast area of plains, forests, lakes, and rivers where Europe meets Asia. Most of their territory is a great plain. This plain, called the **steppe,** begins in Europe and extends eastward into Asia. The steppe has made it easy for invaders from both Asia and Europe to move into Russian territory. It was the first site of Russian civilization. North of the steppe is a thickly forested region. This area was not heavily settled until after the 1200's A.D. However, its secure location soon made it the country's political center.

Throughout Russian history, rivers have been very important. The major rivers of Russia flow from north to south and empty into either the Black Sea or the Caspian Sea. Rivers have been used for trade and transportation and have helped unite the country. The most important centers of Russian history have been located on or near major rivers.

In spite of its many waterways, early Russia was a landlocked country, hundreds of miles from the open sea. In the 1500's A.D. Russia began to expand its borders in order to find outlets to the sea.

Another important geographic feature of Russia is its northern location. Much of the country is located farther north than most other centers of civilization. Because of its interior location, the country is not affected by warm moist winds from the oceans. Instead, freezing arctic winds blow across the land from early fall to late spring. As a result, most of Russia has a climate with great extremes of temperature in summer and winter, short spring and fall seasons, and small amounts of rainfall.

This location and climate have brought many hardships to the Russians. For example, crops are very difficult to grow in many areas due to poor weather conditions. Also, transportation is hindered because most of Russia's waterways are frozen nearly year-round.

Russian Origins

Historians know little about the origins of the Slavs, the larger group to which the Russians belong. Some believe the Slavs came from what is now eastern Poland. Others think they may have been farmers in the Black Sea region. It is known that by 500 A.D., the Slavs had separated

Have students compare the Russian Proverbs (below) with the Sayings of Confucius on p. 46.

into smaller groups and had settled in different areas of eastern Europe. One group, known as the West Slavs, lived in the marshlands, plains, and mountains of east-central Europe. They successfully fought the Germans to the west and the Scandinavians to the north for control of this territory. Today, the descendants of the West Slavs are the peoples of Poland and Czechoslovakia. Another group, known as the South Slavs, settled in the Balkan Peninsula. Today, their descendants are the peoples of Yugoslavia.

The largest group of Slavs, called East Slavs, lived in the land near the Black Sea between the Dniester and the Dnieper Rivers. From 500 to 800 A.D., they moved eastward toward the Volga River. These people gradually intermarried with Asiatic and Nordic peoples who later invaded the area. From the East Slavs came the peoples who are known today as Russians, Ukrainians, and Belorussians.

Early Russians

The early Russians lived in villages made up of related families. They cleared the land for farming and shared their tools and produce. Forests provided the Russians with timber, which they used to build their **izbas,** or log cabins. Many izbas had wooden gables and window frames decorated with painted carvings of flowers and animals. Skilled artisans also used wood to make musical instruments, boats, and images of favorite gods.

The Russians used the many rivers in their area for transportation and trade. They set up trading towns along the riverbanks. By the 800's A.D., a trade route ran from the Baltic Sea in the north to the Black Sea in the south.

Kiev   The early Russians were not warlike. During the second half of the 800's A.D., they relied on the Varangians, a group of warriors and traders from Scandinavia, to protect their trade routes. The Varangians not only provided military support, they also laid the foundations of Russian government.

The arrival of the Varangians is recorded in the *Russian Chronicles,* a collection of Russian history, tales, and legends written in the 1100's A.D.

Russian Proverbs

- The burden is light on the shoulder of another.
- Fear the goat from the front, the horse from the rear, and man from all sides.
- Pray to God, but keep rowing to the shore.
- Don't be so smart; smarter ones than you are in jail.
- A bad peace is better than a good war.
- A kind word is like a spring day.

- A person who has committed a mistake and does not correct it is committing another mistake.
- Happiness is not a horse; you cannot harness it.
- There is more light than can be seen through a window.
- Make peace with men and quarrel with your faults.

The Varangian warriors were known as *russ* in their language. They organized the Slavs, setting up fortified cities called *gorods* along the rivers. The impact of the *russ* was so great that the Slavs came to be known as "Russians."

The grand prince of Kiev accepted tribute and homage from princes and traders. What benefits did the princes and traders hope to derive from this practice?

According to the *Russian Chronicles*, in 862 A.D. the people of Novgorod, a northern town on the Russian trade route, asked a Varangian leader named Rurik to be their prince. Upon Rurik's death, another Varangian named Oleg succeeded him. Oleg moved south and set up the first organized Russian state. He established his capital at Kiev, the southernmost town on the trade route. Kiev stood on a hill overlooking the Dnieper River and was located close to where the forests met the steppe. Kiev was in a good location to protect its merchant ships.

Control of Kiev enabled Oleg to dominate the north-south water trade route. Towns along the route were brought together under his leadership. Kiev soon became the chief political and commercial center among the Russian territories. The rulers of Kiev, known as "Grand Princes," conducted raids against Constantinople. They were attracted by the wealth and civilization of the Byzantine capital. In 911 A.D. a treaty ended these raids and established trade between the Byzantines and the Russians. During the summer months, Russian merchants carried furs, honey, and other forest products by boat to Constantinople. There they traded their goods for cloth, wine, weapons, and jewelry.

Early Russian Government   By 900 A.D. the Russians had organized into a confederation of city-states and **principalities,** or territories ruled by princes. Each region enjoyed local self-government; however, they all paid special respect to the grand prince of Kiev. The grand prince collected tribute from the local princes to support his court and army. The major duties of these princes were to administer justice and to defend the frontiers. The princes were assisted by councils of wealthy merchants and landed nobles, who were known as **boyars. Veches,** or assemblies, represented all free, adult male citizens. They handled daily affairs and had the power to accept or remove princes.

These three institutions—the princely office, the council, and the veche—varied in power from region to region. In the northeastern territories, the princes wielded a great deal of political power. In the southeastern areas, the boyars had the greatest political influence. In Novgorod and a few northern trading towns and cities, the veches overshadowed both princes and boyars. In these areas, the veches came close to establishing a tradition of representative government in Russia. However, later princes limited the powers of the veches.

St. Cyril, apostle of the Slavs, reputedly invented the Cyrillic alphabet in 869 A.D.

Economic Prosperity   During the 1000's A.D., Russian trade prospered and grew as a result of contacts with the Byzantines and Muslims. Kiev's merchants exchanged money for goods and enjoyed a sophisticated urban culture. Archeologists and historians believe that Kiev was an important trading link between Europe and Asia, and between Scandinavia and the Middle East. Recent excavations in Sweden unearthed more than 200,000 Arabic and Byzantine coins. Such a discovery shows the extensive amount of trade that passed through Kiev during this period. By 1050 A.D. Russian civilization was more advanced than the civilizations of any other western or Mediterranean culture. Only the Byzantine and Islamic civilizations surpassed it.

Christianity in Russia

Before the late 900's A.D., the Russians honored nature spirits and ancestors, and worshiped many gods. The most popular gods were Perun, god of thunder and lightning, and the Great Mother, goddess of the land and harvest. Images of the gods were built on the highest ground outside the villages.

Vladimir's Conversion   As a result of contact with the Byzantine Empire, many Russians were influenced by Eastern Orthodoxy. Olga, a princess of Kiev, became the first member of the Russian nobility to accept the faith. After her death, she was made a saint of the Eastern Orthodox Church. Her grandson, Prince Vladimir I of Kiev, decided to abandon paganism and to adopt a new religion that he thought would help the Russians to become more civilized. An old Russian legend states that Vladimir sent observers abroad to examine Judaism, Islam, Roman Catholicism, and Eastern Orthodoxy. They were unimpressed by what they witnessed until they came to Constantinople. There they were awed by the beauty of Eastern Orthodox worship in the Hagia Sophia. When they returned to Kiev, the observers persuaded Vladimir to convert to Eastern Orthodoxy. In 989 A.D. Vladimir ordered the mass baptism of his people in the Dnieper River. He then made Eastern Orthodoxy the official religion in his territories. He also established closer ties between Kiev and Constantinople by marrying the sister of the Byzantine emperor.

Orthodox Russia   Vladimir's acceptance of Eastern Orthodoxy gave the Russians a sense of belonging to the civilized world. The new religion brought Byzantine culture to Russia. Byzantine priests and bishops introduced the Russians to colorful rituals and taught them the art of painting icons. The Russians learned to write their language in the Cyrillic alphabet. Schools were established in the towns for the sons of boyars, priests, and merchants. Byzantine architects arrived in Kiev to build stone cathedrals and churches with onion-shaped domes. Monasteries also were founded in the towns and countryside, and attracted many of the new converts. By 1000 A.D. the Eastern

The most direct expression of Russian folk art was woodcarving and wooden architecture. What architectural styles were adopted from the Byzantines?

Orthodox Church in Russia had developed an organization and had won the support of the people. It became known as the Russian Orthodox Church.

The acceptance of Eastern Orthodoxy, however, contributed to the isolation of Russia from the outside world. Following the schism between the eastern and western churches, Russia was separated from western Europe. Its people lost contact with developments that took place in that area after 1200 A.D. At the same time, the Byzantine practice of translating the Bible and Orthodox church services into local languages had an important impact. Because Russian scholars had translations of some classical and Christian writings in their own language, they did not learn Greek or Latin. As a result, they did not deepen their knowledge of the heritage of western European civilization. Instead, they turned for inspiration to the traditions of their own local culture.

During Yaroslav's rule, many noteworthy buildings were constructed. St. Sophia in Kiev is one of the churches built during his reign. What has been considered Yaroslav's greatest achievement?

Kievan Rulers

Vladimir I, who ruled from 980 to 1015 A.D., was one of the most important grand princes of Kiev. Known for his skills as a warrior, he successfully defended Russia's eastern frontiers against nomadic invaders. He also expanded Russia's western borders by capturing lands in Poland and near the Baltic Sea.

After Vladimir's death, his sons fought each other for the Kievan throne. In 1019 A.D. Yaroslav triumphed over his brothers and assumed full control of the state. During his reign, Kiev reached the height of its cultural and economic development. Skilled artisans and builders transformed the appearance of the city with fortifications, gates, churches, and monasteries.

Yaroslav encouraged the spread of learning and earned the title "the Wise." He collected books and brought scholars from Constantinople to Kiev. Yaroslav was also a skilled diplomat. He negotiated alliances with western European kingdoms. He arranged marriages for his relatives with members of royal families in Poland, Norway, Hungary, and France.

Yaroslav's major achievement was the organization of Russian laws. He asked the clergy to create a code of law based on local Slavic customs and Byzantine law. Written primarily for the princes and merchants, the code made crimes of property more serious than crimes against persons. By the standards of the day, it was exceptionally mild regarding punishments. For example, it did not provide for a death penalty.

Fall of Kiev

Struggles among princes for control of the throne broke out after Yaroslav's death in 1054 A.D. During the next century, Kiev began a slow decline, with only brief periods of recovery. Developments outside of Russia played an important part in Kiev's misfortunes. The Fourth Crusade in 1204 A.D. and the creation of a Latin state in Constantinople disrupted Russian trade with the Byzantines. As a result, Kiev's economy was seriously weakened. The final blow to Kiev took place in 1240 A.D., when Mongol invaders from central Asia captured the city and completely destroyed it.

Point out that the Moscow area was known as Muscovy during this time in its history.

Mongols   The Mongols, or the Tatars as the Russians called them, defeated the armies of the Russian principalities and conquered most of the country. During the invasion, they sacked towns and villages and killed many people. After establishing control, the Mongols allowed the Russians to practice Christianity and to govern themselves. However, the Russian princes had to pay tribute to the **khan,** or Mongol leader. Russians also had to serve in the khan's armies. The Mongol invasion helped the Russians gain a sense of being one people. However, they also became further isolated from the outside world.

During this period the Russian Orthodox Church remained strong and preserved Russian culture. As city life in the south of the country declined, Russian monks began to move into the remote northern forests. There they founded monasteries and churches. The monks were followed by farmers and artisans, who were also trying to escape Mongol rule. These people became settlers in the new towns and villages that soon developed around the monasteries.

Alexander Nevsky   After the fall of Kiev, the political center of Russia shifted north along with the movement of population. In the late 1200's A.D. the principality of Vladimir-Suzdal and the city of Novgorod became the strongest of the Russian territories. They had been less affected by the Mongols than the other Russian principalities and cities. However, they faced powerful enemies along the Baltic coast—the Catholic Swedes and the Teutonic Knights, a crusading order that had been formed in Palestine and later transferred to northeastern Europe. Both groups wanted to force the Russians to accept Roman Catholicism and western European culture.

In 1240 A.D., Alexander, the young prince of Novgorod, defeated the invading Swedes beside the Neva River and won the title *Nevsky,* or "of the Neva." Two years later, he won a great victory over the Teutonic Knights on an icy lake near the Baltic. Alexander Nevsky became known as a war hero. In 1252 A.D. he was made the prince of Vladimir-Suzdal. As prince, he paid visits to the court of the khan, where he negotiated the easing of Mongol controls over his

Nevsky's defeat of the Teutonic Knights on Lake Peipus became one of the first great epics of Russian literature. How was Nevsky honored for his successes?

people. Because of his services to the nation, after his death in 1263 A.D., Alexander Nevsky was made a saint of the Russian Orthodox Church.

In the early 1300's A.D., Nevsky's youngest son Daniel became the ruler of Moscow, a small, prosperous town that was located on important land and water routes. Daniel's successors expanded the territory of Moscow. By the late 1400's A.D., Moscow had become the most powerful city in Russia. It was soon to become the capital of the world's largest Eastern Orthodox Christian state.

1. Identify: West Slavs, South Slavs, East Slavs, Varangians, *Russian Chronicles,* Kiev, Olga, Vladimir, Yaroslav, Mongols, Alexander Nevsky, Moscow.
2. How did geography and climate affect the early history of Russia?
3. Why did the Russians accept Eastern Orthodoxy as their official religion?
4. What effects did the Mongols have on Russia?

CHAPTER 5 REVIEW

Summary

1. The Byzantine Empire began as the Roman Empire in the East. It lasted for almost 1,000 years after the fall of Rome.
2. The Byzantine Empire was a Christian state. Its emperor was regarded as protector of the Eastern Orthodox Church.
3. During the empire's height, Constantinople became the largest and most prosperous Christian city in the world.
4. The emperor Justinian extended the empire's borders to their greatest extent, developed a legal code, and contributed to a cultural awakening.
5. The schism in 1054 A.D. and the Fourth Crusade in 1204 A.D. led to bitterness between eastern and western Christians.
6. The Byzantines preserved and contributed to classical literature, law, and philosophy. They also excelled in iconography, manuscript illumination, architecture, mosaic art, and luxury crafts.
7. Throughout their history, the Byzantines lost territory to invaders such as the Arabs, the Seljuk Turks, and the western Europeans. The Ottoman Turks finally ended the empire by capturing Constantinople in the year 1453 A.D.
8. The Eastern Orthodox Church brought Byzantine culture, including the Cyrillic alphabet, to Russia and to the area of southeastern Europe.
9. The early Russians prospered from river trade and were organized into a collection of city-states and principalities under the grand prince of Kiev.
10. About 1240 A.D., Russia was conquered by the Mongols. Many Russians settled in the northern forests and established monasteries, towns, farms, and villages.
11. By 1400 A.D., Moscow had become the most important Russian city and the center of a new Russian state.

Building Vocabulary

theology	icons	sanctuary	steppe
ethnic group	iconoclasts	iconostasis	izbas
clergy	schism	iconography	principalities
laity	sultan	mosaic	boyars
dowry	hierarchy	illuminated	veches
Greek fire	regents		khan

Reviewing the Main Ideas

1. Why was the eastern part of the Roman Empire able to survive for nearly 1,000 years after the fall of Rome?
2. Why was the establishment of Constantinople important in the rise of the Byzantine Empire?
3. How did ethnic and religious conflicts shape the development of the empire?
4. What role did the empress Theodora play during Justinian's reign?
5. What did Justinian's military campaigns accomplish?

6. How did the crusades affect relations between the Byzantine Empire and western Europe?
7. Why did the Latin Empire in the east collapse?
8. What contributions did the Byzantines make to western civilization?
9. Where did the early Slavs settle?
10. Why was Kiev an important city to the early Russians?
11. What were the major features of early Russian government?
12. What contribution did Alexander Nevsky make to early Russia?

Discussing Important Ideas

1. Was the involvement of Byzantine emperors in church affairs helpful or harmful to the church? to the state?
2. Of the accomplishments of Justinian, which was the most important? Explain.
3. In her actions, was Theodora a typical Byzantine woman? Explain.
4. Did the loss of non-Greek territories in the 600's A.D. strengthen or weaken the Byzantine Empire?
5. Do you agree that the schism between eastern and western churches was caused only by doctrinal differences? Why or why not?
6. If you had been a Byzantine at the time of the iconoclastic controversy, what would have been your position on the use of icons in church worship?
7. What advantages and disadvantages did conversion to Eastern Orthodoxy bring to the Russians?
8. Which ruler—Vladimir I or Yaroslav—made the greater contribution to the rise of Russia? Why?

Map Skills

Refer to the map on page 120 to answer the following questions:
1. The Wall of Theodosius has how many gates?
2. How many churches lie east of the River Lycus?
3. Which structures suggest Roman influence?
4. What three harbors served Constantinople? Describe their locations.
5. How was the city prepared to defend itself against attack?

CHAPTER 6

Mosque and School

> ❝ *Praise the name of thy Lord the Most High, Who hath created and balanced all things, Who hath fixed their destinies and guideth them. . . .* ❞
>
> *Koran, Sura 87.1*

Islam

During the 600's A.D., a new religion known as Islam[1] emerged in the Middle East. The Arabs were the first Muslims, or followers of Islam. Within 100 years they had transformed Islam from a small religious community into a large political empire. The Islamic state that the Arabs created absorbed many peoples and cultures. It encompassed an area larger than the Roman Empire. At its height the Islamic Empire stretched from the Atlantic Ocean in the west to the borders of China in the east.

From the 700's to the 1100's A.D., the achievements of the Islamic Empire were unsurpassed. While western Europe was struggling to emerge from a period of decline following the collapse of the Roman Empire in the West, Arabs and other Muslims were establishing centers of learning and preserving much of the knowledge of the ancient world. They made discoveries in medicine, chemistry, physics, and mathematics. They also made important contributions in the arts. Their knowledge and skills in these fields were later passed to western Europe. As a result, much of early western science and literature was influenced by Islam.

Although the Islamic Empire no longer exists, the faith of Islam still forms a common bond among the people who live in the empire's former territories. Today more than 700 million people consider themselves followers of Islam. They form the majority of the population in the Middle East, North Africa, and various parts of South Asia.

1 Beginnings

The homeland of the Arabs was the Arabian Peninsula, a wedge of land about 1 million square miles (2.6 million square kilometers) in size, situated between the Red Sea and the Persian Gulf. This location placed the Arabs on the margins of the great civilizations of the Middle East. During ancient times, the empires of the region found Arabia uninviting and made no efforts to conquer it. Thus, early Arab culture was only indirectly influenced from outside.

Geography and climate were responsible for the isolation of Arabia. Geographical remoteness kept outsiders from invading the area and allowed the Arabs to develop their civilization. The Arabian Peninsula was made up of two distinct regions. The southwestern area, across from the northeast coast of Africa, had well-watered valleys nestled between mountains. Farming became profitable in this fertile area and supported a large population. The rest of Arabia, however, consisted of arid plains and deserts. High temperatures, scanty rainfall, and sparse vegetation made the region unsuitable for human habitation. However, a few settlements developed around desert oases.

Arabia Before Islam

Like the ancient Hebrews, Phoenicians, and Chaldeans, the Arabs were the descendants of Semitic tribes. Archeologists have traced Arab civilization in the Arabian Peninsula to at least 3000 B.C. Arab peoples are mentioned in the writings of the Hebrews, Greeks, Persians, and Romans.

Around 100 A.D. the prosperous kingdoms in southwestern Arabia traded with Rome, India, and the Far East. At the same time, other Arab kingdoms in northern Arabia came under Roman protection. About 400 years later, all of the Arab kingdoms declined as the Byzantine and Persian empires struggled for control of the Middle East.

Bedouins   During this period, **nomadic,** or wandering groups, of Arabs lived in the Arabian Peninsula. They were known as **bedouins** and roamed the desert in search of pasture and water for their camels, goats, and sheep. Their diet consisted mostly of dates and milk, and their homes were tents woven from camel or goat hair.

The bedouins were organized into tribes, each made up of a group of related families. Arabs valued family ties because they ensured protection and survival in the harsh desert climate. At

---

[1]The Arabic word *islam* means "submission" (to the will of God).

Sheikhs expected absolute obedience from their tribes in warfare and in searching for water.

According to legend, the original Ka'bah had stood in heaven. The first man, Adam, built an earthly Ka'bah modelled on the heavenly one. The town of Mecca grew up around the Ka'bah.

The vast interior of the desert reflects the austere nomadic life of a bedouin woman as she tends the herd. Bedouins depend heavily on camels, not only for transportation, but also for milk, meat, and hair for weaving. What values are emphasized in bedouin tribal life?

the head of each tribe was a **sheikh,** or chief, appointed by the heads of the families. The sheikh was advised by a council of elders and had to respect the customs of the tribe. His rule was based not on hereditary right, but on leadership abilities and the consent of the tribe.

Certain rules regulated the life of a bedouin tribe. A tribe's survival depended on every member obeying tribal rules. If the rules were broken, punishment had to be imposed on the offender. The rules were based on values such as honor, generosity, loyalty, and bravery. These values established a common bond among the members of each tribe.

Arab tribes were warrior societies in which the use of camels, horses, and swords was stressed. Tribes often fought over pastures and sources of water. They also followed the law of retaliation, "an eye for an eye, and a tooth for a tooth." To defend its honor, a tribe would fight another tribe in **blood feuds,** or quarrels in which an injured tribe seeks revenge against an opponent. In order to accumulate wealth, tribes often raided each other and seized **booty,** or war prizes.

The early Arabs also pursued peaceful activities. For example, they took pride in their Arabic language. Composing and reciting poetry were favorite activities. Poems described battles, desert scenes, camels, horses, and love affairs.

Every year, poets from various tribes met to compete in contests.

Mecca   By 500 A.D. many tribes began to settle down to pursue either agriculture or trade. Groups of merchants soon emerged and founded market towns. Camel caravans began to carry goods on trade routes that connected southwestern Arabia to the Mediterranean Sea and the Persian Gulf. One of the largest and richest towns that developed along these routes was Mecca. Located 50 miles (80 kilometers) inland from the Red Sea, Mecca was governed by a merchant tribe called the Quraysh. The Quraysh made Mecca a powerful center of business and commerce.

Mecca was also an important religious center. During the early 500's A.D., the majority of Arabs worshiped some 300 gods and goddesses, who were under the authority of the creator god Allah. Pilgrims came to Mecca to worship at Arabia's holiest shrine, the Ka'bah, which stood in the center of town. The Ka'bah was a simple, cube-shaped building containing statues of the various deities. A small black stone believed to have fallen from heaven was sealed into a corner of the building. Pilgrims kissed the black stone, made offerings before the images, and walked around the Ka'bah seven times. The merchants of Mecca grew wealthy from the business that the pilgrims brought to the city.

Point out that *Allah* is the Arabic term for "God." Mohammed preached that Allah was the same god as the God of the Jews and the Christians.

Rise of Islam

The transition of Arabia from a nomadic to an urban society brought changes to Arabian culture. Business ties began to replace tribal ties. A new code of rules was needed to regulate life in Arab towns. At the same time, Byzantines and Persians were putting pressure on the Arabs. Although Arabs found unity in a common language, they lacked a central government to handle these problems.

Religious ideas also began to change. Through military and commercial contacts with Byzantines and Persians, Arabs learned about the monotheistic religions of Judaism and Christianity. As a result, many Arabs became dissatisfied with polytheism and searched for a new religion. Righteous men known as **hanifs** denounced the worship of idols, lived simple lives, and believed in one god. However, they rejected Judaism and Christianity, preferring to find a uniquely Arab kind of monotheism. All of these developments contributed to the emergence of Islam, an event that would bring Arabs into contact with other civilizations and change the course of their history.

Mohammed   Islam was founded by an Arab merchant named Mohammed, who was born in Mecca around 571 A.D. Muslim traditions state that Mohammed was orphaned at an early age and raised by an uncle. Upon reaching his teens, Mohammed worked as a camel driver on a prosperous trade route. At about the age of 25, he married his employer, a rich 40-year-old widow named Khadija.

Mohammed's marriage relieved him of financial worries and gave him time to reflect on the meaning of life. He became troubled by the greed of Mecca's wealthy class and its mistreatment of the poor. He was also disturbed by the worship of idols and the immorality of city life. As a result, Mohammed began spending time alone, praying and fasting in a cave outside the city.

Revelation and Message   It is believed that in 610 A.D., Mohammed experienced a **revelation,** or vision. He heard a voice calling him to be the apostle of the one true deity—Allah, or God. A short time later, a second revelation commanded him to "rise and warn" the people about divine judgment. Although Mohammed had doubts about the revelations, he finally accepted his heavenly mission.

In 613 A.D. Mohammed began to preach to the people of Mecca. He preached that Allah was the only god, and that people everywhere must worship and obey him. All believers in Allah, Mohammed declared, were equal. Therefore,

In towns and oases along the caravan routes were fortified caravanserai. Built for the safety and refreshment of travelers, a caravanserai was often a huge complex containing a hospital, a hotel, and a mosque. There, traveling merchants were provided with water, food, and sleeping quarters before the real business of trading began. What does the photo reveal about the life of the traders?

By the time the Muslims arrived in Medina, all of the arable land had been occupied. Thus, the Muslims had to work as laborers until they gained wealth by raiding Meccan caravans.

the rich should share their wealth with the poor. Mohammed also preached that Allah measured the worth of people by their devotion and good deeds. People were told to live their lives in preparation for the Day of Judgment, or the last day, when Allah would punish evildoers and reward the just.

Mohammed made slow progress in winning converts to his message. He first won over his wife Khadija and other members of his family. Most other converts came from those of Mecca's poor who were attracted by Mohammed's call for social justice. However, the majority of Meccans rejected Mohammed's preaching. Wealthy merchants and religious leaders of Mecca particularly disliked the prophet's attacks on the images at the Ka'bah. They became concerned that worship of Allah could end pilgrimages to Mecca. Wealthy Meccans believed that the city's economy would then be ruined, and, that they would lose their prestige and wealth. Because of these fears, Mecca's leaders began to persecute Mohammed and his followers.

Mohammed persisted in preaching until threats against his life forced him to seek help outside Mecca. In 622 A.D. he made an agreement with pilgrims from Yathrib, a small town 200 miles (320 kilometers) north of Mecca, to settle a dispute in their city between two Arab tribes. In return for Mohammed's help, the people of Yathrib promised to shelter and protect his followers. Mohammed then sent about 60 Muslim families from Mecca to Yathrib. Later, he and his remaining followers secretly left Mecca and traveled to their new home. This departure of Mohammed to Yathrib is known in Muslim history as the *Hegira*, or the Emigration. Muslims consider this event as the beginning of the Muslim era. Thus, 622 A. D. became the first year on the Muslim calendar.

Islamic Community   The people of Yathrib accepted Mohammed as Allah's messenger and as ruler of their city. Yathrib became the center of Islam and was renamed Madinat al-Nabi, "the city of the prophet," or Medina.

Mohammed proved that he was a skilled political and religious leader. He established a community based on principles that he defined in the Medina Compact of 624 A.D. This document stated that all Muslims were to place loyalty to the Islamic community above tribal loyalties. Mohammed was declared the community's lawgiver and commander-in-chief. All community disputes were to be settled by him. Tribes or individuals could no longer carry out blood feuds and other acts of revenge. The Compact also extended protection to Jews and other non-Muslim minorities who submitted to

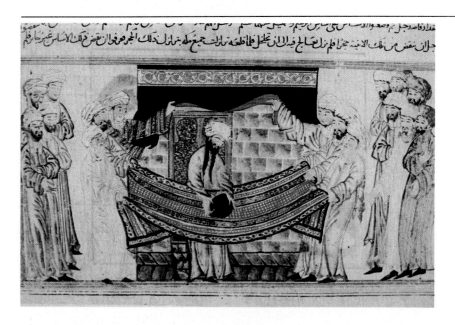

After Mohammed blessed the black stone, it was framed in silver and reset in a wall of the Ka'bah. In what city is this most sacred sanctuary of the Muslim world?

The Koran states that Abraham was a Muslim. Muslims believe that Arabs are descendants of Abraham's son Ishmael and that Jews are descendants of his other son Isaac.

Koran means "recitation," or "that which is to be read." Its final version was compiled in 655.

the political authority of the Islamic community.[2] As a result of the Compact, Islam became a state and a culture as well as a religion. All areas of life were placed under the divine law given to Mohammed. This law was recorded in the Koran, or Muslim holy scriptures.

Although he had become a powerful political leader, Mohammed continued to face opposition from Mecca. He began to lead his followers in raids against Meccan caravans passing through Medina's territory. After two important victories over Mecca's army, Mohammed won increasing support from Arab tribes outside Medina. Many of them accepted Islam and rallied to Mohammed's cause. Mohammed soon became strong enough to force the Meccans to surrender peacefully. In 630 A.D. Mohammed and his followers entered Mecca, encountering little resistance. They destroyed the idols in the Ka'bah and turned the shrine into a place of worship for Muslim pilgrims. The Meccans accepted Islam and acknowledged Mohammed as Allah's prophet. Mecca became the spiritual center of Islam, while Medina remained its political capital.

After taking Mecca, Mohammed and his followers extended their control into other parts of Arabia. In 631 A.D. delegates representing Arab tribes from all over the peninsula came to Medina to show their acceptance of Islam and Mohammed's authority. The Islamic state included all of Arabia and was supported by a strong army recruited from all the Arab tribes.

After a brief illness, Mohammed died at Medina in 632 A.D. He left behind two major achievements: a new monotheistic religion that stood on an equal level with Judaism and Christianity, and a well-organized political-religious community that increased the power and influence of the Arabs.

1. Identify: Islam, Mecca, Ka'bah, Mohammed, Allah, Medina, Medina Compact.
2. What developments in Arabia prepared the way for the rise of Islam?

---

[2]Mohammed had tried to convert the Jews to Islam. But they had rejected his message and continued to practice their own faith. Mohammed broke ties with the Jews completely after some refused to accept the Medina Compact.

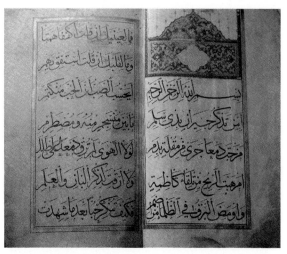

A distinguishing characteristic of Islamic books is the beauty of the writing combined with abstract designs. What is the most important book in Islam?

3. What message did Mohammed bring to the people of Mecca? How was it received?
4. Why is the Hegira important in Islamic history?

2 Islamic Beliefs and Practices

Mohammed set up a basic set of beliefs and practices for his followers. In spite of social and political changes, these beliefs and practices have remained remarkably the same throughout Islamic history.

Koran

According to Muslim tradition, an angel revealed a series of divine messages to Mohammed over a 22-year period. Mohammed's followers wrote down these messages. After the prophet's death, they were collected into the book now called the Koran. Since its creation, the Koran has played a central role in Muslim education and worship. For all Muslims, the Koran is the final authority in matters of faith and practice.

Written in Arabic, the Koran contains stories, legends, and philosophy in verse form. Verses are arranged into 114 chapters called **suras**. Suras vary in length from a few lines to several hundred verses. Following the first one, the suras are grouped according to length so that the longer appear first and the shorter appear last.

Morals   The Koran presents the basic moral values of Islam, which are similar to those of Judaism and Christianity. Honor of parents, kindness to neighbors, protection of orphans and widows, and charity toward the poor are affirmed. Murder, stealing, lying, and adultery are condemned. The Koran also lays down specific rules to guide the daily activities of Muslims. For example, the Koran forbids gambling, eating pork, or drinking alcoholic beverages. It also has regulations affecting marriage, divorce, inheritance, and business practices.

Law   Law and religion are closely related in Islam. Although Islam has no ranked order of clergy, generations of legal scholars and theologians have organized Islamic moral rules into a code of law known as the **shari'a**. The shari'a covers all aspects of Muslim private and public life. It is based on the Koran and the Hadith, or sayings of Mohammed that have been handed down by scholars.

Five Pillars

The Koran presents the Five Pillars, or the five essential duties that all Muslims should fulfill. They are faith, prayer, almsgiving, fasting, and a pilgrimage to Mecca.

Faith   The first pillar is the confession of faith. All Muslims must believe and recite the creed that states, "There is no god but Allah, and Mohammed is his Prophet." This creed summarizes the central Islamic belief in the oneness of Allah, who is all-powerful, just, and merciful. All Muslims are required to submit completely to the will of Allah as written in the Koran.

The creed stresses the role of Mohammed as prophet. Mohammed is not considered divine; Muslims view him as the last and most important of a series of messengers who have brought God's word to different peoples. To Muslims, Allah is the same god as the God of the Jews and the Christians; and Abraham, Moses, and Jesus are considered prophets. However, Muslims regard certain Jewish and Christian teachings as distortions of the original truth. They believe that Islam is the final and complete revelation that has taken the place of other religions.

Prayer   The second pillar involves prayer. Muslims are required to pray five times a day—at sunrise, noon, afternoon, sunset, and evening. They pray while facing Mecca, using a set form of words and motions. The motions involve kneeling, bowing, and touching one's forehead to the ground as a sign of submitting to God. Private prayers can be offered anywhere—at home, in the outdoors, or at a place of work. Group prayer, however, takes place in a mosque at noon on Fridays.[3] There, male believers are led by an **imam,** or prayer leader. Sometimes prayers are followed by a sermon. Any male Muslim with a certain amount of religious education can hold a leadership position, such as imam or preacher.

Alms   The third pillar concerns the giving of alms, or charity. There are two kinds of alms. One is money that Muslims donate on their own. The other, called the **zakat,** is an income tax collected by the state. It is used for schools or to help the poor.

Fasting   The fourth pillar is fasting. The purpose of this duty is to remind Muslims about spiritual values. A season of fasting is observed during Ramadan, the month in which the Koran was first revealed to Mohammed. Every day during that month, Muslims are required to give up food, drink, and other pleasures between sunrise and sunset. The only people who do not have to fast are children, pregnant women, travelers, and the sick. At night, the fast is broken. Special prayers are said, and people can then enjoy a meal or stroll through the streets with family and friends. At the end of Ramadan, elaborate festivities are held for three days to celebrate the end of the fast.

Pilgrimage   The fifth pillar is the annual pilgrimage to Mecca. The pilgrimage, known as the **hajj,** takes place about two months after Ramadan. Every able-bodied Muslim is expected

---

[3]A mosque is not only a place of worship, but also a center of Islamic life. In early times, a mosque served as a court of law, a religious school, a community shelter, and a hospital. In many parts of the world, mosques still provide these services.

to go on a hajj at least once in his or her life. Those who do are especially honored in the community. The hajj involves three days of ceremony, prayer, and sacrifice during which Muslims from all over the world come together. Throughout Muslim history, the hajj has been a visible expression of Muslim unity. It has also allowed for the exchange of ideas among people from different areas of the Islamic world.

1. Identify: Koran, Hadith, Five Pillars, Ramadan.
2. How do Muslims regard the Koran?
3. How does the Koran guide the daily lives of Muslims?
4. When do Muslims worship?

3 Islamic Empire

When Mohammed died in 632 A.D., he left no clear instructions about who was to succeed him as the leader of Islam. Muslims knew that no one could take Mohammed's place as the messenger of Allah. However, they realized the need for a strong political-religious leader who could preserve unity and guide the daily affairs of the community. A group of prominent Muslims met and chose a new type of leader, whom they called *khalifa,* or **caliph,** which means "successor." The first caliph was Abu Bakr, Mohammed's father-in-law and close friend.

Abu Bakr and the next three caliphs were elected for life. They ruled the Islamic state from Medina. All were close friends of Mohammed and linked to him by marriage. They followed the prophet's example, kept in close touch with the people, and asked the advice of other Muslim leaders. For these reasons, Muslims have called them the Rightly Guided Caliphs.

Rightly Guided Caliphs

The Rightly Guided Caliphs had as their main duty the protection and spread of Islam. They conducted a series of military expeditions that carried Islam beyond the Arabian Peninsula to other lands.

Conquests Under the Rightly Guided Caliphs, Arab armies moved against the Byzantine and Persian empires. The Arabs were eager to

The faithful traveled to Mecca bearing palm leaves as a sign they were on a pilgrimage. The hajj is the fifth pillar of faith. What are the other four pillars?

spread Islam and acquire the agricultural wealth of these regions. The population of Arabia was growing, and there was a need for more food and farmland. Arab warriors began making raids into southern Syria. Soon the raids turned into wars of conquest. In the 630's A.D. Palestine and Syria were brought under Arab control. By 650 A.D. Arab armies had also acquired Iraq, Persia, and Egypt. As a result of these conquests, the Byzantine Empire was reduced to Constantinople, Asia Minor, and the Balkans. The Persian Empire disappeared completely and was brought under Islamic rule. All of the conquered territories were united into an Islamic empire.

The Arabs were successful in their conquests for many reasons. Islam united them in a common goal that they viewed as holy—to carry Islam to other peoples, as Mohammed had directed. According to the Koran, Muslims had a religious duty to struggle for the faith, even by armed force. The Islamic state, therefore, viewed the conquests as a **jihad,** or holy war, against **infidels,** or unbelievers. Warriors who died fighting were promised immediate entry into paradise.

Have students scan the dictionary for other English words of Arabic origin.

In 719, the caliph Umar II unsuccessfully tried to reform the tax system. He had decreed that all land owned by non-Muslims should have the highest taxes even if the owners became Muslims.

English Words of Arabic Origin

Arabic	Arabic Meaning	English
amir al	commander of the sea	admiral
al-kimiya	gold-making juice	alchemy
al-kuhl	refined or distilled substance	alcohol
al-jabr	binding of disorganized parts	algebra
Shah mat	the king is at a loss	checkmate
sifr	nil number	cipher, zero
diwan	couch without arms	divan
makhazin	storehouse of goods or munitions	magazine
matrah	square stuffed pad	mattress
sharab	sweet water-ice	sherbert

The Arabs were also fearless fighters whose desert lifestyle had toughened them mentally and physically. Strong military commanders led them on surprise attacks against their enemies. Arab warriors, mounted on camels and horses, fought in small groups. They were lightly armed with lances and swords and carried few supplies. Consequently, they moved very quickly through the desert.

Methods of controlling the lands and peoples they conquered also contributed to Arab success. In the captured territories, caliphs founded military towns. There, Arab soldiers and their families lived and worked, remaining apart from the conquered peoples. The military towns became administrative centers, exercising political control over the non-Arab population.

Caliphs laid down rules for the treatment of non-Arabs. Those who surrendered without a fight had only to pay taxes to the Islamic Empire. In return, the Arabs protected them, excused them from military service, and allowed them to keep their lands. Those who resisted and were defeated not only had to pay taxes, but they also lost their land. In addition, they had to continue farming for the Arabs. The Islamic state controlled the taxes and land gathered from the conquered peoples. From this revenue, the state paid allowances to the warriors who lived in the military towns.

The Arabs did not require the conquered peoples to accept Islam. Most Persians become Muslims, while many Syrians and Egyptians remained Christians or Jews. These religious minorities were treated better under Muslim rule than under the rule of former governments. However, they did not have the advantages that Muslims enjoyed.

About 750 A.D. more non-Muslims began to accept Islam. Some converted because of the religious appeal of Islam. Others changed their faith to escape taxes and to enjoy greater material benefits. Islam soon became the predominant religion in most of the conquered lands.

The caliphs were unprepared to deal with such large numbers of converts. Because of a sharp decline in the number of non-Muslims, the government was receiving less income from taxes. At the same time, Muslim armies were increasing in size, but finding less booty. As a result, the Islamic Empire faced increasing tensions that threatened to pull it apart.

Struggle for the Caliphate During the period of conquests, rival groups fought for control of the **caliphate,** or the office of caliph. In 656 A.D. Muslim leaders made Ali, a cousin and son-in-law of Mohammed, the new caliph. Ali had a strong group of supporters known as Shiites. While most Muslims believed in an elective caliphate open to all members of the

"Shiite" means party or faction in Arabic. Shiites are today the largest Muslim group in Iran, Iraq, and Lebanon.

The map below is the subject of the "Using Maps" section of the Chapter 6 Review.

community, the Shiites claimed that the office of caliph should only be held by members of Mohammed's own family.

Opposition to Ali's caliphate soon arose in Syria. There a military leader named Mu'awiya set up a rival government. He built up a powerful Syrian army to fight Ali and to seize control of the entire Islamic domain.

Although Ali had a stronger army, he refused to fight Mu'awiya. Instead, he tried to arrange a negotiated settlement of their dispute. Ali's action was seen by some followers as a sign of weakness, and they left his ranks. Meanwhile, support for the Shiite cause declined in the Islamic community. In the middle of this confusion, while at prayer in a mosque, Ali was killed by a discontented supporter.

As a result of Ali's murder, Mu'awiya became caliph and established complete control over the Islamic state. The Shiites, however, claimed the caliphate for Ali's son, Husayn. Mu'awiya's son, Yazid, assumed the caliphate after his father's death in 680 A.D. In the same year, Yazid's troops killed Husayn and a small number of Ali's family and followers in a battle at Karbala in Iraq.

The deaths of Ali and Husayn led to a serious schism that permanently divided Islam into two major groups. The Shiites made up one group. Located mostly in Iraq and Persia, they continued to give allegiance to members of Mohammed's family. The Shiites followed a series of leaders who aimed to destroy the existing caliphate and establish a new one in its place. Most Muslims, however, were in the second group. They rejected Shiite goals and followed the tradition of the Rightly Guided Caliphs. This group became known as Sunnis, or "followers of the way."

Umayyads

As caliph, Mu'awiya began a new era in Islamic history. In 661 A.D. he made Damascus the capital of the empire and founded the Umayyad dynasty. From that time on, the caliphate was hereditary. The 14 caliphs who succeeded Mu'awiya were either his sons or

THE EXPANSION OF ISLAM

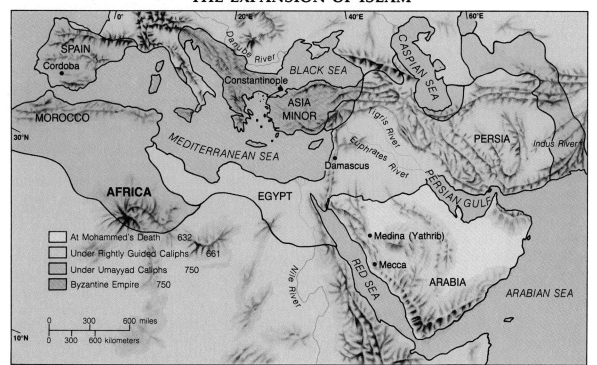

At Mohammed's Death 632
Under Rightly Guided Caliphs 661
Under Umayyad Caliphs 750
Byzantine Empire 750

0 300 600 miles
0 300 600 kilometers

The Dome of the Rock at Jerusalem was built on the site of Solomon's temple. It housed the rock where Abraham was said to have attempted to offer his son Isaac for sacrifice. It also covers the spot where Mohammed was believed to have ascended into heaven.

other members of the Umayyad family. Caliphs began to rule less like tribal sheikhs and more like kings. They stressed the political rather than the religious importance of their office.

The Umayyads built a powerful and united Islamic Empire. They made Arabic the official language throughout their realm and minted the first Arabic currency. As the empire grew, many of the traditions of Arab desert culture were abandoned in favor of the practices of Middle Eastern empires of the past.

Reforms The most significant change under Umayyad rule was the reorganization of the government into a bureaucracy that was closely controlled by the caliphs. Many Arabs were not experienced in working in this type of government. As a result, the Umayyads relied on non-Muslims who had held posts in the Byzantine or Persian governments. Many non-Muslims, mostly Syrian Christians, worked as officials and tax collectors in the Islamic government. Some also served as doctors and tutors in the caliph's court.

The Umayyads also increased Islamic military power. They built the first Islamic navy and improved the organization of the army. The Islamic army became a well-disciplined force that adopted the fighting techniques of the Byzantines and Persians. The army now fought in rows of armed cavalry. It also carried out methods of siege warfare, using battering rams, portable towers, and tunneling.

The Umayyads relied on the reorganized army to enlarge the empire. During the early 700's A.D., Muslim warriors extended the empire's control over central Asia and the lower Indus Valley of India. They also moved west through North Africa to the Atlantic and then into Spain. In 732 A.D. Muslim forces attacked southern France, but were blocked by a Christian European army at the Battle of Tours. This effort marked the limit of Islamic expansion in the West.

Umayyad Culture The Umayyads also developed peaceful ways to hold the empire together. They expanded communications by building postal roads and rest stations. They sponsored public works projects, such as the repair and maintenance of neglected irrigation canals. Thus, many barriers to travel throughout the empire were eliminated. People from different areas could now meet, trade, and exchange ideas. Gradually, an intermingling took place between the Arabs and the people they conquered. This development was aided by the fact that many of the non-Arabs spoke languages similar to Arabic.

Under the Umayyads, a new Islamic civilization emerged that was largely Arab but was also influenced by the cultures of the conquered peoples. Artists and architects from a variety of backgrounds were employed by the Umayyads to build magnificent mosques, palaces, and fortresses. In their work, they drew inspiration from classical Greek and Byzantine cultures. Two famous buildings of this period, the Great Mosque of Damascus and the Dome of the Rock Mosque in Jerusalem, are still standing.

Fall of the Umayyads In spite of their achievements, the Umayyads had social and economic problems that led to their downfall. One problem was the growing friction between the ruling Arab Muslims and the non-Arab Muslims. At this time, non-Arabs had to become **mawalis,** or adopted members of an Arab tribe, in order to become Muslims. Many took this step, but were disappointed that their conversion to Islam did not make them equals with the Arab Muslims. Non-Arab Muslims received less money than the Arabs for serving in the army, and they had to pay higher taxes. Such treatment, they claimed, was a violation of the Islamic belief in the equality of all believers.

Other groups also opposed the Umayyads. Many Arab tribes disliked the strong central government of the Umayyads and hated paying taxes. The Shiites continued to demand a new caliphate. The Persians, many of whom were Shiites, wanted to break away from the Islamic Empire and establish their own state.

All of these dissatisfied groups united under the Abbasids, a branch of Mohammed's family. In 747 A.D. the Abbasids and their allies staged a revolt in Persia against the Umayyads. Three years later they defeated the Umayyad army and became the new rulers of the Islamic Empire.

The legendary deeds of Harun al-Rashid are recorded in the tales of the *Arabian Nights*.

The map below shows only the innermost part of the city of Baghdad.

Abbasids

The Abbasids soon eliminated their Shiite and Persian supporters and established a new dynasty that governed the empire from 750 to 1258 A.D. The Abbasid dynasty reached its height under Caliph Harun al-Rashid, who governed from 786 to 809 A.D. During that time, the Muslims developed an urban civilization that was unequaled anywhere in the world.

Baghdad The Abbasids built a new capital in Iraq called Baghdad. The city lay in a fertile plain on the west bank of the Tigris River. It was situated at the crossroads of the great land and water trade routes that stretched from the Mediterranean to the Far East. Baghdad was well placed for defense because it could only be approached by river or bridge.

Designed by a Jewish astronomer and a Persian engineer, Baghdad was built, over a period of four years, by 100,000 skilled workers drawn from every region of the empire. The city was constructed in the shape of a circle. At opposite points, it had four large gates. The gates were linked by two highways that crossed in the center of the city. The highways, which led to different parts of the empire, divided Baghdad into four pie-shaped sections. For protection, three huge walls surrounded the city.

Within the innermost wall lay the center of Baghdad. It consisted of the caliph's magnificent palace, a grand mosque, and other government buildings. Between the innermost wall and the middle wall were the luxurious homes of courtiers and army officials. City architects provided an open area for defense and a large park for recreation between the middle and outer walls. A deep moat surrounded the outer wall. Beyond this wall and moat were the homes of the common people. During the 900's A.D., about 1.5 million people lived in Baghdad.

Abbasid Politics The founding of Baghdad brought a shift in the empire's center of power from the western to the eastern part of the Middle East. As a result, under the Abbasids significant changes occurred in the empire. The empire kept the Arabic language and the Muslim faith. But in other ways, Arab culture was transformed by contributions of non-Arab Mus-

lims. The name "Arab" no longer meant a person from Arabia, but came to mean any subject of the empire who spoke Arabic.

The Abbasids worked to ensure equality among all Muslims, Arab and non-Arab. They set up a new ruling group that included Muslims of many nationalities. Persians became the dominant group in the government bureaucracy, while Turks became the leading group in the army. Arabs, however, continued to control religious life and administration of law.

The caliphate itself was also changed by the new international character of the empire. Abbasid caliphs strengthened their power in order to hold the empire together. They ruled and lived like Persian kings. Caliphs regarded themselves as God's deputies and took the title "Shadow of God on Earth." They made fewer public appearances so that the people would think of them as powerful and mysterious figures. Court ceremonies became more elaborate, and the few government officials who were allowed to approach a caliph had to bow down before the throne and kiss the floor.

The Abbasids created the government post of vizier. As the caliph's chief minister, the vizier stood between the ruler and the people. The

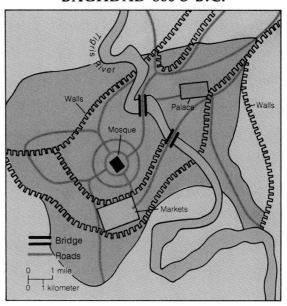

BAGHDAD 800'S B.C.

Tigris River

Walls

Palace

Walls

Mosque

Markets

Bridge

Roads

0   1 mile
0   1 kilometer

Thousands of Arab coins from the Abbasid period have been found as far away as Scandinavia.

Well-known Muslim and Jewish merchants in the Islamic Empire maintained business offices throughout the Mediterranean region and in many of the leading cities of Christian Europe.

vizier took charge of running the empire and appointed the governors of the provinces.

Trade, Commerce, and Culture During the Abbasid caliphate, the wars of conquest ended. More or less permanent borders for the empire were established, and the Abbasids developed peaceful relations with neighboring non-Muslim nations. Trade increased and brought a new period of prosperity. Great camel caravans crossed overland through central Asia to Baghdad on the way to the Mediterranean and North Africa. Ships carried goods between Far Eastern lands and Middle Eastern ports. Baghdad soon became the marketplace of the world. Its merchants sold silk and porcelain from China; rubies, coconuts, and ebony from Spain; drugs and trinkets from the Byzantine Empire; and furs and honey from Russia and Scandinavia.

Increased trade brought changes in the daily life of the empire's people. Persians introduced new games, like polo, chess, and backgammon,

which became popular. Men stopped wearing the traditional robe and began wearing trousers. Women served food on tables rather than on carpeted floors. Many new household items appeared, such as cushions, ovens, frying pans, and silk curtains. The demand for luxury goods became so great that Muslim artisans began producing many of the items themselves.

International trade and payments led to the rise of a banking system. The first bankers were money changers in the markets. They weighed different coins to determine their value and made currency exchanges. Later, they began to keep records and handle more difficult transactions. In the process, they developed a variety of new practices such as the use of checks, receipts, and letters of credit.

International trade also led to a fresh exchange of ideas. Baghdad became the center of an intellectual awakening and attracted poets, philosophers, scientists, and artists. Syrian Christians and Jews translated Greek writings

ABBASID EMPIRE

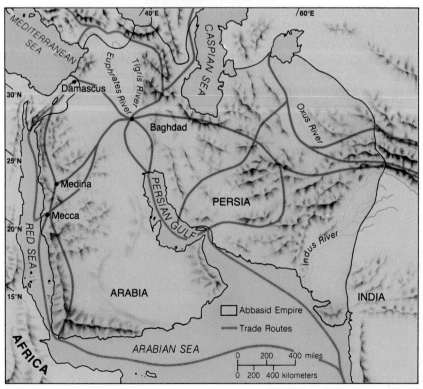

In Islamic society, marriage was considered a duty. A Muslim man usually married for the first time when he was about 20 years old. A Muslim woman usually married between the ages of 12 and 20.

into Arabic. As a result, there was a renewed interest in Greek science and philosophy. At the same time, Persian scholars introduced Arabs and other groups to Persian history and literature. The Persians also brought the philosophy and science of India to the empire.

Abbasid Decline   The Islamic Empire, however, became too large for the Abbasid caliphs to govern effectively. Slowly, it began to split into independent states. Persia in the east, and Morocco, Tunisia, and Spain in the west, fell under the control of local rulers. The caliphs relied on their Turkish bodyguards to rule the rest of the empire. A Turkish group soon set up an independent dynasty in Egypt. All of these developments led to a decline in the caliph's power and influence. Finally, in 945 A.D., the Buyids, a Persian family, seized Baghdad and forced the caliph to accept their rule.

Although its political unity ended around 1000 A.D., Islam still provided cultural and religious unity among its followers. Arab language and traditions were deeply rooted and remained strong in most of the former provinces of the empire. Persia, however, while returning to its old language and culture, continued to accept Islam. Only European areas such as Spain, Portugal, and Sicily gave up both Islam and Arab ways. They returned to Christianity and western European civilization. Yet, even in these lands the period of Islamic rule left a strong imprint on the languages and cultures of their inhabitants.

1. Identify: Abu Bakr, Rightly Guided Caliphs, Ali, Shiites, Mu'awiya, Sunnis, Umayyad, Damascus, Tours, Abbasids, Baghdad.
2. Why were the Arabs successful in their conquests? How did they treat the people they conquered?
3. What changes did the Umayyads bring to the Islamic state?
4. How did increased trade under the Abbasids affect Islamic life?

4 Islamic Culture

During the Islamic Empire, Islam set the guidelines for the way people lived. It laid down rules for family and business life, as well as for religious practices. It also stimulated an interest in scientific knowledge and determined standards for art and architecture.

Islamic Family

The foundation of Islamic society was the family. Islamic households were large because several generations of family members usually lived together. The father or the oldest male was the absolute and undisputed head of the household.

Early Islam stressed the equality of all believers before God; however, in the relationship between the sexes, males and females had distinct roles and rights. The Koran instructed male Muslims that "men are in charge of women." As a result, a woman's social position was defined by her relationship, as wife, mother, daughter, or sister, to the male members of her family. She was rarely viewed as a person in her own right. However, the social position of women in Arabia improved over what it had been in earlier times. Islam forbade the killing of female infants, a common practice among earlier Arab tribes. It also limited **polygamy,** or the practice of a man having more than one wife. A man could have no more than four wives, all of whom were to be treated as equals and with kindness. Although a woman was still subject to the will of her husband, she was given complete control over her own property.

Outside the home, Islamic society was a man's world. Muslim men worked at their businesses or in the fields. When they were not working, they enjoyed various types of recreation. They often went to public baths and coffee houses to relax, talk, and listen to professional storytellers. Men also played chess, practiced gymnastics, or watched horse racing.

Except for shopping, women usually stayed at home, did household tasks, and remained apart from public life. Each married woman was entitled to her own rooms, and cooking and sleeping conveniences. If she was wealthy, she also had household servants. Raised by their mothers or servants, young girls were prepared for marriage and taught how to manage a household.

The lodging houses of merchants were known as caravanserais. They were located on the edge of town or at certain points along trade routes. They consisted of an eating area and sleeping rooms built around a courtyard, where the merchants' animals and goods were kept.

Shoppers met to buy and bargain in the souq, or series of market stalls. The souqs were busy centers of Islamic life. What recreational activities were found there?

City and Country

Though most Arabs lived in rural or desert areas, the leadership of the empire came from the cities. Many cities, such as Damascus, developed as trading centers even before the rise of Islam. Others, such as Kufa, developed from military towns established during the early conquests.

Urban Centers   Islamic cities were divided into distinct business and residential districts. Buildings were constructed close to each other and were separated by a maze of narrow streets. The streets were often covered to protect pedestrians from the hot sun.

The center of a city contained the principal religious and government buildings, sometimes enclosed in fortifications. Mosques with their domes and **minarets,** or towers from which people were called to prayer, dominated the skyline. They were found in every district. Hospitals, and **madrasas,** or theological schools, were usually built near mosques. Another central feature of life in an Islamic city was the **bazaar,** or marketplace. There, merchants sold goods in stalls or shops along the roofed streets. Men met at the bazaar for conversation and business. Nearby were large warehouses and the lodging houses that served traveling merchants.

Buildings in Islamic cities were made of brick or mud. The outsides of most of them were very plain. Because Muslim families valued privacy, homes were built to keep out noise and light. They had few windows, most of which were screened with wood. Each house had a courtyard surrounded by rooms. In wealthy homes, courtyards had fountains and gardens.

The interiors of most Muslim homes were plain and contained few pieces of furniture. They were decorated with beautiful carpets and small art objects. Most people sat on carpets and leaned on cushions or pillows. At mealtime, household members sat in a circle and ate from large trays of bread, meats, and fruits.

Rural Areas   Because of the dry climate water was scarce, and most of the empire's land was not suitable for agriculture. However, good use was made of the few areas that were capable of growing food. Farmers obtained good yields by using irrigation, crop rotation, and fertilizer. Most productive land was held by large landowners who received grants from the government. They had large estates and employed farmers from nearby villages to work the land. A variety of crops, such as wheat, rice, beans, melons, cucumbers, celery, and mint, were grown. Orchards produced almonds, blackberries, melons, apricots, figs, and olives. Farmers also cultivated flowers for use in perfume.

Science

Between the 800's and 1300's A.D., Islamic scientists made significant contributions in several scientific areas, such as mathematics, astronomy, chemistry, and medicine. They based their work on two main intellectual traditions. The first, and most important, was that of Greece. The second was that of India, which came to the Arabs by way of Persia.

The Islamic world experienced a scientific awakening under the Abbasids. During the 800's A.D., Baghdad became a leading intellectual center. In 830 A.D. the caliph Mamun founded the

SCIENCE AND TECHNOLOGY

Islamic Medicine

The Muslims acquired their first knowledge of scientific medicine from the ancient Greeks and Persians. They then went on to develop new methods of explaining and treating diseases. Muslim doctors were the first to discover the functions of internal organs and to diagnose certain illnesses. They also advanced the science of surgery. Head and stomach operations were carried out with the aid of anesthetics, such as opium, to make the patient unconscious. A variety of drugs were used to treat many diseases.

Muslims believed that medicine was a highly technical field that called for a long period of training. Doctors studied in hospitals and medical schools. They learned to base medical treatments upon careful observation of their patients. They also developed skills in diagnosing diseases, prescribing treatments, and performing surgery.

The Islamic medical profession had strict codes of conduct. One physician wrote that a doctor should be kind, understanding, friendly, and able to endure insults and criticism. He also noted that a doctor should have short hair and fingernails, wear clean white clothes, and act with dignity. Before doctors could practice medicine, they had to pass an examination, be licensed, and take the Hippocratic Oath.

Islamic doctors called alchemists tried to turn base metals, such as tin and lead, into gold and silver. Although they were unsuccessful, their efforts led to the practice of making experiments and keeping accurate records of results. Islamic alchemists studied new substances and learned ways to combine them to form compounds. They also produced such laboratory equipment as beakers, flasks, vials, and glass dishes. Their work contributed to the origins of modern chemistry.

Islamic doctors founded the science of optics, the study of sight. They published the first anatomy of the eye and described various eye diseases and treatments. The physician al-Haitham discovered that the eye sees because it receives light from the seen object. This disproved the Greek belief that sight occurs because the eye sends light to the object.

Islamic physicians wrote many medical papers and books. In the 800's A.D., al-Razi authored nearly 200 works, including a medical encyclopedia that described the origin of diseases. He also wrote a handbook that identified the differences between smallpox and measles. A century later, the doctor Ibn Sina produced the *Canon of Medicine*, a monumental volume that attempted to summarize all medical knowledge available at the time. The *Canon* described the circulation of the blood and the functions of the kidneys and the heart. It also offered the diagnosis and treatment for many diseases, as well as advice on diet and hygiene.

Islamic medical practices were unknown in the West during the early Middle Ages. In most of Europe, ignorance, superstition, and prejudice prevented medical advances. It was not until the twelfth and thirteenth centuries that a substantial amount of Islamic scientific and medical knowledge reached western Europe. After that time, Islamic scientific texts were used in European medical schools for more than 500 years.

1. What were some of the accomplishments of Islamic doctors?
2. Why was Islamic medicine important to the West?

House of Wisdom, an institute for the translation of Greek, Persian, and Indian scientific texts into Arabic. Mamun staffed the institute with salaried Christian, Jewish, and Muslim scholars from all over the empire. They used Arabic as a common language, which allowed them to work together and to share ideas from different intellectual traditions. With this support, Muslim scholars and scientists pursued many branches of scientific learning.

Muslim science involved more than just theory; it was put to practical use. For example, mathematics was used to solve daily problems in business and agriculture. Astronomy was used to determine the hours of prayer; the direction of Mecca; and the time period of celebrations, such as Ramadan.

Mathematics Muslims believed that mathematics was the most important of all the sciences. They borrowed from Indian mathematics the 10 numerals 0 to 9, later called "Arabic" by Europeans. These digits were used for the place-value system of writing numbers. In this system, which is used worldwide today, a number's value is determined by the position of its digits.

The number system made possible great achievements in mathematics. Muslim mathematicians developed algebra and expressed equations in terms of curves and lines. They showed an interest in geometry and worked out proofs. Their work in geometry led to the development of trigonometry, which was used to make calculations such as the distance to the stars and the speed of falling objects.

Astronomy and Geography In the 700's A.D., Muslims developed a scientific understanding of the heavens. In 830 A.D. Mamun built an observatory in Baghdad. There, astronomers checked the findings of the ancient Greeks, made observations of the skies, and produced physical and mathematical models of the universe. They accurately described eclipses of the sun and proved that the moon affects the oceans.

Muslim astronomers also produced charts giving distances from the earth to stars and planets. The size and circumference of the earth were measured with a degree of accuracy not achieved again until the twentieth century. From such studies, astronomers concluded that the earth was round. Yet, most Muslim astronomers continued to accept the Greek theory of the universe that heavenly bodies revolve around the earth.

Geographical studies emerged from Muslim astronomy. By the 1100's A.D., Muslim geographers understood the basic outlines of Asia, Europe, and North Africa. They used this knowledge to produce the first accurate maps of the world.

Islamic Arts

Before 600 A.D. the Arabs had little art or architecture. Through their conquests, they learned about the highly developed arts of Persia, Egypt, and Syria. The people in these lands who accepted Islam blended these and other styles into a distinct and colorful Islamic style of art.

Religion determined the form and content of Islamic art. Muslim tradition forbade artists to make images or pictures of living creatures. Theologians feared that people would worship these forms rather than Allah alone. As a result of this ban, Muslim artists drew or sculpted in highly abstract and stylized ways so that figures appeared more symbolic than lifelike. Most of their art consisted of detailed geometric designs entwined with stems, leaves, flowers, and stars. This type of decoration, called **arabesque,** became popular and appeared in an endless variety of shapes and forms. It was used to decorate books, rugs, swords, and entire walls.

Muslims were also skilled in **calligraphy,** or the art of elegant handwriting. They made use of the beautiful Arabic script. Verses from the Koran adorned the walls of religious buildings. Secular quotes appeared on art objects, such as vases and boxes.

Islamic artists did their best work in architecture, particularly in building and decorating mosques. The basic pattern of a mosque consisted of a courtyard surrounded on three sides by shady porches. A large, highly decorated gate was usually built on one of these sides. On the fourth side was an enclosed hall of worship.

Each mosque has to be built in a way that the *mihrab* indicates the exact direction of Mecca, toward which all Muslims are required to pray.

Inside the hall, a **mihrab,** or small arch, was set in the wall nearest to Mecca. The only furniture in a mosque was the **minbar,** a wood or stone pulpit. Some mosques were beautifully decorated with tile work and glass mosaics. Each mosque had one or more minarets, from which a **muezzin,** or prayer crier, called the people to prayer.

Philosophy, Literature, and History

Muslims were actively encouraged to seek out new knowledge. One saying attributed to Mohammed stated that "the ink of the scholars is worth more than the blood of the martyrs." Following such advice, Muslim scholars produced many works in philosophy, literature, and history.

Philosophy and Literature   Muslim philosophers tried to develop systems of thought that would reconcile the teachings of the Koran with Greek philosophy. They believed that religious truths could be analyzed and defended by logic. Many of their works were later translated into Latin and brought a new understanding of philosophy to western Europe.

Muslims made many contributions in literature. Until the 600's A.D., Arabic poetry was passed down orally from generation to generation. The coming of Islam, however, brought the emergence of a written literature. The Koran became the first and greatest work of Arabic prose. Considered by Muslims as divine revelation, it could not be criticized or imitated. Yet, its forceful and eloquent style influenced later works. During the 700's A.D., secular prose appeared that was designed both to instruct and to entertain. The most famous of these writings was *Kalila and Dimna*, a collection of animal fables with moral lessons.

Islamic literature blossomed during the Abbasid period as a result of contact with Greek thought, Hindu legends, and Persian court epics. The upper classes valued elegant speech and the ability to handle words cleverly. Reading and appreciating literature was the sign of a good upbringing. During this period, religious devotion was replaced by a more pleasure-seeking lifestyle. Verses praising wine, women, and

Tales of dancers, princes, genies, thieves, magic carpets, and fabulous birds make up The 1,001 Nights. *Which civilizations contributed to this work?*

song became popular at the caliph's court. Poets became dependent on powerful **patrons,** or sponsors, whom they lavishly praised in highly formal works.

In the eleventh century, Persian joined Arabic as a leading literary language in the Muslim world. Persian writers wrote epics describing warrior heroes of the Sassanid monarchy. Other Persians wrote religious and love poetry. The most famous Persian poet was the mathematician Omar Khayyam. His work, *Rubaiyyat*, has been translated into many languages and is considered one of the finest poems ever written.

The 1,001 Nights, or *The Arabian Nights*, one of the best known Islamic writings, appeared during the declining years of the empire. It is a collection of stories from Arab, Persian, and Indian tales. The stories paint an exciting picture of Islamic life between the 800's and 1500's A.D.

HISTORY and PEOPLE

Maimonides

Moses Maimonides was one of the leading thinkers of the Islamic Empire. As a rabbi, he was an important figure in the empire's Jewish communities. As a doctor, he made lasting contributions to medicine. The influence of Maimonides eventually extended beyond the Muslim world to western Europe.

Maimonides was born in 1135 A.D. in Cordoba, Spain. At that time, most of Spain was part of the Islamic world. Islamic Spain allowed its non-Muslim citizens full religious freedom. However, there were brief periods of persecution. In 1148 A.D. Cordoba came under the rule of a strict Islamic group known as the Almohads. The Almohads forced the Jews of Cordoba to either accept Islam or leave the city.

Due to this persecution, Maimonides and his family moved to neighboring Morocco. In 1165 A.D. anti-Jewish feeling in Morocco forced them to sail to the Middle East. After a brief stay in Palestine, Maimonides and his family finally made their home in Egypt. In spite of these difficult circumstances, Maimonides was able to study Jewish law, Islamic philosophy, and medicine.

While in Egypt, Maimonides became a practicing doctor. His fame as a medical authority spread rapidly. Maimonides soon became the chief physician at the court of the Egyptian ruler. He also carried on a private practice in Fostat, a small town near Cairo. Maimonides wrote a friend describing his daily duties:

> I am obliged to visit the sultan [the Egyptian ruler] every day, early in the morning. . . I must stay the greater part of the day at the palace. . . I do not return to [Fostat] until the afternoon. . . There, I find the antechambers [waiting rooms] filled with people, both Jews and Gentiles. . . I partake of some slight refreshment. . . Then I go forth to attend to my patients [who] go in and out until nightfall.*

Meanwhile, Maimonides became the leader of the Jewish community in Egypt. He taught in synagogues and helped his people with their personal problems. Maimonides wrote letters to Jewish communities in other parts of the world.

Maimonides produced a number of important writings in both Hebrew and Arabic. His medical works included essays on the treatment of diseases and on the use of drugs. However, his most outstanding literary achievement was in the area of religion and philosophy. Maimonides wrote *Mishne Torah*, a 14-volume work on Jewish law and tradition. It was written in Hebrew. His other major religious work, *The Guide of the Perplexed*, sought to reconcile Judaism with the teachings of Aristotle. Written in Arabic, it was later translated into Hebrew and Latin.

Maimonides died in 1204 A.D. and was buried in Palestine. Jews and many Gentiles throughout Europe and the Mediterranean world mourned his passing. Some of Maimonides' ideas had aroused opposition during his lifetime. However, after his death, Maimonides was recognized as one of the great medieval philosophers.

*Maimonides, from a letter to Samuel ben Judah ibn Tibbon as quoted in *Encyclopedia Judaica*, vol. 11, col. 757.

The Spanish Muslim culture was so attractive to young Christian Spaniards that Christian bishops often complained that young people were learning Arabic instead of Spanish. Christians and Jews of Islamic Spain frequently wrote Spanish and Hebrew in Arabic script.

The Alhambra was built by the sultans of Islamic Granada. A fortified palace, the Alhambra was constructed around a series of open quadrangles of which the Court of Lions, shown here, is considered the most beautiful. Which cultures contributed to the Muslim civilization in Spain?

History   Like Judaism and Christianity, Islam traces its origins to historical events. As a result, Islamic scholars developed an interest in writing history. At first, Arab historians wrote history in **chronicles,** or lists of events arranged by year. Later they began to organize events around rulers and people.

Ibn Khaldun was the first Muslim historian to examine history scientifically. He was a diplomat who lived in North Africa during the fourteenth century. Ibn Khaldun looked for laws to explain historical events and human behavior. He believed that history was a process in which human events were shaped by geography, climate, and economics, as well as by moral and spiritual forces. Ibn Khaldun's writings influenced thought in western Europe.

Spain

The most important area where western European and Islamic cultures met was Spain. Islamic armies entered Spain from North Africa in 711 A.D. The invasion occurred very rapidly and was supported by many Spaniards who were dissatisfied with their Visigothic rulers. By 716 A.D. most of Spain was under Islamic rule. Only the extreme northern part kept its European culture and Christian religion.

In 755 A.D. the Umayyad prince Abdul Rahman established an independent dynasty in Spain. Under this dynasty, Spain developed the most prosperous economy in western Europe. The Spanish capital of Cordoba had beautiful mosques, elegant palaces, gardens, lighted streets, and plumbing. During the 800's and 900's A.D., it rivaled Baghdad as the most sophisticated Islamic city in the world.

Between the ninth and fifteenth centuries a brilliant Muslim civilization, which was a blend of Christian, Jewish, and Arab cultures, flourished in Spain. The courts of Islamic rulers included centers for the translation of Arabic works into Latin. European scholars came to Spain to increase their knowledge and learn about Islamic culture. Spanish Muslim poets and musicians developed lyric poetry and romantic songs that soon spread to parts of Christian Europe. European poetry, music, and literature of the Middle Ages were influenced by these Spanish Muslim works.

After 1023 A.D., the Umayyad dynasty was replaced by a number of small principalities under local Muslim rulers. At the same time, Christians from northern Spain moved south and began to reclaim their former lands. To help the Spanish Muslims defend their territory, two

Spain's later Muslim invaders belonged to a North African people known as Berbers. The Berbers accepted Spanish Muslim culture. However as outsiders, they were resented by Spanish Muslims and Christians alike.

Muslim armies from North Africa separately invaded Spain during the twelfth century. Although they set up empires that embraced southern Spain and North Africa, the Muslim forces were unable to stop the Christian advance. By the fourteenth century, most of Spain had returned to Christian rule, except for the small territory of Granada, which remained Muslim. Granada survived until 1492 A.D., when it was captured by Spanish Christian armies. During its last 100 years, Granada developed a rich culture. The rulers of Granada built one of the most outstanding examples of Islamic architecture: the famous palace of Alhambra. Still standing today, the Alhambra is a grand monument to the last flowering of Islamic civilization in western Europe.

1. Identify: House of Wisdom, *Kalila and Dimna, Rubaiyyat, The 1,001 Nights,* Ibn Khaldun, Cordoba, Granada.
2. What contributions did Islamic scholars make in science and mathematics?
3. How did religion affect the style and content of Islamic art and architecture?
4. How did Islamic Spain influence the development of western Europe?

CHAPTER 6 REVIEW

Summary

1. From 300 to 500 A.D., most Arabs were divided into closely-knit tribes that roamed the Arabian Peninsula.
2. By 500 A.D. many Arabs had settled in market towns, the most famous of which was Mecca, a leading pilgrimage center that attracted worshipers from all over Arabia.
3. In 613 A.D. the Arab merchant Mohammed began to preach Islam.
4. In 622 A.D. opposition to Mecca forced Mohammed and his followers to go to Yathrib, where Mohammed founded a community based on the principles of Islam.
5. By 632 A.D. Islam was the principal faith of Arabia and had its spiritual center at Mecca.
6. Islamic faith and practice is based on the Koran and includes the Five Pillars: confession of faith, prayer, alms-giving, fasting, and pilgrimage to Mecca.
7. Under the Rightly Guided Caliphs, the Arabs carried Islam to other lands and succeeded in conquering much of the Middle East.
8. During the seventh and eighth centuries, the Umayyad dynasty, ruling from Damascus, built an Islamic empire that stretched from the Atlantic Ocean to central Asia.
9. In 750 A.D. the Abbasids took control of the Islamic Empire, built a capital at Baghdad, and encouraged trade and the arts.
10. During the 900's A.D., the remote provinces of the empire broke with the Abbasids and became independent states, while the heartland around Baghdad came under the control of the Persians.
11. Between the ninth and fifteenth centuries a brilliant Islamic civilization, which was a blend of Arab, Jewish, and Christian cultures, flourished in Spain.
12. Arabs made many contributions to modern civilization, especially in the fields of chemistry, astronomy, mathematics, and medicine.

Building Vocabulary

nomadic	sheikh	booty	revelation
bedouins	blood feuds	hanifs	suras

shari'a	jihad	minarets	mihrab
imam	infidels	madrasas	minbar
zakat	caliphate	bazaar	muezzin
hajj	mawalis	arabesque	patrons
caliph	polygamy	calligraphy	chronicles

Reviewing the Main Ideas

1. How did the values of the Arab tribes contribute to the spread of Islam throughout the Middle East?
2. How did the coming of Islam change life in the Arabian Peninsula?
3. What beliefs does Islam share with Judaism and Christianity?
4. What was Mohammed's role in the early Islamic community?
5. Why were early Islamic leaders known as the Rightly Guided Caliphs?
6. What problems did the Islamic community face as a result of conquests?
7. What issue divided Sunnis and Shiites?
8. How did the caliphate change over the course of Islamic history?
9. How did outside influences contribute to the development of Islamic science and art?

Discussing Important Ideas

1. Was Islam's development dependent on the existence of towns like Mecca and Medina? Explain.
2. If you had been a resident of Mecca in 613 A.D., would you have believed Mohammed's message? Why or why not?
3. Which factor played a greater role in the Arab conquests—religious zeal or desire for booty? Explain.
4. Could Islam have spread as far so quickly without military conquest?
5. Why are sacred scriptures important in many of the world's religions?
6. Is fasting an important discipline? Why or why not?
7. Would a struggle for the caliphate have been avoided if Mohammed had named a successor before his death?
8. If Mohammed had lived in the 800's A.D., would he have approved of the Abbasid caliphate? Why or why not?
9. How do Muslim attitudes about family life differ from those of the western world? Give examples.
10. Does Islam play an important role in the world today? Explain.

Using Maps

Refer to the map on page 143 to answer the following questions:
1. Describe the western extent of the Islamic Empire at the time of Mohammed's death.
2. Which caliphs extended the Islamic Empire's control into India?
3. Expansion under the Rightly Guided Caliphs gave the Islamic Empire direct access to which new bodies of water?
4. Refer also to the map on page 796. List the modern countries whose territories were part of the Islamic Empire in 661 A.D.

CHAPTER 7

Medieval Castle

> **66** *Of what profit is a good knight? Without good knights, the king is like a man who has neither feet nor hands.* **99**
>
> Díaz de Gámez, Spanish writer (1400's A.D.)

Medieval Europe

Discuss with students the following conditions of the "Dark Ages": constant warfare, social disorganization, political instability, and the dangers of famine and epidemics.

The Middle Ages began in western Europe about 500 A.D. At this time, Germanic peoples controlled many of the lands that once belonged to the Roman Empire of the West. Classical civilization had nearly disappeared. Roads and bridges fell into disrepair. Trade and city life declined. Most people lived in the country and knew little about life beyond their villages. As a result of this decline, the medieval[1] period, especially the early Middle Ages from 500 to 1000 A.D., has often been called the "Dark Ages."

Today, historians who write about the Middle Ages see its positive aspects. Greco-Roman culture, Christian faith, and Germanic practices were gradually combined to form a new western European civilization. After 1000 A.D. the political, economic, and cultural life of western Europe began to move forward. New ideas, institutions, and social groups emerged that laid the foundation of modern western civilization.

1 Early Middle Ages

The Germanic peoples who invaded the Roman Empire in the 400's A.D. were made up of many groups. Each group developed differently. The Vandals, Visigoths, Ostrogoths, and Burgundians set up kingdoms in the heavily populated Mediterranean areas of Europe. Because of their geographical closeness to Rome, these groups accepted many Roman ways. However, none of these kingdoms lasted very long. By 800 A.D. they had either been absorbed by local populations or conquered by outside invaders.

Germanic groups also settled in northwestern Europe, not far from their homelands in Germany. One of these groups, known as Franks, moved into the areas that are now France and West Germany. Others called Angles, Saxons, and Jutes took over most of Britain. These northern peoples were farther from Rome and less influenced by Roman culture. This helped them preserve their Germanic customs. They lived in thinly populated areas that were less attractive to outside invaders. As a result, their kingdoms lasted and eventually became the most powerful states of medieval Europe.

Conversion of Europe

After the fall of Rome in 476 A.D., the Roman Catholic Church emerged as the most important institution in western Europe. With the end of the line of western Roman emperors, the bishop of Rome, now called the Pope, became the leading political figure in Italy. He was also acknowledged as the spiritual leader of Christianity by all of the churches of western Europe. The Pope based his authority on the traditional belief that Peter the Apostle, the first bishop of Rome, had been chosen by Christ to be head of the Church. When Peter died, the authority Christ gave him was passed on to his successors.

Monasteries In spite of its organizational strength, Catholic Christianity had been weakened by the Germanic invasions. Many areas had lost their churches and priests. Also, many western Europeans were not yet Catholic Christians. Led by the Pope, church leaders worked to rebuild the Church and to convert Germanic peoples to the Catholic faith. Their major support in these efforts to strengthen the Church came from the monasteries.

Monasteries had first emerged during the late Roman Empire. They were formed by devout Christians seeking to lead a holy life apart from

---

[1] The term "medieval" was first used by western European scholars during the fifteenth century. It comes from the Latin words *medium*, "middle," and *aevum*, "age." Scholars saw the Middle Ages as a distinct period between ancient and modern times.

157

Before Benedict, monasteries were loosely organized. Monks could come and go at will.

After becoming a Catholic, Clovis benefited from papal support. For the Church, missionary work became easier.

worldly cares. In 520 A.D. a Roman official named Benedict established a monastery at Monte Cassino in Italy. To organize his community, Benedict drew up a list of regulations that later became known as the Benedictine Rule.

Under the Benedictine Rule, monks were required to be celibate, or unmarried, and to lead simple lives. They were closely supervised by an **abbot,** or monastery head. Their most important duties were religious worship and prayer. Monks also performed manual labor.

The Rule proved successful and was soon adopted by other monasteries in western Europe. Benedictine monasteries played an important role in medieval society. They became model centers of Christian living. Monks operated schools and cared for poor people and travelers. They built sturdy stone buildings and introduced new methods of farming. By caring for old manuscripts, monks ensured the survival of western learning.

Tending the sick and counseling the wrongdoer were some of the activities performed by these monks and nuns. What other services did monasteries offer people?

Missionaries Monasteries became the principal centers of missionary activity. In 597 A.D. Pope Gregory I sent Benedictine monks to southern Britain, where they converted Anglo-Saxons[2] to Catholic Christianity. From Britain, Anglo-Saxon missionaries carried Roman Catholicism to pagan, or non-Christian, groups in northern Germany. The missionaries also organized the churches of the Franks and made them obey the Pope.

During the sixth and seventh centuries, monasteries in Ireland sent missionaries throughout the North Atlantic area and western Europe. The Irish Church, however, was independent of the Pope. Its missionary monks were often in competition with Rome. Loosely organized, they were no match for the well-disciplined Benedictines. By 700 A.D. most of northwestern Europe, including Ireland, had accepted Benedictine monasteries and recognized the Pope as head of the Church.

Franks

During the fifth century, the Franks emerged as the strongest of the Germanic groups. Most Franks were free peasants. Agriculture was more important to them than fighting. They set up farms wherever they expanded.

Clovis, the first important Frankish king, created a large kingdom in what is today southwestern Germany and France. He became the first Germanic ruler to accept Roman Catholicism. Clovis's military victories and his religious conversion gave his throne stability.

A century later the Frankish kingdom began to decline. Frankish kings had followed the custom of dividing the kingdom among their heirs. Heirs became rivals and fought each other for land. By 700 A.D. political power had passed from kings to nobles and government officials known as **mayors of the palace.**

Charles Martel By the early eighth century, the Franks once again moved toward unity. In 732 A.D., Charles Martel, a mayor of the palace,

[2] By the 600's A.D., the Angles and Saxons of Britain had become one people: the Anglo-Saxons. The southern part of Britain eventually became known as "Angle-land" or England.

led the Franks to victory against a Muslim army in the Battle of Tours. The Frankish victory helped block Muslim expansion into Europe and ensured that it would remain Christian. This enabled Charles Martel and his family, later known as the Carolingians, to unite the Franks politically. Thus was laid the foundation for a new western European civilization.

Pepin   In 751 A.D. with the backing of the nobles and the Church, Pepin, the son of Charles Martel, became king of the Franks. The Pope anointed, or put holy oil, on Pepin. This made him a divinely-chosen ruler in the eyes of his people.

In return for the church's blessing, Pepin was expected to help the Pope against his enemies. In 753 A.D. Pepin forced the Lombards, a Germanic people, to withdraw from Rome. He then gave Pope Stephen II a large strip of Lombard land in central Italy. In appreciation, the Pope cut his political ties to the Byzantine Empire and looked to the Franks as his protectors. As a result, the fortunes of western Europe and the **papacy,** or the office of Pope, were bound more closely together.

Charlemagne   In 771 A.D., Pepin's son Charles became king of the Franks. He soon emerged as the first important western European monarch. Even in his own lifetime, he was known as Charlemagne, meaning "Charles the Great."

A successful warrior, Charlemagne enlarged the borders of the Frankish kingdom to include what is now Germany, France, northern Spain, and most of Italy. He exercised more authority than the last of the western Roman emperors. As a result of Charlemagne's rule, most western Europeans were united under one government for the first time since the fall of Rome.

Because few western Europeans could read and write, Charlemagne encouraged the formation of schools in churches and monasteries. He gathered scholars from every area of western Europe to teach in a school in his palace. These scholars helped preserve classical learning by making new and accurate copies of ancient manuscripts, such as the Bible, works by the Church Fathers, and the Roman classics. The

The Pope crowned Charlemagne to symbolize the alliance between the Frankish kingdom and the papacy. In what other ways did Charlemagne unite western Europe?

scholars also used a common language—Latin. When knowledge spread from Charlemagne's court to other areas of Europe, western Europeans became united by a common set of ideas.

Christian Empire   One of the ideas that united western Europeans was the creation of a Christian Roman Empire. Church leaders believed that Charlemagne could turn this idea into reality. In 800 A.D. Charlemagne came to Rome to defend Pope Leo III against the Roman nobles. To show his gratitude, Leo crowned Charlemagne the new Roman emperor. As protector of the Church and the ruler of much of western Europe, Charlemagne wanted the title, but he had misgivings about receiving it from the Pope. By crowning a monarch, the Pope seemed to be

Administration of Charlemagne's realm was made difficult by slow transportation and communication.

France and Germany have fought repeatedly—even into the twentieth century—for what was once the middle area of Charlemagne's empire.

FRANKISH EMPIRE

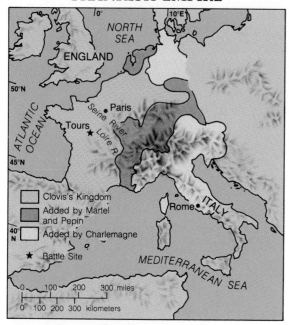

TREATY OF VERDUN

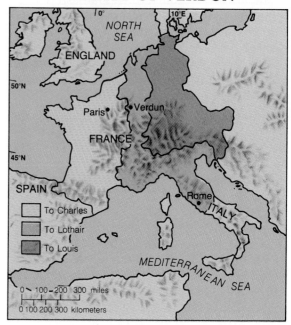

saying that church officials were superior to political leaders.

In spite of his concern, Charlemagne accepted his responsibilities as emperor and worked to strengthen the empire. Because the central bureaucracy was small, he relied on local officials called **counts** to assist him. Each count was carefully instructed on the duties of office. The counts solved local problems, stopped feuds, protected the weak, and raised armies for the emperor. Each year, royal envoys known as **missi dominici** went on inspection tours. They reported to Charlemagne on the performance of the counts and other local administrators. The emperor also traveled throughout the empire observing the work of his officials firsthand.

Collapse Charlemagne's personality, more than any other factor, held the empire together. After his death in 814 A.D., the empire weakened. Charlemagne's three grandsons fought each other for control of territory. In 843 A.D. they agreed to the Treaty of Verdun. This treaty divided the Carolingian lands. Charles the Bald took the western part, an area that is now France. Louis the German acquired the eastern portion, which today is Germany. Lothair became emperor and gained a long strip of land in the middle that stretched from the North Sea to Italy.

Invasions

While internal feuding weakened the Carolingian kingdoms, outside invasions nearly destroyed them. The Muslims seized parts of southern Italy and gained control of the western Mediterranean. The Magyars, or Hungarians, a nomadic group from central Asia, swept into the heartland of Europe. From Scandinavia in the north came the Vikings.

Vikings In the 800's A.D. the Vikings left their overpopulated homelands, which later became the kingdoms of Norway, Denmark, and Sweden. Skilled in sailing and trading, they raided the Atlantic and Mediterranean coasts of Europe. The Norwegians settled the North Atlantic islands of Greenland and Iceland, and even reached North America. The Danes temporarily held England and established the Viking state of Normandy in northwestern France. The Swedes settled in Russia and helped organize its scattered Slavic population.

Negative images of the Vikings prevailed for many centuries because the only written accounts of the Vikings came from Church clerics, the victims of the Viking raids.

European Resistance The people of western Europe suffered at the hands of the Vikings and other invaders. Monasteries and towns were plundered. Many areas lost population and faced economic collapse. In spite of these setbacks, leaders in many areas of Europe were able to resist the invasions.

King Alfred the Great of England defeated the Danes and forced them to give up half the country. By 950 A.D. all of England was united under Alfred's dynasty. At the Battle of Lech in 955 A.D., the Germans, led by King Otto I, halted the Hungarian advance. Seven years later the Pope crowned Otto emperor of the Holy Roman Empire, a large new state consisting of Germany and northern Italy.

France, lacking a strong central authority, had difficulty fighting the invaders. In 955 A.D. a noble named Hugh Capet seized the French throne from the Carolingian family. However, he controlled only a small area surrounding Paris. As a result of royal weakness, French nobles and local officials took over the responsibility of defense. They secured the loyalty of the people in their areas and became virtually independent rulers.

1. Identify: Benedict, Gregory I, Clovis, Charles Martel, Battle of Tours, Pepin, Charlemagne, Treaty of Verdun, Alfred the Great, Holy Roman Empire, Hugh Capet.
2. What impact did monasteries have on medieval Europe?
3. What methods did Charlemagne use to govern his empire?
4. What happened to Charlemagne's empire after he died?

INVASIONS OF EUROPE 8th to 10th CENTURIES

Fiefs freed warriors from farming duties. This enabled them to develop necessary fighting skills.

Discuss with students how feudalism solved two basic problems for the powerful: how to pay for military service and how to insure the loyalty of one's soldiers.

2   Medieval Society

During the Middle Ages, European society was organized into a hierarchy of social groups. Each group had duties to perform for the other groups and for society as a whole. The first group was the clergy, whose duties were to teach Christianity and to help the poor and the sick. The second group was made up of royalty and various ranks of nobles who served as warriors. Their duty was to govern and protect the people. The third group consisted of peasants and a small number of townspeople. Their responsibility was to work for the clergy and the nobles.

Feudalism

To stop invasions and to provide protection, kings and nobles in France developed among themselves a new type of social organization known as **feudalism.** With the weakening of central government, feudalism soon spread to other areas of western Europe. It developed differently in each area, but everywhere it had three common features. These were ties of loyalty and duty among nobles, landholding, and rule by local officials.

Beginnings   Feudalism began about 900 A.D. However, some of its features developed much earlier. For example, landownership and mili-

tary service were tied together in the 700's A.D. At that time, Charles Martel was fighting the Muslims. Muslim soldiers used saddles with stirrups that enabled them to fight on horseback with a sword or lance. Martel wanted to adopt the stirrup and develop a powerful cavalry. However, the cost of keeping such a force required a new type of military system. To support the cavalry, Martel began granting warriors **fiefs,** or estates with peasants. From these fiefs, warriors got the income they needed to buy horses and battle equipment.

Frankish kings later enlarged this system. They gave fiefs to counts and other local officials. In return for the land, these nobles swore an oath of loyalty to the king. They thought of the king as their lord and promised to aid him with arms.

With the Viking invasions of the ninth and tenth centuries, these arrangements fully emerged as feudalism. The nobles who had been granted fiefs were allowed to pass their lands on to their heirs. In return, these nobles, or lords, were expected to supply **knights,** or mounted warriors, for the royal army. In this way, a pyramid of feudal relationships developed. At the top was the king; at the bottom were the knights; and in the middle were various ranks of lords. Each lord was a **vassal,** that is, a noble who served a lord of the next higher rank.

During the Middle Ages, Vikings from northern Europe carried out a series of raids on coastal areas in other parts of Europe. At first these raids were for booty and captives who were sold as slaves to wealthy Muslim kingdoms. Later, however, the Viking raids became centered on conquest to establish settlements. What effect did the Viking invasions have on European society?

As lords and vassals bargained in their self-interest feudal obligations varied from region to region.

Through marriage and inheritance, a person might be vassal to several lords.

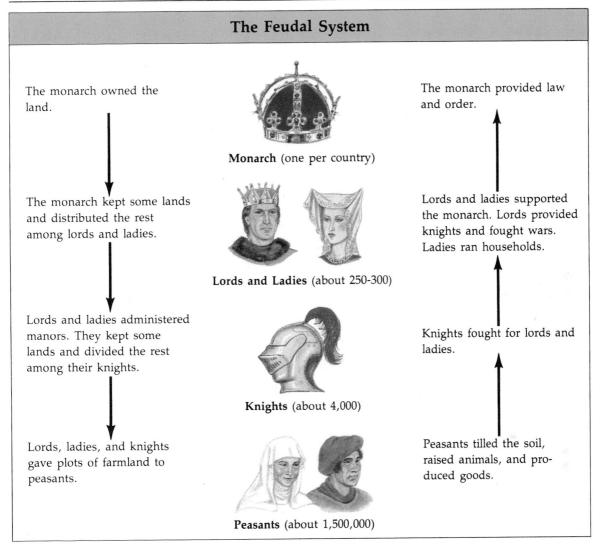

The Feudal System

The monarch owned the land.

The monarch provided law and order.

Monarch (one per country)

The monarch kept some lands and distributed the rest among lords and ladies.

Lords and ladies supported the monarch. Lords provided knights and fought wars. Ladies ran households.

Lords and Ladies (about 250-300)

Lords and ladies administered manors. They kept some lands and divided the rest among their knights.

Knights fought for lords and ladies.

Knights (about 4,000)

Lords, ladies, and knights gave plots of farmland to peasants.

Peasants tilled the soil, raised animals, and produced goods.

Peasants (about 1,500,000)

Feudalism usually weakened a king's power because the loyalty of a lesser vassal was to his own immediate lord and not directly to the king. Powerful nobles soon acquired control over local governments. Nobles judged more serious crimes on their fiefs. Lesser lords under them judged minor crimes.

Obligations Ties between a lord and a vassal were made official in a solemn ceremony known as **homage.** The vassal knelt on the ground, placed his hands between those of his lord, and pledged his loyalty and service. After this ceremony, the lord granted a fief to the vassal.

To hold his fief, the vassal had to perform certain duties. The principal duty was to provide military service to the lord. This usually meant supplying a certain number of knights for 40 to 60 days a year. Other obligations were known as **aids.** For example, the vassal was required to give advice at the lord's court. He also had to contribute money when the lord's son became a knight and when the eldest daughter married. If the lord was captured in battle and held for ransom, the vassals had to pay it. The vassal was expected to provide hospitality when the lord visited his fief. If the vassal did not fulfill his duties, the lord could seize the fief.

The lord could demand from the vassal certain rights known as **incidents.** When the vassal died, his eldest son could inherit the fief only if he made a payment to the lord. If the vassal left a young son, the lord had the right to raise the boy. When the boy became an adult, he was made a vassal and inherited the fief. If the vassal left a daughter, the lord had the right to choose her husband. This man would then become the vassal and inherit the fief. If the vassal died without heirs, the fief was returned to the lord.

Feudal Life

Because of the lack of a strong central government, warfare occurred frequently in feudal society. As a result, every noble built a castle or fortified manor house for defense against his enemies. The earliest castles appeared in the 900's A.D., and were made of wood. By the 1100's A.D., castles were made of stone. They had thick walls and turrets, or small towers. Each castle was built on a hill or mound surrounded by a deep moat. Castles had a square tower called a keep. The keep, located in the strongest part of a castle, contained many rooms, a hall, and a dungeon. Surrounding the keep was a large open area called a bailey. Within the bailey were various buildings, including barracks, storerooms, workshops, and a chapel.

Amusements   When they were not fighting, nobles trained for war by competing in **tournaments,** or special contests among knights. In these matches, they tested their strength, skill, and endurance. Tournaments were often held to celebrate events like the wedding of a daughter or the knighting of a son. They were usually held in a large field near the castle. The most popular event of the tournament was the **joust.** In a joust, two knights in armor rode toward each other with long wooden lances. Each tried to knock the other to the ground.

Another amusement was the chase, or hunt. Nobles hunted deer and other wildlife using dogs and falcons. Often ladies, or noblewomen, joined in the chase. In more leisurely moments, nobles played chess or dice. They listened to the songs of a wandering minstrel, or singer, who entertained in return for a meal or lodging.

Women   Noblewomen often married before they were twelve years of age. They had little say in the choice of a husband. A couple's marriage was usually arranged by the leading men of the two families concerned. Women enjoyed few rights. Their primary duties were to raise children and to take care of the household. However, they often helped their husbands run fiefs and defend the castle during attacks. Ladies developed skills in making cloth and fine embroidery. They also learned to make medicines from plants and herbs. They used this knowledge in caring for the sick and the poor.

Knighthood   Knights were an important part of feudal society. A son of a noble began training for knighthood at the age of seven. He started out as a **page,** or assistant, in the castle of a lord. There, he learned manners and the use of weapons. At 15, he became a **squire.** In addition to attending a lord, a squire spent a large amount of time in military exercises. When sufficiently skilled, he was made a knight in a special ceremony. At this ceremony, the squire pledged to fight for the lord and to protect the weak. Then the lord tapped him on the shoulder with the blade of a sword and pronounced him a knight.

The behavior of knights was governed by a code of **chivalry.** Its purpose was to reduce the coarseness and violence of medieval life. Its rules stated that a knight should be brave in battle, fight fairly, keep his promises, and defend the Church. Chivalry also included standards for courteous behavior toward women of noble birth. Although many knights failed to observe the code, chivalry became the basis for the development of etiquette, or good manners, in western society.

Peasant Life

The feudal world of lords, knights, ladies, and kings was only one part of medieval life. Most western Europeans were peasants who lived in small villages under the protection of a lord. They supplied the food and other services that enabled the clergy to perform religious duties and the nobles to fight wars. At the same time, the peasants were considered inferior to these groups and enjoyed fewer rights.

Typical Manor House and Village

Manor House · Pasture · Church · Autumn Planting · Spring Planting · Fallow Land · Smithy · Mill · Meadow · Bake oven

Manor During the 700's and 800's A.D., peasants had turned their lands over to nobles and clergy in return for protection. The lands were then combined into **manors,** or large estates. Manors varied in size from several hundred to a thousand acres. Knights often owned only one manor, while powerful nobles owned hundreds of them. Many of these manors were often far apart. As a result, lords appointed officials to oversee each manor and its activities. These officials also ran the courts that enforced the lord's law on each estate.

Manors formed the basis of the agricultural system of the Middle Ages known as **manorialism.** While feudalism involved ties among nobles, manorialism concerned agreements between nobles and peasants. In return for the lord's protection and government, the peasants provided a variety of services to the lord. These obligations included farming the lord's land, payments in kind to the lord, and various types of labor, such as road and bridge repair.

Manors were largely self-sufficient. The peasants provided for their own food, shelter, and clothing. They also supplied the needs of the lord and his household. Every manor had its own artisans. Peasant women worked for the lord by making candles, shearing sheep, spinning wool, and making clothes. Only rare luxury items were obtained from outside the manor.

Peasant Groups Part of a manor was reserved as farmland for the lord. Another part was farmed by **freeholders,** or peasants who paid rent and provided the lord with a portion of their harvest. The remaining farmland was used by **serfs,** who were the majority of peasants. Unlike freeholders, serfs were bound to the soil and could not leave the manor without the lord's permission. In return for their land, serfs had to work two or three days a week on the lord's land. They worked extra days during planting and harvesting. Both the serfs and the freeholders had to provide the lord with farm products.

Peasants worked long hours and faced many dangers. Famine and epidemics were commonplace. Wild beasts killed pasture animals and attacked peasant cottages. Nobles, fighting each other or on the hunt, often ruined peasant crops. Though bound to the manor, some serfs fled to the forests, where they joined bands of outlaws. Others escaped to the towns. If they remained in a town for more than a year, serfs were considered free.

In spite of hardships, peasants were able to relax on Sundays and holy days. They enjoyed dancing, singing, and such sports as wrestling and archery. In addition, there were other amusements, such as **mystery plays,** or religious dramas, pageants, and shows by minstrels.

Improvements   The manorial system normally produced only enough food to support the peasants and the lord's household. However, a number of improvements gradually increased the productivity of the land.

The first improvement was a new plow. Since Roman times, western Europeans had farmed with a scratch plow. The scratch plow had a downward-pointed spike. The plow was pulled by two oxen, first in one direction, then crosswise, over a square plot of land. The scratch plow was gradually replaced by a heavier plow, which proved to be more effective in the rich, damp soils of northwestern Europe. The heavier plow made deeper cuts in the ground and had a device called a mould-board that pushed the soil sideways. The plow was set on wheels, drawn by a team of oxen, and used to plow long strips of land rather than square plots. Peasants pooled their oxen and began to farm the land together. The heavy plow allowed them to spend less time in plowing. As a result, farmers were able to develop a better method of planting.

During the ninth and tenth centuries, peasants had used a two-field system. By this method, half of the arable land was planted each year, while the other half lay fallow, or unsown. After 1000 A.D. the two-field system was gradually replaced by a more efficient and productive three-field system. Under the new system, peasants divided the land into three large fields, which were farmed together. Each field was in turn subdivided into long narrow strips. The lord had about one-third of these strips; the rest were held by freeholders and serfs. The lord's and peasants' strips were divided among the three fields to ensure that both the good and bad land was shared equally. One of these fields was planted with winter wheat; a second with spring wheat and vegetables; and the third was left fallow. Each year the crops were rotated and a different field would lay fallow. This helped preserve the fertility of the soil. The three-field system was used in many parts of Europe until the eighteenth and nineteenth centuries.

1. What were the common features of feudalism?
2. What services did a vassal give to a lord?
3. What was the role of the peasants in medieval society?
4. What improvements came to the manor?

3   Catholic Church

The Roman Catholic Church was the center of life for western Europeans during the Middle Ages. It taught that all people had sinned and had to rely on God's grace, or favor, to lead good lives and to win salvation. The only way to receive grace was by taking part in the **sacraments,** or church rituals. The most important of these sacraments was the **eucharist,** or holy communion, which commemorated Christ's death on the cross. People shared in the eucharist at **mass,** or the church's worship service. At each mass, the priest blessed wheat wafers and a cup of wine that stood on the altar. According to church teaching, the wafers and wine became the body and blood of Jesus. The priest then drank the wine, ate one of the wafers, and gave a wafer to each worshiper.

Although people were deeply religious, their understanding of church ceremony was limited. Masses were said in Latin, which few people understood. In many villages priests were poorly educated and could not preach effectively. Many

HISTORY AND THE ARTS

Cathedral Architecture

Magnificent stone cathedrals were the grand masterpieces of the Middle Ages. Rising above towns and villages, they reflected the faith, skill, and dedication of medieval patrons and builders. Nobles, merchants, architects, and laborers gave money, talent, and effort to build cathedrals. It often took many years to finish the largest of them.

The English word "cathedral" comes from the Latin term *cathedra*, meaning "seat." In the Church, the word came to be used for the bishop's seat or throne. Thus, a cathedral is a church containing a bishop's throne. Most medieval cathedrals were built in the shape of a cross. Some scholars believe that this was done as a reminder of the death of Jesus. Others, however, claim that the arrangement reflected a more practical concern for space and balance.

From about 800 to 1100 A.D., medieval cathedrals were built according to the Romanesque style of architecture. Romanesque architecture combined Roman, Byzantine, and other styles. Romanesque cathedrals were massive buildings, noted for their thick stone walls and heavy arches. Other features were dark interiors, arched ceilings, small windows, and horizontal space. Because of their sturdiness, Romanesque cathedrals were called "fortresses of God."

In the twelfth century, new artistic ideas changed cathedral architecture. The French church leader Abbot Suger thought of God as absolute beauty. He believed that humans could come to know God through beautiful things. Suger made a number of revolutionary changes in the construction of St. Denis, his monastery church near Paris. These changes became the basis of a new style of architecture known as Gothic.

In building Gothic cathedrals, architects wanted to create soaring spaces that would direct the gaze of worshipers upward to heaven. To create this visual effect, cathedrals were designed with thinner walls and lighter columns. The columns were extended into the ceiling, where they curved out to form ribbed vaults, or fan-like arched roofs. The vaults were supported by pointed arches and flying buttresses, or arched supports built against the outside walls.

The sides of Gothic cathedrals were filled in with beautiful stained glass windows. These windows let shimmering rays of multicolored light into the nave, or central area of the church. The most magnificent stained glass was the round petal-shaped rose window set above the portal, or church entrance. The blending of colored light with white stone in Gothic cathedrals produced feelings of awe and wonder.

During the thirteenth and fourteenth centuries, Gothic architecture spread from France to other areas of Europe. Each region soon developed its own Gothic style. Cathedrals became larger in size and grander in decoration. Their interiors and exteriors were alive with sculptures of the saints, biblical stories, and everyday events. Every part of the cathedral testified to the medieval sense of the glory of God.

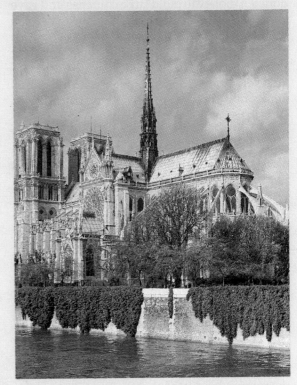

Have students research some of the ways in which Christianity was grafted onto traditional customs.

The episode between Gregory VII and Henry VI is known as the Humiliation at Canossa.

worshipers could not read or write, and few had access to reading materials. What the average person learned about Christianity usually came from the stained glass windows, paintings, and statues found in most medieval churches. As a result, the general population relied on a mixture of Christian and pagan beliefs.

Church and Society

During the Middle Ages, the Catholic clergy helped kings and nobles govern western Europe. Bishops and abbots were an important part of the feudal system. Because many of them came from noble families, they received land from kings in return for military service. But as religious leaders, the bishops and abbots were not supposed to fight. They solved their problem by getting knights to fight for them in exchange for land. This meant that many church leaders were vassals of lords and, in turn, lords of vassals with the same duties as any other noble.

Reform Because of its feudal ties, the Church became very wealthy. Rich nobles donated money to build large churches and gave gifts of land to monasteries. However, the wealthier the Church became, the more church officials grew careless about carrying out their religious duties. Contrary to church tradition, local lords came to control many church offices and lands. They often appointed close relatives as bishops and abbots.

During the tenth and eleventh centuries, a movement for church reform developed in the monasteries and spread throughout western Europe. Devout nobles founded new monasteries that strictly followed the Benedictine Rule. The most famous of these was Cluny in eastern France. The monks of Cluny led simple pious lives and soon won the respect of the people.

Influenced by church reform, a new group of church leaders worked to free the Church from the control of feudal lords. These leaders wanted to make the Church the final authority in western society. In 1059 A.D. they declared that political leaders could no longer choose popes. The election of popes was then placed in the hands of the **cardinals**, or the clergy of Rome. In addition, the reformers insisted that the Pope, not secular rulers, should appoint bishops and priests to church offices.

Gregory VII In 1073 A.D. a reforming monk named Hildebrand became Pope Gregory VII. Gregory believed that the Pope should have complete jurisdiction over all church officials. He criticized the practice of **lay investiture,** in which secular rulers gave the symbols of office, such as a ring and a staff, to the bishops they had appointed.

The attack on lay investiture brought Gregory into bitter conflict with the Holy Roman Emperor, Henry IV. Henry controlled the bishops and abbots of Germany and used them to govern the country. Thus, he believed that Gregory's opposition to lay investiture endangered his hold on Germany. Henry denounced Gregory as an illegally elected Pope and summoned a council of German bishops to remove him from the papacy. Gregory answered by cutting off Henry from the Church. In addition, Henry's subjects were freed from obeying their king.

When the German nobles threatened civil war, Henry decided to make his peace with Gregory. In 1077 A.D., Henry traveled to Italy where he met Gregory at the Castle of Canossa. For three days Henry waited in the snow, seeking the Pope's forgiveness. In the end, Gregory admitted Henry, accepted his promise to obey papal orders, and pardoned him.

The struggle between the Pope and the Holy Roman Emperor continued after Gregory's death in 1085 A.D. Thirty-seven years later, in 1122 A.D., a compromise was reached at the Concordat of Worms.[3] The emperor could still name bishops, but the Pope could refuse to approve those whom he felt were spiritually unqualified. Because no one could hold church office without the Pope's final approval, the Concordat of Worms, in the long run, increased the Pope's authority. With greater responsibilities, the Pope developed a strong bureaucracy in Rome to help him govern the Church.

Innocent III In the early 1200's A.D., the papacy reached the height of its power under

---

[3] A concordat is an agreement between a Pope and a secular ruler. This particular concordat was reached in the German town of Worms.

Innocent III. Innocent declared that the Pope was the final authority in the Christian world. He kept the clergy under tight control and intervened repeatedly in secular affairs. For example, Innocent III placed church penalties on England to make King John accept his choice for Archbishop of Canterbury. Innocent III also judged the elections of Holy Roman Emperors and rejected candidates whom he thought unworthy.

During Innocent III's reign, the Church took steps to stop the spread of heresy. At first, the Church tried to convert heretics through peaceful means such as preaching. But soon force was used. In 1207 A.D. Innocent III sent an army of French knights to southern France to fight heretics known as Albigensians. In spite of fierce resistance, the Albigensians were crushed.

Inquisition   After the Albigensian defeat, heretics in Europe continued to practice their beliefs secretly. In order to seek out and punish them, the Church developed a court known as the Inquisition. The judges of the Inquisition often misused their powers. They accepted rumors as a basis for accusations and used torture to obtain confessions. Heretics who refused to change their beliefs were sentenced to die by burning. At the time, the Church justified these practices, stating that the loss of the heretic's soul was far worse than the killing of the body. The Inquisition largely succeeded in stopping heresy. However, it created an atmosphere of fear and distrust in many areas of Europe.

Friars   During the early thirteenth century, **friars,** or wandering preachers, sought to reform the Church. They emerged at a time when church leaders were being widely criticized for their love of wealth and power. The friars set an example by living simply and owning no possessions. They depended on gifts of food and shelter to survive. For this reason, they were called **mendicants,** or religious beggars. Although they followed monastic rules, the friars did not isolate themselves from the world. Instead, they lived in towns and preached Christianity to the people.

Two well-known **orders,** or church-approved groups, of friars were the Franciscans and the Dominicans. The Franciscans were founded in 1200 A.D. by Francis of Assisi, the son of a wealthy Italian cloth merchant. Francis and his followers sought to follow the simple lives of Jesus and his disciples. They became known for their cheerful trust in God and their respect for nature as a divine gift. The Dominicans were organized in 1220 A.D. by a Spanish priest named Dominic. Like the Franciscans, the Dominicans lived a life of poverty and service to others. However, they also stressed the importance of well-educated, persuasive preachers who could reply to the arguments of heretics. Both the Franciscans and the Dominicans met with immediate success. Through their example and preaching, they kept many western Europeans loyal to the Roman Catholic Church.

Crusades

During the Middle Ages, the Church sponsored a series of holy wars called crusades. The crusades went on for about 200 years. They brought about significant changes in western Europe.

First Crusade   The First Crusade was proclaimed by Pope Urban II in 1095 A.D. at Clermont, France. It was directed against the Seljuk Turks, a Muslim people from central Asia.

Shown here are crusaders preparing to leave for Jerusalem. Despite the failure to recapture the Holy Land, how did Europeans benefit from the Crusades?

The map below is the subject of the "Using Maps" section of the Chapter 7 Review.

Have students analyze Pope Urban's statement to learn about conditions in western Europe and the incentives that the Pope offered to crusaders.

THE CRUSADES

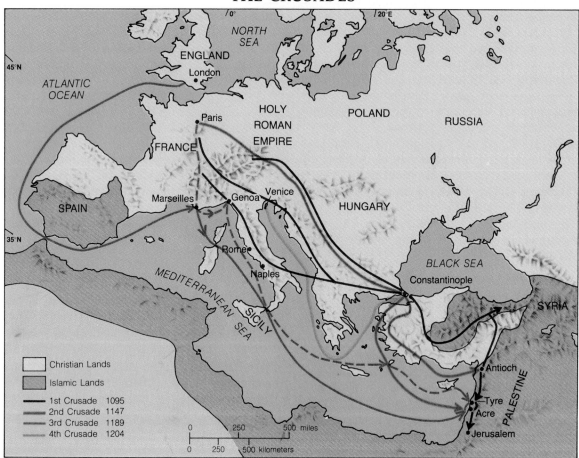

The Seljuks held the Christian shrines in Palestine, including Jerusalem. They were also threatening the Byzantine Empire.

At Clermont, Pope Urban asked for an army to take Palestine from the Seljuks. He said:

> I exhort you . . . to strive to expel that wicked race [the Seljuks] from our Christian lands. . . Christ commands it. Remission of sins will be granted for those going thither. . . Let those who are accustomed to wage private war wastefully even against believers go forth against the infidels. . . Let those who have lived by plundering be soldiers of Christ; let those who formerly contended against brothers and relations rightly fight barbarians; let those who were recently hired for a few pieces of silver win their eternal reward. . . The sorrowful here will be glad there, the poor here will be rich there, and the enemies of the Lord here will be His friends there. Let no delay postpone the journey . . . when winter has ended and spring has come . . . enter the highways courageously with the Lord going on before.*

Thousands of knights and common people responded to the Pope's plea and joined the crusade. Many of them had strong religious reasons for their involvement. As a sign of their religious passion, they adopted the war cry: "Deus vult," which means "It is the will of God." They also wore red crosses on their tunics as a

---

*History of Jerusalem, Fulcher of Chartres, tr. by M. E. McGinty, © 1941 by University of Pennsylvania Press, p. 16.

Two groups of warrior-monks known as Knights Templar and Knights Hospitaller took charge of defense in the crusader settlements. They also protected Christian visitors and helped the sick.

Refer students back to Chapter 5, pp. 117-118, for the account of the Fourth Crusade.

symbol of their obedience to God. Other crusaders saw the holy war as an opportunity to escape problems, seek adventure, or acquire wealth.

Bands of peasants were the first to start out for Palestine. Inexperienced in warfare, most of them either died on the way or were massacred by the Seljuks. The peasants were followed by knights. After a short stay in Contantinople, the knights invaded Asia Minor and marched to Palestine. On their journey, the crusaders suffered from hunger and disease. They were also divided by quarrels among their leaders. In spite of these difficulties, the crusaders won two battles and finally took Jerusalem in 1099 A.D.

The success of the First Crusade reinforced the influence of the Church and strengthened the self-confidence of western Europeans. The religious enthusiasm of the crusaders, however, soon cooled. Many knights returned home. Those who remained set up a series of feudal states in Syria and Palestine.

Second Crusade   Less than 50 years after the First Crusade, the Seljuks conquered part of the crusader states. Pope Eugenius IV then called the Second Crusade to regain the lost territory. The monk Bernard of Clairvaux preached eloquent sermons in support of the crusade. He persuaded King Louis VII of France and Holy Roman Emperor Conrad III to lead armies to Palestine. In spite of high hopes, the Second Crusade failed. The two rulers constantly quarreled with each other. As a result, their forces were defeated by the Seljuks.

Third Crusade   Soon other Muslims came to power in Palestine and conquered crusader lands. The fall of Jerusalem to the Muslim leader Saladin in 1187 A.D. stunned western Europe. In response, Holy Roman Emperor Frederick Barbarossa of Germany, King Philip Augustus of France, and King Richard I of England led the Third Crusade. This "Crusade of Kings" proved to be a failure. Barbarossa died on the way to Palestine, and Philip Augustus returned to France. Richard continued the struggle alone, but his army was not strong enough to defeat Saladin. After three years, Richard gave up and signed a truce with the Muslims. The crusaders

continued to control a coastal strip of Palestine and Syria, but Jerusalem remained Muslim.

Other Crusades   Other crusades followed in the thirteenth century, but none succeeded in winning permanent Christian control of Palestine. In fact, the Muslims slowly conquered all the remaining Christian territories. In 1291 A.D. they captured Acre, the last Christian stronghold in Palestine. By this time, western Europeans had lost sight of the religious goal of the crusades. They were now more concerned about political and economic gain. As a result, European rulers lost interest in regaining Palestine and shifted their attention to other matters.

Effects   Although the crusades failed, they had an important impact on the development of western Europe. At home, they helped break down feudalism. Many of the lesser nobles had to sell their estates to raise money for the crusades. Other nobles died in battle without heirs. Their lands passed to new owners. Taking advantage of such situations, many serfs bought their freedom and became freeholders on the land or artisans in the towns. Meanwhile, kings increased their authority over nobles by raising large armies that replaced the small feudal forces.

The crusades also helped bring western Europe out of its isolation. The crusaders' contact with the civilizations of the Byzantines and Muslims created a demand at home for eastern luxury goods. To meet this demand, European merchants opened up new trade routes. They brought home spices, sugar, lemons, melons, rugs, tapestries, and richly woven cloth. As a result, western European standards of living improved for the first time since the days of the Roman Empire.

The crusades were the first attempt by western Europeans to move into non-European areas. This expansion played an important part in making later European voyages of discovery possible. As a result, Europeans learned to draw more accurate maps and build better ships and weapons. They also developed skills in constructing fortresses, roads, and bridges. European expansion, however, embittered relations with the Byzantine and Muslim worlds.

Venice, Genoa, and other northern Italian cities controlled eastern Mediterranean trade until 1500.

The noble family ruling Champagne found that trade fairs could yield rich profits through rents, sales, taxes, and fines. Other nobles tried to imitate their successes.

1. Identify: Cluny, Gregory VII, Henry IV, Canossa, Innocent III, Albigensians, Inquisition, Francis of Assisi, Urban II, "Crusade of Kings," Acre.
2. What were Gregory VII's goals as Pope?
3. Who were the Dominicans and the Franciscans?
4. What reasons did people have for going on a crusade?

4 Economic and Cultural Revival

Medieval civilization reached its height during the High Middle Ages, or the period between 1000 and 1300 A.D. During this time, feudalism, manorialism, and the Church continued to influence western Europe. New forces, however, shaped medieval society and challenged traditional ways. People gained new confidence in their own abilities. Towns and trade began to flourish, and more complex institutions appeared. Along with these developments, there was an awakening in learning and the arts.

Economic Expansion

Around 1000 A.D. western Europe's economy began to revive. Population increased, and there was an expansion in food production. Improved farming techniques opened up new land to cultivation. Nobles, freeholders, and serfs began migrating into new areas. They cleared forests, drained swamps, and built new farms and villages. In one of the largest migrations of the Middle Ages the Germans moved into eastern Europe, doubling the territory they controlled. This expansion brought the Germans into conflict with the Slavs, who had occupied the region since the 600's A.D.

Towns As agriculture was expanded, the towns of western Europe grew in size and number. Most of them developed along rivers or beside castles and monasteries. For protection, towns were surrounded by walls. As towns grew, additional space was often hard to find. Houses were built close together and often had extra stories that extended over narrow unpaved streets. Shops were located on the first floor of homes, while other floors were used for living quarters. Because most buildings were made of wood, fire was a constant hazard. Contagious diseases were another serious danger. Many spread with deadly speed due to an almost complete lack of sanitation.

Trade Towns furnished markets for agricultural goods and specialized in the production and sale of crafts. This economic activity stimulated trade in all parts of Europe. The most prosperous trading towns developed on the important sea routes that connected western Europe with the Mediterranean Sea, Russia, and Scandinavia. Italian towns, such as Venice, Pisa, and Genoa, controlled Mediterranean trade and brought silks and spices from the East into Europe. On the northwest coast of Europe, the towns of the region called Flanders were the leading centers of trade. These towns specialized in producing woolen textiles. Throughout Europe and the Middle East, markets were found for Flanders' cloth. Other towns grew up along the Baltic coast. They controlled trade between Russia and the North Atlantic. Their major products were furs, timber, and fish.

Overland trade also developed in western Europe. Italian towns sent a steady stream of goods across the Alps to France and Germany. Soon, groups of merchants were traveling along many routes across the continent. These activities led to the rise of inland towns and trade fairs. The most famous fair was held in Champagne, a region of eastern France that served as the crossroads of western Europe. At the Champagne fair, merchants traded textiles and wools from northern Europe for luxury goods from the Mediterranean world.

Banking Before long, merchants at the trade fairs gave up bartering and began to pay for goods with money. The rise of a money economy led to money lending and the growth of banking. Merchants developed procedures for transferring funds from one place to another. They received deposits and made loans, becoming the first bankers in Europe.

The growth of money and banking put the feudal classes in an economic squeeze. Kings, popes, and nobles became dependent on borrowed money from bankers to pay for their steadily rising expenses. To pay off their loans, they had to raise taxes, sell their lands, or demand money payments in place of traditional feudal services.

Guilds Most **burghers,** or townspeople, were merchants, artisans, and workers. Many of them recognized the importance of working together to better their lives. During the twelfth century they organized into business associations called **guilds.** Each type of business or trade was represented by its own guild, whose members lived and worked in the same area of town. Guilds set standards of production and forbade competition. They also made strict rules on prices, wages, and employment to ensure equal treatment. Guild members controlled all business and trade in a town. Outsiders who wanted to sell their goods in the town market had to get permission from the guilds.

Apart from their business activities, guilds provided benefits, such as medical care and unemployment relief, for members and their families. Guilds also organized social and religious life. Guilds sponsored banquets, holy day processions, or parades, and outdoor plays. The meetings and activities of a guild were held in a building called a guildhall.

Guilds for the trades were controlled by **masters,** who owned their own shops and tools. Under them were **journeymen,** experienced workers who received daily wages. A third group was the **apprentices,** or young workers learning the trade. With this close-knit organization, many guilds became politically powerful and often governed towns.

Conflict Conflict soon developed between the landed feudal classes and burghers. City dwellers did not fit into the feudal system and therefore resented owing taxes and services to lords. They wanted to run their own affairs and have their own courts and laws. The feudal lords feared the growing wealth and power of the burghers. They began to strictly enforce feudal laws to keep burghers in their place.

The towns eventually won the struggle. In the twelfth century the towns of Italy formed political groups called **communes.** These groups ended the power of feudal lords, and made the Italian towns independent city-states. In other

The building of many stone castles and cathedrals enabled the masons to establish one of the most powerful medieval guilds. Why were guilds started?

areas of Europe, kings and nobles gave burghers documents known as **charters.** These allowed the burghers to control their own affairs; at the same time, many towns remained a part of a kingdom or a feudal territory.

Learning and the Arts

During the Middle Ages, education was in the hands of the clergy. They set up schools in monasteries and cathedrals. There students prepared to become church officials. They learned subjects such as church music, theology, and Latin. They were also required to study subjects known as the seven liberal arts. They included grammar, rhetoric, logic, arithmetic, geometry, astronomy, and music.

Universities Around 1150 A.D. a new interest in learning developed in western Europe.

Have students discuss whether Abelard would have been supported or opposed by the Church.

Encourage students to read other examples of medieval stories, poems, and folklore. What values and images do these works stress?

Students and teachers began meeting apart from the monastery and cathedral schools. They formed organizations that became known as universities. Universities set rules so that students and teachers would know their obligations toward each other. They also set standards for new teachers and had well-organized courses of study. Classes met at regular times, and students listened to lectures on specific subjects. To qualify as teachers, students had to pass an examination leading to a degree, or certificate of completion.

Church officials and secular rulers supported the growth of universities. They needed educated people to staff their rapidly growing bureaucracies. By the end of the thirteenth century, universities had spread throughout Europe.

Most southern European universities were secular and specialized in law and medicine. They were modeled on the law school at Bologna, Italy. There students hired professors and set rules for them to follow. One rule called for teachers to be punished if absent or late. On the other hand, northern European universities were run by the teachers, who charged a fee to train students and grant degrees. These universities specialized in liberal arts and theology. They were modeled on the University of Paris, the oldest of the medieval universities.

New Learning   At the medieval universities, scholars studied, in great depth, the Latin classics and Roman law. They also acquired new knowledge from the works of Artistotle and the scientific writings of the Arabs. As a result, medieval scholars developed a renewed interest in the physical world that would lead, in time, to the rise of western science.

Many church leaders opposed the study of Aristotle's works. They feared that Aristotle's ideas were hostile to the Christian faith. Some scholars, however, saw no threat from this new knowledge. They applied Aristotle's philosophy to theological questions and developed a system of thought called **scholasticism.** Scholasticism sought to reconcile classical philosophy with church teachings. It emphasized the importance of reason, as well as faith, in the interpretation of Christian doctrine.

One early scholastic teacher was Peter Abelard. He taught theology in Paris during the early 1100's A.D. In his book *Sic et Non*, or *Yes and No*, he collected certain statements from the Bible and the writings of the Church Fathers that showed both sides of controversial questions. Abelard then had his students reconcile the differences through logical thinking.

The most important scholastic thinker of the thirteenth century was Thomas Aquinas, an Italian noble who taught philosophy in Paris and Naples. In his most outstanding work, *Summa Theologica*, or *A Summary of Religious Thought*, Aquinas claimed that reason was a gift from God that could provide answers to basic philosophical questions. Aquinas's teaching and way of thinking were later accepted and promoted by the Roman Catholic Church.

Literature   During the Middle Ages, there was a great outpouring of literature. Songs and epics of the early Middle Ages were written down for the first time. The earliest work was *Beowulf*, an epic poem about an Anglo-Saxon warrior. It was written in England around 700 A.D. Later, French writers composed epic poems, which were called **chansons de geste.** These poems celebrated the courage of feudal warriors. The most famous was the *Song of Roland*. Written about 1100 A.D., it tells of the heroic death of one of Charlemagne's knights after an ambush by a Muslim army.

Romances, or love stories about knights and ladies, became popular during the Middle Ages. These stories usually idealized feudal society. In France, **troubadours,** or musician-singers, produced short lyric poems, which spread to other parts of Europe. In their works, they presented military feats, political satire, and love themes.

Most of these works were written in the **vernacular,** or everyday speech, of the common people. Although Latin was the language of scholars and church leaders, most people spoke early forms of German, French, and English. Vernacular languages were one of the forces that gave each kingdom of Europe its own identity.

During the fourteenth century, writers began to use vernacular languages in their works. The Italian writer Dante Alighieri wrote the *Divine*

Tell students to observe how the struggle for power between monarchs and nobles resulted in three different types of monarchies in England, France, and Germany.

The Middle Ages · 175

Ask students why people of lower birth would be more loyal to the monarch than the nobles would.

In The Canterbury Tales *each of 29 pilgrims, or travelers, was to tell a tale while on the way to Canterbury. Chaucer had completed only 22 of the stories before he died. The tales represent some of the earliest stories written in English. Why did literature of the Middle Ages appeal to the common people?*

Comedy, a narrative poem, in Italian verse. The *Divine Comedy* describes an imaginary journey from hell to heaven and presents the important theological concepts of the Middle Ages. England's Geoffrey Chaucer wrote *Canterbury Tales* in an early form of English. This work is about a group of pilgrims traveling to a shrine at Canterbury, England. The pilgrims represent typical personalities of the medieval period.

1. Identify: Flanders, Champagne, Bologna, Peter Abelard, Thomas Aquinas, *Song of Roland,* Dante Alighieri, Geoffrey Chaucer.
2. What were the features of medieval towns?
3. What did guilds do?
4. What was the aim of scholasticism?

5 Medieval Monarchies

The growth of western Europe's economy and culture strengthened its political institutions. Powerful monarchies emerged in various coun-

tries. Kings began to develop more efficient ways of governing. They checked the lawless tendencies of feudalism and gained the support of townspeople.

France

During the tenth and eleventh centuries, France was a collection of many feudal territories. No institution existed to bind these regions together. France's kings, descended from Hugh Capet and known as Capetians, were weak and did little to increase royal power. They ruled a small area of land between the Seine and Loire Rivers in northern France.

Louis VI   During the twelfth and thirteenth centuries, the authority of the French kings increased. In 1108 A.D. Louis VI became king. Helped by his close adviser Abbot Suger, Louis strengthened royal government. He set up new positions and filled them with loyal persons of lower birth rather than nobles. He punished rebellious vassals and brought greater security to

HISTORY AND PEOPLE

Eleanor of Aquitaine

At the age of 25, Eleanor of Aquitaine accompanied her husband, Louis VII of France, on a crusade to Palestine. She was not going to stay at home and miss all the excitement and glory. It was a typical decision for her.

Throughout her long life, Eleanor was involved in the major political, religious, and cultural events of the day. When she was 15 she became duchess of Aquitaine. Aquitaine was a large region of southwestern France. Eleanor had inherited the territory from her father. Unlike many other parts of Europe, Aquitaine allowed women to inherit property.

On his deathbed, Eleanor's father sent a request to Louis VI of France asking the king to protect his daughter and to find her a suitable husband. Louis was overjoyed with the request. What better way to extend his realm than to have his son marry Eleanor?

The marriage between Eleanor and the future Louis VII, however, proved to be a mismatch. Eleanor was intelligent, assertive, beautiful, and energetic. Louis, on the other hand, was quiet, calm, and serious. Eleanor is believed to have said, "I thought I had married a king, but I find I have married a monk."

To Eleanor, Paris was dreary, dull, and crowded. It was a disappointing contrast to sunny, fun-loving Aquitaine. In the royal household, conflicts soon developed. Eleanor's efforts to advise her husband on politics were viewed as interference by his closest advisers. Her boldness and gaiety were viewed with deep displeasure.

After 15 years of marriage, which produced two daughters and no sons, Eleanor was divorced from Louis in 1152 A.D. She kept her property, returned to Aquitaine, and established an illustrious court. A short time later, she married Henry Plantagenet. He was only 18 years old, but vigorous and worldly. He was also destined to become King Henry II of England. Their marriage embroiled France and England in centuries of conflict, for it gave England more territory and power than France. England now controlled lands from Scotland to the Pyrenees Mountains, including much that the French believed was theirs.

Eleanor's marriage to Henry was successful at first. She bore him eight children, including two future kings, Richard I and John I. Henry's unfaithfulness, however, eventually soured their marriage. Eleanor bitterly turned against him and in 1168 A.D. retired permanently to Aquitaine.

While in Aquitaine, Eleanor set out to restore the glamour of her court and to raise the position of women. She was joined in this effort by her daughter Marie. Marie ordered her chaplain to write the Rules of Love, a code of conduct for knights toward ladies. Then Eleanor and Marie set up a Court of Love, which heard cases and ruled on knights' behavior. Although the court was not taken seriously by Henry II or the other lords of the day, it helped change the behavior between men and women. The court taught that women, instead of being used and abused, should be honored and respected by men. Men were to be gallant, charming, courteous, respectful—in other words, to be chivalrous.

Disputes over royal succession were a common cause of civil wars. William was cousin to Edward the Confessor and had as legitimate a claim to the English throne as Harold.

The *Domesday Book* detailed such information as the amount of arable land and the size of the labor force.

the countryside. Louis also granted charters of self-government to many towns, thus winning the support of townspeople.

Philip Augustus Philip Augustus, also known as Philip II, ruled from 1180 to 1223 A.D. He further strengthened the monarchy. During his reign, Paris was rebuilt and made the center of French government. Philip increased the size of his kingdom through marriage and by acquiring French lands held by the English. In governing his territories, Philip preserved feudal institutions and made them work for the monarchy. Royal agents known as **bailiffs** were appointed to preside over local courts, collect taxes, and command military forces.

Louis IX In 1226 A.D. Philip's grandson became King Louis IX. Louis banned feudal fighting and decreed that only the king, not the nobles, had the right to mint coins. His concern for justice resulted in the dominance of royal courts over feudal courts. Louis' saintly life led to increased moral authority for the French monarchy. His actions caused the French people to regard the king as the source of national unity.

Philip IV Philip IV, Louis IX's grandson, ruled from 1285 to 1314 A.D. Because of his handsome appearance, he was also known as Philip the Fair. Philip increased France's territory and trade by fighting England and Flanders. To pay for these wars, he raised taxes and extended them to new groups, such as the clergy. In 1296 A.D. Pope Boniface VIII forbade secular rulers like Philip to tax the clergy without his consent. Philip, however, was strong enough to force the Pope to back down. The French king's action dealt a blow to the political authority of the Pope.

With the powers of the central government increasing, Philip enlarged the royal bureaucracy. He also formed the Estates-General, an assembly of nobles, clergy, and townspeople, to advise him on important matters. By the time he died in 1314 A.D., Philip had increased royal power over the feudal nobles. He had laid the foundations of a national government in France.

England

During the eleventh century, England's monarchy weakened, and the nobles increased their hold on the country. When the last Anglo-Saxon king, Edward the Confessor, died in 1065 A.D., Harold Godwinson, the most powerful English noble, became the new monarch. Harold's kingship, however, was challenged by William Duke of Normandy. In 1066 A.D., with an army of over 5,000 men, William crossed the English Channel and defeated Godwinson's forces at the Battle of Hastings. As a result of his victory, William became known as "the Conqueror." Later that year he succeeded to the English throne as King William I.

To crush English revolts and maintain the loyalty of his followers, William introduced feudalism into England. He seized the lands of Anglo-Saxon nobles and gave them to soldiers from Normandy. In return for their lands, these soldiers became William's vassals. Unlike French feudalism, the English variety strengthened the monarchy by making all landowners, even lesser vassals, directly loyal to the king.

However, William received advice from a Great Council of royal officials, bishops, and nobles. He also relied on local government officials called **sheriffs** to collect taxes and raise armies. Although he kept many Anglo-Saxon laws and practices, he extended the authority of central government over the entire country. In 1086 A.D. William took a census in order to determine how much to tax his subjects. This census was the first of its kind in western Europe since the Roman Empire. The census figures were later recorded in two huge volumes called the *Domesday Book*.

Henry I The strengthening of royal government was continued by William's grandson Henry I, who ruled from 1100 to 1135 A.D. Henry set up the Exchequer, a special department that handled royal finances. The founding of the Exchequer marked the beginning of government bureaucracy in England. Henry also set up a system of royal courts in which circuit judges traveled about the country to hear legal cases. Their work lessened the power of the feudal courts and emphasized the king's role as keeper of the peace.

Henry II After a period of civil war, in 1154 A.D. Henry I's son became King Henry II of

A well-known episode of Henry II's reign was the king's dispute with Thomas à Becket, the archbishop of Canterbury. In a rage over the right of royal courts to try church officials, Henry ordered the murder of Becket. It took place in the archbishop's cathedral. Henry later mourned the death.

The Magna Charta established the principle that the English monarch was not above the law. In what ways did the Magna Charta limit royal power?

England. During his reign, Henry II ruled England and was a feudal lord in France. In England he restored order and limited the power of the nobles. He also enlarged the activities of the royal courts and used the law to increase his authority. Henry set up a central royal court in London with trained lawyers as judges.

The circuit judges applied the same legal rules in all parts of England, creating a **common law** for the entire kingdom. In each community the judges met with a **grand jury,** or a group of 12 people that submitted the names of people in the area suspected of crimes. Soon a system of trial by jury was developed for determining the guilt or innocence of the accused. The juries in such proceedings became known as **petty juries.**

Richard I and John   Henry's sons Richard I and John were unpopular rulers. Richard I, also known as Richard the Lionheart, became king in 1189 A.D. He neglected England for the crusades and heavily taxed the people. John succeeded Richard ten years later. John lost most of the royal lands in France to the French king. He increased taxes and punished his enemies without giving them trials. The nobles became alarmed and demanded a guarantee of their rights. In 1215 A.D. they forced John to sign the Magna Charta, or "Great Charter."

The Magna Charta placed limits on royal power. A king could no longer collect taxes without the consent of the Great Council. A noble accused of a crime had the right to trial by his **peers,** or equals. If the king broke these promises, his subjects were free to rebel against him. Although the Magna Charta supported the feudal rights of nobles, it later came to be viewed as a step toward democracy. It brought to English government the idea that even a king was bound by the law.

Parliament   After John's death in 1216 A.D., his son became king. Henry III was a weak ruler and allowed the feudal lords to govern England. In 1264 A.D. Simon de Monfort, Henry's brother-in-law, called representatives of the knights and **burgesses,** or important townspeople, to sit in the Great Council. Shortly after this time, meetings of the Great Council became known as **parliaments.**

Henry's son Edward I became king in 1272 A.D. Edward wanted to bring all of Britain under his control. As a result, he devoted much of his reign to the conquest of Wales and Scotland, two lands that bordered England. However, Edward's greatest achievement was the advancement of representative government. In 1295 A.D. Edward called into session the Model Parliament, so called because it set up a system of representation for all classes. The Model Parliament became the example for all future English parliaments.

Following this first session, Parliament became a regular feature of English government. It was the final court of justice in the kingdom. It also advised the king on policy and helped him make laws. Parliament eventually forced the monarch to accept the rule that taxes could be levied only with its consent. By 1400 A.D. Parliament consisted of two separate groups: nobles and clergy met as the House of Lords, while knights and burgesses met as the House of Commons.

Discuss how the involvement of the papacy influenced the power struggle between the Holy Roman Emperor and his opponents.

Barbarossa is a Latin term meaning "red beard."

Holy Roman Empire

During the tenth and eleventh centuries, the Holy Roman Empire was the most powerful state in Europe. Holy Roman Emperors viewed themselves as heirs of Charlemagne and as leaders of Western Christianity. Until 1059 A.D. the emperors even controlled the election of popes. However, after the power struggle between Pope Gregory VII and Emperor Henry IV, the emperors' hold over the empire weakened. German nobles began to rule their domains like independent states. They insisted that the emperors be elected by them at a **diet,** or assembly. At the same time, the towns of northern Italy declared their independence from the feudal lords of the Holy Roman Empire.

In 1152 A.D., Fredrick Barbarossa, a member of the Hohenstaufen family, became Holy Roman Emperor. Frederick, also called Frederick I, took steps to restore the emperor's authority and the empire's unity. First, he forced the German nobles to swear allegiance to him and to work for his government. However, this step proved unsuccessful in restoring his authority. Instead, the nobles grew wealthy from their new government jobs, which further undermined the emperor's power.

Next, Frederick tried to reassert control over northern Italy. There, the communes, led by Milan, formed the Lombard League to oppose him. With the backing of Pope Alexander III, the communes defeated Frederick's armies at the Battle of Legnano in 1176 A.D. Frederick was forced to accept a peace that recognized the independence of the communes.

After Frederick's death in 1190 A.D., his son Henry VI was acknowledged as emperor by the German nobles. Henry married the heiress of the kingdom of Sicily. After he added Sicily to the empire, he spent all of his time in that country. When Henry died in 1197 A.D., his son Frederick II became Holy Roman Emperor.

Born and raised in Sicily, Frederick ignored Germany. He concentrated on building a Mediterranean empire that would extend from Sicily to northern Italy. When Frederick began conquests in Italy, Pope Innocent IV feared that the emperor would seize church lands near Rome. In 1245 A.D. the Pope called a church council that declared a crusade against Frederick. The Pope's attack gave German nobles the opportunity to further break away from the emperor's control. As a result, Germany became a loose confederation of territories under the rule of nobles. The nobles were free to accept or reject the emperor's policies.

In Sicily the Pope was eventually able to replace the Hohenstaufens with the Anjous, a family from France. This move was unpopular with the Sicilians. In 1298 A.D., with the aid of the Spanish, they drove out the Anjou ruler. As a result of the Pope's involvement in this secular concern, he lost much respect as the spiritual leader of western Europe.

1. Identify: Philip Augustus, Louis IX, Philip IV, Battle of Hastings, William I, *Domesday Book*, Henry I, Exchequer, Henry II, Magna Charta, Model Parliament, Frederick Barbarossa.
2. What methods did French kings use to increase their power?
3. How was justice carried out under English monarchs?
4. What problems did Holy Roman Emperors have in governing their empire?

Frederick Barbarossa wanted to restore the power and unity of the Holy Roman Empire. What steps did he take to accomplish this? Was he successful?

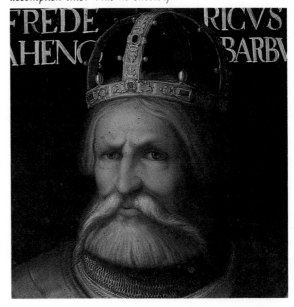

CHAPTER 7 REVIEW

Summary

1. Germanic invasions during the 400's A.D. led to the establishment of a number of kingdoms in western Europe.
2. During the early Middle Ages, Christianity became the dominant religion of Europe, and the Catholic Church gained widespread power and influence.
3. About 800 A.D. the Frankish ruler Charlemagne united most of western Europe into a Christian empire. After his death, the empire was divided into three separate kingdoms, two of which became France and Germany.
4. Magyar, Muslim, and Viking invasions from the 800's to the 900's A.D. brought disorder to western Europe. To stop the invaders and provide protection, a system known as feudalism developed. It divided western Europe into thousands of territories owned and governed by nobles.
5. Feudal society was divided into a hierarchy of social groups—clergy, nobles, and peasants and townspeople.
6. After the Muslim conquest of Palestine in the eleventh century, western Europeans began a series of unsuccessful holy wars called crusades. The crusades helped to break down western Europe's isolation from the Muslim and Byzantine worlds.
7. Increased trade during the 1000's and 1100's A.D. led to the rise of towns and a revival of learning. The power, wealth, and education of townspeople led to a weakening of the feudal system.
8. By 1300 A.D. strong central governments under monarchs were emerging in France and England. The Holy Roman Empire, however, was weakened by conflicts among its emperor, the Pope, and local groups in Germany and Italy.

Building Vocabulary

abbot	joust	cardinals	scholasticism
mayors of the palace	page	lay investiture	chansons de geste
papacy	squire	friars	romances
counts	chivalry	mendicants	troubadours
missi dominici	manors	orders	vernacular
feudalism	manorialism	burghers	bailiffs
fiefs	freeholders	guilds	common law
knights	serfs	masters	grand jury
vassal	mystery plays	journeymen	petty juries
homage	sacraments	apprentices	peers
aids	eucharist	communes	burgesses
incidents	mass	charters	parliaments
tournaments			diet

Reviewing the Main Ideas

1. Why was the Catholic Church important during the Middle Ages?
2. How did Charlemagne advance learning and the arts?

3. What factors led to the development of feudalism?
4. How were women regarded during medieval times?
5. Why did Pope Urban II call for the First Crusade?
6. How did the crusades affect the development of western Europe?
7. How was the economy of western Europe transformed during the later Middle Ages?
8. What was the purpose of guilds?
9. Why did conflict develop between burghers and feudal lords?
10. How were medieval universities established? What impact did they have on medieval society?
11. What forms of literature were popular in medieval Europe?
12. How did medieval monarchs improve government administration?

Discussing Important Ideas

1. Do you believe that Charlemagne deserved his title "the Great"?
2. Compare and contrast the life of a medieval knight with the life of a modern soldier.
3. Compare and contrast medieval European attitudes on marriage, family life, and the role of women with those of today.
4. Did feudalism bring stability or disorder to medieval Europe? Explain.
5. If you had been a peasant living in the Middle Ages, would you have tried to improve your position in life? Why or why not?
6. If you had been a German noble living in 1076 A.D., would you have supported Pope Gregory VII or King Henry IV? Explain.
7. Was the medieval church justified in using force to stop the spread of heresy? Why or why not?
8. Would medieval towns have grown without the spread of trade?
9. Compare and contrast guilds and modern labor unions.
10. What role did monarchs play in medieval Europe? What role do they play in modern European countries?

Using Maps

Refer to the map on page 170 to answer the following questions.
1. Which crusade routes covered both land and sea?
2. How many crusades reached Palestine?
3. Which crusade route avoided mountains entirely? Where did it begin and end?
4. At the time of the crusades, which continents included Islamic lands? Christian lands?
5. The knights of the First Crusade marched from Constantinople to Jerusalem. About how long was their route in miles? In kilometers?

CHAPTER **8**

West African Warriors

❝ *The people are seldom unjust . . . There is complete security in their country. Neither traveller, nor inhabitant in it, has anything to fear from robbers or people of violence.* ❞

Ibn Battuta, Moroccan traveler of the 1300's A.D.
describing the Mali Empire of West Africa

Africa and the Americas

During the ancient and medieval periods, the peoples of Africa and the Americas developed civilizations. However, until early modern times, these civilizations had little contact with the peoples of Europe and Asia. Then, about 1500 A.D., the long period of isolation ended. Increased communication and trade among the continents brought about an exchange of ideas and practices.

In spite of greater contacts, the early history of Africa and the Americas remained largely a mystery to outsiders. One problem was that these civilizations produced few written records of their accomplishments. What remained of their past was in the form of physical objects, such as buildings, pottery, and art work. In recent times, archeologists have uncovered and studied these remains. In addition, linguists have analyzed the languages of modern people in Africa and the Americas to determine the characteristics of the original languages spoken centuries ago. Other scientists have studied **oral traditions,** or legends and history passed by word of mouth from one generation to another. These scientific investigations have greatly increased humanity's understanding of what was once a neglected area of world history.

1 Early Africa

In ancient and medieval times, North Africa had close ties with the Mediterranean world.[1] However, the rest of Africa was isolated from outside contact. Foreigners knew very little about the interior of the continent. They held only half-truths about its inhabitants. In the 400's B.C., the Greek historian Herodotus described the heart of Africa as a place where

> the huge serpents were found [as well as] lions, bears, and horned donkeys. . . Here too are . . . the creatures without heads . . . and also the wild men and wild women and many other less fabulous beasts.*

Even as late as the early twentieth century, Europeans knew very little about African history and civilization. They referred to Africa as the "Dark Continent."

Environment

Geography contributed to Africa's isolation. As the world's second largest continent, Africa spans about 5,000 miles (8,000 kilometers) from north to south. It is almost 4,000 miles (6,400 kilometers) at its widest point from east to west. Within this large area exists a diversity of landscape. The interior of the continent consists of a plateau that drops off sharply at a narrow coastal plain. In Central Africa, the plateau has eroded to form lowlands covered by rain forests. West Africa, however, is largely made up of elevated dry grasslands called **savannas.** Many landscapes—mountain ranges, deep valleys, large lakes, and vast deserts—are found in East and South Africa.

Natural Barriers   Africa's physical landscape has imposed natural barriers that have made travel and communication difficult. One of these barriers is the Sahara Desert. About the size of the United States, the Sahara extends across North Africa from west to east. Before the

---

[1] North Africa was the center of two important ancient civilizations: Egypt and Carthage. Later the region became part of the Roman, Byzantine, and Islamic empires.

*The History of Herodotus, Volume I, Book 4, tr. by George Rawlinson, © 1910 by E. P. Dutton, Inc., p. 362.

Point out that various tropical diseases hindered European exploration of the African interior.

The kingdom of Kush developed in the area of present-day Sudan.

modern period, the Sahara hindered contacts between the Mediterranean world and the interior of Africa. Thus, the civilizations of North Africa developed differently from those in Sub-Saharan Africa, or the region of Africa south of the Sahara Desert.

Africa's coasts and rivers formed another barrier to travel and communication. The coastline of Africa has few bays and coves. Waves dash directly against the shore, making it difficult for ships to approach land. Africa has many rivers, but few are completely navigable. Because of many rapids and waterfalls, ships cannot use the rivers to reach inland areas.

Climate   The climate of Africa has also created problems. In the savanna region, seasons of heavy rainfall are often separated by long dry periods. This uneven rainfall often leads to famine. In the rain forest, swamps and dense vegetation provide obstacles to travel. These places are often inhabited by the tsetse fly and other disease-carrying insects. Before modern times, such unfavorable conditions discouraged outsiders from entering Africa. They also made the task of building civilizations difficult.

AFRICA

Beginnings

Some scientists believe that the earliest humans lived in Africa. Bones and stone tools have been found at many sites in East and South Africa. From these findings, many experts have concluded that Stone Age cultures spread from Africa to other continents.

About 4000 B.C. Africa's climate became drier. The Sahara, once a well-watered grassland, gradually became a desert. Many Saharan people moved east into the Nile Valley, where they settled in villages and became farmers. Their efforts contributed to the rise of Egypt, Africa's first major civilization. Other people traveled south into the interior of Africa. There, they established settlements and learned to farm. However, the Sub-Saharan people were too far from Egypt to benefit immediately from its cultural achievements.

Kush

The earliest African civilizations developed in the area of the continent east of the Sahara Desert. From 3000 to 500 B.C., Egypt was the dominant power in this region. Egyptian rule extended over Kush, a territory in the southern part of the Nile Valley. The Egyptians valued Kush for its gold, granite, and timber. By 1800 B.C. Kush had become an important trade center. The people of the region, known as Kushites, developed their own culture. About 1100 B.C. they broke away from Egypt and became an independent kingdom.

Napata   Kushite kings established a capital at Napata, which became a center of art, learning, and trade. They also formed a strong army and began wars of conquest. During the 700's B.C., the Kushites conquered all of Egypt. Kushite rulers became pharaohs, ruling both Egypt and Kush from the Egyptian city of Thebes.

For nearly 100 years, the Kushites brought peace and prosperity to northeastern Africa. Then in 671 B.C., the Assyrians, armed with iron weapons, invaded Egypt. The Kushites had bronze weapons and were easily defeated. They were forced to leave Egypt and return to Kush.

Point out that the city of Meroë was located southwest of the present city of Khartoum.

By 700 A.D. Arabs controlled the territory of the Axum people. Many converted to Islam.

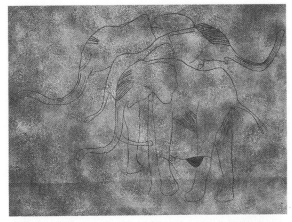

About 4,000 years ago people painted antelopes, lions, ostriches, and other animals on the walls of rock shelters in the Sahara. What do these drawings of elephants reveal about the environment at that time?

Meroë   After their defeat, the Kushites concentrated on strengthening their home territory. From the Assyrians, they learned the skill of making iron weapons and tools. Meroë, the new capital, became one of the earliest centers of iron production in Africa. From Meroë, iron production skills spread to other parts of Africa.

While centered at Meroë, the Kushite kingdom reached the height of its power. Between 250 B.C. and 100 A.D., Kushite merchants controlled trade routes from the Nile River to the Red Sea. They also conducted business throughout the Indian Ocean region. Meanwhile, Kushite warriors, armed with iron weapons, pushed the kingdom's borders farther south into East Africa. At home, Kushite farmers used iron tools to produce more food for a growing population.

Kushite Culture   The Kushite civilization at Meroë at first resembled that of Egypt. Kushite kings were regarded as divine. They built pyramids and monuments to glorify their power. On many of these buildings, messages were carved in a Kushite form of hieroglyphics. As in Egypt, wealthy women played important roles in social and political life.[2] Later, the Kushites mixed Egyptian traditions with Hellenistic and Roman ones.

---

[2] Succession to the Kushite throne may have come through the female side of the family.

Decline   Kush remained a powerful kingdom until the 300's A.D. However, as Kushite armies moved south into East Africa, they faced growing opposition. Axum, the most powerful state in the region was starting to expand. It began to challenge Kush's 1,000-year rule of northeastern Africa.

Axum

Axum's beginnings can be traced to the 600's B.C. During this period, Semitic peoples from Yemen, a region of southwestern Arabia, crossed the Red Sea and settled in northeastern Africa. They established trading settlements along the coast. In time, they mixed with the local population to form one group of people.

Trade and Christianity   Axum, one of the original trading settlements, emerged as a powerful kingdom during the 200's B.C. The kings of Axum controlled trade in the region of the Red Sea. Wealth from trade enabled them to build temples and palaces modeled on those of Hellenistic Egypt.

During the 300's A.D., Axum was strongly influenced by Roman culture and early Christianity. About 330 A.D. King Ezana made Christianity the official religion of the kingdom. A decade later, he defeated the Kushites and brought Yemen under Axum's influence. As a result of these developments, Axum became the dominant power of East Africa for nearly 400 years. During this period, it was able to control the major trade routes that linked Africa with Europe and Asia.

Ethiopia   During the 600's A.D., Axum was threatened by the rise of Islam. Within a century, Muslim soldiers and merchants from Arabia controlled the region of the Red Sea. Axum lost much of its coastal territory and was limited to the mountainous interior of East Africa. There, the rulers of Axum set up a Christian kingdom known as Ethiopia. Ethiopian monarchs worked to spread Christianity throughout Africa. However, they had little success. Civil war and Muslim expansion weakened their kingdom. As a result, Ethiopia remained isolated from world affairs until the nineteenth century.

The early Christians of Ethiopia carved out many churches in the sides of cliffs. These rock churches are still in use today. How did Christianity contribute to Ethiopia's isolation? What Ethiopian ruler promoted Christianity?

Sub-Saharan Africa

Beginning about 700 B.C., black peoples developed a variety of cultures in Sub-Saharan Africa. The earliest of these was the Nok. It was located in West Africa in what is now central Nigeria. The Nok culture flourished between the years 700 and 200 B.C.

Archeologists have unearthed **terra-cotta,** or baked clay, figurines at sites of the Nok culture. They have also uncovered tools, weapons, and jewelry made of iron and other metals. These finds show the importance of metal production in early Sub-Saharan society. Some historians believe that iron metalworking spread to Sub-Saharan Africa from Kush. Others, however, claim that iron production developed independently in the region.

Bantu Migrations   By 100 B.C. the use of iron in Sub-Saharan Africa had brought important cultural changes. With iron tools, farming had become more efficient. This led to greater food production and increased populations. In time, arable land became scarce, causing widespread food shortages. Hunger and starvation forced many black African groups to move from West Africa to less-populated central, eastern, and southern parts of the continent. These peoples were later called Bantu, after the languages that they spoke. The Bantu migrations continued over the next 1,000 years. Historians have considered these migrations to be one of the largest movements of people in world history.

Bantu-speaking peoples at first settled in the forests of Central Africa. There, they used their knowledge of farming and iron production to build stable societies. As the population increased, Bantu groups moved farther south and east. They settled in different areas and changed their economies to suit new conditions. In the highlands of East Africa, the mild climate was suitable for raising livestock. The Bantu who settled there became herders as well as farmers. Those who moved to East Africa's coastal plain grew new crops, such as bananas and yams.[3]

For the most part, the migrations were gradual and peaceful. As Bantu pushed into new areas, they met other black African groups. Some of these people joined the Bantu and adopted their way of life. Others, however, retreated into remote forests or deserts. As a result of their migrations, Bantu-speaking peoples became the dominant group in Sub-Saharan Africa.

Social Organization   Over the years, the Bantu became separate ethnic groups. Each ethnic group had its own territory, language, and way of life and was made up of hundreds of clans. Clans laid down detailed rules in areas such as marriage and family life. They also provided protection and security for their members. All the members of a clan considered themselves to be descendants from a common ancestor.

---

[3] These crops were brought to East Africa from Southeast Asia.

The religion of most Africans at this time can be called animism—the belief in spirits existing in nature.

The savanna region of West Africa is also known as the Sahel, a land that today is often arid.

Villages   The typical Bantu village was made up of several families. Bantu families were large and included all the descendants of one set of grandparents. Family members were expected to be loyal to the **elder,** or family leader, and to help one another. Men of the village farmed and herded, while women prepared food and managed households. In some Bantu groups, property was passed through female members; in others, it was passed through the male line.

The village was ruled by a chief and a council of elders. There was also a supreme clan chief. Supreme chiefs decided disputes, carried out punishments for crimes, and decided times for planting and harvesting crops. Many of them had a great deal of authority. But their powers were limited by local officials and by the customs of the clan. Supreme chiefs also had to seek advice from a council of elders selected from different clan families.

Religion   The Bantu practiced a variety of religions. Each ethnic group had its own beliefs and practices. But most African religions had certain common features. They used myths and proverbs to explain the past and to interpret the meaning of life. They recognized the existence of a supreme god and a number of lesser deities. Another widely held belief was that the spirits of dead ancestors lived among their descendants and guided daily affairs. Bantu worshipers offered prayers, songs, dances, and animal sacrifices to the deities and spirits. The purpose of these activities was to gain such things as good health and an abundant harvest. Women, as well as men, played an active role in many African religions.

1. Identify: Sahara, Sub-Saharan Africa, Kush, Napata, Meroë, Axum, Ezana, Ethiopia, Nok, Bantu.
2. Why did Africa remain unknown to outsiders until modern times?
3. What were the major contributions of Kush and Axum to African civilization?
4. How were Bantu peoples organized?

2   African Kingdoms and Empires

From 300 to 1800 A.D., a series of kingdoms arose in Sub-Saharan Africa. Three of the kingdoms—Ghana, Mali, and Songhai—were located in the savanna region of West Africa. They maintained close contacts with North Africa and the Middle East. As a result, these kingdoms were influenced by Islamic values.

This Bantu village seems to sprout from the landscape like natural growth. Since earliest times people of the savanna regions of Africa have built their dwellings with sunbaked earth and grass-thatched roofs. What type of government did Bantu villages have?

The modern-day country of Ghana takes its name from ancient Ghana. Point out that modern Ghana is a coastal nation, while ancient Ghana was landlocked.

Using the camel as the means of desert transport, nomadic Berbers were able to organize large-scale trading caravans that dealt in salt and gold. Quarried in the desert, salt was highly valued south of the Sahara. West African gold, in turn, flowed north to meet the increasing demands of the Mediterranean world. What other items of trade did caravans carry?

They also prospered from their control of important trade routes that ran from North Africa to the West African coast. Because of their location at the center of this trade, the three territories were known as the Middle Kingdoms.

Ghana

Ghana, the earliest of the three kingdoms, was founded in the 300's A.D. It was centered in an area near the Niger and Senegal Rivers. The people of Ghana at first made their living from farming, fishing, metalworking, and cloth production. Later, trade became their most profitable activity. Forested areas to the south of the kingdom were rich in gold. Ghanian traders carried the gold to trading centers at the edge of the Sahara Desert. There, they made business deals with Arab merchants from North Africa. Gold was exchanged for such items as salt, dried fruits, and tools.

Kings Ghana's name came from the title of its ruler, the *ghana,* or king. The position of king was hereditary and was held only by males. When a king died, the throne was not passed to his own son, but to the son of his oldest sister. Ghanian kings at first claimed to be divine. Later, when they converted to Islam, they gave up this claim. Ghanian kings, however, remained powerful figures.

Ghana was known for its wealth. Its rulers taxed the salt and gold trade to obtain revenue. They also claimed ownership of all the gold found in Ghana. To maintain the high price of gold, they allowed only a limited amount on the market at a given time. Ghanian kings displayed their wealth in public and were surrounded by elaborate ceremony. They held daily audiences to meet their subjects and to resolve disputes.

Empire Between the 800's and 900's A.D., Ghana reached the height of its power. Ghanian armies, equipped with iron weapons, conquered a large empire that stretched from the Atlantic Ocean to the Niger River. During this time, Arab influence was strong, and many Ghanians converted to Islam. Meanwhile, contact was made for the first time with the Christian world. European rulers imported Ghanian gold for the minting of coins. To promote trade, they welcomed Ghanian representatives.

At the end of the 1000's A.D., Ghana's empire declined. The Berbers, a people from North Africa, attacked Ghanian trade centers. Their raids weakened the empire's economy. Changes in climate also contributed to Ghana's downfall. Rainfall decreased, and crops failed. Many Ghanians were forced to migrate to new areas. By the end of the 1200's A.D., Ghana had separated into a number of small independent states.

Ancient Mali is also known as Malinké.

Mali

One of the small states that replaced Ghana was ruled by a people known as the Mandingo. In 1235 A.D. the Mandingo ruler Sundiata Keita defeated his leading rival and began to conquer the surrounding territories. As a result of these victories, the Mandingo state became the dominant power in West Africa. It became known as Mali, meaning "where the king resides." Mali territory spanned from the Atlantic Ocean to what is now Nigeria.

During the fourteenth century, Mali enjoyed a period of peace and prosperity. Merchants traded gold, iron, and copper. Farmers harvested rice, yams, and beans. Artisans produced wooden figures, metal objects, and cloth. By taxing all goods leaving and entering their territory, Mali's rulers became wealthy.

Mansa Musa, who ruled from 1312 to 1337 A.D., is considered Mali's greatest ruler. During Musa's reign, Timbuktu, the Mali capital, became an important center of Muslim art and learning. Throughout Africa, Asia, and Europe, Musa was known for his wealth. In 1324 A.D. he made a pilgrimage to Mecca. Accounts state that he took with him 12,000 slaves and 80 camels, all carrying gold bars. Along the way, Musa gave away so much gold that he brought down the metal's market price.

About 50 years after Musa's death, Mali began to weaken. Berbers attacked from the north, while rebellions broke out within the empire. Many provinces separated from the central government and became independent states.

Songhai

One of the rebellious provinces in the Mali Empire was Songhai. It was located in the Niger River Valley west of Timbuktu. The Songhai people were skilled traders. They profited from trade between North African Arabs and West African blacks who lived along the Atlantic coast.

Because metalworking required considerable skill and knowledge, these West African blacksmiths had special status among their people. Trade in metal led to an increased food supply and wealth for villagers. What metals were in demand by merchants trading in Africa?

The western African kingdoms gained power and wealth through the control of the Saharan gold and salt trade. Such cities as Timbuktu and Gao became busy commercial centers.

AFRICAN CIVILIZATIONS

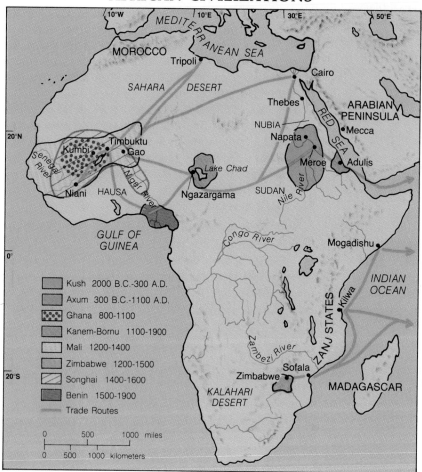

During the late fifteenth century, the Songhai ruler Sunni Ali made Songhai the most important kingdom in West Africa. He fought many wars and expanded Songhai's borders to include most of the savanna region. To effectively control the empire, he set up a central government at Gao.

The Songhai Empire reached its height under Mohammed Askia, who ruled from 1493 to 1528 A.D. As Mohammed Askia conquered more lands, he gained control of the sources of gold and salt. He placed taxes on these products and brought much wealth into the government treasury. Askia also supported learning and restored the cultural splendor of Timbuktu. A devout Muslim, Askia promoted the spread of

Islam. He built mosques and based all the empire's laws on the Koran.

In 1528 A.D. Mohammed Askia was overthrown by his son. A period of disorder followed that led to the empire's decline. Meanwhile, the ruler of Morocco sent his army into Songhai. The Moroccan armies used firearms and cannons. They easily defeated the Songhai forces, who fought with swords, spears, and bows and arrows. Meanwhile, conquered peoples within the Songhai Empire overthrew their rulers. By 1600 A.D. the Songhai Empire no longer existed.

East and South Africa

East Africa also became an important center of civilization. About 900 A.D. Arab and Persian

HISTORY AND CITIES

Timbuktu

From the 1200's to the 1500's A.D., Timbuktu was the most important city in the savanna region of West Africa. It was situated near the southern edge of the Sahara Desert a few miles north of the Niger River. Timbuktu's location was ideal for communications and trade.

Timbuktu was founded about 1100 A.D. At first, it was a camp used by nomads while they pastured their animals. Gradually, the camp's plentiful water supply attracted traders and other travelers passing through the Sahara. Some of these people settled permanently at the site. They farmed the land and eventually established a town.

In the late 1200's A.D., Timbuktu became a part of the Mali Empire. Under Mali rule, the city became a prosperous commercial center. Traders from North Africa gathered there to barter salt, cloth, and horses for gold and slaves. Timbuktu's merchants and artisans grew wealthy from this trade. Meanwhile, the city became a center of government. In 1325 A.D. the Mali ruler Mansa Musa settled in Timbuktu and sponsored many building projects. He had architects construct the large Sankore mosque and a royal palace.

In 1468 A.D., Sunni Ali, the ruler of the Songhai Empire, conquered Timbuktu. Under his successor Mohammed Askia, the city reached the height of its splendor. With the financial support of Ali, the Sankore mosque became a leading center of Islamic studies.

Under Songhai rule, Timbuktu made its first contacts with western Europe. The city became the terminus, or end point, of trade routes that stretched over desert and sea from ports in Italy and Spain. In 1550 A.D., Leo Africanus, a Spanish Muslim writer, passed on to western Europeans the first eyewitness account of Timbuktu.

In the late sixteenth century, Timbuktu began a long period of decline. In 1591 A.D. Moroccan armies overthrew the Songhai Empire and captured Timbuktu. They made the city a part of their kingdom. To end opposition to their rule, Moroccan officials persecuted Timbuktu's scholars and drove them out of the city. Political unrest eventually led to a decline in the city's trade. As a result, Timbuktu became isolated from major centers of civilization.

In the seventeenth century, a series of Berber invasions further weakened Timbuktu. The once-prosperous city became a victim of famine and epidemics. Its population fell from about 50,000 at the beginning of the century to below 10,000 by its end. During the nineteenth and the first half of the twentieth centuries, the French controlled Timbuktu. But the arrival of European civilization had little impact on the city.

In 1960 foreign rule of Timbuktu ended and the city became part of the new African nation of Mali. However, freedom has not brought back Timbuktu's former glory. It remains a small town that time has seemed to pass by. Only a few mosques and monuments bear witness to the city's brilliant past.

1. How did Timbuktu's location influence its economic development?
2. What factors led to Timbuktu's decline?

The Great Zimbabwe was built in the 1300's A.D. when the gold and ivory trade with Arab merchants was at its peak.

In command of the chief routes between the gold mines and the sea, Karanga grew wealthy from trade with the East. These ruins in southeastern Africa still show some of the grandeur of the Great Zimbabwe at the peak of the gold trade. Built of granite slabs fitted without mortar, this sacred stone structure was enclosed by a wall 16½ feet (5 meters) thick and 36 feet (10.8 meters) high. What were the causes of Karanga's decline?

merchants began to settle along the coast of the Indian Ocean. There, they came into contact with traders from the interior of Africa. These traders began sending gold, iron, and other products to the coast. The Arab and Persian merchants then exported these goods to Arabia, India, and the Far East. In return, they received porcelain, pottery, and silk cloth.

By 1200 A.D. the small East African trading settlements had become thriving city-states. The most important was Kilwa, a port for the shipment of gold. Kilwa's wealth from the gold trade was used to build mosques, fortresses, and merchants' homes.

Islam strongly influenced the development of coastal East Africa. Arab and Persian merchants preached Islam and won many converts among black Africans. Many merchants married local women who had converted to the faith. As a result, the coastal city-states developed a civilization that blended Islamic and black African traditions. For example, East Africans began speaking Swahili, a language that was basically Bantu, but contained many Arabic and Persian words.[4] Islamic East Africa reached the height of its prosperity during the fourteenth century.

About 200 years later, it began to decline with the coming of Europeans to the Indian Ocean region.

The Indian Ocean trade contributed to the rise of Bantu kingdoms in Central and South Africa. These kingdoms were rich in mineral resources, such as copper and gold. During the tenth century, they began sending these minerals to the East African coast.

The most famous of the Bantu kingdoms was Karanga. Between the eleventh and fifteenth centuries, the people of Karanga built nearly 300 stone-walled fortresses throughout their territory. The largest was called the Great Zimbabwe. It was the political and religious center of the kingdom.

During the sixteenth century, Bantu states in South Africa and other parts of the continent began to lose their power. Civil wars brought internal disorder and ruined local economies. At the same time, the arrival of Europeans threatened the survival of African civilizations.

1. Identify: Mandingo, Sundiata Keita, Mansa Musa, Timbuktu, Sunni Ali, Mohammed Askia, Kilwa, Swahili, Karanga.
2. Why were Ghana, Mali, and Songhai known as the Middle Kingdoms?
3. How did Islam influence the development of African civilizations?
4. Why did East African city-states prosper?

---

[4] Swahili is still the language of several East African countries.

The early Americans were first called "Indians" by Christopher Columbus. He believed that the lands he explored in 1492 were part of Asia.

Some animals that early Americans hunted are now extinct. Mammoth, musk ox, and long-horned bison.

3 The Early Americas

The world's longest landmass stretching from north to south is the Americas. It consists of two major continents: North America and South America. The narrow southern part of North America is sometimes considered a separate region known as Central America. Within the Americas are found many different physical features. Mountains, plateaus, deserts, forests, plains, and rivers mark the vastness of these two continents.

For a long time, the Americas were isolated from other regions of the world. The Atlantic and Pacific Oceans separated this landmass from other continents. As a result, the Americas were among the last areas of the earth to be settled. People arrived in the Americas long after human cultures first emerged in the Middle East, Africa, and Asia.

The earliest inhabitants of the Americas were Asians. Their descendants came to be known as American Indians, or Native Americans. Over thousands of years, the American Indians developed a variety of cultures and civilizations throughout the region. However, there were no lasting contacts between the American Indians and peoples in other parts of the world until the arrival of Europeans in the Americas around the year 1500 A.D.

Migrations

About 1 million years ago during the ice age, huge glaciers covered the northern regions of the Americas. At that time, many areas that are now under water were dry land. One such area was a narrow land bridge that joined Siberia, the easternmost part of Asia, with Alaska, the westernmost part of the Americas.

About 20,000 to 30,000 years ago, the ancestors of the American Indians began crossing the land bridge from Asia to the Americas. Over the next several hundred years, small bands of them, a few at a time, made the journey. No one knows why they came. However, many historians believe that the earliest Americans were hunters who entered the Americas in pursuit of animal herds.

About 10,000 years later the earth's climate turned warmer and drier. Slowly, water from the melting glaciers raised the level of the oceans. The land bridge joining Asia and the Americas became covered with water. Today this body of water is known as the Bering Strait. It separates Asia and North America by about 50 miles (80 kilometers). With the formation of the Bering Strait, Asian migrations to the Americas came to an end.

Meanwhile, the descendants of the original migrants spread over wide areas. From North America they moved into Central America. By 10,000 B.C. they had reached the southern tip of South America. As they moved from place to place, the Indians of the Americas gathered wild plants and hunted game. They used simple weapons, mainly wooden spears with sharp stone points. Eventually, thousands of separate tribes were formed. Each tribe spoke a different language and followed its own way of life.

About 5000 B.C. changes took place in the ways that American Indians lived. In Mexico, a region north of Central America, food gatherers began growing **maize,** or corn. Gradually the quality of maize improved, and it became the chief source of food. Mexican Indians also raised other crops, like beans, squash, pumpkins, cotton, and sweet potatoes. With a better food supply, they settled permanently in villages and developed arts and crafts. From Mexico, farming and village life spread to Indians living in other parts of the Americas.

North America

Historians believe that about 20 million Indians lived in the Americas around 1500 A.D. Some 1 million of these were in North America. Much of what is known about early North American Indian tribes comes from the work of archeologists. Many archeological teams have uncovered homes, burial mounds, and ceremonial centers containing pottery, stone tools, and the bones of people and animals. Through the study of these and other remains, experts have learned much about North American Indians. Tribes that live in the same region and have similar cultures may be said to belong to a **culture area.** The six

Refer students to the map on p. 199 to locate the major culture areas of North America.

Pueblo is the Spanish word for "village" or "town." The term applies to a group of American Indians as well as their village and their multistoried communal home.

major culture areas of North America are the Arctic and Far North, the Northwest, the California-Great Basin, the Southwest, the Eastern Woodlands, and the Great Plains.

Arctic and Far North   The Indians of the Arctic and Far North lived in the cold northern regions of what is now Canada and Alaska. They consisted of small bands that handled their own affairs without official leaders. The severe climate in the Arctic and Far North was too cold for raising crops. So Indian bands moved about hunting, fishing, and gathering wild plants. Most tools and utensils were made of stone, wood, and animal bones. Clothing was prepared from animal skins and furs.

Northwest   The Indians of the Northwest lived along the Pacific Ocean from southern Alaska to northern California. Their region had a mild climate, thick forests, and rich natural resources. Fish, game, and wild plants were

An Inuit seeks shelter in his qaqmaq, a dwelling with walls of ice roofed with hides. Qaqmaqs were used when it was too cold to live in a hide tent, and too warm to build an igloo. Why did Arctic Indians become nomads?

especially abundant. Tribes settled in villages and were ranked on the basis of wealth and prestige. Wealth was measured in terms of canoes, blankets, sheets of copper and other goods. At a special feast called a **potlatch,** a host's wealth was displayed and distributed to guests. The Indians of the Northwest were skilled wood-carvers. They became known for their **totem poles,** or wooden carvings of people, animals, and mythical beings that represented tribal history and values.

California-Great Basin   The Indians of the California-Great Basin region lived between the Pacific coast and the Rocky Mountains. Those along the coast settled in small villages. They enjoyed a mild climate and an abundance of food, mainly berries, nuts, and fish. Farther inland, the Indians lived in a desert environment. They moved about in small bands, gathering scarce food. Their diet usually consisted of seeds, roots, grasses, rodents, snakes, and insects. The California-Great Basin Indians wove baskets in which they gathered, stored, and prepared food. Many of these baskets were decorated with elaborate designs.

Southwest   The Indians of the Southwest made their home in the rocky desert region that is now Arizona, New Mexico, southern Colorado and Utah, and northern Mexico. Divided into various tribes, they had one of the most advanced cultures north of central Mexico.

One group of Southwest tribes was known as the Pueblo Indians. As farmers, Pueblo people developed irrigation systems and raised crops of maize, beans, and squash. Pueblo artisans made pottery and cloth. Religion was very important to the Pueblo people. They held many elaborate ceremonies in which they prayed for rain.

Each Pueblo village was made up of farmland and a multistoried building that housed the families of the village. The building was made of stone or **adobe,** a sun-dried brick. Sometimes, villages were built under ledges on the sides of cliffs. There, the people could more easily defend themselves against attack.

Other Southwestern Indian groups, such as the Apache and the Navajo, were nomadic hunters and gatherers. They sometimes raided

After the Spanish explorers introduced sheep into the Southwest in the middle 1500's A.D., many Navajo people adopted shepherding as a major economic activity.

A great mound at Cahokia, Illinois, had a base larger than that of Egypt's Great Pyramid.

The Pueblo Indians made beautiful pottery such as this food bowl found in a prehistoric village site in eastern Arizona. What other contributions did Pueblo Indians make to North American Indian culture?

Pueblo communities for food and supplies. Later, many Apache and Navajo groups learned farming and settled in villages. Others, however, did not develop permanent settlements. They continued to depend on food gathering, hunting, and raiding.

Great Plains The Indians of the Great Plains inhabited vast grasslands that stretched from the Rocky Mountains to the Mississippi River. The hard soil of the Great Plains was difficult to farm. So most tribes lived in villages along streams where the soft earth could be easily cultivated. They raised crops of corn, beans, and squash. They also built earth lodges, log-framed homes covered with brush and dirt.

Plains Indians were skilled warrior-hunters who placed a high value on deeds of bravery. In summer, they left their villages to hunt the vast buffalo herds on the Plains. In the fall, the Indians ended the hunt and returned to their villages. They carried the slain buffalo on **travois,** a net or platform attached to two poles and usually pulled by dogs. Upon their return, the Indians harvested the crops and prepared the buffalo. They ate buffalo meat and used buffalo skin for clothing. Buffalo hide covered the wood frames of tepees, the cone-shaped tents used during the hunting season.

Eastern Woodlands The Eastern Woodlands stretched from the Mississippi River east to

the Atlantic coast and from Canada south to the Gulf of Mexico. This region had many forests, lakes, and hills. Winters were cold in the northern part and mild in the southern region. Summers were warm throughout the Eastern Woodlands. The Indians of the area grew crops, such as corn, squash, beans, and tobacco. They hunted in the forests and fished in the streams.

In the Ohio and Mississippi River Valleys, groups of Indians called Mound Builders erected large earthen mounds. Some mounds were used as tombs for leaders. Others served as large bases for ceremonial structures. A number of mounds were made in the shapes of animals. Finely crafted objects, such as shell and copper jewelry and stone pipes and ornaments, have been found in mounds.

Indians living in the northeastern part of North America had a high level of political organization. Around 1400 A.D. five tribes—the Cayuga, Mohawk, Oneida, Onondaga, and Seneca—formed the League of the Iroquois. The purpose of the League was to maintain peace among the tribes. Each of the five tribes sent representatives to a council that discussed and resolved problems affecting league members. Council decisions were binding in matters of war and peace. The League of the Iroquois lasted

In a long severe winter, food from the summer hunt would sometimes not last until spring. A winter hunt was hard and dangerous. What do you think the Plains Indians invented to help them in the snow?

Among the factors common to highly developed civilizations are written language, a system of chronology, a well-organized government, and a division of labor. Have students consider each of these for the most advanced civilizations in the Americas.

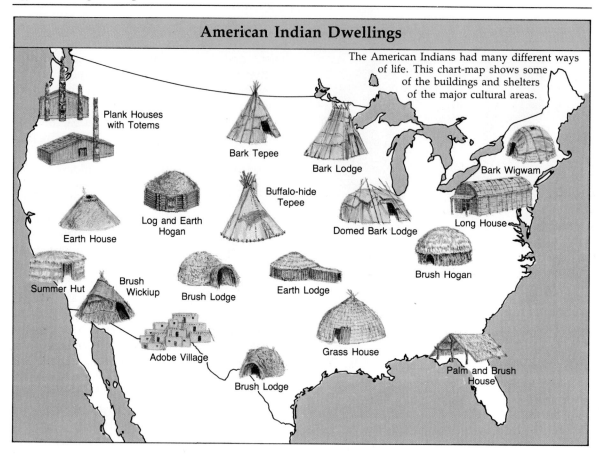

American Indian Dwellings

The American Indians had many different ways of life. This chart-map shows some of the buildings and shelters of the major cultural areas.

Plank Houses with Totems

Bark Tepee

Bark Lodge

Bark Wigwam

Long House

Buffalo-hide Tepee

Log and Earth Hogan

Domed Bark Lodge

Earth House

Brush Hogan

Summer Hut

Brush Wickiup

Brush Lodge

Earth Lodge

Adobe Village

Grass House

Brush Lodge

Palm and Brush House

several hundred years. Through conquest or voluntary agreement, several other tribes in the northeast were brought into the League.

1. Identify: Native Americans, Bering Strait, Pueblo Indians, Apache, Navajo, Mound Builders, League of the Iroquois.
2. How did geography affect the rise of civilization in the Americas?
3. What important changes took place in Mexico around 5000 B.C.?
4. What Indian culture areas have been identified in North America? How did they differ from each other?

4 American Indian Empires

The most advanced American Indian civilizations developed in Mexico, Central America, and South America. In these regions, farmers at an early period produced food surpluses that supported large populations. People built large cities and devoted time to government, religion, and the arts. They also raised armies and established empires. The achievements of the American Indian empires rivaled those of early Asia, Africa, and Europe. They contributed to the growth of later civilizations.

Olmecs

From 1200 B.C. to 1500 A.D., a series of Indian civilizations flourished in Mexico. The earliest of these civilizations was the Olmec. It reached its height during the 800's B.C. The Olmecs were probably ruled by priests. They worshiped a chief god in the form of a jaguar, an animal related to the leopard. Olmec achievements included a counting system and a calendar, both of which were passed on to later Indian civilizations in Mexico.

Have students compare those things that were important to the Maya with those things generally considered important in American society.

Most of what is known about the Olmecs comes from an important archeological discovery. In the 1930's archeologists uncovered the ruins of an Olmec ceremonial center at La Venta near the Gulf of Mexico. The site contained a large stone pyramid and several earthen burial mounds. Four huge heads carved from stone—the largest about 8 feet (2.4 meters) tall—have been found at La Venta. At the site, archeologists have also found pieces of pottery and jade carvings.

Maya

Between 300 and 900 A.D., a civilization known as the Maya flourished in southern Mexico and northern Central America. Influenced by the Olmecs, the Maya built cities consisting of temple-pyramids, houses, terraces, and courts. The largest city was Tikal. It had six temple-pyramids, one of which was 229 feet (69 meters) high. The Tikal population has been estimated between 50,000 and 100,000 persons.

Each Mayan city and its surrounding area formed an independent city-state. Groups of priests and nobles ruled the Mayan city-states. Under these rulers were farmers, merchants, and artisans. Laborers and slaves made up the lowest social group.

Religion and the Arts   Religion was at the center of Mayan life. Festivals were held in honor of particular gods and goddesses. The Maya prayed for plentiful harvests and offered animal sacrifices. Sometimes, in periods of crisis they would sacrifice humans, usually prisoners of war, to their deities. Following prayers and sacrifices, there would be dancing, feasts, and games. One popular activity was a sacred game that resembled basketball. In this game, players tried to hit a rubber ball through a stone ring with their elbows or hips.

The Maya excelled in arts and crafts. Artists decorated the walls of buildings with brightly colored murals of daily life. Sculptors made figurines of humans from stone and clay. The Mayan people also produced elaborately designed pottery.

Economy   The Mayan economy was based on agriculture and trade. Farmers lived in small villages near the cities. They raised crops, such as corn, beans, and squash, and sold their produce at city markets. Mayan merchants set up extensive trade routes throughout Mexico and Central America. They bartered salt, jade, cotton cloth, animal skins, and the feathers of tropical birds. Wheeled vehicles and beasts of burden, such as horses and oxen, were unknown. So goods had to be carried on the backs of laborers or transported on rivers in canoes.

Sciences   The Maya were skilled in mathematics and astronomy. They used a number system based on the number 20. Dots and dashes represented numbers, and a symbol was developed for the concept of zero. From the tops of temple-pyramids, Mayan astronomers observed the movements of heavenly bodies and accurately predicted eclipses. Much of their information was for religious purposes, such as the scheduling of important ceremonies. Mayan astronomers also developed a calendar of slightly more than 365 days, based on the orbit of the earth around the sun. This calendar was more accurate than those used in other civilizations at the time.

Writing   The Maya were one of the first peoples in the Americas to develop a writing system. They used symbols that represented both ideas and sounds. Linguists have not yet deciphered the Mayan language, although meanings for many symbols are now known. Maya wrote inscriptions on buildings and large stone monuments. They carved dates and events on large calendar stones. They also recorded information on astronomy and religious ceremonies in books and manuscripts.

Decline   About 800 A.D. the Mayan civilization began to decline. The Maya stopped building, abandoned many of their cities, and moved to other areas. Scholars do not know the reason for this collapse. Some believe that it may have been caused by factors such as epidemics, drought, famine, and outside invasions. Others claim that Mayan farmers revolted against their rulers and brought about the fall of Mayan civilization.

Discuss why the environment of Central America was suitable for advanced societies.

Toltecs

During the period of the Maya, advanced civilizations also developed in central Mexico. The earliest of these was centered in the city of Teotihuacán. At its height in the 600's A.D., the Teotihuacán civilization influenced the Maya and other Indian peoples. The city itself had nearly 100,000 people. In its center were two large pyramids—the Pyramid of the Sun and the Pyramid of the Moon. These large structures were ceremonial centers, where priests performed animal and human sacrifices to the gods. Made of adobe and stone, the pyramids outlasted the civilization of their builders and still stand today.

About 800 A.D. people called Toltecs gained control of central Mexico. The Toltecs were skilled warriors. Their powerful army conquered territory as far south as the Yucatán Peninsula, where some of the Maya lived. A Toltec empire was established with its capital at Tula.

The massive Toltec pyramids at Tula, and this one at Chichen Itza, belong to an architectural style established much earlier by the Mayas. What was the importance of pyramids to the Toltecs?

The Toltecs expanded trade and mining. They became the first group in the Americas to use gold and silver. In spite of Toltec military and economic strength, by 1200 A.D. internal feuding, disease, and outside invasions had ended the Toltec Empire.

Aztecs

During the final century of Toltec rule, an Indian people called the Aztecs moved from northern Mexico into central Mexico. The Aztecs were probably hunters and gatherers in search of game and better land. To protect themselves, they became skilled warriors and enlarged their territory.

Tenochtitlán   In 1325 A.D. the Aztecs founded a city in central Mexico called Tenochtitlán. They later developed a legend to explain the origins of the city. According to the legend, Aztec priests told their people to settle in the area where they would find an eagle sitting on a cactus and holding a serpent in its beak. After much wandering, the Aztecs finally saw on an island in Lake Texcoco what the priests had described. There, they established Tenochtitlán.

Tenochtitlán's island location made it a unique city. Tenochtitlán was crisscrossed by canals, and raised earthen roads linked the city to the mainland. The people of Tenochtitlán planted corn, pumpkins, beans, tomatoes, and peppers on nearby artificial islands called **chinampas.** These islands were formed by digging up mud from the bottom of Lake Texcoco.

Aztec Empire   By the late fourteenth century, the Aztecs had developed a powerful army. They conquered all of central and southern Mexico. They forced the conquered peoples to pay tribute in the form of gold, silver, jade, and bird feathers. With this wealth, Tenochtitlán became a magnificent city with temple-pyramids, palaces, and market places. By 1500 A.D. the city's population is believed to have reached more than 100,000.

The Aztecs borrowed ideas and practices from those they conquered. The Aztecs learned to use metal, make pottery, and weave cloth. They also adopted the Mayan calendar and number system. At the same time, the Aztecs developed

Use the map below to review the various people who lived in the Americas in the Middle Ages.

INDIANS OF THE AMERICAS

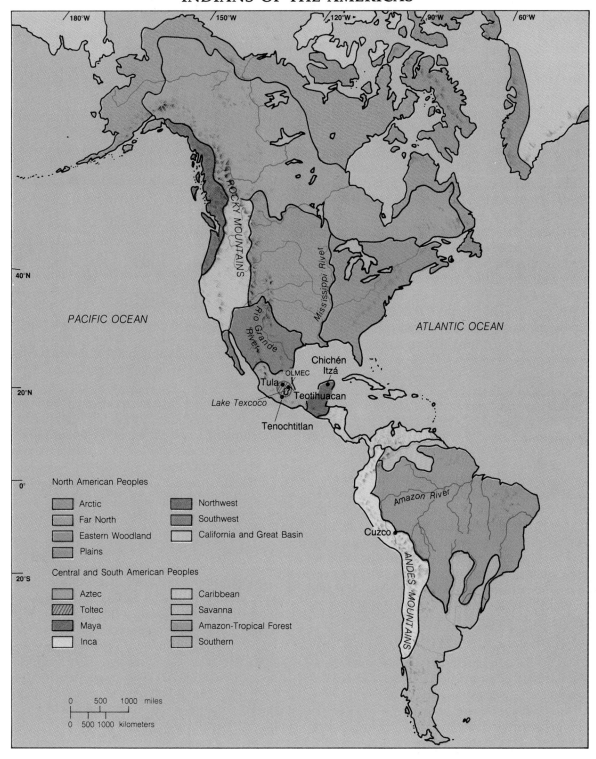

180°W   150°W   120°W   90°W   60°W

ROCKY MOUNTAINS

Mississippi River

40°N

PACIFIC OCEAN

Rio Grande River

ATLANTIC OCEAN

Chichén Itzá

OLMEC

Tula

20°N

Teotihuacan

Lake Texcoco

Tenochtitlan

0°

Amazon River

Cuzco

ANDES MOUNTAINS

20°S

North American Peoples

- Arctic
- Far North
- Eastern Woodland
- Plains
- Northwest
- Southwest
- California and Great Basin

Central and South American Peoples

- Aztec
- Toltec
- Maya
- Inca
- Caribbean
- Savanna
- Amazon-Tropical Forest
- Southern

0   500   1000   miles

0   500 1000   kilometers

their own skills. Farmers cut terraces into the hills to obtain more farmland. They also dug irrigation systems to water their crops. Merchants developed trading skills and sold their wares throughout the empire. They used shells, cacao beans, animal skins, and woven cloth as money. Goods were transported by human labor or by canoe, since wheeled vehicles and beasts of burden were unknown.

Government and Society

The Aztecs developed a complex political system. Their empire was a collection of territories ruled by an emperor. The most important Aztec emperor was Montezuma I. He governed during the early and mid-1400's A.D. and was known for his conquests. Aztec emperors had great power, but they had to consult a council of nobles before making important decisions. Under the emperor were military chiefs, who served as governors in local areas.

The royal family, nobles, military chiefs, and priests formed the most powerful group in Aztec society. Next in importance were farmers, merchants, and warriors. These groups made up the majority of the population. Slaves—mostly prisoners of war, criminals, and debtors—were the lowest social group. They worked the land and were considered the property of their owners.

Religion

Religion was an important part of Aztec life. The Aztecs worshiped many gods and goddesses, who represented the forces of nature. One group of deities was associated with farming. The other group symbolized war and empire. The Aztecs held many religious ceremonies to win the favor of their deities and to guarantee good harvests. To satisfy the war gods, human sacrifices were performed. In many cases, the Aztecs fought wars largely to obtain prisoners to sacrifice to their deities.

Arts

The Aztecs were skilled in the arts. They used stone sculpture to decorate temples, palaces, and other public buildings. One of the best known Aztec works is the Sun Stone, a large circular calendar stone. It shows the head of the sun god surrounded by symbols that represent the days of the Aztec month.

Aztec writing consisted of small picture symbols. Some pictures represented ideas, while others stood for sounds. The Aztecs produced various forms of literature, such as poetry and legendary accounts of their history.

Decline

In the late fifteenth century, the Aztec Empire was at the height of its power. However, it faced many difficult problems. Conquered peoples grew restless under Aztec rule and began to rebel. The Aztecs had to fight repeatedly to maintain their control. In the early sixteenth century, another serious threat to the Aztec Empire came with the arrival of Europeans in the Americas.

Inca

From 100 to 1500 A.D., a series of Indian civilizations arose in the valleys of South America's Andes Mountains. More Indians lived in the Andes than in any other region of the Americas. Mostly farmers, they expanded food production, developed trade, and built cities. They also formed strong central governments and empires. The most famous of these civilizations was the Inca, which was centered in what is now southern Peru.

Inca Rulers

The name *Inca* means "children of the sun." Originally it was the title given to the Inca emperor and his family.[5] According to legend, the emperor was a descendant of the sun god. The first great Inca emperor was Pachacuti. About 1440 A.D. he carried out the first conquests that led to the rise of the Inca Empire. As a monument to his power, Pachacuti made Cuzco, the Inca capital, into a magnificent city.

Expansion

Under Pachacuti's successors, Inca armies continued their conquests. By the early sixteenth century, they had established the largest empire in the Americas. Inca territory extended more than 2,500 miles (4,000 kilometers) along the western coast of South America. The Inca Empire included parts of the modern nations of Colombia, Ecuador, Peru, Bolivia, Chile, and Argentina. The population .of the empire numbered between 4 and 7 million persons.

---

[5] Later, "Inca" was used to describe all of the peoples under the authority of the Inca ruler.

The government of the Incas kept a census of people in each part of the empire. Raise the question of why it is important to keep track of the number of people in a country.

Note the differences in the way the Incas and Aztecs treated people from outside the empire.

Government   The Inca emperor enjoyed supreme power. All land and property legally belonged to him, and every person owed him absolute obedience. Inca rulers used their authority to promote the unity of the empire and its people. They ruled their vast lands through an organized and efficient central government. Nobles were appointed to administer many of the provinces. However, in certain conquered areas, local rulers were left in charge of their own people.

Conquered peoples were allowed a limited degree of freedom if they avoided rebellion and paid their taxes. Those suspected of disloyalty were moved out of their villages. Inca authorities forced them to resettle in new areas among loyal subjects. In time, disatisfaction ended, and most of the conquered peoples accepted Inca rule. Some of them learned Quechua, the Inca language, and adopted many Inca customs and traditions.

Inca Life   The Inca emperor and his officials closely regulated the lives of the people. They assigned citizens to perform certain duties. Men often had to work on government building projects, and women wove cloth that was collected by government officials. Farmers were required to give a portion of their crops to the government.

Grain and other nonperishable produce were kept in government storehouses. In times of drought and famine, the emperor would send these supplies to affected areas. The Inca government controlled trade in metals, jewels, and other scarce items. It decreed that cloth was to be used as money.

Inca cities served as both military fortresses and centers of government. Apart from government officials, most of the people lived in villages located in the valleys or on the steep slopes of the Andes Mountains. The Inca were talented farmers. They made good use of the limited arable land. To grow more food, farmers cut terraces into the sides of mountains. In the dry coastal plain, irrigation systems were used to increase crop yields. Like other Indian civilizations, Inca farmers did not use wheeled vehicles or large work animals. They used human labor.

The Inca were also skilled builders. They erected large temples and fortresses made of stone. Inca engineers developed a paved network of roads that joined the various parts of the empire. Suspension bridges were built to cross rivers and canyons. Merchants used llamas and other small pack animals to carry goods over the roads and bridges. Government messengers traveled the roads, relaying news between Cuzco and other cities.

Andean Indians fish in the waters of Lake Titicaca in boats made from bound totora reed. Early Inca mariners used similar boats to fish the Pacific Ocean. Today only villagers around Lake Titicaca and along Peru's northern coast continue to use such craft. Inca people relied heavily on the fish for food. In what ways did Inca farmers increase the food supply?

The Inca never developed a system of writing. They kept business records by using **quipu,** a rope with knotted cords of different lengths and colors. Each knot and color represented a different item or number.

Religion   Religion played an important role in Inca life. The Inca believed in many deities. The sun god, in particular, was honored because of his association with the royal family. Religious ceremonies were frequently held to mark important occasions. To keep the good will of the deities, Inca priests made offerings of food and sacrificed animals. Human sacrifices were made only in times of emergency.

Inca priests were important in areas of life other than religion. They practiced divination to determine the will of the gods. Their advice often influenced important government decisions.

Inca priests were also doctors. They used herbs to treat illnesses and performed an early form of brain surgery.

Decline   About 1520 A.D. civil war broke out between rivals for the Inca throne. The empire was severely weakened by this struggle. Meanwhile, the first Europeans arrived in South America. Because of its weakness, the Inca Empire was unprepared to meet this foreign challenge.

1. Identify: Olmecs, La Venta, Maya, Tikal, Toltecs, Teotihuacán, Tula, Aztecs, Tenochtitlán, Lake Texcoco, Montezuma I, Sun Stone, Inca, Pachacuti, Cuzco.
2. What were the scientific and cultural achievements of the Maya?
3. What were the major features of Aztec religion?
4. How was the Inca Empire governed?

CHAPTER 8 REVIEW

Summary

1. Until the early 1500's A.D., civilizations in Sub-Saharan Africa and the Americas had few direct contacts with other parts of the world.
2. From 1000 B.C. to 600 A.D., two powerful kingdoms—Kush and Axum—ruled much of northeastern Africa. Kush was known for its production of iron; Axum was a leading center of African Christianity.
3. Bantu-speaking peoples became the dominant group in Sub-Saharan Africa as a result of a series of migrations that lasted over 1,000 years.
4. After the 600's A.D., Islam had an important influence in African life. In East and West Africa, Islam and trade contributed to the rise of empires and city-states.
5. The Middle Kingdoms—Ghana, Mali, and Songhai—controlled the gold and salt trade between North Africa and the West African coast. The rulers of these kingdoms used their

wealth to support building projects, education, and the arts.

6. The first people to settle the Americas came from Asia about 20,000 to 30,000 years ago. Their descendants, the American Indians, established a variety of cultures and civilizations that stretched from North America to South America.
7. Between 1200 B.C. and 1500 A.D., a series of Indian civilizations ruled Mexico and Central America. The most powerful of these civilizations were the Maya and the Aztecs. They built large ceremonial centers that included temple-pyramids, marketplaces, and palaces.
8. The Inca Empire covered most of western South America. A highly organized central government closely regulated the daily life of the Inca people. The Inca were known for their skills in building roads, bridges, fortresses, and terraced farms.

Building Vocabulary

oral traditions	elder	potlatch	travois
savannas	maize	totem poles	chinampas
terra-cotta	culture area	adobe	quipu

Reviewing the Main Ideas

1. What were the technological accomplishments of early Africa?
2. How was early Africa influenced by foreign cultures?
3. Why were the Bantu migrations important in the development of African civilization?
4. What were the common features of Bantu religions?
5. What factors led to the rise of kingdoms and empires in West Africa?
6. How did the earliest settlers reach the Americas?
7. How did Indians farm in the Americas?
8. How did the life of the Plains Indians differ from that of the Pueblo?
9. What form of political organization was developed by the Iroquois? What was its purpose?
10. Why were ceremonial centers important in the Indian empires of the Americas?
11. How was trade carried out in the Indian empires?
12. Why were well-kept roads important for the Inca Empire?

Discussing Important Ideas

1. If Africa and the Americas had been less isolated, would their civilizations have developed differently? What factors enabled early African and American groups to overcome their isolation? Explain.
2. What factors have influenced the spread of ideas and practices from one region to another? Give examples from early African history.
3. Compare and contrast the Indian migrations in the Americas with the Bantu migrations in Africa? How have such large movements of people affected the course of world history?
4. If you had been a ruler of Ghana in the 800's A.D., how would you have governed your kingdom?
5. How did the economies of early civilizations in the Americas differ from those of early civilizations elsewhere?
6. What were the strengths and weaknesses of the Inca Empire? Could it have continued into modern times? Why or why not?
7. Some historians believe that the League of the Iroquois provided a model for the later development of government in North America. Explain.

Using Maps

Refer to the map on page 190 to answer the following questions.
1. In 1324 A.D. Mansa Musa made a pilgrimage to Mecca. About how many miles is Mecca from Timbuktu? How many kilometers?
2. What is the latitude and longitude of Kilwa?
3. Refer also to the map on page 184. In what types of landscape did most of the early African civilizations develop?
4. Why is Africa known as a tropical continent?
5. What geographic characteristics made Kush an important trading center?

UNIT 2 REVIEW

Summary

1. After the fall of Rome in 476 A.D., the eastern Roman Empire became known as the Byzantine Empire. Byzantine civilization was based on Eastern Orthodox Christianity and classical culture.

2. For nearly 1,000 years, the Byzantines defended Christian Europe against invaders from the East. During this period, Byzantine achievements included a code of law and new art forms.

3. About 1000 A.D. the Russians adopted Byzantine religion and culture. They created a civilization centered around Kiev and, later, Moscow. After the fall of the Byzantines in 1453 A.D., Russia became the world's most important Eastern Orthodox nation.

4. In the early 600's A.D., the Arab trader Mohammed founded the religion of Islam and united all of Arabia under his rule. Under Mohammed's successors, the Arabs conquered and ruled an empire that stretched from Spain to central Asia. They also made many contributions in the arts and sciences.

5. During the early Middle Ages, western Europe experienced a cultural decline and failed to achieve lasting political unity. Its most important institution was the Roman Catholic Church headed by the Pope.

6. By the 1200's A.D., the rise of towns and trade in western Europe brought an economic and cultural revival. Monarchs created strong central governments and laid the foundations of the modern nations of western Europe.

7. During ancient and medieval times, powerful kingdoms and city-states flourished in Africa. Under the influence of Islam, many of them developed into important trading and cultural centers.

8. The Americas were settled in ancient times by Asian peoples later known as American Indians. The American Indians established a variety of cultures throughout the region. The most powerful American Indian groups—the Aztecs in Mexico and the Inca in South America—created empires that lasted until the 1500's A.D.

Developing Understanding

1. How did the Byzantine Empire influence the development of European civilization?

2. Compare and contrast the role of the Roman Catholic Church in medieval Europe with the role of Islam in the Islamic Empire. How did both religions affect politics?

3. How did the crusades affect relations between western Europe and the Byzantine Empire? between western Europe and the Islamic world?

4. How did economies differ during the Middle Ages in each of the following areas: the Byzantine Empire, western Europe, the Islamic Empire, Sub-Saharan Africa, and the Americas? Describe the technologies that each area used to support its economy.

Developing Skills

During the crusades, the Byzantine city of Constantinople was the meeting place for crusaders going to Palestine. To the Byzantines, who considered themselves heirs of the Roman Empire, the crusaders were uncivilized. To the crusaders, who saw themselves as the defenders of Christianity, the attitude of the Byzantines was an outrage.

These different points of view are examples of cultural bias, or the way a person's culture affects his or her understanding of an event. Historians and students of history must be sensitive to cultural bias in order to evaluate differing accounts of an event.

In 1096 crusaders led by Godfrey of Bouillon arrived at Constantinople. The Byzantine emperor Alexius, by threatening to cut off their supplies, forced the leaders of the crusade to swear oaths of loyalty to him. What happened after that was described by the emperor's daughter, Anna Comnena. After reading her account, answer the questions that follow and do the suggested exercise.

When they were all gathered together, including Godfrey himself, and the oath had been taken by each Count, one noble had the audacity [boldness] to sit in the chair of the Basileus [Byzantine Emperor] himself. The Basileus suffered this without saying a word, for he had long known the arrogant nature of the Latins; but Count Baldwin intervened and, taking the other by the hand, made him get up, rebuking him sharply. "You should not act in this way," he said, "particularly because you have just promised vassalage to the Basileus. The Basileus are not in the habit of letting their subjects sit where they sit themselves; those who have become vassals of His Majesty must also observe the customs of the country." The man did not answer Baldwin but shot a furious look at the Basileus and muttered a few words to himself in his own language: "See what a boor he is! He alone sits when such valorous [brave] captains remain standing near him."

1. What action by one of the crusaders offended the Byzantines? Why?
2. Why was the crusader offended?
3. In what way did the customs of the two cultures clash?

Suggested exercise: Write an account of this event that expresses either viewpoint.

*From *The Crusades*, ed. by Régine Pernoud, © 1963 by Putnam, pp. 50-51.

Suggested Activities

1. Draw or make a Byzantine icon and an Islamic arabesque. Then write a brief report explaining the major differences between Byzantine and Islamic art.
2. Make a chart comparing the life of a friar, a serf, and a knight in medieval Europe. Include information about their home, clothing, food, daily activities, and education.
3. Taking the role of a North African merchant visiting Timbuktu, write a letter home describing your impressions of the city.
4. Research the Indian groups who lived in your region before the period of European settlement. Find out about their culture, lifestyle, government, and social organization. Report your findings to the class.

Suggested Readings

Dahmus, Joseph, *Seven Medieval Queens*. Garden City, N.J.: Doubleday, 1972. Presents brief biographies of such female monarchs as Theodora and Eleanor of Aquitaine.

Freemantle, Ann. *Age of Faith*. New York: Times, Inc., 1965. Volume from *Great Ages of Man* series. Discusses medieval European life and culture.

Hyams, Edward S. and Ordish, George. *The Last of the Incas: The Rise and Fall of an American Empire*. New York: Simon and Schuster, 1963. Describes the rulers, society, and achievements of the Incas.

Goldston, Robert. *The Sword of the Prophet*. New York: Dial, 1979. A history of the Arab Middle East, including the rise of Islam.

Joseph, Joan. *Black African Empires*. New York: Watts, 1974. Highlights early Africa.

National Geographic Society. *The World of the American Indian*. Washington D.C.: National Geographic Society, 1974. Features the history and cultures of the North American Indians.

Early Modern Times

1400	1450	1500	1550	1600	1650

1400's-1600's Ottoman Empire

1500's-1600's Mogul India

1519-1522 Magellan

1607 Jamestown

1485 End of Wars of the Roses

1555 Peace of Augsburg

1400's Choson dynasty

1521 Córtes

1559 *Institutes of the Christian Religion*

1420 Hussite Wars

1492 Fall of Granada

1530 Henry VIII of England

1589 Henry IV of France

1429 Joan of Arc

1492 Columbus

English expedition to the Pacific

Many changes took place throughout the world during the period from 1000 to 1600. Powerful inland empires emerged in Asia and spread their influence throughout the continent. Trade routes and sea-lanes began to connect the civilizations of Asia and Europe.

During the 1300's and 1400's, the Middle Ages came to an end, and western Europe entered the modern era. European scholars began to question traditional ideas and looked for new sources of knowledge. Reformers challenged medieval Catholicism and developed new religious institutions. Explorers began to learn about the world beyond Europe.

By 1600, western Europeans had laid the foundations of their modern civilization. Their discovery of other continents brought increased trade and wealth. Economic prosperity as well as technology enabled western Europe in the next two centuries to control much of the inhabited world.

CHAPTER 9

Chinese Tapestry

" The universe is like an inn, the passing years are like dust. "
Li Po, Chinese poet (700-762 A.D.)

Asian

Note that from this point in the book the initials "A.D." will not be used to indicate A.D. dates.

Empires

From the eleventh to the seventeenth century, invaders from the steppe of central Asia conquered territories in eastern Asia, the Middle East, and eastern Europe. Originally nomads, the invaders settled in many of the conquered areas. They adapted to the local cultures, advanced trade, and encouraged the exchange of goods and ideas.

During this period, civilizations matured in India, China, Japan, and Korea. Each responded differently to foreign contact. India developed a Hindu-Muslim culture that influenced lands from the Middle East to Southeast Asia. China reached the peak of its cultural development. It was less open than India to foreign influences and relied more on its own traditions. Japan and Korea moved away from reliance on Chinese models. The Japanese, especially, developed a society that successfully combined traditional values with innovation.

1 The Steppe Peoples

At the beginning of the eleventh century, large numbers of nomadic groups roamed the steppe of central Asia. Loosely organized into clans, they depended for their livelihood on the grazing of animals. To protect their pastures and provide for a growing population, they organized under powerful chiefs. The chiefs formed cavalry units of warriors armed with bows and arrows. The nomadic peoples became a military threat to neighboring territories that were more culturally developed. They carried out a series of invasions that transformed the peoples and cultures of eastern Asia, the Middle East, and eastern Europe.

Seljuk Turks

The first steppe people to engage in conquests were the Seljuk Turks. Around 1000, weak Abbasid rulers hired Seljuk warriors to lead their armies. As a result, the Seljuks became powerful and soon controlled the Abbasid government. Meanwhile, many Seljuk groups moved from central Asia into Persia, Mesopotamia, and Syria. There, they formed settlements, converted to Islam, and accepted Islamic ways. The Seljuks also gained control of the main trade routes between eastern Asia, the Middle East, and Europe. They benefited from this trade and used their wealth to build an empire.

The Seljuks next invaded Asia Minor. There, they defeated the Byzantines at the Battle of Manzikert in 1071. The Byzantine emperor feared the loss of Byzantine territory to the Seljuks and appealed to the Pope and western Europe for aid. About 20 years later, the Seljuk conquest of Palestine led to the Pope's calling of the First Crusade.

Though the Seljuks were skilled warriors, they were unable to develop a well-organized government to rule their territories. Seljuk rulers had difficulties holding the empire together. Local officials ignored the central government and acted like independent rulers. They began to fight each other for control of land. As a result, the Seljuks became prey to new nomadic invaders from central Asia.

Mongols

During the late 1100's, the Mongols became the dominant nomadic group in central Asia. Their homeland was Mongolia, a region of forests and steppe northwest of China. In this wild and isolated area, they wandered from pasture to pasture with their herds of sheep, camels, and goats. Because of their nomadic life, the Mongols lived in movable tents called **yurts**. Their principal foods were meat and mare's milk. In a few fertile areas, Mongol farmers established small communities. There, women raised grains while men herded animals.

Genghis Khan   Like other nomads, the Mongols at first were divided into clans. They

209

Long winters and dry summers on the treeless steppes in central Asia forced many clans to move with the seasons in search of pasture for their herds. What were the principal foods of these nomadic clans?

were expert fighters on horseback, using bow and arrow. About 1200 a Mongol leader named Temuchin organized the scattered clans under one government. He brought together Mongol laws in a new code known as the **yasa.** Under Temuchin's guidance, an assembly of tribal chiefs met for the first time to plan military campaigns and to appoint future leaders.

Temuchin's greatest achievement was in military affairs. He organized the Mongol armies into disciplined cavalry units. These units were then placed under the command of officers chosen for their abilities and not for their family ties. These changes made the Mongols the most skilled fighting force in the world at that time. As a result of his efforts, Temuchin was recognized as **khan,** or absolute ruler. Now called Genghis Khan, he set out to create a large empire.

Mongol Conquests   The Mongol armies under Genghis Khan first conquered the other steppe peoples, most of whom were Turks. These victories brought tribute money to the Mongol state as well as new recruits for the Mongol armies. By 1211 the Mongols were strong enough to attack major civilizations. In that year, 100,000 Mongol horsemen invaded China. While fighting the Chinese, the Mongols learned Chinese techniques of siege warfare. Using gunpowder, storming ladders, and battering rams, they won significant victories against their opponents. In spite of Genghis Khan's death in 1227, the Mongols continued their advance. By 1270 all of China was in their hands, and a Mongol dynasty ruled the country.

Under Ogadai Khan, the other Mongol forces moved westward. During the 1230's and 1240's, a Mongol army led by the commander Batu conquered Russia and then crossed the Carpathian Mountains into eastern and central Europe. Upon hearing of Ogadai's death, Batu's army returned to Russia. There they awaited the selection of a new khan. Meanwhile, Ogadai's widow ruled the Mongols.

During the same period, another group of Mongols invaded the Middle East. Using terror to subdue the region, the Mongols destroyed cities and killed large numbers of people. In 1258 the commander Helagu captured Baghdad, the old Abbasid capital, and enslaved its inhabitants. The destruction of the city represented a major setback to Islamic civilization. However, the Mongol advance was finally halted by the Mamluks, a Muslim military group that ruled Egypt.

Mongol Empire   The Mongols created the largest land empire in history. Their territories extended from China to the frontiers of western Europe. Many of the great trade routes between Europe and Asia passed through Mongol lands. During the 1200's, Mongol rule brought peace to the region. This advanced the growth of trade and encouraged closer cultural contacts between East and West.

The Mongols respected the highly advanced cultures of conquered groups and learned from them. In China, the Mongol rulers gradually adopted Chinese ideas and practices. In Persia and central Asia, Mongol settlers converted to Islam and intermarried with the local Turkish population. Turkish became the principal language of the region. The Mongols of Russia, however, kept their traditional customs and lived apart from the Slavs. They settled in the empty steppe region north of the Caspian Sea. From there, they controlled the Russian principalities located in the northern forests.

The unity of the Mongol Empire did not last long. All Mongols gave allegiance to the khan in Mongolia. However, local rulers became increasingly independent. By the end of the 1200's, Mongol territories in Russia, central Asia, Persia, and China had developed into separate and independent domains.

Ottoman Turks

While the Mongol Empire was in decline, Turkish clans under a chief called Osman settled in Asia Minor. Osman founded a dynasty known as the Ottomans and established a strong state.

The Ottomans and their people converted to Islam and adopted the traditions of Middle Eastern civilizations.

Early Expansion   After gaining part of Asia Minor, the Ottomans moved into Byzantine territory in the Balkan Peninsula. They fought against Balkan states who were threatening the Byzantines. In 1389, at the Battle of Kossovo, the Ottomans defeated Serbia, the strongest Balkan state.

Following their Balkan victory, the Ottomans eased taxation on the conquered Christian peoples. They offered estates to local nobles who, in turn, paid tribute and provided troops and civil servants for the Ottoman state. Periodically, Balkan Christian youths were selected to serve at the court of the Ottoman rulers. They converted to Islam. Some were trained at the Palace School to be high administrators. Others were drafted into highly trained infantries known as Janissaries. These soldiers were steadfast defenders of the Ottoman system.

Ottoman Rulers			
Osman	1290-1326	Turkish chieftain; founded the Ottoman state; adopted Islamic institutions	
Murad I	1361-1389	Warrior-sultan; conquered the Balkans; organized the Janissaries; traded with the Italian city-states	Mehmet II
Mehmet II	1451-1481	Known as the Conqueror; made Istanbul (Constantinople) the center of the empire; strengthened government administration; supported Muslim, Greek, and Italian artists and scholars	
Suleiman I	1520-1566	Called the Magnificent; considered the greatest Ottoman ruler; expanded Ottoman control in central Europe, North Africa, and the Middle East	Suleiman I

HISTORY AND PEOPLE

Ibn Battuta

Ibn Battuta was the Marco Polo of the Arab world. During the early and mid-1300's, he traveled to most of the Asian and African empires of his time.

Born in 1304, Ibn Battuta grew up in the Moroccan city of Tangier. There, he was trained as a Muslim scholar. At the age of 21, Ibn Battuta left home on his first trip—a pilgrimage to Mecca. Before reaching the Muslim holy city, he visited Egypt and Syria. While in these lands, he developed a lasting interest in foreign cultures.

For the next 35 years, Ibn Battuta traveled extensively throughout Asia and Africa. After a brief stay in Mecca, he departed for East Africa and later, the Persian Gulf area. By 1335, he had become a well-known figure among educated Muslims. He met many Muslim rulers and received financial support from them. With this income, Ibn Battuta was able to continue his journeys. In the 1340's he settled in India and became a highly respected scholar at the court of the Delhi sultan. The sultan later made him a judge and appointed him ambassador to the Chinese emperor.

Ibn Battuta's voyage to China brought many dangers. He barely escaped with his life when his traveling party was attacked by robbers near Delhi. After sailing from India, Ibn Battuta and his crew were shipwrecked. The traveler-scholar sought shelter in the Maldive Islands, located in the Indian Ocean. There, he served as a judge and married into the ruling family. Finally, when his life was threatened, Ibn Battuta resumed his voyage to China. He landed in the southeastern part of the country and traveled inland as far as Beijing. After a few years, he left China on a long journey home to Morocco.

During his later years, Ibn Battuta served as a judge in Morocco. However, he found time to visit two areas of the Islamic world that he had never before seen: Spain and the Mali Empire. When he was too old to travel, Ibn Battuta had an account written of his travel experiences. This work, called *Travels,* is one of the most famous travel books in history.

Ibn Battuta died in 1368 and was buried in Tangier. During his lifetime, he did not discover new lands, nor did he contribute new scientific information. However, through his travel account, he provided rare insights into the daily life and customs of fourteenth-century Asia and Africa. Historians still rely on Ibn Battuta's work.

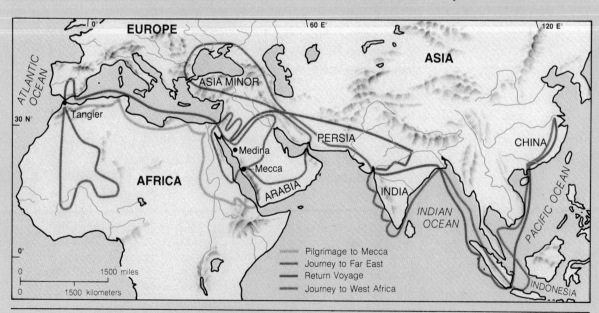

Pope Pius V organized the force that defeated the Ottomans at Lepanto. The armada that defeated the Ottomans was under the command of Don John of Austria.

Tamerlane   While the Ottoman Turks were conquering the Balkans, they faced an increasing threat from the Mongols. In the 1390's a Turkish-Mongol chief named Tamerlane rose to power in central Asia. A devout Muslim, Tamerlane hoped to spread Islam to new areas. His religious zeal also made him oppose Muslims who differed with his understanding of Islam. Claiming descent from Genghis Khan, he united the Mongols and extended their rule over much of the Middle East.

Although Tamerlane was ruthless, the people under his rule created important centers of civilization in central Asia. The most influential city in the region was Samarkand. A wealthy trading and craft center, it became known for its beautifully decorated mosques and tombs.

In 1402 Tamerlane and his armies swept into Asia Minor, defeating the Ottomans at Ankara. However, Tamerlane's effort to acquire territory in Asia Minor never succeeded. In 1405 Tamerlane died, and the huge empire that he had created soon collapsed. The Ottomans were then able to regain their lost lands and continue the expansion of their state.

Balkan Victory   Under Sultan Mehmet II, the Ottomans captured the city of Constantinople in 1453 and ended the Byzantine Empire. The Ottoman armies then advanced farther into Europe. By 1529 they were at Vienna, one of central Europe's most important Christian cities.

Ottoman Life

During the sixteenth and seventeenth centuries, the Ottomans ruled one of the most powerful empires in the world. In addition to their European conquests, they acquired much of the Middle East and North Africa. Along with these gains, the entire eastern Mediterranean came under Ottoman control. The Ottoman Empire became a strong naval power and grew wealthy through trade. Ottoman strength alarmed various Christian states of Europe that bordered the Mediterranean. In 1571 the combined navies of Spain, Venice, and the Papal States of Italy[1] defeated the Ottomans in the

---

[1]The Papal States included Rome and various central Italian territories ruled by the Pope.

Battle of Lepanto off the Greek coast. The Ottomans, however, suffered only a temporary setback. They rebuilt their navy and continued to be an important sea power in the Mediterranean until the 1700's.

Government   Suleiman I ruled the Ottoman Empire from 1520 to 1566. During this reign, the Ottomans reached the height of their power and influence. As sultan, Suleiman enjoyed absolute authority. But to rule effectively, he needed the support of his household officials, the army, and a group of Islamic law administrators called Ulema. Suleiman organized Ottoman laws and became known as "the Codifier." He also sought advice from his **grand vizier**, or prime minister. The grand vizier headed the bureaucracy, which enforced the sultan's decisions throughout the empire. A large number of officials worked in the bureaucracy. Many came from the various nationalities that the Ottomans had conquered. They included Arabs, Greeks, Albanians, Slavs, and Armenians. In spite of national differences, the Ottoman bureaucracy was united by use of the Turkish language and by ties of loyalty to the sultan.

Ottoman Civilization   The Ottomans borrowed from the Byzantines, Persians, and Arabs to create a new Islamic civilization. They particularly excelled in architecture, carpet weaving, and tile decoration. Throughout the Ottoman Empire, skilled architects built fortresses, mosques, aqueducts, and bridges. The most magnificent Ottoman city was Istanbul. Once the Byzantine city of Constantinople, Istanbul was transformed from a Christian into a Muslim city. The Hagia Sophia and the other churches were turned into mosques. New mosques and palaces were built that added to the city's beauty.

Ottoman Groups   The people of the Ottoman Empire were divided into a number of classes. The ruling class consisted of the sultan's family and his high administrators. In the rural areas, **service gentry,** or officials who worked for the state, controlled agriculture. But they did not own the land. They received their estates because of their faithful service to the Ottoman ruler.

Have students refer to the map below when discussing the Ottoman Empire in later chapters.

EXPANSION OF THE OTTOMAN EMPIRE

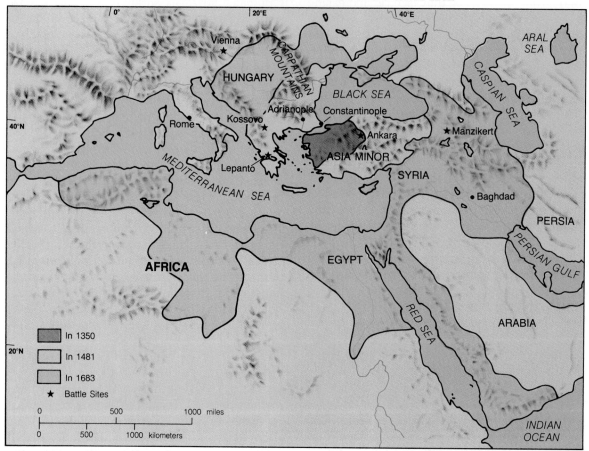

Most of the empire's people were peasants who lived and worked on the agricultural estates. Their lives were regulated by the service gentry or local wealthy landowners. The remainder of the Ottoman population were artisans and merchants who lived in towns.

Christians made up a large part of the Ottoman population. Nonetheless, Islam was the official religion. The Ottoman government allowed non-Muslims to practice their faith in return for payment of a tax. By Ottoman law, each religious group formed a **millet,** or community. The millets ran their own local affairs and chose leaders to present their views to the Ottoman government.

Problems   By 1600 the Ottoman Empire had almost reached the limits of its expansion. A variety of social, political, and economic developments were responsible for changes in the empire. During the 1500's, inflation increased in the Mediterranean world and hurt the Ottoman economy. Meanwhile, the population of the empire increased, putting pressure on Ottoman institutions and resources. In addition, Ottoman armies were fighting on two fronts. One was in Europe, the other in Persia. The opportunity to gain booty and slaves from war decreased. Frustrated soldiers then put pressure on the Ottoman government for salary increases, a demand that the government could not meet. With added demands and less revenue, the government bureaucracy became corrupt and inefficient. Officials began to take bribes and to ignore their duties. The poor performance of the government created discontent among the people, which led to civil war in the provinces.

1. Identify: Seljuk Turks, Manzikert, Mongols, Genghis Khan, Batu, Helagu, Ottoman Turks, Kossovo, Janissaries, Tamerlane, Lepanto, Suleiman I, Ulema, Istanbul.
2. How did the Seljuk Turks gain control of their territory?
3. Why did the Mongol Empire decline so quickly?
4. How was the Ottoman Empire governed?

2 Islamic India

In the early 700's, Islam came to India when Arab invaders occupied the lower Indus Valley. Muslim traders also maintained contacts with Indians along the west coast of India. During the tenth century, the Hindu kingdoms of northwestern India were overrun by Muslim Turkish invaders from central Asia. By attacking India, the Turkish warriors hoped to convert the country to Islam and to acquire booty. Their raids had a destructive effect on the Indian countryside. As strict monotheists, the Islamic invaders disapproved of the sacred idols of the Hindus. Wherever they went, they destroyed Hindu temples and shrines.

By 1030 the Indus Valley was completely under Muslim control. Once order was restored, the area prospered economically and culturally. The Muslim rulers, however, continued to pressure the Hindus to convert to Islam. Nevertheless, traditional Hindu culture survived and blended with Islamic civilization.

About 1200 the Turks set up a **sultanate,** or kingdom, with the capital at Delhi. The Delhi sultanate lasted until the early 1500's. Its officials rejected Hinduism and tried to make Hindus accept Islamic ways. Heavy taxes were imposed on Hindus in an effort to force them to become Muslims. Muslim missionaries, however, sought to win converts by persuasion. Islam rejected the caste system and taught equality. Lower-caste Hindus responded to the message of Islam and converted in large numbers. Many Hindus were bitter at these developments. As a result, clashes often developed in areas where the two religions existed side by side.

Moguls

In the early 1500's, Muslim nomadic warriors known as the Moguls entered northern India from central Asia. The Moguls were descended from Turkish and Mongol groups. Led by a commander named Babur, the Moguls overthrew the Delhi sultanate. Babur became the new ruler and established a strong central government. He founded the Mogul dynasty, which ruled India for the next two centuries.

Akbar   After Babur's death, there was a brief period of chaos and disunity. It ended when Akbar, Babur's grandson, acquired the Mogul throne in 1556. Akbar governed almost 50 years and became the greatest Mogul ruler. A skilled warrior, he completed the Mogul conquest of northern India and extended his dynasty's rule into the southern part of the country. By 1600 he controlled all of India. He was the first ruler to achieve this goal.

Akbar continued his grandfather's work of strengthening the Mogul government. He set up an efficient bureaucracy, creating an orderly system of offices at the district and village levels. Loyal and talented officials were appointed to

MOGUL EMPIRE

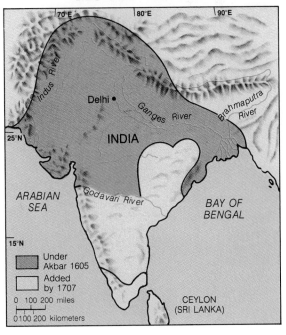

Under Akbar 1605

Added by 1707

0 100 200 miles

0 100 200 kilometers

Akbar's reign was marked by new policies of impartiality among his Hindu and Muslim subjects.

Shah Jahan built the Taj Mahal as a tomb for his wife, Mumtaz Mahal. He had already built the splendid Khass Mahal at Agra for her to enjoy during her lifetime.

government posts. To encourage honesty and faithful service, government workers, for the first time, received salaries. Those caught taking bribes were severely punished. Akbar also worked to lower taxes and to improve government services.

To unite his empire, Akbar tried to end the quarrels between Hindus and Muslims. Although a Muslim, Akbar was curious about all religions. He invited scholars from a number of faiths to his court. He was also tolerant toward his Hindu subjects. During Akbar's reign, many of the harsh penalties and taxes imposed on the Hindus were ended. For the first time, Hindus were appointed to high government posts.

Toward the end of his reign, Akbar came to believe that all religions, regardless of their differences, revealed the same divine truth. He

Under Akbar's rule there was a blending of Persian and Indian art which is reflected in this painting of Akbar greeting a court official. For what type of paintings did Mogul artists become most famous?

tried to set up a new faith that would combine the best in all religions and unify India's religious communities. Akbar's faith, however, did not win lasting support among his people. After his death in 1605, religious conflicts continued.

Mogul Civilization   Under the Moguls, music, painting, and literature flourished. Mogul rulers made their courts centers of art and learning. Akbar established a large library and had painters illustrate its books. Mogul artists excelled in miniature painting, which showed birds, flowers, and scenes of daily life.

Mogul rulers also introduced Muslim styles of architecture. White marble buildings were constructed with domes and minarets. One of the most famous buildings of Mogul India was the Taj Mahal. Still standing today, it was built in the 1600's by the Mogul ruler Shah Jahan to honor his beloved wife.

The Mogul cultural awakening brought Arab and Persian ideas into India. The languages and literature of India underwent changes. In time, a new language emerged known as Urdu.[2] It was based on Hindu rules of grammar but written in Arabic script. Urdu included many Persian and Arabic words.

Muslim influences affected only the upper social groups. The masses of Indians were still Hindu and remained loyal to their cultural traditions. But Hindu customs gradually left their mark on the Muslim minority. Mogul rulers and their nobles ignored Islamic laws that enforced a strict diet as well as modesty in dress. They wore elaborate Indian clothing covered with jewels and enjoyed alcoholic beverages. However, Muslims generally refused to accept Hindu ideas into Islam. One exception was a group known as Sikhs. The Sikhs combined the Islamic belief in one god with the Hindu belief in reincarnation. Their founder Guru Nanak preached the new religion in the early 1500's and won many followers in northwestern India.

Downfall of the Moguls   In spite of its cultural achievements, Mogul India in the 1600's was torn apart by political and religious conflict. At the same time, India entered a long period of

[2]Urdu is still spoken in Pakistan and parts of northwestern India.

By 1669 India experienced the first religious persecutions since Akbar's accession. Under Aurangzeb, the Hindu religion was prohibited and many Hindu temples were destroyed.

The administrative organization of China remained essentially unchanged from the T'ang until 1912.

Architects mixed Persian and Indian styles to produce buildings like the Taj Mahal that had Persian arches and elaborate Indian decoration. By whom and for what reason was the Taj Mahal built?

weak government. Mogul rulers made Islam the official religion and began to persecute Hindus. One ruler named Aurangzeb imposed special taxes on Hindus, destroyed many of their temples, and forced some Hindus to convert to Islam. In reaction, Hindu leaders worked to overthrow the Moguls and began to organize small armies. Meanwhile, disputes among members of the Mogul ruling family led to civil wars. The authority of the central government weakened, and local officials grew more independent. By the mid-1700's, Mogul India was ripe for conquest by foreigners.

1. Identify: Delhi, Mogul, Babur, Akbar, Taj Mahal, Urdu, Sikhs, Guru Nanak, Aurangzeb.
2. How did the Muslim invaders of India regard Hinduism?
3. What were some of Akbar's achievements?
4. How did Islam affect daily life and the arts in India?

3   China

After a long period of disorder, China was reunited about 581 under the Sui dynasty. Sui rulers increased the power of the central government. They restored the Great Wall and built a system of roads and canals. Thousands of forced laborers were used on these projects. As the harshness of Sui rule increased, rebellions occurred throughout China. In 618 the Sui dynasty was overthrown and replaced by the T'ang.

The T'ang

The T'ang dynasty ruled China from 618 to 906. Its rulers reestablished the Chinese empire. Chinese armies moved into central Asia and ended the threat of invasion by nomadic groups. Chinese government officials administered Korea and the northern part of Southeast Asia. Peace came with these military successes and led to one of the most creative periods in Chinese history.

Government and Society   T'ang China was ruled by an efficient government. After a long absence, the examination system was once again used to hire new administrators. In theory, the examinations were open to all males regardless of birth and wealth. In practice, few men could take them unless they belonged to a prominent family or had powerful connections. The examinations took years of study, which no peasant could afford.

In spite of these limitations, there were thousands of bureaucrats organized into ranks. Each rank wore special clothes and caps with a different color badge. Loyal to the emperor, the scholar bureaucrats became the most powerful and privileged group in China. They owned many acres of land, which were leased to peasants. Harsh rule by landowning bureaucrats often led to peasant rebellions.

T'ang rulers, however, tried to keep the bureaucrats from becoming too powerful. The Empress Wu, one of the most influential members of her dynasty, tried to reduce the size of the large estates. She also opened up new agricultural areas and encouraged trade. Other T'ang rulers aided the peasants by reducing taxes in years of crop failure.

Under the T'ang, China had a prosperous economy. It increased its contacts with the outside world. Luxury goods were exported to Japan, India, and the Middle East. The Chinese

During the reign of T'ai Tsung, the Chinese made contacts with Persian and Indian civilizations.

Point out that the method of printing developed by the Buddhists was much like using a large inked stamp or seal.

The real founder of the T'ang dynasty was its second emperor, T'ai Tsung. T'ai Tsung extended his rule over Korea and central Asia. He promoted education by setting up state colleges. His reorganization of the government made China the most developed and sophisticated society in the world at that time. Who was another influential ruler of the T'ang dynasty?

population greatly increased, contributing to the growth of cities. Ch'angan, the former Han capital, was rebuilt as the T'ang capital. It was located at the eastern end of the Asian trade routes.

A well-planned city, Ch'angan was a large metropolis of over 2,000,000 people. It extended five miles (8 kilometers) from north to south, and six miles (9.6 kilometers) from east to west. Within Ch'angan's walls were large markets, parks, temples, and palaces. The main street of Ch'angan was about 500 feet (150 meters) long and stretched the length of the city. It was lined by statues and trees and was always crowded with merchants, bureaucrats, shoppers, and traveling entertainers.

Religion   Under the T'ang, Confucianism, with its emphasis on strong national government, increased in importance. T'ang officials openly preferred it to Buddhism, which they believed encouraged disloyalty to the government. On several occasions the government closed Buddhist temples and monasteries. However, most Chinese were tolerant of religious differences. Many continued to give equal honor to Confucianism, Buddhism, and Taoism.

Learning and Printing   The T'ang period was an age of learning. Scholars compiled encyclopedias and dictionaries. They wrote official histories about court life and the bureaucracy. During the 700's, Chinese Buddhist monks developed the technique of block printing. They carved the text of a page on a single block of wood. The wood was inked then a sheet of paper was pressed on it. Using this method, the Chinese produced the world's first printed books in the 800's.

Later, Chinese scholars began to use movable type. This method was never widely accepted because of the length of time involved in setting the many thousands of Chinese characters.

Literature and the Arts   The T'ang period brought many achievements in literature and the arts. It was especially an age of poetry. Chinese poets, such as Li Po and Tu Fu, aimed to recreate mood and atmosphere in their works. Many of their poems describe brief moments of intense feelings caused by the sight of a natural beauty

HISTORY AND THE ARTS
Chinese Landscape Painting

During the T'ang and Song dynasties, Chinese artists developed a unique form of landscape painting. They painted scenes of nature on silk and paper scrolls. These paintings were done with fine-pointed brushes dipped in black ink. An artist was able to form many kinds of lines on each painting. This was done by adjusting the angle of the brush and the pressure on it.

In their works, Chinese artists did not try to copy nature. Instead, they wanted to express a mood or feeling. Chinese landscape painting stresses the harmony of nature and the human spirit. Most works show towering mountains and vast expanses of water and forest. Human figures, on the other hand, are small in appearance. In this way, it is suggested that human life is only part of a greater whole.

Chinese painting was closely linked with poetry and calligraphy. Poems were often added to landscape paintings as part of the overall design. The painting shown here is called *Spring over the Elixir Terrace*. It celebrates the reunion of two friends, who had been separated during a war. To express joy at meeting his friend, the painter included the following poem:

> For ten years, I wandered, homeless and away
>   from worldly entanglements:
> Now, returning home by the river, I see
>   things differently from most others.
> Jadelike vapors floating in the sky, it is
>   spring but no rain,
> Elixir rays emitted from a well turn to
>   clouds at dawn.
> Standing in the wind I lean on my dragon
>   staff,
> I have long missed hearing your mouth-organ
>   music by moonlight.
> I am happy to be with the venerable
>   immortal,
>   and away from the military strategists;
> We sit looking at paintings and talk about
>   literature.

1. How did Chinese artists paint their works?
2. How did landscape painting express the relationship between humanity and nature?

Tu Fu wrote during a time of artistic attainment comparable to the European Renaissance.

One reform of Wang An-shih was the establishment of state banking and barter offices to control prices for the benefit of Chinese consumers.

spot. One of Tu Fu's poems reveals the Chinese love of nature:

> A few last leaves are falling, blown by
> the breeze;
> The sun sets behind the curving hill.
> How late the solitary crane returns!
> In the twilight the rooks [birds] are already
> flocking to the forest.*

Under the T'ang, there were other cultural achievements. T'ang artisans were the first to add the mineral feldspar to clay before it was molded and fired to produce porcelain. T'ang porcelain was sent to places as far away as Mesopotamia. Architects produced wood or mud brick buildings with tiled roofs that curved gracefully upward at the edges. Court artists developed different styles of calligraphy. They produced texts using fine tinted paper, which they rolled on ivory cylinders tipped with jade, amber, or rock crystal knobs. T'ang painters were the first to use bright colors in their illustrations.

Fall of the T'ang   During the ninth century, the T'ang dynasty weakened as a result of internal unrest and external attacks. The army became more powerful, and military officers soon controlled the central government. Governors in the provinces acted as independent rulers. Meanwhile, corruption and inefficiency increased in the bureaucracy. As the quality of government declined, the common people became restless. By 900, T'ang rulers struggled in vain against widespread rebellions and nomadic raids. In 906 the dynasty came to an end.

The Song

After the fall of the T'ang dynasty, China was divided into territories ruled by military officials. In 960 the Song dynasty came to power in the north and by 980 had gained control of the southern Chinese territories.

The Song rulers restored the bureaucracy and the examination system. Many younger bureaucrats believed that Chinese government and society were too rigid. They wanted reforms that

*Poetry of Tu Fu from *The Rise and Splendour of the Chinese Empire*, René Grousset, 1953 by University of California Press, p. 155.

would bring new talent into the bureaucracy and improve the lives of the common people. One reform-minded official named Wang An-shih favored changing the examinations so that they would test knowledge of practical problems rather than memory of the Confucian classics. He also supported a system of government-funded public schools, redistribution of land, and tax relief for poor farmers. Conservative bureaucrats viewed Wang An-shih as a dangerous radical. They gained the support of court officials and blocked the introduction of his suggested reforms.

Song Achievements   Under the Song dynasty, China's population increased along with trade and commerce. The upper and middle classes enjoyed one of the highest standards of living in the world at that time.

Song rulers encouraged prosperity by pursuing peaceful policies. Instead of raising large armies, they supported public works projects, including the digging of irrigation ditches and canals. They expanded sea trade with foreign lands. Chinese ports were opened to Arab merchants who lived in trading centers. Song rulers were also generous in their support of the arts. Landscape painting was the most popular art form of the Song period.

Two important inventions were made during the Song period: the compass and gunpowder. The compass enabled Chinese shippers to travel beyond their country's coastal waters. Some historians believe that the compass may have

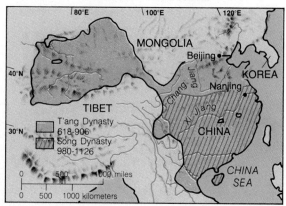

CHINA   618-1126

Although not widely accepted, both Christianity and Islam enjoyed full protection by Mongol rulers.

come to the West from China. The Chinese were the first to use gunpowder, mainly for fireworks. By the 1100's they used it in warfare in the form of small bombs and grenades.[3]

Song Decline   The Song were not strong military rulers. They lost much Chinese territory and were threatened by invaders from the north. About 1126 a nomadic people called the Jurchen conquered all of China north of the Chang Jiang (Yangtze River). They adopted Chinese culture and established a dynasty that ruled northern China. Meanwhile, the Song controlled Chinese lands south of the Chang Jiang.

The Mongols

During the 1200's, the Mongols invaded China and overthrew the Jurchen and Song rulers. They established the Yuan, or Mongol, dynasty. They became the first foreign conquerors to rule the entire country.

Kublai Khan   The first great Mongol emperor of China was Kublai Khan. A grandson of Genghis Khan, he ruled from 1260 to 1294. Kublai Khan extended Mongol rule beyond China's borders. He conquered Korea in the north and part of Southeast Asia. He made two attempts to invade Japan, using Chinese and Korean ships. Both efforts failed because the Mongols were not skilled in naval warfare.

Mongol Government and Society   Mongol rulers at first tried to keep their own culture. Eventually, they accepted many Chinese ways. They established a permanent capital at Cambuluc. With its palaces and parks, Cambuluc was one of the world's most beautiful cities. At its center was the emperor's palace. It was a large building with many courtyards and halls. The grounds of the palace had lakes, hills, orchards, and grassy plains grazed by animals.

The Mongols retained many of the traditional Chinese forms of government. The emperor was regarded as an absolute ruler. He received the advice and assistance of a large bureaucracy. However, the Mongols distrusted the Chinese

and reduced their influence in the government. They ended civil service examinations and excluded Chinese from most government posts. Foreigners of various nationalities were given the most important positions in the emperor's court. The Chinese, however, opposed these policies and wanted freedom from Mongol rule.

The Mongols worked to gain the support of the Chinese. They eventually restored the civil service examinations for some government posts. They provided government funds for schools and temples. They gave charitable aid to the elderly and the sick. Public granaries were maintained to provide food in time of famine. The Mongols also built canals, roads, and irrigation systems.

Under Mongol rule, Chinese civilization broke with past traditions and developed new styles. The most important changes occurred in literature. Because the Chinese were not admitted to government service, scholars turned to creative writing. They developed Chinese drama, in which lively action was combined with realistic portrayals of human characters. Many plays were written in the language of the common people rather than the language of scholars. Chinese theater had little scenery and furnishings. The actors, all of whom were male, wore heavy makeup and elaborate costumes. They sang rather than spoke their lines. An orchestra placed on stage provided background music.

Mongol rulers made Buddhism the state religion. However, they permitted the practice of Confucianism and Taoism. They also allowed the introduction of Christianity and Islam into China. These two religions, however, won only a small number of Chinese converts.

Foreign Contacts   The Mongols established close ties with foreign lands through trade. They built a system of roads that connected China to central Asia, Persia, and Russia. Military posts and inns were set up at frequent intervals along the routes. These enabled merchants to travel in safety and comfort from South China to the Middle East. Arabs, western Europeans, and Russians traded in Chinese cities. At the same time, Chinese and Mongols visited and settled in Russia and western Europe.

---

[3]In the 1300's Europeans developed gunpowder on their own. By producing powerful weapons, such as guns and cannons, they surpassed the Chinese in the skill of making firearms.

Hung-wu is also known as Ming T'ai Tsu, from which the dynastic name is derived.

The Mongol Empire controlled all central Asia and opened, for the first time, trading contact between Europe and the Far East. Italian merchants, in particular, were quick to seize the opportunity for trade. Such merchants as Marco Polo were able to bring tea, spices, pasta, silk, and porcelain directly to European markets. What goods were traded to China in return?

Through these contacts, ideas and practices were exchanged. The Arabs and later Europeans learned about gunpowder, paper, porcelain, and printing from the Chinese. In return, the Chinese received glass, hides, honey, slaves, clothes, silver, cotton, and carpets from the Middle East, Russia, and Europe.

Marco Polo   One of the first western Europeans to visit China was the Italian merchant Marco Polo. Polo arrived in China in 1275 and stayed there for 17 years. During this time, he became an aide to Kublai Khan and served as governor of a Chinese city. Polo also traveled throughout Mongol territory on behalf of the emperor. After returning to Italy, Polo wrote a book called *Description of the World* in which he told of the wealth and splendor of Chinese civilization. In the 1200's Chinese civilization was more advanced than that of western Europe. Polo's writings provided Europeans with their first real information about the Far East.

Mongol Decline   During the 1300's, Mongol rule in China began to decline. Corrupt government officials lived in luxury, while the common people remained poor. The government demanded heavy taxes from the peasants at a time when famine had reduced the food supply. Meanwhile, the Chinese continued to resent Mongol control of their country. All of these grievances led to a series of rebellions. Finally, in 1368, a young Buddhist monk named Hung-wu led an army against Cambuluc and overthrew the Mongol dynasty.

The Ming

After the overthrow of the Mongols, Hung-wu became emperor. He established his capital at Nanjing (Nanking) in southern China. There, he founded the Ming dynasty, which ruled China until 1644.

Government   The Ming dynasty ended Mongol influence in Chinese government. The examination system was fully restored, and Chinese replaced foreigners in government service. Ming rulers also imposed new law codes, reorganized the tax system, and reformed local government.

Ming political reforms led to economic prosperity. Chinese farmers increased their yields and planted new crops, such as cotton, maize, sweet potatoes, and peanuts. As a result, the population increased, bringing more workers into the job market. Ming artisans expanded the production of crafts, tea, silk, porcelain, and cotton cloth.

Chinese architecture reached the peak of its development during the Ming period. Ming emperors built many elaborate gardens, summer

Point out that historians suspect that the Ming developed their navy for commerce and military prestige.

The map below is the subject of the "Using Maps" section of the Chapter 9 Review.

residences, and hunting lodges. They designed graceful pavilions, arched bridges, and tall pagodas. Many Chinese public buildings were known for their curving roofs made of brightly colored tiles.

Exploration   Unlike earlier and later Chinese dynasties, the Ming aimed to make China a sea power. With the support of Ming emperors, the Chinese learned navigational skills and built large fleets. Some of the ships, known as **junks,** measured 512 feet (154 meters) in length and 212 feet (64 meters) in width. Chinese junks usually traveled slowly along the coastline, but they could also venture into open water.

With their strong navy, Ming rulers promoted sea explorations. From 1405 to 1433, they sent out seven expeditions that traveled to India, East Africa, and Persia. One of these fleets had 62 vessels and about 28,000 voyagers. The reasons for these explorations are not known. They may have been efforts to secure new trade routes or to expand Chinese influence overseas. Chinese explorers often forced foreign rulers to pay them tribute and brought back to China many new and luxurious products.

The Ming emperors, however, feared the spread of foreign ideas and practices in China. In 1433 a policy of **isolationism,** or the avoidance of ties with other countries, was adopted. The sea voyages suddenly ended. Chinese shipping was limited to China's coastal waters. The Chinese were also forbidden to leave the country or to contact foreigners.

Ming Decline   In the early 1400's, the Ming dynasty faced many challenges. Weak emperors had difficulty controlling the bureaucracy. They also faced the threats of invaders. To secure the northern frontier, the capital was moved from Nanjing, to Cambuluc, which was renamed Beijing (Peking). In the heart of Beijing, the emperors built a large cluster of palaces known as the Forbidden City. There they lived in isolated splendor and had little contact with daily government business.

Powerful court officials carried out policies on behalf of the emperor. They grew wealthy by selling government offices and taking bribes. They imprisoned many political opponents and seized their lands. In the countryside, landowners refused to pay taxes and placed the burden of payment on the peasants. Those peasants who refused to pay were forced to become serfs or were driven from their lands. Many who were landless fled into the mountains and became bandits. As law and order collapsed, invaders attacked the northern border. In 1644 one of

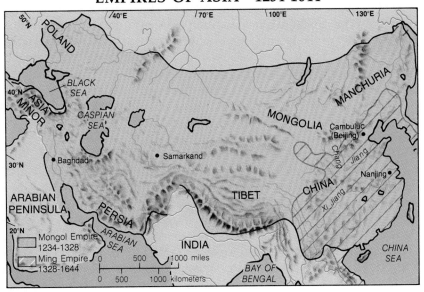

EMPIRES OF ASIA   1234-1644

The most popular type of Japanese court poem was called the *haiku*, an unrhymed verse of three lines containing 5, 7, and 5 syllables respectively.

these groups called the Manchus invaded China and set up a new dynasty.

1. Identify: Sui, T'ang, Wu, Li Po, Tu Fu, Song, Wang An-shih, Jurchen, Kublai Khan, Cambuluc, Marco Polo, Hung-wu, Ming, Beijing, Forbidden City, Manchus.
2. How did the T'ang dynasty establish an efficient government?
3. What were the technological and artistic achievements of the T'ang and Song periods?
4. How did China conduct its relations with the outside world under the Mongols? under the Ming?

4   Japan and Korea

During the late 700's, Japan placed less importance on its ties with China. It began to emerge as a separate civilization. Japanese religion became a blend of Shintoism and Buddhism. The writing system was simplified. Japanese gradually replaced Chinese as the literary language. Writers and artists in Japan began to develop their own themes and styles.

Heian Period

In the 790's the Japanese emperor and his court left Nara and built a new capital called Heian. It was laid out about 30 miles (48 kilometers) north of Nara. Heian, later renamed Kyoto, was the official capital of Japan until the 1800's. The transfer of the capital to a new location marked the beginning of the Heian period, which lasted until 1185.

Emperor and Nobles   During the Heian period, the political authority of the Japanese emperor declined. Although still honored as head of the government, the emperor performed duties that were mainly religious and ceremonial. Nobles took charge of political activities, replacing scholars in the government bureaucracy. They plotted against each other for wealth and power. During the tenth and eleventh centuries, one family of nobles known as the Fujiwara gained control over the emperor and the court. The Fujiwara ran the emperor's estates and made appointments to top government posts.

Fujiwara nobles maintained their authority by marrying their daughters into the royal family. By the tenth century, Japanese women had lost much of their earlier influence and prestige. They now had to follow the wishes of male family members. A Fujiwara daughter often would marry a young emperor. When the royal couple's first son was still a child, the emperor would be persuaded to abdicate, or resign the throne. The Fujiwara empress, under the control of her family, would guide court affairs in the name of the new child emperor.

While nobles asserted their authority in Heian, warlike clan leaders took control of local affairs in the provinces. They ignored the emperor's officials and refused to pay taxes. They supervised the work of the peasants and ran their rice-producing estates like independent territories. The power of the central government weakened considerably. By the end of the Heian period Japan was a collection of small states.

Court Life   Since the emperor and his court had little political power, they had time to develop elaborate court ceremonies and to support the arts. Life at the Heian court was known for its elegance, good manners, and love of natural beauty. Court officials and their wives wrote stories, travel diaries, and essays. They composed poems for special occasions and exchanged them in letters. Japanese court poems were short and skillfully written to convey a mood or emotion.

During the Heian period, women of the court produced Japan's first great prose literature. In the early eleventh century, Lady Murasaki Shikibu wrote *The Tale of Genji*. This work describes the adventures and romances of a Japanese prince. Some literary experts view *The Tale of Genji* as the world's first novel.

Kamakura Period

In 1156 the rule of the Fujiwaras came to an end. A dispute soon developed between two powerful court families: the Taira and the Minamoto. Both families relied on the support of warriors from the provinces. After a series of wars, the Taira defeated the Minamoto. However, the Taira soon lost the backing of the rural

Point out that the title *shogun* is short for *seiidaishogun*. It literally means "barbarian-subduing great general."

Other women ruled China, but Empress Wu was the only one to rule in her own right.

East Asian Leaders

CHINESE

Yang Chien, (541-577), united all of China; distributed grain among the poor; introduced the civil service system.

Empress Wu Hou, (625-705), the first woman to rule China; brought about social reforms; strengthened the T'ang dynasty; conquered Korea.

JAPANESE

Shotoku Taishi, (573-621), established law and order throughout Japan; imported a writing system and calendar from China.

Minamoto Yoritomo (1147-1199), established shogunate in Japan; reorganized local government; strengthened judicial system.

KOREANS

Wang Kon, (870-940), founder-king of Koguryo; centralized the government; freed slaves; encouraged agriculture.

Yi Sun-sin, (1545-1597), invented the iron-clad "turtle boats"; defeated the Japanese in a series of naval battles.

MONGOLS

Temuchin (Genghis Khan), (1162-1227), organized powerful military force; created Mongol Empire; encouraged commerce and cultural exchanges.

Helagu, (1217-1265), grandson of Genghis Khan; led attack on Baghdad in 1258; ruled a Muslim kingdom that reached from Syria to India.

Yang Chien

Shotoku Taishi

Yi Sun-sin

Temuchin

warriors, who were now the most powerful group in the country. The dissatisfied warriors united around Minamoto Yoritomo, the leading member of the Minamoto family. In 1185 Yoritomo and his forces fought and defeated the Taira in the naval Battle of Dannoura.

Shogunate   After his victory, Yoritomo pledged loyalty to the emperor and received from him the title **shogun,** or commander-in-chief. However, Yoritomo was the real ruler of the land. He and his soldiers left the court at Kyoto and settled in the small seaside town of Kamakura in eastern Japan. There, Yoritomo set up a **shogunate,** or military government. The Japanese called the new government *bakufu,* or "tent government," after the shelters in which military officers lived. Yoritomo's soldiers carried out government tasks and managed its country estates. The military replaced court aristocrats as patrons of art and literature.

Mongol Attacks   After Yoritomo's death in 1199, fighting among his heirs weakened the shogunate. In 1219 an aristocratic family called the Hojo took control of the Kamakura government. They named shoguns and ruled through them in the emperor's name.

During the rule of Hojo, the Mongol rulers of China attempted two sea invasions of Japan.

Raise the question, "How do you think the Mongol invasions spurred Japan's national consciousness?"

Another name for the Ashikaga Shogunate is the Muromachi Shogunate.

One invasion occurred in 1274, the other in 1281. On both occasions, bad weather made landings on Japanese soil difficult. In spite of inadequate arms, Japanese warriors forced the Mongols to withdraw. In the second invasion, the Mongol fleet carrying 150,000 soldiers was destroyed by a typhoon. To the Japanese, the typhoon was the *kamikaze*, or "divine wind" of the gods protecting their land from foreign attackers.

Religion By the 1200's Buddhism had spread from the nobles to the common people. Its teachings were simplified and gave rise to many **sects,** or religious groups. The new varieties of Buddhism all taught about a personal afterlife in paradise. The way to paradise, they stated, was through simple trust in Buddha. With salvation so easily available, the influence of priests, monks, and nuns declined. For the first time, the common people began to play an important role in Buddhist life. With widespread support, the sects linked religion with patriotism. Some believed that Japanese Buddhism was the only true Buddhism and that Japan was the center of the universe.

While the common people turned to the new Buddhist sects, the warriors followed their own form of Buddhism called Zen. Brought from China in the late 1100's, Zen taught that the individual had to live in harmony with nature. This harmony, it affirmed, could be achieved through deeper spiritual understanding. In their religious quest, the followers of Zen rejected book learning, logical thought, and religious ritual. Instead, they stressed bodily discipline and meditation. As a method of spiritual training, Zen teachers posed difficult puzzles to their students. The students would then meditate upon these problems. It was believed that long periods of meditation would lead to enlightenment.

Ashikaga Shogunate

By the 1300's Japan was divided by continual warfare among rival groups of warriors. In 1331 Emperor Daigo II led a successful revolt against the Hojo shogunate. His aim was to restore the political authority of the emperor. Daigo was opposed by a warrior named Ashikaga Takauji.

In 1336 Takauji overthrew Daigo and chose another member of the royal family as emperor. He also made himself shogun and established a new military government in Kyoto.

After Takauji's death, political power passed to other members of his family. Ashikaga shoguns, however, could not exercise control over the warriors in the provinces. Many warriors rejected a strong central government and wanted to run local affairs. As a result, the Ashikaga shoguns, like the emperor, lost all political influence and became merely symbols.

Japanese Feudalism During the Ashikaga shogunate, Japan developed a feudal system similar to that of western Europe. Under the emperor and the shogun were warrior landlords called **samurai.** The samurai ran estates that were worked by heavily taxed rice farmers. Some of the most powerful samurai later formed a group of lords known as **daimyo.** Like the medieval knights in western Europe, lesser samurai pledged loyalty and military service to the daimyo.

The samurai fought on horseback with bows, arrows, and curved steel swords. They dressed in loose-fitting armor held together by colored strips of leather. To develop their military skills, the samurai participated in sports. Their activities included judo, karate, and **sumo,** a Japanese form of wrestling. The samurai were as skilled in the arts as they were in battle. They mastered calligraphy, composed poems, and wrote epics. They produced scroll paintings that showed detailed battle scenes.

The samurai followed a strict code of honor called **bushido,** meaning "way of the warrior." Bushido stressed bravery, self-discipline, and loyalty. Unlike European knights, the samurai had no interest in honoring or defending women. They expected women to be self-disciplined and to fight beside them in battle. The samurai were expected to endure suffering, and to defend their honor at all costs. If a samurai's reputation was irreparably damaged, he was expected to commit **seppuku,** or a ritual form of suicide.

The Arts The Ashikaga period saw new developments in the arts. Many artists and

Note that many of the traditions developed during this period of Japanese history are still practiced today by many people in Japan.

Point out that the Choson dynasty of Korea is usually called Yi by Western scholars.

writers were Buddhist monks. They produced a form of drama called Noh. Noh plays developed out of religious dances and were used to teach Buddhist ideas. Noh actors wore masks and elaborate costumes. They danced, gestured, and chanted poetry on a bare stage to the accompaniment of a chorus.

In addition, three art forms emerged that reflected the Japanese love of simplicity, beauty, and nature. One was **ikebana,** or flower arrangement. It began in the temples, where floral offerings were placed before Buddhist images. Later, it developed into an art form that was practiced by Japanese women. The second was landscape gardening. Japanese gardeners tried to copy nature on a small scale. They built artificial hills and ponds, surrounded by trees and flowering shrubs. Some gardens were centers of meditation and reflected the simplicity of Zen. They had carefully placed rocks and raked sand with few plants of any kind. The third art form was the tea ceremony. The Japanese learned tea drinking from the Chinese. Around this daily practice, they developed an elegant ritual for preparing and serving tea.

Economy   In spite of political turmoil, Japan made economic progress during the Ashikaga period. Workshops developed on estates and produced a variety of goods. Each region began to specialize in certain crafts. These goods were transported to other parts of the country. Copper coins soon replaced rice and cloth as the chief means of exchange.

With increased trade, social organization in Japan became more complex. The economic influence of the rural estates declined as new towns developed. A powerful group of merchants and artisans emerged in the urban centers. These business people formed guilds to promote their economic interests and to win greater freedom from feudal lords.

Japanese merchants ended their country's isolation and began trading with China and Korea. They received the support of feudal lords and warriors in many of these ventures. Japanese exports were mainly raw materials like sulphur, lumber, pearls, and gold. But they also included such finished goods as swords and

The rigidly observed, though simple, rites of a Japanese tea ceremony are intended to promote harmony, respect, purity, and tranquility of mind. What other art forms reflect Japanese love of simplicity?

painted fans and screens. During the 1400's, Japanese traders controlled much of the shipping and commerce of East Asia. Economic prosperity later enabled Japan to regain its political unity.

Korea   While Japan prospered, Korea made advances in its civilization. In 1392 a new dynasty known as the Choson came to power. Choson rulers made Seoul the capital of the country. They accepted Confucian teachings and introduced civil service examinations in Korea. They also created a new Korean alphabet.

During the 1500's, Japanese armies invaded Korea and destroyed much of the Choson culture. In time, the Koreans drove out the Japanese, but they faced other invaders seeking to control the Korean peninsula. The Chinese invaded Korea twice in the seventeenth century. For many years afterward, Korea closed itself to all contact with foreign lands. It became known as the "Hermit Kingdom."

1. Identify: Heian, Fujiwara, *The Tale of Genji*, Kamakura, Taira, Minamoto Yoritomo, Dan-noura, Hojo, Zen, Ashikaga Takauji, Noh, Choson.

2. What form of government did Minamoto Yoritomo establish?

3. How did Japan's economy change under the Ashikagas?

4. How did Choson rulers contribute to Korea?

CHAPTER 9 REVIEW

Summary

1. In the eleventh century, the Seljuk Turks became the first of the steppe peoples to establish an empire, which was centered in Asia Minor.

2. During the twelfth and thirteenth centuries, the Mongols of central Asia created the largest land empire in history. They encouraged the growth of trade and cultural contacts between East and West.

3. During the 1400's, the Ottoman Turks established a large empire that included the Middle East, North Africa, and the Balkans. About 100 years later, they were the leading sea power in the Mediterranean world.

4. From 1000 to 1500, the Turks ruled the earliest Islamic state in India. During the 1500's and 1600's, the Mogul dynasty brought all of India under a strong central government. Under the Moguls, a cultural awakening led to the blending of Hindu and Islamic styles.

5. From the 600's to the 900's, the T'ang dynasty ruled a powerful empire in China. It established an efficient government, developed trade with the outside world, and supported achievements in literature and the arts.

6. China's economic and cultural prosperity continued under the Song dynasty, which ruled from the tenth to the twelfth centuries. Political disorders in the late 1100's brought China a period of invasions.

7. In the thirteenth century, the Mongols became the first foreigners to conquer all of China. Under their rule, China broke temporarily with many of its traditions and developed contacts with foreign lands, especially western Europe.

8. The Ming dynasty restored traditional Chinese ways when it came to power in the late 1300's. With its support, China, for a short while, became a sea power. But Ming rulers feared foreign influences and adopted a policy of isolationism.

9. In the late 700's, Japan developed its own civilization apart from China. During the Heian period, the emperor's political authority declined, and power shifted to court nobles and, later, rural warriors. The emperor's court encouraged the arts.

10. During the twelfth century, the Minamoto family restored Japan's political unity under the Kamakura shogunate.

11. After a period of political decline, another shogunate was reestablished by the Ashikaga family in the 1300's. When Ashikaga rule weakened, Japan developed into a feudal society of lords and warriors. In spite of political disunity, Japan's economy and culture made progress during the 1400's.

12. Under the Choson dynasty, Korea made advances in its civilization. After a period of invasions in the 1600's, Korea was closed to all contact with foreign lands.

Building Vocabulary

yurts	millet	shogun	daimyo
yasa	sultanate	shogunate	sumo
khan	junks	sects	bushido
grand vizier	isolationism	samurai	seppuku
service gentry			ikebana

Reviewing the Main Ideas

1. What advantages did the Seljuk Turks gain when they took control of the Abbasid Empire?
2. How did the Mongols live before their conquests?
3. How did Ottoman rulers treat religious minorities?
4. Why did the Ottoman Empire decline in the 1600's?
5. Why did Akbar try to create a new religion?
6. What did T'ang poets express in their works?
7. Why were reforms proposed during the Song period?
8. What changes came to Chinese society under the Mongols?
9. Why was Marco Polo's visit to China important?
10. Why did the Ming dynasty collapse?
11. How did the Fujiwara family maintain its power?
12. How was Japan governed during the Kamakura period?

Discussing Important Ideas

1. What factors led the steppe peoples to expand their territories and to create their empires?
2. What might have occurred had the Mongols continued their military campaign in eastern Europe?
3. Was Suleiman I an absolute ruler? Explain.
4. Could a permanent policy of religious toleration have solved many of India's problems? Explain.
5. Is a strong central government necessary for technological advance and economic prosperity? Why or why not?
6. Would Wang An-shih's reform proposals have strengthened the Song dynasty if they had been introduced? Explain.
7. If you had been a western European visiting Mongol China, why would you have been impressed by the court of Kublai Khan?
8. Was the Ming policy of isolationism beneficial to China? Explain.
9. Why did nobles and shoguns never attempt to overthrow the emperor and establish new dynasties of their own?
10. Why was Korea known as the "Hermit Kingdom" after the seventeenth century?

Using Maps

Refer to the map on page 223 to answer the following questions:

1. What is the relative location of Tibet to China? of Poland to India?
2. Are the empires of Asia in the Northern or Southern Hemispheres? Eastern or Western Hemispheres?
3. In which area of the Mongol Empire was the Ming Empire established?
4. What sea is completely landlocked (surrounded by land with no outlet to other waters)?
5. How many miles is Samarkand from Cambuluc? how many kilometers?

CHAPTER 10

Renaissance Banquet

> **It is a remarkable fact that we all must die, and yet we all live as if we were to live forever.**
>
> Francesco Guicciardini, Italian historian (1485-1540)

Decline
and
Renaissance

During the fourteenth and fifteenth centuries, plague, war, and economic decline weakened medieval Europe. Governments had difficulty keeping law and order. Monarchs lost much of their power to nobles. Church leaders were openly criticized for preferring secular to religious goals. Conflicts among social groups led to rebellion and civil war. At times, it seemed that Europe was falling apart.

In spite of the crises, Europe did not collapse. The failure of medieval ideas and institutions forced Europeans to rebuild their civilization. From about 1350 to 1600, western Europe experienced a profound cultural awakening known as the Renaissance.[1] Due to the Renaissance, educated Europeans developed new attitudes about themselves and the world around them. Although still Christian, they became less concerned with their destiny in heaven and more interested in improving their lives on earth. The changes brought by the Renaissance signaled the end of the Middle Ages and the beginning of the modern period.

1 Medieval Decline

About 1300 medieval Europe entered a period of economic **depression,** or decline. Production in the towns slowed. Rains and floods caused poor harvests, and widespread famines occurred. During this time, known as the Late Middle Ages, Europeans lost much of their security, optimism, and self-confidence.

---

[1]The term "Renaissance" comes from a French word meaning rebirth.

Black Death

Terrible outbreaks of plague heightened Europe's economic crisis. During the mid-1300's, a deadly disease known as the Black Death swept through Europe, killing about one-fourth of the population.[2] Most deaths occurred in crowded and unsanitary towns and cities. Some of the horror of the Black Death can be seen in this account by a priest who visited the French city of Avignon in 1348:

> One-half or more . . . of the people at Avignon are already dead. Within the walls of the city there are now more than 7000 houses shut up; in these no one is living, and all who have inhabited them are departed; the suburbs hardly contain any people at all . . . On account of this great mortality there is such fear of death that people do not dare even to speak with anyone whose relative has died, because it is frequently remarked that in a family where one dies nearly all the relations follow him, and this is commonly believed among the people.*

Doctors could not cure the disease, which further increased public panic. Seeking protection, townspeople fled to isolated rural areas. The decline and shift of population temporarily halted farming production and trade in many areas. Repeated, though less severe, outbreaks of plague occurred for the next 50 years.

---

[2]The Black Death, a form of bubonic plague, began in the Black Sea region and spread southwest across Europe. It was carried by fleas from infected rats.

*Short Chronicle of an Anonymous Cleric, quoted in *The Black Death of 1348 and 1349*, Francis Aidan Gasquet, © 1908, p. 46.

231

Conflicts occurred because nobles and wealthy townspeople wished to buy luxuries from the eastern
Mediterranean. To have items for trade, they put
pressure on workers to produce more.

Social Upheaval

The plague and the economic troubles weakened Europe's monarchies. Taxes brought in less
revenue, and rulers could not meet their
expenses. To raise their income, they fought
wars and conquered more productive lands.
They sold government positions and titles of

*Crowded living conditions and narrow, garbage-filled streets
were the breeding grounds for the Black Death. Because the
nature of contagion was not understood, millions died. What
was the source of the Black Death?*

nobility to the highest bidders. Such practices
lead to an increase in government corruption.
Many Europeans lost faith in their rulers. Social
groups began to fight for political power.

Nobles Nobles often took part in these
upheavals. As monarchies weakened, they
worked to get back their old feudal privileges.
Some exerted their influence through assemblies
and the royal courts. Others formed their own
armies and fought for control of government.
However, once in power, nobles seldom worked
together and split into quarreling groups.

Townspeople Wealthy merchants and artisans in the towns also tried to increase their
influence. Certain groups of them won control of
town governments. While in power, they limited
the political rights of poorer urban dwellers.
They gained control of the guilds and increased
their hold over town economies. Strict regulations were passed that made it difficult for
journeymen to become masters. Enterprising
artisans were discouraged from developing new
methods of production. As a result, many
competing producers and artisans left the towns
and set up new trades in the countryside. There,
they could work and ignore guild restrictions.

Peasants and Workers Despite the economic slump, the living conditions of peasants
and workers generally improved. After the Black
Death, there were fewer laborers to till the fields
and work in the shops. Knowing that their skills
were needed, peasants and workers demanded
and won benefits from their employers. They
received higher wages, paid lower taxes and
rents, and secured the right to move from one
place to another. Also, many of the remaining
serfs gained their freedom.

These changes increased the economic burdens on the upper social groups. The groups
gradually began to take back many of the gains
that the peasants and workers had won. At the
urging of nobles and merchants, governments
passed laws to limit wage increases, raise taxes,
and prevent the movement of workers to new
jobs and places.

Uprisings As a result of these setbacks,
peasants and workers became restless and
unhappy. During the late 1300's, rebellions

In the Peasant's Rebellion of 1381, peasants marched on London and forced King Richard III to abolish serfdom and manorial dues. The rebellion was later put down by the king and his nobles.

The first battle of the Hundred Years' War was a naval encounter in the English Channel near Sluys.

occurred in many areas. Peasants killed landlords, burned tax records, and demanded an end to heavy taxes and other payments. Workers in the towns asked for the right to participate in town government and to form their own guilds. They often rioted when their demands were rejected. In spite of their determination, peasants and workers lacked weapons and were poorly trained in warfare. Thus, nobles and wealthy townspeople were able to crush the revolts.

Results   Although the uprisings failed, they had two important results. First, peasants and workers regained some of their benefits. In western Europe, serfs as a group virtually disappeared. As free laborers, they either moved to the towns or became tenant farmers who paid rent to their former lords for use of the land. Second, the fear of social turmoil brought townspeople and the **gentry,** or lower nobility, closer together. Both of these groups now recognized that strong monarchs were needed to maintain order and to promote economic recovery and growth.

Hundred Years' War

During the 1300's, feudal disputes often led to wars among Europe's monarchs. The most devastating and prolonged of these conflicts was the Hundred Years' War, fought by the kings of France and England.

Causes   In the early 1300's, France and England were bitter enemies despite close cultural and political ties. French kings wanted to annex, or take over, lands in southern France that the English king held as a vassal of the French crown. At the same time, a growing rivalry developed between England and France over Flanders, which was prized for its profitable markets. In 1337 the feud grew worse when Edward III of England declared himself king of France. Philip VI of France then demanded that Edward III pay him homage for the English lands in France. Edward III refused and prepared for war. Two years later, he landed his armies in northern France.

Battles   The English won the most important battles of the Hundred Years' War. They

Bataille de Roosebeque.

Civil strife between Burgundian and Flemish factions undermined France during the Hundred Years' War. The trouble was settled by defeat of the Flemish in the Battle of Roosebeke. What new weapons were used there?

defeated the French at Crécy in 1346 and again at Agincourt in 1415. Several factors were responsible for these victories.

First, the English as a people were more united than the French. English kings appealed to national unity and received financial support from Parliament to fight the war. Second, the English armies developed new tactics. For the first time, foot soldiers fought alongside mounted knights in heavy armor. The foot soldiers used the longbow, a new weapon that was five or six feet (1.5 or 1.8 meters) long and could send steel-tipped arrows a distance of 400 yards (360 meters). In battle, the longbow could send deadly showers of arrows into the air that blocked the advance of mounted French knights.

English forces also experimented with gunpowder.[3] They developed the first portable firearms used in European warfare. The earliest gun consisted of a long tube mounted on a pole; the charge was set off by a match. From models

[3]Europeans may have learned about gunpowder from the Muslims during the crusades.

After the execution of Joan of Arc, an English soldier is said to have whispered to a companion, "We are lost; we have burnt a saint." In 1920, the Roman Catholic Church declared Joan of Arc a saint. Today, she is also a powerful symbol of French patriotism.

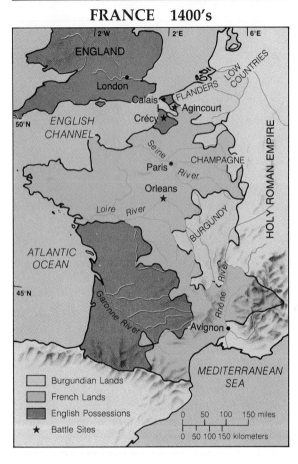

FRANCE 1400's

Burgundian Lands
French Lands
English Possessions
★ Battle Sites

0 50 100 150 miles
0 50 100 150 kilometers

people. They rallied to their king and gradually drove the English out of their country. When the war finally ended in 1453, the port of Calais was the only French territory still under English rule.

Effects   The Hundred Years' War profoundly affected the peoples of England and France. France had suffered more severely than England, since all of the fighting had occurred on French soil. Victory gave the French people a new sense of unity that enabled them to rebuild their country. England had been spared the destruction of its towns and countryside. Yet, defeat led to much bitterness among the nobles who had owned lands in France. For the rest of the 1400's, England was torn apart by social conflict. However, in the long run, the loss of French lands contributed to national unity. The English eventually abandoned permanent claims on the European mainland.

Decline of Feudalism

Since the 1200's, feudalism had been weakened by the growth of towns, the development of a money economy, and the rise of a free labor force. However, the new methods of warfare that emerged during the Hundred Years' War brought about feudalism's collapse. The use of the longbow and firearms made feudal methods of fighting based on castles and mounted knights obsolete. Thus, monarchs relied less on feudal soldiers. Instead they formed national armies made up of mercenaries and **commoners,** or non-nobles.

Maintaining these armies, however, was expensive. Monarchs had to look for new sources of revenue. They turned to the richest members of their realms—the townspeople and the gentry. These groups willingly paid taxes and made loans to monarchs in return for security and good government.

The Troubled Church

During the upheavals of the Late Middle Ages, many people turned to the Church for comfort and reassurance. Religious ceremonies multiplied, and thousands of people went on pilgrimages to the shrines of saints. In spite of this increase in religious devotion, the Church was

of these guns, cannons were later produced. By the end of the Hundred Years' War, cannons had become important weapons in offensive warfare. Their blasts were capable of destroying stone walls. As a result, castles and fortified towns could be easily taken.

Joan of Arc   By 1420 England controlled two-fifths of French soil. They carried on the war from the unconquered southern part of France.

French hopes for victory were raised when a teenage peasant girl named Joan of Arc appeared before King Charles VII. Joan told the king that heavenly voices had called her to save France. With Charles's support, she led a French army to victory at Orléans, a town that had been placed under siege by the English. Soon after her triumph, Joan fell into English hands and was burned as a witch. However, her courage and devotion had a powerful effect on the French

At Avignon, the popes built a magnificent palace that has become known as an architectural masterpiece.

unable to remedy the ills of western Europe. In fact, it was troubled by the same disunity that affected society at large.

Babylonian Captivity　　During the early 1300's, the papacy came under the influence of the French monarchy. In 1309 a French archbishop was elected Pope Clement V. Clement refused to live in Rome because of civil wars that were disrupting Italy. He established his court in Avignon, a small city in southern France. There, Clement and his successors remained until 1377.

This long period of exile is known as the Babylonian Captivity, after the exile of the Jews to Babylon in the 500's B.C. During the Avignon period, the popes worked to improve their administration and to increase church taxes. In the process, they lost much of their moral prestige. Some Europeans believed that the popes had shamefully abandoned Rome, which they felt was the true center of the Church. Others disliked the concern of the Avignon popes for money and efficiency. They believed that the popes had become corrupted by worldly power and were neglecting their spiritual duties.

Great Schism　　Finally, in 1377, Pope Gregory XI left Avignon and returned to Italy. Once again, Rome became the center of the Catholic Church. After Gregory's death a year later, Roman mobs forced the College of Cardinals to elect an Italian as Pope. The cardinals later declared the election invalid, claiming that they had voted under pressure. They elected a new Pope, who settled in Avignon. The Italian Pope, however, refused to resign. As a result, the Church faced the dilemma of having two popes at the same time. One Pope excommunicated the other, and each set up his own College of Cardinals and central administration. When the popes died, in 1389 and 1394, each College elected a new Pope.

This controversy became known as the Great Schism, because it caused serious divisions in the Church. The Great Schism lasted for 40 years. During this time, Europe's secular rulers decided which Pope their people would follow. Rulers in France, Spain, and Scotland backed the Pope at Avignon, while those in England, Italy, Germany, and Scandinavia supported the Pope at Rome.

In 1409, a council met at Pisa, Italy, to unite the Church behind one Pope. It resulted in the election of a third Pope, since neither the Pope at

After the death of Pope Gregory, the Italian archbishop, Bartolomeo Prignano was elected Pope as Urban VI. Before his election Urban VI was a modest and peaceable man; but as Pope, he alienated his political allies through harsh and condemning behavior. It was believed that he killed five cardinals who had plotted against him. How did Urban's behavior contribute to the Great Schism?

Burgundy had fought with the English during the Hundred Years' War. Flanders was one of Burgundy's chief ports. Flemish weavers had close ties with wool merchants in London.

Rome nor the Pope at Avignon would resign. Finally, in 1415, another council met at Constance, Switzerland. It forced the resignation of all three popes. It then elected a new Pope, Martin V, who won the support of all sides.

Results   With the election of Pope Martin V, the Great Schism ended. The long period of division had seriously weakened the organization and moral influence of the Church. At the same time, the secular power of the papacy had declined. By 1400 many Europeans felt a greater sense of loyalty to their monarchs than to the Pope. Also, monarchs for the first time were willing to use military force to make church leaders accept royal commands. Due to these pressures, the papacy had to accept limits on its political authority within each of Europe's kingdoms.

1. Identify: Black Death, Edward III, Hundred Years' War, Joan of Arc, Calais, Avignon, Great Schism.
2. What social and economic problems did Europeans face during the Late Middle Ages?
3. What were the causes of the Hundred Years' War? What effect did the war have on medieval Europe?

2   The Revival of Monarchy

During the 1400's, Europe's monarchs set up stronger central governments. They won the loyalty of their people and began to limit the political influence of the clergy and the nobles. Nobles and church leaders continued to serve in government posts. But monarchs increasingly appointed educated commoners and members of the laity as their closest advisers. These officials, with their legal and record-keeping skills, headed new government institutions that enforced royal authority.

France

During the Hundred Years' War, the French monarchy gained much power and prestige. In the 1440's, Charles VII began imposing taxes with the approval of the Estates-General. He created a standing, or permanent, army under his direct control.

Charles VII's son Louis XI continued to increase the monarchy's power. After becoming king in 1461, Louis set out to unite all the feudal territories in France under the French crown. He especially wanted Burgundy, which included parts of what is now eastern France, western Germany, and the Low Countries. Burgundy was one of the most prosperous areas of Europe. Its ruler, Duke Charles the Bold, had a magnificent court that attracted scholars, musicians, and painters from all parts of Europe. Proud of his territory's accomplishments, Charles wanted to break ties with France and make Burgundy an independent state.

Rather than fight Charles openly, Louis XI encouraged quarrels between Burgundy and the neighboring Swiss. In 1477 Charles fought the Swiss and was killed in battle.[4] Burgundy was then divided into two parts. The northern half, the Netherlands, went to Charles's daughter Mary. The rest became a part of France. After this victory, Louis and his successors won the allegiance of the French nobles. Through treaties and marriages, they were able to acquire the remaining feudal lands.

Louis XI worked to create a French government in which the king had supreme power. He strengthened the bureaucracy, kept a firm hold over the nobles, and promoted trade and agriculture. Louis XI's efforts helped make the monarchy the most powerful institution in France.

England

Like France, England developed a tradition of strong royal government. However, because of the Hundred Years' War, the monarch's power was limited by Parliament. Parliament won the right to levy new taxes, approve new laws, and advise the monarch on important policies.

The monarchy's authority was further eroded as a result of a change in dynasty. In 1399 King Richard II was deposed by a noble, Henry of Lancaster, who became Henry IV. Because he

---

[4]At that time, the Swiss were considered the best soldiers in Europe.

Henry VII hired architects and sculptors to rebuild Westminister Abbey, a London church used for royal weddings and coronations.

The *Reconquista* influenced Spanish literature. A famous work of the period was the *Poem of the Cid*.

had seized the throne, Henry was not widely respected as a ruler. His weak position forced him to rely on Parliament. Henry also had difficulty controlling feuds among influential noble families.

In 1477 a struggle began among the nobles for control of the English throne. Soon England was plunged into a series of battles between the royal house of Lancaster and its rival, the house of York. The conflict lasted until 1485 and became known as the Wars of the Roses.[5]

During the Wars of the Roses, Edward, duke of York, overthrew the weak Lancaster dynasty. He became King Edward IV and founded the dynasty of York. As king, Edward worked to strengthen royal government and to promote trade. Fighting still continued among rival groups of nobles. Before peace could be won, Edward died in 1483. His death brought more uncertainty to England. The heirs to the throne were the late king's two young sons. Edward's brother Richard, however, wanted to be king. He proclaimed himself Richard III and locked his young nephews in the Tower of London. Some historians believe that Richard had the boys murdered.

Because of his questionable title to the throne, Richard III faced much opposition. The last phase of the Wars of the Roses began when Henry Tudor, a Lancaster noble, laid claim to the crown. Henry raised an army and defeated Richard and his supporters at the Battle of Bosworth Field. He then became King Henry VII and founded the Tudor dynasty, which ruled England until 1603.

Henry VII acted to win the loyalty of his people. As a sign of his desire for national unity, he married Elizabeth, the daughter of one of the defeated nobles of York. Henry's hold on the throne was also strengthened because of the decline of the English nobility. Many nobles had died during the Hundred Years' War and the Wars of the Roses. Few of them were now left to challenge the Tudor dynasty. Under Henry VII, the English monarchy became strong once again.

---

[5]The Wars of the Roses received their name because each side supposedly used a rose as its emblem. York's symbol was a white rose, while Lancaster's was a red one.

Henry VII is depicted by an artist of the time as a man of peace. He is holding a red and white rose, symbol of reunion between the houses of York and Lancaster. What did Henry do to gain the affection of the people?

Still, Henry did not enjoy supreme power. He was careful to gain the approval of Parliament in making laws.

Spain

During the late 1400's, Spain emerged as an important European power. Before this time, it had gone through a long period of turmoil and warfare. From 1000 to 1200, the Christian kingdoms of northern Spain had captured most of the country from the Moors. After these military campaigns known as the *Reconquista*, or "the Reconquest," Spain consisted of three Christian kingdoms: Portugal in the west, Castile in the center, and Aragon on the Mediterranean coast. Only the principality of Granada in the south remained Muslim. Portugal became a separate kingdom, but Castile and Aragon eventually united.

Because of their devotion to Catholicism, Ferdinand and Isabella were called the "Catholic Monarchs."

Some of Spain's Jewish refugees settled in the Ottoman Empire, where their skills in weaponry and other technologies helped in the development of the Ottoman economy.

The power of monarchs in Castile and Aragon, however, was limited by local interests and large religious minority groups. During the Reconquista, monarchs had recruited Christian settlers for the territories they reconquered. They gave these settlers land under favorable terms as well as rights of local government. Large communities of Jews and Muslims lived in Castile and Aragon. They had their own laws and elected their own officials. Towns in both kingdoms had **fueros,** or special royal charters, that allowed them to keep their courts and local customs. Above all, the monarchs of Castile and Aragon had to gain approval for their policies from representative assemblies known as **cortes.**

National Unity   In 1469 Prince Ferdinand of Aragon married Princess Isabella of Castile. Within ten years, they became king and queen and established a national monarchy in Spain. However, Castile and Aragon maintained separate bureaucracies. In Castile, the two monarchs strengthened the powers of the crown and reduced local privileges. They sent officials known as **corregidores** to govern the towns and set up special courts in the countryside to enforce royal justice. Ferdinand and Isabella also worked to extend their power over all of Spain. In 1492 their armies forced the surrender of the last Moorish stronghold at Granada.

Shortly after the conquest of Granada, Ferdinand and Isabella ended the traditional policy of toleration for minority groups. They believed that all Spaniards had to be Catholic if Spain was to become truly one nation. In 1492 Spanish Jews were ordered either to become Catholics or to leave Spain. Ten years later the Moors were given the same choice. The departure of many Jews and Moors weakened Spain's economic and intellectual life. Most of the country's important bankers, merchants, and educators were either Jews or Moors. After these groups left, there were few trained Spaniards to take their place.

Inquisition   To help them unite Spain under Catholicism, Ferdinand and Isabella set up the Spanish Inquisition, a court that enforced Catholic teachings. The Inquisition believed that Jews and Moors who had converted to Catholicism still practiced their old religions in secret. It tortured, tried, and punished anyone suspected of heresy. The fear that the Inquisition created further strengthened the power of the Spanish monarchs over their people. However, it limited Spanish contacts with other parts of Europe.

Holy Roman Empire

During the 1300's, the Holy Roman Empire was the largest political unit in Europe. It included mostly German and Slav territories in

Ferdinand and Isabella rode into Granada to accept the surrender of Boabdil, the defeated Muslim ruler. The terms of surrender were generous. The Moors retained the right to bear arms and to keep their property, laws, and religion. A year later Boabdil and his followers were ordered to emigrate to North Africa. What further actions did Ferdinand and Isabella take to make Spain a strong, united nation?

Maximilian's older son, Philip I, married Joanna, the daughter of Ferdinand and Isabella of Spain. His second son, Ferdinand, married Anne of Bohemia and Hungary.

The Teutonic Knights were originally crusaders who had fought in Palestine.

the central part of the continent. The Holy Roman Empire was far from achieving national unity under a strong monarchy. While most European monarchs acquired their thrones through hereditary succession, the Holy Roman Emperor was elected to office by a German diet, or assembly of German princes. The princes governed their local territories as independent rulers. They had the right to accept or reject the emperor's requests for taxes and soldiers.

In the early 1300's, the diet named members of the Luxemburg family to the imperial throne. Under the Luxemburg emperor, Charles IV, the empire enjoyed a brief period of stability and prosperity. Before becoming Holy Roman Emperor, Charles IV had been king of Bohemia, an area that is now part of Czechoslovakia. As emperor, he made Bohemia's capital, Prague, the leading city of the empire and one of the great cultural centers of Europe.

In spite of his overall success as a ruler, Charles IV made one decision that further weakened the imperial throne. In 1356 he issued a decree that limited the number of princes taking part in imperial elections to seven. After Charles IV's death, Holy Roman Emperors were largely dependent on these seven electors. Whenever an emperor died, the electors avoided giving the throne to any powerful prince. They regularly chose as emperor only politically weak nobles with small landholdings.

In the early 1400's, the Hapsburgs, a family of nobles from Austria, gained control of most of the votes in imperial elections. After 1438, a Hapsburg prince was almost always chosen Holy Roman Emperor. Once in power, Hapsburg emperors could not control the German princes and unify the empire. However, they were able to increase their family's prestige by securing other areas of Europe.

One of the most ambitious Hapsburg emperors was Maximilian I. Elected emperor in 1493, Maximilian married Mary of Burgundy and acquired the Low Countries as part of the Hapsburg inheritance. He later married his children into powerful European royal families. Maximilian I's grandson Charles, born in 1500, eventually became king of Spain. In 1519 the German princes elected him Holy Roman Emperor as Charles V. Under Charles, the Hapsburgs became the most powerful European royal family. Their domains included Spain, Austria, Germany, the Low Countries, and Italy.

East Central Europe

The fourteenth and fifteenth centuries saw the rise of kingdoms in East Central Europe, the region between Germany and Russia. The largest and most powerful territories of this region were Poland and Hungary.

Poland   Formed about 900 by West Slavs, Poland had accepted Roman Catholicism and established close ties with western Europe. From about 1000 to 1300, it went through periods of disunity and warfare. During this time, groups of German knights known as the Teutonic Knights took advantage of Poland's difficulties. They expanded eastward and conquered areas of Poland along the Baltic Sea. There, they created farms and founded seaports. Poland profited from the Baltic Sea trade established by German merchants. It soon began to export timber and grain to western Europe.

Many Poles resented German control over parts of their land. They put aside their differences and began to unite. King Casimir III, who ruled Poland from 1333 to 1370, reduced the power of the nobles and formed a strong central government. He also provided shelter to thousands of Jews fleeing persecution in England and France. As a result, Poland had one of Europe's largest Jewish communities by the end of the Middle Ages.

In 1386 Queen Jadwiga, Casimir's successor, married Wadyslaw Jagiello, the duke of the neighboring territory of Lithuania. Their marriage led to a union of Poland and Lithuania, creating one of the larger states of Europe. With this added strength, Poland was able to confront the Germans. In 1410 Polish and Lithuanian forces under Jagiello defeated the Teutonic Knights at the Battle of Tannenburg. This victory halted and eventually reversed German expansion into Poland.

Hungary   To the south of Poland was the kingdom of Hungary. It was made up of different

The map below is the subject of the "Using Maps" section of the Chapter 10 Review.

Louis II had been named king of Hungary by the Hungarian nobles. A Polish-born prince, Louis also ruled Bohemia.

RENAISSANCE EUROPE 1500

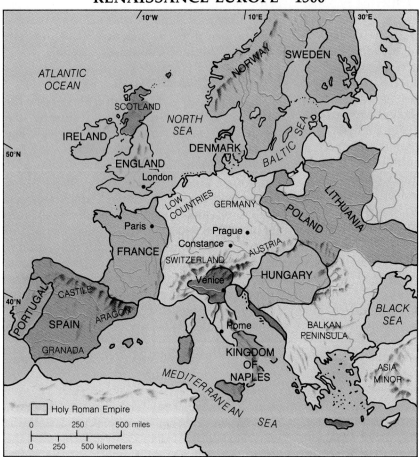

peoples—Magyars, Germans, Romanians, and Slavs. In the year 1000, King Stephen I became a Roman Catholic and introduced his people to western European ways. His family, the Arpads, ruled Hungary until 1301. At that time, the Anjou family from southern Italy took over the Hungarian throne. The greatest of the Anjou rulers was Louis I, who ruled from 1302 to 1308. Louis strengthened the monarchy and encouraged the growth of towns and trade.

After Louis I's death in 1308, Hungary was governed by weak kings, who gave away much of their power to the nobles. In the 1400's the Ottoman Turks expanded into Europe and threatened Hungarian territory. John Hunyadi, a Romanian noble, led the Hungarians in holding back the Ottoman forces. His son Matthias Corvinus became king of Hungary in 1458.

Matthias was a strong ruler who set up a government bureaucracy, encouraged learning, and established a standing army. During his reign, Hungary became the most powerful state in central Europe.

After the death of Corvinus in 1490, the Hungarian monarchy again weakened, and the nobles assumed power. At the same time, the Ottomans resumed their attacks. In 1526 Louis II of Hungary was defeated by the Ottoman ruler Suleiman I at the Battle of Mohacs. After this battle most of the country was occupied by Ottoman armies; the remaining part came under the control of the Hapsburg emperors.

Scandinavia

During the Late Middle Ages, the Viking kingdoms of Scandinavia—Norway, Sweden,

The Hanseatic League was founded in the late 1200's. By the late 1300's, it included almost all of the larger German towns along the North and Baltic seas. One of the greatest contributions of the League was a system of maritime and commercial laws.

and Denmark—became united nations. After the eleventh century, the Vikings followed a more settled lifestyle in their homelands. They accepted Christianity, developed writing systems based on the Latin alphabet, and promoted trade around the Baltic Sea and the North Atlantic. Trade rivalries and boundary disputes led to frequent wars among the Scandinavian nations. Soon a group of northern German trading cities known as the Hanseatic League acquired control of the Baltic trade and began to intervene in Scandinavian affairs.

Wanting to throw off German influence, the Scandinavian kingdoms drew closer together in the 1300's. In 1357 Margrethe I became queen of Denmark. During the next ten years, she also became the ruler of Norway and Sweden. Under her leadership, the three Scandinavian kingdoms joined together as one nation in the Union of Kalmar. Denmark soon dominated the Union. After several unsuccessful revolts against Danish policies, Sweden broke away and became a separate independent kingdom in 1523.

Economic Growth

The strength of royal governments rested on the growth of Europe's economy. During the mid-1400's, the economic slump ended. New, profitable businesses appeared that brought prosperity to new heights. New techniques and inventions increased production. Trade expanded, and Europe's cities increased their wealth.

Metals   Significant changes took place in the making and use of metal. Artisans developed skills in metalworking and made better firearms, tools, machine parts, and housewares. They also developed more accurate measuring instruments. One of the most important of these measuring devices was the mechanical clock. Operated by a system of gears, the mechanical clock permanently altered European lifestyles. With the more precise measurement of time, Europeans began to live more ordered lives. At the same time, they lost much of the spontaneity, or naturalness, of earlier generations.

With a greater demand for metals, the metals business boomed. In mineral-rich areas of central Europe, miners dug deeper mines and used pumps to drain off underground water. Simple blast furnaces were built to enable metalworkers to use the increased supply of ore. Huge bellows, driven by water power, aided the smelting and working of metal.

By the late 1400's, Europeans were producing a variety of metal products. They were also

Johann Gutenberg's design of a printing press using movable type took advantage of the new metal processes. Cast metal letters were arranged in trays, painted with ink, and covered with paper. The press was then screwed down to imprint the words onto paper. When the required number of pages were printed, the letters were rearranged for another page. What other important inventions of the time used metal parts?

Some teachers might wish to review the advances made in printing since the time of Gutenberg.

producing a large amount of silver for coinage. Money became plentiful and further stimulated the economy.

Printing   Advances in metals led to a new development in printing. About 1440 a German craftsman named Johann Gutenberg perfected a printing press that used movable metal type. With this invention, books could be printed quickly by machine rather than slowly by hand. As printing presses became widely used throughout Europe, more books were reproduced at cheaper prices. Through printed books, new ideas spread more rapidly and reached a larger number of people. Learning was no longer an activity limited to the rich and the clergy. With the growth of skilled, educated urban groups, Europe was ready for the Renaissance.

1. Identify: Louis XI, Wars of the Roses, Isabella, Hapsburg, Margrethe I, Johann Gutenberg.
2. How did monarchy develop in France, England, and Spain?
3. What problems did monarchs face in the Holy Roman Empire, in East Central Europe, and in Scandinavia?
4. What economic changes occurred in Europe during the late 1400's?

3   The Italian Renaissance

In the late 1300's, the Renaissance began in the communes, or towns of Italy. Unlike other areas of Europe, Italy had largely avoided the economic crisis of the Late Middle Ages. Italian towns remained important centers of Mediterranean trade and boosted their production of textiles and luxury goods. Economic prosperity brought new wealth and gave Italians a sense of pride in their local communities.

More than other Europeans, Italians were attached to classical traditions. The ruins of ancient Roman buildings, arches, and amphitheaters constantly reminded them of their heritage. Also through trade, Italian towns remained in close contact with the Byzantine Empire. Byzantine scholars preserved the learning of ancient Greece.

Humanism

As newly-discovered works came to their attention, Italian scholars developed an enthusiastic interest in classical writings. This interest in the classics came to be called **humanism,** and the scholars who promoted it were called **humanists.** Humanists improved their understanding of Greek and Latin, studied old manuscripts, and tried to copy the classical writing style.

As they studied, humanists came to admire classical culture and adopted many Greek and Roman beliefs. The most important belief they accepted was the dignity and worth of the individual. As a result, humanism came to mean more than just the study of the classics. It also meant a concern for people and all aspects of human life. Italian humanists, with their stress on individualism, soon brought about the achievements of the Renaissance.

Petrarch   One of the earliest humanists was Francesco Petrarca, or Petrarch, who lived from 1304 to 1374. Known as the Father of Humanism, Petrarch promoted the revival of classical studies, collected ancient manuscripts, and wrote letters in elegant Latin. He influenced the development of Italian literature. Petrarch's style of writing served as a model for writers for more than 200 years. His most noted works were 36 **sonnets,** or short poems, dedicated to Laura, a woman who died during the Black Death.

Boccaccio   Another Italian writer influenced by humanism was Giovanni Boccaccio. Like Petrarch, Boccaccio studied the classics and wrote in Latin. His most famous work is the *Decameron,* a collection of short stories written in Italian. The *Decameron* describes a group of young people who flee from Florence to the countryside during the Black Death. For ten days, they spent their time telling stories. All of these tales present a vivid and colorful account of Italian life during the 1300's.

Italian Renaissance Life

Town life was stronger in Italy than in other parts of Europe. As a result, Italians could easily discard feudalism and other medieval institutions that had their origins in the rural north. Italy did not become unified as did France and

The leading states in Italy were Venice, Milan, Florence, the Papal States, and the Kingdom of Naples. Have students locate these various states on the map on this page.

England. Wealthy and successful, most Italian communes resisted the efforts of emperors, kings, and nobles to control them. They became independent city-states. Each included a walled urban center and the surrounding countryside. With their freedom, Italians were able to carry out new endeavors in a variety of fields.

Social Groups   The Italian city-states developed a new social order in which wealth and ability were more important than aristocratic titles and landownership. Wealthy merchants and bankers replaced the landed nobility as the most powerful social group. Because of their comfortable lifestyle, they were known as the *populo grasso,* or "fat people." Beneath them were shopkeepers and artisans called the *populo minuto,* or "little people." The populo minuto were moderately prosperous and employed large numbers of poor workers. Most of the workers came to urban areas from the countryside. They made up the majority of town dwellers. The lowest social group were the peasants, who worked on the country estates of the populo grasso and supplied the towns with food.

Government   At first, most Italian city-states were republics with elected officials. They were not very stable. Social groups often fought each other for power. Political disputes in particular divided the populo grasso and the populo minuto—the two social groups that could participate in government. Workers, who usually had little or no political influence, often rose in rebellion to demand equal rights. The two upper social groups put aside their differences and worked together whenever their privileges were threatened from below. They were able to crush workers' rebellions and to continue their control of the city-states.

During the 1400's, social conflicts grew worse and paralyzed governments. To end these crises, many city-states turned all political authority over to powerful leaders called **signori.** The signori set up **dictatorships,** or governments controlled by one person or group. They used force to subdue their enemies and to restore law and order. Many signori also worked to win the loyalty of their people. They improved city

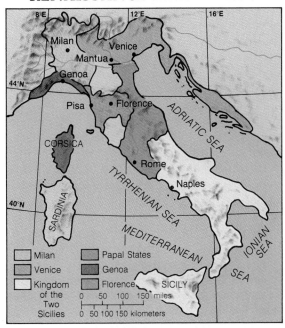

RENAISSANCE ITALY   1400's

services, promoted business, and entertained the poor with parades and ceremonies. They also supported the arts and encouraged learning.

Warfare   While dealing with internal unrest, the Italian city-states fought a long series of wars with each other. They made and unmade alliances and tried to enlarge their territories. Unlike the nobility, the merchants, bankers, and shopkeepers disliked military duty since it interfered with their business and trade. So the signori replaced citizen soldiers with mercenaries known as **condottieri.**

The Italian city-states found that wars were expensive. Thus, they began to seek territorial gain through negotiated agreements. To carry out this policy, the Italian city-states established the first modern diplomatic services. Permanent ambassadors were appointed to stay at foreign courts and represent their home territories. To maintain peace in Italy, the city-states worked out a **balance of power.** That is, they agreed that no one city-state would be allowed to gain enough power to threaten the others. During the 1500's, both of these practices—diplomacy and the balance of power—were adopted by other

HISTORY AND CITIES

Venice

Venice is one of the major seaports of Italy. Built on 118 small islands, it lies in a lagoon at the northern end of the Adriatic Sea. During the Renaissance, this favorable location enabled Venice to control the trade of most of the eastern Mediterranean world.

Venice was founded in the 600's by refugees fleeing the Lombard invasion of the Italian mainland. Isolated from the rest of Italy, Venice avoided wars and turned to the sea for a living. Venetian merchants reached Constantinople and began trading with the Byzantines. Through these contacts, Venice came under the political and cultural influence of the Byzantine Empire. However, by the 700's Venetians were able to establish an independent city-state.

Venice's economy, at first, was based on fishing and the production of salt. Later, fine cloth, glass, and leather goods were produced for export. By 1200 Venice had become a prosperous trading center with ties to both western Europe and the Byzantine Empire.

During the crusades, Venice emerged as a strong sea power. Venetian merchants supplied ships and equipment to the crusaders. In 1204 they helped the crusaders capture Constantinople, and they shared the booty. A network of Venetian colonies and trading centers soon developed throughout the eastern Mediterranean. From these centers, such luxury goods as sugar, spices, and silks were sent in Venetian ships to western Europe.

In the 1300's Venice fought and defeated the city-state of Genoa, its chief Italian rival. This victory enabled the Venetians to gain complete control of the eastern Mediterranean trade. At the height of its power in the 1400's, Venice was known as the "Queen of the Seas." It controlled a commercial empire that included Crete, Cyprus, and the entire Adriatic region.

Peace and prosperity brought Venice many years of political stability. Officially a republic, Venice was governed by a doge, or a duke. Real power, however, was in the hands of a small group of merchant families. They ruled through an executive committee known as the Council of Ten. The Council passed laws and elected the doge.

Venetians were required to place loyalty to the city-state above concern for their families and

After the deaths of the great Venetian painters Titian and Tintoretto, great works of art continued to be studied in Venice, but few were produced there again until the 1700's. In 1720 Giovanni Antonio Canaletto began painting picturesque Venetian scenes, capturing the city's artistic beauty. In his painting of Ascension Day on the Grand Canal, Canaletto shows, in realistic detail, the annual ceremony that symbolizes the marriage of the city and the sea.

friends. They had to report any suspicious behavior to the Council of Ten. Citizens who wanted to make an accusation placed a letter stating the charges in special boxes found throughout the city. Accused persons were immediately arrested and brought before the Council. Council members then met in secret to study the evidence, listen to witnesses, and decide guilt or innocence.

Because of its location, Venice developed features that were unique among European cities. Instead of streets, the city had canals. The largest and busiest was the Grand Canal, which wound through the center of Venice. The Rialto, or business district, lay along a stretch of the canal. There, traders from all over the world crowded the docks to buy and sell goods.

The center of city life was Saint Mark's Square. The Cathedral of Saint Mark, at the east end of the square, was one of Venice's outstanding examples of Byzantine architecture. It was built in the shape of a Greek cross, with a dome over the center and four smaller domes on the arms of the cross. The interior was richly adorned with marble and mosaics. Next to the cathedral was the doge's palace. Built in Gothic style, the palace served as a residence for the doge and as a meeting place for government officials.

Most Venetians, however, had more modest dwellings. Many merchants and shopkeepers lived on the top floors of the buildings that housed their shops. Poor people, who worked for low wages in the shipyards, lived in nearby slums.

Venetian families were close-knit. Most family members lived and worked together in the same neighborhoods. Marriages were arranged as if they were business deals. Men spent long hours at work. They spent their leisure time talking in the piazzas, or public squares, and in taverns. Women stayed at home, ran the households, and raised the children.

Among the Venetians, dress was very stylish. Most men dressed in tights and tunics. Some also wore cloaks and caps. Women dressed in long, flowing dresses with tight bodices and high necklines. Rich people usually wore brightly colored clothing made from expensive silks and velvets.

Venetians loved elaborate parades and ceremonies. Each year a ceremony was held on the Grand Canal to celebrate Venice's mastery of the sea. The ruling doge, dressed in gold robes, traveled down the canal on a gold-covered gondola, or a long, narrow Venetian boat. From the gondola, the doge threw a gold ring into the waters as he said, "We wed the sea in honor of our everlasting rule."

By 1500 Venice's control of the sea had started to decline. The Ottoman Turks captured Venetian trade and colonies in the east. To make up for these losses, the Venetians turned westward. They expanded their territory on the mainland and began to play an important role in Italian diplomacy and commerce.

Meanwhile, the center of European trade shifted to Portugal, Spain, and other kingdoms along the Atlantic coast. As these lands developed new trade routes, Venice's economic strength further weakened.

In spite of economic decline, Venice maintained its position as one of the leading cultural centers of Europe. For centuries it had looked to Constantinople and western Europe for artistic inspiration. As a result, Venice was influenced by a variety of artistic styles, including Byzantine, Romanesque, and Gothic.

In the late 1500's, Venice received the Renaissance artistic tradition. Venetian painters, such as Titian, Tintoretto, and Giorgione, used brilliant oil colors to portray rural landscapes and mythological and religious themes. Architects like Sansovino and Palladio erected buildings in the Renaissance style. As a result, the focus of Italian art shifted from Rome to Venice, making Venice the last great center of the Italian Renaissance.

1. How was Venice governed?
2. What made Venice unique among European cities?
3. What foreign cultures influenced the development of the arts in Venice?
4. What factors brought about the decline of Venice's trade and economy?

Almost a third of the people in Florence made a living by importing wool from agricultural countries and selling finished cloth all over Europe and the Middle East.

Filippo Brunelleschi's dome for the Florence Cathedral was probably the greatest engineering feat of the Renaissance period. The dome still dominates the skyline of Florence, rising over the cathedral's bell tower and the spire of the town hall clock. Under whose rule did Florence become famous for its beautiful buildings?

European states in their relations with each other.

Although the Italian city-states had much in common, each developed its own individual life. Two cities in particular played leading roles in the Renaissance. They were Florence and Rome.

Florence   Florence was the birthplace of the Italian Renaissance. Located in central Italy, its major economic activities were banking and textile production. Originally a republic, Florence in the 1400's came under the rule of a prominent banking family known as the Medicis. Cosimo de´ Medici, the first of his family to rule Florence, favored the lower and middle social groups over the rich. He worked to establish peace between Florence and its neighbors. Because of the popularity of his policies, Cosimo earned the title *pater patrae,* or "the father of his country."

Cosimo's grandson Lorenzo, who ruled from 1469 to 1492, was also a popular leader. During Lorenzo's rule, Florence became known for its splendid festivals, elegant social life, and beautiful buildings. It became a city of art and learning. Lorenzo used his wealth to support artists, philosophers, and writers. As a result of the city's prosperity and fame, Lorenzo was known as "the Magnificent."

During the 1490's, Florence's economic prosperity faded, and the people grew tired of Medici rule. Discontented groups gave their support to a Dominican friar named Girolamo Savonarola. In his fiery preaching, Savonarola accused the Medicis of corruption and called for the reform of Florence's government. In 1494 Savonarola's supporters overthrew the Medicis.

Savonarola believed that Renaissance values encouraged loose living and were ruining Florence. On his advice, the city's new leaders imposed strict regulations on public behavior. Parties, gambling, swearing, and horse racing were banned. Savonarola urged his listeners to repent. For a time, he had crowds make bonfires to burn paintings, fancy clothes, and musical instruments.

Savonarola soon aroused a great deal of opposition. His criticism of church officials angered the Pope. Many people in Florence disliked his strict ways. In 1498 Savonarola was hanged for heresy, and the Medicis returned to power. However, by this time, Florence's greatness had passed.

Rome   About 1500 Rome replaced Florence as the leading Renaissance city. The popes, who were anxious to increase their prestige, rebuilt the city. They had architects construct large churches and palaces with beautiful gardens, fountains, and sculpture. Scholars came from all over Europe to study manuscripts and books in the Vatican Library.

Renaissance popes often placed political goals ahead of religious duties. In ruling the Papal States, they sent ambassadors to other lands, collected taxes, and fought wars. The most

Because of the actions of Church leaders such as Pope Alexander VI, many devout Catholics desired reform for their Church.

Have students use Machiavelli's principles to evaluate major European rulers of this time.

politically-minded Pope was Alexander VI. Elected Pope in 1492, Alexander had bribed the College of Cardinals to vote for him. Once in office, he used the wealth of the Church to support his family, the Borgias. He especially encouraged his son Cesare, who raised an army and conquered much of central Italy.

After Alexander's death in 1503, his successors, Julius II and later Leo X, promoted artistic projects to beautify Rome. Their most notable effort was the rebuilding of St. Peter's Basilica, the largest church in the Christian world.

Italian Renaissance Learning

Italian Renaissance writers and thinkers became the first people to realize that Europe was leaving the Middle Ages and entering a new era. They saw the medieval period as a time of darkness and looked forward to a new civilization based on the long-forgotten ideals of ancient Greece and Rome. Inspired by classical culture, they improved methods of education, developed new styles of literature, and established new rules of conduct.

Scholarship   Italian humanists advanced learning and laid the foundation of modern western scholarship. Instead of promoting a cause, they aimed to be impartial in their search for truth. To help them in their work, they developed new methods of research.

For the first time, western scholars carefully began to analyze and interpret old documents, using their knowledge of classical languages. Their research led them to challenge long-standing traditions about the past. Humanists became concerned about accuracy and legibility in writing. They developed rules for spelling and grammar. They produced dictionaries, textbooks, and other educational materials.

Teaching   Humanists were devoted to teaching as well as to research. They began to replace the clergy as leaders in education. Schools based on humanist principles were set up in the towns to train the sons of wealthy merchants and artisans. In addition to such traditional subjects as reading, writing, and arithmetic, students studied the classics, history, and philosophy.

Humanists called these new studies *studia Humanitatis,* or the humanities. They believed that the humanities would train well-rounded citizens. As part of this program, students also learned good manners and took part in body-building sports such as wrestling, fencing, and swimming.

Literature   The Renaissance emphasis on the individual led to the development of new forms of literature. One of these was the modern autobiography. In the mid-1550's, Benvenuto Cellini, a goldsmith-sculptor, wrote his famous *Autobiography,* in which he described his fast-paced life and boasted about his many various accomplishments.

Another achievement in literature was the writing of political science. In the early 1500's, Niccolò Machiavelli, a diplomat from Florence, wrote *The Prince,* a book which realistically analyzed the politics of Renaissance Italy. According to Machiavelli, rulers must be prepared to use force and deceit in order to hold power. While critics charged that Machiavelli's book justified immoral behavior in politics, *The Prince* appealed to power-hungry Renaissance rulers. It also influenced the political thought and actions of later generations.

Manners   Renaissance writers produced handbooks to instruct townspeople in good manners. The most famous handbook was *The Courtier,* written in 1518 by the diplomat-scholar Baldassare Castiglione. In *The Courtier,* men were taught to be "the ideal gentlemen," skilled in many fields of knowledge, including art, science, sports, and politics. The ideal Renaissance hostess was to be graceful, attractive, courteous, and well educated.

Women   The Renaissance emphasis on education and good manners improved somewhat the position of women. Aristocratic women were given new respect and allowed more educational opportunities. Girls from noble families were taught at home by tutors, some of whom were noted humanist scholars. Merchants' daughters attended schools in convents. No formal learning was provided for daughters of the poor. They were taught to sew, cook, and manage a household.

Donatello's talent was recognized after he sculpted the statues at the churches of Saint Mark and Saint George in the early 1400's.

A number of Renaissance women made outstanding contributions. Isabella d'Este, duchess of Mantua, a small Italian territory, was one of the most intelligent and cultured persons of her day. After her husband was captured in battle, Isabella ruled Mantua with great political skill and attracted artists and scholars to her court. Another famous noblewoman was Lucretia Borgia, daughter of Pope Alexander VI. She became known for her lively parties and her love of music and the arts. She also gained a reputation for poisoning her enemies.

Italian Renaissance Art

Art was an important part of life in Renaissance Italy. The public appreciated works of art and hailed great artists as geniuses. Nobles and townspeople used art to decorate homes as well as churches. They lavishly rewarded artists and gave them a prominent place in society. Having greater security and self-confidence, Renaissance artists developed new forms and techniques based on the classical ideals of beauty, simplicity, elegance, and balance. In their works, they sought to praise human achievement and to win fame for themselves.

Architecture   Italian Renaissance architects departed from the Gothic style and returned to classical architecture. They used domes, columns, and other classical features in the construction of new churches, palaces, homes, and villas. Renaissance architects tried to make their buildings both comfortable and beautiful. They filled them with tapestries, paintings, statues, finely made furniture, and glass windows.

The most famous Italian Renaissance architect was Filippo Brunelleschi. Brunelleschi studied Roman ruins to learn the principles of classical architecture. In 1436 he completed an octagonal, or eight-sided, dome for the cathedral of Florence. The people of Florence considered Brunelleschi's dome to be the greatest engineering feat of the time.

Sculpture   Renaissance sculpture reflected a return to classical ideals. Sculptors were primarily concerned about expressing the beauty of the human body. They carefully studied human anatomy and made lifelike statues that accurately showed muscles, joints, and other body parts. Unlike medieval sculpture, Renaissance figures were usually nude and stood free of any architectural background.

The earliest Renaissance sculptor was Donatello. Donatello worked in Florence, where he sculpted the first statue cast in bronze since ancient times. Another sculptor, Lorenzo Ghiberti, designed bronze doors for the baptistry of Florence's cathedral. His work combined the classical style with a medieval religious theme. The people of Florence greatly admired Ghiberti's doors and called them the "Gates of Heaven."

Painting   Italian Renaissance painters departed from the flat, symbolic style of medieval painting and became more realistic. They tried to show human forms and facial features as they looked in real life. They aimed to portray thoughts, feelings, and action. This realistic style was developed as a result of the careful study of classical art, science, mathematics, the details of nature, and human anatomy.

Biblical, classical, and mythological characters were common subjects in Renaissance paintings. The emphasis on realism also encouraged the painting of portraits, landscapes, and scenes from everyday life.

The new style of painting was first developed in Florence. In the early 1300's, Giotto, an artist-sculptor-architect, did a series of frescoes showing the life of Francis of Assisi. The figures in the frescoes looked like real people with strong emotions.

Later in the 1400's, Masaccio, another artist of Florence, painted *Tribute Money*, a wall painting that portrayed Jesus and his disciples. In painting, Masaccio used light and shade to create rounded figures and to set them apart from the background. He gave his paintings a sense of depth by using **perspective.** That is, figures and objects were made to look smaller as they appeared farther away from the viewer. Masaccio's use of lighting and perspective influenced later Renaissance artists.

High Renaissance   Renaissance art reached its height in Rome during the early 1500's. This period is often called the High Renaissance.

Leonardo da Vinci's design for military machines led to his gaining lucrative jobs as military engineer for both Ludovico Sforza of Milan and for Ceasar Borgia of Romagna.

Perspective

Renaissance artists applied mathematical rules to their paintings. They developed new techniques to portray people, animals, and objects as they appear in real life. The technique of perspective enabled artists to show solid, rounded figures at different distances in their paintings. By changing color tones and arranging lines, artists could create a sense of depth on a flat surface. To perfect their use of perspective, many artists filled sketchbooks with drawings of humans and animals. Others preferred to draw outlines of objects, such as vases and urns.

During the High Renaissance, a number of gifted artists appeared who worked in a variety of fields. In many ways, they represented the Renaissance ideal of the individual.

Leonardo da Vinci   One of the greatest of the High Renaissance artists was Leonardo da Vinci. A citizen of Florence, he did much of his work in other Italian cities, including Milan and Rome. Leonardo is best known for the *Mona Lisa*, a portrait of a strangely smiling young woman of Florence, and the *Last Supper*, a wall painting of Jesus' last meal with his disciples. In both works, Leonardo skillfully portrayed people's personalities, thoughts, and feelings as well as their physical appearances.

Leonardo da Vinci was a scientist as well as an artist. He wrote books on astronomy, mathematics, and anatomy. He made illustrations of inventions far ahead of his time. His drawings include designs for parachutes, flying machines, mechanical diggers, and artillery.

Michelangelo Buonarroti   Another outstanding High Renaissance artist was Michelangelo Buonarroti. Michelangelo began his career as a sculptor in Florence. There, he did the marble statue of *David*, after the biblical charac-

ter. Later in Rome, he sculpted *Pietà*, which shows the dead Jesus in the arms of his mother Mary. Most of Michelangelo's sculptures were awesome in size and suggested controlled but intense emotions.

In 1505 Michelangelo was hired to work at the Vatican, the Pope's court in Rome. Pope Julius II had him paint the ceiling of the Sistine Chapel. Showing scenes from the Old Testament, Michelangelo's completed work was described in glowing terms by the Renaissance biographer Giorgio Vasari:

> *When the work was thrown open, the whole world came running to see what Michelangelo had done; and certainly it was such as to make everyone speechless with astonishment. Then the Pope, exalted by the results and encouraged to undertake even more grandiose enterprises, generously rewarded Michelangelo with rich gifts and money.**

Later Michelangelo painted *Last Judgment* above the altar of the Sistine Chapel. All of Michelangelo's painted figures resembled works

---

**Lives of the Artists*, Giorgio Vasari, tr. by George Bull, © 1965, Penguin Books, pp. 360-61.

Francis I hired the leading Italian artists to decorate his magnificent palace of Fontainebleau.

Michelangelo's ceiling in the Sistine Chapel took four years of arduous endeavor. Michelangelo painted figures such as St. Zacharias while lying on his back on scaffolding raised 70 feet (21 meters) above the floor. Though unable to step back and see the broad effect, he was able to introduce a sense of dimension on his work. Where did Michelangelo begin his career?

of sculpture. They had well-formed muscular bodies that expressed vitality and power. Michelangelo ended his artistic career by designing the dome of the new Saint Peter's Basilica.

Raphael Santi   The last great artist of the High Renaissance was Raphael Santi. Like Michelangelo, Raphael worked at the Vatican. He completed a series of paintings on classical and religious themes for the Pope's apartments. Raphael is most noted for his paintings of Mary, the mother of Jesus. These works were done in bright colors and reflected the Renaissance ideals of grace, harmony, and beauty.

1. Identify: Petrarch, Boccaccio, Lorenzo de´ Medici, Girolamo Savonarola, Alexander VI, Saint Peter's Basilica, Niccolò Machiavelli, Isabella d'Este, Masaccio, Leonardo da Vinci, Michelangelo Buonarroti.
2. Why did the Renaissance begin in Italy?
3. What were the major concerns of the humanists? What contributions did they make?
4. What were the major features of Renaissance art?

4   Spread of the Renaissance

During the late 1400's, the Renaissance spread from Italy to other areas of Europe. Italian artists and scholars traveled to foreign courts and universities. Other Europeans, in turn, went to Italy and studied under Italian masters. Through these contacts, Italian ideas and styles were adopted by the rest of the continent.

France

The Renaissance came to France as a result of renewed warfare in the Italian peninsula. In 1494 the French began a series of invasions of Italy. After a few early successes, they entered into a long conflict with the German and Spanish Hapsburgs, which lasted most of the 1500's. The war finally ended in defeat for the French.

Francis I   The leading supporter of the Renaissance in France was Francis I, who ruled

The van Eyck style of painting influenced many painters north of the Alps in the 1400's.

from 1515 to 1547. While in Italy, he and his nobles were attracted by Italian art and fashions. They brought Leonardo da Vinci and other Italian artists and scholars to their courts in France. They also collected Italian paintings and sculpture. Gradually, with royal and aristocratic support, the French began to develop their own Renaissance based on Italian models.

The French particularly excelled in architecture. Francis I and his nobles hired Italian architects to build **châteaux,** or castles, in the Loire River Valley south of Paris. These châteaux became known for their blend of harmonious classical design and graceful decoration.

Writers   The Renaissance in France led to the growth of French literature. French poets, led by Pierre de Ronsard and Joachim de Bellay, studied classical works and adopted new writing styles from Italian Renaissance poetry. They wrote poems in French, using classical and Italian words to enrich their own language. The most noted French writer in prose was the physician-monk François Rabelais. Rabelais wrote comical tales and satire. In his popular works *Gargantua* and *Pantagruel,* he used adventure stories about two giants to poke fun at the Church, universities, and other institutions of his day. Rejecting the otherworldliness of the Middle Ages, Rabelais believed that humans were naturally good and did not need salvation. Another writer, Michel de Montaigne, was more pessimistic about human nature. In *Essays,* Montaigne pointed out the inconsistencies and flaws in human behavior.

Germany and the Low Countries

The Italian Renaissance was enthusiastically accepted by the wealthy towns of Germany and the Low Countries. Universities and schools promoted humanist learning, and printers produced a large quantity of books. Latin was still the main scholarly language, but writers increased their use of German and Dutch.

Christian Humanism   Unlike Italy, the Renaissance in northern Europe had a more religious tone. Groups of scholars known as Christian humanists emerged. The most famous was Erasmus of Rotterdam.

Erasmus and his colleagues learned Greek and Hebrew so that they could understand the earliest versions of the Bible. Their biblical studies helped them appreciate early Christian beliefs and practices. As a result, they became critical of many church traditions that had developed during the Middle Ages. In his work *Praise of Folly,* Erasmus questioned such practices as monasticism, the worship of saints, and elaborate church rituals.

The Christian humanists wanted reforms in Catholicism that would eliminate abuses and restore the simple piety of the early Church. They believed that humanist learning and Bible study were the best ways to promote these goals.

Painting   Artists in northern Europe developed a style of painting that relied more on medieval than classical models. In the early 1400's, a group of Flemish painters, led by the brothers Jan and Hubert van Eyck, painted scenes from the Bible and daily life in sharp, realistic detail. They developed the technique of painting in oils. Oils provided artists with richer colors and allowed them to make changes on the painted canvas. Painting in oils soon spread to Italy. Meanwhile, Italian Renaissance art reached northern Europe. Dutch artists such as Peter Brueghel combined Italian technique with the artistic traditions of their homeland. They began painting realistic portraits, landscapes, and scenes of peasant life.

England

The Renaissance flourished in England after the Wars of the Roses, which ended in 1485. Henry VII invited many Italian humanist scholars to England. These people encouraged English scholars to study classical literature.

English humanists worked to improve their society. The biblical scholar John Colet admired the Renaissance schools of Italy and founded a school in London to train the sons of nobles and merchants for service in the Church and government. Another humanist, Thomas More, wrote *Utopia,* a book that criticized the society of his day by comparing it with an ideal society in which all citizens are equal and prosperous. More wrote his work in Latin and based it on Plato's *Republic.*

The English Renaissance was especially known for drama. The best known English **playwrights,** or writers of plays, were William Shakespeare and Christopher Marlowe. They drew ideas for their works from medieval legends, classical mythology, and the histories of England and ancient Rome.

Effects of the Renaissance

By the late 1500's, the Renaissance had deeply influenced European life. Its emphasis on intellectual inquiry called into question many long-standing beliefs and practices. Its belief in the importance of the individual led to a growing dissatisfaction with the restraints imposed by traditional political and religious authorities. Although secular in its outlook, the Renaissance did not necessarily contradict Europe's Christian heritage. In fact, a religious revival took place alongside the new interest in the classics. Devout Europeans, in greater numbers, were concerned about the worldliness of the institutional Church and began to search for a more personal faith. This spiritual restlessness soon led to a religious crisis in western Europe.

1. Identify: Francis I, François Rabelais, *Praise of Folly*, Peter Brueghel, Thomas More, William Shakespeare.
2. How did the Renaissance influence French literature?
3. What were the goals of the Christian humanists?
4. How did the Renaissance spread to other parts of Europe?

CHAPTER 10 REVIEW

Summary

1. During the 1300's and early 1400's, western Europe underwent a period of economic decline, religious uncertainty, plague, famine, and war.
2. The Hundred Years' War unified England and France and contributed to the decline of feudalism and the rise of strong royal government in both nations.
3. The kings of France strengthened their monarchy by improving government administration, creating a standing army, and acquiring feudal territories.
4. The English monarchy at first was weakened by the rise of Parliament and disputes among the nobility. After the Wars of the Roses, the Tudor dynasty came to power and strengthened the English throne.
5. During the 1300's and 1400's, national monarchies emerged in Spain, Scandinavia, and East Central Europe.
6. By the mid-1400's, economic conditions improved in western Europe. New inventions, such as the printing press, transformed European society. Meanwhile, western European scholars developed an interest in classical writings and started a new age called the Renaissance.
7. The Renaissance began and flourished in the Italian cities of Florence, Rome, and Venice. There, local rulers used their wealth to support the arts. Italian artists and writers developed new forms of art and literature based on classical models.
8. In the late 1400's and early 1500's, the Renaissance spread from Italy to other parts of Europe. In France, kings and nobles encouraged the development of a uniquely French literature, architecture, and art.
9. In Germany and the Low Countries, scholars studied the Bible and worked for church reforms, while painters developed a realistic and detailed style of painting.
10. In England, scholars worked to improve their society. The English Renaissance was especially known for drama based on classical and historical themes.

Building Vocabulary

depression	cortes	sonnets	balance of power
gentry	corregidores	signori	perspective
commoners	humanism	dictatorships	châteaux
fueros	humanists	condottieri	playwrights

Reviewing the Main Ideas

1. What impact did the Black Death have on western Europe?
2. What inventions appeared in western Europe during the 1300's and 1400's? How did these inventions change western European life?
3. Why did townspeople and gentry support the rise of strong monarchies in western Europe?
4. What problems faced the Roman Catholic Church at the end of the Middle Ages?
5. How did Louis IX strengthen the French monarchy?
6. What were the results of the Wars of the Roses?
7. What was the Reconquista? How did it contribute to the unity of Spain?
8. How did Charles IV's decree of 1356 weaken the throne of the Holy Roman Empire?
9. Why was the Battle of Tannenburg important to East Central Europe?
10. How did the governments of Italian city-states change during the 1400's?
11. What were the Renaissance ideals?
12. How did the Renaissance in northern Europe differ from the Renaissance in Italy?

Discussing Important Ideas

1. If you were a European monarch of the 1300's how would you have responded to the social and economic crises of the period?
2. Some historians believe that the Great Schism and the Babylonian Captivity seriously damaged the moral prestige of the papacy. Explain.
3. Compare and contrast the medieval monarchies of England and France. Which do you think developed the more stable form of government?
4. Do you agree with Ferdinand and Isabella that all the people of a nation should follow the same religion? Explain.
5. Did the invention of the printing press aid the growth of royal government? Why or why not?
6. In what ways was Renaissance thinking different from medieval thinking?
7. Do you agree or disagree with Machiavelli's belief that rulers must be prepared to use force and deceit in order to hold power? Explain the reasons for your answer.
8. Compare and contrast the life of Renaissance women with that of modern women.
9. Which artist or writer made the greatest contribution during the Renaissance period? Explain the reasons for your answer.

Using Maps

Refer to the map on page 240 to answer the following questions:
1. What are the colors used for on the map? Why do some countries have the same color?
2. Do Germany and Austria form the eastern or western boundary of East Central Europe?
3. Which countries made up the Holy Roman Empire in 1500?
4. The term "Scandinavia" applies to which countries on the map?
5. What is the approximate distance from Paris to Rome? from Constance to Prague?

CHAPTER 11

Luther's Bible

> **❝ Faith is a living and unshakeable confidence, a belief in the grace of God so assured that [a person] would die a thousand deaths for its sake. ❞**
>
> Martin Luther, Protestant reformer (1483-1546)

Reformation

During the 1300's and 1400's, the Roman Catholic Church still held the loyalty of almost all western Europeans.[1] However, its leaders failed to adjust to the many social, economic, and political changes taking place in western Europe. As a result, it suffered serious setbacks and lost much of its spiritual influence. Serious abuses continued in the administration of the Church, and the clergy often placed worldly ambition ahead of their spiritual duties.

Around 1500, educated western Europeans were calling for a **reformation,** or a change in the ways the Church taught and practiced Christianity. However, they differed about the types of change needed. Conservative reformers wanted to restore the Church's spiritual health while keeping the best of its medieval traditions. Radical reformers questioned basic Catholic teachings and practices. They called for more preaching and a return to the simpler faith of the early Church. These differences led to a split in western Christianity that has lasted to the present time. By 1600, western Europe and the areas of the world under its influence had many Christian churches. All of these churches competed with each other for the faith and allegiance of the people.

1   Cry for Reform

The 1300's and 1400's in western Europe were still an "age of faith." People were filled with respect and awe for the power of God. Art, literature, and architecture were generally concerned with religious themes. Although Renaissance scholars adopted secular attitudes, they avoided an open break with the Church.

For the common people, life was harsh. Disease, famine, and war were continual threats.

The new learning of the Renaissance had little impact on the average European, whose knowledge of the natural world remained very limited. People often felt helpless in the face of the difficult circumstances. The Church was for many the only source of comfort in a seemingly dark and mysterious world.

Church Abuses

During the Middle Ages, popes had acquired much power and wealth. With the growth of papal authority, serious abuses appeared in the Church. One of the abuses concerned money. The large administrative structure of medieval Catholicism was expensive to maintain. To acquire more funds, the clergy used many money-raising devices that were unpopular and hurt the Church's spiritual life. Fees were charged for almost every kind of church service. **Simony,** or the selling of church positions, was especially disliked since the price of buying an office was passed on to the common people. In addition, one person would often hold several church positions and never carry out any of the responsibilities. Along with these abuses, the popes and higher clergy became increasingly accustomed to living in luxury like secular princes. Their lifestyles further damaged public regard for the Church.

Church Councils

The Babylonian Captivity and the Great Schism aroused great resentment against the powers of the papacy. Many kings, princes, and church scholars called for a reform of church government. The most popular remedy was a general church council. However, there were several problems with this solution. First, such councils were traditionally called by popes. No Pope was willing to call a council that would limit his authority. Yet, the legality of a council would be questionable if it did not receive papal approval. Second, different rulers in Europe

---

[1]The largest non-Catholic minority in medieval western Europe was the Jews. While some Christians recognized Jewish contributions to society, many persecuted the Jews for not accepting Christianity.

supported particular popes for political reasons. Such political divisions made it almost impossible to reach agreement on the site of a council, not to mention the deeper issues involved. Finally, the question was raised: if the Pope could be deposed by a council, who was the real head of the Church?

By 1400 many western Europeans were committed to the idea of a church council. In 1417 a church council at Constance, Switzerland, ended the Great Schism. The new Pope, Martin V, and his immediate successors restored papal authority and limited the use of church councils. Still, the effects of the Great Schism lingered and seriously undermined respect for the papacy.

John Wycliffe

In the late 1300's, papal policies had been strongly opposed in England. There, an Oxford University scholar named John Wycliffe spoke out against the papacy. Claiming that the Bible was the sole authority for religious truth, Wycliffe criticized the Church's wealth and its hierarchy of clergy. He wanted secular rulers to remove church officials who were immoral or corrupt. He also called for an end to church ceremonies that were not mentioned in the Bible.

Wycliffe's most revolutionary act was translating the Bible from Latin into English so that the common people could read it for themselves. Such an act made it more difficult for the Church to keep its monopoly on religious truth. It also led Wycliffe's followers, known as Lollards, to develop a variety of biblical interpretations. To show their dislike of the Church, the more radical Lollards destroyed the images of saints, ridiculed the Mass, and ate communion bread with onions to show that it was no different from regular bread.

Because of widespread anti-papal feelings, the government found it difficult to suppress the Lollards. Wycliffe himself was persuaded to moderate his views and received only a mild punishment. He died peacefully in 1384, and his beliefs continued to spread.

Many influential people in England supported the Lollards. They included Queen Anne, the wife of King Richard II. Born in Bohemia, Anne sent several copies of Wycliffe's writings to her homeland. There, his views became popular.

Jan Hus

During the late 1300's and early 1400's, the Slavs of Bohemia, known as Czechs, strongly backed reforms in the Catholic Church. In addition, they became aware of their own national identity and wanted to end German control of their country. Czech religious and national grievances combined to produce an explosive situation.

The Czechs began to criticize the corruption of leading church officials, many of whom were German. They produced religious pamphlets and copies of the Bible in the Czech language rather than in Latin. The leader of the Czech reform movement was the popular preacher and university professor Jan Hus. The religious views of Hus were similar to those of Wycliffe. His writing and preaching aroused anti-Church and anti-German feelings. When Hus and his works were condemned by church and political leaders, a wave of demonstrations and riots swept across Bohemia.

Hussite Wars Faced with the possibility of a full-scale rebellion against the Church, the Council at Constance in 1415 called Hus before it to defend his views. The Council gave the Czech reformer a promise of protection. It later went back on its word and had Hus burned at the stake as a heretic. Instead of depriving the Czechs of a leader, this act provided them with a hero around whom they could rally. From 1420 to 1436, a series of battles known as the Hussite Wars took place in Bohemia between the supporters of Hus and the defenders of the Church.

During these wars, the Church, with the support of the Holy Roman Emperor, launched five crusades against the Hussites, as the supporters of Hus were called. All of the crusades failed. Hussite soldiers, mostly peasants, were brave fighters. They combined the new firearms technology with the ancient Bohemian tactic of forming defensive walls with farm wagons. The pro-Catholic forces were unable to break the strength and determination of the

Luther had joined the Augustinian order. At the time, it was one of the largest in Europe.

Jan Hus was a noted scholar-preacher. His ideas reached scholars, townspeople, and peasants among the Czech population of Bohemia. The execution of Hus in 1415 united the Czechs against the Roman Catholic Church. Why were Hus's followers able to withstand the crusades supported by church and political authorities?

Hussites. Hussite armies pushed north into Germany, plundering towns and villages all the way to the Baltic Sea.

Peace　By 1436 the Church realized that it could not defeat the Hussites. Representatives of the Pope and the Holy Roman Emperor held talks with the Hussite leaders. Their aim was to keep Hussite beliefs from spreading beyond Bohemia to other parts of Europe. The Hussites, not ready for a complete break with Rome, were willing to compromise. The Church allowed them certain religious liberties in return for allegiance to the Church. Although Hussite military expansion was checked, Hussite ideas spread throughout Europe to influence later and more radical reformers.

1. Identify: Martin V, John Wycliffe, Lollards, Bohemia, Jan Hus.
2. What abuses appeared in the late medieval Church?
3. What reforms did Wycliffe and Hus propose? How did their ideas influence European society?

2　Martin Luther

In the early 1500's, a movement for church reform arose in Germany. It eventually led to a permanent split in the western Church and produced a new form of Christianity known as Protestantism.[2] The series of events that gave birth to Protestantism is known as the Protestant Reformation.

Luther's Early Life

The Protestant Reformation was begun by a German named Martin Luther. Luther, born in 1483, was the son of peasants. His family wanted him to be a lawyer, but he was more interested in religion. In 1506 Luther was caught in a violent thunderstorm and nearly hit by lightning. Terrified by this ordeal, he vowed that he would become a monk.

As a monk, Luther faithfully followed church teachings and practices. Yet he could find no peace of mind. He wondered how God would judge his actions and if he would go to heaven when he died.

While studying the Bible, Luther found the answer to questions that had been troubling him. He decided that trusting in Jesus, rather than doing good works, would save people from their sins. Through faith, people could be certain that God loved them and that they would receive salvation. Luther later stated that because of this

---

[2]Protestantism received its name from the claim of the early Protestants that they were protesting against the corruption of the Catholic Church and affirming basic Christian truths.

Point out that Tetzel was a Dominican. At the time, the conflict between Luther and Tetzel was viewed as little more than a squabble between the Augustinians and Dominicans.

discovery he felt as if he "had been born again and had entered Paradise through wide open gates."

Conflict

In the following years, Luther's ideas quietly matured as he pursued a career as a university professor. They eventually brought him into conflict with the Church. Pope Leo X wanted money to rebuild St. Peter's Basilica in Rome. In order to raise the necessary funds, he authorized the sale of **indulgences.** These were documents issued by the Church that freed their owners from time in **purgatory.** According to Catholic teaching, purgatory is a place of suffering in the life to come. There, people must be purified of their sins before going to heaven.

During the Middle Ages, the fear of purgatory strengthened the appeal of indulgences. Originally, indulgences had been granted to crusaders for their efforts in defending the faith. In time, they were sold to any of the faithful who wanted them. The idea was that the money paid was a sign of repentance and was made holy by being given to the Church. According to Catholic thinking, this was a good practice. However, the Church abused it by using it as an easy way to raise money.

Indulgence sales were especially profitable in Germany. There, no strong central government existed to hinder the Church's effort to raise money and take it out of the country. Such increased fund raising angered many Germans. It made them more willing to listen to criticism of the Church.

The Church's agent for selling indulgences in northern Germany was John Tetzel. Tetzel's method of raising money was somewhat questionable. He told the local peasants that indulgences would relieve them of guilt for future sins and immediately free relatives already in purgatory. He even had a little jingle: "As soon as coin in the coffer [offering box] rings, a soul from purgatory springs."

Ninety-Five Theses   Luther at the time was a university professor in the town of Wittenberg. When asked about indulgences, he claimed that the practice was wrong, since people could not buy God's forgiveness for their sins. Tetzel denounced Luther's opinion about indulgences, and Luther took up the challenge. On October 31, 1517, Luther nailed a placard to the door of the Wittenberg Church. On the placard were 95 **theses,** or statements, that criticized the sale of indulgences as well as other practices. Luther's

Church officials and bankers' agents collected money from devout townspeople in exchange for letters of indulgence. The price of each indulgence varied according to the social class of the buyer. How did the sale of indulgences help the Church?

Because the theses were circulated far and wide, what might have been a local issue became a public controversy discussed all over Germany.

Point out that Luther's case, although important, was only one item on the diet's agenda.

After hearing Martin Luther's defense at the Diet of Worms, the 20-year-old Emperor Charles V said, "A single friar who goes counter to all Christianity for 1,000 years must be wrong. . . . Therefore, I am resolved to stake my lands, my friends, my body, my life, and my soul [to defend the Church of Rome]." For what political reasons did Charles V support the Church's position against Luther?

purpose was to stimulate debate within the Church; it was not to break away from the Church. Nonetheless, the result was a full-scale religious revolt that permanently destroyed Europe's religious unity.

Diet of Worms   Copies of Luther's theses were printed and spread all over Germany, where they found a receptive audience. Indulgence sales fell drastically, and church authorities in Rome became concerned. Papal representatives arrived in Germany and tried to convince Luther to give up his ideas. At first, Luther was open to some kind of understanding. But increasingly he found himself defying the Church. What began as a simple debate over certain church practices had developed into a challenge to papal authority.

In 1521 Pope Leo X condemned Luther's ideas and cut him off from the Church. Luther, however, had widespread support among the German people. With the threat of a church schism in Germany, the Holy Roman Emperor Charles V became involved in the dispute. He feared that religious turmoil would endanger the peace and unity of his realm. Charles also needed the Pope's support in ruling the Holy Roman Empire and in fighting wars against France. Therefore, he acted to stop the spread of

Luther's teachings. A council of German princes, the Diet of Worms, was called in 1521 to consider Luther's case as well as other issues. At the council, the German princes, opposed to the emperor and his policies, backed Luther. Charles was forced to call Luther to the Diet to defend his views.

Luther's friends, fearing the emperor's treachery, urged him not to go. But Luther was determined to go, "though there were as many devils in Worms as there are tiles on the roofs." His trip to Worms was like a triumphal parade as crowds of people came out to see him. Then came the eventful meeting between the Diet and the monk. Luther walked into the crowded assembly hall. A papal repesentative stood next to a table stacked with Luther's writings. He asked Luther if he would take back his teachings. Luther replied:

> *I am bound by the Sacred Scriptures I have cited . . . and my conscience is captive to the Word of God. I cannot and will not recant [take back] anything, for it is neither safe nor right to go against conscience. God help me. Amen.**

*The Reformation, Will Durant, © 1957 by Simon and Schuster, p. 361.

Having defied church and empire, Luther was condemned as a heretic and an outlaw. Hurried out of Worms, he was "ambushed" by his protector, Prince Frederick of Saxony, and hid in a castle for protection. Luther dropped out of public sight for a year. Meanwhile, his reformation spread rapidly across Germany.

Rise of Lutheranism

After Worms, Luther made his final break with Rome and formed the first of the Protestant faiths: Lutheranism. Lutherans, as the followers of Luther were called, did not claim that their faith was a new religion. In fact, it had many of the same beliefs as Catholicism. However, Luther stressed several teachings that distinguished his form of Christianity from the Catholic Church. These teachings were also followed by later Protestant groups.

The most important Protestant teaching developed by Luther was salvation by faith alone. According to Luther, all of humanity is sinful in the eyes of a holy God. No amount of good works, therefore, can win God's approval for salvation; all that people can do to win salvation is trust in God's love and mercy.

Luther's second important teaching was that religious truth and authority lie only in the Bible, not in the institutions of the Church. As a result, Luther and other Protestant reformers simplified church doctrine and rituals to agree with New Testament practice. Instead of priests, Protestant religious leaders were called **ministers.** They did not have the same religious powers as Catholic priests, and they spent more time preaching from the Bible. Protestant worship services were held in the language of the area instead of in Latin. In this way, people could easily understand and share in the services.

Luther also emphasized that the Church was not a hierarchy of clergy, but a community of believers. There was no real difference, he stated, between the clergy and laity in the eyes of God. All useful occupations, not just the priesthood or ministry, were important. They were **vocations,** or callings, in which people could serve God and their neighbors. This view appealed especially to merchants, traders, bankers, and artisans in the towns. Their concern for making profits had been regarded as unethical by the medieval Church. However, by the 1500's they were involved in the commercial revolution sweeping Europe. Business people concerned with secular affairs were glad to find a religious belief that gave respect to their occupations.

Spread of Lutheranism

A technological development that aided the Lutheran revolt was the printing press. Printed copies of Luther's writings were spread far and wide in such numbers that the Protestant movement could not be halted. By 1524 there were 990 different books in print in Germany. Eighty percent of those were by Luther and his followers. By 1546 there were some 100,000 copies of Luther's German translation of the Bible in circulation. Catholic writers in Germany tried to respond to Luther. But they were not as successful as the Lutherans in presenting their arguments and winning public support.

By the mid-1500's, northern Germany was mostly Lutheran. Southern Germany remained Catholic, but even there Lutheranism had made solid gains. There were many reasons why Germans in large numbers supported Lutheranism. One reason was undoubtedly religious conviction. However, non-religious factors also were involved.

German princes often accepted Luther's teachings in order to increase their own power. They made Lutheranism the state religion of their territories, placing it under their protection and control. They also seized lands and wealth owned by the Catholic Church. Townspeople also rallied to the new faith, which agreed with their business principles and practices. Peasants and laborers adopted Lutheranism as a form of protest against the traditionally Catholic ruling classes. Above all, many Germans saw Lutheranism as an opportunity to defy an Italian-controlled Catholic Church that drained so much money from Germany.

With a strong base in Germany, the Lutherans were able to spread their doctrine to other lands. Germany was situated in the geographic and economic center of Europe. German merchants

Refer students to the map on p. 272 to point out the strongholds of the various Protestant sects.

carried religious ideas as well as trade goods all over the continent. From northern Germany, Lutheranism spread to the Scandinavian lands. The monarchs of Denmark and Sweden broke with Rome and established Lutheran state churches in their territories.[3] Luther's ideas also contributed to religious ferment in France, England, and the Netherlands.

Luther's Achievement

As Lutheranism spread, Luther tried to direct his religious movement so that it would not stray from the truth as he saw it. Thus, Luther often denounced Protestant leaders more radical than himself. To protect his movement, he also spoke out on political issues. One of Luther's most controversial political stands concerned a major peasant revolt that erupted in Germany in 1525. Luther saw the German princes as vital to the survival of the Reformation and thus sided with them against the peasants.

Luther died in 1546 at the age of 63. By this time, the Protestant movement had grown too large for him to control. Luther's belief that all people had the right to read and understand the Bible led to a variety of biblical interpretations. New religious viewpoints emerged that were more radical than Luther would have liked. Meanwhile, Luther's hope for the peaceful conversion of Europe to Protestantism was often thwarted by fierce religious hatreds. In many European towns and villages, heated debates and riots often accompanied the removal of the Catholic clergy. Mounting fears of social disorder kept many people loyal to Rome who otherwise would have accepted Protestantism.

Nevertheless, Luther's achievement was significant. As the first Protestant reformer, he had one foot in the past while shaping the future. Despite his opposition to the papacy, he held a largely medieval view of the world. However, his break with Rome shattered Christian unity in western Europe and opened the way for a different kind of European society. With the loss of a common religious viewpoint, western Europeans were able to create new ideas about the world that still shape western civilization today.

1. Identify: Martin Luther, 95 theses, Pope Leo X, Diet of Worms, Frederick of Saxony.
2. Why did Luther post the 95 theses? What impact did his action have on the religious life of western Europe?
3. What were the beliefs of Luther's movement?
4. Why did people support (or reject) Lutheranism?

3 Protestant Growth and Division

The Catholic Church kept western Europe united under one religion for 1,000 years. Protestant unity lasted only about five years.

One example of sixteenth-century social criticism is this cartoon of a legal scholar. It mocks the religious habits of both the Catholic and Protestant middle classes. How is social criticism expressed today?

---

[3]Norway also became Lutheran, but at the time of the Reformation, it was ruled by Denmark.

Have students compare and contrast each of the following religious groups with Lutheranism.

Several reasons were responsible for divisions within Protestantism. First, Luther's successful challenge to the Catholic Church made it easier for other reformers to carry out their goals. Second, the printing press and the vernacular translations of the Bible allowed more people to read and interpret scripture on their own. As a result of these factors, a number of religious groups developed from Luther's reformation.

Huldreich Zwingli

After the rise of Lutheranism, preachers and merchants in Switzerland separated from Rome and set up churches known as Reformed. One of the most important Reformed leaders was Huldreich Zwingli. Born in 1482, Zwingli differed from Luther in background and outlook. While Luther was a monk educated in the medieval tradition, Zwingli was an urban scholar

Zwingli preached that unless a practice of the Church could be supported literally by the Bible, it should be abandoned. In addition to fasting during Lent and the worship of saints, what other practices did he deny?

trained in humanism. As a result, he was more optimistic than Luther about human nature and placed more value on the achievements of the non-Christian, classical civilizations.

Swiss Reformation   Zwingli supported a religious reformation based entirely on the Bible. In 1518 he became a preacher in the Swiss city of Zurich, an important trading center. Zwingli followed Luther's example and spoke out against the sale of indulgences. He also publicly denounced other church abuses and thus began the Swiss Reformation.

Like Luther, Zwingli stressed the importance of faith and denied many Catholic beliefs and practices, such as purgatory, monasteries, and celibacy. Zwingli's goal, unlike Luther's, was to break completely with Catholic tradition. His plan for doing this was to establish a **theocracy,** or church-run state, in Zurich. By 1525 Zwingli had succeeded in this objective. The Catholic mass was banned, and Protestantism enforced. Worship services were conducted in the vernacular. They consisted of sermons and Bible readings. Despite his personal love of music, Zwingli forbade its use in worship. He even smashed church organs. Religious images, which Zwingli regarded as idols, were destroyed. Communion was served in a wooden bowl instead of a silver chalice. Monasteries were closed or turned into hospitals and schools.

Although not persecuted, Catholics had to pay fines for attending illegal masses and eating fish on Fridays (a common Catholic practice). They were also excluded from public office. City officials and clergy closely supervised the morals of Zurich's residents. This emphasis on strict personal behavior was later carried over into other Protestant movements.

Religious Warfare   By 1528 Zwingli's Reformed church had won the support of northern Switzerland; the southern part of the country, however, remained Catholic. Zwingli feared Catholic enemies to the north and south of Zurich. He prepared Zurich for war, trying to unite with the German Lutherans against the Catholics. The proposed alliance between the two Protestant groups never occurred because of theological disagreements.

Point out that John Calvin had studied in Paris, where the Protestant movement had become quite strong under the patronage of King Francis I's sister.

However, Protestants were banished from Paris in 1533 when the rector of the Sorbonne attacked the king and queen as heretics.

Reformed missionary activity in the Catholic areas of Switzerland finally led to war in 1531. Zwingli and his force of 1,500 were destroyed by an army of 8,000 Catholics. An uneasy truce between Swiss Protestants and Catholics followed. Although defeated in battle, Zwingli left a solid religious foundation that ensured the survival of Swiss Protestantism.

John Calvin

In the mid-1500's, the most powerful and influential Reformed group developed in the Swiss city of Geneva. There, John Calvin, a French reformer, set up a theocracy similar to that of Zurich.

Early Life   Born in 1509, Calvin grew up in Catholic France as the first waves of the Reformation hit Europe. Although Protestantism was banned in France, its ideas still filtered across the border from Germany and had an impact on French thinkers. Unlike Luther, who was tormented by the problems of faith, Calvin was a much calmer individual. He seemed to have had few self-doubts and was known for his logical approach to religious issues.

Calvin received a good education in theology, law, and humanism. This background prompted him to read the Bible more carefully. He seems to have had a religious conversion in 1533 as a result of humanist influences and without the inner turmoil that had driven Luther to a similar conversion.

Beliefs   The cornerstone of Calvin's theology was God's all-encompassing power and knowledge. According to Calvin, there was nothing in the past, present, or future that God did not know or control. He also held that from the beginning of time God decided who would be saved and who would be condemned for eternity. This doctrine—that God determines the fate of every human being—is known as **predestination.** Calvin used scripture and local argument to support this belief.

Calvin put forth his religious views in his book the *Institutes of the Christian Religion,* published in its final form in 1559. It was one of the most popular books of its day and influenced religious reformers in western Europe and North America.

Geneva   Calvin went beyond words in trying to advance his religion. In 1536 he took control of the Swiss city of Geneva. At the time, Geneva was in economic decline and known for its moral corruption. Calvin tried to turn the city into a model religious community. His reforms met stiff resistance. The reformer was forced to leave Geneva for a while before being persuaded to resume his work. It took Calvin 20 years to complete the reformation of the city.

Under Calvin's reforms, the city government still functioned. But the Consistory, a church council of 12 elders, exercised real power over the daily lives of the people. All citizens were considered members of the Reformed faith and were required to attend church services three or four times a week. Such acts as fighting, swearing, drunkenness, gambling, card playing, and dancing were outlawed. Members of the Consistory made annual inspections of homes to ensure that moral values were upheld. Punishments in Geneva were harsh, with 58 executions between 1542 and 1564. Most of these were for holding Catholic beliefs or practicing witchcraft. Given such a strict atmosphere, Geneva became known as the "City of the Saints." It attracted reformers from all parts of Europe and became the leading center of Protestant learning.

Calvinism   John Calvin's teaching, known as Calvinism, became the most popular form of Protestantism outside of the Lutheran strongholds of Germany and Scandinavia. Calvinists, as John Calvin's followers were called, later controlled the countries of the Netherlands, Scotland, and England.

Unlike Lutheranism, Calvinism was not linked to a particular nation or form of government. It also had no strong backing from royalty and princes. As a result, Calvinism received widespread support among the common people who disliked the old medieval social structure of Europe.

Of all the Protestant groups, the Calvinists were the most dynamic and missionary-minded. They spread their faith to new areas. As a result of this zeal, they often faced intense persecution. What supported them during these difficulties was the belief that they were God's **elect,** or

Knox had studied under Calvin at Geneva. What does this say about the way Protestant beliefs spread?

chosen people. The Calvinists were also helped by their form of church government. Calvinist church organization was based on local councils of ministers and elected church members. Because of its partially democratic nature, the organization gave participants a stake in its welfare and inspired their loyalty. Since power was distributed among many people, it was harder for enemies to eliminate a few leaders and destroy the movement.

Calvin himself preached obedience to civil authority unless religious conviction forced disobedience. However, he cautioned against open resistance. God alone, he said, would punish evil rulers. Some Calvinists preferred to ignore Calvin's instruction. John Knox, the fiery leader of the Reformation in Scotland, preached the right of moral people to overthrow wicked princes. Other Calvinists were proclaiming that the rights of the people came before those of monarchs. Thus, Calvinism became a dynamic social force in western Europe. Eventually, it contributed to the birth of the early revolutionary movements of the western world.

Protestant Radicals

Once the religious monopoly of the Catholic Church was broken, Protestant leaders had to decide how far they should carry out the Reformation. Luther, Zwingli, and Calvin, despite significant religious differences, shared a common set of beliefs. Among these beliefs were obedience to government authority and respect for the existing social order.

Some reformers, however, demanded more changes and split with the conservative leadership of the Reformation. As a result, numerous religious sects emerged in western Europe apart from the established churches. Although their beliefs differed in detail from one another, these sects were included together under the name of Anabaptists. They received this name because they shared in common the practice of baptizing, or admitting into the Church, only adult members.[4] The Catholic and the established Protestant churches admitted infants into church membership. The Anabaptists disagreed with this traditional practice, claiming that people must be able to make a free choice whether or not to be Christians.

The Anabaptists were more deeply involved in social unrest than the other Protestant groups. The 1500's saw economic difficulties resulting from rising population and inflation. Peasants, artisans, and miners were especially affected. It was they who in large numbers joined the Anabaptists in hope of a better world.

Most Anabaptists honored the Bible as the Word of God. But they also believed that God spoke directly to the human soul. As a result of this belief, Anabaptists often denied the right of civil governments to direct their lives. They refused to hold office, bear arms, or swear oaths. Thus, the Anabaptist movements were regarded with suspicion by government authorities.

Still, most Anabaptists led quiet, peaceful Christian lives. They did not openly resist the authorities. Like the earliest Christians, they helped each other and often held property in common. A few, however, went to extremes in interpreting the Bible literally. They tended to separate themselves from the rest of society which they saw as sinful.

In spite of their peaceful ways, the Anabaptists were often persecuted. They were forced to migrate throughout Europe. In the process, they spread their beliefs throughout Switzerland, Germany, and the Netherlands. In certain areas, the Anabaptist movement turned violent as it accepted revolutionary ideas popular among German and Dutch peasants. The climax of this development occurred in the German city of Münster in the early 1530's.

In Münster, radical Anabaptists seized power. They combined religious fanaticism with a reign of terror that tarnished the reputation of other Anabaptists for years. All books but the Bible were burned. Property was held in common, and polygamy was enforced. John Bockleson, the leader, ruled with a lavish court. He assured his poorer followers that they too would eat from gold plates and silver tables in the near future.

So alarming was this spectacle that Lutherans and Catholics combined forces to crush it. The

---

[4]In the ceremony of baptism, people were either sprinkled or covered with water, a sign of spiritual rebirth.

Point out that not all of the Reformers split from the
Catholic Church. Discuss the reforms of those who
remained within the Church.

Reformers

More
(1477-1535)

Sir Thomas More English humanist who
authored *Utopia*. Presented a plan for perfect
government and sought religious and cultural
reformation.

William Tyndale Welsh humanist who
translated the Bible into English. Convicted of
heresy and burned at the stake.

Olaus Petri Swedish reformer who introduced
Luther's teachings into Sweden. Authored a
Swedish translation of the New Testament.

Tyndale
(1492-1536)

Menno Simons Dutch theologian and
ex-Roman Catholic priest who became the
leader of Anabaptists in the Netherlands.

Stanislaus Hoius Polish cardinal who was a
leader in the Roman Catholic Counter-
Reformation. Drafted a new profession of
the faith.

Servetus
(1511-1553)

Michael Servetus Spanish physician and
theologian who advocated separation of church
and state. Made discoveries on the circulation of
the blood. Burned at the stake for heresy.

John Knox Scottish theologian who established
the strict moral tone of the Church of Scotland
and shaped its democratic form of government.

Teresa
(1515-1582)

Teresa of Avila Spanish nun and writer who
was canonized for her work in restoration of
the convents. The first woman to receive the
title of Doctor of the Church.

Charles Borromeo Italian archbishop who was
canonized for heroic work during the plague.
Endorsed education for all and built colleges.

Borromeo
(1538-1584)

Faustus Socinus Italian theologian who
established a Protestant sect in Poland that
influenced the beginnings of Unitarianism.

Socinus
(1539-1604)

Henry VIII knew that the clergy and the nobility were content with Catholicism, but he saw that many members of Parliament, the merchants, squires, and bankers—the rising middle class—looked upon the old system as an economic burden to England.

Henry VIII broke with the Catholic Church over its refusal to end his marriage to Catherine. What political factors influenced the Pope in his decision not to back Henry?

disciplined resistance of the Anabaptists led to a yearlong siege. The city was finally betrayed, and the Anabaptist leaders killed. An intense persecution of Anabaptists followed. Thousands were killed, and the survivors were hounded from place to place.

Years later, Anabaptist groups would leave Europe for North America. There, they would have a profound influence in shaping two important modern ideas: religious toleration and the separation of church and state.

English Reformation

On the eve of the Reformation, the monarchs of France, Spain, and England had assumed increasing control over the Catholic Church within their lands. As a result, these rulers had few grievances against the Pope. They, however, were hostile to the Protestant Reformation since it threatened their control of religious affairs. Because of their strength, these monarchs were able to limit the spread of Protestantism among the lower classes of their kingdoms. Yet, the Protestant movement was eventually welcomed in England as a result of a political quarrel

between the Tudor king, Henry VIII, and the Pope.

Break With Rome Trouble between Henry VIII and the Pope began in 1526. Henry needed a son to succeed him to the throne. He feared that without a male heir, England might plunge into a civil war similar to that of the Wars of the Roses. Henry's wife, Catherine of Aragon, had one child, Mary. Now that Catherine was older, Henry feared she could no longer have children. Thus, he wanted his marriage ended so he could find a new wife to bear him a son.

Catherine of Aragon was the aunt of the Holy Roman Emperor Charles V. Charles wanted his aunt to remain as queen of England in order to influence the country's policies in favor of the Hapsburgs. Charles was the protector of the Pope, who had the power to grant or refuse Henry's request for an end to the marriage. As a result of Hapsburg pressure, the Pope rejected Henry's request.

Meanwhile, Henry had fallen in love with Anne Boleyn, a young woman of the court. He decided to act on his own to end his marriage with Catherine and to marry Anne. To carry out this plan, Henry, in 1533, started to break England's ties with the Catholic Church. He did this gradually with the backing of Parliament. In using Parliament, Henry wanted to show that his actions were the will of the English people rather than his own whim. Money was no longer sent to Rome, church courts were closed, and Henry was given more authority over the English clergy. In 1534 Parliament finally passed a law that separated the Church of England from Rome and made Henry head of the English Church.

The average churchgoer in England noticed very little difference in the English Church's beliefs and practices as a result of the split with Rome. The Church of England maintained the Catholic faith while denying the Pope. Consequently, most English people accepted it willingly since there were no drastic changes.

Devout Catholics, however, opposed the break with Rome. The most noted of them was Sir Thomas More, the humanist scholar. Accused of high treason, More was condemned by a royal court and beheaded in 1535.

HISTORY AND PEOPLE

Mary Queen of Scots

Mary Queen of Scots was born on December 8, 1542. Within a week, her father died and she inherited the Scottish throne. Four decades later, Mary walked to her execution. The order for her death had been signed by Queen Elizabeth I of England. The two monarchs had never met.

Mary was a cousin to Elizabeth on her father's side of the family. Mary's grandmother and Elizabeth's father Henry VIII were brother and sister. After Elizabeth, Mary was next in line to the English throne. On her mother's side, Mary was related to the Guises, a powerful French family. Following the death of Mary's father, her mother was regent of Scotland until Mary was old enough to rule.

At the age of six, Mary was sent to France for her education. She later married the heir to the French throne. Mary's husband died shortly after becoming king, leaving Mary a widow at the age of 18. Mary then returned to a Protestant Scotland, which wanted her as queen but disliked her Catholicism. In 1565, Mary Queen of Scots married Lord Darnley, a Protestant English noble. Darnley was ambitious for power, and Mary soon came to hate him.

One evening in 1567, Darnley was killed. The house in which he had been staying was blown up. However, evidence appeared that Darnley had actually died from being smothered or strangled. Three months later Mary married the prime murder suspect, the earl of Bothwell. This added to the suspicion that she was to blame for Darnley's death. A casket of love letters supposedly from Mary to Bothwell was produced by her enemies as evidence against her. The Scottish parliament removed her from the throne in favor of her 1-year-old son James. Mary's brother became regent; Bothwell was exiled; and Mary sought refuge in England.

Entering England, Mary fell into Elizabeth's hands. Elizabeth was concerned about Mary's claim to the English throne and her Catholic faith. Many Catholics thought that Mary should be queen. Elizabeth knew that Catholic Spain and France could be counted on to help Mary take the English throne. Therefore, Elizabeth imprisoned Mary for the next 18 years.

Mary did nothing to quiet Elizabeth's fears. She refused to sign away her claim to the throne. Through smuggled letters, Mary supported plans to rescue her and make her England's queen. In the end, she was charged with involvement in a plot against Elizabeth's life. Mary was not allowed to have defense lawyers at her trial. In spite of her denials of seeking Elizabeth's death, Mary was found guilty. Whether she was guilty or not, the facts are not clear. Perhaps Mary's misfortune was that she was a Catholic monarch in an area of Europe that was largely Protestant.

During her five-year reign, Mary I married her cousin, Philip II of Spain, hoping his power and fervent Catholicism would give her support. How did her plans for a Catholic England fail?

Protestant England   When Henry VIII died, his 9-year-old son became King Edward VI.[5] Since Edward was too young to rule, a council of lords governed England for him. Most of the council members were Protestants, and they brought Protestant doctrines into the English Church.

---

[5]Henry VIII married Anne Boleyn, and they had a daughter named Elizabeth. A few years later, Henry had Anne executed for treason. He then married Jane Seymour, who later gave birth to Edward.

Upon Edward's death in 1553, Henry's daughter Mary became queen. A devout Catholic, Mary I restored Roman Catholicism, insisting that all her subjects acknowledge the Pope. When many Protestants refused, she began to persecute them. The English people turned against her, calling her "Bloody Mary." Many people became solid supporters of Protestantism as a result of Mary's persecution.

Mary I died in 1558 without a child to succeed her. Her half sister Elizabeth became queen. Elizabeth I was Protestant and, with the help of Parliament, ended the Pope's authority in the English Church. To unite her people, both Catholics and Protestants, Elizabeth decided that the English Church should be Protestant, but with some Catholic features. The monarch would be head of the Church, which would teach Protestant beliefs. At the same time, however, bishops would handle daily affairs as they did in the Catholic Church. Many rituals would also be similar to those of the Catholic Church.

Most English people were pleased with Anglicanism, as this blend of Protestant belief and Catholic practice was called. The few groups of Catholics who were not pleased remained outside the English Church. Some groups of Protestants also opposed Elizabeth's Church, but they did not leave it. Because they wanted to "purify" the English Church of Catholic ways, they became known as Puritans.

The English Reformation was important for two reasons. First, it made England the leading defender of Protestantism. English support helped preserve Protestantism from possible extinction during a series of religious wars in the late 1500's. Second, the Puritans in the English Church became influential by the early 1600's. As a result of their Calvinist principles, they opposed strong royal authority and wanted to extend the rights of Parliament. Puritan ideas eventually contributed to the rise and spread of democracy in England and North America.

1. Identify: Huldreich Zwingli, John Calvin, Geneva, Anabaptists, Henry VIII, Mary I, Elizabeth I, Anglicanism, Puritans.
2. What factors caused the division of Protestantism into separate groups?

Pope Paul III (1534-1549) was the first in a line of reforming popes following the line of Renaissance popes.

The Inquisition was in a sense a revival of the medieval tribunal for the repression of heresy.

3. Why did Henry VIII break with the Catholic Church?

4. How was the English Reformation different from other Protestant movements?

4 The Catholic Reformation

While Protestantism triumphed in northern Europe, it had limited success in other parts of the continent. Spain and France, the two most powerful European monarchies, remained Catholic. Catholicism also remained strong in Italy, Portugal, Hungary, Poland, and southern Germany.

Although Catholicism had many strongholds, it was still threatened by the growth of the Protestant Reformation. To meet the Protestant challenge, Catholic reformers worked to improve their Church. Through this "Counter Reformation," the Catholic Church eliminated many abuses, clearly defined its theology, and reestablished the Pope's authority over its members.

First Efforts

Since the Middle Ages, the Catholic Church periodically had faced criticism of abuses in its teachings and practices. Several times, reform movements loyal to the Church had made improvements and restored its spiritual life. As a result of their efforts, the Church was able to overcome threats to its survival. Thus, when the Protestant movement began, Catholic leaders felt that reforms alone could halt this latest danger to the Church. They failed to recognize the deeper philosophical and religious issues that Protestantism raised.

In 1536 Pope Paul III established a commission to find out why there was so much protest and what could be done about it. The resulting report, "Advice on the Reform of the Church," blamed church leaders, including popes, for many abuses. It also called for reforms that would convince the Protestants to rejoin the Church.

The reforms undertaken as a result of the report were only partially carried out. During the early 1500's, the Church's financial problems had increased. These included inflation, invasions of the Papal States, and loss of church lands and revenue to the Protestants. Thus, the Church was unable to respond quickly and effectively to the Protestant threat.

A Plan of Action

By the 1540's the Catholic Church had decided on a program: it would introduce reforms and counterattack the Protestants. The counterattack came first. In 1542 the Inquisition was given full powers to uproot Protestantism in Italy. With this crackdown, the Pope's authority was restored all over the Italian peninsula.

The papal triumph put an end to the Italian Renaissance. Italy's vigorous intellectual life was suppressed for the sake of conformity to the Church. The Church censored the press, which

Catholic rulers in Spain, Portugal, and Italy used spies, the police, and the Inquisition to rid their countries of vocal Protestant reformers. How did these rulers control written dissent?

it saw as a threat to established order. In 1543 the Inquisition published the first Index of Prohibited Books, a list of written works banned by the Church. Isolated cases of censorship had existed before the mid-1500's. But the Inquisition's action was the first full-scale effort to limit or destroy a free press in Europe.

Council of Trent   One of the needs of the Church was to clearly state and defend Catholic teaching. In 1545 Pope Paul III called a council of bishops at Trent, Italy, to define official doctrine. The Council of Trent met in several sessions from 1545 to 1563. There was widespread hope that the Council would restore Christian unity, since Protestant representatives attended the sessions for a while. This goal was never realized because the Council took a hard line against Protestantism. Its goals were to strengthen the Catholic Church and restore the Pope's influence in church affairs.

Catholic doctrine was strictly defined so that it could be clearly distinguished from Protestant

Through impressive knowledge and clear, simple sermons, the Jesuits restored respect for the Catholic clergy. As "soldiers" of the Pope, their task was to win back former Catholic lands. In what countries were they most effective?

teaching. Good works, as well as faith, were necessary for salvation. The Latin Vulgate Bible was made the only acceptable form of scripture. In addition, the Church hierarchy alone was to decide the interpretation of the Bible. The elaborate art and ritual of the Church were maintained, since they were considered inspirational for less educated Catholics who had little understanding of church teaching. The mass was to be said only in Latin.

The Council, however, put an end to many church practices that reformers had criticized for centuries. The selling of indulgences was forbidden. Clergy were ordered to follow strict rules of behavior. Each diocese was to build a **seminary,** or a school to train priests. Much of the Pope's power over the Church in various western European lands was restored at the expense of monarchs.

Jesuits   The Council of Trent was in many ways a declaration of war against Protestantism. Now, the Church was prepared to launch a missionary offensive against the Protestants to reclaim formerly Catholic lands. One of the Catholic reformers involved in this effort was Ignatius of Loyola. In 1521 he gave up his life as a Spanish noble to serve the Catholic Church. Ignatius developed a set of spiritual exercises to help people achieve inner peace. After a visit to Palestine, he decided to improve his education in order to preach more effectively. While in school, Ignatius organized a group of followers to spread Catholic teachings. In 1536 the group went to Rome determined to win souls, not by the sword, but by educating the young.

In 1540 Ignatius and his followers founded the Society of Jesus, also known as the Jesuits. Jesuits wore the black robes of monks and lived simply. Organized along military lines, they were expected to show absolute obedience to the Pope. The Jesuits set up schools, helped the poor, and preached to the people. They also taught in universities, worked as missionaries, and served as advisers in royal courts.

The Jesuit order grew rapidly and became known as the "shock troops" of the Catholic Church. They worked hard to strengthen the faith of Catholics and to bring Protestants back to

The terms set at Augsburg signified a victory for the cause of Lutheranism and states' rights.

the Church. As a result of their efforts, the Church retained the loyalty of the people in such areas as southern Germany, Bohemia, Poland, and Hungary.

1. Identify: Pope Paul III, Index of Prohibited Books, Ignatius of Loyola, Jesuits.
2. Why was the Council of Trent called? What did it accomplish?
3. How did the Jesuits serve the Catholic Church?

5 The Age of Religious Wars

By the mid-1500's, the Catholic Church had strengthened itself in opposition to Protestantism. At the same time, the Protestants secured their hold over much of Europe. Each side was ready to prove that its faith was superior. The result was a series of religious wars that swept across Europe from 1545 to 1600.

Germany

After the Diet of Worms in 1521, the Holy Roman Emperor Charles V set out to crush Lutheranism in his domains. However, several factors prevented him from realizing this goal. First, Charles had little control over the German princes, all of whom jealously guarded their liberties. As a result, the emperor could never get effective support from the Catholic states to defeat the Lutherans. Even the Catholic princes feared Charles's power if he should end the Lutheran heresy.

Second, the size of Charles V's empire made it difficult for him to move effectively against the Lutherans. In addition to internal opposition, Charles had to face two powerful foreign enemies: France and the Ottoman Empire. Francis I of France repeatedly stirred up rebellions in Germany, and the Ottomans were a constant menace in the east. Thus, Charles was forced to stop fighting the Lutherans and to defend his borders.

Finally, Charles V had money problems. Several times during his reign, he found himself short of funds while on the verge of a major victory. In an age of mercenary armies, this problem was fatal and forced him to back down, allowing his enemies, especially France, to recover their strength.

All of these factors forced Charles to pursue a relatively mild policy toward the Lutherans for several years. Then, in 1530, the Lutheran and Catholic princes failed to reconcile their differences in a meeting at the German town of Augsburg. After this failure, the Catholic majority pledged that it would suppress Lutheranism. The Lutherans, in turn, formed a defensive alliance known as the Schmalkaldic League.

The Schmalkaldic League declared open resistance to the emperor in order to defend its interests. The formation of the League revealed the disunity of Germany and contributed to its further division. Matters were made worse when French and Ottoman threats forced Charles to come to terms with the League. As a result, Lutheranism was able to further expand its influence in Germany.

Not until 1546 was Charles V able to fight the Schmalkaldic League. At that time, he won a decisive victory. However, the strength of the League prevented Charles from restoring the prestige of his throne or winning all of Germany back to Catholicism. Thus, Charles agreed in 1555 to the Peace of Augsburg, a religious compromise that gave each Catholic and Lutheran prince the right to choose the religion of his realm. Calvinists and Anabaptists were excluded from the agreement. Anyone living in the territory of an opposing religion could move to another area. Therefore, thousands of refugees found themselves on the road searching for new homes.

In the winter of 1555-1556, Charles V, worn out by his difficulties, gave up the throne. The family lands in Austria, as well as the title of Holy Roman Emperor, went to his brother Ferdinand. Charles's son, Philip II, inherited Spain, the Netherlands, parts of Italy, and the Hapsburg overseas possessions.

The age of Charles V gave way to the age of Philip II and Spanish greatness. Philip's reign, which lasted from 1556 to 1598, saw him and Spain at the center of European events and the religious wars that dominated the period.

The map below is the subject of the "Using Maps" section of the Chapter 11 Review.

RELIGIONS OF EUROPE 1560

Revolt of the Netherlands

The Netherlands was one of the wealthiest trading and production areas in sixteenth-century Europe. It was a collection of 17 partially independent provinces.

Charles V had been born in the Netherlands and was popular with its inhabitants. This remained the case even when he drained the area of money for wars and tried to impose his religious policies on it. Philip II, on the other hand, was born and raised a Spaniard. He ruled the Netherlands with a heavy hand.

Philip lived in Spain and never left his homeland after he became king in 1556. A devout Catholic, he claimed that he would rather "die a hundred deaths than rule over heretics." To advance the cause of Catholicism, Philip taxed the Netherlands to pay for Spain's religious wars. At this time, the Netherlands had large Lutheran, Anabaptist, and Calvinist minorities. Philip was determined to remove them from his domain. He brought the Inquisition to the Netherlands and strengthened the power of the Catholic clergy there.

In 1566 angry Protestants in the Netherlands began a series of protests and riots. To restore order, Philip sent 10,000 Spanish troops to the troubled area. Led by the duke of Alba, they almost crushed the uprising. Calvinists were executed, churches were burned, and taxes were raised to levels damaging to trade.

The name *Huguenot* as a description for French Protestants is probably derived from the German word *Eidgenossenschaft*, meaning "oath fellowship."

The Saint Bartholomew's Day Massacre was initiated by Catherine de Medici.

Many Calvinists survived and managed to gain control of several ports in the northern area known as Holland. When word of these Calvinist havens spread, more Calvinists arrived in the region. As a result, the people of Holland, known as the Dutch, became largely Protestant. The Dutch leader against the Spaniards was William Prince of Orange. William became known as "the Silent" because of his ability to hide his intentions. Although an undistinguished general, William was brave and patriotic. His selfless determination provided the revolt with what little unity it had.

The Dutch organized fighting groups known as "Sea Beggars." They attacked the Spaniards by opening up sea dikes and literally flooding the enemy. Spanish attempts to crush the revolt of the "Sea Beggars" brought more support for the rebel cause. In 1581 the rebels finally deposed Philip as their ruler and declared an independent Dutch state in the northern provinces of the Netherlands. They failed, however, to win the largely Catholic south, which remained under Spanish rule.

French Wars of Religion

In the late 1500's, France was ruled by weak monarchs who allowed various groups to tear the country apart. Fighting developed between Catholics and Protestants. Besides the religious struggles, conflicts among nobles and revolts by the old feudal provinces revealed the decline of the French state.

French Protestants, known as Huguenots, made up only 10 percent of the population. However, there were several factors which helped them withstand defeat for over 30 years. Many nobles skilled in government and military service were counted among their number. The Huguenots were located in fortified cities and were well organized. Also, the Catholic opposition was divided and less enthusiastic about its cause.

For 30 years, Catholic and Huguenot armies marched across France destroying fields and homes. Philip II of Spain added to the disorder by actively supporting the Catholics. From 1562 to 1571, there were 18 massacres of Protestants, five massacres of Catholics, and over 30 assassinations in France.

The French Wars of Religion consisted of seven conflicts with occasional periods of peace. The fighting was confused and often involved the slaughter of women and children. The most infamous event of the struggle was the Saint Bartholomew's Day Massacre. On that day—August 24, 1572—the Catholics of Paris suddenly attacked Huguenots, killing 3,000 of them.

Catherine dé Medici, mother of Charles IX and Henry III of France examines the results of the Saint Bartholomew's Day Massacre. Catherine and Catholic nobles plotted the massacre. They misled Charles IX into believing that the Huguenots would soon attack Paris. Attempting to kill the Huguenot leadership, Catholics executed an estimated 20,000 Huguenots throughout France. How long had Catholics and Huguenots been fighting in France?

In 1588, the Catholic leader, Henry of Guise, was murdered by the king, Henry III. Then, a few months later, a fanatical monk killed the king. The Huguenot leader, Henry of Navarre, finally inherited the throne in 1589. However, he was not allowed to become king of predominantly Catholic France because of his Protestant religion. Faced with Spanish threats, Henry decided to renounce Protestantism and become a Catholic in order to receive the French crown.

Despite Henry's obvious political motives, most French people were willing to accept him as King Henry IV. They were tired of constant warfare and yearned for peace. To ensure stability, they were willing to submit to a strong monarchy. This attitude ushered in France's greatest period of royal power and splendor.

1. Identify: Schmalkaldic League, Peace of Augsburg, William of Orange, Sea Beggars, Huguenots, Henry IV.
2. What factors sparked religious conflict in the Netherlands?
3. What was the political outcome of the French Wars of Religion?

CHAPTER 11 REVIEW

Summary

1. In western Europe during the fourteenth and fifteenth centuries, religious reformers like John Wycliffe in England and Jan Hus in Bohemia denounced the Roman Catholic Church for its corruption and abuses.

2. In 1517 a German monk named Martin Luther issued 95 theses in which he criticized the Church for the sale of indulgences and attacked other Catholic beliefs. He began the Protestant Reformation and founded Lutheranism, the first Protestant faith.

3. Luther's ideas spread rapidly and stimulated the development of a number of different Protestant groups.

4. By 1525 Huldreich Zwingli had transformed Zurich into a Protestant theocracy in which Roman Catholic practices were banned. Worship services were based on the Bible and conducted in the vernacular.

5. Beginning in 1536, the French reformer John Calvin began to turn the Swiss city of Geneva into a center of Protestantism. His form of Protestantism, known as Calvinism, spread throughout western Europe.

6. Protestant radicals, known as Anabaptists, controlled the German city of Münster in the early 1530's. Their beliefs contributed to the modern ideas of religious liberty and separation of church and state.

7. The English Reformation began as a political quarrel between Henry VIII and the Pope. In 1534 Parliament separated the Church of England from Rome.

8. After assuming the throne in 1553, Mary I tried to force the English people to return to Roman Catholicism. But, Mary's successor Elizabeth I made the English Church Protestant, with some Catholic features.

9. Between 1545 and 1563, the Council of Trent in Italy reformed many Catholic practices.

10. In 1555 the Holy Roman Emperor Charles V agreed to the Peace of Augsburg, which allowed each German prince to decide whether his subjects would be Catholic or Protestant.

11. Between 1566 and 1581, Protestants in the Netherlands revolted against Spanish rule and established an independent Dutch state.

12. In 1562 the French Wars of Religion broke out between Catholics and Protestants (Huguenots). The Catholics won the struggle, although in 1589 after renouncing Protestantism, a Huguenot leader became Henry IV of Catholic France.

Building Vocabulary

reformation	purgatory	vocations	predestination
simony	theses	theocracy	elect
indulgences	ministers		seminary

Reviewing the Main Ideas

1. Why was it difficult for church councils to meet about reform?
2. Who were the opponents in the Hussite Wars? How was the conflict resolved?
3. Why did Charles V become involved in the dispute between Martin Luther and the Pope?
4. How did Luther's teachings differ from those of Roman Catholicism?
5. How were the beliefs of Huldreich Zwingli and Luther the same? How were they different?
6. What factors helped Calvinists survive in spite of severe persecution?
7. How did the Anabaptists get their name? Why were they viewed with suspicion by government authorities?
8. Why was Mary I called "Bloody Mary"? To what royal family did she belong?
9. For what reasons was the English Reformation important?
10. How did Pope Paul III try to reform the Catholic Church?
11. What factors prevented the Holy Roman Emperor Charles V from stopping Lutheranism in Germany?
12. What conditions helped the Huguenots to survive in Catholic France?

Discussing Important Ideas

1. How did political and economic factors influence the development of the Protestant Reformation? Which do you think were more important?
2. Compare and contrast the religious doctrines of Calvin and Luther.
3. Do you approve or disapprove of the establishment of theocracies in Zurich and Geneva? Why or why not?
4. Why do you think most English people supported Elizabeth I's organization of the English Church?
5. If you had been a Catholic in the mid-1500's, in which European country would you have preferred to live? Why?
6. What were the goals of the Council of Trent? Were they achieved? Explain.
7. Why was the Schmalkaldic League formed? Do you think it was successful in its purpose? Explain.
8. If you had been Henry IV, would you have converted to Catholicism? Explain.
9. Why was religious toleration an unpopular belief in Europe during the 1500's?

Using Maps

Refer to the map on page 272 to answer the following questions:
1. Which religion was the most widespread at this time?
2. Which religions were present as minorities in Bohemia?
3. Where were the Calvinist minorities? the Lutheran minorities?
4. What religions were found in Germany? in England?
5. What city is about 46° north and 6° east?
6. Where did Europe's Jewish population live?

CHAPTER 12

Explorer Departs Europe

❝ The discovery of America, and that of a passage to the East Indies by the Cape of Good Hope, are the greatest and most important events recorded in the history of mankind. ❞

Adam Smith, Scottish economist (1723-1790)

Discovery and Expansion

In the early 1400's, most Europeans were chiefly interested in their own lands and their own problems. Even those who had been fascinated by the tales of Marco Polo and the crusaders did not have the ability or desire to explore foreign continents. European lands were only just beginning to develop into powerful states. They still lacked the energy and resources to exert much influence on the other regions of the world.

By the late 1400's, Europeans had changed their attitude toward foreign areas. They became more self-confident and began to look beyond their own continent. As a result, between 1500 and 1763, Europe entered a new era. This period was a time of discovery when daring European sea captains tested the unknown waters of the Atlantic and Pacific Oceans. It also was a time of expansion when Europeans settled new lands, spread Christianity, and searched for wealth in land and minerals.

Within a lifetime, significant breakthroughs in knowledge led to a new understanding of the planet. The dimensions of the earth were established and the size of its oceans made clear. Maps were made that accurately showed the coastlines of Africa, South Asia, and East Asia as well as the Atlantic coast of the Americas and the Pacific coast of South America. Portions of the interiors of South, Central, and North America were explored.

Europe became the power center of the world, taking over old civilizations and creating new ones. Many Europeans became rich and influential as a result of wealth acquired from Asia, Africa, and the Americas. Old cultures and traditions were shattered as vast numbers of people moved from one continent to another.

There was a borrowing and blending of ideas from many civilizations. At the end of the era, much of the globe became dominated by Europe. The time of limited communication among cultures had come to an end.

1 An Altered World

Until the 1500's, most contacts between civilizations consisted of infrequent, brief visits made by soldiers, seafarers, traders, and missionaries. In-depth involvement between cultures generally took place only between neighboring regions.

In 1400, Europeans had only a limited knowledge of the globe. Most geographers believed that the world was round. But they did not always agree on its size. Their notions of the relationship of Asia, Africa, and Europe were vague. They had no idea that North and South America even existed.

Navigational tools also were limited, and travel on the high seas was rare. Nobody knew the landmarks of the entire globe, and stories of fantastic sea monsters and other horrors were believed by most of the people. As a result, seafarers traveled close to their coastlines, going only where they knew the islands, bays, reefs, straits, tides, currents, and winds.

By the late 1600's, changes had taken place in the European understanding of the world. These changes, which varied in speed and depth, were brought about by several factors and had startling results.

Background for Success

In the late 1400's, improvements began to be made in European ships. Until that time,

277

Point out that the advances of seafarers such as the Phoenicians and Vikings were lost or forgotten.

Indian, Arab, and Chinese sailors had advanced naval technology, yet they did not become global explorers. Have students consider how their motivations differed from those of Europeans.

European ships had been greatly inferior to those of the Indians, Arabs, and Chinese. One improvement was the triangular-shaped **lateen sail.** It had been introduced to the Mediterranean area by Islamic traders. Another was the replacement of the single mast having one large sail by multiple masts having a series of small sails hoisted one above another. Still another was the moving of the **rudder,** the device used to steer a ship, from the side of the ship to the rear. These improvements made European ships easier to handle and enabled them to travel more quickly.

At the same time, improvements were made in navigational tools. Two very important tools were the compass, originated by the Chinese, and the astrolabe, perfected by the Arabs. The **compass,** used to determine geographical direction, made long sea voyages possible. The **astrolabe** allowed ship captains to determine latitude by measuring the angle of the planets and stars.

A third area in which improvements were made was weapons. European sailors were armed with handguns and, for the first time, European ships were equipped with cannons. In time, the effectiveness of the cannons made European ships masters of the sea.

These technological improvements, however, were only one factor that led Europeans to venture farther away from home. Two equally important ones were economics and religion.

Economic Needs The monarchs of Europe were continually in need of money. Frequent wars were financially draining. Another expense was the upkeep of a monarch's court. Since national power was demonstrated by the size and glamour of the court, monarchs were expected to live in grand style. The taxes needed to cover these costs, however, could not be raised without fear of political upheaval. The need for money led monarchs and their advisers to seek more gold and silver.

One means of obtaining gold and silver was through trade. The spices, silks, and jewels that came chiefly from India, China, and the islands of Asia were in great demand. Trading these items could make a country rich. During the early 1400's, Venice controlled Europe's trade with the Far East. European kings, jealous of Venice's monopoly, wanted to share the trade.

Of all the products traded by the Venetians, spices were the most essential and the most profitable. Europeans used them for perfumes, cosmetics, medicines, and most importantly, for flavoring and preserving meat. European grain harvests were not large enough to feed livestock throughout the winter, so most animals were slaughtered in the fall. The only known way to preserve the meat was by smoking it and curing it with spices.

The more valuable and rarer spices were pepper, cinnamon, nutmeg, mace, and cloves. These were grown successfully only in the East Indies, an archipelago of Southeast Asia. The people of these islands traded the spices to Arab,

The development of navigational skills led to many advances in astronomy, physics, and geography. It opened the way for extended sea voyages. What other factors contributed to European exploration?

Have students use the atlas to locate the East Indies. Point out that the present-day country of Indonesia was once called the East Indies.

Have students consider the economic and religious motivations. Which do they think was more important?

EUROPEAN KNOWLEDGE OF THE WORLD

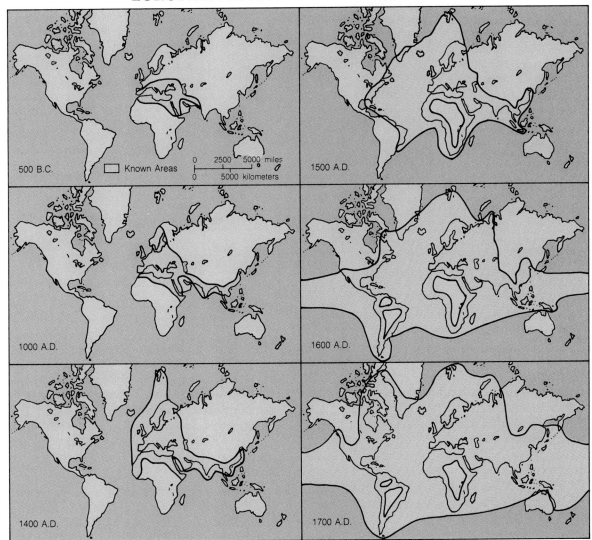

Indian, and Chinese merchants. The spices were then shipped to Egypt for sale to the Venetians. Venice's European rivals wanted to trade directly with the islands. In this way, they could end their dependence on Venetian and Asian merchants. Venice's trade monopoly would end, and profits would shift to their own treasuries.

The desire for profits led some European rulers to finance voyages of exploration to find new sea routes to the islands. Before long, the competition in trade and exploration was fueled by other motives. One was the profitability of such newly

discovered products as gold, silver, sugar, slaves, fish, and furs. A second was the patriotic ambition of one nation to outdo another.

Religious Zeal   The European interest in exploration was also promoted by a desire to spread Christianity and to halt the expansion of Islam. Catholic missionaries, for example, saw in new territories an opportunity to spread their religion and to save souls.

For the Portuguese and the Spanish, halting the spread of Islam was as important as spreading their own faith. Spain had only

Johann Fugger began the Fugger fortune in the 1300's with his small clothmaking business. His heirs diversified the business, trading in silks, spices, and jewels. They traded in Italy, Poland, Hungary, and the Netherlands and set up banking houses throughout Europe.

In the late 1400's, increased trade demanded changes in the organization of commerce. The growth of business was sluggish due to a comparative lack of money and its slow circulation. These obstacles were overcome by advanced banking methods adopted in small exchange banks, such as this one in Florence. What other economic innovations were made during the Commercial Revolution?

expelled the Moors in the late 1400's. Accounts of the advance of other Islamic armies into eastern Europe fed the fear that similar attacks might be launched on Spain and Portugal.

The Portuguese believed that exploration of the African coastline could prevent an Islamic attack. They had heard stories of a Christian kingdom in Africa ruled by a king called Prester John.[1] The Portuguese thought that if they could find Prester John and join forces with him, Christians would be able to attack the Islamic forces from behind. They reasoned that, even if direct military action did not develop, the exploration could still be helpful by cutting Islamic trade routes. This would weaken Islamic economic power which, in turn, would stop the spread of Islam.

New Institutions and Attitudes

The move toward exploration and the expansion of world trade stimulated European economic life. The nation replaced the city and the village as the basic economic unit. Although

[1]Many historians believe that the kingdom referred to in the stories was Ethiopia.

bartering still took place in small local markets, it was too slow and clumsy for large-scale operations. New arrangements developed for investing money, speeding the flow of wealth, and reducing risks in commercial ventures. These changes, which came to be known as the Commercial Revolution, became the roots of modern business life.

Expanded Economic Scene European shippers made many preparations to send trading fleets across the seas. Money was raised; goods, supplies, and crews were assembled; and payment was arranged. Delays were countless. Several years often passed before a fleet returned and investments could be recovered. For this reason, only governments and the richer merchants dared to take part in such ventures, and even they needed help.

At first, assistance came from bankers. One such group of bankers was the Fuggers, a banking family from Augsburg. By the 1500's, these successful merchants and traders had gathered such wealth that they were accepting deposits, making loans, and transferring funds over long distances. They had branches in the

Discuss the advantages of joint stock companies over previous methods for financing trade ventures.

Mercantilism concerned the power of nations rather than the wealth and welfare of its subjects.

important financial centers of Europe and made loans to many European monarchs.

By the 1600's, however, banking families like the Fuggers were beginning to be replaced by chartered banks that accepted deposits of money and issued loans for interest. Before long, they began to provide other services, ones which simplified transactions. They issued bank notes, a much easier form in which to make payments than heavy coins. They acted as money changers, reducing the confusion and other problems associated with many different coins. They provided official exchange rates and used standard weights. Some banks, such as the Bank of Amsterdam, even controlled the minting of coins.

Individual merchants who wanted to invest in exploration often raised money for the business venture by combining their resources in **joint stock companies,** business organizations formed for the purpose of selling stock, or shares. Large and small investors joined together by purchasing shares in the company. Profits were divided among the investors based on the number of shares owned. In case of a loss, investors would lose only the amount they had invested in these shares. In this way, a joint stock company could raise large amounts of money. Further, since the company invested in a series of trading ventures, investors no longer were risking their money on the fate of one ship alone.

Mercantilism As money became more available for large enterprises, ideas changed about the nature and goals of business. Gradually, a system based on the belief that the goal of business was to make profits took shape. Enterprising individuals known as **entrepreneurs** combined money, ideas, raw materials, and labor to make goods. Profits earned from the sale of the goods were used to expand the business and develop new ventures.

A new theory of national economic policy called **mercantilism** also developed. According to it, wealth meant power. In other words, the richer a nation was, the more powerful it was. Wealth was measured by the amount of **bullion,** or gold and silver, a nation owned. One Venetian summed up the feeling about bullion in this way:

[It is] the sinews of all government, it gives it its pulse, its movement, its mind, soul, and it is its essence and its very life . . . . It overcomes all impossibilities, for it is the master, the patron of all; it carries with it the necessity of all things; without it all is weak and without movement. *

Under mercantilism, the economic goal of each nation was to gain as much wealth as possible. This could be done by extracting gold and silver from mines at home or overseas. It also could be done through trade. Nations sought to create a favorable **balance of trade** by exporting more goods than they imported. In this way, the gold and silver received for exports would exceed the gold and silver paid for imports. This greater wealth meant greater national strength.

Colonies served a definite purpose in the mercantilist system. They were the sources of raw materials as well as important markets for finished goods produced by the parent country. Colonies existed to benefit the parent and to help make it self-sufficient. Self-sufficiency, in turn, served to stimulate national production and to keep other countries from benefiting at the expense of a parent country.

Government planning and restrictions were designed to make sure that mercantile goals were achieved. However, mercantilism did not work as well in practice as in theory. One reason for this was that silver and gold could not be held as royal stockpiles. Bullion from Spain and Portugal, for example, flowed to the Far East to pay for spices and silks and to northern Europe to pay for grain, cloth, pottery, and weapons. Bullion also leaked out illegally. The loss from illegal leaks was so great that in the 1500's, Spain often was referred to as "the Indies of other foreign kingdoms."

Another weakness of mercantilism were the monopolies. Even partial ones were costly to maintain. Monopolies fostered illegal trading and raiding that contributed to wars. The wars drained nations of the very wealth they had worked so hard to obtain.

**The Mediterranean and the Mediterranean World in the Age of Philip II*, Vol. 1, Fernand Braudel, © 1972 by Harper and Row, p. 462.

Despite these drawbacks, mercantilism prospered, especially in England. It proved to be a strong motivator, not only in exploration attempts, but also in the establishment of new overseas colonies.

1. Identify: East Indies, Prester John, Commercial Revolution, Fuggers, Bank of Amsterdam.
2. Why were there few contacts between civilizations before the 1500's?
3. What three factors motivated European overseas exploration?
4. What was the goal of mercantilism? How was it to be accomplished?

2 Portugal

One of the first European countries to venture across the seas was Portugal. Between 1420 and 1580, the Portuguese discovered the sea route around Africa to Asia and secured a chain of trading posts in Africa, India, and the East Indies. Portuguese naval power became so strong that other European nations were forced to search the western Atlantic for alternate routes to the East. Portugal's rise to supremacy was due to the efforts of its government. Portuguese officials were the first in Europe to give sustained support to sea exploration.

A Route East

One of the key figures in Portugal's expansion was Prince Henry the Navigator, the brother of the Portuguese king. Although not a sailor himself, Henry provided the inspiration, encouragement, and direction needed for the early voyages of exploration.

In the early 1400's, Henry set up the first European school for navigators in Sagres, Portugal. There he gathered together sea captains, navigators, mapmakers, mathematicians, and astronomers from all over the Mediterranean world. Together these experts worked out objectives for overseas expeditions and saw to it that Portuguese ships had the latest in naval design.

Henry hoped to find gold in Africa and a new route to the Far East, thus extending Portugal's trade and power. To this end, he sent groups of explorers westward into the Atlantic and southward down Africa's western coast. Each group went a little farther than the one before.

The islands discovered on the voyages became supply stations for the expeditions that followed. The gold dust, ivory, and slaves that the Portuguese found along the way stimulated interest in trade. Henry insisted that the logs, charts, and maps from each voyage be carefully guarded. This tight security helped the Portuguese keep their advantage over foreign competitors in the area.

To protect their discoveries against future claims, the Portuguese sought support from Pope Nicholas V. In 1454 the Pope issued a papal bull, or edict, in which he allowed the Portuguese to "occupy and possess in exclusive rights" certain islands, ports, and seas. He stated

Prince Henry the Navigator's interest in exploration kindled in Portuguese sailors the urge to travel and seek adventure. What did Henry hope to achieve by sponsoring overseas expeditions?

Have students locate Albuquerque's bases on a map.

that all of the Portuguese conquests already made, those which "extend to Cape Bajador and Cape Non to the coast of Guinea and all the Orient [are] perpetually and for the future the sovereignty of" Portugal.

Dias   When Prince Henry died in 1460, the Portuguese had traveled a third of the way down the west coast of Africa. By 1473 they had crossed the equator. Their real breakthrough, however, did not come until 1487. Until that time, the Portuguese did not know whether the seas were open around the tip of Africa. Like most Europeans at the time, they based their idea of the world on the works of the Greek astronomer and geographer Ptolemy. Ptolemy believed that Africa was not a peninsula.

Then, in 1487 Bartholomeu Dias sailed around the continent's tip, which he named the Cape of Storms. Dias's voyage showed the Portuguese that they could reach the Far East by sailing around Africa. In honor of this discovery, the Portuguese king renamed the Cape of Storms the Cape of Good Hope.

Vasco da Gama   For several years after Dias's journey, domestic troubles kept the Portuguese from pushing on to India. Finally, in 1495, preparations got underway for an expedition to India to be made by four ships. Two of the ships were specially built to carry a variety of trade goods in addition to the usual cannon and supplies.

In 1497, with the blessing of the king and the Church, the expedition sailed for India. It was led by a Portuguese noble named Vasco da Gama. The chief goal of the voyage was to determine the costs and benefits of direct trade with India.

In 1498 da Gama landed at Calicut on the southwestern coast of India. There, he found the Hindus and Muslims trading fine silks, porcelains, and spices that made the rough woolens, glass beads, and trinkets of the Portuguese appear shoddy. The hostile welcome that da Gama received suggested that the Arab Muslim merchants and Hindu princes saw the Portuguese as a threat to their trade.

Da Gama's voyage took more than two years. Although two ships and half the crew were lost,

the Portuguese viewed the voyage as a triumph. Da Gama had proven that the Indian Ocean could be reached by sea. The route he had taken far out into the Atlantic enabled him to take advantage of the prevailing winds. It soon became the standard route for all ships sailing around Africa. Now the Portuguese could sail to India and the East Indies and bring back the Asian goods the Europeans wanted.

Establishing Control

The Portuguese, not content with only part of the spice trade, took steps to gain a monopoly. Under the leadership of Alfonso de Albuquerque, they set up a string of fortified naval bases at strategic points. One base was Hormuz, at the mouth of the Persian Gulf. Another was Goa, an island along the Indian coast that was used as a trading and administrative center. A third was Malacca, on the southwestern coast of Malaya in Southeast Asia. From these bases, the Portuguese controlled shipping in and out of the Indian Ocean.

Next, the Portuguese expanded farther eastward to the Moluccas, a group of islands in the East Indies. Known as the Spice Islands, they were one of the richest sources of spices in the world. From the Spice Islands, the Portuguese pushed on to China and Japan. The Chinese gave them rights to establish a trading port on an island in the Xi Jiang delta. There, they built the settlement of Macao, which to this day remains under Portuguese control. In Japan, Portuguese merchants traded for Japanese silver and copper; and Portuguese missionaries worked to convert the Japanese to Christianity.

After their success in China and Japan, the Portuguese turned to Sri Lanka (Ceylon), an island off the southeastern coast of India. It served as a source of tea and spices and provided a stopover point between Goa and Malacca. Thus, Portugal was able to dominate the entire trade with the East Indies throughout the 1500's.

The Portuguese became the first Europeans to build an overseas empire. Their main interest lay in Africa and Asia, where they confined themselves to establishing trading settlements. Although they took actions against Asians and

Before plantations were developed in Brazil, settlers sold hardwoods to Europeans.

Explain that even experienced sailors were not accustomed to long stretches on the open seas. Four days outside the sight of land was considered long before 1500.

Africans who interfered with trade, they did not try to establish true colonies in these areas. A major reason for this was that Portugal's population was too small to allow for large-scale emigration to other lands. In addition, the hot, humid climate of the trading settlements did not appeal to most Europeans. Nevertheless, the Portuguese trading posts and forts were eventually made colonies and became the territories of Angola and Mozambique.

Another area that the Portuguese colonized was Brazil. This territory, located in South America, had been discovered in 1500 by the Portuguese captain Pedro Álvares Cabral. Because Cabral found no precious metals, more than 30 years passed before the first permanent settlement was established in Brazil. At that time, Brazil was divided into 15 territorial strips, each of which was granted to a noble Portuguese family. Each family was given the right to establish towns, distribute land, and organize armies.

Large numbers of Portuguese were sent to settle in Brazil. They divided the land into large plantations and concentrated on developing income-producing crops. They introduced sugarcane, then tobacco, coffee, cocoa, and cotton. Since the local population did not supply enough labor for the plantations, slaves were imported from Portuguese ports in Africa. This pattern of colonization was later copied throughout the Caribbean and along the southern coast of the United States.

Portugal's Decline

By the late 1500's, Portugal's trading empire had begun to decline. Portuguese policies had created many enemies in Europe and Asia. The Europeans envied Portugal's wealth. The Asians remembered with bitterness Portuguese brutality. All were eager to take advantage of any Portuguese weakness.

One such weakness was the Portuguese government itself. It was not well organized nor was it strong enough to control its officials at home or in its colonies. A second weakness, which became more serious as time passed and the scale of Portuguese trade increased, was the lack of Portuguese personnel. New sailors were always needed because of the high death rate on board Portuguese ships. As this need grew, so did the scarcity of adequately trained men. The use of poorly trained sailors led to a marked rise in the number of ships lost at sea, which made the Portuguese more vulnerable to attack.

The real turning point for Portugal's trading empire came in 1580 when the Portuguese were defeated by Spain and placed under Spanish rule. Spain limited the amount of trade Portugal could do and paid little or no attention to the Portuguese colonies. At the same time, Portuguese possessions and trade routes became targets for the Dutch and the English, who later captured them. By the 1600's, the only major colonies the Portuguese had left were Brazil, Angola, and Mozambique.

1. Identify: Prince Henry the Navigator, Nicholas V, Bartholomeu Dias, Vasco da Gama, Alfonso de Albuquerque, Pedro Álvares Cabral.
2. Why was the support of the Portuguese Crown important to Portuguese exploration?
3. What caused Portuguese power to decline?

3   Spain

Like Portugal, Spain was interested in the wealth that could be obtained from India and the Far East. King Ferdinand and Queen Isabella were willing to back the expeditions of an Italian navigator named Christopher Columbus. His discovery of a string of islands between North and South America was a turning point for Spain.

Quite by surprise, the Spanish had found two continents the Europeans had never dreamed existed. Within two generations, they created a vast colonial empire in the newly found land. At the same time, they abandoned their attempts to compete with Portugal in the East Indies.

A Route West

At the time the Spanish were able to compete with the Portuguese, the Pope barred interference in Portugal's eastern sea route. This meant that to gain the wealth they sought, the Spanish would have to find a new sea route to Asia. In

Variations on the name Christopher Columbus include Cristoforo Colombo and Cristobal Colon.

When Columbus first talked to Ferdinand and Isabella, he astonished them with his demands: aid to finance the voyage, one-tenth of any profit made, the rank of noble, and the title "Grand Admiral of the Ocean Sea." His request was refused; but, after considering what Spain could gain, Isabella changed her mind and gave Columbus the support he needed. Why did Spain want a new route to Asia?

1492 Christopher Columbus approached Queen Isabella with a plan to reach India by sailing west across the Atlantic. Eager to boost Spain's wealth and prestige, the Spanish monarch was willing to listen.

Christopher Columbus   Before meeting Isabella, Christopher Columbus had been trying for seven years to find backers for a voyage westward to the Indies. By 1492 he had been turned down by the English, the French, and the Portuguese. His cause had not been helped by the fact that he was the poor son of a Genoese weaver and had never captained a ship. He was, however, stubborn, persistent, self-confident, and highly persuasive. Finally, he managed to convince Queen Isabella to support his plan.

In August 1492, Columbus sailed from Spain with three small ships, experienced crews, and some trade goods. At first, it seemed that the ships were making progress in crossing the Atlantic. But as time wore on and no land came into sight, the crews began to despair. When Columbus refused their pleas to turn back, they threatened to **mutiny,** or overthrow the officers and take over the ship. Columbus reluctantly agreed to turn back if land was not sighted within three days.

On the night of the second day, a crew member sighted an island. In the morning,

Columbus and his men went ashore, becoming the first Europeans to set foot in the Caribbean area. Their first impression of the islanders was recorded by Columbus:

> *The islanders came to the ships' boats where we were, swimming and bringing us parrots and balls of cotton thread, and many other things, which they exchanged for things we gave them, such as glass beads and hawk bells. In short, they took and gave of what they had very willingly, but it seemed to me that they were poor in every way. They bore no weapons, nor were they acquainted with them, because when I showed them swords they seized them by the edge and so cut themselves from ignorance. They have no iron; their javelins are reeds without iron points, although some of them are armed with fishes' teeth, and others with other things.**

Columbus, believing the islands to be off the coast of India, called the islanders "Indians." He questioned them about gold and then spent the next three months exploring other islands, including Cuba and Hispaniola, in search of the precious metal. Enough gold was found to raise

---

**Columbus, Cortés, and Other Essays,* Ramón Iglesia, tr. by Lesley Byrd Simpson, © 1969 by University of California Press, p. 13.

The map below is the subject of the "Using Maps" section of the Chapter 12 Review.

Point out on a world map the 1493 line of demarcation and the line drawn in 1494.

Spanish hopes, but no evidence could be found of advanced civilizations.

When Ferdinand and Isabella received Columbus's report of what he had found, they gave him the title "Admiral of the Ocean Sea, Viceroy and Governor of the Islands he hath discovered in the Indies." At the same time, they ordered him to prepare for a second voyage.

Columbus's second expedition, which set out five months later, signaled the direction Spanish policy would take. This time 17 ships set sail carrying 1,500 people. They had all the skills needed to establish a settlement on Hispaniola to serve as a base for further exploration.

Before he died in 1506, Columbus had made four voyages for Spain. He died convinced he had found a new route to Asia. Others, however, did not agree. One such person was an Italian named Amerigo Vespucci, who had taken part in several Portuguese expeditions between 1497 and 1503. He contended that the land Columbus had seen was not Asia but a "New World."

Treaty of Tordesillas   Like the Portuguese, the Spanish turned to the Pope to protect their claims. In 1493, he drew a **line of demarcation,** an imaginary line running down the middle of the Atlantic from the North Pole to the South Pole, dividing the new lands. Spain was to have control of all lands to the west of the line. Portugal was to have control of all lands to the east of the line.

This papal action alarmed the Portuguese. Afraid that Spain might take over their Asian trade, the Portuguese protested the division. In 1494 the Spanish and the Portuguese came to an agreement and signed the Treaty of Tordesillas. The treaty moved the line of demarcation farther west.

Ferdinand Magellan

Eager to explore their new possessions, the Spanish sent out expedition after expedition. In 1513 the Spaniard Vasco Núñez de Balboa crossed the Isthmus of Panama, a neck of land

EUROPEAN VOYAGES OF DISCOVERY

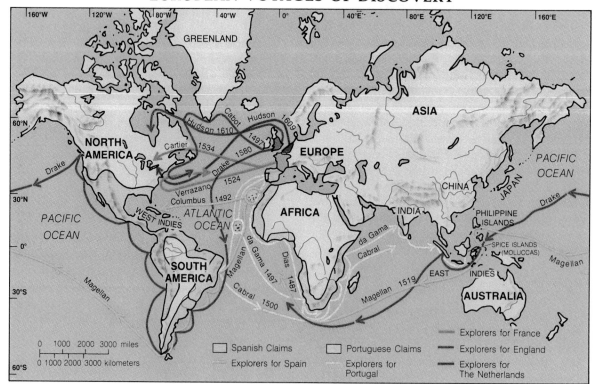

Magellan had no idea that the Pacific Ocean was as large as it is. The Pacific covers nearly one third of the globe, an area equal to all the world's landmasses.

Compare the risks taken by early sea explorers with those taken by modern-day astronauts.

connecting Central America and South America. He became the first European to sight the Pacific Ocean, which he called the South Sea. That same year, another Spaniard, Juan Ponce de León, sailed northward from Puerto Rico and discovered and explored Florida.

In 1519, still another Spanish expedition set out across the seas. This one was led by Ferdinand Magellan, a Portuguese soldier of fortune. Magellan had convinced the Spanish monarchs that he could find a western route to the East Indies. Magellan's expedition, which started out with five ships and 270 men, was plagued from the outset. His Spanish officers did not trust his leadership, and his crews mutinied.

After a frustrating search down the uncharted coast of South America, Magellan finally found the straits that now bear his name. In spite of strong currents, unpredictable winds, and frigid weather, Magellan's ships attempted to travel through the maze of rocky islands in the 300-mile (480-kilometer)-long straits. One ship got separated from the others, and its crew forced its return to Spain. Another was shipwrecked.

Magellan finally passed through the straits into the South Sea. Because the water was so calm, he renamed it the Pacific Ocean. Magellan's exhausted fleet then sailed nearly four months before reaching land. Water and food ran out, and many of the sailors died of **scurvy,** a disease caused by a lack of vitamin C. Those who survived did so on a diet of foul water, wormy biscuits, leather, sawdust, and mice.

Magellan finally reached the island of Guam, where he was able to get fresh provisions. In the Philippines, however, he got involved in a dispute with a local chief and was killed. Nearly 30 of his crew members were massacred. Those remaining escaped to Tidore, one of the spice-growing islands. Fearful of Portuguese attack, they loaded spices into the *Victoria,* the one seaworthy ship that remained, and sailed for Spain.

In 1522 the *Victoria* arrived at Seville, Spain. The 18 survivors of the expedition had been away three years. The spices they brought home with them barely covered the cost of the voyage. Although no one became rich as a result of the

This map of the Pacific Ocean drawn in 1590 shows Magellan's surviving ship, the Victoria, under full sail. What problems did Magellan and his crew encounter on their journey around the tip of South America?

voyage, their expedition did alter scientific thinking. It proved that the world was round and far larger than anyone had believed. It also proved that the oceans of the world were connected and that the lands discovered by Columbus were not Asia.

During the five years after the return of the *Victoria,* two larger fleets were sent to follow Magellan's route. When none of the ships returned, the Spanish decided that the distances were too great for the route to be profitable. As a result, the Straits of Magellan never became a regular sailing route.

In 1529 the line of demarcation was extended around the remainder of the globe. As a result, all of the Western Hemisphere except what is now Brazil was in the Spanish zone. All of the Eastern Hemisphere except the Philippines was in the Portuguese zone. Control of the non-European world was now divided between Spain and Portugal.

Conquering an Empire

Not all Spaniards were motivated by the hope of finding new trade routes. Some were more interested in finding gold. Between 1519 and

In conquering the Aztecs, Cortes depended much on Doña Marina. She was one of his translators.

Hindered by adverse winds on the Pacific, deserts, and mountains, the Spanish did not encounter the Incas until 1530.

Montezuma II reluctantly welcomed Cortés to Tenochtitlán. He thought Cortés was the legendary white god, Quetzalcoatl, returning to the throne. What eventually caused the Aztecs to rise up against Cortés and his Spanish forces?

1550, several thousand Spanish **conquistadores,** or conquerors, in search of riches explored—and seized—much of Central and South America.

Cortés, Mexico, and the Aztecs   One such conquistador was Hernán Cortés, who left Cuba in 1519 with an army of 600 Spaniards to explore Mexico. Of the different groups of Indians who lived in Mexico at the time, the largest and most advanced civilization was that of the Aztecs. It was the wealthy Aztec capital of Tenochtitlán that Cortés sought.

Cortés was a popular but determined and ruthless leader. When he landed at Veracruz, he set fire to his ships to make sure that none of his crew could desert. He hid any signs of Spanish weakness from the Indians. Burials of horses and fallen Spaniards, for example, were carried out only at night. He found out which Indian groups were enemies of the Aztecs and made alliances with them.

The Aztec ruler, Montezuma II, knew the Spaniards were coming. His messengers had described them to him as "supernatural creatures riding on hornless deer, preceded by wild animals on leashes, dressed in iron, armed in iron, fearless as gods." When the Spaniards finally reached Tenochtitlán, they were awed by its order and grandeur. Everything they saw surpassed what they had known in Spain. Montezuma told the Spaniards about a prophecy: the descendants of a former Aztec monarch would return and conquer the Aztec people. Believing that the Spaniards had come to fulfill the prophecy, Montezuma offered to serve them in peace.

The peace did not last long. When Cortés's men massacred some Aztec leaders, the Aztecs turned against the Spaniards. During the fierce fighting that followed, Montezuma was killed and Cortés was forced to flee. But rather than give up, Cortés gathered his Indian allies and returned to Tenochtitlán. He tried to force the Aztecs to surrender by burning and destroying the city as he advanced. The Aztecs, however, refused to yield.

The Spanish were fewer in number than the Aztecs. But they had horses and guns, which were unknown in the Americas. In 1521, after much slaughter and destruction, the Aztecs surrendered. By then, there were more than 50,000 dead, and both Tenochtitlán and the Aztec civilization itself were in ruins.

Pizarro, Peru, and the Inca   Ten years after the Spanish conquest of Mexico, the Spanish conquistador Francisco Pizarro invaded Peru and conquered the Inca Empire. When Pizarro began his attack, the Inca were recovering from a power struggle between two brothers over the Inca throne. As a result, the empire was not prepared for the invasion.

The fate of the Inca was sealed in November of 1532. At the time, the Inca leader Atahualpa walked with an unarmed bodyguard of 6,000 soldiers into the Spanish camp. The Spaniards numbered only about 160 but they were all armed. Most of the Inca were killed, and Atahualpa was taken captive. Not one Spaniard was killed.

Some teachers might wish to have students draw maps showing the routes of the conquistadores.

The boldness of the Spanish attack stunned the Inca. Atahualpa made an agreement with Pizarro to fill two large rooms with gold and silver as a ransom. In return, Pizarro promised to release him. Once the ransom was collected, however, Pizarro had Atahualpa executed. With their leader gone, Inca resistance melted away, leaving the vast riches of the Inca Empire open to the Spanish. Before long, however, civil war broke out between rival factions of Spaniards. Many leaders died violent deaths. One was Pizarro, who was assassinated by his Spanish enemies.

Other Conquistadores and Discoveries

The age of the conquistadores did not end with Pizarro. In 1539 Hernando de Soto sailed from Puerto Rico to Florida and explored westward in search of gold, silver, and jewels. Instead of uncovering wealth, de Soto found the Mississippi River. The following year, Francisco Vásquez de Coronado led an army overland from Mexico into southwestern North America in hope of finding the legendary wealthy Seven Cities of Cibola. Instead of the golden treasure he sought, one of his party discovered the Grand Canyon.

Other conquistadores followed, but none could match the dazzling finds or stunning conquests of Cortés or Pizarro. In the mid-1560's, with Miguel López de Legaspi's conquest of the Philippine Islands, the age of the conquistadores came to an end.

Creating a "Latin" America

Spain now had a huge empire in the Americas. The West Indies, Central America, much of South America, and southern North America all came under Spanish control. Unlike the Portuguese, the Spanish were not content with trading settlements. Instead, they chose to establish colonies, the development of which was carefully planned and directed. Each colony was ruled by a **viceroy,** a representative of the monarch, who was responsible to a council in Spain. The council, in turn, was responsible to the monarch.

While most Spaniards were pleased about the new lands and riches, some were dismayed by stories of the cruelty shown to the Indians. For these Spaniards, the conquests could be justified only if they led to the conversion of the Indians to Christianity. Thus, the Spanish Crown undertook twin goals—to exploit the wealth of the new lands and to convert the Indians to Christianity.

The Indian Debate   Although the Spaniards knew they wanted to convert the Indians, they did not know how to convert them, what rights to allow them, or how to protect them from abuse. Some Spaniards agreed with the view of Bartolomé de Las Casas, a Catholic missionary who came to be known as Protector of the Indians. Las Casas argued that all people were part of a world community ruled by natural law. Spain's role among the Indians, he said, should be limited solely to spreading the gospel. The Indians' personal, economic, and political rights should be protected.

Other Spaniards agreed with the view of Juan Gines de Sepulveda, a noted Spanish thinker. He believed that lesser beings were ruled by higher ones. Although he knew little about Indians, he believed them to be inferior to the Spaniards. Thus, he argued, they should be ruled by Spain, converted to Christianity, and made to adopt Spanish culture. In his view, force was justified to spread Christianity.

Basic religious and economic interests came into conflict where the Indians were concerned. Through this, the Spanish Crown tried to steer a middle course. It proclaimed the Indians subjects of the Crown. They were free, could hold their own lands, keep their own leaders, and sue Spaniards in Spanish courts. At the same time, however, the Indians were to abide by Spanish law and accept Christianity.

The Crown gave conquistadores and later settlers grants which entitled them to the products and services of certain Indian villages. In return, the Spaniards were to provide military protection and to support the local parish priests. Since the Spanish needed Indian labor, forced labor at wage rates set by the government was allowed. The Spaniards saw labor as an important means by which the Indians could be "civilized" and introduced to Spanish culture.

Court records in Mexico show that abuse of the laws protecting Indians was widespread. Indians brought suit against Spaniards for many

Sor Juana Inés de la Cruz, a Spanish-Mexican nun who lived in the late 1600's, was a famous author in colonial Spanish America. Priests, monks, and nuns supervised education in Spain and its empire. What subjects were taught at church mission schools?

reasons. These included extorting excessive labor, bribery, withholding wages, seizing Indian property, grazing Spanish livestock on Indian land, and physical mistreatment. Great numbers of Indians died of overwork, disease, and starvation. Still, Indians received better protection from the Spaniards than did Indian subjects of other later colonial powers.

Spreading the Word   A massive missionary effort was begun in the colonies with the approval of the Pope. The effort was controlled and directed by the Spanish Crown, which hand-picked the earliest missionaries.

The missionaries set out to eliminate old religious beliefs and introduce new ones. In Mexico, they destroyed Indian temples and idols, drove out Indian priests, and banned Indian religious dances. They used Indian labor to build Catholic churches in which they substituted Catholic rituals for the traditional Indian ones. They created mission schools in which they taught Indian children Spanish, religion, and in some cases European trades.

In Mexico, conversion was widespread. In Peru, however, the Indians resisted. Indian religion and culture in Peru persisted alongside the Catholic religion and culture of the Spanish settlers.

Exploiting the Wealth   To the Spanish, the new lands were a source of opportunity and great wealth. Spaniards who settled there tried to recreate or improve upon the lives they had led in Spain. They brought cattle, sheep, and horses with them and converted their large land holdings into ranches.

Exports became the heart of the colonial economy. One export was animal hides, which were sent to Europe to be made into clothing and saddles. Two others were sugar and tobacco, both of which the Spanish had introduced in the Antilles. The most valuable exports by far, however, were silver and gold. In the late 1500's and early 1600's, they accounted for 80 percent of the value of the cargoes shipped to Spain.

At first, the bullion was obtained through plunder or barter. Then the Spaniards turned to panning for gold. Before long, vast silver deposits were discovered. These proved to be the most enduring source of wealth, surpassing gold in total value. At Potosi, a mountain of silver in present-day Bolivia, a boom town of over 100,000 persons grew up at the mine site.

The Crown made every effort to obtain one-fifth of all minerals mined. All discoveries had to be registered. Government officials posted at the mines weighed and tested the minerals and collected the Crown's share. Officials posted at ports watched for smugglers. Gold and silver were shipped only in Spanish vessels, which were allowed to dock only in Seville. The ships sailed in protected convoys with warships escorting the treasure ships.

Despite all these efforts, losses were high. Piracy was one problem. Raids by the Dutch and

HISTORY AND CITIES
Mexico City

After defeating the Aztecs, Cortés completely destroyed their magnificent capital, Tenochtitlán. On its ruins, he planned to build a Spanish city. The new metropolis, known as Mexico City, would become the capital of New Spain, the name the Spaniards gave to their North American empire. In a letter to the Spanish king, Cortés boasted that Mexico City would surpass Tenochtitlán in grandeur.

Cortés immediately set out to fulfill his promise. The central part of what was Tenochtitlán became Spanish, while the surrounding areas were left to the Aztecs and other Indians. With the help of forced Indian labor, Cortés began the building of the new city.

Like other Spanish colonial cities, Mexico City was planned according to strict regulations set by the Spanish Crown. At the city's center was a plaza, or great square. The plaza of Mexico City was laid out on the site of the huge temple-pyramid of the Aztec war god and the palace of the Aztec ruler. On the ruins of the war god's temple, Cortés built a church. To symbolize the triumph of Christianity, broken Aztec idols were used in the church's foundations. In 1553 the church was replaced with a large cathedral.

Cortés's palace was built on the plaza opposite the church. It stood over the ruins of the Aztec royal palaces. Over 7,000 cedar beams and tons of stone were used in its construction. Córtes's palace was later rebuilt on an even grander scale. It became the official residence of the viceroy.

Surrounding the plaza was a grid of streets. By the 1600's the streets were lined with homes, shops, schools, churches, and monasteries. Architects used the baroque style of architecture, which was known for its elaborate decoration. The Indians at first vastly outnumbered their Spanish conquerors. Mexico City had separate Spanish and Indian neighborhoods. However, the Aztecs and Spaniards later intermarried and made Mexico City the first mestizo city.

Under Spanish colonial rule, Mexico City became the economic center of Mexico. The Spaniards rebuilt the principal Aztec roads and canals. With improvements in transportation, agriculture and commerce flourished.

Today Mexico City is one of the fastest growing cities in the world. It is one of the largest cities in the Western Hemisphere. Mexico City continues its tradition as a capital city. Since 1821 it has been the capital of the Republic of Mexico.

The Mexico City metropolitan area is the country's commercial, production, and cultural center. A number of the city's colonial buildings have survived. They include the viceroy's residence and the Cathedral of Saint Francis.

1. How did Aztec influence affect the building and growth of Mexico City?
2. How was Mexico City laid out?

Mexico City was built on an island in Lake Texcoco. Nearly 85 percent of the city's soil contained water. Drainage, therefore, was always a problem. After 30,000 residents died in floods in 1629, the Spaniards improved the Aztec system of canals. Today excess water is pumped out of the soil, causing the ground to sink. Some areas have sunk as much as one foot (30 cm) in one year.

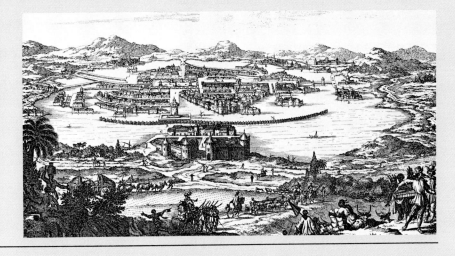

In Mexico alone, the Indian population dropped nearly 90 percent. By 1600, 20 million Indians died.

Inflation experienced in Spain spread to the rest of Europe at a slower and less dramatic rate.

the English was another. Internal corruption was still another. It contributed to "leaks" at every point in the journey from the remote mining sites to Spain.

A Changed Population   Within 100 years after the Spanish invasion, the population of the islands and coastal areas had changed greatly. Indians, who lacked the immunities Europeans had acquired over the years, were wiped out by such European diseases as small pox, malaria, and yellow fever. In the Caribbean, they actually became extinct. The high loss of life among the Indians led the Spaniards to import more and more African slaves. What had been a trickle of smuggled slaves became a flood. By 1700, black Africans made up the largest part of the population in the West Indies.

Gradually a new social structure emerged. At the top were the **peninsulares,** Spaniards born in Spain. Next came the **creoles,** Spaniards born in the colonies. Then came the **mestizos,** those of mixed Spanish and Indian ancestry. After them came the Indians. Lastly were the blacks, which included **mulattos,** those of mixed European and black ancestry, and the **zambos,** those of mixed Indian and black ancestry. These distinctions were very important in colonial Spanish America. They were at the heart of the structure of the government, the economy, and the culture.

Spain's Decline

By 1600 Spain had reached its peak as a European and colonial power. Its easily acquired wealth eventually led to its decline. Spain had spent too much money on religious and dynastic wars with other European countries. It also had pursued economic policies that benefited its enemies more than itself.

Spain's economy was poorly suited to meet the needs of its colonies and to absorb the sudden flood of gold and silver from overseas. Most of the country's merchants and small producers of goods had been expelled when Ferdinand and Isabella drove out the Moors and the Jews. In the years that followed, Catholic Spaniards failed to take their place. The aristocracy, which drew most of its wealth from sheep and cattle raising, had little interest in business and craft produc-

tion. So when the Spanish colonists turned to Spain for such finished goods as hardware, cookware, pottery, and cloth, Spain did not have the resources to provide them.

As the supply of gold and silver rose, the demand for goods increased. Prices skyrocketed and wages climbed. Before long, inflation had reached 400 percent. Spanish merchants became traders for English, Dutch, and French producers who could manufacture better goods at lower prices. Spanish exports to the colonists dwindled to wine and olive oil. Spanish gold and silver flowed directly to northern Europe rather than to Spain.

The government tried to stem inflation by stepping up the production of silver. But this only made the situation worse. Costly wars added to the problem. Because it could not raise enough taxes to finance the wars, the Crown had to borrow from foreign bankers. The bankers responded by raising their interest rates as high as 40 percent. Before long, all the income from the Spanish colonies was assigned to paying off debts.

By 1600 the English were challenging Spanish control of the Atlantic. As a result, Spain's dominance of the New World was weakened. Its trade and colonies were opened to the other European powers.

1. Identify: Christopher Columbus, Amerigo Vespucci, Treaty of Tordesillas, Vasco Núñez de Balboa, Juan Ponce de León, Ferdinand Magellan, Hernán Cortés, Francisco Pizarro, Hernando de Soto, Francisco Vásquez de Coronado, Bartolomé de Las Casas.
2. What factors favored the Spanish in their conquests of the Aztecs and the Inca?
3. What were Spain's goals in the New World? What did the Spanish do to achieve them?
4. Why did Spanish power decline?

4   England, Holland, and France React

The other countries of Europe watched the growing Portuguese and Spanish triumphs first with envy and then with alarm. They had three reasons for their fears. The first was economic.

EUROPEAN CLAIMS IN NORTH AMERICA 1753

The second was religion. Since the Reformation, Catholic Spain had become the archenemy of Protestants in England and the Netherlands. The third reason was dynastic. By 1520 Spain controlled Austria, the Netherlands, Luxemburg, and parts of Italy and Germany. This worried the French, who feared encirclement of their country.

Although the English, Dutch, and French rejected the Pope's division of the world between Portugal and Spain, they did not have the naval strength to interfere in the areas claimed by either power. As a result, they looked for a new trade route of their own to India—a Northwest Passage. When their efforts failed, they decided they would have to challenge the Portuguese and the Spanish in their own waters.

The English

The English began to show an interest in overseas trade as early as 1497. In that year, they commissioned the Italian navigator John Cabot to sail to America by a northern route. Cabot explored the coasts of Newfoundland, Nova Scotia, and New England, giving the English a claim in the New World. But internal problems kept them from developing their claims.

In the mid-1500's, the English made their move. English **sea dogs,** sea captains turned pirates, raided Spanish ships and also sold slaves they had stolen from the Portuguese in the Spanish colonies. In 1576, a sea dog named Martin Frobisher passed through icebergs off the coast of Greenland to discover the bay that today carries his name. In 1580, another sea dog, Francis Drake, became the first Englishman to sail around the world.

The English wanted more than trade. They wanted—and needed—colonies that could provide the raw materials they had to buy from other countries. If it did not have to import so many products, England could become self-sufficient. Colonies also meant more jobs, which were becoming scarce in England. They also meant religious freedom for those who no longer wanted to follow the beliefs of the Church of England.

In 1600 English expansion began in earnest with the establishment of a trading company called the English East India Company. It was chartered by Queen Elizabeth I to trade with the East Indies. The English East India Company set up posts in India, Malaya, and some islands of the East and West Indies. In India, it set up posts at Bombay on the northwestern coast, at Calcutta in the northeast in the delta of the Ganges River, and at Madras on the southeastern coast. The English became overlords in these areas, acting with many of the powers of a sovereign government. They imposed taxes, coined money, built forts, and trained Indians as soldiers.

In the West Indies, settlements were also established. There, the English claimed Jamaica, the Bahamas, and Barbados, three islands unoccupied by the Spanish. In 1640 they introduced sugar to Barbados. It proved to be three times as valuable per acre as tobacco. By the second half of the seventeenth century, Barbados was the most profitable English colony, with the value of its exports surpassing those of England's North American colonies. Rich and poor alike flocked to the islands. More equipment and more labor was needed to grow sugar than the small farmers could provide. Thus, large plantations became the pattern. Using African slaves was cheaper than hiring indentured servants, or people who bound themselves to work for others for a certain time. Therefore, black Africans were brought to the islands as laborers.

At the same time, English attention also focused on North America. In 1606 the English formed the Virginia Company of London, which sent settlers to North America to search for gold and silver. In 1607, they founded the first successful permanent English settlement in America. Called Jamestown, it was located in what is now Virginia. In 1620, a second colony, Plymouth, was founded in what is now Massachusetts by a group of religious dissenters known as Pilgrims.

Gradually the newly arrived English settlers pushed the Indians out who had been living in the areas of settlement. Unlike the Spanish and the Portuguese, the English had no desire to convert the Indians to Christianity. The Indians, on the other hand, had no desire to become the labor force of the English. Slowly the settlers began to expand inland. As they did so, they came into conflict with the Dutch and the French, who had also begun to explore and expand.

The Dutch

In the late 1500's and early 1600's, the Netherlands was a small country on the North Sea. It had few natural resources and limited farmland. The economy of the Netherlands depended heavily on fishing. The Dutch people saw commerce as the key to their survival. In the words of one historian, "Trade not crusade became the Dutch motto."

To be able to underbid their competitors, the Dutch designed their ships for efficiency and economy. Before long, they had a large merchant fleet that could carry larger cargoes with smaller crews than those of other nations. By 1679 the Dutch fleet was larger than those of Spain, Portugal, France, England, Scotland, and Germany combined. Dutch merchants traded in every continent on the globe.

In the middle 1500's, the Dutch sent expeditions to the East and raided Portuguese and Spanish ships. In 1599 their first successful expedition returned from the Far East. Three years later the Dutch government chartered the

Using Hudson as an example, point out that many explorers did not have strong national loyalties. They sailed for any country willing to finance their ventures.

Parallels can be drawn between Holland and present-day Japan. Both had limited natural resources, yet developed into powerful commercial nations.

A Dutch merchant points to ships of the Dutch East India Company docked in Batavia harbor in Java. Through this harbor passed all Dutch trade with China, Japan, India, and Persia. The Dutch developed a network of ports in the East Indies, South Africa, and Ceylon for supplies. What other Europeans sought control of the East Indies?

Dutch East India Company, combining competing Dutch trading companies into one unified company. In this way, it hoped to expand trade and assure close relations between the government and colonial enterprises in Asia.

The Dutch government gave the Dutch East India Company a monopoly in the trade with Africa and the East Indies. It also gave it the power to make war and peace, seize ships, coin money, and establish colonies and forts. In return, the government was to receive customs, or a tax on imports, from the company's trade.

In 1619 the company set up headquarters at Batavia on the island of Java.[2] Before long, it had control of Java, which was heavily populated and rich in sugar, spices, coffee, and tea. Using Batavia as their base, the Dutch pushed forward. By 1625 they had driven out the English and the Portuguese from the East Indies, Malaya, and Sri Lanka. They then claimed for themselves the entire trade of the Spice Islands.

At the same time, the Dutch were expanding into other parts of the world. In 1621 they formed the Dutch West India Company to establish colonies in the New World. Their claim there had been established in 1609 by the explorations of an

English navigator named Henry Hudson. The company gave the Spanish heavy losses and dominated the colonial trade. Its ships carried African slaves and European grain and manufactured goods to the colonies and brought back sugar and tobacco. This Dutch trade caused the English and the French to lose income from duties, or customs, and shipping fees.

The Dutch also tried to gain commercial control in North America. There, they centered their activities at New Amsterdam, a settlement founded on the island of Manhattan at the mouth of the Hudson River in 1625. New Amsterdam served as the clearinghouse for European and colonial trade. Furs from the north; glass, cloth, paper, and other finished products from Europe; and sugar, rum, and tobacco from the Caribbean all funneled through the settlement.

The English reacted to the Dutch commercial success by barring them from English colonial ports. The Dutch, however, continued to smuggle goods. Ships from the Massachusetts and Virginia colonies continued to go to New Amsterdam to buy European goods and avoid paying English duties.

The Dutch also had success on the African continent. In 1652 they founded a colony in South Africa at the Cape of Good Hope to provide fuel, water, and fresh food for ships

---

[2]Batavia was the first Dutch settlement in Asia. Today, it is Jakarta, the capital of the island nation of Indonesia.

sailing to the Far East. The Dutch government encouraged Dutch peasants known as Boers to migrate to the colony. The supplies provided in South Africa saved the lives of thousands of sailors who might have died from scurvy.

By the 1700's, however, Dutch power had begun to decline. Exhausting wars and shipping restrictions among European nations had taken their toll. Before long, the Dutch no longer were able to trade in the profitable markets of the English and French colonies.

The French

During the 1600's, France competed with England and the Netherlands for trade and colonies. In 1524 the French had hired an Italian named Giovanni da Verrazano to find the Northwest Passage. Sailing west to find Asia, da Verrazano explored the North American coast from North Carolina to Maine. He was followed ten years later by a French navigator named Jacques Cartier. Cartier sailed up the St. Lawrence River as far as the present-day city of Montreal. He claimed much of eastern Canada for France.

French exploration did not end with Cartier. In 1608 the French explorer and map maker Samuel de Champlain founded at Quebec the first permanent French settlement in the New World. In 1673 Catholic missionaries Jacques Marquette and Louis Joliet explored the Mississippi Valley to the mouth of the Arkansas River. Nine years later, Robert Cavelier, also known as Sieur de La Salle, sailed down the Mississippi River to the Gulf of Mexico. Claiming the entire inland region for France, he named it Louisiana in honor of King Louis XIV.

To encourage settlements in the new lands, the French Crown granted royal charters to trading companies. The Crown maintained direct involvement in the companies by selecting their directors, raising funds, and providing military support for the settlements. Unlike the English, the French were interested in converting the Indians to Christianity. Jesuit missionaries were sent to work among Indian groups, and emigration to the colonies was limited to Catholics.

Despite these efforts, the French government was more concerned with the dynastic struggles

Canadian Indians traded with French fishermen during the 1500's. They exchanged beaver, fox, otter, and mink pelts for European fishhooks, kettles, and knives. By the early 1600's, the French-Indian fur trade was firmly established in Canada. What did the French government provide to trading companies that encouraged settlement in North America?

Due to differences in English and French colonial objectives, there were ten times more English settlers in New England than French settlers in New France (Canada) by the middle 1700's. This was an important factor in the outcome of the French and Indian War.

in Europe than with the colonies. For this reason, the French companies emphasized trade, which brought quick profits, rather than farming, which required a long-term investment. French explorers gave the Indians blankets, guns, and wine in return for valuable animal skins. They also engaged in fur trapping, fishing, and lumbering. Like trading, these activities brought wealth and did not require large settlements. In this way, the French made allies of the North American Indians and gained a foothold in the heartland of the continent. Thus, when English settlers began to expand inland, they faced not only the Indians but also the French.

The French established footholds elsewhere in India and in the West Indies. In India, they set up a trading center at Pondicherry on the southeastern coast. Like the English, the French became overlords. In the West Indies, the French claimed the islands of St. Kitts, Martinique, and Guadeloupe. As in India, their policy paralleled that of the English. The islands provided France and French sugar and tobacco planters with great fortunes. Like their English counterparts, the French planters formed a company to import African slaves to their islands to work the plantations.

The Treaty of Paris

England soon became alarmed by France's rapid expansion overseas and its dynastic ambitions in Europe. The overseas rivalry turned violent—from 1689 to 1763, France and England waged a series of wars on the continent and abroad.

In North America, the conclusive war was fought between 1754 and 1763 and was known as the French and Indian War. It was part of the Seven Years' War that had erupted in Europe in 1756 and had involved almost every European country. The fighting in North America began over rival French and English claims in the Ohio Valley. To protect their claims, the French built a chain of forts in western Pennsylvania. When the English answered by building their own fort, the French seized it. As the fighting expanded, more than 50,000 English colonial soldiers joined the English regular army.

On September 13, 1759, the English defeated the French at the Battle of Quebec. The English victory had been helped by English superiority on the seas; England had concentrated its resources on its navy and its colonies. While England's German allies fought France on the continent, the English navy cut French relief to its North American territory. France's defeat put an end to the French as a strong power in North America. At the same time, however, it made the English colonies less dependent on England for protection.

In India, war between England and France began in 1756. As in North America, English control of the sea became the key factor. By cutting the flow of French reinforcements, the English navy made it easier for the English army to gain victory on land. In 1761 the French surrendered.

In Europe, the fighting continued until 1763 when the French were defeated and the Treaty of Paris was signed. France lost heavily everywhere. In North America, it lost Canada and all of its territory east of the Mississippi to the English. French lands west of the Mississippi went to the Spanish. In India, the French lost all of their territory to the English. They were, however, allowed to maintain limited trading bases.

With the Treaty of Paris, the first phase of European expansion came to an end. In spite of its setbacks, Spain still held most of South America, and the Dutch kept their position in the East Indies. England had the greatest gains. It now controlled both North America and India. This allowed the English to dominate the next phase of European expansion.

1. Identify: John Cabot, Martin Frobisher, Francis Drake, Barbados, Jamestown, Pilgrims, Henry Hudson, New Amsterdam, Boers, Giovanni da Verrazano, Jacques Cartier, Samuel de Champlain, Jacques Marquette, Louis Joliet, Robert Cavelier.
2. In what ways were the reasons for English and Dutch exploration and expansion the same? In what ways were they different?
3. In what ways did French colonial policies parallel English ones? In what ways did they differ?
4. What were the results of the Treaty of Paris?

CHAPTER 12 REVIEW

Summary

1. During the late 1400's and early 1500's, European nations led by Portugal undertook voyages of discovery that rounded the tip of Africa, found a sea route to the East Indies, discovered the Americas, and circumnavigated the globe.
2. Portugal dominated trade with the East Indies throughout the 1500's. By the 1530's, it had trading settlements in Africa and Asia, and a colony in South America. The Portuguese settlers brought black Africans to Brazil as slaves to work their plantations, a practice used later by other countries.
3. In 1580 Portugal was defeated by Spain. Many of its possessions were seized by the Dutch and the English.
4. In 1492 Christopher Columbus made his first voyage across the Atlantic for Spain. He discovered islands that he believed to be off the coast of India but were actually in the New World.
5. In 1493 the Pope divided the lands of the New World between Spain and Portugal.
6. Between 1519 and 1532, Spanish conquistadores destroyed the Indian empires of Mexico and Peru and established a vast colonial empire in their place. Although the Indians were considered subjects of Spain, abuses to them were widespread.
7. Between 1497 and 1609, the English, Dutch, and French sent explorers to search for a Northwest Passage to Asia.
8. In the mid-1500's, the English and the Dutch challenged the Spanish and the Portuguese domination in trade.
9. In the early 1600's, the English established trading settlements in India, Malaya, the East and West Indies, and North America. The first successful English settlement in the Americas was at Jamestown, Virginia, in 1607.
10. By 1625 the Dutch had taken over the East Indies trade, and in the same year they tried to gain commercial control in North America by establishing New Amsterdam.
11. The first permanent French settlement in the New World was founded at Quebec in 1608. They established trading settlements in North America, India, and the West Indies.
12. In the mid-1700's, conflicting claims in North America and India led to wars that paralleled wars on the European continent. As a result of the Treaty of Paris in 1763, the French lost its colonial empire to England and Spain.

Building Vocabulary

lateen sail	entrepreneurs	line of demarcation	creoles
rudder	mercantilism	scurvy	mestizos
compass	bullion	conquistadores	mulattos
astrolabe	balance of trade	viceroy	zambos
joint stock companies	mutiny	peninsulares	sea dogs

Reviewing the Main Ideas

1. What technological improvements were made in European ships in the late 1400's?
2. How did joint stock companies serve expanded commercial needs?
3. What were some weaknesses of the mercantilist system?
4. What events contributed to Portugal's rise to supremacy in the 1500's?

5. What were the goals of Vasco da Gama's voyage that began in 1497? What did he discover and why was it important?

6. By what means did the Portuguese establish dominance in the spice trade?

7. How did Ferdinand Magellan's expedition alter the geographic knowledge of his time?

8. What was the status of conquered Indians under Spanish rule? under British and French rule?

9. Why did slavery become important to the plantation economies of the English colonies in North America and the West Indies?

10. What did the voyages in search of a Northwest Passage accomplish?

11. Why did Dutch power begin to decline by the 1700's?

12. Why did the French and Indian War begin? What contributed to the English victory at Quebec in 1759?

Discussing Important Ideas

1. In your opinion, what was Prince Henry the Navigator's most important contribution to the voyages of discovery?

2. Which voyage of discovery do you think was most important? Why?

3. How were European nations' goals for trade and settlement similar and how were they different? Did geography, population size, religion, and timing affect their goals? In what ways?

4. Some observers think that space exploration today is motivated by factors similar to those that motivated European overseas explorations. Do you agree or disagree? Why?

5. To what extent did naval superiority determine the progress and outcome of European expansion by 1763?

6. How might history have been changed if the French had held on to its territories in North America?

7. Who benefited the most from the period of discovery and expansion? Who suffered the most?

8. What remnants of European discovery and expansion are still visible today in the Americas? Which European nation has left the most enduring legacy in the New World? Give examples.

Using Maps

Refer to the map on page 286 to answer the following questions:

1. Where is the Cape of Good Hope? the Strait of Magellan? the Isthmus of Panama? Hudson Bay? the Mississippi River? Mexico?

2. What is the longitude and latitude of the West Indies? of the East Indies?

3. How would you describe the route of Francis Drake's voyage?

4. About how far is it from England to the West Indies?

5. Which country made the most voyages of discovery to the Americas?

6. Which country made voyages to India?

UNIT 3 REVIEW

Summary

1. Between the 1000's and 1600's, Seljuk Turks, Mongols, and Ottoman Turks created, in turn, vast empires in Asia, the Middle East, and Europe.
2. Between the 1500's and mid-1700's, a Muslim dynasty known as the Moguls brought all of India under a central government.
3. From the 600's to the 1300's, the T'ang, Song, and Mongol dynasties brought economic and cultural prosperity to China.
4. The Ming dynasty, which ruled from the 1300's to the 1600's, at first engaged in foreign trade. Later, it followed a policy of isolationism.
5. Around 1300, medieval Europe entered a period of turmoil. Struggles during the next two centuries weakened feudalism and led to the rise of strong monarchies.
6. The cultural awakening known as the Renaissance occurred in western Europe from the 1300's to the early 1600's. It laid the foundations of modern western thought and gave the world new forms of art and literature.
7. During the 1500's, reformation in the Church led to the rise of Protestantism and the emergence of a reformed Catholic Church. Western Europe's religious unity ended.
8. During the late 1400's and early 1500's, European nations made voyages of discovery beyond their own continent.
9. European nations established colonies in the New World and the East, leading to intense economic rivalry. Wars in India and North America in the mid-1700's extended Britain's empire at the expense of France's empire.

Developing Understanding

1. Starting in the eleventh century, Asian empires developed and spread their influence far beyond their own borders. Compare this Asian expansion to that of western Europe in the sixteenth century.
2. What factors led to the rise of the modern era in western Europe?
3. A distinctive feature of the Renaissance was the questioning of established ideas and practices. How did this questioning influence religious reform in Europe?
4. What did the lands in the New World offer to the developing European nations?
5. How did Europeans affect other peoples?
6. What problems did European nations face as they expanded into other parts of the world?
7. In what ways had the world been changed by the age of discovery and expansion?

Developing Skills

When historians write history, they bring their own viewpoints, including their assumptions and cultural, political, and personal biases, to their interpretations of data and events. Scholars who hold many of the same viewpoints are said to belong to a *school* of history. Students should be aware of historical schools, because this awareness makes it easier to evaluate a historian's work and identify its underlying viewpoints.

One historical school, for example, concerns itself with the relationship of modern business to the Protestant Reformation. Max Weber, a German sociologist, published *The Protestant Ethic and the Spirit of Capitalism* in the early 1900's. In this and another work, he presented the thesis that modern business attitudes had developed from the Protestant movement, especially Calvinism. He said, "What the great religious epoch of the seventeenth century bequeathed to its [modern] heir was above all a gloriously . . . good conscience in money-making.''

Many historians agreed with Weber, but others did not. Following are three quotations, one or more from historians of the Weber school. Look for the key viewpoint in each quotation and analyze its basic assumptions and biases in order to determine whether or not it supports the Weber school.

1. It cannot be denied, of course, that there were some great [business leaders] among the Puritans. But whether they owed their greatness to Puritan ethics is doubtful. It was probably much more due to their racial qualities or to fortune's guiding hand. (Werner Sombart, *The Quintessence of Capitalism*)
2. However flat and uniform the Middle Ages may have been, they contained currents flowing straight into modern times. [Business enterprise], even if not generalised, was not uncommon in the Middle Ages. It will be difficult, then, to look on it as the product of the Reformation. (H. M. Robertson, *Aspects of the Rise of Economic Individualism*)
3. Calvin himself had a great deal to do with questions of . . . production, and he quite approved of the fact that greater profits were made in trade than in agriculture, since they were simply the reward of carefulness and [hard work]. It is, of course, true that he urged the abolition of certain kinds of business which were questionable from the Christian point of view, such as the manufacture of playing cards, but in general he was in favor of movement and progress. (Ernst Troeltsch, *The Social Teaching of the Christian Churches*)

Suggested Activities

1. Debate the following question: "Which country in South or East Asia underwent the greatest change in its contact with foreign empires?"
2. Make a list of the ideals and characteristics of each art form—literature, architecture, sculpture, and painting—during the Renaissance. Then prepare a brief report on one Renaissance artist and explain how his or her work illustrates the ideals and characteristics you listed for that particular art form.
3. Imagine that you are a reporter in Europe at the time of the religious reformations. Write short articles presenting the religious beliefs and policies of (a) Pope Leo X (b) an Anabaptist (c) Elizabeth I of England (d) a bishop at the Council of Trent (1545) (e) Henry IV of France.
4. Make a table of new products that Europeans obtained outside their continent during the 1700's and identify the sources of each. Explain how the products were used.

Suggested Readings

Birch, Cyril, ed. *Stories From a Ming Collection.* Bloomington, Ind.: University of Indiana Press, 1959. Presents a collection of stories from Ming China.

Bainton, Roland H. *Here I Stand: A Life of Martin Luther.* Nashville, Tenn.: Abingdon Press, 1951. This biography of Luther stresses the reformer's role in the rise of Protestantism.

Hale, John R. *Age of Exploration.* New York: Time, Inc., 1966. Explorations of the 1500's.

Horizon editors. *Lorenzo dé Medici and the Renaissance.* American Heritage, 1969. Emphasizes life in Florence during the rule of the Medicis.

Schulberg, Lucille. *Historic India.* New York: Time, Inc., 1968. Gives a historical overview of the Mogul and other eras of India's past.

From Monarchy to Revolution

1533 Ivan the Terrible	**1603** End of the English Tudors **1605** Cervantes	**1688** Glorious Revolution **1690** Louis XIV of France
1500	**1550**	**1600**	**1650**
	1588 Spanish Armada	**1613-1917** Romanovs of Russia	**1690** Peter the Great
	1598 Edict of Nantes	**1648** Treaty of Westphalia	

UNIT 4

	1776 Declaration of Independence		
	1804 Emperor Napoleon		
	1814-1815 Congress		
1700's Age of Reason	of Vienna	1854 Crimean War	
1700	**1750**	**1800**	**1850** **1900**
1713 Treaty of Utrecht	1789 French	1820 Troppau Protocol	
	Revolution	1829 Greek independence	
1748 *The Spirit*			
of the Laws	1793 Reign of Terror		

Between 1500 and 1700, Europe's monarchies reached the peak of their power. They tightly controlled internal affairs and fought wars beyond their borders to gain wealth and territory.

During the 1700's and 1800's, Europeans in greater numbers opposed strong monarchies. They developed new ideas about society and government. Many of them believed that the people had the right to change governments to meet their needs. They wanted more freedom to choose their leaders and to live without fear of government interference in their daily lives. They became willing to fight for these changes.

In Europe and North America, popular dissatisfaction led to revolution, or a drastic change in society and government. The revolutions did not destroy all of the injustices of the past, but they did bring about political rights for more people.

Naval Battle in the Mediterranean

CHAPTER 13

Royal Court Life

Age

of

Monarchs

Ask students to suggest ways in which the development of nations under absolute monarchs had advantages over political development during the feudal period.

From the 1500's to the 1700's, monarchs reached the height of their power in the countries of Europe. They were backed by merchants and shippers who wanted peace and stability to further trade. To advance their power, monarchs supported a political theory known as **absolutism**. It stated that monarchs held supreme power and were responsible for their actions to God alone. Acting on this theory, monarchs worked to overcome potential rivals among their nobles. They ended the independence of cities and feudal territories. They created strong nations in which the loyalties of all their subjects were directed to the Crown. Government bureaucracies were strengthened to bring many areas of national life under royal control. By 1700 even religious affairs in most countries were subject to the will of monarchs.

During the Age of Monarchs, Europe was in turmoil. Devastating wars were fought over religious, economic, and dynastic issues. Civil strife was commonplace. Yet, instead of returning Europe to the "Dark Ages," these centuries of monarchy resulted in a new, powerful, and creative Europe. Elements of medieval life remained, but the outlines of today's Europe, with its sovereign nations, were emerging.

1 Spain

During the 1500's and early 1600's, Spain was the leading power in western Europe. Its army and navy were considered the strongest, and the riches it obtained from its possessions in the New World were the envy of other European powers.

Philip II

Philip II, who ruled from 1556 to 1598, was the most powerful monarch in Spanish history. A devout Catholic, Philip viewed himself as the leading defender of the faith. His actions to stamp out Protestantism in his domains made him the enemy of all Protestants. A Hapsburg, Philip worked to increase his family's power throughout Europe. As a result, Spain became involved in a number of costly European wars.

Known as the Prudent King, Philip II was cautious, hardworking, and suspicious of others. He built a new granite palace just outside the city of Madrid. Called El Escorial, the palace served as a royal court, art gallery, monastery, and tomb for Spanish royalty. There Philip spent most of his time at his desk, carefully reading and responding to hundreds of documents that poured in from all over the empire. He used councils of bureaucrats to advise him and to handle routine matters. But he made all decisions and signed all papers.

Unrest   Philip II had difficulties ruling both Spain and his vast overseas empire. The provinces of Spain had been formally united when Ferdinand of Aragon married Isabella of Castile. However, these rulers had not created a uniform system of government for the country. Separate laws and provincial authorities were allowed to remain. Gradually, Castile came to dominate Spanish life. In the 1500's it had the most territory, the largest population, and the greatest wealth of all the Spanish territories.

Philip II made Castile the center of Spain and the empire. Madrid, located in Castile, became the capital. The Castilian form of Spanish was

305

Dutch and English historians have traditionally portrayed Philip II in the worst terms.

The defeat of the Spanish Armada broke Spain's hold on the Atlantic trade. Control passed to England and the Netherlands.

spoken at the royal court. Most of Philip's advisers came from Castile. Trade from the overseas empire was controlled by the Castilian city of Seville, and Castilian merchants benefited most from the trade.

Leaders in Aragon and the other Spanish provinces came to resent the dominance of Castile. They were angry at being excluded from a share in Philip's government. In the 1590's Aragon revolted. The revolt was put down, but discontent continued into the following century.

Religious Policy   Philip had to deal with a number of other troubling issues in his domains. In addition to facing rebellious Protestants in the Netherlands, Philip was also concerned about the loyalty of large religious minorities in Spain. The leading suspects were Protestants, Marranos, or Jews who had converted to Christian-

---

For more than 25 years the Dutch rebelled against rule by Philip II of Spain. Eventually the Dutch were successful in this first major challenge to western European absolutism. What other country threatened Philip II's rule?

ity, and Moriscos, or Muslims who had become Christians. Philip gave his wholehearted support to the Inquisition in its efforts to uproot the heresies believed to exist among these groups. He personally attended several **autos da fé,** the elaborate public rituals of sentencing usually followed by executions.[1] The Inquisition was so thorough that Protestantism never took hold in Spain. Its actions, however, led to a revolt by the Moriscos in 1569. The revolt was brutally crushed two years later.

Spanish Armada   Philip's empire faced a growing challenge from Protestant England. In the early years of his reign, Philip had supported Elizabeth I as queen of England, in spite of the Pope's desire to overthrow her. Later, Elizabeth carried out a foreign policy that angered the Spanish king. She aided Protestant rebels in the Netherlands. She also allowed English sailors to attack Spanish fleets carrying silver from the Americas. As a result, Philip turned against Elizabeth and worked for her downfall.

In 1586 Philip decided to invade England. For two years the wealth and talent of the Spanish Empire were thrown into the effort. Finally in 1588, 130 ships and 33,000 men, known as the Spanish Armada, sailed for England.

In late July, the Armada entered the English Channel in crescent formation. The English had more maneuverable ships and longer range cannon than did the Spanish. But they were unable at first to break the solid Spanish formation. English fireboats, however, were able to separate the Spanish ships. Running out of shot and desperately short of water, the Spanish fleet was forced to retreat to the stormy North Sea. About 40 Spanish ships sank near the rocky coasts of Scotland and Ireland. As many as 15,000 Spanish soldiers perished.

Last of the Spanish Hapsburgs

The defeat of the Armada symbolized the beginning of Spain's decline. The cost of wars drained the treasury, and the government was forced to borrow from foreign bankers. Twice Philip's government had to declare bankruptcy.

---

[1]*Autos da fé* is a Spanish phrase meaning "pageants of faith."

In his novel Don Quixote, Miguel de Cervantes Saavedra produced an image of Spain "tilting at windmills," fighting wars it could not win.

Under Edward VI steps were taken to move the Church of England closer to Protestantism.

The Spanish economy suffered from inflation, and industry and agriculture deteriorated. Famine and plague added to Spain's troubles.

Philip II's successors were ill prepared to reverse Spain's decline. Philip's son and grandson, Philip III and Philip IV, lacked his intelligence, enthusiasm, and interest in politics. They turned over most of the affairs of government to nobles. The government was mismanaged, and corruption increased. The royal family and the nobles retreated from national problems by building extravagant homes, holding lavish parties, and wearing expensive clothes.

The war with the Dutch was renewed under Philip IV. Then, Spain became involved in a series of conflicts involving Germany and France. A decade of famine in the 1640's ended with the plague of 1648-1649, in which thousands of Spaniards died. Overburdened and overtaxed, portions of the country revolted. Portugal, a part of Spain since 1580, was one of these areas. The Portuguese struggle continued until 1668, when Spain finally recognized Portugal's independence. The mood of Spaniards slipped from gloom to despair.

Philip IV's son Charles II was the last of the Spanish Hapsburgs. He came to the throne in 1665 at the age of four. No one expected that the sickly Charles would rule very long. When he was older, Charles married but had no children. Thus, most of Europe's monarchs plotted to control the succession to the Spanish throne. After Charles's death in 1700, they went to war to determine how to divide the Spanish Empire.

1. Identify: El Escorial, Madrid, Marranos, Moriscos, Spanish Armada, Charles II.
2. What were the reasons for internal conflict under Philip II's rule?
3. Why did Philip II send the Spanish Armada against England? What was the outcome?
4. What happened to Spain under Philip II's successors?

2   England

England, like Spain, developed a strong monarchy. Its Tudor dynasty, which lasted from 1485 to 1603, brought unity to the country after a long period of decline and disorder. Tudor monarchs were hardworking, able, and popular. They greatly expanded the power and authority of the Crown. However, they never became as absolute in their rule as other European monarchs. Instead, they worked for their goals within such established institutions as Parliament and the courts of law.

Early Tudors

Henry VII, the first Tudor monarch, became king in 1485 after the Wars of the Roses. Henry's claim to the throne was shaky. But he used shrewd maneuvering to disarm his rivals and to increase the prestige of his family. He selected most of his close advisers from among the gentry and merchant classes. Titles were given to these officials, who formed a new aristocracy dependent on the king.

Henry VII helped rebuild England's commercial prosperity. He encouraged the expansion of foreign trade, especially the export of finished woolens to the Netherlands, Germany, and Venice. He promoted the improved collection of taxes as well as careful government spending. In foreign policy, Henry avoided war, using diplomacy and royal marriages to strengthen England's interests abroad. When Henry died in 1509, he left the country peace, prosperity, and an honored throne.

Henry VIII   Henry VIII succeeded his father to the throne in 1509. He fought wars on the European continent and began to make England into a great naval power. Henry's desire for an heir and a happy marriage led him to marry six times. His private life greatly affected the course of the English Reformation.

Henry VIII was the most powerful of the Tudor monarchs. However, he worked through Parliament in obtaining his divorce and in breaking with the Catholic Church. The House of Commons increased its powers during Henry's reign.

Edward VI and Mary I   After Henry VIII's death in 1547, England entered a brief period of turmoil. Edward VI, Henry's son and successor, was only ten years old when he became king. He died in 1553 after a short reign. Protestant nobles then plotted to prevent Edward's Catholic half sister Mary from becoming queen. But the English people rallied behind Mary as the rightful Tudor heir.

Mary I's Catholic policies soon offended the English. Despite strong opposition, Mary married Philip II of Spain in 1554. The next year, she restored Catholicism and burned over 300 Protestants at the stake for heresy. At Philip's urging, Mary involved England in a war with France. As a result, England lost the port of Calais, its final foothold on the European continent. Many English people feared that England would be controlled by Spain. Before this fear could be realized, Mary died childless, and the throne passed to her Protestant half sister Elizabeth.[2]

Elizabeth I

Elizabeth I became queen in 1558 when she was 25 years old. She was shrewd, well-educated, and had a forceful personality. She became known for her sharp tongue, iron will, and personal vanity. But she won the loyalty and confidence of her people. Elizabeth often made journeys throughout the kingdom so that the people could see her. During her travels, she stayed at the homes of nobles who entertained her with banquets, parades, and dances. Elizabeth's reign was one of England's great cultural periods. Poets and writers praised Elizabeth in their works. The theater flourished under playwrights such as William Shakespeare. During Elizabeth's reign, English was transformed into a language with vigor, grace, and clarity.

Marriage   People fully expected that Elizabeth would marry and that her husband would rule. The common attitude of the time was that only men were fit to rule and that government matters were beyond a woman's ability. Elizabeth, however, was slow in seeking a husband. The lesson of her sister Mary had been learned well: to marry a foreign prince would endanger England's interest. At the same time, marrying an Englishman would cause jealousies among the English nobility. In the end, Elizabeth

In the Renaissance spirit, William Shakespeare's plays were filled with human emotion and conflict. In addition to drama, what other cultural advances were made during the Elizabethan period?

refused to give up her powers as monarch for the sake of marriage. To one of her suitors she stormed, "God's death! my lord, I will have but one mistress [England] and no master." Because of Elizabeth's refusal to marry, the country was kept guessing about who would succeed her to the throne.

Court and Government   The queen's household and court were managed by a number of officials. Nobles traveled to London to work in the court and to share in the daily routine of the queen. They sought royal favors, honors, titles, and pensions.

In matters of government, Elizabeth was assisted by a council made up of 12 to 15 nobles.

---

[2]Parliament had barred Philip from inheriting England from Mary.

Discuss the role of the justices in Elizabethan England. Some teachers might wish to discuss the local judiciary in their own communities.

Ask students, "How did lavish royal ceremonies contribute to the popularity of national monarchs?"

With her approval, they drafted proclamations, handled foreign relations, and supervised such matters as the administration of justice and the regulation of prices and wages. These royal advisers were assisted by small staffs of professional but poorly paid bureaucrats.

Parliament was not a policy-making body. It could not command or begin action. However, it did plead, urge, advise, and withhold approval. These powers gave Parliament some influence, especially when it was asked to consider tax laws.

The task of enforcing the queen's law was performed by unpaid respected community members known as **justices of the peace**. Most justices belonged to the gentry or farmer classes. They knew both the law and local conditions. They maintained peace, collected taxes, and kept the government informed of local

Although Elizabeth I always looked like an extravagant monarch, the queen actually had many economic worries. Throughout her reign, she relied increasingly upon Parliament for funds. How did Elizabeth raise additional funds?

crises. Their voluntary participation in support of the government was a key to its success.

Social Policy Elizabeth I believed in the importance of social rank. During the late 1500's, English society was led by the queen and her court. Next were nearly 60 prominent nobles from the great landed families. They were followed by a middle group made up of about 3,000 to 4,000 gentry, merchants, lawyers, and clergy. This group provided the source of Tudor strength and stability. At the bottom were **yeomen,** or farmers with small landholdings, and laborers.

Government laws and policies closely regulated the lives of the common people. The Statute of Apprentices of 1563 declared work to be a social and moral duty. It required people to live and work where they were born, controlled the movement of labor, fixed wages, and regulated apprenticeships. The Poor Laws of 1597 and 1601 made local areas responsible for their own homeless and unemployed. These laws included means to raise money for charity and to provide work for vagabonds.

Economic Policy Elizabeth inherited a monarchy that was badly in debt. Royal revenues were barely adequate to cover annual expenses.[3] Elizabeth, however, spent lavishly on court ceremonies to show the power and dignity of the monarchy. In other matters, she showed the greatest financial restraint, leading many to call her a "pinchpenny."

To raise funds without relying on Parliament, Elizabeth sold royal lands, offices, licenses, monopolies, and the right to collect customs. These measures helped but could not solve the problem. England faced the costs of war and mounting inflation. Thus, Elizabeth was forced to turn to Parliament for funds. Still, she ended her reign badly in debt.

Foreign Policy By Elizabeth's time, England had lost all of its possessions on the European continent. France was too powerful for England to defeat in order to regain its territories.

---

[3]Revenues came from rents of royal lands, fines in court cases, and duties on imports.

Elizabeth I's foreign policy continued to be the basis of British policy until the 1900's.

Religious toleration was an unusual belief in the time of Henry IV. In contrast to Henry's policy, Catholics had no rights under Tudor rule in England.

Although England could not completely withdraw from continental affairs, it developed a foreign policy suitable for a small island nation with limited resources.

For their security needs, the English relied on the advantages of their geographical location. They saw the English Channel as a water barrier that protected their island from European invaders. Therefore, sea power became important in the defense of the nation. Elizabeth continued the efforts begun by her Tudor ancestors to build the navy.

Spain and France posed the greatest naval threats to England. The attack of the Spanish Armada made England realize the dangers of an anti-English alliance between Spain and France. England might be able to defeat one power, but certainly not both. As a result, the English relied on diplomacy as well as sea power.

During Elizabeth's reign, England worked for a balance of power on the European continent. In international affairs, the balance of power principle is concerned with the relative strength of opposing forces. As long as the power of each side is about equal or in balance, then one cannot overpower the other. If one nation becomes more powerful than the other, a third nation can reestablish the balance by throwing its power to the second.

Under Elizabeth, England operated as the third balancing nation. In the early part of Elizabeth's reign, England and Spain feared French power. England cooperated with Spain to keep France out of the Netherlands. Later, when the Netherlands revolted against Philip II, the English supported the rebels and allied with France against Spain. In both cases, the English sided with the weaker power against the stronger one.

Elizabeth also protected English security by ensuring that England's neighbors, Scotland and Ireland, were free of enemy control. In the 1550's Scotland was largely Catholic and hostile to England. Part of Ireland was under English rule, but the rest of the country resisted English armies. Both Scotland and Ireland were open to England's enemies and offered potential bases for a French or Spanish attack on England.

In the 1560's Elizabeth helped Scotland become Protestant and an ally of England. Thirty years later, she carried out military campaigns in Ireland to conquer the Irish. With Scotland and Ireland allied to England, a period of temporary peace came to the British Isles.

In 1603 Elizabeth died at the age of 69. With her death came the end of the Tudor dynasty. King James VI of Scotland, the Protestant son of Mary Queen of Scots, became the new monarch of England. As James I, he founded the Stuart dynasty and united Scotland and England under a common ruler.

1. Identify: Henry VII, Henry VIII, Calais, Elizabeth I, Poor Laws, James I.
2. How did Tudor monarchs restore order and respect for the Crown?
3. What was Elizabeth I's foreign policy?

3 France

At the end of the 1500's, France was exhausted after a long period of civil war. Peace finally came when Henry of Navarre became King Henry IV. Henry founded the Bourbon dynasty, which ruled France until the early nineteenth century. During most of that time, Bourbon kings maintained an absolute monarchy that was imitated by monarchs throughout Europe.

Henry IV

Henry IV was himself a Huguenot, but he converted to Catholicism to quiet his Catholic opponents. Henry believed that people's religious beliefs need not interfere with their loyalty to the government. In 1598 he issued the Edict of Nantes to reassure the Huguenots. The Edict allowed Protestant worship to continue in areas where Protestants were a majority. However, it barred Protestant worship in Paris and other Catholic strongholds. The Edict granted Huguenots the same civil rights as Catholics. Huguenots were able to attend the universities and hold public office. In addition they were permitted to keep about 100 fortified towns under their own armies.

These actions ended religious strife and enabled France to rebuild itself. With the help of

Some radical Huguenots allied with England and Spain in order to win more power from Louis XIII.

the duke of Sully, the minister of finance, Henry restored the Crown's treasury, repaired roads and bridges, and supported trade and industry. He also tried to restore discipline in the army and bring order to the government bureaucracy. All of these royal policies were put into effect without the approval of the Estates-General. In this way, Henry laid the foundation for the absolute rule of later Bourbon rulers.

Louis XIII

Henry's son Louis XIII inherited the throne in 1610 at the age of eight. His mother, Marie de Medici, was regent for the next seven years. In 1617 Louis took over the Crown by force and exiled his mother from the court. A few years later he recalled Marie, and she influenced him to give power to one of her advisers, Cardinal Richelieu.

Gradually Louis gave complete control of the government to the cardinal. Though a member of the clergy, Richelieu set out to build a strong absolute monarchy in France. To realize this goal, he had to reduce the power of the nobles and the Huguenots.

When Louis XIII came to the throne, the nobility was in control of the provinces. Nobles collected taxes, administered justice, appointed local officials, and even made alliances with foreign governments. To end the nobles' power, Richelieu destroyed their fortified castles. He also stripped the nobility of their local administrative functions. The nobility retained their social prestige, while local government affairs were given to agents of the Crown known as **intendants.** Non-nobles, he believed, would not assert themselves and challenge the king's authority.

Richelieu also sought to regain the military and territorial rights given to the Huguenots by the Edict of Nantes. The Huguenots were seen as a threat to the French state. In 1625 radical Huguenots revolted against Louis XIII. After the defeat of the Protestant seaport of La Rochelle in 1628, Richelieu took away the Huguenots' right to independent fortified towns. However, he still allowed the Huguenots to keep their religious freedom.

Having weakened the monarchy's internal enemies, Richelieu sought to make France the supreme power in Europe. He strengthened the French army and took steps to build up the economy. In order to strengthen national unity, he supported French culture. Under Richelieu's direction, France's leading writers in 1635 organized the French Academy. The Academy received a royal charter to establish "fixed rules for the language . . . and render the French

After touring the commercial district of Paris, Cardinal Richelieu lays the cornerstone of a new building. Richelieu strengthened the French economy by promoting the manufacture of glass, tapestry, silk, linen, and woolen cloth. Richelieu gave charters to trading companies that operated throughout the world and established colonies in America, Africa, and the West Indies. What other steps did Richelieu take to make France the strongest European power?

The flamboyant Louis XIV inspects some of the tapestries, vases, carpets, and furniture built at the Gobelins factory in Paris. When the king purchased this factory, he staffed it with expert artisans who created highly ornate furnishings for his royal palace. Even today this elaborate style of furniture bears the name of Louis XIV. How did the king's court reflect this lavish style?

language not only elegant but also capable of treating all arts and sciences." In the following century, French became the language of European diplomacy and culture.

Louis XIV

Louis XIV is recognized as the most powerful Bourbon monarch. He became king in 1643 at the age of five. At first, France was ruled by his two regents—his mother, Anne of Austria, and Cardinal Mazarin, Richelieu's successor. When Mazarin died in 1661, Louis announced that he would run his own government. He was then 23 years old.

The reign of Louis XIV was the longest in European history. It set the style for European monarchies during the sixteenth and seventeenth centuries. During his own lifetime, Louis was known as the Sun King, around whom the royalty and nobility of Europe revolved. He set up a lavish court and surrounded himself with pomp and pageantry. Louis' monarchy had power as well as style. Although Louis relied on a bureaucracy, he was the source of all political authority in France. In one of his audiences, he boasted *"L' État, c'est moi!"* or "I am the State."

Absolute Rule Louis emphasized a strong monarchy because of his fear of disorder without it. As a child, he had lived through the Fronde, a series of uprisings by nobles and peasants that occurred between 1648 and 1652. During the Fronde, royal troops lost control of Paris and mobs rioted in the city. The young Louis and his regents were called to give account of their actions before the Parlement, or supreme court of law. The Fronde was crushed, but Louis never forgot his fear and outrage over this attempt to limit royal power. As king, he intended to never let it happen again.

Louis XIV's feelings about absolute monarchy were later supported by Jacques Bossuet, the leading church official of seventeenth-century France. Bossuet's book on the divine origins of monarchy became one of the most famous justifications of absolute rule. He wrote:

> *What grandeur that a single man should embody so much! . . . Behold this holy power, paternal and absolute, contained in a single head: you see the image of God in the king, and you have the idea of royal majesty.* *

According to Bossuet, subjects had no right to revolt even if the king was unjust. Kings need account to no one except God, but they should act with humility and restraint because "God's judgment is heaviest for those who command."

Court Life After the Fronde, Louis refused to live in Paris. He moved his court and

*Jacques Bossuet, as quoted in *Readings in European History*, vol. II, ed by James H. Robinson, © 1906 by Ginn, pp. 275-76.

government outside of Paris to a new palace that he built at Versailles. The Palace of Versailles was a large, splendid structure. No expense was spared, for Versailles was to demonstrate the wealth, power, and glory of France.

The Palace of Versailles had elegant royal apartments, sweeping staircases, mirrored halls, and lavish formal salons and dining rooms for important state events. There were also offices for government bureaucrats as well as tiny, cramped rooms where the royal officials lived. As many as 10,000 people were housed in Versailles. Outside the palace were vast formal gardens, filled with marble sculptures and fountains.

At Versailles, Louis felt secure from the danger of Parisian mobs. Here, he had the nobility attend his court so that he could control them. Instead of using the nobles in government service, Louis had them wait on him in a round of daily court rituals. The nobility depended on the king's favor for pensions, court posts, and protection from creditors.

Louis freed the nobles from paying taxes. To nobles and non-nobles alike, he sold many offices with guaranteed salaries. Between 1698 and 1709, 40,000 new positions were created. The sale of offices provided needed royal income but became a long-term drain on the treasury.

Government Reform   Louis continued the efforts of Henry IV and Richelieu to strengthen the power of the monarch and the state. He followed the tradition of Richelieu and chose his top advisers not from the nobility, but from middle-class families. Sons often succeeded their fathers in government service.

Although Louis was an absolute monarch, he could not end all of the traditions of the feudal past. Legal systems varied throughout France. Private tolls and customs were levied on goods moving from one province to another. Weights and measures were not uniform. There were separate authorities and districts for financial, judicial, religious, and administrative affairs.

If Louis had tried to change these feudal practices, he would have disrupted the kingdom and endangered his throne. Instead, the king kept the old ways, but added to them new administrative offices and practices. Two key people aided Louis XIV in his efforts—Jean Baptiste Colbert and François Michel Le Tellier, Marquis de Louvois. Colbert believed that the government had to direct the economy. He became Louis' leading economic and financial adviser. Louvois served as minister of war and improved France's military strength.

Economic Policy   Louis, however, failed to reform the complicated tax system. Based on medieval customs, tax rates varied from province to province. The system was also unjust. The poor carried most of the tax burden, while nobles, clergy, and government officials were

Louis XIV expanded his father's hunting lodge into a luxurious royal palace. Acres of orange groves bordered the spacious grounds. The maintenance of Versailles and the new additions that continued throughout the king's lifetime consumed one-half of Louis XIV's yearly income. Why did he build his residence outside the city of Paris?

HISTORY AND PEOPLE

Jean Baptiste Colbert

Jean Baptiste Colbert, the son of a wool merchant in Rheims, France, had a strong interest in economics and a talent for organization and detail. From 1662 to 1683, he was Louis XIV's minister of finance. Some historians think he was the most remarkable government minister France ever had.

As a young man, Colbert worked for a banking firm that had business with Cardinal Mazarin. Colbert straightened out the cardinal's financial affairs and impressed Mazarin with his abilities. Colbert remained in Mazarin's service for many years. It was reported that Mazarin, on his deathbed, said that he was leaving his king a gift more valuable than money or jewels. That gift was Colbert.

After Mazarin died in 1661, Louis XIV depended on Colbert. The finance minister taught the king how to keep accounts. Within two years, Colbert had improved France's financial standing. During the next decade, he doubled the national revenue by reforming the tax system and raising taxes.

Colbert ran every government department except the department of war. He created the French navy, built roads and canals, and worked tirelessly to develop commerce and manufacturing. To develop trade, Colbert also encouraged settlement of France's empire in the New World.

Colbert wanted France to have more exports and he taxed imports heavily. He set up factories to make linen, glass, lace, and other luxury items. To advertise French goods, sample products were sent to foreign visitors at Versailles. Worried that France did not have enough workers, Colbert prohibited artisans from leaving France. He also gave tax exemptions to large families and raised the age at which young people could enter religious orders. Although a Catholic, Colbert opposed government restrictions on Protestants. He realized the importance of their merchants to France's economy.

Colbert was not a likeable man. He seldom smiled and seldom talked. He worked 15 hours a day and never took a vacation. His only passion, he said, was for work. However, he was interested in science and the arts, since they could be used to promote trade. He founded an observatory and a scientific academy. Colbert was responsible for choosing much of the artwork for Versailles.

Colbert hated war, but not because he was humane. He disliked it because it cost so much money and deprived France of so many workers. He also hated Louvois, the war minister. The two men were archrivals. It amused Louis to play one against the other.

Louvois influenced Louis to undertake the wars that made it impossible for Colbert to keep France on a sound financial footing. Even the brilliant Colbert could not raise enough money to pay for constant war. When Colbert died in 1683, France was deeply in debt despite all his efforts.

Before the repeal of the Edict of Nantes, Huguenots were barred from various professions. Marriages between Huguenots and Catholics were declared void. The French military also housed its soldiers in the private homes of Huguenots without the permission of the owners.

After 1678, Louis XIV destroyed many Protestant churches, denied certain professions to Huguenots, and even took Protestant children from their parents to be raised as Catholics. Soldiers could demand lodging in Protestant homes, treating the owners as cruelly as they wished. Rather than endure this persecution, most Huguenots fled to other countries. Where were they welcomed?

exempt from many payments. Independent tax collectors often made large profits from their work. But they were allowed to continue this practice since the money they provided was needed to support the army.

The unreformed tax system aggravated the economic differences between the regions of France. Since any visible improvement in one's farm or household might lead to higher tax payments, there was little incentive to improve one's output. The system encouraged people to move from heavily taxed regions to regions with lower taxes. As a result, heavily taxed areas became poorer.

Religious Policy   Louis regarded the Huguenots as a threat to his absolute monarchy. Many Huguenots were military leaders and prosperous merchants. They often controlled local commerce. In spite of their high social standing, the Huguenots faced mounting persecution from Louis' government. The king wanted the Huguenots to accept Catholicism. He believed that, in this way, they would prove their loyalty to the throne. In 1685 the Edict of Nantes was repealed. Huguenots could no longer practice their religion, and their children had to be educated in the Catholic faith.

Many historians consider Louis' repeal of the Edict as the turning point in his reign. The result of the king's policy was the emigration of almost 100,000 Huguenots. The loss of these talented people was a blow to the production, trade, and military strength of the country. The exiled Huguenots found welcome in the Netherlands and England. Tensions increased between France and Protestant Europe.

Expansion   Louis XIV pursued a bold and active foreign policy. His goal was to expand the glory and power of France. Other European rulers were fearful of Louis' desire for expansion. They allied together in opposition to France.

At the end of Louis XIV's reign, Europe was concerned about the succession to the Spanish throne. It was expected that Charles II of Spain would die without an heir. Both France and Austria had claims to the throne. The rest of Europe was alarmed that the balance of power would be disrupted if France inherited Spain's vast empire. In advance of Charles II's death, the European powers worked out a plan to divide the Spanish Empire. Charles II's will upset their plans. It stated that the entire empire should remain intact and pass to Louis XIV's grandson, Philip of Anjou. Louis XIV accepted the provisions of the will. When Charles II died in 1700, Philip of Anjou became King Philip V of Spain. As a result, Europe was plunged into the War of the Spanish Succession.

Conflict   The War of the Spanish Succession lasted from 1702 to 1713. During the conflict, England, the Dutch Netherlands, and Austria led a Grand Alliance of European nations against

Louis XIV extended France's borders toward the Rhine, but failed to win the port of Antwerp.

France and Spain. Although Spain was the real object of the war, most of the battles were fought in Italy, Germany, and the Netherlands. In addition, the English and French fought each other in North America.

Peace was finally restored with the Treaty of Utrecht in 1713. England and the Dutch Netherlands recognized Philip V as king of Spain, on the condition that France and Spain never be united under one crown. England received the fortress of Gibraltar, which controlled the western entrance to the Mediterranean. The English also won the right to provide slaves to the Spanish American colonies. Spain lost the Spanish Netherlands to Austria, a European power not feared by the English and the Dutch. For protection, the Dutch Netherlands was allowed to build forts along the northern border of France.

As a result of the treaty, France gained trade advantages with the Spanish colonial empire. However, it was forced to surrender the North American provinces of Nova Scotia and Newfoundland to England. The War of the Spanish Succession profoundly affected the internal affairs of France. It drained the country's treasury, brought increased poverty, and created opposition to Louis' rule.

Louis XIV's Legacy France enjoyed one of its most brilliant cultural periods under Louis XIV. Builders and artisans designed and decorated palaces and churches. Artists and playwrights portrayed the daily life of the king's court, the nobility, and the lower classes. Louis' extravagant building projects and his wars, however, left the country near financial ruin. The ways in which Louis weakened the nobility also had their costs. The nobles lost the ability to rule effectively, but not the desire for power. The peasants and the middle class resented the social privileges and wealth of the nobles. After Louis XIV's death in 1715, the nobility sought to expand its power under Louis' great-grandson, Louis XV. Conflicts between the nobles and the lower classes brought France to the brink of revolution.

1. Identify: Henry IV, Edict of Nantes, Richelieu, Fronde, Louvois, Treaty of Utrecht.

2. How did Henry IV try to bring religious peace to France?
3. What were Richelieu's goals? How did Richelieu reduce the power of the nobility? of the Huguenots?
4. What were the successes and failures of Louis XIV's reign?

4   The German States

While the Bourbons were building the strongest monarchy in Europe, the Hapsburgs of Austria were trying to strengthen their control over the Holy Roman Empire. As a result of their effort, the German states became involved in a devastating war. Known as the Thirty Years' War, this conflict eventually involved all of the major European powers except England. But most of the fighting took place in Germany.

Thirty Years' War

Conflicts between Catholics and Protestants continued in Germany after the Peace of Augsburg in 1555. These disputes were complicated by the spread of Calvinism, which had not been recognized by the peace settlement. Furthermore, the Protestant princes of Germany resisted the rule of the Catholic Hapsburgs.

The Thirty Years' War began in Bohemia, where Ferdinand of Styria became king in 1617.[4] Ferdinand was a sworn enemy of Protestantism. Wanting to strengthen Hapsburg authority, he began by curtailing the freedoms of Bohemian Protestants, most of whom were Czechs.

In 1618 the Czechs rebelled. They captured two of Ferdinand's most hated Catholic advisers in the palace at Prague and threw them out a window. The two advisers survived the fall, but the rebels took over Prague. Soon the rebellion developed into a general war—Ferdinand and the German Catholic princes against the German Protestant princes. Philip III of Spain, a Hapsburg, sent aid to Ferdinand.

The Czechs were crushed by 1622 and, over the next ten years, were forcefully reconverted to Catholicism. But the war did not end. Denmark

---

[4]Ferdinand was also the Hapsburg heir to the throne of the Holy Roman Empire.

HAPSBURG POSSESSIONS IN EUROPE 1560

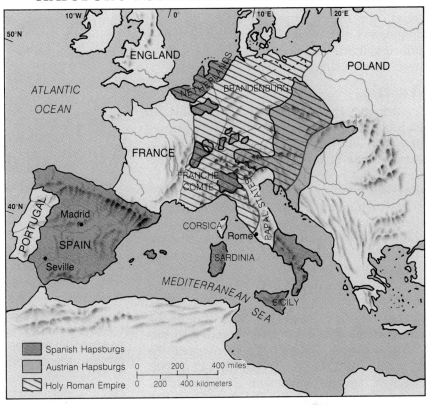

fought against the Hapsburgs, hoping to gain German territory. But the Danes were defeated and obliged to withdraw. Then Sweden, led by King Gustavus II Adolphus, entered the war to defend Protestantism. By this time the war had lasted for 17 years, and religious issues had taken second place to political ones. In 1639, Catholic France, under Cardinal Richelieu, took up arms against the Catholic Hapsburgs to keep them from becoming too powerful.

For 13 more years the war dragged on—Spain and the Holy Roman Empire against France and Sweden. Rival armies plundered the German countryside, and entire towns were destroyed. Historians estimate that Germany lost about one-third of its population.

Treaty of Westphalia

In 1648 the Thirty Years' War finally ended. An international peace conference met at Westphalia in Germany to work out an agreement. The Treaty of Westphalia extended the Peace of Augsburg by adding Calvinism to the list of recognized religions. The Holy Roman Empire remained divided into over 300 separate states. Although the Hapsburgs still controlled Austria and Bohemia, they ruled the other German states in name only. Their hope of establishing an absolute monarchy in Germany was permanently ended.

Other provisions of the peace recognized Switzerland and the Dutch Netherlands as independent states, gave Sweden parts of northern Germany, and allowed France to acquire Alsace and Lorraine.[5] The Treaty of Westphalia confirmed the outcome of the Thirty Years' War: Germany was further weakened, and France had become Europe's leading power. Above all, the Treaty of Westphalia made

---

[5] Alsace and Lorraine were two territories along France's eastern border with Germany.

Point out that Maria Theresa ruled Austria for 40 years.

The Junkers made up the officer class of Prussia's army. Their emphasis on duty, obedience, service, and sacrifice for country deeply influenced many of the Prussian people.

necessary a balance of power among the European states. By banding together, weaker states could prevent a more powerful one from dominating the continent. The balance of power principle influenced relations among the European states for the next 300 years.

Austria

After the Thirty Years' War, the Austrian Hapsburgs concentrated on building a strong monarchy in Austria, Hungary, and Bohemia. Austria was still the most powerful of the German states. In 1683, the Austrians, aided by the Poles, lifted an Ottoman siege of Vienna. By 1739, Austrian armies had regained territory in the Balkan Peninsula from the Ottomans. As a result of the War of the Spanish Succession, the Austrians received the Spanish Netherlands and acquired lands in Italy.

In 1740, 23-year-old Maria Theresa inherited the throne of Austria from her father, Holy Roman Emperor Charles VI. According to law and custom, no woman was permitted to rule Austria. But in 1713 Charles convinced the monarchs of Europe to sign the Pragmatic Sanction. By this agreement, Europe's rulers promised not to divide the Hapsburg lands and to accept Maria Theresa as the monarch.

Maria Theresa had not received any training in political matters. Nevertheless, she proved herself to be a clever and resourceful leader. Overcoming the opposition of the nobility and most of her ministers, she greatly strengthened the Austrian central government. Under Maria Theresa's direction, the central government accepted responsibility for such services as public health, prisons, and roads.

Maria Theresa also understood that the unity of her empire depended on a strong economy. She set up a government office to deal with the economy of the empire as a whole. This office made trade agreements with foreign lands and encouraged exports. Maria Theresa used government funds to encourage the production of textiles and glass.

Prussia

Maria Theresa faced a number of enemies in Europe. One of these was France, the traditional rival of the Hapsburgs. In the 1700's a new rival appeared: Brandenburg-Prussia, a territory in northeastern Germany. Brandenburg-Prussia was ruled by the Hohenzollern family. The Hohenzollerns had been rulers of Brandenburg since the 1400's. During the Thirty Years' War, they gained control of Prussia and other widely scattered lands in Germany.[6]

Great Elector   One of the greatest of the Hohenzollern monarchs was Frederick William. He held the title "Great Elector." After the Thirty Years' War, Frederick William increased the strength of Brandenburg-Prussia by creating a permanent standing army. To meet the cost of his army, he proposed raising taxes. However, the Junkers, or nobles, opposed this plan. Frederick William then worked out a compromise with them. He permitted only Junkers to be landowners, freed them from taxes, and gave them full power over the peasants. In return, the Junkers agreed that Frederick William could tax townspeople and peasants. The townspeople and peasants were too weak to organize and oppose this increased burden. In 1663 the Junkers further strengthened their ties to the Hohenzollern family. They pledged allegiance to Frederick William. As a result of this alliance with the Junkers, Frederick William was able to become an absolute ruler.

Frederick William was succeeded by his son Frederick I. Frederick aided the Austrian Hapsburgs against Louis XIV in the War of the Spanish Succession. As a reward, Frederick was given the title of king. However, he was a weak ruler who did little to strengthen his country.

Frederick William I   Frederick William I, who ruled from 1713 to 1740, was a powerful leader. He centralized the Prussian government, uniting all functions into one bureaucracy under his direct control. He supported production and trade and brought more revenue into the government treasury. Known as the Royal Drill Sergeant, Frederick William I devoted his life to the Prussian army and made it the most efficient fighting force in Europe. Royal agents recruited men from the rural areas of Germany. They even

---

[6]Thereafter, Brandenburg-Prussia became known as Prussia.

The seizure of Silesia doubled the population of Prussia and gave it important industries. It made Prussia one of the great powers of Europe.

kidnapped foreigners and had them serve in the Prussian army. Frederick William I especially delighted in recruiting tall soldiers. He formed a special "regiment of giants" that he drilled himself.

Frederick II   In 1740, Frederick II, Frederick William I's son, became king of Prussia. Frederick II was opposite in personality from his father. As a boy, he had preferred music and art to horseback riding and military drills. Frederick was whipped and even imprisoned by his father for failing to conform to military life. However, when he became king of Prussia, Frederick followed his father's example. He became the most powerful ruler in Prussian history and was given the name Frederick the Great.

Soon after becoming king, Frederick set out to expand Prussian territory. He rejected the Pragmatic Sanction and seized the Austrian province of Silesia. The attack began a conflict called the War of the Austrian Succession.

Prussia's forces were stronger than those of Austria. To avoid conflict, Maria Theresa's ministers advised her to give up Silesia in return for Frederick's promise not to attack her other territories. Instead, the Austrian ruler turned to her Hungarian subjects and persuaded them to send her military aid. Spain and France then backed Prussia. To preserve the balance of power, England and the Dutch Netherlands supported Austria.

After seven years of fighting, the European powers in 1748 signed the Treaty of Aix-la-Chapelle. The treaty officially recognized Prussia's rise as an important nation. Frederick was allowed to keep Silesia; but Maria Theresa was able to hold the rest of her domains. The Austrian ruler, however, was determined to recover Silesia. To achieve this goal, she switched alliances from England to France and Russia, two nations alarmed at Prussia's rising power. The English, in turn, supported the

EUROPE AFTER TREATY OF WESTPHALIA

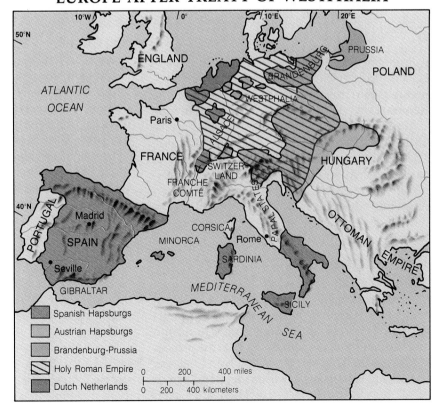

Have students consider the differences between Russia and western Europe in terms of geography and political, social, and economic development.

Prussians. This "diplomatic revolution" set the stage for a new war.

War between Austria and Prussia erupted again in 1756. This war, the Seven Years' War, became chiefly a struggle between England and France. They fought each other in North America, where the war was known as the French and Indian War. They also fought in India. At the Treaty of Paris in 1763, France gave up Canada and all its lands east of the Mississippi River to England. England also replaced France as the leading European power in India.

In the same year, Austria and Prussia signed a separate peace agreement. In the end, Frederick still kept Silesia. Maria Theresa gave up her dream of regaining the province.

1. Identify: Ferdinand of Styria, Peace of Westphalia, Pragmatic Sanction, Hohenzollerns, Junkers, Royal Drill Sergeant, Silesia.
2. What caused the Thirty Years' War?
3. How did Maria Theresa strengthen the central government in Austria?
4. What were the results of the Seven Years' War?

5 Russia

From the 1200's to the early 1700's, Russia was isolated from such western European developments as the Crusades, the Renaissance, and the Reformation. It developed its own unique civilization based on the values of the Eastern Orthodox Church and the Byzantine Empire. The Russian monarchy became all-powerful and easily crushed its opponents. The Church, the nobility, the towns—all of which had posed repeated opposition to royal authority elsewhere—never posed the same challenge in Russia.

Rise of Moscow

After the fall of Kiev in 1240, the city of Moscow gradually emerged as the political center of Russia. It began as a trading center. Its location gave it good strategic access to Siberia and the Baltic and Black Seas. By 1300 the princes of Moscow had become powerful. Ivan I, known as Kalita ("Moneybag"), was made grand prince of all Russia by the Mongol khan after Ivan

promised to extract more tribute from the Russians. Ivan's leadership gained increased recognition when the Russian Orthodox Church added its support to Moscow. The head of the Church moved to Moscow in 1328.

Ivan I expanded his political and territorial control with the backing of the Mongols. Using Mongol troops, he defeated areas that tried to avoid paying taxes to the khan. He acquired other territories by treaty, colonization, purchase, and seizure.

The next important grand prince, Ivan III, ruled from 1462 to 1505. Known as "the Great," Ivan continued the process of territorial expansion. He conquered formerly semi-independent areas such as Novgorod and Tver; and in the east, he drove out the Mongols. Mongol rule over Russia came to an end in 1480, and Russia became an independent state.

Ivan also sought to expand into other countries. He seized territories along the border of Catholic Lithuania, claiming Russia's right to regain lost Eastern Orthodox lands. The right to reclaim lost lands became a part of Russian foreign policy.

The Church   The Russian Orthodox Church gave its full support to the growth of Russian absolutism. Joseph Sanin, an influential abbot living during Ivan III's reign, wrote that "although the [ruler] was like other men in his physical characteristics, in his power he was similar to God in heaven."

The Church claimed that Ivan III was a descendant of "Pruss, the brother of the Roman Caesar Augustus." Further, it claimed that Moscow was the Third Rome, the successor to Constantinople. Moscow was proclaimed to be the rightful new leader of the Eastern Orthodox faith. To make a more direct link to Constantinople, Ivan III married Sophie Paleologue, the niece of the last Byzantine emperor. Ivan took the title of **tsar,** or Caesar, and made the two-headed Byzantine eagle the symbol of Russia.

In contrast to the Catholic Church in western Europe, the Russian Orthodox Church always stressed obedience to the state. It taught the Russian people that submission to authority was

During the reign of Ivan III, the grand prince of Moscow, the Kremlin was enlarged and given brick walls to resist fire. After adding 19 brick towers, the imposing white bell tower of the tsar was refurbished. Why did Ivan III adopt the title of tsar?

a Christian duty. The Catholic Church, through its use of Latin, encouraged classical as well as religious learning. The Russian Church, on the other hand, used the Russian language rather than Greek or Latin. Thus, Russian priests and scholars did not develop the language skills needed to participate in the growing secular intellectual life of western Europe. Russian rulers, however, encouraged the development of a unique national style of icon painting and building construction. Ivan III rebuilt the Moscow Kremlin, or fortress, filling it with beautiful onion-domed churches and ornately decorated palaces.[7]

Ivan IV   The most powerful of the early tsars was Ivan IV. Ivan, who ruled from 1533 to 1584, was known as "the Terrible" or "the Awesome." Ivan was at once learned, pious, and cruel. He became tsar at the age of three. While growing up, he was caught between rival groups of boyars who sought to rule the country. He witnessed much cruelty and was never able to rid himself of his early memories. As an adult, Ivan saw treason everywhere and arrested, exiled, or executed many of his closest advisers. In a fit of rage, he even killed his own son.

Ivan took steps against the boyars to reduce their potential threat to his throne. He seized their scattered lands and placed them under his direct control. This land was known as **oprichnina.** The former owners were uprooted and dispersed. On the oprichnina, which made up about one-half of the country, Ivan placed his own loyal people, called Oprichniki. They became a secret police and terrorized the rest of the country.

Russian Expansion   Under Ivan IV, Russia increased its trade and contacts with western Europe. Ivan imported artisans and doctors from Germany and England. He introduced the first printing press into Russia. Russian ties to the West further expanded after English traders found a northern sea route to Russia in 1553. Ivan IV gave England's Moscovy Company a monopoly on trade with Russia.

Ivan used his armies to expand Russia's borders in all directions. Despite Russia's vast size, it had few seaports, none of which was free of ice throughout the year. Gaining access to the sea for trade was a long-standing goal of Russian rulers.

During the 1550's, Ivan IV annexed Kazan and Astrakhan, Mongol lands east and south of Moscow. In the west, he waged a 25-year war with Poland, Lithuania, and Sweden for control of Livonia, a territory that would have given Russia an outlet to the Baltic Sea. This effort failed, and Russia lost the land to Sweden.

Time of Troubles   In 1584 Ivan IV died and was succeeded by his son Fedor. Fedor was a feeble ruler who died without an heir. After

---

[7]Today the Kremlin in Moscow is the center of government for the Soviet Union, the nation that replaced the Russian Empire in 1917.

Point out that the Time of Troubles did not alter the political structure of Russia.

Raise the question, "How did Peter the Great aid cultural diffusion?"

Fedor's death in 1598, palace intrigue became commonplace. It marked the beginning of a period known as the Time of Troubles, which lasted from 1598 to 1613. During this period, the succession to the Russian throne was contested. Foreign powers intervened in Russian affairs. It was also a time of famine, epidemic, and peasant revolts. The country seemed to be falling into anarchy.

In 1598, Boris Godunov, Fedor's regent and brother-in-law, was elected tsar by a representative assembly known as the Zemski Sobor. Faced with mounting social unrest, Boris returned to the terrorist tactics used by Ivan IV. After his death in 1605, the throne was held by a series of nobles. Sweden and Poland intervened in support of their candidates for the throne. Order was finally restored in 1613, when Michael Romanov was elected tsar. Michael founded the Romanov dynasty, which ruled Russia until 1917.

Social Changes   During the Time of Troubles, many changes took place in Russian life. Unlike western Europe, Russia had never developed a feudal system. Princes and boyars owned property without owing military service to a lord above them. Peasants also had their own land. In the 1500's and 1600's, the freedoms enjoyed by Russia's social groups were gradually destroyed. Princes, boyars, and peasants became tied to the service of the tsar. The influence of townspeople declined, and peasants became serfs, bound to the land for tax purposes. Many Russians escaped government control by moving to the borderlands south of Moscow. There, in a region called the Ukraine, they formed into groups of pioneers known as Cossacks. The Cossacks established self-governing communities and became skilled fighters. Other Russian pioneers moved eastward into Siberia, some of them reaching the coast of the Pacific Ocean.

Peter the Great

In 1689, Peter I, or "the Great," came to the Russian throne. He was a towering figure, nearly seven feet (2.1 meters) tall. Peter had boundless energy and volcanic emotions. During his reign, he wanted to bring Russia into the mainstream of western European civilization.

Encounter with the West   As a youth, Peter was fascinated with practical subjects, such as mechanics, geography, and military strategy. He sought out tutors among the foreign community in Moscow to learn the basic skills of navigation and shipbuilding. He discovered that Russian knowledge of the outside world was badly limited. Most Russians were illiterate peasants; only a few members of the nobility were well educated.

After he became tsar, Peter took an 18-month study tour of England and the Netherlands. He visited shipyards, factories, mills, and laboratories. He learned carpentry and developed enough skill in surgery and dentistry to want to practice on others.

When he returned home, Peter forced Russians to adopt the ways of western Europe. He ordered members of his court to wear western clothing. Men entering Moscow were forced to shave their beards or pay a fine. Women, who had always been excluded from social gatherings, were ordered to attend parties.

Peter sent Russians abroad to study shipbuilding, naval warfare, foreign languages, and mathematics. He invited foreign experts to train Russians. He established a naval academy and schools for artillery and engineering. His greatest effort to open Russia to Europe was the building of a new capital called Saint Petersburg. Saint Petersburg was located near the Baltic Sea in northwestern Russia. It was considered a "Window to the West."

Foreign Policy   Peter's goal was to make Russia a European power. He expanded Russia's boundaries in the south, east, and northwest. In 1689 Russia forced China to recognize Russian claims to Siberia. In 1721 the Russians defeated the Swedes in a long war for control of the Baltic coastline. But their fight against Turkey for a warm-water port on the Black Sea failed.

The Russian failure to win a Black Sea port convinced Peter of the need to create a professional army and navy. Raising the money and developing the necessary talent and resources led Peter to undertake widespread changes.

HISTORY AND CITIES

Saint Petersburg

When Peter the Great founded Saint Petersburg in 1703, the city was considered an absolute ruler's folly. It was located in a remote, marshy area near the Baltic Sea. Superhuman effort and a vast outpouring of money were needed to make the place suitable for habitation.

Peter's original plan was to build a fort that would protect Russian access to the Baltic. Later he decided to construct a capital city that would link Russia to the West. To realize his goal, the energetic tsar had to battle against the forces of nature. The site of the planned city was situated in the far north of Russia, where the winters were long, cold, and damp. It spread over a number of islands formed by the delta of the Neva River as it entered the Gulf of Finland. The islands were swampy, barren, and only a foot above sea level. Floods occurred each year.

Peter, however, was determined to win over nature. He had workers, food, and construction materials brought in from hundreds of miles away. To offset the disadvantages of the climate, workers built raised streets, dug canals, and constructed bridges. Buildings were given stone foundations because wood pilings easily rotted in the damp, spongy ground.

Peter used his awesome authority to force the building of the city. The tsar placed special taxes on the Russian people to pay for the city's construction. Tens of thousands of laborers were drafted to work on the project. Work crews were brought from villages all over Russia for six-month periods. Many of them died.

Once Saint Petersburg was built, Peter worked to guarantee its success. He tried to attract trade from other Baltic ports by sharply reducing tolls for goods entering Russia by way of Saint Petersburg. He forced reluctant nobles and bureaucrats to build homes in the city. Shopkeepers, merchants, and artisans were also ordered to live in Saint Petersburg.

From these harsh beginnings, a magnificent city developed during the next three centuries. Russian tsars hired foreign architects to beautify Saint Petersburg. They built government buildings, palaces, cathedrals, parks, and public squares along the Neva River and the canals that crisscrossed the city. Careful zoning separated government, residential, and working districts. In the center of the city, the major buildings blended harmoniously. They were built in the monumental style of classical architecture. They included St. Isaac's Cathedral, the Admiralty Building (the headquarters of the Russian navy), and the Winter Palace (the Saint Petersburg residence of the tsars).

Saint Petersburg had an atmosphere of spaciousness and dignity. Its stately buildings and broad avenues seemed suspended between vast expanses of blue sky and icy gray water. Many Russians and foreigners alike had mixed feelings about Saint Petersburg. They considered it an elegant but coldly artificial city.

For nearly 200 years, Saint Petersburg was the political and cultural center of Russia. After the 1917 Revolution, Russia's new Communist rulers moved the capital back to Moscow. In the 1920's, Saint Petersburg was renamed Leningrad in honor of the famous revolutionary leader Lenin. Leningrad is today the most important city in the Soviet Union after Moscow.

1. Why was Saint Petersburg viewed as artificial?
2. Could Saint Petersburg have been built in any other country?

The map below is the subject of the "Using Maps" section of the Chapter 13 Review.

Point out that westernization does not always mean modernization. Ask students, "How was this true in Russia during the reign of Peter the Great?"

Government Service   To provide needed leadership, Peter created a new class of loyal nobles called **dvorianie.** He ruled that, in return for government service, the dvorianie would be allowed to own hereditary landed estates. A noble's duty to the tsar started at age 15 and continued until death. Records were kept to ensure good performances. Harsh measures were taken against nobles who tried to avoid government service.

Peter set up a Table of Ranks, which created a hierarchy of positions in both the military and civil service. People were to start at the bottom level and work up to the top as far as they were able. Talented but unlanded people were al-lowed to enter the ranks and were given estates for their service. Thus, ability and service rather than birth became the basis of the dvorianie. Though aristocrats were allowed time to oversee their estates, most of the year was spent at the capital or on the battlefront. Thus, they could not maintain strong ties to their land or to the people who worked for them.

Peter used privileges and force to make the old nobility accept government service. Nobles were given full control over the peasants who worked on their estates. While peasants had gradually increased their freedom in western Europe, the opposite was true in Russia. By the mid-1700's, most Russian peasants had become serfs.

Administration   In the early 1700's, Peter set out to reform the Russian government. He used ideas borrowed from France and other lands to bring more order into his administration. A central bureaucracy was established, and local government was placed completely under the tsar's control. Peter also brought the Church under his direct authority. When the patriarch of Moscow died in 1700, Peter never named a successor. Instead, he established the Holy Synod, a council of bishops responsible to a secular government official appointed by the tsar.

Peter also introduced new tax policies. Formerly the main tax had been placed on each household. The result was that several families often lived under one roof. To increase government income and efficiency, Peter replaced the household tax with a poll, or head, tax on each adult male. Under the new plan, the nobility did not have to pay. As in France, taxes fell on the poorer social groups.

Economy   To stimulate economic growth, Peter brought agriculture and craft production under strict government control. Incentives were provided to increase production in favored areas such as mining and metalworking. New production centers were provided with land, money, and workers. Most of the workers were tied to their trades as the serfs were to the land.

Effects   Peter's reforms strengthened Russia's role in foreign affairs. Russian military triumphs against Sweden forced the European

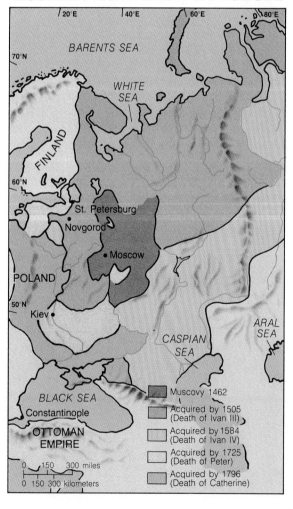

RUSSIAN EXPANSION IN EUROPE

20°E · 40°E · 60°E · 80°E
70°N
BARENTS SEA
WHITE SEA
FINLAND
60°N
St. Petersburg
Novgorod
• Moscow
POLAND
50°N
Kiev •
ARAL SEA
CASPIAN SEA
BLACK SEA
Constantinople
OTTOMAN EMPIRE

Muscovy 1462
Acquired by 1505 (Death of Ivan III)
Acquired by 1584 (Death of Ivan IV)
Acquired by 1725 (Death of Peter)
Acquired by 1796 (Death of Catherine)

0   150   300 miles
0 150 300 kilometers

Catherine was brought to Russia at the age of 15. From that time until she was monarch of Russia 17 years later Catherine became fluent in the Russian language and knowledgeable in politics.

powers to recognize Russia as one of their own. But in his own country, Peter had only limited success. His domestic policies destroyed the Eastern Orthodox culture that had united nobles and peasants. Beginning in Peter's reign, a split occurred between the few who accepted European ways and the many who clung to traditional values. An observer noted: "The tsar pulls uphill alone with the strength of ten, but millions push downhill." Many of Peter's reforms were incomplete and hasty. But his drastic changes did much to bring Russia into contact with developments in the West.

Catherine the Great

After Peter's death in 1725, Russia was governed by a series of weak or ordinary monarchs. The next notable ruler was Catherine II. In 1762, she seized the throne from her husband, Peter III, who had ruled for only six months. Catherine was born a German princess; however, she easily adopted Russian ways and earned the respect of her people.

As monarch, Catherine came under the influence of leading western European thinkers. She studied their works and corresponded with a number of them. For a time, she came to believe that all people were born equal and that "it is contrary to the Christian faith and to justice to make slaves of them."

Early in her reign, Catherine considered freeing the serfs. However, a peasant rebellion threatened her rule and made her change her mind. To ensure the continued support of the nobles, she released them from the government service that Peter the Great had required. Catherine also allowed the nobles to treat their serfs as they pleased. During Catherine's reign, more peasants were forced into serfdom than ever before, and their conditions worsened. The common people of Russia had fewer rights than those in any other part of Europe. When groups of them revolted, Catherine brutally crushed the uprisings.

Catherine received the title "the Great," because of her successful foreign policy. She greatly expanded Russia's borders to the south. She achieved the goal of Peter the Great for a

Catherine II's need for noble support prompted her to call a constitutional convention. The resulting document, however, was never implemented. For what achievements did she earn the title "the Great"?

warm-water port on the Black Sea. In making this gain, she defeated the Ottoman Turks. Catherine also gained from the Ottomans the Sea of Azov and the Crimean Peninsula.

In the west, Catherine acquired territory from Poland. Poland was suffering from feuds among its nobility and gentry. As a result, it was prey to conquest by neighboring powers. In 1772 a quarter of Poland's land was divided among Russia, Prussia, and Austria. Another division took place in 1793, with Russia and Prussia each taking more Polish territory. The third division took place in 1795. Russia, Prussia, and Austria took the rest of Poland, which then ceased to exist until 1919.

Catherine was the last of the great absolute monarchs of the eighteenth century. By the time of her death in 1796, new ideas of liberty and equality had spread throughout western Europe. They directly challenged the age-old institution of monarchy.

1. Identify: Ivan III, Third Rome, Ivan IV, Oprichniki, Livonia, Time of Troubles, Boris Godunov, Zemski Sobor, Cossacks, "Window to the West," Table of Ranks, Holy Synod.

2. How was the rise of Moscow aided by the Russian Orthodox Church? How did the tsars add to the importance of the city?

3. Why did Russia want additional access to the sea? How did Ivan IV and Peter the Great try to achieve this objective?

4. How did the lives of Russian serfs change under Catherine the Great? Why did Catherine change her policies?

CHAPTER 13 REVIEW

Summary

1. The Age of Monarchs refers to the period between 1500 and 1700 when the European monarchies were at their height and the outlines of the modern European states emerged.

2. Between 1556 and 1700, Philip II and the other Spanish Hapsburgs were faced with the difficulties of ruling a vast, scattered empire and a country periodically torn by political and religious revolts.

3. In 1588 the Spanish Armada was sent by Philip II to invade Protestant England. It was soundly defeated, thus marking the beginning of Spain's decline. Inflation, costly wars, famine, and economic weakness added to Spain's troubles.

4. After the Wars of the Roses in 1485, Henry VII became king of England, beginning the Tudor dynasty that ruled England until Elizabeth I's death in 1603. During this period, the Tudors built a solid monarchy backed by the English gentry.

5. In the late 1500's, Henry IV founded the Bourbon dynasty, which ruled France until the early nineteenth century. The French Bourbons unified and strengthened France, becoming the strongest monarchy in Europe at the time.

6. Following Louis XIV's reign and the War of the Spanish Succession, France was near financial collapse and political revolution.

7. The Hapsburgs of Austria failed in their effort to increase their power over the German states. After the Thirty Years' War ended in 1648, Austria and Prussia were the two most powerful German states.

8. In 1741 and again in 1756 Austria and Prussia engaged in wars. By 1763 their dispute had finally ended.

9. After 1300 the grand princes of Moscow began to rule all of Russia. In 1613 the Russian Romanovs inherited a vast state in which power was tightly centralized under the tsar.

Building Vocabulary

absolutism
autos da fé
justices of the peace

yeomen
intendants

tsar
oprichnina
dvorianie

Reviewing the Main Ideas

1. Why were kings and nobles often in conflict with each other? What were some of the methods kings used to curb the opposition of the nobility?
2. Why did the middle class often support the increase of royal power?
3. What factors contributed to Spain's decline?
4. How was the monarchy in England different from those in Spain and France?
5. How did Elizabeth I protect England from potential outside threats?
6. Why did France become the most powerful nation in Europe?
7. Why did the monarchs of Europe imitate Louis XIV?
8. What led to the War of the Spanish Succession? How did it affect the internal affairs of France?
9. Why did Germany remain divided after the Thirty Years' War?
10. How did the War of the Austrian Succession begin? What was its outcome?
11. How did geography and religion affect Russia's development?
12. What steps did Peter the Great take to open Russia to western ideas?

Discussing Important Ideas

1. How did the governments and states created by absolute monarchs differ from the governments existing in medieval times? What advantages did absolute monarchies bring to European life? What disadvantages?
2. Could absolute monarchs achieve all they set out to do? What practical aspects limited their actual power?
3. How did the power of Peter the Great compare to Louis XIV and Elizabeth I? Which monarch had the greatest impact on the average person's life? Explain.
4. Why did some monarchs insist on the theory of absolutism?
5. Were wars essential for the development of the modern state? Use examples from one of the dynasties you studied to support your answer.
6. Do you think religious toleration was incompatible with absolute monarchy? Why or why not?
7. How did royal patronage encourage the growth of the arts? Do you believe great wealth is needed to support the development of fine art? Explain.
8. How did language change during this period? Was the development of a national language important to the growth of the state? How?
9. How was serfdom in Russia different from serfdom in other parts of Europe? What factor(s) accounted for the difference?

Using Maps

Refer to the map on page 324 to answer the following questions:
1. Which ruler added the most area to the Russian Empire?
2. By 1796 what territories and sea outlets had Russia gained?
3. In what general direction does a traveler from Saint Petersburg go to reach Moscow?
4. What two Russian cities are between 20°E and 25°E parallels of longitude?
5. What geographic features made up the southern boundary of Russia by 1796?

Eighteenth Century Scholars

❝ *Once your faith persuades you to believe what your intelligence declares to be absurd, beware lest you likewise sacrifice your reason in the conduct of your life.* **❞**

Voltaire, French writer (1694-1778)

Age
of
Reason

The chapter opening picture on p. 328 is the subject of the "Using Illustrations" section of the Chapter 14 Review.

During the 1600's a scientific revolution took place in Europe. New technology, combined with new approaches to seeking knowledge, made science a main force in the progress of civilization.

The great strides made in the field of science laid the groundwork for a philosophic movement of the 1700's called the Enlightenment. People began to examine age-old institutions and values with the tools of reason and observation. Thus, the 1700's is known as the Age of Reason.

By the end of the century, certain key thinkers had taken a close look at science and reason and found that they could not solve all the world's problems. Nevertheless, many of the ideas developed during the Age of Reason had a profound effect on the political history of the western world and have become a part of today's intellectual heritage.

1   Scientific Revolution

For hundreds of years, European ideas about the universe had been based upon the teachings of ancient Greeks. The Greek astronomer Ptolemy had taught that the earth was at the center of the universe and that all the other spheres revolved around it. The Ptolemaic system included complex mathematics that had been developed over the years to explain the movement of the heavenly bodies.

In the 1500's a Polish astronomer and mathematician, Nicholas Copernicus, began to question the mathematics behind Ptolemy's system. He came up with a new mathematical hypothesis to explain the movement of heavenly bodies. The ideas of Copernicus led to a dramatic change in the way human beings viewed the universe.

Copernicus to Galileo

Copernicus was afraid to publish his ideas. Therefore, his book *On the Revolutions of Heavenly Orbs* did not appear until after his death in 1543. In this book, Copernicus held that the sun was the center of the solar system and that the earth revolved around the sun.

The next step was taken by a German mathematician, Johannes Kepler. Kepler showed that the planets move, not in circles, but

Galileo added support to the Copernican theory when he saw through telescopes he had made, four moons circling Jupiter. What was the reaction of church leaders to Galileo's findings?

Tycho Brahe, the great authority on heavenly bodies after Copernicus, did not accept Copernican ideas.

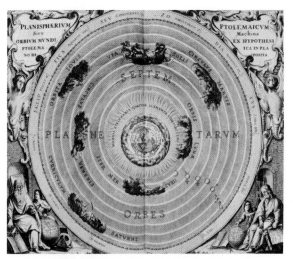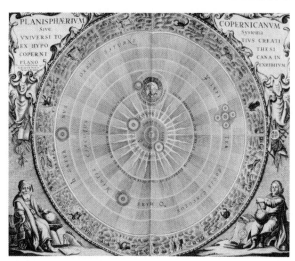

Ptolemy's theory of the universe (left) was refuted by Copernicus's system (right). In the Copernican theory planets retain their circular orbits but they revolve around the sun, not the earth. Who proved planets move in ellipses?

in oval paths called **ellipses,** while the sun stays in place. He also found out that each of the planets does not always move at the same speed. A planet moves faster as it approaches the sun and slower as it moves away from it. Kepler discovered that there is a mathematical relationship between the time a planet takes to orbit the sun and its distance from the sun.

Then, in 1609, the Italian mathematician Galileo Galilei built a telescope. What he saw through the telescope convinced him that the Copernican theory was correct, and he published his findings. The idea that the earth was not at the center of the universe was contrary to the teachings of the Catholic Church. Church leaders were so alarmed by this idea that Galileo was brought before the Inquisition and forced to read the following oath:

> *I, Galileo Galilei . . . swear that with honest heart and in good faith I curse . . . the said heresies and errors as to the movement of the earth around the sun and all other heresies and ideas opposed to the Holy Church; and I swear that I will never assert or say anything either orally or in writing, that could put me under such suspicion.**

---

*Galileo Galilei, as quoted in *Europe from the Renaissance to Waterloo,* ed. by Robert Ergang, © 1954 by Heath, p. 364.

Galileo spent the last years of his life experimenting with the motion of objects on earth. One law he discovered was the **law of inertia,** which says that an object remains at rest or in straight-line motion unless acted upon by an external force. Many historians consider Galileo to be the founder of experimental science.

Bacon and Descartes

During the same period that Galileo was studying the laws of motion, two thinkers were developing a new philosophy of knowledge. One was the English philosopher Francis Bacon, who urged people to set aside traditional beliefs and superstitions and to rely on observation and experiment. He also insisted that it was important to use very precise words in order to avoid errors that result from vague thinking.

The second thinker was the French scholar René Descartes. In 1637 Descartes published an essay, *Discourse on Method,* to explain his philosophy. Descartes began his search for knowledge by doubting everything except his own existence. "I think, therefore I am," Descartes explained. Like Bacon, he believed that truth must be reached through reason. Descartes was also a mathematician. He understood the importance of mathematics to science.

In his *Principia*, Newton showed that all motion that could be timed and measured, whether on the earth or in the solar system, could be described by the same mathematical formulae.

From Monarchy to Revolution · **331**

Point out that natural law was used to justify *both* constitutional and absolutist governments.

Newton

Another great mathematician, Isaac Newton, was born in England in 1642, the same year that Galileo died. When he was in his early twenties, Newton went home to his mother's farm to escape an epidemic at Cambridge University, where he was teaching. During the next 18 months, he began developing his theories in mathematics and physics.

Newton perfected a new kind of mathematics, differential calculus[1], and used it to figure out the theory of gravity. Newton's theory explained why the planets did not fly off in straight lines away from the sun, as they would according to Galileo's law of inertia. The theory of gravity reconciled the idea of inertia with Kepler's idea that the planets travel in ellipses.

Newton published his theory in 1687 in his book *Mathematical Principles of Natural Philosophy*, often called simply the *Principia*. This amazing work had a tremendous impact on the European world. It showed that the universe was orderly and could be described by mathematical formulas. Thus, it seemed to prove that science was the hope of the human race. Someday human beings would understand and master nature, as Bacon and Descartes had predicted.

Spread of the Scientific Movement

Interest in science grew rapidly. It was not confined to one or two groups or countries. Scholars, aristocrats, bureaucrats, and merchants all over Europe were soon exploring the various fields of natural science with the aid of the microscope, the thermometer, and many other new inventions. Many members of the aristocracy and the upper middle class built home laboratories for scientific experiments.

Monarchs founded scientific academies, observatories, and museums. Charles II of England founded the Royal Society of London in 1666. Louis XV of France gave his support to the French Academy of Science, founded in the same year. These societies brought scientists together

to work as teams and gave financial support to scientific work. They provided scientific information, published and translated books and journals, and coordinated scientific efforts in various fields.

1. Identify: Nicholas Copernicus, Johannes Kepler, Francis Bacon, René Descartes, *Principia*, Royal Society of London.
2. Why did the Catholic Church object to the Copernican theory?
3. How did Newton reconcile the theories of Galileo and Kepler?
4. What role did scientific societies play in the scientific revolution?

2 Impact of Science

Advances in science confirmed the idea that much could be known through the use of human reason. If the universe was governed by systematic laws, it followed that not only physical but also political, economic, and social relationships could be understood. The field in which science had the greatest impact was political theory.

Political Theory

One of the most important ideas in political philosophy was the idea of **natural law.** According to this idea, there is a universal moral law, which, like physical laws, is knowable by reason.

Hobbes The English philosopher Thomas Hobbes used the idea of natural law to justify absolute monarchy. In his book *Leviathan*, published in 1651, he argued that this was the best form of government—not because of the divine right of monarchs, but because only an absolute ruler could maintain order and allow natural law to prevail.

Hobbes said that human beings are naturally violent and disorderly. To obtain order, they form a contract or agreement to completely obey a government. Without an absolute government, there would be chaos. According to Hobbes, people do not have the right to rebel against their government, no matter how unjust it might be.

Locke Another English philosopher, John Locke, also based his theories on the idea of natural law. But he came to an entirely different

[1]The German mathematician Gottfried Wilhelm von Leibniz developed the same method independently and published it in 1675.

SCIENCE AND TECHNOLOGY

Telescopes and Microscopes

Inventions and improvements of scientific instruments made it possible for scientists of the 1600's and 1700's to observe new phenomena and collect more accurate data. Two of the most important inventions were the telescope and the microscope.

The magnifying power of lenses was known as far back as 2000 B.C., but their use was not widespread until the invention of printing led to a need for spectacles. In the late 1500's or early 1600's, several people may have developed telescopes and microscopes independently.

When Galileo heard of the telescope, he built one of his own that magnified objects to a power of three. Soon he was making larger telescopes and modifying the curvature of the lenses. His largest had a magnifying power of 32.

Galileo used his telescope to make amazing discoveries. He saw the craters of the moon and observed that Venus goes around the sun, as the theory of Copernicus predicted. Because telescopes gather light as well as magnify, he was also able to see the dim moons of Jupiter and the large number of stars in the Milky Way.

Galileo's discoveries with the telescope advanced scientific knowledge. In addition, they helped to prove the Copernican theory and contributed to the work of Newton, leading to a revolutionary change in the way people understood the universe.

The microscope also had a great impact on understanding human life. Microscopes in the 1600's and 1700's were of two kinds, simple and compound. The simple or one-lens microscope had been used since the 1400's. The compound microscope, using two lenses, was developed in the Netherlands around 1600.

Some of the most remarkable discoveries with the microscope were made by a Dutch draper and haberdasher, Anton van Leeuwenhoek, who had a hobby of grinding lenses. Leeuwenhoek made hundreds of high-quality lenses for simple microscopes, but he kept his methods secret. His strongest lens had a magnifying power of 300. Because he observed things that required much greater magnifying power, it is thought that he must have had some technique for improving the effectiveness of the lens.

In 1674 Leeuwenhoek, using a microscope, became the first person to observe bacteria and protozoa, which he called "little animalcules." He studied the life cycles of weevils and fleas, showing that they were hatched from eggs. His discoveries helped to disprove the prevailing theory of spontaneous generation—the idea that certain forms of life arose from lifeless matter, such as maggots from rotten meat, fleas from sand, and frogs from mud.

1. How was the invention of printing related to the development of telescopes and microscopes?
2. How did Leeuwenhoek's work help to disprove the theory of spontaneous generation?

Point out that Locke carried over many ideas of the Middle Ages. Medieval philosophy had never favored an absolute monarch.

Meetings in salon society usually took place at the home of a prominent person.

conclusion. Like Hobbes, Locke said that government was based on a contract. Unlike Hobbes, he said that people in a state of nature are reasonable and moral, and that they have natural rights to life, liberty, and property. These rights exist apart from any government, and people have the right to break their contract if their government fails to uphold their natural rights.

Locke published his ideas in 1690 in *Two Treatises of Government*. His writings became widely read and had a great influence on European and American thinkers. Locke became a major source of inspiration for the dawning Enlightenment.

The Scientific View

The scientific view of the world carried over to other areas of life besides political theory. People began to doubt traditional beliefs and values. Old understandings about human life were reexamined, and new ones proposed.

Law In the area of law, people began to look for principles that could meet scientific standards. Less value was placed on hearsay and on confessions made under torture. Since these were the chief kinds of evidence in cases of witchcraft, the scientific view helped bring trials for witchcraft to an end.

The first attempts to create some kind of international law were made in the 1600's. People like William Penn, founder of the Quaker colony of Pennsylvania in America, and Hugo Grotius, the Dutch jurist, called for an international code based on natural law. They also supported the creation of international courts to help the cause of world peace. Certain principles, such as freedom of the seas and protection for diplomats, were suggested.

Faith in natural law also led to a demand for humanitarian reforms. For example, slavery was condemned. Denmark in 1792 became the first country to prohibit the slave trade. Social reformers throughout Europe also called for prison reform and an end to torture and capital punishment.

History In the field of history, scholars began to look for evidence to support accounts of the past. They examined manuscripts for evidence of forgery, studied old coins, and analyzed historical inscriptions on buildings. A new interest developed in chronology and in finding a way to relate the dating systems of different peoples.

Religion Religion was another area in which traditional beliefs were questioned. Many people turned away from the established religions. Europe became a more secular society. Religious toleration spread. Most people still had faith in God, but were less certain that their religion was the only truth.

A number of intellectuals joined a movement known as **deism**. Deism began in England in the late 1600's when some aristocrats and clergy began to question the Christian belief in miracles and the supernatural. Deists called for a religion based on reason and natural law.

1. Identify: *Leviathan*, John Locke, Hugo Grotius.
2. How did Hobbes's philosophy differ from Locke's?
3. How did the scientific view affect the law?
4. Why did religious toleration increase?

3 Enlightenment

During the 1700's many Europeans believed that reason could solve every problem. They thought that their age was enlightened compared to an uncivilized and superstitious past.

Enlightenment thinkers were known as the **philosophes,** the French word for "philosophers." They were primarily writers who wrote for the public and spread Enlightenment thought and ideas.

Salon Society

Although the Enlightenment was an international movement, its center was in Paris. Here the intellectuals depended on an institution called the **salon.** These were meetings of writers, artists, and educated people who were interested in discussing the latest Enlightenment ideas. Wealthy individuals, usually women, supported salons and acted as patrons for artists and writers.

Use the illustrations below to review the various contributions of the thinkers who are listed.

Thinkers of the Age of Reason

Cervantes (1547-1616)

Bacon (1561-1626)

Locke (1632-1704)

Pope (1688-1744)

Rousseau (1712-1778)

Miguel de Cervantes Saavedra, Spanish novelist, poet. Where there is music there can be no evil. *Don Quixote*

Sir Francis Bacon, English philosopher, statesman. Some books are to be tasted, others to be swallowed, and some few to be chewed and digested. *Essays*

Pierre Corneille, French playwright. To win without risk is to triumph without glory. *The Cid*

John Locke, English philosopher. Reading furnishes the mind with materials of knowledge; It is thinking that makes what we read ours. *Of the Conduct of Understanding*

Jean Racine, French playwright. Love is not dumb. The heart speaks in many ways. *Britannicus*

Alexander Pope, English poet, satirist. We may see the small value God has for riches by the people he gives them to. *Thoughts on Various Subjects*

Moliere (Jean Baptiste Poquelin), French playwright. People can be induced to swallow anything, provided it is sufficiently seasoned with praise. *The Miser*

Jean-Jacques Rousseau, Swiss philosopher, novelist. Men always love what is good, . . . it is in judging what is good that they go wrong. *The Social Contract*

Karl von Clausewitz, Prussian army officer, writer. It (war) is not merely a political act but a real political instrument. *War, Politics & Power*

Antoine Rivaroli, Italian journalist. There are men who gain from their wealth only the fear of losing it. *L'Esprit de Rivarol*

Madame de Staël (Anne Louise Necker), Swiss writer. A nation has character only when it is free. *De la littérature*

French philosophes who contributed to the *Encylopedie* sometimes were collectively called the Encyclopedists.

Voltaire   Perhaps the most celebrated of the literary figures to frequent salon society was François Marie Arouet, known to the world as Voltaire. He wrote poetry, plays, articles, and books. His writing was witty and easy to read. A deist, Voltaire poked fun at hypocrisy and attacked the established churches that persecuted people who believed differently. Above all, he proclaimed the importance of science and reason.

In his youth Voltaire was twice imprisoned for writing works that criticized the royal court of France. Later he moved to England and became an admirer of England's practice of greater religious freedom. He wrote, "An Englishman, as one to whom liberty is natural, may go to heaven his own way." Voltaire also admired John Locke and popularized Locke's ideas throughout Europe.

Montesquieu   The most learned of the philosophes in political matters was Charles Louis de Secondat, baron de Montesquieu. His master work, *De l'Esprit des Lois (The Spirit of the Laws)*, appeared in two volumes in 1748. In this work, Montesquieu classified governments according to three categories: monarchy, despotism, and republicanism. Monarchy, Montesquieu stated, was based on honor—that is, on honors awarded to outstanding subjects by the monarch. A despotism was based on fear, while a republic rested on civic virtue. He thought that republics worked best in small countries or city-states. Monarchies were better for medium-sized countries, and despotisms were suitable for large countries in hot climates.

The second part of his work is possibly the best known because of its influence on the Constitution of the United States. It discussed the need for dividing political power into three separate branches: executive, legislative, and judicial.

Encyclopedie   The biggest project of the Enlightenment was the *Encyclopedie,* a 17-volume encyclopedia to which all of the most prominent philosophes contributed. The first volume was published in 1751 and the last in 1772.

The great *Encyclopedie* was first conceived by its publisher as a French translation of a 2-volume English encyclopedia. But its young editor, Denis Diderot, made it into a giant reference work, containing all the current knowledge about science, technology, and history. It presented Enlightenment ideas and criticized society and government from an Enlightenment viewpoint. Although banned by the Catholic Church, the *Encyclopedie* was widely read throughout Europe.

The more noted French intellectuals of the Enlightenment held private courts in the salons of such well-known women as Madame Geoffrin, Mademoiselle de Lespinase, and Madame du Deffend. A virtual institution was made of the intimate gatherings where serious and stimulating conversation was the order of the day. What city served as the center of salon society?

One of the most notable physiocrats was Robert Turgot, finance minister to Louis XVI.

Frederick the Great, like other enlightened despots, justified his authority on grounds of its usefulness to society. He called himself "first servant of the state."

Physiocrats One group of Enlightenment thinkers, called Physiocrats, was concerned with economic ideas. The Physiocrats criticized mercantilism because it involved too much government interference in the economy. They believed in the doctrine of **laissez faire,** meaning "leave it alone." In other words, the government should leave the economy alone.

The Physiocrats also disagreed with the mercantilist idea that gold and silver were the source of the nation's wealth. They said that the true source of wealth was the land. Farming created wealth. On it depended both production and trade.

Enlightenment Thought

Enlightenment thinkers did not all think alike. They criticized each other as much as they criticized society. However, they shared certain attitudes in common.

One outlook that they had in common was skepticism. "Doubt is a disagreeable state of mind," said Voltaire, "but certainty is an absurd one." The philosophes agreed that the word of authority alone was not a suitable basis for accepting a belief or theory. According to them, reason and experience were far more important.

They admired freedom of all kinds. They were especially aware of the need for freedom of speech and freedom of the press. These freedoms were important to them because they had to work under the restrictions of government censorship. Another major concern was religious freedom. The philosophes called for religious toleration and an end to wars of religion.

Whatever their concerns, the philosophes shared a faith in progress. They believed that society could be changed for the better, and they looked to the state, rather than the church or any other institution, to accomplish this goal.

Montesquieu thought that the ideal form of government was a limited monarchy such as England's. Others thought that more progress could be made in a republic. Still others, such as Voltaire, favored **enlightened despotism—** monarchies in which rulers had absolute powers and used those powers to reform society.

Enlightened Despots

Enlightened despots did not claim to rule by the will of God, for such a claim would not have been believed during the Age of Reason. Instead, they justified their rule on the belief that society needed enlightened rulers. They believed that both their rule and the welfare of their people would best be served by measures that increased prosperity and made government more efficient.

Prussia The most famous of the enlightened despots was Frederick the Great of Prussia. He wrote poems and essays and had a reputation as a minor philosophe. He greatly admired Voltaire, who lived at the Prussian court for two years at Frederick's invitation.

Frederick believed that a king was the "first servant to the state." He once wrote to Voltaire:

> *My chief occupation is to fight the ignorances and the prejudices in this country. . . . I must enlighten my people, cultivate their*

Frederick II of Prussia discussed many of his poems with Voltaire, his writing teacher. It was Voltaire who first called Frederick "the Great." What reforms did Frederick institute that supported that title?

Raise the question of whether or not the American Revolution could have been avoided if there had been an enlightened ruler on the British throne. Ask students, "In what way was American independence a result of the Age of Enlightenment?"

manners and morals, and make them as happy as human beings can be; as happy as the means at my disposal permit me to make them.*

Frederick took a number of steps that were considered enlightened. He reformed Prussia's judicial system, abolishing the use of torture except in cases of treason and murder. He urged religious toleration, although he discriminated against the Jews. After the Seven Years' War, Frederick tried to help the peasants by giving them seed and using state funds to rebuild houses and barns.

Austria   Maria Theresa was a devout Catholic and did not accept the thinking of the philosophes. However, she introduced a number of Enlightenment reforms. She tried to help the serfs by issuing codes to govern the relationship between lords and peasants, protecting peasants' rights. She freed the peasants who lived on land owned by the Crown. In 1774 she set up schools for all children between the ages of 6 and 13. These schools were supported by local and national funds.

In 1775 Maria Theresa's husband died, and their son Joseph became co-ruler. Joseph II was a great admirer of Enlightenment ideas. He was impatient with his mother's slow, practical measures. After her death in 1780, he began to make sweeping reforms. He abolished serfdom and made land taxes equal for peasants and nobles. He took property from the Catholic Church and used the money to support hospitals. He granted complete freedom to the press. One reform decree followed another in quick succession.

Despite Joseph's good intentions, most of his reforms failed. He made changes too abruptly and antagonized too many people. By the time he died in 1790, Joseph had been forced to repeal many of his reforms because of rebellion by the nobles. He was succeeded by his brother Leopold II. Leopold revoked most of Joseph's laws, but allowed the peasants to keep their freedom.

---

*Frederick the Great, as quoted in *Europe from the Renaissance to Waterloo,* loc. cit., p. 502.

Other Nations   Spain, Portugal, Denmark, and Sweden each had rulers who were interested in Enlightenment ideas. Catherine the Great of Russia was also a follower of the Enlightenment in some respects, although she was able to make only very limited reforms. In France, the nobles frustrated every effort at reform made by the government. Almost everywhere, enlightened despotism was limited by the vested interests of the aristocracy and the churches. On the whole, the enlightened monarchs failed to make the reforms that might have stopped the violent revolutions to come.

1. Identify: Voltaire, *The Spirit of the Laws*, Denis Diderot, Joseph II.
2. What function did the salons serve in the Enlightenment?
3. For what reason did the Physiocrats criticize mercantilism?
4. How did enlightened despots justify their rule?

---

4 Challenge to the Enlightenment

Although Enlightenment ideas were widespread, not everyone agreed that human reason alone could explain the universe. Among those who questioned Enlightenment philosophy were some of the philosophes themselves.

Critics of the Enlightenment

Rousseau   One of the most important philosophes, Jean Jacques Rousseau, criticized what he believed was excessive reliance on reason. Born in Geneva to a French Huguenot family, Rousseau led an unhappy life, always feeling like an outsider. He suffered from chronic physical illness and possibly from mental illness as well. Nevertheless, he was a leading thinker and one of the most profound writers of his day.

Rousseau's unhappy life convinced him that human beings were naturally good but that civilization was evil. People's good qualities, he said, came from their emotions. Their bad qualities came from reason. He urged people to throw off civilization and return to nature, as far as that was possible.

Rousseau wanted a state in which all persons had a sense of membership and participation.

Following a trend to return to nature, it became popular for nobles to dress and act in an idealized version of happy peasants enjoying the peaceful bliss of country life. What noted critic of the Enlightenment urged a return to simple rural life?

In 1750 Rousseau won an essay contest with a *Discourse Concerning Science and the Arts*. This essay, which attacked science and the arts for corrupting morals, made him famous. In 1760 Rousseau published *La Nouvelle Heloise*, a novel that described the beauties of nature and the pleasures of a simple country life. The book had so much influence that all kinds of people started trying to live a simple life like that of the characters in the book. Even the queen of France, Marie Antoinette, had a cottage built for herself at Versailles, where she enjoyed pretending to be a milkmaid.

A second book, *Emile* (1762), was a treatise on education in novel style. In it Rousseau called for education that would preserve a child's natural goodness. This book, too, was highly influential. In the same year, Rousseau published his most famous work, *The Social Contract*. It began, "Man is born free, and everywhere he is in chains." Rousseau wrote that society existed because people came to an agreement, a social contract, to give up their individual rights to the "general will."

Unlike Locke, who had thought that the agreement was between the people and a ruler, Rousseau thought the agreement was among the people themselves. Therefore, **sovereignty,** or the power to rule, belonged to the people. Governments, therefore, received their authority from the people. According to Rousseau, people were "in chains" because governments had taken away individual freedoms and broken the contract. To regain their freedom, Rousseau said, people had a right to change governments.

The Social Contract was little read during Rousseau's lifetime. However, after his death it became a major influence on French politics.

The word *baroque* comes from the Portuguese. It literally means "an irregularly shaped pearl."

Hume The Scottish philosopher David Hume was another philosophe who questioned the value of human reason. Hume pointed out that there was no proof of the existence of natural law. In *An Enquiry Concerning Human Understanding* (1748) he said that reason was no better than faith as a source of knowledge. "A total suspense of judgment," said this total skeptic, "is our only reasonable recourse."

Kant Hume's ideas were taken up by the German thinker Immanuel Kant. Kant thought that reason could not explain problems of **metaphysics,** or those aspects of philosophy that deal with universal, eternal questions, such as the existence of God and the limits of knowledge. In his most important work, *The Critique of Pure Reason* (1781), he said that human feelings about religion, beauty, and morality were real even though science and reason could not explain them.

Kant believed that science was valuable, but limited. It could not provide a guide for morality. As a moral principle, he put forth what he called the **categorical imperative**—"categorical" meaning "absolute" and "imperative" meaning "command." Kant's categorical imperative meant that a person's actions should be such that he or she would be willing to have them become universal laws.

Religious Reaction

Ordinary men and women as well as philosophers found something wanting in the rationalism of the Enlightenment. Deism, the religion of reason, was not enough for many people. They wanted a religion that was more emotionally satisfying.

In Germany, Count von Zinzendorf established a new sect called the Moravian Brethren, which emphasized the emotional and mystical side of religion. In England, a movement called Methodism, led by John Wesley, likewise stressed personal religious experience. North America went through a period of religious revival called the Great Awakening.

The need for a religion with more feeling also led to a Catholic revival known as Jansenism in France and a movement called Hasidism among eastern European Jews. All of these movements rejected reason in favor of an enthusiastic faith.

1. Identify: Jean Jacques Rousseau, David Hume, Immanuel Kant, Count Von Zinzendorf.
2. What was Rousseau's opinion about the effect of science on morality?
3. What principle, according to Kant, should guide a person's actions?
4. What did the Moravian Brethren, the Methodists, the Jansenists, and the Hasidic Jews have in common?

5 Art and Literature

The Enlightenment was one of many movements that affected art and literature during the 1600's and 1700's. During this period the influence of the Renaissance declined. The Age of Reason combined with and overlapped other forces, including the Counter Reformation and the Age of Absolutism, to bring about new styles.

Mannerism

One of the first steps away from the Renaissance was taken by artists called **mannerists.** The mannerists rejected Renaissance principles of balance and perspective. They preferred to portray people and scenes as they saw them subjectively.

Mannerists were influenced by the intensely emotional piety of the Counter Reformation. One of the greatest mannerists was the Cretan painter Domenikos Theotokopoulos, known in Spain as El Greco or "The Greek." He painted the saints in distorted figures that showed strong religious feelings.

Baroque

Other artists thought that mannerism was too subjective. They developed a new style called **baroque,** meaning bizarre.

Baroque had many aspects. It was intended to be more realistic than mannerism. At the same time it was grand, elaborate, formal, and emotional. Much baroque art was religious. It was encouraged by the Catholic Church as a way to inspire religious feelings. On the other hand, much of it was very worldly. The great monarchs

HISTORY AND PEOPLE

John Wesley

John Wesley, born the son of an Anglican minister in 1703, learned to read the Bible at a very young age. When he was five years old, his home caught fire, and he narrowly escaped being burned to death. After that he called himself "a brand plucked out of the burning."

Wesley studied at Oxford University, and in 1728 was ordained as a priest in the Church of England. The next year, he returned to Oxford to fulfill the requirements of a fellowship. Meanwhile, John's brother Charles, who later became well known as a hymn writer, had started a group called the Holy Club at the university. Members of the club were called "Methodists" because they tried to live Christian lives through method, or discipline. They held frequent services, fasted for two days a week, and performed social services for prisoners and the poor. John joined the group and soon became its leader.

In 1735 John and Charles Wesley went as missionaries to the colony of Georgia in North America. Their mission was not very successful.

They did not succeed in converting the North American Indians they met, and John developed some misunderstandings with the Anglican colonists. They returned to England in 1738, feeling that they had failed.

Soon after his return, John Wesley met a Moravian, a disciple of Count von Zinzendorf, who told him that faith alone was all he needed. At a Moravian meeting, he experienced a religious conversion. "I felt my heart strangely warmed," he wrote. "I felt I did trust in Christ, Christ alone, for salvation. . . ."

After this experience, Wesley began to preach the idea of salvation by faith. He attracted huge crowds with his enthusiastic sermons and was able to arouse strong emotions in his listeners. He wrote, "The power of God came so mightily among us that one, and another, and another, fell down as thunderstruck."

At first he worked through the Church of England, but the Anglican clergy did not approve of his zeal or the fact that his listeners often reacted by screaming, fainting, and going into convulsions. When pulpits were closed to him, he began to preach anywhere and everywhere he could—on street corners, in courthouses, and private homes, and to large outdoor gatherings. With tremendous will and energy, he spent the rest of his life traveling, preaching, and organizing Methodist societies. He traveled many miles on horseback and preached more than 40,000 sermons, some to crowds of up to 20,000 persons.

Wesley always maintained that he did not intend to start a new denomination. "I live and die a member of the Church of England," he said. However, he ordained lay ministers and organized societies in various places. At the time of his death in 1791, at the age of 88, the Methodist movement had about 175,000 followers and over 600 lay preachers. After he died, the Methodist Church broke away from the Anglican Church. Eventually the Methodist Church attracted millions of members in many parts of the world.

Some teachers might wish to play recorded baroque music in the classroom, noting how the visual image of baroque is transferred to sound.

Velasquez's paintings exemplify the baroque ideal of realism. His portraits of the Spanish royal family had a strong influence on later portrait painters. Why did the great monarchs encourage baroque artists?

of Europe encouraged it as a way to advertise their glory and power and to inspire feelings of patriotism.

Painting   In painting, Peter Paul Rubens of Flanders was a master of the baroque style. He painted highly emotional religious scenes. Another master was the Spaniard Diego Velázquez, who painted portraits at the Spanish court.

Architecture   In architecture the best example of baroque is Louis XIV's palace at Versailles. Another good example is the public square of St. Peter's Basilica in Rome, which is enclosed by two great semicircles of columns. Baroque

architects used elaborate decorations with many cherubs and angels, curves and swirls, colored marbles and gilt, twisted columns, and formal gardens.

Music   Baroque music was elaborate, overflowing, and emotional. The opera, created by Italian composers such as Alessandro Scarlatti, was a baroque form. Two Germans, Johann Sebastian Bach and George Frederic Handel, were among the great baroque composers.

Literature   Literature also went through a baroque period. Writers used rich, emotional language and emphasized drama and tension. The use of many similes and metaphors and exclamations was typical.

Many Renaissance writers showed elements of the baroque. Milton's *Paradise Lost* is an example,

Baroque architecture dominates the older regions of Bavaria. An excellent example is this church in Ottobeuren, Bavaria. What are some of the major characteristics of baroque architecture?

as are Shakespeare's later plays. Miguel de Cervantes Saavedra of Spain also wrote about baroque themes. His novel *Don Quixote,* written in the early 1600's, is considered by some critics to be the greatest novel ever written.

Rococo

Toward the end of the 1600's, a new style called **rococo** began to grow out of baroque. Most popular in France, it reflected the tastes of French aristocrats. Rococo was elaborate like baroque, but less grand. Instead, it was lighter, more delicate—almost dainty.

Rococo painters such as Jean Antoine Watteau portrayed playful rather than serious subjects.

Gulliver's Travels *was one of the major novels written during the Age of Reason. Though it contains some of Swift's most savage satire, it has become a favorite among children. Who were other novelists of the period?*

Rococo architecture, on a smaller scale than baroque but extravagantly decorated, was used for palaces, churches, and houses belonging to the nobility. Rococo music was light, gay, and intricate.

"Realism"

In contrast to the baroque and rococo styles, painters in the Netherlands developed a realistic style. The Protestant Dutch were not as interested in religious themes as painters in Catholic countries. Frans Hals and Jan Vermeer portrayed scenes of everyday life. Still life paintings were popular.

Most brilliant of the Dutch realist painters was Rembrandt van Rijn. Although he followed no particular faith, he was deeply interested in the spiritual side of life and often chose religious subject matter.

Neoclassicism

In the late 1700's, Europe experienced another return to classicism—**neoclassicism,** or new classicism. To leaders of the Enlightenment, Greek and Roman classicism represented the order and reason they strived for in European life.

Architecture　　In the mid-1700's, archeologists began to dig out the ancient Roman cities of Pompeii and Herculaneum, which had been buried by a volcano. Discoveries there helped to inspire a new interest in classical styles of architecture. Neoclassical architects used simple forms, such as squares and circles, rather than the elaborate swirls of the baroque style of architecture.

Literature　　In literature, too, the models for the Age of Reason were the Greek and Roman classics. Writers tried to achieve perfect form, and were not concerned with emotions. The English essayist and poet Alexander Pope and the French dramatists Corneille, Molière, and Racine, were among the important classicists of literature.

A very important development in the 1700's was the beginning of the modern English novel. Daniel Defoe's *Robinson Crusoe* (1719), Jonathan Swift's *Gulliver's Travels* (1726), Samuel Richard-

Ludwig van Beethoven is considered to be the greatest composer of classical symphonies. He also composed chamber music, oratorio, opera, and piano music.

During the 1700's, the piano replaced the harpsichord in popularity because of its tone and versatility. The piano served not only as a solo instrument but also for accompaniment in concerts. What other changes were made in music in the 1700's?

son's *Pamela* (1740), and Henry Fielding's *Tom Jones* (1749) were among the earliest examples of this form of literature.

Music Music also entered a classical period after 1700. Classical music stressed balance, contrast, and a refined expression of emotion. The greatest composers of this period were the Austrians Joseph Haydn and Wolfgang Amadeus Mozart. The German composer Ludwig van Beethoven began his musical career in the 1790's.

Painting By the late 1700's, the rococo painting admired by aristocrats was declining. Neoclassicism was becoming more important, especially in France. Jacques Louis David and Jean Auguste Dominique Ingres of France were the recognized leaders of the movement. Neoclassical painting was simple, balanced, and clear. It expressed the values of the coming period of revolution—values such as patriotism, duty, and sacrifice.

1. Identify: El Greco, Peter Paul Rubens, Diego Velázquez, Alessandro Scarlatti, *Don Quixote*, Jan Vermeer, Rembrandt van Rijn, Daniel Defoe, Jacques Louis David.
2. How did mannerist painting differ from Renaissance styles?
3. How did the rococo style of painting differ from baroque?
4. What artistic style was favored by leaders of the Enlightenment?

CHAPTER 14 REVIEW

Summary

1. The Copernican theory, published in 1543, that the sun was the center of the solar system, led to a dramatic change in the way human beings viewed the universe.
2. Advances in science encouraged the use of scientific approaches to other fields of knowledge, particularly in the area of political theory.
3. Interest in science increased, and scientific organizations supported the study and spread of scientific knowledge.
4. In the late 1600's, Isaac Newton showed that the physical universe could be explained by mathematical laws.
5. A new philosophy of knowledge was developed, emphasizing observation, experiment, and reason rather than faith and tradition.
6. During the 1700's, Europe experienced a movement called the Enlightenment, in which reason was seen as the solution to the problems of society.
7. Several European rulers, known as enlightened despots, attempted to put Enlightenment ideas into practice.
8. The Enlightenment's emphasis on reason led to a reaction that stressed the value of emotion and the limits of reason.
9. New styles developed in art, literature, and music, reflecting the influence of the Enlightenment and other major forces of the 1600's and 1700's.

Building Vocabulary

ellipses	philosophes	sovereignty	mannerists
law of inertia	salon	metaphysics	baroque
natural law	laissez faire	categorical imperative	rococo
deism	enlightened despotism		neoclassicism

Reviewing the Main Ideas

1. What new philosophy of knowledge developed in the 1600's?
2. Why did Newton's work have a significant impact on the world of thought?
3. How did the idea of natural law affect political philosophy?
4. How was the field of history affected by the scientific view?
5. How was religion affected by the Age of Reason?
6. What attitudes did Enlightenment thinkers share?
7. How did enlightened despots put Enlightenment ideas into effect? Did they succeed in their efforts? Explain.
8. How did Rousseau's ideas compare to Locke's?
9. Why did the Catholic Church and absolute monarchs encourage baroque art?
10. What style of painting did artists in the Netherlands develop? What was its subject matter?
11. How did neoclassicism reflect values of the Enlightenment?

Discussing Important Ideas

1. Do scientific laws apply to society in the way that they apply to the physical universe? Why or why not?
2. Do you agree or disagree with Montesquieu that different kinds of government work best in different kinds of societies? Explain.
3. How does the government of the United States show the influences of Locke and Montesquieu?
4. Do you agree or disagree with Rousseau that human beings are naturally good?
5. Does science have the effect of corrupting or of purifying morals?
6. Bishop Bossuet said that the skepticism of the philosophes was "an unending error, a risk-all boldness, a deliberate dizziness, in a word, a pride that cannot accept its proper cure, which is legitimate authority." Do you agree or disagree? What did Bossuet mean by "legitimate authority"?
7. Were the 1700's truly an age of enlightenment? Why or why not? Give examples to support your opinion.
8. Has science fulfilled the promise of progress it seemed to hold in the 1700's? Why or why not?

Using Illustrations

Study the picture on page 328, read the caption, and answer the following questions:

1. Who is the main subject of this painting? How do you know?
2. What scientific objects are in the room?
3. How would you describe the central activity being illustrated?
4. Do you think any of the figures in the painting are scientists? Why or why not?
5. Do you think the women standing in the corner of the room are included in the central activity? Why or why not?
6. What does the painting illustrate about the scientific movement?

CHAPTER 15

Paris During the French Revolution

❝ The form of government in any state cannot be altered without apparent danger of ruin to that state. ❞

John Pym, English political leader (1584-1643)

Age

of

Revolution

James I of England was also James VI of Scotland. He was a philosopher of royal absolutism, having written a book on the subject called *The True Law of Free Monarchy.*

In the 1600's most of the countries of Europe were ruled by absolute monarchs. But the forces of change were building. By 1688 England had undergone two revolutions that significantly limited the powers of the monarch. During the late 1700's, England's American colonies and France went through revolutions that eliminated monarchy entirely. A new political age was dawning.

1 Revolution in England

Elizabeth I, who ruled from 1558 to 1603, was a strong monarch. But she did not have absolute power. Her authority was limited by Parliament, which grew more independent during her reign. Parliament was made up of two houses. In the House of Lords, nobles inherited their positions. In the House of Commons, members were elected by a small group of landowners. Most members of the Commons belonged to either the landowning gentry or the rising merchant class. As a group, the gentry, or "country gentlemen," were becoming the most influential in England.

Elizabeth was tactful in her relations with Parliament. She was skillful at getting what she wanted, but she avoided confrontations. For its part, Parliament was willing to defer to the popular queen. After she died in 1603, Parliament—especially the Commons—was determined to increase its control over national policy.

James I

James I, the son of Mary Queen of Scots, was already king of Scotland when he inherited the throne of England from Elizabeth in 1603. He was a learned man, but he was a poor judge of people and political situations. His background in dealing with the weak Scottish Parliament did not prepare him for dealing with the English Parliament. James interfered with the business of the English Parliament. He also scolded its members for actions he opposed.

James believed strongly in the **divine right of kings,** the idea that the power of monarchs came from God and was absolute. He did not hesitate to tell Parliament about his viewpoint. James declared that a good king should act according to law, but he is not bound to it and should act according to "his own good will." Such statements caused resentment in Parliament, and conflicts soon developed with the Crown.

James's greatest weakness in these conflicts was his need to ask Parliament for money. He was extravagant both in his own spending and in the gifts he lavished on his favorite advisers at court. When Parliament refused to vote him enough funds, the king resorted to other means of raising money, such as the sale of titles.

Foreign policy was another source of conflict with the Parliament. Having a genuine desire for peace, James ended a war with Spain that had lasted nearly 20 years and had put the Crown greatly in debt. However, many English people disliked Spain and did not want peace. When James tried to arrange a marriage between his son Charles and a Spanish princess, the Protestant English were appalled. They were afraid that a Catholic queen would bring up the heir to the English throne as a Catholic. When plans for the marriage collapsed, the Protestants were pleased.

In the early 1600's, most English people were members of the Church of England. One group of dissenters, or opponents, within the Church was the Puritans. They wanted the Church to be "purified" of remaining Catholic rituals and symbols. James, as head of both church and state in England, thought that anyone who criticized the Church was not a loyal subject. When he refused to support the Puritan cause, the Puritans turned against him.

Because Puritans were well represented in the Commons, bitterness between the king and Parliament increased. James threatened the Puritans, saying that he would "harry [force] them out of the land." Because of James's policies, many Puritans left England and settled in North America.

Charles I

In 1625 James died, and his son Charles became king. Like his father, Charles I believed in the divine right of kings and opposed the Puritans. The church official whom he appointed as Archbishop of Canterbury was William Laud, a hated enemy of the Puritans. Furthermore, the king married the Catholic sister of France's King Louis XIII, Henrietta Maria. To please his bride, Charles promised to ease the laws against Catholics in England.

Charles badly needed money for a new war with Spain and had to call a meeting of Parliament to ask for funds. The Commons voted to give him less than a quarter of what he needed. Then it changed the subject of debate to religion. Commons members wanted strict enforcement of the laws against Catholics. They also asked for laws to promote Puritanism. Charles refused and dissolved, or ended, Parliament. A new Parliament was chosen. It too was dissolved after refusing to grant money to Charles.

Charles then tried to raise money by collecting taxes without Parliament's consent. He began levying "forced loans." Those who would not pay were put in jail. Some of the persons who were imprisoned applied for **writs of habeas corpus,** saying that they had not been specifically accused of any crime. Such writs were issued to bring a person before a judge and to show cause for imprisonment.

Charles I was the model gentleman: devout, prudent, and scholarly. But his scolding of the House of Commons like a schoolmaster was not well received. How else did Charles I handle his relationship with Parliament?

The judges, who did not want to admit that the people were in jail for refusing to lend money, sent them back to jail without giving a reason. Many citizens were alarmed that the king could put people in jail without just cause. They were also very concerned that the judges had allowed him to do it.

Another grievance of the people was that Charles began to **billet,** or board and lodge, his troops in private homes. Charles also declared martial law in some areas. Thus, discontent was high when the king called his third Parliament in 1628.

By this time England was at war with both France and Spain. Charles needed money desperately. But the new Parliament was not

One of Charles I's ministers hated by the Puritans was Thomas Wentworth, the earl of Strafford. He had once been a leader of the king's opposition party; now he was seen as a traitor.

about to grant it without major concessions from him. In the end, the members of Parliament forced Charles to agree to a Petition of Right, which had four main points. First, the king could not collect taxes or force loans without Parliament's approval. Second, nobody could be imprisoned without cause being shown. Third, troops could not be billeted in private homes against the owner's will. Fourth, martial law could not be declared in time of peace.

Even after Charles signed the Petition of Right in return for a large grant of funds, there was no peace between king and Parliament. Charles finally dissolved Parliament in March 1629 and vowed never to call it again.

For the next 11 years, the king ruled without Parliament. During this time he continued to offend many of the gentry by the ways he raised money. They also disliked the persecution of the Puritans, which was carried out by Archbishop Laud.

In 1639 Charles and Archbishop Laud tried to force the Calvinist Church of Scotland to accept a new prayer book based on the Church of England's *Book of Common Prayer*. The king wanted to break the power of the Scottish Church. The Scots shared the same religious beliefs as the Puritans. They considered the Anglican Church to be too much like the Catholic Church. As a result, they rebelled against Charles's religious policies.

The Long Parliament

In order to put down the rebellion in Scotland, Charles was forced to call Parliament once again. He asked for money, but the Commons demanded that he first hear their grievances. Charles dissolved this Parliament after only three weeks. Still without money, he soon had to call another meeting. The Parliament that was summoned in November 1640 was known as the Long Parliament because it continued to meet for 20 years.

The Long Parliament began its attack on the king by overthrowing his ministers. Archbishop Laud was imprisoned and later executed. Parliament then passed the Triennial Act, which said that there should be no more than three years between each meeting of Parliament. It also passed an act that prohibited Charles from dissolving the current Parliament without its consent. Finally, Puritan leaders in the Commons drew up the Grand Remonstrance, a long list of grievances against the king.

As the Puritans grew stronger, a **royalist,** or pro-monarchy, party began to form in Parliament. It was made up of moderates who wanted Parliament to control the Church but who did not want Anglicanism to be replaced by Puritanism. They also thought that the king had suffered enough. As time went on, debates between the Puritans and the royalists became more heated.

Despite resistance by the royalists, Parliament in June 1642 sent Charles "Nineteen Propositions" that made Parliament the supreme power in England. When Charles refused to agree to its demands, Parliament raised an army against the king. Charles withdrew to Nottingham with his royalist followers. The English Civil War had begun.

Civil War

The English Civil War split the country in two. Most of the nobles took the side of the king, but some, especially those who were Puritans, took the side of Parliament. The gentry were divided, with a small majority backing the king. Yeomen generally followed the lead of their local gentry, while the peasants generally took neither side.

Many people found themselves fighting against friends and relatives. One of Parliament's generals, Sir William Walker, wrote: "God, who is the searcher of my heart, knows with what reluctance I go upon this service and with what perfect hatred I look at war without an enemy. . . ."

Because the king's forces included a strong cavalry, his supporters were called Cavaliers. Parliament's supporters were known as Roundheads because they cut their hair short. The first two years of the war were indecisive. Then Parliament reorganized its forces under the leadership of Oliver Cromwell.

Cromwell was a very religious man and a brilliant military leader. He stressed rigorous training and firm discipline. Religious men were

Soldiers in Cromwell's New Model Army often marched into battles singing the psalms.

Charles I was a realist in religious matters. He had advised his son, the future Charles II, never to accept Catholicism if he wished to rule England.

chosen for Cromwell's New Model Army. They regarded Cromwell as a hero and gave him their solid support. The New Model Army eventually defeated Charles, forcing him to surrender in May 1646.

Charles was tried for treason and sentenced to death. Just before he was beheaded, on February 9, 1649, he made the following statement:

> *For the people I desire their liberty as much as anybody whomsoever; but I must tell you that their liberty and freedom consists in having government, in those laws by which their life and goods may be most their own. It is not by their having a share in government; that is nothing pertaining to them.**

Many people, both in England and abroad, were shocked by the execution of the king. Charles I was seen as a martyr and the Puritans as villains.

Commonwealth

After the execution, Parliament abolished both the office of king and the House of Lords. England was declared to be a commonwealth, a state having a republican form of government. Parliament was now the supreme authority in the land. But it was surrounded by enemies. It had to deal with not only the defeated royalists but also the more radical revolutionaries. One of the most important groups of radicals was the Levelers, who called for religious freedom and **universal manhood suffrage,** or the right of all males to vote. Another group, known as the Diggers, wanted the common people to take over ownership of the land. Both of these groups were put down by Parliament.

The Commonwealth also faced rebellions in Ireland and Scotland. After Charles I was executed, the Catholic Irish proclaimed his son, Charles II, as their king. Actually, they did not care about having a king as much as they wanted to be rid of England and Protestantism. Oliver Cromwell, as commander in chief of the army, led his troops into Ireland and defeated the rebels. He treated the Irish with extreme

harshness and soon crushed the rebellion. By 1652 a third of the Irish population had died. Lands of the Catholic rebels were confiscated, and anti-Catholic laws were enforced.

In Scotland, the Calvinists also proclaimed Charles II as their king. In 1650 Cromwell defeated the Scots in their own land. The next year, the Scots invaded England and were again defeated.

Cromwell was now the most powerful person in England. He and the army were dissatisfied with the Long Parliament, which quarreled over various reforms and made little progress. They wanted a new, more stable government to take its place. But the members of Parliament did not want to give up their power. They refused to hold elections for a new government. Finally, in April 1653, Cromwell lost his patience. He led his soldiers into the Commons and drove out the members by force.

For the next five years, Cromwell ruled as a military dictator with the title of Lord Protector.

Oliver Cromwell was noted for military skill and strength of character. In all that he did, he was convinced he was performing God's work. How was life in England changed during Cromwell's rule?

---

*Charles I, as quoted in *A History of England*, David Harris Willson, © 1967 by Holt, Rinehart, and Winston, pp. 410-411.

The army tried to broaden its base of power while protecting republicanism and tolerating the various sects. It failed because most of the people preferred a king and were suspicious of radical sects.

From Monarchy to Revolution · 351

Between 1665 and 1667, England experienced war with Holland, a plague, and the London fire.

Under Cromwell the English people were forced to accept a strict Puritan moral code. Drinking, dancing, gambling, and other popular activities were forbidden. However, Cromwell allowed a limited kind of religious toleration for different branches of the Protestant faith.

When Cromwell died in September 1658, his son Richard was proclaimed Lord Protector. Richard did not have the support of the army, and he resigned after only nine months. By this time, most of the English were tired of Puritan rule and opposed the military dictatorship. Army leaders, looking for a stable government, recalled the Long Parliament.

Restoration

Members of the Long Parliament began negotiations with Charles II, who had been living in exile in Europe. The two parties agreed to restore both the monarchy and Parliament. In 1660 Charles II returned to England.

Although England once again had a king, the Crown had lost many of its powers. All the acts of Parliament to which Charles I had agreed, such as the Petition of Right, were still in effect. The restoration thus gave England a **constitutional monarchy**—a monarchy limited in its powers by a constitution. Rather than being a single document, England's constitution was made up of many—such as the Magna Charta and the Petition of Right—plus other laws and customs.

Charles II was charming and witty. He was not about to make a stand on any matter of principle, because he was determined to avoid his father's fate. He was interested in art, science, and entertainment. During his reign, Puritan rules were abandoned. People again enjoyed dancing, sports, and theater.

Outwardly, Charles accepted the Church of England. Secretly, however, he leaned toward Catholicism, his mother's religion. He admired it because it supported absolute monarchy. He hoped for a policy of religious toleration that would include Catholics. But the decision depended on Parliament. Charles had agreed to let Parliament settle the religious question before he became king.

In 1661 a new Parliament was elected. It was known as the Cavalier Parliament because it contained a majority of royalists. During the next few years this Parliament passed a series of acts known as the Clarendon Code. The effect of these laws was to make the Church of England once again the state religion. Only Anglicans, or members of the Church of England, could attend the universities, serve in Parliament, or hold religious services. Hundreds of non-Anglican clergy were driven from their churches. Despite discrimination, however, many people remained "Nonconformists," or Protestants who did not conform to the Church of England.

Charles became involved in a conflict with Parliament because his brother James, the heir to the throne, was openly a Catholic. In 1679 Parliament tried to pass an Exclusion Bill to keep James from becoming king. During this conflict, those members of Parliament who wanted to exclude James from the throne received the name Whigs. Those who defended James were called Tories. Eventually these two groups developed into England's first political parties.

To keep the Exclusion Bill from being passed, Charles dissolved Parliament. He ruled without calling it again until he died in 1685. As a result, the English throne passed to a Catholic king, James II.

The Glorious Revolution

James II did not accept the fact that England had a limited monarchy. He wanted to rule as an absolute monarch. Furthermore, he wanted to bring back Catholicism. In defiance of the law, he appointed Catholics to government and university positions. He said he had the power to suspend the law. He issued a Declaration of Indulgence, granting religious toleration to Catholics and Protestant dissenters.

Members of Parliament were alarmed, but they tried to be patient. They were waiting for James to die and for the throne to pass to his Protestant daughter Mary, who was married to William of Orange, leader of Holland. But in 1688 James had a son by his second wife, who was a Catholic. The prince would be heir to the throne and would certainly be brought up as a Catholic.

Suddenly it looked as if England might have a long line of Catholic kings. Unwilling to accept this, a group of Whig and Tory leaders invited William of Orange to invade England. He landed with a small force in November 1688 and headed toward London. James fled to France. William and Mary were offered the Crown on condition that they accept a declaration of rights. These events were called the Glorious Revolution because they occurred without bloodshed.

In 1689 the declaration of rights was passed into law as the Bill of Rights. It said that the king could not raise taxes or maintain an army without the consent of Parliament and could not suspend laws. It also said that no Catholic or anyone who married a Catholic could become king. Further, it said that Parliaments should be held often and that there should be freedom of debate in Parliament.

The Bill of Rights was important because it put these ideas in written form so that Parliament's power could not be challenged in the future. In addition, the bill guaranteed the rights to appeal to the king, bear arms, and have a trial by jury. Thus, the Bill of Rights protected certain individual rights as well as the role of Parliament in English government. Later the same year, Parliament further protected individual rights by passing the Act of Toleration,[1] which gave religious freedom to all Protestants, including "Nonconformists."

In 1701 Parliament passed the Act of Settlement. It stated that the throne of England could not be inherited by a Catholic. It also established the order of succession to the throne.

Parliament and Crown

The Bill of Rights and the Act of Settlement made it clear that Parliament had won in the long battle with the Crown. England was still a monarchy, but a king or queen could not rule without Parliament's consent.

However, England was not a democracy. Although members of the Commons were elected, only about 250,000 people out of six million had the right to vote. Suffrage was restricted to male property owners. Democratic ideas such as those of the Levelers generally disappeared in England, or were held by people who had no political power. Parliament was controlled by people of property—nobles, gentry, merchants, and clergy.

William of Orange, known as William III, was a strong monarch who did his best to keep power in his own hands. He insisted on having complete control over the army and foreign affairs, but he was willing to let Parliament handle domestic policy.

William was succeeded by his sister-in-law Anne in 1702. To govern the country she relied on a **cabinet,** a small group of advisers selected from the Commons. Thus the power of Parliament increased. In 1707, during Anne's reign, England was united with Scotland by the Act of Union, which was passed by the Parliaments of both countries. After that Scotland gave up its own Parliament and the Scots were represented in the British Parliament.[2] However, Scotland was able to keep its own religion and laws.

In 1714, under the terms of the Act of Settlement, Anne was succeeded by her closest Protestant relative, the German prince George I of Hanover. George did not speak English and made no attempt to learn it. His chief minister was the Whig leader Robert Walpole, who took control of the cabinet.

When George I died in 1727, Walpole managed to remain in power under the king's son, George II. Both Georges, unfamiliar with the way British government worked, allowed and even encouraged the growth of the cabinet's powers. Walpole was considered to be Britain's first **prime minister**—the chief executive of a **parliamentary government.** In this form of government, the prime minister is the head of the party that wins a majority in the Parliament. The prime minister forms a cabinet, and together they make up the executive branch. They are responsible to Parliament, the legislative branch.

---

[1] Catholics and other religious groups were excluded from the Act of Toleration. Restrictions on them lessened over the years; however, their civil rights were not guaranteed by law until the early 1800's.

---

[2] Together, England, Scotland, and Wales are known as the United Kingdom. The country is also called Great Britain or Britain.

Point out that the American phase of the Seven Years' War was known as the French and Indian War.

Have students draw maps of the 13 colonies. This can serve as a review of American colonial history.

George I and George II relied upon Robert Walpole's expertise in finance and diplomacy. Thus, the power of the British monarchy declined in the early 1700's. What powers does the British prime minister have?

In 1760, George III, grandson of George II, became king at the age of 22. During his reign the British Empire was greatly expanded by its victory over France in the Seven Years' War. In North America, Britain gained Canada and all of France's territory east of the Mississippi River. But the cost of the war—and the ways in which George III and his ministers tried to deal with that cost—led to a rebellion in Britain's American colonies.

1. Identify: James I, William Laud, Petition of Right, Long Parliament, Oliver Cromwell, Levelers, "Nonconformists," Whigs, Act of Settlement, William of Orange, Robert Walpole.
2. What grievances did the Puritans have against Charles I?
3. Why did the English people rejoice when Charles II was restored to the throne?
4. How did parliamentary government develop after the Glorious Revolution?

2 Revolution in America

By the mid-1700's, Britain had 13 thriving colonies on the eastern coast of North America. By the end of the Seven Years' War in 1763, the population of the colonies had grown to over 1.5 million, most of whom were British. Thus, the people had a common language and a common political background.

In Britain, the ideas of the Levelers and other radical groups—ideas about universal suffrage, liberty, and equality—had died out. But some of these radicals had fled to America, and there the old ideas stayed alive. In the colonies there was no aristocracy. The hardships of life on the frontier and the easy availability of land tended to blur class divisions. Each colony had a representative assembly, and the colonists were used to governing themselves.

Navigation Acts

Except for regulating trade, the British government generally left the colonies alone. In the mercantilist view, the American colonies were valuable to Britain only to the extent that they benefited Britain's balance of trade. The role of the colonies was to produce goods—mostly raw materials—that could not be produced in Britain and to provide markets for British manufactured goods.

To ensure that the colonies fulfilled this role, Parliament in the 1600's passed a number of acts known as the Navigation Acts. These acts forbade the manufacture of certain goods in the colonies and listed certain colonial products that could be sold only to Britain.

New Policy

After the 1750's, Britain began to interfere more actively in the colonial economy. The French and Indian War had freed the colonists from the French threat, but it had left Britain in debt. Furthermore, the land won from France in Canada and in the area west of the Appalachian Mountains would have to be defended. It was estimated that 10,000 troops would be needed to guard it, at an expensive cost.

Britain used admiralty courts because juries in colonial
courts often acquitted smugglers.

The first step to solve these problems was
taken by George Grenville, whom George III
appointed First Lord of the Treasury in 1763.
Grenville issued a proclamation that said the
colonists could not, for the time being, settle in
the lands west of the Appalachians. This move,
he hoped, would avoid Indian wars until Britain
had the area under control and could gradually
open the land to settlers. But the colonists were
eager to move westward, and they did not
appreciate the attempt to stop them.

Next, Grenville decided that it was only fair for
the colonists to help pay the cost of their own
defense. Thus, he set about enforcing the
Navigation Acts. Customs officials were sent to
America to collect duties. Warships went along
to assist them. Smugglers were hunted down by
the navy and tried in admiralty courts—without
juries—instead of in colonial courts.

In 1765, under Grenville's leadership, Parliament passed the Stamp Act. This act said that
stamped paper, on which a tax had to be paid,
was to be used for all legal documents, newspapers, ships' papers, and advertisements. Next,
Parliament passed the Quartering Act, which
said that British troops could be billeted with the
colonists.

Colonial Protests

All of Grenville's measures were resented by
the colonists, but it was the Stamp Act that gave
them a common cause against the British
government. Nowhere could it be enforced.
Radicals opposing the act formed an organization known as the Sons of Liberty. Rioters
burned stamps and attacked stamp agents. Nine
colonies sent delegates to a Stamp Act Congress,
which issued a "Declaration of Rights and
Grievances" saying that Parliament did not have
the right to tax colonists.

Boston Tea Party   The Stamp Act was
repealed in 1766, but at the same time Parliament
passed a Declaratory Act. This act stated that
Parliament had the right to make laws for the
colonists. The next year new duties were placed
on glass, lead, paper, and tea, leading to
renewed protests in the colonies. Customs
agents in Boston called on Britain to send soldiers

*In protest against the Stamp Act, American colonists hung
British stamp agents upon posts, subjecting them to public
harassment. What did the Stamp Act require from the
colonists?*

to protect them. In March 1770, in a fight
between the soldiers and Bostonians, five Bostonians were killed.

After this incident, known in the colonies as
the Boston Massacre, Parliament repealed all
duties except the one on tea. For a time, the
colonists were contented. But in May 1773
Parliament passed a Tea Act that allowed the
East India Company, Britain's trading company,
to ship tea directly to American retailers. Because
the tea did not have to go through British and
American wholesalers, it could be sold at a lower
price. The measure was intended to help the
East India Company, which was close to
bankruptcy.

Raise the question, "Who benefited most from the Tea Act?" Point out that many of the people protesting British tax policies in the colonies were merchants and traders.

From Monarchy to Revolution · 355

Some teachers might wish to have a class reading and review of the entire Declaration.

American wholesale merchants were afraid that the East India Company would acquire a monopoly on the tea trade. They stirred the colonists to alarm. In Boston, colonists disguised as Indians dumped tea into the harbor.

This so-called Boston Tea Party was quickly punished by the British government. The port of Boston was closed, the governor's council was to be chosen by the king instead of by the Massachusetts assembly, and town meetings were forbidden except to elect town officers. A new Quartering Act allowed British troops once again to be stationed in Boston.

The Quebec Act was also passed. It was not intended to punish the colonists, but that is the way the colonists interpreted it. The act established a new government in Canada and annexed to Quebec the territory north of the Ohio River, thus closing the area to the colonists.

In the Declaration of Independence, the authors Benjamin Franklin, Thomas Jefferson, Roger Sherman, John Adams, and Robert Livingston listed grievances against George III. How did the Declaration reflect Enlightenment thought?

Continental Congress   The colonies reacted by calling the First Continental Congress. The Congress met in Philadelphia in the fall of 1774. It resolved that the "English colonists . . . are entitled to a free and exclusive power of legislation in their several provincial legislatures." In other words, only the colonial assemblies should have the right to make laws in the colonies. However, the Congress recognized Parliament's right to regulate trade.

Meanwhile, some colonists prepared for war. In the spring of 1775, the first skirmish took place at Lexington, Massachusetts, when the British tried to seize the colonists' firearms and ammunition. In response, the Second Continental Congress meeting in Philadelphia named George Washington commander in chief of the continental army.

Even at this point, many colonial leaders hoped to avoid a complete break with Britain. But extremists called for independence. In January 1776 the radical Thomas Paine published his pamphlet *Common Sense*. In highly emotional terms, he called on colonists to join the struggle for freedom: "Ye that dare oppose not only the tyranny but the tyrant, stand forth!" His words persuaded many moderates to the cause of independence.

Declaration of Independence

In June the Congress appointed a committee to prepare a declaration of independence. On the committee was Thomas Jefferson of Virginia, who wrote the first draft. Like many colonial leaders, he was familiar with the works of John Locke and the Enlightenment thinkers. Jefferson's declaration reflected the ideas of natural law and the social contract. He wrote:

> *We hold these truths to be self-evident, that all men are created equal, that they are endowed by their Creator with certain unalienable rights, that among these are life, liberty, and the pursuit of happiness. That to secure these rights, governments are instituted among men, deriving their just powers from the consent of the governed; that whenever any form of government becomes destructive of these ends, it is the right of the people to alter or abolish it . . .*

The map below is the subject of the "Using Maps" section of the Chapter 15 Review.

Have students write short biographies of the many notable people who lived during the time of the American Revolution.

The Congress adopted Jefferson's Declaration of Independence on July 4, 1776. A few days later, George Washington had it read to his troops to inspire them and give them hope.

The War of Independence

The War of Independence was long and bitter. Although the Americans did not have an army that could face the British in the open field, they had a skillful general in Washington. They also had help from the French in the form of arms and ammunition. The French were eager for an American victory, hoping to revenge the losses of the Seven Years' War. However, they did not actively join forces with the Americans until victory seemed certain.

The British had the disadvantage of trying to fight a long-distance war. Furthermore, they had to conquer the whole country to win. The Americans had only to hold out until Britain admitted defeat.

The turning point came in October 1777 with a British defeat at Saratoga. This American victory persuaded France to come in on the American side. Spain followed in 1779. Faced with a naval war against France and Spain, Britain became less interested in defeating its rebellious colonies. In August 1781, Britain's largest army was forced to surrender at Yorktown. For the Americans, the war was virtually over. Britain, however, continued to fight France and Spain for the next two years.

By the terms of the Treaty of Paris in September 1783, the United States was recognized as an independent nation. Spain regained Florida, which it had lost to Britain in the Seven Years' War. France won some West Indian islands, but was left with a huge debt.

A New Nation

The Americans now faced a task more difficult than winning a war: forming a stable government. Each of the colonies had already drafted a state constitution that gave most political power to a representative legislature. Between 1781 and 1787 the United States was a **confederation,**

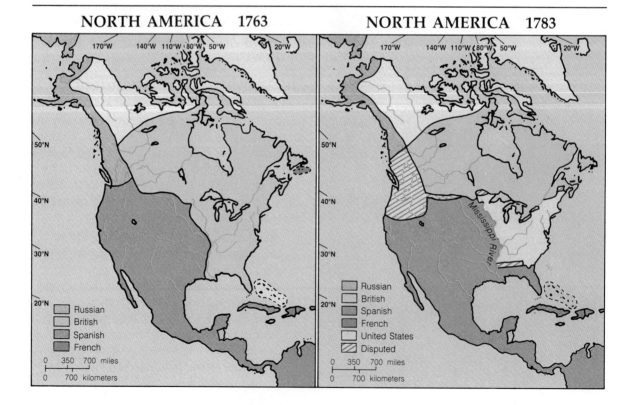

NORTH AMERICA 1763

- Russian
- British
- Spanish
- French

0   350   700 miles

0   700 kilometers

NORTH AMERICA 1783

- Russian
- British
- Spanish
- French
- United States
- Disputed

0   350   700 miles

0   700 kilometers

The Articles of Confederation provided for a confederacy to be known as The United States of America.

or league of independent states, under an agreement called the Articles of Confederation. The Confederation government was weak because it could not tax or regulate commerce.

These weaknesses led to calls for a stronger central government. In 1787 Congress called a convention to revise the Articles. At the convention, the delegates scrapped the Articles and wrote a new constitution.

The United States Constitution set up a **federal system,** or a government in which power is divided between a central and regional (state) governments. Following the recommendations in Montesquieu's *The Spirit of the Laws* (1748), political power was also divided among three branches of government—the executive, the legislative, and the judicial.

Under the new constitution, the United States was a republic. Elections were held in 1788, and George Washington became the first president of the United States. One of the first steps taken by Congress was the development of a Bill of Rights, which was added to the Constitution in the form of ten amendments. The Bill of Rights protected individual liberties such as freedom of religion, freedom of speech, and trial by jury. It also protected states' rights.

Significance of the Revolution

The success of the American Revolution proved to the world that Enlightenment ideas could actually work in practice. The Constitution of the United States was an example of a social contract—the division of powers among the branches of government, sovereignty of the people, and the protection of natural rights. The United States was idealized as a land of opportunity, and Europeans who hoped to achieve that ideal in their own countries looked to the example of the American Revolution.

1. Identify: Navigation Acts, George Grenville, Quebec Act, Thomas Paine, Saratoga, Yorktown, Articles of Confederation, Bill of Rights.
2. Why did Grenville decide to enforce the Navigation Acts?
3. What advantages did the Americans have in their war with Britain?
4. What kind of government was set up by the United States Constitution?

3 The French Revolution

The French watched the American Revolution closely. In France, absolute monarchy was at its height. But there were many who hoped for change. A traveler in France in 1787 described "a great ferment amongst all ranks of men, who are eager for some change, without knowing what to look for, or to hope for; and a strong leaven of liberty, increasing every hour since the American Revolution."

Unlike the American colonies, France had long been a nation with a strong central government. Indeed, France was the richest and possibly the most powerful state in Europe. All Europe looked to France for manners, literature, clothing styles, art, and ideas. Paris was the center of the Enlightenment. Yet, there were problems. Social inequalities imposed hardships on the masses. Expectations for change were rising, but they were not fulfilled.

Background of the Revolution

In France everyone belonged to one of three **estates,** or orders of society. The First Estate was the Catholic clergy; the Second Estate was the nobility; and the Third Estate was everyone else. The estates determined a person's legal rights and status in society. Estates were also political divisions. The Estates-General represented not individuals, but the collective interests of the estates. However, no Estates-General had been called since 1615.

The First Estate made up about 1 percent of the population. Bishops and abbots, though only a small part of this group, controlled between 5 and 10 percent of the land of France. Thus, they had at their disposal not only the **tithe,** or 10 percent of a believer's income, but also large revenues from their properties. Much of this money was used to support schools, poor people, church employees, and the upkeep of church property. The rest paid for the wealthy lifestyles of many bishops and abbots. The clergy were one of the chief targets of Voltaire, who repeatedly referred to the Church as *l'infame,* meaning "that infamous institution."

French kings had purposely weakened the Second Estate by requiring the nobility to spend much of each year away from their own land, attending the royal court in Versailles. Meanwhile, control of the provinces continued in the hands of intendants, the special agents of the Crown. After Louis XIV's death, the nobles once again began asserting their privileged position in the provinces. The nobility, like the clergy, did not have to pay taxes. Although they made up about 2 percent of the population, the nobles controlled about 20 percent of the land.

About 97 percent of the French population belonged to the Third Estate. This class was divided into three subgroups: the **bourgeoisie,** or middle class, artisans, and peasants. The bourgeoisie generally lived in the city and was made up of doctors, lawyers, merchants, and business managers. This group had been growing in numbers and strength. They made up about 5 percent of the population and were the most outspoken and well-to-do group of the Third Estate. They had read the writings of the Enlightenment and believed in freedom and social justice. They deeply resented the privileges of the nobles.

Thousands of artisans lived in the slums of Paris. They were employed in such places as the government-owned tapestry and carpet factories. They worked for low wages under poor conditions. These workers were often at the mercy of wage fluctuations.

The peasants were the largest group of non-nobles. They were better off than most European peasants, and owned about two-fifths of the land. However, they had to pay feudal dues, fees, and fines to the nobles, as well as the church tithe and the **taille,** a tax on land. In the 1700's, the nobles, facing an increasing cost of living, needed more money. Therefore, they put increased pressure on the peasants by collecting dues more diligently. The nobles also charged the peasants higher fees for using such things as their mills and wine presses.

Financial Crisis

By the time Louis XV came to the throne in 1715, there was a growing disillusionment on the part of all classes of society. This trend became particularly acute as the national debt reached crisis proportions.

The century had begun with debts from the wars of Louis XIV. The extravagant court of Louis XV further increased the debt. In the 1770's and 1780's the debt was doubled again by France's support of the American Revolution. At the end of his reign, even Louis XV recognized the depth of the crisis and exclaimed, *"Après moi le déluge!"* ("After me [comes] the flood!")

The new king, Louis XVI, recognized that he faced a serious crisis. Therefore, he appointed an able finance minister, Robert Turgot. Turgot curbed expenses at the palace, reduced internal customs duties, and pushed reform of the guilds. But his attempt to tax the nobles led to his dismissal in 1776. New taxes required the approval of the courts, which were in the hands of the leading aristocrats. The nobles were not prepared to vote taxes for themselves.

By 1786 no one would lend money to the government. When the privileged classes refused to aid the king, he made a bold choice. He

In France, peasants and other members of the Third Estate bore the costs and burden of the privileged classes. The wealthy felt the poor "should eat grass, like . . . horses." What fees and taxes did peasants pay?

Point out to students that the nobles of France unwittingly began the changes of the French Revolution by calling for a restoration of their feudal rights.

In an indoor tennis court at Versailles, members of the Third Estate and a few clergy and nobles pledged never to adjourn until they had given France a new constitution with the freedoms and representation that the French people demanded. How did the nobles' demands for change differ from those sought by the Third Estate?

summoned the Estates-General to meet in May 1789.

Immediately a debate began about the organization of the Estates-General. The nobles wanted some liberal reforms—constitutional government and freedom of speech and press—and some were even willing to give up their exemption from taxes. In return, however, they expected to control the government. For this reason they called for an Estates-General with three separate chambers. One would be for the nobles, one for the clergy, and one for the Third Estate. Each estate would have a single vote. In this way the upper estates could easily dominate the assembly.

Members of the Third Estate had something else in mind. They did not want to be governed by nobles. Claiming that they had more right to represent the French nation than either the clergy or the nobles, they called for a mass meeting of the three estates, with each delegate voting as an individual. Because the Third Estate was as large as the other two estates combined, this would give the Third Estate dominance. The case for the Third Estate was made by a member of the clergy, the Abbe Sieyès, in a pamphlet entitled *What Is the Third Estate?* He wrote:

Who then shall dare to say that the Third Estate has not within itself all that is necessary for the formation of a complete nation? It is the strong and robust man who has one arm still shackled. If the privileged order should be abolished, the nation would be nothing less, but something more. Therefore, what is the Third Estate? Everything; but an everything shackled and oppressed. What would it be without the privileged order? Everything; but an everything free and flourishing. Nothing can succeed without it, everything would be infinitely better without the others.*

National Assembly

When the king refused the Third Estate's request for a mass meeting, its delegates on June 17 declared themselves the National Assembly. They stated that they had the right to prepare a constitution for France. In response, the king's troops locked the delegates out of their meeting place. The delegates of the Third Estate, joined by reform-minded clergy and nobles, then met on a nearby tennis court.

At this point, on June 20, 1789, the delegates swore the Tennis Court Oath, agreeing to remain in session until a constitution was completed.

*"What Is To Be Done?," Abbe Sieyès as quoted in *Translations and Reprints from the Original Sources of European History*, vol. VI, by University of Pennsylvania Press, pp. 33-35.

The king now saw the danger of letting the Third Estate draw up a constitution alone. Therefore, he ordered all three estates to negotiate together in the National Assembly.

Discussions among the estates were heated. The upper clergy and nobility wanted to keep their privileges, while extremists of the Third Estate called for complete equality and the abolition of titles. All of this activity disturbed the king. He assembled his troops at Versailles, where the delegates were meeting.

Fall of the Bastille The people of Paris immediately suspected that Louis would try to disband the National Assembly. In addition, the people were angry about food shortages and high prices. Poor harvests had caused the price of bread to double. In protest, on July 14 a mob stormed the Bastille, a large prison in Paris where countless prisoners, even the writer Voltaire, had been locked up. When the cells were opened, however, only seven prisoners were found.

The storming of the Bastille gave the signal for other spontaneous uprisings in the provinces. Peasants broke into manor houses, robbed the granaries, destroyed feudal records that showed what they owed in dues, and drove out some of the landowners.

Declaration of Rights These events prompted the National Assembly to hasten its work. Seeing the threat of anarchy, the clergy and nobility joined with the Third Estate to produce significant reforms. Clearly the king would have to accept a constitutional monarchy. On the night of August 4, feudal dues and tithes were abolished. By the end of August, the Assembly had adopted the Declaration of the Rights of Man and Citizen.

Following the ideas of Locke, Montesquieu, and Rousseau, the Declaration stated that neglect of natural rights had caused public misfortune and the corruption of governments. It guaranteed freedom of speech, press, and religion. It also provided freedom from arbitrary arrest and punishment. The Declaration further declared that people are equal and that "social distinctions may be based only upon general usefulness."

March to Versailles After passing the Declaration, the National Assembly began the difficult task of writing a constitution. Meanwhile, it faced growing opposition from the royal court. Louis XVI refused to accept the decrees of August 4 and the Declaration of Rights. The people of Paris feared that the king would act against the revolution. Rumors of a crackdown stirred mobs to action. In October 1789 an angry crowd of women marched to Versailles and forced the king and the queen, Marie Antoinette, to return to Paris where they could be watched.

Soon the National Assembly also moved to Paris. Later this move was recognized as a mistake, because the delegates could now be subjected to pressure from the streets. Every day

In 1788 a harvest failure caused a 50 percent rise in the price of bread. Since people could buy fewer products, manufacturing declined. Nearly one-fourth of Parisians were out of work by the summer of 1789. By that fall, these intolerable conditions, as well as the fear of royal interference with the new National Assembly, caused 7,000 Parisian women to march on Versailles. What did the march accomplish?

The king did not really accept the acts of the Assembly. In June, 1791, he and his family tried to escape from France. They were recognized at Varennes and were brought back to Paris.

Many countries still had absolute monarchs. They distrusted the French revolutionary movement, fearing its spread to their territories.

the galleries were filled with unruly crowds, who booed and hissed when they disapproved of what the delegates were saying.

Constitution of 1791

During the next two years the Assembly made sweeping reforms. It kept the monarchy, but limited the powers of the king. It set up a **unicameral,** or one-house, legislature whose members were to be chosen by voters. Although equal rights were declared for all, only males who paid a minimum tax had the right to vote.

The National Assembly next seized lands belonging to the Catholic Church.[3] This action offended many devout Catholics. In 1790 the Assembly passed the Civil Constitution of the Clergy, placing all church affairs under state control and allowing the election of bishops and priests by the voters. As a result, Pope Pius VI condemned the revolution. The Assembly then required the clergy to take a loyalty oath. About half of them refused. There were now two churches in France—one loyal to the government, the other loyal to the Pope.

In September 1791 a constitution that included the assembly's reforms was proclaimed. Three months earlier, Louis XVI and Marie Antoinette had tried to flee France in disguise. Recognized at a road stop, the royal couple was arrested and returned to Paris. Louis then reluctantly accepted the new limited monarchy.

Many French people were not happy with the Constitution of 1791. For some, it went too far; for others, not far enough. Delegates were seated in the legislature according to their political beliefs. The royalists, who believed the revolution had gone too far, were seated on the right. Moderates, who favored the constitutional monarchy, sat in the middle. The radicals, who wanted to replace the monarchy with a republic, sat on the left.[4] The extreme radicals, demanding a "true democracy" in which all males could vote, were called Jacobins.

---

[3] Government debts were paid with special bank notes that could be used to buy church lands. Since the government owed money to the bourgeoisie, this class acquired most of the church properties sold.

[4] This seating arrangement is still followed today in many legislatures. From it comes the political terms "right," referring to conservatives, and "left," describing liberals.

War

News of the French Revolution spread to neighboring countries and unrest developed in the German states and the Austrian Empire. French **émigrés**, or nobles who left France, tried to convince these governments that they should overthrow the revolution if they wanted to remain in power. Meanwhile, French revolutionary leaders felt that a patriotic war would unite France behind its new government. In April 1792 the National Assembly declared war on Francis II, the Austrian emperor. Austria was soon supported by other monarchies, like Prussia and Sardinia.

The French army at first fought badly because most of the former officers had been nobles who had fled the country. As enemy forces approached Paris, however, the French army rallied around the cry of *"Liberté, Egalité, Fraternité!"* ("Liberty, Equality, Fraternity!") In September the German duke of Brunswick, who had threatened to burn Paris, was defeated at Valmy. The enemy advance was halted.

The Second Revolution

The war produced an unexpected turn of events in France. It gave the Jacobins a chance to rise in revolt. On August 10, 1792, even before the enemy was defeated, a mob and provincial troops took over the government of Paris and declared a new administration, the Commune. Next, the king and queen were threatened, causing them to flee to the Assembly for protection. But the radicals seized control of the Assembly, removed the king from office, and imprisoned the royal family. They killed over a thousand people whom they claimed were **counter-revolutionaries,** or enemies of the revolution. The radicals then called for a national convention to rewrite the constitution.

Execution of Louis XVI

The Convention, led by Jacobins, immediately abolished the monarchy and declared France a republic. When a trunk of secret letters indicated that Louis was plotting with émigrés to overthrow the revolution, the Convention convicted him of treason and sentenced him to death. The king was beheaded on January 21, 1793, by a machine called the guillotine.

HISTORY AND THE ARTS

Revolutionary Music

Revolutionaries frequently use music to spread their message. Revolutionary music has the ability to stir people to action. Like the charge played at football games, or a trumpeted cavalry charge, revolutionary music is inspirational. It helps individuals overcome fear and raises their emotions to a higher pitch, so that they may be united with a larger group. Sacrifice and commitment to a greater cause become easier.

During the American Revolution, the thoughts and emotions of the colonists were expressed in popular songs. Many of the songs were verses set to familiar tunes—often British tunes. Ballads were written describing the boycott of British tea, the siege of Boston, and every issue that aroused the colonists. Lyrics were hastily made up and quickly circulated on broadsides—single sheets of print that were used to spread news.

The first political music of the American Revolution was probably "The Liberty Song." It was written by John Dickinson, who said, "I have long renounced poetry, but, as different songs are very powerful on certain occasions, I venture to invoke the deserted muse [inspirer of music]." The Sons of Liberty adopted his words as their official song:

In Freedom we're born, and in Freedom we'll live,
Our purses are ready,
Steady, friends, steady
Not as slaves but as Freemen our money we'll give.*

The most famous and enduring of the American revolutionary songs was "Yankee Doodle." The British had used the term "yankee" as an insult. They sang "Yankee Doodle" as they marched to Lexington, to show their scorn for the American soldiers. But the colonists sang it back and made it a battle cry for freedom.

"The Marseillaise" was the song that called people to take part in the French Revolution. The music was composed by Claude Joseph Rouget de Lisle, a captain of the army engineers. It originally had a different title, but it came to be called "The Marseillaise" because it was sung by the troops from the city of Marseilles. In 1795 the song became the national anthem of France.

"The Marseillaise" was only one of many works of music inspired by the French Revolution. Nor was all of the music based on popular song. Beethoven began to write his Third Symphony, or Eroica, as a tribute to Napoleon. The composer, however, tore up the dedication page when Napoleon proclaimed himself emperor. Beethoven composed his only opera, *Fidelio*, as a joyous hymn to freedom. First produced in 1805, *Fidelio* tells of a woman's efforts to free her husband, who was a political prisoner in Spain.

Revolutionary groups and protest groups have continued to use music to arouse public opinion and to build support for their causes. During the 1800's, "The Internationale" became the revolutionary song of many workers around the world. In the United States, "We Shall Overcome" became a unifying force in the civil rights movement of the 1960's.

1. Why is revolutionary music powerful?
2. What are some examples of revolutionary music?

---

*All the Years of American Popular Music, David Ewen, © 1977 by Prentice-Hall, p. 12.

The Committee of Public Safety sent hundreds and hundreds of suspected counter-revolutionaries to the guillotine for execution.

The Reign of Terror has been the theme of many famous novels, including *A Tale of Two Cities* by Charles Dickens.

The reaction to Louis' execution was immediate. In March 1793, the Netherlands, Britain, and Spain joined in the fight against France. In France, meanwhile, many people were starving. Under such conditions, counter-revolutionaries emerged to plot against the Convention.

Reign of Terror   The Convention recognized the desperate situation and formed the Committee of Public Safety, an emergency government with the powers of a dictatorship. Maximilien Robespierre, a brilliant young Jacobin lawyer, became its head. He was a fanatical idealist who swayed audiences by his eloquence and his continual reference to a "Republic of Virtue." By this he meant a democratic republic made up of honest people and good citizens.

In order to stop the counter-revolutionaries, the Committee began what was known as the Reign of Terror. Revolutionary courts were set up that could try anyone who was suspected of being disloyal. Orders went out for the arrest of those who had "not constantly manifested [shown] their attachment to the Revolution."

About 500,000 people were arrested during the next year. Of these, as many as 40,000 were executed. Among the victims of the Reign of Terror were Marie Antoinette and a number of revolutionary leaders who disagreed with the Committee on matters of policy. Most of the victims—at least two-thirds—were peasants and workers.

Republic of Virtue   Meanwhile, the Committee went about setting up the "Republic of Virtue." Because Catholicism was seen as counter-revolutionary, a program was begun to do away with Christianity. Churches were closed or turned into "temples of reason." Later this policy was changed to allow worship of a Supreme Being. A new calendar did away with Sundays and church holidays, gave new names to the months of the year, and named the first year of the republic Year I.

All symbols associated with monarchy were rejected. Simple, classical styles were in fashion. Men wore working-class trousers instead of knee breeches. Women wore long dresses in the style of the Roman Republic. Natural hairstyles replaced wigs. People addressed each other as *citoyen* ("citizen") and *citoyenne* ("citizenness") rather than *monsieur* and *madame*.

Even playing cards were redesigned, with pictures of kings and queens replaced by pictures of workers and soldiers. But only one lasting change came about. This was the development of the metric system, a simplified system of weights and measures.

Mobilizing for War   The Committee of Public Safety also had to deal with the war. France faced invading armies on several fronts. To meet this threat, the Committee proclaimed a **levée en masse** ("mass mobilization"), which called on every man, woman, and child to aid in defeating the enemy. Soon France had the largest army in Europe—800,000 men in arms.

The Committee also prepared the French economy for war. It took control of food distribution and arms production. Price controls were put into effect to check inflation and help the poor. The war effort was successful, and by the end of 1793 the French had driven out their enemies. By the spring of 1794, France had taken the offensive.

End of the Terror   With the Republic out of danger, the Reign of Terror no longer seemed necessary. Some members of the Convention called for an end to the bloodshed. But Robespierre saw to it that they too were sent to the guillotine. Other members of the Convention, beginning to fear for their own safety, turned against Robespierre. On July 28, 1794, he went to the guillotine himself, along with a number of his followers.

After Robespierre's death, the Jacobins lost power and the Reign of Terror came to an end. A reaction against Jacobin ideas began, and the wealthier **bourgeois,** or members of the bourgeoisie, took control of the Convention. Even royalists came out of hiding. Fashions changed as people rebelled against the "Republic of Virtue." Once again, people wore knee breeches, luxurious dresses, and wigs. Many Catholic churches reopened. Price controls were relaxed; and prices rose sharply, causing hardship for the poor. Riots broke out, but the leaderless lower classes were easily put down by the army.

In 1796, Napoleon married Josephine de Beauharnais, a wealthy Creole from the West Indies. Her first husband had been killed during the Reign of Terror.

The Directory Although the wealthier bourgeois were more conservative than the Jacobins, they did believe in a written constitution. In 1795 the Convention put into effect a new one called the Constitution of the Year III. It was a constitution that gave the middle and upper classes control of the government. Only those who paid taxes or who had served at the front could vote. The voters chose electors, who had to be well-to-do property owners. The electors then chose members of a legislative assembly, which in turn selected five men who made up the executive body, called the Directory.

The Directory faced enormous problems. It was surrounded by enemies—royalists on one side, radicals on the other. The French economy was in chaos. The treasury was empty, and inflation was out of control. The inability of the Directory to solve these problems made it increasingly unpopular.

Rise of Napoleon Meanwhile, France was still at war with Austria, Sardinia, and Britain.[5] In 1796 command of the French army in Italy was given to a young general, Napoleon Bonaparte. Napoleon soon defeated the Austrian and Sardinian armies. When he returned to Paris, he received a hero's welcome. Next, Napoleon decided to strike at the British by attacking their forces in Egypt. This action, he hoped, would cut off Britain's trade with India.

Alarmed by Napoleon's invasion of Egypt, the European powers formed a new alliance against France. A new war began, and the French suffered defeats in both Germany and Italy. These losses led to increased dissatisfaction with the Directory. The Directory soon faced the threat of a **coup d'etat,** or sudden use of force by a small group to overthrow a government.

1. Identify: Third Estate, Robert Turgot, Abbe Sieyès, Tennis Court Oath, Bastille, Jacobins, Maximilien Robespierre, the Directory.
2. Why did Louis XVI call a meeting of the Estates-General?
3. What reforms were made by the National Assembly?
4. Why was the Reign of Terror instituted?

---

[5] Peace had been made with the Dutch Netherlands, Prussia, and Spain before the creation of the Directory.

4   The Napoleonic Revolution

Napoleon Bonaparte, the son of an aristocratic Corsican family, became a French subject when Corsica was acquired by France in 1768. After attending a military school in Paris, he received his first commission at the age of 16. Brilliant and ambitious, he always seemed to have a sense of his destiny.

Overthrow of the Directory

Napoleon once quipped, "I found the crown of France lying on the ground and I picked it up with a sword." When he heard of the Directory's troubles, Napoleon decided that the time was ripe for him to act. Leaving his army in Egypt, he returned to Paris and offered his help to those seeking to overthrow the Directory.

After a successful coup d'etat in 1799, another new constitution, the Constitution of the Year VII, was written. It set up a new government that

---

This unfinished portrait of the young Napoleon suggests his intelligence and determination. French army life inflamed his ambition; by age 28 he was a national hero. For what accomplishment did Napoleon earn his first fame?

In 1802, Napoleon founded the Legion of Honor, a medal to honor soldiers and civilians who had made contributions to France. The Legion of Honor is still France's highest award.

From Monarchy to Revolution · **365**

was actually a dictatorship, although it called itself a republic. The executive branch was a committee of three members, called consuls. Napoleon was named First Consul for ten years. He became the most powerful person in France.

Domestic Policy

One of Napoleon's chief concerns was to bring order to the country. Ever since the beginning of the revolution, bands of robbers had roamed the land, attacking travelers and raiding villages. In a few months, Napoleon's soldiers wiped out most of these bands. Another problem was a royalist rebellion in western France, which Napoleon soon suppressed.

Religious Reform   Napoleon also made peace with the Catholic Church. Realizing that many French people were strongly against the Civil Constitution of the Clergy, he began to negotiate with Pope Pius VI. In an agreement called the Concordat of 1801, freedom of religion was given to all French Catholics. Napoleon retained the right to name all bishops, and they had to swear allegiance to the state. The Pope agreed to accept the loss of church lands and gave up the right to ask for tithes. In return, the state agreed to pay salaries to the Catholic clergy. Napoleon also paid the salaries of Protestant ministers, to make sure that no one thought that Catholicism was the state religion.

Thus, Napoleon was able to get the backing of French Catholics and the Pope. At the same time, he kept the Church under the control of the state. "With the aid of Catholicism," he said, "I should easily attain all my great results."

Napoleonic Code   One of Napoleon's most important achievements was putting a new law code into effect. The old feudal and royal laws were often confusing and contradictory. As a youth, Napoleon had studied and admired Enlightenment thinkers. He wanted to rewrite the laws on the basis of reason and natural law.

The Napoleonic Code made the law clear and consistent. It preserved some reforms of the revolution, such as making all men equal before the law. The rights of women, however, were reduced. Freedoms of speech and press were also curtailed.

Other Reforms   Many other reforms were made. Education was placed under the control of the national government. Secondary schools called **lycées** were set up; and plans were made for a public school system, to be financed by taxes. Taxes were collected by professional tax collectors, and there were no exemptions. A national bank was established to receive the taxes and to make loans to businesses. Gradually, it brought inflation under control.

Napoleon's strong government and the accomplishment of peace and order made him well loved even though he was a dictator. In 1802 voters approved when he named himself First Consul for life. They approved again when he became Emperor of the French in 1804.

Napoleon's Empire

Although Napoleon proved that he was an able administrator, he was more interested in building an empire. Soon after becoming First Consul, Napoleon defeated both Italy and Austria. He also persuaded Russia to withdraw from the war. Though Napoleon was not able to defeat the British navy, the British were ready for peace because their commerce had suffered during the war. The two powers signed the Treaty of Amiens in March 1802.

Third Coalition   The peace lasted little more than a year. The British were angry because Napoleon had put a high tariff on British goods. They became alarmed by Napoleon's obvious appetite for conquests. In May 1803 England declared war on France once again.

During the next two years, William Pitt, the British prime minister, put together another alliance against France. It was the third such attempt since 1792. Britain, Austria, Russia, and Sweden were allied against France and Spain. But the allies were unable to halt Napoleon's advance.

Within a few years, Napoleon had expanded his empire to include much of Europe. He became king of Italy, his brother Joseph became king of Naples and Sicily, and his brother Louis became king of Holland. The Holy Roman Empire came to an end. In its place Napoleon created the Confederation of the Rhine, a loose

EUROPE AT HEIGHT OF NAPOLEON'S POWER 1812

organization of the German states, and made himself its "Protector." This led Prussia to declare war on France, but the French easily crushed the Prussian army.

After the Prussian defeat, Tsar Alexander I of Russia decided to negotiate with Napoleon, and Russia became an ally of France against Britain. Meanwhile, the British navy under Admiral Horatio Nelson had inflicted a stunning defeat on the French and Spanish fleets in the Battle of Trafalgar in October 1805. As a result, it seemed impossible for Napoleon to invade England. Therefore, he turned to economic warfare.

Continental System   Napoleon's plan, called the Continental System, was to destroy British trade by shutting British goods and shipping out of all European ports. He issued the Berlin Decree, forbidding imports of British

goods in all the ports of Europe he controlled. He also required Russia and Prussia to go along with the blockade. When Portugal refused to agree to it, Napoleon attacked the country. Spain, France's ally, also refused to support the Continental System. In order to control Spanish ports, Napoleon forced out the Spanish king and made his brother Joseph king of Spain.

At this point Napoleon's fortune began to turn. With British help, the Spaniards and Portuguese both were able to force out the French. Meanwhile, Britain had responded to the trade blockade with a counter threat: any ship on its way to a continental port had to stop first at a British port. Napoleon responded that he would seize any ship that did so.

This economic warfare led the British into a conflict with the neutral United States known as

Point out that the retreat from Russia proved to be the beginning of the end for Napoleon. The French leader's reputation as a military genius suffered, and opposition emerged in countries that had been under his rule.

the War of 1812. It was France that suffered the most, because Britain was able to increase its trade with non-European countries. British control of the seas meant decreased trade for continental ports and increased costs for shipping goods overland.

Russia's trade was being hurt as well. By 1812 Alexander I felt strong enough to defy the Continental System. Napoleon had to subdue Russia or other countries might also rebel.

Invasion of Russia   The long French march on Russia began in May 1812. The Russians refused to yield to Napoleon's threat. Burning everything as they went, the Russians retreated into the interior and allowed the French forces to capture Moscow in September.

The day after the French entered Moscow, a giant fire, probably started by Russian patriots, destroyed most of the city. Winter was coming, and the French army could not stay in Russia without shelter. But Napoleon delayed too long before ordering a retreat. The terrible Russian winter caught him and his troops on the borders in late November. The Russians then relentlessly attacked the disorderly French troops. The retreat became a rout. About four-fifths of Napoleon's army—500,000 men—died or were captured before the army reached Prussia. Prussians and Russians followed the retreat toward France and were joined by Austria and Sweden. Meanwhile, Britain was pushing into France from Spain.

Napoleon's Defeat   Napoleon raised a mixed army of young and old to meet the invaders. He tried to strike his enemies separately as before. But Napoleon was no longer able to outfight them. The allied armies defeated Napoleon at Leipzig, Germany, in October 1813. By March 1814 the allies were in Paris.

The victors restored the French throne to a member of the Bourbon family, the brother of Louis XVI. Napoleon was exiled to Elba, an island off the coast of Italy. The boundaries of France were reduced to those of 1792.

The Hundred Days   After thousands of young French soldiers had died all over Europe, it seems strange that many French people wanted Napoleon to make a comeback. Yet Napoleon appealed to their desire for order and national greatness. On March 1, 1815, Napoleon returned to France and won widespread support. The troops of the restored Bourbon king, Louis XVIII, deserted to their former commander. Napoleon took Paris by storm on March 20. He remained in power for 100 days.

Because he wanted to avoid war, Napoleon announced that France wanted no more territory. But the European governments were terrified that Napoleon might regain his former strength. Immediately Prussia, Britain, and the Netherlands, under the command of the duke of Wellington, advanced toward France. Napoleon met them at Waterloo in the Austrian Netherlands in June 1815. The French were decisively defeated. Napoleon was then placed under house arrest on the island of St. Helena in the South Atlantic. He died there in 1821.

Napoleon's Legacy

It is impossible to separate Napoleon's impact from that of the French Revolution. When he came to power, he promised to make the changes of the revolution secure, and he spread revolutionary reforms throughout Europe. On the countries he controlled, Napoleon imposed his code of law, including the principles of equality before the law and religious freedom. The Catholic Church lost its political influence, church lands were taken, and tithes were ended. There was one principle of the revolution, however, that Napoleon did not follow. He did not allow true representative government.

Although Napoleon's empire collapsed, many Europeans wanted to keep the benefits of the French Revolution. They did not forget their taste of freedom from absolute monarchy. Monarchs, nobles, and clergy were not strong enough to restore things to the way they had been before 1789.

1. Identify: Concordat of 1801, Napoleonic Code, Treaty of Amiens, William Pitt, Confederation of the Rhine, Alexander I, Horatio Nelson, Continental System, Elba, Waterloo.
2. Why was Napoleon unable to defeat Britain?
3. Why was the invasion of Russia a disaster for Napoleon?

CHAPTER 15 REVIEW

Summary

1. During the 1600's and 1700's, forces were building to bring an end to the age of absolute monarchy.
2. In England, James I and Charles I aroused the enmity of Parliament by trying to rule as absolute monarchs.
3. In 1642 a civil war broke out between Charles I and Parliament. The king was executed and the Protestant general Oliver Cromwell seized power from Parliament.
4. After Cromwell's death, the monarchy and Parliament were restored, but with more limits on the monarch's power.
5. Both Charles II and James II quarreled with Parliament over religion. In 1688 William and Mary were invited to take the throne. During the next several decades, England developed a parliamentary government.
6. After the Seven Years' War, Parliament began taxing England's American colonies to help pay for the colonists' defense. The colonies rebelled and declared their independence in 1776.
7. After winning its War of Independence, the colonies became the United States and set up a republican government under a written constitution.
8. The Constitution of the United States reflected Enlightenment ideas and inspired Europeans who wanted republican governments of their own.
9. In 1789 a financial crisis forced Louis XVI to call the Estates-General, opening the way for constitutional reform and revolution in France.
10. In 1792 radicals overthrew the revolutionary government and instituted the Reign of Terror. Two years later, the wealthier bourgeois regained control of the government, but they were unable to solve France's military and economic problems.
11. In 1799 the government was overthrown by the general Napoleon Bonaparte, who later became the ruler of France. Napoleon's military conquests created a French empire and spread reforms throughout Europe.
12. After Napoleon was defeated in 1814, the French throne was restored and the boundaries of France were reduced to what they had been before the revolution.

Building Vocabulary

divine right of kings
writs of habeas corpus
billet
royalist
universal manhood suffrage
constitutional monarchy
cabinet
prime minister

parliamentary government
confederation
federal system
estates
tithe
bourgeoisie

taille
unicameral
émigrés
counter-revolutionaries
levée en masse
bourgeois
coup d'etat
lycées

Reviewing the Main Ideas

1. What were some of the conflicts between James I and Parliament?
2. What were the results of the English Civil War?

3. How did Parliament limit the powers of the king after the Glorious Revolution?
4. Why did Britain begin to interfere with the colonial economy after the Seven Years' War?
5. What events led to the Boston Tea Party?
6. How did the beliefs and experiences of the American colonists contribute to their desire for independence?

7. What were the results of the war between the American colonists and the British?
8. How did the American Revolution affect the French Revolution?
9. What role did the bourgeoisie play in the French Revolution?
10. What were the weaknesses of the Directory?
11. How did Napoleon spread the ideas of the French Revolution?

Discussing Important Ideas

1. What were the virtues, if any, of absolute monarchies? What were the defects of absolute monarchies?
2. How did religious issues affect the conflict between Parliament and the Crown in England?
3. How was the influence of the Enlightenment reflected in the American Revolution and the French Revolution?
4. Was it unfair of the British government to tax the American colonists? Why or why not?

5. Why did the American Revolution lead to a stable government, whereas the English Civil War and the French Revolution did not?
6. How did class structure affect the English Civil War? the French Revolution?
7. Can liberal reforms be made without a violent revolution? Why or why not?
8. What similarities and differences do you see in the Glorious Revolution, the American Revolution, and the French Revolution?

Using Maps

Refer to the maps on page 356 to answer the following questions:
1. What do the maps illustrate?
2. What is the most significant difference between them?

3. Which countries gained land in North America between 1763 and 1783? Which lost land?
4. Which nations in 1763 occupied territory that today is part of the United States? in 1783?

CHAPTER 16

Paris Uprising, 1848

66 *Now peace returns comforting us,*
And our minds return faithfully to the old,
To build up, what strife and passage of
    armies destroyed,
To secure, what a good spirit has preserved. 99

Johann Wolfgang von Goethe, German poet and dramatist (1749-1832)

Reform
and
Reaction

Some teachers might wish to compare the Congress of Vienna with recent gatherings of leaders of the world's industrial, communist, or nonaligned nations.

European political affairs immediately after the defeat of Napoleon were generally harmonious. The five leading powers were Austria, Britain, Prussia, Russia, and France. They agreed that little good had been accomplished by the long struggle with Napoleon. They were determined to avoid future wars by maintaining the balance of power.

In 1814 and 1815, the nations of Europe met in Vienna to restore peace and stability to their continent. The settlements of this peace conference revealed the importance given to international cooperation and avoidance of conflict. Delegates at the conference aimed at suppressing two powerful forces released in Europe by the French Revolution. These forces were **nationalism,** the demand by national groups for independent states of their own, and **liberalism,** the desire to change governments on the basis of democratic ideals.

By the mid-1800's, clashes had developed throughout Europe between conservatives and liberals. Conservatives wanted to limit the effects of the French Revolution, while liberals wanted to extend them. Instead of peace, Europe entered a new era of revolution and disorder. The spirit of European cooperation broke down, replaced by suspicion and rivalry.

1 Restoring Peace and Stability

In the fall of 1814, diplomats from all over Europe gathered in Vienna for a peace conference known as the Congress of Vienna. Their goal was to restore the old order of Europe after more than 20 years of war. Most of the diplomats were conservative aristocrats. They believed that Europe would have peace only if it returned to the traditions of strong royal government that had existed before the French Revolution. Therefore, the boundaries of European states were drawn up to reflect the wishes of the rulers rather than those of the people they governed. To protect the settlements reached at the Congress, the diplomats created alliances among the powerful European states.

Congress of Vienna

The five great powers of Europe dominated the Congress of Vienna, which lasted for nearly eight months. Delegations from the great powers included some of the most famous diplomatic leaders of the nineteenth century. The chief British delegate was Foreign Secretary Viscount Castlereagh. King Frederick William III and Prince Karl von Hardenberg headed the Prussian delegation. Tsar Alexander I and Count Karl Robert Nesselrode represented Russia. Charles Maurice de Talleyrand decided matters for France. Clemens Prince von Metternich, chief among all the delegates, represented Austria.

Metternich served as host to the conference and presided over it. More than any other delegate, Metternich was able to influence the outcome of the Congress. He made sure that the settlements reached at Vienna were guided by the three principles: compensation, legitimacy, and balance of power.

The great powers excused France from making financial payments to them for the costly wars against Napoleon. However, they did expect some **compensation,** or payment, in the form of territory. Britain, for example, was permitted to retain areas that it had seized during the wars.

371

Louis XVIII came to the French throne in 1814. But in 1815 he was forced to flee Paris when Napoleon suddenly returned to France from exile in Elba.

Discontent with the Bourbon restoration enabled Napoleon to win popular support. The Congress supported legitimate, not popular, rule.

These included strategic outposts in the North Sea, Mediterranean Sea, Caribbean Sea, South Africa, and South Asia. As part of the settlement at Vienna, Austria gained the rich Italian provinces of Lombardy and Venetia as well as territory on the eastern coast of the Adriatic Sea.

At the conference, Prussia and Russia made it known that they wanted to expand their borders. Neither Britain nor Austria was happy about this situation. Both feared that increased Prussian and Russian influence in central Europe would lead to an imbalance of population and resources among the great powers on the continent. To put pressure on Prussia and Russia, Britain and Austria concluded an agreement with France. The agreement bound the three powers to resist Prussian or Russian territorial expansion by armed force if necessary. In the end, a compromise was reached. Prussia was given extensive territories along the Rhine River and almost half of the kingdom of Saxony for its compensation. Russia received most of the Polish territory formerly held by Prussia and Austria. This added to the Polish territory already held by Russia. A new kingdom of Poland was then formed under the rule of the tsar.

Once the crisis over territorial compensation was settled, delegates at the Congress of Vienna turned their attention to stabilizing European governments. Believing that divine-right monarchy was necessary for proper order, the delegates sought to restore the absolute monarchs who ruled Europe before Napoleon. The Congress reestablished royal dynasties in France, Spain, Portugal, Sardinia, Naples, and Sicily. In France, the Congress officially recognized the Bourbon heir Louis XVIII as the **legitimate,** or legal, ruler.

To safeguard other ruling dynasties, the Congress placed further controls on the French. It reduced France to the borders that it had held in 1790. **Buffer,** or neutral, states were established around French territory. To the north of France, the Austrian Netherlands and the Dutch Netherlands became a single country under the Dutch ruler. Thirty-nine independent German states formed the German Confederation headed by Austria. Switzerland regained its neutrality and independence as a federal league of states. The Italian kingdom of Piedmont united with the Mediterranean island of Sardinia.

Possibly the greatest accomplishment of the Congress of Vienna was that it reestablished a balance of power among the great nations of Europe. That is, the arrangements made at Vienna prohibited any one state from being allowed to increase its possessions without the consent of the others. In doing so, the conference

As host to the Congress of Vienna, Francis I of Austria was obliged to entertain a horde of royal consorts, family members, ladies-in-waiting, and delegate aides. Plays, musicals, and balls helped to make Vienna the center of European society at that time. Who was the chief delegate of each of the five major powers in attendance?

Have students compare the map below with the map of Europe at the height of Napoleon's power. It appears on p. 366.

The map below is the subject of the "Using Maps" section of the Chapter 16 Review.

EUROPE AFTER CONGRESS OF VIENNA 1815

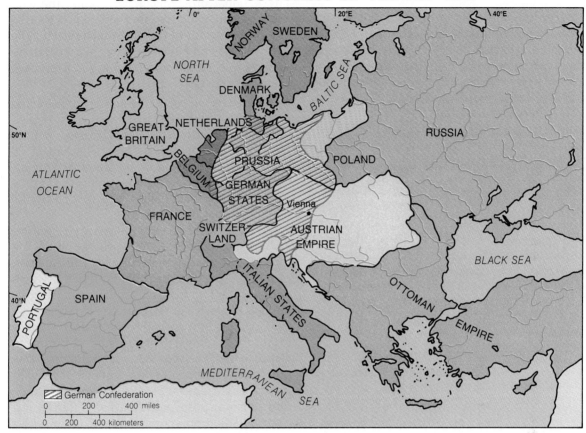

German Confederation

0   200   400 miles

0   200   400 kilometers

offended none of the great powers and tried to avoid any problems that would lead to war.

Two Alliances

Determined to protect the settlements made at Vienna, the great powers signed two additional agreements. These were the Holy Alliance and the Quadruple Alliance.

Holy Alliance   Tsar Alexander I of Russia conceived the Holy Alliance as an attempt to establish international order based on the principles of "Justice, Christian Charity, and Peace." Issued in the name of the tsar, the king of Prussia, and the emperor of Austria, all Christian rulers in Europe were asked to pledge cooperation as a Christian union of monarchs.[1]

Metternich dismissed the idea as "a loud-sounding nothing." Nevertheless, all the invited rulers joined the Holy Alliance except Pope Pius VII and the future king George IV of Britain, then acting as prince regent. The Pope had commented that "from time immemorial the papacy had been in possession of Christian truth and needed no new interpretation of it." The future British king excused himself on the ground that his signature on such an alliance would be in violation of the British constitution if it did not have the approval of Parliament.

Quadruple Alliance   The Quadruple Alliance represented the more substantial diplomatic agreement of the two. By it, Britain, Austria, Prussia, and Russia joined together to maintain the settlements of Vienna. The four powers concluded the alliance in November 1815. France was admitted three years later, when the

_____

[1]The only European ruler not invited to join the Holy Alliance was Mahmud II, the sultan of the Ottoman Empire. He was a follower of Islam.

Have students consider the possibilities of the congress system working in the world today.

members of the alliance met for the first time at Aix-la-Chapelle.

According to the alliance agreement, representatives of the great powers were to meet periodically to discuss the security of Europe. Their special concerns were the preservation of territorial boundaries set at Vienna, the exclusion of Napoleon Bonaparte and his heirs from French rule, and the prevention of any revolutionary movements from taking hold in Europe. The major role of the alliance was the establishment of policies for maintaining the **status quo** in Europe or, maintaining the existing state of political affairs in Europe.

The Congress System

During most of the mid-1800's, the great powers met "for the purpose of consulting upon their common interest and for the consideration of the measures most salutary for the maintenance of the peace of Europe." By doing this,

To make the agreements reached at the Congress of Vienna long lasting, Prince von Metternich pushed for the creation of the Quadruple Alliance. What countries made up the Alliance, and what was its major role?

they introduced a new system for settling international problems. It was called the **congress system,** which became better known as the Concert of Europe or the Metternich system. The congress was an advisory body, not a decision-making one, made up of representatives from the great powers.

Metternich   Just as Metternich of Austria had dominated the negotiations at the Congress of Vienna, he also dominated European politics through the congress system. For almost 30 years, Metternich used the system to achieve his own political goals. These were to oppose liberalism and nationalism and to defend the political status quo in Europe.

Metternich had become his country's minister of foreign affairs in 1809 at the age of 36. He remained in that post until 1848. The Austrian prince possessed a great political talent, which permitted him to have a long diplomatic career. He had a particular genius for reconciling the conflicting interests of particular nations in order to gain peace and stability for general European interests. He was very vain and pompous. This often led to difficulties in his relations with Austrian citizens. "In 1848," French Prime Minister François Guizot related, "during our common sojourn in London he said to me with a half smile which seemed to excuse his words in advance: "Error has never approached my spirit."

Challenges to the Congress   The political goals of Metternich and his Concert of Europe did not go unchallenged. The first major challenge appeared in Germany, where university students demonstrated for liberal reforms and national unity. Metternich, who was alarmed by this revolutionary activity, convinced King Frederick William III of Prussia to pass a series of repressive measures in 1819. These so-called Carlsbad Decrees imposed strict censorship on all publications and suppressed freedom of speech. Metternich, through the Prussian king, managed to end student agitation in Germany, but new challenges to the status quo arose in other areas.

Early in 1820, the great powers faced their most serious problem—a revolt against the

Have students keep in mind as they read section 2 the importance of *1848* in the era of revolutions.

government in Spain. In January, reformers forced the Bourbon king of Spain, Ferdinand VII, to accept a liberal constitution. As news of that revolt spread, reformers in Naples attempted to force their own Bourbon king, Ferdinand I, to accept a similar constitution in July. By October, Metternich called a meeting of the great powers to discuss responses to the uprisings. At Troppau, Metternich, Tsar Alexander I, and the Prussian representative drew up a statement asserting that they would never recognize the right of a people to revolt against their ruler. At successive meetings in the following years, Austria, Russia, and Prussia decided to enforce the so-called Troppau Protocol by intervening in Spain and Naples to prevent the spread of liberalism. In 1821 Austrian troops marched into Naples to restore the monarchy. In 1823 French forces aided the king of Spain. Because it opposed armed intervention in these countries, Britain withdrew from the congress system. It developed its own foreign policy.

Meanwhile, as royal authority was reestablished in Spain and Naples, the American colonies of both Spain and Portugal were in revolt. Also, the Greek people began fighting for independence. It was in Greece that nationalism won its first triumph during the years of the Concert of Europe.

Greece had been subject to Ottoman rule since the capture of Constantinople in 1453. In 1821, Greek nationalists revolted. In 1825, Tsar Nicholas I, upon succeeding his brother, Alexander I, was joined by Britain and France in supporting the Greek cause. Four years later, after a show of military force by the European powers at Adrianople, the Ottoman Empire sued for peace and recognized Greek independence.

The Greek war for independence was followed in 1830 by revolts in other European countries. In the former Austrian Netherlands, a national uprising against the Dutch led to the creation of a new nation known as Belgium. In Poland, a liberal revolution was successfully crushed by the Russian tsar.

1. Identify: Clemens Prince von Metternich, German Confederation, Concert of Europe, Carlsbad Decrees, Troppau Protocol.

2. Which nations dominated the negotiations at the Congress of Vienna? What leaders represented each of these nations?

3. What was the major accomplishment of the Congress of Vienna?

4. What was the purpose of the Holy Alliance? the Quadruple Alliance?

2 A New Era of Revolutions

The success of the Greek war for independence strengthened the hopes of many liberals and patriots throughout Europe. A series of revolutions, beginning in 1830 in Belgium and Poland, seemed to illustrate that the ideals of the French Revolution continued to inspire a desire for reform. In France, Austria, Italy, and Prussia, liberal reformers attempted to upset the status quo created at the Congress of Vienna.

Revolt in France

With the Congress of Vienna, Louis XVIII was returned to the throne of France. Time appeared to have been turned backward with the restoration of the Bourbon monarchy. In 1830 and 1848, however, middle-class liberals and workers joined forces to attack the return of the old order and to establish their own right to political authority.

July Revolution During his reign, Louis XVIII sought a compromise between monarchists and republicans. Although he did speak of himself as king "by the grace of God," Louis XVIII accepted the French constitution of 1814. He also granted a Charter of Liberties, guaranteeing equality before the law and individual liberties. But the Charter also affirmed that "all authority in France rests in the king."

In general, the constitutional monarchy of France was acceptable to a majority of the people. That was until the return of the extremely conservative émigrés. This group of aristocrats, who had fled during the Revolution of 1789, returned to France in hopes of ignoring the accomplishments of the revolutionary era. It was their desire to reestablish the old order in all its phases. These **ultraroyalists,** so called be-

Louis Philippe also called himself the Citizen King. Although his heart was not with them, he felt that his policies were directed toward the middle class instead of the nobility.

The return of Louis XVIII to Paris was met with jubilation by many people. During his reign, Louis succeeded in maintaining peace and prosperity while paying off the country's war debts and freeing France of armies of occupation. He was, however, never a popular figure because of the peoples' fear of ultraroyalists. Who were the ultraroyalists?

cause they were more conservative than Louis XVIII, were led in their efforts by the king's brother. Upon the death of Louis XVIII in 1824, his brother succeeded him as Charles X.

Charles X eagerly set out to restore absolute royal authority by proposing extremely conservative measures to the French legislature. Supported by the clergy and the aristocracy, he introduced bills such as one to give émigrés compensation for property lost during the Revolution, and another to restrict individual liberties of citizens. But opposition to these measures was great in the legislative assembly.

Charles X reacted to the opposition by dissolving the legislature and calling for new elections in 1830. Angry voters, however, returned a decisive majority of liberals to the legislature. Unable to control the country's lawmakers, the king issued the July Ordinances. This proclamation dissolved the newly elected legislature, restricted voting rights, and established strict censorship of the press.

On July 28, 1830, Paris mobs protested the ordinances, starting a national uprising. Workers, students, artisans, and merchants took to the streets as they had done in 1789. When several regiments of the king's soldiers deserted to the rioters, Charles X **abdicated,** or gave up his right to govern, and fled to Britain.

The July Revolution ended with the establishment of a new constitutional monarchy. Louis Philippe, duke of Orleans and a cousin of Charles X, succeeded to the throne. The new monarch was acceptable to middle-class liberals, although many of them had preferred the creation of a republic. They feared, however, that if France became a republic, the great powers of Europe might intervene to restore the Bourbon monarchy. Because the new French king had the support of the middle class, he became known as the Citizen-King.

Revolution of 1848   During the period from 1830 to 1848, many French people experienced a growing discontent with Louis Philippe's government. At heart, the Citizen-King favored the wealthy, and many middle-class citizens demanded further reforms beyond those established after the July Revolution.

In general, opposition to the government of Louis Philippe was led by two groups, the republicans and the socialists. Both groups demanded an extension of voting rights. Republicans regarded this as a means for establishing a French republic. Socialists regarded this as a step toward a wider political and economic reorganization. According to socialist reformers such as Louis Blanc, the political and economic ideas of **socialism** would end private ownership of

Point out that Paris and Vienna were very much alike as the two greatest cities in Europe.

property. A socialist government, argued Blanc, would represent society as a whole rather than the special interests of private individuals.

In 1847, Louis Philippe boldly stated, "There will be no reform; I do not wish it. If the deputies vote for it, . . . my veto still remains." That year, republicans and socialists joined with liberal monarchists in a campaign for voting rights and against the government of Louis Philippe. To gain popular support, opposition organizers planned numerous public banquets. At these banquets, opposition speakers presented their ideas for reform.

Trouble came in 1848, when Prime Minister François Guizot canceled a banquet and parade scheduled for Paris. Guizot feared that the Paris banquet would lead to a disorderly demonstration. But the cancellation order came too late. On February 22, great crowds poured into the streets of Paris anyway. Many sang "The Marseillaise" and shouted protests against Guizot.

To restore order, Louis Philippe called out a middle-class military group known as the National Guard. But it was in sympathy with the demonstrators. On February 28, the National Guard joined in fighting the regular French army. Over the next few days, fighting resulted in the death or wounding of at least 52 civilians. Louis Philippe dismissed Guizot. Then, under public pressure, the Citizen-King himself abdicated. The Revolution of 1848 came to an end with the rebels proclaiming France a republic.

Other Uprisings

Inspired by events in France, reformers in many parts of Europe fought against their absolutist governments. Political discontent in Austria, Italy, and Prussia was particularly significant in the changing political climate on the continent. In these areas, however, the status quo was more or less maintained.

Revolution in Austria　News of the February Revolution of France sparked riots in the streets of Vienna. In March 1848, university students, workers, and middle-class artisans and merchants demanded a constitution, the removal of Metternich, and the end to absolutist rule in the Austrian Empire.

Banners throughout Vienna proclaimed, "In a month Prince Metternich will be overthrown! Long live constitutional Austria!" Public opinion and private pressure from the Austrian aristocracy forced the powerful Metternich to resign as foreign minister, and he left the country. To

The reign of Louis Philippe (seated) was favorable to business and mercantile interests. The right to vote was limited to men over 25 who owned property. Those who were not content included the workers, who felt betrayed, and intellectuals, whose actions were restricted and writings censored. What groups organized to fight for needed reform?

To gain worldwide support for Hungarian nationalism, Kossuth toured the United States and other countries.

Uprisings in Italy and Prussia eventually led to the creation of the modern countries of Italy and Germany. Italian and German nationalism is discussed in detail in Chapter 20.

satisfy the demonstrators in Vienna, Emperor Ferdinand I granted some concessions. He abolished censorship, appointed liberal ministers, and summoned the Austrian parliament back into session.

The Vienna uprising was only one of many revolts in the Austrian Empire in 1848. In Hungary, Magyar nationalists, led by Louis Kossuth, demanded their own constitution and a separate Hungarian parliament. Czechs in Austrian-ruled Bohemia wanted equality with the Germans living in the area. Other rebellions took place in Slovakia, Galicia, Dalmatia, and Transylvania. In Italy, Italian nationalists in Lombardy and Venetia also revolted against Austrian rule.

In responding to these revolts, Ferdinand I granted the demands of the Magyars and the Czechs. However, other national groups who lived in Hungary resented being under Magyar control. Croatians, Serbs, Slovaks, and Romanians organized to resist Maygar authority in Hungary. Meanwhile, the Germans of Bohemia remained loyal to the Hapsburgs and opposed the Czechs. They requested the Austrian military occupation of Prague in June 1848. By October, Austria had defeated the Czechs. It regained its control of Bohemia with local German support.

Overwhelmed by revolution in his empire, Ferdinand I abdicated on December 1, 1848, in favor of his nephew, Francis Joseph. Under the new emperor, the reconquest of Hungary became an important priority for restoring order to the empire.

Before becoming directly involved itself, Austria supplied weapons to an army of Croatian patriots fighting a war of resistance against Hungary. The Croatians won an initial success by occupying Budapest in January 1849, but by February they were forced out of Hungary. At that time, the Magyars confidently proclaimed Hungary a free republic.

In June 1849 Francis Joseph accepted the offer of Tsar Nicholas I of Russia to aid in suppressing the Hungarian revolution. The tsar wanted to restore order in eastern Europe as much as the emperor wanted peace in the Austrian Empire. In August 1849 a Russian army invaded Hungary. Kossuth and other Magyar leaders were defeated and fled into the Ottoman Empire.

Revolution in Italy   A revolutionary wave spread across Italy in 1848. Beginning in January, revolutionaries in Sicily overthrew their king. This stimulated similar action in Naples, where the king was forced to approve a constitution based on the French Charter of Liberties. In other Italian states, such as Tuscany, Piedmont, and the Papal States, people pressured their rulers into accepting liberal constitutions. In the duchies of Parma and Modena, the ruling dukes were forced to flee their thrones altogether.

Friction between Italian nationalists and Austrian authorities led to violence in Austrian-controlled Lombardy and Venetia in 1848. In Milan, Italian patriots attacked Austrian troops, forcing them to leave the city. In Venice, local citizens proclaimed their city a free republic and forced the Austrian garrison and fleet out of the region.

By the summer of 1848, numerous local revolts and open warfare against Austrian forces temporarily weakened the Austrian hold on the Italian peninsula. The Italian states, however, failed to present a strong, united opposition to Austria. As a result, many of the uprisings in Italy were crushed. The old order was restored in Italy with Austrian help. Only Piedmont managed to keep the liberal constitution that it had won in 1848.

Revolution in Prussia   Louis Philippe's fall in France ignited widespread discontent throughout the German states. As in Hungary and Italy, the revolutionary movement in Germany was both liberal and national. In many German states, rulers granted constitutions and other reforms. In Prussia uprisings were often violent and change did not come easily.

In March 1848 the Prussian capital of Berlin became a riot scene as soldiers and police clashed with workers and middle-class artisans demanding reform. King Frederick William IV, who came to the throne in 1840, however, was convinced that the trouble was caused by foreign agitators. He sought an immediate solution by proclaiming "to his dear Berliners" a promise of democratic reforms.

Leaders of the revolts throughout Germany met at Frankfurt to outline their demands. The

Compare realpolitik with the political philosophy that Machiavelli outlined on p. 247.

A wave of revolution hit Europe in 1848. Though economic problems and a need for social reform sparked much unrest, political rights were the first demand of revolutionaries. Political uprisings and revolutions occurred in what European countries in 1848?

reformers called for the election of a national assembly to draw up a constitution for a united Germany. With the Prussian king's approval, the Frankfurt National Assembly convened on May 18, 1848. Disagreements developed, however, between representatives of the working class and those of the middle class. Division over the plan for national unity and selection of a ruler eventually led to the Assembly's dissolution. By April 1848 Frederick William IV regained absolute rule of Prussia and German unification was delayed. The status quo was restored.

1. Identify: Charter of Liberties, July Ordinances, Citizen-King, Louis Blanc, François Guizot, Louis Kossuth, Francis Joseph.
2. What prompted a revolt against the reign of Charles X in France?
3. Which groups in France favored an extension of voting rights? Why did they oppose the government of Louis Philippe?
4. What were the results of the 1848 revolutions in Austria, Italy, and Prussia?

3 Breakdown in European Cooperation

Throughout the new era of revolutions, the general peace of Europe had been maintained. Although many of the great powers experienced internal disorder, no major war occurred among them. This was largely due to the efforts of Britain and Russia, the two powers not seriously affected by revolution at home. The revolutions, however, bred distrust and suspicion among all the great nations of Europe in the 1850's.

Diplomacy and Revolution

The revolutions brought in a new era of European diplomacy. According to historian Gordon A. Craig,

> . . . the revolutions had the effect of shaking the validity of all of the values of the past, and this was true of the field of diplomacy as in any other. For one thing, the revolutions marked the entrance into politics of a generation of European [diplomats] who were much less responsive to arguments in favor of restraint and compromise than their successors and who were more ruthless in their methods.*

Chief among the new diplomats was Prince Felix Schwarzenberg of Austria. Schwarzenberg advanced the practice of **realpolitik**, politics based on practical rather than theoretical goals. Realpolitik meant a willingness on the part of a group or nation to use any means in order to promote its interest. These means often included

*Europe Since 1815, Gordon A. Craig, © 1961 by Holt, Rinehart and Winston, p. 163.

violence and the repudiation of established laws. After 1848, force replaced diplomacy as a means for solving international problems.

The Crimean War

Prince Schwarzenberg had many followers among European nationalists and heads of state.[2] Tsar Nicholas I was one. It was the tsar's efforts to extend his control over Ottoman territory that contributed to the Crimean War, the first conflict between the great powers since 1815. A significant result of the Crimean War was that it permanently destroyed the Concert of Europe.

Causes of the War   On the surface, it appeared that the Crimean War was a dispute between Britain and Russia over the holy places in Palestine, which was part of the Ottoman Empire. Essentially, however, there were three major causes for the war. First, there was Russia's realpolitik approach to territorial expansion and the tsar's failure to appreciate its effect on the other great powers. Second, Britain and France feared that Russian expansion toward the Mediterranean would endanger their trade in the Middle East. Third, there was the inability of the British government to establish a well-defined foreign policy without falling victim to the pressures of British public opinion. The tragedy of the Crimean War was that its purpose could have been accomplished by diplomacy instead of by force.

In 1852 a dispute arose regarding the privileges of religious orders in certain holy places in Palestine. The Ottoman sultan Abdul Mejid I, under French pressure, granted the Roman Catholic orders certain rights that seemed to infringe on the rights already granted to the Eastern Orthodox clergy. Tsar Nicholas I regarded himself as the defender of Eastern Orthodoxy. He demanded that the Ottoman sultan respect the rights of the Orthodox clergy in Palestine. In doing so, moreover, he insisted that it was Russia's duty to protect all Eastern Orthodox people living within the predomina-

tely Muslim Ottoman Empire. When the sultan refused to comply with the tsar's demands, Russian troops were ordered to occupy Ottoman territory along the Danube River in Wallachia and Moldavia.

Meanwhile, Tsar Nicholas I had approached Lord George Seymour, the British ambassador at Saint Petersburg, suggesting that the Ottoman Empire was "a very sick man." At that time the tsar made a bid for an agreement with Britain to dismember the Ottoman Empire. Although the tsar was willing to share selected parts of the empire with Britain, British officials saw the tsar's plan as a threat to them. If Russia took control of the Dardanelles, for example, British naval interests in the Black Sea area would be endangered. From this point, Anglo-Russian relations began to deteriorate. While a major element of British foreign policy became the preservation of the Ottoman Empire, Russia pushed for the empire to be dismembered.

The international controversy concerning the Ottoman Empire became known as the Eastern Question. Regarding the Eastern Question, British leaders were divided between two plans of action. Prime Minister Lord Aberdeen and Foreign Secretary Lord Clarendon believed in secret diplomacy. They wanted to quietly involve the other great powers in a congress to arrange a settlement. However, Lord Palmerston, a former foreign secretary, believed in answering Russian force with British force. With no unified policy, British intentions in the Ottoman Empire appeared obscure.

British public opinion strongly sided with Lord Palmerston. Ever since the late 1840's, the British people had developed a great affection for the Ottomans and their culture. Pro-Ottoman and anti-Russian feelings were further encouraged by the British press, which portrayed Russia as an expansionist villain. When the Ottomans declared war on Russia in October 1853, pro-war sentiment in Britain became intense.

Tsar Nicholas I had hoped that the war would be limited to Russia and the Ottoman Empire. In March 1854, however, both Britain and France declared war on Russia. France joined the fighting because it did not want to be left out of

----

[2]Schwarzenberg's most gifted "students" included Count Camillo di Cavour of Piedmont and Otto von Bismarck of Prussia. These two leaders will be discussed later in Unit 5.

HISTORY AND PEOPLE

Florence Nightingale

Florence Nightingale won lasting fame for her service during the Crimean War. She was the subject of the British soldiers' legend of the "Lady with the Lamp." The legend tells of a night nurse who glided down the dark corridors of hospital wards, answering the cries of the sick and comforting the fears of the dying.

This gentle image was only a shadow of the real Florence Nightingale. She had a brilliant mind and keen organizational ability. Born into the aristocracy in 1830, Nightingale received a classical education. She wanted to be of service to others. At a time when nursing was not considered a noble profession, she went against her family's wishes and became a nurse, eventually becoming director of a women's hospital in London.

In 1854 British Secretary of State at War Sidney Herbert asked Nightingale to lead a group of nurses to the Crimean War. When she arrived at the battle zone on November 5, she found conditions appalling. While troops suffered fearfully from cold, dysentery, and cholera, the hospitals were filthy, unventilated, overcrowded, and understaffed. They lacked the most basic of supplies, such as furniture, clothing, and bedding. Within six months, Nightingale transformed the situation, ignoring slow-moving bureaucratic procedures and appealing directly to the secretary of state at war when needed.

Nightingale's efforts in the Crimean War sharply reduced the death rate in British army hospitals and won her worldwide fame. But, the two years of service permanently damaged her own health. After the war, Florence Nightingale seldom left her home in London.

Her handicapping condition did not diminish her mental activity, however. With support from her staff, she planned strategies that were to reform hospital administration and the nursing profession. Her *Notes On Hospitals*, published in 1859, revolutionized the management of hospitals by calling for improved sanitation and more attention to the emotional health of patients. As a result of her work, numerous nurses' training schools were established that stressed medical and personal approaches to caring for patients. In 1864 she helped inspire the organization of the International Red Cross.

Florence Nightingale was the only person to gain a heroic reputation from the Crimean War. Her activity made the nursing profession a respected public career for women. It was a first step toward equality for women in public life.

Florence Nightingale had an errand of propaganda as well as mercy. She was sent by Herbert to the battlefront with the responsibility of breaking down prejudices against female nursing. Under her charge, clean water, fresh air, and nourishing food began to flow into Barrack Hospital. Such measures saw the death toll fall from 42 per 100 to 22 per 1,000. Thus, Nightingale accomplished her purpose.

Some teachers might wish to assign the entire poem by Tennyson for student reading.

The Crimean War was the first major conflict recorded by photography and the first to receive extensive coverage by newspapers. War correspondents throughout Europe wrote about the battles from firsthand observations. The stories were sent by telegraph from the battlefield to newspaper offices far removed from the scene. What were the major causes of the Crimean War?

any peace settlement involving territorial changes. Britain was swept up by a desire to take some action in the Ottoman dispute. Its decision to declare war, however, was influenced by public pressure. The British public wished to see Britain reassert its influence in European affairs.

After Britain declared war, writer Thomas Carlyle entered the following comment into his diary. In it, he emphasized the role of the press and public opinion in involving the British in the Crimean War.

> *It is the idle population of editors, etc. that have done all this in England. One perceives clearly that the Ministers go forward in it against their will. . . . Poor Souls! What could the Ministry do after all?**

In addition to Britain and France, Piedmont joined in the war against Russia in 1855. Austria and Prussia, however, remained neutral.

The War   Most of the fighting in the war took place in the Crimean Peninsula, which juts into the Black Sea from southern Russia. Cholera and other deadly diseases proved to be the greatest battlefield enemy for both sides. More deaths were caused by sickness than by injuries.

Newspaper stories about the horrible conditions in Crimea inspired many private citizens, including Florence Nightingale of Britain, to set up field hospitals to care for the sick and wounded.

Newspaper accounts also told of brutal battles, such as those at Alma River and Inkerman. These stories attempted to counterbalance more romantic portrayals of the fighting that many British people preferred to read. Perhaps the most frequently remembered conflict of the Crimean War was the Battle of Balaklava. It was here that a misunderstanding of orders sent 600 British soldiers charging directly into the deadly fire of Russian artillery. The drama of the error inspired Alfred Lord Tennyson to write his well-known poem, "The Charge of the Light Brigade." The poem begins:

> *Half a league, half a league,*
> * Half a league onward,*
> *All in the valley of Death*
> * Rode the six hundred.*
> *"Forward, the Light Brigade!*
> *Charge for the guns!" he said:*
> *Into the valley of Death*
> * Rode the six hundred.**

*Thomas Carlyle, as quoted in *Europe Since 1815*, Gordon A. Craig, Ibid., p. 1169.

*"The Charge of the Light Brigade," Alfred Lord Tennyson, as quoted in *Literature II*, by Albert R. Kitzhaber, © 1968 by Holt, Rinehart and Winston, pp. 69-70.

After the British capture of the Russian fortified port of Sevastopol, Russia offered to make peace. In early 1856, the Crimean War came to an end. The number of casualties during the war has been estimated at 250,000. It was a costly war for all the participants.

Effects of the War Negotiations for a peace settlement opened in Paris on February 25, 1856. Delegations from Britain, Russia, France, Austria, Piedmont, Prussia, and the Ottoman Empire attended. The treaty, concluded on March 30, resulted in no major territorial changes in Europe. Also, it did not force financial payments from Russia. Nevertheless, the tsar viewed the military defeat and the treaty as humiliating for Russia.

The Treaty of Paris was based on war goals set by Britain and France as early as August 1854. It guaranteed the independence and territorial integrity of the Ottoman Empire. It renounced both any right of intervention in Ottoman internal affairs and Russia's claim to be protector of all Eastern Orthodox Christians. Other provisions in the treaty guaranteed **autonomy,** or self-government, to Wallachia and Moldavia. These two territories later became the nation of Romania. The treaty also declared the waters and ports of the Black Sea to be neutral, opening them to all nations for trade.

Another result of the peace conference was the Declaration of Paris. By it, the great powers meeting at Paris sought to establish international rules for governing sea trade during wartime. Among other principles, the declaration stated that free ships make free goods. This meant that warring nations were not to interfere with neutral sea commerce. This later became a point for conflict among the great powers.

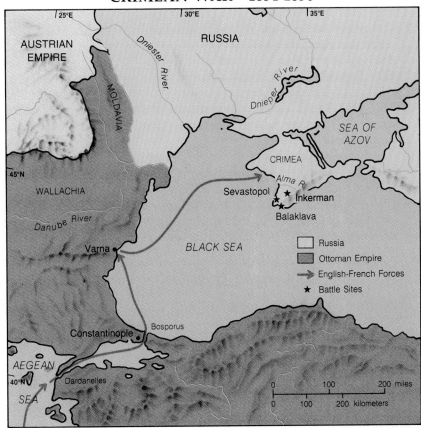

CRIMEAN WAR 1854-1856

In general, the Paris peace conference seemed to reaffirm the ideals of the Concert of Europe. But this was a misleading sign for future events. During the years immediately following the conference, the Concert was to prove ineffective. The ambitions of certain European powers and the political weakness of others brought about a breakdown in European cooperation in diplomatic affairs.

1. Identify: Felix Schwarzenberg, Lord Aberdeen, Lord Clarendon, Lord Palmerston, Crimean Peninsula, Florence Nightingale, Battle of Balaklava, Wallachia and Moldavia.
2. How did the new era of revolution affect diplomacy in Europe?
3. What reason did Tsar Nicholas I use to start a war with the Ottoman Empire?
4. Who was mainly responsible for involving Britain in the Crimean War?

CHAPTER 16 REVIEW

Summary

1. Austria, Britain, France, Prussia, and Russia dominated the negotiations and worked out the settlements of the Congress of Vienna. Metternich presided over the peace conference and greatly influenced the proceedings.
2. The major settlements at Vienna involved territorial compensation for losses during the Napoleonic wars, restoration of absolutist monarchies, and establishment of a balance of European political power.
3. The Quadruple Alliance introduced the Concert of Europe as a means for settling international disputes.
4. The objectives of the Concert of Europe were to oppose liberalism and nationalism and to defend the political status quo in Europe.
5. Major challenges to the Concert of Europe occurred in Germany in 1819 and in Spain and Naples in 1820. Diplomatic intervention

by Metternich in Germany and military intervention by Austria, Prussia, and Russia in Spain and Naples restored the status quo.
6. A new era of political revolutions began in 1830 and lasted through 1848. Revolts during this time were both liberal and national in nature.
7. The French Revolution of 1848 resulted in the creation of a republic. Liberal and national revolts in Austria, Italy, and Prussia were generally unsuccessful.
8. The revolutionary movement of 1848 weakened the Concert of Europe by introducing diplomats who favored force rather than restraint and compromise in international relations.
9. The Crimean War, which chiefly involved Britain and Russia, permanently disrupted the cooperation of the Concert of Europe.

Building Vocabulary

nationalism	legitimate	congress system	socialism
liberalism	buffer	ultraroyalists	realpolitik
compensation	status quo	abdicated	autonomy

Reviewing the Main Ideas

1. What general principles guided the settlements at the Congress of Vienna?
2. How was France affected by the settlements at Vienna?

3. Which European rulers did not join the Holy Alliance? Why?
4. What challenge to the congress system was successful in the 1820's?
5. Why did the people of France turn against the constitutional monarchy in the early 1800's?
6. What was the result of the 1830 July Revolution in France?
7. Why did both socialists and republicans oppose the government of Louis Philippe?
8. Who led the Magyar nationalists in their revolt against Austria? What were the nationalist demands?
9. Why was the Frankfurt National Assembly elected?
10. What caused the Crimean War?
11. What impact did the Crimean War have on the Concert of Europe?
12. What were the major settlements reached at the Paris peace conference of 1856? How did they affect the peoples of the Balkans?

Discussing Important Ideas

1. Compare and contrast the diplomatic philosophies of Metternich and Schwarzenberg.
2. Why did the Austrians and Russians want to maintain the status quo?
3. How successful were the five leading European powers in suppressing nationalism and liberalism in the early to mid-1800's?
4. How did Charles X bring on the July Revolution of 1830? What political attitudes did he hold?
5. Why do you think Louis Philippe was chosen as king of France?
6. Why do you think revolutions broke out in Austria, Italy, and Prussia immediately after the Revolution of 1848 in France?
7. How did revolutions from 1830 to 1848 influence relations in Europe?
8. How do you think the purpose of the Crimean War could have been accomplished by diplomacy rather than by force?

Using Maps

Refer to the map on page 373 to answer the following questions:
1. Which nations on the map are included in the German Confederation?
2. What political units formed France's eastern boundary at this time?
3. Which of the five major powers attending the Congress are located in central Europe?
4. Which empire ruled Greece in 1815? ruled Poland in 1815?
5. What is the relative location of the Crimean Peninsula to Great Britain?

UNIT 4 REVIEW

Summary

1. The Age of Monarchs in the 1500's and 1600's was an unsettled time marked by civil unrest and wars fought over religious, economic, and dynastic disputes. European monarchies reached the height of their power and the outlines of the modern European states emerged.

2. A scientific revolution took place in Europe in the 1600's. Through observation and experimentation, scholars found that the universe could be understood by natural laws.

3. Other thinkers applied reason and observation to the institutions and values of society. This resulted in the Enlightenment movement of the 1700's, in which reason was seen as the solution to society's ills.

4. In reaction to the Enlightenment, new styles in art and literature emphasized emotion and the limits of reason.

5. By 1688 England had been through two revolutions, which eventually led to a parliamentary form of government.

6. Britain's American colonies revolted in 1776 and formed the United States—a nation with a republican government based on a written constitution that reflected Enlightenment ideas.

7. Constitutional reforms were established in France in the late 1700's, but by the end of the century France was once again governed by an absolute ruler.

8. Austria, Prussia, Russia, Britain, and France sent representatives to Vienna in 1814 to restore peace and stability to Europe. For the next three decades, most of these powers acted to suppress nationalism and liberalism in Europe.

9. Between 1830 and 1848, a new era of political revolutions occurred in Europe. France became a republic, but revolts in Austria, Italy, and Prussia were unsuccessful.

10. The Crimean War during the mid-1800's shattered cooperation among the major powers of Europe.

Developing Understanding

1. How did European rulers strengthen their authority during the Age of Monarchs?

2. What factors led to Spain's decline in the 1600's and France's rise to prominence?

3. Why is the eighteenth century in Europe called the Age of Reason?

4. In what ways did European art and literature change in the 1600's and 1700's?

5. How did the balance of power principle affect European political relations between the mid-1500's and 1815?

6. What were the consequences of the Glorious Revolution, the American Revolution, and the French Revolution?

7. How did the major powers maintain the status quo in Europe between 1815 and 1848?

Developing Skills

When historians go about writing history, they generally sort through a large number of facts and ideas. Because it is not in human nature to be completely objective, they tend to be biased in their choices of which facts and ideas to write about or emphasize. The result is, almost inevitably, a more or less slanted account.

The collection of facts from which historians choose is itself a product of bias. Over the centuries, people have recorded certain statistics and put into writing their interpretations of the facts. In doing so they have made choices about what is important to be saved. History is more likely to be that of the victors than that of the vanquished; of the literate rather than the illiterate; of the powerful rather than the weak.

Below are 10 facts about Napoleon Bonaparte. To see how the selection of facts may produce a slanted account, choose 4 or 5 of those facts and write a paragraph with one of the following topic sentences:

   a) Although Napoleon carried on some of the ideals of the French Revolution, he reversed many of its reforms.
   b) Although Napoleon reversed some of the reforms of the French Revolution, he carried on many of its basic ideals.

1. The Napoleonic Code retained some of the basic ideas of revolutionary law, such as equality before the law and freedom of religion.
2. Napoleon did not allow true representative government.
3. Napoleon severely limited freedom of the press.
4. The Napoleonic Code gave France a uniform system of civil law, which had long been a goal of the revolution.
5. Under Napoleon the police system was greatly extended.
6. The Napoleonic Code included many provisions for the protection of middle-class property, which was contrary to revolutionary ideals.
7. Napoleon submitted his Constitution of the Year VIII to a popular vote, and an overwhelming majority voted in favor of it.
8. After Napoleon took over as First Consul, he proclaimed, "Citizens, the revolution is established upon the principles which began it."
9. The Napoleonic Code completely wiped out the privileges of the feudal aristocracy.
10. Unlike revolutionary law, the Napoleonic Code did not give women equal rights with men.

Suggested Activities

1. Prepare a chart on three of the royal dynasties you have studied. Show the lines of succession and the countries each monarch ruled.
2. Describe the best system of government according to each of the following: Hobbes, Locke, Montesquieu, and Rousseau. Take the role of one of these figures in a panel discussion on whether or not the United States has the best possible system of government.
3. Develop a list of factors that contributed to the revolutions described in this unit. Then write a few paragraphs to answer these questions: a) Why were the scientific advances in the 1600's called a *revolution?* b) Is the women's movement of the present a *revolution?*
4. For each of the revolutions that occurred in Europe in the 1840's, write newspaper headlines that trace events from the outbreak of the revolution to its end.

Suggested Readings

Barbary, James. *Puritan and Cavalier: The English Civil War.* Nashville: Thomas Nelson Publishers, 1977. Discusses the two sides in the English Civil War.

Hanff, Helene. *Queen of England: The Story of Elizabeth I.* New York: Doubleday, 1969. Presents the life of Elizabeth I of England.

Liverside, Douglas. *The Day the Bastille Fell.* New York: Watts, 1972. Presents the dramatic opening events of the French Revolution.

Siedel, Frank and James M. *Pioneers in Science.* Boston: Houghton, 1968. Presents short biographies of leading scientific figures from the Age of Reason to the present.

The Rise of Modern Europe

		1733 Kay's flying shuttle		1776 *The Wealth of Nations*	1800 Ireland and Britain united
1700's Industrial Revolution begins					1800 New Lanarck
1700	**1725**		**1750**	**1775**	**1800**
	1708 Newcomen's steam engine				1793 Whitney's cotton gin
	1709 Darby's coke-smelted iron			1764 Hargreaves' spinning jenny	1807 Fulton's *Clermont*

1829 Stephenson's *Rocket*	**1854** *Hard Times*	**1876** Bell's telephone **1878** Edison's light	**1907** Women's suffrage in Norway
1830's Morse Code, Gramme's dynamo	**1861** Italian unification	**1880's** Post-impressionism	

1825	**1850**	**1875**	**1900**	**1925**

	1844 *The Three Musketeers*	**1870** Franco-Prussian War	**1885** Daimler's gasoline engine
	1848 *The Communist Manifesto*	**1871** German unification	**1890** Fall of Bismarck **1896** Marconi's wireless

Derby Day in England

I n the eighteenth century, a series of changes transformed Europe's economy. These changes involved a shift from animal and human power to machine power. New methods and inventions were developed that had a lasting impact on the economy.

By the middle of the 1800's, these economic changes had drastically altered the pattern of European life. People in large numbers moved from rural areas to the cities. The middle and working classes increased in size and importance. They became loyal to their nations and demanded a voice in political affairs. Monarchs who tried to stamp out democratic and national feelings failed. They were forced to accept constitutions, parliaments, elections, and the creation of new nations. Under popular pressure, governments passed reforms to deal with the social problems resulting from the new economy.

Early Industrial Site

66 *Steam and electricity have conquered time and space to a greater extent during the last sixty years than all the preceding six hundred years witnessed; so that a [person] may now cram into ten years as much experience as [his or her grandparent] could have done in fifty.* **99**

London journalist, 1897

The Industrial Revolution

In the 1700's and early 1800's, a series of changes occurred in Britain's economy that would transform the way people had lived for centuries. Although the changes began slowly, they grew in momentum as one development led to another. Among the earlier changes were improved methods of farming, key technological inventions, and new sources of power. These, in turn, led to changes in the way products were made. Machines were developed to perform work that once had been done by hand or by animal labor. Entrepreneurs brought the machines and workers together in factories. Soon there was division of labor, mass production, and large-scale efficient operations. By the 1850's the changes had become so widespread that people realized they were entering a new age.

This economic and social transformation has been called the Industrial Revolution by historians. It started in Britain during the 1700's without anyone realizing what was happening. Many years passed before British society felt its full effects. By the late 1800's, however, the Industrial Revolution had spread beyond Britain to other areas of Europe, North America, and Japan. It is now transforming other parts of Asia, Africa, and Latin America.

The Industrial Revolution is one of the most significant developments in modern human history. It changed much of the world from a rural and agricultural society to an urban and industrial one. It also led to the rise of modern culture and brought to the forefront such concerns as crowded cities, environmental pollution, job safety, worker satisfaction, and comprehensive care for the poor and disadvantaged. The impact of the Industrial Revolution has been so vast that one esteemed historian believes it is comparable only to the Neolithic Revolution, when early humans learned to domesticate animals and raise crops.

1 Pre-Industrial Life

Before the 1700's, life in Europe, as in the rest of the world, was geared to the seasons of the year. Changes came slowly. People moved at a slower pace and had access to less information than they do today. Towns and cities retained some of their rural character, and only a small minority of people lived in them. London, which had a population of 750,000 in 1750, was the largest city in Europe. The center of the city, however, was only a few miles away from outlying agricultural fields.

About 75 percent of Europeans lived in rural villages of 200 to 600 inhabitants. The tallest structure in the village was the church with its steeple. The church was the physical and spiritual center of the community. In the villages, home life and work were closely related as most work was done in nearby fields or in a worker's cottage or adjoining workshop. Thus, the family was an economic as well as a social unit.

Family and Land

In the villages of Europe, most people lived in small cottages with earthen floors and inadequate light and air. The already crowded quarters often were shared with livestock. All members of a family had to work hard to ensure survival. Husband, wife, and children worked alongside each other from morning to night.

Life expectancy in today's industrialized nations is over 70 years.

Point out that prior to the Industrial Revolution most people had no expectations of change in their lives. Have students compare this attitude with feelings about change today.

Before industrialization in the 1700's, survival depended upon each family member contributing to the farm's production. In eastern Europe, peasants were still serfs, having to share the harvest with the lord and having to pay taxes to the crown and a tithe to the Church. In western Germany and France, peasants actually owned the land and could pass it on to their children. How did inheritance traditions differ for sons and daughters?

Sons assisted their fathers, who labored as farmers or artisans. Daughters helped their mothers, who did household and farm chores.

Life expectancy was slightly over 40 years. Since most people married in their mid-to-late twenties, they could expect to live together only five to ten years before one of them died. Since people often remarried, households with half brothers and half sisters were common. For most of these people, life was not only relatively short but harsh. Although most women bore many children, families generally were small due to deaths brought on by disease, famine, and war. One baby in three died in the first year of life. Only one in two reached the age of 21.

For all classes, from peasant to artistocrat, family, village, and soil were closely tied together. Land was the source of livelihood and well-being. Having sufficient land on which to subsist, or survive, was essential. Thus, traditions concerning land guided daily life. These traditions were designed to ensure the stability and welfare of the community. Marriage and inheritance were geared to keeping a family's property intact.

Marriages were arranged by parents to maintain or better the economic status of their sons and daughters. A man generally had to own enough land on which to support a family before he could marry. It was not unusual for a man to postpone his marriage until he inherited the family property. In some areas, younger sons were not permitted to inherit. Daughters in some cases inherited land but the law usually did not allow them the full rights of ownership. All the land was generally inherited by the eldest son, while younger sons received cash payments. Younger sons could continue, however, to work the land provided they remained single. In other areas, a son could buy the land over time while his parents were still alive. This arrangement ensured a type of welfare for the elderly.

Agriculture

The main occupation of the pre-industrial community was farming. All other activities revolved around it. Tradition, rather than innovation, determined farming practices. Farmers used simple methods and tools inherited from the Middle Ages. Since they knew little about fertilizers, they had to depend on nature to restore nutrients to the soil. Nature, however, was not reliable, and famine and natural disasters were accepted as facts of life.

In many villages, private and public lands were not separated and fenced off. Families owned or leased small strips of land in several areas of the village. This ensured a fair distribution of land and protected farmers in the event disaster struck any one field. The strips of land were so small that they were worked cooperatively. Farmers jointly decided what crops to grow and where and when to plant and harvest them.

In addition to private plots, each village had a **commons,** or public land, consisting of woodlands, pastures, and less desirable land located near the village. All village farmers had the right to pasture their animals and gather wood in the commons. The poorer peasants, who did not own plots of land, depended on the commons for tending sheep, gathering wood, or raising a few crops.

The village economy was limited largely to the local area. Villages were connected only by rough dirt wagon tracks that became impassable when it rained. As a result, transport was often slow, and trade beyond the local community was difficult. People lived at subsistence levels, producing only a small amount of food for sale to nearby towns. They made their own clothes, furniture, tools, and homes from products raised in the fields or gathered in the forests. Thus, villages were fairly self-sufficient. And as long as the population remained stable and tradition and custom held sway, little was likely to change. Pre-industrial farmers had little **incentive,** or motive, to increase production.

Industry

Before the Industrial Revolution, small manufacturing and mining operations were spread throughout rural areas. They were designed primarily to serve local needs. They employed small numbers of workers and were closely tied to the agricultural cycle. When the harvest took place, for example, nail makers, miners, and other such workers joined farmers in the fields. During the slow winter months, some farm workers turned to industrial trades. This close relationship between agriculture and industry guaranteed labor adequate to fill basic needs.

Most rural manufacturing was done by a method known as the **domestic system.** Under this system, poor rural families used raw materials supplied by a merchant to produce goods in their cottages by hand or by waterwheel. The merchant gathered the finished

This 1783 engraving shows a family at home in County Down, Ireland, spinning flax into linen. After the raw fiber was prepared and spun, it was wound on a clock-reel and immersed into a vat of boiling dye. The yarn was then woven into cloth and sold by merchants locally or abroad. Rural families supplemented their income through these small "cottage industries." How else were industry and agriculture interrelated before the Industrial Revolution?

Make sure that students understand the terms *birthrate* and *death rate* in discussing population growth.

products and sold them in small-town markets. Rural families owned or rented the equipment needed to make the products and received payment from the merchant for completed work. Production by this system involved many long hours of work. Workers, however, controlled the rate and times at which they worked. The system provided work during times of agricultural distress, saving many from starvation.

In Britain, the domestic system played an important part in the production of woolen fabric and in coal mining. These were two of the country's chief industries, and both were linked to agriculture. Since the Middle Ages, the British woolen industry was second only to agriculture in the numbers of people it employed and the volume of trade it created. Making woolen fabric involved a number of steps, many of which could be performed in a farm laborer's cottage. Women and children were responsible for sorting, cleaning, and spinning the wool; men did the weaving. These simple rural domestic practices later became the basis on which the technology and skills of the Industrial Revolution were built.

In the case of coal mining, the coal pits or hillsides from which the coal was extracted belonged to the landowners of the farm property on which they were situated. The people who worked the mines often became farm laborers during the harvest. Farm horses pulled the wagons that carried the coal from the pits. In some districts, women and children performed heavy labor, carrying the coal up to the surface in baskets on their backs.

The manufacture of luxury goods took place in towns. There, artisans under the guild system made and sold goods in shops. They used hand tools to produce weapons, furniture, clothing, jewelry, and other goods. Some of these goods were sent abroad to pay for imports. The rest were traded for food in the surrounding farms and villages.

1. Where did most people live in pre-industrial times?
2. Why was land so important? What traditions worked to keep a family's land intact?
3. What was the chief occupation of the pre-industrial community? What role did tradition play in its practice?

2 Sources of Change

In the 1700's, Britain's pre-industrial economy and society began to change. Population began to grow rapidly, and production improved and increased. The stage was set for the coming of the Industrial Revolution.

Population Growth

In 1750 the population of Europe was about 125 million persons. By 1800 it had climbed to 187 million. By 1850, it had reached 266 million. This rapid increase was the result of several factors.

One factor was a change in the birthrate and death rate. Before 1700, the birthrate was high. It was matched, however, by an equally high death rate. In the 1700's, the pattern changed. The number of births increased, and the number of deaths decreased.

The drop in the death rate was due to a number of developments. One was an increased supply of better food. Farmers adopted new feed crops, such as the turnip, which enabled livestock to live through the winter. This meant that for the first time fresh meat was available year-round. Farmers also introduced new crops that were rich in vitamins and minerals and grew well even in poor soil. One of these was the potato which, by the end of the 1700's, was standard fare for many people. One historian noted that:

> Day after day, three times a day, people ate salted boiled potatoes, probably washing them down with milk, flavoring them, if they were fortunate, with onion or a bit of lard, with boiled seaweed or a scrap of salted fish.*

Better nutrition meant fewer deaths. More children survived beyond infancy, and more adults resisted dangerous illnesses.

Also contributing to the drop in the death rate were better hygiene and improved sanitation. The development of cheap soap and inexpensive cotton underwear lessened the dangers of infection. The use of brick instead of timber for walls, and slate instead of thatch for roofs,

---

*"The Population Revolution," William Langer, in *The Other Side of Western Civilization: Readings in Everyday Life*, Vol. II, ed. by Peter N. Stearns, © 1979 by Harcourt Brace Jovanovich, p. 97.

Crop failures in Ireland in the 1840's forced many Irish people to emigrate to other countries.

reduced the number of disease-carrying insects and the danger of fire. The improvement of drainage and the supply of running water in larger towns also aided public health.

The growth in the birthrate, on the other hand, seems to have stemmed chiefly from a change in the age at which people married. In the 1700's, new lands were opened for cultivation in eastern Europe. This meant that young people did not need to wait so long for sufficient land to start new households. At the same time, the domestic system began to spread in western Europe. This gave people an opportunity to earn an income independent of the land. As a result, couples began marrying in their teens and having families at an earlier age than in the past. Only those individuals dependent solely on farming adhered to the traditional practice of late marriages.

The population explosion had an important impact on European life. It led to a much greater demand for land, jobs, food, and other commodities. It created increased tensions within families as fathers lived longer and were not able to provide adequately for increased numbers of children. Further, because there were more people to feed, any widespread crop failure could have devastating effects.

Some of the pressure was taken off in the late 1700's and early 1800's as people became more mobile. Many Europeans left their homelands to build new lives in the Americas, Australia, New Zealand, and, eventually, South Africa. Many of those who remained in Europe migrated to areas within their own countries where new methods in industry were being developed. There, they provided the skills and labor force needed to make industry grow.

Agricultural Prosperity

The population boom caused concern for many educated people in Britain. One of these people was Thomas Malthus, a member of the clergy who believed that population growth would lead to disaster. In 1798 Malthus published a book entitled *An Essay on the Principle of*

Malthus's Principles of Population

According to Malthus's theory, the human population would increase as the following numbers do: 1, 2, 4, 8, 16, 32, 64, 128, 256,—a geometric increase. The food supply, however, would increase at an arithmetic rate: 1, 2, 3, 4, 5, 6, 7, 8, 9. In two centuries the ratio between population and food supply would be 4,096 to 13. This theory, of course, assumes no ability to increase food production or create new food sources.

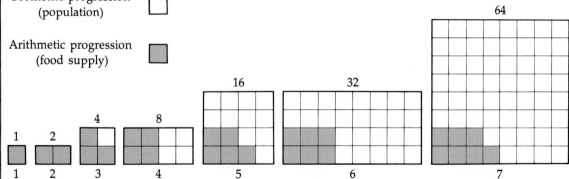

Regarding Malthus's theory, each block represents world population, while the shaded area of each block represents the food supply. Population increases faster than the food supply; therefore the white squares represent the percentage of people who would be without food.

Population. In it, he argued that population would increase so rapidly that it would outstrip society's ability to provide the necessities of life. Therefore, unless people limited the size of their families, poverty, famine, and social collapse were unavoidable.

Malthus's predictions were not fulfilled. Instead of leading to social collapse, the increased demand for food and the rising prices led to increased production as wealthy landowners seeking to improve their incomes promoted agricultural change. They began an agricultural revolution that transformed rural areas and turned farming into a profit-making business.

The first thing the landowners did was to end the open field system and bring the land under their direct control. The system had gradually been giving way to private ownership since the 1100's. But now the trend, known as the **enclosure movement,** gained momentum. In the late 1700's, the British Parliament passed laws that allowed small individual plots and common lands to be enclosed with hedges or fences and combined into larger estates under private management.

The goal of the enclosure movement was to increase agricultural efficiency and productivity. Although the goal was achieved, some historians point out that it was done by violating the rights of the poor. Many small farmers did not have the money or fields to make agricultural improvements. Yet, they did not want to become tenant farmers. As a result, they and the landless often were displaced, some of them forcibly removed from their homes by wealthy landowners.

In spite of the injustices, agricultural efficiency was increased, as were crop yields. As fewer laborers were needed to produce food, more people were free to join the industrial labor force. At the same time, landowners had to cope with fewer restrictions and could use the land as they wished. Because joint agreement no longer had to be reached, more effective work could be done on larger blocks of land. Less time was spent traveling between the fields. Because landowners could limit the size of their herds, their pastures were not overgrazed so they had larger and healthier livestock.

The second thing the landowners did was to introduce new methods of farming. They increased the amount of usable land by rotating crops over a four-year cycle instead of the traditional three-year one. Along with wheat and barley, they planted new soil-enriching crops such as turnips, clover, and beets, carefully planning the order in which the crops followed one another in the field. The new system of rotation allowed farmers to use all their arable land instead of only two-thirds. At the same time, new drainage procedures were developed. They helped increase even further the amount of available land.

The third thing the landowners did was to conduct scientific experiments to increase yields. They used fertilizer and introduced such new tools as the seed drill to till the soil and to plant seed in orderly rows. They also experimented with using the better animals as breeding livestock to produce larger sheep, fatter cattle, and more powerful horses.

New and improved farm implements, such as Jethro Tull's seed drill and horse-drawn iron-tipped hoe, were featured in Diderot's Encyclopedie. *What other scientific advances increased agricultural production?*

The changes in agriculture increased supplies of grain, meat, and dairy products. They also contributed to improvements in transportation. As lands were enclosed, landowners set aside portions for the building of new roads. The new roads helped link rural areas more closely to urban markets, making production for markets beyond the local area more tempting. As trade increased between different areas, each was able to specialize in producing its best products rather than having to produce a wide range of goods. Innovation and competition rather than tradition gradually became the accepted way. Farms were able to meet the demands of a growing population for food, and agriculture became a booming profit-making business.

British Advantages

Agricultural prosperity and a large labor force were only two of the factors that led Britain into an industrial revolution and made it the world's first industrial nation. Britain also had three other key elements needed for industrialization—capital, natural resources, and talent. While other European countries had some or all of these, Britain was the first country in which they all came together.

Capital   One of the elements any country must have to industrialize is **capital**—money to invest in labor, machines, and raw materials to produce goods and services. During the 1700's, capital was plentiful in Britain. Many British aristrocrats had increased their wealth through agriculture, wars, the slave trade, and overseas commerce. At the same time, a sizeable middle class of merchants, artisans, and shopkeepers had emerged and prospered from trade. Both groups sought other ways to use their wealth in addition to buying land and spending for personal pleasures. In their search for profit, these people became interested in industrial development. As **capitalists,** or investors, they played an important role in the financing of the Industrial Revolution.

At the same time, the banking system in Britain grew stronger. The number of banks had been increasing since the 1600's. The banks offered credit, much of it on a long-term basis, thus creating new capital. They allowed funds to be transferred from one banking institution to another and from one area to another. This made it possible for one area to draw on another for money for industry. By the 1800's, London had 70 banks and had become the undisputed financial center of the world.

The availability of capital became linked to the political stability of the country. The British had confidence in their government, and business people were willing to take risks. The government encouraged economic expansion and had favored the promotion of trade since 1688. It also protected the rights of private property and gave more freedom to merchants and business people than most other countries in Europe. British investors who in the past had invested in government bonds were eager to earn more profit than the bonds could bring. So they turned to industry, which promised faster and more profitable returns.

Natural Resources   Britain had important natural resources in the form of coal and iron ore. What gave Britain the edge over countries such as Germany and Russia, which also had large deposits of coal and iron ore, was its rivers.

Britain had many navigable rivers that provided the British with links among coal and iron ore fields. Many of the rivers, which flowed abundantly year-round, provided water power for manufacturing. Above all, the rivers provided a cheap and convenient way to transport both raw materials and finished goods. To further increase access to natural resources and to cut transportation costs, British engineers deepened rivers and built harbors and canals.

Britain also had access to the many natural resources in its colonies and could take advantage of external as well as internal resources. In addition, British colonies and trading stations in the Americas, Africa, and India could be depended upon to supply such raw materials as cotton, tea, and spices. The colonies also provided a guaranteed market for such finished goods as cloth and iron utensils.

Talent   Finally, Britain was rich in the human talent needed to bring together labor, capital, and natural resources. British society

With Thomas Newcomen's invention it was possible for coal to be mined in and below water layers under ground.

was ready for a change. As one observer at the time wrote, "The age is running after innovation. All the business of the world is to be done in a new way. . . ."

Science was directed toward the solution of practical rather than abstract problems. For many upper- and middle-class people, it was a hobby. This popularity encouraged many inventors, most of whom were amateurs. Mostly middle class and from a variety of backgrounds, they were members of the clergy, lawyers, doctors, barbers, and innkeepers. Their combined efforts eventually led to such inventions as the steam engine, locomotive, and power loom.

Along with inventors, entrepreneurs became more numerous and more active than they had been in the past. Some entrepreneurs came from the gentry and the commercial-financial middle class. Others rose from the ranks of rural and urban workers. As a group, they organized and directed the growth of industry by bringing together labor, capital, and inventions.

1. Why did the disasters predicted by Thomas Malthus fail to occur?
2. What developments affected the death rate in the 1700's?
3. What three things did wealthy landowners do in the 1700's to increase agricultural production?

3   Industrial Expansion

Beginning in the early 1700's, a series of mechanical inventions were developed and applied in the small manufacturing centers of Britain. At first, the new machinery depended on running water as its energy source. Then, steam replaced water. The combination of steam and machinery led to industrial growth and stimulated improvements in transportation. It also brought about many social changes.

Early Breakthroughs

For hundreds of years, technical problems had limited output in coal, iron, and textiles—Britain's three basic industries. In the 1700's, breakthroughs in several industrial techniques opened the way to create new products and to increase output. Before long, coal, iron, and textiles had become the pillars of the world's first modern industrial economy.

By 1700, adequate fuel supplies had become a problem in Britain. Since the 1500's, Britain had had a serious shortage of wood. The British used wood to heat their homes and to make charcoal for the **smelting,** or melting, of iron ore. As Britain's iron industry grew, more and more forests were used up. To ease the situation, many people turned to coal, most of which was carried by boat from northeastern England to London and other urban centers. But, before coal production could be more significant, other problems had to be solved.

As the demand for coal increased, deeper mines were dug. These new mines presented a number of problems that limited production. Most were filled with poisonous dust and gases, and the miners lived in constant fear of fire and underground explosions. Often, a large bellows was used to keep the air circulating and to disperse the gases.

Safe lighting also was a problem. Visibility in the pits generally was poor, so some mines used phosphorescent wood to provide light. Other mines hired boys to stand near working miners and create sparks of light with a flint and a small-toothed wheel.

The major concern, however, was that deep mines generally filled with water. At first, the water was raised from the mines by hauling it out in buckets, by working hand pumps, or by using pumps that were powered by windmills, waterwheels, or donkeys. But these methods were slow and expensive. Then, around 1708, a British ironsmith named Thomas Newcomen developed an engine that used steam pressure to force a piston up and atmospheric pressure to bring it down. Newcomen's engine was the first practical application of steam power. The engine solved the problem of water in the mines by drawing it out through a pipe in the mine shaft. By the mid-1700's, improvements had been made in the engine, and it was in wide use in the mines of Britain.

During the 1800's, other improvements came to the coal industry. Safety lamps increased visibility, and dust control made the mines safer.

Contrast mining in the 1700's with the industry today. Note advances made in mine safety.

The picture below shows James Watt's steam pumping engine at work during the 1790's.

As deeper mines were dug, devices to pump out groundwater had to be installed. Horsepower generated the early pumps. If the mine was large, however, hundreds of horses were needed. By the early 1700's, primitive steam engines took the place of the horse. What improvements helped to make coal mining safer during the 1800's?

Coal was brought to the surface more efficiently and transported more quickly and cheaply. These and other technological changes resulted in a large increase in coal production. It rose from 2.5 million tons (2.25 million metric tons) a year in 1700 to 10 million tons (9 million metric tons) in 1800 to over 200 million tons (180 million metric tons) by the end of the century. Since coal was the basic energy source, its greater availability boosted expansion in other industries.

Iron and Steel The jump in coal production had a huge impact on the iron industry. In pre-industrial Britain, workers smelted iron ore in the rural areas of the country, using wood charcoal for fuel. Since it took several tons of fuel to **refine,** or remove the impurities from, one ton (0.9 metric ton) of ore, refineries had to be located at the edge of woodlands near the ore deposits. In the early 1700's, because of the shortage of wood, iron workers tried to use coal instead of wood charcoal in the smelting process. The coal, however, did not burn hot enough, and its high sulfur content polluted the ore and made the refined iron flawed and brittle.

In 1709, a father and son team of iron manufacturers, both named Abraham Darby, devised a process by which coal could be used effectively. The Darbys burned coal to make a substance known as coke. They then used the coke to smelt iron in their blast furnaces. The coke-smelted iron not only proved to be as workable as the charcoal-produced iron but was cheaper as well. The process soon spread all over Britain. It helped make coal and iron the principal raw materials of the Industrial Revolution. It also led to a shift in the location of refineries and **foundries**—buildings in which molten metals are cast into products—from the edge of woodlands to the coal fields.

Advances were also made in other areas of iron production. "Puddling," or stirring, the molten iron ore removed more impurities and produced higher quality iron. Rolling the iron allowed manufacturers to flatten it, make it workable, and fashion it into a variety of shapes ueful for machine construction. As a result, by the early 1800's, most machine parts were made of iron instead of wood.

Even with all the improvements, iron was still too brittle or soft for such products as rails, bridge supports, and drive shafts. This led manufacturers to turn to **steel,** iron mixed with carbon to remove impurities. Steel could withstand the stresses and strains created by new machines operating at high speeds and could support heavier loads. At first, however, the known techniques for making steel from iron were too costly to be used widely.

Steel prices dropped 50 percent between 1856 and 1870.

Because weavers were paid by the piece, they were motivated to find ways to increase production.

Then, in 1856, a British inventor named Henry Bessemer developed a process of producing inexpensive steel. It consisted of blasting compressed air through molten iron to burn out the extra carbon and other impurities. The process also greatly reduced the time needed to turn iron into steel. Ten years later, Sir William Siemens, a German-born Englishman, developed the **open hearth process,** another method of producing inexpensive steel. Siemens then joined with Emile and Pierre Martin, two French brothers, to improve the original process.

As a result, the price of steel dropped drastically and steel manufacturing expanded rapidly. The advances in the refining of iron into steel made construction on a gigantic scale possible. Bridges, ships, and buildings larger than people had dreamed of could now be built.

Textiles   Developments in the production of steel transformed the scale of construction. But advances in the textile industry transformed methods of production. It was in the manufacture of textiles that the transformation was most rapid.

In the 1700's, cool, colorful cotton cloth was in great demand in both Britain and overseas. When the domestic system could not meet the demand, cotton cloth merchants set out to expand production. At the time, spinning was slow and tedious work. It took five or six spinners to keep pace with one weaver. Weaving too was laborious. Weavers had to push a shuttle back and forth across the loom by hand. Then, they had to beat the **woof,** the threads that run crosswise, down tightly against the previous row. The width of the fabric was limited by the distance a weaver could "throw" the shuttle.

In 1733 a British clock maker named John Kay made an important improvement in the loom. He invented the fly shuttle, a shuttle mounted on small rollers so that it could roll back and forth on a wooden rail. By pulling a cord that caused wooden hammers to hit the shuttle, one weaver could send it quickly from one side of the loom to the other. Thus, wider fabrics could be woven at a faster pace.

With weavers producing cloth more rapidly, spinners now had to produce more yarn. To do this, they needed a more productive machine. That machine appeared around 1764. It was devised by a British weaver-carpenter named James Hargreaves and was called a spinning jenny. The jenny did not cost much to build, was small enough to be used in a worker's cottage, and did not take a lot of strength to operate. In its early stages, the jenny made it possible for one person to spin six to seven threads at a time. With later refinements, a person could spin as many as 80 threads at once.

Within 20 years, the spinning jenny had been improved by ingenious British inventors and expanded into a power loom, capable of weaving bolts of cloth in textile factories. By 1800 the factory system had replaced the domestic system. What was the factory system?

James Hargreaves named his invention the "spinning jenny" in honor of his wife.

Diversification of energy sources gave industrialists flexibility in selecting factory sites.

The next major breakthrough came in 1768 with Richard Arkwright's water frame, a machine that used water power to do spinning. Unlike the spinning jenny, the water frame could not be operated by muscle power and could not be used in a worker's cottage. The water frame was followed in 1784 by a power loom invented by Edmund Cartwright, a British poet and a member of the clergy. Cartwright's loom could be operated by horse, water, or steam power. Not too long after, a weaver named Samuel Crompton invented the "mule," a spinning machine that combined the best features of the spinning jenny and the water frame. It produced a fine, strong thread which could be used to make all kinds of cloth. It was especially adapted to use in fine muslins, which until this time had to be imported from the East.

These and other improvements greatly increased the demand for raw cotton. Cotton, however, was hard to process because of the seeds that had to be removed from each ball. By hand, a person could clean one to six pounds (0.45 to 2.7 kilograms) of cotton a day. In 1793, Eli Whitney, an American, overcame this last hurdle with the cotton gin, a cotton cleaning machine. It could remove cotton seeds 50 times quicker than it could be done by hand.

These developments led to the mechanization of the textile industry and the decline of the domestic system. The new machines were too large, heavy, and costly for most workers to use in their homes. In addition, some depended on large quantities of water power that the small streams and creeks in rural areas could not supply. As a result, cloth manufacturing gradually began to move out of workers' cottages into factories, which were built near major waterways. This marked the beginning of the **factory system,** an organized method of production that brought together workers and machines under the control of managers. The waterways provided power for the machines and transportation for raw materials and finished cloth.

Under the factory system, all steps in the production process were designed to increase production and cut costs. Each worker performed a particular part of the operation. Roles and responsibilities were clearly defined and separated. As a result, in time, workers and managers became distinct classes.

The success of the mechanized British cotton industry soon attracted the attention of people in other industries. As the advantages of mechanization became apparent, other countries also began to adopt similar methods.

Steam Power

At the heart of much of the change that took place in industry was the discovery that steam power could be used in manufacturing. During the early years of the Industrial Revolution, water was the major source of energy that ran the factories. But, with the development of heavy machinery, water proved to be ineffective. A more reliable and constant source of energy was needed. This new source also had to be plentiful and inexpensive.

In the 1760's, James Watt, a Scottish mathematician and instrument maker, was asked by a professor at the University of Glasgow to repair a classroom model of Newcomen's engine. Although the best machine of its kind at the time, the Newcomen engine wasted too much heat and used a lot of fuel. Upon investigating the model, Watt discovered the engine's chief defect. For the next 15 years or so, he worked to improve the engine. In 1782 he made an improvement that enabled the steam engine to run machinery. Watt's invention was slowly introduced into industry and became the essential power for heavy machines. Since the engine used steam created by heating water with coal and, later, gas and oil, industrialists no longer had to depend exclusively on power generated from running water. This gave them greater flexibility in deciding where to build their factories.

With steam power came new forms of transportation on water and on land. In 1807, using a British steam engine, an American inventor named Robert Fulton designed the first practical steamboat. Called the *Clermont,* it set a record by making the trip from Albany to New York in five days. Most oceangoing ships, however, for a long time did not use steam because they could not carry the large quantities of coal needed. An

George Stephenson, inventor of the *Rocket*, also invented the mining safty lamp mentioned on p. 398.

As railroad construction increased, travel times decreased and long-distance travel became affordable for most people.

George Stephenson, inventor of Rocket, *surveyed and constructed the 40-mile (64-kilometer) railroad line between Liverpool and Manchester. Stephenson, known as the Father of Railways, acted as consultant on many railroad projects, solving problems of roadway construction, bridge design, and locomotive manufacture. What industries grew as a result of the railroad?*

increase in steamboats for trans-Atlantic trade did not take place until the 1880's, when fuel-efficient engines were developed.

On land, steam played a large part in the development of the railroad. The first British rail systems were near coal mines. Coal and iron ore from the underground mines were loaded into wagons that were pulled along wooden rails by men on horses. Later, iron rails replaced the wooden ones. Horses were used to pull trains of wagons along the rails to canals and seaports.

Then, in the early 1800's, an English inventor named Richard Trevithick devised a high-pressure steam engine that had wheels and was designed to run on rails. This was the first successful **locomotive,** or movable steam engine. It was not until 1829, however, that steam transport really came into its own. That year, a British mining engineer named George Stephenson used his locomotive, *Rocket,* to pull a train on the first modern railroad, the Liverpool and Manchester Railway. The *Rocket,* which traveled at an average speed of almost 14 miles (22.4 kilometers) per hour, proved that steam power on rails was a workable idea. It started a railroad-building boom in Britain that soon spread to the rest of the world.

The steamship and the railroad brought a tremendous change in nineteenth-century life.

They increased economic growth in the coal and steel industries. They also provided cheaper and faster transportation that increased the flow of goods and people over long distances. The growth of transportation on a global scale laid the foundations of a world economy and opened up new forms of investment.

1. Identify: Thomas Newcomen, Abraham Darby, Henry Bessemer, Sir William Siemens, Emile and Pierre Martin, John Kay, James Hargreaves, Richard Arkwright, Edmund Cartwright, Samuel Crompton, Eli Whitney, James Watt, Robert Fulton, Richard Trevithick, George Stephenson.
2. How did the jump in coal production affect the iron industry?
3. Why was textile manufacturing moved out of workers' cottages into factories?
4. How did the development of steam power affect transportation?

4 Spread of the Industrial Revolution

At first, Britain made a strong attempt to keep its industrial inventions and processes secret and maintain a monopoly. Parliament passed laws restricting the flow of machines and skilled workers to other countries. By the late 1820's,

Point out that industrial advances occurred in a variety of political circumstances. For example, Britain and the United States industrialized with little government participation. The governments of Germany and Japan, however, took strong, active roles in guiding their nations' industrial growth.

however, many trained mechanics and technicians were leaving Britain to seek business opportunities and to spread their skills in other lands.

By the mid-1800's, British financiers were playing a major role in funding industrial development in other countries. In India, Latin America, and North America, for example, the British financed the construction of railroads. In European countries, British industrialists set up factories and machine shops. They supplied equipment and technical staff as well as capital. Before long, Britain became known as "the workshop of the world."

Industrial Advances

Other countries began to take what they had learned from the British and use it to build their own industries. In most areas, however, large-scale manufacturing based on the factory system did not really begin to take hold until 1870 or later. The major exceptions were Belgium, France, Germany, and the United States.

Belgium Belgium was one of the first European countries to industrialize. As early as 1799, the first wool-carding and wool-spinning machines in continental Europe were built there by a British mechanic and inventor named William Cockerill.

By the 1830's, Belgium had begun to industrialize in earnest. In 1834 the Belgian government adopted a plan for the construction of a national system of railways. The plan had been drawn up by the British inventor George Stephenson, and the construction was financed with loans from British banks.

By the 1850's, 10 percent of Belgium's population was engaged in the production of chemicals, iron machinery, and linen and woolen textiles. Due in part to its rich deposits of coal, iron, zinc, and marble, Belgium's rate of industrial development soon compared with that of Britain. By 1870

Railroad Mileage 1830-1870

	1830	1840	1850	1870
Europe	60	2,800	14,000	65,000
Great Britain	60	1,800	6,600	15,600
Germany	—	400	3,500	11,150
France	—	260	1,800	10,750
Belgium	—	200	540	1,800
North America	—	2,800	9,000	56,000
United States	—	2,800	9,000	53,000
Asia	—	—	200	5,100
South America	—	—	—	1,800
Africa	—	—	—	1,100
Australia	—	—	—	1,000
World Total	60	5,600	23,200	130,000

The chart below is the subject of the "Using Charts" section of the Chapter 17 Review.

The German government encouraged close cooperation between industrialists and academic scientists.

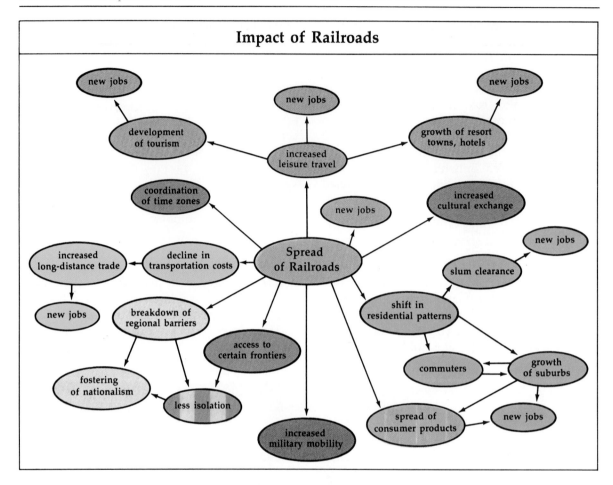

Impact of Railroads

Belgium was a nation of foundries, factories, and mines. Most Belgians lived in cities and earned a living from industry or trade.

France The next European country to industrialize was France. The process there was slower and less complete than in Britain or Belgium. There were several reasons for this. For one, the internal tolls on rivers and between provinces made it costly for merchants to distribute goods. For another, the Napoleonic Wars had strained the country's economy and had cost it the lives of much of its work force. Also, the French continued their emphasis on the production of luxury and hand-crafted items.

The first industries in France affected by industrialization were mining and metallurgy. Then, in the 1840's, railway construction was intensified with the aid of the British, and power-driven machinery began to compete with

handwork in the textile industry. By 1870 a network of major railway lines radiated in every direction from Paris, and many of the French were urban factory workers. Unlike in Belgium, however, most of the people remained agricultural workers.

Germany The next country in Europe to industrialize was Germany. Some machinery was brought in from Britain before 1830. A few factories were built as well. In 1839 British capital was used to build the first important railway from Dresden to Leipzig. In Britain, Belgium, and France, railway building speeded up the construction of foundries and factories. In Germany, it preceded the real beginnings of industrialization and helped create the need for foundries and factories.

Thus, industrialization did not really get underway in Germany until the 1840's. At that

Some teachers might wish to discuss the chemical revolution that also took place between 1870 and 1910. At this time coal by-products became important in the manufacture of dyes, medicines, perfumes, and flavors in foods. Nitrates were developed into fertilizers, too.

time, coal, iron, and textile industries began to emerge. They were supported by German banks and foreign investment. Once Germany became a united country in 1871, the government began direct funding of industrial development, and industrialization blossomed rapidly.

United States   The northeastern part of the United States was the other area most affected by the new industrialization. This was due chiefly to two factors. One was the capital and machinery exported from Britain. The other was a good deal of mechanical invention.

In the late 1700's, Eli Whitney's concept of a way to organize mass production and his introduction of standardized and interchangeable gun parts revolutionized industry in the United States and abroad. In the early 1800's, Cyrus McCormick's invention, the mechanical reaper, did the same for agricultural methods and production. In time, shoe and textile factories geared for large-scale production flourished along the rivers of New England, and coal mining and iron working became dominant in Pennsylvania. By 1870, the United States was well on its way to becoming as industrialized as Britain, Belgium, or Germany.

Science and Technology

Between 1830 and 1870, the Industrial Revolution had almost completely swept through Britain and had made inroads in western and central Europe and the eastern part of the United States. From 1870 to 1910, the movement accelerated and spread. Industries already largely mechanized produced more goods. New industries emerged. The industrial population grew larger while the agricultural one grew smaller. This was true not only in Britain, Belgium, Germany, and the United States, but to some degree in all the countries of Europe as well as in Russia and Japan.

Much of the new growth in industrialization came about because of the application of science to technology. In the mid-1800's, scientific knowledge brought new ideas and created new disciplines such as bacteriology, psychology, and applied science. The first truly comprehensive theories of science were developed and combined. Science became established in university curriculums. Elaborate research labs were founded. More importantly, scientists and inventors discovered that science and technology were useful to one another.

Electricity   Much of the progress made and many of the new industries that arose stemmed from an increasing knowledge about and use of electricity. Electricity, in turn, had come about because of general advances in physics and chemistry. Once the theories governing electricity were understood, it became possible to put them into use.

One invention followed another. In the 1830's, Zénobe Théophile Gramme, a Belgian, developed the first commercially successful **dynamo,** or generator. At about the same time, Samuel F. B. Morse, an American, invented the first successful electric telegraph. He also devised the Morse Code, a communication system of dots and dashes based on long and short vibrations. For many years, it served as the basis for the international telegraph code. By 1866 telegraph cable had been laid under 2,000 miles (3,200 kilometers) of the Atlantic, creating a revolution in the sending of news and business information. In 1876, communications took another giant step forward. That year, an American named Alexander Graham Bell invented the telephone. It was modified and improved, and adopted throughout the United States and Europe.

In 1878, another American, Thomas Alva Edison, invented the incandescent electric light. He demonstrated it the following year at his laboratory in Menlo Park, New Jersey. *New York Herald* headlines informed the public, "It Makes a Light Without Gas or Flame, Cheaper Than Oil." Edison did much to make electricity into an everyday commodity. Prior to his invention, electricity had been limited for the most part to special purposes. The chief reason for this was that it had to be generated at the place where it was used. Before long, Edison lights were illuminating public buildings, factories, and homes all over the world.

In 1881 the first regular electric streetcar system began operation in Germany. It had only one car. But, by the end of the decade, most

HISTORY AND PEOPLE

Eli Whitney

Eli Whitney is best known as the inventor of the cotton gin. He is equally important, however, as the originator of the idea of interchangeable parts, which greatly contributed to industrial growth.

Whitney was born and raised on a Massachusetts farm. At an early age, he showed his talent as a mechanical genius. Stories tell how young Eli disassembled his father's watch and successfully put it back together without anyone's knowledge. Whitney later studied law at Yale University and paid for his education by using his mechanical abilities in repair work. Whitney's graduation finally brought the creative opportunity that would make him famous. He became the inventor of the cotton gin.

The development of the cotton gin is an exception to the rule that inventions are the products of many people who struggle long and hard in their work. Whitney built the machine in a short time while visiting a cotton plantation in Georgia. There, he learned about the locally

grown green seed cotton. Because of the time needed to clean it, the cotton did not bring growers many profits.

Whitney turned his genius to the solution of the problem. Within a few weeks during the winter of 1792-1793, he developed a working model of a cotton gin. Because of its efficiency, the machine was highly successful; and public demand for gins surpassed Whitney's ability to produce them. The gin was so easy to build that others quickly copied it. Whitney brought lawsuits against his competitors. Although his sole right to a patent on the invention was upheld by the courts, Whitney never benefited from these legal decisions. Congress refused to renew the patent when it expired in 1807. In response, Whitney stated that "an invention can be so valuable as to be worthless to the inventor."

During his long legal struggles, Whitney began a new venture that would transform manufacturing. He built a factory in New Haven, Connecticut, where he applied the idea of interchangeable parts to the production of firearms. Until Whitney's innovation, skilled workers made by hand all of the parts and assembled them into a complete weapon. Each gun was produced differently, and replacements for broken parts had to be specially made. Whitney designed machine tools that produced standard parts which would fit any musket.

To show the value of the new method, Whitney promised the United States government 10,000 muskets in two years. At a demonstration, skeptical government officials were astounded when Whitney assembled 10 complete muskets from parts drawn at random from various piles. Illnesses and delays in supplies, however, forced Whitney to wait nine years before fulfilling his government contract.

Nevertheless, the success of the idea of interchangeable parts was assured. It led to the rise of mass production, a development which made the United States a leading industrial power.

Have students compile a list of automobile pioneers from around the world.

Many inventors contributed to the auto industry. Rudolf Diesel (left) patented an engine that operated on cheaper, less refined fuel. Charles Goodyear (right) discovered how to vulcanize rubber. What country first led in auto manufacturing?

European and American cities had, or were getting ready to have, electrically powered street railway systems. In 1896, Guglielmo Marconi, an Italian engineer, patented in Britain a practical system of wireless telegraphy. Two years later, radio communication was established across the English Channel. In 1901 it was established across the Atlantic.

By the twentieth century, electricity was becoming a household reality. Not only were there electric lights and telephones, but there were also vacuum cleaners, sewing machines, and washing machines, powered by small electric motors.

Internal-Combustion Engine   Another factor that hastened the pace of industrialization between 1870 and 1910 was the creation and perfection of two engines. One was the **steam turbine,** a rotary motor in which a current of steam, air, or water directly rotates the shaft in its bearings. Its use for a steam engine was devised by a British engineer named Sir Charles Parsons, who first patented his steam turbine in 1884. By 1910 turbines manufactured by Parsons at a factory in Britain were widely used to run electric dynamos and steamships.

The other engine was the **internal-combustion engine,** a device that uses a gas explosion behind a piston to transfer energy directly into mechanical power. In 1885 and 1886, a German engineer named Gottlieb Daimler designed a small, portable internal-combustion engine fueled with light oil. Daimler's "gasoline engine" could propel vehicles and boats. In 1892, Rudolf Diesel, another German engineer, patented the first oil-burning internal-combustion engine. By 1910 it was being used in generating plants, ocean liners, and locomotives.

Most dirigibles were filled with hydrogen, a highly explosive gas. Travel in them was risky.

Some teachers might wish to trace the growth of industrialization and urbanization in countries other than Britain.

The steam-turbine and internal-combustion engines ushered in a new era in transportation. In the late 1880's and during the 1890's, motor cars were introduced in France, Germany, Britain, and the United States. At first, more cars were manufactured in France than anywhere else. But, in 1902, an American mechanic named Henry Ford founded a motor car company in Detroit. In 1909 he began to produce low-priced cars on a fairly large scale. By 1910, three-quarters of the cars produced in the world were being made in the United States. In 1913 Ford applied the idea of an electrically powered moving assembly line to the production of cars. As a moving belt or chain carried the "growing" car past them, workers performed their specific tasks. In this way, a car could be assembled in half the time it used to take. This led to lower prices and helped usher in the era of mass automobile ownership.

Cars were not the only form of transportation made practical by the gasoline engine. It also had a startling effect on aviation. A German, Count Ferdinand von Zeppelin, and a Brazilian, Alberto Santos-Dumont, designed and built dirigibles, or motorized airships, airplanes lighter than air. At the same time, mechanics and engineers were experimenting with other flying machines, motor airplanes heavier than air. Among the most successful in this area were two American brothers, Orville and Wilbur Wright. They made their first successful flight in 1903.

The growth in transportation led to the emergence and growth of two other industries—petroleum and rubber. In 1860 the world output of crude oil was one-half million barrels. By 1910, it was 325 million barrels. In 1970 the world's production of crude rubber was 10,000 tons (9,000 metric tons). In 1910 it was 75,000 tons (67,500 metric tons). Much of the growth in the rubber industry could be traced to the growing demand for rubber tires for cars.

1. Identify: William Cockerill, Eli Whitney, Cyrus McCormick, Zénobe Théophile Gramme, Morse Code, Alexander Graham Bell, Thomas Edison, Guglielmo Marconi, Sir Charles Parsons, Gottlieb Daimler, Rudolf Diesel, Henry Ford, Ferdinand von Zeppelin, Alberto Santos-Dumont, Orville and Wilbur Wright.

2. Why was the process of industrialization slower and less complete in France than in Britain or Belgium?
3. What did scientists and inventors find out about science and technology? What effect did this have on the Industrial Revolution?

5 Life Transformed

The Industrial Revolution brought many changes in people's lifestyles. The changes appeared first in the new industrial cities of Britain. From there, they spread to other areas of the country and then to the rest of the world.

Many of the changes brought on by the Industrial Revolution were not expected. Some of them were unwelcome. In general, people looked upon the changes with a mixture of awe and dismay.

Growth of Cities

Industrialization caused a dramatic shift in where people lived. In Britain, for example, most people had lived in rural areas, mainly in the south. But, by 1850, the situation had changed. The rural landscape became transformed as new manufacturing cities displaced farms and villages. Factory smokestacks and their plumes of black smoke soon dwarfed church steeples. Railroads cut through crowded city neighborhoods, bringing noise, soot, and blight.

New coal, textile, iron, and steel industries arose in northern England and in the center of Scotland. As more and more people from southern England migrated north seeking jobs, new cities emerged and grew.

Industrial cities, shipping ports, and commercial centers bulged with new inhabitants, while towns and cities without adequate transportation or resources lost much of their population. Manchester, the center of Britain's cotton industry, and Liverpool, a leading port, were classic examples of urban growth. Manchester grew from a city of 25,000 in 1772 to one of 367,000 in 1851. Liverpool's population soared from 77,000 in 1801 to 400,000 in 1851. In 1785, only three British cities had populations over 50,000. By 1860, 31 cities had populations that size.

HISTORY AND CITIES

Manchester, England

Manchester is located in northern England. It developed where three easily bridged rivers, the Irk, Medlock, and Irwell, come together. Early records show that Manchester was a Roman fort in the first century A.D. During the Middle Ages, it became an important trade and religious center in northern England.

In the sixteenth century, Manchester became a leading textile center. Merchants living in the city passed out raw materials to peasant weavers and collected their finished cloth products for shipment to Liverpool, London, and foreign ports.

Although the city grew rapidly during the eighteenth century, it still had a quiet atmosphere. People enjoyed sailing on the Irwell. Cattle grazed close to the center of town, and orchards dotted the banks of the Irk. Pigs roamed the unpaved, narrow, barely lit streets. Leading merchants had their homes in the center of town close to their businesses. There were no great commercial or industrial buildings.

By the early 1800's, the impact of the Industrial Revolution on Manchester was apparent. Between the late 1780's and 1800, the population rose from 40,000 to over 70,000. A boom in the newly mechanized cotton industry created a small class of wealthy industrialists. It also resulted in a new working class made up, in large part, of immigrant workers from surrounding English counties and from Ireland.

During this period, the appearance of Manchester changed. Mills and warehouses, the city's new architectural landmarks, replaced private homes and shops in certain areas. With the coming of the railways, industrialists built large mansions on the outskirts of the city, leaving the city center to working-class slums. The Irwell became so badly polluted that it was described as "a flood of liquid manure."

In 1835 Alexis de Tocqueville, a French writer and political philosopher, visited Manchester and gave his impressions of the city:

> . . . .*Thirty or forty factories rise on the tops of the hills. . . . The wretched dwellings of the poor are scattered haphazard around them. . . . The roads which connect the still-disjointed limbs of the great city show, like the rest, every sign of hurried and unfinished work; the incidental activity of a population bent on gain. . . . Here humanity attains its most complete development and its most brutish; here civilization works its miracles, a civilized [person] is turned back almost into a savage.**

Others, however, were more optimistic about Manchester. *The Edinburgh Journal*, a leading British magazine, stated in 1858 that

> *Manchester streets may be irregular, its smoke may be dense, and its mud ultra-muddy, but not any or all of these things can prevent the image of a great city rising before us as the very symbol of civilization, foremost in the march of improvement, a grand incarnation [embodiment] of progress.*

1. What were the causes of Manchester's transformation from a small trading town to a large industrial city?
2. Do you think that what happened to Manchester can be called "progress"? Why, or why not?

Journeys to England and Ireland, Alexis de Tocqueville, tr. by G. Lawrence and K. P. Mayer, © 1958 by Arno, pp. 105-108.

Case studies can be used to compare and contrast urban problems past and present.

Profound physical changes took place to accomodate growing urban populations. Villages, hamlets, and early industrial sites swelled into cities, while cities founded in medieval times expanded beyond their old walls to include rural areas. Such growth, however, was not without problems. Many cities were unprepared and ill equipped to support their growing populations.

One major problem was housing. Because additional housing could not be built fast enough to meet the flood of migration from rural areas, workers often had to live in poorly constructed and overcrowded homes. In the words of one official at the time, new housing built especially for the workers often was "of the commonest materials, and with the worst workmanship . . . altogether unfit for people to live in." Houses were jammed next to each other on all sides. As a result, rooms often were dark and airless. Since rents were high and always increasing, many poor families were forced to live in cramped attics and damp cellars.

Another problem confronting many cities was poor sanitation. Sewers most often were open trenches running down the middle of unpaved streets. Pure water was a luxury, if it existed at all. Factories created dumps of industrial refuse, polluted waterways with chemical wastes, and filled the air with smoke and dangerous gases. These conditions fostered the spread of disease. Consequently, in the early years of heavy industrialization, life expectancy in the city was sharply lower than in the countryside.

A New Way of Life

Cities thrust upon new industrial workers a way of life that was unfamiliar, confusing, and always changing. Traditional values and beliefs no longer seemed to be reliable guides for the future. Sons no longer carried on in the jobs of their fathers. In fact, some of those jobs no longer existed because machines had made some trades obsolete. Older family members and the church, which in the past had provided support and guidance, often were missing. Some workers managed to adapt successfully to their new lives. Others, however, could not. The strain on them was reflected by increases in the levels of alcoholism, prostitution, divorce, and crime.

A great amount of the strain placed on the city dweller came from work situations. New and old values clashed. Industrial workers had no property of their own, and there was no use for their rural skills. Thus, they were entirely dependent for their survival on the factory owners. Under the domestic system, workers could produce at their own pace. Under the factory system, discipline and precision were required for efficient production. This forced workers to produce faster.

Working hours in the factories were long—six days a week, 12 to 19 hours a day. There were few safety regulations, and many workers were injured or killed in accidents on the job. Women and children who labored as unskilled workers worked 10 hours a day or longer. Since children could be paid less and were easier to train than adults, employers preferred to hire them.

This scene of Wentworth Street in London shows the despair of the urban poor in the late nineteenth century. Overcrowding led to poor sanitation and poor health. How did factories contribute to poor sanitation?

Have students write brief fictional accounts of a day in the life of the person in the picture below.

At first, workhouses for delinquent children were the main source of child laborers. By the mid-1800's, however, the pressures and high costs of city life forced many parents to allow their young children to work. Why were children preferred as workers?

Wages were kept low so employers could realize a good profit. Many workers did not earn enough to provide their families with the necessities of life. During economic slumps, many workers lost their jobs or faced cuts in pay. In some cases, whole districts dependent on one trade were plunged into unemployment. The upper and middle classes tended to blame the unemployed workers for being out of work, accusing them of laziness. Since governments did not provide aid programs for the needy, unemployed workers had nowhere to turn for relief except to charity or the poorhouse.

All of this had an effect on family life. Under the domestic system, home and work place generally were one and the same. Industrialization changed that. This separation of home and work place broke the tradition of the family as a cooperative unit. In middle-class families, fathers became the sole breadwinners while mothers assumed the major responsibility of raising children. Thus, male activities centered in the work place while female ones centered in the home. In working-class families, although most members continued to work, they labored apart and had little time together. By the end of the 1800's, they too came under the influence of changes affecting middle-class family life. During this period, stereotypes emerged that created and reinforced the idea that men and women occupied different roles based on differences in their characters.

1. How did the Industrial Revolution affect where people lived?
2. What were two major problems confronting city dwellers?
3. What were working conditions like during the early years of the Industrial Revolution?
4. What impact did the separation of home and work place have on the family unit?

CHAPTER 17 REVIEW

Summary

1. In pre-industrial times, most people lived in rural areas where life was geared to the seasons and change was slow.
2. The family was a cooperative economic unit using marriage and inheritance customs to ensure that successive families would have enough land on which to subsist.
3. Village life was based around growing and producing for local consumption. No incentive existed for increasing production.
4. The sudden population growth in the 1700's strained all aspects of social, economic, and political life. However, it provided both an incentive for increased agricultural productivity and, later, a pool for industrialization.
5. Among other factors, Britain had the right combination of capital, accessible resources, and talent to lead the Industrial Revolution.
6. The Industrial Revolution began with innovations in the textile, coal, and iron industries. These changes transformed the methods of production, the scale of construction, and the sources of energy used to power machines. They eventually led to the rise of new forms of transportation.
7. Great Britain initially tried to protect its industrial secrets; but, in the 1800's it provided capital and machinery for industrialization in Europe and the United States.
8. The Industrial Revolution shifted the bulk of the population from rural to urban areas, causing the rapid growth of some cities and the decline of others.
9. Traditional family values and relationships were altered by the separation of home and work place.

Building Vocabulary

commons
incentive
domestic system
enclosure movement
capital
capitalists

smelting
refine
foundries
steel
open hearth process

woof
factory system
locomotive
dynamo
steam turbine
internal-combustion engine

Reviewing the Main Ideas

1. How were agriculture and industry related during pre-industrial times?
2. How was the family an economic as well as a social unit in pre-industrial society?
3. How did marriage and inheritance customs protect the family's welfare?
4. What caused Europe's sudden growth of population in the 1700's? What were the effects of that growth?
5. What did the enclosure movement accomplish? What were its negative effects?
6. Why did Britain become the leader of the Industrial Revolution? How did British industrial ideas spread to other nations?
7. What benefits came from improvements in mining coal and in refining iron and steel?
8. How did changes in the British textile industry alter the traditional methods of production?
9. Why was the development of steam power so important to industry? What effects did it have on transportation?

10. In what ways did electricity, the steam turbine, and the internal-combustion engine quicken the pace of industrialization?

11. What were some of the immediate consequences of the Industrial Revolution? What were some of its long-term consequences?

Discussing Important Ideas

1. The first half of the nineteenth century has been called the "age of coal and iron" and the "age of the railroads." Which name do you think is most appropriate? Why?
2. Do you think the Industrial Revolution would have taken place if there had been no sudden growth in the population? Explain your answer.
3. Can Thomas Malthus's views on population growth be of any value in the twentieth century? If so, how?
4. How can consumer demand influence technological development? Give examples from your text and from the world today to support your answer.
5. What technological development during the Industrial Revolution had the most sweeping impact? Why?
6. Britain had several key elements that led it to industrialize before other nations. Which element do you think was the most critical?
7. If you had lived in a nineteenth-century British industrial city, what aspects of city life would you have liked and disliked?
8. What were the advantages and disadvantages of the Industrial Revolution?

Using Charts

Refer to the chart on page 404 to answer the following questions:
1. What do the arrows on the chart indicate?
2. What does the chart indicate about the relationship between commuters and the growth of suburbs?
3. What were the ten most direct impacts of the spread of railroads?
4. Why are two of the oval-shaped entries on the chart striped?
5. What kinds of jobs are represented by the "new jobs" entries on the chart?

CHAPTER 18

"Summer Evening" by Vincent Van Gogh

❝ *The whole mass of previous ideas and conceptions that tied the world together are dissolved and collapse in the vision of a dream.* ❞

Georg Wilhelm Friedrich Hegel, German philosopher (1770-1831)

Response to the Industrial Revolution

In time, the Industrial Revolution sparked deep change in all aspects of life in Europe. Population began to grow rapidly. Improved medicine and health care, better sanitation and safer water, and better nutrition led to a sharp cut in the death rate. Goods began to be produced for a large market. Prices went down, and wages went up. More people could pay for manufactured products than ever before. The dramatic material advances gave people hope that poverty, illness, and misery could be overcome.

The era of the masses, or common people, was launched. Education, traditionally offered only to the upper classes, was extended to people of other classes as well. New schools, libraries, and universities were founded. Newspapers, magazines, and other reading material began to enjoy wide circulation.

The working classes began to exert more political and economic influence. The domestic system had kept industrial workers apart. The factory system brought them together and led them to form trade unions to promote their common interests. Since such unions were not legal in Britain in the early 1800's, the first ones often were secret societies that posed as social or funeral clubs. Not until 1824 did the British Parliament recognize the right of workers to organize unions. In time, and with some struggle, the labor unions grew in size and number. They soon became a major force not only in Europe but in other parts of the world as well.

All these changes, however, did not take place at once. While there was pride in early accomplishments and great expectations for the future, there also was frustration. And with the frustration often came doubt and a loss of confidence in the future. To explain what was happening, people sought new ideas and new answers. They hoped these would give them the guidance they needed for the future.

1 The Capitalist Response

Capitalism, an economic system in which the means of production are privately owned, had begun to develop with medieval commerce and the rise of a bourgeoisie, or middle class. The understanding of capitalism was furthered in the mid-1700's by the French physiocrats and their philosophy of laissez faire. As the Industrial Revolution progressed, new philosophies emerged. Some of these were based on the work of earlier thinkers. All of the new philosophies sprang from a desire to understand and reform society.

Laissez-Faire Economics

By the mid-1700's, nobles, gentry, and merchants knew from experience that their particular country was enriched by trade with other countries. What most of them did not know, nor had anyone been able to explain satisfactorily, was how or in what manner. The explanation came in 1776 with the publication of a book called *The Wealth of Nations*. Its author, a Scottish professor named Adam Smith, offered a doctrine which revolutionized European society.

Adam Smith   In *The Wealth of Nations*, Adam Smith spoke out against mercantilism and the controls it placed on the individual. Basic to the mercantilist system were several beliefs. One was that **bullion,** or money, was wealth.

Another was that national power was more important than individual welfare. The more bullion the state had, the more powerful it was. At the time, most bullion came through foreign trade. As a result, commerce and industry were closely regulated and controlled by government. Tariffs and taxation were in wide use.

Smith did not agree with these beliefs. In his view, labor, not money, was the source of wealth. Individual welfare, not national power, should be the goal. Smith argued that the major economic drive of any individual was self-inter-

est. Smith did not think this was all bad. He believed there was a natural order in the universe that made all the individual strivings for self-interest add up to the social good. In the end, the greatest good for society as a whole would be achieved. Competition, along with a free market price system, would act as an "invisible hand" and guide resources to their most productive use. Thus, said Smith, the best economic policy was the one that allowed individuals to act freely without government interference.

Smith's ideas met with great response from the commercial and industrial class. Merchants and manufacturers did not like all the controls placed on them. Smith's work gave them a reason for their desire to change existing government policy. This was especially true in Britain, where the economy was growing rapidly. British industries really did not need any protection or special help. Britain was so far in advance of the industrial and trade capacities of other countries that free trade would have been to its advantage.

Smith wrote *The Wealth of Nations* before the Industrial Revolution was well under way. As the Revolution developed, some of his theories were discarded. Even so, *The Wealth of Nations* had a great influence on other European thinkers. It introduced science into economics and presented the idea that wealth was created by labor.

David Ricardo One British economist influenced by Smith was David Ricardo. Like Smith, he believed in laissez faire and felt that government interference in business would only upset the natural order.

Ricardo set forth some of his theories in his book *Principles of Political Economy and Taxation*, published in 1819. One theory, known as the Iron Law of Wages, was that wages could not rise above the lowest level needed for subsistence.

Ricardo believed that wages were determined by supply and demand. When labor was plentiful, wages would be low. When labor was scarce, wages would be high. When workers received higher wages, they would have more children. This would increase population, which would mean a larger work force. With more people competing for jobs, employers could

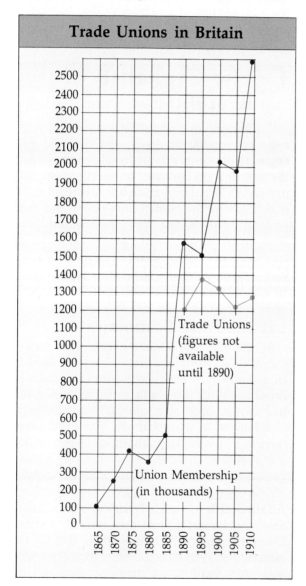

Trade Unions in Britain

Trade Unions (figures not available until 1890)

Union Membership (in thousands)

David Ricardo's Law of Rent chiefly concerned the rents that tenant farmers paid landlords.

Be certain that students are able to distinguish among the ideas of Smith, Ricardo, Bentham, and Mill.

lower wages and still find people willing to work. Lower wages would encourage workers to have fewer children. This, in time, would lead to a shortage of workers. With fewer workers available, employers would have to pay higher wages. Workers could not escape this cycle, which condemned them time and again to periods of low wages and misery.

Ricardo also analyzed other issues. One was why property owners, capitalists, and workers received the share of income they did. From this came the Law of Rent, which said that rent is a result, not a cause, of price. Another issue concerned the value of goods. Ricardo concluded that the value of goods was measured by the amount of labor it took to produce them. This came to be known as the **labor theory of value.**

Ricardo painted a far gloomier picture of the economic future than had Adam Smith. His views, along with those of Thomas Malthus, led people to call economics "the dismal science."

Need for Reform

Other British thinkers took some of the ideas of Adam Smith and David Ricardo and extended them. They believed also in laissez faire. But they did not agree that poverty and misery had to exist. Believing that British society should—and could—be improved, they called for reform. Two of these British thinkers were Jeremy Bentham and John Stuart Mill.

Jeremy Bentham Jeremy Bentham developed the concept of **utilitarianism.** It was a philosophy based on Bentham's belief that the rightness of any action, law, or political institution should be measured by its usefulness. How useful each was could be judged by the contribution it made to human happiness and to the reduction of human misery.

In Bentham's view, the purpose of all legislation was to promote "the greatest happiness of the greatest number." Two things were needed to achieve that happiness. For one, the administration of the state had to be made more efficient. For another, the individual had to be allowed to act freely without governmental restrictions.

Bentham crusaded for a better code of law, education for all, a public health service, and

Jeremy Bentham promoted the idea of the secret ballot as early as 1809. No government used this ballot until 1856 when Australia adopted it. Other electoral reforms Bentham supported were annual elections and widespread suffrage. What other reforms did Bentham suggest?

changes in the electoral system. He also made plans for a new constitutional code, a model prison, and perpetual peace.

John Stuart Mill Another British thinker who wanted to correct the problems caused by industrialization was John Stuart Mill. He made contributions in the areas of logic, ethics, philosophy, politics, and economics.

Mill's book *Principles of Political Economy* was published in 1848. In it, Mill set out to revise the ideas of Adam Smith and David Ricardo. Unlike Smith and Ricardo, he did not believe that goods and services were distributed by natural law. He believed instead that once wealth was produced,

Utopian socialists were devoted idealists and humanitarians. They hoped that the ruling classes could be persuaded to see that most reforms would be to their benefit, too.

its distribution depended "on the laws and customs of society." If governments chose to, they could tax wealth, take property, or ban inheritances.

Mill reasoned that since distribution was controlled by human laws, progress was possible. Technological change could help the working class improve its standard of living and have a brighter future. To assure that future, however, laissez faire would have to be altered. Government had to provide protection against monopolies and preserve competition. It also had to safeguard the rights of the individual.

Mill believed strongly in the rights of the individual. To him, individual liberty was a basic human right. In his work *On Liberty*, published in 1895, he argued that freedom of thought was the key to progress and that freedom of discussion was the wisest course. Government, he said, should guarantee individual liberty.

Mill favored taxing rents and inheritances. He also advocated free trade, the formation of workers' cooperatives, and universal suffrage. The government, said Mill, should work for the well-being of all its citizens.

1. Identify: *The Wealth of Nations*, Adam Smith, David Ricardo, *Principles of Political Economy and Taxation*, Iron Law of Wages, Jeremy Bentham, John Stuart Mill, *Principles of Political Economy*.
2. How were Adam Smith's views different from those of the mercantilists?
3. On what did David Ricardo base his belief that the poor never would escape poverty?
4. In what ways did John Stuart Mill want laissez faire altered?

2 The Socialist Response

Not everyone in Europe agreed in full with the capitalist way of thinking in the early 1800's. Some people called socialists believed that the means of production should be operated to benefit all of the people rather than just some of the people. The reforms they sought tended to be different in nature from those sought by others. These "reformers" hoped to end the misery of the poor by changing the structure of society.

Utopian Socialists

Most of the early socialist schemes centered around **utopias,** or ideal societies. In these utopias, the abundance of the industrial age would be shared equally by all. All people would be treated fairly. There would be no poverty.

Saint-Simon and Fourier   Among the early utopian socialists were Claude Henri de Rouvroy, comte de Saint-Simon, and Charles Fourier of France.

Saint-Simon was an aristocrat who fought in the American Revolution. He also supported the French Revolution, and in 1783, gave up his title. Saint-Simon believed that workers, not the "idle class," should get the highest income. He also believed that the controlling forces of society were in industry and science. He concluded, therefore, that to establish a better social order, industrial and scientific leaders should reorganize and direct the state.

Although Saint-Simon set up no program to achieve his goals, his ideas inspired others. His disciples took them and modified them. They advocated a society run by engineers and scientists with public ownership of the means of production. They also favored the end of individual inheritance rights and the gradual emancipation of women.

Charles Fourier was the son of a French shopkeeper. He believed that if people's natural passions were channeled properly, there would be social harmony. Before this could happen, however, the artificial restraints of civilization had to be destroyed. Unlike Saint-Simon, Fourier had detailed plans to achieve his goal. He regrouped society into **phalansteries,** model communities of about 1,600 people. All the members of a community would live together in community buildings. Each member would work at what he or she did best. Profits would be distributed on a formula based on the amount of labor, capital, and talent contributed by each person. The highest rewards would go to the labor force. Those who did the unpleasant jobs would receive more than those who did the enjoyable ones. Although several phalansteries were set up in France and in the United States, none had lasting success.

One of Owen's ideas was that of the consumer cooperative, where food and clothing were purchased wholesale and distributed at low cost to members of the cooperative.

The Rise of Modern Europe · **419**

Other names given to "scientific socialism" are "radical socialism" and "Marxist socialism."

The school in Robert Owen's community of New Lanark was one of the first to provide education for children under six. Half of the schoolday was spent in instruction and half of the day in play. The curriculum stressed exercise, and classes were even held outdoors. Sharing and cooperation were emphasized, and no form of punishment was permitted. How do these practices reflect Robert Owen's beliefs?

Robert Owen   The first move in the direction of practical socialism was made by Robert Owen, a wealthy Scottish manufacturer. Owen believed that a person's character was molded in great part by his or her environment. Therefore, character could be changed. Since in Britain at the time, the mainspring of a person's social life and economic activities was competition, Owen believed that competition was at the root of many existing problems. Thus, he reasoned, if competition were replaced by cooperation, the condition of life would change for the better.

In 1800 Owen set out to prove this point and to show employers that it paid to treat their workers well. That year, he moved to New Lanark, a grim mill town in Scotland. In time, he turned the town into a model industrial community. Although Owen did not turn the town's textile mill completely over to the workers, he greatly improved their living and working conditions. Workers received fair wages and good housing and sanitary facilities. Children were sent to schools rather than into the factories. The stores in which the workers traded sold quality goods at low prices. The mill made a profit, and the workers prospered. Before long, New Lanark became famous both in Britain and abroad. Much of the success was due to Owen's determination and personality.

In 1826 Owen sold New Lanark and sunk his wealth into New Harmony, Indiana, a larger model community in the United States. There he tried to set up a voluntary and freely self-governing cooperative community. New Harmony, however, did not meet with the same success as New Lanark.

Scientific Socialism

As the Industrial Revolution spread, workers grew in number and in potential strength. At the same time, some socialists began to argue that the ideas of the utopians were foolish and futile. Primary among those who felt this way were two German philosophers, Karl Marx and Friedrich Engels. They believed that the important thing was not to conceive of ideal systems but to work to dissolve the existing one. They formulated a "scientific socialism." It was based on the premise that the history of society is the history of the struggle between classes.

Karl Marx and Friedrich Engels   Karl Marx was the son of a prosperous German lawyer. He studied law at the Universities of Bonn and Berlin. In 1842 he earned a doctorate in history and philosophy. Because of his radical views, however, he could not get a teaching position. So instead he took a position as the editor of a newspaper. Before long, his writings, which were critical of events in Prussia, were suppressed by the government, and he was forced to leave the country.

Eventually, Marx went to Paris. There, in 1844, he met Friedrich Engels. Engels was the son of a German manufacturer. He was passing through

Marx called his process "dialectical materialism." He borrowed the process of change from Hegel and added materialism to emphasize his own economic interpretation of history.

Paris on his way to Manchester, England. There, he was to take a position in a textile factory in which his father had an interest.

Engels was horrified by the conditions he found in Manchester. In 1845 he published his findings in a book entitled *The Condition of the Working Class in England in 1844.* The book attracted wide attention. Among those impressed by the work was Karl Marx.

Marx and Engels became lifelong friends and collaborated on several works. In 1849, Marx, exiled from most of the major centers of Europe, settled in London. The following year, Engels did the same. Marx worked off and on as the London correspondent for the *New York Tribune.* This, however, did not earn him enough to maintain his family. They lived in poverty, often on the edge of starvation. Engels, on the other hand, was a successful business person. He provided Marx with the financial aid he needed. This made it possible for Marx to devote his life to research and writing.

Engels (left) and Marx (right), shown with Marx's daughters, had different talents. While Engels was brilliant at promoting their works, Marx was the superior theorist. What were their occupations?

Marx's Theories

Marx based his theories in great part on the teachings of the German philosopher Georg Wilhelm Friedrich Hegel. Hegel taught that changing ideas were the major force in history. As ideas clashed, new ideas emerged. This produced new changes, conflicts, and ideas. The process was never ending.

Like Hegel, Marx believed that history advanced through conflict. But, in his view, economics was the major force. Production was at the base of every social order. Laws, social systems, customs, religion, and art all developed in accord with a society's economic base.

The most important aspect of the economic base was the division of society into classes. The class that controlled production became the ruling class. No ruling class would willingly give up its control of production. The only way to make the ruling class give it up was through revolution. Therefore, conflict between classes was inevitable. This conflict, which Marx called "class struggle," was the force that pushed history forward.

Marx argued that Europe had moved through four stages of economic life—primitive, slave, feudal, and capitalist. During the primitive stage, people produced only what they needed to live. There was no **exploitation,** or unfair use, of a person for one's own advantage. But once tools were developed and people could produce a surplus, they became exploitable. From then on, history was the story of class struggle. One class was pitted against another—master against slave, lord against serf, capitalist against worker. In each case, it was the "haves" against the "have-nots."

During the feudal period, for example, classes were divided into nobility, clergy, merchants, artisans, and serfs. When commerce expanded, it brought the bourgeoisie into conflict with the landholding nobles and clergy. The bourgeoisie destroyed and replaced the unproductive feudal nobility and established a new industrial order.

Capitalism, then, was not a permanent state of humankind. It was merely the latest phase of historical development. Another revolution would cause the downfall of capitalism. This time the class struggle would be between the

The alienation of workers and the loss of human dignity, which occurred in the industrial setting, formed the basis of Marx's objections to capitalism.

The picture below is the subject of the "Using Illustrations" section of the Chapter 18 Review.

bourgeoisie, or capitalists, and the **proletariat,** the newly created class of factory workers whose main asset was their labor. As the makers of goods, the proletariat was the true productive class.

Like David Ricardo, Marx believed in the labor theory of value. That is, the value of any item is equal to the amount of labor needed to produce it. At the time, however, workers were not paid wages equal to the full value of their labor. Therefore, argued Marx, the worker was being exploited by the capitalist. Marx called the difference between what the workers were paid and the real worth of their labor **surplus value.** It became the capitalist's profit.

Under capitalism, said Marx, worth was measured only in terms of money. The labor of workers was treated like any other item to be bought or sold. While the capitalists flourished, the workers suffered. They had no power, no responsibility, and no say. They had no control over their time, their jobs, their working conditions, or the products they created.

Since workers were not being paid the full value of their labor, in time they would not be able to afford to buy what was being produced. The result would be a great amount of unsold goods on the market. Then production would be cut back, and workers would be laid off. Prices would fall, and there would be less profit. The economy would stop growing. There would be a **recession,** a period of decline in economic activity. Once all the unsold goods were disposed of, prices would rise and profits would grow. Then the whole economic cycle would begin again.

With each cycle, the capitalists would gain more money and power. At the same time, the workers would suffer more and grow poorer. They would become more enslaved to the capitalists. The gap between rich and poor would widen, and workers and capitalists would grow more hostile toward one another. In time, the workers would unite and revolt. They would sweep aside the capitalist system.

Marx believed that the revolution would take place in a highly industrialized country where the crises of capitalism had advanced. Once the

This pyramid, which mocks a capitalist society, illustrates Marx's theories on class struggle. All of Marx's ideas about changing society revolve around this struggle. According to Marx, when did the struggle begin?

workers had control, they would begin to build a society in which the people as a whole owned everything. Since there would be no private property, there would be no exploitation. In time, class distinctions would disappear. Everyone would become equal, and society would be classless. Government, which in Marx's view was created to protect the exploiters from the exploited, would "wither" away. So would family and religion. In the end, each individual would find true fulfillment.

Marx's Writings   The broad views of Marx and Engels were set forth in *The Communist Manifesto,* which was published in 1848. In it, Marx and Engels expressed their general view of the class struggle and their belief that revolution was inevitable.

The *Manifesto* served as the platform for the Communist League, which Marx joined in 1847.

Point out that Marx was not well known during his lifetime. He was neither a popular speaker nor a popular writer. However, according to historian Isaiah Berlin, "no thinker in the nineteenth century has had so direct, deliberate and powerful an influence upon mankind as Karl Marx."

He encouraged revolution and said that the Communists could help bring it about in several ways. One was by bringing about an international union of workers. Another was by supporting whatever political party favored the "momentary interests of the working class." In *The Communist Manifesto*, Marx announced:

> The Communists disdain to conceal their views and aims. They openly declare that their ends can be attained only by the forcible overthrow of all existing social conditions. Let the ruling classes tremble at a Communist revolution. The proletarians have nothing to lose but their chains. They have a world to win.*

In the *Manifesto*, Marx and Engels urged, "Working men of all countries, unite!" In 1864 the first step was taken toward this goal. Representatives of British, French, German, Polish, and Italian workers met in London to organize the First International Working Man's Association.

In 1867 the first volume of Marx's work *Das Kapital* was published. It expanded on the ideas set forth in the *Manifesto*. Marx died in 1883 while working on the remaining volumes of *Das Kapital*. After Marx's death, Engels edited the remaining notes and drafts. They were published as volumes II and III of *Das Kapital* in 1885 and 1894. The three volumes became the foundation of international socialism.

Impact on Workers   At the time Marx and Engels put forth their theories, capitalism was in its early stages. Many workers were being exploited, and their poverty contrasted sharply with the luxury enjoyed by industrialists and landowners.

By 1900, however, conditions had begun to change in western Europe. Workers could buy much more with their wages than they could 50 years earlier. As workers gained the right to vote, they were able to exert enough pressure through elections and laws to correct the worst social ills. In some areas, the gap between the rich and poor had narrowed. Many workers began to see that through gradual reform they could share in the wealth. They did not think that violent revolution, as preached by Marx, was necessary.

As workers became more of a force in capitalist society, they had less reason to join a revolutionary movement of workers. The ties of class became less important and those of language and place more important. Workers preferred to keep their loyalties to their own countries rather than unite with workers of other countries in a revolutionary struggle. They became bound by nationalism rather than by internationalism.

1. Identify: Comte de Saint-Simon, Charles Fourier, Robert Owen, Karl Marx, Friedrich Engels, Georg Wilhelm Friedrich Hegel, *The Communist Manifesto, Das Kapital*.
2. What were the goals of utopian socialism?
3. On what premise was scientific socialism based?
4. Why did Karl Marx believe that revolution was inevitable?

3 The Creative Response

Economists, industrialists, and philosophers were not the only ones who responded to changes brought on by the Industrial Revolution. Many European writers and painters also reacted. From the late 1700's to the early 1900's, the world of arts was in a constant state of change with one movement following another.

Artists interpreted the events of the times and mirrored the mixed feelings of the general public. They conveyed what the philosophers and others were demonstrating in other ways with other methods. They showed that an old order was rapidly disappearing and that, because of the many changes, the people were in a state of confusion. At the same time, these artists laid the foundations for the art and literature of more modern times.

Romanticism

During the middle and late 1700's, some European writers began to object to the Enlightenment's stress on reason, form, and the

---

The Communist Manifesto, Karl Marx and Friedrich Engels, as quoted in *The Marx-Engels Reader*, tr. by Robert C. Tucker, © 1972 by Norton, p. 362.

Explain that many romantics were strongly influenced by the American and French revolutions as well as the Industrial Revolution.

Many romantics were troubled by the present and looked nostalgically to the Middle Ages.

The romantic movement influenced the architecture of the early 1800's. To capture the past, architects studied Gothic structures from the late Middle Ages and copied the designs accurately. Thus, when a fire damaged the Houses of Parliament in 1834, the buildings were reconstructed in a Neo-Gothic style. The beauty and grandeur of this style appealed to Britons. What criticisms of industrialization did the romantics make?

classics. They objected to the spread of industrialization as well. They felt that the world—and the arts—had become cold, overly rational, and machinelike. Their movement became known as **romanticism,** and they took their basic ideals from the French philosopher Jean-Jacques Rousseau. He emphasized the senses and emotion over the intellect and reason. He also believed in the goodness of humankind.

The romantics wanted a return to nature. They glorified its energy, awesome powers, and quiet beauty. For them, nature was a source of protection and solace. They stressed the unity of humans with nature, the past, and myths. They felt compassion for the weak and oppressed and paid attention to the "simple peasant." They also admired the violently self-centered hero and rediscovered the artist as an individual creator. Individual freedom, love, and life were themes that occurred over and over again in their works.

In music, Romantic composers used ballads and folk tales in their work. They created a new range of sound, increasing the size of the orchestra as well as emphasizing the role of individual performers. Romantic music became universal. It was performed, understood, and appreciated regardless of national boundaries. Among the great Romantic musicians were Germany's Ludwig van Beethoven, Austria's

Franz Schubert, Poland's Fréderic Chopin, France's Hector Berlioz, and Italy's Gioacchino Rossini.

Germany and France In Germany, the romantic movement developed for the most part under the guidance of two men. One was Friedrich von Schiller. In his works, Schiller idealized heroic deeds, high ethical principles, and nobility of spirit. He insisted on freedom and made much of those who struggled to gain it. The other leading romanticist was Johann Wolfgang von Goethe. His many works expressed a mystic feeling for nature and his country's medieval past.

In France, the romantic movement had many followers. The French artists and painters chose to deal with times and places distant from the industrial scene. They were more interested in the Middle Ages than in the present. François de Chateaubriand was one of the founders of romanticism in French literature. Much of his work focused on the mysteries of Christianity and its victory over paganism. For him, the common people had a "holy innocence" that was the most sublime, or exalted, beauty of the universe.

Aurore Dupin, better known as George Sand, wrote novels distinguished by a romantic love of nature and a moral idealism. One of the first to

SCIENCE AND TECHNOLOGY

Age of the Scientist

Beginning in the late 1700's, great advances began to be made in the world of science. In chemistry, laboratory experiments became more refined. By 1880, Aristotle's theory that all matter was made up of earth, air, water, and fire had been discarded. Scientists had begun to draw up a list of basic chemical elements. The change in attitude was due in great part to the work of a French chemist-physicist, Antoine Lavoisier, and a British theologian-chemist named Joseph Priestley.

Progress was rapid too in the physical sciences. In 1810, John Dalton, a British schoolteacher, formulated the first practical atomic theory of matter and a table of atomic weights. In the 1840's, the work of Hermann von Helmholtz, a German scientist, and of James Joule, a British physicist, showed that one form of energy, such as electricity, could be converted into another form of energy, such as heat. Helmholtz also formulated the law of the conservation of energy. It stated that energy can be changed from one form into another but cannot be created or destroyed. Several years later, William Thomson (Lord Kelvin) explained that even though the total energy of the universe remained constant, the amount of useful energy did not.

The pace of the developments sped up between 1870 and 1914. During that period, the German scientist Wilhelm Conrad Röntgen discovered and studied X rays. The French husband-wife team of Pierre and Marie Curie discovered, among other things, the highly radioactive metallic element of radium and showed that it emits energy. These discoveries led the scientific world to conclude that light, electricity, the X ray, and all other forms of energy are very much the same. Then, in 1905, Albert Einstein, a German-born American physicist, formulated his special theory of relativity and in 1916, his general theory of relativity. These theories presented a unified explanation of the phenomena of the physical world. Together, these discoveries helped destroy the concept of nature that had served as the foundation of much of science since the time of Newton.

The greatest development, however, came in the medical and the biological sciences. In medicine, one discovery followed another. In 1776, Britisher Edward Jenner discovered the vaccination for smallpox. In 1842, Crawford W. Long, an American doctor, gave a patient ether before an operation. The ether made the surgery more bearable for the patient. It also allowed Long more time to perform his task. The end result was a greater number of successful operations. In 1847, Ignaz Semmelweis, a Hungarian physician, reduced greatly the number of deaths from obstetrical operations by washing his hands in antiseptic solutions before performing surgery. About 20 years later, a British physician, Joseph Lister, extended the idea to all kinds of surgery.

A major milestone of medical progress—the germ theory of disease—came about in the 1800's mainly through the efforts of Louis Pasteur, a French chemist, and Robert Koch, a Prussian doctor. They demonstrated that microscopic organisms, germs, often caused disease. Now other scientists had a target at which they could aim, and medical achievements multiplied at a rapid rate. By the early 1900's, Jokichi Takamine, a Japanese chemist, had isolated a glandular secretion called adrenalin and had shown it could be used to regulate the action of the heart. Before long, a beginning was made in the study of certain glands and in the discovery of vitamins.

Medical experimenters also made great inroads in their knowledge of the mind. In the mid-1800's, they began to concentrate on the relationship of physiology to psychology, a new science dedicated to the study of emotional and behavioral characteristics. Some scientists, like the Russian Ivan Pavlov, experimented with animals to see what effects outside stimuli had on their behavior and reflexes. Others, like the Viennese doctor Sigmund Freud, formulated theories about the unconscious. Psychology as a

In 1831 British scientist Michael Faraday discovered through experimentation in his laboratory that an electric current flowed through a wire when he waved a magnet near it. This discovery inspired Faraday to invent the dynamo, an electric generator which turns mechanical energy into electrical energy. Other scientists of this era contributed to the invention of the electric motor. From these two discoveries, all electrical machines and appliances have developed.

science was not widely accepted at first. Many people were not yet willing to believe that humans were driven by motives that lay beneath the conscious mind and did not always have rational control of their environment.

Even more disturbing to some people were developments in the biological sciences. At the center of the controversy were the theories put forth by Charles Darwin, a British naturalist, in his book *On the Origin of Species by Means of Natural Selection, or the Preservation of Favoured Races in the Struggle for Life.* Darwin believed in a theory of evolution based on natural selection. In his view, new species of plants and animals developed from existing ones. Factors in the environment caused variations in each species' offspring. In the struggle for existence, only those who were better adapted to the environment survived and reproduced. In 1871 Darwin furthered his theories in another book, *Descent of Man.* In it, he traced human evolution from animal species.

Darwin's theories were not totally new. In 1794, his grandfather, Erasmus Darwin, had suggested that all warm-blooded animals might have originated from one living stock. In 1809 French naturalist Jean Lamarck had theorized

that structural changes capable of being inherited were caused by adaptive responses to environment. The controversy about Darwin, then, stemmed not from the newness of his theories but because most theologians and scientists of the time accepted the view of creation set forth in the Bible in the Book of Genesis. To these people, Darwin's theories were "scientific atheism" that ignored divine purpose.

Other developments in the biological sciences, not as controversial as evolution, were as important. Among these were the German biologist Theodor Schwann's cell theory and Louis Pasteur's discoveries in microbiology. In 1835 Schwann pointed out that all plants and animals were composed of tiny structural units, or cells, the division and multiplication of which caused growth and maturity. Around 1865, Pasteur proved that all existing forms of life were reproduced only by living things.

1. What changes took place in the fields of chemistry and the physical sciences between the late 1700's and early 1900's?
2. What effects do you think medical and biological developments had on the average person of the period?

The map below shows the countries of origin of the most prominent musicians of the era.

Some teachers might wish to inform students when classic movies such as *The Hunchback of Notre Dame* are being shown on television.

EUROPEAN MUSICIANS 1800's

make peasants and laborers the heroes of fiction, she wrote of a picturesque country life full of charm. Alexander Dumas, on the other hand, found his inspiration in the past. He is best known today for his novels *The Three Musketeers* and *The Count of Monte Cristo.*

The foremost French romanticist was Victor Hugo. In what are considered by many his two greatest novels, *The Hunchback of Notre Dame* and *Les Miserables,* he portrayed the sufferings of humanity with great compassion and power. For many years, he represented the living voice of French romanticism.

French painters also had a great nostalgia for the past and a preference for exotic themes. They avoided the classical forms and rules of painting. Instead, they tried to represent and capture in their art the emotional, the spiritual, and the ideal. Two of the foremost painters of the time were Eugène Delacroix, whose works depict dramatic scenes from history, and Jean Baptiste Camille Corot, who specialized in lush and highly romanticized landscapes.

Britain It was in Britain, however, that romanticism had the strongest hold. The Scottish

novelist Sir Walter Scott won a wide following with his historical works *Ivanhoe, Quentin Durward,* and *The Talisman.*

The English poet and painter William Blake presented a highly personal, mystical vision in his works. He demonstrated the pride he felt for his country and his awe of industrialism in his play *King Edward the Third.* In the following lines, he described how King Edward, looking back on Britain from his wars with France, sees

commerce fly around
With his white wings, and sees his golden London
And her silver Thames, throng'd with shining spires
And corded ships, her merchants buzzing around
Like summer bees, and all the golden cities
*In his land overflowing with honey.**

The Scottish poet Robert Burns showed a deep feeling for nature and a tenderness for the simple things of life. In his poems, he expressed a sympathy and respect for the common person who had to work to survive.

---

*"Complete Writings," William Blake, ed. by Geoffrey Keynes, © 1966 by Oxford University Press, p. 19.

Bring various art books to class to show examples of art when discussing "A New Era in the Arts."

The same themes filled the works of poets Samuel Taylor Coleridge and William Wordsworth. Together they published the volume *Lyrical Ballads*. It began the romantic movement in British literature. Both Coleridge and Wordsworth believed that nature was the embodiment of a universal spirit that united all things. Wordsworth, in particular, believed that by revering nature, people could attain a deeper awareness of life's nobility. At the same time, they could increase their love and compassion for their fellow creatures. Wordsworth blamed industrialization for brutalizing the human spirit. He also believed it had caused a decline in religious faith and the loss of traditional values.

Of all the British romantic poets, the most typical were John Keats, Percy Bysshe Shelley, and George Gordon, better known as Lord Byron. In his poem, "Ode on a Grecian Urn," Keats summed up the heart of the romantic philosophy: "'Beauty is truth, truth beauty,'—that is all/Ye know in earth, and all ye need to know."

A New Era in the Arts

As the century advanced, some painters and writers began to reject the sentimentality, exaggeration, and unreality of the romantics. They wanted to portray life in a more realistic and scientific manner, to deal with the world in a more down-to-earth way. These artists wanted change, not escape.

Realism   The new movement in the arts became known as **realism.** Realists advocated human freedom and wanted a better world. During the 1850's and 1860's, they began to portray the character of the new industrial society. They focused in great part on the problems of the bourgeois as they struggled in search of material success.

Many realists pushed for social reform by vividly picturing the injustices of society. They hoped in this way to make clear the need to do away with poverty and wars.

Realism in art grew in France in the 1850's. The first painter there to accept the term "realism" and to apply it to himself was Gustave Courbet. He thought art should be a reflection of the artist's own experience. "Painting," he said, "is essentially a concrete art and does not consist of anything but the presentation of real and concrete things." Courbet and the others who followed him did not portray their subjects with photographic accuracy; they simply presented the facts of contemporary life. In doing so, these artists called attention to the more unfortunate members of society and the difficult circumstances of their lives.

Courbet painted large, somber canvases showing French life. His painting *Burial at Ornans* portrayed a group of grief-striken peasants from Courbet's hometown standing around the grave of a loved one. Courbet did not sentimentalize the peasants or make them appear like carefree souls content with their lot in life. He portrayed them honestly, suggesting that the suffering of the peasants was as much the artist's concern as the lifestyles of the rich and the famous. Courbet told his friends that the real title of the work was *The Burial of Romanticism*.

In his 1851 work, *The Stone Breakers*, Courbet portrayed workers with sweat-covered bodies, misshapen hands, and weary faces. The directness and lack of sentiment gave a sense of heroism to heavy labor. Another work, *The Painter's Studio*, released in 1855, offered yet another message—the difficulty that the gifted individual has in relating to society. The canvas shows Courbet at work surrounded on one side by intellectuals and the wealthy, and on the other by the destitute and the exploited. Out of the entire group, only the model looking over Courbet's shoulder and the child looking up from his knee seem to take notice of what is happening.

By the end of the 1850's, other painters besides Courbet were involved with realism. Notable among these were Honoré Daumier and Jean François Millet.

The realist movement also flourished in literature. In France, Honoré de Balzac brutally and frankly showed what he viewed as the stupidity, greed, and baseness of the bourgeoisie. He greatly enjoyed revealing what went on behind the scenes in "respectable society." Gustave Flaubert used his novel *Madame Bovary*

In his novel David Copperfield, *from which this illustration comes, Dickens' sense of optimism accompanies concern with humanity's selfishness and brutality. Dickens' comic spirit and sharp wit have made such novels as* Oliver Twist, A Tale of Two Cities, *and* A Christmas Carol *very popular to this day. What was the general subject of Dickens' novels?*

to depict in minute detail the deadening life of a young woman married to a dull provincial doctor and her dreams for happiness. His portrayal pointed out the tragic conflict between the dreary realities of everyday existence and romantic dreams. The novel created such a stir among the middle class that the French government sued Flaubert for having committed an "outrage to public morals and religion."

In Britain, among the first to use the methods of realism was William Makepeace Thackeray. His target was the middle and upper classes. He poked fun at the showy display and vanity of people in high places. Mary Ann Evans, who wrote under the name of George Eliot, used her novels to show how women had not been allowed to develop their talents.

Foremost among British writers was Charles Dickens, who spoke on behalf of the poor. Much of what Dickens wrote about was based on his own life and experiences. He knew well the life of the child in the factory and the brutality of the slums. In his novels, he brought alive a vast gallery of London characters, making clear his anger toward those of the middle class who allowed or fostered the horrible state of the poor. He painted vivid pictures of the sad conditions in the prisons, hospitals, poorhouses, law courts, and other institutions of London.

In his novel *Hard Times*, published in 1854, Dickens attacked the impersonality and the cold materialism of the fictional city of Coketown:

It was a town of red brick, or of brick that would have been red if the smoke and ashes had allowed it; . . .

It was a town of machinery and tall chimneys, out of which interminable serpents of smoke trailed themselves for ever and ever, and never got uncoiled.

It had a black canal in it, and a river that ran purple with ill-smelling dye, and vast piles of buildings full of windows. . . . It contained several large streets all very like one another, and many small streets still more like one another, inhabited by people equally like one another, who all went in and out at the same hours, with the same sound upon the same pavements, to do the same work, and to whom every day was the same as yesterday and tomorrow, and every year the counterpart of the last and the next.*

Dickens touched people's consciences with his descriptions of the day's social ills. His works did much to speed up the progress of social reform in Britain.

Naturalism   In the mid-1800's, a new movement emerged in literature known as **naturalism.** Naturalist writers took an almost scientific approach to their art, describing everything with objective precision. They analyzed reality in terms of heredity, environment, physical drives,

---

*Hard Times, Charles Dickens, © 1907 by Dent, p. 19.

Édouard Manet painted the portrait of Emile Zola below. Manet is described on p. 431 as a painter of controversial portraits. Zola was a zealous supporter of the impressionists, who were often treated with hostility by the general public.

and other natural forces. Their concern was with the factual, harsh, and miserable aspects of life.

While most western European writers were still portraying the shifting social scene, some Russian writers began to take into account heredity, environment, and the human spirit as well. Ivan Turgenev was one of the first to do this. As early as 1852, in a series of essays called *A Sportsman's Sketches*, he wrote of walks through the woods and fields of his home and of the conversations he held with the peasants he met. The work had an explosive effect because of the way in which Turgenev presented the peasants. He portrayed them as wise and intelligent people with lively imaginations and a sense of dignity. This was contrary to the prevailing view of the peasant. Many people believed Turgenev's work had an influence on Tsar Alexander II's decision in 1861 to free the serfs.

Count Leo Tolstoy's works also showed great compassion for the serf. His writings combined deep character study with a penetrating analysis of social customs. They reflected his deep concern for and understanding of the effects that government, social structure, and popular beliefs had on people's characters. Two of his major works were *War and Peace*, a novel set during the 1812 invasion by Napoleon, and *Anna Karenina*, the tragic story of a woman's faith in romantic love.

Feodor Dostoevsky concentrated on human crime and guilt. An intellectual revolutionary, he believed that no matter how horrible a person was, he or she could be redeemed. In 1866 his novel *Crime and Punishment* was published. On the surface, it was the story of a poor student who murdered an old pawnbroker for money. On a higher plane, it was an intense psychological study, a portrait of sin, remorse, and redemption through suffering.

In France, one of the earliest and leading naturalists was Émile Zola. He believed that the novelist should examine without passion what went on in life and then arrive at conclusions. As a result, he carefully observed and studied all aspects of the society of his day and developed a deep sympathy for the less fortunate, and a strong zeal for social justice. Zola's novels dealt with such social problems as alcoholism, "bad" heredity, poverty, and disease. Between 1871 and 1893, he wrote *Les Rougon Macquart, The Natural and Social History of a Family Under the Second Empire*. The 20 novels of the series told the story of various branches of a family. Although all of the branches had hereditary traits in common, because of social environment, each branch developed differently.

Naturalism also took hold in the United States. Two of its foremost advocates were Stephen Crane and Theodore Dreiser. Crane, one of the first to introduce realism into American literature, is believed by many to be the first modern American writer. He is best known today for his novel *The Red Badge of Courage*. Written in 1895

Émile Zola's scientific fiction analyzed human weaknesses. His novels have a poetic quality, unknown in works by other naturalists. To what possible influences would Zola attribute human vices?

Point out that both Crane and Dreiser were not popularly read during their lifetimes.

and set during the American Civil War, the work traces the emotions of a young soldier through various stages from fear to quiet heroism.

Dreiser's novels reflected his belief that people were the victims of forces over which they had no control—forces such as economics, society, and chance. In his view, behaving virtuously and being moral did not necessarily bring material success or happiness. Dreiser also believed that novelists had the right to portray life as they saw it. He exercised that right in *Sister Carrie* and *Jennie Gerhardt*, both of which were attacked as immoral because they focused on women whose lifestyles ran counter to what polite society thought was proper.

Henrik Ibsen, a Norwegian, brought naturalism to the theater. Until he was eight years old, Ibsen and his family had led a comfortable life. Then, his father went bankrupt, and the town in which the family lived shunned them. This instilled in Ibsen a lifelong dislike for hypocrisy, or pretense, and a tendency to rebel against society's rules. Ibsen brought contemporary life to the stage. He dramatized the tensions behind family strife. His characters portrayed human passions experienced by people all over the world. Very often, this meant unveiling truths society would rather have kept hidden. Two of Ibsen's strongest works were *A Doll's House*, produced in 1879, and *Hedda Gabler*, produced in 1890. In both cases, he brought into the open the feelings of the nineteenth-century woman caught between her inner nature and the role society expected her to play.

Symbolism   Some writers and intellectuals soon became disgusted with what they viewed as the increasing ugliness of European society. To escape from the brutal realities of industrial civilization, they created a world of shadowy images evoked by symbols. Their movement, called **symbolism,** began in France under the leadership of the poet Stéphane Mallarmé.

Mallarmé believed that "to name an object is to destroy three quarters of the enjoyment of a poem, which is made up of the pleasure of guessing little by little." Thus, he and his followers, who included Paul Verlaine and Arthur Rimbaud, sought in their works to convey impressions by suggestion rather than by direct statement.

Symbolism soon spread to the other arts and to other countries. In all cases, the symbolists wanted to achieve the "total experience." They used the exotic and the unknown, suggesting the world of the spirit through imagery. Intellectuals applauded their efforts. The average person, on the other hand, had a hard time trying to understand them.

New Trends in Painting

By the 1860's, changes were taking place in art as well as in literature. At the time, an artist's drawing had to be considered "correct" and subject matter "proper" by London's Royal Academy of Art or Paris's École des Beaux-Arts (School of Fine Arts). Without their acceptance and a place in their yearly exhibitions, chances of professional success were very slim.

In 1863, the École turned down more than 3,000 of the 5,000 works submitted for its approval. This was the highest proportion of rejections anyone could remember. The French emperor, Napoleon III, heard of the large number of rejections and decided to hold an exhibit to let the public see the refused paintings for themselves. The exhibit was a great success, which gave many of the rejected painters hope for their futures.

Impressionism   In 1874, a group of painters whose work had been rejected over and over again by the École held their own independent exhibition in Paris. They gave the people what they wanted—art that did not delve into social problems or try to convey a universal or moral message. They wanted art that was pleasant to look at, was not exotic, and was a little sentimental. The new movement was called **impressionism.** It took its name from a painting entitled *Impression, Sunrise, 1872* by the French artist Claude Monet.

The impressionists abandoned the three "rules" on which the academic painters had based their art—line, perspective, and studio lighting. Fascinated by the effect of color and light, they used them to create an impression. These artists sought to present the immediate

Claude Monet resented the label "impressionism." He preferred "instantaneity," since his art form depicted the spontaneous as well as the changing effect of light on color from one instant to another.

Monet's Impression, Sunrise *is an early example of impressionist art. Rather than mixing color first on a palette, the impressionist artist applied different hues of color directly on the canvas in short brush strokes. Only from a distance did the colors blend to form a distinct image. Who were the leading impressionists of the late 1800's?*

impression of their senses. Their figures generally were distorted with only a few significant details used to represent an entire object.

The impressionists sought to capture the fleeting moment—the sparkle of sunlight on a river, the wind stirring flags, the joy of people dancing at an open restaurant. They discarded perspective and detail and moved their work from the studio to the out-of-doors or into the bourgeois world of the theater, dance halls, and cafés. They took their subject matter from real life. But they rid their painting of social significance and moral themes and avoided the vulgar and ugly.

The individual personalities of the impressionist artists differed greatly. This was reflected in the subject matter of their paintings. Édouard Manet, whose portraits were the focus of controversy and scandal, chose classical and traditional themes. But he treated them in a novel and direct way. Edgar Degas painted ballet dancers, women putting on their make-up or fixing their hair, café life, and racetrack scenes. Influenced by photography and Japanese prints, he introduced into his works off-center subjects, unusual angles, and cut-off views—all of which seemed to be that way by accident.

Pierre Auguste Renoir painted idealized portraits of women and children and lush landscapes and outdoor scenes. Claude Monet was considered one of the foremost landscape painters in the history of art. He would paint the same subject over and over again to show the variations of light and atmosphere brought on by changes in the time of day and the seasons. Camille Pisarro, another landscape painter, concentrated on a free and vital interpretation of nature. Alfred Sisley also painted landscapes, but his had a certain longing and sensibility not found in those of his contemporaries.

Post-Impressionism   In the late 1880's, some artists began to turn away from impressionism. They found it lacking in form and discipline. They believed that art should reproduce reality as closely as possible. To do this, they felt discipline had to be applied to structure and to composition.

These painters, known as post-impressionists, developed their styles independently. They were united only by their belief that impressionism should be rejected. Their art was an expression of the chaos and the growing complexity of the machine age. It symbolized the restlessness and confusion of the times. It was

Note the balanced distribution of the characters in the painting below. Point out that Georges Seurat used parallelism in their placement.

the beginning of what is now known as modern art.

One of the leaders of the post-impressionists was Paul Cézanne. The son of a French banker, Cézanne was persuaded by his friend Émile Zola to paint instead of pursuing the study of the law. In the 1860's, Cézanne had committed himself to romanticism. By the 1870's he had tired of it and had begun to show his paintings with the impressionists. In the 1880's, he laid the foundations for post-impressionism, declaring, "I do not want to reproduce nature, I want to re-create it." Others who agreed with Cézanne were Georges Seurat, Paul Gauguin, Vincent van Gogh, and Henri de Toulouse-Lautrec.

Seurat found his inspiration in industrial society, painting scenes from contemporary life. Fascinated by science, he applied it to his paintings. The figures he painted were arranged according to strict laws of composition. Their silhouette-like form made them appear fixed rather than in quick motion. Seurat refined the broken color of the impressionists by calculating mixtures of color strictly for their effect on the viewer. The technique he devised was called pointillism, which consisted of painting in small dots of pure color. The dabs of paint were to be mixed by the eye of the viewer to produce intense color effects. This can be seen in his canvas, *A Sunday Afternoon on the Island of La Grande Jatte*, which took him a year to paint. It is made up of thousands of differently colored dots. To the viewer, red and blue dots appear as purple, while blue and yellow ones appear as a mass of green.

Gauguin, on the other hand, was a noncon-formist who preferred to live apart from society. When he was 35 years old, he left his family to go

Across the huge canvas of A Sunday Afternoon on the Island of La Grande Jatte, *Seurat's scientific style and his keen sense of light and shadow make a casual day at the beach very formal. How was Seurat's use of color original?*

Some art historians view impressionism as an artistic response to the invention of photography. With photography many portrait and landscape painters in particular lost business. Photography moved painters toward new directions of creativity.

In his paintings and posters, Toulouse-Lautrec defied the traditional concepts of line, color, and perspective. Toulouse-Lautrec used freely drawn lines and uneven perspective to create a powerful sense of movement and rhythm. His characters in motion were rarely drawn anatomically correct. How did Toulouse-Lautrec differ from Seurat in the use of color?

to the French province of Brittany to paint. There he produced *The Vision after the Sermon,* one of the first applications of modern art to a biblical scene. Still not content, Gauguin went to the Pacific island of Tahiti. There he painted what are considered some of his finest paintings, using nature as a starting point from which to abstract figures and symbols. In 1897, he painted *Where do we come from? What are we? Where are we going?* It portrayed islanders of all age groups from the very young to the very old in vibrant colors. It represented Gauguin's attempt to find through the symbols of a non-industrial culture the universal truths which he thought the people of industrialized societies had forgotten.

Van Gogh was one of the few post-impressionists who was not French by birth. The son of a Dutch minister, he led a short, turbulent, and unhappy life. After leaving a theological seminary without graduating, he went to Belgium. There he tried to preach to oppressed miners and their families. They laughed him out of town. He then turned more to painting, saying, "I paint as a means to make life bearable. . . . Really we can speak only through our paintings." Within a little over two years, he produced the majority of the paintings for which he is remembered. Using

brilliant colors and distorted forms, he made his art an instrument of intense personal expression. In 1888, Van Gogh killed himself. He had sold only one of his paintings during his lifetime.

Toulouse-Lautrec was the son of a wealthy noble. He set up his own studio when he was 21 years old. An admirer of Degas, he concentrated at first on depicting sporting events. He then turned to the Parisian music halls, circuses, brothels, and cafés. He painted the life and the people of these places in vivid detail. He used overly bright and artificial colors to catch the atmosphere of the people and type of life he was portraying. The changes Lautrec made in technique and color created a greater freedom and a new directness in poster design. His posters of the dancers and personalities of the Moulin Rouge café in Paris attracted world attention.

1. Identify: Jean-Jacques Rousseau, Johann Wolfgang von Goethe, George Sand, Victor Hugo, William Wordsworth, *Madame Bovary,* Charles Dickens, Ivan Turgenev, Emile Zola, Stephen Crane, Henrik Ibsen, Claude Monet.
2. How did the romantics regard nature?
3. With what were realists concerned?
4. In what ways were the paintings of the impressionists different from earlier painters?

CHAPTER 18 REVIEW

Summary

1. The Industrial Revolution brought about a great many changes in political, social, and economic thought and life in Europe.
2. Adam Smith put forth a doctrine of laissez faire which met with great response from the mercantile and industrial classes and revolutionized European society.
3. David Ricardo expanded Adam Smith's ideas but, at the same time, concluded that workers would not be able to escape low wages and misery.
4. Among those who believed in laissez faire were Jeremy Bentham and John Stuart Mill, both of whom argued that British society could be improved through reform.
5. Early socialists thought the way to improve society was to change its structure and create utopias in which everyone would share equally in the benefits of the industrial age.
6. The first move in the direction of practical socialism was made by Robert Owen, a wealthy manufacturer who created a successful model industrial community at New Lanark, Scotland.
7. Two German philosophers, Karl Marx and Friedrich Engels, formulated a scientific socialism based on the premise that the history of society has been the story of the struggle between classes.
8. Karl Marx argued that a revolution between the bourgeoisie and the proletariat was inevitable and that capitalism would be swept aside and replaced by a classless society in which the means of production would be controlled by the people.
9. Between the late 1700's and early 1900's, writers and painters interpreted and conveyed the state of confusion that existed in society as a result of the changes wrought by the Industrial Revolution.
10. Romanticists reacted to industrialization by glorifying nature, the humble people of the earth, the emotional, the spiritual, and the ideal.
11. Realists and naturalists rejected the escapism of the romanticists and vividly depicted life as it actually was in the hope of bringing about reform.
12. In the 1870's a group of artists called impressionists abandoned the rules that governed traditional art and portrayed scenes from daily life in a colorful, pleasant, and slightly sentimental manner.
13. In the late 1880's, painters known as post-impressionists, who believed that structure and composition had to be disciplined to reproduce reality, laid the foundations for modern art.

Building Vocabulary

capitalism	utopias	surplus value	naturalism
bullion	phalansteries	recession	symbolism
labor theory of value	exploitation	romanticism	impressionism
utilitarianism	proletariat	realism	

Reviewing the Main Ideas

1. What were some of the changes sparked in Europe by the Industrial Revolution?
2. What effect did *The Wealth of Nations* have on the field of economics?

3. On what was the philosophy of utilitarianism based?

4. How did Jeremy Bentham think the greatest happiness of the greatest number of people could be achieved?

5. On what did John Stuart Mill believe the distribution of wealth depended?

6. What did each of the utopian socialists think was wrong with society?

7. What did Robert Owen do in New Lanark?

8. Why did Karl Marx think that the worker was being exploited by the capitalist?

9. What happened to make Marx's theories less desirable to many workers?

10. What four movements emerged in literature between the late 1700's and the early 1900's?

11. What did writers like Charles Dickens do to help bring about reform?

12. What kind of art did the people want in the 1870's?

Discussing Important Ideas

1. Do you agree with Adam Smith that the major economic drive of any individual is self-interest and that a natural order in the universe will make all the individual strivings add up to the social good? Explain.

2. What were the differences and similarities between Adam Smith's and John Stuart Mill's conception of laissez faire? Which view do you think is the most prevalent in society today? Give reasons for your answer.

3. Both David Ricardo and Karl Marx believed in the labor theory of value. Do you? Why or why not?

4. Karl Marx maintained that, in time, class distinctions would disappear and there would be no need for government. Why do you think this has never happened even in modern-day Communist countries like the Soviet Union?

5. In what way was the society envisioned by Karl Marx different from that envisioned by the utopian socialists?

6. How did the various movements in literature and art affect the nineteenth-century view of the working class? What effect do you think this had on society as a whole?

7. How did artists and writers react to the changes produced by the Industrial Revolution? Support your answer with examples from the chapter.

Using Illustrations

Study the illustration on page 421, read the caption, and answer the following questions:

1. Which groups are represented at each level of the pyramid?

2. Do you think there are more people at the bottom or near the top of the pyramid? Why?

3. What is meant by the labels: "We work for all" and "We feed all"?

4. What is the relationship between the people at the base of the pyramid and capitalism?

5. What would the pyramid look like in an ideal socialist society?

CHAPTER 19

British Political Rally

❝ *Democracy is like a rising tide; it only recoils to come back with greater force, and soon one sees that for all its fluctuations it is always gaining ground. The immediate future of European society is completely democratic; this can in no way be doubted.* **❞**

Alexis de Tocqueville, French politician and author (1805-1859)

Democracy in Western Europe

Point out that the shift away from direct royal rule was hastened during the ineffective reigns of George III, George IV, and William IV. Critics of the monarchy expected it to fade away totally.

The governments of western Europe responded quite differently to the challenges of the nineteenth century. Industrialization and the rise of the middle class sparked the need for reform. During the 1800's, governments were under growing pressure to extend democracy. They were also called upon to improve the generally poor living conditions in which most people lived and worked.

Some governments showed an ability to adjust their policies and institutions to changing times. Others were less able. For each government, the path to democracy varied. Britain, for example, was satisfied with the prospect of gradual reform. It restricted the authority of the monarchy and ruling aristocracy, while slowly giving voting rights to more citizens and making social changes. Meanwhile, countries such as France sought rapid reforms by violent revolutions.

1 Political Reform in Britain

Political change in Britain took place slowly. Though there were some demonstrations for faster change, the British government generally moved toward greater democracy through a process of evolution rather than revolution. Actions by Parliament in the middle 1800's led the British people to believe that their government could be made responsive to their needs.

British Government

By the 1800's Britain had a mixed form of government, containing elements of monarchy, aristocracy, and a parliamentary system. Monarchs were under a constitution and no longer claimed to rule by divine right. Their authority in government was limited. It consisted of the rights to encourage, to warn, and to be consulted by those who really governed Britain. Real executive power belonged to the cabinet led by the prime minister. Legislative authority was held by Parliament.

Executive Authority The prime minister and cabinet carried out the executive duties of British government. Together, they made foreign policy and oversaw administration of domestic programs. Both the prime minister and cabinet members were closely tied to Parliament. The prime minister had to be a member of Parliament, and cabinet officials were traditionally chosen from the legislature. Walter Bagehot in his classic study, *The English Constitution*, described the British cabinet as "a *hyphen* which joins, a *buckle* which fastens, the legislative part of the state to the executive part of the state. In its origins it belongs to the one, in its functions it belongs to the other."

Legislative Authority Parliament consisted of the House of Lords and the House of Commons. Members of the Lords inherited or were appointed to their positions. Representatives in the Commons were elected by qualified voters. Together both houses passed laws. They also selected and could dismiss the prime minister.

The British aristocracy as a class made its influence felt through the House of Lords. British aristocrats believed that they possessed a "superior fitness" for governing. Not only did they have the political resources of wealth, education, and leisure time, but they also boasted a strong sense of social responsibility as well. British historian Barbara Tuchman writes that government service was "considered in England as nowhere else the proper and highest profession of a gentleman."

The House of Commons was considered the democratic side of British government. In theory, it represented the British people in government, although only 6 percent of British men actually had voting rights. Members of the

Britain was not totally spared from the violence that plagued Europe. An incident at St. Peter's Field in 1819 ended in soldiers killing 11 demonstrators and wounding about 400. Radicals called the episode the Peterloo massacre in derisive comparison with the battle of Waterloo.

Because both a district's wealth and population determined representation under the Reform Act of 1832, the new House of Commons continued to be dominated by landowners. Who benefited the most from the reforms?

Commons, too, had to be men of wealth, education, and leisure time, if not nobility. Only wealthy individuals could afford to campaign for a seat in the House of Commons. Since representatives received no pay, men who were not rich could not afford to serve. In the early 1800's, aristocratic titles and wealth were the keys to political power in Britain.

Electoral Reforms

In the early 1800's, the system of representation in Parliament reflected great political inequalities. British government did not reflect the social and **demographic,** or population, trends that were taking place in Britain as a result of the Industrial Revolution. Political power remained in the hands of the wealthy landed aristocracy, while much of the growing industrial and commercial class had no voting rights. Some rural districts were well represented in the House of Commons, while growing industrial centers had little representation. Without changing the structure of British government, a series of reforms, however, slowly changed Britain into a more democratic state by the end of the 1800's.

Reform Act of 1832   The British counterpart to the political revolutions sweeping the continent in the 1820's and 1830's began with the Reform Act of 1832. It set a precedent for political change through legislative action rather than mob action. The bill provided for a redistribution of election districts and a change in the conditions of the **franchise,** or right to vote.

The Reform Act of 1832 gave densely populated industrial cities, such as Manchester and Bristol, greater representation. At the same time, many of the so-called rural "rotten boroughs" lost representation. In the rotten boroughs, population had decreased or even disappeared since the time the districts were first created in the 1600's. Nevertheless, over two centuries the rotten boroughs still sent representatives to the House of Commons.

The Reform Act of 1832 increased the total electorate from about 800,000 to nearly a million by extending the franchise to nearly all middle-class men. But industrial workers, artisans, farmers, and lower middle-class merchants remained without the vote. In spite of the act, most of the urban population remained **disfranchised,** or without voting rights. The most important result of the Reform Act of 1832 was that it started a shift in the balance of political power in Britain. With the middle class becoming active in politics, power began to move from the landed rural aristocracy to the urban industrial and commercial class. The passage of the Reform Act of 1832 also sparked a greater political awareness among the other classes.

Use the list of Reform Acts below in discussing the life of workers in Britain before these new laws.

Reform Movements   Disappointed that the Reform Act of 1832 did not do enough for them, industrial workers and their employers demanded further political reforms. Each group developed new forms of organization to take action. The two most important groups were the Chartists and the Anti-Corn Law League.

The Chartists were largely workers unhappy with the political situation and wanting relief from economic hardship. They took their name from a document, which they drew up in 1838, called the People's Charter. It outlined the group's major demands for extending democracy. These included passage of legislation to give the vote to all adult men, to use the secret ballot, to eliminate property qualifications for members of Parliament, to pay representatives, and to set up equal electoral districts. The Chartists hoped such laws would extend political participation to all male citizens in Britain. The Chartists, however, had little immediate success; and their movement faded by the late 1840's. By that time, economic conditions for industrial workers had greatly improved by other means.

Industrial Reform Acts

In the early 1800's, social reformers in Great Britain began to demand regulation of industrial working conditions. The main acts passed to improve working conditions were:

1833	The Textile Factory Act	prohibited the employment of children under 9 years old; limited the hours of children aged 9-13 years to 9 a day; limited the hours of teenagers aged 13-18 to 12 a day
1842	The Mines Act	women and children were not to work underground; no child under 10 years old could be employed in a mine
1844	The Factory Act	reduced the hours of children aged 9-13 years to 6½ a day; introduced a 12-hour day for women and for teenagers 13-18 years old; introduced compulsory fencing of machinery
1847	The Ten Hours Act	introduced a ten-hour day for females and for boys under 18 years old
1850	The Act of 1850	fixed the working day from 6 a.m. to 6 p.m. with 1½ hours off for meals, and with a free Saturday afternoon. Thus, the 60-hour week was gained by men
1860	Coal Mines Regulating Act	stopped the employment of boys under 12 in coal mines
1864	The Factory Act	extended the provisions of the textile acts to other industries
1874	Disraeli's Factory Act	introduced a 56½-hour week
1876	Merchant Shipping Act	introduced to protect seamen by ensuring the safe loading of ships
1897	Workmen's Compensation Act	brought in a new principle by providing for the payment of compensation to workers incapacitated by industrial diseases or accidents

The Anti-Corn Law League felt that repealing the Corn Law would lower the price of bread, giving workers more money to buy British goods. The League sent 800 speakers on tour to urge repeal. What other methods did the League use?

Meanwhile, the middle class threw its support behind the Anti-Corn Law League. The League promoted a single-point program: repeal of the Corn Law. The law, passed in 1815, put a duty on all imported grains. The League believed that the duty raised the price of food for city dwellers and that only wealthy landowners benefited from the tax. In 1846 a crop failure forced the British to import large amounts of grain. The Anti-Corn Law League increased its pressure on the government through public rallies and the press. Finally, in response to this effort, Parliament repealed the unpopular law. The success of the League demonstrated what it was possible to gain when a group properly organized to meet a political goal.[1]

Reform Act of 1867   Passage of the Reform Act of 1867 moved Britain farther on the road to democracy. By lowering property qualifications, this second Reform Act proved more sweeping than the first Reform Act of 1832. It extended the vote in the cities to all male homeowners and to most men who rented. In rural areas, the act gave the vote to every man owning property and to some tenant farmers. The result was an increase in the electorate from roughly 1 million to 2 million. However, large groups in Britain remained disfranchised. Members of the armed forces, most rural workers, and all women did not have voting rights.

Political Parties

One consequence of electoral reform was the creation of a more elaborate organization of political parties in Britain. Before 1800 both major parties—the Tory party and the Whig party—represented wealthy landowners. They had no formal organization. Rather, they were loose groups of politicians who happened to have common interests. As more middle-class men gained voting rights, the old parties had to reorganize to win support from the new voters. After 1832 the Tory and Whig parties began changing into the modern Conservative and Liberal parties.

By 1859, the Conservative and Liberal parties developed their own well-defined political beliefs. The Conservative party believed in government regulation of trade and industry in order to have growth and prosperity. The Liberal party supported free trade and opposed government interference.

Support for the Conservative party generally came from the landed aristocracy and members of the old Tory party. The new industrial and commercial classes and members of the old Whig party formed the foundation of Liberal party support. Both parties, however, actively competed for middle- and working-class votes.

---

[1]The Anti-Corn Law League used a variety of methods to promote its cause. It was most effective in the use of new means of communication, such as the penny postcard.

Political Leadership

Distinct differences in party philosophy and policy were in part the products of dynamic leadership in the middle and late 1800's. William Gladstone led the Liberal party during much of this period, while Benjamin Disraeli led the Conservative party. These famous politicians dominated their parties and much of British political life. Although they did not always agree on how to run the government, both leaders and their parties believed that Parliament alone should make political changes. Through their efforts Britain continued down a gradual path toward democracy.

Gladstone William Gladstone once defined the liberalism of his Liberal party as "Trust in the People, qualified by Prudence." For 50 years Gladstone led his party. He served as prime minister four times—1868 to 1874, 1880 to 1885, 1886, and 1892 to 1894.

Gladstone's first term as prime minister became known as the "Great Ministry" because of its many social changes. Gladstone directed reform legislation in such areas as civil administration, education, and elections. A civil service reform of 1870 made appointments to most civil service positions dependent on competitive examinations. The Education Act of 1870 divided the country into school districts, which were maintained by local control. With the Ballot Act of 1872, Gladstone satisfied the old Chartist demand for the secret ballot. He also changed election districts. The Redistribution Act of 1885 divided Britain into electoral districts that were almost equal in population.

Disraeli Benjamin Disraeli, the first earl of Beaconsfield, gained fame in Britain first as an author of novels and later as a politician. He served as prime minister twice, once in 1868 and again from 1874 to 1880.

Disraeli believed that the Conservative party could save aristocratic traditions while cautiously adopting democratic reforms. He realized that blocking change would be damaging both to the party and the country. To increase support for his party, Disraeli often associated himself and the Conservatives with popular legislative efforts. It was Disraeli, in fact, who introduced the Reform Act of 1867 and secured its passage, in spite of opposition by many Conservatives.

The intense rivalry between Gladstone (left) and Disraeli (right) led to a consolidation of many small political interest groups into two unified parties. What programs did the Liberal and the Conservative parties adopt to broaden their appeal to voters?

The Fabians were sometimes called "gas-and-water socialists" because they advocated government ownership of utilities.

In the long run, Disraeli gained support for his party among voters in all classes. The Conservative party under Disraeli's leadership particularly appealed to many workers by supporting legislation for improved working conditions and shorter working hours.

1. Identify: Reform Act of 1832, People's Charter, Anti-Corn Law League, Reform Act of 1867, William Gladstone, "Great Ministry," Redistribution Act of 1885, Benjamin Disraeli.
2. How were the British people represented in government in the early 1800's?
3. Why was the British parliament in need of reform by 1830?
4. What groups supported the Liberal party? the Conservative party?

2 Growth of British Democracy

The British government continued to change in the last quarter of the 1800's. As slow steps were taken toward democracy, groups such as the working class, women, and Irish Catholics tried to influence political life.

Role of Labor

Britain's Chartist movement of the 1840's had been a product of political unrest caused by distressful economic conditions. Support for the Chartists faded when growth in the British economy brought a better standard of living for industrial workers. As conditions became worse once again by the 1870's, workers supported a growing organized labor movement.

Parliament had lifted many restrictions on organized labor during the 1820's. By the time of Gladstone's "Great Ministry," unions were common features of British industrial life. As the British economy soured after 1870, union membership and activity increased greatly. Numerous demonstrations and strikes tried to defend benefits gained during better economic times. To many industrial workers, these methods were the best ways to protect their interests.[2]

[2]The late 1880's and 1890's were a period of numerous industrial strikes, ranging from the London dockers' strike of 1889 to the engineers' strike of 1897.

By 1867, most British workers could vote, and membership in trade unions, such as the Associated Shipwright's Society, gave workers even more political power. What actions did unions take in the 1870's? Why?

While labor unions grew stronger in Britain during the late 1800's and early 1900's, socialism also gained many followers. In 1884, a group of middle-class socialist thinkers formed the Fabian Society. The Fabians, as they were called, supported democracy to gradually improve conditions for workers. Elected political leaders, they believed, could be won to socialism. Parliament would then bring Britain's industries under greater government control and give social security to workers. Unlike the labor unions, Fabian socialists favored parliamentary action over strikes and demonstrations.

At first, Fabian socialists worked through established political parties. They found their greatest support in the Liberal party. In time they hoped to send several Liberals to the House of Commons to speak for workers' interests. With increased political activity, however, workers themselves were able to elect their own candidates to Parliament. In 1901 they formed their own organization, later called the Labor party. In the 1906 election, 29 seats in Parliament were won by Labor party members.

The 1906 election also brought a reform-minded Liberal government to power. With the backing of the small Labor party, the Liberals introduced measures that improved the position of workers. In 1909 Parliament passed an old-age pension act that offered benefits to all qualifying British citizens. Unemployment offices also were set up to help find jobs for those out of work. In 1911 the National Insurance Act provided health and unemployment insurance. By 1912, laws established a minimum wage and extended compensation benefits to workers who became ill or had an accident on the job.

Status of Women

Like the workers, the women of Britain spoke out for equality and a better life. A militant demand for basic legal rights and the extension of the vote to women had its origins at this time.

Women in nineteenth-century Britain generally had few rights. Women could not vote or hold public office. They were restricted in their access to education and employment. Married women could not own property. If a married woman left her husband, she risked being arrested. Alfred, Lord Tennyson summed up many nineteenth-century British attitudes toward women in his poem, "The Princess."

> Man for the field and woman for the hearth:
> Man for the sword and for the needle she:
> Man with the head and woman with the heart:
> Man to command and woman to obey.*

Early challenges to the existing status of women in Britain came mainly from the middle class. Through the efforts of many different groups of middle-class women, legislation such as the Married Women's Property Acts of 1870

---

*"The Princess," Alfred, Lord Tennyson, as quoted in *Modern Classics*, n.d. by Houghton Mifflin, pp. 112-113.

and 1882 gave women limited control over their own lives. Before greater gains were possible, however, women realized they needed voting rights first.

Britain's first voting rights association was formed in 1867. The National Society for Women's Suffrage succeeded in convincing Parliament to allow women to vote in local elections. However, it failed in its effort to win for women the right to vote in national elections. In 1903 Emmeline Pankhurst and her two daughters, Christabel and Sylvia, founded the Women's Social and Political Union (WSPU) to lead a voting rights campaign on behalf of all

In 1907, Emmeline and Christabel Pankhurst spent six weeks in jail. Their demonstrations for women's suffrage involved them in frequent struggles with the police. When did British women win the right to vote?

HISTORY AND PEOPLE

Queen Victoria

When Queen Victoria came to the throne in 1837, the British people had little love or respect for their monarchy. By the time of her death in 1901, Victoria had succeeded in bringing the throne and the people closer together. Victoria became so closely associated with her subjects that she became the symbol of a period in British history called the Victorian Age.

Victoria became queen at the age of 18. For a monarch, she had few political abilities. Yet, she more than made up for this lack of understanding with her dedication to raising the position of the British monarchy. In time, she learned her role as a constitutional monarch, avoiding political issues and conflicts. However, she played an important part in shaping policy by representing the views and interests of common

British citizens to their elected government officials.

Assisting Victoria in her tasks was her husband, Prince Albert. Known as the Prince Consort, Albert devoted himself to science and the arts. He took a lively interest in the first world's fair—the International Exhibition of 1851. Victoria and Albert enjoyed a happy family life. They had five daughters and four sons, many of whom married into other European royal houses.

The 60-year reign of Victoria created a new kind of monarchy, different from the kind that was typical in the age of absolute monarchs. Victoria adapted to the fast-paced political and economic changes of the 1800's. In response to these changes, she reshaped the monarchy to new standards and ideals.

The British monarchy before Victoria had been closely tied to the rural, landed aristocracy. Victoria chose to identify herself more with the middle class. The middle class was responsible for the activity and wealth that was transforming Britain into a modern, democratic, and industrialized nation.

Victoria's royal court remained as magnificent as those in the past. There were public ceremonies and grand parties in London. The royal family also went on long vacations in the Scottish Highlands and on the Isle of Wight. However, under Victoria, the British monarchy directed its attention to serving the people and earning their loyalty.

In turn, the British people began mirroring the queen's own personal tastes in literature, music, and art. Above all, they adopted her strict moral standards as well as her high regard for family life. After Victoria's death in 1901, it was recognized that she had brought both dignity and popularity to the British Crown at a time when monarchies, in general, had neither. Her example has been followed by most of her twentieth-century successors, including the present monarch, Queen Elizabeth II.

The Irish struggle can be seen as one small part of a larger global struggle by various national groups for self-determination in the late 1800's and early 1900's.

The theme of the Great Exhibition of 1851 was "Progress." The London fair displayed the "Works of Industry of All Nations," though over one-half of the exhibits showed Britain's technological superiority. The Crystal Palace, a structure of iron and glass covering 19 acres (7.6 hectares) of Hyde Park, housed the exhibits. Its extraordinary greenhouse design was very popular with Queen Victoria and the British people. The fair's chief promoter throughout Europe was German-born Prince Albert. In what other areas did Prince Albert assist the queen?

British women. To attract attention to its cause, the WSPU held street demonstrations and hunger strikes in prison. However, its occasional use of violence cost the WSPU much public support. Nevertheless, the women's suffrage movement continued to grow and have an impact on British society. In 1918, after World War I, Parliament granted British women over 30 years of age the right to vote. A decade later, it gave the vote to all women over 21.

The Irish Question

Unlike the working class and women, Irish Catholics did not want greater participation in the British government. They wanted to govern themselves. More than any other political issue, the Irish Question dominated the parliamentary scene in late nineteenth-century Britain.

Since the 1500's, Ireland had been treated as a colony by its English rulers. The English government encouraged Protestants from England and Scotland to settle Ireland. By the 1600's and 1700's, Protestant immigrants had gained almost total political and economic control over the Irish population.

Predominantly Catholic, the Irish people objected to English laws. One such law forced them to contribute to the support of the Church of England. The Irish people also opposed the Act of Union of 1800, which joined Ireland and Britain. This was in spite of the fact that the Act of Union gave Ireland representation in Parliament and that later laws made it possible for Irish Catholics to be elected to office in Ireland.

Economically, the Irish people objected to the control of Irish land by British landowners. Irish tenants could be driven from their lands if they failed to pay the rent—a frequent occurrence in hard times.

Irish hatred of British rule became more intense as a result of a disastrous famine in the 1840's. The British government failed to aid Ireland. Thousands of Irish people died of starvation, and over a million died of other diseases. Millions more fled Ireland altogether. Many moved to the United States.

Various groups formed to fight for Irish rights. In Parliament, Irish representatives strongly backed Irish nationalist interests. Under the leadership of Charles Stewart Parnell, Irish nationalists disrupted parliamentary proceedings. Other forms of protest, such as boycotts and street demonstrations, took place all over Ireland. They all demanded immediate **home rule**, or self-government, for Ireland. For years, Parliament refused the idea of Irish home rule because it wanted to protect Ireland's Protestant minority. Given home rule, the Catholic majority

Some teachers might wish to discuss the problems that most governments face in approving budgets.

Bitterness toward England mounted among the Irish during the 1800's. Half the land in Ireland was owned by 700 Britons. Land and homes were leased from British absentee landowners. Tenants were often evicted on short notice. Irish Catholics also resented paying a tithe to the Church of England. After the famine of 1845, which led to many deaths and massive emigration, the Irish rallied around the issue of self-government. What two leaders in parliament sought passage of an Irish home rule bill in the late 1800's?

would regain political and economic control of Ireland.

In response to strong Irish protests, Parliament granted some concessions. The Disestablishment Act of 1869 freed Catholics from paying taxes to support the Church of England. Through the Land Acts of 1870 and 1881 many tenants were able to regain their land. These actions, however, did not completely satisfy Irish nationalists.

Prime Minister Gladstone became convinced that granting Irish home rule was the only way to end the conflict. In 1886, Gladstone introduced a home rule bill in Parliament, against the will of his Liberal party. The bill would have given Ireland major control of its domestic matters, while Britain would retain control of foreign policy, defense, trade, and the coinage of money. Gladstone's action split the Liberal party. When the bill finally came to a vote, it was defeated.

In 1893 Gladstone tried again to push Irish home rule legislation through Parliament. Again the bill failed. It passed the Commons but was defeated by the Lords. Finally, long after Gladstone's death in 1898, Parliament passed a home rule bill in 1914, but it never went into effect. Protestants threatened to fight British troops if Parliament demanded enforcement.

Constitutional Crisis

Throughout the nineteenth century, the House of Lords repeatedly attempted to thwart the many reform measures initiated by the House of Commons. Since legislation in the British government had to pass both houses, the aristocrats of the House of Lords often blocked or amended reforms they considered threatening to them. In a confrontation over the controversial government budget of 1909, the House of Lords eventually lost some of its authority to the House of Commons.

The so-called People's Budget proposed by David Lloyd George, minister of the treasury, aimed to shift the tax burden from workers and the middle class to wealthy landowners. To do this, Lloyd George wanted income and inheritance taxes, levies on unearned income, and heavy rates on unproductive land. The budget narrowly passed in the Commons and was soundly defeated in the Lords. Facing a financial crisis, the Commons denounced the action of the Lords as a violation of the constitution.

Divisions ran deep among factions, interest groups, and socio-economic classes in France. Some groups even experienced divisions in their own ranks.

In 1910 the People's Budget was again presented for a vote in Parliament. This time, the Commons passed it, and the Lords also reluctantly agreed to it. But with the budget matter settled, the Commons was now determined to curb the authority of the Lords. The 1911 Parliament Act narrowed the powers of the Lords by removing money bills from their control. With this act, the British government took another step toward full democracy. Real authority in the British government shifted from the aristocrats in the House of Lords to the popularly elected representatives of the House of Commons.

1. Identify: Fabian Society, Labor party, Emmeline Pankhurst, the Irish Question, Act of Union of 1800, Charles Stewart Parnell, David Lloyd George, 1911 Parliament Act.
2. What social reforms were passed by Parliament after the 1906 Labor party victory?
3. What legal and political rights did British women gain in the nineteenth century?
4. What grievances did the Irish people have against the British government? Why did Parliament oppose home rule for Ireland, and what concessions did it make?

3 Political Change in France

Political change in France followed an indirect and often painful path between the years 1848 and 1871. During that time, the French government changed in form from monarchy to republic to empire to republic once again. Democracy was greater and lesser at various times as a result.

From Republic to Empire

The Second Republic of France emerged from the bitter political turmoil of the revolution of 1848. Louis Philippe abdicated, and a republic was proclaimed at the insistent demand of the people of Paris. The new government placed legislative authority in a unicameral assembly. Executive authority was in a president, to be elected for one four-year term by universal manhood suffrage.

The French elected a variety of representatives to the National Assembly. Moderate republicans held a majority with some 500 representatives. Leftists, who advocated swift changes in government policies, had fewer than 100. Legitimists, who backed the old Bourbon monarchy, had about 100 representatives. Orleanists, supporters of the fallen Louis Philippe, had nearly 200.

A presidential election gave Louis Napoleon, nephew of Napoleon Bonaparte, an overwhelming victory. A newcomer to French politics, Louis Napoleon had not joined any of the rival groups in the Assembly. His popularity came more from his name than for his political skills. After all, the name "Napoleon" brought to the minds of the French people the greatness of their country under the first Napoleon.

With such favorable support, Louis Napoleon sought to overthrow the republic and make himself emperor. To guarantee popular support for this goal, Napoleon moved to further endear himself to the French people. In 1849, for example, he convinced the predominantly Catholic French population that he was their ally. Under Louis Napoleon's orders, French troops went to Rome and restored the Pope's government, which had been overthrown by Roman revolutionaries. For the next 20 years, Louis Napoleon's support helped the Pope keep political authority in central Italy.

Meanwhile, in 1849 demonstrations once again filled the streets of Paris. Leftists, opposing French support of the Pope, led the disturbances. Alarmed at the renewed mob action, the National Assembly adopted restrictions on civil liberties and other measures to keep law and order. The National Assembly also retreated from universal manhood suffrage by passing laws disfranchising about a third of the voters.

Louis Napoleon used the restrictive measures of the National Assembly to convince the people that the republic was a failure. He then decided to take total control of the French government. On December 2, 1851, the anniversary of the coronation of Napoleon I in 1804, Louis Napoleon directed a coup d'etat. He dissolved the National Assembly and arrested some 70 of his

Under Louis Napoleon, the legislature was only a rubber stamp for executive decisions.

Some historians describe Napoleon III as a listener who "gave illusions of depth that was not there." Others view him as an "amiable adventurer," not an inspiring leader.

Louis Napoleon's pamphlets, "Napoleonic Ideas" and "The Elimination of Poverty," were effective campaign handbills. A landslide victory secured his position as president of France. What was his greatest achievement in the 1850's?

political opponents. He also reestablished universal male suffrage and called for a **plebiscite,** or national vote, to approve or reject his actions. On December 20, the people of France approved his actions and authorized him to change the constitution.

The new constitution allowed Louis Napoleon to be president for 10 years with nearly complete legislative and executive authority. The constitution provided for a legislative body, the Corps Législatif, but its power was sharply reduced.

In another plebiscite in 1852, the people voted to change the French republic into a hereditary empire. Accordingly, Louis Napoleon was proclaimed Napoleon III, Emperor of the French, and his government was known as the Second Empire.[3]

[3]When Louis Napoleon adopted the name Napoleon III, he was honoring the first Napoleon's son, who never ruled. The first Napoleon had renounced the title for himself and his heirs.

The Second Empire

Some historians consider Napoleon III to be Europe's first modern dictator. His strong rule as emperor rested on an illegal seizure of authority. As a result, Napoleon III was often less sure of his authority than the absolute rulers that governed before him. This insecurity bothered Napoleon III, and he tried to adopt measures to guarantee his control of France.

Napoleon III's insecurity was reflected in the many contradictions of his regime. The first years of his rule were **authoritarian.** That is, Napoleon III governed with strict authority. The final years of his empire, however, were more liberal.

Authoritarian Years The empire from 1852 to 1860 demanded unquestioning obedience from its citizens. To ensure this obedience, vocal opponents of Napoleon III remained in prison. The government also kept strict control of the press. Newspapers could be established only by government permission. In some cases, government officials hired and fired editors. During this part of Napoleon's rule, civil liberties were limited.

But the authoritarian years were not without their successes. The most striking achievement of the authoritarian years was economic growth. During this time, France experienced vigorous economic expansion. This was due to Napoleon's direct intervention and his creation of a favorable climate for free enterprise.

In a speech given in 1852, Napoleon III rallied his listeners to the cause of French prosperity.

> *We have enormous uncultivated territories to clear, routes to open, harbors to deepen, rivers to make navigable, canals to finish, and our network of railroads to complete. . . . Such are the conquests which I meditate, and all of you who surround me, who wish, like myself, the welfare of our [country], you are my soldiers.**

During the decade of the 1850's, French industrial growth doubled and foreign trade

*Napoleon III, as quoted in *Select Documents of the History of France,* ed. by Frank Maloy Anderson, © 1904 by Russell and Russell, pp. 559–560.

The Franco-Prussian War is discussed in greater detail on p. 471.

tripled. Meanwhile the use of steam power and railroad mileage increased dramatically. French money and engineers built numerous bridges, railways, docks, and other ambitious public works projects. The largest and most famous project was the reconstruction of Paris.

The success of France's economic growth was closely tied to the availability of credit. Napoleon encouraged the formation of investment banks, such as the Péreire brothers' Crédit Mobilier. These banks sold shares of stock to the public in order to raise capital for industrial projects. In a similar way, other banks helped finance farm improvements. The surge of French enterprise eventually extended beyond its borders. French money financed projects throughout much of continental Europe in the 1850's.

Although French influence expanded greatly, Napoleon III assured the French people and the powers of Europe that "the Empire means peace." Nevertheless, Napoleon III involved France in the Crimean War in 1854. The dispute between Britain and Russia over the declining Ottoman Empire brought France into the war on the side of Britain.

Napoleon III emerged from the Crimean War with greater recognition from the other European monarchs, who had little regard for the emperor before the war. The French were on the winning side, and Napoleon served as host for the Paris peace conference that ended the war in 1856. Napoleon now seemed assured that his hold on France was secure.

Liberal Years By 1860, Napoleon III had achieved a number of economic and foreign policy successes. His growing self-confidence led him to ease his tight-fisted grip on the country. Napoleon also realized that the French had developed politically to such an extent that they would no longer tolerate an authoritarian government.

From 1860 to 1870, the empire became more liberal in tone. Napoleon agreed to numerous measures that ended many government restrictions. The Corps Législatif once again was permitted to function as a legislature. It debated bills and regained some control over the national budget. Other liberal measures allowed open and fair elections, lifted some restrictions on the press, and allowed labor unions and strikes. The "liberal empire" might have evolved further had it not been for growing opposition to the emperor in the legislature.

Napoleon's political opposition, silenced since 1851, took advantage of liberal reforms. They won 35 seats in the Corps Législatif in the 1863 elections. Effective opposition leaders, such as the Orleanist Adolphe Thiers and the republican Jules Favre, attacked the government for not carrying reform far enough. A downward turn in the French economy also worked in favor of the opposition.

Mistakes in foreign policy also added to Napoleon's troubles. In the 1860's, Napoleon intervened in Mexico. There, he hoped to establish a government under Archduke Maximilian of Austria. His attempt failed and nearly led to a war with the United States. But the most costly error in judgment came when Napoleon involved France in a war with Germany in 1870.

Few French or foreign observers anticipated the quick and relatively easy defeat of France in the Franco-Prussian War. Declaring war on July 19, the French armies were slow to mobilize, and German forces crossed into France with little armed resistance. On September 1, the Germans won a decisive victory at Sedan, where Napoleon III was taken prisoner. When news of the defeat reached Paris on September 4, crowds filled the streets and forced the collapse of the Second Empire. The city of Paris endured a German siege for four months before a truce was signed.[4]

The Commune of Paris

A new National Assembly, dominated by royalists, was elected to make peace with Germany. The National Assembly accepted a large indemnity to pay Germany for its losses during the war. The peace treaty also gave the French provinces of Alsace and Lorraine to Germany. German forces further humiliated France by staging a triumphal march through Paris.

---

[4]With Paris under siege by German forces, the new French government moved from Paris to Bordeaux in the south and later to Versailles.

To defend themselves against French troops, the Communards set up barricades in the streets of Paris. During the clash, the Communards destroyed a statue of Napoleon I and burned public buildings, including Tuileries Palace. Some historians view this uprising as the first organized revolt of the working class against capitalism. What happened to the supporters of the Commune?

The first task of the National Assembly after making peace with Germany was to restore order in France, particularly in Paris. The National Assembly abruptly ended the suspension of rent and debt payments, which existed during the siege of Paris. It also stopped payments to the National Guard, which was the only source of income for most workers during the siege. These measures primarily hurt the urban working class. They led to an uprising among the workers of Paris. During the revolt, the workers established a socialist government known as the Commune of Paris. The leaders of the Commune refused to recognize the National Assembly and called for the conversion of France into a decentralized federation of free cities.

In a bitter civil war, the National Assembly, under the leadership of Adolphe Thiers, reasserted its control over Paris by besieging the city. The National Assembly arrested and killed over 20,000 suspected Communards, supporters of the Commune of Paris. Others were put in prison or exiled. The horror of the events of the rebellion set back advances made by workers and caused distrust between the middle and working classes.

1. Identify: Louis Napoleon, Corps Législatif, Napoleon III, Crédit Mobilier, Adolphe Thiers, Sedan, Commune of Paris, Communards.

2. What were the main provisions for authority under the constitution of the Second Republic?
3. How did the French economy grow during the reign of Napoleon III?
4. What events led to the decline and fall of the Second Empire?

4 The Third French Republic

After the fall of the Commune of Paris, the French people had to decide on a definitive form of government. For a time it looked as if France would return to a monarchy, since the royalists held a sizable majority in the National Assembly. The Crown was offered to the aging Bourbon count of Chambord. However, he strongly believed in absolute royal authority and refused to accept constitutional limitations. It appeared a republic was the only acceptable alternative. So, in 1875 the National Assembly, before it dissolved itself, adopted a series of laws that together formed the constitution of the Third Republic.

Government Structure

The constitution of the Third Republic provided for legislative authority to be held by a **bicameral,** or two-house, legislature. The French

The dominance of the Chamber over the president was the result of an early crisis. In 1877, MacMahon dissolved the Chamber, calling for new elections. His hopes of bringing more royalists into the legislature failed when republicans won most of the seats. MacMahon then resigned.

legislature consisted of the Chamber of Deputies and the Senate. The Chamber of Deputies was considered the democratic side of French government. The Senate, which served as a check on the Chamber of Deputies, was reserved for the aristocracy.

Members of the Chamber of Deputies were elected by qualified voters, by universal male suffrage. The Deputies presented all money bills. No other legislation could be passed without their approval. The Chamber of Deputies was set up to assure the French people a say in government. It kept the aristocracy and the wealthy industrial and commercial classes from controlling the government.

Members of the Senate were chosen by an electoral college made up mostly of delegates from different towns across France. Small towns and villages had an equal vote with large cities. This ensured control of the Senate by the wealthy rural landowners, who ran the small towns and villages.

The two houses elected a president, whose chief duty was to represent the state or the nation as a whole. The extent of the authority and duties of the French executive was like that of the British monarchy. Marshal MacMahon, a royalist, became the first president of the Third Republic.

Cabinet ministers, appointed by the president with legislative approval, acted with the consent of the Chamber of Deputies and the Senate. Whenever any cabinet lacked legislative support, however, it had to resign in favor of a new cabinet that was agreeable to the legislature. Because of party rivalries, this situation resulted in a very unstable executive branch of government. The average life of a cabinet between 1875 and 1920 was less than ten months. Over this time, the Third Republic had 102 cabinets.

A large multiparty system also contributed to the instability of the Third Republic. More often than not, no single party was strong enough to control the government by itself. Two, and sometimes as many as six, parties were needed to form a **coalition,** or alliance, to govern and approve a cabinet. If any one party withdrew its support of the coalition, the result was the fall of the cabinet and the disruption of government.

Advances and Setbacks

Even though the French government lacked structural stability, it made some significant advances in extending democracy. Between 1879 and 1885, it safeguarded individual civil liberties, protected the rights of public meetings, and lifted restrictions on the press. It also gave more authority to local governments and allowed the formation of trade unions.

The most important education reforms of the Third Republic were those that began free compulsory primary education and opened secondary education to women. These laws reduced illiteracy to less than 10 percent of the population. The education reforms were perhaps the most lasting achievements of the Third Republic.

The republican-dominated Chamber of Deputies reformed the structure of public education in an attempt to reduce the influence of the Catholic Church. Republicans viewed the Church as an obstacle to modernization and its traditionally strong hold on the educational system as a threat to the republic. Some laws kept religious orders from running schools. Other laws expelled certain religious groups from France altogether. Issues that brought the state into conflict with the Church often resulted in street demonstrations by supporters of both sides.

In addition to the problems between church and state, the government faced severe troubles with the national economy. Critics blamed the regime for the economy's poor performance and lack of direction. The rate of industrialization had slowed since the time of Napoleon III, and France remained largely agricultural as late as 1914. This, the critics felt, was due mainly to the high percentage of French capital invested in other countries—a practice begun during Napoleon III's Second Empire.

Threats to the Republic

The late 1800's saw three crises that threatened to force the collapse of the Third Republic. These crises were the Boulanger case, the Panama scandal, and the Dreyfus affair.

Boulanger Case   The first threat to the Third Republic came from General George Boulanger,

HISTORY AND CITIES

Paris

Visitors have long been enchanted by the special atmosphere of Paris. It is lively and cosmopolitan. The French author Victor Hugo recognized the special qualities of Paris in the nineteenth century when he stated that "this city does not belong to a people, but to peoples . . . the human race has a right to Paris."

The grandeur and vitality of modern Paris have resulted from government actions since the Middle Ages. From that time, Paris, or nearby Versailles, has been the seat of national government. Monarchs, emperors, and republican rulers all adopted policies and programs to centralize important national activities in Paris. Under government patronage, Paris became the cultural as well as the political capital of France. Government support also stimulated industrial growth in the city.

Physically, the face of Paris changed over centuries. However, much of what the visitor sees today stems from the efforts of Napoleon III and his building prefect Baron Georges Haussmann in the nineteenth century.

In 1850 Paris still had a medieval quality. Many small houses lined a maze of winding streets. It did not have sidewalks and sewers. Violent revolutions had scarred or destroyed many buildings. The rapid growth of industry and an increase in population influenced Napoleon and Haussmann to replan the city. In doing so, they changed many features of the city. They destroyed the cramped quarters and built wide boulevards and broad squares. During the reign of Napoleon III, the central markets were rebuilt. The city was also given a modern water and sewage system.

Napoleon and Haussmann sought to add more glory and security to Paris by rebuilding it. It has been said, however, that Napoleon was a person of mixed motives. The openness of his building plan has often been attributed to a desire to make barricade building difficult in the event of another revolution. Nevertheless, modern Paris owes more to the 18 years of Napoleon III than the centuries of rulers who preceded him. He succeeded in improving living conditions, providing for the increasing traffic of Paris, and making his capital a more beautiful city.

1. Why can it be said that Paris is the most important city in France?
2. What changes were made to Paris during the reign of Napoleon III?

Haussman's system of avenues radiating from wider boulevards gave Paris the grandeur and beauty of a great city. This street scene by German artist Adolf Menzel shows the vitality and color of a city that drew artists from all over the world. But Paris was not just a cultural center—all commercial, political, cultural, and industrial roads in France led to the metropolis of Paris.

In the Dreyfus Affair, many French people believed that national security and prestige were more important than the life of one individual.

a popular French war hero. Boulanger had been made minister of war in 1886 but was forced to resign when his popularity became threatening to the republic. Upon his dismissal in 1888, Boulanger launched a political campaign demanding the election of a new Chamber of Deputies. He won enthusiastic public support and aid from royalists and other anti-republicans. In 1889 supporters urged Boulanger to overthrow the Third Republic with a coup d'etat. When the government ordered him arrested for treason, Boulanger fled to Belgium. The Boulangist movement collapsed without the direction of its popular leader.

Panama Scandal   A second crisis arose for the Third Republic over a financial scandal surrounding the construction of a canal in the Central American territory of Panama. Ferdinand de Lesseps, builder of the Suez Canal and president of the Panama Company, was suspected of corruption when the company collapsed and thousands of shareholders lost all of their money. An investigation later revealed that company directors had bribed a large number of politicians and journalists to get more money for the Panama Company. Company directors and several members of the Chamber of Deputies and the Senate were brought to trial in 1893. Revelations during the trial caused widespread distrust of the government when it was learned that the government had attempted to silence the whole scandal.

The Panama scandal partly benefited France's growing socialist movement. In 1893 almost 50 socialists won seats in the Chamber of Deputies.

Dreyfus Affair   The 1890's saw the Third Republic's greatest crisis—the Dreyfus affair. In 1894, Captain Alfred Dreyfus, a Jewish army officer, was arrested for selling French military secrets to the Germans. In a military court, he was tried and sentenced to a life term at France's most feared prison on Devil's Island off the coast of French Guiana in South America.

The Dreyfus family and a few other people believed Dreyfus was innocent. They complained that defense attorneys were not allowed to see important evidence during the trial. They were later joined by republicans and socialists

For 12 years the Dreyfus trials tested the survival of the Third Republic. The case's racial prejudice, bribery, and the press's sensationalism horrified many French people. Who supported the Dreyfus conviction?

who viewed the Dreyfus conviction as a miscarriage of justice. For royalists, Catholics, anti-Semites—those hostile to Jewish people—and other critics of the republic, justice had been done.

By 1898 bits and pieces of new evidence favoring Dreyfus began appearing in the newspapers. This renewed the controversy over the case. Calls for a retrial, however, were resisted at first by top army officials.

The crisis over the Dreyfus affair reached its peak between 1898 and 1899. Émile Zola, one of France's leading novelists, wrote an explosive letter to the newspapers. Headlined *"J'accuse"* ("I accuse"), Zola accused military leaders of forgery, suppression of evidence, and other crimes related to the Dreyfus case. The published letter enraged the French people. Even families split over the issue as international attention focused on France because of the case.

In 1898, the real spy, Major Ferdinand Esterhazy, fled to England. In 1899 a second military trial found Dreyfus guilty once again because the army would not admit that it was wrong in convicting Dreyfus in the first trial. This

Have students compare and contrast democracy in Switzerland with that of the United States government and individual state governments.

time Dreyfus won a presidential pardon and did not have to return to prison. In 1906 Dreyfus was fully cleared by a civilian court.

The Dreyfus affair was an important event in modern French history. It not only deeply impressed a generation of French people but also proved that the republican form of government was able to survive in France. After the Dreyfus affair, republicans directed their attention toward other pressing issues. Among them, there was the separation of church and state in 1905.

1. Identify: Count of Chambord, Marshal MacMahon, George Boulanger, Ferdinand de Lesseps, Alfred Dreyfus, "J'accuse."
2. What caused political instability in the French government of the Third Republic?
3. What actions did the Third Republic take to guarantee civil liberties and reform education?
4. Describe the three major crises that threatened to disrupt the Third Republic.

5 Other European Democracies

Democracy advanced at a varied pace elsewhere in western Europe. The strength of traditional forms of government, the rate of industrialization, and other individual circumstances accounted for the differences.

The Low Countries and Switzerland

By the late 1800's, democratic governments had developed in the Low Countries—Belgium and the Netherlands. Meanwhile, Switzerland continued on a journey toward democracy that had begun during the Middle Ages.

Belgium   The people of Belgium (the former Austrian Netherlands) came under Dutch rule in 1815. They gained their independence in 1830 and established a constitutional monarchy. Leopold I was the first king of Belgium. A bicameral legislature was chosen by voters, who qualified on the basis of tax payments.

Like Britain, Belgium moved gradually toward democracy. During the 1890's, it carried out its most important electoral reforms. In 1893, the constitution was amended to grant voting rights to all male citizens over 25 years of age. In 1899, all political parties were granted representation in the legislature based on the percentage of votes each received in elections.

The Netherlands   In the Netherlands, progress toward democracy was slower. The Dutch did not have a constitution until 1849. Royal authority remained strong, with the monarch having power to veto all legislation. Suffrage in the Netherlands was limited until the late 1800's. In 1896 only 14 percent of the population was franchised. Universal manhood suffrage was approved only in 1917. By this time, real executive power was held by a prime minister and cabinet responsible to the legislature. The Dutch monarch became less a political figure and more a symbol of national unity.

Switzerland   By contrast, Switzerland developed the most advanced democracy in western Europe. The Swiss government was based on a tradition of democracy that dated back to the Middle Ages. The country traditionally was divided into a number of districts called **cantons.** Swiss citizens in the cantons enjoyed many civil liberties and a wide franchise.

Unlike other European citizens, each Swiss citizen was expected to play an important role in political matters. Some cantons were direct democracies. In a **direct democracy,** voters make their own decisions without having representatives act for them. The principle of direct democracy was carried over into the Swiss central government, which was established in 1848. Under the revised constitution of 1874, defense and trade were placed under the federal government. Provisions were also made for the popular referendum and the initiative. A **popular referendum** is one in which voters can demand that a bill passed by the legislature be approved by them in a plebiscite. The **initiative** allows citizens to propose legislation to be considered by the national legislature.

Scandinavia

During the late 1800's and early 1900's, the kingdoms of Denmark, Sweden, and Norway moved toward democratic government. The

The map below is the subject of the "Using Maps" section of the Chapter 19 Review.

NEW NATIONS IN EUROPE IN THE 1800'S

suffrage was extended, and political parties developed on the basis of social class. Farmers and workers used peaceful means to persuade governments to pass social reforms.

Denmark   In Denmark, the largely peasant population was ruled by a monarch. During the second half of the 1800's, the Danish monarch kept nearly absolute authority over an ineffective parliamentary government. By 1900, however, demands for political reform were being advanced. But it was not until 1915 that the reform movement succeeded in gaining political reforms. These reforms provided for an extension of the suffrage to all men and most women and for greater authority to be given to the Danish legislature. At the same time, social legislation was passed, providing old-age pensions and health insurance for all citizens.

Norway and Sweden   As for Norway and Sweden, both countries were united under one monarch for most of the 1800's. Norway, which once had a parliamentary government, was taken over in 1814 by Sweden, which had an absolute monarchy. Differences in political development produced tensions that led Norway

to break the union in 1905. Norway then became an independent constitutional monarchy. As in Britain, the role of the monarch was chiefly ceremonial. The legislature had the real authority. In 1907 Norway became the first sovereign state to give the vote to women.

In Sweden, constitutional laws in 1864 set up a bicameral legislature to limit royal authority and the influence of the aristocracy. In 1909 universal manhood suffrage was introduced for elections to the lower house of the legislature, and property qualifications were reduced for elections to the upper house. Shortly after 1909, voting rights were extended to women. All political parties were given legislative seats based on the percentage of votes each received.

Spain and Portugal

Spain and Portugal were unlike the rest of the nations of western Europe. They made little progress toward democracy before the twentieth century.

Spain   During the 1800's Spain, in theory, was a constitutional monarchy. However, the army and wealthy landowners shared in governing the country. A number of groups wanted reform, but Spain was too deeply divided by regional, class, and political differences. These divisions hindered progress in Spain's several attempts to set up a republic during the 1800's. Competing social and political groups resisted any compromises. They often resorted to violence to guarantee their influence in the Spanish government.

Spain did not have many of the national characteristics that had contributed to the spread of democracy elsewhere in western Europe. Industrialization was limited, so Spain did not develop a large middle class devoted to political change. For fear of losing its power, the influential Catholic Church opposed government reforms. In 1898 revolts in Spain's overseas colonies of Cuba and the Philippines seriously weakened the Spanish government. Calls for reform came from leading Spanish writers and thinkers. But the country was too deeply divided to accept any drastic changes in its political structure.

Portugal   Portugal's constitutional monarchy also experienced division and instability. In addition, the Portuguese were plagued by economic troubles. Political violence resulted in the assassination of King Carlos I and his eldest son in 1908. Two years later, Carlos's heir King Manuel was overthrown and fled the country. A revolutionary mob proclaimed a republic, but the republic could not bring economic or political stability to Portugal. By 1914 Portugal's new democracy was near collapse.

1. Identify: Leopold I, Cuba, Philippines, Carlos I.
2. What accounted for differences in democratic development throughout western Europe?
3. What hindered the extension of democracy in Spain and Portugal?

CHAPTER 19 REVIEW

Summary

1. British government in the nineteenth century contained elements of monarchy, aristocracy, and a parliamentary system.
2. Britain became more democratic as more people gained voting rights and election districts were redistributed to give equal representation.
3. Electoral reform in Britain brought about the creation of political parties that represented certain well-defined political beliefs.
4. While democracy evolved in Britain, the working class, women, and Irish Catholics often used militant means to speed up the reform process.
5. French government in the nineteenth century changed in form from monarchy to republic to empire to republic.
6. The Second Republic of France served as a stepping-stone from which Louis Napoleon launched the Second Empire of France.
7. The most striking achievement of the Second Empire of France was economic growth. The Second Empire collapsed as a result of the Franco-Prussian War.
8. The Third Republic of France lacked a strong executive branch of government and was structurally unstable. It survived three major crises—the Boulanger case, the Panama scandal, and the Dreyfus affair—that all threatened its collapse. The most enduring achievements of the Third Republic were its safeguards of civil liberties and education reforms.
9. Some western European countries, in addition to Britain and France, moved toward democracy and the adoption of social changes by the start of the twentieth century. Other countries, such as Spain and Portugal, adopted democratic structures but did not actually practice democracy.

Building Vocabulary

demographic	home rule	bicameral	direct democracy
franchise	plebiscite	coalition	popular referendum
disfranchised	authoritarian	cantons	initiative

Reviewing the Main Ideas

1. What major electoral reforms were achieved in Britain between 1832 and 1914?
2. How did the balance among monarchy, aristocracy, and democracy change in Britain from 1830 to 1914? Which element dominated government in 1830? in 1914?
3. Who benefited most from the changes in the British political system?
4. What aspects of modern political party organization were adopted following the extension of the franchise in Britain?
5. How did British labor unions attempt to defend their economic benefits? How did the Fabian socialists seek to achieve their goals?
6. What was the outcome of the constitutional crisis over the budget bill of 1909?
7. What major political factions, parties, and interest groups existed in France in the 1800's? What were the goals of each?
8. How was the authority of Napoleon III expanded under the Second Empire?
9. What role did the French government play in the economic growth that occurred during the Second Empire?
10. How was legislative and executive authority distributed in the Third Republic of France?
11. What was the significance of the Boulanger case, the Panama scandal, and the Dreyfus affair?
12. How did democracy evolve in the Low Countries, Switzerland, Scandinavia, Spain, and Portugal?

Discussing Important Ideas

1. Why did many people fear democracy in the nineteenth century?
2. How can a monarchy exist in a parliamentary system of government?
3. Why was the Reform Act of 1832 so important to the development of democracy in Great Britain?
4. Why did the fact that Louis Napoleon was Napoleon Bonaparte's nephew help Louis Napoleon win the election for president of the Second Republic in France?
5. Evaluate the foreign policy of Napoleon III.
6. Why can it be said that Napoleon III was Europe's first modern dictator? Was he more or less secure in his authority than the divine-right monarchs who ruled before him?
7. Why was the Dreyfus affair a trial for all French patriots?
8. What important social legislation was passed by the beginning of the twentieth century? Do you think this legislation would have been enacted without progress toward democratic development in western Europe?

Using Maps

Refer to the map on page 455 to answer the following questions:

1. What do the dates below some of the nations' names represent?
2. What does it mean if a nation has no date below its name?
3. Which western European nations are not part of continental Europe?
4. What Scandinavian nations are shown?
5. What do the colors on the map represent?
6. Why would this map be called a political map? Is it also a relief map?

CHAPTER 20

National Celebration in Italy

❝ *Liberty does not fail those who are determined to have it.* ❞

Giuseppe Garibaldi, Italian patriot (1807-1882)

Unification of Italy and Germany

The map below and the map on p. 465 are subjects of the "Using Maps" exercise on p. 477.

From the Middle Ages to the nineteenth century, central Europe was made up of numerous kingdoms, principalities, and free cities. These territories lay in areas now occupied by the nations of Italy and Germany. Over centuries, the rival powers of France, Spain, and Austria conspired and fought to keep Italy and Germany weak and divided.

Stimulated by the desire for economic growth and by the success of the American and French revolutions, Italian and German nationalists worked to unify their countries. The manner in which they formed governments and developed policies in their new nations had a powerful impact on Europe and the world as a whole. The creation of a united Italy in 1861 and a united Germany in 1871 changed the European balance of power. The consequences of Italian and German unification were made clear in World Wars I and II. They also underlie the concern for European security in the twentieth century.

1 Unification of Italy

The Italian peninsula had not been united under one government since ancient times. In 1815 it was still made up of individual states. A Bourbon monarch ruled the Kingdom of Naples and Sicily in the south. The Pope controlled the Papal States in the center of the peninsula. Hapsburg dukes ruled Modena, Lucca, Parma, and the Grand Duchy of Tuscany in the northwest. The Savoy dynasty ruled Piedmont, which bordered France, and held title to the Mediterranean island of Sardinia. Lombardy and Venetia in the north were legally part of the Austrian Empire.

In addition to varied political allegiances, cultural and economic division discouraged the unity of Italy. Different dialects of the Italian language were spoken throughout the peninsula. Trade barriers and poor transportation separated one region from another. Along the Po River, for example, there were 22 toll stations. Because railway lines did not always cross state borders, it sometimes took eight weeks for goods to be moved from Florence to Milan. This was a distance of only 200 miles (320 kilometers).

Many of these cultural and economic divisions continued into the twentieth century. However,

ITALIAN STATES 1815

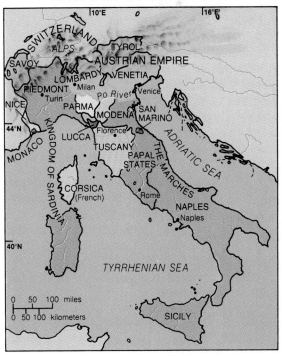

the political divisions were swept aside in a move toward unification that dominated Italian history for much of the nineteenth century.

Early Unification Efforts

Before the 1800's, "Italy" existed for many people as a cultural ideal. Famous painters and scholars as well as the glories of Rome had long been considered significant elements in the history of the Italian people. After 1815, interest grew in the prospects of national unification.

Interest in unity was primarily inspired by a growing desire among Italian intellectuals and the middle class to end foreign control of the peninsula. In 1815 the Congress of Vienna had given Austria possession of Lombardy and Venetia. It also supported Austria's actions against liberal and national movements throughout the peninsula. Austria's brutal suppression of reform demonstrations in 1820 and 1821 led many Italian people to regard the expulsion of Austria as their major goal.

Unity Movements   One of the earliest organizations against foreign rule in Italy was the Carbonari, or the Society of Charcoal Burners. Its members, however, were not workers, but middle-class people who formed branches throughout Italy. The Carbonari had led revolts in the cities of Naples and Turin in 1820 and 1821. The failure of these uprisings revealed the weaknesses of the Carbonari. There was no central organization to coordinate its efforts. Also, the Carbonari was unable to gain popular support throughout the peninsula. After Austrian troops had reestablished order in Naples and Turin, many Carbonari members were imprisoned or exiled.

In 1831 exiled Carbonari member Giuseppe Mazzini founded Young Italy, a new society formed to correct the weaknesses of the Carbonari. Young Italy was intended to be a broadly based people's movement, under the direct control of Mazzini. It was dedicated to the creation of a united and free Italian republic by means of revolution.[1]

[1]Reformers and revolutionaries in other lands shared Mazzini's admiration of republican government. Societies called Young Poland, Young Germany, and Young Switzerland were modeled after Young Italy.

Because they were compelled to meet in secret, the Carbonari took their name symbolically from charcoal, which is black, but when lit burns with a bright flame. What was the major goal of the Carbonari society?

Mazzini was the most effective speaker for Risorgimento, the movement for Italian unity. Although Young Italy was not much more successful than the Carbonari, Mazzini's writings profoundly influenced those that were to achieve unity in later years. Mazzini encouraged people in Italy to think of themselves as Italians rather than Romans, Venetians, or Piedmontese. He helped build the sense of national identity that was necessary for political unification to take place.

According to Mazzini, the **nation-state,** which is a political organization containing one as opposed to several nationalities, was very important. Through it, people in one unified country could best contribute their efforts to the good of all humanity. As Mazzini wrote in his essay, "The Duties of Man":

In laboring according to true principles for
our Country we are laboring for Humanity;
our Country is the fulcrum of the lever which

we have to wield for the common good. If we give up this fulcrum we run the risk of becoming useless to our Country and to Humanity. Before associating ourselves with the Nations which compose Humanity we must exist as a Nation.*

Unity and the Pope   Mazzini's call for a republican Italy bothered some supporters of Italian unity. Those in Piedmont, for example, believed that Italy should be unified under the monarchy of Piedmont, which contained about one-fifth of the total population of the Italian peninsula. Other supporters of unification called for an Italy under the leadership of the Pope.

In 1843 the movement to unite Italy under papal rule was given strength by the publication of Vincenzo Gioberti's *On the Moral and Civil Primacy of the Italians*. In this 700-page volume, Gioberti, an Italian scholar, outlined a federation of all Italian states under the papacy.

While Gioberti's idea appealed to many people, there were sceptics who pointed out some problems. Popes, they stated, had been for a long time an obstacle to unification. The papacy lacked the political power to unify Italy itself. Yet, it was powerful enough to block any other group from doing so. Repeatedly, popes had called upon other Catholic countries in Europe for armed support against their opponents in Italy. In addition, the administration of the Papal States was known to be corrupt as well as inefficient.

These problems did not hinder support for the administration of Pope Pius IX, a liberal who seemed bent on reform. Soon after his election in 1846, Pius IX introduced progressive reform measures, such as freedom of speech and the press. This action encouraged many Italian people who wanted the Pope to rule all of Italy. However, papal support for this plan did not last.

1848 Revolts   In January 1848, Mazzini-inspired nationalists led a republican revolution in Sicily. This prompted the Sicilian monarch to reluctantly grant a constitution and other re-

forms. Some weeks later, news of larger revolutions in France and Austria sparked uprisings throughout the Italian peninsula. When fighting began against Austrian forces in Lombardy and Venetia, King Charles Albert of Piedmont hastily granted a constitution and joined the war to expel the foreigners. Popular pressures also forced the rulers of Naples, Tuscany, and the Papal States to send troops.

By April 1848, it seemed that the united Italian forces would drive the Austrians from the peninsula. Then, the Pope suddenly announced the withdrawal of his troops. He stated that he opposed any offensive war against troops from another Catholic country. As a result, Naples also withdrew its troops, and the army of Charles Albert was defeated. The Austrians then easily reestablished their control.

Italian nationalists were displeased with Pius IX's decision not to fight Austria. Angry mobs finally forced the Pope to flee the city in November 1848. Revolutionaries proclaimed Rome a republic and called Mazzini to the capital to head the government. The explusion of the Pope from Rome, however, aroused the Catholic

Mazzini was a ceaseless fighter for Italian unification. His writings helped build a sense of unity in Italy, and served as a source of inspiration to other European republicans. What society did Mazzini originate?

**The Duties of Man and Other Essays*, Guiseppe Mazzini, © 1907 by Dutton, pp. 54-55.

Review the concept of realpolitik introduced in Chapter 16 on p. 379.

After Pius IX disappointed the citizens of Rome by proclaiming his neutrality in the war with Austria, the people rioted. The pope was then forced to withdraw to Naples where he appealed to Catholic nations for aid. Pius IX is shown here blessing the troops who came to help bring about his return to Rome. What governments sent soldiers to help the pope?

governments of Naples, Spain, and France. They came to the aid of Pope Pius IX. Louis Napoleon sent a French army to Rome to restore papal authority. The unsuccessful defense of Rome was conducted by Giuseppe Garibaldi, a bold adventurer dedicated to Mazzini's plan for an Italian republic.

Lessons of 1848   In the events of 1848 there were strong lessons for Italian nationalists. Mazzini's republic failed, discrediting his approach to unity. The creation of a federation under the Pope also seemed unlikely. The only winner appeared to be Piedmont. The brave stand that Charles Albert, and after him his son Victor Emmanuel II, made against the Austrians won much popular support. As a result, nationalists looked to the ruler of Piedmont for leadership in their cause. Even Gioberti, the champion of the federation led by the Pope, stated, "Except for the young sovereign who rules Piedmont, I see no one in Italy who can undertake our emancipation." Hope for unification thus fell to King Victor Emmanuel II and his adviser, Count Camillo di Cavour.

Piedmont and Count Cavour   After 1848, Italian unification became the essential task of the Piedmont government. Victor Emmanuel worked to keep popular support. In addition, Count Cavour displayed a political shrewdness that was to serve the unity movement well.

Cavour became a member of the Piedmont cabinet in 1850, after years of experience as a successful industrialist, banker, and landowner. He started in a minor post as minister for agriculture, industry, and commerce. By the time of the Crimean War in 1854, Cavour had risen to dominate the king's council of ministers. He was known as a master of realpolitik. His objectives were to increase the political and material strength of Piedmont and to achieve Italian unity.

In economics, Cavour favored free trade and free enterprise. In politics, he was deeply impressed by the British approach to reform. He wanted Piedmont to carry out slow, orderly reform under a limited monarchy. He feared that further outbreaks of mob violence would only delay Italian unity. Cavour felt that unity could only come after Piedmont had driven the Austrians from the peninsula.

Austria's defeat of Piedmont in 1848 convinced Cavour that the aid of a foreign power was needed to expel Austria. To win such aid, Cavour supported France and Britain in the Crimean War. Historian William Roscoe Thayer called this action "one of the most brilliant strokes of statecraft in the nineteenth century." By sending an army to the Crimea, Piedmont established a claim to equality with the other warring nations. This also admitted Piedmont to

Remind students of France's internal situation. See pp. 448 and 449.

the Congress of Paris, which settled treaty matters after the war. At Paris, Cavour discussed the condition of Italy and denounced the influence and misgovernment of Austria in the peninsula. He found Napoleon III willing to give him a sympathetic hearing.

Achievement of Unity

Although the Risorgimento had been gaining support through the first half of the nineteenth century, no one dreamed that unity could be achieved quickly. Yet in the few decisive years between 1858 and 1861 this is what happened. Unification became a reality and a framework for national government was created. During this time, Count Cavour was the key figure in Italy's struggle to win freedom from one foreign power without falling victim to another.

Plombières Agreement   In the summer of 1858 Cavour met secretly with Napoleon III at Plombières-les-Bains in France. There, Napoleon

Camillo Cavour, shown here, owned the newspaper, Il Risorgimento, the Resurrection. It gave its name to the movement for Italian independence and unification. Why was Cavour considered a master of realpolitik?

promised to aid Piedmont in expelling Austria if Piedmont found itself at war with Austria. In the event of victory, Piedmont was to receive the northern and central portions of Italy, while France was to be rewarded with Savoy and Nice.

Cavour's task now was to force Austria to make a declaration of war against Piedmont. He accomplished this by supporting anti-Austrian groups in Lombardy. Austria then insisted that Piedmont cease its military build-up. When Piedmont refused, Austria declared war in April 1859. The fighting began when Napoleon III personally led a force of 120,000 soldiers to aid Piedmont.

War and Peace   The war between Piedmont and Austria was short, lasting from April to July 1859. In June the combined forces of France and Piedmont inflicted severe defeats on Austrian troops at Magenta and Solferino. Success in removing Austria from the peninsula seemed within reach. However, Napoleon III suddenly withdrew from the fighting. French losses were numerous, and Napoleon III feared further French deaths if he continued in the war. In addition, French Catholics pressured Napoleon III not to actively support a government that wished to weaken papal authority in Italy.

Without consulting Cavour, Napoleon III concluded an **armistice,** a temporary halt of hostilities by mutual consent, at Villafranca on July 8 with Emperor Francis Joseph of Austria. By the terms of the treaty that was signed in Zurich on November 10, Austria gave Lombardy to Piedmont. Austria, however, retained control of Venetia. As a concession to French Catholics, Napoleon III agreed that the rest of Italy would eventually be united under the Pope.

News of the armistice was a blow to Cavour. He insisted that Victor Emmanuel II continue to fight, and he resigned his office in a rage when the king refused. Victor Emmanuel II accepted the settlement because he realized that victory was impossible without France. Cavour later returned to office to continue his struggle for Italian unity.

Central Italy   Stirred by the war, Tuscany, Parma, Modena, and Romagna (the northern part of the Papal States) revolted against their

Romantic writers enhanced Garibaldi's popular reputation with exaggerated tales of his bold courage, compassion, and desire to end oppression.

Garibaldi decided to free Italy from the south, using his Red Shirts in the hit and run tactics of guerilla warfare. From what city did Garibaldi launch his expedition? In what year?

rulers. Their revolutionary governments declared for union with Piedmont. To gain consent for such a large territorial expansion, Cavour had to appease, or satisfy, Napoleon III. He did this by surrendering Savoy and Nice to France. Victor Emmanuel II then accepted the central territories into his kingdom in April 1860. Piedmont now represented nearly half the population of the Italian peninsula.

Conquest of Naples The success of the national movement in northern and central Italy encouraged its supporters in the south. Until this time, southern Italy had remained aloof from events occurring elsewhere in the peninsula. Ferdinand II, king of Naples and Sicily, refused to join the war against Austria. But when Ferdinand II died and his young, inexperienced son, Francis II, came to the throne in 1858, conditions seemed promising for a revolution. In southern Italy, revolution was led by Giuseppe Garibaldi.

As a young man, Garibaldi was inspired by Mazzini and joined Young Italy. Forced into exile after participating in uprisings in the 1830's, he went to South America for a time. There, he fought in several revolutionary wars, gaining an expert knowledge in **guerrilla fighting,** a method of warfare using hit-and-run tactics. Garibaldi

returned to Italy in 1847, taking part in the short-lived Roman Republic in 1848. He was then forced to flee a second time.[2]

When Garibaldi believed the time was ready for revolution in Naples and Sicily, he returned to Italy. In 1860 he collected a thousand volunteers in Genoa and landed an expedition in Sicily. With only light opposition, Garibaldi gained total control of the island in a few weeks. He then crossed to the mainland and advanced easily to Naples. The army of Naples was unable to match the guerrilla fighting of Garibaldi's "Red Shirts," so called because of the color of their uniform shirts. Naples fell and Francis II fled.

Meanwhile, Cavour became nervous over Garibaldi's success in the south, even though Victor Emmanuel II secretly supported the expedition. It seems that the king of Piedmont believed that Garibaldi could free him from his dependence upon Cavour in the matter of unification. Victor Emmanuel II believed he had nothing to lose and all of Italy to gain if Garibaldi proved successful.

---

[2]Garibaldi's military skills were recognized worldwide. In 1861 the United States offered him command of a Union force at the outbreak of the American Civil War. Garibaldi refused the offer.

Have students compare and contrast the problems of Italian unity with those problems experienced in the United States after the American Revolution.

The map below and the map on p. 459 are subjects of the "Using Maps" exercise on p. 477.

To prevent Garibaldi from further victories in southern Italy, Cavour sent most of Piedmont's army into the Papal States. On September 18, the forces of Piedmont defeated the papal army at Castelfidardo, then entered the state of Naples. Defeating the last of the Bourbon forces at Gaeta, Cavour's military action kept him in control of the campaign for national unity. It actually did little, however, to block Garibaldi.

By October 1860, popular support for unity was overwhelming in southern Italy. After voters in Naples, Sicily, The Marches, and Umbria backed union with Piedmont, Garibaldi surrendered his conquests to Victor Emmanuel II. By February 1861, the whole peninsula except Rome and Venetia had become united under one government. Victor Emmanuel II was declared king of the newly created constitutional monarchy of Italy.

The New Italy

Three months after the unification of Italy, Count Cavour died. It was reported that his dying words were "Italy is made. All is safe." At the same time, another politician, Massimo d'Azeglio, more realistically stated "Italy is made. We still have to make the Italians." Difficult tasks lay ahead in the years immediately following unification. There remained the issue of breaking down old cultural and economic divisions and of uniting Venetia and Rome to the rest of the nation.

Nation Building In the 1860's Italy was a country of 22 million people. National unification, however, had not erased cultural and economic divisions that had developed over centuries. But, rather than having these divisions form the basis of a loose confederation, a strongly centralized government was formed under the leadership of Piedmont. Piedmont's laws and customs were often forced on the other states in the name of national unity. This was not always accepted.

Relations between northern states and southern states proved to be a very difficult problem. There was often discontent over the economic situation. The south was poor and agricultural, while the north was newly industrialized.

Discontent, too, was fanned by former rulers, such as Francis II of Naples and Sicily, who hoped to regain their thrones. Bloody civil wars were frequent during Italy's early national period. Fighting in these wars caused a much greater loss of life than occurred in the wars for unification.

Effective national government was needed to encourage and guarantee unity. Gradually a unified military force and a national educational system were developed. Also, a railroad network was built, linking the south with the north and the rest of Europe.

Venetia and Rome Count Cavour had called Rome the "star of Italy . . . our polar star . . . around which 25 centuries have accumulated all the glories of the world. [It] must be the capital of Italy." At the same time, Cavour wanted to take Venetia from the Austrians. To achieve these goals, he had to depend on foreign assistance.

In 1866 Italy allied with Prussia in a war against Austria. As a reward for fighting on Prussia's

ITALIAN UNIFICATION 1872

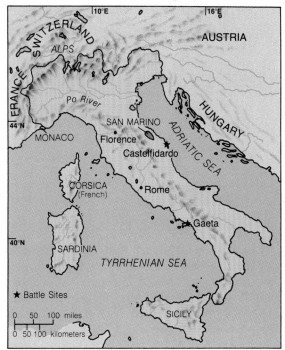

Point out that after Pius IX, Popes gradually became more active in Italian politics.

side, Italy was promised Venetia. In the confict, Italian forces were defeated by the Austrians. Nevertheless, the Prussian victory in the war was so overwhelming that Italy received Venetia anyway.

In 1870 war between France and Prussia provided Italy the opportunity to win Rome. Napoleon III found it necessary to withdraw his forces, which had been protecting the Pope. As a result, Italian troops were able to enter Rome without much resistance. The last political territory of the papacy was lost. Pope Pius IX sought refuge behind the walls of his Vatican palace. From there, he continued his opposition to the government that now controlled the entire peninsula.

In 1872 Victor Emmanuel II moved the national capital from Florence to Rome. The unification of Italy was complete, but many problems remained to divide the Italian people. One of the most difficult problems was the gap in the standard of living between the industrialized north and the agricultural south. Another was the inability of the Italian government to satisfy the demands of the workers for social reform.

1. Identify: Carbonari, Giuseppe Mazzini, Young Italy, Risorgimento, Vincenzo Gioberti, Pius IX, Charles Albert, Giuseppe Garibaldi, Victor Emmanuel II, Count Camillo di Cavour, "Red Shirts."
2. What obstacles blocked early efforts to unify Italy?
3. What was Mazzini's goal for Italy? What method did he favor for achieving national unity?
4. What was Cavour's goal for Italy? What method did he favor for achieving national unity?

2 Unification of Germany

Germany was the last of the great European powers to achieve political unity. Germany, like Italy, had been divided into many states for a long time. Geographically, 39 German states stretched north and south from the Baltic Sea to the Alps, and east and west from the Rhine River to Russia. In 1815 these numerous independent states were under the influence of both Austria and Prussia.

While Great Britain and France were developing as nations and growing commercially for most of the nineteenth century, Germany remained divided and economically disadvantaged. Past experiences, such as the Reformation and the Thirty Years' War, contributed to Germany's social and economic divisions. Some of the German states were Protestant. Others remained predominately Catholic. Antagonisms between northern states and southern states ran deep.

When Germany finally became united in 1871, many German people wanted to overcome the numerous divisions of their past. The manner in which the Germans achieved unification and formed their government had a great impact on events in the twentieth century.

Beginnings

When the Congress of Vienna created the German Confederation in 1815, the first major step toward German political unity had been taken. After the Congress of Vienna, the establishment of closer economic ties paved the way for greater political union.

German Confederation The object of the confederation was to guarantee the independence and internal order of its member states. The confederation was formed to protect German monarchs against foreign intervention from Russia and France and to maintain the political status quo in each state.

The German Confederation loosely tied together the numerous German states with a diet sitting at Frankfurt. The diet of the confederation was a diplomatic congress, not a representative lawmaking body. Members of the diet were delegates of the various governments. In accord with its position as head of the diet, Austria dominated the confederation. This eventually brought it into conflict with Prussia, the military and economic power of northern Germany.

Prussia was the largest of the German states. Since the time of Napoleon's Confederation of the Rhine, it held much important territory in northern Europe. Prussia's government was well

The Junkers' influence in Germany caused contempt and fear among German radicals. Junkers valued military might and unquestioning obedience to authority.

In discussing Bismarck, compare his political methods with those of Cavour.

organized, and its economy was strong. Political power in Prussia was in the hands of the aristocratic landowners called Junkers.

Zollverein   The Junkers called for a Zollverein, or an economic union to reduce trade barriers among German lands. The large holdings of the Junkers produced abundant farm goods. But because of tariffs and other trade restrictions set up by various German states, these goods seldom moved beyond Prussian borders.[3] There were even tariffs on items shipped from one Prussian territory to another. The multiple tariff systems among the German states hampered hopes of economic growth in Prussia.

On the insistence of the Junkers, the Prussian government moved in 1819 to establish a uniform tariff for all its territories. It began that year to sign tariff treaties with other German states. By 1834, when the official Zollverein was formed, most of Germany, except Austria and a few other states, was included in the economic union.

The Zollverein benefited its members by making prices lower and more uniform. It led to an improved transportation and communication network. Members also adopted common systems for currency, weights, and measures. Thus, an economic unity was achieved before political unity in Germany.

By forming this close economic union, Prussia had won a political victory over Austria. Just as Piedmont led Italy toward unification, Prussia now was to direct events that would eventually unite Germany.

Prussia and Bismarck   In January 1861, William I became king of Prussia, succeeding his brother Frederick William IV. After serving as regent since 1858, William's ascension to the throne was hailed as the beginning of a new era. This was despite the fact that William was 64 years old when he became Prussia's ruler.

William I had little liking for liberal institutions. He merely tolerated the Prussian assembly that had been established under pressure during

This cartoon from Kladderadatsch, *a German satirical journal, depicts Germany as it would be if the Zollverein was discontinued. In what ways were member states benefitted by joining the Zollerein?*

the revolutionary years of 1848 and 1849. William I did like the military, and he planned an expansion of the Prussian army. He was convinced that Prussia could firmly establish its position of leadership in Germany only with a large army. Liberals in the lower house of the Prussian assembly, however, saw no use for a large army except to maintain strict control over the Prussian people. They believed the king should adopt more democratic principles to gain support from the other German states.

The bill to enlarge the army passed in the Junker-controlled upper house, but was rejected overwhelmingly in the lower house. In frustration, the king threatened to abdicate. But, rather than give up hope, he recruited Otto von Bismarck, a brilliant negotiator and practitioner of realpolitik. Bismarck carried out the king's military program in spite of the opposition.

[3]A merchant traveling from Austria in the south to Hamburg in the north crossed through 10 states, paying a duty at each border.

William I (left) relied upon Bismarck (right) to make the Prussian army the largest and most efficient fighting machine in Europe. Why did William want Prussia to have a strong military force?

Before becoming the king's prime minister in 1862, Bismarck had served in the diet of the German Confederation, in the Prussian assembly, and in Russia and France as the Prussian ambassador. Bismarck was a conservative Junker politician who shared the king's convictions that Prussia did not need more democracy; it needed a strong army to lead the German people to unity.

On September 30, 1862, Bismarck delivered one of his most famous speeches, revealing his plans for uniting Germany. To the finance committee of the lower house, Bismarck announced the following:

> *Germany is not looking at Prussia's liberalism, but [its] power. . . . The great questions of our time will not be decided by speeches and majority decisions—that was the mistake of 1848 and 1849—but by Blood and Iron.**

---

*Die politischen Reden des Fürsten Bismarck (The Political Speeches of Prince Bismarck), ed. by Horst Kohl, Vol. II, Berlin, © 1892, p. 30, Sept. 30, 1862.

When the lower house again refused to approve the army budget, Bismarck pushed through the program by simply raising the necessary taxes. Bismarck continued to bully and outmaneuver the lower house to gain more power for himself. Like Cavour in Piedmont, Bismarck was to become the real ruler of Prussia, dominating German political life for almost 30 years.

Three Wars

To further the cause of German unity, Bismarck had to convince opponents of Prussian power that Prussia was the best leader for unification. He also needed to separate Austria from its many supporters, among whom were many southern Germans. Bismarck began this process with the Danish War.

Danish War In the last months of 1863, Bismarck convinced Austria to join Prussia in upholding the autonomy of Schleswig-Holstein. These were two territories located on the border between Germany and Denmark. They were ruled by the Danish king, but they were not a part of Denmark. Holstein's population was entirely German. Schleswig's population was a mixture of Germans and Danes.

In 1863 King Christian IX of Denmark moved to make Schleswig a Danish province. This action was opposed by Germans in both territories, who called on German people elsewhere for support. When the Danish king refused to back down, Prussia and Austria declared war on Denmark. Denmark was defeated after three months of fighting.

Some Germans viewed the military victory as a victory for German nationalism. Bismarck, however, thought the Danish War was important for three other reasons. First, the war tested the Prussian army and its commanders, who were later to fight Austrian and French forces in wars of greater significance. The Danish War also aroused patriotic support in Prussia for the new army. In addition, the war made Europe aware of Prussia's military might and its political dominance in Germany.

The treaty that ended the Danish War gave Schleswig and Holstein to Prussia and Austria to

SCIENCE AND TECHNOLOGY

Telegraph

During the nineteenth century, the invention of the telegraph revolutionized long-distance communication. Until its invention, messengers served as the chief means of transmitting information over a distance. In the 1790's, the French inventor Claude Chappe had set up a system of semaphores, or visual signals, that relayed messages throughout France. However it was too inefficient to be used for any but the most urgent messages. Only with discoveries in electricity were inventors able to develop successful telegraphs. These devices were able to change coded messages into electrical impulses and send them over wires.

The development of the telegraph as a practical device for transmitting messages over great distances is particularly associated with the names William Cooke and Charles Wheatstone. Although a variety of forms of telegraphs had been designed and demonstrated before theirs, these two British scientists were the first to prove the value of the invention.

By 1845, the partners had installed a demonstration line between Paddington and Slough in England for the Great Western Railway. The line and its possibilities for expanding communication attracted enormous publicity when a suspected murderer was seen boarding a London-bound train at Slough. The news was quickly telegraphed to police in Paddington where he was arrested on arrival.

The 1840's were a period of rapid expansion of telegraph service. This resulted in Britain from the success of the Paddington to Slough line. In the United States, Samuel Morse, who invented the universal telegraph code of dots and dashes, completed the first American telegraph line, linking Baltimore, Maryland, with Washington, D.C., in 1844. The line was in service one day before it carried to Washington the results of the Democratic presidential convention meeting in Baltimore. Four years later, Florida was the only state east of the Mississippi River not to be part of the American telegraph network. In addition to Britain and the United States, telegraph systems were also expanding across the European continent.

In 1846 Wheatstone proposed a submarine cable to link Britain with the European network. This was completed in 1851 after numerous failures in laying cable across the English Channel. Seven years later, Europe and North America were first joined by telegraph. The first submarine cable across the Atlantic, however, broke down shortly after it was put into service. Not until 1866 were the two continents linked with regular service.

By the late 1860's, the world's telegraph system covered almost 150,000 miles (240,000 kilometers), including 95,000 miles (152,000 kilometers) in Europe and 48,000 miles (76,800 kilometers) in the United States. In 1872 the first telegrams were exchanged between the mayors of London, England, and Adelaide, Australia. The countries of the world grew closer together by way of a web of telegraph lines, the first step in a worldwide communication network.

1. Who demonstrated the first practical use of the telegraph in Britain? in the United States?
2. What technological achievement allowed telegraph communication between Britain and continental Europe and between North America and Europe?

Although called the Seven Weeks' War, the actual fighting lasted only five weeks and three days.

Have students consider the impact of advances in military technology on foreign relations and the balance of power.

govern jointly. After a bitter debate ending in the Convention of Gastein, Prussia took control of Schleswig. Austria took over the administration of Holstein. This arrangement led to further strains in the relationship between the rival powers.

Seven Weeks' War   Bismarck gained public support for his efforts in the Danish War. At the same time, he began taking action to strip Austria of its allies in the event of an Austro-Prussian war. Bismarck befriended Russia in 1863 by offering Tsar Alexander II help in putting down a Polish uprising. He gained the support of France in 1865 by offering Napoleon III possible "compensations" in the event of conflict with Austria. He satisfied Italy in 1866 by offering King Victor Emmanuel II the Austrian province of Venetia if Italian forces would support Prussia in a war with Austria.

Meanwhile in Schleswig-Holstein, Austria began promoting the claims of the young duke of Augustenburg, who maintained that he was the rightful heir of the two territories. This prompted

Bismarck to order troops into Holstein, because he felt that Austria was planning an alliance against him. Austria then asked the diet of the German Confederation to take military action in Schleswig-Holstein. Bismarck considered this act a declaration of war. In response, he dissolved the confederation and moved the Prussian army against Austria on June 15, 1866.

The war between Austria and Prussia lasted only seven weeks. For Bismarck it was a limited war with limited objectives. Its purpose was to separate Austria from Germany and end the chance for a united Germany under Austrian control. In the end, Bismarck did not want to destroy Austria with a harsh peace settlement. He knew that he would probably need an Austrian alliance in the future.

The treaty ending the Austro-Prussian war was negotiated at Prague. The settlement permanently dissolved the German Confederation and surrendered Holstein to Prussia. As previously arranged by Bismarck, Italy took over Venetia. France, however, made no gains. The

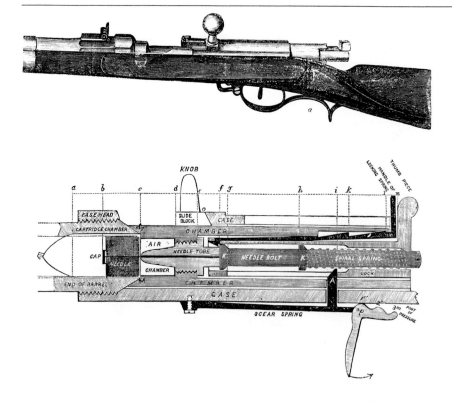

Under Bismarck the Prussian army was strengthened and made more efficient. Its soldiers were provided with the Dreyse military rifle, also known as the "needle gun." This gun could be loaded through the breech, the back of the barrel, instead of through the muzzle, the front end. It could fire four bullets in the time it took to load and fire an old-fashioned muzzle-loader. Which war made Europe aware of Prussia's military might?

Review the impact of the Franco-Prussian War on the French. See pp. 449 and 450.

Treaty of Prague also called for "a new organization of Germany without the participation of Austria."

The "new organization" became the North German Confederation in 1867. It embraced all the German states north of the Main River. The constitution of the confederation, which was drawn up by Bismarck, allowed for each state to remain self-governing. Supremacy, however, was given to the king of Prussia. Each state was to manage its domestic affairs. Foreign policy and national defense were to be in the hands of the Prussians. Legislative authority was vested in a federal council composed of representatives from the various governments and a diet elected by universal manhood suffrage.

The establishment of a strong confederation by Germany made Bismarck a popular hero among German nationalists. Even liberals supported him. But, Bismarck's work of unifying Germany was not finished.

Franco-Prussian War The southern German states, which were largely Catholic, remained outside the confederation. Most of them feared Protestant Prussia's military strength, and its control of Germany. The kingdoms of Bavaria and Würtenburg, in particular, steadfastly opposed German unification under Prussian rule. They would accept German unification only if Prussia gave up some of its authority in a united government. Prussia would not agree to this, however.

France, Austria, and Italy all had their reasons to oppose the creation of a united Germany in the center of Europe. Yet, France posed the most serious obstacle to Germany in the late 1860's. Napoleon III was determined not to accept German unification unless France received some territory—its "compensation" for not joining Austria in the Seven Weeks' War. To resolve the situation, war with France seemed the most effective course of action for Bismarck.

Some historians believe that Bismarck was solely responsible for the Franco-Prussian War. In his memoirs, Bismarck had written "that a Franco-German war must take place before the construction of a united Germany could be realized." But if Napoleon III had not wanted war as much as Bismarck, the war may never have taken place.

Bismarck knew that he could not directly invade France. He had to lure France into war, taking advantage of Napoleon III's weakness in foreign policy and of the French public's anti-German feeling. Bismarck's excuse for the war came in 1870 in connection with the Hohenzollern candidacy for the Spanish throne.

A revolution in 1868 had deposed Queen Isabella of Spain. In search of a new ruler, the Spanish government offered the throne to Prince Leopold of Hohenzollern, a Catholic cousin of William I of Prussia. The French feared that Leopold's acceptance of the throne would lead to a Spanish-German alliance against France. Napoleon III protested the offer by sending a representative to William I, who was vacationing at the German resort of Ems. The French wanted the Prussian king, as head of the Hohenzollern family, to order Leopold to reject the Spanish throne. William refused the demand, but Leopold later withdrew his acceptance voluntarily.

In July 1870, the French further demanded from William I a promise that a Hohenzollern would never sit on the Spanish throne. Word of this new demand was sent by telegraph from William I to Bismarck. Bismarck altered the famous Ems Telegram to make the French demand seem more threatening. According to Bismarck, France was now attempting to interfere in German affairs. In response, the French declared war on Prussia.

The southern German states, more anti-French than anti-Prussian, decided to join Prussia in the fighting that began July 19, 1870. With the easy defeat of the French, Bismarck gained support from all the German states for the unification of Germany under Prussian control.

Formation of the German Empire

On January 18, 1871, William I was proclaimed emperor of a Germany that now stretched from the Baltic Sea in the north to the Inn River in the south. Bismarck became the German **chancellor,** or chief minister.

The new empire united 25 German states into one federal union. Its government was patterned after that of the North German Confederation.

GERMAN CONFEDERATION 1815

GERMAN UNIFICATION 1871

There was a federal council and a legislative assembly. Each state had its own ruler for domestic affairs. The national government controlled defense, trade, commerce, and foreign affairs. At the head of the national government was the emperor, called the **kaiser.** The kaiser had authority to make appointments, command the military, and determine foreign policy.

The German constitution, according to Bismarck's design, strongly favored Prussia. It stated that the kaiser had to be the king of Prussia. Since Prussia was the most populous state, it also controlled the central government. Real political power in the German Empire remained in the hands of the Prussian Junker aristocrats. Unification did not make Germany a model democratic state.

1. Identify: Zollverein, William I, Otto von Bismarck, Convention of Gastein, North German Confederation, Prince Leopold, Ems Telegram.
2. Why did Bismarck fight the Danish War?
3. How was German unification advanced by the Seven Weeks' War?
4. Why did Bismarck feel that war between France and Prussia in 1870 was important?

3 Germany from 1871 to 1914

Unity won on the battlefield during the Franco-Prussian War did not unite the German people. Religious, economic, social, and political divisions remained. After 1871, new national loyalties had to be forged in Germany.

Although German unification had been achieved, German leaders still had to instill a spirit of unity in their people. Bismarck became the key figure in early German nation building. With the support of Kaiser William I, Bismarck took charge of policy in the German Empire. In the early years of the new empire, he faced several direct challenges to the German nation-state and his own political authority.

The Kulturkampf

Bismarck faced a challenge from the Catholic Church in the so-called *Kulturkampf,* or "cultural struggle," between church and state. The conflict began over the question of whether German Catholics were loyal to the empire or to the Pope.

Threatened by the May Laws, many religious orders sought refuge in countries such as the United States.

Its immediate causes were the Pope's condemnation of secular authority and his efforts to strengthen his spiritual authority over Catholics.

In 1864 Pope Pius IX published the *Syllabus of Errors,* in which he condemned liberalism, socialism, nationalism, and many other nineteenth-century views. The Pope claimed for the Church the control of all cultural and educational activities that involved Catholics. He also declared the complete independence of the Church from state control.

In 1870 bishops from all over the Catholic world met at Rome for the First Vatican Council. The Vatican Council stated that the Pope, when he speaks on matters of faith and morals, is **infallible,** or free from error. This teaching of the Church marked a triumph of the papacy over local church officials. It also appeared to be an attempt to raise the papacy above all secular states and to extend papal authority to the political domain.

Furthermore, in 1870, Catholic elements in Germany organized the Center party during the first elections of the legislature. In general, the Center party represented Catholic interests in opposition to the predominantly Protestant Prussians. The pro-papal attitude of the Center party irritated and alarmed members of the majority Protestant National Liberal party. Concern was especially heightened when the Center party insisted that the German Empire should intervene in Italy in order to restore the pope's landholdings.

Bismarck was annoyed at the growing popularity of the Center party in Germany and believed that the Church was backing resistance to the empire. He also feared that the Center party would make alliances with Catholic powers, such as Austria and France. In the Protestant-Catholic dispute, Bismarck joined the Protestants against the Catholics.

According to Bismarck, the Jesuits were papal agents at work to destroy the German Empire. So Bismarck launched his campaign against the Church by removing the Jesuits from Germany in 1872. Beginning in 1873, the German legislature passed a series of laws aimed at destroying Catholic influence in Germany. These so-called May Laws placed the education of the clergy under the control of the state, deprived bishops of much of their authority, ended the Church's right of self-government, and dissolved religious orders. They also required that weddings be performed by secular officials. In response, the Pope declared the laws invalid and broke diplomatic ties with Germany. He threatened to expel from the Church any Catholic obeying the May Laws.

Bismarck soon realized that he was fighting a losing battle. Instead of weakening the Center party, Bismarck's repressive measures seemed to strengthen it. The Center party gained even more seats in the legislative elections of 1877. The Kulturkampf also forced the Junker-controlled Conservative party to oppose Bismarck. The conservatives feared any policy that attacked an organized religion.

In 1878, Pope Pius IX died. His successor Pope Leo XIII made it easier for Bismarck to reach an accord, or agreement, with the Catholic Church. In practice, the Kulturkampf had ended by 1881. Most laws directed against Catholics were repealed before the end of the decade. The German government, however, kept control over education and marriage.

Bismarck and Socialism

Just as the conflict with the Catholic Church dominated the first decade of the empire, a conflict with socialism filled the second. In Germany, a brand of socialism favoring gradual reform rather than violent revolution developed during the 1870's. In 1871 socialists held only two seats in the legislative assembly. In 1874, they won 10. By 1875, the socialist position became stronger through the merger of two socialist organizations into one Socialist Workmen's party. This party officially became the Social Democratic party in 1890.

Although most German socialists were not revolutionaries, Bismarck believed that any form of socialism posed a serious threat to the empire. To destroy socialism in Germany, Bismarck set out to crush its organization. He also aimed to win over its working-class supporters by making them dependent upon the state.

To win the support of moderates, Bismarck included sickness benefits, unemployment pay, and old-age pensions in his legislative program. These measures effectively reduced the desire of many workers to join unions, particularly when the union movement was represented in the Reichstag through the Social Democrat Democratic Party. Why was Bismarck opposed to the Social Democrats?

Bismarck launched his campaign against the socialists in 1878. In part, his campaign was in response to an attempt on the life of Kaiser William I. The attack had been linked to a socialist organization, causing Bismarck to introduce a bill to ban all socialist activities. It was not passed, however. Bismarck then dissolved the legislature, called for elections, and appealed directly to the voters for support. The newly elected legislature was more conservative than the one before it. It passed Bismarck's antisocialist bill in modified form. The new law banned all socialist meetings and publications. It did not outlaw the party itself. But it did end the public activities of the socialists.

Bismarck's efforts to suppress the socialists met with only temporary success. While the voting power of the party sank in 1878, the party continued to exist in secret. Gradually, it won back popular support and gained 24 seats in the legislature that was elected in 1884.

Meanwhile, Bismarck tried to show the workers that the government, and not the socialists, had their true interests at heart. In 1883 he directed the passage of the Sickness Insurance Law, which gave limited compensation to those who missed work because of illness. The Accident Insurance Law, passed in 1884, provided for the care of workers injured in industrial accidents. In 1889 the Old Age Insurance Law protected workers in retirement.

Although Bismarck's social reforms provided comfort and security for most Germans, it became evident that his efforts were not successful in ending the popularity of the socialists. In the 1890 election, the Social Democratic party won 35 seats in the legislature. With strong socialist backing, the legislature refused to renew Bismarck's antisocialist law. Bismarck responded by demanding the immediate dissolution of the legislature. The legislature, however, stayed in session. Bismarck's policy of strong government in Germany was thus broken. This marked the beginning of the end of Bismarck's political career.

The Fall of Bismarck

In 1888 Kaiser William I died at the age of 91. His son, who took the name Frederick III, succeeded him. Frederick III was a liberal and an admirer of the British political system. This may have been because he was married to the oldest daughter of Britain's Queen Victoria. Frederick III was also critical of Bismarck's repressive measures against Catholics and socialists. Once Frederick became kaiser, liberals in Germany looked forward to a new progressive era. Unfortunately, Frederick III ruled for only 91 days before dying. His son William II then became emperor at the age of 29.

William II was a man of great energy and strong opinions. Like his grandfather, William I,

Ask students to explain the cartoon below.

he favored a powerful military. He believed in the absolute authority of the emperor and the divine right of his Hohenzollern family to rule Germany. He disliked the German constitution and the legislature. Because of William II's belief in a strong monarchy, he quickly came into conflict with Bismarck. Bismarck wanted the kaiser to stay out of political affairs.

The first clash between William II and Bismarck came over a disagreement on antisocialist laws. Bismarck demanded continuing restrictions on the socialists. The kaiser proposed a milder approach. Feuding continued as a result of William II's demand that cabinet officials report directly to him and not to Bismarck.

After steering the German ship of state for 30 years, Bismarck resigned. This cartoon was published upon Bismarck's departure from office. What is the cartoon saying about Bismarck's relationship with William II?

DROPPING THE PILOT.

Under William I, Bismarck often was able to get his way by threatening to resign. When Bismarck offered his resignation to William II in 1890, the kaiser accepted it. Much to Bismarck's surprise, William "sent the veteran pilot over the side" and began his own personal rule of the German Empire.

Bismarck's policies had left Germany strong but they frustrated the German people. His strict rule prevented the development of a parliamentary democracy. The growing middle and working classes in a rapidly industrializing Germany were never permitted effective participation in political affairs.

Germany Under William II

During his reign, William II encouraged development in many areas. Among these was the military. William II insisted that a strong army was the best support for royal authority. He also believed that a strong army would serve to **deter,** or discourage, other European nations, particularly France, from war. By 1913 Germany's standing army numbered over 800,000 soldiers. There were nearly 6 million men in the military reserves.

The most striking development during the reign of William II was the growth of industry. This economic expansion may be best measured by increases in coal and iron production. Between 1891 and 1913, coal output doubled. Between 1888 and 1910, the amount of unrefined (pig) iron produced tripled. Production in these two areas exceeded all other European countries, including Britain. In addition, Germany's electrical and chemical industries, which had been practically nonexistent in 1882, ranked among world leaders in 1914. By 1914, Germany had become one of the world's major industrial powers. Only Britain produced more manufactured goods.

Commercial growth accompanied Germany's industrial expansion. Between 1871 and 1914, the value of German exports increased fourfold. Imports increased about three and one half times. The Germans developed a huge merchant fleet to carry external trade. A highly efficient network of railways and canals was built to move goods inside Germany.

Bismarck had often stressed to the other great powers that Germany was content with the status quo and would not try to increase its power. With his *weltpolitik*, William II reversed Bismarck's position. This new policy increased tensions in Europe.

Rapid economic growth brought changes to German life, too. The nation's population dramatically shifted from country to town. Primarily rural in 1871, 60 percent of the Geman people lived in urban centers in 1914. There were also fewer people leaving Germany during this period. In the early 1880's, emigrants moved out of Germany at an annual rate of 221,000. That dropped to 18,500 by 1912.

Rapid military and economic development formed a strong base for the modern German nation. It led Kaiser William II to change the course of Germany's foreign policy. During much of his reign, he advocated **weltpolitik,** or a "world policy." Germany under William II moved to take its place as a leader in global affairs.

1. Identify: *Syllabus of Errors*, First Vatican Council, Center party, National Liberal party, Conservative party, Pope Leo XIII, Social Democratic party, Frederick III, Kaiser William II.
2. What events resulted in a Kulturkampf between the German state and the Catholic Church?
3. What did Bismarck plan to achieve by securing passage of the May Laws?
4. What military and economic developments occurred during the reign of William II?

CHAPTER 20 REVIEW

Summary

1. In the middle of the nineteenth century, present-day Italy and Germany consisted of many small independent states.
2. To achieve political unification, Italy had to expel Austria from the Italian peninsula and overcome papal opposition and local apathy.
3. Giuseppe Mazzini, Giuseppe Garibaldi, and Count Camillo di Cavour were key figures in Italian unification. They generated interest in the cause of unity and gained the military support needed to expel Austria and unite southern Italy with the rest of the peninsula.
4. Italy became a constitutional monarchy in 1861 under the leadership of Piedmont. Its first king was Victor Emmanuel II.
5. Germany was united economically through the customs union called the Zollverein before it gained political unification.
6. Otto von Bismarck was the main figure in German political unification. Bismarck directed the development of a strong Prussian army. Prussia's military victories helped to win the support of the German people for the cause of unity.
7. Germany became united as the German Empire under the leadership of Prussia. In 1871 William I became the first emperor. However, Bismarck became the most important person in the new government.
8. The constitution of the German Empire provided for a democracy, but the new government was controlled by the autocratic regime of Bismarck and William I.
9. Bismarck discouraged the development of strong parliamentary leadership. However, his efforts to destroy Catholic and socialist parties failed and eventually led to his resignation.
10. During the reign of William II, Germany made great strides in economic development, built a large military, and took a more active role in world affairs.

Building Vocabulary

nation-state	guerrilla fighting	kaiser	deter
armistice	chancellor	infallible	weltpolitik

Reviewing the Main Ideas

1. What contributions to the cause of Italian unity were made by Mazzini, Garibaldi, and Cavour?
2. How were France and Austria involved in the matter of Italian unification?
3. What role did the Pope play in the process of unifying Italy?
4. How did Venetia and Rome finally become part of Italy?
5. How did the German Confederation and the Zollverein contribute to the development of German unity?
6. What three wars were crucial to German unification? What were Bismarck's objectives in these wars?
7. What "new organization" in Germany was created by the Treaty of Prague in 1866? How did it contribute to unification?
8. What provisions in the constitution of the German Empire allowed Prussia to dominate the new nation?
9. Which rival powers competed for the leadership of a united Germany?
10. How did Bismarck attempt to curb the influence of the Catholic Church and the socialists in Germany?
11. How did Bismarck plan to end the influence of socialism in Germany?
12. How did Bismarck's influence in the German Empire end when William II became kaiser?

Discussing Important Ideas

1. Why had Italy failed to become a united nation before 1860? Explain your answer.
2. How was the participation or actions of foreign powers crucial to Italian unification?
3. Were Mazzini's goals achieved in the Italy created by Cavour? Explain.
4. How does a policy of realpolitik differ from an idealistic approach to politics? Do you think nations today operate according to realpolitik or idealism?
5. Do you think Cavour or Bismarck had the easier task of uniting his country?
6. What impact did the unification of Germany have on the European balance of power?
7. What prevented the development of strong democratic rule in the German Empire?

Using Maps

Refer to the maps on pages 459 and 465 to answer the following questions:

1. What Italian states did the cities of Milan, Turin, Venice, Florence, Rome, and Naples belong to in 1815?
2. Which Italian states were united into one nation by 1872?
3. Which parts of the Austrian Empire became part of a united Italy? Which did not?
4. What was the status of San Marino and Sardinia following Italian unification?
5. What states and geographic features defined the shape of Italy in 1872?
6. What was the status of Monaco in 1872?

UNIT 5 REVIEW

Summary

1. In pre-industrial Europe, the basic economic unit was the family, and agriculture was the main occupation. Some manufacturing was carried out, but families generally produced only enough to meet their own needs.

2. Stimulated by rapid population growth and agricultural prosperity, the Industrial Revolution began in the 1700's with innovations in the British textile, coal, and iron industries. By the late 1800's, the Industrial Revolution had spread throughout Europe and to North America and Japan.

3. The Industrial Revolution brought about many changes. Foremost were population shifts from rural to urban areas, changes in traditional family life, and the emergence of social problems unique to an urban society.

4. Important philosophies based on capitalism and socialism arose during this period out of a desire to understand and reform the problems caused by industrialization.

5. Artistic reaction to the Industrial Revolution reflected the confusion of the times. Response ranged from escapist romanticism to reform-motivated realism.

6. Britain became more democratic as it underwent reforms such as the development of political parties, the establishment of labor unions, and the extension of suffrage. France's government changed from a monarchy to republic to empire to republic. Countries such as Spain and Portugal adopted democratic structures but did not actually function as democracies.

7. Italy became united in 1861 after decades of struggle to expel Austria and to overcome papal opposition. Germany achieved unification in 1871 under the leadership of Otto von Bismarck and Kaiser William I. Rapid military and economic development moved Germany into a position of world leadership during the reign of William II.

Developing Understanding

1. What roles did capital, resources, and talent play in industrialization?
2. What social and economic changes occurred in Europe during the transformation from pre-industrial societies to industrial ones?
3. How did nineteenth-century capitalists and socialists differ in their response to the Industrial Revolution?
4. What major political reforms were instituted in Britain in the 1800's? How were these achieved?
5. What progress was made toward democracy in France between 1848 and 1871?
6. What were the main obstacles to Italian and German unification? How were these obstacles overcome?

Developing Skills

One of the best sources of historical information is statistical data. For example, historians of the Industrial Revolution would be interested in statistics dealing with banking, imports and exports, population, and the output of agricultural and industrial products. These data could provide valuable clues to when and where economies began to change.

It is important for students of history to be able to analyze and interpret statistical data. Examine the table on population growth and compare it with the table on page 403 showing railroad mileage. Then decide which of the following statements are true or false based on the evidence in the tables, and which may be judged true or false based on logical inference.

THE GROWTH OF POPULATION*
(millions)

	1800	1850	1900
Europe	187.0	266.0	401.0
Great Britain	16.1	27.5	41.8
Germany	24.6	35.9	56.4
France	27.3	35.8	39.0
Russia	37.0	60.2	111.0
Spain	10.5	—	16.6
Italy	18.1	24.3	32.5
Sweden	2.3	3.5	5.1
Belgium	—	4.3	6.7
Netherlands	—	3.1	5.1
North America	16.0	39.0	106.0
United States	5.3	23.2	76.0
South America	9.0	20.0	38.0
Asia	602.0	749.0	937.0
Africa	90.0	95.0	120.0

*The European World: A History, Jerome Blum, Rondo Cameron, Thomas G. Barnes, © 1966 by Little, Brown and Company, p. 563.

1. Railroad mileage increased more in countries that were more industrialized.
2. Population growth in France was slower because it did not build enough railroads.
3. All the European countries whose populations more than doubled between 1800 and 1900 were countries that experienced a high rate of industrialization during this time.
4. The most highly industrialized countries (Great Britain, Germany, and the United States) showed high rates of population growth between 1800 and 1900.
5. Great Britain, France, Germany, and Belgium were the only European countries that had railroads by 1870.
6. In general, there was more construction of railroads and more population growth after 1850 than before 1850.
7. By 1870, the major countries of Europe were connected by railroads.
8. In the United States, the greatest amount of railroad construction took place after the Civil War.
9. The continents with the greatest railroad mileage (Europe and North America) were the continents that showed the greatest percentage increases in population.
10. The most significant cause of population growth in the 1800's was industrialization.

Suggested Activities

1. Study an industry, other than the railroad, to understand its impact on society. Make a chart similar to the one on page 404 to graphically display what you have learned.
2. Look at three paintings by Honoré Daumier or Jean François Millet. What does each work communicate about life during the Industrial Revolution?
3. Prepare a report on one of the following topics: (a) organized labor movement in Britain (b) women's suffrage in Europe (c) the Irish Question.
4. Imagine you are Otto von Bismarck in 1890, shortly after you had resigned. Write a newspaper article titled: "The Successes and Failures of My Administration."

Suggested Readings

Ashton, T. S. The Industrial Revolution. London: Oxford University Press, 1971. Gives an introduction to the Industrial Revolution in Britain.

Berlin, Isaiah. Karl Marx: His Life and Environment. New York: Galaxy, 1959. Discusses the life and ideas of Marx and their impact.

Longford, Elizabeth. Queen Victoria: Born to Succeed. New York: Harper and Row, 1965. A biography of Victoria during the early years of her reign.

Tuchman, Barbara. The Proud Tower. New York: Macmillan, 1965. A social and political narrative of Europe from 1870 to 1914.

Imperialism and Modernization

1803 Louisiana Purchase	**1823** Monroe Doctrine	**1850-1864** Taiping Rebellion
1804 Haitian independence	**1825** Decembrist Uprising	**1855-1881** Tsar Alexander II

1800	**1815**	**1830**	**1845**

	1830-1914 Partition of Africa	**1857** Indian Mutiny
1810-1825 Liberation of Latin America	**1830's-1920's** Age of the Caudillos	

1861-1865 U.S. Civil War	1878 Treaty of San Stefano	1898 Spanish-American War
	1882 Egypt invaded by Britain	1899-1900 Boxer Rebellion
		1910 Mexican Revolution
1860	**1875**	**1890**	**1905**	**1920**
1867 Dominion of Canada		1904-1905 Russo-Japanese War	1911 Chinese Republic
1867 Ausgleich		1905 Freedom Manifesto
1867-1912 Meiji Japan		

During the 1800's, the ideas and practices of the West spread to other parts of the globe. Their impact was first felt in eastern Europe, where nationalism, liberalism, and industrialization threatened to undermine the traditions of the ruling dynasties. Later, western contacts forced the peoples of Asia and Africa to end centuries of isolation and to open their lands to trade.

In the Americas, the United States built a stable democracy, expanded its territory, fought a civil war, and became a world industrial power. The Spanish and Portuguese colonies farther south became independent. Democracy in these lands, however, suffered setbacks as landowners and military leaders controlled political life and restrained economic development.

Toward the end of the century, Europe and the United States continued a policy of building empires. They enlarged their trade and protected their interests in many parts of the world.

Europeans in Tokyo procession

Cartoon of Balkan Rivalries

&& *Experience shows that the most dangerous moment for a bad government is usually when it begins to reform itself.* **99**

Alexis de Tocqueville, French politician and author (1805-1859)

Multinational Empires

The goals of most revolutionaries were similar almost everywhere in Europe: constitutional government, abolition of feudal dues, and freedom of religion, press, and assembly.

Throughout the nineteenth century, much of eastern Europe was divided among the Austrian, Russian, and Ottoman empires. Each was a **multinational empire,** containing varied ethnic and religious groups who spoke different languages and dialects.

The major unifying force in each multinational empire was the ruling dynasty. The Hapsburgs had ruled Austria for about 600 years. The Romanov tsars had controlled Russia since the 1600's. The Ottoman dynasty had dominated the land bridge between Europe and the Middle East since the 1400's.

By the late 1800's, the dynamic forces of liberalism and nationalism were having an impact on eastern Europe. This situation threatened the unity of the Austrian and Ottoman empires. It also posed a challenge to the rule of the tsars in Russia.

1 The Austrian Empire

The Hapsburg empire of Austria consisted of about 20 distinct nationalities. The largest of these were the Germans of Austria and Bohemia, and the Magyars of Hungary. Other national groups included Czechs, Serbs, Croatians, Slovaks, Romanians, Poles, Italians, Slovenes, and Ukrainians.

During 1848 and 1849, uprisings throughout the empire revealed mounting dissatisfaction with Austria's centralized, absolute rule. Opponents of the Austrian system of government felt that it did not take seriously the historical rights and cultural differences of the nationalities within the empire. Some proposed a federal structure to replace the centralized one. This, they believed, was the best means to transform the empire into a modern state. Such a federal plan would divide authority between the central government in Vienna and a number of regional governments. The idea, however, was completely disregarded by Emperor Francis Joseph and his chief minister, Prince Felix Schwarzenberg. The Austrian government opposed all reform and set out to strengthen the emperor's rule that had been weakened by revolution.

Francis Joseph

Francis Joseph became emperor in 1848, when he was 18 years of age. His coming to the throne was part of an effort to restore absolute rule in Austria. Schwarzenberg, however, was the real head of government. Under Schwarzenberg, the old order was restored in Austria and opposition to domestic reform was made government policy.

Bach System   After the revolutions of 1848 and 1849 had been crushed, Schwarzenberg established a strong bureaucracy to enforce government decisions. The bureaucracy was made up of nonelected officials who were sent to every part of the empire to exercise judicial and administrative functions in the emperor's name. In the event of local uprisings, these civil servants were supported by the emperor's army and a force of secret police. The secret police kept government officials informed about the activities of revolutionaries.

The bureaucracy was directed primarily by the minister of the interior, Alexander Bach. It was sometimes called the Bach system. The Bach system proved to be very unpopular throughout the empire. People lived under the constant threat of military force and feared the activities of the secret police. The non-German nationalities, in particular, associated the Bach system with the emperor's policy of "Germanization." "Germanization" meant making German the official culture and language of the empire and enforcing its use. This policy represented the effort

Viennese society made the city one of the cultural centers of Europe and gave it a reputation for gaiety that persisted long after Vienna's "golden age" had vanished. This painting by Wilhelm Gause, of a ball in the Hofburg Palace, reflects the lightheartedness of Viennese nobility. Francis Joseph, in his white military uniform covered with medals, represented the unifying force of the Austrian Empire. Who was the real head of government?

of the government to undermine national movements within the Austrian Empire.

Those leading the opposition to the Bach system were mostly non-German nobles and middle-class thinkers and professionals. The nationalist movements in the Austrian Empire generally were not well supported by the lower classes. The large peasant class, for example, more often than not remained loyal to the Hapsburg ruler.[1]

The peasants of the empire were mostly Roman Catholic, and the Hapsburg dynasty had long been considered the "greatest Roman Catholic power in the world." To guarantee peasant support and the favor of Catholic nations outside Austria, Francis Joseph concluded a concordat with the Pope in 1855. This agreement gave the Catholic Church increased

authority particularly in matters of education throughout the Austrian Empire. With the concordat, the Austrian government acted to counter the revolutionary spirit in the schools and to give greater uniformity to the empire's institutions.

Critics of the concordat of 1855 and the Bach system pointed to the expanded role of the emperor's army, the bureaucracy, the Church, and the secret police in maintaining the empire's unity. Adolph Fischof, one of the principal leaders of the 1848 Vienna uprising, stated that the domestic policy of Francis Joseph created "a standing army of soldiers, a sitting army of officials, a kneeling army of priests, and a creeping army of [informers]."

The leading center of opposition to the emperor's absolute rule was in Hungary. There, Magyar nationalists were regrouping after the defeat of Louis Kossuth's Hungarian Republic in 1849. The Magyars were the strongest of the non-German groups within the empire. Unrest among the Magyars eventually led the Austrian

---

[1]Austria's peasants looked to the emperor to guarantee their freedom. Under revolutionary pressure in 1848, Francis Joseph had ended forced labor by peasants on aristocratic estates. Nobles, now dependent on free labor to farm their lands, did not share common interests with the peasants.

The map below shows the distribution of *majority* populations in each area. Point out that one group did not make up the total population in its area.

government to scrap the Bach system and seek a compromise with the national groups.

Austrian Weakness   Austria had depended on Russia to crush the Hungarian revolt of 1849. This was the first in a series of events that revealed the weakness of the Austrian Empire. Austria's role in the Crimean War from 1854 through 1856 further undermined its international position.

During the Crimean War, the emperor and his foreign minister, Count Ferdinand Buol-Schauenstein, agreed to help Britain and France prevent Russia's territorial expansion. Austria, however, had planned its own expansion by annexing the Danube principalities of Wallachia and Moldavia. Austrian forces occupied the principalities and remained there during the war and for a time afterwards. This move angered Britain and France as well as Russia. Britain and France wanted Austria to be active in the fighting. Russia viewed Austria's occupation of

the principalities as a threat to its interests in the Balkans. The result was a disaster for Hapsburg prestige in Europe. The Crimean War also brought the empire close to financial ruin through the prolonged **mobilization,** or war readiness, of its troops.

Furthermore, Austria lost control of the province of Lombardy in Italy. The war also forced Austria out of the Danube principalities. The Austrian government was reluctant to commit large numbers of its troops in both Italy and the Danube principalities when there was danger of internal revolt in Hungary.

Territorial losses and internal unrest forced Francis Joseph to strengthen his support at home. Appealing to his German subjects, Francis Joseph took steps to unite all of Germany under Austrian leadership. This effort, however, led to great humiliation for the emperor.

When Francis Joseph called a meeting of all German princes in Frankfurt in 1863, Prussia,

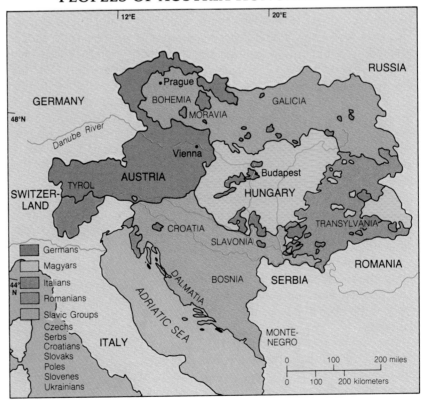

PEOPLES OF AUSTRIA-HUNGARY 1914

Review the results of the Schleswig-Holstein War and the Seven Weeks' War on pp. 468 to 471.

which was Austria's rival for German leadership, refused to attend. Without Prussia, the meeting was a failure. In the following year, however, Austria found itself allied with Prussia in the Schleswig-Holstein war, which further weakened Austria financially. While some Austrian forces fought in Denmark, others were needed in Venetia to maintain Austrian control of that Italian province. The consequences of this situation made Austria an easy victim for Prussia in the Seven Weeks' War of 1866. By its defeat in this war, Austria was forced out of any plan for German unity. At the same time, it also lost control of Venetia. These setbacks in foreign policy forced Francis Joseph to realize that changes had to be made within his empire in order to prevent it from breaking apart.

The Dual Monarchy

Francis Joseph's efforts to strengthen his authority were effectively challenged by the Magyars of Hungary. After Austria's defeat in the Seven Weeks' War, the emperor sought a compromise with Hungary. Austria needed peace with Hungary to keep the empire together. Hungary agreed to a compromise because it seemed to be the only way to preserve its own national existence.

Compromise of 1867 Austrian officials had been negotiating with Hungarian leaders during most of the 1860's. However, neither side was moved to compromise until the Austrian defeat at Sadowa in the Seven Weeks' War. Some time after this crucial battle, Francis Joseph sent for Francis Deak, the Hungarian leader, and asked him what the people of Hungary wanted. Historian Robert Ergang reports that when Deak answered that they wanted "their rights," the emperor replied, "I suppose it must be as you insist." After a long series of further negotiations, the so-called *Ausgleich,* or "Compromise," was reached between Austria and Hungary. It created the state that became known as Austria-Hungary.

The compromise provided for the restoration of Hungary's independence, which had been abolished in 1849. Hungary now had its own prime minister and a separate parliament mod-

eled on that of Austria. Thus, Hungary was free of Austrian interference in its internal affairs.

Jointly, Austria and Hungary decided matters on foreign policy, defense, and finances for the empire. They had common ministries of foreign affairs, war, and finance. Other matters of mutual concern were handled by a system of committees. Members of these committees were elected by the Hungarian parliament, meeting at Budapest, and the Austrian parliament, meeting at Vienna.

Under the Ausgleich, Francis Joseph remained ruler of both areas. He kept his title as emperor of Austria, and the Hungarians[2] crowned him king of Hungary. The new state became a **dual monarchy:** the empire of Austria and the kingdom of Hungary.

Joint Economies While Austria and Hungary had separate political institutions, their economies were linked. Industrialized Austria supplied manufactured goods for the dual monarchy. Agricultural Hungary supplied food products. Disputes, however, developed between the two regions over foreign trade, tariffs, and currency.

Austria's industrial growth during the mid-1800's was generally slow. However, after the creation of the dual monarchy, Austrian production of coal, iron, steel, and manufactured goods grew from year to year. Bohemia and Moravia became the leading industrial centers, producing machine tools, textiles, armaments, shoes, and chemicals. The concentration of industry in Bohemia and Moravia meant more rapid **urbanization,** or the growth of cities, there. This development, in turn, greatly affected the political climate of the dual monarchy by the early years of the twentieth century.

After the Ausgleich

Nationalist movements continued to disrupt Austria-Hungary after the Ausgleich of 1867. Each part of the dual monarchy faced this problem in different ways.

---

[2]The term "Hungarians" refers to those people living in the area known as Hungary. These included Romanians, Slovaks, Croatians, and Serbs as well as Magyars.

This early photograph shows some of the Magyar nobles who exacted recognition of Hungary from Francis Joseph in the Compromise of 1867. Although the Compromise was far less than many Hungarians demanded, it was far more than Francis Joseph would have consented to before the war with Prussia. Who was the leader of the Hungarian nationalists?

Nationalism in Hungary

After 1867, the Magyars of Hungary assumed absolute control over the Slavs in their territory. Magyar leaders reluctantly granted the Croatians limited home rule but moved to **assimilate,** or absorb, the other Slavic nationalities. In 1868 the Hungarian parliament passed a bill stating "the official language of the government in all government services is and will remain Magyar." Four years later, Francis Deak emphasized in a speech to the diet:

> *If we wish to win over the nationalities we must seek at all costs to Magyarize them; this can only happen if we create in them love and attachment for Hungarian conditions. Two things are clear to me: to exterminate them would be . . . barbarism, even if they were not in any case too numerous for this to be possible. And to make them our enemies is not in our interest.**

During the late 1800's, Magyar language and culture completely dominated all areas of life in Hungary. In fact, many non-Magyars legally changed their names to win social acceptance.[3]

---

*Francis Deak, as quoted in *Europe Since Waterloo*, Robert Ergang, © 1967 by Heath, p. 313.

[3]For a few pennies people with names like Rosenberg, Meier, Schmidt, or Blitzstein could acquire common Magyar names such as Hunyadi, Petöfi, and Fejervary.

Social pressures and strictly enforced laws prevented the other national groups from effectively challenging Magyar control.

Nationalism in Austria

The Austrian half of the dual monarchy included Germans, Italians, and Slavic groups, such as the Czechs, Slovenes, Poles, and Ukrainians. The Germans formed less than half the total population, but they held a dominant position. The Slavic majority was often at a disadvantage. After 1867, the Slavs began to demand more autonomy.

With greater industry and urbanization, Austria faced a more complex national situation than did predominantly rural Hungary. Members of the Austrian middle and working classes organized according to their nationalities and became politically active. The most outspoken of the national groups in the Austrian half of the dual monarchy were the Czechs.

After the demands of the Magyars had been met by the emperor in 1867, the Czechs fully expected to receive the same treatment. They particularly wanted equal rights for Bohemia in Austria-Hungary. But members of the Austrian government did not want to split the empire further. In addition, the Magyars were not willing to share power with the Czechs or any other Slavic group. Lack of government action led to protests in the Czech areas of Bohemia.

The method of planting seeds shown below is called broadcasting. Have students determine if this is an effective way to plant seeds.

Francis Joseph feared that nationalist rivalries would lead to the collapse of his dynasty. He spent the final years of his reign trying to reconcile the claims of the many nationalities under his rule. In fact, the emperor became one of the few unifying forces in the dual monarchy. In 1907 he personally sponsored a reform that introduced universal manhood suffrage in his Austrian domain. The emperor hoped that passage of the bill would appease the various nationalities, and it did for a time. His wish that the dual monarchy would be a strong political unit, however, was disappointed. By 1914, nationalist feuding had paralyzed Austria-Hungary's system of government.

1. Identify: Francis Joseph, Bach system, "Germanization," Francis Deak, Ausgleich.
2. Why did Austria's multinational groups oppose the centralized, absolute rule of the emperor?
3. Why did Austria and Hungary agree to a dual monarchy?

About 90 percent of Russia's population were peasants who eked out a bare existence by primitive agricultural methods and were at the mercy of landowners. What were the two major features of life in Russia?

2   The Russian Empire

In the early 1800's, the Russian Empire was by far the largest state in the world. It spanned both Europe and Asia. From its borders with Prussia and Austria in the west, the empire stretched to the Pacific Ocean in the east. It extended from the Baltic Sea and Arctic Ocean in the north to the Black and Caspian Seas in the south.

This vast territory consisted of more than 60 nationalities, speaking over 100 different languages. Nearly two-thirds of the population were Slavs. The predominant Slavic groups were the Russians, Ukrainians, and Belorussians. Their homelands were in the European part of the empire. Other European groups included the Lithuanians, Latvians, and Estonians along the Baltic coast. There were also Germans, Jews, Finns, and Poles in parts of European Russia.

In the south toward the Middle East, Armenians, Azerbaijanis, and Georgians lived in the region of the Caucasus Mountains. Farther east were Asiatic peoples like the Mongols, Turks, Mordovians, Chuvashes, and Bashkirs. They lived in such varied areas as the steppe of central Asia, the Volga and Oka river basins, and the Ural Mountains.

Two main features of life in the Russian Empire were absolute rule by the tsars and manual labor by peasant serfs. Together they guaranteed the traditional order in both the economy and government. Essentially a creation of the Romanov dynasty, this order became threatened by the same forces of reform that were at work in the rest of Europe during the nineteenth century.

Monarchy in Crisis

During the early 1800's, Russian tsars discussed political and social reforms with their advisers. But in practice, they resisted change. Alexander I, who ruled from 1801 to 1825, granted a constitution to Russian-ruled Poland. Yet he rejected constitutional government for Russia itself. He also permitted the liberation of some serfs. However, further reforms were postponed because of the many wars in which Alexander became involved.

The brightest period in the reign of Alexander I came when his troops defeated those of Napoleon in 1812. Thereafter, the tsar played a major role at the Congress of Vienna.

Decembrist Uprising   Alexander's policies led to mounting opposition among younger army officers who had accepted western liberal ideas. After 1817 many secret political societies were formed in the army. All of these societies wanted freedom for the serfs, but they differed regarding political goals. Some favored gradual reforms and a constitutional monarchy. Others supported revolution and the creation of a republic.

In 1825 Alexander I died without heirs. The Russian throne passed to his younger brother, who became Nicholas I. General uncertainty about the transfer of power provided an opportunity for a military revolt by several of the radical societies. This revolt, known as the Decembrist Uprising because it took place in the month of December, was ill planned. Also, many of its participants were halfhearted about opposing the government. Thus, Nicholas I was able to crush the uprising in a single day. Of the revolt's leaders, several were executed; the rest went into exile in Siberia. In spite of its failure, the Decembrist Uprising inspired later Russian revolutionaries.

Nicholas I   Nicholas I believed in an absolute monarchy and firmly opposed the spread of liberal ideas. During the 1830's and 1840's, he intervened in Poland and Hungary to crush liberal and nationalist uprisings. At the same time, Nicholas extended Russian territorial claims in the Balkans and in central Asia.

Reform in Russia

Despite Nicholas I's efforts to resist change, demands for reform persisted. Russian losses in the Crimean War underlined the fact that the empire was in serious trouble. Nicholas, however, was too ill to begin any serious reforms. Following Nicholas's death in 1855, this task was left to his son, Alexander II.

Russia's Problems   Russia's humiliating defeat in the Crimean War revealed the extent to which Russia lagged behind other European nations. Russian soldiers lacked up-to-date weapons. Military leaders had no efficient means to rapidly transport troops into battle and to maintain battlefield communications. Russia, by

European standards, had shown itself to be a poor, backward country.

When Alexander II became tsar in 1855, Russia was almost totally agricultural. The middle class was small, and industry was practically undeveloped. There were only about 483,000 industrial workers in a country with over 60 million people. All of Russia had a mere 650 miles (1,040 kilometers) of railway.

One major reason for Russian backwardness was the system of serf labor that embraced most of the population. With the support of the government, landowners kept the majority of the serfs illiterate, unskilled, and tied to the land. Also, a large number of serfs, known as domestic serfs, worked as servants in the homes of nobles. Serfs were usually not free to move to urban centers where the factories were located. Entrepreneurs hoped to make Russia a modern, industrial power. They wanted the serfs freed for use as a cheap labor force in the factories.

Alexander II wanted to catch up to Europe in military and industrial strength yet preserve the old autocracy in government. What was the major cause of Russia's industrial backwardness?

Ask students, "What is the difference between a serf and a slave?"

Freedom for the Serfs   Alexander's first major reform as tsar was to free the serfs. It had been clear to him that serf labor was one of the greatest obstacles to progress in the empire. At the same time, many landowners began supporting reform because they feared that the serfs might rise in revolt. During the reign of Nicholas I, there had been more than 500 uprisings in the countryside.

The **emancipation,** or freeing, of the serfs was decreed on March 3, 1861.[4] This measure gave the serfs personal freedom and the right to obtain land purchased by the state from the landowners. The landowners, however, benefited the most from emancipation. They had a choice of keeping their best land and selling wasteland. They also received a generous compensation from the government for the lands they relinquished to the state.

For the serfs, emancipation was actually a mixed blessing. By law, they had been granted new rights. In reality, the great majority of the newly freed serfs became dependents of the government that had freed them. In return for their land, the serfs were expected to make payments to the state. To make certain that this debt was paid, the government bound individual peasants to **mirs,** or village communes. The communes then saw that the peasants worked the land and made payments to the government from their earnings.

Many peasants gave up their land rather than return to bondage. They were generally the poorest and least skilled of their social group. Landless peasants usually moved from the farms to the cities, adding to the growing numbers of unskilled urban workers.

For the peasants who remained in the mirs, life was difficult. Commune officials often decreased land allotments as the peasant population grew. With smaller parcels of land on which to grow crops, peasant families could not grow enough food to pay back their debt. At times, peasant farmers had trouble growing enough food to eat.

With conditions similar to those that existed before the emancipation decree, the peasants lost faith in government reforms. They blamed "evil-minded" landowners and bureaucrats for interfering with the will of the tsar. As peasant expectations were disappointed, many uprisings took place in rural areas. Local officials, landowners, and military forces, however, easily crushed these rebellions.

Other Reforms   The emancipation decree of 1861 had an effect on the structure of Russian local government. With it, landowners lost absolute control over the provinces. This caused a need for a new system of local government.

In responding to this need, Alexander II gave limited home rule to 33 provinces in European Russia. By a law decreed in 1864, the **zemstvos,** or local councils, were created. Each zemstvo consisted of representatives for nobles, peasants, and villagers. It had charge of local matters, such as starting schools, improving roads, and hiring doctors and teachers. Once a year, the local zemstvos of each province sent deputies to an assembly to discuss matters affecting the province as a whole. In 1870 Alexander II allowed greater self-government to the cities. Municipal councils were set up that performed the same functions in the urban areas that zemstvos carried out in the rural areas.

Tsar Alexander II became known as the Tsar Liberator for his many reforms. In addition to those already mentioned, he limited the use and authority of the emperor's secret police. He eased restrictions on the press. He also expanded the educational system, increasing the number of universities and granting schools some measure of autonomy. But his most notable reforms came in the judicial system, where he introduced the jury trial in criminal cases and appointed judges to lifetime terms of office.

In 1874 Alexander II began a reorganization of the Russian army. Under his plan, military service was required for men of all social classes. Before this time, the Russian army consisted mostly of **conscripted,** or drafted, serfs. With the reorganization, the period of military service was reduced from 25 years to six years. Military training was modernized. Harsh punishments

---

[4]The emancipation decree of Tsar Alexander II was issued two years before President Abraham Lincoln's Emancipation Proclamation in the United States.

Russian expansion was continental. Point out that Russia was not active in overseas expansion.

The map below is the subject of the "Using Maps" section of the Chapter 21 Review.

RUSSIAN EXPANSION   1801-1914

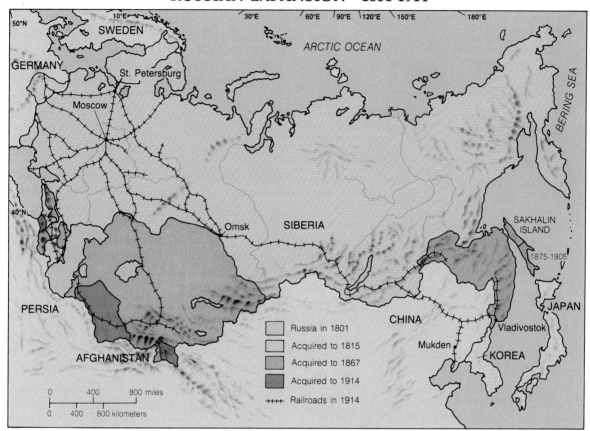

Russia in 1801
Acquired to 1815
Acquired to 1867
Acquired to 1914
++++ Railroads in 1914

0   400   800 miles
0   400   800 kilometers

were reduced. Officers and soldiers were provided with a basic education. It was chiefly in the new army that Russia's peasants and urban workers learned to read and write.

Reaction to Reform

The reforms of Alexander II did not please many upper- and middle-class groups that wanted more change. The opposition to the tsar's measures ranged from reformers who demanded peaceful, democratic programs to revolutionaries who wanted the complete destruction of all authority and institutions.

Reformers   People who supported improvements in government were generally divided into two major groups of reformers. One group was called the Westerners. They represented the interests of liberal-minded nobles and the small, but growing, middle class. They called for a constitution that would establish a limited monarchy and guarantee rights similar to those in western Europe. Many of these moderates supported greater participation in government by all social groups.

The other group were called Slavophiles. They did not want to borrow from the West. Instead, they felt that Slavic tradition, the Orthodox Church, and the leadership of the tsar could provide the inspiration needed for reform.

Revolutionaries   A revolutionary movement known as Populism emerged in the 1870's. Made up of intellectuals and students, it believed that eventually the peasants would lead a revolution, overthrow the tsar, and establish a socialist state. To prepare for this goal, the Populists worked to better the conditions of the peasants. Groups of students felt that it was their duty to educate the peasants. They went to the

HISTORY AND THE ARTS

Nationalist Composers

In 1869 Modest Petrovich Mussorgsky completed what has since become Russia's most famous opera, *Boris Godunov*. Its story centers around the figure of Tsar Boris, but the opera's true hero is the Russian people. In *Boris Godunov*, Mussorgsky sought to express the soul of Russia by portraying the poor condition of the nation's common people.

At the time, Mussorgsky was one of a group of European composers who became known as nationalist composers. Through their music, they helped to build a national identity by voicing their frustrations over the oppression of their peoples.

The nationalist composers seldom had formal musical training. They rebelled against the classical tradition established by German composers. Instead, they turned to the folk songs and dances of their own nationalities for inspiration. They created original music, capturing the style, rhythm, melody, and harmony of their ethnic groups.

In Russia, nationalist composers Alexander Borodin and Nikolai Rimsky-Korsakov were as famous as Mussorgsky. Borodin is remembered for the opera *Prince Igor* and its "Polovtsian Dances." Rimsky-Korsakov composed many operas, including *The Snow Maiden*, and the symphonic suite *Scheherazade*.

The first Czech to use folk music in his work was Bedřich Smetana. His opera *The Bartered Bride* sparkles with charming melodies and dances popular in the Czech villages of Austrian-ruled Bohemia. *The Moldau*, also by Smetana, describes life along a Bohemian river. The great popularizer of Czech music, however, was Anton Dvořák. He delighted audiences around the world with his *Moravian Duets* and *Slavonic Dances*. In 1892 Dvořák was invited to the United States to head the newly created National Conservatory of Music, which was founded to stimulate the growth of nationalism in American music. While he was in the United States, Dvořák composed his famous Symphony No. 9 (*From the New World*).

By the end of the 1800's, music by nationalist composers had become popular in many different European countries. Norway and Spain, in particular, provided settings for numerous nationalist compositions.

1. What is a nationalist composer?
2. Who were the most famous nationalist composers in the Russian and Austrian empires?

Mussorgsky felt that music should have the natural flow of human speech. He used the poetic repetitions in Russian folk tales, the dignity of church chants, and the sounds of nature in his music. His opera, Boris Godunov, was not accepted at first by the public. It had no female leading character, and it was too radically different from popular operas of the time with their lilting soprano arias. After Mussorgsky's death in 1881, his friend, Rimsky-Korsakov, revised Boris and included a leading female role. The revised version has become the most popular Russian opera.

Compare the "Russification" policy of Alexander III with the "Magyarization" policy in Hungary.

Toward the end of the 1800's, Russian nationalism and the official policy of "Russification" contributed to the growth of militant antisemitism. The "Black Hundreds" destroyed Jewish shops and homes and beat defenseless children and the aged. These gangs enjoyed the active support of many Orthodox priests, bureaucrats, workers, and peasants. Why was the policy of "Russification" enforced by Alexander III?

villages to prepare the peasants for the revolution. The peasants, however, distrusted the students and refused to accept radical ideas. As a result, many revolutionaries turned from peaceful persuasion to violence.

Radical reformers, such as Michael Bakunin, wanted **anarchy,** no government or institutions at all. Bakunin called for the destruction of the state, the family, law, property, and all other institutions. Some young people rejected all traditions, believing that nothing was sacred. Hence, they became known as **nihilists** (from the Latin *nihil,* which means "nothing").

The nihilists were determined to strike at the tsarist government by killing key officials. In 1866 they made their first attempt to assassinate Alexander II. In response to the growing influence of the nihilists, Alexander II decided in 1881 to establish a popular assembly to give his subjects participation in national government. But before the measure became public, a young nihilist killed Alexander II with a bomb.

Unrest under the Last Tsars

If Russian revolutionaries believed that the Romanov dynasty could be destroyed by assassinating Alexander II, they were mistaken. Autocratic rule continued under Russia's last tsars, Alexander III and Nicholas II.

Alexander III   Alexander III succeeded his father as tsar, vowing to maintain the old order in its strictest form. He warned his subjects that he would not tolerate a constitution. He blamed too much freedom for the death of his father. Thus, he reduced the authority of the zemstvos, abolished autonomy in the schools, censored the press, and arrested nihilists.

To strengthen his hold on the empire, Alexander imposed a strict policy of "Russification." This meant that anyone who questioned the authority of the tsar, spoke a language other than Russian, or followed a religion other than Eastern Orthodoxy was to be considered unloyal to Russia. "Russification" was an attempt to make the empire's many nationalities into one. But instead of bringing unity, the policy stirred unrest among the subject nations. In areas such as Poland and Finland, the tsar's policy was resisted. However, most of the people reluctantly accepted it because they feared that the Russian army would be used against them.

Among the most hated policies of Alexander III was the persecution of certain non-Russian groups. The Jewish people, in particular, were singled out for cruel treatment. During the early months of the new tsar's reign, Alexander III issued a number of decrees. These decrees deprived Russian Jews of their freedom of

Some teachers might wish to discuss Nicholas and Alexandra in greater detail, mentioning the influence that the monk Rasputin had on the royal family. See p. 593.

movement by forcing them to live in only one area within the empire. This area, known as the Pale, was made up of 15 provinces in the southwestern part of the empire. In some cases, enforcement of the decrees resulted in bloody **pogroms,** or massacres, of Jewish people.

Meanwhile, discontent among the peasants grew under the rule of Alexander III. Since the emancipation, the population of the mirs had grown at a fast rate. Between 1860 and 1897 the peasant population of European Russian grew from 50 to almost 80 million. With this increase, individual peasant landholdings were proportionally reduced. Because of little or no modern farm equipment, crop yields were small, probably less than any other country in Europe. Peasant demands for more land brought continuing rural unrest.

Nicholas II   When Alexander III died in 1894, most Russian people expected more liberal rule under his son Nicholas II. But Nicholas's words and actions proved them wrong. Like his father, Nicholas II regarded the preservation of the status quo as his duty. However unlike Alexander III, Nicholas lacked a strong-willed personality to make absolute rule effective. He and his wife Alexandra were isolated by court life from their people. They had little understanding of Russia's desperate plight.

Toward the Revolution

During the reign of Nicholas II, a revolutionary mood swept over Russia. While the peasants in the mirs showed dissatisfaction with their lot, political forces in the cities began opposing the tsar's government. Middle-class merchants, artisans, manufacturers, and professionals called for the immediate establishment of a constitutional monarchy. Other liberal middle-class reformers called for the government to take land from the nobles and give it to the peasants.

Nicholas II is shown here with the Tsarina Alexandra and his daughters, the Grand Duchesses Marie, Tatiana, Olga, and Anastasia. His son, the Grand Duke Alexis, is seated at his mother's knee. Nicholas was a weak and autocratic man who could find little sympathy for, or understanding of, the people's demands for change. What did Nicholas II consider his main duty?

Apart from the socialist parties, there was an important liberal party called the Constitutional Democrat party, or simply CADET. It derived its support from the zemstvos.

Rise of the Workers   For the first time, the proletariat in large numbers opposed the government. Although slower in organizing than the middle class, the urban workers proved to be the most influential political force in Russia. Their success was due to Russia's swift industrial development since the reign of Alexander II.

After the emancipation of the serfs in 1861, many landless peasants had moved to the cities, where they formed a large force of cheap, unskilled labor. At the same time, Russia's rich natural resources began attracting foreign investors. These foreigners wanted to use Russia's huge labor force in mining and large-scale industry. The combination of cheap labor, abundant resources, and foreign investment sparked Russian industrial expansion.[5] One result of this development was the rapid growth of a politically active working class in Russia.

Conditions in Russian factories in the late 1800's and early 1900's were generally bad. Lighting, ventilation, and sanitation were poor. The workday was usually longer than 12 hours. Workers often lived in dirty barracks that resembled prisons. Less skilled than workers in western Europe, Russian workers were often mistreated by factory owners and the government. Many workers, who had learned to read and write in the army, were able to compare their situation with that of workers in western Europe. They realized that their situation was worse and decided to take action.

Russian Marxism   By the 1890's, groups of middle-class thinkers and radical workers had accepted Marxism, or the teachings of Karl Marx. They believed that the working class, and not the peasants, would lead the revolution. Marxist organizers worked to coordinate labor activity against the government. In 1898 the Marxists formed the Russian Social Democratic Labor party to act on behalf of the urban workers. The party, however, split in 1903 because of differences of opinion. One group, made up of

The rout of their troops at Mukden was one of the many defeats suffered by the Russians during the Russo-Japanese War. How did defeat contribute to unifying the various revolutionary factions in Russia?

moderates, believed that Russia needed to develop an industrial state with a sizeable working class before a socialist revolution could occur. According to them, socialism's triumph would be the work of the masses. The other more radical group was led by an activist-thinker named Vladimir Ilyich Ulyanov, also called Lenin. Lenin and his supporters believed that a socialist society could be introduced immediately by force. They claimed that a small group of dedicated revolutionaries would carry out the revolution with the help of a small working class allied to the peasants.

Members of the moderate group became known as Mensheviks, while members of the radical group were called Bolsheviks. Both groups were active in rousing opposition to the government of Nicholas II in the early 1900's.

Russo-Japanese War   The peasants, urban workers, and the small middle class all opposed the continued **autocracy,** or absolute rule, of the tsar. However, it took Russia's defeat in a war with Japan to unite them in a common revolutionary struggle.

---

[5]Russia's industrial development during the late 1800's and early 1900's was best seen in the extension of its railroad network. By 1904 the Trans-Siberian railroad linked Moscow with the eastern part of the empire.

Refer students to a map of the Russo-Japanese War on p. 541.

For his role in arranging the peace settlement in the Russo-Japanese War, President Theodore Roosevelt was awarded the Nobel Peace Prize.

To bolster Russian prestige in Asia, Nicholas II attempted to expand his empire's territory in the Far East. There, he came into conflict with the Japanese. By moving into Manchuria and Korea, Russia threatened what Japan had considered its sphere of influence. Japan struck out against Russia by attacking the Russian Pacific fleet at Port Arthur on February 8, 1904. This action began the Russo-Japanese War. Nicholas II then sent Russian soldiers into battle to protect his empire's ports on the Pacific coast.

Russia could not easily supply its troops and send reinforcements. The recently completed Trans-Siberian railroad had only one track. In 1904 it did not have a link to the Pacific coast. When a Russian fleet attempted to deliver supplies and reinforcements, many of its ships were sunk by the Japanese. Russian land forces experienced a major setback with their defeat in the Battle of Mukden in Manchuria.

Domestic uprisings also hindered Russia's war effort. In 1905 Nicholas II agreed to accept the mediation of United States President Theodore Roosevelt in arranging peace with Japan. A treaty ending the war was signed on September 5, 1905, in Portsmouth, New Hampshire.

Revolution of 1905   The strain of war on the Russian economy had raised domestic food prices, while workers' wages had not changed. To protest the price increases, spontaneous strikes broke out in many cities throughout the Russian Empire. On Sunday January 22, 1905, workers marched on the tsar's Winter Palace in Saint Petersburg. In a confrontation with guards, many workers were killed. The so-called Bloody Sunday demonstration sparked strikes in most industrial centers and a wave of political activity against the government.

Middle-class organizations drew up programs for political reform. The zemstvos issued lists of demands. In the spring of 1905, the first **soviets,** or workers' councils, were formed to voice workers' grievances. The most important of the soviets was in Saint Petersburg, where Leon

Lenin (left) saw the Revolution of 1905 as a forerunner of the coming conflict between workers and the tsar. By 1917 he had consolidated the soviets, and Trotsky (right) had organized the Red Army. What was the name given to Lenin's radical group?

With the formation of a constitutional government some institutions had changed for the better. Education budgets were increased to a point where 150,000 primary schools were functioning in 1914. The Duma also set up health and accident insurance programs for workers in 1912.

In the months that followed Bloody Sunday, dissatisfaction spread. The spirit of revolution flared throughout the country. Students marched through the streets of many cities carrying red flags, street barricades were set up, and fighting became intense. Though most of the revolutionary goals were not realized in the Revolution of 1905, what concessions were forced from the tsar?

Trotsky, a socialist writer, was its leader. The general cry throughout the empire was for the establishment of a representative government to be elected by universal suffrage.

When disorder in the cities and the rural areas continued, Nicholas II announced a law providing for the election of a national **duma,** or legislature. Rather than being a legislative assembly, the tsar proposed that the Duma serve him as an advisory council. Instead of appeasing the tsar's subjects, this measure set off a series of nationwide strikes. In October 1905, workers seized control of cities such as Saint Petersburg and Moscow. One observer at the time reported:

> *Telegraph and telephone lines ceased to work; electric lights went out; street cars stopped running; newspapers suspended publication; the postal service came to an end; and even such classes of men as lawyers, druggists, bank clerks, and the clerks of the circuit courts stopped work as a means of showing their sympathy with the revolutionary movement.**

The events of October 1905 finally forced Nicholas II to yield to the demands of his people. The tsar issued the Freedom Manifesto, also known as the October Manifesto. It granted

**Europe Since Waterloo*, Ibid., p. 292.

individual rights to citizens and allowed the Duma to make laws. In theory, Russia had become a constitutional monarchy. But in practice, Nicholas II continued to act like an absolute ruler. He supported many stern measures to restore order in the empire. In some places, pogroms were directed against Jews, and peasant leaders and labor organizers were arrested.

By the time the first elected Duma met in 1906, it became clear that Nicholas did not want limits placed on his autocratic rule. He responded by restricting the powers of the new Duma. Furthermore, the tsar assumed the right to make laws while the Duma was not in session. When the Duma asked for public support, it was quickly dissolved by the tsar. Later, other dumas that were not of the tsar's liking were also dissolved. Fearing punishment if they opposed Nicholas, many Russians reluctantly accepted restrictions of their liberties.

The tsar's ability to silence opposition was only temporary. Russia's troubles had not been resolved. On the eve of World War I, peasants, workers, and middle-class people in Russia supported renewed revolutionary activity in growing numbers.

1. Identify: Decembrist Uprising, Tsar Liberator, Westerners, Slavophiles, Michael Bakunin, "Russification," Pale, Marxism, Social Demo-

The Indochina War was more commonly known as the Vietnam War in the United States.

The Indonesians won their freedom in 1949 after fighting a four-year conflict against the Dutch.

cratic Labor party, Lenin, Bloody Sunday, Leon Trotsky, Duma, Freedom Manifesto.

2. What were the major reforms of Alexander II?
3. How did the views of the Bolsheviks and Mensheviks differ?
4. What role did the proletariat play in the Revolution of 1905?

3 The Ottoman Empire

During most of the 1800's, the Ottoman Empire included Asia Minor, the central portion of the Balkan Peninsula, Tripoli in North Africa, and the Mediterranean islands of Crete and Cyprus. The empire was made up of a collection of religious communities as well as nationalities. The largest of the religious millets, or communities, was Muslim. Muslims were subdivided into the dominant Sunnis and smaller groups such as Shiites, Druses, and Wahabis. The empire also had many Jews and Christians. In parts of the Balkans, Eastern Orthodox Christians formed the majority of the population.

In the Ottoman Empire, the Turks were the ruling class. Islam was the state religion. Each individual millet, however, followed its own laws and customs under the direction of its own religious leader. The various religious leaders—Muslim, Jewish, or Christian—had a great deal of civil authority in their communities. The Eastern Orthodox Patriarch of Constantinople, for example, controlled nearly all of the Romanian provinces. There, any person excluded from the Eastern Orthodox Church was considered an outlaw.

Reform and Reaction

Prompted by its dependence on the West in the Crimean War, the Ottoman government moved to strengthen its authority and modernize the economy and society. In 1856, Sultan Abdul-Mejid I issued the Hatt-I Humayun, a far-reaching reform decree.

The decree created a national citizenship by taking away the civil authority of the empire's religious leaders. It tried to get rid of cultural and religious divisions by making people from all cultures and religions eligible for public office.

Reforms of taxes, property rights, and the military followed. Between 1856 and 1876, Abdul-Mejid I and his successor, Abdul-Aziz, encouraged liberalism and nationalism in order to make reform a reality.

Powerful resistance to change grew among the religious leaders, who had lost civil authority in their own communities. Although many Muslim, Jewish, and Christian leaders protested reform, merchants and artisans in the individual communities welcomed it.

Non-Turkish groups, such as Armenians, Bulgarians, Macedonians, and Serbs, however, had little interest in reforming the empire. They began to think of themselves as separate nationalities and wanted nation-states of their own.

The Hatt-I Humayun generally did not have the broad-based support needed to guarantee its success. The Ottoman reform movement also lacked strong leadership. To gain public support, determined reformers known as the Young Ottomans overthrew the weak sultan Abdul-Aziz and replaced him with Abdul-Hamid II.

At first the new sultan went along with the reform movement. In 1876 he proclaimed a new constitution. He affirmed the unity of the empire and promised individual liberties for his subjects. In 1877 the first Ottoman parliament met in Istanbul. But later that same year Abdul-Hamid II decided to resist reform. He suddenly dissolved the parliament and ended constitutional rule. The sultan believed that moving the Ottoman government toward liberalism would lead to ruin. To further protect the empire from change, he drove many of the Young Ottomans into exile. Then he imposed autocratic rule.

Abdul-Hamid II

Abdul-Hamid II reigned as sultan of the Ottoman Empire from 1876 to 1909. During this entire period, his rule was strict and uncompromising. The sultan particularly used harsh measures against the rebellious non-Turkish nationalities. In 1876 peasants in Bulgaria revolted and were put down with brutal force. In 1894 Ottoman troops crushed an Armenian uprising by killing thousands of people.

Have students use the map below to draw a time line illustrating the Ottoman decline.

Meanwhile, the exiled Young Ottomans, who lived in Paris, London, and other European capitals, plotted the overthrow of the sultan. In this way, they hoped to rebuild the Ottoman Empire as a modern state. However, while the Young Ottomans worked for reform, many European governments wanted the empire dissolved. The great European powers looked to the Ottoman Empire as an open territory for expansion. Abdul-Hamid II ruled in fear of both the Young Ottomans and the European powers, especially Russia.

The Russo-Turkish War

In the 1870's Russia began a war of expansion against the Ottoman Empire. Known as the Russo-Turkish War, the conflict was declared by the Russians in the name of Pan-Slavism. Pan-Slavism was a political and cultural move-

ment emphasizing unity among all Slavic peoples. Russia considered itself the leader of the Slavs. It backed Slavic groups in the Balkans that wanted independence from the Ottomans.

The Pan-Slav movement had developed in the 1840's among Slavs living outside Russia and the Ottoman Empire. These Slavs included Czechs, Slovaks, and Poles who had accepted liberal ideals and opposed Russian autocracy. By the 1860's many Russians had embraced Pan-Slavism. They became the leaders of the movement and used it to justify their expansion into the Balkans. As for the Slavs in the Ottoman Empire, they favored Russian involvement. They did not approve of Russia taking territory. But they did look to Russia to defeat the Ottomans so that the Slavic territories could gain their freedom.

British Concern   When Russia declared war on the Ottoman Empire in 1877, many of the

DECLINE OF OTTOMAN EMPIRE   1699-1914

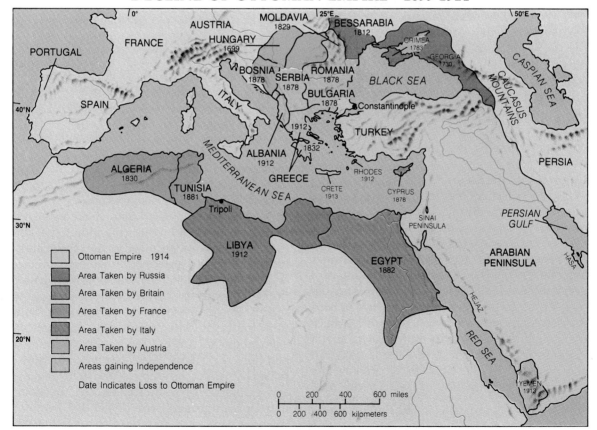

great European powers showed concern. Britain, in particular, was prepared to fight to prevent Russian expansion. As news of Russian victories over the Ottomans reached Britain, public opinion cried out for war. A popular slogan in Britain at the time gave a new word—"jingoism"—to the English language.

*We don't want to fight, but by jingo, if we do, we've got the men, we've got the ships, we've got the money too.**

Jingoism describes an extreme demonstration of patriotism usually provoked by some foreign threat. In this case, it was the threat of Russian territorial expansion.

San Stefano   The treaty ending the Russo-Turkish War was signed at San Stefano near Istanbul on March 3, 1878. It established a large Russian-controlled Bulgarian state in the Balkans. The new country was to be so large that the Ottoman sultan would have retained only a small strip of territory in Europe.

The great European powers protested the Treaty of San Stefano. Britain and Austria-Hungary were the most vocal. They demanded that the treaty be reviewed by a congress of European leaders. It would be the task of the congress to finalize a peace settlement. Britain and Austria-Hungary were so insistent on a review of the treaty that they both were ready to declare war on Russia to see that the treaty's terms would not be enacted.

Congress of Berlin   In the end, a congress of European leaders met in Berlin to revise the treaty. Otto von Bismarck presided over the meeting that began in June 1878. The representatives of the great powers divided Bulgaria into three parts, a part of which was to remain under Ottoman rule. The Congress of Berlin also decided that Montenegro, Serbia, and Romania were to become independent states, free of both Russian and Ottoman control. To further curb the ambitions of Russia, Britain was given authority over the island of Cyprus. Austria-Hungary gained the right to administer the Ottoman Balkan provinces of Bosnia and Herze-

*A History of the Modern World, R. R. Palmer and Joel Colton, © 1950 by Knopf, p. 632.

govina. As a result of the Congress of Berlin, Russian war gains were lost. The Ottoman Empire lost much of its European territory.

Ottoman Decline

The Russo-Turkish War was followed by three decades of social unrest in the Ottoman Empire. Abdul-Hamid II failed to master the crisis. In 1908 reformers known as the Young Turks staged a revolution.

Young Turks   The major objective of the Young Turk Revolution was the overthrow of the autocratic and inefficient government of the sultan. In its place, they proposed a constitutional, parliamentary system. To achieve their objective, the Young Turks undermined the sultan's power base by winning the support of the army. Without military backing, the sultan was forced to accept the program of the Young Turks; and the revolution was accomplished with little bloodshed. In December 1908, elections were ordered. In early 1909, Abdul-Hamid II went into exile. He was succeeded by his brother Mohammed V.

With the change in government, certain national groups saw the opportunity to break ties with the empire or seize some of its territory. Prince Ferdinand of Bulgaria, for example, proclaimed his country completely independent from Turkey. The rulers of Crete broke ties with the Ottoman Empire and formed a union with Greece. Francis Joseph of Austria-Hungary annexed Bosnia and Herzegovina.

Despite further territorial reductions, the Young Turk Revolution gave hope that the empire could be modernized. Under the restored constitution, personal liberties were guaranteed and certain restrictions were abolished. Unfortunately, many of the reforms never became reality. Inexperience on the part of the Young Turk leadership often resulted in many discussions about reform but few programs for it. In addition, the Young Turks began to promote a policy of making the empire Turkish in language and culture. This plan offended the remaining non-Turkish groups, who demanded freedom. In some parts of the empire, changes brought

The Young Turks, or the Party of Union and Progress, was formed originally in 1889 and was inspired by the liberal writings of the Young Ottomans.

Abdul-Hamid II was averse to any reduction of his power and therefore suspended the freedoms granted in the reform movement of 1876. His actions led many officials and officers to join the Young Turks, a rebel organization that ultimately forced Abdul-Hamid from his throne. The victorious Young Turks then marched through the streets of Pera. What was the major objective of the Young Turk revolution?

chaos and anarchy. The new leaders lacked the strict methods of enforcement that characterized the rule of the sultan.

Ottoman Breakup   Internal disorder coupled with an uncertain foreign policy hastened the decline of the Young Turk movement. It also made possible the breakup of the Ottoman Empire.

In 1912 Italy began the process of dismembering the empire. By occupying Tripoli, Italy forced the Ottoman government to surrender its last province in North Africa. That same year, a group of Balkan states moved to free members of their respective nationalities from Ottoman rule. By the fall of 1912, the Balkan League, made up of Bulgaria, Greece, Montenegro, and Serbia, had begun a war against the Ottoman Empire. As a result of the war, the empire lost all of its European territory with the exception of Istanbul and a small surrounding area.

Balkan Conflict   Unity among members of the Balkan League was short-lived. No sooner had the Balkan states won the war when they began to fight among themselves over the lands they had gained. Before the war with the Ottomans, Serbia and Bulgaria had secretly arranged for land distribution in case of a victory. Once the war ended, Bulgaria refused to go along with the plan. The Bulgarians did not want to give up territory won directly in battle. To keep their land, the Bulgarians attacked Serbian and Greek forces in the disputed area. In this second Balkan War, Montenegro and Greece sided with Serbia against Bulgaria. Romania joined the fighting when it saw the opportunity to win land from Bulgaria. The Balkan conflict brought new hope to the Ottomans. Seeing an opportunity to recover its own lost European territory, the Ottoman Empire attacked Bulgaria.

The fighting ended in 1913 with the Treaty of Bucharest, and the disputed land was redistributed. Bulgaria, which lost the war, had to surrender the lands that it had gained in the conflict with the Ottomans. Serbia and Greece obtained most of this territory. For its part, the Ottoman Empire acquired the city of Adrianople from Bulgaria.

The Treaty of Bucharest, however, did not bring a lasting peace to the Balkans. In 1914 events in the region brought many of the world's great powers into a global conflict. The coming of World War I increased the rivalry of the European powers for control of the Ottoman Empire.

1. Identify: Hatt-I Humayun, Young Ottomans, Young Turks, Abdul-Hamid II, Pan Slavism, San Stefano, Congress of Berlin, Balkan League, Treaty of Bucharest.

2. Why did local religious leaders in the Ottoman Empire oppose centralized rule?

3. What did Russia use as a pretext for war with the Ottoman Empire in 1877? What was the outcome of the war?

4. Why did Britain and Austria-Hungary demand an international review of the terms of the treaty of San Stefano?

CHAPTER 21 REVIEW

Summary

1. The major unifying forces within the Austrian Empire were the Hapsburg ruler, the army, the bureaucracy, and the Catholic Church.

2. The most significant weaknesses of the Austrian Empire were its fragmented national populations, its foreign policy, and its lack of internal administrative unity.

3. To prevent the Austrian Empire from breaking up, a compromise was reached with the Magyars. It resulted in the creation of the state of Austria-Hungary.

4. To respond to the weaknesses revealed by the Crimean War, Tsar Alexander II initiated numerous reforms in the Russian Empire. Reforms affected chiefly serfs, local governments, the judiciary, and the military.

5. While reaction to reform in the Russian Empire was generally favorable, groups such as the nihilists called for the total destruction of the tsarist government.

6. Tsar Alexander III responded to the nihilist assassination of his father by reestablishing the strict autocracy of the tsar. Preservation of the old order also was the objective of Nicholas II. Rule under the last tsars resulted in political unrest in the Russian Empire.

7. The rise of the urban proletariat created a major political force in the Russian Empire. More than any other social class, the industrial workers had the greatest influence on bringing about change and limiting the absolute rule of the tsar.

8. Before 1856, the Ottoman Empire was characterized by the decentralized authority of individual religious leaders. An imperial edict attempted to centralize authority and create national unity.

9. The Young Turk Revolution succeeded in changing the Ottoman government from an autocracy to a parliamentary system. It failed, however, to transform the empire into a modern state.

10. As central authority declined, the Ottoman Empire was slowly dismembered by internal as well as external forces. By 1914 the Ottoman Empire had lost most of its European territory.

Building Vocabulary

multinational empire	dual monarchy	assimilate	mirs
mobilization	urbanization	emancipation	zemstvos

| conscripted | nihilists | autocracy | duma |
| anarchy | pogroms | soviets | jingoism |

Reviewing the Main Ideas

1. What was the chief purpose of the Bach system in the Austrian Empire?
2. What events weakened Austria's foreign prestige by 1900?
3. How did the nationalities situation change in Austria and Hungary after 1867?
4. What were the results and consequences of the emancipation of the serfs in the Russian Empire?
5. Which groups opposed Alexander II's reforms and what were their views?
6. How did the working class become an important political force in Russia?
7. How did the Hatt-I Humayun affect the Ottoman Empire?
8. What features characterized the rule of Abdul-Hamid II?
9. How was the Ottoman Empire reduced in size from 1877 to 1913?
10. What was the major objective of the Young Turk Revolution?
11. How did Italy participate in the breakup of the Ottoman Empire?
12. What led to the first Balkan conflict? How were the Balkan wars resolved? What countries gained from the wars?

Discussing Important Ideas

1. How did Austria's imperial bureaucracy both unite and divide the empire?
2. What were the advantages and disadvantages in forming Austria-Hungary?
3. Why did the existence of serfdom in Russia impede industrial progress?
4. How had Russia changed by the end of Alexander II's reign?
5. Compare and contrast the reigns of the last tsars of Russia: Alexander III and Nicholas II.
6. Why did the Russian Revolution of 1905 fail to achieve its goals?
7. How did the views of the Young Turks differ from most European governments?
8. How was the Young Turk Revolution a success? How was it a failure?

Using Maps

Refer to the map on page 491 to answer the following questions:

1. In which span of time did Russia gain the most territory—1801-1849, 1850-1866, or 1867-1913?
2. What Russian seaports are on the map?
3. Which Russian city had the most rail service in 1914? Which had the least?
4. What was the shortest distance between Moscow and Omsk by rail in 1914?
5. What states and geographic features limited Russian expansion to the north?

CHAPTER 22

Struggle for Mexican Independence

&& *Two great examples lie before our eyes: the American Revolution and the French Revolution. Let us discreetly imitate the first; let us most carefully avoid the disastrous effects of the second.* &&

Francisco de Miranda, Venezuelan patriot (1750-1816)

The Americas

For 300 years Spain and Portugal held empires in the Americas without facing serious threats to their rule. In the early 1800's, however, the situation changed. Inspired by revolutions in the United States and France, Spanish Americans rebelled and threw off colonial rule. During the same period, the Portuguese colony of Brazil enjoyed a peaceful transition to independence.

Once independence was achieved, the countries of Latin America faced the much larger task of bringing order out of chaos. They had to create political systems suited to their own needs. Meanwhile, the United States was developing from a struggling young nation into a major world power that exerted considerable influence in Latin America.

1 Struggle for Independence

Enlightenment ideals, such as natural rights, liberty, and equality, took root in the Americas during the 1700's. They were embodied first in the American Declaration of Independence and in the creation of the United States of America. The lesson of American independence was not lost on the leaders of Latin America. Next came the French Revolution, whose radicalism affected not only politics, but also social and economic life. Within a few decades, similar revolutions swept Latin America.

Haiti

The first Latin American country to win independence was Haiti. The country at first was a French colony named Saint-Domingue. It occupied the western third of the island of Hispaniola in the Caribbean Sea. The Spanish colony of Santo Domingo occupied the eastern part of the island.

When the French Revolution began in 1789, Saint-Domingue had about half a million people. About 85 percent were black slaves. The rest were mulattos and Europeans. Leaders of the colony were very much aware of and influenced by the French Declaration of the Rights of Man. In 1791, the slaves, many of whom worked on sugar plantations, revolted and proclaimed themselves free. They were led by François Dominique Toussaint L'Ouverture, a former slave from a hill plantation.

The revolt was successful and by 1799 Toussaint was recognized as the ruler of Saint-Domingue. In 1801 Toussaint freed the slaves in neighboring Santo Domingo. He then brought the former colony—it had been surrendered to France in 1795—under his rule. Thus, Toussaint controlled the entire island. He wrote a constitution and organized a new government.

Toussaint tried to maintain friendly relations with the leaders of the French Revolution. He never declared actual independence. But when Napoleon Bonaparte took over in France, a French army came to Saint-Domingue and restored direct French control. The French commander deceived Toussaint, lured him into a trap, and sent him to France, where he died in 1803.

Leadership of the revolution was taken over by Jean Jacques Dessalines, a black general who had served under Toussaint. Aided by a yellow fever epidemic, which killed thousands of French soldiers, Dessalines defeated Napoleon's army. In 1804 he proclaimed the independence of Saint-Domingue and renamed it Haiti,[1] an Indian word meaning "place of mountains." However,

---

[1] By treaty in 1814, Spain regained Santo Domingo. Today, Hispaniola is divided into the nation of Haiti in the west and the Dominican Republic in the east.

HISTORY AND PEOPLE

François Dominique Toussaint L 'Ouverture

François Dominique Toussaint L 'Ouverture was born a slave in the French colony of Saint-Domingue in 1743. Half a century later, he would become known throughout the world as the liberator of Haiti. Toussaint's major goals were to eliminate black slavery and to establish Haitian independence. He accomplished both.

The son of black slaves, Toussaint was said to be the grandson of an African king. From Jesuit priests, Toussaint gained a limited knowledge of French. He also became a devout Catholic. As a slave, Toussaint worked on a plantation herding livestock. Later, he became an assistant to the plantation manager. In 1777 he was freed.

On August 24, 1791, influenced by the French Revolution, the slaves in Saint-Domingue suddenly revolted. At first, Toussaint was uncommitted. He even helped his former master escape. But soon he joined the revolutionaries. Toussaint, however, became disenchanted with the revolt's leaders. He began to train his own guerrilla band and was soon the mastermind of the rebellion.

In 1793 France and Spain were at war. For a brief time, Toussaint joined the Spaniards of Santo Domingo against the French of Saint-Domingue. It was at this time that Toussaint gained his nickname L'Ouverture (The Opening). It referred to his remarkable ability to open holes in the French lines of defense. While Toussaint's forces were winning in the north, the British allied with the Spanish and invaded Saint-Domingue's coastal towns. The French were close to surrender. But, in May 1794, without warning, Toussaint switched sides. One reason he gave for joining the French was that France had recently freed all the slaves. Toussaint's support for the French eventually spelled the end for the British and Spanish occupation of the island.

The governor of Saint-Domingue made Toussaint lieutenant governor of the colony and commander in chief of the Haitian forces. While he directed brilliant military operations against the British and the Spanish, Toussaint also worked for reform.

In 1796 Toussaint became governor of Saint-Domingue. Three years later, he forced the British to sign a treaty and withdraw. In January 1801, Toussaint invaded Santo Domingo, the former colony of Spain. He freed the slaves there and secured control of the entire island.

Toussaint tried to convince Napoleon Bonaparte of his loyalty. But Napoleon wanted to restore not only the French colony, but slavery as well. In January 1802, a huge French force landed on the island. After weeks of intense fighting, Toussaint agreed to a truce in exchange for the French general's promise that slavery would not be reestablished. Toussaint was allowed to retire to a plantation. But a few weeks later, he was accused of plotting an uprising. He was seized and sent to the French Alps. There he was imprisoned until his death on April 7, 1803. His brave life and tragic death made him a symbol of the fight for liberty.

Ferdinand VII was restored to the Spanish throne as a result of the Congress of Vienna.

Mexico's national holiday celebrating independence is September 16. Independence was granted in 1821.

the war had destroyed the new nation's plantations and irrigation works. Haiti became a poverty-stricken country, easily controlled by tyrannical rulers.

Spanish America

In Spanish America, as in Haiti, events in Europe and North America had a profound effect. The works of Rousseau and other Enlightenment writers, although forbidden by the Inquisition, were secretly printed and read. The American Revolution had set an example of how to win independence, and the French Revolution had spread the ideas of liberty and equality. In 1808, when Napoleon invaded Spain and placed his brother Joseph on the throne, many Spanish-American leaders saw a chance for the colonies to achieve independence.

The rigid class divisions of colonial society contributed to the desire for independence. The privileged position of the Spanish-born peninsulares was a source of envy and frustration to the American-born creoles. One step lower on the social scale were the mestizos of mixed European and Indian blood. It was this class that had the greatest interest in independence. They did not enjoy the social and political advantages of the creoles or the peninsulares, although they were better off than the mulattos and zambos. Each of these groups had suffered under the colonial system. Many people were ready to support a revolution.

Spanish territories in the New World were divided into **viceroyalties,** or administrative regions ruled by a viceroy. There were four viceroyalties by the end of the 1700's: New Spain, New Granada, La Plata, and Peru. Each of these regions developed an independence movement in the early 1800's.

Mexico

One of the earliest uprisings occurred in Mexico, which was a part of New Spain. It was led by a parish priest named Miguel Hidalgo. Hidalgo had worked among the Indians and mestizos and developed a deep sympathy for their plight. On September 16, 1810, Hidalgo began his revolt with an army of untrained Indians and mestizos. Despite Hidalgo's disap-

proval, the rebels massacred many peninsulares. They marched to the city of Guadalajara, in western Mexico, and made it their center of government.

Hidalgo's movement was more than an effort to win independence. It was a **social revolution**—an attempt to change the structure of a society, not just its leaders. The rebel government introduced reforms that freed the slaves and returned land to the Indians. Because of these measures, it was not supported by the upper-class creoles, even though they wanted independence.

Lack of discipline and military training among the rebels weakened their government. The upper classes of Mexico sided with their colonial rulers and supported an attack on Guadalajara. A Spanish army routed the rebel forces. Hidalgo was captured and executed.

After Hidalgo's death, another priest, José María Morelos, took over as leader of the revolution. In 1813 he called a conference that declared Mexico's independence from Spain. Morelos's forces fought the Spanish and were defeated in 1815. Morelos was then taken prisoner and executed.

Independence　Meanwhile, developments occurred in Europe that profoundly affected Mexico and the rest of Spanish America. In 1815 Napoleon Bonaparte was defeated, and King Ferdinand VII of Spain was restored to his throne. Ferdinand introduced oppressive policies that cost him many of his supporters both in Spain and in Spanish America. In 1820 an uprising in Spain forced Ferdinand VII to accept a liberal constitution and reforms.

Upper-class royalists in Mexico feared that the liberal government of Spain would enforce reforms ending their own privileges. To prevent change, they declared Mexico's independence from Spain. Ironically, their leader was Agustín de Iturbide, the army officer who had crushed Morelos's movement. Iturbide made himself emperor in 1822. Opposition to his oppressive rule developed. He was soon deposed and Mexico became a republic.

Central America　When Mexico became a republic, the Central American provinces that

Consider some of the problems that the Spanish encountered in administering this vast territory.

were part of New Spain decided to become free. At a meeting in Guatemala, representatives declared the region independent and established the United Provinces of Central America. After a civil war in the 1830's, Central America was divided into the independent nations of Costa Rica, El Salvador, Guatemala, Honduras, and Nicaragua.

New Granada

The struggle for independence in New Granada was begun by a creole named Francisco de Miranda. As a young man, Miranda had fled his homeland after being accused of a crime. For nearly 30 years, he traveled in Europe and the United States. During his journeys, he developed plans to free the Spanish colonies in the Americas. In 1806 he sailed with a small army to Venezuela, one of the provinces of New Granada. To his disappointment, the Venezuelans gave him no support. Miranda then returned to exile in Europe.

LATIN AMERICA 1790

Bolívar   Another supporter of independence for New Granada was Simón Bolívar, a young and wealthy creole from Venezuela. Bolívar's early life had been marked by tragedy. His parents died when he was a child. Within a year after his marriage, his young bride died. Following this loss, Bolívar turned from his personal grief and dedicated his life to the liberation of his country.

Bolívar was a well-educated person who admired the Enlightenment and the French Revolution. He became acquainted with European ways and developed political skills. Bolívar's personality and qualities of leadership attracted many followers to his cause.

During the period of Napoleon's wars, New Granada supported Spain's King Ferdinand VII against the French emperor. In 1810 liberal creoles, with Bolívar as their leader, organized a **junta,** or council, in the city of Caracas. The junta ousted the local officials and formed a government that was loyal to Ferdinand VII.

A group within the junta, including Bolívar, wanted full freedom for their country. To achieve this goal, Bolívar traveled to England to seek support. There, he persuaded Francisco de Miranda to return to Venezuela and join the junta.

On July 5, 1811, the junta proclaimed the independence of Venezuela and chose Miranda to head the new government. However, Miranda did not stay in office for long. A Spanish army defeated the Venezuelan forces in 1812. Miranda, believing that the situation was hopeless, accepted a surrender agreement. Then, he tried to escape. Bolívar and other patriots were angry with Miranda and accused him of treason. They allowed the Spaniards to capture him. Miranda was taken to Spain, where he died in 1816.

In 1813 Bolívar again revolted against the Spanish. He was able to take Caracas, which shortly afterward was lost to the Spanish army. Bolívar fled Venezuela, took refuge in British-ruled Jamaica, and then traveled to independent Haiti. In exchange for Bolívar's promise to free the slaves in Venezuela (a promise he kept), the president of Haiti helped him equip another small force.

Independence brought political chaos to most new countries. This discussion begins on p. 511.

In his address to the Venezuelan congress in Angostura in 1819, Bolívar pleaded for unity. His dream was to unite the liberated states of South America under a single ruling body. However, freedom gave way to nationalism, and each newly freed nation preferred its own government. How long did the Republic of Gran Colombia stay united?

Independence   By 1817 discontent with the oppressive Ferdinand VII was widespread in New Granada. Bolívar took advantage of this situation and returned to Venezuela. Instead of moving against Caracas, Bolívar decided to make a dramatic march across the Andes Mountains. With a few thousand volunteers, he made a successful, but costly, crossing and surprised the Spanish forces near Bogota. At the Battle of Boyacá in 1819, Bolívar's troops defeated the Spaniards and ended Spanish rule in New Granada. Within two years, Bolívar had driven the Spanish from Venezuela. He proclaimed a new nation: the Republic of Gran Colombia, or Great Colombia. Bolívar became the first president of Gran Colombia. The new republic extended over the present-day countries of Colombia, Venezuela, Panama, and Ecuador.[2]

La Plata and Chile

Like New Granada, the viceroyalty of La Plata had remained loyal to the Spanish king during Napoleon's wars. In 1810 the creoles of La Plata overthrew the local government and set up a junta in the town of Buenos Aires. In 1816 they established a confederation, calling it the United Provinces of La Plata. Later, the United Provinces of La Plata became known as Argentina.

An important leader in the Argentine independence struggle was José de San Martín. San Martín was born in La Plata in 1778. At the age of seven he went with his family to Spain. There San Martín later attended military school and became an officer in the Spanish army. In 1812 he returned to his homeland with a desire to assist in its liberation. He offered his services to the Buenos Aires junta.

For several years thereafter, San Martín recruited and trained an army to invade Peru, the stronghold of Spain in South America. By the end of 1816 San Martín's troops were ready for action. They were joined by a force of soldiers under the leadership of Bernardo O'Higgins. San Martín and O'Higgins led their army through the difficult mountain passes of the Andes. They attacked and defeated the Spanish forces near Santiago.[3] After its victory, the patriotic army marched into Santiago, where O'Higgins was made the head of the new republic of Chile. Chile's independence was assured in 1818 when San Martín and O'Higgins decisively defeated the Spanish army.

---

[2]During the 1830's, Gran Colombia divided to form the independent republics of Colombia, Venezuela, and Ecuador. Panama became independent of Colombia in 1903.

[3]Santiago was the largest town in Chile, the name given to the southern part of the viceroyalty of Peru.

Between 1807 and 1821 Rio de Janeiro became known as Portula, capital of the Portuguese government in exile.

Peru and Bolivia

After the independence of Chile, San Martín began preparation for the invasion of Peru. With the aid of a former British naval officer, he assembled a small fleet and used it to transport his forces to southern Peru in August of 1820. A year later he secured a victory, entered the city of Lima, and proclaimed the independence of Peru. However, San Martín's rule was shaky. The Spanish army was still in the hills, and San Martín needed military help to defeat it. He hoped to get help from Bolívar.

In July 1822, the two liberators of South America met at the port of Guayaquil in Ecuador. Differences over strategy and policy separated the two men. The help offered by Bolívar was not enough to meet San Martín's needs. Their styles and personalities were also very different, as the following description shows:

> On the night of 27 July a ball was given for San Martín. Bolívar, as usual at affairs of this kind, thoroughly enjoyed himself. San Martín remained cool and aloof and seemed depressed. At one o'clock in the morning he called his aides, and told them he wanted to leave because he could not stand the noise. His luggage was already on board, and, unobserved, he left the hall, went to his ship, and set sail from the port.*

San Martín decided to withdraw from the scene and allow Bolívar to take command. After stops in Chile and Argentina, San Martín left for France, where he spent the rest of his years in retirement.

Bolívar continued the fight against Spain. In 1824 the Spaniards were finally defeated in Peru. The following year saw the liberation of northern La Plata by one of Bolívar's trusted generals. The area was declared a republic and was named the Republic of Bolívar, or Bolivia. Spanish America was finally liberated.

Brazil

Brazil achieved its independence without the bloodshed that accompanied the liberation of Spanish America. Unlike the Spaniards, the Portuguese were more tolerant colonial rulers. Therefore, the discontent of the Brazilians was not as strong as that of the Spanish Americans.

When Napoleon invaded Portugal in 1807, the Portuguese royal family escaped from Lisbon. Under British protection, they sailed to Brazil and settled in the city of Rio de Janeiro. Rio was declared the capital of the Portuguese Empire under Prince João, ruling as regent for his mother, who was ill. When she died, he became King João VI.

João introduced reforms in the government of Brazil. He took various steps to improve the country's agriculture, mining, and industry. Before, Brazil had been allowed to trade only with Portugal. Now João opened Brazilian ports to world trade. The British were given special trading rights. Industry grew and commerce flourished. In 1815 João made Brazil a self-governing kingdom within the Portuguese Empire.

After he was ordered by the Portuguese government to return to Lisbon in 1822, Pedro received a petition signed by 8,000 Brazilians that urged him to stay. Who else advised him to remain in Brazil to lead the independence movement?

*Simón Bolívar, Gerhard Masur, © 1948 by University of New Mexico Press, p, 482.

Have students list the "Common Problems" for later reference in discussing Latin America.

João liked Brazil so much that he remained there after the defeat of Napoleon in 1815. In 1820, liberals took over the Portuguese government in Lisbon. João faced the loss of his throne if he stayed in Brazil. Therefore, he returned to Portugal. Before he left Brazil, João appointed his 23-year-old son Pedro as regent of the country.

The new Portuguese government in Lisbon took measures to make Brazil into a colony again and ordered Pedro to return to Portugal "to complete his education." But João advised Pedro to remain in Brazil and lead the Brazilians if they demanded their independence. As the Brazilians grew more defiant and restless in the face of Portuguese pressure, Pedro defied Portugal and declared the independence of Brazil.

Pedro was crowned Emperor Pedro I of Brazil in December 1822. João would not allow the Portuguese government to send an army against his son. To protect its special trading privileges, Britain pressured Portugal to recognize Brazil's independence. Portugal did so in 1825. Brazil became the only independent South American country to choose monarchy as its form of government.

1. Identify: Saint-Domingue, Jean Jacques Dessalines, Miguel Hidalgo, Guadalajara, José María Morelos, Agustín de Iturbide, Francisco de Miranda, Gran Colombia, United Provinces of La Plata, Bernardo O'Higgins, Pedro I.
2. In what way was the Hidalgo-Morelos revolution different from other independence movements in Latin America?
3. What was the purpose of the meeting in 1822 between José de San Martín and Simón Bolívar? What occurred afterward?
4. How did the policies of the Portuguese government after 1820 affect the future of Brazil?

2 Nation Building

By the mid-1820's, most Latin American countries had won their independence. Their next task was to achieve national unity and stable government. These goals, however, were difficult to reach. Simon Bólivar, who had dreamed of uniting all of northern South America into one powerful state, became so disillusioned that he wrote, "Those who have toiled for liberty in South America have plowed the sea."

Common Problems

In trying to build stable and prosperous nations, Latin Americans faced a number of problems. One obstacle was the geography of Central and South America. High mountains and thick jungles made transportation and communication difficult, hindering trade and economic growth. Vast areas of fertile land remained undeveloped. Population centers, separated by physical barriers, became rivals.

Other problems were part of Latin America's colonial heritage. Spanish and Portuguese rule had given the Latin Americans little practice in self-government. Instead, they were used to authoritarian government, which was not responsible to the people and demanded obedience from them.

In the colonial system, political power was in the hands of the executive branch of government. The judicial branch was weak and limited, and the legislative branch was practically nonexistent. Latin Americans had strong well-educated leaders, but they had no experience in the legislative process. Simon Bolívar complained that the colonial system had kept his people in a state of "permanent childhood" with regard to government. "If we could have at least managed our domestic affairs and our internal administration, we could have acquainted ourselves with the process and machinery of government," he wrote.

Another part of the colonial heritage was the rigid class structure of Latin American society, which independence did not change. The dominant group was now the creoles instead of the peninsulares. They owned most of the good land and controlled business and government. Their privileged position was resented, especially by the mestizos.

Soon after independence, political conflicts increased. Liberals called for separation of church and state, breakup of large estates, higher taxes on land, public social services, and civilian control of government. Most of the liberals were mestizos, intellectuals, or merchants who wanted free trade. Opposed to this group were the conservatives, who drew most of their support from the creole aristocracy, rich landowners, church leaders, and military officers.

Another issue that sharply divided the people was the question of how much power the central government should have. The creoles, who tended to live in the cities, favored a strong central government. The mestizos favored a weak central government that allowed the provinces to control local matters themselves.

Rise of Caudillos

The wars of independence had created economic and political chaos. The creoles who tried to run the government had little political experience. They drew up constitutions modeled after the United States Constitution, but they were unable to enforce the laws. Disorder and instability made many Latin American countries ripe for military takeovers.

Latin Americans had traditionally responded more to personal leaders than to abstract theories of government. This tradition led them to accept the rise of **caudillos**—"strong men," or military dictators—many of whom had been leaders of the independence movement. In most regions of South America, the Age of the Caudillos lasted for several decades.

Mexico

Nowhere did the Age of the Caudillos lead to more violence than in Mexico. For 30 years after independence, Mexico was beset by revolutions and counterrevolutions. The dominant group was the creoles, and the most important political figure was an army officer, General Antonio Lopez de Santa Anna.

Santa Anna   Santa Anna was the son of a wealthy creole. He joined the Spanish army as a youth and fought against patriots who demanded independence. Later he shifted sides and fought with the patriots.

In 1833 Santa Anna marched his troops into Mexico City and had himself "elected" president. For the next 20 years, he played the key role in determining Mexico's political fate. He was ousted from power several times, but each time he returned and took over again.

Texas   When Santa Anna first came to power, Texas was part of Mexico. Many Texans, however, had originally come from the United States, and their number was continuing to rise.

During the 1800's, Mexico's most dreaded threat to travelers was the banditti, *groups of highway robbers. One young English traveler on a 40-mile (64-kilometer) journey by coach through silver mining country observed more than 15 crosses by the roadside, each marking the spot where a treacherous murder had taken place. Criminals were treated leniently during this period. A thief was jailed for only a few days, and a murderer might be imprisoned for only a year or two, depending on the wishes of the authorities. Why did disorder and violence follow Mexico's war of independence?*

Have students research the national holidays for each
of the countries listed on the map below.

LATIN AMERICA 1828

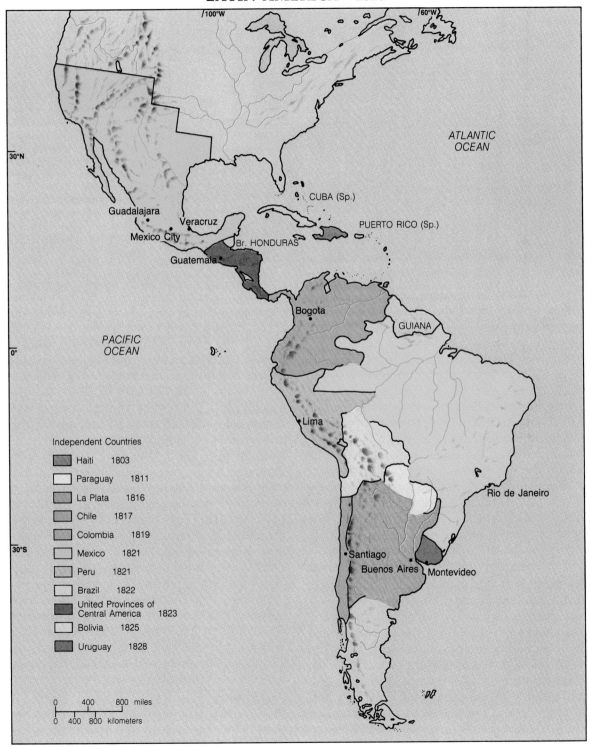

ATLANTIC
OCEAN

CUBA (Sp.)

PUERTO RICO (Sp.)

Guadalajara
Veracruz
Mexico City
Br. HONDURAS
Guatemala

Bogota

GUIANA

PACIFIC
OCEAN

Lima

Rio de Janeiro

Santiago
Buenos Aires Montevideo

30°N

0°

30°S

100°W

60°W

Independent Countries

Haiti   1803
Paraguay   1811
La Plata   1816
Chile   1817
Colombia   1819
Mexico   1821
Peru   1821
Brazil   1822
United Provinces of
Central America   1823
Bolivia   1825
Uruguay   1828

0   400   800 miles
0   400 800 kilometers

Among the defenders at the Alamo in 1836 were American frontier fighters Jim Bowie and Davy Crockett. Shortly after the fall of the Alamo, Texans and American volunteers defeated the Mexican army at San Jacinto, the battle in which Santa Anna was captured.

Texan general Sam Houston and his army of Texan and American volunteers surprised Santa Anna's forces at the San Jacinto River. Within 18 minutes, the battle was over. Although wounded, Houston led the charge for victory. Since Houston's men had destroyed an escape bridge, Santa Anna and his troops fled through a swamp. The Mexican general was captured, and taken to Houston. Houston sent Santa Anna to Washington, D.C., to negotiate with President Andrew Jackson. Santa Anna soon returned to Mexico. Under what condition was he released?

In the 1830's Mexico suspected that the United States wanted to acquire Texas. The Mexican government passed a law forbidding Americans to settle in Texas. The law also provided for Mexico's military occupation of Texas. Opposed to this action, Texas rebelled against Mexico in 1835. Santa Anna led his troops against the rebels. In San Antonio, he laid siege to a mission called the Alamo, where a small number of Texans refused to surrender. When the mission fell, he killed the defenders, an act that fired the anger of other Texans.

Meanwhile, Texas had declared its independence from Mexico. A few weeks later Texan troops under General Sam Houston defeated the Mexican army and captured Santa Anna. In return for his freedom, Santa Anna signed a treaty recognizing the independence of Texas.

Mexican War   Texas remained independent until 1845, when the United States Congress approved its annexation and made it into a state. Disputes over the Mexico-Texas border and Mexican resentment of United States settlers in California soon led Mexico into a war with the United States. Santa Anna was again defeated, and Mexico City was captured. In February 1848, a peace treaty was signed between the two warring countries. Mexico received $15 million but lost vast territories in the north.

The humiliating defeat forced Santa Anna out of office. But after several years of trouble and chaos, conservatives took over the government and invited Santa Anna to head it. Needing money for his lavish expenses, Santa Anna sold a strip of land to the United States for $10 million in 1853. Known as the Gadsden Purchase, the deal brought under American control about 50,000 square miles (130,000 square kilometers) of land in what is now southern Arizona.

Reform and Civil War   In 1855, reform-minded liberals ousted Santa Anna and took over the government. Benito Pablo Juárez, a Mexican-Indian, became president. The liberals had three goals. First, they wanted civilian rather than military control of government. Second, they wanted to limit the power of the Church. Third, they wanted to break up the great estates of the creoles and return the land to the Indians.

Outraged conservatives revolted and took Mexico City. However, the liberal government was able to escape and establish headquarters in Veracruz. In the civil war that followed, the liberals won and returned to power. Juárez was again elected president in 1861.

Foreign Invasion   When Juárez returned in 1861, Mexico was nearly bankrupt. One of the steps Juárez took was to stop making payments on foreign debts. Britain, France, and Spain

Hoping to increase farm production, Díaz ordered a land reform in which the land was divided among rich landowners. One result was that many Mexicans left farm areas to go to cities in order to find jobs. Overcrowding in the cities brought unrest.

responded by landing troops in Veracruz. However, the British and the Spanish withdrew when they realized that Napoleon III wanted to conquer Mexico.

The French emperor sent reinforcements along with a European prince, Maximilian of Austria, to be crowned as emperor of Mexico. The coronation took place in 1864. In 1867, Napoleon III decided that conquering Mexico was too diffcult and expensive. He withdrew his troops and Maximilian was left to defend himself. He was soon captured by Juárez's troops and executed. Juárez returned to power and remained president until his death in 1872.

Porfirio Díaz   The next caudillo was Porfirio Díaz, a mestizo who became the president of Mexico in 1877. His administration was one of the longest in Mexican history. It lasted until 1911. Early in his career, Díaz favored the liberals. However, once in office, he became concerned with maintaining law and order. To achieve this goal, he relied on his army and on strict measures that stifled individual freedoms.

Díaz encouraged foreign investors to bring their capital to Mexico. He offered many benefits and privileges to entice them. In this respect, he was typical of caudillos in the 1900's. They sought the support of business interests—especially foreign business—as well as the support of the military. The foreign companies that took advantage of this atmosphere made good profits and enjoyed stable political conditions. Unfortunately for the Mexican people, most of the profit was spent outside the country. Wealthy Mexicans also enjoyed the fruits of stability, which made them richer. However, the conditions of the Indians and mestizos grew worse.

Mexican Revolution   A revolt led by the Indians and mestizos broke out against Díaz in 1910. For several years civil war raged in Mexico. Finally, in 1917, a new constitution was written. Under the constitution, large estates were divided and sold to peasants. Workers won the right to form unions, strike, and engage in **collective bargaining,** or negotiations between employers and employees about wages and working conditions. A basic education was required for all children aged 6 to 15.

In the late 1920's, the revolutionaries organized into a political party known as the PRI, or Partido Revolucionario Institucional. Mexico's government has since remained stable under the 1917 constitution and the dominance of one political party.

This cartoon from the 1890's shows Díaz bestowing upon himself the additional powers usually granted to a cabinet of advisers. Behind Díaz are objects that symbolize the caudillo's attitude toward more representative government. Free suffrage is depicted as a skull, whereas, the sovereignty of the states appears as chains. Freedom of expression is represented by a padlock. Public expenditures is seen as a sharp fork. The pope's miter [pointed hat] suggests the Church's acceptance of Díaz's government in exchange for more freedom. What policies of Díaz led to his downfall?

Britain was one of the first countries to recognize Argentine independence. It was with British assistance that the cattle industry was introduced and railroads were built to carry beef from the central plains to the coastal markets.

Argentine gauchos originally came from Peru to settle the fertile area along the Andes Mountains. Their livelihood depended upon raising cattle on the pampas, or plains. The gauchos were a rugged, self-sufficient people, who fiercely resented the Spanish authorities in Buenos Aires. The porteños were descendants of European traders, soldiers, and government officials who had come to live in southeastern South America. How did gauchos and porteños differ in the type of government they wanted in Argentina?

Argentina

In Argentina, as in Mexico, independence was followed by the rule of caudillos. During most of the 1800's, sharp political conflict divided the two leading social groups in the country. One group was the **gauchos,** or cowboys of mixed Spanish and Indian ancestry, who lived in rural beef-producing provinces. The other was the **porteños,** or the middle and upper classes who lived in Buenos Aires. The gauchos wanted a federal form of government, with most of the power belonging to the provinces. The porteños favored a strong central government administered from Buenos Aires.

Most of the Argentine provinces were ruled by local caudillos who had no desire to be governed by Buenos Aires. In 1829, the supporters of federalism were able to take control of the central government. Their leader, Juan Manuel Rosas, became president.

Rosas   Although called a president and a federalist, Rosas ruled as a caudillo, with much of the government's power concentrated in his own hands. He censored newspapers, closed schools, and ruthlessly crushed rebellions. In 1852, a combined force of Argentines, Brazilians, and Uruguayans attacked Buenos Aires and overthrew Rosas.[4]

---

[4]Brazil and Argentina fought over the land on the eastern bank of the La Plata River, which is today Uruguay. In 1828 they signed a treaty that made Uruguay an independent buffer state.

Constitutional Government   Justo Urquiza, a provincial governor, became the new leader of Argentina. He called for a meeting of delegates to write a constitution for the country. But the porteños would not accept Urquiza's rule. All the provinces except Buenos Aires sent delegates to the constitutional assembly.

The new constitution, proclaimed in 1853, established a confederation. Soon after, war broke out between Urquiza's forces and the army of Buenos Aires, led by General Bartolomé Mitre. After several rounds of fighting, Urquiza was defeated. However, the two sides compromised their differences. Buenos Aires entered the confederation in 1861.

Mitre was elected president in 1862 and the name of the country was officially changed from the United Provinces of La Plata to Argentina. Gradually the provincial gauchos were subdued and the government became more centralized, with its headquarters in Buenos Aires.

In the late 1800's, Argentina had several outstanding presidents who helped their country develop modern institutions. The first of these presidents was Domingo Faustino Sarmiento, who was elected in 1868. Sarmiento was an educator and a writer who had traveled in Europe and the United States. He had been imprisoned for criticizing previous governments. Sarmiento's presidency introduced many agricultural, educational, and political reforms. Economic growth was stimulated by the building

Slavery was abolished in Brazil in 1888.

of railroads and the immigration of many Europeans, mainly Spaniards and Italians.

Another outstanding president was Roque Sáenz Peña, who was elected in 1910. In 1912, he put through a law that made voting free, secret, and compulsory for all men over 18. Government reform and economic growth continued until 1930, when army officers seized control of the government.

Brazil

The experience of Brazil was different from that of other Latin American countries. There had been no violent revolution and therefore there were no military leaders to become caudillos. The Brazilians also had experienced administrators to help them through the change from a colony to an independent nation. However, they suffered from some of the same political conflicts as other Latin American countries.

When Pedro I became emperor of independent Brazil, he faced opposition from those who wanted a republican government and also from those who wanted a weak central government and more power for the provinces. Pedro defeated his opposition. In 1824, he proclaimed a constitution that gave Brazil a strong central government, with power mostly in the emperor's hands. Soon, however, he began to drift toward absolutism, acting more and more like a dictator and ignoring his own constitution. Discontent began to grow.

Pedro II   By 1831, Pedro I had become so unpopular that he was forced to abdicate in favor of his five-year-old son, Pedro II. A series of competent regents took over the country and supervised the training of young Pedro. Able tutors made sure that he received an excellent education. In the meantime, public opinion in the country was sharply divided. Some people supported a strong, conservative monarchy. Some wanted a republic, and others favored a limited monarchy. Regional conflicts and division over issues threatened the unity of the country. Finally, in 1841, Pedro II was crowned emperor.

Pedro II was determined to improve the lives of the Brazilians. He ruled with a strong hand,

but he allowed the Brazilian congress to meet regularly and to make decisions. Individual freedoms were more respected in Brazil during his reign than in any other place in South America.

The long reign of Pedro II, which lasted until 1889, was a period of growth and prosperity for Brazil. Within a few years of his coronation, Pedro II was able to establish a strong central government and to end unrest in the provinces. His policies encouraged economic development in agriculture, industry, and trade. Coffee became a major export and eventually replaced sugar as the leading crop. The discovery of new uses for rubber and new ways to process it gave the Brazilian economy a great boost. The construction of railroads, factories, ports, and roads proceeded at a high pace. This development created new demands for labor, which was supplied by European immigrants, particularly from Italy and Germany.

End of Slavery   The question of slavery divided public opinion in Brazil as it did in other countries. Pedro II favored the abolition of slavery and so did a large segment of the population. But plantation owners depended on slaves for farming their land. They opposed any move for emancipation. A compromise was struck in 1871 with the Law of Free Birth. It stated that children born to slaves would be freed at the age of 21.

The abolitionists, or those who favored an end to slavery, were led by a very capable politician, Joaquim Nabuco. He and his followers pressed the governments of the provinces to abolish slavery. Some of these governments responded favorably. Finally, while Pedro II was on a visit to Europe, the Brazilian congress pased a bill of abolition. Pedro II's daughter Isabel, who was ruling in his name, quickly and gladly signed the bill into law.

Shortly after Pedro II's return from Europe, an unlikely combination of plantation owners who were unhappy with emancipation, liberals who wanted a republic, and army officers who wanted to play a role in politics overthrew the emperor and sent him into exile. The loss of Pedro II left a serious vacuum in Brazilian public

Some teachers might wish to discuss how territorial growth in the U.S. caused problems for Indians.

life. The country was declared a republic, but a series of army officers took over the government, ruling as dictators. Brazil's history as a republic was marked by many internal conflicts and revolutions.

1. Identify: Antonio Lopez de Santa Anna, Alamo, Gadsden Purchase, Benito Pablo Juárez, Maximilian, Porfirio Díaz, PRI, Juan Manuel Rosas, Domingo Faustino Sarmiento, Pedro II, Joaquim Nabuco.
2. Why did Mexico go to war with the United States?
3. Why did the people of Buenos Aires resist constitutional government in Argentina?
4. What steps were taken to end slavery in Brazil?

3 The United States and Latin America

While the Latin American countries were struggling to win their independence and build strong nations, the United States was growing in size, wealth, and power. During the 1800's it became a dominant force in the Western Hemisphere. Latin Americans referred to the United States as the "colossus of the North" and began to regard their northern neighbor with a mixture of envy and resentment.

Rise of the United States

The territorial growth of the United States was phenomenal. In 1803, Napoleon sold the Louisiana Territory to the United States for $15 million, which he needed to finance his European wars. Thus, in one stroke, the size of the United States was doubled.

Other new territories were acquired by annexation (Texas, Hawaii), by treaty (Florida, Oregon Territory), by purchase (Gadsden Purchase, Alaska), and by victory in war (California and the Southwest). By the end of the century, the nation had reached its present-day boundaries. The United States also saw rapid growth in its population, due to a high birthrate and immigration from Europe, Asia, and Africa.

At the same time, the American economy was expanding rapidly. The Industrial Revolution, which began in England, spread quickly to the United States. However, it affected the regions of the country in different ways. Industrialization took place chiefly in the North, where immigrants supplied a large unskilled labor force. The agricultural South became the chief producer of raw cotton for British textile mills.

The differences in their economies led the two regions, North and South, to take widely different positions on various issues. The most divisive issue was slave labor, upon which the South depended. The South wanted to expand slavery into the territories gained during the Mexican War. The North wanted these new areas to remain free.

In 1860, Abraham Lincoln was elected president. The South feared that he would try to do away with slavery. Eventually, 11 Southern states **seceded,** or withdrew, from the Union. The North insisted that the South did not have the right to secede and that the Union must be saved at all costs. By 1861, the North and the South were fighting the Civil War. The North won the Civil War in 1865. The Northern victory preserved the Union, and slavery was banned throughout the United States.

After the Civil War, industrialization continued with new vigor. Railroads were soon to provide every region of the country with access to the markets of the others. By the end of the 1800's, the United States was on its way to becoming the industrial leader of the world. As such, it became more involved with the economies of other countries and began to take a more active role in international affairs, especially in Latin America.

Monroe Doctrine

Even before the independence of all the Latin American countries was well established, Spain had sought the support of other European powers in reconquering its former colonies. Both the United States and Britain opposed Spain's plan. The United States did not want a strong European power so close to its borders. Britain had developed good trade relations with the South Americans and did not feel that its commercial interests would be served by the return of Spanish control to the colonies.

Review the means by which each state became part of the United States.

The map below is the subject of the "Using Maps" section of the Chapter 22 Review.

TERRITORIAL EXPANSION OF THE UNITED STATES

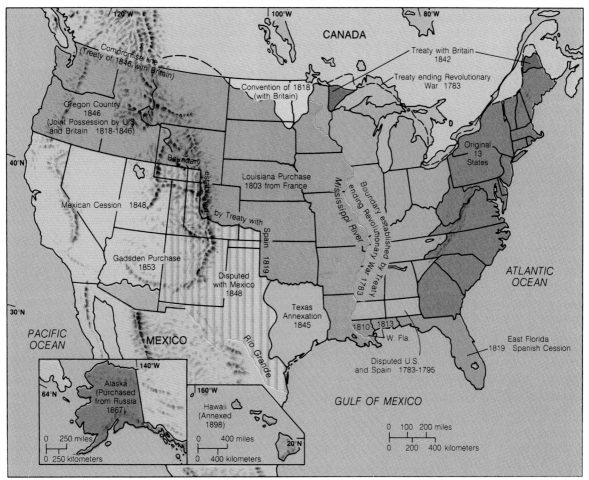

Britain suggested to the United States that a joint warning be issued to various European powers. However, President James Monroe and Secretary of State John Adams decided to act alone. In 1823, Monroe warned the European powers not to interfere in the countries of the Western Hemisphere:

> *The American continents . . . are henceforth not to be considered as subject for future colonization by any European powers . . . we should consider any attempt on their part to extend their system to any portion of this hemisphere as dangerous to our peace and safety.*

This statement came to be known as the Monroe Doctrine. At that time it was not clear what the United States would do if European powers tried to conquer any part of Latin America. However, the support of the British navy ensured that the infant states of Latin America would remain free to determine their own destinies.

Growing Involvement

As the United States grew in strength and stature after the Civil War, it began to make its power felt in Latin America. In 1889, the first Pan-American Conference met to discuss matters of general concern to American countries. It was presided over by James Blaine, the American secretary of state.

"Remember the Maine" became the American battle cry in the Spanish-American War.

Point out that proposals for a canal across Nicaragua were also considered. They were rejected in part because of the numerous volcanoes in that area of Central America.

Six years later, when Britain was in conflict with Venezuela over the boundaries of British Guiana, the United States urged that the dispute be submitted to **arbitration,** or settlement by a third party that is agreeable to both sides. Appealing to the Monroe Doctrine, the United States Department of State issued a strong warning to Britain to pressure it into accepting arbitration. Aware of the power of the United States and involved with other problems, Britain agreed to a peaceful settlement.

Spanish-American War

Soon after the Guiana border dispute was settled, the United States turned its attention toward Cuba. In 1895, the island was still a colony of Spain. Cuban patriots demanding independence launched a struggle that attracted much sympathy in the United States.

Press stories about cruelty and killings in Cuba, often exaggerated, were widely read. American businesses were concerned about the safety of their investments on the island. After the battleship U.S.S. *Maine* was mysteriously blown up in the harbor of Havana, war broke out between Spain and the United States.

The Spanish-American war lasted for three months and ended with a victory and new territories for the United States in the Pacific and the Caribbean. Puerto Rico and the Philippine Islands became American territories. Cuba was recognized as independent but came under the protection of the United States.

Panama Canal

Victory in the Spanish-American War made the United States a world power. It became important for the United States to be able to move its fleet quickly between the Pacific and Atlantic Oceans. What was needed was a canal across the Isthmus of Panama, which connected Central America and South America.

At the time, Panama was part of Colombia. In 1903, Colombia refused to lease the land that the United States required for digging the canal. Soon afterward, a rebellion occurred in Panama. With help from the United States Marines, the rebels declared Panama's independence from Colombia.

After quickly recognizing the new nation, the United States signed a lease with the Panamanian government. This action angered many Colombians. Nevertheless, the digging began in 1904. Work was hampered by a high death rate due to yellow fever and malaria. But this problem was solved by a sanitation program to control

French engineer Ferdinand de Lesseps was the first to tackle the Panama Canal project. In 1881 his crew began excavations. In many areas, the canal was literally cut through mountains. Unfortunately, de Lesseps' efforts were not enough. Diseases, landslides, and floods caused his company's failure in 1889, after a staggering 78 million cubic yards (59.3 million cubic meters) of material had been excavated. The American company that took over in 1904 also had a problem with diseases. How were yellow fever and malaria controlled?

The Hay-Bunau-Varilla Treaty gave the United States the right to build the Panama Canal, a lease on land along the canal, and sole control of the canal area "forever." Note recent changes.

AMERICAN INVOLVEMENT IN THE CARIBBEAN 1895-1918

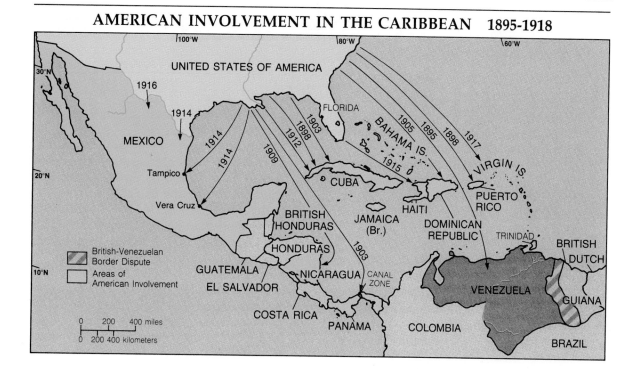

disease-carrying mosquitoes. The canal, which took seven years to build, was considered a great engineering feat.

Roosevelt Corollary

Possession of the Panama Canal gave the United States even more of a stake in Latin America. Thus, the United States continued to exert its power in the region throughout the early 1900's. In 1904, the Monroe Doctrine was extended by President Theodore Roosevelt. Some Latin American countries had been unable to pay back foreign loans, and European powers threatened to collect their debts by force. Roosevelt announced that the United States would act as a police power to force Latin American countries to honor their debts. Thus, the United States would not only stop European powers from intervention, but would itself actively intervene in Latin America.

The Roosevelt Corollary was first applied in 1905. At that time the United States took charge of the customs service of the Dominican Republic, receiving duties and distributing them to that country's creditors. Beginning in 1916, United States Marines occupied the Dominican Republic for eight years to keep order. Likewise, the Marines occupied Haiti and Nicaragua for long periods. In Nicaragua, the American-trained National Guard, headed by General Anastasio Somoza, took over the government, and Somoza ruled as a dictator.

The United States hoped that its Marines would provide stability and prepare the way for democracy. However, most Latin Americans interpreted American actions as moves to turn their countries into "colonies" of the United States and to protect foreign businesses that were using their resources. The Roosevelt Corollary produced much resentment in Latin America toward the United States.

1. Identify: Monroe Doctrine, James Blaine, *Maine*, Roosevelt Corollary, Anastasio Somoza.
2. What factors contributed to the United States Civil War?
3. Why did the United States and Great Britain oppose Spain's plan to reconquer its colonies?
4. How did the United States acquire land for the Panama Canal?

CHAPTER 22 REVIEW

Summary

1. Enlightenment ideals influenced Latin Americans, especially after the success of the American and French revolutions.
2. Haiti became the first independent nation in Latin America, winning its freedom from France in 1804.
3. After a period of social and political unrest, Mexico became an independent republic in the 1820's.
4. Simón Bolívar led successful revolts in northern South America and set up the Republic of Gran Colombia (later Colombia, Venezuela, Ecuador, and Panama).
5. José de San Martín and an army of patriots liberated a large area of Peru. Joined by Bernardo O'Higgins, San Martín's forces also freed Chile from Spanish rule.
6. In 1825 Brazil separated from Portugal and established its own independent monarchy. In spite of a period of stable government under Pedro II, Brazil in 1889 chose to become a republic.
7. The newly independent Latin American countries lacked experience in self-government. As a result, most were ruled by caudillos during the late 1800's.
8. In the early 1800's, the territory of the United States more than doubled in size. Following the Civil War, the United States began to develop into a strong industrial nation.
9. Upon issuing the Monroe Doctrine in 1823, the United States acted to keep European nations from expanding their control in Latin America.
10. Beginning in the 1890's, the United States increased its influence in Latin America. It won territory from Spain in 1898 and leased land from Panama to build the Panama Canal in 1903. The Roosevelt Corollary was used to justify American involvement.

Building Vocabulary

viceroyalties
social revolution
junta

caudillos
collective bargaining
gauchos

porteños
seceded
arbitration

Reviewing the Main Ideas

1. How did the ideas of the American Revolution and the French Revolution affect the people of Latin America?
2. Why was the Battle of Boyacá important in the Latin American struggle for independence from Spain?
3. Who were the liberators of Spanish America? What was the final event that resulted in each liberation?
4. What difficulties prevented Latin Americans from developing stable governments?
5. Why did the people of Texas quarrel with the Mexican government? What role did the United States play in this dispute?
6. What happened to Mexico's territory during the rule of Antonio Lopez de Santa Anna?
7. What were the goals of Benito Juárez and his liberal supporters in Mexico?

8. What political conflict divided Argentina during most of the late 1800's?
9. How did Brazil's political experience differ from that of other Latin American nations?

10. How did the United States make its power felt in Latin America during the late 1800's?
11. What were the results of the Spanish-American War?

Discussing Important Ideas

1. How does conflict among social classes affect political stability? Give examples from nineteenth-century Latin American history.
2. Did caudillos help or hinder the development of Latin America? Explain.
3. Do you think a nation can develop without a democratic government? Why or why not?
4. If you had lived in Brazil in 1889, would you have supported a monarchy or a republic? Explain.
5. Compare and contrast the political careers of Santa Anna, Benito Juárez, and Porfirio

Díaz. Which leader do you think had the greatest impact on Mexico? Explain.
6. How did immigration affect the economic development of both the United States and Latin America?
7. Compare and contrast the United States and Brazil regarding the steps taken to end slavery in each country.
8. Did United States ownership of territories following the Spanish-American War conflict with its political ideals? Support your answer.

Using Maps

Refer to the map on page 519 to answer the following questions:
1. By what year was the eastern seaboard of the United States completely acquired? the western seaboard below Canada?
2. Which countries in 1785 claimed lands in the present-day United States? in 1898?

3. In what two years did the United States gain the most territory west of the Mississippi River? from which countries?
4. When did the United States acquire the region around the Great Lakes?
5. What present-day states form the border with Mexico?

CHAPTER 23

Japanese Rural Scene

❝ Today the alien barbarians of the West . . . are dashing about across the sea, trampling other countries underfoot, and daring . . . to override the noble nations. ❞

Aizawa Seishisai, Japanese nationalist (1782-1863)

East Asia

In the 1600's and 1700's, imperial China and Japan largely concentrated on domestic affairs. In China, the Ming dynasty was overthrown by invaders from the north, and a new dynasty was established. In Japan, the feudal domains were united under a strong central government.

Both countries deliberately isolated themselves from the world as much as possible, trying to protect their civilizations from foreign influences. In the 1800's, however, both were forced to bow to pressures from western powers to increase their foreign contacts. China was weakened by these contacts, but Japan used them to strengthen itself until it was able to meet the western powers on equal terms.

1 Imperial China

By the early 1600's, the Ming dynasty in China was in serious decline. Corruption and incompetence had sapped the strength of the government. The last Ming emperor, Ch'ung-chen, tried to reverse the decline, but it was too late. Soon after he came to the throne in 1628, a terrible famine struck in Shangxi province. Starved peasants ravaged the countryside. At the same time, soldiers mutinied because they had not been paid for a long time. The rebellion grew. Meanwhile, the Manchus, invaders from Manchuria, moved southward to attack Beijing. They stopped only when they reached the Great Wall.

In 1644 Chinese rebels entered Beijing. The desperate Ming commander asked the Manchus for help and opened the narrow pass that controlled access from Manchuria. The Manchus swept in and defeated the rebels. Once in Beijing, however, the Manchus refused to leave.

Qing Dynasty

After several years of struggle, the Manchus defeated the Ming and set up a new dynasty, known as the Qing (Ch'ing) dynasty. They successfully maintained control for almost 300 years, during which time they extended their empire to the north and west, to include Manchuria, Mongolia, Sinkiang, and Tibet. They also conquered neighboring countries, such as Korea, Burma, and Vietnam. The island of Taiwan was added to the empire in 1683.

Qing Emperors   The Qing were fortunate in having a series of able emperors in its first two centuries of rule. The period of their reign brought prosperity to China. Qing emperors tried to improve the lives of the Chinese. They worked to lighten taxes and undertook public works projects, such as flood control on the Huang He River. They also supported the arts. Some of the emperors were scholars, poets, and painters.

Qing rulers imposed new regulations on the Chinese. A Chinese man was required to wear Manchu clothing and shave his head, leaving a pigtail. A Chinese woman was not allowed to follow the traditional practice of binding her feet. However, this rule could not be enforced.

Otherwise, Qing rulers did not try to alter the basic elements of Chinese culture. They used Chinese institutions and traditions to govern the country. They also took steps to win Chinese support, such as lowering taxes. These policies worked well, and most Chinese came to accept Qing rule. Eventually Chinese culture was adopted by the Manchus, who came to think of themselves as Chinese.

Economic Life   The Manchus made few basic changes in China's economy. The Qing policy of internal peace and government-spon-

Porcelain from southeast China became very popular in Europe during the 1700's.

sored work projects contributed to the economic prosperity of China in the 1700's. So too did agricultural improvements. Chinese farmers brought additional land under cultivation. They planted new crops, such as sweet potatoes, corn, and peanuts, that came from the Americas. They also developed faster-growing varieties of rice. These changes contributed to a population explosion. The population of China jumped from about 150 million in 1600 to 350 million in 1800. China became the most populated country in the world. It has remained so through the twentieth century.

This scene of the Qing conquest of China is described in three languages used in China during the 1600's—Manchu, Chinese, and Mongol. What other elements of Chinese culture did the Qing emperors permit?

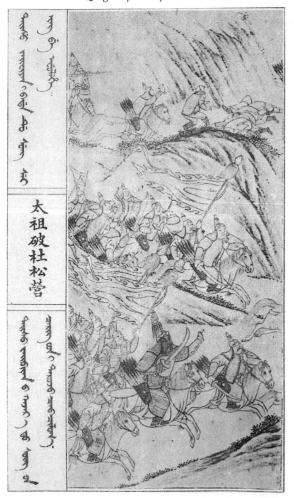

Under the Qing dynasty, three-quarters of the Chinese people lived in rural areas. In the south of China, a few powerful landlords owned most of the land. They increasingly placed heavy demands on their tenant farmers. In the north, landlords had relatively less influence. Landownership was held by many peasant farmers. The peasants divided plots of land among family members. The plots became smaller over successive generations. The average peasant holding was two and one-half acres (one hectare).

Land was carefully tended during the Qing period. Many farm workers, using simple tools, built and maintained terraced fields and irrigation systems. This type of agriculture was known as **labor intensive,** as it relied on labor more than capital. Since capital was scarce and labor plentiful, there was no incentive for developing laborsaving devices.

Internal trade in China flourished during the Qing period. There was a lively exchange of goods within and between regions. Great merchant families arose and made fortunes trading salt, grain, silk, fish, timber, cloth, and luxury goods. Guilds were created to bring merchants together and make interregional trade easier.

Different regions of China specialized in a particular product. The southeastern region was the center of the porcelain and pottery industries. The central coastal area was known for textiles. Other regions produced cotton, silk, and sugar. Economic expansion aided China's population growth.

In China, commercial activity did not lead to an industrial revolution, as it did in England. China had different traditions and values. The merchant class was considered the lowest social group. It was believed that merchants produced nothing of value. Instead of investing in trade and production, wealthy merchant families used their money to gain social status. They educated their sons to become scholars and officials. They purchased aristocratic titles and collected art objects. Thus, although the merchants had a great deal of capital, China did not develop an industrial economy.

Other factors were also involved. Traditions of inheritance and family needs divided or drained

Guangzhou has been the site of foreign trade in China for over 1,000 years. In 1685 the British East India Company set up a hong at Guangzhou, which consisted of business offices and homes for foreign traders. Throughout the 1700's, 13 hongs were located on the waterfront. The ships shown here are from Denmark, Great Britain, the United States, and British-ruled India. What restrictions were placed on foreign trade in China during the eighteenth century?

family fortunes within two or three generations. There was little money available for investment. In addition, Chinese scholars concentrated on literary, artistic, and philosophical pursuits rather than on scientific research.

Foreign Contacts

The Chinese believed that they had the most prosperous and most advanced civilization in the world. Foreigners were considered "barbarians." China's contacts with neighboring countries confirmed this sense of superiority. The Qing were able to establish their **hegemony,** or dominance, over much of Southeast Asia, Tibet, Mongolia, and Korea.

China's relations with its vassal states and foreign lands were carried out through a system of tribute. Under this system, important foreign visitors were required to pay homage to the Chinese emperor. They brought gifts and performed a ritual ceremony known as the **kowtow.** This involved kneeling before the emperor and touching the head to the floor. Performing the kowtow later became a point of conflict in China's dealings with western nations. Westerners resented being treated as inferiors.

Early contacts with Europeans did little to change Chinese attitudes. About 1680, the Qing emperor developed a system to handle trade with the West. The system lasted until the middle of the 1800's. All western trade was funneled through the port of Guangzhou (Canton). Specific Chinese merchants were granted monopolies to deal with western traders. Foreigners were restricted to a small area of Guangzhou and placed under Chinese law.

Westerners repeatedly tried to better their position in China. In 1793 the British sent a mission to Beijing under the leadership of Lord George Macartney. The Chinese emperor accepted British gifts but refused to alter the trade system. His letter to Britain's King George III reflected China's sense of superiority and its security in its own ways.

> Swaying the wide world, I have but one aim in view, namely, to maintain a perfect governance and to fulfill the duties of the state: strange and costly objects do not interest me. If I have commanded that the tribute offerings sent by you, O King, are to be accepted, this was solely in consideration for the spirit which prompted you to dispatch them from afar. Our dynasty's majestic virtue has penetrated unto every country under heaven, and kings of all nations have offered their costly tribute by land and sea. As your Ambassador can see for himself, we possess all things.*

*Emperor Ch'ien Lung as quoted in *Modern Chinese History, Selected Readings,* Harley Farnsworth MacNain, © 1923 by Commercial Press, Ltd., pp. 2-9.

Arabs and Turks first introduced opium to China in the late seventh or early eighth century. The Chinese used it chiefly as medicine to relieve pain.

1. Identify: Ch'ung-chen, Manchus, Qing, Lord George Macartney.
2. What contributions did the Qing dynasty make to China during the first two centuries of its rule?
3. What relationship did the Qing have with neighboring countries?

2 Decline and Humiliation

In the 1800's China began to decline. Its growing population strained the country's resources. Later Qing emperors lacked the wisdom, vigor, and leadership skills of earlier Chinese rulers. During the second half of the 1800's, China received a number of devastating blows. Famine and rebellions weakened China's government. At the same time, the Qing dynasty suffered humiliating losses to the increasingly powerful nations of the West.

The Opium War

Western pressures to break the Chinese trade system at Guangzhou reached a peak in the 1840's. The immediate issue was trade in **opium,** a drug made from poppies.

There were few products that China was interested in buying from the West. The Chinese preferred to receive silver for their tea, silks, and porcelain, which Great Britain was buying in increasing quantities. This drain of silver was unsatisfactory to the British. Then, they found that there was a market in China for opium.

Opium from British-ruled India became commercially profitable and an important source of revenue to British merchants. Because opium smoking is so addictive, it soon became widespread in China. Silver started flowing out of China to pay for the rising imports. "If the opium traffic is not stopped," said a Chinese official, "the country will become poorer and poorer and its people weaker and weaker." But Chinese efforts to halt the opium trade failed. Opium was smuggled into the country, and government officials were bribed to ignore the illegal trade.

In 1839 the Qing emperor sent a personal representative to Guangzhou to stop the opium trade. Over 20,000 chests of opium were seized and publicly burned. This action gave the British a cause for war. The British wanted to continue the opium trade and expand their commerce in China. The Chinese sought to end opium imports and to maintain the trade system at Guangzhou. It was a clash between two civilizations that held fundamentally different views of social order and international relations.

The so-called Opium War involved only a few one-sided encounters along the coast of China. Chinese defenses, some of which dated back to the early Ming period, were no match for British gunboats.

In 1840 Great Britain sent 16 warships to the mouth of the Guangzhou River. It demanded that China resume the opium trade and lift trade restrictions. In the following year, when the Qing emperor balked, the British attacked Guangzhou and the surrounding area. The Chinese had no effective defense against British naval strength. They recruited local militia to join the imperial troops, but both forces were powerless against the British. What action prompted the Opium War?

A precedent for British extraterritoriality was set by
medieval Arab traders at Guangzhou. They were
governed by their chieftains and were not subject to
Chinese laws.

Imperialism and Modernization · **529**

Unequal Treaties

The Treaty of Nanjing (Nanking), signed in
1842, ended the Opium War. It abolished the
Chinese monopolies of foreign trade at Guangzhou. The island of Hong Kong was ceded to the
British and five additional ports were opened to
British trade. The Chinese government was
forced to grant **extraterritoriality** to British
merchants in China. This removed them from
the jurisdiction of Chinese law. A British citizen
who murdered a Chinese would be tried and
punished in British courts rather than in Chinese
ones. China also had to give Britain **most-favored-nation status.** This meant that any additional privileges given to any other power would
automatically be given to the British.

The Treaty of Nanjing was the first in a series
of treaties known as the "unequal treaties."
Other powers, threatening the use of force, soon
demanded the same or even better trade
conditions. All of the treaties included most-favored-nation clauses, so that new privileges
were extended to all. China was unable to defend
itself against these demands.

Internal Rebellions

As the nineteenth century advanced, conditions worsened in China. Droughts, floods, and
famine added further blows to the already
strained Chinese economy. Many peasants
became homeless refugees and faced starvation.
Banditry, uprisings, and rebellions became
widespread. The Qing dynasty was unable to
halt the disturbances.

An uprising known as the Taiping Rebellion
climaxed these internal disorders. It threatened
to topple the Qing dynasty and to sweep aside
traditional Chinese ways. The rebellion began in
1850 in the south, where Qing control had
always been weak. Its leader was Hung Hsiu-
ch'uan, a scholar who had failed to pass the civil
service exams. He came in contact with Christian
missionaries and developed his own version of
Christianity. Hung believed that he was a
younger brother of Jesus Christ.

Under Hung's leadership, the Taiping rebels
developed a set of beliefs and an organization.
Their program combined Christianity and tradi-

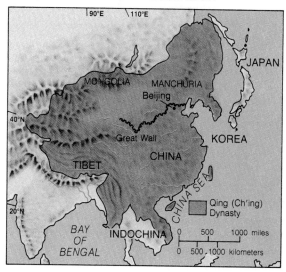

CHINA 1644-1911

tional Chinese values. They sought to end the
Qing dynasty, replacing it with a "Heavenly
Kingdom of Great Peace."[1] They planned to
upset the existing social order in China and to
create a new society based on equality and
shared property.

The Taiping Rebellion lasted until 1864. Its
eventual defeat was due to a number of factors.
First, the rebels had lost much of their revolutionary drive by the late 1850's. Many Taiping
leaders were killed in a coup d'etat, and weaker
leaders took their place. Second, the opposition
became stronger. The scholar-gentry class remained loyal to the Qing dynasty and organized
effective armies against the Taiping rebels.
Third, the foreign powers, who had earlier
remained neutral in the rebellion, decided to aid
the Qing. They feared that the rebellion would
threaten the trade advantages won in the
"unequal treaties."

Despite the defeat of the rebels, the decline of
the Qing was clear to Chinese and foreigners
alike. Although dissatisfied with the dynasty,
many Chinese rallied to its defense. They
believed that the greater danger to China came
from its contact with foreigners.

---

[1]From the first word of this phrase in Chinese, the rebels
received their name: Taiping.

The Chinese stressed classic traditions. New ideas were viewed as a threat to their whole structure.

1. Identify: Opium War, Treaty of Nanjing, Taiping Rebellion, Hung Hsiu-ch'uan, "Heavenly Kingdom of Great Peace."
2. Why was opium economically important to the British?
3. Why was the Taiping Rebellion a threat to the Qing dynasty and to Chinese tradition?
4. Why did the Taiping Rebellion fail?

3 China's Struggle to Survive

By the 1860's many Chinese came to believe that China had to acquire the advanced technology of the West, if it was to meet the "foreign threat." For the first time, the Chinese were beginning to think that they might have something to learn from the "barbarians." However, they still believed in the superiority of China's political and social structures.

Self-Strengthening

After the Taiping Rebellion, the Chinese government started a program of reform known as "self-strengthening." This reform had two aims. The first was a revival of the Confucian values of hierarchy, social order, and harmony. The government gained renewed respect as it enforced traditional discipline, increased tax revenues, and cut spending. The second area of reform involved borrowing ideas and practices from the West. This was a more controversial matter that threatened to divide Chinese society.

Reformers believed that western technology could be grafted onto the Confucian system. To move in this direction, a school was established to train Chinese students in western languages and sciences. A heated dispute over this school showed the depth of Chinese resistance to change. Conservatives argued that engineering, mathematics, and other technical subjects were not as important as the classics and that they should not be made part of the civil service examination system. Many people feared that western subjects would corrupt traditional Chinese culture.

Nevertheless, the emperor supported the reform effort and increased its pace. A foreign office was formed to handle relations with foreign nations. Chinese officials began to read the western press to learn about the West and its intentions in China. Shipyards and arsenals were built to make western steamships and weapons. Western scientific texts were translated into Chinese.

However, these efforts had little success because of the strong opposition to western ways. In 1874, for example, a railroad was built by the British between Shanghai and Sungkiang. The Chinese objected to the railroad because it destroyed the natural harmony of the landscape. Public protest was so strong that the government bought the railroad and wrecked it.

Sino-Japanese War

China's failure to modernize was costly. For hundreds of years, China and Japan had been rivals for ownership of Korea. The Qing dynasty had claimed suzerainty, or political control, over Korea since the 1600's. But in 1876, Japan occupied some Korean islands and forced Korea to open two ports to Japanese trade. At that time, China was too weak to do anything except persuade Korea to open its ports to western countries as well. In this way, the Chinese hoped to check Japanese influence in the country.

Japan was determined to detach Korea from China. China was just as determined not to let Japan gain a foothold on the Asian mainland. In 1894, the two rivals went to war. In this conflict, known as the Sino-Japanese War, China's navy was easily beaten by the smaller, but better-equipped Japanese fleet. China was forced to recognize Korea's independence. It also lost some of its territory—the island of Taiwan and the Liaotung Peninsula—to Japan. Japan gained all of the trade concessions in China won by the western nations plus additional ones.

The Sino-Japanese War was a turning point for the Chinese. Many reformers began to seek the reasons for China's weakness. They called for a reform that would go beyond the principles of the "self-strengthening" program.

Hundred Days Reform

In 1898, during a period known as the Hundred Days Reform, Emperor Kuang-hsu

Boxers were particularly hostile to missionaries because the Boxers resented the invasion of Christianity under the protection of gunboats.

In the final battle of the Sino-Japanese War, Japan's modern navy torpedoed China's two principal ships. Japan's swift victory amazed the rest of the world. Japan was subsequently seen as the emerging power in the East. What territory did China lose to Japan?

issued a series of decrees calling for drastic changes in Chinese life. They included modernizing the schools and the examination system; improving agriculture, mining, and medicine; and strengthening the military forces. The decrees also wanted steps taken to put an end to extraterritoriality.

Conservatives opposed these reform measures. They supported the emperor's aunt Tz'u-hsi, who became known as the Dowager Empress. Tz'u-hsi seized power from the emperor in a coup d'etat. Thus, the possibility of peaceful change with the support of the dynasty ended. The empress's court became increasingly corrupt and backward-looking.

Boxer Rebellion

In 1899 another major rebellion broke out. It was led by a secret organization called the Society of Righteous and Harmonious Fists. Known in English as the Boxers, the members of the society believed that the ancient Chinese arts of self-defense would give them supernatural protection against western guns. The Boxers had

been gaining strength for two years, as China endured another period of drought, flood, and famine.

The Boxers believed that China's problems could be solved if foreigners and their "evil influences" could be expelled. They became violently anti-Christian, killing missionaries and thousands of Chinese converts throughout the country.

The Qing leaders had mixed feelings about the Boxers. Secretly, they hoped the Boxers would be successful. Empress Tz'u-hsi resisted western demands to take firm measures against them. She said, "China is weak; the only thing we can depend upon is the hearts of the people. If we lose them how can we maintain the country?"

Late in 1899, the Boxer Rebellion became a war against all foreigners in China. Boxers besieged the foreign **legations,** or diplomatic residences, in Beijing for nearly two months. Finally, in August 1900, the arrival of foreign troops broke the siege and defeated the Boxers.

An agreement known as the Boxer Protocol ended the Boxer Rebellion. It provided for the

HISTORY AND PEOPLE

Tz'u-hsi

Tz'u-hsi, who lived from 1835 to 1908, was the most powerful woman in the history of China. She ruled China for nearly half a century. Westerners called her the Old Buddha and the Dowager Empress.*

In 1851, at the age of 16, Tz'u-hsi became a wife of Emperor Hsien-feng. Five years later, she gave birth to the emperor's only son and heir. When Hsien-feng died in 1861, the boy became emperor. Tz'u-hsi became a regent and ruled China with the assistance of powerful friends at court.

The Taiping Rebellion and foreign intervention made Tz'u-hsi opposed to reform and suspicious of foreigners. She rejected the advice of Prince Kung, her brother-in-law, for reforms to end government corruption and to modernize the country.

In 1873 Tz'u-hsi's grandson became emperor. However, the Dowager Empress remained in control of political affairs. In 1875 the young emperor died. Many people believed that Tz'u-hsi encouraged the emperor to lead a wild life, which caused his health to decline. Ignoring the traditional rule of succession to the throne, Tz'u-hsi adopted a three-year-old nephew, Kuang-hsu, and installed him as emperor. A new regency was established that gave her absolute power over the government. Again, the Dowager Empress blocked reforms. She used a large sum of money, which the government had set aside for the Chinese navy, to build a magnificent summer palace outside Beijing.

The Chinese defeat in the Sino-Japanese War (1894-1895) aroused new demands for modernization. By this time, Kuang-hsu had come of age and began to rule. He began to support the reform movement and issued decrees promoting change. But the alarmed conservatives rallied behind Tz'u-hsi and used the army to block the emperor's measures. They confined Kuang-hsu to his palace and began to reverse the reforms.

One of the conservative groups backing the Dowager Empress was the Boxers. Tz'u-hsi allowed them to carry out violent attacks against westerners, especially Christian missionaries. The Boxers cut telegraph wires, destroyed railroad tracks, and eliminated other signs of western influence. In 1900 the rebellion reached its peak. About 100 foreigners were killed, and foreign embassies in Beijing were surrounded. Foreign troops, however, soon seized the city. Tz'u-hsi was forced to accept humiliating peace terms.

When westerners put down the Boxer Rebellion, Tz'u-hsi had no choice but to accept the long overdue reforms. She stayed in power until her death in 1908. A woman of great charm and intelligence, Tz'u-hsi used her abilities to outmaneuver her political opponents. She succeeded in maintaining power, but her efforts blocked the dynasty's last chance for peaceful change.

---

*A dowager is a widow who assumes her dead husband's title and privileges.

Sun viewed Chinese history as a cycle of division, disorder, unification, and despotism. Each period of disorder was followed by a fierce struggle for the throne during which the country and its people suffered. To break the pattern, it was necessary to replace the monarchy with a republic.

This cartoon drawn during the Qing era shows the hostility China felt toward westerners who increasingly intruded upon Chinese affairs. By 1899 these strong anti-foreign feelings climaxed in the Boxer movement. The Boxers appealed particularly to poverty-stricken peasants and unemployed soldiers and farm workers who saw foreigners as the main source of their troubles. In the cartoon, the Chinese serpent and dragon are defending themselves against many European attackers. How did foreign governments punish China for the Boxer Rebellion?

execution or imprisonment of leading Qing officials who had supported the Boxers. Foreign powers were given the right to station troops at legation sites, and an indemnity of about $333 million was placed on the Chinese government. The Qing dynasty continued to rule, but only with the backing of the foreign powers. China's existence would have ended if the powers had been able to agree on how to divide the country among themselves.

Revolutionary Movements

By 1900 many Chinese were studying abroad. Their despair over China's decline turned into hatred for the Qing dynasty. Revolutionary groups developed, funded by donations from Chinese living overseas. They were also given encouragement by the Japanese. Two rival leaders, Liang Ch'i-ch'ao and Sun Yat-sen, emerged.

Liang Ch'i-ch'ao Liang Ch'i-ch'ao, a member of the scholar-gentry class, was the most influential writer of the period. His training included the Chinese classics and foreign travel. Liang favored gradual reform and the development of popular education, nationalism, and loyalty to the state rather than to an emperor. He argued for a constitutional monarchy rather than a republic.

Sun Yat-sen Born in southeastern China in 1866, Sun Yat-sen was a professional revolutionary from a peasant background. He studied abroad, adopted Christianity, and received a medical degree. His education was in sharp contrast to the traditional scholarly education of those Chinese who wished to become members of their country's civil service.

Upon returning to China, Sun opposed traditional Chinese ways. He turned to revolution and formed a secret society in Guangzhou. Forced to flee China, Sun visited Japan, the United States, and Britain. He organized the overseas Chinese into a movement known as the Alliance for the Chinese Revolution. Sun called for rapid revolution, following the ancient saying, "Make one all-out effort and be forever at ease." His goal was a constitutional republic. Sun's approach won more followers than Liang's.

Fall of the Qing Dynasty Revolutionary groups were successfully suppressed by the Qing until 1911. Then, a small anti-Qing rebellion sparked revolts throughout the country. Provinces in southern, central, and northwestern China declared themselves independent. Qing army officers joined the revolutionaries. In 1911 Sun Yat-sen, who had been in the United States, returned and was elected as the president

The popular novel *Shogun* by James Clavell describes the encounter of an English sea captain and a Japanese shogun whose character was based on the life of Tokugawa Ieyasu.

Sun Yat-sen, shown here with his wife, Soong Ching Ling, had more knowledge of the West than his rival, Liang. To the Chinese people, Sun symbolized modernization. How were his plans for change different from Liang's?

of the new Chinese Republic. The Qing dynasty and the centuries-old Chinese monarchy were officially ended in the following year.

1. Identify: Hundred Days Reform, Tz'u-hsi, Boxers, Boxer Protocol, Liang Ch'i-ch'ao, Sun Yat-sen.
2. What types of reform were involved in the effort of "self-strengthening"? Who opposed them and why?
3. What was the cause of the Sino-Japanese War? What effects did the war have on China?
4. What did the Boxers want to achieve?

4 Tokugawa Japan

During the 1300's and 1400's, Japan had no unified government. The daimyo controlled their own districts and warred against their rivals. Toward the end of the 1500's, three generals reunited the country. They first defeated the weaker daimyo and brought them under their control. Then, they took on the more powerful ones.

One of the generals, Oda Nobunaga, began the process of Japan's reunification. He led his army against the capital city of Kyoto in 1568. After this victory, he moved against Osaka, where he defeated a powerful Buddhist sect after a ten-year siege of its stronghold. Shortly thereafter Nobunaga was murdered. He was quickly replaced by his best general, Toyotomi Hideyoshi, a man of humble origin but great personal ability. By 1590 virtually all of Japan was united under Hideyoshi's rule.

After Hideyoshi's death in 1598, one of his leading vassals, Tokugawa Ieyasu, seized control and completed the work of uniting Japan. At the Battle of Sekigahara in 1600, Ieyasu put down the last major challenge to his rule. He asked the emperor to name him shogun and took measures to ensure that the title and power stayed in the Tokugawa family. Under Tokugawa leadership, Japan had 250 years of peace and stability.

New Order

Ieyasu established the headquarters of his government at the fishing village of Edo.[2] There, he built a vast fortress protected by high walls and moats. Meanwhile, the Japanese emperor continued to live in Kyoto and remained the official political leader of Japan. In fact, the emperor was the head of government in name only. Real power was held by the shogun.

Social Classes Before 1600 there had been some social mobility between classes. Hideyoshi and Ieyasu had both risen to the top from humble backgrounds. To maintain social stability and limit future rivals, they introduced measures that froze the social structure.

Under Tokugawa rule, the Japanese were divided into four classes. At the top were the samurai who held all political power. As a symbol of their authority, the samurai alone were permitted to wear swords. They lived apart

---
[2]Edo later became known as Tokyo.

Just as samurai alone were permitted to wear swords, only nobles in medieval Europe had the right to wear swords.

from the rest of the population. Marriage was forbidden among the samurai and the three lower classes: peasants, artisans, and merchants. Merchants, as elsewhere in Asia, were considered the lowest class because they were believed to be nonproductive.

Class status governed all social relations and could not be changed. Rules barred class members from performing tasks that belonged to another class. For example, farmers and their descendants were limited to farming. They could not become artisans, and artisans could not engage in farming. All class positions were hereditary.

Political System   The Tokugawa political structure was joined to the old feudal system. In theory, the daimyo were allowed to have complete authority within their own lands. In practice, the shogun had absolute control.

To ensure the political and military security of Japan, Ieyasu reassigned daimyo lands. The daimyo were divided into three groups: Tokugawa relatives, long-time supporters of the Tokugawa, and recent allies of the family. Tokugawa relatives and their long-time supporters were given the most productive lands near Edo. The others, many of whom were considered potential enemies, received less desirable lands in the far northern and western areas of Japan.

After his victory in 1600, Ieyasu demanded the absolute loyalty of the daimyo to the Tokugawa shogunate. He required that each daimyo travel to Edo every other year to provide tribute and service to the shogun. This system was known as **sankin-kotai,** or attendance by turn. When the daimyo returned to their country estates, they were required to leave their families in Edo as hostages. Guards on the roads approaching Edo watched for the passage of women and children. They also searched for weapons that could be used in a plot against the shogun.

The daimyo spent large amounts of their income traveling to and from Edo and maintaining several households. The system kept them obedient to the shogun and reduced their ability to mount a rebellion against his government.

In the late 1500's, Hideyoshi built many castles for the daimyo in his attempt to conquer and unify all of Japan. One of the most breathtaking is the "White Heron" castle at Himeji, built in 1577. Its five-story watchtower and high stone walls made it a formidable military fortress. Hideyoshi's castles exemplify the vast power and wealth of sixteenth-century samurai leaders. Hideyoshi was aided in some of his conquests by his vassal Ieyasu. In 1590 Hideyoshi ordered a council of daimyo to enforce a policy of national unification. Ieyasu pursued this goal when he became shogun in 1603. How did Ieyasu strengthen the power of the shogun?

Have students compare the Tokugawa system with that of Louis XIV.

The Tokugawa family and a select group of daimyo controlled the government. Together they made up the Council of Elders, the leading administrative body. Assisting the Council, as the "eyes and ears" of the state, was a group of officials known as the **metsuke.** The metsuke toured the country and reported on possible uprisings or plots against the shogun. A genuine bureaucracy began to develop, working on the principles of joint decision making and promotion based on talent and status.

Ethics   Tokugawa ethics placed loyalty to the shogun above loyalty to the family. Duty and honor became the central values. Individuals had to develop strict inner discipline to live up to the requirements of their assigned place in life. These values gradually spread from the samurai through all social classes in Japan.

Over the course of time, Tokugawa rules for personal conduct evolved into complex rituals and etiquette. Minute details came to have heavy symbolic meaning. They became a way to maintain conformity and control. This was important for a society that had a large population and only a small area of productive land.

Early Western Contacts

In 1543 the Portuguese became the first Europeans to reach Japan. Jesuit missionaries quickly followed. Francis Xavier was the earliest and most famous of the Jesuit missionaries who came to Japan. After Xavier won the support of some local daimyo, Christianity spread more rapidly and widely than it did in China. Because of language and cultural barriers, the Jesuits encouraged the training of Japanese priests and the creation of a native Christian church. By 1614, there were 300,000 Japanese converts.

Tokugawa rulers, fearing that Christianity was a threat to their power, began to persecute Christians. Missionaries were killed or forced to leave Japan. Thousands of Japanese Christians had to renounce their faith or face death. By 1638, Christianity in Japan had been almost completely wiped out.

The Tokugawa also ended Japanese contacts with the European world. The Japanese were not allowed to live abroad. Those who returned from schooling, trading, or exile abroad were usually killed. Construction of ships large enough for long-distance voyages was banned.

All western Europeans except the Dutch were barred from Japan. Unlike the Spanish and Portuguese, the Dutch were only interested in trade, not conquest or conversion. Therefore, the Tokugawa considered them safe. In 1641 the Dutch were confined to a tiny island in the harbor of Nagasaki. There, they and a few Chinese were permitted to carry on tightly regulated trade. Once a year, Dutch merchants were allowed to bring tribute to the shogun. Through them, a small amount of information about the West continued to flow into Japan.

Economic and Social Changes

Despite Japan's isolation and the efforts of the Tokugawa rulers to prevent change, Japan's society and economy continued to develop. During the early Tokugawa period, the Japanese economy was largely based on agriculture. The wealth of the daimyo was measured by the amount of rice their lands produced. The daimyo and samurai were economically and socially better off than any other class.

In the next 200 years, significant changes took place. National unity and peace increased internal trade. Merchants grew wealthy and became the dominant social group. The daimyo and samurai borrowed from the merchants and became a debtor class. With the expansion of commerce, towns grew in size and importance.

The rise of the merchant class and the growth of commercial activity was stimulated by sankin-kotai. Merchants provided the goods and services needed by the daimyo on their journeys to Edo. Roads were built, and post stations often grew into towns.

At the same time, the demands of the shogun for increased taxes led the daimyo to develop better farming methods and increase their yields. As agriculture became more efficient, fewer people were needed for farming. Unemployed farm workers moved to the towns and cities seeking work as artisans. In Japan's urban centers, the rigid social order began to break down and class distinctions blurred.

All roles in kabuki dramas are played by men. There are no women kabuki actors even today. Some of the most famous kabuki actors have been honored in recent years as exceptional performers.

The delicate manner and exquisite dress of the geishas made them models of traditional Japanese femininity. The word geisha means "art person." In what arts were geishas trained?

Beginning in the 1700's, Japanese cities began to dominate the cultural life of the country. Social life in the cities revolved around amusement centers, where there were bathhouses, restaurants, theaters, and other forms of entertainment. Here Japanese merchants and samurai could relax in the company of **geishas**, women who were professional entertainers, trained in the arts of singing, dancing, and conversation. Rigid etiquette prevented Japanese men from bringing their wives to the centers.

Cities became the leading centers of Japanese culture. The arts flourished in an urban setting because townspeople had money to spend on leisure activities. A new form of theater known as **kabuki** developed. Kabuki became popular for its portrayal of historical events and emotion-filled domestic scenes. The amusement centers provided material for playwrights, novelists and poets. Artists loved to paint scenes showing beautiful geishas and scenes of family and city life.

During the 1700's and 1800's, the ban on foreign contacts was gradually relaxed. The Japanese began to read western books and study western ideas. In 1771 two Japanese doctors discovered that the Dutch knowledge of anatomy was more accurate than that of the Chinese. Their translations of a Dutch medical text created a wave of interest in "Dutch learning." Through the Dutch at Nagasaki, other Japanese scholars studied European texts on advanced gunnery, smelting, engineering, shipbuilding, map making, and astronomy.

Reopening of Japan

Some of the Japanese scholars who studied western science wanted the country opened to overseas trade. Many foreign countries, including Russia, Britain, and the United States, sought access to Japan. However, most Japanese did not want foreigners in their country. The Tokugawa rulers continued to oppose a change in policy.

In 1853 the American government decided to force Japan to end its isolation. Commodore Matthew Perry sailed into Edo Bay and demanded that Japan grant trading privileges to the United States. He also wanted refueling stations for American whalers and protection for shipwrecked sailors. Perry threatened war if Japan did not agree.

Within a year, Perry returned for Japan's answer. In an unprecedented move, the shogun had consulted the daimyo and the emperor. Government opinion was divided. Unable to rally the nation behind him, the shogun bowed to the American demands. The Treaty of Kanagawa granted the United States two remote ports for refueling, good treatment for shipwrecked Americans, and permission for a United States **consul,** or diplomatic official, to live in Japan. It also included a most-favored-nation clause.

By 1858, Japan had signed treaties with the United States, the Netherlands, Britain, France, and Russia. These countries were allowed to trade in several Japanese ports, set import and export tariffs, and have the right of extraterritoriality. The door to Japan was now wide open to the rest of the world.

This nineteenth-century Japanese portrait of Commodore Perry shows how foreigners appeared to the Japanese. How was the artist's perception of the American officer influenced by his eastern culture?

Fall of the Tokugawa

The American demand for trade and diplomatic relations threw the shogunate into a turmoil from which it never recovered. Its decision to open Japan to foreigners aroused fierce opposition at home. Many Japanese did not want foreign influences to enter their country.

The leaders of the opposition were young samurai from remote districts in northern and western Japan. They joined a movement "to restore imperial rule and repel the barbarians." In 1867 they succeeded in ending the shogunate and won the support of Emperor Mutsuhito, a boy of fifteen.

1. Identify: Oda Nobunaga, Toyotomi Hideyoshi, Tokugawa Ieyasu, Battle of Sekigahara, Council of Elders, Francis Xavier, Matthew Perry, and Mutsuhito.

2. What means did Ieyasu use to maintain political and social stability in Japan?
3. How was Japan's isolation ended?

5 Meiji Japan

Mutsuhito, who ruled from 1867 to 1912, became known as the Meiji Emperor, meaning "Enlightened Emperor." He moved his capital from Kyoto to Edo and renamed it Tokyo, or "eastern capital."

Although the Meiji Emperor gave his name to this period of Japanese history, he remained the symbolic leader of the Japanese rather than their actual ruler. Real power was held by the samurai who had overthrown the Tokugawa. The new leaders were flexible, tough, and extremely able. With the emperor's support, they made profound changes in Japan.

Meiji Reforms

The Meiji leaders sought to make Japan a great power capable of competing with the West. Adopting the slogan, "Rich country, strong military," they began sweeping reforms to modernize Japan's government and society. To help in their planning, high-ranking Japanese delegations visited western nations, carefully studying their strengths and weaknesses.

Social Change   The Meiji leaders decided to end restrictions based on social class. All people were declared equal. Universal military service was established in 1873. Samurai privileges were abolished, and the samurai were ordered to stop wearing their swords. Some conservative samurai revolted, but they were crushed by the government. Samurai class distinctions faded within several generations. The daimyo were persuaded to turn over their lands to the emperor. Later, the government paid them for their loss. Thus, feudalism came to an end in Japan. However, samurai and daimyo families adapted to change and continued to influence Japanese life.

Education   The Meiji leaders established a system of universal education designed to produce loyal, skilled citizens ready to work for

The Japanese educational system was very successful in meeting goals for literacy. Within 30 years, the literacy rate was over 90 percent.

Japan's modernization. Six years of schooling were required for all Japanese. Education at higher levels, however, was restricted. Women who wanted more than an elementary education had to attend private schools. In addition, universities were open to only a small number of promising students. In this way, the Japanese hoped to create a new ruling class based on talent rather than birth.

Industrialization   In the 1870's, Japan began to industrialize to protect its home market from foreign competition. The Japanese carried out this task with little outside assistance. They were reluctant to borrow capital from the West, fearing foreign takeovers if loans could not be repaid. In any case, most western banks were not interested in making loans to Japan. They considered the country a poor financial risk. Japan sought the help of foreign technical advisers. But the high wages that the foreigners demanded encouraged Japan to develop its own talent as quickly as possible.

The Japanese government laid the groundwork for industrial expansion. It revised the tax structure to raise money for investment. It developed a modern currency system and supported the building of postal and telegraph networks, railroads, and port facilities.

The government also understood the need to educate the Japanese people in western ways. Many Japanese students were sent abroad to study and borrow western ideas and methods. They concentrated on learning the strengths of each country.

Beginning in the late 1880's, Japan's economy grew rapidly. With the support of the government, large business enterprises, such as Mitsui and Mitsubishi, controlled entire industries. A growing population provided a continuing supply of cheap labor. The combination of western methods and cheap labor allowed Japan to produce low-priced goods. Wars at the turn of the century further stimulated Japan and enabled it to take over many western markets.

When the Meiji leaders abolished the class system in Japan, the samurai lost their power and prestige. The government gave them interest-bearing bonds as a form of pension, but inflation quickly lessened their value. Nearly 2 million Japanese, the samurai and their dependents, thus faced the prospect of poverty. After the samurai lost control of the military, many revolted throughout the country. The final revolt was at Satsuma. Saigo Takamori, one of the leaders who had overthrown the Tokugawa shogunate, led 40,000 samurai against the new Japanese army. Despite the army's modern equipment, the samurai fought six months before they were defeated. How was the government wiser in handling the daimyo class?

The Japanese Diet consisted of a House of Representatives and a House of Peers.

Even though Meiji leaders sought equality between social classes, they developed a loyalty to the emperor that was based on Shinto worship. Under Meiji rule, the emperor was viewed as divine and the supreme symbol of Japan. At the age of 16, the emperor Mutsuhito in 1868 granted his first imperial audience to a minister from the Netherlands. Since Mutsuhito was considered sacred and inaccessible to the common people, he sat on a raised throne, enclosed by a canopy. To make Japan an industrial and military power equal to western nations, Mutsuhito, in 1871, sent a party of 100 government observers to the United States and Europe to study foreign institutions. However, the Meiji leaders did not rely on the West for financial assistance in their efforts to modernize. Why?

Japan soon became one of the world's leading industrial nations.

Political Change   After studying European political constitutions, Japan adopted its own in 1889. It was closer to the German autocratic model than to the British democratic one. The emperor was the source of all authority. A bicameral legislature known as the Diet had the power to vote taxes and approve the budget.

Japan gradually adjusted to western forms of government. It developed a system of cabinet rule led by a prime minister. The Diet expanded its powers as it gained more control of government finances. Meanwhile, samurai, merchants, and peasants demanded a greater voice in political life. Each of these groups formed political parties to express its views.

Japan as a World Power

By the 1890's, the Meiji leaders had achieved their goal of creating a modern nation. Japan had acquired an efficient government, a vigorous economy, and a strong army and navy. Needing more natural resources to increase its strength, Japan began to compete with the western powers in establishing colonial empires. The Japanese began to expand into the Pacific area.

In the next few years, the western powers began to recognize Japan as an equal. The British agreed to give up their right of extraterritoriality, and other powers followed that example. Japan also regained the right to control its own tariffs.

During the 1890's, tensions developed between Japan and China. Despite Chinese protests, the Japanese had annexed the disputed

Refer students back to pp. 495 and 496 for reviewing the Russo-Japanese War.

The map below is the subject of the "Using Maps" section of the Chapter 23 Review.

Ryukyu Islands in the Pacific. They also became involved in Korea, which the Chinese regarded as their sphere of influence. In 1894, Japanese troops were sent to Korea when Chinese forces entered the country to put down a rebellion. The Japanese refused to withdraw after the revolt was crushed. Hostilities developed between Japan and China, leading to the Sino-Japanese War. China was defeated in the conflict, and Japan assumed the dominant role in East Asian affairs.

After China's defeat, Japan faced growing rivalry with Russia for control of Korea and Manchuria. To face a possible challenge from Russia, Japan began looking for allies. In 1902, Japan made a military alliance with Britain, the first between a western and non-western nation. Each nation agreed to aid the other in the event of an attack by two or more powers, while remaining neutral if the other was at war with a single power. Thus, Britain was not obliged to aid Japan against Russia unless Russia was supported by another power.

In 1904 Japan became involved in a war with Russia over control of Korea and Manchuria. The Japanese victory in the Russo-Japanese War forced Russia to withdraw its troops from Manchuria and to recognize Japan's interests in Korea.

After the war, Japan was free to carry out its goals in Korea. A series of unequal treaties transformed Korea into a Japanese territory. Also, the Korean king was forced to abdicate, and the Korean government came under the control of Japanese officials. In 1910, Japan formally annexed Korea and began a program of modernization. Under Japanese rule, the Koreans lost many of their liberties. They began to resist the Japanese. However, the Japanese easily crushed Korean opposition.

By 1914, Japan had achieved equality with the West and was now recognized as a world military power. As a result of this achievement, the Japanese people had developed strong feelings of patriotism and nationalism. Their gains inspired nationalist movements in other Asian countries.

1. Identify: Meiji Emperor, Mitsubishi, Diet, Russo-Japanese War.
2. Who were the real rulers of Meiji Japan?
3. What steps did the Meiji leaders take to reduce the privileges of the samurai class?
4. How did the Japanese government encourage industrialization?

RUSSO-JAPANESE WAR   1904-1905

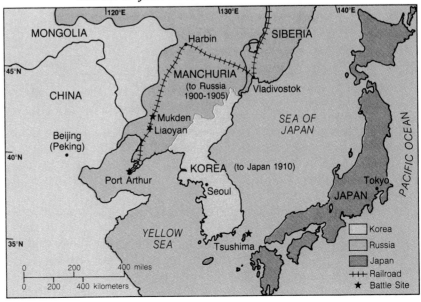

CHAPTER 23 REVIEW

Summary

1. In the early 1600's, the Ming dynasty in China was overthrown by the Manchus, invaders from Manchuria.
2. The Manchus set up a new dynasty, the Qing, which lasted for nearly 300 years.
3. The Manchus adopted Chinese traditions and institutions and became largely assimilated into Chinese culture.
4. The Chinese regarded their culture as vastly superior and attempted to limit contacts with western countries.
5. Following the Opium War in the 1840's, China was forced to make major concessions to western countries.
6. China tried to modernize in order to meet the threat from foreign countries, but resistance to change by the people made the attempt unsuccessful.
7. Failure to modernize, defeat by the Japanese, and internal problems led to the fall of the Qing dynasty and the establishment of the new Chinese Republic in 1911.
8. In the late 1500's, Japan was united under the Tokugawa shoguns.
9. In an effort to preserve their power, the Tokugawa leaders maintained a rigid social structure and enforced a policy of isolation from foreign contacts.
10. In 1853 the United States forced Japan to open its doors to western countries.
11. The failure of the Tokugawa leaders to protect Japan from foreigners led to their overthrow in 1867 and a new period in Japanese history, known as the Meiji period.
12. The Meiji leaders succeeded in modernizing Japan and making it a world military power.

Building Vocabulary

labor intensive	opium	legations	geishas
hegemony	extraterritoriality	sankin-kotai	kabuki
kowtow	most-favored-nation status	metsuke	consul

Reviewing the Main Ideas

1. What were the important values of the Chinese during the Qing dynasty?
2. What prevented China from developing an industrial economy?
3. How did the Chinese attempt to limit contacts with foreigners?
4. How did China view itself? How did the Chinese view outsiders?
5. What were the results of the Opium War? How did it extend western influence?
6. What was the outcome of the Sino-Japanese War?
7. How did the Boxer Rebellion differ from the Taiping Rebellion?
8. What caused the downfall of the Qing dynasty?
9. What was the class structure of Tokugawa Japan?
10. What ethical values were stressed by Tokugawa leaders?
11. What kind of government evolved in Meiji Japan?
12. How did the Russo-Japanese War affect Japan?

Discussing Important Ideas

1. What were the main cultural differences separating China and Japan from the West?
2. Why was fundamental reform resisted for so long in China? Compare reform in China to reform in Japan.
3. Was it necessary to overthrow the Qing dynasty in order to modernize China? Explain.
4. Why were the Japanese able to modernize more quickly than the Chinese? How were Japanese traditions affected by the Meiji reforms?
5. Were Japan's leaders, drawn from the military class, better suited to judging the western threat than China's scholarly elite?
6. What are the advantages and disadvantages of a fixed social structure compared to social mobility? Give examples from the history of East Asia to support your position.
7. Why did the United States force Japan to end its isolationist policy? Do you agree or disagree with the action it took?
8. Did Japanese dominance of East Asia have a positive or negative impact on the area?

Using Maps

Refer to the map on page 541 to answer the following questions:

1. Where were most of the battle in the Russo-Japanese War fought?
2. What is the relative location of Japan to Korea? Manchuria to Korea?
3. Which regions were connected by a railroad?
4. How far is Vladivostok from Tokyo?
5. Which two cities are located at almost the same latitude?
6. What large landmass lies across the Pacific east of Japan?

CHAPTER 24

The British in India

❝ No nation can claim rights without acknowledging the duties that go with the rights. ❞

Theodore Roosevelt, United States President (1858-1919)

Empire Building

Refer students to the map on p. 547. It shows the partitioning of Africa by 1914.

The nineteenth century was not only a period of nation building but also a period of empire building. By the late 1800's, the world's most powerful nations competed with one another for territorial claims over much of the globe. The various national policies for establishing authority over other areas in the world is known as **imperialism.**

Nations generally gained control of other areas by means of treaty, purchase, or military force. The most common forms of maintaining control were colonies, protectorates, or spheres of influence. A colony was directly ruled by an imperial authority. A **protectorate** kept its own government for domestic decisions but relinquished foreign policy to an imperial authority. A **sphere of influence** was a territory that kept its own government but whose trade was controlled by a foreign power.

The great powers of the nineteenth century built empires for various reasons. These reasons were political, economic, and even social. Political rivalries and military concerns often motivated governments to expand their territories overseas. Government and industry worked together to secure new markets and new supplies of raw materials. Some groups of people also wanted to introduce their ways of doing things to people whose cultures were different.

Nations that built empires had certain things in common. Each possessed a developed industrial economy and a powerful military force. Countries that were subjected to imperialism generally were not industrially developed, and they lacked a strong military force to resist invaders. These countries could not be considered underdeveloped in any other sense, however. They possessed rich cultural traditions, and their levels of technological development were usually adequate to meet their own needs. They rarely welcomed change from outside their country.

1 Imperialism in Africa

At the middle of the nineteenth century, the continent of Africa was largely unknown to most Europeans. In the 1600's and 1700's, Dutch and Portuguese traders had established outposts along the African coast. These posts generally formed a network of stops for traders as they moved to and from major markets in Asia. Britain and France also had set up African trading posts. By 1914, however, the great powers—chiefly Britain, France, and Germany—had **partitioned,** or divided, the continent into numerous large possessions.

Conquest of North Africa

At the beginning of the 1800's, North Africa west of Egypt was made up of several Arab-Berber territories: Tripoli, Tunis, Algiers, and Morocco. Tripoli, Tunis, and Algiers officially owed allegiance to the Ottomans. Morocco, however, was completely independent. In reference to North Africa's Berber heritage, the Europeans called the North African lands the Barbary Coast.

The North African territories received much of their income from fees placed on foreign trade. Using swift sailing ships, Barbary sailors raided European and American merchant ships traveling through the Mediterranean. The Europeans regarded these actions as piracy.

In 1830 France invaded Algiers (present-day Algeria). It used the Barbary raids as an excuse for the invasion. Algerian resistance to French occupation was fierce and lasted for many years. In 1881 the French invaded Tunis (now called Tunisia). About 30 years later, they occupied Morocco.

Egypt   Meanwhile, British interest in North Africa began peaking in 1859. That year, a French company headed by Ferdinand de Lesseps

545

Egypt's financial crisis was brought on by its ruler Khedive Ismail. Because of his extravagant spending on schools, shipping, roads and other public works, he bankrupted his state.

The Suez Canal was opened in 1869 with lavish ceremony attended by most of the rulers of Europe. The first convoy to sail through the canal was led by a French ship carrying the French Empress Eugénie. At first, Great Britain opposed the canal. However, after it was built, the British recognized its crucial role in the route to India, and their holdings in the Pacific. How did Great Britain gain control of the Suez Canal?

started to build the Suez Canal through Egypt. The waterway connected the Mediterranean and Red Seas, creating a short transportation route between Europe and Asia. The British viewed the canal as an important lifeline from Europe to their colonies in Asia and the Pacific.

When the canal was finished in 1869, Egypt had complete ownership of the canal company. A few years later, the Egyptian government was forced to sell shares of stock in the canal company in order to meet a financial crisis. To expand British influence in the area, Prime Minister Benjamin Disraeli secured sufficient shares of stock to gain partial control of the canal.

Egypt's poor financial situation eventually provided Britain with an excuse to intervene militarily. In 1882 a British force moved into Egypt. It defeated an Egyptian army led by the nationalist leader Ahmed Arabi. After this victory, Egypt became a protectorate of Britain.

Sudan　In securing its control of Egypt, Britain moved to take possession of the headwaters of the Nile River in Sudan. In 1898 a combined Anglo-Egyptian force defeated resisting Sudanese nationalists and seized control of most of the Nile Valley. Britain's presence in Sudan brought it into direct conflict with France.

A French expedition had reached the Nile at Fashoda in hopes of advancing France's claims to the area. Under public pressure at home over the Dreyfus affair and to avoid war, the French government yielded to British claims in Sudan. The Fashoda incident, nevertheless, pointed out the very real possibility that empire building could drag the great powers into conflict.

Morocco　For years after the Fashoda incident, Britain and France quarreled over rights to the Nile Basin. However, an agreement was reached between the two powers in 1904. In exchange for French recognition of British claims in the Nile, the British recognized French claims for a sphere of influence in Morocco. Britain also guaranteed that it would not protest any French effort to take over political control of Morocco.

The agreement between Britain and France angered the German emperor William II. Viewing any improvement in Anglo-French relations as a threat to Germany, William II boldly proclaimed Germany's support for an independent Morocco. In the end, however, the crisis over Morocco was settled by an international conference of European powers in 1906. All of the great powers recognized the French sphere of influence in Morocco.

Compare the map below and a current map of Africa.
Note the colonial names for modern nations.

IMPERIALISM IN AFRICA 1914

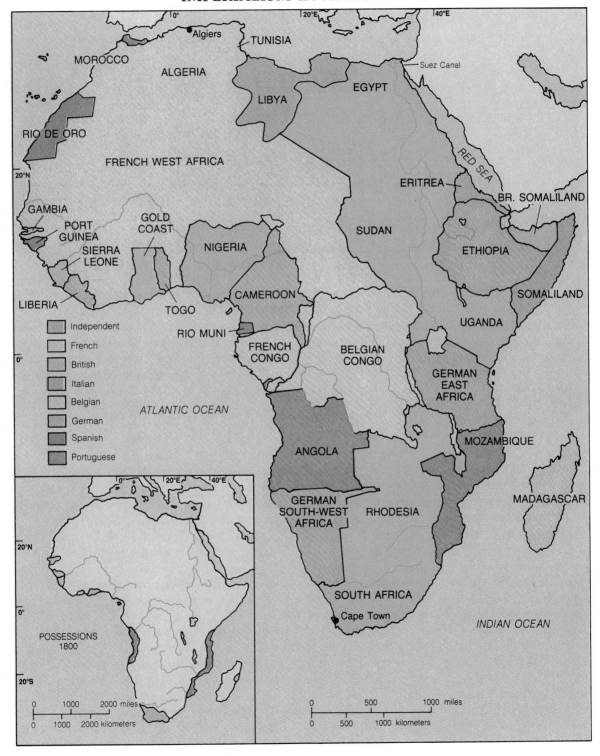

MOROCCO

Algiers

TUNISIA

ALGERIA

LIBYA

EGYPT

Suez Canal

RIO DE ORO

FRENCH WEST AFRICA

RED SEA

20°N

ERITREA

BR. SOMALILAND

GAMBIA

PORT GUINEA

GOLD COAST

NIGERIA

SUDAN

ETHIOPIA

SIERRA LEONE

LIBERIA

TOGO

CAMEROON

SOMALILAND

RIO MUNI

UGANDA

Independent

French

British

Italian

Belgian

German

Spanish

Portuguese

FRENCH CONGO

BELGIAN CONGO

GERMAN EAST AFRICA

0°

ATLANTIC OCEAN

MOZAMBIQUE

ANGOLA

MADAGASCAR

GERMAN SOUTH-WEST AFRICA

RHODESIA

SOUTH AFRICA

Cape Town

INDIAN OCEAN

POSSESSIONS 1800

20°N

0°

20°S

0   1000   2000 miles

0   1000   2000 kilometers

0   500   1000 miles

0   500   1000 kilometers

Italian forces occupied coastal Libya in 1911 but failed to pacify the interior until 1930.

Stanley was sent to Africa to establish trading posts along the Congo River and sign treaties with Bantu chiefs of the region. A chief named Mazamboni greeted Stanley and entertained him with an impressive dance performed by 1,000 warriors. What association sent Stanley to the Congo River Basin?

Tripoli   In 1911 Italian troops invaded Tripoli, which was wedged between French North Africa and the British protectorate of Egypt. The Italians defeated resisting Turkish troops and set up the colony of Libya. By controlling Libya, the Italians ended further British and French expansion in North Africa.

Partition of Africa

The scramble for African possessions south of the Sahara Desert began in the 1870's, when Belgium, Britain, France, Germany, Italy, and Portugal rushed to establish claims. Many of these claims were based on treaties concluded by European missionaries and individuals who had been exploring the African interior.

David Livingstone   One of the most prominent people whose work drew international attention was David Livingstone. Livingstone was a Scottish medical missionary turned explorer. He traveled through areas that had never been seen by Europeans. He also mapped the areas where he traveled. Among Livingstone's achievements was his exploration of the Zambesi River and his search for the source of the Nile River. In this latter endeavor, he spent the last seven years of his life.

Accounts of Livingstone's travels were published in many European and American newspapers. At one point during his journey to the source of the Nile, Livingstone suddenly stopped sending dispatches to the newspapers. James G. Bennett of the New York *Herald* presumed he was lost and commissioned explorer Henry Morton Stanley to find Livingstone. Stanley's story of how he found Livingstone in 1872 excited a widespread popular interest in Africa. Stanley's further travels in Africa also excited the interest of the great powers.

Congo   Support for Stanley's later expeditions came mainly from the International Association for the Exploration and Civilization of Central Africa, later called the Congo Association. King Leopold II of Belgium formed the association as a private venture aided with funds from other countries interested in Africa. Leopold II directed Stanley to explore the Congo River Basin and gain trading rights from the various peoples living in the area. Based on Stanley's explorations for the association, Leopold II claimed the entire Congo River Basin as a sphere of influence.

The British, French, Germans, and Portuguese took exception to Leopold II's claim. They believed that he posed a threat to their own claims on the continent. Sensitive to the pressures building over Africa, German Chancellor Otto von Bismarck called an international conference at Berlin in 1885. Fourteen nations, including the United States, attended.

HISTORY AND PEOPLE

The Mahdi and Gordon

During the 1880's, Sudan was in the hands of a nationalist army led by a religious prophet known as the Mahdi. The Mahdi's forces temporarily halted British and Egyptian advances in the region. They represented one of many groups in Asia and Africa that resisted the spread of European colonial rule. In 1882 Mohammed Ahmad had declared himself the Mahdi, or messiah, of his people. He urged his fellow Sudanese to rise up against the British-led forces that were attempting to capture the headwaters of the Nile. The Mahdi called for a holy war to keep the foreigners out of Sudan.

Sudanese resistance to imperialism was based in part on Islam. By declaring a "holy war," the Mahdi was able to motivate his soldiers to defend their country as they would defend their faith. In accord with Islamic teaching, the Mahdi promised his troops that anyone dying in the holy war would go directly to heaven. The result of this was the defense of Sudan at all costs. Bitter fighting led to numerous battlefield deaths.

In August 1882, Joseph Ohrwalder, a Catholic missionary-priest, witnessed the attack of 30,000 Sudanese soldiers on the town of El Obeid. El Obeid was a provincial capital controlled by the British-led Egyptians. Ohrwalder spent ten years as a captive in the Mahdi's camp after the siege of El Obeid. In his memoirs he wrote about the Mahdi's advance:

> masses of [Sudanese] rolled like waves through the deserted streets; they did not advance through these alone, but hurrying on from house to house, wall to wall, and yard to yard, they reached the ditch of the Mudirieh, and like a torrent suddenly let loose, regardless of every obstacle, with . . . shouts they dashed across it and up the ramparts . . .*

Believing that Sudan could not be held against the Mahdi, the Gladstone government urged British and Egyptian forces to abandon the country and evacuate the capital at Khartoum. In 1884 the British government sent General Charles George Gordon to direct the evacuation of Khartoum. Gordon was the former British governor of Sudan and a hero of military campaigns in North Africa and China.

Once in Khartoum, Gordon tried to hold the capital against the Mahdi instead of evacuating it. But his attempt was futile. With a British relief column on its way, the Mahdi attacked the city in the fall of 1884. When the column under the command of Sir Herbert Stewart reached Khartoum in January 1885, the bodies of Gordon and 11,000 British and Egyptian troops were found.

After Gordon's defeat, Sudan remained under the Mahdi's control until 1898. At that time, Sir Horatio Herbert Kitchener and his British-Egyptian army defeated the Sudanese nationalists at the Battle of Omdurman. This battle effectively broke nationalist power in Sudan. Sudan remained under foreign rule until 1956.

*Ten Years' Captivity in the Mahdi's Camp, Joseph Ohrwalder, ©1892 by Wingate, p. 37.

Point out that much of Africa was impenetrable for European explorers and settlers until quinine was discovered as an antidote for malaria. Many Africans had developed a natural immunity to most forms of malaria, so they were not susceptible to the disease.

The Berlin conference accomplished two things. First, it drafted an international code governing the ways in which the great powers were to proceed in acquiring African territory. It also set up the territories of the Congo Association as an international state, the Congo Free State. The Berlin conference specified that the state was to be neutral and open to international trade.

In 1889 the great powers reassembled in Brussels at the request of Leopold II. The Brussels conference worked to suppress slavery and the slave trade in Africa. It also undertook to protect the rights of the African people during European expansion.

The great powers' attempts at internationalizing Africa failed because they had no way of enforcing the decisions made at Berlin and Brussels. In the end, Leopold II went his own way in the Congo. To make it a complete Belgian concern, the king personally paid back all the contributions his international Congo Association received from non-Belgians. By 1890 Leopold II had taken over the Congo Free State—not as a Belgian colony, but as his own private plantation.

Leopold II was a harsh ruler and his actions in Africa became an international scandal. For example, African workers who failed to bring a specified amount of rubber and other products to the king's trading posts in the Congo were beaten severely. Protests from around the world resulted in the Belgian government taking over the Congo Free State in 1908. It then became known as the Belgian Congo.

While the Belgian government controlled nearly 900,000 square miles (2,330,100 square kilometers) in the heart of Africa, other European nations partitioned much of the remaining continent. By 1900 the Portuguese had annexed all of Angola and Mozambique in southern Africa. The Italians took over Somaliland and Eritrea in the horn of Africa, the northeastern corner of the continent near the Red Sea.

Ethiopia   Aware of European plans for expansion into the horn of Africa, Ethiopian Emperor Menelik II bought modern weapons and trained his army to use them. In a battle at Adowa in 1896, the Ethiopians defeated the Italians. It was the first time that Africans had successfully defended themselves against European forces. The Battle of Adowa discouraged further invasions of Ethiopia for nearly 40 years. Ethiopia in eastern Africa and Liberia in western Africa were the only two African nations not to experience European colonial rule.[1]

European Rivalries   Elsewhere on the continent, the Germans established colonies in East and West Africa. Germany also ruled the huge desert area of modern-day Namibia. In the early 1900's, the territory was known as German Southwest Africa.

Soon after the Battle of Adowa, Menelek II brought all the Ethiopian highlands under his control, founding modern Ethiopia. What other African country remained free of European colonial rule?

---

[1]In 1816 freed slaves from the United States settled territory in western Africa. They called their land Liberia and named their capital Monrovia to honor United States President James Monroe. Monroe was serving as president when the settlement of Liberia began.

The British had taken control of the Cape Colony during the Napoleonic wars.

In 1835 the Afrikaans-speaking Boers of the Cape Colony set out on a "great trek" to escape British rule. The Boers reached the rich farmlands they wanted, but only after bloody opposition by the Zulu. What names did the Boers give to the new settlements?

The French controlled most of West Africa from Algiers across the Sahara to various ports along the Atlantic coast. They also occupied a small area on the Red Sea that became known as French Somaliland. French economic influence grew in Ethiopia after the Italian defeat there in 1896. The French government's imperialist policy included plans for a French belt of influence across Africa from Dakar in the west to the Gulf of Aden in the east. This policy received a major setback with Britain's own plan for a British Africa stretching from the Cape of Good Hope to the Suez Canal.

The main sponsor of the British plan was Cecil Rhodes, a British administrator and financier. He proposed the building of a major railroad to link the British Cape Colony in the south with Egypt in the north. The railroad was to establish British control and dominance in Africa.

The British in South Africa

In 1488 the Portuguese arrived in South Africa. However, the area was not settled by Europeans until the Dutch set up the Cape Colony in 1652. The African Dutch, or Afrikaners, had been in the country over 140 years when the British took over the Cape Colony. The Cape Colony at the southernmost point of Africa was the only area in which Europeans settled in large numbers.

The Afrikaners strongly resisted British rule. They opposed British laws outlawing slavery. The Afrikaners had long made slaves of the black Africans they called Bushmen and Hottentots. Afrikaners also followed **apartheid,** a strict social policy separating the races.

Rather than tolerate British colonial rule, the Afrikaners decided to leave the Cape Colony. They made a "great trek" to an area north of the

The Great Trek brought Afrikaners into Zulu territory where conflicts developed between the two.

Cecil Rhodes had gained a monopoly on diamond and gold production in South Africa. He used his wealth to check Afrikaner expansion and to forward British imperial interests.

Militarily, Zulu warriors were as vigorous and disciplined as the North American Iroquois, and far more numerous. British expansion into South Africa was halted for some time by the Zulu, who had already inflicted great losses on the Boers. The strength of the Zulus rested on the skilled leadership of Cetywayo, who defeated the British in the Battle of Isandhlwana. What was the major reason for the eventual British conquest of the Zulus?

Orange River, establishing two independent republics. One they called Transvaal; the other was known as the Orange Free State.

In 1870 diamonds were discovered at Kimberley in the Transvaal. Sixteen years later gold was found in nearby Witwatersrand, also in the Transvaal. The discovery of these two important minerals worsened the conflict between the British and the Afrikaners, whom the British called Boers (from the Dutch word for farmers).

After 1870, thousands of people, mostly British, rushed to southern Africa to strike it rich. Many pushed into the Transvaal to stake their claims. Friction between the British newcomers and the Afrikaners brought about wars in the early 1880's and from 1889 to 1902. The last of these wars is referred to as the Anglo-Boer War.

One immediate cause of the Anglo-Boer War can be traced to 1895 when Cecil Rhodes ordered a secret invasion of the Transvaal. Rhodes, prime minister of the Cape Colony, sent a small party of volunteers, under British administrator Leander Jameson, into the Transvaal. The so-called Jameson raid failed to raise a revolt among British settlers in Boer territory. However, it did cause an outcry in Europe. After news of the raid reached Germany, William II sent a telegram to Paul Kruger, president of the Transvaal. The emperor congratulated Kruger on his success in

driving out the British "without having to call for the support of friendly powers." By "friendly powers," he meant Germany.

The Kruger telegram created an acute crisis in British-German relations. It also resulted in the resignation of Rhodes as prime minister of the Cape Colony. Four years after the Jameson raid, continuing tensions in South Africa led to the outbreak of the Anglo-Boer War. Lasting three years, the conflict consisted of a series of brutal, bloody encounters between British forces and Boer farmers turned guerrilla fighters.

The Treaty of Vereeniging ended the Anglo-Boer War in 1902. Under the terms of the treaty, the Afrikaners accepted British sovereignty. The British, in turn, promised to maintain certain Afrikaner institutions and practices. Among these was the recognition of Afrikaans, along with English, as an official language in South Africa. The British also agreed to follow apartheid. In 1910 the Union of South Africa was formed, formally joining the Afrikaner republics with the British territories of Cape Colony and Natal.[2] The Union became an independent nation with close ties to Britain.

British expansion in southern Africa also brought it into conflict with the Africans of the

---

[2]Natal had become a separate British colony in 1856.

Refer students to an atlas map showing the modern nation of Indonesia. Review the major islands that make up the former Dutch East Indies.

region. One of the most violent confrontations resulted in the Zulu War of 1879. The Zulus formed one of the largest groups of Bantu-speaking people in southern Africa. Under their king, Cetywayo, the Zulus defeated the British in the Battle of Isandhlwana, hoping to halt British advances. Several months later, the British captured Cetywayo and made peace with the remaining Zulu chiefs.

By 1914 Britain had secured its territorial holdings in Africa. British Africa included Bechuanaland, Rhodesia, Nyasaland, and the Union of South Africa in the south. In the east, the British held Egypt, Sudan, Uganda, Kenya, and British Somaliland. Along the west coast, the British held various areas, including Nigeria, Gambia, Sierra Leone, and the Gold Coast.

1. Identify: Barbary Coast, Ahmed Arabi, David Livingstone, Henry Morton Stanley, Congo Association, Leopold II, Battle of Adowa, Menelik II, Cecil Rhodes, Boers, Leander Jameson, Zulu War.
2. Why were the British interested in controlling Egypt?
3. Where were the major African possessions of Britain, France, and Germany in the early 1900's?
4. What factors led to the Anglo-Boer War? How was the conflict resolved?

2 Imperialism in Asia

In the late 1800's, the Dutch, British, and Russians acquired control in much of Asia. While the Russians expanded their continental territory, the Dutch and British established overseas colonies. Other great powers, including Germany and France, also competed for colonies and spheres of influence in Asia.

The Dutch East Indies

In the 1800's, the Dutch established a colony in the East Indies to replace the chain of trading stations that they had set up in the region during the 1600's. The Dutch East Indies consisted of four large islands, about 13,000 small islands, and half the island of New Guinea. The four large islands were Java, Borneo, Sumatra, and Celebes. Java was the center of the Dutch colonial economy.

The Dutch East Indies was thought to be one of the world's ideal colonies in the nineteenth century. The Dutch colony had rich and varied natural resources. It consistently proved profitable, exporting far more goods than it imported. The products of the East Indies were largely tropical and did not compete with those of Europe. The East Indies also proved to be an ideal possession because no foreign power directly challenged Dutch rule in the region.

The Dutch at first used a system of forced labor, called the **culture system,** to run the economy of the East Indies. Under the culture system, Dutch colonial authorities required local farmers to deliver a tax in kind of specified amounts of certain crops. These crops were usually sugar and coffee. After 1870, the culture system was abandoned. It was replaced with a less rigid system of using local labor and resources.

In the East Indies, the Dutch at first faced little open opposition to their rule. They lessened resistance by discouraging **westernization,** or the spread of European culture. The local Malay culture was protected. As a result, western ideas of nationalism and liberalism entered the colony slowly.

The greatest resistance to the Dutch eventually came from Islam, the major religion of the Dutch East Indies.[3] By 1914 the people of the East Indies were attracted to a global Pan-Islamic movement. Pan-Islamism was a political and cultural movement emphasizing the common bonds of all Muslims and opposing the colonial rule of the European powers. This movement somewhat weakened the Dutch hold on the colony, but not enough for the Dutch to consider granting self-government to the East Indies.

British India

The major British colonial possession in Asia was India, a wealthy source of tea and other tropical goods. In the nineteenth century, British India included all of the territory now occupied by the nations of India, Pakistan, Bangladesh, and Burma.

---

[3]The former Dutch East Indies, now Indonesia, has the largest Muslim population of any country in the world today.

Suttee was an ancient Hindu custom requiring a widow to die on her husband's funeral pyre. Hindus cremate or burn the dead.

The victory at Plassey secured Bengal, India's richest province. This helped fund future conquests.

Gaining Control   Before 1800, few Europeans were concerned about acquiring all of India. Up to that time, the interior was part of the declining Mogul Empire. However, rivalry for profitable coastal trading stations led to a war between Britain and France in 1756. Actually, the war between the two great powers in India was part of the global Seven Years' War in which battles were fought in Europe and North America as well as in Asia.

When the war came to India, British forces in the region were led by Robert Clive. Clive had come to the subcontinent as a clerk and had risen rapidly through the military ranks. During the war, Clive and his troops gained a decisive victory in the Battle of Plassey in Bengal on June 23, 1757. At the same time, the British fleet routed the French at sea. Britain's superior naval forces in the Indian Ocean gradually cut off the French outposts in India from Europe. British victories on land and sea opened the way for the establishment of a British colony in India under the control of the British East India Company.

East India Company   In 1757, the colony of the East India Company comprised territory along much of India's coastline. The vast interior of India was ruled by local princes. Treaties with the princes protected British trade with the interior.

During the first two decades of the 1800's, the British East India Company's hold on India was uncertain at best. During the Napoleonic Wars, the French supported numerous local princes who were hostile to the British. This threat, and the many failures of local princes to honor treaty obligations, angered officials of the East India Company. To secure more control of the subcontinent, they moved militarily.

The first surge of British expansion was ordered by Governor General Richard Colley, Lord Wellesley. By wars, annexations, and treaties, Wellesley took over the Ganges Valley and brought most of southern India under the control of the East India Company. Between 1816 and 1818, the British defeated the powerful Maratha chiefs and occupied the interior of India. By the 1840's, the East India Company ruled the subcontinent's peoples with the exception of the Sikhs, who lived in the Punjab region of northwestern India.

The Sikhs were led by a warrior named Ranjit Singh. With the help of the French, Singh had formed a modern army capable of holding off the British advances in the region. As long as Singh was alive, the British and the Sikhs were at peace. But when Singh died, there was a fierce war between the two military forces. As a result of victories in these wars, the East India Company was able to annex the Punjab territory in 1849. By doing so, British dominance over the entire subcontinent was secured.

Cultural Conflicts   Various groups of Indians resented the rule of the East India Company. Under the company's control, many local princes and landowners unfriendly to the British lost their authority and property. In addition, the British disrupted many aspects of Indian culture, offending both Muslims and Hindus.

Many of the controversial British measures were carried out under the administration of Governor General James Andrew Dalhousie. Dalhousie had little regard for Indian civilization. Under his rule, many Indian practices were suppressed and British customs were introduced. Among other things, Dalhousie outlawed suttee and permitted Hindu widows to remarry. English replaced Persian as the language of the law courts, and Christian missionaries were granted special privileges to travel throughout the subcontinent. One British official even suggested that the British had a plan to abolish the caste system.

Indian Mutiny   The people of India did not always welcome western changes, and a clash between cultures developed in 1857. That year, the British faced a dangerous rebellion, called the Indian Mutiny. The mutiny began among the **sepoys,** Indian soldiers who served in the British army in India. One cause of the revolt was the introduction of rifles in which the cartridges were supposedly lubricated with the fat of cows and pigs. The greased cartridges offended both Muslim and Hindu sepoys. Muslims considered the pig "unclean," while Hindus regarded the cow as sacred.

Local British garrisons were unprepared for the mutiny of the sepoys. Many British regulars had been sent to duty in the Crimean War before the rebellion began.

Social and economic changes made in India by the British were basically responsible for the outbreak of the Indian Mutiny. According to some Indians, canals were an insult to their river gods, and demons inhabited telegraph lines. The immediate cause of the mutiny came when the Enfield rifle was issued to the sepoys. Its cartridges, which had to be bitten before they could be fired, were allegedly greased with cow or pig fat. Why did the greased cartridges offend the sepoys?

To settle the problem, the British assured the sepoys that the grease used on the cartridges was a compound of mutton fat and wax. The sepoys did not believe this explanation. After refusing to accept the cartridges, the sepoys were arrested and imprisoned. This set off the mutiny.

The rebellion began at Meerut in Bengal on May 10, 1857, when several sepoys killed their British officers. Then, the sepoys marched on the city of Delhi, the capital of the Moguls. There, a new Mogul empire was proclaimed in opposition to British rule. Revolts in support of the sepoys broke out in other parts of India. The Indian mutiny lasted over six months, during which time brutal killings were committed by both sides. The British successfully crushed the uprisings. In doing so, they realized that direct rule from London was needed to prevent future rebellions.

British Rule One of the most important results of the Indian Mutiny was the decision of the British Parliament in 1858 to end the rule of the East India Company in India. Much of central India remained as semi-independent princely states, but ultimate authority was transferred directly to the British government. A viceroy was sent to India to represent the British Crown. In a proclamation establishing the new Indian government, Queen Victoria stated:

*When . . . internal tranquility shall be restored, it is our earnest desire to stimulate the peaceful industry of India, to promote works of public utility and improvement, and to administer its government for the benefit of all our subjects resident therein. In their prosperity will be our strength, in their contentment our security, and in their gratitude our best reward.**

To carry out this new policy, the British spent a great deal of money for economic development in India. As a result, India's total railway system increased by 30,000 miles (48,000 kilometers). By 1900 India had more than 50,000 miles (80,000 kilometers) of paved roads. To further unite India, a postal service was established and telegraph lines were built.

Under British colonial rule, the Indian educational system was improved. Elementary schools were set up in most villages; and universities were opened at the major cities of Calcutta, Bombay, Allanabad, Madras, and Lahore.

In spite of all the tangible advances made by the British, there remained a deep anti-British feeling in India. This was because the Indian

---

*Proclamation for Crown Rule in India (1858), *The Annual Register, 1858*, p. 259, as quoted in *Pageant of Europe*, ed. by R.P. Stearns, © 1961 by Harcourt Brace Jovanovich, Inc., p. 641.

Many members of India's educated class were trained in western schools.

INDIA UNDER BRITISH RULE

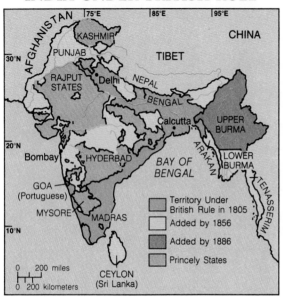

people basically opposed any foreign domination, no matter how generous. By 1900 the demand for national self-government had spread among members of India's educated classes. Some Indians wanted the complete end of British rule in their country. Others sought the more limited goal of Indian home rule within the British Empire.

In the first years of the twentieth century, self-government became a demand of the masses. Seeking to calm the cries for autonomy, the British decided to increase Indian representation in government. The India Councils Act of 1909 gave Indians an active voice in the decisions of newly created provincial and central legislative councils. This reform, however, did not satisfy the demands of the growing nationalist movement in India. India became one of Britain's major overseas concerns after World War I.

Russian Expansion

Russian expansion in central and eastern Asia was generally political in nature. The Russians demanded neither new markets nor more natural resources. What they wanted was a warm water port. Several times during the 1800's, the Russians fought the Ottomans to gain

an outlet to the Mediterranean Sea by way of the Black Sea and the Dardanelles. When these attempts failed, the Russians put pressure on the Chinese, Persians, and Indians.

During the Crimean War, the Russians made inroads into Chinese territory in the valley of the Amur River. In 1854, Nicholas Muraviev, the governor general of Eastern Siberia, founded the city of Khabarovsk beside the Amur River.[4] By the late 1850's, Russia had joined the other great powers in taking land from the Chinese. Russian territorial expeditions in East Asia led to the establishment of numerous coastal cities and the founding of Vladivostok in 1860. Located on the Pacific coast, Vladivostok, which means "lord of the east," was 5,700 miles (9,120 kilometers) from the centers of Russian culture in Saint Petersburg and Moscow.

In the 1860's the Russians took over Turkestan, a Muslim territory east of the Caspian Sea in central Asia. This move put pressure on Persia to the south. However, increased British involvement in Persia during this period limited Russian expansion. While the Russians took the city of Tashkent in 1864, the British completed the first Persian telegraph line as part of a network extending from Europe to India. British business investments in Persia followed.

Persia's strategic location in the Middle East as well as its rich oil reserves brought the Russians into direct confrontation with the British. The result was a 1907 British-Russian compromise by which a Russian sphere of influence was recognized in northern Persia and a British sphere of influence was recognized in the south.

The Russians also met British opposition in Afghanistan. There the British had already fought two wars against the Afghans to keep the territory as a free zone between Russia and India. In 1874 the Russians moved into Afghanistan. Another British-Russian compromise averted war and set up a buffer zone of 20 miles (32 kilometers) to separate the Russian Empire from British India. Both the Persian and Afghan

---

[4]While Russia expanded in Asia, it gave up holdings in North America that had been acquired during the 1700's. In March 1867 Russian territory in Alaska was transferred by treaty to the United States for a sum of $7,200,000. At the time, the sale was unpopular in the United States and regretted in Russia.

The Treaty of Nanjing in 1842 resulted in the ceding of Hong Kong to Britain and in the opening of five major Chinese ports to European traders. A second treaty in 1858 opened China further to the European powers and the United States.

compromises halted further Russian and British advances in central Asia.

Indochina and Siam

In Southeast Asia, British expansion was limited by the French. After taking over Burma in 1886, the British encountered a growing French presence farther east. Between 1859 and 1893, the French laid claim to areas of Southeast Asia including Tonkin, Laos, Annam, Cambodia, and Cochin-China. This whole region became known as French Indochina.

Squeezed between the two growing blocks of British and French territory in Southeast Asia lay the independent kingdom of Siam.[5] In 1893 the French moved to take Siam, sending forces into the capital city of Bangkok. The British strongly opposed this French action. Armed conflict, however, was avoided when the two powers agreed to define their spheres of influence in Southeast Asia. As a result of the agreement, Siam remained independent and the European powers promised not to interfere in its affairs. British advances north from Singapore through the Malay Peninsula also were halted. Above all, an acceptable boundary was drawn between British and French territory. Through the early twentieth century, the French continued to control Indochina, while the British ruled Burma and the Malay Peninsula.

Foreign Impact on China

The Opium War had opened China to foreign influence in the 1840's. During the last half of the nineteenth century, China signed a number of treaties with such powers as Britain, France, Germany, Japan, and the United States. Taking advantage of China's military weakness, the imperial powers, with the exception of the United States, divided the country into spheres of influence.

Spheres of Influence   Britain leased the port of Kowloon opposite Hong Kong. France took control of Guangzhou Bay in southern China. Germany leased Jiaozhou (Kiaochow) Bay and a port on the Shandong (Shantung) Peninsula. Russia obtained a lease on the southern Liaodong (Liaotung) Peninsula, including Port Arthur, and acquired rights to build railroads in Manchuria. Japan secured rights in Fujian (Fukien) province across from Taiwan. Within each sphere of influence, the controlling power set up trade restrictions that kept out other countries. Limitations were also placed on the sovereignty of the Chinese government.

Open Door   The United States opposed the creation of spheres of influence in China. It looked for ways to limit further expansion and to maintain the integrity of the Chinese government. The United States also wanted equal economic opportunity so that American businesses could trade freely in China. In 1899 and 1900, American diplomats sent to the imperial powers the so-called Open Door Notes. These notes proposed that the trading rights of all nations be respected within each sphere of influence. They also called for international efforts to bolster the shaky Chinese government.

Although the imperial powers eventually agreed to the American proposals, the Open Door policy did not bring lasting stability to China. With continuing foreign involvement in Chinese affairs, the Chinese felt deep humiliation and resentment. Anti-foreign feeling contributed to such disorders as the Boxer Rebellion

---

[5]Today, Siam is known as Thailand.

CHINA   1900

The aboriginals arrived some time during the Ice Age. They probably got to Australia by way of New Guinea across a land bridge, which is now covered by the Torres Strait.

(1899-1900). It also caused many Chinese to turn against the weak monarchy, which was overthrown a decade later.

1. Identify: Java, Pan-Islamism, Robert Clive, Lord Wellesley, Sikhs, Ranjit Singh, James Andrew Dalhousie, India Councils Act of 1909, Vladivostok, Turkestan, Indochina, Open Door Notes.
2. Why was the Dutch East Indies in the nineteenth century considered an ideal colony?
3. What was the major area of conflict between the Indians and the British? How did this bring about the Indian Mutiny of 1859?
4. What was the major reason for Russian expansion in Asia?

3 Oceania

The largest region into which the western imperial nations expanded was Oceania. This region contains Australia and New Zealand as well as the vast area of the Pacific Islands.

Australia and New Zealand

British claims to both Australia and New Zealand were based on the expeditions of the sea captain James Cook. Cook first explored the South Pacific in 1769 and 1770. During his voyages, Cook mapped all of New Zealand and sailed along the east coast of Australia.[6] As a result of Cook's explorations, Australia and New Zealand became exclusively British domains.

Australia   In 1770 James Cook claimed Australia for Britain and named it New South Wales. The British government decided to settle the territory in 1786, after it had lost its American colonies. In 1788 Britain established New South Wales as a **penal colony,** or settlement for criminals. Many of Australia's earliest British settlers had been jailed in Britain. They gained freedom on the condition that they move to Australia. This practice, known as **transportation,** helped relieve overcrowding in British jails.

Captain Arthur Phillip founded the first settlement, which was the beginning of the city of Sydney. Gradually, colonial government in New South Wales began granting small tracts of land to military officers and freed convicts. During the 1790's, the first free settlers began arriving. By the 1820's the people of New South Wales had developed a strong colonial economy based on the production of wool for export to Britain. The colonial population of New South Wales, however, was no greater than 400,000 in 1850.

In 1851 the discovery of gold in New South Wales and in a neighboring area called Victoria greatly influenced the development of colonial Australia. Immigrants from Britain poured into the territory by the hundreds of thousands. Some became rich finding gold. Most of the unsuccessful prospectors, however, could not afford to return to Britain. So they stayed. As a result, the free population of New South Wales soared. In 1860 there were over 1.1 million people. The increase in population eventually forced the British to end the transportation of convicts to Australia in 1868.

With more people came the demand for a better administration of colonial Australia. By the late nineteenth century, Australia was ruled as six separate British colonies—New South Wales, Victoria, Queensland, Tasmania (an island off the southeastern coast), Western Australia, and South Australia. In 1901 the British government made Australia a **dominion,** or self-governing territory independent of Britain but owing allegiance to the British monarch. The British approved a constitution that united the colonies and created the Commonwealth of Australia. The Commonwealth included the former colonies plus a region known as the Northern Territory.

Many of the conflicts of imperialism that the British experienced elsewhere were avoided in Australia. This was possible because the British settlers, at first, had little resistance from the local people. The **aboriginals,** as the original Australians are called, were forced into the dry, harsh interior with the gradual advance of British settlement from the coasts. In addition, the

---

[6]At the time of Captain James Cook's first voyage, no one knew if Australia actually existed. Scientists in the 1700's argued for its existence because they thought a large continent in the Southern Hemisphere was necessary in order to balance the known landmasses of the Northern Hemisphere.

The first Europeans to see New Zealand were Dutch sailors. They sighted the islands in 1642 but were prevented from landing by Maori warriors. The Dutch explorers, led by Adel Tasman, named the islands *Nieuw Zeeland* for a province in the Netherlands.

Growth of the wool industry was a vital factor in the development of Australia. "The Golden Fleece," a painting by Tom Roberts, symbolizes the importance of wool to the Australian economy. What other products attracted immigrants to Australia?

British government showed a willingness to grant a large degree of self-government to British colonists. In other regions of the world, the British were reluctant to grant autonomy.

New Zealand The first Europeans to land in the islands of New Zealand were part of James Cook's expedition in 1770. During the 1790's, hunters from Britain and the United States set up whaling stations in New Zealand. The islands also attracted traders interested in timber.

The arrival of foreigners brought many problems to the local Maori people. The introduction of firearms, for example, increased warfare among the Maori tribes. Foreigners also brought diseases to which the Maori had no resistance. As a result of tribal warfare and disease, the Maori population dropped from about 200,000 to nearly 100,000 by 1840.

In an effort to provide law and order for the Maori and the settlers, British naval officers and a group of Maori chiefs concluded the Treaty of Waitangi. Signed on February 6, 1840, the treaty provided for British protection of Maori rights, including property rights, while the Maori gave the British sovereignty over New Zealand.

Late in 1840, the first permanent British settlements were founded at Wellington and Wanganui. Their economies developed, based on wool exports to British markets.

As in the case of Australia, New Zealand's British population was relatively small until the discovery of gold brought many immigrants. The discovery of gold in 1861 also brought conflict between the newcomers and the Maori.

Prospectors not finding gold in New Zealand remained on the islands to farm. In an effort to

The map below is the subject of the "Using Maps"
section of the Chapter 24 Review.

gain more land, they violated Maori land rights, those guaranteed by the Treaty of Waitangi. During the so-called Maori Wars, the New Zealand government sided with the newcomers and seized some areas of Maori land for public use.

The colonial government of New Zealand exercised much self-government throughout the late nineteenth century. Britain had granted it a constitution in 1852. One reason for New Zealand's autonomy may have been the problems of administration encountered by the British government which tried to rule it. New Zealand was the most remote of the British holdings. In 1907 New Zealand became a dominion within the British Empire.

The Pacific Islands

Britain, France, and the Netherlands were the most active powers in the Pacific during the late 1800's and early 1900's. In addition, Germany and the United States had joined the race for colonies by 1900. Historian Gordon A. Craig has said:

> Collecting Pacific islands became as favored an occupation of the powers as annexing African colonies. The initiative was taken, as in Africa, sometimes by traders or missionaries

IMPERIALISM IN THE PACIFIC 1914

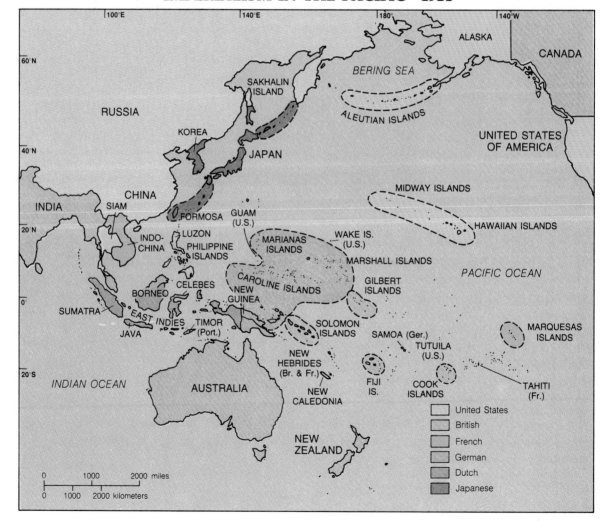

Point out that the Pacific Islands can be divided into three parts: Melanesia, Micronesia, and Polynesia. Have students identify these parts and name the major islands in each.

Some teachers might wish to discuss the history of Hawaii in greater detail.

*and sometimes by governments themselves, for the islands often had more value as coaling stations and strategical points than as trading posts . . .**

For reasons of strategy, the British wanted those islands that were natural approaches to Australia and New Zealand. One of the most important acquisitions in this plan was New Guinea. The British also were interested in establishing a naval station in the Fiji Islands.

The British annexed the Fijis in 1874 during the Disraeli administration. They had to share New Guinea, however, with the Dutch and the Germans. In 1884 New Guinea was partitioned among the three powers. The Dutch got the western half as an extension of their East Indies colony. The Germans got the northeastern corner. The British received the territory of Papua in the southeastern corner, which faces Australia. The British also took over the Cook Islands in 1888 and the Gilbert and Ellice Islands in 1892.

French imperialism in the Pacific began in 1880 when Tahiti was made a French colony. By 1900, the French had occupied the Society Islands, the Marquesas, and the Tuamotu Archipelago. France, however, was more interested in developing its holdings on the Asian mainland than in developing those in the Pacific.

In addition to its share of New Guinea, Germany took over the Bismarck Archipelago, a group of islands northeast of New Guinea. In 1885 Germany annexed the Marshall Islands. It later purchased from Spain the Carolines and the Marianas, including Saipan and Tinian. In 1889, Germany, Britain, and the United States arranged for the joint administration of Samoa. The Germans used their island possessions for strategic as well as commercial purposes. They were responsible for organizing and developing the **copra,** or coconut products, industry in the Pacific.

German purchases from Spain of the Carolines and the Marianas came as a consequence of the defeat of Spain in 1898 in a war with the United States. The Spanish-American War started from

troubles in Spain's colony of Cuba and resulted in Spain's loss of many overseas possessions. This included the ceding of the Philippine Islands and Guam to the United States in 1898.

The same year that the United States secured the Philippines and Guam, it annexed Hawaii. In 1900 the Hawaiian Islands were organized as a territory of the United States. They became important as a coaling station for the American Pacific trade and the American navy in the region. The expansion of the sugar and pineapple industry in Hawaii also benefited the United States as a source of revenue. American conquests in the Pacific, particularly in the Philippines, brought the United States into the very heart of Asian affairs and the race for colonies.

1. Identify: Oceania, James Cook, New South Wales, Arthur Phillip, Commonwealth of Australia, Treaty of Waitangi, Wellington, Maori Wars.
2. What was the basis for Britain's claim to Australia and New Zealand?
3. What brought about dramatic increases in the populations of colonial Australia and New Zealand?
4. Why were the Hawaiian Islands important to the United States?

4 British North America

In 1823, the United States boldly announced the Monroe Doctrine, declaring that no European power should undertake further colonization in the Western Hemisphere. But for many years, no European power recognized it. Largely for their own reasons, the Europeans did not move to establish new colonies in the Western Hemisphere as they had done in other parts of the world. European relations with existing colonies in the Americas were redefined. While Spain and Portugal granted independence to its colonies in Latin America, Britain's role in Canada was changing.[7]

---

*Europe Since 1815, Gordon A. Craig, © 1961 by Holt, Rinehart, and Winston, Inc., p. 450.

[7]British holdings in the Western Hemisphere during the nineteenth century included Bermuda, the Bahamas, Turks and Caicos Islands, Grenada, Barbados, Trinidad, Tobago, British Honduras, British Guiana, and the Falkland Islands. Britain also had major capital investments in Nicaragua and Argentina.

Have students draw a time line showing the most important events in Canadian history. Have students cite events in United States history corresponding with events in Canada.

Upper and Lower Canada

By the middle of the nineteenth century, Canada consisted of a number of British colonies unconnected with one another. In varying degree, each was dependent on the British government. The colonial population was equally divided. One part was French, another part immigrant British, and a third part descendants of United Empire Loyalists—people from the former American colonies who had remained loyal to Britain during the American Revolution. The British and Loyalists lived chiefly in Nova Scotia, New Brunswick, and around the Great Lakes. The French, Canada's earliest European settlers, lived in the Saint Lawrence River Valley.

In 1763 the British gained control of Quebec, the territory that included most of French Canada. It was a prize for victory in the Seven Years' War. From that time, the French in Quebec had firmly resisted British rule. The predominantly Catholic French were particularly irritated by the flow of British immigrants, English-speaking and Protestant, that began about 1780.

As a solution to the growing English-French problem in Quebec, the British government passed the Constitutional Act of 1791. This law divided Quebec into two colonies, Lower Canada and Upper Canada. Lower Canada remained officially French-speaking, but Upper Canada became English. Each colony had a locally elected assembly whose laws were subject to veto by a governor-general appointed by the British government in London. This arrangement worked well until internal political differences brought rebellion in each colony.

By the late 1830's, the French in Lower Canada began to feel threatened by the growing English-speaking minority. Meanwhile, in Upper Canada, a division over political authority occurred between the established aristocracy of United Empire Loyalists and more recent British immigrants. In 1837 unrest triggered rebellions in both colonies.

Uprisings in both Upper and Lower Canada convinced the British government that it had a serious problem in North America. In 1838 the British Parliament ordered Lord Durham to Canada to investigate the situation. In a report to Parliament, Durham urged the granting of virtual self-government and the introduction of the British parliamentary system to Canada. Durham insisted that the real authority in Canada should be an elected assembly, not a British-appointed governor-general or the British government in London. With acceptance of the Durham Report by the British Parliament, a pattern of colonial self-government developed in Canada. This pattern was later adopted by other territories of the British Empire.

The Dominion of Canada

After self-government, the next step in the development of Canada was federation. In 1867 the British Parliament passed the British North America Act. This law joined Upper Canada (Ontario), Lower Canada (Quebec), and the Maritime Provinces of Nova Scotia and New Brunswick in a federation called the Dominion of Canada.[8] This act became the basis of the modern nation of Canada. In that same year, Canadian voters elected their first parliament. The first Canadian prime minister was John A. Macdonald, a Scottish-born lawyer.

At first, the Dominion of Canada consisted of four provinces clustered in the southeastern corner of the country, from the Great Lakes east to the Atlantic Ocean. However, in 1869 the Dominion acquired from the old Hudson's Bay fur-trading company the vast Northwest Territory, which extended to the Pacific. From this territory, the province of Manitoba was formed in 1870. In 1871, British Columbia, including Vancouver Island on the Pacific coast, became a province. In 1873 Prince Edward Island on the Atlantic coast joined the Dominion of Canada.

To link the eastern provinces with the western ones, the Canadian Pacific Railway was completed in 1885. This made possible the settlement and development of the Canadian prairies. In

---

[8]The Canadians originally decided to call their union the Kingdom of Canada. The British government, however, suggested the term "dominion." The British felt that "dominion" was less offensive to the United States, which objected to the existence of monarchies in the Americas.

Compare Canadian growth with that of the United States. Refer students to the map of the United States on p. 519.

The discovery of gold in the Northwest Territory in 1896 led to a gold rush that drew fortune hunters, merchants, artisans, and farmers. They established settlements like this throughout the territory. What else helped the settlement of western Canada?

1905 the prairie provinces of Saskatchewan and Alberta were added to the Dominion. They became important grain-producing areas.

Canada became the first example of successful **devolution,** or granting of self-government, within one of the European colonial empires. Canada was then followed as a dominion in the British Empire by Australia in 1901, New Zealand in 1907, and the Union of South Africa in 1910. Each of these colonies was mainly made up of European settlers.

Decades later, Britain's plan of creating dominions was applied to its colonies made up of non-European peoples. Of these, India and Pakistan were the most notable. Through the dominion system, Britain led the retreat from empire in the 1900's, just as it had led the scramble for empire a century before.

1. Identify: United Empire Loyalists, Lower Canada, Upper Canada, Lord Durham, British North America Act, John A. Macdonald, Canadian Pacific Railway.
2. Why did the French settlers of Canada object to British rule?
3. What was accomplished by the Constitutional Act of 1791?

CHAPTER 24 REVIEW

Summary

1. Empire building was begun in the 1600's by traders and missionaries. In the 1800's governments themselves began to build empires for political, military, economic, and social reasons.

2. Each imperialist nation possessed a developed economy and a powerful military force. Countries subjected to imperialism generally were not economically developed and lacked a strong military force.

3. While the Dutch and Portuguese were the first to establish African trading outposts, the major rivals for Africa were France and Britain. Britain, France, Germany and Belgium participated in partitioning Africa into colonies.

4. The Dutch colony of the East Indies was considered one of the world's ideal colonies in the nineteenth century.

5. India was one of Britain's most important colonies. Internal conflicts, however, between the British and the subject Hindu and Muslim Indian population caused unrest.

6. Unlike the other powers in Asia, the Russians did not expand to gain new markets and more resources. The Russians stretched into Asia to secure warm water ports.

7. The heart of French imperialism in Asia was in the region now known as Indochina.

8. European imperialism in China resulted in the partitioning of that country into exclusive spheres of influence. The Open Door Policy sought to end this development.

9. The race for colonies in Oceania was led by Britain, which held Australia and New Zealand. The numerous islands of the Pacific were targets of British, French, German, Dutch, and American imperialism.

10. British colonial policies in Canada set an example for granting self-government to overseas colonies settled and controlled by Europeans. The British policy of granting dominion status to colonies was later applied to European colonies of non-European peoples.

Building Vocabulary

imperialism	apartheid	sepoys	dominion
protectorate	culture system	penal colony	aboriginals
sphere of influence	westernization	transportation	copra
partitioned			devolution

Reviewing the Main Ideas

1. Which European country was the first to invade North Africa and seize territory for a colony?
2. How did the British gain control over Egypt?
3. How did the Fashoda incident and the crisis over Morocco bring European powers into conflict?
4. Why was the 1885 Berlin conference held? What were its results?
5. Which two African nations did not experience European colonial rule?
6. How did British expansion in South Africa bring Britain into war with the Afrikaners and the Zulus?

7. How did the British gain control in India?
8. How was Russian expansion in the late 1800's and early 1900's limited by other nations?
9. In what areas did European nations come into conflict with one another in Asia? How were most of these conflicts settled?
10. How was China gradually opened to foreigners?
11. How did Britain, France, Germany, and the United States gain each of their major possessions in the Pacific?
12. What was the Durham Report? What was its significance?

Discussing Important Ideas

1. Contrast British and Dutch attitudes and policies regarding the cultures of their subject peoples in India and the East Indies.
2. What made some regions of the world more attractive to European settlement than others?
3. What are two examples of successful resistance to imperialism? How do you account for these successes?
4. How did the policy of apartheid develop in South Africa? Is it still practiced today?
5. Why do you think European powers were more willing to grant self-government to European settlers in the overseas colonies than to non-European subject peoples?
6. How did competition for colonies contribute to worsening relations among European powers? How important were colonial possessions to European economies?
7. On what basis do you think European powers chose to use colonies, protectorates, or spheres of influence in their empire building?
8. Does imperialism exist today? Support your answer. If imperialism exists today, does it differ from nineteenth-century imperialism?

Using Maps

Refer to the map on page 560 to answer the following questions:
1. Which Pacific islands were controlled by Britain in 1914? by Germany?
2. Who controlled the East Indies? the Philippines? Timor?
3. Which islands lie predominantly in the Western Hemisphere?
4. What mainland Asian territories were controlled by foreign powers in 1914?
5. Which country appears to have had the most extensive Pacific holdings?

UNIT 6 REVIEW

Summary

1. By the late 1800's the forces of industrialization, liberalism, and nationalism brought challenges to the Austrian, Russian, and Ottoman empires.

2. In 1867 Austria reached a political compromise with Hungary, resulting in the dual monarchy of Austria-Hungary. By 1914 the new state had grown weak from internal nationalist conflicts.

3. In Russia, Tsar Alexander II freed the serfs and attempted other reforms to modernize the empire. But his successors Alexander III and Nicholas II reaffirmed autocracy. The 1905 revolution forced Nicholas to announce reforms, but he continued his absolute rule.

4. In 1856 the Ottoman ruler Abdul-Majid I tried to establish constitutional government. But 20 years later autocratic rule was restored. In 1908 the reform-minded Young Turks set up a parliamentary government. However, they were unable to prevent the dismemberment of the empire.

5. In the early 1800's, many Latin Americans threw off colonial rule. For several decades after independence, most of the new nations were ruled by military dictators.

6. During the 1800's the United States developed a stable democracy and emerged as an important world power. Its influence and involvement in Latin America increased late in the century.

7. For nearly 300 years China prospered under Qing rule. But, in the 1800's China was forced to break its isolation. A combination of internal and external events led to rebellion and the formation of the Chinese Republic in 1911.

8. For 250 years Tokugawa Japan enjoyed peace and stability. Gradually, during the 1700's and 1800's, Japan relaxed its ban on foreign contacts. In 1853, under pressure from the United States, it gave up its policy of isolation. During the Meiji era, Japanese leaders modernized the country. By 1914 Japan had become a world military power.

9. During the nineteenth century, imperialism spread throughout much of Africa, Asia, Oceania, and British North America. In the mid-1800's, Britain granted self-government to Canada, thus beginning a slow trend by the European powers away from empire building.

Developing Understanding

1. How did industrialization, liberalism, and nationalism affect the Austrian, Russian, and Ottoman empires during the nineteenth and early twentieth centuries?

2. What inspired the Latin American struggles for independence in the early 1800's? What problems faced the independent nations?

3. Why did western nations want China and Japan to give up their isolationist policies? How did contacts with the West affect the two countries differently?

4. How did imperialist nations differ in their reasons for empire building during the period of the 1800's?

Developing Skills

Historians rarely rely on a single source of evidence in order to explain developments and events. Instead, they gather many pieces of evidence and look for multiple factors, verification of hypotheses, and overall patterns.

Study the following sources to find explanations for the rise of imperialism in the 1800's. Also examine the illustrations in the unit. Then make a list of every factor suggested by these sources as a cause of imperialism.

The first source is a statement made by German political writer Heinrich von Treitschke:

For a nation that suffers from continual over-production, and sends yearly 200,000 of her children abroad, the question of colonization is vital. . . . It is also easy to calculate that our population, provided its growth continues as before, must, in no distant future, rise to a hundred millions and more; then their fatherland would be too narrow for the Germans. . . .[1]

The second source comes from a speech made in 1898 by American Albert J. Beveridge, who later became a United States Senator:

But today we are raising more than we can consume. Today we are making more than we can use. Today our industrial society is congested; there are more workers than there is work; there is more capital than there is investment. We do not need more money—we need more circulation, more employment. Therefore we must find new markets for our produce, new occupation for our capital, new work for our labor.[2]

The third source is an 1837 report of the British House of Commons:

It is not to be doubted that this country has been invested with wealth and power, with arts and knowledge, with the sway of distant lands and the mastery of restless waters for some great and important purpose in the government of the world. Can we suppose otherwise than that it is our office to carry civili[z]ation and humanity, peace and good government, and above all, the knowledge of the true God, to the uttermost ends of the earth?[3]

[1]*Treitschke: His Doctrine of German Destiny and of International Relations*, Adolf Hausrath, © 1914 by G.P. Putnam, pp. 197, 205-207, 209-210, 215.

[2]Speech by Albert J. Beveridge, September 16, 1898, Indianapolis, Indiana, quoted in *The Library of Oratory*, ed. by C.M. Depew, © 1902, XIV, pp. 438-440.

[3]Quoted in *Two Centuries*, by J.J. Cosgrave and J.K. Kreiss, © 1969 by Sydney, Whitcombe and Tombs Pty. Ltd., p. 239.

Suggested Activities

1. Study the Pan-Slav movement in the 1840's and the 1894 conflict between the Turks and the Armenians. Make a list of the cultural and historical factors that led to each.

2. Debate the following statement: "Freeing the serfs in Russia was primarily an act of social justice."

3. Participate in a round-table discussion on how life in the United States would change if the government adopted a strict policy of isolation.

4. Make a map similar to the one on page 521 to show United States involvement in Latin America today.

5. Take the role of a foreign correspondent in India in 1900. Write an article on self-government that reflects the views of Indians who do and do not want an end to British rule.

Suggested Readings

Crankshaw, Edward. *The Fall of the House of Hapsburg.* New York: Penguin Books, 1983. Discusses the Hapsburg dynasty in the nineteenth and early twentieth centuries.

Forster, E. M. *A Passage to India.* New York: Harcourt, Brace, 1949. A novel about life in India under British rule.

Hann, Emily. *China Only Yesterday, 1850-1950: A Century of Change.* Garden City, N.Y.: Doubleday, 1963. A history of China from the Opium Wars to the twentieth-century Communist revolution.

Prago, Albert. *The Revolution in Spanish America: The Independence Movements of 1808-1825.* New York: Macmillan, 1970. Discusses the leaders and early events of Latin American independence, as well as the challenges faced in establishing independent nations.

World in Conflict

1930 Gandhi's Salt March	1934 The Long March	1938 Munich Pact		1943 Battle at Stalingrad
	1935 Nuremberg			1944 D-Day
1931 Commonwealth of Nations	Laws	1939-1945 World War II		
	1936 Popular Front			1945 V-E Day

1930	1934	1938	1942	1946

1933-1945 Hitler's Germany		1941-1945 The Holocaust	1945 United Nations
1936-1939 Spanish Civil War			
1933 Good Neighbor policy		1941 Pearl Harbor	1945 V-J Day

By 1900, the most powerful nations of the world were those of the West. They were industrial nations that controlled world trade. Several also ruled large empires in Asia and Africa. Each nation tried to protect its economic interests and colonies.

In 1914 these countries became involved in a world war. Their leaders vowed it would be the last. However, 25 years later, they entered another. The two world wars diminished western Europe's role in global affairs. European colonial empires weakened, and nationalist movements emerged in Asia, Africa, and Latin America.

The two wars led to a world divided between nations that supported democratic ideals and those that followed political philosophies favoring dictatorships. By 1945, two nations influenced by western Europe—the United States and the Soviet Union—had become the most important powers in the world.

Harvest of Battle by C.R.W. Nevinson

CHAPTER 25

Trench Warfare

❝ *It is a fearful thing to lead this great peaceful people into war, into the most terrible and disastrous of all wars, civilization itself seeming to be in the balance.* **❞**

Woodrow Wilson, United States President (1856-1924)

World War I

In the summer of 1914, an assassination took place in the Austro-Hungarian province of Bosnia in the Balkans. Although some people mourned, there was no broad sense of outrage or alarm. There had been other assassinations in the recent past with no major consequences.

Within weeks, it became apparent that this assassination was different. By August, the major European powers were at war with each other. The war was to last for four years; it led to the development of new weapons that changed warfare forever. By the time it was over, the war had involved most nations of the world and was the largest that the world had ever seen.

It was known as the Great War, the "war to end all wars." Later, it came to be known as World War I. The name by which it was called was not important. The changes it brought about were. The way of life that had existed before the war was destroyed. Empires were destroyed, and governments toppled. European dominance of the world was shaken. The war marked the close of a long era of international peace.

1 The Seeds of Conflict

Since the mid-1800's, rivalries had been building up and intensifying among some of the countries of Europe. For the most part, economics, imperialism, and nationalism were at the heart of the rivalries.

Economics and Imperialism

As western nations industrialized, each sought the most favorable conditions for its economic growth. This led to intense competition. As industrialization spread, the competition grew keener. One by one, Britain, France, Germany, Austria-Hungary, Russia, and Italy sought to establish and expand empires.

Britain wanted to maintain the lifelines of its empire and keep open the sea-lanes it needed for trade. It also wanted to make sure no other nation became strong enough to attack it. France wanted to add mineral-rich Morocco to its African empire. Germany wanted to gain economic control of the declining Ottoman Empire. Austria-Hungary hoped to gain passage through the Balkans to the Aegean Sea. Russia wanted control of the Bosporus and the Dardanelles and to extend the control it already had over Manchuria.

Competition turned to conflict as one power crossed another in its efforts to accomplish its goals. In 1898, for example, Britain and France confronted one another over rival claims in Egypt and the Sudan. The following year, Germany started to build the Berlin-Baghdad railway, which created resentment among both the British and the Russians. The British feared that the railroad would interfere with their interests in India and reduce traffic through the Suez Canal. The Russians thought the railroad interfered in their traditional areas of interest. In 1905, 1908, and 1911, Germany and France came close to war over control of Morocco.

In each case, the disputes were smoothed over. But the suspicion, resentment, and bitterness grew and festered.

Nationalism

Contributing to the tension was a growing spirit of nationalism. Nationalism had unified Germany and was rapidly becoming popular in France. There, French nationalists sought revenge against Germany for depriving France of Alsace and Lorraine in the 1870-1871 Franco-Prussian War.

The French novelist Victor Hugo urged France to "have but one thought: to reconstitute her forces, gather her energy, nourish her sacred anger. . . . Then one day she will be irresistible. Then she will take back Alsace-Lorraine." This put the Germans on their guard. They were well

Refer students to the map of the peoples of Austria-Hungary on p. 485.

By 1910 British and French military leaders believed that war with Germany was likely. They developed a plan to defend France against a German invasion through Belgium.

aware that the issue of Alsace-Lorraine was not settled permanently.

In Austria-Hungary, nationalism was creating the most violent tensions in Europe. The empire's Slavs were attracted to Pan-Slavism. Slavic nationalists in neighboring Serbia supported the Slavs of Austria-Hungary. They wanted their own country to be the center of a South Slav, or Yugoslav, nation. This new Slavic state would be formed out of Slavic territories in Austria-Hungary.

Austria-Hungary was alarmed by Serbian activities in the Balkans. It feared that the idea of a Yugoslav state would attract restless Slavic groups in Austria-Hungary. Such a development would harm the security of the empire and lead to its breakup.

In 1908 Austria-Hungary annexed the Slavic territories of Bosnia and Herzegovina, once provinces of the Ottoman Empire. Angered at the Austro-Hungarian move, Serbia called on Russia, its traditional protector, for help. Russia, however, still was weak from the Russo-Japanese War and was not ready to fight again. In addition, Russia had made a secret deal with the Austro-Hungarians. The Russians had agreed to let Austria-Hungary have Bosnia in exchange for the right for Russian warships to go through the Dardanelles. So, Russia persuaded the Serbians to restrain themselves. Then, Russia discovered that Austria-Hungary had made its move before Russia could get its part of the deal. As a result, the Russians were bitter.

The first Balkan war in 1912 further inflamed the Serbians. One of Serbia's war aims had been to acquire Albania, a small territory along the Adriatic coast. This would give Serbia the access it wanted to the sea. When, after winning the war, Serbia did not get Albania, Serbian resentment grew even stronger.

In 1913 a second Balkan war broke out. Albania was made independent, frustrating once again Serbian passions. In this war, as in the last one, the Russians had not been able to support Serbia. This upset the Serbians and humiliated the Russians. Austria-Hungary, meanwhile, became increasingly worried about its future role in European affairs.

Militarism and the Alliance System

As tensions began to rise, so did **militarism,** the policy of aggressive military preparedness. The European powers assessed each other's military strength and studied population figures and growth rates. They compared military training programs and levels of spending. They also looked at levels of industrialization and tried to estimate how fast a nation could mobilize its troops.

Diplomats maneuvered to win new allies. Military leaders argued for increased military spending and more arms. After 1870, all the powers but Britain adopted conscription and universal military training. They were sure that their national security depended almost entirely on the technology, skill, and readiness of their military forces.

Each nation's actions caused a reaction in the other nations. For example, when Germany decided in 1898 to expand its navy, Britain felt threatened. The Germans argued that they needed a larger navy to protect colonial and merchant shipping and "for the general purpose of greatness." Britain argued that as an island nation that depended on trade for many vital supplies, it had to be able to control the seas. To do this, said the British, they had to maintain a navy as large as the combined fleet of their two nearest rivals.

Along with militarism came a hardening of the **alliance systems,** or international combinations of states. In 1872 Otto von Bismarck created the League of the Three Emperors, which united Germany, Austria-Hungary, and Russia. His purpose was to isolate France by attaching all of its possible friends to Germany. The Emperors' League, however, did not last very long because of Austro-Russian rivalry in the Balkans. Bismarck then created a new and stronger alliance with Austria-Hungary.

In 1882 Italy joined the Austro-German alliance, and it became known as the Triple Alliance. Italy joined because it wanted allies against France. The Italians were angry with the French for occupying Tunisia. They also were afraid that the French might send an army to

Tell students that many people feared a large-scale modern war. Polish banker Ivan Bloch wrote a six volume study and predicted terrible destruction.

Bloch's work contributed to the convening of two international peace conferences in the Netherlands in 1899 and 1907.

defend the Pope, with whom they were having a dispute. The three powers of the Triple Alliance agreed that if any one member became involved in a war with two or more enemies, the others would provide support.

In 1890 another alliance began to evolve as Russia and France developed friendlier relations. In 1894 Russia and France signed a secret military alliance in which they agreed to come to each other's aid in case of an attack by either Germany or Austria-Hungary, or by both powers. This was followed in 1904 by the Entente Cordiale, a friendly agreement between France and Britain. Three years later, Britain and Russia settled their conflicting ambitions in Persia and central Asia.

All of these agreements developed into the Triple Entente, a loose alliance between France, Russia, and Britain. Russia, an autocratic monarchy, and France, a democratic republic, were willing to ally out of a common fear of Germany and Austria-Hungary. Britain, a democratic monarchy, was willing to join because it was alarmed by Germany's naval-building program. It felt hard pressed to protect its empire on its own.

Thus, by 1907, the great powers of Europe had aligned themselves in two opposing combinations. On one side stood the Triple Alliance. On the other stood the Triple Entente.

1. Identify: Albania, Triple Alliance, Entente Cordiale, Triple Entente.
2. What were the three major causes of the rivalries that built up between European nations?
3. Why was Austria-Hungary alarmed by Serbian activities in the Balkans?
4. What led to the formation of the Triple Alliance and the Triple Entente?

2 The Outbreak of War

Until 1914 a false optimism prevailed in Europe regarding peace. Although the arms race and the military buildup continued, most Europeans did not really think there would be a major war. Major wars had been avoided for a long time. Most countries were enjoying industrial-

ization and economic prosperity. A war would destroy what had been built up over the years.

Despite this optimism, war did come, triggered by the assassination in the Balkans. That event set in motion the diplomatic moves that ended in war.

The Assassination

On June 28, 1914, Archduke Francis Ferdinand, nephew and heir to the aging Austrian emperor Francis Joseph, paid a formal visit to Sarajevo, the capital of Bosnia. Francis Ferdinand planned, upon becoming emperor, to give the Slavs a more equal role in the Austro-Hungarian government. This would have defused much of the support for Slavic independence.

As Francis Ferdinand rode in a motorcade down the streets of Sarajevo, a bomb was thrown at his

The assassination of Archduke Francis Ferdinand and his wife proved to be a fateful event. Within a month, the continent of Europe was ablaze with war. What was the reaction of Austria-Hungary to the deaths?

Have students consider alternatives to Austria's actions against Serbia.

As diplomacy failed, political leaders turned to the military and its preplanned schedules for armed mobilization. Political leaders believed that delays in mobilizing benefited the enemy.

car. Although it missed Francis Ferdinand's car, it injured some of the people in the car behind him as well as about a dozen spectators.

A little later, another attempt was made. This one was successful and resulted in the deaths of Francis Ferdinand and his wife Sophie. The assassin who shot and killed the royal couple was a 19-year-old Bosnian student named Gavrilo Princip. He was one of seven assassins who had lined the parade route in the hope of killing the archduke. All seven assassins were members of a secret Serbian nationalist-terrorist society called Union of Death, or the Black Hand.

The Failure of Diplomacy

Although the assassination had not taken place in Serbia, Austro-Hungarian leaders held the Serbians responsible. They were encouraged in this line of thinking by their German allies and by Count Leopold Berchtold, the Austro-Hungarian foreign minister. On July 5, Berchtold sent an envoy to Berlin to talk to the German emperor, William II. William assured the envoy that Germany would give its full support to any actions Austria-Hungary might take against Serbia. The next day, the German chancellor officially repeated this promise. In effect, Germany handed Austria-Hungary a "blank check" to do with Serbia as it pleased.

Declaration of War   On July 23, Austria-Hungary gave Serbia an **ultimatum,** a statement of terms that must be accepted. Serbia had 48 hours in which to agree to all the terms or Austria-Hungary would declare war. Berchtold bluntly stated that the ultimatum "would be wholly impossible for the Serbs to accept."

The Serbian government did not like the ultimatum but knew that Serbia was not ready for war with Austria-Hungary. So, it answered the ultimatum in conciliatory terms. However, it refused to agree to the demand that Austro-Hungarian officials take part in the investigation and trial of those involved in the assassination. That, the government said, would interfere with Serbian sovereignty.

The Serbian answer did not satisfy Austria-Hungary. It was not willing to delay any longer or negotiate any further. On July 28, 1914, exactly one month after the assassination, Austria-Hungary declared war on Serbia.

From the time the ultimatum was issued until war was declared, the other powers tried to find a way to avoid a war. None met with success. Russia was the first to act once war was declared. It had lost face too many times before and had to support Serbia now. The tsar was convinced that Germany would become involved in the war. So he mobilized against both Austria-Hungary and Germany.

On July 31, Germany gave Russia an ultimatum. Russia had to halt its moves. On the same day, Germany also gave France an ultimatum. France had 18 hours in which to declare that it would stay neutral if Germany went to war with Russia. France's answer was to give its support to Russia. Russia gave Germany no answer at all. As a result, on August 1, Germany declared war on Russia. Two days later, it declared war on France.

Invasion of Belgium   The British, meanwhile, still hoped to avoid war through negotiations. They did not make it clear whether or not they would support France and Russia. Germany hoped Britain would stay neutral.

The same day that Germany declared war on Russia, the German army marched into Luxemburg. The Germans then demanded passage across Belgium. Belgium was a neutral country whose borders and neutrality had been guaranteed in an 1839 treaty signed by Britain, Russia, France, and Germany.

The Belgians refused the Germans entry and appealed to Britain for help. On August 3, the Germans invaded Belgium. Britain protested, sending an ultimatum to Germany that demanded withdrawal from Belgium. The German chancellor responded by calling the 1839 treaty "a scrap of paper." This left the British little choice. On August 4, Britain declared war on Germany.

1. Identify: Sarajevo, Francis Ferdinand, Gavrilo Princip, Black Hand, Leopold Berchtold.
2. How did Austria respond to the assassination of Archduke Francis Ferdinand?
3. Why did Russia enter the conflict between Austria-Hungary and Serbia? What effect did this have on Germany and France?

Make sure students know which countries fought on each side. Refer students to the map on p. 589.

Have students consider the difficulties in fighting a two-front war.

Wartime propaganda was used by many nations. In Great Britain this poster (left) urged men to join the army. A German poster (right) called for enlistment in the navy. Why was it necessary for these countries to encourage enlistment in the armed forces?

3 A World at War

In August 1914, the major powers lined up against each other. Germany and Austria-Hungary, joined by the Ottoman Empire and Bulgaria, became known as the Central Powers. Britain, France, Russia, Serbia, Belgium, and later Japan and Montenegro, became known as the Allied Powers, or Allies. Certain nations, such as the United States, were neutral.

None of the armies were really prepared for what lay ahead. Cavalry and horse-drawn vehicles were the chief mode of transportation. Certain French uniforms, which were designed during the Franco-Prussian War, included highly visible red trousers. Most of the Austro-Hungarian army could not understand the language of their German-speaking officers.

The Russian army was badly trained and poorly equipped. Many of the Russian officers had received their ranks because of their social class rather than for their military competence. None of the armies had stockpiled enough weapons, ammunition, supplies, or basic materials to last for more than six months.

The Schlieffen Plan

Germany's invasion of Belgium had been part of the Schlieffen Plan, a war strategy drawn up in 1905 by Alfred von Schlieffen, chief of the German generals. The plan assumed that Russia would be slow to mobilize. That meant that Germany would not have to concentrate on a western front and an eastern front at the same time. It could throw its full weight against France on the western front.

In discussing specific battles, refer students to the maps on p. 578.

For the German military, the victory at Tannenberg hid the importance of the defeat at the Marne.

Schlieffen planned for an overwhelmingly strong right wing of the German army to smash through Belgium and Holland, bear down on Paris from the west, and encircle the French army. Meanwhile, a weaker left wing would take care of the French in the Alsace-Lorraine area in the south. Schlieffen believed the Germans could accomplish all this in six weeks. Then they could move on to the eastern front and fight against Russia.

Schlieffen's plan ran into problems at the start. First, the German commander, Helmuth von Moltke, weakened the right wing by taking forces from it to reinforce the left wing. Then he decided not to send the German army through neutral Holland. As a result, the army had to pass through an area of Belgium that was heavily fortified.

Lastly, Schlieffen's plan assumed that the Belgians would offer little or no resistance. To the German's surprise, the Belgians heroically resisted the invasion, defending their cities, towns, and villages. The Germans had to pound the country with their biggest guns before the Belgians finally surrendered.

After the surrender, the Germans swung toward France. In the coal-mining center of Mons, they met the British Expeditionary Force, which they eventually forced to retreat. Despite the retreat, the British viewed their action at Mons as a success. Britain's battle medal for the early days of the war became known as the Mons Star, while veterans of the British Expeditionary Force came to be called Mons Men.

At the same time the German right wing was fighting at Mons, the left wing was attacked by the French at Alsace-Lorraine. While the casualties were heavy, the battles seemed inconclusive. Finally, the Germans emerged victorious. The French offensive collapsed, and the French army retreated.

Battle of the Marne   France struggled to recover. The French chief of command, General Joseph Jacques Joffre, strengthened the troops facing the advancing German right wing. Under the leadership of General Joseph Simon Gallieni, Paris was evacuated. Reinforcements were sent to the front in Parisian taxis.

On September 5, the French and German armies collided in northeastern France in the Battle of the Marne. The battle consisted of a series of widely separated, hard-fought actions that resulted in terrible losses on both sides. After four days of shelling, the French finally pushed back the Germans.

The German retreat at the Marne signified the abandonment of the Schlieffen Plan. It also made it clear that neither side was capable of defeating the other quickly or easily.

Eastern Front   Russia, meanwhile, kept its word to the French and sent troops into battle even before its military was fully mobilized. The speed with which the Russians moved surprised Germany and Austria-Hungary. By August 13, the Russians had invaded East Prussia from the south and from the east. This forced Germany to regroup, alter its leadership, and call for reinforcements from the western front. At the same time, the Russian invasion relieved German pressure against the West during the first critical weeks of the war.

Russian success, however, did not last long. At the end of August, the Russians and the Germans came together at Tannenberg in present-day northeastern Poland. There, in a series of independent actions that covered 60 miles (96 kilometers) and went on for four days, the Russians suffered a disaster from which they never fully recovered.[1]

The Germans had learned of Russian plans by accident. In the pockets of a dead Russian soldier, they found papers that outlined the proposed movements of the Russian armies. They found out even more when they intercepted uncoded messages sent on Russian field wireless sets connecting the three main Russian headquarters.

Thus, at Tannenberg, the Germans were able to encircle and destroy the Russian army. More than 92,000 Russians were taken prisoner and more than 30,000 were killed. The German casualties, on the other hand, numbered about 13,000.

---

[1] Ironically, Tannenberg was the site of the famous medieval battle in which Slavs had defeated Germans.

Make sure that students understand the importance of the first month of the war. After September 1914, few advances were made by either side.

Refer students to the casualties list on p. 586. Conditions in the trenches caused numerous deaths.

In response to France's appeal for action against Germany, Russia formed two armies to invade East Prussia. Russian artillery forces like this struck along the eastern front. What effect did Russia's actions have on Germany's Schlieffen plan?

Years of Deadlock

By 1915 the war had reached a stalemate. In the west, the Germans controlled almost all of Belgium and the richest part of France. After the Marne, they had continued their advance toward the ports of Dunkirk and Calais. They were stopped by the British at Ypres, a town in southwestern Belgium. The battle that took place there had cost the British more than 50,000 casualties, almost half of its force. In the east, where the last Austrian forces had been pushed out of Serbia, the Germans were getting ready to take over Poland.

All of the **belligerent,** or fighting, nations had been forced to shift their plans. To produce the needed ships, guns, food, ammunition, and medicines, entire populations had been thrown into the war effort. To raise morale, even the smallest victories were given big headlines, while **propaganda,** or ideas, facts, and rumors used to help or harm a cause, presented the enemy in the worst light.

Western Front   By 1915 the war on the western front had turned into a deadly war of **attrition** with each side trying to wear down the other. To protect themselves, soldiers on both sides dug **trenches,** or ditches. Eventually, two parallel opposing trenches stretched in an unbroken line from the Swiss border to the North Sea. Each was fortified by land mines and barbed wire. The land that separated friendly and enemy lines was known as "no man's land."

Soldiers lived in the trenches for weeks on end with the terror of bombardment hanging over them. They endured wet feet, the cold, poison gas, mud, rats, and dysentery. To advance from one position to another, the soldiers charged "over the top" of one line of trenches and ran to another. As attackers struggled to get through the barbed wire, they were mowed down by heavy artillery and machine guns. The generals, however, kept ordering new offensives in the hope of a breakthrough.

Throughout 1915, battle followed battle— Neuve-Chapelle, St. Mihiel, Ypres, Artois, Champagne. At Ypres, the Germans introduced a new weapon—poison gas. From cylinders in their trenches, they released chlorine gas. The wind carried the deadly gas into the French trenches. The gas caused choking, gasping for breath, and vomiting. It ripped lungs and killed.

Some teachers might wish to discuss in detail battles
not mentioned in the narrative.

WORLD WAR I 1914-1918

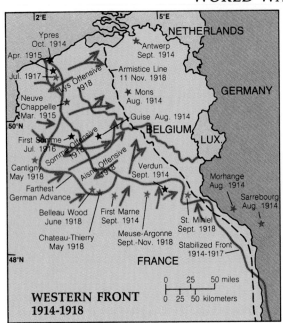

WESTERN FRONT 1914-1918

EASTERN FRONT 1914-1918

☐ Allied Powers	★ Allied Victory	← Allied Offensive
☐ Central Powers	★ Central Powers Victory	← Central Powers Offensive
☐ Neutral Nations	★ Indecisive Battle	

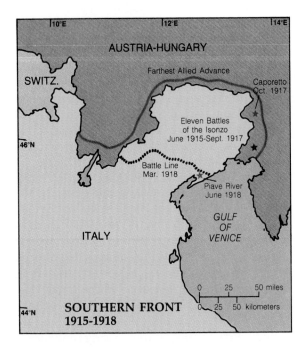

SOUTHERN FRONT 1915-1918

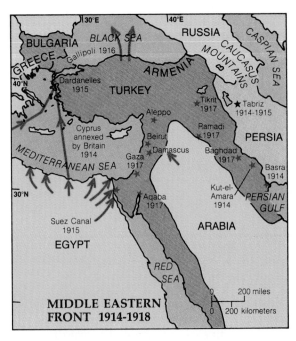

MIDDLE EASTERN FRONT 1914-1918

Italy was neutral at the beginning of the war, declaring that Austria broke a treaty obligation by attacking Serbia. Italy bargained with both sides before joining the Allies.

The value of the tank was generally unappreciated until late in 1917 when many flaws were corrected.

The year 1916 opened with the war still at a stalemate. In May of the year before, Italy had denounced the Triple Alliance and entered the war on the Allied side. To get Italy on their side, the Allies had promised that if they won the war, they would give Italy Trieste, South Tyrol, and former Ottoman lands in Asia Minor and Africa. By 1916, although the Italians had fought four battles against the Austro-Hungarians near the Isonzo River, little ground was gained. Except for the British and Japanese conquest of most of Germany's overseas colonies, 1916 opened with a dark outlook for the Allies.

In February 1916, the Germans, commanded by Crown Prince Frederick William, made their move. They staged a surprise attack against the French at Verdun, the French fortress in northeastern France on the Meuse River. There, the French, under General Henri Pétain, rallied to the cry, "They shall not pass." More than 2 million soldiers took part in the battle, the longest and one of the bloodiest of the war. More than 750,000 French and German soldiers lost their lives. When the fighting finally stopped, the line of the western front had moved less than 10 miles (16 kilometers) in either direction.

Later, the British, aided by a small French force, launched an offensive against the Germans in the valley of the Somme River in northern France. There, the British introduced another new weapon—the tank. The clumsy armored vehicle, mounted on caterpillar tracks, had been designed to survive machine-gun fire as it demolished barbed wire. But even with the tank, little ground was gained. The battle turned out to be an even greater struggle of attrition than Verdun.

Eastern Front   In the east, the war was more mobile. The front was longer and less trenched. Still, neither side could really claim victory there either.

By mid-1915, the Russians had had to give up territory greater than the whole of France. They had lost many soldiers as well as ammunition and guns equal to the amount they had had on hand when the war began. The Allies were afraid that Russia would make a separate peace with the Central Powers. So they promised that if the

Allies won the war, they would give Russia Constantinople and control of the straits connecting the Mediterranean to the Black Sea.

Meanwhile, Bulgaria signed a treaty with Germany. In it, Bulgaria agreed to take part in an invasion of Serbia. The Serbians appealed to the Allies for help. The French and British agreed to send troops to Serbia. But the troops got no further than Salonika, Greece. There they landed, and there they stayed.

By October, Serbia was overrun by Austria-Hungary, Germany, and Bulgaria. The Serbian army, along with some Serbian refugees, fled into the mountains of Montenegro and Albania. In January 1916, the remnants of the army who had fought their way to the coast were rescued by Allied ships and taken to the Adriatic island of Corfu. There, after reorganizing and rearming, they took up positions on the Salonika front in Greece. The Austro-Hungarians, meanwhile, took over Montenegro.

During this time, the Russians had been rebuilding and re-equipping their armies. In March, they launched an offensive against the Germans but made no headway. A few months later, they turned their attention to the Austro-Hungarians. They captured many cities and took several hundred thousand prisoners. But they paid a heavy toll. They lost more than a million men and used nearly all of their available supplies.

Although Russian morale was greatly undermined, their effort had helped the Allied effort in the west. The Germans had been forced to transfer divisions from the west to the east, which hampered them at Verdun.

Dardanelles Campaign   As the war progressed and casualties soared, each side tried to find alternatives that would turn the war in its favor. In Britain, Winston Churchill, First Lord of the Admiralty, asked, "Are there not other alternatives than sending our armies to chew barbed wire in Flanders?" Churchill favored opening an offensive on the Dardanelles, the "soft underbelly" of the enemy. From there, the Allies could take Constantinople and possibly put the Ottoman Empire out of the war entirely. This would make it easier to supply Russia and to

U-boat is short for the German *unterseeboot*, literally "undersea boat."

Point out that as the war raged in Europe some Americans demanded that the United States prepare for war itself. Others feared that preparedness would make United States entry more likely.

strengthen Serbia. It might also lead to the collapse of Austria-Hungary.

Churchill's idea had merit. But when it was put into effect, it failed for lack of coordination, planning, and troops. Through most of February and March of 1915, an allied naval squadron took the offensive on the Dardanelles. It nearly succeeded, but the loss of almost one-third of its ships led it to return to Alexandria. This gave the Turks time to strengthen their defenses.

In April, the Allies followed up with a land attack on the peninsula of Gallipoli. They were driven back by Turks led by Mustafa Kemal. Even with reinforcements, the Allies could not make headway. Added to the strong enemy resistance was the heat, dysentery, and malaria. On January 9, 1916, the Allies gave up the effort and withdrew the last of their troops from the area. The evacuation was the only successful operation of the whole campaign.

On the Seas   The British, meanwhile, had been using their naval superiority to dominate the seas. They were determined to keep the Germans from invading Britain and to keep war materials from reaching the Central Powers by sea. The Germans were just as determined to disrupt Allied shipping. Both Britain and Germany depended heavily on the seas for their food and war materials. Without those goods, neither country could continue the war.

Britain blockaded all ports under German control. The blockade was so effective that Germany had to receive most of its supplies through neighboring neutral Holland, Denmark, Sweden, and Norway. The Germans protested that the blockade was against international law and called it "the hunger blockade." The British also stopped ships they suspected of carrying **contraband,** or prohibited goods. They escorted the ships into port, seized their cargoes, and allowed the ships to move on.

Submarine Warfare   The Germans found a new way to counter the British blockade and to wear down British sea power. They instituted submarine warfare. German submarines, or U-boats, struck without warning, disregarding all rules of naval warfare. At the time, the naval code stated that enemy ships had to give warning before attacking a non-military target so the passengers and crew could be evacuated. The attacking ship was expected to take on board the evacuees. The Germans, however, said that their submarines would be easy targets if they surfaced to give warning. Further, they had no space for passengers or contraband cargo.

These Berlin women are searching for food. The Germans maintained that the British "hunger blockade" was the cause of Germany's food shortage. In reality, the blockade was only part of the cause. Germany's conscription laws left only the young and aged to work the farms. The shortage of labor and high prices encouraged farmers to sell their cattle and pigs. Supplies ran short, and a poor harvest in 1916 contributed to the shortage. Germany was then forced to get supplies past Britain's blockade. How did Germany meet the blockade?

As a result of the *Lusitania* incident, President Wilson asked the United States Congress for more money to increase the size of the army and navy.

Among other ersatz foods was a flour made from potatoes.

World War I gave impetus to the development of new and more effective means of warfare. Poison gas, machine guns, cannons, and tanks were improved and used with devastating results on land. Various types of aircraft began to dominate the skies. Submarines, regarded until 1914 as solely defensive, were developed by Germany to become long-range vessels of aggression at sea. Where did Germany first use submarines in World War I?

German submarines patrolled the North Atlantic, which had been declared a military area. All ships had been warned that any ship traveling in the area did so at its own risk. The Germans made it clear that because British ships often flew the flags of neutral nations, all vessels headed for Allied ports would be attacked.

On May 7, 1915, a German submarine torpedoed and sank the British luxury liner *Lusitania* off the Irish coast. The *Lusitania* carried over 1,000 passengers and a secret cargo of munitions bound for Britain. Most of the people died in the attack, including 120 Americans. The American public was shocked and outraged. When President Woodrow Wilson protested, the Germans argued that they had warned the passengers not to sail on the *Lusitania*. They had been given orders to sink submarines on sight. Nonetheless, the Germans secretly ordered submarine commanders not to attack passenger vessels. When the attacks stopped, the Americans were somewhat appeased.

Three months later, German submarines sank the British passenger liner *Arabic*. Once again the American president protested. Once again submarine activity stopped. Then, in March 1916, German submarines torpedoed the French steamer *Sussex*. Although the ship did not sink, several American passengers were killed. This led the United States to issue an ultimatum to the Germans. It threatened to sever diplomatic relations if Germany did not agree to stop attacking passenger and freight vessels. The Germans responded by ending unrestricted submarine warfare for a while.

The Critical Year: 1917

By 1917 the war had expanded to include even more countries. The campaigns on the western front had been hard and costly. They also had been inconclusive, bringing about no real change.

Morale had become a serious problem among soldiers and civilians alike. The winter had been bitter. Food shortages were so serious that food had to be rationed in some areas. The German people especially were in serious straits. They began to make **ersatz** food, food made out of synthetics and wood pulp. Disillusionment and despair seemed to spread everywhere. Then, suddenly, two events occurred that broke the deadlock of the war.

Collapse of Russia   The first event was Russia's withdrawal from the war. By 1917 morale in the Russian army had reached bottom. As many as a quarter of the Russian soldiers had no weapons of their own and were reduced to picking up the guns of those who had fallen in

The British deciphered the Zimmermann telegram in January 1917. To protect their intelligence, they waited until February 24 to give it to President Wilson. It was published on March 1.

front of them. Food shortages, which were grave to start with, were made worse by inadequate transport.

The problem was not confined to the army. In March, there were food riots, mutinies, and strikes. The tsar's government fell, and a **provisional,** or temporary, government was set up in its place. In the midst of these internal problems, Germany pulled its troops back to the Hindenburg Line, a shorter line in the west that was easier to defend. This allowed the Germans to step up their pressure on Russia. They even spread special leaflets to the Russian soldiers. The leaflets had been designed to weaken Russian resolve.

Russian socialists campaigned for peace. But the provisional government, under pressure from the Allies, agreed to stay in the war and launch a new offensive. The offensive was launched in July. When it failed, Russian morale cracked, discipline broke down, and soldiers mutinied and deserted. As the Germans advanced, the pressure within Russia grew, fanned by the socialists.

In November, the Bolsheviks, the most radical group of Russian socialists, seized power. The Bolshevik leader Lenin had spent the earlier years of the war in exile in Switzerland. With the help of the Germans, he and some other exiled revolutionaries had returned to Russia in April.[2]

The new Bolshevik government was determined to bring an end to Russia's participation in the war. It began immediately to call for an armistice. In December, the Russians opened talks with the Central Powers in the Polish fortress town of Brest-Litovsk. On March 3, 1918, the Russians signed the Treaty of Brest-Litovsk in which they agreed to give up Finland, Poland, the Baltic States, and a large part of the Ukraine to Germany.

Russia's withdrawal from the war allowed Germany to shift some of its forces from the eastern to the western front. For the first time, the Germans now outnumbered the Allies on the western front.

---

[2]The Germans helped in Lenin's return, hoping that he would spread revolution in Russia and force the government's withdrawal from the war.

Entrance of the United States The second event to affect the war was the American decision not to remain neutral any longer. Until this point, Americans had mixed feelings about the war. Many Irish-Americans were staunchly anti-British, and many German-Americans sided with the Central Powers. Many other Americans favored the Allies. The majority of Americans, however, agreed with President Wilson that the war was strictly a European conflict. While incidents such as the sinking of the *Lusitania* angered them, they were not ready to take an active part in the war.

The Germans did not want the Americans in the war. At the same time, however, they were determined to break the British control of the seas. They believed that the way to do this was to follow a policy of unrestricted submarine warfare. They thought that even if the United States entered the war, Germany would win it before the Americans could become a real threat. So Germany announced that beginning February 1, it would sink on sight any merchant ships heading to British or western European ports. President Wilson responded to the announcement by breaking off relations with Germany.

In March, American newspapers published the Zimmermann Note, a telegram sent to the Mexican government by Arthur Zimmermann, the German foreign minister. The British had found, decoded, and passed on the note to the Americans. In it, Zimmermann proposed a secret agreement with Mexico. He promised that if Mexico allied with Germany, upon victory Mexico would be given New Mexico, Texas, and Arizona. Zimmermann also proposed that Mexico talk to Japan about joining the alliance.

That same month, the Germans sank four American merchant ships. Thirty-six lives were lost. For the Americans, this was the final blow. On April 2, 1917, President Wilson asked Congress for a declaration of war. He called upon Americans to help make the world "safe for democracy."

The American entry into the war raised Allied morale. It also gave the Allies much needed resources, both industrial and human. The Americans threw themselves into the war effort.

HISTORY AND PEOPLE

Elizabeth Kenny

Elizabeth Kenny was one of the outstanding medical pioneers of the twentieth century. Born in Australia in 1886, she later became known for a method of treating polio that is still used today.

As a child, Kenny lived in the outback, the isolated rural areas of Australia. Although she had little schooling, Kenny enjoyed reading medical books. This curiosity about medicine led her into nursing. Her first assignment was in the bush, or frontier country, where professional nurses were in short supply.

In 1910 the young nurse Kenny faced a serious outbreak of polio in the area. There was no known cure for polio, and medical help was difficult to obtain. Thus, Kenny had to rely on her own ingenuity in dealing with the crisis. She discovered that hot woolen strips wrapped around patients' arms and legs could relieve the muscle spasms caused by polio. Through her efforts, many were saved from the crippling effects of the disease.

Kenny went on to develop a method for treating polio victims. The method included the use of heat packs, massages, and muscle exercises. Kenny set up a small clinic where she applied her treatment.

In spite of the proven success of the Kenny method, Australian medical authorities remained skeptical. They continued to support the traditional practice of using splints, though only a small number of patients who received this treatment ever regained the use of their limbs. Many doctors refused to adopt any approach that questioned the dominant medical thinking of the day. They also did not want to admit that a major medical breakthrough could come from a woman, particularly one who was not a qualified doctor.

During World War I, Kenny served overseas as a nurse in the Australian army. At war's end, she said: "I have spent more time on dark ships in danger zones than any other woman in the world." Because of her bravery, Kenny was called "Sister," a title given to distinguished head nurses in the British and Australian armies.

After the war, Sister Kenny returned to her work in Australia. She wrote books and articles explaining her treatment of polio. When opposition from medical authorities continued, Kenny left Australia and eventually came to the United States. There, for the first time, her method won official acceptance. During the following years, the Kenny method was used to control polio epidemics in many large cities of Europe and North America. However, it was not until the late 1940's that Kenny's work was fully accepted in Australia. In 1950 Sister Kenny returned to her homeland to resume her work. Illness, however, cut short her efforts. She died in November 1952.

After Kenny's death, vaccines were developed to prevent polio epidemics. Nevertheless, the disease continues to strike many victims. No drug has yet been found to kill the polio virus or prevent its spread in the body. The Kenny treatment remains the only effective method of curbing the crippling effects of the disease.

Some teachers might wish to discuss American war mobilization in greater detail.

One of the most romantic phases of the Great War was the fighting in the air. Have students research some of the more popular stories, including the ones about Germany's "Red Baron."

A Selective Service System was instituted to draft soldiers into the army. The British and the French urged the Americans to speed up their arrival on the continent. They did not want to launch any more offensives without reinforcement from the Americans.

It took time to build and train an army, but the American navy was of immediate help. The German U-boat campaign was growing more effective daily. By April, Britain was down to a six-week supply of food. American Admiral William S. Sims went to London to discuss with the British how to deal with the submarines.

In London, Sims introduced the idea of the **convoy technique.** Under this system, merchant ships crossed the Atlantic in clusters of a hundred or more, surrounded by a small number of warships to protect them. The first trial convoy sailed from Gibraltar in May. It arrived safely in London three days later. Before long, the system was used for all ships crossing the Atlantic.

At the same time, mines and underwater explosives began to be used more effectively. So did air **reconnaissance,** or surveying. The airplane had started to come into its own earlier in the war. At first, airplanes had been used only for scouting, photography, and dropping markers. In time, they came to be used to bomb enemy military and civilian positions.

Turning the Tide   The fighting along the trench lines continued. In April 1917, a French offensive stalled. It led to losses so great that French soldiers mutinied. Thousands deserted, leaving great areas of the front undefended. Almost half of the French army was out of action.

Flanders   The British, in an effort to keep the Germans from taking advantage of the French weakness, launched an offensive. Their plan was to capture German U-boat bases in Flanders. Early heavy rains repeatedly halted the British advance. The heavy clay soil of Flanders turned into an impassable expanse of mud. In November, the fighting finally came to an end at Passchendaele. Casualties were enormous, and both the British and the Germans were reaching the end of their reserves.

Farther south, at Cambrai, the British massed more than 300 tanks and surprised the Germans. The success was short-lived, however, as the Germans managed to push the British back to where they had started and farther.

Southern Front   Meanwhile, in Italy, the Germans joined forces with the Austro-Hungarians to give the Italians a crushing defeat at the Battle of Caporetto. The war-weary Italians panicked. They fled from the front, sweeping up the reserves behind them. Tens of thousands deserted. The defeat signaled the end of a deadlock that had lasted more than two years.

Middle Eastern Front   The war was also being carried on in the Middle East. The Arabs, seeking independence from the Ottomans, turned to the British for help. In October 1915, Britain had pledged its support for an indepen-

Aerial warfare captured the imagination of the public. Ace aviators, pilots who had shot down five or more enemy planes, were romanticized by the press as heros. For what purpose were planes being used by the end of the war?

Thomas Edward Lawrence was popularly known as Lawrence of Arabia.

Have students analyze why the war came to an end in 1918.

dent Arab state. The following year, however, Britain signed the Sykes-Picot Agreement with France and Russia. It provided for the division of the Ottoman Empire among the three powers.

While the war on the western front was stalemated, the Allies advanced in the Middle East. There, the British stopped a Turkish drive on the Suez Canal and then went on to destroy the Ottoman Empire. In December 1917, they occupied Jerusalem. British efforts in the Middle East were aided by Arab fighters who sought independence from the Turks. Arab guerrilla raiders, led by a young British officer named T. E. Lawrence, harassed the Turks and gave the British valuable information about important Turkish locations.

End of Fighting   In the spring of 1918, the first unified Allied command in the west was created under French General Ferdinand Foch. At about the same time, the Germans mounted a series of offensives. Their aim was to split the Allies and drive the British into the sea. They almost succeeded. They came to within 37 miles (59.2 kilometers) of Paris before they were stopped by the Allies.

By then, the Germans had lost valuable time and were out of reserves. Their morale was extremely low. The Allies, on the other hand, had strong reserves. Tanks were in good supply, and each month 25,000 fresh American troops were arriving in France. General Foch ordered a counterattack that pushed the Germans back to the Hindenburg Line. The push continued with the British advancing in the north and the Americans and the French attacking through the Argonne region of France.

The resistance of the other Central Powers collapsed in other areas. The Allied troops in Salonika finally broke out and drove through the Balkans. On September 30, Bulgaria surrendered. A month later, Turkey asked for peace. On November 4, following an Italian victory at Vittorio Veneto, Austria-Hungary surrendered.

Although the German army still stood firm, morale in Germany gave way. In Bavaria and the Baltic ports, mutinies led to revolution. On November 9, Kaiser William II abdicated. The following day, he fled to Holland. On November

T.E. Lawrence led bands of Arab guerrillas against the Turks in the Middle East. Lawrence's soldiers wrecked ammunition trains, blew up bridges, and dynamited railroads. How else did they help the British?

11, the Germans signed an armistice. At 11:00 a.m. on the eleventh day of the eleventh month, the fighting stopped. In the words of one newspaper reporter, "The fires of hell have been put out." The war had ended without a single truly decisive battle having been fought. Germany had lost the war while its troops were still occupying territory from France to the Crimean Peninsula.

1. Identify: Central Powers, Allied Powers, Schlieffen Plan, Helmuth von Moltke, Joseph Jacques Joffre, Joseph Simon Gallieni, Henri Pétain, Winston Churchill, *Lusitania, Sussex,* Treaty of Brest-Litovsk, Zimmermann Note, Sykes-Picot Agreement, Ferdinand Foch.
2. What effect did the rapid Russian mobilization have on the Germans?
3. At the end of 1916, which side was winning the war?
4. What two events helped break the deadlock of the war?

Some teachers might wish to discuss the Fourteen Points in greater detail.

Point out that since Bolshevik Russia was in the middle of a civil war, the Allies treated their former ally as an outcast after the war. Both France and Britain were anti-Bolshevik.

4 Restoring the Peace

The fury of the war had shattered Europe. Ten million soldiers were dead, and another 20 million were wounded or disabled. Governments were almost bankrupt, and revolution threatened much of eastern Europe. The old aristocratic political order was dead. A new Europe had to be forged. Boundaries of parts of the Middle East, Asia, and Africa had to be redrawn.

The attention and hope of many people focused on United States President Woodrow Wilson. Wilson's speeches before the end of the war had uplifted the war-weary masses. He made them believe that the sacrifices of the war were not in vain. Wilson had put forth his Fourteen Points, a peace plan whose terms included international recognition of freedom of the seas and of trade, limitation of arms, and an end to all secret alliances. It also called for just settlements of colonial claims, the right of self-determination for all nations, and the establishment of a "general assembly of nations" to settle future problems peacefully. It was these Fourteen Points that Germany thought would be the basis of peace negotiations.

For the most part, everyone seemed to agree that Wilson's points should be the guiding framework for the peace settlement. There were only two major reservations. One was held by Britain. Control of the seas had been a major British war aim vital to British interests. Britain, therefore, objected to the idea of open seas. The other reservation was held by France. Wilson had stated that there should be "no annexations, no contributions, and no punitive damages" as a result of the war. France believed that some statement demanding **reparations,** or payment for damages, should be included in any peace settlement.

The Paris Peace Conference

In January 1919, delegates from 27 nations gathered in Paris to work out five separate peace treaties known together as the Peace of Paris. Representatives from the defeated Central Powers and Russia were not invited. In a break with tradition, heads of state attended the conference. President Wilson represented the

Military Casualties	World War I	
Country	Killed and died of wounds or disease	Wounded
Russia	1,700,000	4,950,000
Germany	1,773,000	4,216,000
France	1,385,000*	4,266,000
British Empire	908,400	2,090,200
Austria-Hungary	1,200,000	3,620,000
Italy	650,000	947,000
Turkey	325,000	400,000
Serbia and Montenegro	48,000	143,000
Belgium	14,000	44,700
Romania	335,700*	120,000
Bulgaria	87,500	152,400
United States	116,516	234,428
Greece	5,000	21,000
Portugal	7,200	13,800

* Includes missing. All figures approximate to the nearest round number. (Civilian casualties caused by military action, famine, and disease were estimated at 17,000,000.)

The mandate system was under the administration of the League of Nations.

The "Big Four" powers at the Paris Peace Conference were represented by (left to right) Vittorio Orlando, Lloyd George, Georges Clemenceau, and Woodrow Wilson. Upon his arrival, President Wilson was received with enthusiasm by the people of Paris. To them, he represented a new idealism in international relations. How did the other powers obtain compromises from Wilson?

United States; Prime Minister Georges Clemenceau, France; Prime Minister David Lloyd George, Britain; and Prime Minister Vittorio Orlando, Italy. Most of the major decisions were made by these "Big Four."

It soon became clear that there were basic differences between the idealistic goals of Wilson and the nationalistic goals of the French, British, and Italian leaders. Lloyd George and Clemenceau were determined to make Germany pay for the war. Wilson's chief aim was to secure acceptance for his idea of an international assembly of nations, a League of Nations. The League became a bargaining point. The other powers used it to exact compromises from Wilson. Time after time, Wilson gave in on other issues to ensure that the League was included in the treaties.

Treaty of Versailles   In the end, military, territorial, and economic provisions that punished and weakened Germany were agreed upon, and the Treaty of Versailles was drawn up. Militarily, the German army was greatly reduced, and conscription was prohibited. The German navy was limited to a very few ships and no submarines. Germany was forbidden to have an air force or to build major weapons of aggression.

Territorially, Germany also was reduced and restricted. Alsace-Lorraine was returned to France. France also received control for 15 years of the coal-rich Saar Basin. The Rhineland, which France had also hoped to control, was to be occupied for 15 years by Allied troops.

In the east, Germany was forced to repeal the Treaty of Brest-Litovsk. An independent Poland was reestablished out of lands formerly held by Germany, Austria-Hungary, and Russia. So that it could have access to the Baltic Sea, Poland was given the Polish Corridor, a strip of land separating East Prussia from the rest of Germany. The Polish-German city of Danzig was made a free city, and Germany was barred from trying to unite with other German-speaking peoples in Austria and other parts of central Europe.

In addition, Germany was stripped of all of its colonial possessions. All of its overseas territories were given over to the Allies as **mandates,** territories administered by other countries.

Have students use these maps to explain how the map of Europe changed as a result of World War I.

EUROPE IN 1915

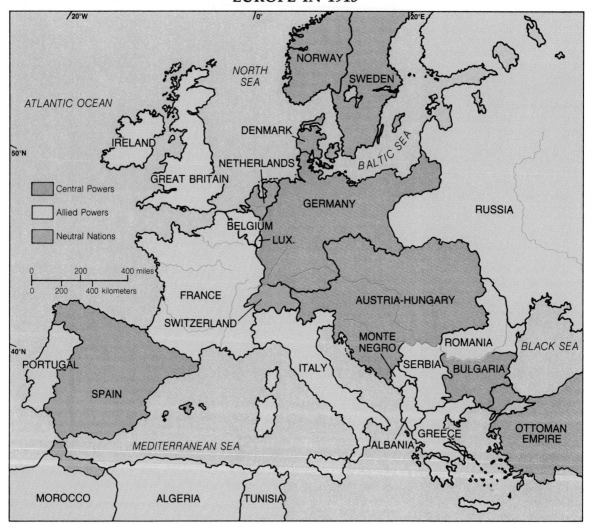

Britain and France divided Germany's African colonies. Australia and New Zealand split the German Pacific islands south of the equator. Japan was given mandates for the German Pacific islands north of the equator. Japan also received many concessions in China.

France and Britain, however, still were not content. Germany was forced to accept responsibility for causing the war. The Allies insisted that Germany be forced to pay for the property damages it caused during the war, for the costs to the Allies of fighting the war, and for soldiers' pensions.

The treaty-signing ceremony was held in the Hall of Mirrors at Versailles on June 28, 1919, the fifth anniversary of the assassination of Archduke Francis Ferdinand. Only four of Wilson's Fourteen Points and nine supplementary principles emerged intact in the treaty. The Covenant of the League of Nations was one of these.

Other Settlements   Separate peace treaties were signed with Austria, Bulgaria, Hungary, and Turkey. In them, the greatest attention was given to territorial matters. The Allies recognized the breakup of Austria-Hungary. Austria was left a small, economically weak country. Italy

Ask, "Which countries in 1919 no longer exist today?"

EUROPE IN 1919

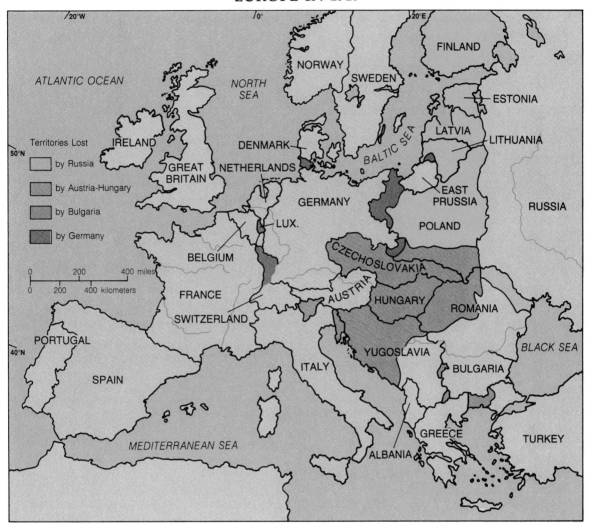

received from Austria territory near the Brenner Pass in the Alps. This area included many German-speaking people. Italy also wanted the port of Fiume on the Adriatic, but President Wilson refused to agree. As a result, the matter was not resolved in the treaties.

New nations emerged in eastern Europe from the ashes of the old Russian and Austro-Hungarian empires. These nations included Finland, Estonia, Latvia, Lithuania, Poland, Czechoslovakia, and Yugoslavia. The Allies, particularly France, regarded them as a **cordon sanitaire,** or quarantine line, that would serve as a buffer

against any potential threat from Russia or Germany.[3] In the creation of Yugoslavia, the Serbs achieved their goal of forming a nation of South Slavic peoples. Hungary lost territory to Yugoslavia, Czechoslovakia, and Romania, while Bulgaria lost land to Yugoslavia, Greece, and Romania.

In the Middle East, the Ottoman Empire was divided. The Arabs did not get the independence

[3]The Allies were concerned that the new Bolshevik government of Russia would try to spread its revolutionary ideas to the rest of Europe. They also feared a future revival of militarism in Germany.

Some historians argue that given the conditions under which the negotiators worked, the settlement was the best that could have been achieved. Others argue that it was the result of "nationalism, greed, and diplomatic bungling."

they were promised by Britain. Instead, Palestine, Transjordan, and Iraq were made British mandates and Lebanon and Syria were made French mandates.

Legacy of the War

The war and the peace settlements left Europe and the rest of the world troubled. Europe's civilization was in ruins. Throughout the world there was disillusionment, anger, and despair. Slogans such as "the war to end all wars," "make the world safe for democracy," and "make a nation fit for heroes" proved to be empty. Because so many had died and so many others had become scarred psychologically, the generation who fought in the war became known as the "lost generation."

The peace settlements not only failed to heal old wounds but opened new ones as well. The settlement was harsh and punitive and had been arrived at through secret negotiations. Freedom of the seas was not assured. Economic barriers were not lowered. Only the defeated powers were disarmed to levels needed for internal security only. The provisions against Germany were too harsh to expect a reconciliation with Britain and France. At the same time, they were not so harsh that they destroyed the country of Germany completely.

1. Identify: Fourteen Points, Peace of Paris, Woodrow Wilson, Georges Clemenceau, David Lloyd George, Vittorio Orlando, League of Nations, Treaty of Versailles, Polish Corridor.
2. What major points did Woodrow Wilson's peace plan include?
3. What were the goals of Wilson, Clemenceau, and Lloyd George during the Paris Peace Conference in 1919?
4. What were some of the reasons the peace settlements were resented?

CHAPTER 25 REVIEW

Summary

1. Economic competition, rivalry for colonies, and nationalism led to mistrust and hostility among European nations. This, in turn, led to militarism and the hardening of alliance systems.
2. By 1907, the great powers of Europe were in two opposing alliances.
3. The 1914 assassination of Archduke Francis Ferdinand by Serbian nationalists caused Austria-Hungary to declare war on Serbia. Within a month, the major powers of Europe were involved.
4. The war stalemated for three years in deadly trench warfare while each side tried futile offensives, introduced new weapons and methods of warfare, and searched for alternative means to break the stalemate.
5. In 1917 the deadlock of the war was broken by Russia's withdrawal from the war and the United States' entry into the war.
6. The war came to an end in 1918 as German offensives failed to defeat Britain and France before fresh American troops and supplies arrived in force.
7. Woodrow Wilson's Fourteen Points offered ways in which nations could be organized and relate to each other so that conflict could be resolved peacefully.
8. The Treaty of Versailles, signed on June 28, 1919, imposed harsh military, territorial, and economic penalties on Germany, which was blamed for the war. At the same time, it included a Covenant of the League of Nations.
9. In the separate treaties signed with Austria, Bulgaria, Hungary, and Turkey, the Allies concentrated mostly on territorial matters.
10. The peace settlement was resented and thought to be disappointing and unfair by many.

Building Vocabulary

militarism	propaganda	ersatz	reconnaissance
alliance systems	attrition	provisional	reparations
ultimatum	trenches	convoy technique	mandates
belligerent	contraband		cordon sanitaire

Reviewing the Main Ideas

1. What did nationalism, colonialism, militarism, and alliances each contribute to the tensions that ended in World War I?
2. Why was Archduke Francis Ferdinand assassinated in 1914?
3. What were the consequences of the German invasion of Belgium?
4. On what assumption was the Schlieffen Plan based? What happened to the plan during the first month of the war?
5. What did the Battle of the Marne indicate to both sides involved in the war?
6. What methods or alternatives did each side use to try to break the stalemate?
7. Why was trench warfare so deadly?
8. In what ways did unrestricted submarine warfare disregard the existing rules of naval warfare? How did the Germans justify this?
9. Why did Russia withdraw from the war? What difference did the withdrawal make in the outcome of the war?
10. What incidents led the United States to abandon its neutrality and enter the war?
11. What part did the Fourteen Points play in the Paris Peace Conference?
12. What did the Treaty of Versailles do to weaken Germany militarily, territorially, and economically?

Discussing Important Ideas

1. What purpose did the alliance system serve? Do you think World War I could have been avoided had the system not existed?
2. Do you think Serbia should have agreed to all the terms of Austria-Hungary's ultimatum? Why or why not? What might have happened if it had agreed?
3. Why were the Allies eager for America to enter the war? Do you think the outcome would have been different if it had remained neutral? Explain.
4. In what ways was World War I the transition between traditional and modern warfare?
5. How did Woodrow Wilson's goals for peace differ from those of the French and British leaders? What effect did this have on the peace settlement?
6. How do you think the Germans felt about the Paris Peace Conference? Give reasons for your answer.
7. Why did the Paris Peace Conference fail to make World War I "the war to end all wars"?

Using Maps

Refer to the maps on page 578 to answer the following questions:
1. Which has the larger scale (closer to reality): the map of the southern front or the Middle Eastern front?
2. While the Schlieffen Plan was being launched on the western front, what was happening on the eastern front?
3. In what year did the Central Powers achieve their farthest advance on the western front?
4. How does the western front map show the line of opposing forces during the stalemate?
5. Which map shows the Allied effort to open supply lines to Russia?
6. By 1918 which side appeared to have the upper hand on the southern front?

CHAPTER 26

Hitler's Totalitarianism

❝ *The great masses of the people . . . will more easily
fall victims to a big lie than to a small one.* ❞

Adolf Hitler, German dictator (1889-1945)

Totalitarianism and Democracy

The two decades after World War I brought sweeping changes to the West. At first, the Allies hoped that the Treaty of Versailles and the League of Nations would ensure years of peace. They believed that the overthrow of autocratic governments would spread democracy throughout the world.

But instead of peace and democracy, the years following the war saw bitter conflict and a restriction of individual rights. Political, economic, and social upheavals shook the world's industrialized nations. Long-established democracies, such as the United States and Britain, managed to survive. Weak or young democratic governments in Russia, Italy, and Germany, however, collapsed. In these lands, hard times helped bring to power a new form of dictatorship known as **totalitarianism.**

Totalitarianism has become the leading challenge to democracy in the twentieth century. It takes its name from the word "total," since a totalitarian government has total control over almost every aspect of people's lives. Under totalitarianism, the individual is considered a servant of the state and is permitted few personal freedoms. A totalitarian government controls not only all political and economic decisions but also all sources of information. Books, radio, newspapers, the arts, and the educational system are used to promote the government's **ideology,** or political philosophy.

Totalitarianism grew out of World War I. To fight such a massive, total war, democratic and autocratic governments alike had temporarily assumed extraordinary powers to mobilize their resources. After the war, totalitarian dictatorships adopted such government controls and extended them to all areas of life. They used their vast authority to remodel entire societies, transform economies, and conquer other lands. In their quest for greatness, totalitarian governments came into conflict with each other and with the western democracies. Their actions set the stage for the beginning of World War II.

1   Russian Revolution

The twentieth century has been called the century of revolutions. Of the many revolutions that occurred during this era, none was as important as the Russian Revolution of 1917. Within a few months, Russia was transformed from a centuries-old autocratic monarchy into the world's first Marxist state.

The First Revolution

World War I proved to be the breaking point for tsarist rule in Russia. In 1916 the Duma criticized the government's conduct of the war, and Tsar Nicholas II ended its sessions. The tsar and his wife Alexandra became unpopular for other reasons. Their only son and heir had an incurable disease. His condition forced the royal couple to rely on the alleged healing powers of a disreputable monk named Rasputin. Rasputin was soon influencing government policies. His political incompetence alarmed many conservatives, who feared that the monarchy was being endangered. In December 1916, several close relatives of the tsar assassinated Rasputin.

Fall of the Tsar   Rasputin's death did not solve the monarchy's problems. Public anger against the government mounted as a result of

Bolsheviks originally differed from Mensheviks mainly on matters of organization and tactics. Russian Marxists referred to each other as "hards" and "softs."

Bolsheviks were the "hards." Mensheviks were the "softs."

The storming of the Winter Palace in Petrograd by the Bolsheviks resulted in the overthrow of Kerensky's provisional government. The Bolshevik party, after years of training in secret, was now ready to end Russian democracy and to build the world's first Communist nation. What was Lenin's slogan? What did it promise the Russian people?

food and fuel shortages. On March 8, 1917, food riots broke out in Petrograd (Saint Petersburg).[1] The crowds demanded food and shouted, "Down with the Tsar!" Troops called out to put down the riots refused to fire on the people. Many soldiers joined the rioters. The tsar ordered his generals at the front to crush the rebellion. However, the generals told him that any troops they sent would also join the rioting. With the country in chaos, the tsar finally abdicated, ending the 300-year-old Romanov dynasty.

Provisional Government   After the tsar's abdication, political authority in Russia passed to a provisional government. The provisional government called for elections later in the year to choose a constituent, or constitutional, assembly. The constituent assembly would then establish a permanent government.

The provisional government, which consisted of middle-class Duma representatives, soon had a rival for power—the Petrograd Soviet of Workers' and Soldiers' Deputies. Members of the Petrograd Soviet were workers and peasants belonging to different socialist and revolutionary groups. The majority were either Mensheviks or

Social Revolutionaries. A smaller, more radical group was the Bolsheviks.

Soviets   The Petrograd Soviet became a model for the founding of other soviets in towns and villages throughout Russia. Together the soviets called for an immediate peace, the transfer of land to the peasants, and the control of factories by workers. This three-point program gained great popularity among the Russian masses.

Throughout the summer of 1917, Russians continued to suffer from the war. The provisional government, under pressure from the Allies, had decided to stay in the conflict. Preoccupied with war policy, the provisional government could not carry out the social reforms proposed by the soviets. In failing to act, it lost much popular support.

Lenin   Vladimir I. Lenin, the head of the Bolsheviks, decided to take advantage of the chaos. He had been in exile in central Europe when the revolution began. A shrewd revolutionary, Lenin returned to Russia in the spring of 1917. His goal was to organize the Bolsheviks and seize power from the provisional government in Petrograd.

Lenin realized that the provisional government could not maintain support of the soldiers, peasants, and workers. He won them over with

---

[1] At the outbreak of war in 1914, the German-sounding name "Saint Petersburg" was changed to the Russian name "Petrograd."

The Julian calendar was used in Russia until 1918.

the slogan, "Peace, Land, and Bread!" In other words, Russia was to leave the war, the peasants were to gain land, and the Russian people were to receive adequate food supplies. Another point in Lenin's program was that the soviets should be the only government. This was summed up in the slogan, "All power to the soviets!"

Bolshevik Revolution

During the summer of 1917, the Bolsheviks gained control of the Petrograd Soviet. In November 1917, they staged a coup d'etat in Petrograd against the provisional government. Bolshevik soldiers, workers, and sailors took over the main post office, the telephone system, electrical generating plants, and train stations. In the harbor of Petrograd, the warship *Aurora* turned its guns on the Winter Palace, the seat of the provisional government. The government ministers surrendered with only a few shots being fired.

This second phase of the revolution is called by various names: the Bolshevik Revolution, or either the October or November Revolution. The Bolshevik seizure of power occurred on November 7 according to the Gregorian calendar followed in the West. But in 1917 the Russians were still using the Julian calendar, which is several days behind the Gregorian calendar. So in Russia, November 7 was actually October 24.

In November, elections to the constituent assembly were held in spite of the Bolshevik coup. Four hundred twenty seats went to the Social Revolutionaries; only 225 went to the Bolsheviks. When the assembly met in Petrograd in January 1918, it was immediately dissolved by Bolshevik soldiers. In this way, Lenin showed his dislike for western-style democracy and majority rule.

Civil War

After the end of the constituent assembly, the Bolsheviks were challenged by many different groups in Russia. There were royalists, who favored the restoration of the monarchy; middle-class liberals, who supported a capitalist democracy; and moderate socialists, who wanted democracy and a state-controlled economy.

RUSSIAN CIVIL WAR 1918-1922

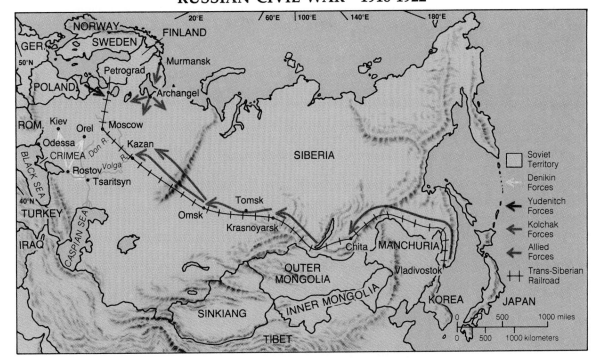

The Bolsheviks used foreign intervention to appeal to national patriotism.

Compare the so-called Red Terror with the famous Reign of Terror in France in 1793. Point out that in each case the Terror was in part a response to a civil and a foreign war.

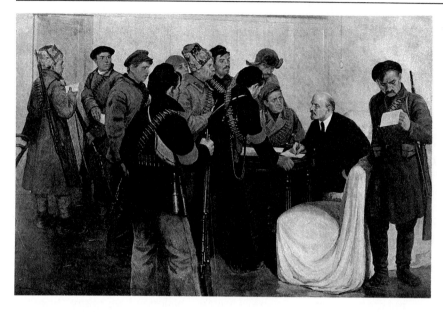

When the Germans threatened Petrograd, Lenin moved the government to Moscow. There, Lenin (seated at right) worked tirelessly to build the Red Army and to establish state control of all food supplies and industries. What other means did Lenin use to strengthen Communist control of Russia?

With such diverse groups, Russia's political situation was highly unstable. In 1918 the country slipped into a devastating civil war between the Bolsheviks and their opponents.

Reds and Whites   In March 1918, Lenin kept his promise to remove Russia from World War I. Russia signed the Treaty of Brest-Litovsk with Germany, giving up a large part of Russian-controlled territory. However, there was no peace in Russia itself. Groups opposed to the Bolsheviks joined together and fought to gain power. These groups were called the Whites. The Bolsheviks at this time began to call themselves Communists. Since they favored the red flag of revolution, they were also called the Reds. They and their supporters throughout the world formed the Communist party. Their political ideology, based on the ideas of Marx and Lenin, became known as **communism.**

The Allies, including the United States, sent soldiers and military aid to help the Whites. They wanted to defeat the Reds quickly and get Russia back into the war against the Central Powers. Lenin's government, however, was determined not to yield power. Under the Communist leader Leon Trotsky, the Red Army was organized to defend the Communist state. It restored discipline to Russian military ranks and fostered loyalty to communism among the soldiers.

The Whites had many soldiers and arms, but they were not united. Royalists were suspicious of middle-class liberals. Both royalists and liberals thought that moderate socialists were as dangerous as the Communists. As a result, the Whites could not easily crush the Reds as they had planned. For three grim years, the fighting raged. Both sides slaughtered civilians. When the Whites captured an area, they killed all people suspected of Communist sympathies. The Reds did the same against "counter-revolutionaries" in territories that they conquered.

Terror   During the upheaval, Lenin used terror as a political weapon against his opponents. In keeping with communism's anti-religious viewpoint, he placed severe restrictions on the Russian Orthodox Church. In July 1918, Communist soldiers killed the imprisoned tsar and his family. To further strengthen his control, Lenin set up the Cheka, a secret police force. Anyone opposed to the Communist state was arrested. Many socialists who had backed Lenin's revolution now withdrew their support and fled Russia to escape punishment. By 1921 Lenin had strengthened his control. The White armies and their allies were defeated.

1. Identify: Nicholas II, Rasputin, Petrograd Soviet, Bolshevik Revolution, Whites, Communist party, Reds, Cheka.

The establishment of a federal system was intended to solve the nationalities problem.

2. Why did Russia stay in World War I after the fall of the tsar?

3. What was Lenin's slogan for winning support? What did it mean?

4. Who challenged the Bolsheviks for power in 1918?

2 The Communists in Power

During the Civil War, Lenin moved the capital of Russia from Petrograd to Moscow. With the end of the fighting, he was able to put his plans for the new Communist state into action.

U.S.S.R.

In 1922 the Communists changed the official name of their country from Russia to the Union of Soviet Socialist Republics (U.S.S.R.).[2] The new name revealed, and yet hid, much about the identity of the new Communist state.

Socialist State   First the U.S.S.R. was to be a socialist country. In theory, this meant that the means of production were in the hands of the state, which was to build the future, classless society. This state, called the **dictatorship of the proletariat,** was controlled by workers under the leadership of the Communist party. Therefore, the party came to enjoy a monopoly of political and economic power in the country.

Party and State   Second, the Communist party would rule the nation through a federal system of individual republics and a central government in Moscow. From the beginning of Communist rule, the people elected representatives to soviets on the local, republic, and national levels. However, real power was held by the leaders of the Communist party. Like the government system, the party was also organized at local, republic, and national levels. Decisions were made by a small group at the top, passed down the party hierarchy, and enforced at the appropriate level. Government officials, most of whom were Communists, dutifully carried out party decisions. Thus, when voters cast their ballots, they were only endorsing government candidates and policies already chosen by the party.

Nationalities   Like the tsar's government, the Communist state had to deal with the country's many nationalities. Resenting years of oppression under the tsars, the non-Russian nationalities hoped that the Communists would allow them to determine their own futures. However, Lenin's government was not willing to see the complete breakup of the old Russian Empire into independent states. Instead, it gave each major nationality its own republic within the Soviet Union. Each republic had its own soviet and bureaucracy as well as the right to its own language and cultural traditions. However, important decisions were still made by the central government in Moscow under the direction of the Communist party. In spite of the Communist goal of equality for all nationalities, the Russians remained the dominant group in the Soviet Union and largely determined its policies.

RUSSIA   1914-1922

---

[2] The U.S.S.R. is also called the Soviet Union.

A severe drought and a breakdown of transportation contributed to the agricultural chaos.

Lenin's embalmed remains are permanently on view in the Kremlin. After Lenin's death the city of Petrograd was renamed Leningrad.

Economic Policy

During the Civil War years (1918-1921), the economic policy of the Communist government was known as **war communism.** Under war communism, the government **nationalized,** or took over, the entire economy. Problems with agriculture in this period were especially severe. Peasants hoarded their food rather than sell it for worthless currency. Starving townspeople armed themselves and went into the countryside to force peasants to sell them food. Fighting inevitably resulted. In the chaos, agricultural production fell drastically. More than 4 million people died in the famine that followed.

In 1921 Lenin tried to bring order to the Russian economy. He announced a plan called the New Economic Policy, or NEP. In a startling departure from Marxist theory, Lenin allowed some private businesses to operate in order to stimulate the economy. Basic industries, like steel, railroads, and large-scale manufacturing, remained under government control. But small manufacturers and farmers were permitted to own their own businesses and to sell for a profit. Foreign capitalist nations were encouraged to invest in the Soviet economy. Lenin justified the NEP by saying that for socialism to grow it was necessary to take "one step backwards."

Trotsky and Stalin

An attempted assassination and two strokes had left Lenin disabled. He died in 1924 at the age of 54. During this time, a struggle for power developed that continued during most of the decade.

The two main rivals to succeed Lenin were Leon Trotsky and Joseph Stalin. Next to Lenin, Trotsky had been the most important person in the Communist party. He had played a key role in the Bolshevik Revolution and had built the Red Army into a powerful organization. Trotsky came from a middle-class background and was a scholar who had contributed many new ideas to the Marxist movement. He was also a speaker of great power and eloquence.

Stalin was the son of artisans and came from Georgia, a territory south of Russia. A seminary student in his youth, Stalin later renounced

Stalin was a master of political infighting. By the mid-1920's he had eliminated his rivals and consolidated his position as leader of the Communist party. What, according to Stalin, was the purpose of the Communist movement?

Russian Orthodoxy and became a Marxist revolutionary. Unlike Trotsky, Stalin was a skilled administrator who saw to the details of party organization. In 1922 he rose to the important post of secretary general of the Communist party. As secretary general, Stalin was in charge of appointments to party posts. He made sure that his own followers received party positions so that they would back him in his quest for power.

Trotsky and Stalin were more than rivals for power. They also had a fundamentally different view of the path that the Soviet Union should follow. According to Marx and Lenin, socialism was only a stage of development leading to the ideal society of communism. Trotsky believed that before socialism could be built in the U.S.S.R., revolution had to be spread all over the world. This idea was known as **permanent revolution.** Stalin, on the other hand, believed in "socialism in one country." By this he meant that

While in exile Trotsky wrote and spoke in favor of a permanent revolution. He cited what he called "Stalinism" as a betrayal of Marxism-Leninism. This angered Stalin.

In addition to fearing dependence on foreign lenders, the U.S.S.R. could not borrow because of bad credit.

the Soviet Union should concentrate on growing strong first, before it tried to spread revolution around the world. According to Stalin, the purpose of the Communist movement in other countries was to defend the Soviet Union. The battle between Stalin and Trotsky was waged in an organization called the Comintern, or Communist International. The Comintern was an organization of Communist parties from all over the world, founded by Lenin in 1919.[3]

Trotsky was better known than Stalin and was closer to Lenin. But in the years following Lenin's death, Stalin was able to outmaneuver Trotsky. Using his post as secretary general, Stalin succeeded in gathering strength within the Communist party. Trotsky remained more popular, but the race for power was not a democratic election. By 1928, Stalin, through his control of the party bureaucracy, was securely in power. Trotsky was exiled, first to Siberia and later to Europe and Mexico. In 1940 he was murdered in Mexico by a man who probably acted on Stalin's orders.

The Five-Year Plans

In 1928 Stalin declared an end to the NEP and announced the first Five-Year Plan for the Soviet economy. Under the plan, all aspects of industrial and agricultural production were to be controlled by the government. It set goals over a five-year period to boost output. It also provided for housing, health care, and other services.

In order to make Russia into a leading industrial power, great sacrifices were demanded of the Soviet people. The first Five-Year Plan concentrated on building heavy industry. Consumer goods, like clothing, shoes, and furniture, were produced in small amounts. They were usually of inferior quality.

The plan was very detailed and tightly controlled by bureaucrats in Moscow. For example, it took careful administration to have the right number of goods delivered at the right factory on the right day. Breakdowns in the plan did occur, but in general the first Five-Year Plan was a success in spurring industrial growth.

Collective Farms   In agriculture, the plan called for **collectivization,** or farmland to be owned collectively, or jointly, by the peasants. The idea was that large collective farms would lead to increased and more efficient production. In addition peasants, unable to afford expensive farm machinery, would be able to rent equipment from the government.

The idea of collective farms soon led to conflict between the government and many of the peasants. Most opposition came from the **kulaks**—peasants who had become productive farmers. The kulaks had prospered under the NEP and did not want to give up their private property in land, livestock, and machinery to the collectives. Rather than surrender their livestock, many kulaks slaughtered them, creating meat shortages.

Fighting broke out in the countryside, as military forces and poor peasants wanting collectives forced the kulaks off the land. Thousands of kulaks and their families were killed or arrested and sent to labor camps in Siberia. By 1929 the kulaks were completely wiped out as a group. Collective farms became a lasting feature of Soviet agriculture, with the government controlling the output.

Results   In 1933 the first Five-Year Plan was declared fulfilled. It was followed by a second and a third, and more. Five-Year Plans are still in effect in the U.S.S.R. today. Though they caused tremendous hardship and chaos in Soviet society, the early plans were successful in rapidly building the Soviet Union into an industrial power. They, however, were unable to revive Soviet agriculture.

The U.S.S.R. Under Stalin

Stalin ruled the Soviet Union until his death in 1953. In the first decade of Stalin's rule, the U.S.S.R. made tremendous gains in industrial growth. It also became one of the most brutal dictatorships that the world had ever seen.

Secret Police   Stalin's methods were not subtle. He demanded complete obedience and used terror to obtain the loyalty of his people. Stalin increased the powers of the secret police, so that no one in the country felt safe from him.

---

[3] The Comintern was founded to spread communism, by peaceful or violent means, in other parts of the world.

Point out that Mussolini was fond of the glories of ancient Rome. His use of the term "fascism" shows this.

Every aspect of social and political life was under the scrutiny of the secret police. A climate of fear spread through Soviet society. Workers were encouraged to tell on each other; children were even praised for informing on their parents. Those people accused of disloyalty were either shot or sent to labor camps in Siberia, where only the hardiest survived.

Purges Members of the Communist party did not escape the reach of Stalin's secret police. In 1934 a high party official was assassinated. The killer was probably from the secret police and carried out the murder on Stalin's orders. In any case, Stalin used the killing to rid himself of opponents and strengthen his hold over the party. Hundreds of Communist party members and officials were expelled from the party, arrested, and shot.

Stalin then turned against a group called the Old Bolsheviks. These officials were associates of Lenin and Stalin's old revolutionary colleagues. Some of them had sided with Trotsky and were in disgrace with the Stalin-controlled party. In 1936 Stalin moved to **purge,** or remove, them from any position where they could threaten his leadership. These officials were put on trial in Moscow. In open court before foreign reporters, they pleaded guilty to false charges of treason, murder, and other serious crimes. During the trials, the Old Bolsheviks showed no signs of mistreatment and seemed to be in full possession of their faculties. Western experts have since concluded that psychological torture was used to break their wills. The real truth, however, has never been established.

The purge trials succeeded in eliminating any threat to Stalin from within the Communist party. All of Lenin's old associates who could have challenged Stalin were executed. By 1939, Stalin had established his dictatorship of fear as a way of life in the Soviet Union.

1. Identify: New Economic Policy, Leon Trotsky, Joseph Stalin, Comintern, Five-Year Plans, Old Bolsheviks.
2. How was the Soviet Union organized?
3. How did Stalin defeat Trotsky?
4. What methods did Stalin use to strengthen his control?

3 Fascist Italy

In World War I, Italy had fought on the Allied side. However, although a victor nation, Italy faced many problems. These problems included 600,000 soldiers killed, massive war debts, economic depression, and unemployment. Italy was also plagued by social unrest and political instability. The democratic government was unable to control the situation. Out of the chaos emerged a political leader who had fought in the Italian army as a corporal. His name was Benito Mussolini, and his plan for governing Italy led to the creation of a new type of totalitarianism.

Rise of Fascism

Born in 1883, Mussolini came from a working-class family. As a young man, he worked as a journalist and was active in socialist politics. World War I brought about a decisive change in Mussolini's life. He abandoned socialism and became an ardent nationalist.

During the war, Mussolini developed new ideas about government. He called his theories **fascism.**[4] Fascism was a political creed that supported the unity of all social groups under the control of the nation-state. Mussolini later defined it as "the dictatorship of the state over many cooperating classes."

Fascism gave the state absolute authority and the right to rule by force. Like communism, fascism was a totalitarian system of government. But unlike communism, to which it was bitterly opposed, fascism backed capitalistic principles. It supported the economic goals of the upper and middle classes.

In addition, fascism was extremely nationalistic. According to its principles, the cause of the nation was to be advanced at all cost. War and conquest were glorified as means of achieving national goals.

Road to Power

After World War I, Italy faced many strikes in its leading industries. Inspired by the Bolshevik

---

[4] The term "fascism" comes from the Latin word *fasces,* a bundle of sticks that was the symbol of power in ancient Rome.

While fascism became popular in Italy, the rest of the world was slow to understand it.

Mussolini wrote that fascism "was born of the need for action." Ask students to explain this.

Fascists adopted the fasces, *the ancient Roman symbol of strength through unity, and greeted each other with the Roman salute. What did this poster intend to convey about Mussolini to the Italian people?*

Revolution, workers often shut down production and took over factories. In the rural areas, peasants seized land from wealthy landowners. Tenant farmers refused to pay their rents. As a result of this unrest, the upper and middle classes feared a Communist revolution. However, the Italian Communist party was not strong enough to be a threat in Italy.

Dissatisfaction was also widespread among rightists. Ex-soldiers and Italian nationalists were bitterly disappointed with the results of the peace conference at Versailles. Italy had expected to receive huge portions of territory from the Central Powers. Instead, it only gained a small part of Austrian territory.

Mussolini was a clever politician. He played upon Italian fears of communism, emphasizing a tough law and order program. He vowed to end social unrest and protect private property. He pleased nationalists by pledging to restore Italy's greatness. To woo workers from revolution, he promised full employment and workers' benefits, such as old-age pensions and insurance.

By 1921 fascism had become a major political movement in Italy. Mussolini adopted the black shirt as part of the uniform of the Fascist party. The Black Shirts, as Mussolini's young followers were called, did more than talk. Squads of them beat up their political opponents on the streets. They also broke up political rallies and labor strikes. Legally elected officials opposed to fascism were driven from office.

When the democratic government failed to act against the Black Shirts, Mussolini grew bolder. In October 1922 the Fascists staged a huge march on Rome. From all directions, Fascists descended on the capital. To many Italians, it appeared that the Fascists were planning to seize power. Mussolini stayed behind in Milan, waiting to see how the government would react.

The government, largely made up of middle-class officials, was caught in its own trap. It had not moved on the Fascists, believing that fascism was useful in controlling the socialists and the workers. Now Mussolini was turning against the government. The cabinet asked King Victor Emmanuel III to declare martial law, or rule by the army—in order to meet the Fascist threat. The king refused and the cabinet resigned. Instead of calling for new elections, the monarch named Mussolini as prime minister.

Mussolini's Dictatorship

Mussolini set out to end Italian democracy. In a 1924 election, the Fascists won a majority in the Italian parliament. Their victory was helped by the brutal tactics of Black Shirts at the polls who made sure that Italians voted for Fascist candidates. With a Fascist-controlled parliament, Mussolini was able to gain sweeping powers that gave his decrees the force of law. Mussolini began calling himself Il Duce, "The Leader." He was now dictator of Italy.

As dictator, Mussolini crushed all opposition to his rule. Non-Fascist parties and political organizations were banned. Books and newspapers were censored, and freedom of speech was ended. All labor unions were brought under the control of the government.

Corporate State   Mussolini reorganized the Italian government, calling it the **corporate state.** Under the new system, the practice of representation by political party and geographical area

During Mussolini's rule, the Pope recognized Italian unity. In return, Italy set up Vatican City in the heart of Rome as an independent state under the Pope.

The Spartacist League was named for Spartacus, a slave of ancient Rome who led a rebellion in 72 B.C.

was ended. Instead, **syndicates,** or corporations of workers, employers, and government officials, were formed in each industry. They sent representatives to a legislature in Rome that set policies on wages, production, and distribution. Under the corporate state, Mussolini hoped to bring labor and employers together and to end the political quarreling that he associated with democracy. In theory, the corporate state was a new form of democracy; in practice, it was a political tool for fostering Mussolini's power.

Reaction   Fascism was popular in Italy during the 1920's and 1930's. Many Italians believed that Mussolini had brought order to the nation and had prevented a Communist revolution. They said that he "made the trains run on time." Mussolini's policy of strengthening the armed forces helped solve the unemployment problem. Other Italians, however, were saddened by the loss of democracy and were bitterly opposed to fascism. During Mussolini's rule, thousands of them were arrested, beaten, and murdered.

Foreign Affairs   Mussolini favored an Italian foreign policy based on conquest and military glory. He made himself commander in chief of the armed forces. All of Italy's economic and human resources were used to make Italy a "great power." Mussolini told Italians that it was their destiny to recapture the greatness of ancient Rome. Many Italians enjoyed the increased feelings of patriotism and nationalism that were part of the Fascist program. In doing so, they ignored the course toward war that Mussolini's government had taken.

1. Identify: Benito Mussolini, Black Shirts, Victor Emmanuel III, Il Duce.
2. What problems faced Italy after World War I?
3. How did the Black Shirts undermine democracy in Italy?
4. Why was fascism popular with the Italian people?

4   Nazi Germany

After World War I, the Allies wanted to make sure that Germany would never again threaten the European balance of power. The Versailles treaty limited the size of the German armed forces and required the Germans to form a democratic government.

The German people, however, had no experience with democracy. When faced by economic crisis, they turned to a strong leader who promised to restore Germany's greatness. As a result, German democracy was destroyed by one of history's most brutal totalitarian dictatorships.

The Weimar Republic

After World War I, political chaos swept Germany. A provisional government, which had taken over after William II's abdication, did not have strong support. In January 1919, a Communist group called the Spartacist League tried to seize power. The uprising was soon crushed, but it brought fear to Germany. Many Germans believed that revolution from Russia would spread throughout Europe.

In early 1919, elections were held for an assembly to write a democratic constitution for Germany. The meetings were held in the city of Weimar. In July, work on the constitution was completed, establishing a democratic republic. The republic, which lasted from 1919 to 1933, was called the Weimar Republic.

Trials of Democracy

The Weimar Republic faced many challenges. The German economy suffered from high unemployment and inflation. Political instability and violence threatened the young democracy.

The republic's first test came in 1920. A group of royalist army officers tried to overthrow the government. Like many Germans, they claimed that the democratic parties had betrayed the nation by accepting the Versailles treaty. The revolt was put down, but it showed a major weakness of the republic. Democracy in Germany did not come from the free choice of the people but was imposed by military defeat.

Reparations   Under the terms of Versailles, Germany had to make reparations to the Allies. In 1921 it was decided that Germany owed the Allies $35 billion—an impossible amount to repay. In 1922 the German government announced that it would not be able to pay.

Point out that the Allies—Britain, France, and Belgium—could not pay their war debts to the United States unless they collected reparations from Germany.

After the war Munich swarmed with many secret societies led by people discontented with the republic.

France, however, insisted that Germany meet its obligations. In 1923 French troops marched into Germany's industrial Ruhr Valley and took control of the coal mines and steel mills. Angered at the French invasion, German workers went on strike while their government paid them. With income from Ruhr industries going to France, Germany had lost an important asset.

Inflation   To meet expenses, the German government kept printing paper money at a fast rate. The result was inflation at a dizzying level. Soon German money became worthless. Before World War I, four marks, or German units of currency, equaled one American dollar. By the end of 1923, it took 4 trillion marks to equal one dollar.

The inflation had severe consequences in Germany. To members of the middle class, it was a disaster. In a short time, their hard-earned savings became worthless. To people who owed money, the inflationary spiral was a welcome relief. They could pay off debts with worthless money. However, in general, the German economy was disrupted by the chaos; middle-class confidence in democracy was badly shaken.

Brief Recovery   The middle and late 1920's saw some relief in Germany from economic and political troubles. By 1924 economic order had been restored. The French left the Ruhr after a compromise was reached that eased German reparations payments. Freed of debt and strengthened by American loans, Germany entered a five-year period of prosperity.

During this period, Germany saw its position in foreign affairs improve. In 1925 it signed treaties at Locarno, Switzerland, with France and Belgium. The Locarno agreement guaranteed each country's borders and opened the way for friendlier relations between Germany and its western neighbors.

Rise of Nazism

Among the many new political parties that appeared in Germany after the war was a small nationalist group called the National Socialist Workers' party. From the German pronunciation of the first two syllables of the word "national," the party got a shorter name—Nazi.

Inflation was so high in Germany, that workers demanded their pay daily because money lost value and bought less each succeeding day. In 1923, how many marks were needed to equal the value of one United States dollar?

One of the first recruits to the new party was a World War I veteran named Adolf Hitler. Born in Austria in 1889, Hitler as a young man failed to make a career for himself as an artist. After serving in a German regiment during the war, Hitler settled in the southern German city of Munich. There, he joined the Nazi party and soon became its leader.

Brown Shirts   Under Hitler's direction, young German veterans and street thugs formed a private army. They were known as the Brown Shirts because of their uniform. In 1923 Hitler and the Brown Shirts tried to seize power in Munich. In a beer hall, with armed Brown Shirts outside, Hitler jumped on a table, fired a gun at

Hitler was sentenced to five years but only served less than one year before his release.

the ceiling, and announced "The national revolution has begun!" The Brown Shirts then marched on the government buildings, but the police stopped them and made arrests. For his part in the Beer Hall Putsch,[5] Hitler spent ten months in prison.

Nazi Beliefs   While in prison, Hitler wrote an autobiography, *Mein Kampf (My Struggle)*. In the book, Hitler described the main ideas of nazism. He believed that the Germans were better than any other people. According to Hitler, they were a "master race" that deserved to rule the world. Bitter at Germany's defeat in World War I, Hitler blamed the Jews and other racial and political minorities for Germany's problems. He stated that the German people had not caused their own defeat. They had been "stabbed in the back" by Jews and Communists, who had surrendered the country to the Allies.

Depression   In the four years after Hitler's imprisonment, Weimar Germany gradually recovered and the Nazis had little influence. Once out of jail, Hitler resumed leadership of the party. At this time, an economic depression struck Germany and the rest of the industrialized world.

The depression brought Hitler and the Nazis back into the center of German politics. Millions of Germans were out of work. Hitler blamed the depression on the Jews, and many Germans began to listen to him. In an election in 1928, the Nazis won only 12 seats in the Reichstag, or German parliament. In 1932 they won 207 seats and became the largest party in the Reichstag, although still far short of a majority.

In early 1933, political stalemate developed among Germany's many political parties. To resolve the crisis, the president of Germany asked Hitler to become chancellor. Through entirely legal means, the Nazis had come to power in Germany.

Hitler in Power   After Hitler assumed power, the Nazis were still a minority in the Reichstag. Hitler planned to hold a new election. A week before the election, the Reichstag building mysteriously caught fire and burned to

the ground. Without any evidence, Hitler claimed that the fire was the work of Communists who wanted to seize power. He hoped to reduce Communist support among workers.

Through pressure by the Brown Shirts, German voters were forced to back the Nazis in the election. Although Hitler still did not have a solid majority, he won enough support to carry out his program. As soon as the new Reichstag met, Hitler had the legislators vote him emergency powers to deal with the "Communist threat." He became dictator of Germany and began the Nazi revolution.

The Third Reich

Hitler called his government the Third Reich.[6] *Reich* is the German word for empire. Hitler boasted that the Third Reich would last for 1,000 years. As head of Germany, Hitler took the title of "The Leader," or *Der Führer* in German. He banned all political parties except the Nazi party. The constitution of the Weimar Republic with its guarantees of freedom of speech, assembly, religion, and press was also discarded. Labor unions and other organizations were placed under Nazi leadership.

Hitler directed his most bitter attacks against the Jews. In 1935 the Nuremberg Laws were announced that stripped Jews of their citizenship. Jews were no longer allowed to hold public office or any government post. They were forbidden to marry non-Jews. Jewish students were barred from schools. Jewish businesses were strictly controlled or destroyed. All Jews were forced to wear a yellow star on their clothing when out in public.

These measures were only the "official laws" against the Jews. Nazi thugs routinely terrorized Jews. They attacked them on the streets and vandalized their businesses, homes, and synagogues. Hitler's secret police, the Gestapo, arrested Jews and other opponents of the government by the thousands. Many were shot. Others were sent to large prisons called **concentration camps.**

---

[5] *Putsch* is a German word meaning "overthrow."

[6] The First Reich was the Holy Roman Empire in the Middle Ages. The Second Reich was the German Empire from 1871 to 1918.

By the middle 1930's Hitler gained the support of most elements of German society, including Junker landowners, the military, and industrialists. Most thought that Hitler could be useful to them. However, they soon discovered that they could not control Hitler.

The Nazis developed the art of propaganda and used it on an unprecedented scale to persecute Jews. Hitler claimed that all of the world's evils were due to the Jews who corrupted the values of a pure German society. In this exhibition of anti-Semitic posters, Jews were accused of being capitalists, yet communists; moneylenders, yet unemployed dependents living on German charity; controllers of the universities, yet uneducated rabble. How did the Nuremberg Laws reflect Nazi anti-Semitic policies?

Hitler was determined that there would be no opposition to his rule. Like Stalin, he was suspicious of even his closest supporters. Hitler particularly feared radical members among the Brown Shirts and set out to purge their ranks. One night in 1934, Hitler had the leaders and hundreds of Brown Shirts arrested and shot.

Assured of absolute power, Hitler began a program to make Germany a strong military power. The Treaty of Versailles had limited the size of the German army and the number of weapons it could have. But Hitler openly attacked the treaty and ignored its provisions. Under his orders, German factories began turning out guns, ammunition, airplanes, tanks, and other weapons. Hitler made no secret of his ambitions to expand Germany's territory. One Nazi slogan stated, "Today, Germany; tomorrow, the world!"

1. Identify: Weimar Republic, Ruhr Valley, Locarno, Nazi party, Adolf Hitler, Brown Shirts, Beer Hall Putsch, *Mein Kampf*, Reichstag, Third Reich, Der Führer, Nuremberg Laws, Gestapo.
2. Why did Germans form a democratic government after World War I?
3. Why did French troops march into the Ruhr?
4. How did inflation affect Germans?

5   Western Democracies

The victorious Allies paid a heavy price in winning World War I. Victory had drained the total resources of each nation. The peace conference at Versailles was dominated by one idea—that such a war should never happen again.

Peace, however, did not bring easy times to the leading western democracies: Britain, France, and the United States. In each country, the return of millions of soldiers to civilian life created unemployment and economic instability. Britain and France were seriously weakened after four years of fighting. The two decades that followed the war brought increasing economic and political strains. Though prosperity came to each country in the mid-1920's, it was quickly followed by a devastating economic depression. The depression further weakened the democracies. It hindered their ability to counter the rising totalitarian threat in Italy and Germany.

Britain

Britain faced a number of problems after World War I. These problems involved more than just a difficult adjustment to peace. The war had

Unemployment was so bad that there were some towns in which not a single wage earner had a full-time job.

brought a drastic change to Britain's place in the world. Before World War I, Britain was a leading economic power. British banks in London lent money to many countries all over the world. The war, however, brought the British heavy costs that they could not meet. As a result, Britain became a debtor instead of a creditor nation, with most of its debts being owed to American banks.

The war also cost Britain its privileged position in world trade. American and Japanese companies had captured many of Britain's overseas markets in the war years. Britain became hampered by the age of its factories. Countries that had industrialized later, like the United States and Japan, had newer factories that could produce goods at a lower cost. With the loss of overseas markets, unemployment soared in Britain. By 1921, more than 2 million British workers were out of work.

General Strike   Britain's economic woes reached a crisis in 1926. Coal miners had been engaged in a bitter strike for higher wages. The miners could not win their demands from the coal companies. However, they were successful in persuading more than half of the union

workers in Britain to join in a **general strike**. A general strike is one in which all or a large number of workers participate in order to bring pressure on the government. In the General Strike of 1926, the British government declared a state of emergency. Troops were called out to keep order and to run essential services. Soldiers drove buses, mined coal, delivered food, ran electrical power stations, and performed other jobs.

In the end, the general strike failed, and the workers' demands were not met. In 1927 Parliament passed the Trades Disputes Act, which made general strikes illegal and restricted the political activities of unions.

Political Changes   In spite of the failure of union activity, the working class in the 1920's changed the politics of Britain. During the decade, the Labor party replaced the Liberals as the second leading party of the country after the Conservatives. In 1924 and 1929, Labor governments were elected to office. Each time, King George V named the Scottish labor leader Ramsay MacDonald as prime minister. While in office, the Labor party did not have a clear

The General Strike of 1926 in Great Britain involved almost 3 million trade union members. During the strike, troops were sent to unload ships, convoy food supplies, and maintain other essential services. After nine days, the unions called off the strike with the understanding that negotiations between the workers and mine owners would be initiated. Though unsuccessful, the strike played an important role in Britain's trade union movement. How did the Trades Disputes Act affect trade unions?

Refer students back to the discussion on the Irish Question on pp. 445 and 446.

majority. It had to depend on Liberal votes to pass legislation in Parliament.

The election of Labor governments heartened British workers. It at first alarmed the Conservative party, which had the support of the upper and middle classes. However, once in power, MacDonald and other Labor leaders tempered many of their radical demands and proved to be moderate socialists.

Ireland   During and after the war, the British had to face the centuries-old Irish Question. Parliament had passed a home rule act for Ireland in 1914, but the law was never enforced. Meanwhile, Irish nationalists began to demand complete independence. During the Easter season of 1916, they staged the Easter Rebellion against British rule. In doing so, the Irish hoped to take advantage of Britain's preoccupation with the war. British forces put down the rebellion, but fighting resumed in 1919.

By 1921 the British had grown tired of fighting the Irish and agreed to a compromise. A treaty signed that year granted dominion status to the Catholic southern part of Ireland, which became known as the Irish Free State. The largely Protestant counties in the northern part of Ireland remained part of Britain. They were known as Ulster, or Northern Ireland.

In 1937 the Irish Free State received a new constitution. The name of the country was changed to Eire. Eire however remained a dominion with close military and economic ties to Britain.[7]

Empire to Commonwealth   During the 1920's and 1930's, Britain's empire underwent significant changes. After the war, Britain not only retained control of its colonial territories but even added more to its far-flung domain. However, the dominions, like Canada and Australia, emerged as completely independent states. Their involvement in the war in Britain's behalf had increased their sense of nationhood. After the mid-1920's, Britain recognized the right of the dominions to conduct their own foreign policies. In 1931 the British Parliament passed the Statute of Westminster. This law established

the Commonwealth of Nations, a voluntary association linking Britain and the dominions on an equal basis. The only tie binding the Commonwealth nations was a common allegiance to the British monarch, who was acknowledged as "Head of the Commonwealth."

France

Many battles of World War I had been fought in France. The French endured the destruction of their farmlands, forests, villages, and cities. France also suffered horrible casualties. Half of the French males who were between the ages of 18 and 32 in 1914 were killed in the fighting during World War I.

Troubled Years   Like Britain, France faced severe economic troubles after the war. It was badly in debt to the United States for war loans. French industry and agriculture were disrupted by the conflict. Unemployment and inflation brought hardships to the French people.

The 1920's and 1930's were marked by great political instability in France. Many political parties competed for votes. Each received seats in the national legislature according to its percentage of the vote. Since no party ever came close to a majority, governments were formed by coalitions of parties. Because of the number of parties involved in the government, prime ministers and cabinets changed frequently during this period.

France was also troubled by political extremism on both the left and the right. Communists and Socialists struggled for power against right-wing Fascist admirers of Mussolini. Both the left and the right viewed each other as the great enemy of the nation. Political violence became commonplace in many areas of France.

Popular Front   The political crisis reached a head in 1934. A government scandal caused a Fascist group to riot in Paris. Several people were killed. Left-wing groups rallied to defend the republic. Socialists and Communists came together in a political movement known as the Popular Front.

In a 1936 election, the Popular Front won enough votes to form a government. Leon Blum, the Socialist leader, became prime minister.

---

[7] In 1949 Eire ended its dominion status and became the Republic of Ireland.

The Maginot Line was built under the direction of André Maginot, French minister of war.

Maginot Line

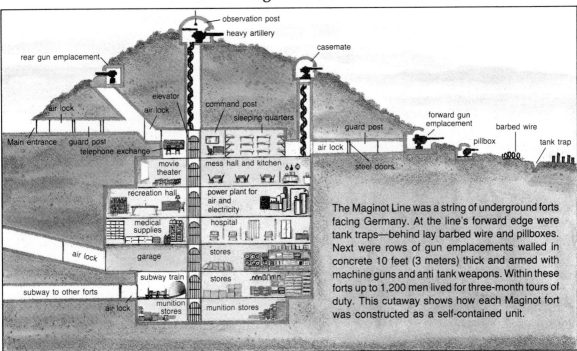

observation post
heavy artillery
casemate
rear gun emplacement
elevator
air lock
air lock
command post
sleeping quarters
forward gun emplacement
barbed wire
guard post
air lock
pillbox
tank trap
Main entrance
guard post
telephone exchange
steel doors
movie theater
mess hall and kitchen
recreation hall
power plant for air and electricity
hospital
medical supplies
stores
air lock
garage
stores
subway train
subway to other forts
munition stores
air lock
munition stores

The Maginot Line was a string of underground forts facing Germany. At the line's forward edge were tank traps—behind lay barbed wire and pillboxes. Next were rows of gun emplacements walled in concrete 10 feet (3 meters) thick and armed with machine guns and anti tank weapons. Within these forts up to 1,200 men lived for three-month tours of duty. This cutaway shows how each Maginot fort was constructed as a self-contained unit.

The Popular Front ruled for less than a year. But in that short time, many new laws were passed that helped French workers and farmers. Workers won wage increases; unions were able to negotiate with employers on an equal basis; farmers were able to sell their surplus wheat to the government.

Foreign Policy   In foreign affairs, France had one goal: to prevent another war. To protect its national security, France backed the League of Nations and worked to create a system of alliances that would restrain Germany. However, the French also sought friendly ties with the Weimar Republic. In 1928 France signed a series of treaties at Locarno, Switzerland, with other European countries, including Germany. These agreements guaranteed existing national boundaries. They also rejected war as a means of settling differences.

As insurance against any future German invasion, France built a series of fortifications 200 miles (320 kilometers) long called the Maginot Line. This stretch of concrete bunkers and trenches extended along France's border with Germany. French military leaders boasted that the Maginot Line could never be crossed and was an effective barrier to any invader. However, they neglected to mention that each past German invasion had come through the neutral country of Belgium, whose border with France was virtually undefended.

The United States

The United States was involved in only the last two years of World War I. No battles were fought on American soil. American casualties were far fewer than those of the other major powers. Like the other belligerent nations, the United States had mobilized all of its people and resources for the conflict. Yet, its physical distance from the fighting and its late entry helped the United States avoid the economic losses that affected other lands. In fact, the United States emerged from the war in a much stronger position.

Foreign Ties   In the four years of World War I, the United States had changed its financial

All through October 1929 stock prices slipped. On October 29, 1929, the stock market "crashed."

relationship to Europe. Before the war, it owed European nations about $4 billion. After the war, European countries owed the United States $10 billion. American banks had lent billions to the Allies to fight the war. While French and British industry were weaker after the conflict, American industry and agriculture had grown tremendously during this time.

America's war involvement and strong economy increased its influence in foreign affairs. President Wilson proposed a greater world role for the United States by having it join the League of Nations. However, the Treaty of Versailles, which established the League, was rejected by the United States Senate. Many Americans still supported the policy of isolationism that had been introduced during the early years of the republic.

Isolationism meant that the United States was to avoid becoming involved in alliances with European nations. But in 1919 the United States was a very different country from what it had been in 1797. After World War I, it was an industrial and military power upon which the rest of the world depended. The absence of the United States from such international organizations as the League of Nations made those bodies significantly weaker.

Social Changes   Beginning in 1919, Americans largely concentrated on their own internal affairs. The war had opened new prospects for economic development at home. During the following decade, new technology and consumer goods changed the lifestyles of many Americans. In the 1920's, cars, telephones, radios, and movies all brought Americans closer together. Before this time, the United States had been a country of different regions. Now it had acquired a more national culture.

The 1920's were a time of prosperity for many Americans. Buying on credit, a system previously reserved for the rich, came into general use. People bought cars, appliances, and other goods on the installment plan. Many people made money on the stock market. They bought stocks on credit. The plan was called **buying on the margin.** The buyer paid a small amount of the total worth of the stocks, hoping that the stock

market would continue to go up. If it did, the buyer would pay for the stock bought on the margin and make a profit, too. If the market went down, the buyer immediately had to pay in full for the stock bought on the margin—a **margin call.** But, in the 1920's, it seemed that the market could only go in one direction—up. Americans were confident that the good times would last forever.

The Crash   In October 1929, the unthinkable happened: the stock market crashed. Within a few weeks, stocks lost more than 40 percent of their value. Billions of dollars were lost. The whole economy came down like a house of cards.

With the development of sound movies in the late 1920's, movies and movie stars became an important part of American life. What other technological advances of the period changed the lifestyles of many Americans?

SCIENCE AND TECHNOLOGY

Mass Communications

The 1920's and 1930's were the beginning of the age of mass communication. During this time, radio brought major changes in daily life throughout the western world. It brought a tremendous variety of information and entertainment to millions of people for the first time. It enabled people to learn about news and sports events as they occurred or shortly afterward.

Radio broadcasting began on a large scale in North America and Europe during the 1920's. Networks developed that linked radio stations in various cities. In the United States, radio programs were paid for by advertisers who sponsored commercials. In most other countries, radio received most of its funds from the government.

The period from 1925 to 1950 is often called the golden age of radio broadcasting. Radio became the major source of family entertainment. Every night families gathered in their homes to listen to comedy skits, adventure dramas, sportscasts, and music. Radio started the careers of leading show business personalities.

Political leaders understood the importance of radio. In democratic countries, they used radio to take government policies directly to the people. United States President Franklin D. Roosevelt held informal talks on the radio called fireside chats. The talks did much to help gain public support for the New Deal. In totalitarian countries, radio and newspapers were controlled by governments to spread propaganda and enforce loyalty. Hitler and Mussolini appeared at large outdoor rallies and gave rousing speeches, which were broadcast throughout their nations.

During this period, another device of mass communication—television—was invented. Since the late 1800's, electrical engineers had tried to send pictures through the air. A working television system was finally developed in 1926 by John Logie Baird, a Scottish engineer. Experimental television broadcasts were made in Britain and the United States during the 1930's. However, it was not until after World War II that television replaced radio as the leading source of news and entertainment.

1. Why are the 1920's and 1930's known as the golden age of radio?
2. How did political leaders use radio?

In 1920 the first major radio broadcasts were made in Europe and in the United States. Within a short time the varied interests of people were catered to as listening to the radio became a major leisure time activity. Direct reporting of the World Series and football "bowl" games captured sports fans. Famous comedians, like Jack Benny and Bob Hope, entertained tens of thousands weekly, while the music of famous band leaders, like Harry James and Duke Ellington, was brought into most American homes.

Have students draw up a list of questions to be used to interview people who lived through the depression. Use the interviews as the basis of a class discussion.

During the Great Depression, millions of unemployed lost their homes. Shanty towns like these in the United States (left) and Germany (right) sprang up in most industrialized countries of the world. In what year did the depression reach its peak?

Millions of shareholders were faced with margin calls that they could not meet. They lost everything. People who had made millions found themselves penniless almost overnight.

The stock market crash was only the beginning of the economic collapse. From 1929 to 1932, thousands of banks were forced to close when they could not pay their depositors. People lost all their savings. Few people had the money to buy consumer goods, so manufacturers were left with huge inventories they could not sell. Factories closed, and people lost their jobs. The downward spiral continued, reaching its worst point in 1932 when more than 25 percent of American workers were unemployed. From the good times of the 1920's, the United States had entered the worst economic depression in its history.

The depression quickly spread from the United States to other areas of the industrialized world. Trade and production declined, and millions suffered hardships.

Causes The depression caught many people by surprise, but several causes were soon evident. First, the American prosperity of the 1920's was largely an illusion. Americans did make money in the stock market. But throughout the decade workers' wages lagged behind rising prices. Second, the buying power of American consumers was based on credit, not real strength in the economy. The liberal use of credit was based on the idea that the economy would continue to grow. Third, American farmers had a particularly hard time in the 1920's. Farm prices were so low that farmers often lost money on their crops. They were forced to borrow more and more just to stay in business.

Fourth, in the 1920's, the United States had economically isolated itself from the rest of the world. It had the highest tariffs in its history, making foreign goods very expensive. Real prosperity requires the unrestricted flow of goods between nations. But, in the 1920's, the United States and other industrial powers were more concerned about foreign competition. To protect their own farms and industries, they imposed high tariffs on imports.

Government Reaction In the first years of the depression, the United States government did very little to remedy the problem. American politicians and business leaders believed that the bad times "had to be ridden out" and that government should not interfere in business affairs. There were no government programs to provide relief. Great Britain and Germany had national programs of unemployment insurance

There were two types of New Deal programs, emergency measures and long-range planning.

Countries represented at the Washington Conference on the Limitations of Armaments included the United States, Great Britain, France, Belgium, Japan, Holland, Portugal, and China.

Roosevelt's New Deal was often strongly criticized. Some thought the New Deal did too little, while others believed it did too much. When it failed to bring a quick end to the depression, criticism increased. Many Americans wre concerned about the trend toward big government and a welfare state. Some business people and conservatives even expressed fears that, if not checked, the New Deal could lead to totalitarian rule in the United States. What was the major accomplishment of the New Deal?

and help for the needy. But similar programs did not exist in the United States.

In the opinion of many American political leaders, direct relief was not the responsiblity of the national government but of the individual, the family, and the local community. Government-funded relief, they believed was a step towards socialism. It would destroy American self-reliance and self-esteem. In their view, it would also put a halt to voluntary action and many democratic institutions.

The New Deal   In 1932, American voters elected a new president, Franklin D. Roosevelt. Roosevelt had campaigned on the promise of "a new deal" for the American people. Believing that the economic crisis was worse than any other in American history, he decided to involve the Federal Government in aiding the economy and providing relief to the unemployed.

In the first 100 days of his administration, Roosevelt sent a number of bills to Congress that quickly became law. These measures regulated the banks and the stock market. They established production guidelines for industry and agricul-

ture. Programs were also created that helped put people back to work. The United States government began public works projects to build roads, dams, bridges, homes, and parks. Later New Deal legislation provided for social security, unemployment insurance, and the right of unions to organize and negotiate with management.

Roosevelt's New Deal policies were not entirely successful in ending the depression. In 1938 production fell and unemployment rose again. But the New Deal did much to restore the confidence of the nation and lessen human suffering. The New Deal had an impact in other ways. It expanded the role of the Federal Government in American society. It also made both government and business responsible for the performance of the economy.

Foreign Affairs   Despite its rejection of the Versailles Treaty, the United States was active in diplomacy in the 1920's and 1930's. In 1921 an international conference was held in Washington, D.C., to promote **disarmament,** or the reduction of military weapons. The United States

The Kellogg-Briand Pact, also known as the Pact of Paris, gave people around the world hope that there would be no more war.

signed a treaty with Japan and Britain limiting the growth of naval warships. The leading powers at the Washington conference agreed to respect one another's island possessions in the Pacific. They promised to settle disagreements that occurred in that area by conciliatory negotiations rather than by military means. They also pledged to guarantee China's independence and to respect the Open Door Policy in that country.

In 1928 the United States and France signed an agreement called the Kellogg-Briand Pact. The agreement said that war would be an illegal means of settling international disputes. Eventually, 62 nations signed the agreement, but it was nothing more than a statement of intentions. It had no powers of enforcement.

During the 1930's, Americans were hopeful of avoiding a future world war. But, like the other democracies, they were not prepared to act once the aggressive aims of Germany, Italy, and Japan became known.

The graphs below are subjects of the "Using Graphs" section of the Chapter 26 Review.

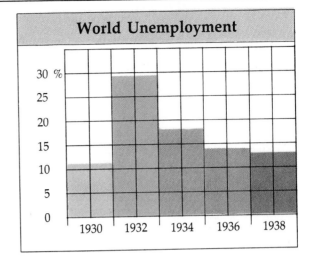

1. Identify: Trade Disputes Act, Ramsay MacDonald, Easter Rebellion, Irish Free State, Ulster, Popular Front, Leon Blum, Maginot Line, Franklin D. Roosevelt, New Deal, Kellogg-Briand Pact.
2. Why did British workers engage in a general strike in 1926?
3. Why did the French build the Maginot Line? What was its weakness?
4. Why did the United States Senate reject the Treaty of Versailles? How did the United States conduct foreign policy after 1919?

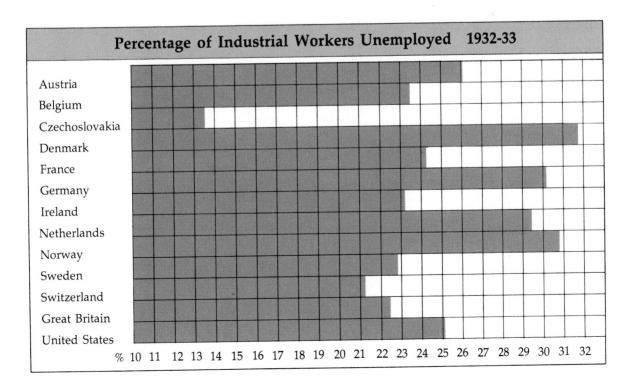

CHAPTER 26 REVIEW

Summary

1. Following World War I, totalitarian governments arose in Russia, Italy, and Germany, which challenged the western democracies.
2. Two revolutions took place in Russia in 1917. The tsar was replaced by a provisional government in March, and the Bolsheviks seized power from the provisional government in November.
3. The Russian Civil War in 1918 pitted the Reds (Bolsheviks) against the Whites. The Red Army prevailed despite aid given to the Whites by the United States and other nations.
4. Vladimir I. Lenin changed the name of Russia to the Union of Soviet Socialist Republics (U.S.S.R.) and introduced his New Economic Policy (NEP).
5. Joseph Stalin won the struggle with Leon Trotsky to succeed Lenin. He introduced Five-Year Plans that centralized industry and agriculture. Stalin created a dictatorship of fear.
6. In 1922 Benito Mussolini came to power in Italy. His Fascist government crushed all opposition and introduced the corporate state to Italy. Mussolini rearmed Italy and prepared for war.
7. From 1919 to 1933, Germany was ruled by a democratic government called the Weimar Republic. In 1923 the republic survived attempted takeovers and terrible economic conditions.
8. In 1933, Adolf Hitler, leader of the Nazi party, was named chancellor of Germany. Hitler demanded emergency powers and made himself dictator. His government, the Third Reich, eliminated any opposition and violently persecuted the Jews. Hitler began to rearm Germany.
9. After World War I, Britain lost its dominant position in world trade, and it was tested by labor struggles and political changes.
10. France went through a period of political instability after World War I. It built the Maginot Line in hope of preventing another German invasion.
11. The United States emerged from World War I as the leading financial and industrial nation in the world.
12. The stock market crash of 1929 brought on the worst economic depression in history. Promising Americans a "new deal," Franklin D. Roosevelt was elected president in 1932.

Building Vocabulary

totalitarianism
ideology
communism
dictatorship of the proletariat
war communism
nationalized

permanent revolution
collectivization
kulaks
purge
fascism
corporate state

syndicates
concentration camps
general strike
buying on the margin
margin call
disarmament

Reviewing the Main Ideas

1. How did Lenin come to power in Russia during the Russian Revolution?
2. Why were the Reds successful in the Russian Civil War?

3. How did the Communist state deal with the nationalities question?
4. What was the main dispute between Trotsky and Stalin?
5. How did Stalin turn the U.S.S.R. into an industrial nation?
6. What was the role of the state under a fascist government?
7. What role did Communists play in Mussolini's and Hitler's rise to power?

8. How did World War I affect Britain's position in world trade?
9. What was the source of hostility between Ireland and Britain?
10. Why were there so many changes in government in France after World War I?
11. What were the causes of the depression?
12. How did the New Deal change the relationship between business and government in the United States?

Discussing Important Ideas

1. In what ways did the Russian Revolution of 1917 differ from revolutions in the United States and France?
2. Do you think the U.S.S.R. was more a socialist state under Lenin, or under Stalin?
3. If Trotsky had defeated Stalin, do you think his administration would have ruled differently? If not, why not? If so, in what ways?
4. What factors led to the emergence of totalitarian states in the Soviet Union, Italy, and Germany after World War I?

5. What were the strengths and weaknesses of the totalitarian states under Stalin, Mussolini, and Hitler?
6. Do you think war was an inevitable result of Mussolini's and Hitler's policies? Explain your answer.
7. How did the existence of many political parties in France and Germany weaken democracy in both countries?
8. What were the effects of the depression on governments in Germany, Italy, and the United States?

Using Graphs

Refer to the graph at the bottom of page 613 to answer the following questions:
1. What does each horizontal bar represent?
2. What do the numbers along the bottom of the graph represent?
3. Why do you think the period between 1932 and 1933 is used for this graph in this chapter?

4. In which country was unemployment the highest? the lowest?
5. What was the unemployment rate in Germany, France, Great Britain, and the United States between 1932 and 1933?
6. What does this graph suggest about the condition of industry in western Europe between 1932 and 1933?

CHAPTER 27

Battle Against Colonialism

" In the construction of a country it is not the practical workers but the idealists and planners that are difficult to find. "

Sun Yat-sen, Chinese nationalist (1866-1925)

Nationalism Between the Wars

In 1914 nearly 85 percent of the world's land was under the economic or political control of the West. However, by the end of World War I, it seemed that European influence throughout the world was in decline. As a result, many national leaders in Asia, Africa, and Latin America hoped that their lands would gain greater freedom from foreign control.

The United States officially disowned imperialism and began to back the spread of democracy to other lands. In 1918 United States President Woodrow Wilson supported **self-determination,** or the right of national groups to set up independent nations. After the war, the principle of self-determination was applied only to Europe. However, peoples elsewhere expected that it would soon be applied to them. During the 1920's and 1930's, struggles for independence took place in South and East Asia, the Middle East, Africa, and Latin America.

1 Nationalism in South and East Asia

Throughout Asia, opposition to colonial rule dramatically increased after World War I. Organized independence movements emerged that resisted and disrupted the policies of European colonial rulers.

India

During World War I, India had provided 1.5 million soldiers and furnished large sums of money for the British war effort. These contributions, together with Allied support of self-determination, gave many Indians the hope of obtaining **swaraj,** or independence. After the war, the Indian National Congress party, the leading nationalist group, staged demonstrations throughout India.

To maintain control, the British passed the Rowlatt Acts in 1919. These laws gave police in India the right to jail without trial anyone suspected of anti-British activities. Angered by the Rowlatt Acts, Indian nationalists successfully persuaded Indians to strike and fast in nonviolent protest.

Amritsar Massacre Throughout India, the protests against British policies were generally peaceful. However, violence occurred in the northern Indian city of Amritsar. There, several Britons were killed or injured. British soldiers responded by using force against a crowd of Indian demonstrators. In what became known as the Amritsar Massacre, British General Reginald Dyer ordered his troops to fire into the unarmed gathering until the ammunition ran out. The result was that 379 Indians were killed and over 1,200 Indians were wounded. The tragedy at Amritsar strengthened the determination of Indian nationalists to achieve independence.

Gandhi During this period, Mohandas K. Gandhi became the leading Indian nationalist. Born in India of middle-class parents in 1869, Gandhi had been educated in England. He later practiced law in South Africa, where he and other Indians experienced mistreatment because of their dark skin. Until 1914, Gandhi lived in South Africa and led protests against racial discrimination. He was a **pacifist,** or a person opposed to war or violent conflict. In keeping with his beliefs, Gandhi used protest methods,

Gandhi was a member of the Jain sect of Hinduism. See pp. 37 and 38 to explain Gandhi's non-violence.

Gandhi revived the art of homespinning and weaving cloth as a symbol for Indian unity. Gandhi himself wore nothing else. He hoped that Indians would develop their own textile industry to rival the British.

In 1924 Gandhi spoke to his followers in Calcutta, following his failed efforts to settle a dispute in the Indian National Congress party. He then fasted for three weeks to dramatize to the Indian people his methods of non-violence. In 1932 Gandhi fasted in jail to protest British discrimination against the "untouchables," members of the lowest Hindu caste. The Indian public rose to the support of their respected leader, forcing the British government to revise its policy. What changes did the British make in the mid-1930's that moved India toward self-government?

such as the boycott and **civil disobedience,** or the refusal to obey laws that are considered unjust. When Gandhi returned to India, he led a nonviolent movement for self-government and for greater tolerance among the country's many social and religious groups.

Gandhi's understanding of India's problems made him popular throughout the country. The Indian people called Gandhi *Mahatma,* meaning "Great Soul." His doctrine of moral nonviolent protest, known as **satyagraha,** or "soul force," won him international attention. "I personally would wait, if need be, for ages," he said, "rather than seek to obtain the freedom of my country through bloody means."

Using satyagraha, Gandhi hoped to convince the British to leave India. He and his followers refused to cooperate with the British administration. They decided not to participate in the local legislative assemblies that the British had introduced to appease the Indians. Gandhi also led boycotts against British control of the Indian economy. In support of the local textile industry, he convinced Indian people not to buy or use cotton goods made in Britain. This stand had a profound influence on the British, who exported much of their cotton cloth to India. Gandhi revived the art of spinning and weaving as a

symbol of Indian national unity. Homespun was widely proclaimed as the only proper dress for real Indian patriots. Gandhi himself wore nothing else.

Toward Independence   In 1930 Gandhi carried out one of his most dramatic acts of civil disobedience. He led hundreds of followers on a 200-mile (320-kilometer) march to the sea, where they made salt from seawater. This action was a protest against the Salt Act, which made it a crime to possess salt not bought from the government. The march was followed by widespread civil disobedience.

Under pressure from Gandhi's movement, the British began to make changes. In 1935 Parliament passed the Government of India Act. This measure placed agriculture, education, public health, and public works under the control of 11 provincial councils. The British government retained control of national lawmaking, finance, defense, and foreign affairs.

The majority of Indian nationalists at first rejected the act, wanting complete independence. However, the Indian National Congress party, at the insistence of Gandhi, finally accepted it as a first step toward self-government. The Indian historian K. M. Panikkar states that with the Government of India Act, "British

There was a period of political turmoil in China after the overthrow of the Manchu dynasty and the death of provisional President Yuan Shih-kai.

Chiang had studied military science in Japan where he served in the Japanese army for two years.

authority in India was in full retreat, in the administrative field no less than in the political and economic fields." Nevertheless, independence was not yet won.

Hindu-Muslim Relations   Bitter relations between Hindus and Muslims posed the most difficult internal issue for Indian independence. The large Muslim minority feared being ruled by the Hindu majority. In 1937 the Indian National Congress party, controlled by Hindus, won election majorities in eight of the eleven provinces of India. Muslims came to power in the others. This heightened bitter feelings. The Muslim League, under Mohammed Ali Jinnah, split with the Congress party. It demanded a separate Muslim nation for the millions of Muslims in India. The Hindus, led by Jawaharlal Nehru, a follower of Gandhi, wanted a united India. Although a Hindu, Gandhi was concerned at the deepening rift between Hindus and Muslims. His pleas for toleration were largely ignored by both groups.

China

Near the close of World War I, China abandoned its neutrality and backed the Allies. When the war ended, Chinese leaders hoped that their stand in the conflict would give China equal status with the West. Their hopes were crushed at the Paris peace conference. China lost both prestige and territory. The peace conference handed over to Japan the northern Chinese province of Shandong, formerly controlled by Germany. Other major foreign powers were allowed to maintain extraterritorial rights in China. Deeply embittered, the Chinese refused to sign the Treaty of Versailles.

Kuomintang   Meanwhile, political turmoil swept China. The national government had no real power. Local military officials called **warlords** fought each other for control of the provinces. In southern China, the revolutionary leader Sun Yat-sen tried to establish order through his Kuomintang, or Nationalist, party. In 1924 Sun established a base of power at Guangzhou.

Sun Yat-sen realized that he needed his own army to defeat the warlords and to unite China.

To establish a military force, he turned to the Soviet Union. With the help of Soviet advisers, a Kuomintang army was organized in 1924. Sun appointed a young officer named Chiang Kai-shek to head the new army. Chiang succeeded to the leadership of the Kuomintang upon Sun's death in 1925.

Chiang hoped to establish a single national government in China under the Kuomintang. In a series of military campaigns, Chiang defeated the warlords. By 1928 the Kuomintang army had won control of the entire country. A new national government was set up at Nanjing.

Chinese Communists   While Chiang was gaining control of China, he had to deal with a rival political organization: the Chinese Communist party. The Chinese Communists, made up of intellectuals and urban workers, had organized in 1921. Many members of the party also belonged to the Kuomintang. In 1927 the Communists tried to win control of the Kuomintang, but failed. This led to a break between the two parties. To prevent any future takeovers,

In 1927 Kuomintang leader Chiang married Soong Meiling, the sister of Sun Yat-sen's wife. Chiang pledged to fulfill Sun's dream of a united nationalist China. How long did it take Chiang to honor his pledge?

Point out that estimates vary for the number of marchers and deaths during the Long March. Ask students how they think the Long March gave greater unity to the Communist movement in China.

Chiang's supporters purged the Kuomintang of Communists and Soviet advisers. Many Communists and suspected Communists were killed. Those that survived were forced into hiding. The Soviets fled home to the Soviet Union, while the Chinese Communists sought refuge in the mountains of southeastern China.

In its mountain retreat, the Communist leadership rebuilt the party and formed the Chinese Red Army. The two most powerful Communist leaders were Mao Tse-tung and Chu Teh. Mao was a former librarian, teacher, newspaper editor, and union organizer. Chu had studied in Europe and was a former commander in the Kuomintang army. Under their guidance, the Chinese Communists gained widespread support in rural areas. The party seized land from wealthy landlords and gave it to the peasants. Revising Marxist theory, Mao claimed that peasants, not workers, would lead the future Communist revolution in China.

Long March   Under Chiang Kai-shek, the Kuomintang had the backing of the upper and middle classes in China's cities. To regain control of certain rural areas, the Kuomintang began a series of military attacks against the Communists. At first the Chinese Red Army fought off Kuomintang forces. But in 1934 the Kuomintang army succeeded in removing the Communists from their mountain bases. To escape Chiang's army, Mao Tse-tung and about 90,000 followers retreated from southeastern China into the northeastern part of the country. Later known as the Long March, the Communist retreat covered over 5,000 miles (8,000 kilometers). Only 7,000 people survived the ordeal.

By marching to the northeast, the Chinese Communists were closer to Soviet supply lines and farther removed from Chiang's army. In this remote area, the Chinese Red Army regained its military strength. Mao emerged as the undisputed leader of the Chinese Communist Party.

In spite of their differences, Mao and Chiang had a common enemy in the Japanese. When the Japanese threat to China increased in the mid-1930's, the two Chinese leaders were forced into an uneasy alliance.

Japan

In World War I, Japan had fought on the side of the Allies. During the conflict, the Japanese supplied weapons to their European partners, particularly to Russia. At the same time, they took advantage of the war to expand their

On the Long March, the Communists were constantly pursued by the Kuomintang. They suffered great losses from daily bombings by Chiang's air force. Though he was seriously ill with a fever, Mao led the Communist retreat. He and his followers were plagued by heavy rains, flooded rivers, and marshes on the first half of their journey. Later, as they neared Tibet, thousands did not survive the 18 mountain crossings and the bitter cold. What advantages were there for the Communists in making the Long March?

Point out that changes in U.S. immigration policy were not directed toward the Japanese alone. Laws limited the number of European immigrants but barred all Asian immigration.

economic and political influence in East Asia. In addition to ruling Korea and Taiwan, Japan pressed for an enlargement of its role in China. In 1915 Japanese diplomats forced the Chinese government to accept a list of Twenty-one Demands. The Twenty-one Demands, in effect, made China a Japanese protectorate.

Japan and the West   When World War I ended, Japan received Germany's Pacific islands north of the equator as mandates from the League of Nations. The Japanese also entered into a series of military and commercial agreements with the western powers. Yet, in spite of these gains, the Japanese were bitter toward the West.

First, Japan felt that the West did not accept it as an equal. In 1919 the League of Nations, dominated by western powers, refused to accept a Japanese demand for a statement on racial equality in the League's charter. The Japanese regarded this rejection as a humiliation. In 1924 the United States banned further Japanese immigration to its shores. In response, the Japanese staged demonstrations and boycotted American goods.

Furthermore, the Japanese were angered over the West's refusal to support Japanese policy in China. While Japan wanted to tie China closer to itself, the West wanted to retain the Open Door policy. As a result of western pressure, Japan had to abandon the Twenty-one Demands and recognize western interests in China.

Internal Problems   After World War I, Japan faced mounting social and economic problems at home. Of major concern was a population explosion. Japan's population had increased from nearly 35 million in 1872 to about 60 million in 1925. This rate of increase was a problem because of the already high density of population on the Japanese islands. Since emigration was cut off to such places as the United States, the Japanese looked for other ways to cope. They placed renewed emphasis on manufacturing and foreign trade. It was hoped that new factories and markets would provide employment for larger numbers of people.

During the 1920's and 1930's, Japan's industry grew rapidly, and Japanese manufactured goods

To show their commitment to modernization, some Asian leaders granted voting rights to women after their countries became independent. However, Japanese women did not gain suffrage until 1945. What year could all Japanese men vote?

began to flood world markets. Increased manufacturing, however, stimulated the need for raw materials. Since Japan had few mineral resources of its own, it was forced to look overseas for them.

Meanwhile, Japan's working class increased in importance. Labor unions became more powerful and increased their membership to a third of a million members by the end of the 1920's. At the same time, steps were taken toward greater democracy. In 1925 the Japanese parliament granted universal male suffrage; voters increased from three to 14 million.

In spite of these gains, democracy remained very limited in Japan. Political power was in the hands of nobles and urban industrialists. The emperor, Hirohito, was a constitutional monarch. However, he was a powerful symbol of traditional authority. Behind the emperor was an influential group of military leaders, who were opposed to democratic reforms.

Militarism   During the 1930's, Japan's leaders became frustrated with their increasing

Refer students to the map of Japanese territorial expansion on p. 652.

In the picture below Kemal is wearing an astrakhan, not a fez. The hat is of Russian origin. It is made of wool.

problems at home and abroad. As a result, the government no longer followed a policy of democratic reform and cooperation with the West. Instead, it became more authoritarian and nationalistic. Attempts were made to limit western cultural influences. Increased attention was given to traditional Japanese values, such as physical courage and strict obedience to authority. Politicians lost their influence, and the military became the dominant group in the government. Under its new military leadership, Japan began to build up its military forces. It set out on a program of territorial expansion on the Asian continent. Japan's primary target was China, weakened by civil war and a backward economy.

1. Identify: Amritsar Massacre, Mohandas K. Gandhi, Salt Act, Government of India Act, Mohammed Ali Jinnah, Jawaharlal Nehru, Kuomintang, Chiang Kai-shek, Mao Tse-tung, Long March, Twenty-one Demands.
2. How did Gandhi seek to end British rule in India?
3. What actions did Chiang Kai-shek take to unite China?
4. How did Japan deal with the problems it faced during the 1920's and 1930's?

After World War I, the Ottoman sultan was unable to protect his empire from the Allies. Because of this, the Turks supported Mustapha Kemal's fight for independence. What did Kemal gain from the Allies in 1923?

2 Nation Building in the Middle East

After World War I, nationalism became a vital force in the Middle East. New nations—Turkey, Iran, and Saudi Arabia—developed in the region. They began to modernize their societies and economies. Other areas, mostly Arab, came under western European control. In Arab lands, strong nationalist movements developed to end western influence and win independence. In one region—Palestine—rivalry between Palestinian Arabs and Jewish immigrants for the same territory led to prolonged civil war.

Turkey

The end of World War I saw the breakup of the Ottoman Empire. Middle Eastern Arab lands, such as Syria, hoped for independence. Instead, they came under French or British rule. In Asia Minor, the Turks faced the threat of Allied occupation. British, French, and Italian troops captured parts of Asia Minor and landed forces in Istanbul. Meanwhile, a Greek army advanced into western Asia Minor, claiming a large area for Greece.

Turkish Nationalism   In August 1920, the sultan's government signed the Treaty of Sèvres with the Allies. The treaty formally ended the Ottoman Empire, reducing Turkish rule to Istanbul and part of Asia Minor. As a result of the agreement, the sultan's popularity declined. Mustapha Kemal, a Turkish war hero, quickly formed a republican nationalist movement in Asia Minor and rallied the country behind him. In September 1922, Kemal's nationalist forces drove the Greek armies from Asia Minor. A year later, the National Assembly abolished the Ottoman sultanate and proclaimed the Republic of Turkey. Kemal became its first president.

With a nationalist government firmly in power, Turkey sought better terms from the Allies. In 1923 it signed with them the Treaty of

As the first modern Middle Eastern leader, Atatürk set an example that many subsequent Middle Eastern leaders would attempt to follow.

Reza Khan led the Cossack Brigade, a palace guard set up by Tsar Alexander III in 1879 for the shah.

Lausanne. This agreement allowed the Turks all of Asia Minor and led to the withdrawal of Allied troops from the region.

In the new Turkish republic, the Turks were the dominant nationality. At the end of the struggle against the Greek army, the Turks had forced over a million Greeks in Asia Minor to move to Greece. This migration caused great hardship to the Greeks. However, the Turks regarded it as a necessary step to unite the country and to end foreign control.

Reforms   As president, Mustapha Kemal undertook sweeping changes. The Turks drew up a constitution and established a legal system based on western models. Turkey in theory became a democracy. It had a freely elected parliament and universal suffrage. To unite the country, the capital was moved from Istanbul to Ankara, a city with a central location in the heart of Asia Minor.

In his effort to modernize Turkey, Kemal reduced the influence of Islam. He ended Islam's status as a state religion and limited the authority of Muslim religious leaders. The government did away with some old traditions, such as the wearing of the veil by women and the **fez** by men.[1] It also outlawed polygamy and allowed women the right to vote and to hold public office.

Kemal and the nationalists introduced other changes. They adopted the western calendar, the Latin alphabet, and the metric system. They required all Turks to choose a family name, a western practice not previously used in Turkey. Kemal himself took as his last name Atatürk, which means "father of the Turks."

During the 1930's, the Turkish government introduced economic reforms. It raised tariffs to protect local industries and to reduce dependence on western imports. It began a five-year plan to increase industrial production. Though the plan was modeled on that of the Soviet Union, Atatürk refused to accept communism or any other foreign ideology. He and the Turkish nationalists wanted Turkey to be independent of foreign control.

---

[1] The fez is a brimless hat. It was popular among the upper classes of the Ottoman Empire. Turkish nationalists regarded the fez as a symbol of the old order that had to be discarded.

Iran

Like Turkey, Persia underwent swift political, economic, and social change after World War I. At the end of the war, Persia was still divided into British and Soviet spheres of influence. In separate treaties, signed in 1919 and 1921, Britain and the Soviet Union recognized the independence of Persia. But these agreements, according to Persian nationalists, still gave the British and the Soviets too much control over the affairs of the country. The nationalists wanted an end to all foreign influence.

In 1921 nationalist reformers backed an army officer named Reza Khan in an attack on the corrupt Persian monarchy. With 3,000 troops, Reza marched on Tehran, the capital, and

Once Reza Khan ascended Persia's celebrated Peacock Throne, he immediately lessened foreign control over the country. Why did the shah renegotiate oil contracts with foreign companies?

Jewish independence in Palestine had been destroyed by the Romans in 68 A.D.

established a new government. He wanted to set up a republic on the model of Atatürk's Turkey. However, Persia's powerful Muslim religious leaders opposed a secular republic. They feared that it would take away their authority over the people. In response, Reza threatened to resign his leadership. Fearing national chaos without Reza, the Majles, or Persian parliament, gave him the powers of a dictator. In 1923 Reza forced the **shah,** or king, to give up his throne. Two years later, Reza proclaimed himself shah and changed his family name to Pahlavi, the name of the ancient Persian language.

Reza Shah Pahlavi began a program of modernization similar to that of Atatürk. However, he was careful not to offend the religious leaders. The new shah moved to strengthen his authority by improving the military, building railroads, and paving highways. As a result of these measures, communication increased among the country's many ethnic and tribal groups.

Reza Shah also profited from the West's interest in Persia as a source of oil. Before World War I, western oil companies had acquired rights to drill for oil in the southern part of the country. Reza Shah renegotiated Persia's oil contracts in an attempt to gain higher revenues and to assert greater control over foreign companies. To emphasize his desire for a new modern country, Reza Shah supported the renaming of Persia. In 1935 the country became officially known as Iran.

In 1937 Iran concluded treaties with the neighboring countries of Afghanistan, Turkey, and Iraq. The four nations formed an alliance that worked to keep foreign influences out of the region. The alliance was shattered, however, with the beginning of World War II. Britain and the Soviet Union reentered Iran in 1941 to block German interests. They forced Reza Shah to abdicate. The British and the Soviets established a new Iranian government, one that cooperated with them during the war. The Iranian throne was given to Reza's 22-year-old son, Mohammed Reza Pahlavi. The new shah signed a treaty with Britain and the Soviet Union that permitted them to keep troops in Iran until the end of World War II.

Palestine

The Ottoman territory of Palestine came under the control of British forces during World War I. After the war, the Treaty of Sèvres made Palestine a British mandate under the League of Nations.

Promises   During the 1920's and 1930's, Palestine was claimed by both Arab and Jewish nationalists. Their claims were based on promises that the British had made to each during World War I. In 1915 the British had made vague promises of independence to the Arabs in return for their support against the Ottomans. The Arabs interpreted these promises to mean that all of Palestine would be Arab.

The British government had also sought Jewish support for the war effort. In 1917 the British government adopted the Balfour Declaration, named for the foreign secretary, Lord Arthur Balfour. The Declaration called for

> the establishment in Palestine of a national home for the Jewish people . . . it being clearly understood that nothing shall be done which may prejudice the civil and religious rights of existing non-Jewish communities in Palestine.

The British announcement encouraged the Zionists, or Jewish nationalists who wanted a homeland for their people.[2] In fact, when the Declaration was issued, there were already over 50,000 Zionists living in Palestine. Most of them had migrated there from eastern Europe before World War I. Nonetheless, they made up about 10 percent of the population, most of which was Arab.

Rivalry in Palestine   In 1920 the British set up a mandate government in Palestine. They soon faced a growing conflict between the Palestinian Arabs and the Jews. Arab nationalists opposed continued Jewish immigration and the purchase of Arab lands by Jewish settlers. They called upon Britain to stop the flow of Jewish

---

[2] In 1897 the Zionist movement was established by an international congress of Jewish leaders. Its chief organizer was an Austrian named Theodor Herzl. The term "Zionism" derives from the word "Zion," the name of a hill in Jerusalem on which the royal palace of David stood.

The map below is the subject of the "Using Maps" section of the Chapter 27 Review.

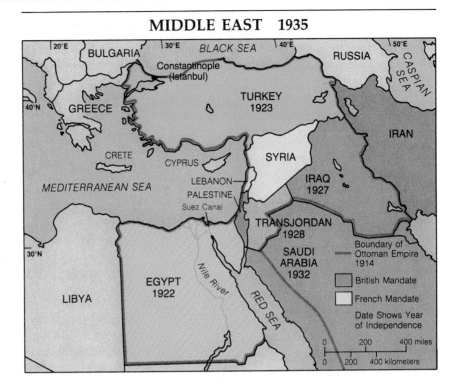

MIDDLE EAST 1935

immigrants. However, the British agreed only to limit it. This decision pleased neither Jews nor Arabs. The Arabs staged protests and attacked Jewish settlements. The Jews armed themselves against these attacks and rioted against the British restriction of immigration.

The Arab-Jewish rivalry in Palestine increased in bitterness during the 1930's. After 1933, many Jews began arriving in Palestine to escape Nazi persecution in Europe. By the mid-1930's, almost one-third of Palestine's population was Jewish. The Arabs feared that the Jews would eventually take over the region. They stepped up their attacks on Jewish settlements and businesses.

In 1936 the British government appointed a commission under Lord William Peel to investigate the situation in Palestine. The Peel Commission concluded that the country should be divided into separate Arab and Jewish states. Britain was to retain a mandate only over Jerusalem, Bethlehem, and a corridor to the sea. The British government refused to commit itself to this plan. Both Arab and Jewish leaders denounced it. The League of Nations accepted the plan and criticized British administration of the area. But it was powerless to enforce any changes. Palestine moved closer to civil war.

Saudi Arabia

During the 1920's and 1930's, the only independent Arab ruler in the Middle East was Abd al-Aziz Ibn Saud. He ruled a large portion of the Arabian Peninsula. Known as Ibn Saud, he was also head of the Wahabis, a strict sect of Sunni Muslims.

Before World War I, Ibn Saud's base of power had been the Nejd, a region in eastern Arabia. After the war, he conquered more territory and extended his authority throughout the peninsula. In 1925 Ibn Saud captured the holy cities of Mecca and Medina as well as the port of Jidda. After these victories, he proclaimed himself king. In 1932 he renamed his kingdom Saudi Arabia, after his family.

During the early years of Saud's rule, Saudi Arabia remained poor and undeveloped. Nearly 98 percent of its territory was desert or wasteland. However, in 1933 Ibn Saud allowed an

American corporation to search for oil in his country. A major discovery was made in 1936. After World War II, Saudi Arabia began to develop into a major oil-producing country.

1. Identify: Treaty of Sèvres, Mustapha Kemal, Treaty of Lausanne, Ankara, Reza Khan, Majles, Balfour Declaration, Zionists, Peel Commission, Ibn Saud, Wahabis.
2. What changes did Atatürk introduce in Turkey?
3. How did Reza Shah Pahlavi become ruler of Iran?
4. What two national groups claimed the right to live in Palestine? On what basis did each make its claim?

3   Africa

After World War I, the first stirrings of nationalism occurred in Africa. Many African leaders hoped that their continent would receive greater political freedom. Their hopes turned to disappointment when the peace settlements enlarged rather than reduced the size of European empires. During the 1920's and 1930's, groups of European-educated Africans emerged in support of nationalism.

North Africa

After World War I, nationalist movements arose in British and French territories in North Africa. Egypt wanted to break its ties with Britain and become an independent kingdom. In French North Africa—Morocco, Algeria, and Tunisia—the Arab majority began to demand freedom.

Egypt   After World War I, nationalism became a powerful force in Egypt. The strongest nationalist party, the Wafd, had grown tremendously after the war. It particularly attracted the support of the emerging middle class. To counter the Wafd, the British exiled the party's leader, Saad Zaghlul, to the Mediterranean island of Malta in 1919. In doing so, they hoped to prevent Zaghlul from presenting Egypt's case for complete independence at the Paris peace conference.[3] The exile of Zaghlul was followed by strikes and riots in Egypt.

[3] Saad Zaghlul eventually was allowed to attend the Paris peace conference, but he failed to win support for Egypt's cause among the delegates.

Early in 1920, the British Parliament sent a commission headed by Lord Alfred Milner to Egypt to investigate the disorders. The Milner Commission's report recommended Egyptian independence. It proposed the establishment of a constitutional monarchy and a parliament. Independence, however, was to be limited by an alliance with Britain. The alliance was to guarantee British interests, permitting the British army to stay in Egypt to defend the Suez Canal.

In 1921 Zaghlul returned to Egypt to direct the cause for complete independence. In London, British and Egyptian leaders met and conducted negotiations toward this goal. The discussions collapsed over the question of keeping British forces in Egypt. Following the conference, the Wafd party proclaimed a policy of nonviolent resistance to the British.

In 1922 Britain declared Egypt independent. This decision was made without consulting the Egyptians. In acting on its own, the British government was able to set its own terms. British troops were to remain in Egypt in spite of Egyptian opposition.

In the same year, Egypt held its first elections, which resulted in a strongly nationalist government headed by the Wafd. Tensions continued over the next decade between Egypt and Britain. However, the growing threat of Mussolini's Italy to the eastern Mediterranean eventually brought the two countries closer together. In 1936 Egypt and Britain signed a defense treaty that withdrew all British troops from Egypt, except for those in the Suez Canal zone. It admitted Egyptians into Sudan, which had been off limits to Egyptian settlement since the British conquest of the area in 1896. The British-Egyptian treaty was a step toward Egypt's full independence.

French North Africa   During the 1920's and 1930's, Tunisia and Morocco were French protectorates. Algeria was a French colony. Nationalism became a major force among the Arab-Berber population in all three areas. However, Algeria, with its strongly pro-French European minority, became the major center of conflict between colonial officials and the nationalists.

Various organizations promoted nationalism in North Africa. They drew much of their

HISTORY AND THE ARTS

African Art: Its Impact on Europe

Since the late 1400's, finely carved wooden masks and statues from Africa had been finding their way to Europe. Explorers brought them back as mementos of their dangerous journeys. Missionaries displayed them to show the lifestyles of the cultures that they sought to convert. Only a few Europeans viewed these objects as valuable pieces of art that were worthy of being collected and preserved. Most Europeans dismissed African art as bizarre and unusual.

About 1900, a group of young painters living in Paris "discovered" African art. They found numerous masks and other objects in the city's curiosity shops. These European painters saw in African art an expressive power that they thought was missing in their own art. At the time, most European artists were largely concerned with showing the outward appearance of the world. But these "exotic" African objects clearly represented a different artistic approach. The African artists who made them were primarily interested in giving shape and form to a spiritual reality or an abstract idea.

The encounter with African art directly influenced the work of such modern artists as Georges Braque, André Derain, Henri Matisse, Pablo Picasso, and Maurice de Vlaminck. Their paintings reflected the angles, lines, and shapes of African sculpture. This art is characterized by long, square, disproportionate human features.

European fascination with African art led to an artistic movement known as "primitivism." An outgrowth of this type of art became known as modern European abstract art.

1. How was African art different from European art?
2. What impact did African art have on European painters at the turn of the century?

inspiration from the nationalist movement in Egypt. In the mid-1920's, the North African Star party and the Religious Teachers' Association were founded in Algeria. Both organizations instilled in their followers a sense of national pride and a devotion to Islamic culture. Similar groups were formed in Morocco and Tunisia. Together, these organizations laid the foundation for the independence struggles of later decades.

Sub-Saharan Africa

After World War I, the European colonial powers strengthened their hold over Sub-Saharan Africa. In most British and French colonies, representative forms of government were established, although ultimate authority remained with European officials. Colonial economies improved with the building of railroads and paved roads. Yet, most of these economic improvements benefited European businesses, not African ones.

Nationalist Movements   During this time, an influential minority of Africans were educated in missionary schools and European universities. They accepted western ideas on democracy and the self-determination of peoples. Many of them opposed European rule of their lands and developed an appreciation of their local cultures. Some led or became involved in nationalist activities.

In British-ruled Kenya, Harry Thuku formed the Gikuyu Association in 1921. The association was largely made up of young educated East Africans. It made its nationalism known through newspapers, journals, and pamphlets. In spite of its growing popularity, the Gikuyu Association eventually collapsed under British pressure. Thuku himself was arrested by the British authorities and accused of plotting to overthrow the colonial government.

In West Africa, nationalist leaders, such as B. N. Azikiwe of Nigeria, formed organizations that demanded self-government. Their ideas spread rapidly among western-educated Africans living in urban areas. The most influential nationalist movements emerged in French-ruled Senegal and the Ivory Coast and British-ruled Nigeria and the Gold Coast. However, British and French officials in these areas were slow in responding to African demands.

Rivalries   Throughout Africa, rivalries among ethnic groups often hindered the unity of nationalist movements. This problem of internal African conflict developed as a result of European colonial policies. European diplomats had largely ignored the territorial spread of African ethnic groups when establishing colonial boundaries. Members of the same ethnic group were often separated from each other by artificial borders. Under European rule, they were linked to other ethnic groups with whom they had nothing in common. Following a policy of "divide and conquer," European colonial officials supported one group of Africans against another. In doing so, they were able to establish control over their colonies more easily.

Azikiwe used his chain of newspapers to promote independence in West Africa. His leadership in the political Nigerian Youth Movement earned him many followers. What African group was most receptive to nationalist ideas?

Jomo Kenyatta's people were the Gikuyu. A common European way of spelling this word is "Kikuyu."

African Writers   In spite of its early weaknesses, nationalism in Sub-Saharan Africa led to a rebirth of African culture. Many nationalist leaders were thinkers and writers who did most of their work outside Africa. In France, Leopold Senghor of Senegal published poems and articles expressing pride in his African heritage. In Britain, Jomo Kenyatta of Kenya published a book in 1938 called *Facing Mount Kenya: The Tribal Life of the Gikuyu*. In this work, he attempted to explain the traditional culture of his people to European readers. He also described the effects of European rule on his homeland. Kenyatta concluded

> *They [Europeans] speak as if it was somehow beneficial to an African to work for them instead of for himself, and to make sure that he will receive this benefit they do their best to take away his land and leave him with no alternative. Along with his land they rob him of his government, condemn his religious ideas, and ignore his fundamental conceptions of justice and morals, all in the name of civilization and progress.**

Kenyatta, Senghor, and other African thinkers hoped to unite their people by giving them an appreciation of Africa's rich cultural heritage.

1. Identify: French North Africa, Wafd, Saad Zaghlul, Milner Commission, North African Star, Harry Thuku, B. N. Azikiwe, Leopold Senghor, Jomo Kenyatta.
2. How did Egypt gain its independence?
3. What were some of the beliefs of the educated African nationalists?

4   Latin America

After World War I, a new wave of nationalism swept Latin America. Cities and industries grew. A new type of political leadership emerged that was based on the support of urban workers rather than on that of landowners. Latin Americans acted to restrict foreign influences in the region. For many of them, the greatest foreign threat came from the United States. To counter

growing anti-American feeling, the United States attempted to change many of its policies in Latin America.

National Leaders

During the 1920's and 1930's, strong political leaders ruled in many Latin American countries. These leaders included Lázaro Cárdenas of Mexico, Hipólito Irigoyen of Argentina, Getúlio Vargas of Brazil, and Juan Vicente Gómez of Venezuela. Their goals were to build strong industrial economies and to modernize their societies.

Mexico   Lázaro Cárdenas became president of Mexico in 1934. His government carried out reforms in the spirit of the 1910 revolution. First, Cárdenas directed the redistribution of vast tracts of land to landless peasants. He formed cooperative farms to boost agricultural production. Cárdenas's main goal was to make Mexico economically independent of foreign countries. In the late 1930's, Cárdenas nationalized the foreign-controlled railroads and oil companies. The foreign owners, mostly British and American, received little compensation.

Argentina   In Argentina, Hipólito Irigoyen became president twice between 1916 and 1930. Irigoyen's support came chiefly from urban workers and the middle class. They elected him president because of his party's success in achieving electoral reforms, such as universal male suffrage. During his first administration, Irigoyen carried through social reforms that improved factory conditions, boosted workers' wages, and regulated working hours.

Irigoyen's second term of office aroused widespread opposition. Accused of being a dictator, Irigoyen was overthrown by an army-backed coup d'etat in 1930. With the coming of the depression, Argentina was split between leftist and rightist political movements. To maintain social order, the army began to assume an important role in the Argentine government.

Brazil   In Brazil, Latin America's largest nation, President Getúlio Vargas came to power in 1934. Three years later, Vargas proclaimed a new constitution that gave him full dictatorial powers. To gain working-class support, the

Facing Mount Kenya, Jomo Kenyatta, © 1938 by Random House, Inc., p. 305.

Vargas administration increased wages, shortened working hours, and gave unions the right to organize. Like Argentina, Brazil was divided by feuding between the political left and right. Vargas, however, was able to maintain control with the support of the army.

Venezuela   From 1908 to 1935, Venezuela was ruled by President Juan Vicente Gómez, who had dictatorial powers. During this period, oil was discovered along Venezuela's Caribbean coast. By the late 1930's, Venezuela had become the third largest oil-producing nation in the world. British, Dutch, and American oil companies, however, controlled the Venezuelan oil industry. They backed the Gómez government in order to maintain their rights to drill for oil.

Oil meant prosperity for Venezuela. However, the increased national wealth was enjoyed only by the upper classes. The large majority of the population remained poor. Gómez used the oil profits to strengthen his government. He paid off his country's huge national debt to European bankers and created a strong army. He also used some of the profits for his personal benefit. Gómez's spending policies led to greater corruption in the government.

During the 1930's, opposition to the Gómez dictatorship increased. Venezuela's industrial development had led to the rise of a working class. Many workers and students actively opposed the Gómez government. When Gómez died in 1935, riots spread throughout the country. Army leaders then took power and ruled the country under a new constitution. The army continued to control Venezuelan politics for the next several decades.

Mexican artist Diego Rivera, well known for his murals in public buildings, presents in this 1931 fresco a study of industrial life and the working class. What benefits did the working class achieve in Latin America during the 1930's?

Some teachers might wish to discuss current United States policies in Latin America.

United States and Latin America

During the 1920's and 1930's, the mineral wealth of Latin America attracted American businesses, which invested heavily in the region. To protect American economic interests, the United States intervened militarily in Central American and Caribbean countries.

During the 1920's, United States forces occupied Haiti and established control over its economy. The United States also intervened in Nicaragua. There, rebel forces led by General Augustino César Sandino resisted the Americans and tried to force a United States withdrawal. To help the American soldiers, the United States government trained a loyal Nicaraguan army called the National Guard. By the mid-1930's, the National Guard was able to defeat the rebels. Its leader, Anastasio Somoza, seized power in 1936. From that time until 1979, the Somoza family ruled Nicaragua with American support.

The growth of American economic and military influence in the region was resented by many Latin Americans. Latin American nationalists particularly opposed the Roosevelt Corollary. They stated that no country had the right to interfere in the affairs of another. They also claimed that, while the United States was exploiting their raw materials, Latin America was getting few economic benefits in return. Anti-Americanism was especially strong during the worldwide depression. At this time, world market prices for raw materials fell sharply. This decline increased hardships among Latin Americans dependent on trade with North America and Europe.

Aware of the growing resentment, the United States tried to improve relations with its southern neighbors. Following his election in 1928, United States President Herbert Hoover went on a goodwill tour of Latin America. He hoped to show that the United States regarded its Latin American neighbors as equals. At the same time, Secretary of State Joshua Reuben Clark began to restate the meaning of the Monroe Doctrine. In a memorandum issued in December 1928, Clark held that the Doctrine's warning that European powers could not interfere in Latin America did

During Hoover's tour of Latin America, he said his visit was that of "one good neighbor to another." This phrase laid the foundation for Roosevelt's Latin American policy. What changes in policy did Roosevelt make?

not mean that the United States had the right to interfere.

In 1933 President Franklin D. Roosevelt announced the Good Neighbor policy toward Latin America. He renounced past United States military intervention in the region. To prove his good intentions, Roosevelt ended American restrictions on the sovereignty of Cuba. He also ordered the withdrawal of American troops from Haiti and Nicaragua. In spite of the changes in American policy, many Latin Americans remained suspicious of the United States.

1. Identify: Lázaro Cárdenas, Hipólito Irigoyen, Getúlio Vargas, Juan Vicente Gómez, Augusto César Sandino, Good Neighbor policy.
2. What reforms were carried out in Mexico, Argentina, and Brazil after the war?
3. How did United States policies in Latin America change after the war?

CHAPTER 27 REVIEW

Summary

1. World War I contributed to growing nationalism among the peoples of Asia, Africa, and Latin America.
2. After the war, national disturbances increased throughout India. Followers of Mohandas K. Gandhi, leader of the Indian independence movement, employed nonviolent methods to protest the British administration of their country.
3. Two separate groups of nationalists competed for the loyalty of the Chinese people. Chiang Kai-shek led the Kuomintang party. Mao Tse-tung became the most prominent leader of the Chinese Communist party. The common enemy of both parties were the Japanese.
4. President Mustapha Kemal sought to end foreign influence in Turkey so that Turks could build a strong, modern nation. Kemal, later known as Atatürk, introduced numerous political and economic reforms as well as changes in cultural traditions that did not fit with his goals for modernization.
5. Like Atatürk in Turkey, Reza Shah in Iran introduced many reforms to modernize and strengthen his nation.
6. In the period between the wars, Arabs and Jews claimed the right to live in Palestine. Both groups fought bitterly to realize that claim.
7. The most powerful leader of the Arabian Peninsula was known as Ibn Saud. He was responsible for forming the modern nation of Saudi Arabia.
8. Egypt became independent in 1922 after the emergence of a nationalist movement.
9. As a result of colonial rule, numerous subject peoples were exposed to western ideas and education. In the 1920's and 1930's, an educated African group began to emerge. These intellectuals formed the basis for the major African nationalist movements after World War II.
10. Two significant changes took place in Latin America. First, a new type of leadership emerged based on the support of urban workers rather than wealthy landowners. Second, the period was marked by the changing attitudes of the United States toward Latin American countries. The United States was the dominant power in the Western Hemisphere after World War I.

Building Vocabulary

self-determination
swaraj
pacifist

civil disobedience
satyagraha

warlords
fez
shah

Reviewing the Main Ideas

1. What did Gandhi and his followers hope to accomplish for India?
2. What difficulties did Sun Yat-sen encounter in creating a new China?
3. Why were the Chinese Communists forced on the Long March?
4. Why was Japan bitter toward the West after the war?

5. What major political, economic, and cultural changes were made by Kemal in Turkey?
6. How did Reza Shah try to modernize the country of Persia?
7. How did Ibn Saud gain control of the Arabian Peninsula?
8. What discovery transformed the economy of Saudi Arabia?
9. What events led to Egyptian independence? What role did Britain play in the events?
10. Why did the British insist on maintaining a military presence in Egypt?
11. What nationalist activity took place in Sub-Saharan Africa in the 1920's and 1930's?
12. How did the nature of leadership change in Latin America after the war?

Discussing Important Ideas

1. Why was World War I an important stimulus to nationalist movements in Asia and Africa?
2. Compare and contrast nationalist activities in India, Turkey, and Algeria.
3. How do you account for the different types of nationalist movements and leaders in the world in the 1920's and 1930's?
4. Why was Saudi Arabia almost overlooked by the major world powers until the 1930's?
5. How did educated Africans try to strengthen African nationalism?
6. Why do you think the United States moved from a policy of military intervention in Latin America to a Good Neighbor policy?

Using Maps

Refer to the map on page 625 to answer the following questions:
1. What nations' territories in 1935 lay within the 1914 boundaries of the Ottoman Empire?
2. What Middle Eastern countries in 1935 bordered the Mediterranean Sea? Palestine?
3. What nation occupied the peninsula of Asia Minor in 1935? the Arabian Peninsula?
4. What European nations in 1935 still controlled lands in the Middle East?
5. What country was formerly known as Persia?

CHAPTER 28

Amphibious Assault

" You cannot organize civilization around the core of militarism and at the same time expect reason to control human destinies. "

Franklin D. Roosevelt, United States President (1882-1945)

World War II

Little more than 20 years after the Treaty of Versailles, a wider and far more devastating war than World War I swept the globe. Once again, the world was divided into two separate and opposing alliances. On one side was the Axis—Germany, Italy, Japan, and seven other supporting countries. On the other side were the Allies—Britain, France, the Soviet Union, the United States, and 29 other supporting countries. In all of Europe only five countries—Ireland, Sweden, Switzerland, Spain, and Portugal—remained neutral.

In 1945 the Allies defeated the Axis and their supporters. The world at the end of the war was drastically different from the one that had existed at the beginning of the conflict. Exhausted by the struggle, Europe could no longer dominate world civilization as it had since the 1800's. In its place were two superpowers, the United States and the Soviet Union. Along with this change and the many others brought about by the war came the new and awesome force of nuclear weapons.

1 The Slide into War

In the 1930's the democracies of the West watched uneasily as authoritarian leaders rose to the forefront in Europe and Asia. Despite their concern, the democracies could not agree on their **collective security,** or what was needed to defend their common interests against enemy attack. Conflicting feelings about the dangers of militarism, fascism, nazism, and communism contributed to their indecision.

For most people, the memories of World War I were still fresh. Many people wanted to avoid a war at all costs. Some had become pacifists,

vowing never to fight again under any circumstances. Anti-war feeling was especially strong in the United States. There, isolationism was the dominant mood. Many Americans were convinced that Europe was a region of bitter quarrels and hatreds of which they wanted no part.

At the root of much of the world's problems were the peace settlements made at the end of World War I. For the most part, Britain, France, and the United States were satisfied with the settlements. Germany, Italy, and Japan were not. They believed that many of their difficulties stemmed from the settlements, and they were bitter about the situation. They were willing to risk war to revise the treaties and to improve their position in the world.

Japanese and Italian Expansion

Japan made the first move in 1931. The Japanese depended heavily on foreign sources for raw materials and on markets for finished goods. To remain industrially strong, Japan had to gain new territory that would provide it with the materials and markets it needed.

One of the areas in which Japan had some extraterritorial privileges was Manchuria, an area in northeastern China rich in natural resources. In September 1931, Japanese army units stationed in Manchuria used an explosion on the South Manchurian Railway as an excuse to overrun the area. The Japanese government had not approved, or even known about, the army's actions. The Chinese, who were not in a position to protest the action militarily, responded by boycotting Japanese goods. To force the Chinese to drop the boycott, the Japanese sent troops into the Chinese port of Shanghai.

The Japanese government separated Manchuria from China and made it independent,

635

renaming it Manchukuo. They then set up a puppet ruler who allowed them to control all important activities.

China protested Japanese actions in the League of Nations. In March 1932, the League named Japan an aggressor and told it to return Manchuria to China. The Japanese ignored the League's decision and continued to make military and economic gains in China. On May 27, 1933, they announced their withdrawal from the League.

The ease of Japan's success encouraged Italy to try similar moves. In 1934 Italian and Ethiopian forces clashed in a disputed zone on the frontier of Italian Somaliland in Africa. The Italians demanded an apology and reparations. Instead, the Ethiopians asked the League of Nations to investigate the matter to determine who was responsible for the incident. It was decided that since each side viewed the area where the incident took place as its own territory, neither side was to blame. This did not satisfy the Italian dictator Mussolini, who was looking for an

Haile Selassie appealed to the League of Nations for decisive action against Italian aggression in Ethiopia. But League members Britain and France were afraid to alienate Mussolini. The League's inaction led to its downfall. Why were the League's sanctions against Italy ineffective?

Chinese soldiers protected their position at Shanghai until these well-trained and well-equipped reinforcements joined the Japanese army in the Hongkew sector of that port city. Why did the Japanese attack Shanghai?

excuse to send troops into Ethiopia. He thought that an Ethiopian colony would offset economic problems in Italy. Further, an Italian victory in Africa would build up Italy's image as a world power.

In October 1935, Mussolini invaded Ethiopia. The Ethiopian emperor, Haile Selassie, appealed to the League of Nations for help. The League condemned the action and declared Italy an aggressor. At the same time, it voted certain **sanctions,** measures designed to inflict economic losses, against Italy. League members were forbidden to give trade credits to Italy or to sell it arms and certain raw materials. Members were allowed, however, to sell Italy oil, coal, and iron, which it needed to make war.

The League's actions did not stop Mussolini. In May 1936, he completed his conquest of Ethiopia after much resistance. Ethiopia was formally annexed to Italy and with Eritrea and Italian Somaliland was organized as Italian East Africa. The king of Italy took the title of "Emperor of Ethiopia."

When Hitler successfully reoccupied the Rhineland
and built fortifications known as the Siegfried Line, he
altered the strategic balance of Europe. France now
was not able to aid its allies in Central Europe.

Rhineland

In March 1936, at the height of the Ethiopian crisis, Adolf Hitler sent troops into the Rhineland of western Germany. Since 1919, the Versailles treaty had forbidden German troops in the region in order to protect French security. By invading the Rhineland, Hitler gambled that France and Britain would not do anything to stop him.

When Hitler won the gamble, he put an end to the Versailles treaty and to collective security. Germany began to rearm at a rapid pace. In October 1936, Hitler signed a political and military pact with Mussolini called the Rome-Berlin Axis. The next month, Hitler signed the Anti-Comintern Pact, an anti-Communist alliance that included Germany, Japan, and Italy. Stalin, afraid that the new alliance threatened Soviet security, urged the western powers to unite against Germany and its allies. Fearful that such a union would lead to war, they refused. However, Communist and Socialist parties in most countries condemned inaction. They formed alliances against the Nazi threat. Such alliances, known as "popular fronts," won control of France and Spain during the 1930's.

Anschluss

Hitler, meanwhile, grew bolder. He had dreamed for a long time of Anschluss, the annexation of Austria to Germany. In *Mein Kampf,* Hitler wrote: "German-Austria must return to the great German mother country. . . . One blood demands one Reich."

In 1934 Hitler had tried to take over Austria. But he backed down when Mussolini responded by mobilizing Italy's troops. In 1938 Hitler tried again. He invited the Austrian chancellor to Berchtesgaden, his mountain retreat in Bavaria, and bullied him into appointing Nazis to key posts in Austria.

The Austrian chancellor appealed to Britain and France for help, but neither country was willing to become involved. In March 1938, Hitler annexed Austria. He insisted that he was only promoting political stability by uniting German-speaking peoples. Once again, the western democracies refused to act.

Munich Crisis

Austria was the first victim of Hitler's policy of German expansion. Czechoslovakia was the next. In the late 1930's, Czechoslovakia was the only democracy in central Europe. Its standard of living was second only to that of Germany. It held the key strategic position in the region. Czechoslovakia also had a strong army and alliances with France and the Soviet Union.

About 3 million Germans lived in the Sudetenland, a heavily fortified region in northwestern Czechoslovakia bordering on Germany. On September 12, 1938, Hitler demanded that the Germans of the Sudetenland be given the right of self-determination. The Czechoslovak government responded by proclaiming martial law. In an effort to avert an international crisis, British Prime Minister Neville Chamberlain suggested to Hitler that they meet to discuss the matter. Chamberlain was supported in his efforts by the French government.

Chamberlain met with Hitler twice without any agreement being reached. The Czechoslovak government, meanwhile, had ordered full mobilization of its troops. On September 29, a third meeting was held in Munich. Also attending this time were French Premier Édouard Daladier, Mussolini, and several others. Czechoslovakia and the Soviet Union were not represented. Britain and France agreed to the Munich Pact, which gave Germany control over the Sudetenland. In return, Hitler promised to respect Czechoslovak sovereignty. He also promised not to take any more European territory and to settle future disputes by peaceful negotiation.

Chamberlain returned home to cheering crowds, proclaiming that he had ensured "peace in our time." He trusted Hitler and believed that the Nazis would cause no more trouble. He thought that a policy of **appeasement,** granting concessions to maintain peace, would stabilize Europe. Stalin, who had not attended the conference, had a different view. He thought Hitler should be opposed, with force if need be. He viewed the Munich agreement as a British and French attempt to turn Hitler away from western Europe and eastward toward the Soviet Union.

Be sure that students see Czechoslovakia's key strategic location in Europe. See the map on p. 640.

Some teachers might wish to assign readings from Ernest Hemingway's *For Whom the Bell Tolls* and George Orwell's *Homage to Catalonia*. Both discuss experiences in the Spanish Civil War.

In 1936 Hitler announced a second four-year plan. The plan's hidden goal was to make the German armed forces and economy ready for war. In 1933 Germany's army consisted of 100,000 soldiers. By 1938, 850,000 regulars and 900,000 reserves served Hitler. After saluting columns of German storm troopers at the Nazi party rally in 1938, Hitler made an inflammatory speech about the destiny of Sudetenland Germans. Riots followed throughout that region of Czechoslovakia. What events before 1938 could have warned European leaders of Hitler's intentions?

On March 15, 1939, Hitler sent his armies into Czechoslovakia and took control of the western part of the country. The eastern part, Slovakia, became a German puppet state. Although alarmed by Hitler's action, the western democracies and the Soviet Union were unable to reach agreement on how to deal with Hitler.

Spanish Civil War

A civil war broke out in Spain that further inflamed the international situation. In 1931 a republic had replaced the monarchy. The republican government began a program of social reforms. It limited the Catholic Church's authority in education and redistributed land among the peasants. As a result, many right-wing groups in Spain opposed the republic and wanted to restore the old order. In July 1936, right-wing army chiefs staged a revolt in Spanish Morocco. The uprising soon spread to Spain. For three years, the right-wing Spanish Nationalists, led by General Francisco Franco, and the Loyalists, or Spanish republicans, battled one another.

At an early stage in the fighting, foreign powers began to interfere, and Spain became the battleground of the rival ideologies of fascism and communism. While the Soviets gave aid to the Loyalists, the Germans and Italians supported the Nationalists.[1] Idealistic sympathizers from Britain, France, and the United States joined the International Brigades to fight alongside of the Loyalists.

Hitler saw the civil war in Spain as a way to strengthen ties with Italy and to secure a future vital supply of Spanish iron ore and magnesium. Hermann Göring, the head of the Luftwaffe, or German air force, saw in the war a chance "firstly, to prevent the further spread of Communism; secondly, to test my young Luftwaffe in this or that technical aspect."

Under Göring's direction, the Condor Legion was formed. It was an air and ground force made up entirely of Germans. Eventually, some 6,000 Germans operated planes, tanks, and antiaircraft units in Spain. They used Spanish towns and cities as testing grounds for new war techniques. They tested the combined use of fire and high explosive bombs and other new weapons. Much of what the Germans learned militarily in Spain was later put to use in World War II.

In March 1939, the Spanish Nationalists decisively defeated the Loyalists. Francisco

---

[1]The western democracies feared a larger conflict, so they remained neutral in the Spanish Civil War.

Franco entered Madrid and established a right-wing dictatorship, friendly but not allied to Hitler and Mussolini. After three years, the Spanish Civil War finally ended. Several hundred thousand Spaniards died in the fighting, and much of Spain lay in ruins.

Nazi-Soviet Pact

In March 1939, Hitler turned his attention to eastern Europe. He threatened to take over the Baltic port of Danzig and the Polish Corridor. This threat led the British and the French to increase their military spending and to make new alliances. They pledged to help Poland, Greece, Romania, and Turkey defend their borders if it became necessary.

All along, Stalin had tried to urge the western powers to do something about Hitler. Although Chamberlain now realized that he had been wrong about Hitler, he still did not trust Stalin's motives. The British prime minister feared that Stalin wanted to extend Soviet influence in eastern Europe. He also questioned the fighting ability of the Soviet army. Despite this, Britain and France asked the Soviet Union to join them in an alliance to contain nazism. Stalin said he would do so in return for western acknowledgement of the Soviet right to occupy a broad zone stretching from Finland to Bulgaria. Chamberlain refused Stalin's request. This deepened Stalin's suspicion that the West would like nothing better than to have Germany and the Soviet Union destroy one another.

In *Mein Kampf*, Hitler spoke of creating **lebensraum,** or "living space," for German settlers in the rich agricultural areas of eastern Europe. This convinced Stalin that Germany eventually would move eastward toward the Soviet Union. He doubted that the West would come to his country's aid if it were threatened by Germany. So he began secret talks with the Germans. On August 23, 1939, the Soviet Union and Nazi Germany made the Nazi-Soviet Non-aggression Pact. In the agreement, the two nations pledged to remain neutral if either were attacked by someone else. Stalin and Hitler also secretly agreed to create spheres of influence in eastern Europe. Germany would occupy the western part of Poland, while the Soviet Union would govern the eastern part. In addition, Finland and the Baltic republics of Estonia, Latvia, and Lithuania would be recognized as part of the Soviet sphere of influence.

Neither Stalin nor Hitler had any illusions about their agreement. Stalin still believed that war with Germany was inevitable. But he thought the pact would serve to increase Soviet security. If nothing else, it would buy the Soviets time to prepare and improve their strategic position. Hitler saw the pact as a means of securing Germany's eastern border. Without having to worry about fighting the Soviets, the Germans would be free to act where they wanted. Leaders in the West were shocked and outraged. They realized Stalin's deal destroyed the last barrier to war.

On September 1, 1939, Hitler, believing that the West would not act, invaded Poland. Two days later, Britain and France declared war on Germany. World War II had begun.

1. Identify: Axis, Allies, Manchukuo, Haile Selassie, Rome-Berlin Axis, Anschluss, Neville Chamberlain, Édouard Daladier, Munich Crisis, Francisco Franco, International Brigades, Hermann Göring, Luftwaffe, Nazi-Soviet Non-aggression Pact.
2. Why did Japan invade Manchuria, Italy invade Ethiopia, and Germany invade the Rhineland?
3. What issue brought civil war to Spain? How was Spain's government affected by the war?
4. Why did Stalin agree to the Nazi-Soviet Pact? What was the Pact's outcome?

2 Germany on the Offensive

The Luftwaffe began bombing Poland on September 1, 1939, spreading confusion and panic. Panzers, armored tank divisions, followed quickly. Next, the infantry, a million and a half strong, moved into Poland in motorized vehicles. This was **blitzkrieg,** "lightning war," a new German strategy aimed at taking the enemy by surprise.

The blitzkrieg worked with speed and efficiency, devastating Poland within a few short weeks.

AXIS EXPANSION IN EUROPE   1935-1941

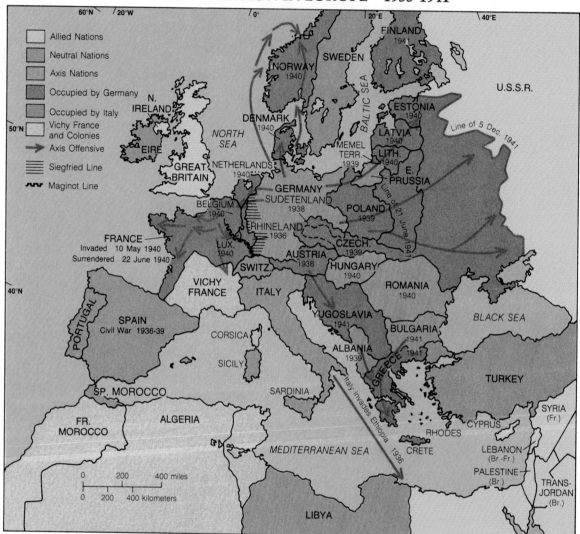

The speed of the victory took Britain and France by surprise. They could not move fast enough to send troops to Poland. Stalin, just as surprised as the western powers, moved quickly to occupy eastern Poland. He did not want to give Hitler a chance to go back on the terms of their non-aggression pact.

On September 25, Stalin and Hitler signed an agreement that divided Poland between them. A few weeks later, Stalin forced the Baltic republics to accept Soviet military bases on their soil. When he tried to do the same with Finland, war broke out between Finland and the Soviet Union. The Finns held out until March before they were finally forced to surrender. Their defeat moved the Soviet frontier 70 miles (112 kilometers) to the west, which provided protection for the exposed Soviet city of Leningrad.

Western Front

The western front was quiet all through the winter and spring of 1939-1940. This was a period of **sitzkrieg,** "sitting war," also called "phony war." On April 29, 1940, the sitzkrieg ended as

HISTORY AND CITIES

Warsaw

Warsaw, Poland's capital, suffered more than any other European city during World War II. In 1939 the Germans held Warsaw in a three-week siege that left much of the city in ruins. More than 10,000 Poles died and another 500,000 were wounded before Warsaw surrendered.

The German occupiers tried to reduce Warsaw to a small insignificant town. They removed Warsaw's cultural treasures to German cities. Many of Warsaw's people were sent away to concentration camps. About 400,000 Polish Jews were confined in one area of Warsaw. In 1942 alone, nearly 300,000 of them were killed by the Germans or died of hunger and disease. In spite of Nazi terror, Warsaw refused to admit defeat and became the center of the Polish underground resistance.

By the summer of 1944, Soviet armies, now on the Allied side, had pushed the Germans out of Russia and had reached the outskirts of Warsaw. The people of Warsaw rose against the Germans. However, the Soviets did not come to the city's aid. The Germans crushed the Polish resistance and evacuated the entire population of Warsaw. They destroyed all of the buildings that still stood. As a result of the uprising and its aftermath, nearly 150,000 to 180,000 Poles died. When Soviet troops finally entered Warsaw in January 1945, they found the city deserted and in a state of total destruction.

After World War II, Polish survivors returned and began to rebuild Warsaw. Today, a new city has arisen on the ruins of the old one. The population of Warsaw has grown, and the city has emerged once again as Poland's leading urban center.

The people of Warsaw have carefully reconstructed the Old Town, which contains many of their city's historic buildings. The famous landmarks in this district include the Cathedral of Saint John, the Church of Saint Anne, the Royal Palace, and the ancient city walls, all of which date from the Middle Ages or the Renaissance.

Alongside the Old Town has arisen a modern city of new housing developments, stores, and office and government buildings. The city's skyline is dominated by the Palace of Science and Culture. This building is a Gothic-style skyscraper built by the Soviet Union and given as a "gift" to the people of Poland. Modern Warsaw also has spacious parks and fine libraries, museums, and theaters.

In addition to being the political and cultural heart of Poland, Warsaw is also a major center of Polish industry, most of which is located in the outskirts of the city. The people of Warsaw, who number about 1,500,000, are proud of their accomplishments. They believe that they have fulfilled the city's ancient motto, "It defies the storms."

1. How did World War II affect Warsaw?
2. How did the people of Warsaw fulfill their city's ancient motto?

The rapid defeat of France stunned most of the world.

Military leaders dominated World War I. Political leaders dominated World War II. Discuss the varied personalities of Churchill, Roosevelt, Hitler, Stalin, and Mussolini.

Hitler's army, the Wehrmacht, invaded Denmark and Norway. The defeat of Denmark took only a few hours. The defeat of Norway took longer and considerably reduced the strength of the German naval fleet.

The British and the French watched and waited in France along the Maginot Line. However, a German attack never came. The Maginot Line was impressive, but it had a flaw—a 50-mile (80-kilometer) gap in the Ardennes. The French believed that the forests, swamps, and hills of the Ardennes were a sufficient barrier, so they built no fortifications in the area. However, it was through Belgium and the Ardennes that the Germans had invaded during World War I. A French tank commander, Charles de Gaulle, pointed this out and pleaded for more tanks and planes. The French command insisted that France need not fear because the Maginot Line was impenetrable. De Gaulle's response was: "Peering between the battlements of our fortifications, we shall watch the enslavement of Europe."

Before dawn on May 10, 1940, the Germans attacked the Netherlands from the air. The Dutch, surprised and shaken, managed to resist for only a few days. At almost the same time, the Germans attacked Belgium along the Meuse River and through the Ardennes. Gathering momentum, they broke into France, bypassing the Maginot Line. By mid-May, the French line was broken. The battle for France was being lost in the air and on the ground. The trapped Allied forces fell back to Dunkirk, a port city in northern France. Beginning on May 26, about 800 British civilian and naval boats, shielded by Britain's Royal Navy and Royal Air Force (RAF), crossed the English Channel. Over the next nine days, they evacuated more than 300,000 troops, two-thirds of which were British.

On June 10, Mussolini declared war on France and Britain. On June 14, the Germans entered Paris. Rather than allow the city to be destroyed by bombing, the French surrendered it to the Germans. On June 22, France signed an armistice with Germany. By its terms, Germany occupied all of northern France and the Atlantic coastline to the Spanish border. Southern France, which the Germans did not occupy, was to be governed by the French. A puppet government was set up in the town of Vichy under French Marshal Henri Pétain.

The Battles of Britain and the Atlantic

The month before France fell, Winston Churchill had replaced Neville Chamberlain as prime minister of Britain. On May 13, 1940, he gave his first speech before the House of Commons. He told the Commons that he had "nothing to offer but blood, toil, tears, and sweat." He ended the speech as follows:

> You ask, what is our policy? I will say: It is to wage war, by sea, land, and air, with all our might and with all the strength that God can give us: to wage war against a monstrous tyranny, never surpassed in the dark, lamentable catalogue of human crime. That is our policy. You ask, What is our aim? I can

Paris fell quickly to the Nazis. Some historians attribute this to French fears that the Luftwaffe would destroy the city's beautiful architecture. What were the terms of the armistice France signed with Germany?

Through lend-lease the United States came to be known as the "arsenal of democracy."

*answer in one word: Victory—victory at all costs, victory in spite of all terror; victory, however hard and long the road may be; for without victory, there is no survival.**

Hitler knew that Germany did not have the capacity to mount a full-scale invasion of Britain. So he launched an offensive from the air in hope of destroying British airfields and vital industries. In early August, the Luftwaffe began bombing the southern coast of Britain. By the middle of the month, there were more than 1,000 German planes in the air, ranging as far north as Scotland. In early September, the Luftwaffe launched its great **blitz,** or series of air raids, against London. Bombs dropped continuously. In November, German bombing almost totally demolished the industrial city of Coventry in northern England.

Despite the shattered cities, destroyed factories, and large number of dead, the Luftwaffe was not able to defeat the RAF or break the morale of the British people. Churchill spoke for all the British people when he said about the RAF that "never in the field of human conflict was so much owed by so many to so few."

By the autumn of 1940, Hitler knew that he had lost the Battle of Britain. It was his first major defeat. He decided that if he could not bomb the British into submission, he would starve them. Without food, the British would have to surrender. German submarines had been sinking ships in the Atlantic since 1939. After the Battle of Britain, they stepped up their efforts, sinking merchant ships bound for Britain faster than new ones could be built. When the British began to use the convoy system, the Germans countered with **wolf packs,** clusters of submarines that shadowed convoys during the day and attacked them at night.

Churchill declared that the submarines had become a greater menace than the bombers and appealed to the United States for help. United States President Franklin D. Roosevelt agreed to provide 50 old destroyers in return for rent-free leases of certain British naval and air bases in the North Atlantic and the Caribbean.

----

*Their Finest Hour, Winston S. Churchill, © 1949 by Houghton Mifflin, pp. 25-26.

Throughout the rest of 1940, the British imported food and armaments from the United States on the basis of **cash and carry.** They paid cash for the goods and transported them across the Atlantic in their own ships. In 1941, in response to other appeals from Churchill, cash and carry was replaced by **lend-lease.** This program enabled the United States to lend war equipment to any country whose defense was deemed vital to the defense of the United States.

In August 1941, Churchill met face-to-face with Roosevelt off the coast of Newfoundland in the North Atlantic. Jointly they issued an eight-point program called the Atlantic Charter. Similar in content to Wilson's Fourteen Points, it emphasized freedom of trade and the right of peoples to choose their own governments. The Charter called for "the final destruction of Nazi tyranny."

Meanwhile, the Battle of the Atlantic continued. It did not come to an end until 1945.

Invasion of the Soviet Union

Having failed to defeat Britain, Hitler turned to the Soviet Union, which he thought he could defeat quickly. His goal of lebensraum could be fulfilled only by conquering the vast Soviet steppe. In addition, he wanted the wheat of the Ukraine and the oil supplies of the Caucasus. Hitler ordered his generals to destroy the Communist state and make the Soviet people slaves of Germany.

On June 22, 1941, the Germans launched their attack on the Soviet Union. Despite British warnings and the massing of German troops along the border, the Soviets were taken by surprise. As German divisions rapidly advanced into Soviet territory, Stalin appealed to his people to resist the invasion. He called for a **scorched-earth policy.** As the Soviets retreated into the interior of the country, they were to destroy everything that could be of use to the invaders.

By November 1941, German armies had pushed 600 miles (960 kilometers) into the Soviet Union. Forty percent of the Soviet population was under German control. Leningrad was under siege, cut off from any land connection

Because of Stalin's purges of the military, no one was sure how the Soviet army would fight.

Believing in the slogan "Asia for Asians," many people in Asia welcomed the Japanese advance at first. The Japanese occupation, however, left many Asians bitter toward Japan.

The powerful German Panzers were no match for the Soviet winter of 1941. The intense cold froze lubricating oil and cracked engine cylinders. What were other problems the German divisions encountered during that winter?

with the rest of the Soviet Union. Kiev had fallen, and the Germans were on the outskirts of Moscow. Yet, the Soviets were not ready to surrender. Young fighters defending Moscow rallied to the cry, "Behind us is Moscow—there is no room left for retreat!"

In December, winter set in. The Germans, not used to the bitter cold and snow of a Soviet winter, were forced to dig in and wait for spring. One German soldier described conditions in this way:

> We had no gloves. We had no winter shoes. We had no equipment whatsoever to fight or withstand the cold. . . . We lost a considerable part of our equipment, guns, heavy and light equipment in general. Due to the cold we lost a lot of people who got frost-bitten, and we had not even the necessary amount of ointments, or the most simple and primitive things to fight it. . . . Guns didn't fire anymore. Even our wireless

equipment didn't work properly anymore because the batteries were frozen hard. . . . We were afraid to become wounded and to become just the prey of a very bad winter climate or the prey of the enemy. . . A good number, when it came to a decisive moment, tried not to stick their heads out as much as they might have done otherwise.*

1. Identify: Panzers, Wehrmacht, Ardennes, Charles de Gaulle, Vichy, Battle of Britain, Atlantic Charter, Battle of the Atlantic.
2. Where did the Germans receive their first major defeat? What had Hitler gained to that point?
3. How did the United States aid the British in 1940 and 1941?

3 The Japanese and the Americans

While Germany was on the move in Europe, Japan was reaching out in East Asia and the Pacific. In 1937 the Japanese invaded China. The result was a full-scale, though undeclared, war. In the end, the Chinese government under Chiang Kai-shek retreated to the interior of the country, leaving the Japanese in control of northern China. In March 1940, a Japanese-dominated government was established in China at Nanjing.

Japanese Expansion

The Japanese thought their best interests lay in East and Southeast Asia. These areas could provide the raw materials Japan needed. Many of those materials lay in Dutch, British, and French possessions, which the western powers had left virtually undefended.

In July 1940, the Japanese government announced its plan to achieve a "new order in Greater East Asia." It adopted the slogan "Asia for the Asiatics" and claimed that its goal was the establishment of a Greater East Asia Co-prosperity Sphere. Its first move was to demand the right to build airfields and station troops in northern

*German Lieutenant Maurer, quoted in *The World At War*, Mark Arnold-Foster, © 1973 by Thames Television Limited (Stein and Day, U. S. Publishers), p. 132.

The fervor of these Japanese pilots on graduation day illustrates the confidence the Japanese had in gaining control of the Pacific. What led to Japan joining forces with Gemany and Italy in the Tripartite Act?

French Indochina. Its next move was to invade Tonkin Province in Indochina. This led the United States to extend a loan to China and to put an embargo, or ban, on scrap iron to Japan.

Japan retaliated on September 27, 1940, by signing a Tripartite Pact with Germany and Italy. The pact stated that world peace depended on the right of every nation to "receive the space to which it is entitled." The three powers pledged to cooperate to reach that goal in Europe and in East Asia. They also pledged to come to each other's aid in the event of attack.

Pearl Harbor

On July 24, 1941, the Japanese occupied southern Indochina. President Roosevelt told them that if they withdrew, he would help them find access to the raw materials they needed. When they refused the offer, Japanese-American trade came to an abrupt halt. To resolve the matter, negotiations opened between Japan and the United States.

While the negotiators were meeting, the Japanese government decided on war with the United States. According to the Japanese, the United States stood in the way of their plans for expansion in the East. To seize the territory they wanted, they had to knock out the United States Pacific Fleet based at Pearl Harbor in Hawaii.

The American government believed that Pearl Harbor was safe from attack. So did most Japanese. But Admiral Isoroku Yamamoto, the commander of the Japanese navy, did not agree. He convinced Japanese leaders that Japanese bombers taking off from aircraft carriers could accomplish a successful surprise attack on Pearl Harbor.

In December 1941, the Japanese put Yamamoto's plan into effect. The Japanese fleet approached Hawaii from the north and from the east. Early on the morning of the seventh, they launched their bombers. The attack was even more successful than the Japanese had hoped. Within two hours time, they had disabled or sunk 19 American ships and destroyed 188

Though the two destroyers protecting the U.S.S. Pennsylvania (rear) were gutted by Japanese aircraft during the Pearl Harbor attack, the flagship was hit only once. To what extent was the American fleet damaged?

In the five months following Pearl Harbor, Japan conquered an empire of 100 million people.

planes. They also had killed more than 2,400 people and wounded an additional 1,100 or more.

The Japanese thought the attack on Pearl Harbor would show the Americans how strong and powerful they were and make the United States see that it would be wise to allow them to proceed with their expansionist plans. In this, the Japanese miscalculated. The day after the attack, President Roosevelt addressed the United States Congress. He called December 7 "a date which will live in infamy." He asked for and got a declaration of war against Japan.

From Neutrality to Commitment

Until the attack on Pearl Harbor, isolationist opinion in the United States had kept America from participating in the war in Europe. Most of the country's early actions had been designed to prevent American involvement. Neutrality Acts, passed after Mussolini attacked Ethiopia, prohibited arms shipments, loans, and credit to

Demands for arms created thousands of jobs in munitions factories. As most young men left for war, women filled the gap by joining the work force. How did the Neutrality Acts affect munitions shipments?

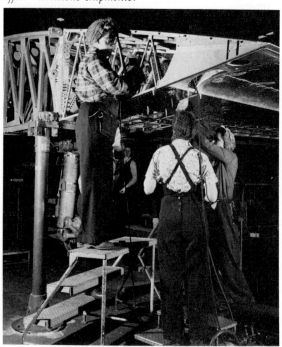

belligerents. They also forbade Americans to travel on belligerent ships. After the Spanish Civil War began, the export of munitions, or armaments, "for the use of either of the opposing forces in Spain" was banned.

By 1939, President Roosevelt had become convinced that Germany's expansion had to be stopped. He believed that the United States could help in this task by supplying France and Britain with the arms and ammunition needed to do the job. Roosevelt convinced Congress that a cash-and-carry policy would allow the United States to supply the British and French without risking the loss of American neutrality.

The German blitzkrieg in Poland and Mussolini's declaration of war on France and Britain turned American neutrality into American **nonbelligerency.** This meant that while the United States would not actively enter the war, it would extend the democracies as much material aid as possible. In 1940 Roosevelt made the "destroyers for bases" deal with the British. This signaled another change in United States policy. The United States went from nonbelligerency to limited participation in the war.

The United States became more deeply involved in the war after Hitler extended the German war zone in March 1940 to include Iceland and the waters between Greenland and Iceland. Since both Greenland and Iceland commanded the American sea-lanes to Britain, the United States responded by allowing American ships to patrol far out into the Atlantic.

The Japanese attack on Pearl Harbor put an end to American doubts and brought the United States officially into the war. On December 11, 1941, Germany and Italy honored the pledge they had made to Japan in the Tripartite Pact by declaring war on the United States. Britain, in support of the United States, declared war on Japan.

Allied Cooperation

The attack on Pearl Harbor united Britain, the United States, and the Soviet Union in the war. Though mistrust still lingered between the western democracies and the Soviet Union, both sides ended their criticism of the other. They

The cartoon below is the subject of the "Using Illustrations" section of the Chapter 28 Review.

Cuban artist Conrado Massagver's view of World War II is a deadly game of dominoes between Allied and Axis leaders, (clockwise, from left) the United States' Roosevelt, Germany's Hitler, Japan's Tojo, Britain's Churchill, the Soviet Union's Stalin, and Italy's Mussolini. In the real war, what strategy did Stalin suggest to the other Allies to take pressure off the Soviet Union?

prepared to pull together, yet each nation continued to have its own interests and concerns. Churchill, Roosevelt, and Stalin had to consider economic, political, and military factors as they decided how best to wage war. They agreed to support the aims of the Atlantic Charter and not to make separate peace agreements with any of the Axis countries.

Churchill and Roosevelt agreed that the defeat of Japan was secondary to the defeat of Germany. There were several reasons for this decision. As Churchill pointed out, "the defeat of Germany . . . will leave Japan exposed to overwhelming force, whereas the defeat of Japan would by no means bring the World War to an end."

Germany posed a more direct threat than Japan to the Western Hemisphere. And, of the two, the Germans were the more likely to develop new, more powerful weapons that might help the Axis win the war.

Stalin urged the Allies to help reduce German pressure on the Soviet Union by opening a second front in Europe quickly. While Churchill and Roosevelt agreed there would have to be a second front, they did not feel they were strong

enough to open one right away. They planned instead to conduct campaigns in North Africa, the Middle East, and the Mediterranean to divert and weaken Germany.

1. Identify: Greater East Asia Co-prosperity Sphere, Tripartite Pact, Pearl Harbor, Isoroku Yamamoto, Neutrality Acts.
2. What were Japan's goals in Asia and the Pacific?
3. Why did the Japanese attack Pearl Harbor? What effect did the attack have on the United States?
4. Why did the Allies decide to concentrate on the defeat of Germany before the defeat of Japan?

4 The World at War

By late summer of 1942, the war was being fought in western and eastern Europe, Italy and the Mediterranean, Burma and China, and the Atlantic and the Pacific. The future looked bleak for the Allies as the Axis scored victory after victory.

The Italians had invaded Albania, Egypt, and Greece. The Germans had occupied Estonia and the Soviet cities of Sebastopol and Rostov. They also had invaded Greece, Yugoslavia, and Crete.

The Battle of Stalingrad was one of the most costly battles of the war. Soviet losses were greater at Stalingrad (now known as Volgograd) than American losses throughout the entire war.

In North Africa, Germany's Afrika Korps, led by Field Marshal Erwin Rommel, "The Desert Fox," had defeated the British time and time again.

The Japanese had even greater success. In the East, Malaya, Singapore, and Burma all had fallen to them. When they took Burma, they cut the Burma Road, the only remaining overland route for shipping war supplies to the embattled Chinese government. In the Pacific, they had captured the Dutch East Indies, Guam, Wake Island, and the Philippines.

Only on the seas had the Allies been able to make much of a gain. Neither side had been able to claim victory in the Battle of the Coral Sea, the first naval battle fought entirely in the air by carrier-based aircraft. But, in the Battle of Midway, the Americans gave the Japanese navy its first major defeat. The battle put an end to Japanese naval superiority in the Pacific.

In occupied Europe, the Germans had maintained tight control. To keep the Nazi war machine supplied, Hitler's subordinates were draining the occupied countries of their wealth, food, raw materials, and manufactured goods. Many civilians had been sent to Germany to work as slave laborers in factories and on farms. In many of the countries, **resistance groups,** underground organizations that engage in secret operations and sabotage against an enemy, had emerged. These groups, which were made up of people from all classes of society, grew in importance as the war progressed.

The Soviet Union

In July 1942, an angry Stalin protested to the other Allies. He wanted to know why the Soviets were still fighting alone in eastern Europe. At a conference held in Moscow in August, Churchill told him that the second front could not be opened for another year.

On August 22, the Germans attacked Stalingrad. Stalingrad was a major industrial center on the Volga River, one of the Soviet's chief communication arteries. Since the city was named after Stalin, its loss would have been a severe blow to the Soviets for symbolic reasons. Stalin ordered that the city be held at all costs. Hitler was as determined to take the city as Stalin was to hold it.

In September, the Soviets launched a counterattack and encircled the Germans holding Stalingrad. They cut off German air and land supply lines and gradually tightened a trap around the Germans. Hitler refused to allow his troops to evacuate. The Soviets and the frigid winter weather closed in on them. When the winter was at its coldest, the encircling Soviet armies met. On February 1, 1943, the Germans finally surrendered. Only a third of them had survived. The defeat at Stalingrad destroyed the best of the German army.

War in the Desert

Since 1940 the desert war in Africa had no real victors. Neither side could decisively defeat the other. Then, in the spring of 1942, Rommel nearly defeated the British. It appeared that the Germans would soon control Egypt. If they did, the whole Allied position in the eastern Mediterranean would collapse.

In 1939 China opened a 717-mile (1147-kilometer) road through the Himalayas to Burma, which includes the treacherous "21 curves" at Annan. How did Japanese control of the Burma Road during the war hurt the Chinese?

Plans for reducing the Axis powers to "unconditional surrender" were discussed at Casablanca.

To regain the initiative, the British built a last line of defense at the railway junction of El Alamein, about 70 miles (112 kilometers) from Alexandria. At this point, General Bernard Montgomery was given command. He carefully waited until he had superiority in tanks and soldiers. Then, in late October 1942, he launched an attack on Rommel's forces. Within ten days, the Germans were forced to retreat. For the next two months, the British pushed them back across the Egyptian-Libyan frontier. At the end of January 1943, Montgomery captured Tripoli, the capital of Libya. Now neighboring Tunisia was open to Allied conquest.

The advance from Egypt was the eastern half of a "pincers movement" the Allies had planned to regain North Africa from the Axis. The western half began with a series of landings at Casablanca in Morocco and at Oran and Algiers in Algeria. When the Allies landed in these areas, they met heavy resistance from the Vichy French who governed French North Africa. To end the fighting, Allied commander Dwight D. Eisenhower made an agreement with Admiral François Darlan, a third-ranking Vichy official. In return for Allied support of his claim to French North Africa, Darlan ordered an end to the fighting. On November 11, 1942, an armistice was concluded. Now the Free French[2] were able to join the Allies in capturing Tunisia, the last German stronghold in North Africa.

In December 1942, Darlan was killed by an opponent. Shortly after, General de Gaulle succeeded him. Meanwhile, the pincers were pushing in on Tunisia. In the early spring of 1943, the Allies attacked from the east and the west. In May, Axis forces in Tunisia surrendered to the Allies.

Conferences

In January 1943, Churchill and Roosevelt met with other Allied leaders in a conference at Casablanca, French Morocco. Stalin had been invited but could not attend. During the confer-

---

[2]The Free French, led by General Charles de Gaulle, made up the anti-Nazi French government-in-exile. Headquartered in London, the movement coordinated the activity of French forces fighting on the Allied side.

EASTERN FRONT 1941-1944

ence, it was decided that the Allies would fight until the Axis surrendered unconditionally.

In May, at a British-American conference in Washington, D.C., Roosevelt, Churchill, and various British and American military officials discussed the opening of a second front in Europe. They decided that in the spring of 1944 they would invade Normandy, a region of northwestern France on the English Channel. In August, at a conference in Quebec, the date for the invasion was reconfirmed. Three months later, Stalin, Churchill, and Roosevelt met in Tehran, Iran. At the four-day meeting, Stalin agreed to the British-American invasion of western Europe. He promised to open a Soviet offensive on the eastern front at the same time.

The Campaign in Italy

At the Casablanca Conference in early 1943, the Allies had discussed what they could do to secure the Mediterranean. They decided they could attain this goal by invading Sicily and then, if the outlook were favorable, Italy itself.

The fall of Mussolini ended the 21-year period of fascist rule in Italy.

In October 1943 the Badoglio government declared war on Germany. Point out that the Badoglio government represented the south, while German troops controlled the north.

NORTH AFRICAN AND ITALIAN CAMPAIGNS 1942-1944

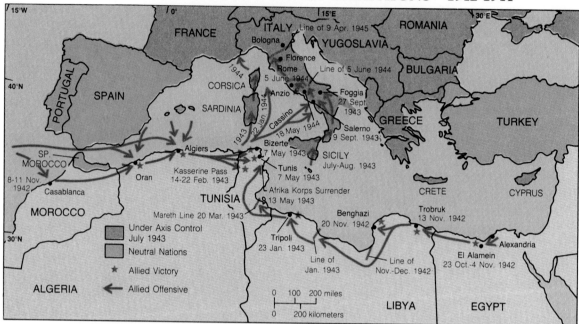

In July 1943, the Allies, under the command of General Eisenhower, began a combined air and sea attack on Sicily. By August 17, they had reached Messina, a seaport on the extreme northeastern tip of Sicily, where they expected the Germans to escape to the Italian mainland. Although the Allies already had taken the rest of Sicily, they could not prevent the evacuation of some 39,000 German soldiers, 70,000 Italians, and all their equipment.

The conquest of Sicily led quickly to the downfall of Mussolini. On July 25, King Victor Emmanuel III of Italy fired Mussolini, had him arrested, and sent him to prison. Marshal Pietro Badoglio became the new prime minister of Italy. Badoglio promised Hitler that Italy would keep fighting. At the same time, however, he ordered that the Fascist party be dissolved, and on September 3, he signed a secret act of surrender to the Allies.

The Allied forces crossed the Strait of Messina and landed in Calabria on the Italian mainland. On September 8, news of Badoglio's unconditional surrender was announced. Two days later, the Germans occupied Rome, and the king and

Badoglio withdrew to southern Italy. The Germans rescued Mussolini and put him in control of northern Italy. Southern Italy remained under Badoglio.

A new, more bitter phase of the war began for Italy. For a year and a half, the Allies fought their way up the peninsula. As preparations were underway for the Normandy invasion, reinforcements could not be spared to break the stalemate in Italy.

The Germans set up their defenses at Monte Cassino, the sixth-century monastery that had been the birthplace of the Benedictine Order. Located on a mountain top, the monastery dominated the road the Allied forces would have to take to Rome. When the Allies could not penetrate the German defenses at Monte Cassino, they landed behind the German lines at Anzio, about 30 miles (48 kilometers) south of Rome. They thought the landing would force the Germans to withdraw from Monte Cassino and open the road to Rome.

Not until May did Allied troops dislodge the Germans from Monte Cassino. In the process, they bombed and destroyed the monastery.

Point out that the Allies entered Rome from the south. It was the first time in its long history that the city had been captured from the south.

They did not know that the Germans had let the monks remain inside the monastery and had set up their fortifications outside the monastery wall.

The British and the Americans broke out of Anzio and headed north. On June 4, 1944, the Allies entered Rome, which the Germans abandoned without a fight.

The Normandy Invasion

Operation Overlord was unmatched during World War II. No other offensive was as large and as carefully planned as this operation to open the second front. General Eisenhower organized close to 150,000 soldiers, 5,300 ships, and 12,000 planes to take part in the invasion. The invading force and all of its equipment and supplies assembled in southern England to prepare for the invasion.

The Germans knew there would be an invasion, but they did not know when or where it would occur. So they spread their forces thinly along the English Channel coast of France and strengthened their defenses of the Normandy beaches.

The Allies had intended to launch the invasion in May, but they postponed the day of attack, D-Day, until June. Bad weather and choppy seas nearly delayed it yet another month. On June 6, the weather cleared and the Allied forces invaded a 60-mile (96-kilometer) stretch of the Normandy coast.

By the beginning of July, more than 1 million troops had landed on the continent, and massive numbers of fresh forces and supplies poured in through northern France. On July 25, the Americans began a breakthrough at St. Lô. By early August, American tank commander General George Patton and his forces were in open country racing across northern France. Within a month and a half, almost all of France had been liberated.

At this point, General de Gaulle ordered his forces to advance on Paris, where ten days earlier the French Resistance had risen up against their German occupiers. On August 25, 1944, de Gaulle, whom the French already considered their liberator and leader, entered Paris. By the next day, Paris was a free city for the first time in four years.

While the German high command knew an Allied invasion of occupied France was imminent, it disagreed on whether the Allies would choose Pas de Calais near Dunkirk or Normandy. Allied counter-intelligence played on this indecision by feeding the Germans false information about dummy troop installations across the English Channel from Pas de Calais. The installation was complete with unoccupied barracks and mockups of tanks and planes. The deception worked—the Germans were caught ill prepared for the massive amphibious assault at Normandy. How long did it take for the invading Allied forces to liberate Paris?

Refer students to the map of the Eastern Front on p. 649.

On May 7, 1942, Allied naval and air forces stopped a possible Japanese invasion of Australia by winning the battle of the Coral Sea. The victory made possible the U.S. offensive campaign in August.

Soviet Advances

Meanwhile, the Soviet army kept advancing, recovering one Soviet city after another. In January 1944, it relieved the siege of Leningrad. More than 800,000 of the city's inhabitants had died of cold or starvation or had been killed by Germans during the 890-day siege. By spring of 1944, the Soviets had fully liberated the Crimea and the Ukraine. In July, they crossed the Polish frontier and soon were on the outskirts of the capital city of Warsaw.

On August 1, however, the Polish Resistance rose up against the Germans and fought them in the streets of Warsaw. In retaliation, the Germans burned and destroyed much of the city. Two hundred fifty thousand Poles were killed in the 60-day struggle. Because the Polish resisters were anti-Communist, Stalin did nothing to help them. Nor would he allow the British to use behind-the-lines airfields to airlift supplies to them. This embittered the Poles and renewed western suspicions of Stalin's motives. The West feared that Stalin wanted eastern Europe.

On August 23, Romania had surrendered to the Soviets. This opened the Balkans to the advancing Soviets. Shortly after, Bulgaria sued for peace and joined the war on the Soviet side. By October 1944, almost all of East Central Europe was under Soviet control.

The Struggle for the Pacific

The battle continued to rage in the Pacific. In early August 1942, the Americans launched a campaign in the Solomon Islands. While troops under General Douglas MacArthur attacked the Japanese on land, naval forces under Admiral Chester W. Nimitz confronted them on the seas.

In the Solomon Islands, the Americans built their own airstrip. Shortly after, they attacked

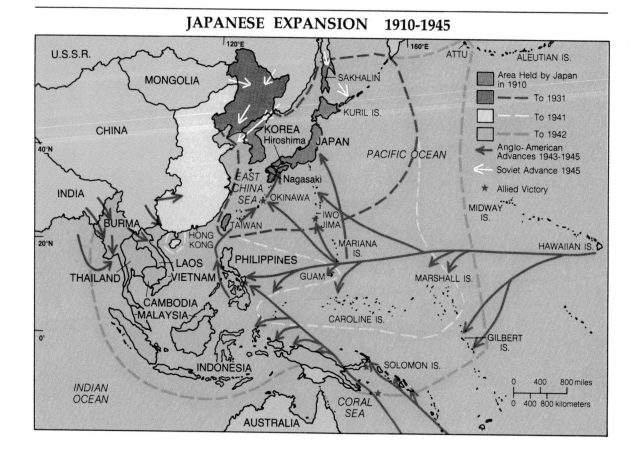

JAPANESE EXPANSION 1910-1945

the rough volcanic island of Guadalcanal. The six-month land, naval, and air battle for control of the island ended in victory for the Allies. It was the first in a series of battles fought by the Americans as they made their way north toward Japan. Their strategy was to leapfrog, capture some islands and bypass others. Those bypassed would be isolated, cut off from supplies, and would "wither on the vine."

By early November, the Americans had taken the largest island in the Solomons. They also had defeated the Japanese at the naval battle of Empress Augusta Bay. As the Americans advanced toward Japan, Japanese military leaders called upon their soldiers to die for their homeland. Pilots known as **kamikazes** volunteered for suicide missions against the Americans, crashing their bomb-laden aircraft into Allied bases and ships. The Japanese were far from ready to give up.

1. Identify: Erwin Rommel, Battle of Midway, Stalingrad, Casablanca, Normandy, Tehran, Warsaw, El Alamein, Bernard Montgomery, Dwight D. Eisenhower, François Darlan, Pietro Badoglio, Anzio, Operation Overlord, D-Day, George Patton, Douglas MacArthur, Chester W. Nimitz.
2. How did the Soviets plan to defeat the Germans at Stalingrad?
3. What strategy did the Allies use to try to bring the war in North Africa to an end?
4. What plans did the Allies make at the Tehran conference in 1943?
5. What did the Americans hope to do with their leapfrog strategy in the Pacific?

5 1945: War's End

In February 1945, Roosevelt, Churchill, Stalin, and their chief advisers met at Yalta, a resort in the southern Crimea. By then, it was clear that Hitler would be defeated shortly. Critical matters had to be resolved concerning postwar Europe.

Churchill and Roosevelt feared that Stalin intended to establish Communist governments in eastern Europe. Under their pressure, Stalin agreed to hold free elections in Soviet-occupied eastern Europe. In return, the Soviet Union was to get the eastern half of Poland.

Other agreements were made at Yalta. At the war's end, Germany was to be disarmed and divided into four zones that would be occupied and administered by Britain, France, the United States, and the Soviet Union. Berlin also was to be jointly administered and divided into zones. Poland was to be compensated for loss of eastern territory to the Soviet Union by receiving former German land.

It also was agreed that France and China would be invited to help sponsor a conference to form the United Nations, a permanent international organization that would maintain peace and security after the war. The groundwork for a charter for it had been laid at a conference at Dumbarton Oaks just outside Washington, D.C.

Victory over Germany

Before Yalta, in early September 1944, the Allies had launched an attack on Germany. As they advanced from the east to the west and bombed German cities, Hitler insisted that Germany would never surrender. Although most of the German people still remained loyal to Hitler, resistance to his leadership had grown among his chief generals and others. Two months earlier, a group of his top generals had even made an unsuccessful attempt to assassinate him.

Hitler was convinced that a surprise offensive through the lightly defended Ardennes would reverse the Allied advance. In spite of his generals' objections, this last and desperate offensive was launched in mid-December 1944. The battle that followed was known as the Battle of the Bulge because the Germans broke through the Allied lines, causing a dangerous "bulge" in them. The Allies finally checked the German drive at Bastogne, Belgium. By January 1945, they were ready to storm the Rhine River, the historic defensive barrier of Germany. By April, the British and the Americans had reached the Elbe River. That same month, they met with Soviet troops at Torgau on the Elbe.

On May 8, 1945, V-E (Victory in Europe) Day, the war in Europe formally came to an end. Germany had surrendered unconditionally. By then, Mussolini had been caught by Italian

On May 1, 1945, German radio announced that Hitler had died and that Karl Doenitz had succeeded him.

Between May and August 1945 United States battleships shelled Japan's major cities, while the air force bombed the Japanese industrial centers.

partisans and shot and hung. Hitler had committed suicide in his **bunker,** a fortified underground chamber, in Berlin.

Victory over Japan

Like Germany, Japan held out well after it was clear it could no longer win. Before the end of 1944, American planes were bombing Japan, and the Japanese prime minister and his cabinet had resigned. In the Battle of Leyte Gulf, the last naval engagement of the war, the Japanese lost what remained of their sea power.

Still, they fought on. In 1945 two of the fiercest battles in the Pacific were fought for control of two islands. Iwo Jima, the largest of the Volcano Islands, was 750 miles (1,200 kilometers) from Tokyo. Okinawa, the largest of the Ryukyu Islands, was 360 miles (576 kilometers) off the southern tip of Japan. These islands were vital because they put Japan within easy reach of attack. The Japanese lost both battles.

On July 26, 1945, the United States issued an ultimatum to Japan to surrender. When the Japanese refused, the United States decided to

ALLIED OFFENSIVE IN EUROPE   JUNE 1944–MAY 1945

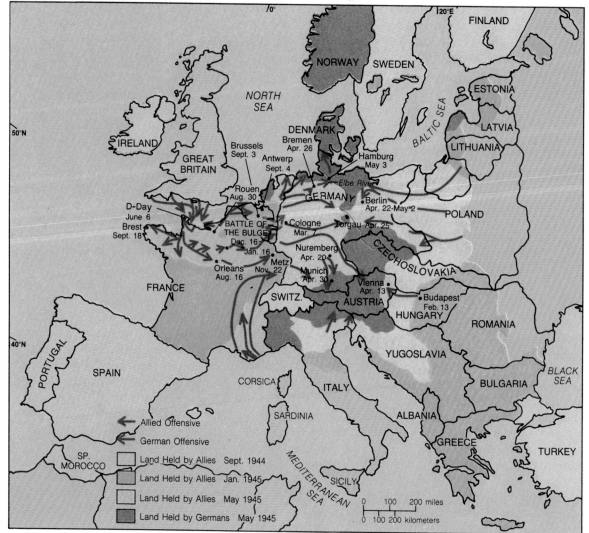

The Soviets declared war on Japan on August 8, 1945, immediately invading Manchuria.

This photo was taken a few hours after the atomic bomb exploded in Hiroshima. Victims waited to receive first aid from doctors and nurses who were injured themselves. Since nearby army posts experienced little damage, soldiers were the first to begin relief measures. Hospitals filled quickly, and public schools became first aid stations. Those who survived the explosion were badly burned and suffered radiation sickness. A black rain of mud, ash, and other radioactive fallout lingered long after the attack. How many Japanese were killed by the atomic bomb?

use a new secret weapon—the atomic bomb—to bring an end to the war. The bomb had the explosive force of 20,000 tons of TNT. Harry Truman, who had become president in April 1945 after the death of Roosevelt, received the news that the bomb had been tested successfully while he was at a conference in Potsdam, Germany. He and the other Allied leaders there were finalizing the plans they would put into effect after the war was over.

On August 6, 1945, the first atomic bomb was dropped on Hiroshima, a center of the Japanese munitions industry. The devastation was far greater than anyone had anticipated. Within moments of the blast, over 60 percent of Hiroshima was leveled. When the Japanese still refused to surrender, the Americans dropped another bomb three days later on the port city of Nagasaki. The destruction there was even greater than Hiroshima. In both cities, about 200,000 Japanese were killed.

Japan's Emperor Hirohito issued a radio message saying that "the unendurable must be endured." On August 14, 1945, Japan agreed to surrender unconditionally. President Truman declared August 15, V-J (Victory over Japan) Day. On September 2, the surrender was made official in a formal ceremony aboard the battleship *Missouri* in Tokyo Bay. The war was over.

The Aftermath

More than 70 million people had fought in World War II. Between 15 and 17 million had died, and many more were wounded or psychologically scarred. As many as 12 million were refugees or displaced persons. In addition, large parts of Europe and Asia lay in ruins. Because of heavy aerial bombing and shifting battlelines, the devastation was far more widespread than in World War I.

Holocaust The most appalling horror of the war was the Holocaust,[3] or the mass murder of European Jews by the Nazis. As part of his plan for world conquest, Hitler had set out to eliminate the Jews. When the Nazis advanced throughout Europe in 1939 and 1940, Jews in conquered territories were forced to live in special areas called **ghettos.** They also had to work as slave laborers. In 1941 the Nazis began their campaign of mass murder. Millions of Jews were immediately shot or were imprisoned in concentration camps. The most infamous camps were Auschwitz and Dachau in Poland and Buchenwald in Germany.

In the concentration camps, the captives lived and worked under horrible conditions. Many died of starvation and disease; others were the

[3]Holocaust means "widespread destruction."

Some teachers might wish to devote several lessons to the study of the Holocaust.

Jewish artist Felix Nussbaum was imprisoned in Auschwitz, where he painted The Condemned. *He and his wife perished in this camp in 1944. How did the Allies react to initial reports of Nazi brutality toward Jews?*

victims of cruel experiments carried out by Nazi doctors. A large number of prisoners were marched into gas chambers in which they were killed with poison gas.

The Nazis tried to keep the concentration camps secret from the general population and from the rest of the world. Even Jews in the ghettos at first were unaware of the fate in store for them. But once they became aware of Nazi intentions, Jews fought back in Warsaw and other European cities. However, Jewish resistance groups were outnumbered and lacked arms to fight the Germans. In spite of their heroic efforts, Jewish resisters were easily defeated.

During the war, rumors had reached the Allies about the Nazi treatment of the Jews and other groups. However, little action was taken, since many governments disbelieved the rumors and devoted their primary attention to winning the war. The truth about the Holocaust became clearly known when Allied forces liberated the concentration camps at the end of the war. The horrors they uncovered sickened and outraged the world. More than 12 million people had been slaughtered by the Nazis. Six million were Jews—about two-thirds of Europe's Jewish population. The other 6 million victims belonged to minority and ethnic groups, such as the Slavs and the Gypsies, whom Hitler had despised and had vowed to eliminate.

Nuremberg Trials After the war, the Allies began to address the wrongs committed by the Nazis. It was decided at the Potsdam conference that Nazi leaders would be tried and punished for pursuing "aggressive war" and for "crimes against humanity."

Have students research more fully the organization of the League of Nations and compare it to the United Nations.

Between November 1945 and September 1946, trials were held at Nuremberg to bring justice to the guilty and to rid Germany of Nazi influence. Twenty-one top level Nazis were tried. Eleven were sentenced to be hung, seven were sent to prison, and three were acquitted. The trials raised important questions about one's personal responsibilities when ordered to commit a crime during a war.

United Nations   As planned at the Yalta conference, representatives from 50 nations met in San Francisco on April 25, 1945, to draft the Charter of the United Nations (UN).

The Charter was completed in early June. Although it provided for six major bodies, it assigned the bulk of power to only two of them—the Security Council and the General Assembly. The Security Council, which decided diplomatic, political, and military disputes, was made up of 11 members. The five permanent members were Britain, China, France, the United States, and the Soviet Union. Each was given the right to veto any Security Council decision. The other six members served two-year terms. The General Assembly, the policy-mak-

ing body, was made up of representatives from all the member nations of the organization. Each nation had one vote.

The third, the Economic and Social Council, was created to oversee the fight against poverty, ignorance, and disease. The fourth, the International Court of Justice, was established to deal with international legal disputes. The fifth, the Trusteeship Council, was created to promote the welfare of people in colonial territories and to help them toward self-government. The sixth, the Secretariat, was created to handle the administrative work of the United Nations.

The Charter of the United Nations was signed by all 50 nations on June 26, 1945.

1. Identify: Yalta, United Nations, Dumbarton Oaks, Battle of the Bulge, V-E Day, Battle of Leyte Gulf, Iwo Jima, Okinawa, Harry Truman, Potsdam, Hiroshima, Nagasaki, V-J Day, *Missouri*, Holocaust, Nuremberg.
2. What was decided at the Yalta conference?
3. How effective was the German offensive through the Ardennes? What happened afterwards?
4. How did the Americans convince the Japanese to surrender?

From the ten-month trials at Nuremberg, 42 volumes of testimony and documentary evidence were recorded. The proceedings were highly criticized by legal authorities who claimed that the procedures followed in the trials were unprecedented in an international court of law. The accusers in the trials, the Allied nations, served as judges, and defense attorneys for the Nazi officers were prevented from introducing evidence against the Allied powers. On what charges were the Nazis tried?

CHAPTER 28 REVIEW

Summary

1. Dissatisfaction with and bitterness about the peace settlements made at the end of World War I was a primary factor in the willingness of Japan, Italy, and Germany to go to war again.

2. Europe and Asia slid toward war as Britain, France, and the United States refused to oppose the expansionist moves of Japan into Manchuria, Italy into Ethiopia, and Germany into the Rhineland, Austria, and Czechoslovakia.

3. The Soviet Union, convinced that the West was not interested in its welfare, allied itself with Germany in 1939.

4. World War II began on September 1, 1939, when Hitler invaded Poland, whose borders had been guaranteed by France and Britain. Hitler's blitzkrieg of Poland devastated the country and resulted in its being divided between Germany and the Soviet Union.

5. By late June 1940, Hitler's forces had taken Denmark, Norway, the Netherlands, Belgium, and France; and Italy had declared war on France and Britain.

6. When Hitler could not bomb the British into submission during the Battle of Britain, he tried to starve them out by sinking their ships in the Atlantic. This brought the United States to Britain's aid.

7. After his first major defeat in the Battle of Britain, Hitler reneged on his non-aggression pact with Stalin and invaded the Soviet Union.

8. Japan's goal to establish a Greater East Asia Co-prosperity Sphere led it to expand into China and Indonesia, ally itself with Germany and Italy, and attack Pearl Harbor. The Japanese attack on Pearl Harbor on December 7, 1941, brought America into the war on the side of Britain and France.

9. From 1941 to 1944, the Allies and the Axis fought one another in western and eastern Europe, Italy and the Mediterranean, Burma and China, and the Atlantic and Pacific, with most of the early victories going to the Axis.

10. The war in Europe came to an end formally on May 8, 1945, when Germany surrendered unconditionally. The war with Japan did not come to an end until August 14, 1945, after the United States had dropped two atomic bombs on Japanese cities.

11. After the war, some Nazis were tried at Nuremberg and punished for their actions during the war.

12. The United Nations was established after the war to maintain peace and to help solve the economic, social, and cultural problems of the nations of the world.

Building Vocabulary

collective security	blitzkrieg	cash and carry	resistance groups
sanctions	sitzkrieg	lend-lease	kamikazes
appeasement	blitz	scorched-earth policy	bunker
lebensraum	wolf packs	nonbelligerency	ghettos

Reviewing the Main Ideas

1. Why were Japan, Italy, and Germany bitter after World War I?

2. What effect did Chamberlain's policy of appeasement have on Czechoslovakia?

3. What reason did Hitler give for annexing Austria and taking control of the Sudetenland? How did Britain and France react to these actions?
4. Why did Stalin sign a non-aggression pact with Hitler instead of allying with France and Britain?
5. Why were the French so sure that France was safe from Hitler?
6. Why did Hitler decide to invade the Soviet Union? What was the result?
7. Why did the Allies invade Sicily?
8. How successful was Operation Overlord in 1944?
9. Why was Roosevelt willing to make concessions to Stalin at Yalta?
10. How did the Germans feel about Hitler by the fall of 1944?
11. What impact did the Holocaust have on Europe's Jews?
12. What were the six major bodies of the United Nations? What was the purpose of each?

Discussing Important Ideas

1. What did Japan's actions in Manchuria and Italy's actions in Ethiopia reveal about the League of Nations?
2. What do you think might have happened if Churchill, rather than Chamberlain, had been prime minister of Britain when Hitler invaded the Rhineland and Czechoslovakia and annexed Austria? Give reasons for your answer.
3. If you had been in Stalin's position, would you have turned to Hitler? What would have been your options? Explain your answers.
4. Of what importance to the rest of Europe was the Spanish Civil War?
5. The Soviet Union has always maintained that it was dealt with unfairly during World War II. Do you agree? Why or why not?
6. Had the Japanese not bombed Pearl Harbor, do you think the United States would have continued to stay out of the war? Explain.
7. Do you think the war could have been avoided? If so, how?
8. What lessons do you think the world should have learned from World War II?

Using Illustrations

Study the cartoon on page 647, read the caption, and answer the following questions:
1. What does the dominoes game represent?
2. What can you tell from the way the six figures are arranged around the table?
3. Whose "turn" is it?
4. Why do you think Hitler is shown glaring at Roosevelt?
5. Which players appear to be winning?
6. What do you think the cartoon explains?

UNIT 7 REVIEW

Summary

1. In the late 1800's and early 1900's, the industrialized nations of Europe came into conflict as they extended their empires. The rise of nationalism and militarism increased their rivalries. By 1907, Europe had divided into two opposing military alliances.

2. In 1914 the assassination of the heir to the Austrian throne triggered World War I. The Central Powers—Germany, Austria-Hungary, Bulgaria, and the Ottoman Empire—fought against the Allies—Britain, France, Russia, Serbia, Belgium, and later, Japan, Montenegro, and the United States.

3. During most of the war, each side suffered heavy casualities, but won no decisive victories. In 1918 World War I finally ended. The peace settlements punished and weakened Germany and the other Central Powers. National boundaries were altered, and the League of Nations was established.

4. Following the war, totalitarian dictatorships arose in Russia, Italy, and Germany, alarming the western democracies. In Asia, Africa, and Latin America, nationalist movements demanded independence from foreign influence or control.

5. World War II began in 1939 when Hitler invaded Poland. During the war, the major world powers were once again divided into two opposing alliances: the Axis (Germany, Italy, and Japan) and the Allies (Britain, France, the United States, and the Soviet Union).

6. Eleven months after the invasion of Normandy in 1944, the Germans surrendered. The war with Japan did not end until the Unted States dropped atomic bombs on Japan.

7. As the Allies liberated Europe, the truth about the Holocaust was revealed. More than 12 million people, half of whom were Jews, had been slaughtered by the Nazis.

8. In 1945 the United Nations was established as an international organization for peace.

Developing Understanding

1. What conditions in Europe led to World War I? What was the turning point in the war?
2. How did totalitarian governments come to power in Russia, Italy, and Germany?
3. What were the causes and impact of the depression of the 1930's?
4. What did nationalist movements in Asia, Africa, and Latin America accomplish?
5. How did the World War I peace settlements contribute to the outbreak of World War II?
6. Why do you think the Allies were victorious in World War II?

Developing Skills

Primary sources—firsthand accounts or evidence such as letters, business contracts, government documents, photographs, and diaries—provide valuable information about historical events and developments. Historians and students of history must learn how to analyze a primary source.

The following reading is an example of a primary source. It was originally written by Benito Mussolini for the *Encyclopedia Italiana* (1932). Mussolini was aided by Giovanni Gentile, the editor of the encyclopedia, who was known as the "philosopher of Fascism." To analyze the source, answer the questions at the end.

Fascism . . . believes neither in the possibility nor the utility of perpetual peace. . . . War alone brings up to its highest tension all human energy and puts the stamp of nobility upon the peoples who have the courage to meet it. . . .

. . . . Fascism combats the whole complex system of democratic ideology. . . . [It] denies that the majority, by the simple fact that it is a majority, can direct human society; it denies that numbers alone can govern by means of a periodical consultation, and it affirms the immutable, beneficial, and fruitful inequality of mankind. . . . The foundation of Fascism is the conception of the State, its character, its duty, and its aim. Fascism conceives of the State as an absolute, in comparison with which all individuals or groups are relative. . . .

For Fascism, the growth of empire . . . is an essential manifestation of vitality. . . . Fascism is the doctrine best adapted to represent the tendencies and aspirations of a people, like the people of Italy, who are rising again after many centuries of abasement and foreign servitude. But empire demands discipline, the coordination of all forces, and a deeply felt sense of duty and sacrifice: This fact explains many aspects of the practical working of the regime, the character of many forces in the State, and the necessarily severe measures which must be taken. . . .*

1. What qualifications did the author have to write on this subject?
2. When, where, and for what purpose was the article written?
3. What information does the article give you about fascism? What are its main points?
4. How could this information be verified by other sources?

---

*"The Political and Social Doctrine of Fascism," by Benito Mussolini, quoted in *International Conciliation*, January 1935, No. 306, pp. 7-9, 13-16.

Suggested Activities

1. Which of Wilson's Fourteen Points should have been included in the Treaty of Versailles? Participate in a dramatization of the conference negotiations to arrive at an answer.
2. For one week, record the activities you do outside your home. Then, consider how each might be affected if you lived in a totalitarian state.
3. Read several poems or stories by twentieth-century African writers. Discuss how the authors view the relationship between traditional lifestyles and modern ones.
4. If you had been a military adviser for the Allies in World War II, which recommendation would you have given for ending the war with Japan? Would you have proposed an invasion of Japan or dropping the bomb?

Suggested Readings

Appel, Benjamin. *The Age of Dictators.* Crown, 1968. Looks at the rise of totalitarianism in Europe during the twentieth century.

Feis, Herbert. *Churchill, Roosevelt, and Stalin.* Princeton, 1966. Studies the careers of the three main Allied leaders from 1941 to 1945.

Paradis, Adrian A. *The Hungry Years: The Story of the American Great Depression,* Chilton, 1967. Discusses the causes of the depression and its impact on the American people.

Remarque, Erich Maria. *All Quiet on the Western Front.* Fawcett, 1979. Novel about a young German soldier in World War I.

Schnabel, Ernst. *Anne Frank: A Portrait of Courage.* Harcourt, 1958. Story about a young Jewish girl living in Nazi-controlled Europe.

The Contemporary World

662

1966	1970	1974	1978	1982	1986

1967 Six-Day War

1969 Americans land on the moon

1970's Détente

1972 Nixon in China
1972 SALT I

1978 Camp David Agreement

1979 Iranian revolution

1980 Outbreak Iran-Iraq War
1980 Solidarity

1983 Military coup in Nigeria

1984 Soviets boycott Olympics

After World War II, democracy thrived in North America, Western Europe, and Oceania. Communism was dominant in Eastern Europe and parts of East Asia. Newly independent nations in Asia, Africa, and Latin America did not align themselves with either the East or the West.

In the mid-1980's, the world's nearly 180 independent nations differed widely in size, population, government, and culture. In spite of differences, they became increasingly interdependent. That is, the actions and decisions of one country had an impact on other countries. Global interdependence increased as nations relied more and more upon the natural resources and manufactured goods of other nations. In the process of becoming more interdependent, nations have often come into conflict. However, they have also developed new ways to cooperate.

Tokyo skyline

CHAPTER 29

The Berlin Wall

66 *A shadow has fallen on the scenes so lately lighted by the Allied victory.* **99**

Winston Churchill, British Prime Minister (1874-1965)

East-West Relations

W orld War II had weakened the countries of Europe to the point where their influence in world affairs was greatly diminished. The United States and the Soviet Union emerged as the most powerful nations in the world. Differences in ideology and policy soon pulled the two countries apart and led to a struggle between them known as the **cold war.**[1] In the cold war, each superpower sought world influence by means short of total war, such as the threat of force, the use of propaganda, and the sending of military and economic aid to weaker nations.

1 Postwar Developments

The cold war became the focus of international relations during the late 1940's and the early 1950's. This period is often called the era of **bipolarism,** or the domination of world affairs by two superpowers. The superpower rivalry divided much of the world into two blocs: one led by the United States, the other by the Soviet Union.

Soviet and American Goals

When World War II ended, the Soviet Union was economically devastated. It lost nearly 20 million casualties, which was a large part of its human resources. Stalin could have made the economic reconstruction of the Soviet Union his primary goal. Instead, he devoted his attention to territorial expansion as well as economic reconstruction. Stalin did not trust the western

---

[1]The term "cold war" was first used during the 1930's to describe Nazi Germany's use of threats and terror against small nations. In the late 1940's, American political commentators adopted the term to describe the struggle between the United States and the Soviet Union.

Allies. He believed that the capitalist countries of the West were out to destroy the Soviet Union. Therefore, Soviet strategy after World War II was to expand communism and weaken the capitalist countries.

In 1945 the United States looked forward to an era of tranquility in foreign affairs. As a World War II victor, it had unequaled military strength and a productive industrial economy. It also was the only nation in the world to have the atomic bomb. Most Americans, however, were tired of war and did not want to assume the burden of world leadership. Public opinion was strongly in favor of using the United Nations for resolving international disputes peacefully. American diplomats and political leaders expected that friendly relations with the Soviet Union would continue in the postwar period. However, this optimism about Soviet-American ties soon faded as a result of various Soviet actions in eastern Europe.

Eastern Europe

Eastern Europe became the first region where Soviet and American interests came into conflict. During the closing months of World War II, Soviet troops had captured much of eastern Europe from the Nazis. At the Yalta and Potsdam conferences, the Allies recognized the region as a Soviet sphere of influence. Stalin claimed that the Soviet Union needed a friendly eastern Europe as protection against any future western attack. Roosevelt and Churchill were willing to grant his request, but they expected Stalin to fulfill the Yalta promise to allow political freedom for such nations as Bulgaria, Poland, Hungary, and Romania. Stalin, however, feared the emergence of anti-Soviet governments in eastern Europe. He did not want the West to control the region, and therefore he refused to accept the western interpretation of the Yalta agreements.

Discuss the literal and figurative meaning of the phrase "iron curtain."

In February 1945, Allied leaders, Winston Churchill, Franklin Roosevelt, and Joseph Stalin met at Yalta on the Crimean Peninsula. They discussed Soviet entry into the war against Japan, the Allied occupation of Germany, the political freedom of eastern European countries, and the creation of an international organization for peace. The Yalta agreements broke down almost immediately. What became the major area of dispute between the West and the Soviet Union?

Soviet Satellites   Beginning in the spring of 1945, communism gained widespread influence in eastern Europe. In Albania and Yugoslavia, local Communist parties, which had led the resistance against Axis forces in their countries, took control with little help from the Soviets. In Poland, Romania, and Bulgaria, where Soviet troops were in full command, the Soviet Union aided in the formation of coalition governments that included Communists and left-wing non-Communists. Soon the Soviets further tightened their grip. They refused to allow free elections and eliminated freedoms of speech, religion, and the press in Bulgaria and Poland. In the next few years, the same tactics were used in other countries of eastern Europe. Non-Communists were ousted from governments, and the Communists gained complete control. Contacts between the West and eastern Europe were gradually curtailed. By 1947 most of the nations of the region had become Soviet **satellites,** controlled by the Soviet Union.

Western Response   President Roosevelt had believed that postwar cooperation with the Soviets was possible. But a few weeks before his death in April 1945, he realized that Soviet policies in eastern Europe were undermining the spirit of the wartime alliance. Roosevelt's successor, Harry Truman, began to take a hard line toward the Soviets. He received the backing of British Prime Minister Churchill. In March 1946, Churchill, in a speech given in Fulton, Missouri, said that an "iron curtain"—a Soviet-made barrier—had fallen across Europe.

> Nobody knows what Soviet Russia and its Communist international organization intend to do in the immediate future, or what are the limits, if any, to their expansive . . . tendencies. . . . From Stettin in the Baltic to Trieste in the Adriatic an iron curtain has descended across the continent of Europe.*

*Struggle for the World, Desmond Donnelly, © 1965 by St. Martin's Press, p. 211.

Point out that it had long been a Russian goal to control the Dardanelles. Refer students to the discussion of the Crimean War on p. 380.

Some teachers might wish to discuss the status of the arms race today.

Churchill, in effect, recognized that Europe was now divided into two distinct parts: non-Communist Western Europe and Communist Eastern Europe. He urged cooperation among the western democracies to stem the tide of Soviet expansionism.

Iran and Turkey

While the main area of dispute between the West and the Soviet Union was Eastern Europe, an East-West rivalry also developed in the Middle East. This region was valued by both sides for its oil. In 1946 the Soviets pressured the government of Iran for a share in that country's oil resources, which were largely controlled by the western democracies. The Soviets kept their army in northern Iran in violation of a 1942 treaty with the Allies.

Threatening the use of force to protect western interests in the region, the United States appealed to the United Nations Security Council for the withdrawal of Soviet troops from Iran. A few weeks later, the Soviet Union and Iran announced the withdrawal of Soviet troops in return for Iran's sale of oil to the Soviet Union. After the Soviet departure, the Iranian government gained control of Azerbaijan, a northern province held by Iranian Communists, and announced that it would not sell the Soviets the promised oil.

In the same year, the Soviet Union laid claim to Turkish territory. It also pressured Turkey for joint Turkish-Soviet administration of the Dardanelles. Soviet ships passed through the strait to the Mediterranean, and the Soviet government wanted some control over the area. The United States, however, saw the Soviet move as an attempt to dominate Turkey, Greece, and the Middle East. When the United States sent an aircraft carrier into Turkish waters, the Soviets backed down.

Atomic Energy

In late 1945, the United States proposed that the United Nations supervise all nuclear energy production. The following spring, United States Atomic Energy Comissioner Bernard Baruch offered a plan to ban atomic weapons. Under this plan, the United Nations would be allowed to inspect atomic facilities anywhere in the world to make sure that no country was secretly making bombs. Each country would also have to give up its veto power over United Nations' decisions dealing with atomic energy. When such an international control system had been set up, the United States would destroy its stockpile, or reserve supply, of atomic weapons.

The Soviets rejected Baruch's plan. Suspicious of the strong western influence in the United Nations, they stated they would not allow United Nations' inspectors into the Soviet Union nor would they give up their veto power. Instead, they demanded that the United States destroy its bombs at once. Unwilling to trust the Soviets, the United States refused to agree. In 1949 the Soviets successfully exploded their first atomic bomb. International tensions increased as the two superpowers engaged in an **arms race,** or a competition to strengthen their armed forces and weapons systems.

1. Identify: "iron curtain," Azerbaijan, Bernard Baruch.
2. What were Soviet and American goals after World War II?
3. How did the West respond to postwar Soviet expansion into Eastern Europe and the Middle East?
4. What plan was offered in 1946 to control nuclear weapons? Why was this plan not implemented?

2 Containment in Europe

During 1947 the Truman administration developed a new American foreign policy to deal with the Soviet Union and other Communist countries. This policy was known as **containment** because its purpose was to contain, or hold back, the spread of communism. Through a display of firmness, Truman hoped to keep communism inside its existing borders and to encourage its leaders to compromise with the West. He planned to carry out the containment policy by increasing American military strength, sending military aid to countries threatened by Communist takeover, and giving economic aid to needy areas overseas.

Kennan Article

The idea of containment was first presented in early 1947 by George Kennan, a State Department expert on the Soviet Union. In an article in the *Journal of Foreign Affairs,* Kennan said that the Soviets believed that communism would triumph over capitalism all over the world. In their desire to reach this goal, the Soviets would seek to expand their territory at the West's expense. However, Kennan thought the Soviets did not want a war with the West and were willing to take their time in pursuing world conquest. Therefore, he proposed that the United States pursue a "policy of firm containment, designed to confront the (Soviets) . . . at every point where they show signs of encroaching upon the interests" of the West. Kennan's ideas were accepted by the Truman administration and became the basis of American foreign policy for the next 30 years.

The Truman Doctrine

In the spring of 1947, Truman applied the containment policy for the first time in the eastern Mediterranean. In Greece, local Communists were fighting a guerrilla war against the pro-western monarchy. The West feared that the fall of Greece to communism would endanger western influence in the eastern Mediterranean region. British troops had checked the Communist advance in 1946 and continued to assist the Greek monarchy afterward. But aid flowed to the Greek Communists from neighboring Yugoslavia, Bulgaria, and Albania. Meanwhile, economic weakness at home prevented the British from continuing their commitment in Greece. In February 1947, Britain informed Truman of this fact and asked the United States to assume British responsibilities in the area.

Truman and Secretary of State George Marshall decided that the United States would take Britain's place in defending the eastern Mediterranean. In March, Truman asked Congress for a $400 million aid program for Greece and Turkey. In asking Congress for support, Truman made a new statement of foreign policy that became known as the Truman Doctrine. He stated:

> I believe that it must be the policy of the United States to support free peoples who are resisting attempted subjugation by armed minorities or by outside pressures. . . . If we falter in our leadership, we may endanger the peace of the world—and we shall surely endanger the welfare of our own nation.

Congress approved Truman's aid request. With the acceptance of the Truman Doctrine, the United States took on international responsibilities as the leader of the western world. American

During the German occupation of Greece, organized guerrillas provided strong resistance. Forming one of the forces were these men and women of the Communist controlled E.L.A.S. The E.L.A.S. reorganized in 1946 to fight a savage civil war against the pro-western Greek government. What factors persuaded Truman to assist the Greek government against the E.L.A.S. guerrillas?

The chart below is the subject of the "Using Charts" section of the Chapter 29 Review.

The Soviets insisted that the Marshall Plan was a device for the U.S. to gain control of Europe.

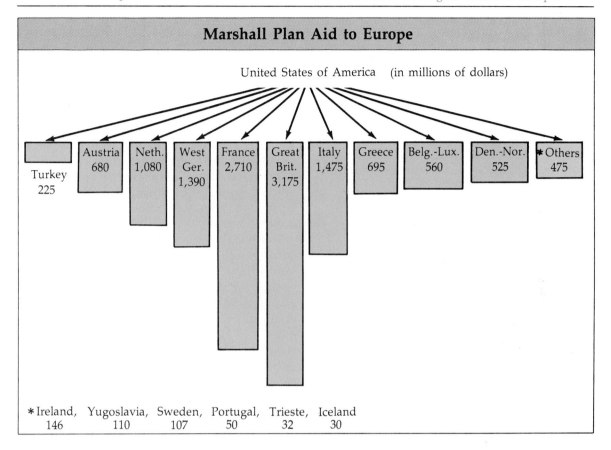

Marshall Plan Aid to Europe

United States of America   (in millions of dollars)

Turkey 225	Austria 680	Neth. 1,080	West Ger. 1,390	France 2,710	Great Brit. 3,175	Italy 1,475	Greece 695	Belg.-Lux. 560	Den.-Nor. 525	*Others 475

*Ireland, Yugoslavia, Sweden, Portugal, Trieste, Iceland
   146   110   107   50   32   30

military aid would now be available to any nation threatened by communism. As a result of American assistance, Greece was able to defeat the Communist guerrillas.

The Marshall Plan

Later in 1947, Truman applied the containment policy to Western Europe. World War II had dangerously weakened Europe's economy and social structure. The United States feared that a European economic collapse would open the area to communism. It believed that its own military and economic security depended on a strong and free Europe.

Therefore, the United States government devised a new approach to provide aid to Europe. Speaking at Harvard University on June 5, Secretary of State Marshall proposed a European aid program that became known as the Marshall Plan. Its purpose, he said, was to restore "the confidence of European people in the economic future of their own countries." In order for the plan to work, Marshall urged a united European effort to determine where Europe's economic needs lay and how the United States could help.

Western European countries responded enthusiastically to the Marshall Plan. However, the Soviet Union turned down the chance to participate in the plan and forced its satellites to do the same. Despite their great need for economic aid, the Soviets felt they could not afford to give out information about their economy and standard of living. They also opposed linking their socialist economy with the largely capitalist ones of Western Europe.

The Marshall Plan proved to be a great success. Western European nations worked together to boost productivity, reduce trade barriers, and use resources efficiently. They received about $13 billion in aid from the United States during the next four years. By 1951, Western European

The establishment of two German governments marked the unofficial recognition of respective areas of control for the Soviets and the western Allies.

economies were prospering, and the influence of communism in these nations had declined.

The Marshall Plan extended American influence in Western Europe and helped unite the region into a single economic bloc to counter the Soviets. In reaction to the Marshall Plan, in 1949 the Soviet Union set up a rival plan known as the Council of Mutual Economic Assistance, or COMECON. Eastern Europe was thus formed into a single economic bloc under the leadership of the Soviet Union.

Germany

As part of its containment policy, the United States wanted to incorporate Germany into the Marshall Plan. But Germany was still divided into zones of foreign occupation. As tension increased between the Soviet Union and the West, it was becoming obvious that no final peace agreement would be reached about Germany.

The Germans in the western zones, with assistance from the western Allies, moved quickly to rebuild their area. The British, French, and Americans believed that a strong democratic western Germany would be an asset in any confrontation with the Soviet Union. Free

elections for local governments were held in the western zones. In Berlin, the American, British, and French zones of the city were joined into what became known as West Berlin.

Berlin Blockade The three western powers also planned to set up a West German state by joining their zones of occupation. The Soviets, fearful of a reunited Germany, were determined to prevent this step. In June 1948, the Soviets acted to force the West to give up its plan. They blocked land routes from the West into West Berlin, which lay well within the Soviet zone of occupation.

The West's response was to launch a massive airlift to supply the city's needs. Several thousand tons of food, fuel, and other necessities were flown in every day for 11 months, with planes landing and taking off every three minutes in West Berlin's two airports. The morale of the 2 million West Berliners was boosted by this show of western support. As a result of the airlift, the Soviets finally lifted the blockade in May 1949.

Two Germanies Following the Berlin blockade, the western powers carried out their plans for the formation of an independent West

OCCUPATION OF GERMANY AND AUSTRIA 1945

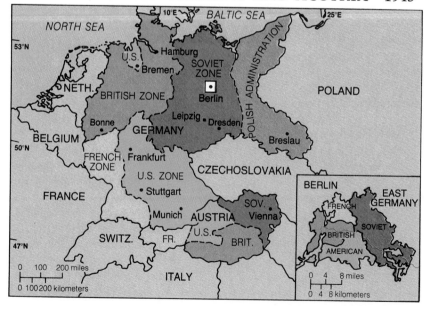

Stalin reimposed controls on the Soviet people after a period of relative freedom during the war.

After the Soviets blockaded the corridor to Berlin, supplies were airlifted by the American and British air forces. Over seven tons of medical and food supplies were flown into Templehoff Airport each day for eleven months. Some American pilots instituted an informal "Little Berlin Airlift" by dropping candy tied to handkerchief parachutes to the children who waved to them from rooftops. Why did the Soviets establish the blockade?

German state. In May 1949, a constitution was approved that set up a federal system of 11 states. In the fall of that year, the Federal Republic of Germany, or West Germany, was proclaimed, with its capital at Bonn. The Soviets then set up the German Democratic Republic, or East Germany, with its capital at East Berlin. Thus, Germany was divided into two different countries.

Alliances

Just before the Berlin blockade, another crisis had occurred in Europe. In February 1948, Czechoslovakia was taken over by Communists and became a Soviet satellite. The Czechoslovak and Berlin crises increased western concern about military defense. In April 1949, shortly before the end of the Berlin blockade, the North Atlantic Treaty Organization (NATO) was formed by Belgium, Britain, Canada, Denmark, France, Iceland, Italy, Luxemburg, the Netherlands, and the United States.[2] Members of this military alliance agreed that an attack on one would be considered an attack on all. In response to NATO, the Soviet Union and its Eastern European satellites signed a military alliance in 1955 known as the Warsaw Pact.

[2]In 1952 Greece and Turkey also joined the alliance.

1. Identify: George Kennan, Truman Doctrine, George Marshall, COMECON, West Berlin, Bonn, East Berlin, NATO, Warsaw Pact.
2. What was the purpose of the Marshall Plan?
3. Why did the Soviet Union impose a blockade on Berlin in 1948?

3   The Soviet Bloc

The cold war affected the internal policies of the Soviet Union and its Eastern European allies. Stalin believed that a full-scale conflict with the West was inevitable. To guard against the West, the Soviet ruler increased his control over the Soviet Union and Eastern Europe. He purged Communist parties of officials suspected of disloyalty. He also forbade writers and artists to use western ideas in their works.

The Soviet Union

After the war, Stalin worked to reconstruct heavy industry and boost the military might of his country. The Soviet Union surpassed its prewar rates of production in several major products, including coal, steel, and oil. It continued a high level of military spending and exploded its first nuclear bomb. To aid Soviet citizens, the government rebuilt the many towns

Refer students to the map of Europe on p. 589. Note the changes that have occurred between 1919 and 1945.

Stalin had been in power 29 years.

and villages that were destroyed during the war. However, the needs of consumers for better food, clothing, and housing were not met.

Stalin died on March 5, 1953. He was succeeded by a collective leadership of top Communist party officials. The new Soviet top command included Georgi Malenkov (prime minister), Vyacheslav Molotov (foreign minister), Lavrenti Beria (secret police chief), and Nikita Khrushchev (Communist party secretary). After a struggle for power, Khrushchev emerged as the dominant leader in 1955.

De-Stalinization In the following year, the 20th Congress of the Soviet Communist Party was held in Moscow. At a secret session, before Soviet delegates as well as representatives of every Communist party in the world, Khrushchev delivered a controversial speech. He denounced Stalin for the purges of the 1930's, in which thousands of loyal party members had been tortured and condemned to death or sent to labor camps. Stalin was also accused of creating a "cult of personality," in which he boosted his own honor at the expense of the Communist party.

In attacking Stalin, Khrushchev ignored his own role in assisting Stalin in the purges. His anti-Stalin speech was primarily designed to

EUROPE 1945-1955

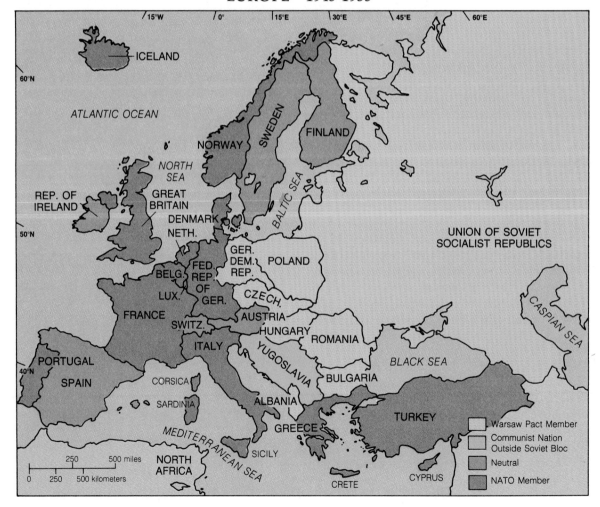

In 1959 the Supreme Soviet chose Khrushchev as premier. By doing this it reunited control of the party and control of the governmnt in the hands of one person.

To celebrate Soviet Navy Day in 1950, sailors formed a star around this banner that reads, "Glory to Great Stalin." Only three years after Stalin's death, Khrushchev denounced any such activity as a "cult of personality," and stated that there must be a return to the principle of collective leadership in the Communist party. What major changes were made in the Soviet Union by Khrushchev's de-Staliniza-tion program?

strengthen his own power and to appease a growing restlessness among the Soviet people. Now that Stalin was gone, many Soviets wanted a relaxation of government controls and a better standard of living. Khrushchev hoped to meet these demands without weakening the leadership of the Communist party.

From 1956 to 1964, Khrushchev carried out a program of de-Stalinization, or a reversal of some of Stalin's policies. While keeping Stalin's program of Five-Year Plans and collective farming, Khrushchev ended certain restrictions. He gave artists and intellectuals more freedom. He also reduced the terror of the secret police and freed many political prisoners from labor camps. Soviet citizens were promised better wages and more consumer goods.

In smaller ways, too, Khrushchev acted to remove Stalin's influence from Soviet life. Streets, cities, and public places that carried Stalin's name were changed. Stalin's career was given less emphasis in Soviet history texts. His embalmed body was even removed from an elaborate tomb in Moscow's Red Square, where it had been displayed near that of Lenin.

Khrushchev Era

One of the major achievements of the Soviet Union under Khrushchev was the continued development of Soviet mili-

tary might. In the late 1950's, the Soviets successfully tested long-range rockets known as **intercontinental ballistic missiles** (ICBM). In October 1957, they launched the first artificial earth satellite, Sputnik I. These events added to the prestige of the Soviet Union and its leader.

Khrushchev tried to raise sagging agricultural production by reorganizing collective farms and bringing new lands under cultivation. However, under the centrally planned Soviet economy, so much capital was invested in the defense industry that there was not enough to invest in agriculture. As a result, farm output continued to be below expectation. Industrial production in certain areas, such as consumer goods, also suffered as a result of the government's emphasis on heavy industry and the military.

These economic troubles contributed to Khrushchev's downfall. In October 1964, Khrushchev was forced into retirement and replaced by a two-man leadership. Leonid Brezhnev became the Communist party secretary and Aleksei Kosygin served as prime minister.[3] In time, Brezhnev became the more powerful of the two.

---

[3]Since the Khrushchev era, changes of leadership in the Soviet Union have been relatively peaceful and bloodless. Such changes during Stalin's time would have sent many to an execution squad.

Although Poland today is a satellite of the Soviet Union, Polish nationalism remains strong.

Brezhnev During the mid-1960's, Brezhnev introduced economic incentives for farmers to increase food production. Farmers continued to work on collective farms. However, they were allowed to own small private plots, which they farmed in their spare time. Also, more capital was invested in farm equipment and agricultural training. More food was available, but collective farm production still fell short of the goals set by Five-Year Plans.

In many cases, central planning of the Soviet economy was proving to be inefficient. However, the government refused to allow individual enterprises a greater say in economic decision making. It feared that such freedom would weaken Communist party controls. With few reforms, the Soviet economy became sluggish by the end of the decade. Many Soviet citizens were annoyed about shortages. They continued to hope for more and better consumer goods.

Soviet political life under Brezhnev experienced changes. Brezhnev reversed Khrushchev's program of de-Stalinization, and the Soviet system became more repressive. Although secret police terror was not as ruthless as it was under Stalin, Soviet officials tightened controls over artists and intellectuals. **Dissidents,** or opponents of government policies, were arrested and sent to prison or labor camps. Some eventually were exiled to the West.

Soviet Satellites

During the height of the cold war, the Soviet Union maintained tight control over its satellites in Eastern Europe. The peoples of these nations resented Soviet domination, but were largely powerless to change their situation. Only the Balkan states of Yugoslavia and Albania were able to establish their independence from the Soviet Union.

East Germany During the 1950's and early 1960's, industrial East Germany was the most prosperous of the Soviet satellites. However, its people were deeply dissatisfied with Soviet controls. After Stalin's death in 1953, they let loose their frustrations. In 1953, a workers' uprising occurred in East Berlin. Soviet troops stationed in East Germany put down the rebellion with little difficulty.

In the years that followed, many East Germans fled to West Berlin, which was easily accessible to them. The population of East Germany declined by about 2 million during the 1950's as a result of this migration. Then, in an attempt to stop the drain of its work force, the East German government built the Berlin Wall in August 1961. The Wall, a tall concrete structure that separated the eastern and western halves of the city, shut off the flow of refugees and raised tensions between East and West. It became the symbol of the "iron curtain."

Poland Under Communist rule, Poland became industrialized. Like East Germany, it was restless under tight Soviet controls. Khrushchev's program of de-Stalinization raised hope in Poland for greater freedom. However, the Communist government of Poland did not make changes fast enough to suit the Polish people. In June 1956, workers rioted in the industrial city of Poznan. Their action was followed by upheavals throughout the country. Poland's Communist leaders decided that some concessions had to be made. Polish supporters of Stalin were removed from office. The popular Communist leader Wladyslaw Gomulka, who under Stalin had been accused of anti-Soviet activities and jailed, came to power.

In the late 1950's, the Soviets allowed Poland greater freedom to run its internal affairs. Many political prisoners were freed; the secret police lost some of its powers; and farmers were allowed to own their own farmland. The Roman Catholic Church, which had the loyalty of most Poles, was able to carry out its activities with little interference. However, the Communist party kept its hold over the country and maintained close ties to the Soviet Union. By the mid-1960's, the party had eliminated many of the Polish freedoms that had been won a decade earlier.

Hungary Hungary, a largely agricultural nation, experienced harsh Communist rule after 1947. Large estates were broken up and given to poor farmers. But the Communist government forced the farmers to combine their new proper-

Both Yugoslavia and Albania in Eastern Europe are not Soviet satellites, yet they are communist.

Hungarian freedom fighters armed with guns were ineffective against the Soviet troops and tanks that attacked in force to crush the rebellion. What events led to full-scale revolution in Hungary?

ties into collective farms. Great stress was placed on industrialization, often at the expense of workers' living standards. Communist opposition to religion led to restrictions on the Roman Catholic Church, Hungary's largest religious group. By 1950, even many Communist leaders were accused of disloyalty to the Soviet Union and were executed.

When de-Stalinization was introduced in Hungary, it led to a full-scale revolt in the fall of 1956. As in Poland, worker uprisings brought a liberal Communist government to power. However, Imre Nagy, the new Hungarian prime minister, went further than the Polish leaders. He supported Hungary's withdrawal from the Soviet bloc and its declaration of neutrality. The Soviets at first seemed willing to accept this change. However, too much was at stake for them to let Hungary go on its own. A neutral Hungary would eventually mean the breakup of Soviet control in Eastern Europe.

In November 1956, Soviet troops and tanks poured into Hungary, crushing the revolt.

Realizing that intervention could cause World War III, the western powers sympathized with the Hungarians, but did nothing to help. Order in Hungary was restored under a Soviet-controlled government led by János Kádár. More than 150,000 refugees fled the country to the West.

Czechoslovakia   Czechoslovakia, with its developed industry and democratic traditions, was the last Eastern European country to become Communist. After the 1948 Communist takeover, Czechoslovakia based its industrial economy on the Soviet model. The Communist government crushed political opposition and acted to destroy the influence of the Roman Catholic Church. At the same time, it carried out purges against its own officials. These were the bloodiest purges outside the Soviet Union. After Stalin's death, Czechoslovakia refused to promote de-Stalinization. Under President Antonin Novotny, it had one of the most rigid Communist governments in Eastern Europe.

Bulgaria and Romania   Bulgaria and Romania remained loyal to the Soviet Union during the early postwar period. Bulgaria, with a Slavic culture very close to that of Russia, was a natural Soviet ally. Romania, however, had been traditionally linked to the West. By the early 1960's, it had developed its own independent economic and foreign policies. The Romanian government, in particular, opposed Soviet efforts to have Romania remain solely a supplier of raw materials to the Soviet bloc. Instead, it wanted to develop heavy industry.

Romania's success in preserving its independence was due to its Communist leader, President Nicolae Ceausescu. Ceausescu also promoted close Romanian ties with nations in Europe and Asia that the Soviets regarded as enemies. However, he kept Romania in the Warsaw Pact and was careful not to push the Soviet leaders beyond their point of tolerance.

Yugoslavia   After World War II, Yugoslavia became the only large Communist state in Eastern Europe to resist Soviet domination. Its popular leader Josip Broz Tito had led the resistance against the Nazis and was as much a Yugoslav nationalist as a Communist. Despite

Discuss the impact of Sputnik I on American education during the late 1950's.

To improve relations with Yugoslavia, Khrushchev (left) made a state visit to Belgrade in 1955 where he met formally with Tito (right). What was the major cause of friction between Yugoslavia and the Soviet Union?

Yugoslavia's close outward ties to the Soviet Union, Tito went his own way in making policies for his country. Stalin was angered by Tito's independent attitude. Relations between the Soviets and the Yugoslavs worsened. Finally, in 1948, the Soviets expelled Yugoslavia from the international Communist movement. Throughout Eastern Europe, they waged a propaganda war against what they called Titoism, or the tendency of some Communists to place their national interests above those of the Soviet Union. With the support of his people, Tito was able to resist Soviet pressures and to develop his own brand of communism. Under Tito, Yugoslavia declared itself neutral in the global struggle between East and West. Although adhering to communism, the Yugoslavs received economic and diplomatic aid from the West.

1. Identify: Nikita Khrushchev, Leonid Brezhnev, Aleksei Kosygin, Berlin Wall, Wladyslaw Gomulka, Imre Nagy, Nicolae Ceausescu, Josip Broz Tito, Titoism.

2. What changes were brought about in the Soviet Union as part of de-Stalinization? Why were they more successful?
3. Which countries had some success in resisting the Soviet Union?
4. How did the Soviet Union justify interference in the affairs of other Communist countries?

4 The West

The West, led by the United States, underwent significant changes after World War II. The West enjoyed one of its greatest periods of prosperity. At the same time, the cold war heightened concern about the spread of communism.

The United States

After World War II, the United States entered an era of economic growth that brought material wealth to a larger group of Americans. Businesses boosted production, and new industries emerged. As a result of higher wages and better benefits, more Americans had more money to spend on goods. The desire to make up for wartime shortages increased market demand. A soaring birthrate added to the number of consumers.

During the late 1940's and the 1950's, the United States played a leading role in science and technology. Americans in greater numbers received a university education, contributing to a "knowledge explosion." American technical skills brought the United States into competition with the Soviet Union in the exploration of outer space.

Anti-communism   During this time of prosperity, the cold war gave rise to deep divisions in the United States. Conservatives blamed government leaders for allowing communism to make gains overseas. They also charged that Communists were serving in high government positions. The charges led to widespread investigations of the influence of communism on American life. Conservatives believed that the investigations were needed to save the country from communism. Liberals charged that the conservatives were violating civil liberties, by trying to fix guilt on people without evidence.

SCIENCE AND TECHNOLOGY

Space Exploration

The 1950's and 1960's saw the beginning of space exploration. However, the preparation for space travel began a few decades earlier. During the 1930's, scientists in Germany, the United States, and the Soviet Union explored the possibility of using liquid-fueled rockets for space flight. A decade later, the German, American, and Soviet governments became interested in the use of rockets. Germany took the lead in rocket development with its V-2 guided missile, used in the bombing of Britain. After the war, German scientists went to the United States and the Soviet Union to continue their work on rockets.

In the late 1950's, the United States and the Soviet Union began programs to explore space. They launched rockets that placed artificial satellites into orbit around the earth. In the following years, hundreds of satellites were sent into space and made possible the development of a worldwide communications and weather information network. Scientific probes were also sent to the moon and the planets, and around the sun.

In the early 1960's, humans began to travel in space. In April 1961, the Soviet cosmonaut Yuri Gagarin became the first human in space, making a two-hour orbit of the earth. John H. Glenn, Jr., the first American to orbit the earth, made three turns around the planet in February 1962. In June of that year, Soviet cosmonaut Valentina Tereshkova became the first woman in space, orbiting the earth for almost three days.

As part of their cold war rivalry, the superpowers carried out a "space race." They rivaled each other to be the first to place a human on the moon. The United States finally won the race. In July 1969, Neil A. Armstrong and Edwin M. Aldrin, Jr. became the first humans to explore the moon.

The space voyages of the 1950's and 1960's paved the way for later achievements. In the early 1970's, American scientists and engineers developed the space shuttle, a reusable spacecraft that could take off like a rocket and land like an airplane. With the space shuttle, astronauts could launch, retrieve, and repair satellites while in space. In April 1981, *Columbia*, the first space shuttle, was launched. Two years later, Sally Ride became the first American woman to travel in space. She and three other astronauts made a six-day flight on the space shuttle *Challenger*. During their voyage, they launched two communications satellites from the shuttle and conducted a variety of scientific experiments. In the future, crews of astronauts will use space shuttles to build and maintain space stations in earth orbit.

1. What made space exploration possible?
2. How did the cold war affect the exploration of outer space?

Domestic Unrest   The United States experienced other forms of domestic troubles. In spite of general prosperity, many Americans—including a high number of blacks and other minorities—faced discrimination in jobs, housing, education, and other areas. A lack of education and jobs made poverty among these groups widespread.

During the late 1940's and 1950's, blacks, joined by whites and other groups, began a movement for civil rights. This effort resulted in several United States Supreme Court decisions that attacked discrimination. In the best-known case, *Brown* v. *Board of Education of Topeka, Kansas* (1954), the Supreme Court ruled that **racial segregation,** or separation of the races, in public schools was illegal. Dwight D. Eisenhower, who had become president in 1953, ordered federal agencies to enforce the Supreme Court decision.

In August, 1963, over 200,000 people marched on Washington, D.C. They gathered at the Lincoln Memorial and heard King deliver his powerful "I have a dream" speech. How did King seek to gain equal rights for all Americans?

The civil rights struggle became the leading domestic issue in the United States. In 1955, Martin Luther King, Jr., a Baptist minister, used nonviolent means to protest discrimination in housing, public facilities, and voting. In spite of opposition, he was able to convince many Americans of the injustice of racial discrimination. John F. Kennedy, who became president in 1961, urged Congress to pass legislation outlawing racial discrimination. After Kennedy's assassination in 1963, President Lyndon B. Johnson persuaded Congress to pass many major civil rights laws. At the same time, he supported reforms in education and social welfare to achieve what he termed the "Great Society."

Canada

Canada became an important economic power after World War II. It ranked as one of the world's ten leading industrial nations. With its increased economic prestige, Canada played a larger role in international affairs. In 1945 it was one of the founding members of the United Nations. Three years later, it signed the North Atlantic treaty forming NATO. NATO was the first military alliance Canada had joined in peacetime. Beginning in the mid-1950's, Canadian soldiers participated in UN-sponsored peacekeeping forces in various troubled areas of the world.

In internal affairs, Canada struggled to find its own national identity. While breaking many of their traditional ties to Europe, Canadians found themselves increasingly influenced by American ideas and practices. This "Americanization" tied the Canadian economy closely to that of the United States. Canadians resented the growing influence of their powerful southern neighbor; however, they still worked to maintain a close relationship with the United States.

Canada became more **pluralistic** during the postwar years. That is, its population was made up of many different groups. More than a million people from Central Europe, Eastern Europe, and Asia settled in Canada's largest cities. Although keeping much of their ethnic cultures, they became a part of English-speaking Canada.

Increasing "Americanization" caused concern among French Canadians, who feared that their

Today about 30 percent of Canada's people are of French ancestry.

The breakup of European colonial empires is discussed in detail in Chapter 30.

In order to curb the separatist movement in Quebec, the Official Languages Act was passed in 1969. Under the act, all official notices are to be in both French and English. Street signs, public notices, and official documents are now written in both languages. To accomodate customers, businesses and stores also use French and English. Why are many French-Canaians concerned by a trend toward "Americanization"?

culture would be engulfed by the English-speaking one. In the early 1960's, they began a movement to increase their political power. One of their demands was that French be made an official language along with English. In Quebec, many began to support efforts to make their province an independent nation.

Western Europe

After World War II, the non-Communist nations of Western Europe were concerned about two major issues: economic development and military security. They came to realize that only through united action would they be able to improve their economies, strengthen the western alliance, and contribute to world affairs.

European Unity   Western Europeans established several organizations to reach the goal of European unity. In 1951, six nations—France, Italy, West Germany, Belgium, the Netherlands, and Luxemburg—set up the European Coal and Steel Community. The purpose of the organization was to create a tariff-free market for European coal and steel products. By ending trade barriers and developing uniform standards, the European Coal and Steel Community would further European industrial growth.

The Community was so successful that the same countries decided to integrate, or bring together, the rest of their economies. In 1957, the six nations signed the Treaty of Rome, creating the European Economic Community (EEC), also known as the Common Market. They planned to abolish all tariffs among themselves and form a single economic market by 1970. They also set up the European Atomic Energy Community to coordinate their atomic energy capabilities.

In 1959 Britain, Sweden, Denmark, Austria, Switzerland, and Portugal created the European Free Trade Association (EFTA). EFTA was a looser union than the Common Market and allowed its members to give special treatment to non-members. This was done so that Britain could keep its trade agreements with its former colonies in the Commonwealth. However, EFTA was not as successful as the Common Market. In 1961 Britain applied for admission to the Common Market. France feared the growth of British influence in continental affairs. Two years later, it vetoed British entry into the Common Market.

Britain   After World War II, Britain's position as a world power further declined. Many of its important Asian and African colonies became independent. With the loss of empire, Britain no longer had easy access to markets and sources of raw materials. British industries, often inefficient and outdated, had difficulty competing in world markets that were increasingly dominated by the

The constitution for the Fifth French Republic was approved by more than four to one in a popular referendum.

United States, Japan, and other Western European nations. Because of its economic weakness, Britain had to pass on many of its international obligations to the United States. However, it maintained a strong military role in the western alliance, developing its own nuclear force.

In internal affairs, Britain underwent many changes. In 1945 Churchill and the Conservatives were voted out of office. They were replaced by the Labor party, which appealed to many Britons who wanted greater social equality. Under Prime Minister Clement Attlee, the Labor government continued wartime restrictions to improve the economy. However, it also promised a better standard of living for all British citizens.

Carrying out a moderate socialist program, the Labor government nationalized the coal, steel, and transportation industries. Greater freedom was given to labor unions to strike and to participate in political activities. Free education was provided to all people up to the age of 16. In the area of social welfare, the Labor government introduced a national health service that provided free medical care for everyone.

As the economic situation improved in the early 1950's, the Conservatives returned to power and ruled until 1964. Although they ended many government controls over the economy, Conservative prime ministers, such as Winston Churchill, Anthony Eden, and Harold Macmillan, did not eliminate the social welfare programs introduced by the Labor party.

In 1952 the popular wartime monarch George VI died and was succeeded by his daughter Elizabeth. As queen, Elizabeth II had little, if any, power. However, for many Britons, she became a reassuring symbol of traditional British values during a period of rapid, and sometimes discouraging, change.

France   German occupation of France during World War II had ended the Third French Republic established in 1870. Following the war, a coalition government of moderates and leftists came to power under General Charles de Gaulle. De Gaulle had difficulty working with the leftists. In 1946 he resigned when they opposed his plan for a strong presidency. Later that year,

a new constitution was approved establishing the Fourth French Republic. It closely resembled that of the Third French Republic, having a strong legislature and a weak presidency.

In spite of economic growth, France in the 1950's was plagued with domestic and international problems. The existence of many political parties undermined hopes for stable government. No single political party was strong enough to obtain a working majority in the National Assembly. Cabinets were formed by coalitions of several parties. When one of the parties disagreed with established policy, the cabinet members had to resign and form a new government.

Overseas, France fought financially draining wars against nationalist movements in its colonies. The leading centers of resistance to French rule were Indochina and North Africa. In the mid-1950's, France gave up control of Indochina but refused to yield its major North African colony, Algeria. As a result, a civil war broke out in Algeria between Algerian nationalists and European settlers.

The Algerian conflict deeply divided French society. In 1958 French military officers and their European supporters seized control of the colonial administration in Algeria. This action led to a crisis that toppled the Fourth French Republic. To restore stability, de Gaulle was asked to come out of retirement and head an emergency government.

De Gaulle asked the French people to approve the creation of a strong presidency elected directly by the people. French voters responded overwhelmingly to de Gaulle's appeal. Thus, the Fifth French Republic was born.

De Gaulle was chosen the first president of the Fifth Republic. His political party, the Gaullist Union, formed a working majority in the National Assembly. As president, de Gaulle recognized that France could not stubbornly hold on to its empire against strong nationalistic opposition. In the early 1960's, he allowed France's African colonies, including Algeria, to become independent.

With the loss of France's empire, de Gaulle worked to strengthen French cultural and

France exploded its first atomic bomb in the Sahara in 1960.

On a visit to Cologne in 1962, Charles de Gaulle tried to restore friendly relations with West Germany. De Gaulle became a close ally of Konrad Adenauer, and they worked together for a Franco-German treaty of reconciliation and economic cooperation. What was de Gaulle's relationship with other Western leaders?

economic influence throughout the world. His strongly nationalistic policies angered France's allies, especially the United States and Britain. In the mid-1960's, de Gaulle withdrew France from NATO's military command, while maintaining political ties with the western alliance. Under de Gaulle, France built its own nuclear strike force. It also sought to compete with the United States and the Soviet Union by giving economic aid to poorer nations.

West Germany During the postwar years, West Germany rebuilt its economy and became Western Europe's leading industrial nation. Many experts called West Germany's reconstruction an "economic miracle." New industries used the latest in modern equipment, and industrial production more than tripled in the 1950's. Prosperity enabled West Germany to absorb more than 10 million refugees from the Soviet bloc, and over a million workers from the rest of Europe.

West Germany's democratic political system was dominated by two major parties: the Christian Democrats and the Social Democrats. The Christian Democrats, under the leadership of Konrad Adenauer, formed the first West German government in 1949. They were com-

mitted to a largely capitalist economy and a close relationship with the West. In 1955 West Germany became a member of NATO and began to establish its armed forces.

As chancellor, Konrad Adenauer was known as a strong leader devoted to the western alliance, European unity, and the reunification of Germany. During his term of office, West Germany developed into one of the world's most stable democracies. Adenauer retired in 1963. He was succeeded as chancellor by Ludwig Erhard, who served until 1966. Erhard had been economics minister in Adenauer's government.

During the 1960's, the Christian Democrats lost support to the Social Democrats, a moderate socialist party. The Social Democratic leader was Willy Brandt, the mayor of West Berlin. The Social Democrats maintained strong support for NATO. However, they also wanted to improve relations with the Soviet Union and its Eastern European allies.

Italy After World War II, Italy emerged once again as a democratic nation. In June 1946, it held its first free election in 20 years. Italians voted for a republic to replace the monarchy that had been linked to fascism. A new democratic constitution was adopted in 1947.

Three political parties—the Christian Democrats, the Communists, and the Socialists—were powerful in the Italian republic. Most Italian governments, however, were controlled by the Christian Democrats in a coalition with smaller parties. From 1948 to 1953, the Christian Democratic leader, Alcide de Gasperi, was prime minister. Committed to the western alliance, he excluded Communists from the government. De Gasperi favored a capitalist economy, supporting industrial growth and agricultural reform.

During the 1950's, the Italian economy grew impressively. Its rate of growth ranked among the highest in Europe. By the 1960's, industry had replaced agriculture as the backbone of the economy.

The rapid changes in Italy's economy, however, brought many problems. Most of the country's economic growth occurred in the north. As a result, the gap between the poor regions of the south and the prosperous regions of the north widened. Many people moved into urban areas from the countryside, creating overcrowded conditions. Workers demanded social reforms and a greater share of the national wealth. In response to these demands, the Christian Democratic government broadened its base of power. In 1962 a political agreement gave the Socialists a role in the ruling coalition. The Christian Democratic-Socialist alliance set out to reform the tax system, improve education, and expand social welfare programs.

Benelux   Though small in size, Belgium, the Netherlands, and Luxemburg played important roles in European affairs. All three nations were democratic monarchies with prosperous industrial-agricultural economies. Their economic strength made them leading supporters of European unity. In 1948 Belgium, the Netherlands, and Luxemburg formed an economic union called Benelux. This union later became the basis of the Common Market.

Switzerland   After World War II, Switzerland continued the traditional policy of neutrality that had kept it out of modern Europe's conflicts. It did not join the UN, but Geneva, Switzerland, became the UN's European headquarters. The city also became a noted international conference center. Switzerland enjoyed a prosperous economy and was a leading banking center of the world. However, its democratic system was slow in granting political equality to women. Only in the late 1950's were Swiss women allowed to vote in local elections. They did not achieve full political rights until the 1970's.

Scandinavia   Sweden, Denmark, and Norway enjoyed economic prosperity after World War II. They ranked among the world's most prosperous nations. Scandinavian governments developed social welfare systems that spread a high standard of living to all income groups. Critics of government social policies claimed that "cradle to the grave" welfare made people so secure that they lost initiative and became bored. Many Scandinavians also resented the high taxes that paid for social welfare. But they continued to support the system, believing that its benefits outweighed its disadvantages.

Although alike in many ways, the Scandinavian nations had differences in foreign policy. Denmark and Norway were members of NATO, while Sweden was neutral. Sweden's neighbor, Finland, also followed a neutralist policy because of its location next to the Soviet Union.

Spain and Portugal   After World War II, Spain and Portugal were ruled by dictators and remained largely isolated from democratic Western Europe. Francisco Franco continued to govern Spain. His government at first was rejected by the western democracies because of its links to fascism and nazism during the war. However, with the onset of the cold war, Franco's anti-communism enabled the West to ease its stand. Western nations wanted Franco's help in the defense of Western Europe against the Soviet bloc.

During the 1960's, Spain enjoyed one of the highest rates of economic growth in the world. Franco ended his country's isolation and encouraged foreign investments in Spanish industry. He also eased some of the restrictions on personal freedom. Protests soon erupted against the dictatorship, especially in several regions that wanted greater control over their local affairs. One region, the Basque Provinces,

The Basque people speak a language different from any other in Europe. Their history is very long, but it is of obscure origin.

wanted independence from Spain. A nationalist Basque organization formed and began a campaign of **terrorism,** the use of violence to achieve political aims. Under Franco, Basque terrorists and other dissidents were arrested.

In Portugal, dictator Antonio de Oliveira Salazar, who came to power in the 1930's, crushed all opposition to his rule. His economic policies favored the wealthy, making Portugal one of Europe's poorest countries. Unlike the other European colonial powers, Portugal refused to give up its colonies in Asia and Africa. Portuguese troops were sent to Africa to fight black nationalist guerrillas. Thousands on both sides were killed, and the cost of the fighting drained Portugal's already weakened economy.

Greece   After the defeat of the Communists in 1949, Greece went through a period of economic growth, although it remained one of Europe's poorest countries. Much of this growth came about as a result of American aid. Greece also enjoyed political stability under the conservative prime minister Constantine Caramanlis, who came to power in 1955.

In the mid-1950's, tensions arose between Greece and Turkey over the British-ruled island of Cyprus. Greeks made up 80 percent of the population, while the rest were Turks. The Greeks of Cyprus wanted to unite with Greece. They organized a revolutionary movement with the support of the Greek government. Turkey and the Turks of Cyprus opposed this move. After a period of difficult negotiations, an agreement among Britain, Greece, and Turkey led to independence for Cyprus in 1960.

In the early 1960's, Greece entered a period of political turmoil. Wanting social reforms, Greek voters moved to the political left. At the same time, the Caramanlis government came into conflict with its long-standing supporter, the powerful right-wing monarchy. In 1963 King Paul I and German-born Queen Frederika withdrew support from Caramanlis, and the Caramanlis government fell. Later that year, George Papandreou, the liberal opposition leader, became prime minister. He won a landslide election victory in 1964, ending nearly two decades of conservative rule. Paul I died in 1964

The conflicting interests of Greeks, Turks, and Cypriots, who wanted self rule, sometimes led to violent confrontations. To help prevent such outbursts, British security forces stopped all traffic into cities to search for weapons. When and how did Cyprus gain its independence?

The "Spirit of Geneva" meant the willingness of the top leaders to work together in peace.

and his son came to the throne as Constantine II. Constantine soon clashed with Papandreou over the political role of the monarchy. The king dismissed Papandreou, leading to a period of shaky government and political unrest.

1. Identify: Martin Luther King, Jr., "Great Society," EEC, EFTA, Clement Attlee, Konrad Adenauer, Willy Brandt, Alcide de Gasperi, Benelux, Antonio de Oliveira Salazar, George Papandreou.
2. What domestic problems did the United States and Canada face in the 1950's and early 1960's?
3. How did the Labor party change postwar British society?
4. What were the reasons for political instability in France between 1945 and 1958? How was stability finally achieved?

5   Era of Peaceful Coexistence

By the mid-1950's, both the United States and the Soviet Union had developed **hydrogen bombs,** nuclear weapons that were many times more powerful than atomic bombs. The terrible threat of nuclear war led leaders of both countries to seek ways of relaxing cold war tensions. The superpowers gradually opened contacts with each other through diplomatic channels and **summit conferences,** or high-level meetings of political leaders.

A Temporary Thaw

Under Khrushchev, the Soviets adopted a new policy toward the West known as **peaceful coexistence.** This meant that they would compete with the West but would avoid war.

The first sign of a thaw appeared in May 1955. In that month, the western powers and the Soviet Union signed a peace treaty with Austria, ending the post World War II occupation of the country. All western and Soviet troops left the country, allowing Austria to become an independent neutral nation.

United States President Dwight D. Eisenhower agreed to a diplomatic summit meeting with Soviet leaders. At Geneva in July 1955, Eisenhower, British Prime Minister Anthony

Eden, and French Prime Minister Edgar Faure met with Khrushchev and his colleague Nikolai Bulganin to discuss disarmament and German reunification. Although the meeting produced no specific results, observers noted a reduction of tensions that was promptly called the "Spirit of Geneva." The summit conference placed the cold war on a different basis. The superpowers admitted that a nuclear stalemate had developed and that the current balance of power between East and West had to be accepted. Following Geneva, the rivalry between East and West increasingly shifted to the emerging nations in Asia, Africa, and Latin America. There, the superpowers sought influence.

As tensions eased, individual countries within the two power blocs acted independently of American and Soviet policies in certain areas. At the same time, newly independent countries in Asia and Africa declared themselves **nonaligned,** or neutral, in the cold war and began to exert their own influence in world affairs. In April 1955, representatives of 29 Asian and African nations met at Bandung, Indonesia, and adopted resolutions on world peace and self-determination for all nations.

By the late 1950's, the bipolar world had been replaced by a more diverse one of regional groups. Both superpowers continued to play leading roles in world affairs, but they no longer could control events to their liking.

Continuing Tension

In the late 1950's and early 1960's, the "thaw" in the cold war continued despite occasional setbacks. The Soviets shifted their course in foreign policy during this period. Although Khrushchev continued to seek closer contacts with capitalist countries, he sometimes followed a hard line with them. He tried to gain an advantage over the West by encouraging unrest in trouble spots of the world. In Asia and Africa, the Soviets backed **"wars of liberation,"** or revolutionary movements against western political and economic influence.

Meanwhile, the United States remained committed to the containment policy, while increasing contacts with the Soviet Union. In September 1959, Khrushchev visited the United States and

Plans for the Bay of Pigs invasion were worked out during the Eisenhower administration.

met with Eisenhower. Another summit meeting was to be held in Paris in May 1960. Eisenhower had planned to visit the Soviet Union during that year also. But shortly before the conference, the Soviets shot down an American U-2 spy plane over their territory and captured its pilot. Khrushchev used the occasion of the summit to launch a propaganda attack on the United States. He also canceled Eisenhower's planned visit to the Soviet Union.

Kennedy's Foreign Policy   In 1961 Eisenhower was succeeded by John F. Kennedy, who wanted to have a dynamic foreign policy that would impress the Soviets with American strength and boost United States prestige abroad. Under Kennedy, the United States increased its military budget and built up its armed forces. At the same time, it also used peaceful means to extend American help and influence overseas. The Alliance for Progress, for example, aided economic development in Latin America, while the Peace Corps sent Americans to other countries as teachers, farmers, and technicians to promote economic development.

Bay of Pigs   In 1959 a young guerrilla fighter named Fidel Castro overthrew a right-wing dictatorship in Cuba. Castro set up a Marxist government and established close relations with the Soviet Union and other Communist nations. The United States became concerned about the spread of communism from Cuba to the rest of Latin America.

After becoming president, Kennedy approved an invasion of Cuba by American-trained Cuban exiles. In April 1961, the invaders landed at the Bay of Pigs on Cuba's southern coast. But the local population did not aid them, and the United States did not provide air support. The Bay of Pigs invasion failed, causing a loss of prestige to the United States and a closer connection between Cuba and the Soviet Union.

Cuban Missile Crisis   The American setback in the Bay of Pigs invasion encouraged Khrushchev to adopt a more aggressive position in the cold war. In the summer of 1962, the Soviets started to build missile sites and launching pads in Cuba. By October, Soviet missiles and bombers capable of carrying nuclear weapons were stationed on the island, only 90 miles (144 kilometers) from the United States coast.

In October, Kennedy put a blockade on all military shipments to Cuba, and threatened to

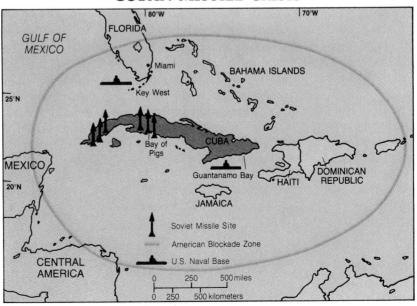

CUBAN MISSILE CRISIS

Use the map on p. 685 to show the closeness of Cuba to the United States. Discuss the problems presented by missiles so close to American shores.

extend it to other types of cargo. He demanded that the Soviet weapons in Cuba be removed.

Soviet ships were on their way to the Caribbean island, and American naval forces were ready to challenge them. The whole world watched nervously to see what would happen. Finally, Khrushchev backed down. He agreed to dismantle and remove the missiles in exchange for American promises to lift the blockade and to refrain from invading Cuba.

In the short run, the crisis led to a reduction of cold war tensions. Both the United States and the Soviet Union had faced the prospect of nuclear war and were not willing to face it again. As a result, a new period of American-Soviet relations began. In 1963 a telephone "hot line" linked Washington and Moscow for the first time, so that leaders of both nations could instantly communicate with each other. In the same year, the United States, the Soviet Union, and other world powers signed a treaty banning the testing of nuclear weapons in the atmosphere. For the next few years, the Soviet Union and the United States maintained a relationship of mutual understanding and respect, although they disagreed sharply on Eastern Europe, the Middle East, and Southeast Asia.

1. Identify: Anthony Eden, "Spirit of Geneva," Bandung, John F. Kennedy, Alliance for Progress, Peace Corps, Fidel Castro.
2. Why did the summit conference of May 1960 fail?
3. What happened after the Bay of Pigs invasion?
4. How was the Cuban missile crisis resolved?

CHAPTER 29 REVIEW

Summary

1. After World War II the Allies split into two opposing camps: the western bloc, led by the United States; and the eastern bloc, led by the Soviet Union.
2. The Soviet Union used the presence of its armies in Eastern Europe to establish Soviet-dominated Communist regimes.
3. To halt Soviet expansion, the United States provided economic and military aid to its allies and other non-communist countries.
4. Soviet attempts to isolate West Berlin failed despite a long land blockade.
5. The Allied zones in postwar Germany evolved into two separate German states.
6. After Stalin's death in 1953, the new leaders of the Soviet Union denounced some of his policies. This led to a crisis for Soviet rule in several countries of Eastern Europe.
7. Eastern European countries largely failed to free themselves from Soviet dominance during the 1950's and the 1960's.
8. In spite of internal problems, western countries prospered economically and achieved relative political stability.
9. Soviet-American relations improved briefly in the mid-1950's, followed by increased tension that came to a head with the Cuban missile crisis in 1962.

Building Vocabulary

cold war
bipolarism
satellites

arms race
containment
intercontinental ballistic missiles

dissidents
racial segregation
pluralistic

terrorism
hydrogen bombs

summit conferences
peaceful coexistence

nonaligned
"wars of liberation"

Reviewing the Main Ideas

1. How did the world power structure change after World War II?
2. Why did conflict develop between the Soviet Union and its former allies?
3. How did Communist governments come to power in Eastern Europe after the war?
4. What policy did the United States adopt in response to Soviet expansion?
5. Why did Germany become divided into two countries following the Berlin blockade?
6. How did Khrushchev's policies differ from Stalin's?
7. How did Soviet economic and political policy change under Brezhnev?
8. What attempts did Eastern European countries make to free themselves from Soviet control?
9. Why was the Common Market formed? Who were its original members?
10. What were the conditions of the postwar economies of West Germany, Spain, and Italy?
11. Why did Khrushchev support the idea of peaceful coexistence?
12. In what ways did the Soviet Union and the United States compete—short of war?
13. What steps did the Soviet Union and the United States take to end tensions?

Discussing Important Ideas

1. How would you evaluate the rule of Stalin in terms of its impact on the Soviet Union and the world?
2. Are communism and capitalism compatible? Why or why not?
3. Some analysts of the cold war believe that the United States should have exploited the Soviet Union's weakness right after World War II, when only the Americans had the atomic bomb. Do you agree or disagree with this belief?
4. How do you think the cold war affected domestic affairs in western bloc countries?
5. How has the existence of nuclear weapons affected the cold war?
6. What roles have other countries played in the struggle between the Soviet Union and the United States?
7. Do you think the United States-backed invasion of Cuba in 1961 was justified?
8. How effective are summit conferences in solving world problems?

Using Graphs

Refer to the graph on page 669 to answer the following questions:
1. What is the chart designed to show?
2. Why are the boxes different sizes?
3. What do the arrows indicate?
4. How many countries are represented?
5. How much money did West Germany receive? Over how many years?

CHAPTER 30

Chinese Parade

66 *We fought the colonialists in order to uplift the living standards of our people.* **99**

Jomo Kenyatta, African nationalist (c. 1894-1978)

Postwar Asia, Africa, and Latin America

The First World refers to the world's industrialized democracies, such as the United States and Canada. The Second World refers to the Communist bloc of nations, including the Soviet Union and Poland.

After World War II, numerous nations gained independence in Asia, the Middle East, and Africa. These new nations, as well as those in Latin America, have experienced rapid growth and development in the postwar era.

Many of the countries of these regions have come to be called the Third World. The term "Third World" applies to those newly independent countries that officially refuse to support either the Soviet Union or the United States. Third World nations are generally in the early stages of industrialization. Many of their people still make a living from the land, using traditional methods of farming. Third World nations often depend on the superpowers for economic and military aid.

Not all of the nations of Asia, Africa, and Latin America are considered part of the Third World. For example, Japan, South Korea, Turkey, Israel, South Africa, Brazil, and Argentina have characteristics that distinguish them from Third World nations. These countries have well-developed industrial economies. They also tend to be pro-western in foreign policy.

1 East Asia

The decade after World War II brought sweeping changes to East Asia. Defeated in war, Japan went through a brief period of American military rule. Civil war in China resulted in the defeat of the Kuomintang army and the establishment of a Communist government. Korea was divided between the United States and the Soviet Union. It became the scene of the first major conflict since World War II.

Japan

At the end of World War II, Japan was ruled by an American army of occupation. The United States set out to end Japanese militarism and reestablish democracy.

American Occupation   After Japan surrendered on September 2, 1945, American forces occupied Japan. The United States Army supervised the disarmament of the Japanese military and the surrender of military centers on the Japanese islands.

With formal surrender, Japan was placed under the authority of General Douglas MacArthur, Supreme Allied Commander in the Pacific. MacArthur's task was to set up a new government and reorganize the economy.

Upon taking charge, MacArthur's most immediate action was to break Japanese links to their imperial past. In a series of decrees, MacArthur restored civil liberties, freed political prisoners, and dissolved the secret police. Under MacArthur's rule, Japanese women gained voting rights, education was liberalized, and local government and labor unions were strengthened. One of the most important breaks with the past, however, came when Emperor Hirohito renounced the divinity attributed to him by Japanese tradition.

MacArthur introduced democratic reforms within the existing Japanese political structure. The postwar Japanese government consisted of the emperor, a legislative diet, and a prime minister with a cabinet. The first election took place in 1946, bringing Shigeru Yoshida to power as prime minister.

In 1947 a new Japanese constitution went into effect. It formally ended the political powers of the emperor and transformed him into a "symbol of the state." The new constitution also safeguarded individual rights, renounced militarism, and introduced a greater measure of local self-government.

In the Meiji era industry and commerce were concentrated in the hands of a few powerful business houses—the *zaibatsu*—such as Mitsubishi and Yasuda.

Although the treaty permitted rearmament, Japan did not rearm.

As a young soldier, MacArthur (left) had visited a Japanese infantry unit during the Russo-Japanese War. He was profoundly impressed with how devoted the Japanese people were to their emperor. After the war, MacArthur directed Emperor Hirohito (right) to command the imperial forces to submit to the Allied occupation. In this way, the Japanese and their government accepted MacArthur's authority over Japan more readily. In return, the Allied commander retained the emperor and most of the Japanese civil service during the six-year occupation. What other concession did MacArthur require?

To guarantee moderation in the new government, MacArthur ordered a series of purges against all active supporters of Japanese nationalism. The policy ultimately affected more than 1.5 million people, including many intellectuals and business people. In addition, a military tribunal was set up to try and punish Japanese war criminals.

American occupation authorities also supervised the reorganization of Japanese industry and agriculture. The large factory and banking combinations collectively known as the **zaibatsu** were dissolved, and new forms of economic organization were approved. In agriculture, a sweeping program of land redistribution was begun. Owners with large landholdings were forced to sell much of their property to the government at low prices. In turn, the government offered the land to previously landless peasants.

The postwar economic reorganization of Japan went a long way in restoring the country's industrial might. Conservative pro-business groups began playing a dominant role in national life. When Douglas MacArthur ended his administration of Japan in 1951, these groups assumed full political control. As a result of the American occupation, they were now committed to democratic principles.

Peace Treaty   In January 1951, Japanese and American envoys opened talks on a peace treaty between the Allies and Japan. The final treaty was approved and signed by Japan and 48 other nations at San Francisco on September 4, 1951.

In the peace settlement, Japan benefited from cold war tensions between the Communist and western blocs. The United States wanted to ensure that Japan would support the West. The peace treaty, largely determined by the Americans, placed no reparations on Japan. The Japanese were allowed to rearm to guard East Asia against Communist expansion. In addition, full sovereignty was restored to Japan. Japanese territory, however, was reduced to the four home islands and some minor islands. This was the territory controlled by Japan in the 1800's, before it began to dominate East Asia and the Pacific.

The treaty signed at San Francisco was not entirely acceptable to all the nations that signed it. Australia and New Zealand feared future aggression by Japan because it was able to rearm. The new island republic of the Philippines denounced the treaty for its failure to force the Japanese to pay reparations to it and other countries that had been occupied during the war. Nevertheless, the peace treaty was hailed as "a

The Soviet Union supported Chiang Kai-shek in order to preserve its wartime solidarity with the Allies.

Viewed as Mao's heir in 1949, Liu Shao-ch'i soon fell from favor when the two disagreed over policy.

treaty of reconciliation." United States President Truman called it "a treaty that will work. It does not contain the seeds of another war."

In addition to the peace treaty, the United States and Japan concluded a mutual security agreement. Aimed at defending East Asia from communism, the defense treaty permitted United States troops to remain indefinitely in Japan. It stirred controversy in Japan, where a vocal peace movement staged protests. The peace movement hoped to make Japan neutral in the East-West struggle.

With an American military presence in Japan, the Japanese government spent relatively little on defense. Thus, it was able to help Japanese industry. Government support led to tremendous growth in the Japanese economy. By the mid-1960's, increases in the **gross national product** (GNP)—the total value of goods and services produced in a year—and foreign trade had brought prosperity to much of the Japanese population.

Communist China

Within a few years after the end of World War II, a civil war gave control of mainland China to the Chinese Communists. For the next two decades, China experienced numerous economic, social, and political changes.

Civil War At the height of World War II, there existed a Nationalist China, a Communist China, and a Japanese-occupied China. After the defeat of the Japanese, the Nationalists, or the Kuomintang supporters, and the Communists fought each other for control of the areas once held by Japan.

In this struggle, the Nationalists had three times as many soldiers as the Communists. The Nationalist leader, Chiang Kai-shek, also had the advantage of American aid. The Allies, including the Soviet Union, recognized Chiang's government as the only legal authority in China. On the other hand, the Communists had wide support among Chinese peasants who benefited from Communist land reform policies.

Fighting between the two groups broke out in 1945 when Mao Tse-tung, the Communist leader, refused to surrender the northern prov-

inces to the Nationalists. Mao also rejected Nationalist control over the rest of China. Although the United States helped negotiate a temporary truce, efforts for a permanent peace between the two sides failed. In 1946 Chiang Kai-shek increased the fighting with a massive attack on Communist strongholds in the north.

In the early years of the civil war, the Nationalists controlled all of the major cities, while the Communists held mainly the rural areas. Chaotic economic conditions, corruption, and poor military strategy, however, contributed to the defeat of the Nationalists. The major city of Beijing fell to the Communists in January 1949. Within nine months, the Communists drove the Nationalist armies off the Chinese mainland. Chiang Kai-shek and a large number of his supporters fled to the island of Taiwan, where they set up a capital at Taipei.

On October 1, 1949, Mao Tse-tung officially proclaimed the People's Republic of China at Beijing. In the new government, Chou En-lai, a noted intellectual and revolutionary leader, became prime minister. Mao, as chairman of the Communist party, was the most powerful government official. Liu Shao-ch'i, Mao's closest adviser, was considered his heir apparent.

People's Republic In spite of some opposition, the new Communist government enjoyed wide support in China. Internationally, the People's Republic of China was immediately recognized by the Soviet Union and its satellites. Burma, India, and Britain soon followed. In 1950 the Chinese signed a treaty of "friendship, alliance, and mutual assistance" with the Soviet Union. It was followed by a series of economic agreements between the two countries.

In 1953 the Chinese began receiving considerable aid from the Soviet Union to build up their industry. That year, the Chinese announced their first five-year plan and designated the period of its operation as a "transition to socialism." The plan stressed heavy industry and collectivization of agriculture. Private enterprise was practically ended as the government nationalized banking, industry, and commerce.

In 1958 a second, more ambitious five-year plan was begun. Mao heralded it as the "Great

In discussing population growth refer students to the section on population growth on p. 394.

China's role in the Korean War is discussed on p. 694.

Over 77 percent of the total budget for the first five-year plan of the People's Republic had been earmarked for heavy industry. New industrial centers, such as this gas refinery in Yümen, were built in northwestern and southwestern China. In the next plan, the "Great Leap Forward," the government pressed for more record-breaking industrial production, instead of balancing growth by concentrating on other vital areas of the economy. The result was economic failure. What other factor hindered economic growth in China?

Leap Forward." During this time, large farm areas were consolidated into rural cooperatives called **communes**. Members of each commune were divided into production brigades with responsibilities that ranged from farming to weaving.

Communal farming replaced the traditional Chinese farm structure. However, the commune system did not meet its immediate goals. As early as 1959 it became clear that the "Great Leap Forward" was heading for failure. Food shortages, mismanagement, and peasant resistance to the communes brought unrest.

Despite setbacks in agriculture, the Chinese economy made significant progress toward industrialization under Communist rule. In the years before the Communist regime, for example, annual steel production had never reached 1 million tons. By 1960, Chinese steel mills produced over 18 million tons. Total industrial output in the 1960's placed China among the top ten industrial nations in the world.

The Communists faced one serious problem that hindered overall economic growth in China. The growth of the economy could not keep pace with China's expanding population. By 1965 an estimated 700 million people lived in China. In addition, the population was growing at a rate of 2 to 3 percent each year.

Nevertheless, the Communists succeeded in transforming life in many ways for the Chinese people. Public sanitation and health were greatly improved. Illiteracy was reduced. Women were given full equality with men.

While the first years of the People's Republic boasted accomplishments, they were not without many other serious problems. Power struggles and public opposition were met by the Communist regime with repression. So-called enemies of the people, or political opponents, were routinely jailed or executed. In the first seven years of Communist rule nearly 1 million "enemies" had been executed.

In 1956, Communist repression increased opposition to the government. "Tens of thousands of persons went out to the streets to oppose the People's Government," wrote Mao. To ease tensions, he declared, "Let a hundred flowers blossom; let a hundred schools contend." He called on his opponents to state their opinions about government policies and their plans for reform. Mao, however, was unprepared for the severe criticism he actually received. In 1957 Mao ended the "hundred flowers" policy of free speech.

Mao's Communist regime followed a foreign policy as active and aggressive as its domestic policy. In 1950 the Chinese intervened in Korea.

The roots of the Sino-Soviet split lie partially in the precommunist period, when tsarist Russia laid claim to Chinese territory.

Elements of Mao's philosophy are contained in the "little red book," *Quotations from Chairman Mao Tse-tung.*

A year later, they occupied Tibet, a mountainous country between India and western China. When Tibetan nationalists revolted in 1959, the Chinese harshly suppressed them. Chinese actions in Tibet led to strained relations with India. Border disputes with India resulted in an undeclared war in 1962.

Sino-Soviet Split　　Friendly relations between the People's Republic of China and the Soviet Union began to sour by the late 1950's. What once was described as a "lasting, unbreakable, and invincible" friendship turned into a bitter feud over Communist ideology and for leadership among the world's Communist countries.

The feud between China and the Soviet Union developed as a result of the Soviet Union's policy of de-Stalinization. Since 1949, Mao had encouraged a personality cult of his own. That is, he promoted the idea that he embodied the ideals of Chinese communism. When Khrushchev denounced Stalin's personality cult in 1956, Mao took this to be an attack on him and his leadership in China.

The Sino-Soviet split grew wider as Mao became convinced that the Chinese Communists, not the Soviets, provided the best example of a Marxist-Leninist system in action. Mao denounced Khrushchev as abandoning Marxist-Leninist ideals. Mao viewed China as the role model for world communism.

Angered by Mao's challenge to their leadership of the Communist movement, the Soviets began withdrawing support from China. They did not back Chinese actions in Tibet or India. They also reduced the amount of economic aid given to the Chinese. The Chinese became particularly angry with the Soviets when they did not help China develop atomic weapons[1] and did not support China's intentions to invade Taiwan. A war of words was launched by both sides during the early 1960's. The Soviet Union eventually canceled all economic and technical programs in China, recalling its advisers and specialists.

[1]China exploded its first atomic bomb in 1964. It became the fifth world atomic power, following the United States, the Soviet Union, Britain, and France.

Cultural Revolution　　The failure of the "Great Leap Forward" and the Sino-Soviet split gave rise to more **pragmatic,** or practical, leadership in China. Chief among the pragmatists were Liu Shao-ch'i and Teng Hsiao-p'ing. Both Liu and Teng favored realistic goals to solve the country's urgent economic and foreign dilemmas. Mao, however, remained the idealist, insisting on maintaining the ideology of revolution rather than on introducing practical reforms.

Before they were able to introduce reforms, the pragmatists were challenged by the followers of Mao. The result was a purge of the pragmatists during the so-called Cultural Revolution. With the help of Chinese Red Army units under Defense Minister Lin Piao, leaders of the Cultural Revolution ousted Liu and Teng.

The Cultural Revolution was a time of massive civil disorder and confusion throughout China. All forms of foreign and traditional Chinese culture were banned. Schools closed; factory production dropped; violence erupted. During the chaos, various factions within the Chinese Communist party clashed with one another. The most violent of these factions was the Red

Chinese ballet and opera companies in the 1950's related the Communist party's past and reinforced Mao's teachings. How did the cult of Mao, which such performances promoted, cause conflict between China and the Soviet Union?

Guards made up of students loyal to Mao's philosophy. The Red Guards freely roamed China terrorizing opponents of Mao.

The Cultural Revolution was brought to an end under pressure from Mao and Chou En-lai. At the same time, a common dislike for the Soviets helped to unite the Chinese. In March 1969, Chinese and Soviet forces clashed over disputed territory along their common border.

Conflict in Korea

During World War II, the Allied powers agreed that Korea was to be temporarily occupied. At the end of the war, Soviet troops moved into the northern part of Korea down to the 38th parallel. United States forces occupied the southern area. The occupation was to end as soon as a Korean government could be freely elected.

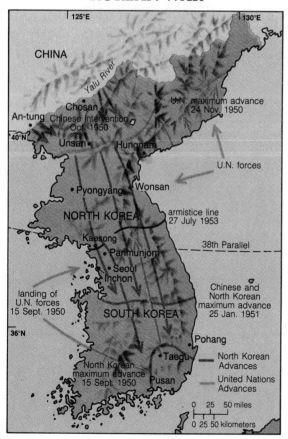

KOREAN WAR

In the months after the war, the Soviets and Americans failed to agree on procedures for the election. As a result, two separate governments were formed by 1948. The Soviets created in the north a Communist government similar to those of its Eastern European satellites. Elections in the south established a republican administration under the presidency of Dr. Syngman Rhee. By 1949 both Soviet and American occupation troops were withdrawn from Korea.

In June 1950, the North Korean government tried to reunite Korea by launching an invasion of the south. South Korea immediately appealed to the United Nations. In response, the Security Council, in the absence of the Soviet Union, passed a resolution committing combat units to the defense of South Korea. In the summer of 1950, United States troops arrived in Korea and were subsequently joined by troops from other nations.[2]

For many weeks during the early period of the war, United Nations troops under the command of General Douglas MacArthur were forced to retreat. They were nearly expelled from the peninsula. However, the tide of battle turned when MacArthur staged a surprise landing from the sea at Inchon behind North Korean lines. Now on the offensive, the United Nations forces were able to push the North Koreans out of South Korea. They advanced into North Korea, reaching the Yalu River at the border with Communist China.

At this point in the war, Communist China entered the fighting. Chinese troops crossed into Korea in such large numbers that United Nations forces were forced to retreat once again to the south. Communist forces captured the South Korean capital of Seoul on January 4, 1951. United Nations troops recaptured it on March 12. A stalemate was reached in the area of the original line of division at the 38th parallel.

In July 1951, truce negotiations began between the warring parties. These talks dragged on until July 27, 1953, when an agreement was reached and a truce was signed. Korea was once again divided near the 38th parallel.

---

[2]Fifteen nations in addition to the United States joined the UN force in the Korean War.

Refer students to the map on p. 698 to locate the countries of India and Pakistan.

The Korean War brought tremendous social problems to Korea. There were thousands of war-widows, orphans, and unemployed. The North and South Korean governments were unable to handle their problems alone. While the Chinese aided in rebuilding the North, the United States and other western countries helped South Korea. Despite corruption in its government, South Korea developed a strong capitalist industrial economy by the mid-1960's. In contrast, North Korea developed along the Communist model. The government abolished all private ownership of industry and trade, and it collectivized agriculture.

1. Identify: Third World, Shigeru Yoshida, Taipei, People's Republic of China, Chou En-lai, Liu Shao-ch'i, "Great Leap Forward," Teng Hsiao-p'ing, Cultural Revolution, Red Guards, Syngman Rhee, Inchon.
2. How did the new Japanese constitution guarantee democracy?
3. What were the results of the Chinese Cultural Revolution?
4. What events led to the creation of two Koreas?

Whereas Gandhi had appealed to the Indian masses, Nehru, a wealthy intellectual, gained the support of the upper-class members of the Indian National Congress party that ruled independent India. How long did Nehru lead India?

2 South and Southeast Asia

During the European race for empire in the 1800's, much of South and Southeast Asia became European colonies. Britain ruled India, the largest and most populous of the colonial areas. The Dutch controlled much of the island territory in Southeast Asia. The French held Indochina. At the end of World War II, the European powers began a retreat from empire by granting independence to many of their subject peoples in Asia.

The Indian Subcontinent

After World War II, Britain finally agreed to give India its independence. The preparations for Britain's withdrawal, however, were complicated by growing political disunity throughout the subcontinent.

Division The British had ruled the subcontinent under one government. They wanted the region to remain united after independence. However, as the time for independence approached, Hindus and Muslims began to fight each other. Hundreds of thousands of people were killed in bloody clashes throughout India.

Fearing a civil war, the British arranged for a division of the subcontinent into two separate nations: India and Pakistan. On August 15, 1947, the Dominion of India was proclaimed at New Delhi. Jawaharlal Nehru became India's first prime minister. He led a predominantly Hindu nation that occupied most of the subcontinent. That same day, the Dominion of Pakistan, a Muslim state, was proclaimed at Karachi. Liaqat Ali Khan became prime minister. Pakistan was made up of two disconnected regions separated by a thousand miles (1,600 kilometers) of Indian territory. West Pakistan was located on the northwestern side of India, while East Pakistan was situated at the delta of the Ganges River near Burma. Although East Pakistan made up only 15 percent of Pakistan's territory, it contained 55 percent of the country's population.

Nehru sent Sikh soldiers to defend Kashmir's Hindu ruler, when neighboring Pakistanis crossed the border to aid a Muslim revolt. What actions were taken to reduce conflict over Kashmir?

After independence, nearly 10 million people migrated from one country to the other. Hindus in Pakistan moved to India. Many Muslims in India moved to Pakistan.[3] With such a large movement of people, tensions increased. Nearly 500,000 persons were killed in religious riots. During this violent period, Mohandas K. Gandhi was assassinated by a Hindu nationalist who opposed Gandhi's efforts to bring peace between Hindus and Muslims.

Conflicts also developed over the decisions made by local rulers to join either India or Pakistan. In Kashmir, the Hindu ruler decided to make his region a part of India, although a majority of his subjects were Muslim. In Hyderabad, the Muslim ruler ignored the wishes of

[3]Although numerous Hindus migrated to India and many Muslims migrated to Pakistan, some 40 million Muslims remained in India after the division. This helped keep India a multireligious state with Hindus, Muslims, Buddhists, and smaller groups of Christians and others.

the predominantly Hindu population and joined Pakistan. Both areas were claimed by Pakistan and India. Full-scale war was avoided in 1949 when India and Pakistan accepted a UN-sponsored cease fire. Kashmir eventually was divided between the two nations, and Hyderabad became a part of India.

During the 1950's and early 1960's, India and Pakistan remained bitter enemies. A war broke out between them in 1965, but there was no decisive winner. In 1966 a peace agreement was signed in the Soviet city of Tashkent. The agreement had been negotiated with the help of Soviet Premier Aleksei Kosygin.

India   In 1950 India became a republic in the Commonwealth of Nations. In spite of wars, poverty, famine, and internal disputes, India remained committed to parliamentary democracy. The Indian constitution aimed to unite the diverse groups that made up the country. It established the equality of all people under the law and granted universal suffrage. Caste distinctions were banned and discrimination against untouchables and outcastes became illegal. By making Hindi the official national language, the government hoped to further national unity.

In 1950 the Indian government introduced a series of five-year plans for economic development. The plans set up a **mixed economy,** one in which some businesses are privately owned, while others are under the control of government. The Indian government backed large projects, such as road building, factories, irrigation systems, and energy plants. India, however, remained largely a nation of farmers who worked their own small plots of land.

In world affairs, India became the leader of the nonaligned nations. It was one of the first non-Communist states to develop close relations with Communist China. These ties, however, were disrupted in 1962 when China laid claim to Indian territory in the Himalayas and sent troops into the region. India suffered a loss of prestige and appealed for outside help. When the United States and other countries provided military aid to India, the Chinese withdrew their forces from the disputed area.

Some teachers might wish to discuss in greater detail United States involvement in Indochina.

India enjoyed political stability under Jawaharlal Nehru. The National Congress party dominated Indian politics on the national and local levels. After Nehru's death in 1964, Lal Bahadur Shastri served as prime minister. When Shastri died in 1966, Indira Gandhi, Nehru's daughter, was elected to the office. She continued a policy of nonalignment and received military and economic aid from both the Americans and the Soviets.

Pakistan   After independence, Pakistan allied itself with the West in opposition to India, which chose nonalignment. In 1956 Pakistan ended its dominion status and became a republic. Fighting among various political factions led to political instability.

The geographical separation of the country provided additional problems. Islam was the common bond that held Pakistan together. But aside from religion, there was little else that provided a sense of national unity. The people of East Pakistan resented control of their region by West Pakistan, where the national capital, Karachi, was located. East Pakistanis found it difficult to influence the government bureaucracy and the army, which were largely run by West Pakistanis. There were also cultural differences that heightened the growing rift between the two regions. The people in the eastern part were mostly Bengalis, sharing a common culture with the people of eastern India. Those in the western part had close cultural ties to the Middle East and western India.

Friction between the two regions as well as government corruption and inefficiency led to a military coup d'etat in 1958. A new leader, General Mohammed Ayub Khan, ruled Pakistan until 1969. Khan, however, had no better success in holding the two Pakistans together. Throughout the 1960's, tensions grew as the Bengalis in East Pakistan demanded a greater share in governing the country.

Southeast Asia

After World War II, independence movements increased in strength in Southeast Asia. In response to this pressure, the European colonial powers slowly withdrew from the region.

Indochina   During World War II, Japanese forces had occupied much of French Indochina. At this time, nationalist forces in the eastern region of Vietnam waged a guerrilla war against the Japanese. At war's end, the Vietnamese nationalists, known as the Vietminh, proclaimed an independent republic under their leader, Ho Chi Minh. Ho was a dedicated Communist who blended Vietnamese nationalism with Communist ideology.

Between 1946 and 1954, the French tried to regain their control over Vietnam. At first they were willing to grant self-government to the Vietnamese. However, negotiations broke down; and active fighting began. The costly war dragged on for seven years during which time the French received substantial aid from the United States. The United States government hoped that the French would be able to prevent a Communist takeover.

In 1954 French forces suffered a disastrous defeat at the fortress of Dien Bien Phu. Realizing that their cause was lost, the French negotiated a truce with the Vietminh. Later that year, an international conference at Geneva, Switzerland, concluded several agreements to determine the future of Vietnam and the rest of Indochina. One of the agreements provided for a temporary division of Vietnam. The division, made at the 17th parallel, created a Communist state in North Vietnam and a pro-western government in South Vietnam. The country was to be reunited when a national election could be held. The rest of Indochina—the territories of Laos and Cambodia—became independent monarchies free from French control.

After the Geneva settlement, Communist North Vietnam began to work for the reunification of the country. Communist guerrilla forces were still scattered throughout South Vietnam. They were prepared to use force to realize the goal of a united, Communist Vietnam. Preparations for a "war of national liberation" were increased after South Vietnamese President Ngo Dinh Diem refused to hold a referendum on national reunification. In 1960, groups of South Vietnamese Communists, known as the Vietcong, formed a united guerrilla movement. A civil war soon broke out between the Vietcong, aided by North Vietnam, and the South Vietnamese government.

In 1961 the United States increased its support of the South Vietnamese government, providing more financial aid, weapons, and military programs. It also attempted to make South Vietnam more democratic by insisting on various political reforms. At the same time, the Soviet Union increased its aid to North Vietnam and the Vietcong.

Indonesia   In 1945 the people of the Dutch East Indies declared their independence. This was soon after the Japanese had withdrawn and before the Dutch could reestablish control. Achmed Sukarno, the nationalist leader, became the president of the new nation, which became

known as Indonesia. In 1949 the Dutch recognized Indonesia's independence.

As president, Sukarno established a united nation, overcoming divisions among the islands. In foreign policy, he pursued neutrality in the East-West struggle. However, by the early 1960's, Sukarno came under the influence of the Indonesian Communist party, one of the largest in Asia. As a result, he began drawing closer to the Communist bloc for support. Sukarno's pro-Communist policies angered Muslim groups and the armed forces. In 1965 the Indonesian Communists planned to seize power. However, the military became aware of these plans and staged a coup d'etat before the uprising could be carried out. The coup resulted in much bloodshed and forced Sukarno and his followers into

INDEPENDENCE IN SOUTH EAST ASIA

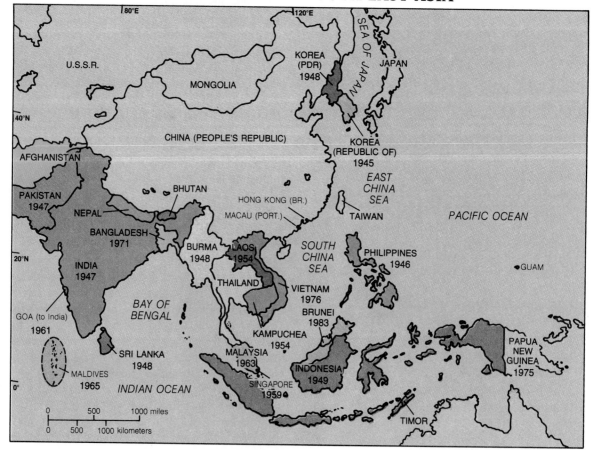

The Philippine economy expanded rapidly after World War II. Its free enterprise system and natural resources attracted many American investors.

exile. In 1968, General T. N. J. Suharto, the leader of the coup, was elected president of Indonesia. Under Suharto's leadership, Indonesia aligned itself with the West.

Burma and Malaysia   Elsewhere in Southeast Asia, Burma became fully independent from Britain in 1948. In 1957 the British-protected sultanates and territories in the Malay Peninsula became the independent country of Malaya. Six years later, Malaya and the former British territories of Sarawak and North Borneo joined together to form the Federation of Malaysia. In 1965 the city of Singapore seceded from Malaysia and became an independent nation.

Philippines   The Philippines, another Southeast Asian nation, gained its independence from the United States in 1946. It established a democratic republic based on the American model. To improve the economy, a long-range program of industrial expansion was begun. However, government economic plans were disrupted by the outbreak of a Communist uprising in the central region of Luzon, one of the larger islands in the Philippines. During most of the 1950's, the government carried out a military offensive against the Communist guerrillas. The Communists received much of their support from landless peasants. To help defeat the Communists, the government introduced reforms to break up large estates and redistribute land to the peasants. By 1960 the Communist guerrillas had been brought under control.

Thailand   A strong anti-Communist nation in the region was Thailand, formerly known as Siam. Thailand experienced considerable political upheaval after World War II. Elected governments were often overthrown in military coups. However, social stability was maintained as a result of the people's devotion to Buddhism and the Thai monarchy.

SEATO   To block Communist expansion in Southeast Asia, Thailand joined other governments in forming the Southeast Asia Treaty Organization (SEATO). Established in 1954 on the initiative of the United States, SEATO linked Thailand and the Philippines with Australia, New Zealand, and the United States in a defensive alliance.

The Hagana, a Zionist military organization, defied British immigration policy to help thousands of Jews enter Palestine. This ship was stopped and boarded by British soldiers. Why did Zionists gain worldwide support?

1. Identify: New Delhi, Karachi, Lal Bahadur Shastri, Indira Gandhi, Mohammed Ayub Khan, Vietminh, Ho Chi Minh, Dien Bien Phu, Ngo Dinh Diem, Vietcong, Achmed Sukarno, T. N. J. Suharto, Burma, Malaysia, Luzon, Thailand, SEATO.
2. What were the aims of India's constitution?
3. Which Southeast Asian nations achieved independence in the postwar era?

3   The Middle East

Before 1945 much of the Middle East was either under the direct control of western colonial powers or under their influence. By 1960, however, most of the countries in the region were independent. Between 1945 and 1965, the Middle East became the focus of ongoing struggles between Arabs and Jews.

Arab-Israeli Conflict

The end of World War II saw no improvement in the relations between Arabs and Jews in Palestine. Nazi persecution of Europe's Jews increased worldwide support for the Zionist movement. Jews in large numbers came to

After its creation in 1948, Israel was promptly recognized by the Soviets and the Americans.

The map below is the subject of the "Using Maps" section of the Chapter 30 Review.

MIDDLE EAST CRISES 1945-1963

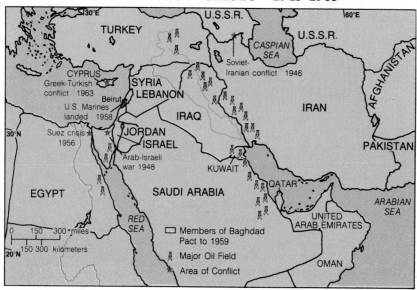

Palestine to help in the building of a Jewish state. Increased Jewish immigration and Zionist goals heightened Arab hostility. Both Jews and Arabs stepped up terrorist activities against each other and the British mandate government. British authorities found it impossible to maintain order in the region.

UN Plan   In 1947 the British government announced that it planned to pass on the problem of Palestine to the United Nations. On the basis of a UN commission report, the Security Council voted for the division of Palestine into Jewish and Arab states. Jerusalem was to be under UN supervision. Zionists favored the plan. Arab members of the United Nations opposed it, declaring their support for Arab control of Palestine.

Creation of Israel   On May 14, 1948, Britain withdrew from Palestine. The Jews of the region immediately set up an independent republic. They called it Israel with its capital at Tel Aviv.[4] Israel's first elections in 1949 made David Ben-Gurion prime minister. Chaim Weizmann became president. The legislative body was known as the Knesset.

---
[4]Israel moved its capital from Tel Aviv to Jerusalem in December 1949, ignoring a UN resolution to place the city under international control.

Israel's Arab neighbors refused to recognize the new nation. Egypt, Syria, Lebanon, and Iraq united their military forces and invaded Israel in the spring of 1948. This first Arab-Israeli war was fought until the beginning of 1949. Well-organized Israeli forces easily defeated the Arab armies.

Palestinian Arabs   The United Nations mediated the cease-fire and armistice that ended the fighting in 1949. The peace settlement resulted in more land for Israel. At the same time, nearly three-quarters of a million Palestinian Arabs were forced to leave the country that had been their homeland.

Many of the Palestinian refugees moved to makeshift camps in nearby Arab countries. Terrorist groups were organized among the more radical elements of these refugees. By 1964, various Palestinian Arab groups and agencies merged to form the Palestinian Liberation Organization (PLO). The PLO served as a government in exile. Through military and diplomatic means, it promoted the interests of the refugees in regaining their territory from Israel.

Israeli Development   After the Arab-Israeli conflict of 1948-1949, Israel developed its economy with the help of loans from western nations,

HISTORY AND PEOPLE

Golda Meir

Golda Meir was one of the most distinguished women in recent Jewish history. She was born Golda Mabovitch in Kiev, the Ukraine, in 1898. The Mabovitch family, along with other Jews in the Russian Empire, faced persecution from anti-Semitic mobs. In 1906 Golda and her family left Kiev and sought a new life in the United States.

Golda Mabovitch grew up in Milwaukee, Wisconsin, and became a school teacher. In 1917 she married Morris Myerson, a Jewish immigrant from Russia. Memories of pogroms and news of continued anti-Semitic activities in Eastern Europe made her a devoted Zionist. In 1921 the Myersons emigrated to Palestine. Even though Golda Myerson loved her husband and children, marriage and motherhood were not enough to fulfill her. She and her husband separated, and she devoted herself full time to Zionism. During the 1920's and 1930's, she became a leading figure in the Palestinian Jewish labor movement.

With the coming of World War II, Golda Myerson pressured British officials to admit more Jews from Nazi-ruled Europe into Palestine. Although the British refused entry to adults, Myerson's efforts aided in bringing many children into the country. After the war, she visited the United States, raising more than 50 million dollars for the Zionist cause.

As British withdrawal from Palestine neared in 1948, violent clashes mounted between Palestine's Jews and Arabs. In a dramatic move for peace, Golda Myerson, in disguise, met secretly with Jordan's King Abdullah. The king reportedly told her that the Jews were too impatient in wanting to establish their own nation. Myerson answered: "We have been waiting for 2,000 years. Is that hurrying?" Four days later, the Jewish state of Israel was proclaimed.

Golda Myerson served in the new Israeli government. In keeping with the rule that Israeli officials should bear Hebrew names, she changed her last name to Meir. As Israel's labor minister from 1949 to 1956, Meir backed unrestricted Jewish immigration and carried out programs of housing, irrigation, and road construction. In 1956 she was appointed foreign minister, a post that she held for nine years. Meir finally became prime minister in 1969 at the age of 70.

As prime minister, Meir worked for peace between Israel and its Arab neighbors. Her efforts, however, were thwarted by the Yom Kippur War of 1973. Accepting responsibility for the high casualties, she retired from public life the following year.

After her retirement, Golda Meir's efforts for peace paid off in better relations between Israel and Egypt. By the time of her death in 1978, she was widely respected as a courageous, honest, and practical political leader.

Have students explain why the Arabs viewed Israel as a new form of western imperialism in the region.

Compare and contrast Nasser and Atatürk as Middle Eastern leaders.

German reparations, and collections from Jewish communities worldwide. To promote agricultural growth, the Israelis continued a practice that had begun during the early period of Zionist settlement in Palestine. They built special communities known as kibbutzim and moshavim. **Kibbutzim** are collective farm settlements in which the land is held in common. **Moshavim** are cooperative settlements in which farms are individually owned, although farmers share agricultural equipment and general costs. A similar arrangement was used in industry. Some businesses were owned by the state; others were privately owned.

In internal affairs, the most difficult problem facing Israel was that of making a united nation from the different Jewish groups that had settled the country. The two major groups of Jews in Israel were the Ashkenazim and Sephardim. The Ashkenazim were Jews from Eastern Europe. The Sephardim were Jews who migrated to Israel from North Africa and other parts of the Middle East and Asia. Each group had its own cultural tradition.

The greatest foreign problem for the Israelis was the threat of further attacks from Arab neighbors. To improve their defense, the Israelis increased the size and training of their armed forces. They also spent large amounts of government revenues for weapons.

Arab States

During the postwar years, nationalism grew with intensity in the Arab states as did the idea of Pan-Arabism. Pan-Arabism was a political and cultural movement emphasizing ties among all Arab peoples. The creation of Israel, in particular, promoted Arab unity in the Middle East. To many Arabs, the existence of Israel seemed like a new form of western influence in the Middle East.

Egypt   Until the early 1950's, Egypt was ruled by its monarchy and a class of wealthy landowners. In addition, British influence remained strong. British troops were stationed in Egypt to protect the Suez Canal. Since independence in 1922, Egyptian nationalists had been demanding the complete withdrawal of British

forces from their country. After the Egyptian defeat in the first Arab-Israeli war, many Egyptians turned against the monarchy and wanted an end to western influence in their country. In 1952 a military coup d'etat removed King Farouk and gave Egyptians hope that the British would leave Egypt.

The leader of the military takeover was a young army colonel named Gamal Abdel Nasser. Nasser and his military colleagues proclaimed a republic. Within a year, Nasser had complete power as president. Under his rule, Egypt emerged as the leading Arab state.

Nasser's government moved quickly to win the support of Egyptians. It introduced land reform that reduced the estates of the landowners and gave land to the peasants. It also negotiated a British withdrawal from the Suez Canal zone and Sudan. In 1953 an Anglo-Egyptian agreement was reached leading to Sudanese independence.[5] A year later, the Egyptians and the British set a timetable for British troops to leave the canal zone. However, British and French stockholders still retained ownership of the canal.

Suez Crisis   Having accomplished land reform and the expulsion of the British, Nasser turned to two new goals. He wanted to strengthen his armed forces and build a large dam at Aswan in Upper Egypt. Nasser wanted the Aswan High Dam to improve agriculture and produce electricity in the Upper Nile Valley.

At first, Britain and the United States agreed to loan money to Nasser for financing the Aswan project. However, Nasser also wanted the western powers to supply him with new weapons so he could fight Israel. When they refused, Nasser openly negotiated with the Soviet Union for arms. At the same time, he spoke out against the Baghdad Pact, an alliance of Britain, Turkey, Iraq, Pakistan, and Iran aimed at blocking Soviet expansion in the Middle East.[6]

---

[5]Nasser had wanted the Sudanese to unite with Egypt once the British had gone. The Sudanese, however, voted for independence and remained a separate country.

[6]After Iraq withdrew from the Baghdad Pact in 1959, the alliance was reestablished as the Central Treaty Organization (CENTO).

Christian groups enjoyed the most power in Lebanon by controlling much of the government and economy.

In 1956 Nasser waved in response to cheering Egyptians as he moved through Port Said, the Mediterranean outlet of the Suez Canal. Nasser raised the Egyptian flag over the port during a ceremony in which Egypt formally nationalized the canal. After this action, Nasser became a worldwide symbol of the Arab people. His familiar cry "I am an Arab" encouraged many Arab countries to look toward Egypt for leadership and protection from outside intervention. What attempt did Nasser make to unify Arab countries?

Opposed to Nasser's pro-Soviet policies, Britain and the United States withdrew support for the Aswan project. Nasser responded in 1956 by nationalizing the Suez Canal and securing Soviet aid to build the dam. As a result, a second Arab-Israeli war broke out. In the conflict, Israel helped Britain and France in an unsuccessful attempt to regain control of the canal by force. The United States opposed the invasion, and the Soviet Union threatened military intervention. In the face of this pressure, the three invading nations removed their troops from Egypt. With the crisis concluded, a UN emergency force moved into the Sinai Peninsula to patrol the Egyptian-Israeli border.

Nasser and Arab Unity   As a result of the Suez crisis, Nasser's Egypt won respect throughout the Arab world. It had successfully rallied much of world opinion against two western powers and Israel. Riding a wave of popularity, Nasser began to promote Arab unity under Egypt's leadership. In 1958 he forged a brief union between Egypt and Syria, naming it the United Arab Republic.

By the 1960's, Nasser's popularity had begun to decline. Many conservative Arab leaders believed that Nasser was using Pan-Arabism to promote his own personal ambitions. They began to withdraw their support from the Egyptian leader. Radical Arab organizations, such as the PLO, however, remained loyal to Nasser. They depended on him for leadership in their struggles against Israel and conservative Arab governments.

Lebanon   After 20 years as a French mandate, Lebanon gained independence in 1943. Lebanon's population was almost evenly divided between Muslims and Christians. Among these two groups were various sects. The Christians comprised members of the Maronite, Eastern Orthodox, and Armenian churches. The Muslims included Sunni, Shiite, and Druze sects. Each religious group had representation in the government. However, the Christian groups enjoyed the most power.

During the 1950's and 1960's, Lebanon prospered as a leading center of business and trade in the Middle East. However, many Muslim Lebanese were excluded from these economic benefits as well as from political power. In 1958, radical Muslims staged an uprising against the pro-western Christian President Camille Chamoun. Chamoun appealed to the United States for help. In response, United States President Eisenhower ordered American troops to Lebanon to bolster the Chamoun administration.

Following the election of a new Lebanese president later in the year, American forces left the country. The 1958 Lebanese uprising revealed the desire of many Arabs to keep western influence out of the Middle East.

Syria   Like Lebanon, Syria had been ruled as a French mandate before World War II. In 1946, it became an independent nation. At that time, the Syrians elected their first parliamentary government. Then, in 1949 the military ousted the elected government, blaming its leaders for Syria's defeat in the first Arab-Israeli war. Two other military coup d'etats took place before civilian government was restored in 1954.

In 1958 Syria formed the United Arab Republic with Egypt. But many Syrians resented the growth of Nasser's influence in their country. In 1961 Syria broke with Egypt and formed its own government. By 1963, the leftist Ba'ath party had gained power in Syria. Over the next three years, it set up a socialist economy and established close ties to the Soviet Union. Many of the Ba'ath party's policies were directed against western influence in the Middle East. Dedicated to Arab nationalism, Ba'ath party leaders remained distrustful of Israel.

Iraq and Jordan   During much of the 1950's, Iraq and Jordan were close allies. Both countries were ruled by monarchs of the Hashimite family and had many interests in common. In early 1958, Iraq and Jordan formed a federation, coordinating their domestic and foreign policies. Once British protectorates, they maintained close ties with Britain. Because of their links to the West, Iraq and Jordan came under bitter attack from Nasser and his supporters.

On July 14, 1958, a group of pro-Nasser army officers led by General Karim el-Kassem seized power in Iraq. The new rulers killed the pro-western king Faisal II and his advisers. They set up a one-party government similar to that of Egypt. One of their first acts was to end Iraq's close relationship with the West.

In Jordan, Arab nationalists forced King Hussein I to end his government's close ties to Britain.[7] After the 1958 revolution in Iraq,

Hussein feared that pro-Nasser groups would try to overthrow him. He called for British military help to maintain order in his country. When stability was restored, the British forces withdrew.

During the 1960's, Hussein was less pro-western, but he continued to oppose radical Arab policies. Jordan, with a large population of Palestinian refugees, became a natural base for guerrilla attacks on Israel. Without denying Palestinian grievances, Hussein tried to limit the activities of the guerrillas that endangered his throne. He relied on the United States for military support and on Saudi Arabia for backing in the Arab community of nations.

Saudi Arabia and the Gulf States   King Ibn Saud died in 1953. He was succeeded by Saud, one of his many sons. During most of King Saud's reign, real power was exercised by the king's brother Faisal. In 1964 Faisal deposed Saud and became ruler of the oil-rich country. Faisal strongly opposed Nasser's brand of Arab nationalism. But he did not exert any influence in the Arab world until the late 1960's.

Elsewhere on the Arabian Peninsula, Kuwait, Oman, the island of Bahrain, the peninsula of Qatar, and the seven Trucial states[8] were all ruled by sheikhs. Kuwait gained independence in 1961. It became the first of these territories to become completely independent of Britain. In the southern part of the Arabian Peninsula were the independent state of Yemen and the British protectorate of Aden. During the early 1960's, pro-Nasser forces overthrew Yemen's monarch and established a republic.

Turkey and Iran

Although not part of the Arab world, Turkey and Iran were subject to the same tensions that were felt in other parts of the Middle East. During the 1950's and early 1960's, both nations experienced nationalistic upheavals. They also faced the issues of modernization and democratic reform.

---

[7]After the assassination of his grandfather King Abdullah, Hussein, at the age of 17, became king of Jordan in 1952.

[8]The Trucial States are located along the eastern coast of the Arabian Peninsula. They now form a union known as the United Arab Emirates, which includes Abu Dhabi, Ajman, Dubai, Fujairah, Ras al-Khaimah, Sharjah, and Umm al-Qaiwain.

One method that Turkey used to attract foreign capital was denationalizing the oil industry. Ask students how they think Turkey was able to benefit from denationalization.

Explain how various countries have used nationalization of certain industries for economic reform.

Turkey   After World War II, the Soviet Union demanded territorial concessions from Turkey. Soviet pressure forced the Turkish government of Prime Minister Ismet Inönü to seek aid from the western powers. Under the terms of the Truman Doctrine of 1947, the United States supplied Turkey with military and economic aid to block Soviet advances. This aid allowed Turkey to keep out the Soviets and to introduce internal reforms.

In the early 1940's, Turkey's democracy had been replaced by a one-party system. As a result of public pressure, the ruling People's party at the end of the decade allowed the formation of opposition parties. In 1950 the People's party's chief rival, the Democratic party, won an overwhelming majority in the general elections. Jelal Bayar became president, and Adnan Menderes prime minister. The new administration favored a capitalist economy and encouraged foreign investments in Turkey. It also adopted a pro-western foreign policy, joining NATO and the Baghdad Pact.

During the 1950's, the Menderes administration became dictatorial and oppressive. It was finally ousted in 1960 by a military coup d'etat. The following year, the Turkish parliament elected Jemal Gürsel president, and Ismet Inönü became prime minister again. Under the new government, Turkey continued to support western alliances. However, relations with the West were sometimes strained. In 1964 the United States temporarily stopped sending military aid to Turkey. This was a protest against Turkish actions in a crisis with Greece over the island of Cyprus.

Iran   Shah Mohammed Reza Pahlavi continued to govern Iran after World War II. Fearing Soviet expansion into his country, the shah turned to the United States for military and economic aid. He also increased his powers over the Iranian government.

In 1950 anti-shah members of the Majles, the Iranian parliament, named Mohammed Mossadegh prime minister. Mossadegh was a strong Iranian nationalist and an opponent of the shah. He particularly opposed the shah's moderate approach in dealing with the western powers

that controlled Iran's oil production. In 1951 Mossadegh's government announced the nationalization of the oil industry. It declared that future oil revenues were to be used for social and economic reforms within Iran. In response, Britain and other western countries boycotted Iranian oil. Iran's economy suffered, and bitterness toward the West increased.

In January 1953, Mossadegh gained from the Majles increased authority to govern Iran. Viewing Mossadegh as a threat to the monarchy, the shah in August moved to dismiss the prime minister. Mossadegh refused to give up his authority and finally forced the shah to flee the country. A few days later, an American-backed coup brought down Mossadegh's government, and the shah returned to the Iranian throne.

Upon returning to Iran, the shah repealed many of Mossadegh's anti-western measures. In 1955 Iran joined the Baghdad Pact, restoring its links with the West. To win public support, the

In Iran, the 1960's marked not only the crowning of Empress Farah, but also the shah's "White Revolution," which called for rapid economic development and social reforms. What assured Iran's stability during the 1960's?

Refer students to the map of African Independence on p. 710.

Refer students to the discussion on French domestic issues on pp. 680 and 681.

shah in 1962 introduced land reforms designed to aid Iran's landless peasants. With a reform program and strong army support, the government of Shah Mohammed Reza Pahlavi remained stable throughout the 1960's.

1. Identify: David Ben-Gurion, Knesset, PLO, Pan-Arabism, Gamal Abdel Nasser, Baghdad Pact, United Arab Republic, Ba'ath party, Faisal II, Hussein, Kuwait, İsmet İnönü, Adnan Menderes, Mohammed Mossadegh.
2. What plan for partition did the United Nations approve for Palestine?
3. What events led to the first and second Arab-Israeli wars?
4. How did Pan-Arabism affect the governments of Syria, Iraq, Jordan, and Lebanon?

4 Africa

After 1945, Britain, France, and Belgium began to yield to African nationalist demands for freedom. Portugal alone refused to grant its colonies independence. At the close of the war, Egypt, Ethiopia, Liberia, and South Africa were the only sovereign states in Africa. By 1965 there were over 30 independent nations.

French Retreat

The French retreat from Africa was slow and undertaken reluctantly. In the late 1940's, the French brutally crushed nationalist uprisings throughout its African empire. However, by the mid-1950's, the French government recognized that it did not have sufficient resources to put down these independence movements. The first French African territories to become independent were in North Africa. In 1956 the French granted freedom to Tunisia and Morocco. However, the French made a special effort to retain Algeria, their last North African territory.

Algeria The situation in Algeria was very different from that in France's other African colonies. The French considered Algeria a part of France, not a colony. There were at least 1 million European **colons,** or settlers, in Algeria. Most of them were French. So when Algerian Muslims began fighting for independence, many French viewed this resistance as an act of treason. After the loss of Indochina in 1954, the French government particularly wanted to keep Algeria in order to bolster sagging national pride.

The Algerian war for independence lasted for seven and a half years. Considered the most violent anticolonial uprising, it resulted in nearly 1 million casualties. The Algerian conflict was responsible for the collapse of the Fourth Republic and twice threatened to topple the Fifth Republic. When the Algerians gained their freedom in 1962, they were highly respected in the Third World. Ahmed Ben Bella, the first president of Algeria, became a leader in the non-aligned movement of African and Asian states.

Sub-Saharan Territories While the French fought in Algeria, the rest of their African empire began to dissolve. In 1958 President Charles de Gaulle offered all of the Sub-Saharan colonies a choice. They could become self-governing in a French-sponsored community of nations or decide for complete independence. Only the West African territory of Guinea chose complete separation. In taking this step, Guinea had to give up French economic aid. Its leader Sékou Touré turned to the Soviet Union for assistance.

De Gaulle feared that other French Sub-Saharan colonies would follow Guinea in concluding agreements with the Soviets. To prevent this, de Gaulle granted them complete independence along with French assistance. Under these terms, the remainder of France's African colonies became independent nations. Madagascar became the Malagasy Republic in 1960. That same year, French West Africa was replaced by the new nations of Mauritania, the Ivory Coast, Togo, Dahomey, Niger, Upper Volta, and Mali. Also, French Equatorial Africa became the states of Chad, Gabon, the Central African Republic, and the Congo Republic. In addition, the French gave up control of their United Nations trusteeship in Cameroon. French Somaliland, located in the horn of Africa, was the last French colony on the continent. It became the independent nation of Djibouti in 1977.

British Retreat

By the mid-1960's, Britain's African empire was coming to an end. The transition from

For a time during the Nigerian civil war, the Ibo established their own nation called Biafra.

colonial rule to independence was generally peaceful; however, the pace of transition varied from region to region.

West Africa   In Britain's West African territories, conditions were favorable for independence. There were many experienced African leaders and few European settlers.

In 1957 the Gold Coast became the first British African colony to gain its independence. It became known as Ghana. In 1960 Nigeria became independent as a federal state. Even under the most favorable circumstances, however, a peaceful transition to independence did not guarantee political stability in these new nations. Ghana and Nigeria both underwent internal upheavals. President Kwame Nkrumah established a dictatorship in Ghana. After Nkrumah's overthrow in 1966, Ghana was ruled by a series of military and civilian governments. In Nigeria,

tension grew between the Muslim north and the largely Christian south and east. This division was further complicated by hostility between various ethnic groups. In 1966 an ethnic group called the Ibo broke away from the central government and established the Republic of Biafra in the east. The Nigerian central government, controlled by a rival group known as the Hausa, fought the Ibo for three years.

East and Central Africa   In the British territories of East and Central Africa, conditions for independence were not always favorable. Kenya, Tanganyika, and Southern Rhodesia had large European minorities that were reluctant to see independent African governments established in the territories.

In Kenya, an African movement called the Mau Mau led attacks against European settlers and their African supporters. The goal of the

Although the Nigerian federal army was strengthened by British, Soviet, French, and Spanish arms, these resilient Ibo soldiers fought courageously for Biafra's right to sovereignty. How long did the Nigerian civil war last?

Kenyatta's ties with the Mau Mau movement were never established.

Mau Mau was to drive out the Europeans. In response, the British government declared a state of emergency, arresting and jailing all African nationalists suspected of aiding the Mau Mau. Among those arrested was the nationalist leader Jomo Kenyatta.

By the mid-1950's, British forces had crushed the Mau Mau. However, the British recognized that their days in Kenya were numbered. They began to loosen their hold on the colony and prepared its African leadership to receive power. In 1963 Kenya became independent with Jomo Kenyatta as its first president.

Britain relinquished its rule in the rest of East Africa. Tanganyika achieved independence in 1961. A few years later, it united with the offshore island of Zanzibar to form the nation of Tanzania. Under the leadership of President Julius Nyerere, Tanzania developed a form of African socialism. Under this system, villages were organized into agricultural units similar to cooperative farms. In 1962, Uganda, a British protectorate, became independent. Tensions among rival ethnic groups led to the overthrow of several Ugandan governments during the rest of the decade.

In Central Africa, Britain granted independence in 1964 to Nyasaland, which became known as Malawi. In that same year, Northern Rhodesia became the independent state of Zambia. Southern Rhodesia, however, remained a British colony under its large European minority. It became known as Rhodesia.

During the early 1960's, the Europeans of Rhodesia united under the leadership of a political party called the Rhodesia Front. The goal of the Rhodesia Front was to bar African participation in the government and to retain

Kenyatta was released from prison by the British government in 1961, after his Kenya African National Union party won parliamentary elections and refused to assume power without their leader. What position did Kenyatta hold in the republic of Kenya?

The purpose of South African apartheid, an Afrikaan word meaning apartness, is to segregate the country's four major racial groups—white, African, colored, and Indian—in every aspect of their lives. The groups live in separate residential areas. Their children attend different schools and universities. Choice industrial and service occupations are reserved for whites. Wages for whites can be as much as 12 times the amount non-whites earn in the same position. Whites and non-whites use separate public facilities and transportation. How did South Africa respond to the British Commonwealth's objections to the apartheid?

European dominance in the colony. In 1962 the Rhodesia Front took control of the colonial government. When the British in 1965 pressed the Rhodesia Front to share political power with the Africans, the party declared Rhodesia's independence. Britain, along with the majority of the world's nations, opposed this move. The UN called on all nations to withhold recognition and aid to the Rhodesian government.

South Africa   Until the 1960's, the Union of South Africa was the only independent state in the southern part of the continent. Its government was controlled by the Afrikaners. In 1948 the Afrikaner policy of apartheid was made official throughout the country. In addition, the black majority and non-white minorities were denied civil rights and not regarded as citizens. Opposition to South Africa's apartheid policy grew around the world during the 1950's. In response to Commonwealth pressures for change, South Africa broke its ties to the British monarchy. It chose to become a republic outside the Commonwealth of Nations.

Belgian Retreat

In 1959 the Belgian government announced a phased withdrawal from its colony, the Belgian Congo. The Belgians had hoped to avoid the problems of the French in Indochina and Algeria. But what was planned as a withdrawal to last over a generation was crowded into a short 18 months. Violent riots in the Congo forced the Belgians to grant independence in 1960 much sooner than expected.

Almost immediately, the new Republic of Congo fell into chaos. The government of Prime Minister Patrice Lumumba was challenged by Moise Tshombe, the leader of the mineral-rich Congo province of Katanga. In the dispute, Katanga declared its independence from the Congo.

A civil war broke out in the Congo that soon took the form of an East-West conflict. Many western powers, interested in the Congo's mineral wealth, either supported or sympathized with Tshombe, while many Communist and nonaligned nations backed Lumumba's government. To prevent the involvement of the superpowers, the United Nations intervened. It sent a multinational emergency force of about 20,000 troops to restore order. In the fighting, the pro-Soviet Lumumba was captured by his enemies and killed. In early 1963, the Katanga secession ended, and order was restored.

AFRICAN INDEPENDENCE

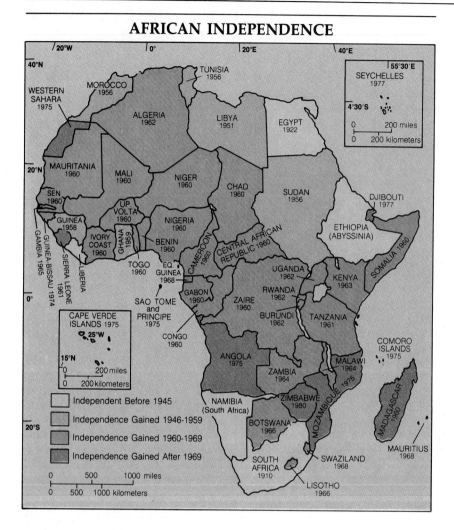

20°W · 0° · 20°E · 40°E

40°N

TUNISIA 1956

55°30'E
SEYCHELLES 1977

4°30'S

0   200 miles
0   200 kilometers

WESTERN SAHARA 1975

MOROCCO 1956

ALGERIA 1962

LIBYA 1951

EGYPT 1922

20°N

MAURITANIA 1960

MALI 1960

NIGER 1960

CHAD 1960

SUDAN 1956

DJIBOUTI 1977

SEN 1960

UP. VOLTA 1960

NIGERIA 1960

GUINEA 1958

GAMBIA 1965

GUINEA-BISSAU 1974

IVORY COAST 1960

GHANA 1959

BENIN 1960

SIERRA LEONE 1961

LIBERIA

TOGO 1960

EQ. GUINEA 1968

CAMEROON 1960

CENTRAL AFRICAN REPUBLIC 1960

ETHIOPIA (ABYSSINIA)

SOMALIA 1960

UGANDA 1962

KENYA 1963

RWANDA 1962

GABON 1960

SAO TOME and PRINCIPE 1975

ZAIRE 1960

BURUNDI 1962

TANZANIA 1961

0°

CAPE VERDE ISLANDS 1975

25°W

15°N

0   200 miles
0   200 kilometers

CONGO 1960

ANGOLA 1975

ZAMBIA 1964

MALAWI 1964

COMORO ISLANDS 1975

MADAGASCAR 1960

20°S

Independent Before 1945

Independence Gained 1946-1959

Independence Gained 1960-1969

Independence Gained After 1969

NAMIBIA (South Africa)

ZIMBABWE 1980

MOZAMBIQUE 1975

BOTSWANA 1966

MAURITIUS 1968

SOUTH AFRICA 1910

SWAZILAND 1968

LISOTHO 1966

0   500   1000 miles
0   500   1000 kilometers

In 1964 the United Nations force was withdrawn. That year, a government of reconciliation was formed in the Congo. This government included Tshombe, who became prime minister. However, rebels loyal to the memory of Patrice Lumumba initiated a guerrilla war against the new government. As a result of this ongoing struggle, the Congo remained a world trouble spot throughout the decade of the 1960's.

1. Identify: Ahmed Ben Bella, Sékou Touré, Djibouti, Ghana, Kwame Nkrumah, Mau Mau, Tanzania, Julius Nyerere, Rhodesia Front, Patrice Lumumba, Moise Tshombe.
2. How did the Algerian crisis affect the French government and its colonial policies?
3. What conditions favored a successful transition from colony to independent nation in West Africa?
4. Why were civil wars fought in Nigeria and the Republic of Congo?

5 Latin America

After 1945 the nations of Latin America struggled for political stability and for social and economic progress. The postwar period was a time of revolutionary change in the area. It brought Latin America into the mainstream of world affairs.

The Organization of American States was set up on April 30, 1948, as a regional organization under the UN. Discuss other regional organizations and their impact on world affairs.

Inter-American Relations

Following World War II, the nations of the Americas committed themselves to greater cooperation. In September 1947, a regional defense pact was signed at Rio de Janeiro, Brazil. The following year, the Organization of American States (OAS) was founded to encourage closer political and economic ties among the nations of the Western Hemisphere.

The United States, the most powerful nation in the Western Hemisphere, officially sought good relations with its southern neighbors. However, this ideal was not always achieved. At the beginning of the cold war, the United States largely neglected Latin America. Lack of indus-

try and poor agricultural methods were widespread in the region. Corrupt governments controlled by the military and the wealthy classes did little to promote economic progress and improve living conditions. Radical Latin Americans accused the United States of supporting these governments, while conservative Latin Americans blamed the United States for not supplying enough economic aid.

In the 1950's, the United States, concerned with the spread of communism, directed its attention to Latin America once again. In 1954 the Central Intelligence Agency (CIA) helped to overthrow the leftist government of Jacobo Arbenz Guzmán in Guatemala. In the following

In 1954, after receiving criticism from Latin American leaders, the United States increased its economic aid, particularly in financing industrial and agricultural development. What other concern caused the United States to assist Latin America?

Perón had been a military attaché in Italy during the Mussolini era. Influenced by fascism, Perón believed in a dictatorship based on the working class.

Juan Perón saluted the crowds after taking the oath for a new presidential term in 1952. Within months, his wife Eva died of cancer. Without his strongest supporter and publicist, Perón's conflicts with his many opponents, particularly the Church, intensified. In a country whose population is predominantly Catholic, Perón pushed bills through the legislature that legalized divorce. The Perón-controlled assembly also enacted other legislation that formally separated church and state, and subjected all religious institutions to taxation. What group finally ousted Perón from office?

years, in order to prevent Communist takeovers, the United States often supported unpopular conservative or military governments in Latin America. Anti-American feeling grew throughout the region and became part of several growing revolutionary movements.

Latin American Governments

During the 1950's and 1960's, Latin American countries experienced a variety of political systems ranging from the authoritarian right to the Marxist left. When one system failed to solve a nation's problems, another system was introduced, often through revolution. Argentina, Brazil, and Cuba provide examples of Latin America's political upheaval.

Argentina In Argentina, Juan Perón ruled as a dictator from 1946 to 1955. Perón's government dealt harshly with its opponents, yet its social programs won it wide support among Argentine workers. Perón also aroused nationalistic fervor by nationalizing foreign-owned businesses. His wife Eva, a former film and radio star, increased Perón's popularity. She skillfully used public appearances and the mass media to promote her husband's programs.

In spite of Perón's popularity, the dictator's government was opposed by the Roman Catholic Church and the Argentine upper classes. Inflation and neglect of agriculture weakened the economy. In 1952, Eva Perón died. With her death, Perón's popularity declined. Finally, the army, which had grown fearful of Perón's authority, overthrew him in 1955. A series of civilian and military governments followed, and Argentina remained politically divided between pro-Perón and anti-Perón factions for the next two decades.

Brazil From 1945 to 1964, Brazil was ruled by democratic governments. However, economic weakness and quarreling between the political left and right undermined Brazilian democracy. In the early 1960's, President João Goulart introduced land reforms for the peasants and greater income benefits for workers. Conservative opposition to Goulart's reforms led to a military takeover in 1964. The new military government abolished all political parties and suspended civil liberties.

Cuba During the 1950's, the most important Latin American revolutionary movement since the 1910 Mexican Revolution developed in Cuba. Beginning in 1953, guerrilla forces led by Fidel Castro, a young Cuban lawyer, conducted a war against the government of dictator Fulgencio Batista. Batista, who had ruled Cuba since 1933,

Ask students what they think Khrushchev meant by his statement on the Monroe Doctrine.

had refused to carry out reforms. To keep order, he used an American-equipped army. In 1959 Castro overthrew Batista and established a revolutionary government.

Castro promised democratic reforms and a better standard of living for the Cuban people. His government enjoyed widespread support among Cuban workers and peasants. In time, the people benefited from improvements in welfare, education, and health care. However, Castro failed to establish democracy in Cuba. This lost him much support in the United States.

Within a year after seizing power, Castro revealed his dislike of the United States and its Latin American policies. He angered the American business community by seizing American property in Cuba. He offended American respect for civil liberties by persecuting his opponents. Castro won enemies among upper-class Cubans, who opposed his programs to nationalize factories and sugar plantations. Thousands of upper-class Cubans fled to the United States to escape the Castro government.

Revolutionary Cuba became a dictatorship and formed close ties with the Soviet Union. In February 1960, Cuba negotiated a trade agreement with the Soviet Union that enabled the Soviets to obtain Cuban sugar at low prices. The United States responded by banning the import of Cuban sugar to the United States. Khrushchev then promised Soviet protection to Cuba, claiming that the Monroe Doctrine had "outlived its time." By the end of 1961, Castro's government was openly Communist and had become popular in many Latin American countries.

Other Latin American Nations During the 1950's and 1960's, not all Latin American countries were ruled by military or Communist dictatorships. Mexico, for example, was governed by a stable, elected government. Military rule in Venezuela ended in 1959 and was replaced by a civilian democratic government. Nonetheless, these countries shared similar social and economic problems with the other countries of Latin America during the postwar years.

1. Identify: OAS, CIA, Jacobo Arbenz Guzman, Juan Perón, Eva Perón, Getulio Vargas, João Goulart, Fidel Castro.
2. What major problems faced many Latin American nations in the postwar years?
3. What did Castro do that lost him support in the United States?

Soon after his forces controlled Cuba's government, Castro formally announced that he would make Cuba a socialist state. Castro had kept his Communist sympathies quiet during the revolution for fear his guerrilla army would lose support. Those followers who protested his Marxist goals were soon forced into exile. By the second year of his rule, Castro and his economic adviser, "Ché" Guevara, visited Moscow. What assistance did the Soviet Union give Castro's Cuba?

CHAPTER 30 REVIEW

Summary

1. Japan restructured its political and economic institutions during the American occupation after World War II. Within two decades, Japan had developed a stable democracy and a strong economy.

2. Following World War II, the Chinese Communists defeated the Nationalists and established the People's Republic of China. China passed through two turbulent decades after the Communist takeover.

3. After the war, Korea became divided into two separate countries. The cold war and a war between the two Koreas transformed what was intended to be a temporary division into a permanent division.

4. The Indian subcontinent gained independence from the British in 1947. The British divided the subcontinent into two countries: India and Pakistan. The physical and cultural separation between East and West Pakistan caused problems for the new nation.

5. Much of Southeast Asia, including Vietnam, Cambodia, and Laos, was a battleground for independence during the postwar era. Elsewhere in the region the transition from colonial rule to nationhood progressed more peacefully.

6. Most of the countries of the Middle East became independent after World War II, although unresolved conflicts between Arabs and Jews in Palestine resulted in wars and the displacement of many Palestinian Arabs.

7. Between 1945 and 1965, the number of independent African nations increased from three to 30. Once they achieved independence, the African states turned their attention to unity and economic development.

8. Although most of Latin America had been independent for a long time, many nations struggled with political and economic instability in the middle years of the twentieth century.

Building Vocabulary

zaibatsu
gross national product
communes

pragmatic
mixed economy
kibbutzim

moshavim
colons

Reviewing the Main Ideas

1. What social, political, and economic changes were made during the American occupation of Japan?

2. Why was the Japanese economy growing rapidly by the mid-1960's?

3. How did the rise of Communist rule in China affect the Chinese government, society, and economy?

4. What caused the Sino-Soviet split?

5. Why did the "Great Leap Forward" fail?

6. What was the postwar situation in Korea?

7. Why was the Indian subcontinent divided at the time of its independence? What problems developed as a result?

8. What were some of the major events in each successful Southeast Asian independence movement?

9. What events led to the partition of Vietnam?

10. What were the results of the two Arab-Israeli wars?
11. What major problems did Turkey and Iran face after World War II?
12. How was the postwar situation in Africa different from that in Latin America? How were events in these areas of the world affected by the East-West struggle?

Discussing Important Ideas

1. How did the East-West conflict affect Japan?
2. What major problems did the Communists face in ruling China? How successful was the new government in solving the problems?
3. Why was India more united than Pakistan after the division of the subcontinent in 1947?
4. Why do you think Pan-Arabism was often anti-western?
5. Why did some African countries peacefully gain independence, while others experienced problems during the transition?
6. What was the basis for anti-American feeling in Latin America following World War II?
7. Do you think Cuba under Castro was a threat to the United States? Why, or why not?
8. How successful was the UN in maintaining peace in the Third World? Explain.

Using Maps

Refer to the map on page 700 to answer the following questions:
1. Who were Israel's neighbors at the time of statehood?
2. Which crisis occurred in the Sinai Peninsula? Which arose over the island of Cyprus?
3. Which crisis involved the U.S.S.R.? When and where did it occur?
4. Where did the United States send armed forces in 1958?
5. What three nations had developed the most major oil fields before 1964?

United Nations in Session

❝ The management of a balance of power is a permanent undertaking, not an exertion that has a forseeable end. ❞

Henry Kissinger, American Secretary of State (1923–   )

Global

Dimensions

A quick review of the summaries for Chapters 24, 27, and 30 is helpful to students before discussing the material in Chapter 31.

In the late 1960's, drastic changes began to take place in the international situation that had prevailed since World War II. As the years wore on, the changes affected greater numbers of people throughout the world.

One thing, however, did not change. War continued to be accepted by large and small nations alike. By many, it was—and still is—used as an instrument of foreign policy. World peace was maintained, mainly out of fear of the fatal consequences of a total war. But rebellion and revolution, and civil war and regional war, continued to break out all over the world. In the new interdependent world of the 1970's and 1980's, war of any kind in one area eventually meant tensions, misunderstandings, and complications in many other areas.

Above all—to this day—looms the rivalry of the superpowers. Many people believe that until the United States and the Soviet Union come to a deeper understanding and a mutual trust, there can be no true and lasting peace in the world.

1   The Middle East

Over the years, the nations of the Middle East have experienced a great many political, economic, and social changes. Along with these changes have come unrest and conflict.

Although many factors have contributed to the discord, three stand out. One is the Arab-Israeli conflict, which has been going on since Israel became a state in 1948. A second is oil, which has brought great wealth to some Middle Eastern countries. At the same time, however, it has led the superpowers to become involved in the affairs of the Middle East. A third factor is the conflict between the modern and the traditional. In their efforts to modernize, some Middle Eastern governments have altered or cast off traditional religious and political values and customs. Some Middle Easterners resent and oppose this.

The Arab-Israeli Conflict

On June 5, 1967, Israel entered a third war with its Arab neighbors. The month before, Syria and Israel had stepped up hostilities against each other. Pressured by other Arabs to support Syria, Egyptian leader Gamal Abdel Nasser ordered the United Nations troops, which had been policing the Egyptian-Israeli border since 1956, to evacuate the Sinai Peninsula. As soon as the troops left, Egyptian forces equipped with Soviet tanks, jets, and weapons moved in and closed the Gulf of Aqaba to Israel. This cut off Israel's vital oil supplies. Israel responded by launching an all-out attack on Arab airfields in Egypt, Jordan, and Syria.

By June 10, the war was over. During this Six-Day War, the Israelis destroyed most of the Egyptian and Syrian air forces and cleared the path to the Suez Canal. They also took the Golan Heights from Syria, the eastern half of Jerusalem from Jordan, and the West Bank of the Jordan River.

PLO   The area occupied by Israel in 1967 was home to more than a million Palestinians who were seeking self-determination. The Arab defeat in the war led them to move away from reliance on Arab states and to strike out on their own. The Palestine Liberation Organization elected Yasir Arafat as its leader. The PLO was determined to carry out its own armed struggle against Israel. It demanded that an independent Palestinian state be established on the West Bank. The UN asked Israel to withdraw from the occupied territories. Israel said it would not withdraw until a permanent peace settlement in which the Arab states recognized its legal existence as a country was negotiated.

717

Both Ramadan and Yom Kippur are traditionally observed with fasting and prayer.

Discuss the impact of the 1973 oil embargo on most of the world's industrialized nations. Bring to class news photographs showing long gasoline lines.

During the Six-Day War Israel managed to overrun territory along the Syrian and Jordanian borders. Since that time, there have been periodic attacks by both sides and no lessening of Arab-Israeli tensions. This Israeli patrol is checking in at a guard post on the Golan Heights. What other territory was occupied by Israel in the Six-Day War?

In 1969 and 1970, tension mounted. Israel annexed the eastern part of Jerusalem, Old Jerusalem, to their section, West Jerusalem. In response, the PLO mounted guerrilla attacks on the Israelis. The Israelis invaded adjacent Arab land and bombed Syrian and Egyptian territories. Finally, in the summer of 1970, a cease-fire went into effect.

The cease-fire, however, did not ease the tension. The PLO, which continued its fight against Israel, clashed with Jordanian forces in a bloody civil war. The war forced many Palestinian fighters to leave Jordan. They moved to Lebanon and from there carried out a series of attacks on Israel. Not even Israeli citizens outside of Israel were safe. This was shown in the summer of 1972 when the PLO killed 11 Israeli athletes taking part in the Olympics in Munich, Germany.

October War   In 1973 the Israelis and the Arabs went to war for the fourth time. The Arabs wanted to regain the territories they had lost during the Six-Day War. On October 6, which coincided with the Jewish holy day of Yom Kippur and the Muslim holy month of Ramadan, the Arabs attacked Israel. While Egyptian invasion forces crossed the Suez Canal, Syrian forces attacked the Golan Heights. After nearly three weeks of fighting, the United Nations arranged

for a cease-fire. United States Secretary of State Henry Kissinger used **shuttle diplomacy,** going back and forth between Egypt, Israel, and Syria, to mediate. Largely due to his efforts, Syria and Egypt agreed to stop the fighting.

During the war, the United States and the Netherlands had provided the Israelis with weapons and supplies. To get them to withdraw their support, the Arab oil-exporting countries imposed an oil embargo on them. At the same time, the Arabs cut back their production of oil. This created oil shortages in many countries of the world. The Arabs hoped the shortages would lead other nations to pressure Israel to withdraw from the occupied territories. The oil shortage caused the price of oil products, such as gasoline, to rise sharply. The oil embargo only lasted about four months. When it was over, everyone expected oil prices to go down. But because other oil-producing countries had taken advantage of the shortage and quadrupled the price of a barrel of oil, prices did not fall.

A Separate Peace   The end of the October War did not bring an end to the Arab-Israeli conflict. All efforts made to bring about peace seemed to end in failure. Then, in November 1977, Anwar el-Sadat, who had become president of Egypt after Nasser's death in 1970, accepted an invitation to visit Israel and address

Ask students, "Why do you think most Arab states did not welcome Sadat's move to negotiate with Israel?"

The map below is the subject of the "Using Maps" section of the Chapter 31 Review.

the Knesset. Sadat became the first Arab leader to negotiate with Israel. He called for acceptance of Israel, a just solution to the Palestinian issue, and an end to the state of war.

While most countries of the world welcomed Sadat's move, many Arab states did not. They responded by severing diplomatic relations with Egypt. They were even more displeased when, at the invitation of American President Jimmy Carter, Sadat met with Israeli Prime Minister Menachem Begin at Camp David, the American presidential retreat in Maryland. Out of this meeting, which took place in September 1978, came the Camp David Agreement and the framework for a formal peace treaty between Egypt and Israel.

In March 1979, in Washington, D.C., Sadat and Begin signed the peace treaty, the first ever signed between an Arab nation and Israel. For the first time, an Arab country recognized the legal existence of Israel.

The peace was hailed in most countries as a great step forward. But within the Arab and Islamic worlds, it only increased Sadat's isolation. The Arabs thought that by making a separate peace with Israel, Sadat was destroying Arab unity. Despite this, in 1980 Egypt and Israel established formal diplomatic relations.

A year later, Sadat was dead, the victim of an assassination by Muslim extremists. Vice President Hosni Mubarak became the new president of Egypt. Since he took office, he has improved Egypt's relations with other Arab and Islamic countries. Early in 1984, Mubarak met with King Hussein of Jordan and American President Ronald Reagan to discuss the current state of affairs in the Middle East.

Unresolved Issues   Two of the issues not resolved in the 1979 peace treaty were the Palestinian issue and the future of some of the territories occupied by Israel during the Six-Day War.

The Arabs want independence and statehood for the Palestinians of the West Bank and the Gaza Strip. The Israeli government claims that the West Bank is part of historic Israel and vital to Israel's defense. It has encouraged the establishment of Israeli settlements there. The Arabs view the settlements as part of an Israeli plot to force them out.

The Arabs also want control of East Jerusalem and the Golan Heights returned to Syria. Most of the inhabitants of East Jerusalem are Muslim and Christian Palestinians. The area contains Jewish, Christian, and Muslim holy places. Followers of all three religions feel very strongly about their rights to the city. However, the Israeli government has stated that the future of East Jerusalem is not subject to negotiation.

Civil War in Lebanon

Another area of the Middle East in which peace has been elusive is Lebanon. When Lebanon became independent in the 1940's, Christians were in the majority, so they received a majority of seats in the parliament and controlled the presidency. By the 1970's, only about 45 percent of the people were Christians,

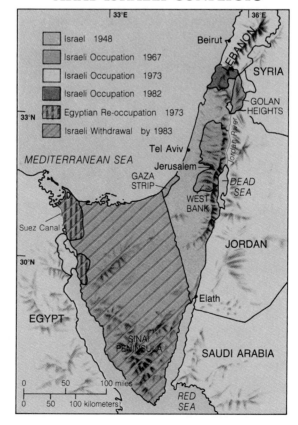

ARAB-ISRAELI CONFLICTS

- Israel 1948
- Israeli Occupation 1967
- Israeli Occupation 1973
- Israeli Occupation 1982
- Egyptian Re-occupation 1973
- Israeli Withdrawal by 1983

but they still maintained the majority in the government. Demands for reform of the system led two Christian parties, the Phalangists and the Liberals, to form armed militias. The Druze and the Sunni and Shiite Muslims also formed militias. Secular political parties soon followed suit.

The situation was further complicated by the presence in Lebanon of some 400,000 Palestinians, many of them members of the PLO. Using Lebanon as their base, the PLO launched violent attacks on Israeli towns and citizens. In return, the Israelis bombed and invaded Lebanese territories. Most Lebanese Muslims supported the Palestinians and the PLO. Most Christians did not. The Phalangists asked the Palestinians to leave Lebanon. When they would not, open clashes between the Phalangists and the PLO broke out. When Muslim and Druze forces joined with the PLO, clashes turned into civil war.

After several months of fighting, the Arab League and the Lebanese asked Syria to send in troops to restore order. In 1976 order was restored and a cease-fire accepted. In 1977, Syria closed ranks with the PLO and its allies, while the Phalangists and their allies received encouragement from the Israelis. Once again, civil war raged in Lebanon.

In June 1982, the Israelis invaded Lebanon. Their intent was to wipe out PLO bases for reasons of Israeli security. In August, the PLO agreed to withdraw its forces from Lebanon. To monitor the pullout, the United States, France, and Italy sent a multinational peacekeeping force to Lebanon.

Internal fighting in the PLO led to new fighting. In the winter of 1984, the multinational peacekeeping force withdrew from Lebanon, and the civil war broke out again.

Iran and Iraq

Discord also prevailed in Iran and Iraq. For many years, the two countries had been engaged in disputes over their borders and over control of islands in the Persian Gulf. In 1975 they finally signed an agreement settling their differences.

Iranian Revolution   The Iranians, meanwhile, were having internal problems. Their ruler, Shah Mohammed Reza Pahlavi, was spending great amounts of oil revenues on construction projects in the cities, lavish ceremonial events, and defense. Many villages still were without running water and other basic facilities. In his efforts to modernize, the shah promoted westernization programs and often disregarded religious and traditional Iranian and Islamic values.

The struggle between the various political groups in Lebanon increased in 1982. In August of that year, troops of a multinational peacekeeping force arrived in the country in an attempt to restore peace. The small size of the peacekeeping forces, however, made their efforts difficult. The strength of anti-government Muslim groups finally prompted the withdrawal of the multinational troops in March 1984. This photo shows Italian troops on patrol in Beirut. What other countries made up the multinational peacekeeping forces?

The case of the shah illustrates a split that existed in American attitudes regarding Iran. Many Americans opposed the shah's rule because of violations of human rights. Others supported the shah as a strong ally against the Soviet Union.

Mass demonstrations in support of Ayatollah Khomeini took place throughout Iran. Khomeini's supporters denounced all foreign influences, and many women returned to traditional Muslim clothing. Why were Iranian feelings of hostility toward the shah transferred to the United States?

Silent opposition to the shah grew until, in January 1978, it broke into strikes and antigovernment demonstrations. By 1979 the unrest forced the shah out of the country. The Iranians who opposed the shah had rallied around Ayatollah Ruhollah Khomeini, an Iranian Shiite Muslim leader living in exile in France. He advocated the overthrow of the shah, ridding Iran of all foreign influences, and returning the country to strict Islamic traditions.

After the shah was deposed, the Iranians invited Khomeini to return to Iran and rule in the shah's place. Khomeini declared Iran an Islamic republic and put into effect policies that would return the people to strict Islamic traditions. Meanwhile, the anti-shah feelings of the Iranians were transferred to the Americans, who had for years supported the shah. The United States allowed the shah, after he was forced out of his own country, to go there for medical treatment for a terminal illness.

The Iranians demanded that the shah be returned to Iran to stand trial for his "crimes against the Iranian people." When the United States refused, anti-American sentiment grew. On November 4, 1979, a group of young Iranians stormed the United States Embassy in Iran and held more than 50 Americans hostage. As the United States pressed for the hostages' release,

its relations with Iran further deteriorated. The hostages were not released until January 1981.

Iran-Iraq War Khomeini appealed to Iraqi Shiite Muslims to follow Iran's example. Tension mounted between the two countries until September 1980, when a full-scale war broke out. The Iranians and Iraqis bombed each other's installations, and Iraqi troops marched into Iranian territory. The war, which had already claimed the lives of more than 300,000 persons, was still being fought in the mid-1980's. It has strained the resources of both Iraq and Iran and hurt their internal development. It has also had global ramifications. Iran has threatened to block the Strait of Hormuz and prevent the flow of oil if other countries aid Iraq. This has aroused the fear of Japan and the western countries that depend on imported oil.

1. Identify: Six-Day War, Golan Heights, West Bank, October War, Henry Kissinger, Arab League, Anwar el-Sadat, Jimmy Carter, Menachem Begin, Camp David, Hosni Mubarak, East Jerusalem, Phalangists, Ayatollah Ruhollah Khomeini, Strait of Hormuz.

2. What were some of the consequences of the Six-Day War and the October War?

3. What events led to the outbreak of civil war in Lebanon?

4. Why did the Iranians rise against the shah? What was the result of their actions?

President Mobutu of Zaire is shown here in Kampala for a summit meeting of the OAU (Organization of African Unity) in July 1975. When and why did Mobutu change the name of the country to Zaire?

2 Africa

By the late 1960's, more than 50 African nations had won their independence. By 1980, independent African nations totaled one-third of the membership of the United Nations. Many of those nations discovered that independence did not necessarily mean freedom from economic problems or political strife.

From Colony to Military Rule

Many African nations have been subject to military rule at one time or another since becoming independent. Three that stand out are: the Republic of Congo, known today as Zaire; Uganda; and Nigeria.

The Congo   The Belgian Congo was one of the first African nations to become independent. Rival leaders began to fight one another shortly after independence was declared. Finally, United Nations troops were sent in to restore order.

In 1965, General Joseph D. Mobutu, later known as Mobutu Sese Seko, moved in and established a dictatorship. His plan was to "Africanize" the country. In 1970 Mobutu was elected president. The following year, as part of his Africanization policy, he changed the name of the country to Zaire.

Since then, Mobutu has kept a tight reign on the country, putting down any revolts that have arisen. In 1979 he announced that there "will be no second political party in Zaire as long as I am here." In recent years, Zaire has been having economic problems. Despite this, Mobutu's regime remains in control and insists it will continue to do so.

Uganda   In 1971 the government of Uganda was taken over by General Idi Amin, who established a military dictatorship. He kept tight control, and his treatment of Ugandans was often brutal.

In 1972 Amin ordered all Asians[1] to leave the country. He accused them of sabotaging the economy and claimed he was waging "economic" war. He was supported by many Ugandans who resented the prosperity enjoyed by the Asians. Amin confiscated the homes, businesses, and other assets of the departing Asians. Most of the 74,000 or so people of Asian descent in the country at the time had been in commerce and had dominated domestic trade. After they left, Uganda's economy began to suffer.

In 1979, after many months of fighting, troops made up of Tanzanian soldiers and Ugandan refugees captured the capital city of Kampala and toppled Amin's regime. In 1980 elections were held, and Milton Obote became president of Uganda. Obote's government has managed to make some progress, but guerrilla groups opposed to Obote continue to threaten Uganda.

Nigeria   After its civil war with Biafra, Nigeria was reorganized into many small states, but the country was still run by the military. In 1979 national elections were held and civilian rule restored. A new constitution was drawn up, and the government set about restoring stability. At the same time, it worked to regain the position of leadership Nigeria had held in Africa.

---

[1] Most of the Asians in Uganda were Indians. Some had arrived in the 1700's as traders and merchants; others had been brought in the 1800's by the British as laborers.

Many African problems have their origin in the colonial/pre-independence period. For example, many ethnic conflicts are the result of the artificial national boundaries set up by Europeans. Europeans also established the one-item (crop or mineral) economies that are subject to fluctuations of world markets.

By 1980 Nigeria was the wealthiest nation in black Africa. The bulk of its wealth came from oil revenues. When large surpluses of oil in the world market caused oil revenues to fall off, Nigeria began to experience economic problems. At the same time, civil and religious problems accelerated.

In January 1983, the government ordered more than 2 million illegal aliens, many of whom were teachers or skilled workers, to leave the country. This, however, did not solve the problems. On December 31, 1983, the military deposed president Alhaji Shehu Shagari and took over the government. This brought to an end Nigeria's position as the fourth largest democracy in the world.

The Struggle for Black Rule

In the 1950's, the West African poet Dennis Osadebay included these lines in a poem he wrote:

> Let me play with the white man's ways,
> Let me work with the black man's brains,
> Let my affairs themselves sort out.
> Then in sweet rebirth
> I'll rise a better man,
> Not ashamed to face the world.
> Those who doubt my talents
> In secret fear my strength;
> They know I am no less a man.
> Let them bury their prejudice,
> Let them show their noble sides,
> Let me have untrammeled growth.*

These lines express the feelings of the many Africans who have struggled to attain black rule in their countries. Two examples of this struggle can be seen in Rhodesia, known today as Zimbabwe, and in the Republic of South Africa.

Rhodesia   In 1972 civil war broke out in Rhodesia. The major cause of the war was the makeup of the government. Although the majority of the Rhodesian population was black, the government consisted entirely of whites.

For seven years, black nationalists fought to bring down the white minority government. In 1978, while the struggle was still continuing, a new government was formed. Whites remained in the government, and Bishop Abel Muzorewa became prime minister. He was Rhodesia's first black prime minister. The government, however, was still not recognized internationally; and the fighting continued.

In 1979 a cease-fire finally went into effect. The Muzorewa government was forced to hold free elections, which would be supervised by the British. In 1980, Robert Mugabe, a black nationalist leader, became prime minister by an absolute majority. Britain declared Rhodesia to be independent, and the country was renamed Zimbabwe.

South Africa   In the Republic of South Africa, the struggle for black rule is still going on. The government and the economy continue to be controlled by the white minority, and the policy of apartheid remains in effect. In recent years, however, some young blacks have turned to violence and urban guerrilla warfare.

In 1979 a few of the restrictions on blacks were lifted. For the first time, blacks were allowed to enter white restaurants. In certain sports, they were allowed to play on the same team with whites. But they still were not allowed to live in the same areas as whites. Nor were they allowed to take part in politics.

In 1980 a riot by blacks in Cape Town was put down by force as were other rebellions that followed. In 1983 a car bomb set off outside the South African Air Force headquarters in Pretoria killed 18 people and wounded 200 others. A representative of a black nationalist group announced that armed struggle had been forced on black South Africans "as a result of the apartheid [government]." The group went on to say that the armed struggle would increase and would "make itself felt among an increasing number of those who have chosen to serve in the enemy's forces of repression."

Several weeks before the bombing, the government had submitted a new constitutional plan to the parliament. It would have given Asians and colored, those of mixed blood, a limited voice in government for the first time. Blacks, however, would still be excluded. In

---

*"Young Africa's Plea," by Dennis Osadebay, as quoted in *An Anthology of West African Verse*, ed. by Olumbe Bassir, © 1957 by Ibadan University Press, Nigeria, p. 57.

African countries that had some colonial self-rule made the smoothest transition to independence.

Isabel Perón was Juan Perón's second wife. The popular Eva Perón, his first wife, died in 1952 at the age of 33.

November 1983, white voters overwhelmingly approved the new plan.

1. Identify: Zaire, Mobutu Sese Soko, Idi Amin, Milton Obote, Alhaji Shehu Shagari, Abel Muzorewa, Robert Mugabe, Zimbabwe.
2. What form of government was set up in the Congo and Uganda?
3. What led to the 1983 military takeover in Nigeria?
4. What was the result of the civil war in Rhodesia?

3   Latin America

During the last 20 years, the nations of Latin America have continued to work toward more stable government, economic growth, and an improved standard of living. The task has proved enormous. It has been complicated by such natural disasters as earthquakes, by rapid population and urban growth, by existing extremes of wealth and poverty, and by dissenting political views within each country.

Chile

In 1970, Salvador Allende, a Socialist, was elected president of Chile. He was the first Marxist to come to power in Latin America through peaceful means.

During his campaign, Allende had promised sweeping political and economic changes. As soon as he took office, he raised everyone's wages 35 percent and froze prices. He organized farm workers into cooperatives and speeded up land reforms. He also nationalized industries and utilities. When Allende nationalized the copper mines, he angered North Americans, who owned most of them.

After a time, the economy, which at first had boomed, began to fail. Upper-class Chileans, afraid of the changes taking place, invested less; and government funds began to decline. At the same time, farm and factory workers blamed the government for the high cost of living. They also felt the government had not brought about the promised changes quickly enough.

In 1972, tension between Allende and his opponents was growing. There were angry strikes and demonstrations. The unrest and tension grew until 1973, when the military, funded by the U.S. Central Intelligence Agency, overthrew the government. In the process of the fighting, Allende was killed.

Since 1973, Chile, which was the oldest democracy in South America, has been ruled by a military dictatorship. At its head is General Augusto Pinochet. Pinochet dissolved the Congress, issued a new constitution, did away with civil liberties, and canceled all of Allende's economic policies.

In May 1983, Chile saw its first antigovernment demonstrations since Pinochet took power. They were the start of a series of protests that continued through the summer and into the fall. Government efforts to stop the protests led to violence. The unrest in Chile still continues.

Argentina

Another country of South America experiencing difficulties is Argentina. From 1955 to the early 1970's, the country was ruled by the military. In 1972 ex-President Juan Perón returned from exile and was elected president. A few months after he took office, Perón died. The vice-president, his widow Isabel Perón, became the new president. She was the first woman to hold that office in Latin America.

Argentina, however, was suffering from high inflation and unemployment, which Perón could not bring under control. In 1976 the military ousted the government and took control of the country.

By 1981, the country was suffering from economic chaos. Production was falling, and unemployment was on the rise. The new government of General Leopold Galtieri tried to resolve these problems but failed. This led to oppression and the abuse of human rights.

In March 1982, in an attempt to win popular support and unite the country, Galtieri brought attention to the 17-year-old Anglo-Argentine dispute over the Malvinas, also known as the Falkland Islands. The islands were settled by the British in 1833, and the nearly 2,000 inhabitants were British farmers and sheepherders. Despite this, Argentina had never recognized British sovereignty over the islands.

HISTORY AND CITIES

Brasilia

One of the most remarkable twentieth-century cities is Brasilia, the capital of Brazil. In 1956 Brasilia did not even exist; it was only an architect's idea. Today, Brasilia is a thriving city of over 270,000 people. It contains some of the most striking modern architecture in the world.

Since the early 1800's, Brazilians had wanted to move their capital inland from the coastal city of Rio de Janeiro. In this way, they hoped to develop the economically backward interior. However, political problems delayed the planning of a new capital until the 1950's. Then, the site that became known as Brasilia was chosen. It lay in a wilderness area about 600 miles (960 kilometers) northwest of Rio de Janeiro. The government began to build the city in 1956.

By the early 1960's, the main government buildings had been completed, and the national government moved to Brasilia. Scientific, business, and cultural offices, as well as foreign embassies, were opened in the new city. Residential areas of modern homes and apartment buildings arose to house the growing number of settlers. Highways were built to link Brasilia with the rest of the country.

Brasilia is one of the world's leading examples of large-scale urban planning. It is designed in the shape of a drawn bow and arrow. The bow, running north to south, is made up of residential and business areas. The area spanning from east to west consists of national and city government buildings. At the eastern tip lies the Plaza of the Three Powers, around which are located the buildings of the legislative, executive, and judicial branches of the Brazilian government. An artificial lake lies east of Brasilia. It separates the city from outlying suburban communities, where many government officials live.

In addition to being the seat of government, Brasilia is the headquarters of many Brazilian businesses and associations. It is also a leading educational and cultural center. The University of Brasilia is one of the principal institutions of higher learning in the country. The National Theater, located in Brasilia, has auditoriums for dramatic performances and concerts. In all of its activities, Brasilia represents Brazil's determination to develop its resources and become a leading world power.

1. Why did Brazil move its capital from the coast to the interior?
2. What does the creation of Brasilia express about Brazil's goals in the twentieth century?

Oscar Niemeyer, renowned Brazilian architect, designed most of the government buildings in Brasilia, including the National Theater (far right). The theater's two auditoriums hold 1,700 seats in which international artists perform plays, symphonies, and operas. Along with traditional architectural elements, Niemeyer integrates modern, decorative shapes within the building's structure. Niemeyer was greatly influenced by Brazil's colonial baroque art, as well as French architect Le Corbusier, one of the earliest modern architects.

Using the map below, note the number of democracies
in Latin America.

GOVERNMENTS IN LATIN AMERICA   1984

On April 2, 1982, Argentine troops invaded the Falklands and defeated the British troops stationed there. Argentinians hailed the invasion as a great victory. Most Western Europeans, however, considered it an outrage. Even many Latin American countries, which supported Argentina's claim to the islands, spoke out against the invasion. The British decided they had to act. At the end of April, a British naval force landed in the Falklands. After a few weeks of fighting, the British defeated the Argentine troops and took control of the islands.

On June 17, Galtieri resigned as head of the Argentine government, and a **de facto,** or actual, military government ruled. In October 1983, elections finally were held. Raul Alfonsín became Argentina's first civilian president in almost eight years. Shortly after, he announced that nine generals and admirals, including Galtieri, would be tried in a military court for the "terror, pain, and death" they had caused since 1976 while ruling the country. The officers in question were **arraigned,** or brought to court to answer charges, in 1984.

Much of the disruption and violence in Central America has been caused by outside involvement, including that by Cuba and the United States.

The Sandinistas are named for former rebel leader Augustino César Sandino. Refer back to p. 631.

Central America

Of all the areas of Latin America, Central America has suffered the most disruption and armed violence over the past few years. Poverty is at the root of much of the problem. Examples of the strife in the area can be seen all too clearly in El Salvador and Nicaragua.

El Salvador   In 1977 General Carlos Umberto Romero became president of El Salvador. Leftist and rightist guerrillas alike reacted with violence. In 1979, however, Romero was still in office, and the violence was still going on. That same year, the Inter-American Commission on Human Rights accused Romero and his government of torturing and murdering political opponents. At the same time, other groups charged them with violating the human rights of their citizens.

In October 1979, the Romero government was overthrown. This, however, did not bring a stable government or put an end to the civil war. Elections held in 1982, in which Dr. Álvaro Magaña Borjo became president, did not solve the problem either. Terrorist groups continued to wage war. This has led almost 20 percent of the population to flee.

In May 1983, in an effort to bring the civil war to a halt, the Salvadoran Assembly unanimously passed an amnesty law. It offered **amnesty,** or a general pardon, to some 250 political prisoners and any leftist guerrillas surrendering within 60 days. At the time, five guerrilla organizations were fighting to bring down the government.

Three months later, government and guerrilla representatives met face-to-face for the first time. The government promised to hold national elections the following year and asked the guerrillas to take part, but they refused.

In May 1984, José Napoleon Duarte was elected president of El Salvador. He promised to hold negotiations with the guerrillas. However, the guerrillas still refused to accept the government. As a result, the civil war is still going on.

Nicaragua   In July 1979, the Sandinista National Liberation Front, a leftist guerrilla group, overthrew the government of Nicaraguan dictator Anastasio Somoza Debayle. This put an end to the 40-year rule of the Somoza family. It also slowed down the civil war that had been raging for seven weeks.

The Sandinistas, whose motto was "A free country or death," set up a five-member provisional junta. It was to govern the country until order could be restored, the economy could be revived, and elections could be held. Although some progress was made, by mid-1981 the country was placed under what the government called "a state of economic and social emergency." Harsh penalties were handed out for acts "contrary to economic and social stability." Such acts included strikes, unauthorized occupation of land, and obstruction of production.

By 1982 elections still had not been held, and the civil war was picking up speed. By 1984, more than 8,000 rebels called **contras** were waging war on the Sandinistas from their base in Honduras. This not only created disruptions at home but increased tension between Nicaragua and the United States government. To ease the situation, the Sandinista government announced that elections for president, vice-president, and the National Assembly would be held early in 1985. Shortly after, however, the government announced that the elections would have to be put off until early November. The unrest continues.

1. Identify: Salvador Allende, Augusto Pinochet, Isabel Perón, Leopold Galtieri, Falkland Islands, Raul Alfonsin, Carlos Umberto Romero, Álvaro Magaña Borjo, José Napoleon Duarte, Sandinista National Liberation Front, Anastasio Somoza Debayle.
2. Why was Salvador Allende overthrown by American-backed military forces?
3. Why did Salvadoran guerrillas refuse to take part in national elections?
4. What did the Sandinistas do after they took power in Nicaragua?

4   Asia

More than half the world's population today lives in Asia. Some experts believe that Asia is the fastest growing and most dynamic area on the globe. To illustrate their claim, they point to

Indira Gandhi is the daughter of former prime minister Jawaharlal Nehru.

Point out that because of the size and diversity of India's population, its government faces a difficult challenge in ruling the world's largest democracy.

Japan. By 1980, Japan was second only to the United States in world industrial production. In a period of about 35 years, Japan grew from a defeated nation ravaged by war to a world leader. Most experts agree that this "miracle" can be attributed to a highly skilled and dedicated work force, devotion to economic development, and a government policy of aid to industry and tariffs on imports.

Other countries of Asia, however, have not been able to develop in the same way or to the same degree as Japan. While the effort toward progress is being made, much of the area still suffers from economic and political instability.

South Asia

One of the areas of Asia that has experienced political instability and turmoil in recent years is South Asia. The area is dominated geographically by India. As a result, what happens in that country affects strongly what happens in all of South Asia.

India   In 1971 Indira Gandhi was reelected prime minister of India. That same year, she signed a treaty of friendship with the Soviet Union. It severely limited India's policy of neutrality in the East-West struggle.

In 1975 Indira Gandhi was convicted of irregularities in her 1971 election campaign. This,

combined with the country's economic problems and growing student unrest, led her opponents to call for her resignation. Her answer was to declare a constitutional state of emergency and to suspend civil liberties.

The state of emergency was not lifted until 1977. New parliamentary elections were held, and Indira Gandhi and the Indian National Congress party were voted out of office. Three years later, after promising to be more moderate in her policies, Gandhi once again was elected prime minister.

In recent years, Gandhi's efforts to rule India have been influenced by unrest in several states. In two states, Assam and Punjab, religion is at the root of the problem. When the government announced early in 1983 that it would hold elections in Assam, the Hindu population there protested. They were afraid that the millions of illegal Muslim immigrants in Assam would gain political rights. Weeks of rioting followed. To restore order, Gandhi sent in troops. The rioting, however, continued. Finally, a new chief minister of Assam was sworn in.

In Punjab, the violence continues. In 1983 the central government declared that since the local government could not control the violence between the Sikhs and the Hindus, it was taking direct control of the state. The Sikhs, who

Indira Gandhi is shown here speaking at a political rally. It has been alleged that such rallies were carefully staged by her followers. Despite accusations of corruption in her administration, she has retained a considerable political following. How did Gandhi try to resolve the problems in Assam and Punjab? What is the basic cause of conflict in those two states?

Sikhism was founded about the year 1500 A.D. Its followers accept some beliefs common in both Islam and Hinduism. There are approximately 13 million followers of Sikhism in India today.

The people of Bangladesh are mostly Bengalis, speaking the same language as most people in eastern India.

Helicopters played a significant role in the Vietnam war. Besides their effectiveness in pinpointing enemy positions, helicopters were used in transferring troops and supplies and transporting the wounded to hospitals. What other kinds of military tactics were used by the United States in Vietnam?

account for about half of the state's population, want to establish an autonomous state called Khalistan. In March 1984, Gandhi, in an effort to appease the Sikhs, offered to officially recognize Sikhism as a separate religion. To date, it has been designated as a sect of Hinduism. When the Sikhs turned down the offer, Gandhi put into effect a law that allows a person to be imprisoned for two years without standing trial.

Pakistan and Bangladesh   In 1970 Pakistan still was divided in two parts, West Pakistan and East Pakistan. That year, floods ravaged part of East Pakistan. When relief supplies were slow in coming, the East Pakistanis blamed the central government. The government was dominated by West Pakistanis, a fact that had been resented for a long time by the East Pakistanis.

At the end of 1970, elections were held, and the East Pakistanis won a majority of seats in the national assembly. The West Pakistani leaders refused to convene the assembly. When protest riots broke out in East Pakistan, the government sent in troops.

In 1971, civil war broke out. Pakistanis trying to escape the war fled to India. Indian troops invaded East Pakistan to help the East Pakistanis defeat the West Pakistani troops stationed there. It did not take them long to accomplish their

goal. As a result, in December 1971, East Pakistan officially became an independent nation—the People's Republic of Bangladesh. West Pakistan retained the old name of Pakistan.

In 1973, India, Pakistan, and Bangladesh signed a peace settlement. In 1977, General Zia-ul-Haq seized power in Pakistan. He promised free elections and a return to democracy. As yet, Pakistan has had neither. In Bangladesh, there were 18 attempted coups between 1975 and 1981. There was a short experiment with civilian government, but in March 1982, the military under Lieutenant-General Hussein Mohammed Ershad took over the country.

Southeast Asia

Events in Southeast Asia over the last several decades have made headlines in most parts of the world. Much of this has stemmed from events in Vietnam.

Vietnam   In 1964 United States President Lyndon B. Johnson claimed that American warships had been attacked in the Gulf of Tonkin by the North Vietnamese. This led the United States Congress to pass the Gulf of Tonkin Resolution, which gave the president broad war-making powers. In early 1965 Johnson used those powers to authorize bombing raids over

With the establishment of the Socialist Republic of Vietnam, Saigon was renamed Ho Chi Minh City.

The Tet Offensive was a turning point in the Vietnam War. Due to it, the U.S. realized that it could not defend South Vietnam from Vietcong attacks.

VIETNAM WAR

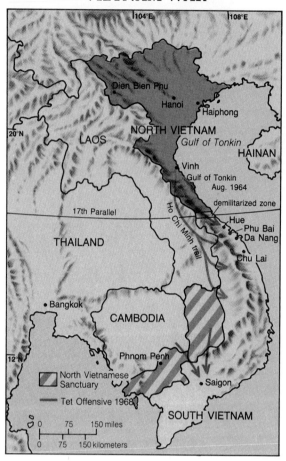

In March 1968, the United States called a limited halt to the bombing of North Vietnam. In April, the North Vietnamese agreed to hold preliminary peace talks. In October, the United States called a full halt to the bombing, and peace talks got underway in Paris.

While the peace talks dragged on, the war continued. In 1969 the newly elected American President Richard M. Nixon began his "Vietnamization" program. Under it, American troops were to be replaced gradually by South Vietnamese forces. The United States would train and supply the South Vietnamese forces to the point where they would be able to defend their own land. The United States would continue to provide military assistance and air support.

Between 1969 and 1973, when the last of the American troops withdrew from Vietnam, the war expanded. North and South Vietnamese troops continued to fight each other for control of South Vietnam. The North Vietnamese and the Vietcong penetrated more deeply into Laos and Cambodia. In pursuit of them, American and South Vietnamese troops entered Cambodia, and the South Vietnamese, supported by the United States, invaded Laos. When the North Vietnamese launched a broad offensive in the early spring of 1972, the United States replied by bombing Vietnam and mining Haiphong harbor.

Early in 1973, agreement was finally reached at the peace talks in Paris, and the Paris Accords were signed. The accords led to an end of American involvement in the Vietnam War. But they did not stop the Vietnamese from fighting. Without the Americans, however, the South Vietnamese army was not able to hold the south. On April 30, 1975, North Vietnamese troops entered Saigon, the South Vietnamese capital. That same day, the city fell to them, and the war came to an end. In 1976 North and South Vietnam were united and became the Socialist Republic of Vietnam.

In 1979, forces from the People's Republic of China invaded Vietnam. Many ethnic Chinese living in Vietnam fled north to China by land. Others fled by water in makeshift boats. They were joined by South Vietnamese who had found life in Vietnam too difficult. These

North Vietnam and over Communist-controlled areas in South Vietnam. This included the Ho Chi Minh Trail, the system of supply routes used by the North Vietnamese. Since the supply system cut through the neighboring countries of Laos and Cambodia, it eventually involved them in the war. The United States thought the bombing raids would lead the North Vietnamese government to make the Vietcong stop fighting in the south.

The Vietcong, however, did not stop, and the war took on broader dimensions. By 1965 close to 200,000 Americans were fighting alongside the South Vietnamese in Vietnam. By 1968 the United States was supporting more than 1 million combat soldiers in the area. Half were Americans. The rest were Vietnamese.

refugees became known as "boat people." Many of them did not survive their journey.

Cambodia and Laos   The Vietnamese war affected several neighboring countries. One was Cambodia. In 1975 North Vietnamese troops and the Vietcong based in Cambodia encouraged and aided the Khmer Rouge, the Cambodian Communists, in overthrowing the American-backed government of Cambodian ruler Lon Nol. In its place, they set up a Communist government under Pol Pot. Pol Pot imposed a reign of terror and forced many Cambodians to move from the cities to the countryside. At the same time, he became involved in border disputes with Vietnam. In 1978 the Vietnamese responded by invading Cambodia. They overthrew Pol Pot and set up a new government friendly to Vietnam. They also changed the name of the country to the People's Republic of Kampuchea.

Another country affected by the Vietnam War was Laos. During the war, the North Vietnamese moved their supplies through Laos. In 1975 Laos, like Cambodia, became a Communist country. When anti-Communist forces in northern Laos started hostilities, the government turned to Vietnam for help. By 1979 there were more than 30,000 Vietnamese troops in Laos.

Philippines   In 1965, Ferdinand E. Marcos became president of the Philippines. During Marcos's term, unrest grew among leftists and Muslims. To counter the turmoil, Marcos in 1972 declared martial law and established a dictatorship. Nine years later, he ended martial law, believing that the country had returned to stability. However, opposition to the Marcos government steadily grew. In 1983, a liberal opposition leader was assassinated. Marcos appointed a commission to investigate the murder, but his opponents charged that the government had played a role in the killing. In the 1984 parliamentary elections, Marcos allowed his opponents to participate, and they won much support. Marcos, however, refused to relax his grip on the nation.

The People's Republic of China

By 1969, China's Cultural Revolution was at an end, and China had begun to change its attitude toward the West. There were several reasons for this. For one, a rift had begun to develop between China and the Soviet Union, on whom China had depended for technological support for many years. China needed to improve relations with other industrial countries. For another, the more friendly relationship between the Soviet Union and the United States led Chinese leaders to fear that the two superpowers might work together against China.

In 1971 the Chinese invited the American table tennis team to China. That same year, secret

These women are making electrical components in one of the new industries that are part of China's Four Modernizations plan. Since women were given full equality, their role in all aspects of industry, science, agriculture, and technology has become increasingly important. What effect has Teng's Four Modernizations plan had on China's foreign policy?

In discussing this survey of Europe, some teachers might wish to explain in detail the major events leading up to these present-day situations.

talks began between American Secretary of State Henry Kissinger and Chinese leaders. At the same time, the People's Republic was admitted to the United Nations.

In 1972, at the invitation of the Chinese government, President Nixon visited Beijing. At the end of his visit, he and his Chinese hosts issued the Shanghai Communique. In it, they pledged to work toward the improvement of relations between their countries. They also agreed to establish diplomatic offices. In 1975 another American president, Gerald Ford, visited China. He reaffirmed his support of the Shanghai Communique.

The following year, Chinese leaders Mao Tse-tung and Chou En-lai died; and China entered a period of internal unrest. As Mao had not named a successor, a power struggle broke out among the remaining leaders. The moderates won and took control of the party and the government. Mao's wife and three other radicals, known as the "Gang of Four," tried to seize control from them. The radical revolt failed, and by the end of 1976 the moderates seemed to be firmly in power.

The moderates, led by Teng Hsiao-p'ing, hoped to completely modernize China by the year 2000. To do this, a plan known as the Four Modernizations was put into effect. It stressed modernizing four areas—agriculture, industry, the military, and science and technology. The plan brought China into closer contact with Japan and the industrial nations of the West.

In 1979 China established formal diplomatic relations with the United States. Teng Hsiao-p'ing, now the senior deputy prime minister, visited the United States on a goodwill tour. He was the first high-ranking official in the history of the People's Republic of China to make such a visit.

In the early 1980's, Chinese leaders continued to work to modernize their country and to improve China's relations with both developed and developing nations. Teng and other Chinese leaders carried out overseas visits. Their purpose was to strengthen China's economic and political ties with foreign countries. China also worked to close the rift between it and the Soviet Union.

1. Identify: Khalistan, Zia-ul-Haq, Hussein Mohammed Ershad, Gulf of Tonkin Resolution, Ho Chi Minh Trail, "Vietnamization," Paris Accords, "boat people," Khmer Rouge, Lon Nol, Pol Pot, Ferdinand E. Marcos, Shanghai Communique, Four Modernizations.
2. How did Indira Gandhi's government handle the problems in Assam and Punjab?
3. What events led East Pakistan to become the independent nation of Bangladesh?
4. What effect did the Vietnam War have on Laos and Cambodia?

5 Europe

Throughout the years, Europe has been a leading agricultural and industrial center of the world. The governments of some of its nations have ranked among the leading global powers. While these facts remain true today, in recent years the continent has been beset by problems.

Western Europe

Since the oil embargo of 1973, most of the countries of Western Europe have suffered from rapid inflation, slow economic growth, and rising unemployment. These economic problems have greatly affected their internal politics and personal growth. They have also strained European unity and relations among the industrialized nations of the West.

Britain   In the late 1960's, Britain was ruled by a Labor government headed by Prime Minister Harold Wilson. Wilson hoped to modernize the British economy. However, problems at home and abroad undermined his efforts. By 1970, Britain was in deep economic difficulty. A series of strikes in 1972 by miners and dockworkers only made the country's economic problems worse. In January 1973, in an effort to help its lagging economy, Britain joined the Common Market. But membership in the market did not solve its economic woes.

In 1979, a new prime minister, Conservative party leader Margaret Thatcher, took office. She was the first woman in British history to become prime minister. Thatcher worked to reduce government spending. In time, the rate of inflation began to slow. At the same time,

Refer students back to the discussion of the Irish Question on pp. 445 and 446.

however, unemployment rose greatly. Despite this, in 1983, Thatcher and her party again won the parliamentary elections, this time by a landslide.

Two major problems that faced the Thatcher government in 1984 were not related to internal or economic difficulties. One was British relations with Libya. Terrorist activities in Britain by Libyan and anti-Libyan groups resulted in a number of deaths, the expulsion of Libyan diplomats, and the breaking off of relations between the two countries. Libyan leader Colonel Muammar al-Qaddafi accused the British of harboring his opponents whom he called "Libyan terrorists." He warned that the severing of diplomatic relations by the British would be "bound to have repercussions on the ordinary Libyan and British citizen." Some western leaders do not think Qaddafi's threats should be taken too lightly. They view him as a terrorist, one who could ignite a major war.

The other problem confronting the government was the status of Northern Ireland, which has been a self-governing part of the United Kingdom since 1921. In the 1960's the Protestant majority there firmly controlled the government and the economy. Members of the Catholic minority began to protest. They criticized British rule in Northern Ireland and wanted to join the region to the largely Catholic Republic of Ireland. In 1969 civil rights demonstrations turned into violent confrontations between Catholics and Protestants. When the British sent in troops to restore order, matters got worse. In 1972 the British government suspended Northern Ireland's government and took control. Throughout the 1970's, terrorist groups from both sides continued to carry out bombings and other violent activities. In the early 1980's, the problem remained unresolved.

France   France has also had its problems since the late 1960's. In 1968 students discontented with educational policies rioted in the streets of Paris. Other students soon began their own protests. At the same time, thousands of workers all over France went on strike. They demanded higher wages and new work rules. Many of the demonstrators called on President Charles de Gaulle to resign. To put an end to the strikes and demonstrations that were paralyzing the country, the de Gaulle government promised to reform the universities and to raise workers' wages.

At the same time, de Gaulle dissolved the National Assembly. In June, elections were held, and the Gaullist party won. Less than a year later, after the French people voted down several of his proposals for reform, de Gaulle resigned.

The civil rights movement in Northern Ireland began as a protest of injustices by the Catholic community. The movement soon led to a series of terrorist activities fostered by Irish Republican Army extremists. The IRA's aim has been to publicize its cause by creating incidents of terrorism that attract international attention. What steps have been taken by the British government in the attempt to restore order to Northern Ireland?

Have students prepare a table listing the countries of Eastern and Western Europe and their leaders.

De Gaulle was succeeded by Georges Pompidou, who maintained de Gaulle's policies. When Pompidou died in 1974, Valéry Giscard d'Estaing, who had been Pompidou's finance minister, became the new president of France. Giscard encouraged women's rights. He also raised the minimum wage and increased worker benefits. But under Giscard, France, like many other countries of Europe, suffered from inflation, a slowdown in industry, and unemployment.

In the 1981 elections, Socialist leader François Mitterand defeated Giscard. The Mitterand government, the first leftist government in France in almost 50 years, announced its plans to nationalize more of the economy and to decentralize political power. By early 1984, Mitterand's government was in trouble. Steelworkers, truck drivers, and farmers were striking in protest of Mitterand's economic plans. Students were marching in protest of planned educational reforms. Even reforms intended for the press and the police have become the object of criticism by some.

West Germany In 1969, Willy Brandt, ex-mayor of Berlin and leader of the Social Democrats, became chancellor of West Germany. For the next five years, he furthered his policy of Ostpolitik, or Eastern Policy. It was intended to improve West Germany's relations with the Soviet Union and the other nations of Eastern Europe. Toward this end, Brandt in 1970 signed treaties of nonaggression and cooperation with the Soviet Union and Poland. This led to an agreement among the Soviet Union, the United States, France, and Britain to improve access to West Berlin. In 1972 Brandt signed a treaty with East Germany that laid the groundwork for the establishment of full diplomatic relations between the two countries. The following year came a treaty with Czechoslovakia. That same year, West Germany became a member of the United Nations. For his role in improving East-West relations, Brandt won the Nobel Prize for peace.

In 1974, after it was revealed that an East German spy had been on his personal staff, Brandt resigned. He was succeeded by Helmut Schmidt, his finance minister. Under Schmidt,

West Germany remained the strongest economic power in Western Europe.

In March 1983, Helmut Kohl, the head of the Christian Democrats, was elected chancellor. Despite cabinet scandals and antinuclear protests, Kohl was as popular more than a year after his election as he had been on election day. One of his major goals was the maintenance of West Germany's strong economic position.

Greece In 1967 a group of right-wing army officers known as "the Colonels" took over the government of Greece. They suspended the constitution and imposed rigid controls on the Greek people. International protests against their dictatorial ways were ignored. In 1967 King Constantine tried in vain to overthrow Greece's military rulers and then fled into exile. In 1973 "the Colonels" formally abolished the monarchy and made Greece a republic.

A year later, Turkish troops invaded Cyprus, which Greece continued to claim. The invasion separated the northern third of the island, inhabited by Turks, from the southern part of the island, inhabited by Greeks. As a result of the invasion, some western nations cut back on the aid they had been giving Turkey. They hoped this would force Turkey to withdraw its troops. The Turks, however, would not withdraw.

Greece's military government was surprised by the Turkish invasion. Unprepared to fight the Turks, it suffered a deep humiliation. In July 1974, it yielded power to a civilian government headed by the former prime minister Constantine Caramanlis. Democratic rule was restored; and in November Caramanlis's party won in the first free elections held since the 1960's. In 1981 Greece became a member of the Common Market. That same year, the Socialists won in parliamentary elections. Their leader, Andreas Papandreou, the son of George Papandreou, became prime minister. Although Greece remains a member of NATO, the Papandreou government pursues a nonaligned foreign policy and often criticizes NATO actions.

Portugal In 1968 Portugal's dictator Antonio de Oliveira Salazar died. He was replaced by Marcello Caetano, who began to ease government restrictions. Many Portuguese, however,

Thomas Masaryk was Czechoslovakia's first president from 1918 to 1935. He hoped that his new country would serve as a link between Western and Eastern Europe.

The Contemporary World · 735

Ask students, "How was the authority of the Soviet Union threatened in Czechoslovakia in 1968?"

were dissatisfied with the slow pace of Caetano's reforms. In 1974 left-wing military officials took control of the government, proclaimed a return to democracy, and granted freedom to most of Portugal's colonies.

Portugal's return to democracy was sometimes violent. Conflict developed between the political parties of the right and the left. In addition, the country faced severe economic problems. In 1982 a new constitution went into effect, ending the role of the military in the government.

Spain   In 1975, Spanish dictator Francisco Franco died. The monarchy was restored under Juan Carlos, the grandson of the last Spanish monarch. King Juan Carlos I began a process of establishing a new democratic government. Political parties were allowed; and in 1977 Spain held its first free elections since the 1930's. A year later, a democratic constitution was approved.

Most Spaniards favored the move toward democracy; however, Franco's followers remained active and wanted a return to authoritarian government. In February 1981, right-wing military officers tried to overthrow Spain's young democracy. King Juan Carlos opposed their plans, and the coup collapsed.

In 1982 Spain strengthened its ties with the democracies of Western Europe and joined NATO. In that same year, the Socialists won the parliamentary elections in Spain. Their leader, Felipe González, became prime minister. He led Spain's first leftist government since 1939.

Eastern Europe

The countries of Western Europe were not the only ones on the continent to suffer economic problems and undergo change. Some of the countries in Soviet-dominated Eastern Europe also experienced upheaval. Predominant among these were Czechoslovakia and Poland.

Czechoslovakia   In 1968, Alexander Dubček became the leader of the Communist party in Czechoslovakia. He began to "democratize" the country by introducing more liberal reforms than were allowed in any other Communist state. He eased press censorship and began to allow some political groups to meet freely. He also cut back restrictions on intellectuals and educators.

In 1975, the monarchy was restored in Spain. King Juan Carlos I and Queen Sophia are shown here reviewing a military parade in Madrid, the nation's capital. What other changes were made in Spain during the 1970's?

Dubček assured the Soviets that Czechoslovakia was still loyal to the Warsaw Pact and the principles of communism. Before long, however, many Czechoslovak intellectuals demanded more freedom. Soon there were hints that opposition parties might be allowed to operate and that Czechoslovakia might withdraw from the Warsaw Pact. This alarmed the Soviet Union. The Soviets viewed the liberal Czechoslovak policies as a threat to their security.

On August 20, 1968, about 500,000 troops from the Soviet Union and its Warsaw Pact allies invaded Czechoslovakia. They seized Prague and sent Dubček and other Czechoslovak leaders to Moscow. Most of Dubček's reforms were withdrawn and a new constitution put into effect. In April 1969, Dubček was replaced as party leader. In 1970 he was expelled from the

Have students recall the major events in relations between the U.S. and U.S.S.R. from 1918 to the present.

party entirely. Since then, the Soviets have maintained a tight rein on Czechoslovakia.

Poland   In the 1980's Poland made its bid for reform. Suffering from economic problems, the country was plagued by debt, high prices, and shortages of food and raw materials. Poles had to wait in lines for hours to get basic food staples. At times, after their long wait, they were told to come back another time as no food was available.

To protest these and other conditions, workers banded together to form a new union, independent of Communist party control. In October 1980, the government officially recognized the union, which was called Solidarity. Until this time, independent trade unions such as Solidarity had not been allowed to exist in Communist countries.

Under the leadership of a union leader named Lech Walesa, Solidarity led workers in demonstrations and strikes. In the fall of 1981, it called for free elections. The Polish government of Prime Minister Wojciech Jaruzelski responded by demanding that strikes and other "anti-state" activities be banned. That December, Solidarity called for a vote to determine whether or not Poland should continue to be governed by the Communist party. The government responded by declaring martial law. Thousands of people were arrested, and Solidarity was suspended.

These actions forced Solidarity to continue its activities underground.

Martial law was not lifted until July 1983. Meanwhile, the unrest continued despite a government show of force. In 1984, Solidarity continued to protest government restrictions by threatening strikes and boycotts.

1. Identify: Harold Wilson, Margaret Thatcher, Muammar al-Qaddafi, Northern Ireland, Georges Pompidou, Valéry Giscard d'Estaing, François Mitterand, Willy Brandt, Ostpolitik, Helmut Schmidt, Helmut Kohl, "the Colonels," Andreas Papandreou, Juan Carlos I, Felipe González, Alexander Dubček, Solidarity, Lech Walesa, Wojciech Jaruzelski.
2. What prompted terrorist activity in Britain during the 1970's and 1980's?
3. Why did the Soviets invade Czechoslovakia in 1968? What were some of the results of the invasion?
4. What major issues confronted Poland in the early 1980's?

6   The Superpowers

Between the late 1960's and the present, relations between the superpowers—the United States and the Soviet Union—have gone through many changes. In the late 1960's, relations became strained almost to the breaking point by

Lech Walesa is shown addressing members of Poland's independent labor union, Solidarity. Walesa's negotiations with the government led to recognition of Solidarity in 1980. But late in 1981, the government declared martial law and outlawed the union. Many of its members, including Walesa, were arrested. When martial law was officially ended, many controls over people's freedom were retained. For example, strikes and other kinds of protests were forbidden. What prompted the Polish government to declare martial law?

The Greek ship Constantia *is shown loading 500,000 bushels of grain for transportation to the Soviet Union. It was only a small part of the millions of bushels of wheat and corn that the Soviets purchased from foreign markets. What other products did the Soviet Union have to buy from markets abroad?*

American involvement in the Vietnam War and by the Soviet invasion of Czechoslovakia. Then, in the early 1970's, the situation reversed. **Détente,** a period of mutual understanding and relaxation of tensions, prevailed. Then, in the late 1970's, hope and optimism faded as the superpowers entered another period of cold war. In the 1980's relations between the United States and the Soviet Union were seriously strained as a result of their conflicting global interests.

The Soviet Union

In the late 1960's, the Communist party leadership under Leonid Brezhnev increased restrictions on the Soviet people. It worked to end the protests of small dissident groups at home and in the satellites. It became increasingly distrustful of the West.

The Soviet Union, in particular, feared a lessening of its hold on Eastern Europe. In ending reforms in Czechoslovakia in 1968, the Soviets announced a new policy for Eastern Europe. Known as the Brezhnev Doctrine, the policy stated that any threat to communism in one Warsaw Pact country would be militarily opposed by the others. The Brezhnev Doctrine was meant to prevent other satellites from taking the same liberties as Czechoslovakia.

By the late 1970's, the Soviet Union was stronger than ever as a military power. At the same time, some attempts had been made at reform. Much of the reform was in agriculture. A limited attempt had also been made to introduce market forces into the economy. Although economic growth was slower than before, it was steady.

In 1982 Brezhnev died. By then, the Soviet economy had taken a turn for the worse. Several poor harvests in a row had led to a shortage of grain, and a decrease in the production of meat and dairy products had resulted in a shortage of food. This, in turn, had forced the government to make huge food purchases abroad.

After Brezhnev's death, Yuri Andropov became the new leader of the Soviet Union.[2] With the exception of Brezhnev, he was the only Soviet leader to be both general secretary of the Soviet Communist Party and president of the Soviet Union. Shortly after assuming control, Andropov announced that the government would experiment with economic reforms.

A few months after Andropov took office, he stopped making public appearances. Rumors began to spread that he was seriously ill. The

---

[2] Before becoming the Soviet leader, Andropov had been head of the KGB, the Soviet security and intelligence agency.

Discuss the ERA. Trace the movement for women's rights going back to the 1800's.

government tried to deny the rumors at first. But on February 9, 1984, Andropov died of kidney failure. Four days later, Konstantin Chernenko was elected to replace him. Chernenko promised to continue Andropov's program of economic and political reforms. At the same time he pledged to strengthen the country's defenses.

The United States

In the late 1960's and early 1970's, the United States, like Western Europe, was plagued by unrest and economic problems. Student protests were daily occurrences. Equal treatment of minorities and women was a major issue. The assassination of black civil rights leader Martin Luther King, Jr., shocked and saddened many Americans. In some areas, it triggered riots. At the same time, it prompted the passage of several civil rights acts and a number of other laws intended to aid minorities.

An even more explosive issue during this period was the Vietnam War. A great many Americans became opposed to United States participation in the war. Opposition to President Lyndon Johnson's Vietnam policies was a major factor behind his decision not to run for a second term as president in 1968.

In 1968 Richard Nixon was elected president of the United States. He pledged to end the war in Vietnam and bring the American people together. His decision in 1970 to invade Cambodia, however, led to antiwar protests on college campuses all over the United States. In May, the National Guard fired on demonstrating students at Ohio's Kent State University and killed four. At Jackson State University in Mississippi, two more lives were lost.

In 1972 Nixon ran for a second term and was reelected. That same year, an Equal Rights Amendment (ERA) was passed by Congress. It proposed to amend the Constitution so that equality of rights under the law could not be denied or abridged on account of sex. It was **ratified,** or approved, by 35 states—three short of the number necessary. ERA advocates vowed to continue their fight.

Nixon's second term in office was marked by scandal. Vice-President Spiro Agnew was ac-

cused of taking bribes when he was governor of Maryland; he was forced to resign. Then the president himself came under fire. A security guard at the Watergate Hotel in Washington, D.C., discovered burglars in the Democratic party headquarters. The burglary was traced to President Nixon's reelection committee. A special investigating committee set up by the United States Senate discovered that the White House knew of the burglary and tried to cover it up. Although the president denied the cover-up charges at first, tapes of White House conversations proved that he had had knowledge of the cover up. In 1974, faced with impeachment, President Nixon resigned. He became the first American president to resign from office. He was succeeded by Vice-President Gerald Ford. Two years later, Ford was replaced by a new president, Jimmy Carter.

Throughout the 1970's, the American economy performed poorly. It faced problems such as low productivity, strong foreign competition, and **stagflation,** the combination of rising prices and high unemployment. In 1979 the economy hit a new low. In addition, more and more Americans began to protest the buildup of nuclear weapons and the construction of nuclear power stations.

In 1980 Ronald Reagan was elected president. He promised to balance the federal budget by cutting government spending and lowering taxes. Under Reagan, inflation began to slow and the economy began to improve. However, due to increased military spending, the budget deficit reached a new high. Unemployment rose.

Understanding and Rivalry

In May 1972, three months after his visit to China, United States President Richard Nixon journeyed to Moscow to meet with Soviet leader Leonid Brezhnev. It was the first time since World War II that an American president had visited the Soviet Union. At the time, the Soviets were concerned about the growing friendship between the United States and the People's Republic of China. At the end of the visit, Nixon and Brezhnev agreed to accept the principle of peaceful coexistence, to resolve disputes

Have students use old newspapers to research public opinion regarding American and Soviet foreign involvement throughout the 1970's.

through negotiation, and to work to prevent nuclear war. At the same time, the Strategic Arms Limitation Talks agreement, SALT I, was approved. It limited the number of nuclear warheads and missiles each country could maintain.

Détente   For the next several years, the United States and the Soviet Union continued to cooperate in many areas. In August 1975, the heads of government of the United States, Canada, and all the countries of Europe except Albania met in Helsinki, Finland, to sign the final act of the Conference on Security and Cooperation in Europe. There, they officially recognized Eastern Europe as a Soviet sphere of influence. They pledged to work for peaceful cooperation in Europe, to give the United Nations their support, and to respect human rights. In the view of many, the conference marked the high point of East-West relations during the decade. It was followed in 1979 by the signing of a SALT II agreement.

Détente did not put an end to the rivalry between the two countries. Nor did it stop the Soviet Union and the United States from stockpiling conventional weapons, building up their armed forces, or placing their military in other countries.

Global Intervention   Throughout the 1970's, despite détente, the United States and the Soviet Union competed against each other in various parts of the world. In 1973, during the Arab-Israeli War, for example, the United States supported the Israelis while the Soviets backed the Arabs.

In Africa, especially, the two superpowers carried out their rivalry. The newly independent nations there needed financial and technical aid. Both the United States and the Soviet Union rushed in to help. Cuban troops and advisers were sent to Mozambique, Namibia, and Angola to train and fight with pro-Soviet groups determined to install Marxist governments in their countries. One by one, the groups achieved their Marxist goals.

In the horn of Africa, made up of the countries of Djibouti, Kenya, Ethiopia, and Somalia, the Soviets were both successful and unsuccessful.

In 1974 the Ethiopian emperor Haile Selassie was overthrown, and a socialist government came to power. A pro-Soviet government was already in power in Somalia. The Soviet Union provided both countries with military aid and advisers. In 1977 Ethiopia and Somalia clashed over Ogaden, a region ruled by Ethiopia but whose people wanted independence. When the Soviet Union sided with Ethiopia, Somalia expelled Soviet advisers from the country. The Somalis accepted aid from the United States and gave it access to naval bases that had been used by the Soviets. Meanwhile, the Soviets strengthened their ties to Ethiopia.

With the aid of Soviet advisers and Cuban troops, Ethiopia in early 1978 staged a major offensive in the Ogaden. This led to the withdrawal of Somali troops from the region. By the early 1980's, the fighting had significantly declined.

As Cold War tensions eased in the early 1970's, friendlier relations developed between the United States and the Soviet Union. What was the high point of East-West relations during the 1970's?

THE ODD COUPLE

Discuss the current state of Soviet-American relations.

While all of these incidents caused tension between the superpowers, détente prevailed. In 1979, however, the situation changed. The year before, a Soviet-backed military coup had overthrown the government of Afghanistan. The Afghanis, led by Muslim fighters known as Mujahidin, organized armed resistance against the new regime. The Soviet Union, afraid that the uprising of Muslims in Afghanistan might spread and threaten its security, stepped in. In August 1979, Soviet troops invaded Afghanistan and set up a new government. In the spring of 1984, the fighting was still going on.

The Soviet action against Afghanistan drew sharp criticism from all over the world. The United States responded quickly. Its Senate refused to ratify the SALT II agreement. Sale of grain and high technology to the Soviets was halted. A call was put out to boycott the 1980 Summer Olympic Games in Moscow. Détente had come to an end.

The 1980's When Ronald Reagan became president of the United States, he stiffened policies toward the Soviet Union. He increased military spending. He also placed a new system of nuclear missiles in Western Europe. Although this was done with NATO support, the action drew protests from many Western Europeans and Americans. It also aroused fear and suspicion within the Soviet leadership.

Reagan accused the Soviets of aggression all over the globe. The United States began to provide support to any anti-Communist government, regardless of its stand on human rights. In 1982 Reagan announced plans for a massive aid program for Central American and Caribbean countries professing to be anti-Communist. In 1983 he sent American troops, supported by

Guerrillas like these have resisted the Soviet invasion of Afghanistan. In the West it was feared that the Soviet invasion was a stepping-stone to gain control over Middle East oil supplies. What was the American reaction to Soviet aggression?

Pictured below are German Chancellor Helmut Kohl (far left), Canadian Prime Minister Pierre Trudeau (third from left), French President François Mitterand (fourth), American President Ronald Reagan (center), Japanese Premier Yasuhiro Nakasone (third from right), British Prime Minister Margaret Thatcher, and Italian Premier Amintore Fanfani (far right).

In 1983, the leaders of the United States, Japan, West Germany, France, Great Britain, Italy and Canada met in Williamsburg, Virginia, to discuss world economic issues and to seek ways to achieve arms reduction through international control. What was the outcome of the Strategic Arms Reduction Talks in Geneva several months later?

troops from six Caribbean countries, to the island of Grenada, where they overthrew a new leftist regime.

As the 1980's progressed, relations between the superpowers grew more tense. In the fall of 1983, a Soviet fighter plane shot down an unarmed South Korean commercial airliner flying from Alaska to Seoul. The plane had been flying off course over sensitive Soviet military installations. The Soviets declared that the plane had been on a spy mission for the United States. Later, they admitted that their fighter pilot had thought the airliner was a military reconnaissance plane. The pilot had made a mistake when he shot it down.

A few months later, the Soviets walked out of the Strategic Arms Reduction Talks being held in Geneva. After two years, the talks were still at a standstill. In May 1984, the Soviets and all Soviet bloc countries except Romania announced that they would boycott the Summer Olympic Games in Los Angeles. The month before, Soviet leader Chernenko stated in an interview with Tass, the official Soviet news agency, "Alas, the situation in the world is not improving. It remains very dangerous."

1. Identify: Brezhnev Doctrine, Yuri Andropov, Konstantin Chernenko, Politburo, ERA, Salt I, Helsinki, Mujahidin, Grenada.
2. What reforms were made in the Soviet Union under Brezhnev and Andropov?
3. What effect did the burglary at the Watergate Hotel have on the American government?
4. What agreements strengthened détente in 1972?
5. Why did tensions increase between the superpowers after the late 1970's?

CHAPTER 31 REVIEW

Summary

1. Since the late 1960's, hostility between the Israelis and Arabs has led to two major wars. One exception to the prevailing tension was the 1979 peace treaty between Israel and Egypt.
2. Elsewhere in the Middle East, civil war divided Christians and Muslims in Lebanon. In Iran, a revolution in 1979 established an Islamic republic. Tension between Iran and Iraq led to a prolonged war.
3. Many newly independent African nations faced economic difficulties and came under military rule. The struggle for black independence continued in southern Africa.
4. Latin American nations were ruled by a variety of governments ranging from right-wing military dictatorships to democracies to left-wing revolutionary states. Central America, the trouble spot of the region, became a battleground between non-Communist governments and leftist guerrillas.
5. The United States was directly involved in the Vietnam War from 1964 to 1973. After American withdrawal from Indochina, the region came under the control of the Communist governments.
6. The People's Republic of China pursued a pragmatic policy of modernization and opened up contacts with the West. At the same time, relations with the Soviet Union remained strained.
7. Japan became the leading economic power of Asia. Another Asian democracy, India, was divided by political conflict between the ruling party and opposition parties as well as by hostility between the Hindu majority and religious minorities.
8. The democracies of Western Europe experienced economic difficulties and devoted themselves to security issues. The continuing East-West arms race caused growing concern among many Western Europeans.
9. Eastern European nations, such as Czechoslovakia and Poland, grew restless under Soviet control and pressed for reforms. The Soviet Union, however, used force or the threat of force to keep its satellites loyal.
10. During the early 1970's, the United States and the Soviet Union entered a period of détente. However, mutual suspicion led to an onset of the cold war by the end of the decade.

Building Vocabulary

shuttle diplomacy	arraigned	contras	ratified
de facto	amnesty	détente	stagflation

Reviewing the Main Ideas

1. What three factors have contributed the most to conflict in the Middle East?
2. Why was the Egyptian-Israeli peace treaty a milestone in Arab-Israeli relations?
3. What happened in Uganda and the Congo after they were granted independence?
4. How are the governments of Nigeria and Zimbabwe organized?

5. What effect did the 1983 South African constitution have on apartheid?

6. How did the governments of Chile and Argentina change between 1970 and the mid-1980's?

7. Why did the Argentine government decide to invade the Falkland Islands?

8. How has Prime Minister Gandhi attempted to quell disturbances in Assam and Punjab?

9. What factors led China to broaden its relations with other countries?

10. What major problems have confronted Western Europe since the early 1970's?

11. What events led to the collapse of détente?

Discussing Important Ideas

1. How does the Arab-Israeli conflict reflect global interdependence?

2. Do you approve or disapprove of the British response to the Argentine invasion of the Falkland Islands? Why?

3. Could the United States have withdrawn from the Vietnam War sooner than it did?

4. What economic problem in Western Europe has had the most serious consequences?

5. Evaluate the actions taken by the United States in response to the Soviet invasion of Afghanistan. Should more have been done?

6. Do you think the United States should continue to provide military support to countries that oppose communism, regardless of their records on human rights?

7. Why do you think the superpowers continue their rivalry?

Using Maps

Refer to the map on page 719 to answer the following questions:

1. What territories did Israel gain as a result of the Six-Day War in 1967? Which Arab nations were affected?

2. Which Arab nations lost territory to Israel in 1973? 1982?

3. When did Egypt recover the Sinai Peninsula?

4. Where do the Palestinian Arabs seek to establish statehood?

5. How would you describe the physical location of Tel Aviv? Jerusalem?

6. What is the distance between Beirut and Tel Aviv?

CHAPTER 32

Computer Graphics

❝Make it new.❞
Ezra Pound, American author (1885-1972)

Twentieth-Century Culture

Discuss the Ezra Pound quotation on p. 744. Encourage students to find their own quotations that best describe their understanding of the twentieth century.

Change itself has been the most constant aspect of the twentieth century. In addition to political and economic upheavals, there have been revolutionary scientific and technological developments. Scientists have learned many of the secrets of life, sent people to the moon, and developed the capacity to destroy humanity. Inventions such as automobiles, airplanes, telephones, televisions, and computers have altered lives. They have broken down local and regional barriers. They have made possible the spread of a common culture throughout the globe.

The intellectual and artistic achievements of the century have been as diverse and, at times, as revolutionary as the forces that created them. There has been widespread experimentation. Points of view have often been in sharp disagreement. The views of the **avant-garde**—those who create new ideas and techniques—have often been at odds with those of the general public. Some of the new ideas have gained wide acceptance. Others await the verdict of history.

1 Beginnings of the Modern Era

World War I was the great divide between the old and the new. The disillusionment caused by the long, terrible war led artists and intellectuals to a restless search for something new. The postwar period was a time for breaking with tradition and experimenting with new styles in politics, society, and culture.

After the strains of war, there was a general desire for pleasure and entertainment. Some people had prospered from the war and had plenty of money to spend. This was especially true in the United States, where business boomed and the era became known as the "Roaring 20's." The age was symbolized by young women known as flappers, who wore their hair and their skirts short, smoked and drank, and danced the Charleston.

New Technology

Prewar inventions began to have a major impact in Europe and North America during the 1920's. Assembly lines turned out cars, like the American Ford and the French Citröen. These cars were inexpensive enough so that workers could buy them. The automobile enabled people to travel more easily. It also changed the landscape, leading to the building of highways and the further growth of cities.

Another invention that came into wide use was the radio. Families gathered around their sets, listening to news and entertainment shows. Radio helped to produce a more **homogeneous,** or uniform, culture. It also stimulated advertising and contributed to a rise in spending for consumer goods.

The movie was a third invention that came into its heyday in the 1920's. During World War I, the European film industry had been disrupted, while the American film industry grew. After the war, Hollywood productions dominated the movie screens of the world. Silent films were produced at first. Then, in 1927, talking pictures were introduced. Whether silent or sound, movies attracted large audiences.

Automobiles, radios, and movies helped break down economic, local, and regional barriers. They introduced millions of people to postwar

745

ideas about psychology, music, fashion, and political and social issues.

The Unconscious Mind

Before the war only a few medical specialists knew about the Austrian doctor Sigmund Freud. After the war, Freud became one of the towering influences of the twentieth century with his theories on the working of the human mind. His ideas brought new methods in psychology, education, and sociology, and they provided new themes for artists and writers.

Freud established the theory that unconscious motives control much of human behavior. He also formed ideas about the origin and treatment of mental illness. Freud's technique in studying and treating the mind became known as **psychoanalysis.** This method involved listening to patients discuss whatever thoughts came into

Freudian terms, such as "Oedipus complex" and "sublimation," became part of everyday language when Freud's theories were popularized during the 1920's. What methods did Freud use to treat mental illness?

their minds. By analyzing memories, dreams, and random statements, a **psychiatrist,** or doctor who studies the mind, could help patients determine the unconscious causes of their behavior. In knowing the reasons for their actions, patients would be able to find relief from their mental problems.

Freud believed that a person's unconscious denial of his or her sexual feelings was responsible for mental illness. This was one of his most controversial opinions. Many interpreters of Freud used his theories to justify a loosening of sexual standards. In this way, Freud's ideas contributed to the changes in sexual behavior that occurred during the twentieth century.

Some of Freud's closest followers disagreed with his views on sex and formed their own theories. Carl Jung, a Swiss psychologist, believed in a "collective unconscious" that was the sum of all human experience and that showed itself in common emotional responses to certain symbols and images. Alfred Adler, an Austrian psychologist, thought that life was a struggle to overcome the powerlessness of childhood, to gain control and superiority. Both these lines of thought have won followers.

New Artistic Directions

The break between old and new was perhaps sharpest in the arts. In painting, music, literature, and dance, traditions that had been evolving since the Renaissance were abandoned. The avant-garde experimented widely with new styles, media, and subject matter. Often their pioneering efforts were greeted with cries of shock and protest.

Literature   Many of the period's most thoughtful writers were deeply disillusioned by World War I and its aftermath. In the United States, F. Scott Fitzgerald captured the sense of disillusionment and the pleasure seeking of the 1920's in *The Great Gatsby* and other novels. Another American writer T. S. Eliot expressed a dissatisfaction with the postwar world in his poems, "The Waste Land" and "The Hollow Men." In Britain, a group of intellectuals known as the Bloomsbury Group met in various homes in the Bloomsbury section of London. They

In discussing Picasso, refer students back to the special feature, "African Art: Its Impact on Europe," p. 627.

included the novelist Virginia Woolf, the economist John Maynard Keynes, and a number of other academic and literary figures. The Bloomsbury Group stressed the importance of reason in finding truth and criticized the status quo in art, literature, and philosophy.

In the 1920's, France dominated the literary scene. Aspiring writers from many countries lived there, including Americans such as Ernest Hemingway, Gertrude Stein, and John Dos Passos. Their experiences of war cut them off from traditional values and middle-class society. They sought the meaning of life in writing.

In Paris, the Irish writer James Joyce found a publisher for his novel *Ulysses,* an account of a day in the lives of three ordinary people in Dublin, Ireland. *Ulysses* was a landmark in the development of the modern novel. Joyce studied Freud's theories and applied them in his works. He developed a style known as "stream of consciousness" in which the inner thoughts, rather than the external actions, of his characters are presented. Joyce's psychological emphasis and his frank, earthy language raised a storm of protest and led to a number of court battles over censorship.

The 1920's also saw a blossoming in American black literature. Writers James Weldon Johnson, Langston Hughes, and Claude McKay, among others, explored the black experience and used it as a theme for novels, poems, and plays. Because the movement was centered in New York City's Harlem district, it was known as the Harlem Renaissance.

Picasso   In the visual arts, the greatest innovations were made by the Spanish painter Pablo Picasso. Picasso was endlessly creative and versatile throughout his 91 years of life. He never settled into one style, but was constantly experimenting with new styles, new techniques, and new media. He was intrigued by African tribal masks and sculptures, which reduced human figures to their simplest planes. Some of Picasso's works reflected his interest in classical mythology.

In 1907 Picasso painted *Les Demoiselles d' Avignon.* Shocking at the time, the painting is now recognized as the first example of **cubism,**

Joan Miró's painting Person Throwing a Stone at Bird *(1926) expresses a feeling that people often experience in dreams, of having a distorted or expanded body. How did surrealist painting reflect the influence of Freud?*

an abstract art form that uses intersecting cubes and cones. It created a revolution in the art world. Painters no longer tried to be realistic. Cubist painters transformed their subjects by flattening them, cutting them up, rearranging different portions, and altering shapes and colors to fit their own vision. Picasso said: "Art is a lie that makes us realize the truth."

Gradually cubist works became more and more abstract and geometric. Artists gave up trying to represent objects. Dutch artist Piet Mondrian created abstract paintings showing geometric arrangements of lines and blocks of primary colors.

Surrealism   Another new artistic development was **surrealism,** which used dreamlike images and unnatural combinations of objects to explore the unconscious mind. Surrealist painters were influenced by Freud. People did not know what to think of the bizarre, often haunting, quality of surrealist paintings. The Spanish painter Salvador Dali created such realistically impossible, but striking, images as limp watches set in bleak landscapes and fantastic rock formations. Other surrealist painters, such as Paul Klee of Switzerland and Joan Miró of Spain, painted fantasies and strange collections of objects and symbols.

The Fagus Works, a shoe factory, was the first large building to be constructed from the designs of Walter Gropius. Built in 1911, it had a steel frame and freestanding glass walls. What goals did students of the Bauhaus school seek to achieve in their designs?

Bauhaus   The most influential school of architecture and interior design in the twentieth century was the Bauhaus. Established in Germany in 1919, its founders worked to develop art forms appropriate to modern technology and materials. Beauty was linked to practicality. The followers of the Bauhaus method designed furniture, glassware, tableware, and graphics that could be mass produced. They also designed buildings that made use of concrete and steel.

Under the leadership of architect Walter Gropius, the clean severe Bauhaus style refashioned the exteriors and interiors of buildings throughout the world. Sleek glass and steel skyscrapers and modern kitchens with storage cabinets above and below counters were both products of the Bauhaus.

Dance   The twentieth century saw a transformation in the art of dance. The American dancer Isadora Duncan revolutionized dance with her personal style of performing barefoot in a loose tunic rather than in a classic ballet costume. Another American dancer, Martha Graham, expanded on Duncan's style and turned modern dance into a striking art form.

Another innovation in dance came from the Russian Sergei Diaghilev and his company, the Ballets Russes. Their work led to the birth of modern ballet. Diaghilev was an **impresario,** or

sponsor, who pulled together the talent in the Ballets Russes that created dazzling and shocking ballets. The Russian composer Igor Stravinsky wrote *The Rite of Spring* (1913) for Diaghilev and his dancers. Stravinsky's modern music was a turning point for ballet. The leaping dance steps performed to Stravinsky's music by ballet star Vaslav Nijinsky created a sensation. The further blending of modern dance and classical ballet was carried on by another Russian, George Balanchine. Balanchine, founder and director of the New York City Ballet, had begun his career as a **choreographer,** or dance arranger, with the Ballets Russes.

Classical Music   In the early twentieth century, Eastern Europeans made significant contributions in classical music. The work of Russian composer Sergei Prokofiev was considered revolutionary in the 1920's. His most famous composition is the children's symphony *Peter and the Wolf* (1936). He was called the "age of steel" composer. Prokofiev's music often seemed driving and **dissonant,** or lacking in harmony. It also had links to the traditions of nineteenth-century classical music.

Radical changes in music theory were developed by Arnold Schönberg, a self-taught Austrian composer. Instead of harmonies based on the traditional eight-note scale, he proposed

In studying the music of the 1920's, have students who are interested in the subject develop a "Name That Tune" game for the era's music in review.

Have students research the life of Einstein.

new musical arrangements based on 12 equally valued notes. His ground-breaking composition, *Pierrot Lunaire* (1912), used stark, dissonant, heavily symbolic music to express what he regarded as the decay of civilization. Audiences were outraged by performances of Schönberg's works.

Only after World War II did many composers become interested in following Schönberg's theories. One early follower, Austrian Alban Berg, wrote two powerful, heavily psychological operas *Wozzeck* (1922) and *Lulu* (1934), which have only recently gained critical acceptance.

Jazz   American jazz was the characteristic music of the 1920's. Jazz developed from a mixture of American folk and religious music, European classical harmonies, and African rhythms. The music of American blacks—spirituals and work songs from the days of slavery—was a major source.

In the 1920's jazz began to develop into a more sophisticated form and to reach a wider audience through phonograph records. Among the outstanding jazz artists were trumpet player and bandleader Louis Armstrong, blues singer Bessie Smith, and pianist-composer Jelly Roll Morton. It was not until the 1940's, however, that interest in jazz spread beyond the United States.

Science

The early twentieth century was also a time of revolutionary changes in the field of physics. Polish-born Marie Curie and her French husband Pierre did research on the element radium. British scientist Ernest Rutherford and Danish scientist Niels Bohr developed the first models of the structure of the atom. In 1938 Austrian physicist Lise Meitner explained the occurrence of atomic reactions. Her work focused on the splitting of uranium atoms with subatomic particles called neutrons.

These discoveries led to a great number of useful applications in chemistry, medicine, geology, archeology, astronomy, electronics, and physics. Science affected daily life more than ever before.

Einstein   In 1905 the German physicist Albert Einstein published his book, *Special Theory of*

Relativity. Einstein's **theory of relativity** shattered the view of the universe held since Newton's time. It says, in essence, that there are no absolutes in measuring time and space. Time and space depend on the relative motion of bodies in space. For example, the speed of two passing trains appears differently to bystanders on the station platform than it does to passengers on the trains.

Einstein also developed his now famous formula $E = MC^2$. The formula states that the speed of light is constant, or unchanging. All matter has energy, and if matter could be broken down and changed into energy, the amount of energy would be enormous. Einstein's formula was supported in 1945 when scientists tested the first atomic bomb in New Mexico.

Relativism   Einstein's theory of relativity had an impact beyond the area of physics. It was confusing and unsettling, but fascinating to the general public. As the theory was translated into popular terms, it seemed to reinforce the belief

Although Einstein was a poor student as a child, he was fascinated by science. He was 26 years old and employed as a patent examiner when he published his theory of relativity. How did the theory affect the general public?

Many of the popular films of the 1930's are often shown on television. Notify students when some of them are aired.

that there were no absolutes in any field of knowledge or in moral values. For many people, good and evil became relative terms. That is, judgments about morality depended on the circumstances of time and place. For example, abuse of political prisoners might be judged evil in a democracy, but judged necessary and acceptable in a country trying to restore political stability. This philosophical viewpoint, known as **relativism,** grew out of Einstein's strictly scientific idea of relativity.

1. Identify: Bloomsbury Group, Harlem Renaissance, Salvador Dali, Bauhaus, Isadora Duncan, Sergei Diaghilev, Igor Stravinsky, Louis Armstrong, Lise Meitner.
2. What did Freud contribute to twentieth-century understanding?
3. In what ways were the creations of Joyce, Picasso, and Schönberg different from nineteenth-century works?
4. How did Einstein's theories affect popular thought?

2   Time of Upheaval

The 1930's and 1940's were a brutal shock after the prosperity and gaiety of the 1920's. The economic depression, the Spanish Civil War, the rise of Hitler, and World War II raised grave doubts about the future. Artists and intellectuals turned from personal interests and became committed to social and political causes. In the U.S.S.R. and Nazi Germany, their work was carefully controlled by the government. Yet, the period was not a time of total despair and gloom. Big dance bands and movies provided some relief during the troubled times.

Popular Entertainment

The 1930's were the golden age of American film. The big Hollywood studios made comedies, dramas, musicals, and historical epics. It was the era that produced such classics as *Gone With the Wind, Snow White and the Seven Dwarfs,* and *Top Hat.* Public attention was focused on movie stars such as Clark Gable, James Cagney, Fred Astaire, Greta Garbo, Bette Davis, and Katharine Hepburn. Movie houses showed double features and changed them weekly.

The content of most European films was not markedly different. Movies in general were escapist, designed to make viewers briefly forget the terrible strains of the depression and the growing political turmoil. In the 1940's filmmakers promoted the war effort in all countries involved in World War II. Films were used to

Clark Gable and Vivien Leigh starred in the 1939 Hollywood production of Margaret Mitchell's best-selling novel Gone With the Wind, *an epic on the American Civil War from a southern point of view. What functions did movies serve in the 1930's and 1940's?*

Have students compare and contrast the economics of the 1930's with the economics of other eras. For example, refer students back to the discussion of Adam Smith beginning on p. 415.

strengthen the resistance of the people against the enemy.

The New Economics

Economists and government leaders were baffled by the depression. The shock of the crash and the inability of governments to solve the economic slump raised grave doubts about the capitalist system. In desperation, many young Americans and Europeans turned to Marxism as a solution.

In the 1930's it became clear that business would not pick up again by itself. With so much of the work force unemployed, there was little demand for consumer goods. Production reached a low point, and there seemed no way to improve the situation. Workers could be hired only if consumption drastically improved. That would occur only when more people were employed.

A means to rescue the capitalist system was proposed by British economist John Maynard Keynes. In his book *The General Theory of Employment, Interest, and Money* (1936), Keynes stated the revolutionary idea that governments should "prime the pump," or get the economy moving again through massive spending.

This idea was opposed to both traditional capitalist theory, which held that the government should stay out of business, and socialist theory, which advocated government ownership of business. However, Keynes's theories gradually gained acceptance. Government support of the economy through spending became standard practice in capitalist countries.

Government and the Arts

During the 1930's and 1940's, some governments became actively involved in the arts. This participation varied significantly from country to country.

Soviet Union   In the 1920's artists in the Soviet Union had enjoyed much freedom. Painters, musicians, writers, and filmmakers had shared in a ferment of ideas. In the 1930's, under Stalin, all artists were directed to help in the effort to build the new Communist society. Restrictive limits were placed on their creative activity as individuals.

In 1934, Maxim Gorky, one of the Soviet Union's leading writers, promoted **socialist realism,** a new method of art that received the support of the government. In following socialist realism, writers were to present reality from the standpoint of Communist ideology. They were required to focus on Soviet heroes and to be uplifting and positive in their conclusions. All other forms of writing—religious inquiry, pure poetry, and pessimism—were discouraged. Literary criticism was limited to praising works of socialist realism and attacking works that deviated from the rules. The government-controlled Soviet Writers' Union acted as a censor of all works submitted for publication.

The rules of socialist realism were extended to filmmaking, musical composition, painting, and the theater. Composers were forbidden to use Schönberg's musical theories in their compositions. Abstract painting was branded as a corrupt art form. Artists who violated the rules lost their jobs and privileges. Their works went unpublished, unexhibited, or unperformed. Artists faced exile and death in Soviet concentration camps. In addition to restrictions on individual creativity, contacts with the outside world were cut off. Foreign publications were barred. Foreign radio broadcasts were jammed, or interrupted by the government.

All these changes had a chilling effect on Soviet artists. Most Soviet works became predictable and uninspiring. However, there were some exceptions. Mikhail Sholokhov's *And Quiet Flows the Don* was a masterful novel about the Cossacks during the Russian Revolution. Sergei Prokofiev managed to compose some excellent works. Filmmaker Sergei Eisenstein made powerful films, like *Alexander Nevsky* and *Ivan the Terrible,* that were based on Russian history. A few people wrote secretly and circulated their works underground.

Nazi Germany   Hitler tightly controlled intellectual and artistic activity in Nazi Germany. The experimentation that had flourished during the 1920's was ended. The Bauhaus school of architects was forced to close. Many of the century's most talented individuals fled from Germany. They included people in all fields of

Discuss the contributions to American society made by those people who fled Germany in the 1930's.

Lithuanian artist Ben Shahn's painting Red Stairway *(1944) shows a disabled man, perhaps representing all of humanity, climbing a surrealistic stairway that goes up only to descend again into a scene of destruction. The figure in the lower right represents the perpetual struggle to rebuild civilization. Why did social realists paint scenes depicting human suffering?*

learning. Among them were Sigmund Freud, Albert Einstein, Walter Gropius, and Arnold Shönberg. Many of these people eventually settled in Britain or the United States.

Hitler imposed his own ideas on the arts. He made plans to rebuild Berlin according to the styles of monumental classical architecture. In this way, he hoped to glorify nazism. Nazi films, however, were not always devoted to propaganda; they could also be entertaining. Notable exceptions were two brilliant, but controversial, documentaries directed by filmmaker Leni Riefenstahl. Her film *The Olympiad* is about the 1936 Olympics, and *Triumph and the Will*, is a record of Hitler's mass party rallies at Nuremberg. Nazi painters glorified Hitler in their works.

United States   During the administration of Franklin D. Roosevelt, the United States government created a variety of projects for artists. Under the Farm Security Administration, photographers recorded the plight of farmers during the depression. Through the Works Progress Administration (WPA), artists painted murals in post offices and other public buildings. Composers and playwrights wrote music and dramas, while touring theatrical groups performed in small towns across the country. Writers recorded oral histories and compiled state histories.

With or without government backing, many American artists became actively involved in social causes during the 1930's. John Steinbeck wrote the novel *The Grapes of Wrath*, the story of poor, oppressed Oklahoma farmers who settled in California. John Dos Passos's trilogy *U.S.A.* is a broader criticism of conditions in American society during the period. Richard Wright's *Uncle Tom's Children* studied racial problems.

Artists such as Ben Shahn, Moses Sayer, and Peter Blume became known as **social realists.** They were publicists and reformers who painted to draw attention to injustice, corruption, and human suffering caused by the depression. They used a variety of techniques to make their point, drawing on expressionist, cubist, and surrealist traditions as well as realism. Many of the social realists continued to attack social ills in the decades after the 1930's.

The Reaction to Tyranny

The Spanish Civil War was a turning point for intellectuals and artists. French author Albert Camus wrote:

It was in Spain that men learned that one can be right and yet be beaten, that force can vanquish spirit, that there are times when courage is not its own recompense. It is this, doubtless, which explains why so many men,

George Orwell was the pseudonym, or pen name, for Eric Blair. Ask, "Why do you think some writers during this period used pen names?"

Compare the intellectual reaction after World War II with that after World War I.

*the world over, regard the Spanish drama as a personal tragedy.**

Pablo Picasso painted his powerful cubist antiwar painting *Guernica* after the Nationalist bombing of the pro-Loyalist Basque village of Guernica. Novelists fighting with the Loyalists wrote novels sympathetic to the republican cause. They included the Britons George Orwell and Arthur Koestler and the American Ernest Hemingway.

During World War II, artists and writers were concerned about the war effort. Intellectual or artistic criticism of their particular nation's allies was avoided. As a result, western writers and artists did not deal with Soviet injustices until the late 1940's. At that time, the cold war was at its height and had an impact on literary themes. Arthur Koestler, a Hungarian-born writer who became a British citizen, wrote *Darkness at Noon*, showing the violation of individual liberties by Stalin's government during the Soviet purges. George Orwell presented a satire of Stalin's system in *Animal Farm*. In the novel *1984*, Orwell made clear how the use of language can control peoples' thoughts.

1. Identify: John Maynard Keynes, Maxim Gorky, Mikhail Sholokhov, Sergei Eisenstein, Leni Riefenstahl, *The Grapes of Wrath*, *Guernica*, George Orwell.
2. What kinds of movies were popular during the 1930's? Why?
3. In what ways did the United States, the Soviet Union, and Nazi Germany differ in their involvement in the arts?

3 The Postwar Period

The years following World War II saw rapid change. Some countries recovered quickly and reached new heights of prosperity. Elsewhere conditions worsened for many, as growing populations strained limited resources.

The late 1940's and 1950's were similar to the 1920's. Both postwar eras were times of rebuilding and recovery. Most people sought a rapid return to prosperity and the "good life." This

*Great Events of the Twentieth Century, ed. by Reader's Digest, © 1977 by The Reader's Digest Association, p. 264.

came most quickly in the United States, where war had not been fought on its soil. Americans went on a spending spree, buying consumer goods unavailable during the war.

Recovery elsewhere was slower and more painful. Rationing continued in Britain until the mid-1950's. Portions of cities in many countries remained unreconstructed for years. It took time for refugees to find and make new homes. Yet, by the late 1950's, it was clear that a remarkable recovery also was taking place in Western Europe and Japan.

The Search for Meaning

Despite outward prosperity, there were signs of stress and uncertainty in the postwar West. As in the 1920's, some people rejected the emphasis on material goods. They turned away from science and reason, which had created the weapons of war, and looked elsewhere for the meaning of modern existence.

Beat Generation　In the United States, one reaction came from a small group of nonconformists. They felt alienated by American prosperity and material values. They became known as beats, or **beatniks.** The novelist Jack Kerouac and the poet Allen Ginsberg were the spiritual leaders of the beat generation.

Beatniks wanted to be open to experience and sensation. They tried not to direct their lives toward set goals. Their sandals, jeans, and black turtlenecks became symbols of their refusal to conform to middle-class society. Beat writing opposed traditional rules of writing and was intended not to be easily understood. By experimenting with drugs and rejecting authority, beatniks increased official pressure against them.

Though the beat communities broke up by the end of the 1950's, they had some lasting influence. Beat vocabulary, such as "cool" and "hip," became part of everyday speech. Many writers were influenced by them. In the late 1960's, the beat generation was reborn in the hippie movement, in reaction to the Vietnam War.

Existentialism　A similar questioning about the meaning of life came from France's leading philosopher and writer, Jean Paul Sartre. In his

Poetry readings at bars and coffee houses were part of the beat scene in the 1950's. Beat poets thought that poetry had become too refined, and they tried to restore its vigor by writing in a free, unstructured style. What values were rejected by the beats?

plays and novels, Sartre developed a philosophy which was called **existentialism.** In reaching these ideas, he had been strongly influenced by experiences in the French resistance in World War II.

According to Sartre, each human being is alone. The essence of each person is the freedom to act, to choose, to say "no" or "yes." Sartre denied the role of unconscious forces. A person is what he or she chooses to be. Life is essentially painful, because human beings are forced to create their own values and ethics rather than being able to find guidelines in traditional religion or rational philosophy. He wrote:

> *The existentialist frankly states that man is in anguish. His meaning is as follows—when a man commits himself to anything, fully realizing that he is not only choosing what we will be, but is thereby at the same time a legislator deciding for the whole of mankind—in such a moment a man cannot escape from the sense of complete and profound anxiety. There are many, indeed, who show no anxiety. But we affirm that they are merely disguising their anguish or are in flight from it.**

---

*John-Paul Sartre as quoted in *Existentialism from Dostoevsky to Sartre*, ed. by Walter Kaufmann, © 1956 by Meridian Books, pp. 292, 310, 311.

Sartre's philosophy influenced many thinkers in Western Europe and the United States. The vision of humans being alone, isolated, and alienated was picked up by artists and playwrights.

Theater of the Absurd   Two French writers, Irish-born Samuel Beckett and Romanian-born Eugene Ionesco, and American Edward Albee were some of the playwrights influenced by existentialism. Their plays have been labeled the Theater of the Absurd for their view of life as meaningless and irrational.

Beckett's play *Waiting for Godot* (1953) is an example of the Theater of the Absurd. There is little plot, little action, just two tramps talking and waiting for somebody or something. By the end, it is still not clear who Godot is or what Godot stands for. However, the vision of modern life as rootless, painful, and empty of friends, faith, and traditions is an unmistakable one.

The Soviet Orbit

The cultural life of Eastern Europe and the Soviet Union developed separately from that of the West. During World War II, Soviet artists had been allowed more freedom, but with peace came the return of censorship.

After the death of Stalin in 1953, writers began to push for greater freedom. The novelist Ilya

Discuss the reasons why the state of international relations influences Soviet policies toward artistic freedom.

Ehrenburg argued that writers had a duty to explore inner feelings as well as to describe social and economic accomplishments. Under Khrushchev, restrictions were eased. More truthful, sensitive works were allowed to be published. Poems by the once-disfavored poet Anna Akhmatova appeared, as well as new poetry by the younger generation of writers, such as Andrei Voznesensky and Yevgeny Yevtushenko. Many formerly forbidden western works were allowed into the Soviet Union.

Still, restrictions remained. Boris Pasternak won a Nobel Prize in 1958 for his novel *Doctor Zhivago*, but he was not allowed to journey to Stockholm to receive the prize. International events, such as the Hungarian invasion in 1956, brought tightened literary restrictions.

By 1966 the "thaw" had ended. Dissident writers secretly sent their works abroad to be published. The government reacted with harsh measures. Other writers courageously resisted the government. International publicity was brought to the cases of Andrei Sinyavsky and Yuli Daniel, and later to that of scientist-writer Andrei Sakharov. In 1974 the Soviet Union forced its greatest living novelist, Alexander Solzhenitsyn, into exile after he wrote works critical of the Soviet prison camp system.

Some Soviet artists fled their homeland so that they could develop their talents more fully in the West. In 1961 ballet dancer Rudolf Nureyev **defected,** or escaped, to Britain. A few years later, Mikhail Baryshnikov and Natalia Makarova also defected to the West. All three have contributed to the recent rapid growth of interest in ballet in the West.

The Information Explosion

In the postwar period, changes in the arts have been outpaced by changes in science and technology. There has been an explosion of information. So much information is now available that it has become nearly impossible to stay up-to-date on any subject. For example, there have been more books and articles published about Shakespeare than one person could read in a lifetime.

Causes   The increased pace of learning has been due to several factors. The first involves population. Twenty-five percent of all human beings ever living are alive now. Ninety percent of all scientists are living now. Second, research

Mikhail Baryshnikov, who defected from the Soviet Union in 1974, is known for a style of dancing called bravura *(brilliant and daring). In 1980 he became artistic director of the American Ballet Theater. How did other Soviet artists react to government repression?*

and development is now carried on by teams financed by corporations, universities and governments, rather than by isolated individuals supporting themselves.

Third, computers increase the speed and complexity of analyses that can be performed. Fourth, knowledge is spread quickly through international publications and conferences. Data from computers can be shared worldwide.

Genetics   One area that has been affected by the information explosion is the field of genetics. In the 1860's Gregor Mendel had identified the gene as the basic unit of inheritance. In 1953 James Watson and Francis Crick, building on the work of others, made the next important achievement. They identified the double helix,

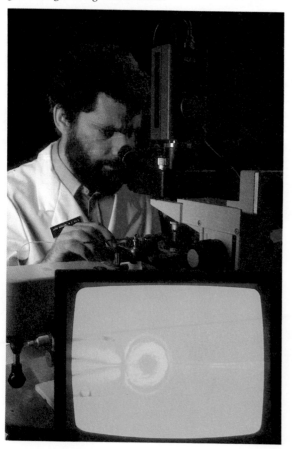

A genetic researcher inserts a human gene into a mouse embryo. Scientists are learning to identify disease-causing defects in genes and can even synthesize new genes. Why is genetic engineering controversial?

or spiral structure of the genetic molecule DNA. Once the structure of DNA was known, scientists learned much about how cells reproduce themselves. Their findings have applications for research into the origins and cure of cancer and causes of mutations and birth defects.

The discovery of DNA has also led to the new and controversial field of genetic engineering. Research in this field poses unknown potentials and dangers. It may lead to cures for deadly diseases and new strains of protein-rich plants. It could result in new and dangerous diseases.

Emerging Groups

The postwar period was also an era of social change, marked by the growing influence of women, minority groups, and Third World peoples. Writers, poets and political leaders from these groups captured world attention. They made people more aware of the situations of their respective groups.

Women's Movement   After women won the right to vote in a number of countries following the end of World War I, **feminism,** or the movement supporting women's rights, faded. During World War II, women took over men's jobs for the duration of the war, then "retired" once the soldiers came home. During the 1950's, most women's lives were centered around home and family.

The limits placed on a woman's role were attacked in 1963 by the feminist leader Betty Friedan. Her book *The Feminine Mystique* inspired the rebirth of the women's movement. Women began to organize women's **consciousness-raising,** or self-awareness, groups. These groups enable women to appreciate their talents and to counter sex stereotyping and sex discrimination. They work for equal access to jobs and education and for equal pay.

By 1975 the women's movement had made much progress. That year was declared International Women's Year by the United Nations. Women from all over the world met in Mexico City to identify barriers to equal rights and to develop national 10-year plans of action. They set up programs in such areas as politics,

In discussing Third World writers, review a list of winners of the Nobel Prize for literature. Excerpts of the winning works by Third World writers might be assigned for student reading.

Women's Suffrage Around the World

New Zealand	1893	Luxemburg	1919	Salvador	1939
Australia	1902	United States	1920	Quebec, Canada	1940
Finland	1906	Ecuador	1929	Dominican Rep.	1942
Norway	1907	South Africa (white		France	1945
Denmark	1915	only)	1930	Guatemala	1945
Iceland	1915	Spain	1931	Japan	1945
Canada (except		Thailand	1932	Argentina	1946
Quebec)	1917	Ceylon	1934	Belgium	1946
USSR	1917	Brazil	1934	Mexico	1946
Netherlands	1917	Cuba	1934	China	1947
Austria	1918	Turkey	1934	Liberia	1947
Czechoslovakia	1918	Uruguay	1934	India	1949
Poland	1918	Burma	1935	Uganda	1958
Britain	1918	Romania	1935	Nigeria	1960
Germany	1919	Philippines	1937	Switzerland	1971

Women now have the right to vote in all but a handful of nations. Kuwait and Liechtenstein are two of the countries that still deny suffrage to women.

education and training, housing, health and nutrition, families, and mass communications. The women meeting in Mexico found many common bonds, despite their various national differences.

Third World Writers   Third World writers developed a distinctive voice in the postwar era. Over the course of the century, they relied less on western models and turned to their own cultural heritages. They developed a literature that drew on rhythms, images, traditions, and experiences separate from the western tradition.

In Africa, traditional literature was oral, and written literature was a new African art form. The first modern African writers were French-speaking poets of the late 1940's and early 1950's, such as Leopold Senghor. They strongly identified themselves as black writers and wrote to protest French rule.

Modern African literature exists in several African languages and in the languages of the European powers that colonized Africa—France, Britain, Spain, and Portugal. Many African works explore the continent's rich cultural heritage and its conflicts with western culture. For example, Ghanian playwright Ama Ata

Aidoo in *The Dilemma of a Ghost* (1965) describes the conflicts that arise when a young Ghanian man marries an Afro-American woman. Africa's best-known playwright, Wole Soyinka of Nigeria, wrote *A Dance of the Forests* (1963) to celebrate Nigerian independence.

Latin American writers also broke away from European influences and tapped the richness of their own cultures. A number of them have achieved international fame. The first Latin American to win the Nobel Prize for literature was Chilean poet Gabriela Mistral in 1945. Another Chilean poet, Pablo Neruda, won the prize in 1971. The most recent Nobel Prize winner is Colombian author Gabriel García Márquez. He wrote *One Hundred Years of Solitude* (1967), which traces the history of Latin America through the story of the mythical town of Macondo and the six generations of a family that lived there. His work combines a strong element of fantasy with realism.

The Family

Since 1945, families have been forced to react to the rapidly changing world around them. In industrialized countries, families have become

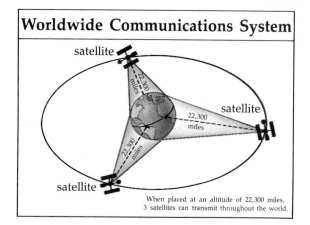

Worldwide Communications System

satellite

22,300 miles

satellite

22,300 miles

22,300 miles

satellite

When placed at an altitude of 22,300 miles, 3 satellites can transmit throughout the world.

smaller. Having only two children is common. Day-to-day contacts with relatives other than the immediate family are rare. Often, grown children live at great distances from their parents and from each other.

Traditional family relationships and responsibilities have changed. Mothers are increasingly finding work outside the home. Many are forced to take jobs for economic reasons. Others are doing so by choice. Some roles performed by mothers have been divided among the family members.

Other roles have been taken over by outside enterprises and institutions. Child care centers, nursery schools, and after-school programs have filled some of the needs for child care. Producers of convenience foods and fast-food chains have reduced cooking burdens. Synthetics and easy-care fabrics have cut ironing time. Nursing homes provide care for the elderly. Traditional responsibilities of families and churches to educate and provide values are being placed on schools and governments.

Divorce has become increasingly common, as societal and legal barriers have fallen, and as the emphasis on romantic love and personal fulfillment has increased. The number of children raised by single parents or related by second marriages is increasing.

In the Third World, families are under stress, too. As modernization has spread, old values have been challenged. Many daughters are seeking more education rather than early marriages. Arranged marriages are declining.

The struggle for economic survival has left many children in the care of one parent. Less fortunate children simply have been abandoned as parents are unable to care for them. Without adequate food, clothing, shelter, and a chance for education, these homeless children face troubled futures. They are appearing in growing numbers in the cities of the Third World.

1. Identify: Jean Paul Sartre, Samuel Beckett, Boris Pasternak, Rudolf Nureyev, James Watson, Francis Crick, Betty Friedan, Wole Soyinka, Gabriel García Márquez.
2. In what ways were the 1920's and the 1950's similar?
3. What did the 1975 International Women's Year conference in Mexico City accomplish?
4. How have families changed since World War II?

4 The Globalization of Culture

Even as colonial empires have vanished, western ideas and learning have spread around the globe. At the same time, contributions from the nonwestern world have been carried to the West, providing new inspirations and blends of ideas.

Though underlying cultural and national characteristics have remained strong, surface differences are changing and, in some cases, disappearing. International airports have a sameness around the world. Cities are losing their distinctive qualities as sleek "international-style" skyscrapers and expressways have been constructed. A person's nationality is often hard to identify from the clothes he or she is wearing.

Technology

Technology has played a large part in the process of global blending. Communications satellites have enabled people around the world to watch international events at the same time. As many as 2 billion people watched the 1984 Winter Olympic games. Popular American television series such as *All in the Family* and *Dallas* are shown in many countries. In areas without television, contact with the larger world has been made possible by small transistor and short-

Use a large world map on a bulletin board to mark with pins and yarn all the direct contacts between your community and other parts of the world.

wave radios. Cheap, widely available cassette recorders enable people to hear their favorite national and international pop music stars.

Commercial jet air travel has increased contacts between foreigners. Remote areas have been made accessible by the spread of motorcycles, jeeps, and pickup trucks. Business people, scientists, and educators meet in international conventions and exchanges. Music and dance companies regularly make tours to other continents. Athletes participate in international competitions. Tourists search out new and different settings to explore.

All these groups bring back impressions and influences of places they have seen: photographs; new tastes in foods, clothing, and the arts; souvenirs; and memories of conversations. The people and places visited are also influenced by these contacts.

The Beatles, the most popular rock group of the 1960's, experimented with new forms of musical expression and were widely imitated by other composers and performers. How do superstars contribute to the globalization of culture?

John Paul II, the first non-Italian Pope since 1523 and the first from a communist country, has made more visits abroad than any other Pope in history. How has his election affected politics in Poland?

Music

Music has always been able to cross language barriers. Now there is a clear blending of many different styles. Jazz and rock have become international favorites. Local singers have adapted jazz and rock to their own music. Superstars, such as the Beatles in the 1960's, the Bee Gees in the 1970's, and Michael Jackson in the 1980's, have won massive worldwide followings. Their lifestyles as well as their music have had a strong influence on youth.

Regional musical traditions have spread beyond their localities. Popular Caribbean music has been carried to the United States. Jamaican reggae, for example, has spread to North America and Europe. Composers have tried adapting Oriental musical rhythms, harmonies, and instruments to western compositions.

Religion

Religion reflects the impact of global changes, too. As secular viewpoints have spread, many people no longer accept traditional religious teachings. Numerous critics claim that religions have lost touch with modern human needs and

The diagrams below are the subject of the "Using Diagrams" section of the Chapter 32 Review.

GLOBAL DIMENSION

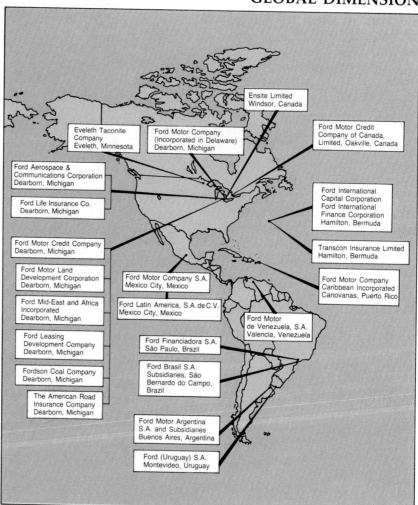

problems. However, religious belief is still important to many people. In addition, many religious groups have sought to update their traditional teachings and apply them to twentieth-century problems. Some of these religions have actively promoted human rights issues and have called for an end to the nuclear arms race. Another major development is the rise of the ecumenical movement, which seeks to promote greater understanding among the world's religions. However, conflict between rival religious groups persists in areas such as Northern Ireland, Lebanon, and India.

Religion has played an important role in recent social and political movements. In Iran, Shiite Islamic religious leaders under Ayatollah Ruhollah Khomeini led the 1979 revolution against the shah. Once in power, they proclaimed Iran an Islamic republic and sought to replace western secular values with traditional Islamic ones.

In Poland, Roman Catholicism became the leading source of opposition to the Communist Polish government. The election of the Polish-born Pope John Paul II in 1978 and his visit to Poland in 1979 heightened Polish yearnings for freedom. Roman Catholic clergy and laity were

Have students compile a list of multinational corporations. Discuss the influence of these corporations in local and global affairs.

OF A MULTINATIONAL COMPANY

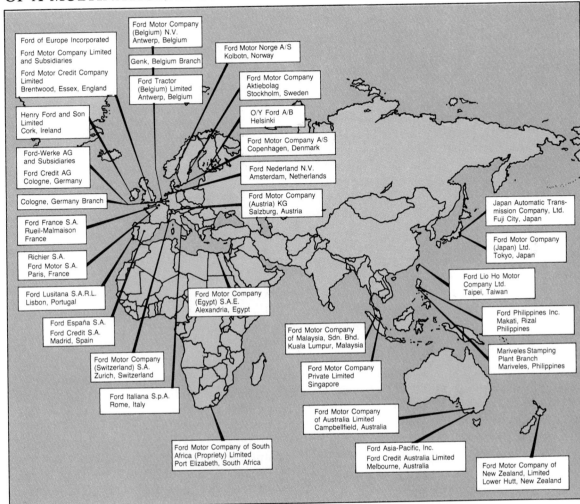

active in the formation of Solidarity, the independent trade union movement.

Multinational Corporations

A different type of change has been brought about by **multinational corporations.** Multinational corporations are western-based businesses that produce or market in more than one country. Examples are multinational oil companies, automobile manufacturers, banks, and fast-food chains.

In the Third World, these companies have brought with them their technology, business organization, and values. Multinational companies hire local people to work on construction projects, in offices, shops, and assembly plants. While many western ideas have been learned in the process, successful multinational corporations have found that the exchange is not just in one direction. Sometimes products and marketing techniques have been geared to local customs and wants. Successful management practices developed in one country have been used by others. However, many Third World countries claim that multinational corporations exploit their resources while ignoring local needs.

Some teachers might wish to discuss the methods of protest that Mohandas Gandhi used in India.

Have students imagine life without machines. Some students might wish to write a brief summary of a day without machines.

Protest

Protest has become an international phenomenon. There have been two broad types of protest. First, widespread intellectual dissent has arisen to established social and political practices. Protests of this sort have been voiced in literature, the popular media, and the press. The second type has involved organized confrontation with ruling groups on specific issues. It has included parades, strikes, sit-ins, vigils, and massive nonviolent demonstrations. Continued mass demonstrations against the shah of Iran brought about his fall in 1979. In the summer of 1982, participants from many nations joined in a mass demonstration in New York City against the nuclear arms race.

The second type of protest has also included violent terrorist activities, such as kidnappings, assassinations, hijackings, and bombings. The level of international terrorism grew rapidly in the 1970's and 1980's. Terrorists have taken advantage of new technologies, remote control devices, jet travel, and television. Funds, weapons, and terrorist personnel travel with little difficulty across national boundaries. These developments have raised troubling questions about what measures can and should be undertaken to reduce terrorism. International legislation has proved inadequate, as some countries are still willing to give sanctuary to terrorists.

1. How have television and jet travel contributed to the globalization of culture?
2. How have multinational corporations brought change?
3. How are the blending of East and West, North and South apparent in music and religion?
4. Why is protest and terrorism an international phenomenon?

5 The Frontiers of Change

Change has continued in the 1980's, posing new challenges, new decisions, and new adjustments for people to make. As with so much of the century's changes, scientific and technological changes are at the heart of these developments.

Home and Work Place

Homes, offices, and factories are acquiring new technologies. Relationships, jobs, and the quality of life are being affected.

Home Television is becoming an even more important item in homes. Cable and satellite networks have greatly increased the choice of programming. Through the addition of computers and video tape, televisions are becoming home video terminals that have increased educational and entertainment possibilities.

New computer applications are being developed and tried in test markets. People can request information such as sports scores, airline schedules, food and stock market prices, and texts of newspapers and books. They can express opinions and make mail-order purchases. The video terminal may eliminate the need for personal trips to stores and libraries. Publishers, movie producers, and marketing industries are trying to anticipate the effect of the video-computer market on them.

Work Place Since the 1970's, there has been increasing concern about the quality of life at the work place. This concern has been a reaction to trends that began in the industrial revolution— the efforts to fragment production and increase **automation,** or the use of machines.

In the 1970's, Volvo, the Swedish automobile manufacturing company, pioneered new ways of organizing assembly work to increase worker participation and responsibility. The company reorganized and enlarged tasks to reduce boredom. Teams were formed to complete assignments and were given responsibility for inspection, maintenance, and job assignments within the team. Unions, workers, and management cooperated in developing the changes. Companies in the United States and elsewhere have experimented with similar reforms.

The latest generation of technology is now spreading into offices and factories. Office workers are using computers and word processors. Robots have proven successful in assembly plants in Japan. These sophisticated office and manufacturing machines will reduce the numbers of workers needed, force the learning of new skills, and affect the quality of life.

Victor Vasarely's painting Arcturus II *is an example of an international art movement of the mid-twentieth century known as op art, which deals with optical illusions. Op artists create the illusion of movement with interactions of color and geometric forms. Why are new art forms sometimes not accepted by the public?*

Medicine and Ethics

Throughout the twentieth century, there have been phenomenal advances in medicine. It continues to be one of the fastest areas of change. Revolutionary devices are enabling doctors to diagnose conditions and perform surgery that was impossible only a few years before. Hearts, kidneys, and livers can be successfully transplanted. Artificial hearts are in the experimental stages.

Life support and life-sustaining operations for people of all ages from the extremely premature infant to the elderly are raising complex ethical and moral decisions. Families, doctors, lawyers, hospitals, churches, and governments are struggling over matters such as the rights of the patient, the rights of the family, and the obligations of society and the government in extreme medical situations.

Technology and the Arts

Technology and the arts have been increasingly intertwined. Artist Robert Raushenberg has tried huge experimental events combining lights, television, drama, and electronic music. Audiences have become participants in productions. Artists and engineers collaborate in mixing sounds, lasers, and video and audio tapes. Other artists experiment with creating computer art and computer music.

These diverse productions have at times amused, confused, and angered audiences. History shows that understanding new art forms is a long process.

1. How have some companies experimented with improving the quality of life on assembly lines?
2. What are some of the ethical and moral issues created by recent breakthroughs in medicine?
3. How have technology and the arts combined?

SCIENCE AND TECHNOLOGY

Today's Technological Revolution

Since 1945, the world has undergone a technological revolution. The most significant and rapid change has occurred in the field of electronics. The term "electronics" refers to devices that use electrical pulses or signals to operate equipment. Electronics is the basis for such items as radio, television, radar, video equipment, and computers.

Computers are at the heart of today's technological revolution. They are electronic machines that carry out calculations and process information at an amazing speed. The first computer, introduced in 1946, weighed 30 tons (27 metric tons) and performed 5,000 calculations per second. Today's computers are a hundred times more powerful, cost a fraction of the original computer, and can be carried by one person. Future computers will be even smaller, more powerful, and less expensive.

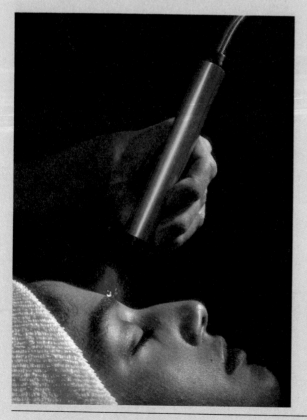

Over the past two decades, computers have become important in business and industry. Since the late 1970's, thousands of consumers have bought computers for use in their homes. Before the end of the century, computers will be as common in the industrialized world as telephones and televisions. Mass produced and relatively inexpensive, computers will also be available to consumers in the Third World.

The "brain" behind complex electronic operations is the microchip, a unit of interconnecting circuits etched on a tiny wafer of silicon. Invented in 1959, the microchip, or chip, became widely used after the early 1960's. Each chip contains thousands of microscopic transistors, or materials that transmit electrical signals. Since the microchip's invention, engineers have doubled the number of transistors on a single chip. At this rate, by 1990, they expect to place 10 million transistors on a chip that will carry out thousands of calculations per second and store information for thousands of text pages. One hundred years from now the amount of information contained in a microchip will probably approximate that in the brain.

Even today, microchips are being used in many different areas. In medicine, experts use chips to move electronic limbs worn by accident victims. Chips are also placed behind the ears of people with hearing problems. In the future, scientists hope to attach chips to the nervous system to check body functions and to correct chemical imbalances and many other medical problems.

The use of microchips is expected to transform industrial production. In certain industries, chip-operated robots will eventually perform operations such as spraying paint, assembling machines, welding steel, loading vehicles, and navigating planes and ships. Today, there are about 60,000 robots in the world. Nearly half of them are in Japan. By 2000, there will be hundreds of thousands of robots. Some will be used in industry; others will perform household tasks.

The intense heat generated by lasers (opposite page) removes diseased body cells with little damage to surrounding tissue. Robots in Japan's Nissan Motors factory (right) replace human labor for many tasks. Robots work efficiently for extended periods of time and display exceptional physical strength. Some robots today can be programmed to complete as many as 180 commands.

Scientists are also discussing the development of biochips, or tiny computerlike units made of organic material that responds to electronic stimuli. Experts state that eventually a limit will be reached beyond which the circuits of the silicon chip will be so crowded that they may overheat and melt. Organic material, they believe, will prove to be a better construction material than silicon.

The development of biochips will have far-reaching effects. Biochips may be linked to the brain to correct mental disorders caused by nerve damage. Certain types of paralysis and blindness may be healed. Biochips connected to the brain may also aid memory and boost intelligence.

Another product of the late twentieth-century technological revolution is the laser. A laser is a device that concentrates light and releases it in a thin narrow beam. The light is released in pulses so short in duration that they are measured in picoseconds, a millionth of a millionth of a second. The laser beam can be focused as narrowly as 0.0001 inch (0.00025 centimeter), producing an intense heat of over 10,000 °F (5,500 °C).

Invented in 1960, the laser is capable of welding miniature metal parts for electronic instruments, removing diseased tissue from the eye, and transmitting voice and visual signals efficiently over a long distance. Nevertheless, many scientists believe that the laser has the potential for even further uses. In the coming years, the laser will play an important role in industry, medicine, and communication.

Today's technology has helped people gain control over nature and so build a more civilized way of life. It has increased the production of goods and services. It has made labor easier and has given people better health and higher standards of living. But the advance of technology also presents enormous challenges. For example, new machines will continue to free workers from routine and boring jobs. However, some of these workers may then face the hardships of unemployment. With help from government and industry, they can be retrained to enter more highly skilled and more interesting careers. Also, devices designed to improve memory and body function may, in the wrong hands, be used to alter the beliefs and actions of people against their will. Thus, ways will have to be found to ensure that new technology is directed toward humane goals.

1. How has electronics transformed life since 1945?
2. What role has the laser played in industry, medicine, and communication?
3. What do you think are the benefits and dangers of today's technological revolution?

CHAPTER 32 REVIEW

Summary

1. Scientific and technological advances coupled with political and economic upheavals have altered the pace, the quality, and the meaning of life in the twentieth century.
2. Revolutionary ideas in psychology, physics, and the arts that developed around the turn of the century gained wide followings after World War I.
3. The 1930's became a time for commitment to political and social causes, as artists, writers, and others joined to fight the misery and injustices of the depression, the Spanish Civil War and the rising tyranny of fascism and communism.
4. The post-World War II era was a time of recovery and returning prosperity, during which some people sought a good time while others sought the meaning of existence.
5. Under Khrushchev there was an easing of Soviet restrictions on artistic freedom, but by the late 1960's extreme measures were again taken to force artistic conformity.
6. An explosion of information has been produced in the postwar period. This is often accomplished by teams of researchers who are supported by corporate, university, and government sponsors.
7. Since World War II, women, minority groups, and Third World groups have found powerful voices to raise issues and fight for recognition and equal rights.
8. Families in developed countries have changed in size, roles, and responsibilities, while in developing countries, traditional family ties have been strained and tested by modernization and limited economic opportunities.
9. Modern telecommunications, transportation, and multinational corporations have contributed to the globalization of culture.
10. New technology continues to alter people's lives, affecting the home and work place, raising difficult moral and ethical questions, and providing new artistic media for artists.

Building Vocabulary

avant-garde	surrealism	relativism	defected
homogeneous	impresario	socialist realism	feminism
psychoanalysis	choreographer	social realists	consciousness-raising
psychiatrist	dissonant	beatniks	multinational corporations
cubism	theory of relativity	existentialism	automation

Reviewing the Main Ideas

1. What new technologies had a major impact on society after World War I?
2. How do modern art and modern music differ from nineteenth-century art and music?
3. What achievements in physics were made in the early part of the twentieth century?
4. Why were movies popular during the depression years?
5. Why was Keynes's idea that governments should "prime the pump" important?
6. What was the impact of the 1930's and 1940's on artistic creativity?

7. Why did the search for the meaning of life become important to people in the postwar period?
8. Why has there been an explosion of information in the twentieth century?
9. What are some concerns of the women's movement?
10. What are some themes addressed by postwar Third World writers?
11. What forces have contributed to the globalization of culture?
12. What technological changes are altering conditions at home and in the work place? What impact will they have on people?

Discussing Important Ideas

1. What is the difference between relativity and relativism?
2. What do you think beatniks and existentialists were trying to communicate to the postwar world?
3. What should be the role of the artist in relation to the rest of society? What should be the role of government toward the artist?
4. Do you think the quality of human life has been improved or worsened as a result of this century's scientific and technological changes? Explain.
5. What changes do you think have been the most important during the century? Give reasons for your opinion.
6. Who do you think has made the most significant contribution to the twentieth century? Why?
7. Are you optimistic or pessimistic about the future? Explain.

Using Diagrams

Refer to the diagram on pages 760 and 761 to answer the following questions:
1. What is the purpose of this diagram?
2. Which two continents have the greatest number of Ford operations?
3. Is Ford located behind the "iron curtain"?
4. Are there more Ford operations in the Western or Eastern Hemisphere?
5. What kinds of businesses does Ford own besides those in automotive manufacturing?

CHAPTER 33

Nuclear Explosion

❝ This must be the context of our thinking—the context of human interdependence in the face of vast new dimensions of our society. . . ❞

Adlai Stevenson, American political leader (1900-1965)

Challenges of Tomorrow

In presenting this chapter, teachers should stress the positive efforts being made to deal with the world's problems.

Today the nations of the world face a bewildering array of international issues. These include promoting peace, using natural resources effectively, protecting the environment, ending hunger and disease, and improving the world's standard of living. How these issues are resolved will decide the very survival of the human race.

No one can really predict the future, but an analysis of present conditions can be the basis for making intelligent guesses. Some **futurologists,** or forecasters of the future, are pessimistic, while others are optimistic. Many hold to a mixture of opinions. *The Global Report to the President of the United States* predicted in 1979:

> *If present trends continue, the world in 2000 will be more crowded, more polluted, [and] less stable . . . than the one we live in now.* *

However, the report stated that this prediction will probably occur only if "very real problems are ignored," and "if national policies . . . remain essentially unchanged through the rest of the century." Fortunately, the report adds that "policies are beginning to change" and "there is reason for hope." The kind of future that emerges will in large part depend on humanity's ability to adjust to rapid changes and to use new technology to better human conditions.

1 War and Peace

Humanity has survived many wars, including two world wars. In modern times, each major war has tended to be more costly in lives and

---

The Global 2000 Report to the President of the United States, Vol. 1: The Summary Report, © 1980 by Pergamon Press, Inc., p. 1.

materials than the previous one. Today, a major concern is the continued growth in the military power of countries. In 1983 the nations of the world spent more than $600 billion for military purposes. This expenditure is ten times greater than what countries spent for humanitarian aid.

The reason given for armaments is that nations must protect themselves, doing all in their power to increase their physical security. However, the modern world has become so interdependent that a regional conflict could easily become a world war. In the nuclear age, a world war would most likely mean the destruction of the planet and the extinction of human civilization. To avoid catastrophe, nations must seek ways of eliminating or controlling nuclear weapons. At the same time, efforts must be undertaken to resolve international disputes through peaceful means.

Nuclear Arms

Since 1945, nuclear weapons of tremendous destructive power have been developed. A one-megaton bomb, equal to 1 million tons (0.9 million metric tons) of TNT, can destroy a city of 2 million people. The combined explosive power of all nuclear weapons is 1 million times greater than the bomb dropped on Hiroshima. The superpowers possess thousands of nuclear warheads targeted at each other's cities. These warheads are stationed on a variety of delivery systems, such as land missiles, submarine missiles, and bombers. Because of their large numbers, nuclear arms are capable of **overkill.** That is, they can destroy the world several times over in a matter of hours.

Many experts believe that the destructive power of nuclear weapons has served to prevent war between the superpowers. This prevention

The graph below is the subject of the "Using Graphs" section of the Chapter 33 Review.

Before discussing nuclear weapons, some teachers might wish to review *Understanding Nuclear Weapons and Arms Control* by Teena Mayers, © 1983. It is available through the National Council for the Social Studies.

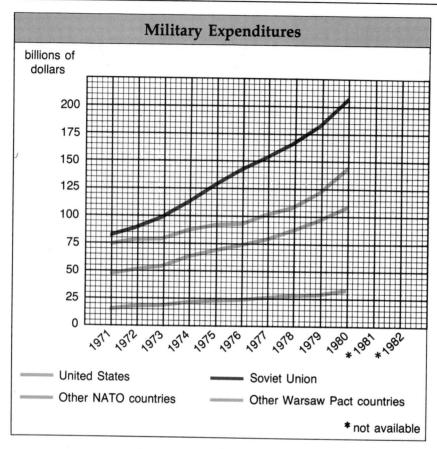

Military Expenditures

billions of dollars

United States
Other NATO countries
Soviet Union
Other Warsaw Pact countries

* not available

is called **deterrence.** However, there is the growing fear that, as long as nuclear weapons exist, there is the danger that someday they will be used. Only recently some world leaders have talked seriously about the limited use of nuclear weapons in a future conflict. But many experts claim that a "limited" nuclear war is not possible. They believe that once such a nuclear exchange is started, it will prove difficult to contain. Each side will go all out to defeat the other.

In spite of the danger, the superpowers continue to stockpile their supply of nuclear weapons and to develop new ones. In doing so, each side hopes to build an effective deterrent that prevents either side from attempting an attack.

Arms Race Since the beginning of the cold war, the United States and the Soviet Union have been competing in an arms race. During the 1950's and 1960's, the United States was the

dominant nuclear power, but the Soviet Union worked to build up its supply of nuclear weapons.

Beginning in the late 1960's, the Soviets made dramatic increases in their military strength, especially in the category of nuclear warheads. By 1981 they had more launchers, submarines, ships, tanks, artillery, and aircraft than the United States. It has been argued, however, that American weapons are technologically superior. Although the Soviets have more and larger land missiles, the American missiles are believed to be more accurate and maneuverable. Thus, fewer numbers may be offset by quality.

In general, many experts today believe that the military advantages of each country tend to balance out, resulting in a broad **parity,** or equality, between the two nations. However, as each superpower makes further changes in its arsenal, the other reacts by adding to its own military program. This competition leads to the increasingly destructive power of nuclear weapons and a greater ability in getting these weapons to their targets.

Arms Control   During the 1960's and 1970's, the superpowers negotiated a variety of arms control agreements. **Arms control** refers to limiting the use of weapons in certain locations and under certain conditions. Under these agreements, the United States and the Soviet Union placed **ceilings** on some of their nuclear forces. That is, they agreed that they could increase the numbers of their weapons only to a certain level. They also agreed to reduce stockpiles of other weapons. Limits were placed on the testing and development of certain kinds of nuclear arms. The superpowers also improved crisis communication to prevent accidental war.

Arms control agreements, however, did not end the arms race. Tensions increased between the United States and the Soviet Union in the late 1970's and early 1980's. New agreements were difficult to achieve, and existing ones were placed in jeopardy. In late 1983, all superpower arms talks were suspended. Meanwhile, both sides continued to build their military forces.

By the mid-1980's, many people in the United States and Western Europe feared the further heightening of the arms race. They demonstrated and called for arms control talks to begin again. Many also supported a **nuclear freeze,** in which the superpowers would agree not to increase the weapons they already have. However, the success of such goals depends on the willingness of the superpowers to improve their relations and to trust each other.

Nuclear Proliferation

Another issue affecting war and peace is **nuclear proliferation,** or the spread of nuclear weapons to previously non-nuclear countries. Nuclear technology has become more readily available throughout the world. As a result, the superpowers no longer hold a monopoly on nuclear weapons. More and more nations are ready to join the "nuclear club." By the mid-1980's, four other nations—Britain, France, China, and India—had successfully exploded nuclear devices. Several other nations have the ability to develop nuclear weapons. These include Israel, South Africa, and a number of Western European countries.

In 1968 the United States, the Soviet Union, Britain, and 60 other nations signed the Nuclear Nonproliferation Treaty. This agreement was designed to prevent the spread of nuclear

In the 1980's, growing numbers of people began protesting the heightening of the arms race by the superpowers. Demonstrations in support of arms control and nuclear bans were increased throughout Europe and North America. This New York protest was organized by the World Peace Council to criticize the nuclear buildup and to demand new arms control agreements. On what does the success of arms control depend?

Emphasize the peaceful use of nuclear reactors.

weapons to those nations that did not have them. In time, over 100 nations signed the treaty. France, China, and a number of countries wanting to develop nuclear weapons refused to sign the agreement.

The 1968 treaty has a major weakness. It does not ban nations from buying or selling nuclear technology or **nuclear reactors,** that is devices for generating power through the release of atomic energy by a controlled chain reaction. Thus, many nations who want to develop their own weapons are able to acquire the necessary technology from nuclear nations, many of which are signers of the treaty.

As nuclear weapons spread to more nations, "limited" regional wars are more likely to develop into a nuclear holocaust. To prevent such a disaster, proposals have been made to encourage more nations to sign the 1968 treaty. These include guarantees of territorial borders and the creation of nuclear-free zones, or areas where nuclear weapons are banned. Another suggestion is that nuclear nations set an example of restraint by reducing their existing stockpiles. In this way, nuclear weapons will be less desirable to nations seeking ways to increase their status in the world. Many experts recognize that, unless the spread of nuclear weapons is brought under control, the chances of nuclear war will steadily increase.

Arms Trade

Global tensions in the 1970's and 1980's have led to a vast worldwide trade in military weapons. In 1980 the sale of arms among the nations of the world was valued at $30 billion and was increasing by $5 billion a year. More than 75 percent of the world arms trade goes to Asian, African, and Latin American nations.

An issue facing many nations is whether or not to become involved in the arms trade. Policy-makers in nations that export arms, such as the United States and the Soviet Union, must consider a number of questions. Is it right to sell arms to poorer nations with serious economic and social needs? If friendly nations are not armed, will their national security, as well as the security of the supplier nation, be endangered?

How much economic benefit does a nation receive from arms sales abroad? The answers are not clear.

The United States and the Soviet Union compete with each other by backing and arming opposing sides in various disputes among Asian, African, Middle Eastern and Latin American nations. From 1974 to 1979, the United States supplied $27 billion worth of arms to these areas; the Soviet Union, $23.4 billion.

Many nations profit from the arms trade and use that profit to pay for imports. For example, France's weapons exports pay for a quarter of its oil imports. Other nations involved in the arms trade include Britain, West Germany, Czechoslovakia, Brazil, South Korea, and Israel. While benefiting supplier nations, the arms trade puts a strain on the economies of poorer nations that buy arms. In addition, it contributes to the heightening of local conflicts in various parts of the world.

1. Why is nuclear arms control an important international issue?
2. What steps have been taken to reduce the spread of nuclear weapons?
3. Why do some nations export arms? Why do other nations buy arms?

2 Global Wealth

Another issue facing the global community is the gap between the world's richer and poorer nations. As more nations have become independent since 1945, a debate has emerged about how to reduce this gap and to distribute the world's wealth more evenly.

Developed and Developing Nations

The world's wealthiest nations include the United States, Canada, Japan, Australia, New Zealand, and most of the nations of Western Europe. They form the group of nations known as the western bloc. Countries in this group are **developed nations.** They are highly industrialized and have well-developed economies.

Other developed nations belong to the eastern, or communist bloc of nations. This includes

HISTORY AND CITIES

Bombay

Bombay is a major metropolitan area of India. Located on the western coast, it is one of India's leading seaports. Bombay's 8 million people are divided into numerous religious and linguistic groups. Besides the Hindus, who are the largest of the religious groups, there are Muslims, Buddhists, Christians, Sikhs, Jains, Parsis, and Jews. The people of Bombay speak 15 major Indian languages and more than 150 other tongues and dialects, including about 50 non-Indian ones.

A traveler approaching Bombay from the sea has a magnificent panoramic view. In the foreground are the wide harbor, several small islands, and many ships. Behind them is the skyline of a busy industrial and commercial center. In the far distance rise the mountains of the Western Ghats. Once in the city, the visitor faces a colorful sea of humanity moving through streets lined by buildings of many architectural styles, both eastern and western. Near the city's center are housing developments, huts, and shacks in which the poorer Bombay residents live.

Indian rulers, Hindu and Muslim, governed the area of Bombay until 1534, when the Portuguese established a trading post in the region. In the late 1600's Britain obtained control of the trading post, which became known as Bombay. The British established municipal services, built fortifications, and made Bombay an important trading center.

Under British rule, Bombay became one of India's leading cities. During the 1850's, British engineers built roads and railroads linking Bombay and the interior of India. Raw cotton grown in rural areas was brought to spinning and weaving plants in the city. When the American Civil War (1861-1865) disrupted the flow of American cotton to Europe, Bombay's textile industry soared. The opening of the Suez Canal in 1869 further helped Bombay's economy by shortening the shipping time between India and Europe.

Today, Bombay is still a leading textile manufacturing city. However, its economy is more varied, producing chemicals, machinery, and food products. Bombay is also the financial hub of India and is the center of India's motion picture industry.

In the past 30 years, Bombay's population has grown tremendously. Most of this increase is due to a steady migration to the city from rural areas. Rural migrants leave their villages because the cultivated areas cannot support their growing numbers. They move to Bombay seeking better economic opportunities. People from the same village or district live near each other in this continually growing city. They bring their own lifestyles and maintain many of their rural ways in the big urban center. To reduce overcrowding, the city government has steadily expanded Bombay's area into surrounding fields and villages.

1. How has Bombay's economy developed over the centuries?
2. What major problem does Bombay face today?

For the graph below, the figures through 1982 are based on United Nations data. United Nations projections are used for figures beyond 1982.

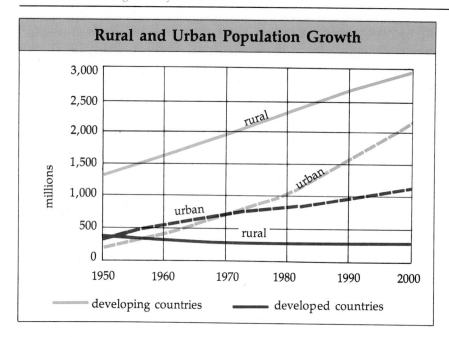

Rural and Urban Population Growth

developing countries   developed countries

the Soviet Union, the People's Republic of China, and other Communist states. Like the western bloc, these nations have industrial-agricultural economies. Progress has been made in their economic development, but they are not as economically prosperous as the western bloc.

The **developing nations** are economically poor and primarily agricultural, although some are becoming industrialized. They share common problems such as poverty, hunger, disease, and lack of economic development. They are located mostly in Africa, Asia, Latin America, and the Middle East. Although politically independent, the developing nations are subject to the economic systems of the developed nations. They supply raw materials to the developed nations in exchange for manufactured goods.

Some developing countries have resources, but until recently, lacked the economic skills to develop them. Some are beginning to become more prosperous. Oil-rich Arab countries in the Third World are among the world's richest nations in total income. Yet, this new wealth has not reached all of their people, many of whom are still poor.

Some developing countries, on the other hand, have few natural resources. They are the world's poorest and least developed nations.

Often, they rely on the financial resources of richer nations to survive.

Demands for Change

Since the 1960's, developing countries have been demanding changes in the world's economy to improve their standards of living. They no longer accept poverty as unavoidable and want an increased share in the world's resources. This desire for economic improvement by developing countries is known as the **revolution of rising expectations.**

Developing countries often feel that developed countries, in controlling the world's market, have discriminated against them. For instance, they state that the developed countries have imported natural resources from them at low prices. At the same time, the developed nations have charged developing nations high prices for the manufactured goods produced from the same raw materials.

Developing nations also point out the unequal distribution of the world's wealth. Rich nations, they state, have the finances and skills to build factories, roads, ports, and bridges. Poor nations lack adequate money and human resources to improve their economies. Trade, a source of national wealth, is limited because the poor

Third World indebtedness to United States banks can prove to be a threat to world financial stability.

Ask students "How do you think efforts to increase wealth in developing nations is hampered by expanding populations?"

countries cannot borrow money to open new markets.

Developing countries also want fairer terms of trade with the developed countries. Many Third World countries have not yet acquired a diverse economy. They produce only one major item for export. This export may be an agricultural product, such as sugar, or a mineral, such as copper. The prices of these products are often unsteady on the world market. When they fall, the economies of poor nations suffer. At the same time, many developing nations are dependent on developed nations for manufactured goods. It is difficult for them to pay for these goods because of declining national incomes.

Population Growth

The twentieth century has seen a sharp rise in total world population and in its rate of increase. Today, the world has about 5 billion people. If current projections stand, the number of people in the world will be more than 6 billion by the year 2000. This means there will be twice as many people as there were 20 years ago.

The increase in world population has been the result of both higher birthrates and lower death rates. More babies survive their years of infancy today than babies did at any time in the past. The use of medicines and the elimination of many epidemics have increased children's chances of living.

Many social scientists insist that a marked reduction in the rate of population growth is necessary if the world is to survive hunger and famine. The developed countries of Europe and North America have been successful in reducing the rate of their population growth. But the population of developing countries in Asia, Africa, and Latin America continues to rise at a high rate. In only a few nations, like China, have governments attempted to and been successful in slowing the birthrate.

High birthrates in many developing countries are due to religious objections to the means of population control. Another important reason is the fact that parents in agricultural areas need many children to help them work in the fields. In addition, they depend on their offspring to support them in old age. Large families also are desired because they provide aid during emergencies. This situation will probably continue until suitable systems of health care and social security are established in these countries.

Urban Growth   The problems arising from world population growth are not only related to numbers. They also involve where and how this

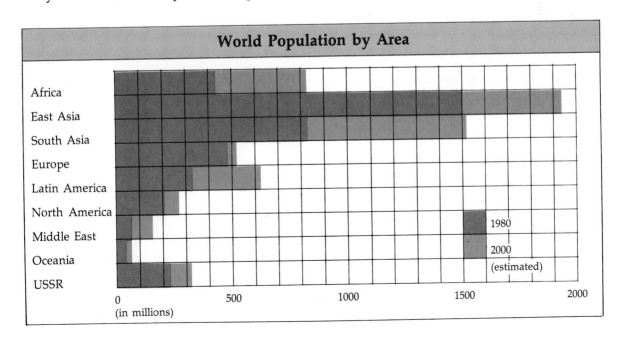

World Population by Area

Africa
East Asia
South Asia
Europe
Latin America
North America
Middle East
Oceania
USSR

1980
2000
(estimated)

0   500   1000   1500   2000
(in millions)

Many people in the world's developing nations move to the cities in order to find jobs. However, many are unable to gain employment. The growing number of urban unemployed is a worldwide problem.

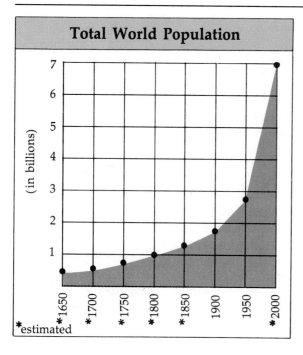

Total World Population

(in billions)

*1650 *1700 *1750 *1800 *1850 1900 1950 *2000

*estimated

growth is taking place. In 1800 about 3 percent of the world's population lived in cities. By the year 2000, more than half of the world's people will be living in urban areas. The rate of urban growth between 1920 and 1980 was two and a half times greater than the rate of increase for the total population.

In developing countries, urban areas are experiencing a population explosion. While the urban population of the developed countries tripled between 1920 and 1980, that of the developing countries rose tenfold. Migration from rural to urban areas is a major factor in this jump in urban population. This trend will probably continue into the twenty-first century. According to United Nations estimates, 25 metropolitan areas in the world will each have more than 10 million people by 2000. Twenty of the 25 urban areas are located in developing countries. Mexico City will lead the way with 30 million people.

With growing populations, the world's cities are already facing enormous social problems. This is especially true in developing countries. Housing in the Third World has not kept up with the population increase. As a result, more than half the residents of urban areas live in slums.

There, they dwell in misery, lacking the basic necessities of life. Within sight are wealthy neighborhoods and bustling modern business districts.

The social and political effects of such conditions are disturbing to many governments. Efforts have been made to rid urban areas of slums and to improve city services. But political leaders often face a dilemma. The more they do for their cities, the more the cities attract migrants from rural areas. As a result, urban overcrowding increases.

Food Crisis An adequate balance between population and food supplies is an important issue that concerns the world's nations, both rich and poor. The fact that some people starve while others are well fed is a problem that demands a solution. Many experts claim that if the food and population crises are not met chaos will disrupt many countries.

It is estimated that more than 500 million of the world's population do not have an adequate diet. Studies in developing nations show that nearly 40 percent of preschool children are undernourished. Since 1950 the production of food has been rising at an annual rate of 2.5 percent. However, the demand for food has been rising at a rate of over 3 percent a year. The number of hungry people in the world could increase to over 1 billion by the year 2000.

The problem of hunger is not caused by a worldwide shortage of food. Instead, it is due to the unequal distribution of wealth and technology between the world's rich and developing nations. The rise in world food production has been taking place mostly in developed countries. Governments in some of these countries pay farmers to cut production to keep prices stable. The developed countries export surplus food, which is sold to countries that are able to pay the price. Many poor people in the Third World remain hungry, because their governments do not have the money to buy the food. In addition, foreign economic aid has fallen short of what is required to eliminate hunger.

A rise in food output has occurred in several developing countries, such as Mexico and India. However, the growing populations in these

Have students brainstorm for ways in which they can influence change.

lands consume all of this additional food without providing much more per person. In some cases, developing countries have turned from exporting food to importing it. For example, the African country of Zaire was a food exporter 20 years ago. Now it buys more than $300 million worth of food from other countries each year. Its population rose by about 70 percent during the same period. Fourteen other African countries underwent a growth rate in population that surpassed their rate of growth in food production.

In recent years, agricultural scientists have worked to further increase world food production. They have set up programs to improve farming methods and to provide higher yields. They also have developed new types of grain that can be produced in greater abundance. However, much still has to be done. Many farmers in the Third World lack fertilizers and use primitive equipment and methods. Thus, there is a great need in developing nations for modern agricultural training and equipment.

Responsibility for Change

Many people today believe that the governments of the industrialized countries have a responsibility to help in solving the problems of the developing countries. They believe a determined effort should be made to share the earth's resources and to cooperate with the developing nations in planning the world's economic future. They stress the fact that both developed and developing nations are already dependent on each other. They must learn to work together to lessen the gap between them.

Others, however, stress that the industrialized countries have a primary responsibility to meet serious needs among their own people. They feel that the poverty of developing nations must be overcome. But, they state, the developed nations cannot be held accountable for achieving economic growth in developing countries. Poorer nations, themselves, through their own efforts have to improve their economic and social standards of living.

1. What characteristics distinguish developed from developing nations?
2. What factors have caused the sharp rise in world population during this century?
3. Why does hunger exist in today's world?

In 1983, central Africa suffered a devastating drought. Western foreign aid agencies distributed grain in an attempt to prevent famine. What programs have been set up to help developing countries increase their food supplies?

3 Natural Resources

In the past decade, there has been major concern about whether the amount of the world's natural resources is decreasing. The energy crisis of the 1970's highlighted this concern. At first attention was focused on petroleum oil. But before long, it was extended to other mineral resources. According to many experts, the **proven reserves** of most minerals, that is, the known mineral deposits that are profitable to mine, will be exhausted within one or two generations. This estimate is based on the present rate of consumption, or usage, of these mineral resources.

Point out that most machines use energy inefficiently. An average automobile engine, for example, uses only 20 percent of the energy available in gasoline. The rest is burned as wasted heat. Note that it is the challenge for future engineers to develop more efficient machines.

Experiments with underwater farming aimed at raising the productivity of the oceans is proving to be successful. Fish hatcheries and floating kelp farms will soon be able to add to world food resources. What other resources are being taken from the oceans?

Proven reserves, however, are only a small fraction of what the earth really has of these minerals. If new technology is developed and the costs of mining are lowered, engineers will be able to exploit new deposits. Also, if the relative prices rise, the amount of proven reserves will rise. On this basis, at the current rate of use, the world has enough oil and natural gas to last for more than 2,000 years. Iron will last for more than 4 million years and aluminum for more than 200 million years.

Oil

Since World War II, global demand for energy has increased due to the spread of industrialization and higher standards of living. Oil at first was relatively inexpensive, clean, and an easily attainable source of energy. As a result, the rate of increase in the demand for oil was higher than that for other energy sources. When oil prices jumped sharply during the 1970's, people were pressed to conserve their use of oil and to search for other energy-producing products. Many governments also developed plans to ration oil.

Unless oil is conserved or replaced with other sources, its production costs will steadily rise. Soon prices will reach a point at which oil will be too expensive to afford. Tar sand, shale rock, natural gas, and coal (all of which are plentiful in North America) can provide billions of barrels of liquid fuel. But, with current technology, the cost of extracting and processing these resources is becoming increasingly expensive. Perhaps in the future, scientists and engineers will develop ways that will make the use of these energy-producing products less costly. But until that time, the sensible choice is conservation and the use of alternate sources.

Studies show that in 40 minutes the sun delivers to the earth's surface enough energy for the world to use in a year. However, the energy is spread over too vast an area to be efficiently collected.

The oceans contain almost every mineral found on land.

Other Energy Sources

Researchers have been exploring old and new sources of energy for heating, lighting, and power. Special emphasis has been placed on providing renewable and clean energy.

Nuclear Power   During the past two decades, nuclear power plants have been built in more than 20 countries. The safety of these plants, however, has been questioned. During the late 1970's, several near accidents occurred in a few of them that could have been disastrous. The type of nuclear plants currently in use rely on **fission,** or the separation of nuclear particles, to generate energy. But nuclear fission also produces dangerous radioactive waste that is difficult to dispose of.

Nuclear **fusion,** or the combination of nuclear particles, produces far more energy and much less waste than nuclear fission. But the technology to harness this energy and to convert it into electricity is still in the stage of research and development. It may take 10 to 20 years or even more before it is ready for public use.

Solar Power   Solar energy is another option to which people have turned in recent years as a source of energy. Solar panels have been installed on houses and public buildings. These devices gather sunlight and convert it into usable energy for heating. However, there is still much to be done before solar technology can become a widely used source of clean and reliable energy.

Natural Sources   Researchers are also exploring new ways to improve our use of wind and water power. They also have developed resource recovery plants that burn solid waste and use the heat to generate electricity. These plants are operational and available to local communities at reasonable prices. Research is also underway to harness power from ocean tides and geothermal, or hot underground, springs.

Ocean Floor

An area that scientists have considered as a rich source of important minerals is the ocean floor. The world's oceans are estimated to contain 240 million tons (216 million metric tons) of cobalt, 6 billion tons (5.4 billion metric tons) of manganese, and 290 million tons (261 million metric tons) of nickel, to name just a few.

However, seabed mining is often very difficult. This is due not only to a lack of technology and high cost but also to international politics. In 1982, after many years of difficult negotiations, the UN Law of the Sea Conference approved a treaty. The treaty included provisions dealing

The increasing demand for the development of new sources of energy has led to research in a variety of areas. The solar furnace shown here is located in France. It is the most powerful in the world, having a capacity of one megawatt (1,000 kilowatts) of thermal energy. An arrangement of mirrors focuses the sunlight on an opening in the tower where temperatures of 7,000°F (3,870°C) can be produced. What other sources of energy are being explored?

Discuss the possibilities of gaining new natural resources by way of outer space development.

with the exploitation of minerals in the oceans. The nations supporting the treaty regard the seabed as the common heritage of humanity. They want to regulate its use so that the benefits of seabed mining are spread among the developing and developed nations alike. On the other hand, the United States and several western industrialized nations oppose the treaty. They claim that their private companies have been spending a great deal of money on research and development of sophisticated technology to mine the ocean floor. According to the United States, it would not be profitable for these companies to share the proceeds with others.

The Environment

The pressures of population and the growth of industry have had undesirable effects on the earth's physical environment. The building of dams and canals to irrigate dry, but fertile, land has increased the amount of crops. However, in many cases, such use threatens to ruin the soil. Salts and minerals accumulate in the stored water. As the water evaporates, salt and mineral deposits are left that often destroy the soil's fertility. Land has been ruined also as a result of overgrazing. In this case, animals have eaten or trampled the plant life that holds the topsoil in

place. When the wind blows, the topsoil is scattered, and the land eventually turns into desert.

Another problem is the widespread use and disposal of chemicals. Chemical products are used as pesticides, or agents to eliminate insects and animals that endanger crops. However, they also have destructive effects on other animals and humans. In addition, chemical wastes from factories and other sources have polluted, or poisoned, the air and water in many areas. One deadly form of pollution is **acid rain,** or rainwater containing poisonous industrial wastes. Acid rain has damaged forests and polluted lakes and rivers. It and other forms of pollution have killed animals as well as vegetation. Pollution in heavily industrialized regions has become a serious hazard to the health of humans.

A movement to halt the damage to the environment gathered force during the 1960's and 1970's. It was successful in arousing the concern of people in many countries. Laws were passed to check or reverse many of the destructive effects on the environment. Nevertheless, much still needs to be done in this area, particularly on the international level. All nations are affected by environmental problems; and developments in one country have a definite

The problem of acid rain is worldwide. Natural resources like lakes in Sweden and forests in Germany, as well as such human-made things as ancient sculptures in China, have all been adversely affected. Environmental protection groups are insisting that governments enact laws to check the burning of sulphuric coal, which causes 86 percent of the pollutants in acid rain. Many governments have anti-pollution laws, but environmental groups argue that the programs move too slowly. What are other causes of environmental pollution?

Analyze the literacy chart below. Have students determine ways to improve world literacy.

influence on another. An example is the dispute between the United States and Canada over acid rain. Canadians have complained that industrial pollution from the United States is destroying some of their country's forests, lakes, and wildlife. They urge the United States to impose stricter pollution controls on American industry. The United States government believes that Canadian claims are exaggerated. It refuses to take responsibility for what it views as Canada's problem.

1. What is the energy crisis, and what are its causes?
2. What alternative sources of energy are researchers investigating?
3. What are some of the present dangers to the physical environment?

4 Human Rights

In recent decades, the struggle for human rights has captured the attention of world governments and public opinion. Attitudes toward human rights, however, vary considerably around the globe. Nations often disagree about which rights are the most important to protect.

Since the end of World War II, the United Nations has been the principal organization involved in defining human rights. In 1948 the United Nations adopted the Declaration of Human Rights. In this document, the world organization requests member nations to strive to attain equal rights and better standards of life for all people.

Education

Until the last two decades, the majority of the world's population throughout history was illiterate. Furthermore, the majority of the illiterate were women. In this century, gains in education were made in Europe and North America long before they were made in Asia, Africa, and Latin America. Since the 1960's, however, rapid progress in education has been made in the Third World. Today, the majority of the world's people are literate. Education has ceased to be only a privilege and has become a right to all citizens of the globe. It has become an important means to achieve modernization.

Literacy Around the World

country	percent literate
Africa	
Algeria	25
Egypt	44
Ethiopia	5
Nigeria	38
South Africa (Africans)	50
South Africa (white)	99
Asia	
Bangladesh	24.3
India	29
Indonesia	66
Iran	37
Japan	99
Korea, South	90
Korea, North	90
Pakistan	24
Philippines	83
Thailand	82
Turkey	62
Europe	
France	97
Germany, East	99
Germany, West	99
Hungary	97
Italy	94
Netherlands	98
Poland	98
Romania	98.5
Spain	97
Great Britain	98.5
Yugoslavia	80.3
North America	
Canada	99.7
Mexico	74.5
United States	99
South America	
Argentina	85
Brazil	83
Chile	90
Colombia	73.5
Peru	47.5
Venezuela	74
Australia	99
Soviet Union	99

based on 1980 figures

During the 1960's and 1970's terrorists became a growing problem in many areas of the world. Terrorist groups supporting a variety of causes staged dramatic events in order to attract public attention. These Middle Eastern guerrillas proudly pose in front of a hijacked airplane flown to a desert airstrip in Jordan. Why has there been no international agreement on how to deal with terrorists?

Terrorism

Terrorism has emerged as a development that will shape events for the rest of this century. It has been called "the ultimate violation of human rights." Ordinary citizens are often harmed or killed by terrorist actions. A few of the victims are well-known business persons and diplomatic personnel. Many national groups in Western Europe, Latin America, Africa, and the Middle East live constantly with the danger of terrorist activity.

Terrorist acts sometimes have been carried out by an individual to satisfy a personal grievance. Most, however, are committed by political groups demanding certain rights on behalf of a people or a cause. Terrorists in these groups usually believe that they cannot achieve their goals by normal political means, so they resort to violence.

Terrorist Tactics   The purpose of terrorism is to scare opponents and force them to accept terrorist demands. Hijackings, bombings, kidnappings, murders, and armed attacks on embassies and government buildings are the common methods used by terrorists to achieve their goals.

In some cases terrorists have the support of large groups of people. They are often viewed as freedom fighters rather than terrorists. Most terrorists are linked to an international network that supplies training, weapons, money, and forged documents.

International terrorists hold many differing political opinions. Some are anarchists. Others support a new social order based on Marxist ideas. Many terrorists represent ethnic, religious, and nationalistic causes.

Although most people are not affected directly by terrorism, it has had an indirect influence on their lives. Regular searches of clothing and baggage take place before boarding a plane. Security measures for world leaders have been tightened, making them less accessible to the public. Business people and diplomats may be restricted in work and travel.

Policies Toward Terrorism   Governments have worked out different ways of dealing with terrorists. Some have followed a policy of giving in to terrorist demands in order to save lives. A more common tendency today is to follow a hard-line policy of refusing to cooperate with terrorists. This often involves answering force with force. Many countries, such as Britain, Israel, and Germany, have special police and army units to deal with the problem.

Most governments officially want to end terrorism, but no international agreement exists on how to deal with it. Government officials cannot agree whether terrorists should be treated as criminals or political offenders.

Political differences among nations also cloud the issue of terrorism. Many nations claim that they are opposed to terrorist acts in principle no matter what the terrorist motives might be. They want international agreements to punish the offenders. However, in certain instances, they will support terrorist groups that might seem to advance their interests. Other nations openly admit their belief that some terrorist acts are legitimate if the cause is just. They often view terrorism as a tool of revolution against outside influence and control.

Refugees

Since 1900, wars and various other upheavals have uprooted millions of people. In fact, the twentieth century has sometimes been called "the century of refugees." Refugees flee from one place to another to find protection and safety. Cubans, Poles, Southeast Asians, and Palestinians are only a few of the groups that have been refugees from their homelands in the past few decades. Some have found new homes. Others, such as the Palestinians and Southeast Asians, have spent years in refugee camps. That is, they have been people without a country.

In the past, most refugees were seeking to escape persecution on account of their race, religion, or politics. In recent years, most refugees are seeking to escape the poor economic conditions in their homelands brought about by war, social upheaval, or merely lack of economic development.

Developed nations, however, have become ever more reluctant to accept the increasing flow of refugees, immigrants, or aliens of any type. Here, developed nations often make a definite distinction between refugees and immigrants. Refugees flee their homeland, frequently in large numbers. Often they lack passports and other legal documents necessary to travel between countries. Immigrants, on the other hand, have gone through a legal process to move and become a resident, perhaps a citizen, of another country.

For the nations of the world, the problem is one of controlling their borders, their popula-tion, and the possible burden on their economies that refugees and immigrants may impose. In Germany, Britain, and the United States alike, growing numbers of citizens have charged that their nations can no longer afford to accept a flood of people. Yet, others argue that democratic societies have an obligation to accept newcomers seeking freedom from political oppression or economic distress.

The Shape of Tomorrow

Many scientists refer to current changes in science and technology as the "technological revolution." These developments are called a revolution because of the great impact they are having on nearly every aspect of our lives.

As new technology is developed, it raises the general level of productivity. It also eliminates

The "boat people" endure many hardships in their efforts to reach safety. If they are resettled within a year or two, they are fortunate. Why are some developed nations unwilling to accept these refugees into their countries?

old jobs and creates new ones at a pace faster than any that the world has ever experienced. The results of this process affect both economic and social relations. There will be fewer traditional and manufacturing jobs. More leisure time will be available. The average workweek may drop to 30 or fewer hours, making vacations longer and more frequent. People will have to consider how they will use their "free time." Will they enjoy themselves with visual entertainment, sports, and travel, or will their lives be filled with boredom? Opportunities for personal growth and advancement will broaden the scope of rights that people may claim as their own. Some people are beginning to speak of rights to have a job, medical care, decent housing, and an adequate diet. There is mounting pressure to increase public expenditures to provide equal opportunities to everyone, wherever they live.

The earth is not short of resources and people are not short of resourcefulness. Humanity has survived and progressed in spite of adversities and serious setbacks. Hopefully, this can be a source of optimism as people face the challenges of the future.

1. Why has terrorism been called "the ultimate violation of human rights"?
2. How have governments tried to deal with terrorism?
3. Why has the twentieth century been called "the century of refugees"? What problems have twentieth-century refugees faced?

CHAPTER 33 REVIEW

Summary

1. The nations of the world face many important international issues that will affect the development, and even the survival, of human civilization.
2. Since 1945 the superpowers and other nations have competed in an arms race. This race continues in spite of arms control agreements; it has produced widespread concern about the dangers of nuclear war.
3. Another nuclear danger is the proliferation, or spread, of nuclear weapons to previously non-nuclear countries.
4. Global tensions have led to a worldwide trade in military weapons. The United States and the Soviet Union are major suppliers of military weapons to Third World countries.
5. Vast differences in wealth exist among the nations. The economically developed nations belong to either the western or the Communist blocs. The economically developing nations of Asia, Africa, Latin America, and the Middle East belong to the Third World.

6. The world's cities, particularly in the Third World, are facing enormous social problems due to their growing populations. Food and other population-related crises place many burdens on developing nations and threaten their economic development.
7. Industrialized nations depend on developing nations for raw materials and the export of manufactured goods.
8. Developing nations are demanding changes in the world economy that will end the unequal distribution of the world's wealth and improve their standards of living.
9. The energy crisis has led to a search for alternative energy sources. Attempts have also been made to begin to protect the environment from industrial pollution.
10. The protection of human rights has become a major concern in the last half of the twentieth century. Governments are seeking ways to check the worldwide growth of terrorism. Another human rights issue is that of refugees.

Building Vocabulary

futurologists	arms control	nuclear reactors	proven reserves
overkill	ceilings	developed nations	fission
deterrence	nuclear freeze	developing nations	fusion
parity	nuclear proliferation	revolution of rising expectations	acid rain

Reviewing the Main Ideas

1. Why do the superpowers engage in an arms race in spite of the increased danger of nuclear war?
2. Why have Third World nations been able to increase their supply of weapons?
3. Where does the population growth reach its highest level in the world? Why?
4. What changes do developing countries want to make in the global economy?
5. Why did the consumption of petroleum oil rise rapidly after World War II?
6. What happens to the proven reserves of minerals if their relative prices increase?
7. Why did the United States object to the Law of the Sea treaty?
8. What positions do the United States and Canada take regarding the harmful effects of acid rain?
9. How has terrorism affected people's lives?
10. How have people in nations such as Germany, Britain, and the United States responded to the arrival of refugees?

Discussing Important Ideas

1. Do you favor a continuation of nuclear arms talks between the United States and the Soviet Union? Explain.
2. If you were a world political leader, what steps would you take to lessen the dangers of nuclear war?
3. What do you think can be done to reduce the economic gap between the developed and developing countries?
4. In your opinion, how should the world deal with the problems of housing and hunger?
5. Is nuclear power a desirable source of energy? Why or why not?
6. Do you feel that terrorism can ever be justified? Explain your answer.
7. How should the world's nations handle the refugee problem?
8. What is your forecast for the future?

Using Graphs

Refer to the graph on page 775 to answer the following questions:
1. What do the horizontal bars represent? Why are they different colors?
2. About how many persons were living in East Asia in 1980? in Latin America?
3. What area of the world had the highest population in 1980?
4. What area is projected to more than double its population between 1980 and 2000?
5. Which area's population is growing at the slowest rate?

UNIT 8 REVIEW

Summary

1. After World War II, the United States and the Soviet Union emerged as superpowers and competed for global influence by means short of total war.
2. In the late 1940's and early 1950's, the United States helped rebuild Western Europe and Japan, which soon developed prosperous economies. Western Europe and Japan became allies of the United States in seeking to contain communism and to advance democratic values.
3. During the late 1940's, the Soviet Union set up Communist governments in Eastern Europe. Eastern Europeans have been restless under Soviet controls, and the Soviets often have had to use force to put down opposition to the government.
4. In the post-World War II era, Communist governments came to power in China and other Asian lands. Feuding between China and the Soviet Union led China to improve its relations with the West and to modernize its economy without Soviet aid.
5. After World War II, European empires ended in Asia and Africa. Former colonies became independent. They declared themselves nonaligned in the cold war and be-

gan to develop their economies with aid from western and Communist nations.
6. Since the late 1940's, nationalism—often anti-American in tone—has grown in Latin America. While many leaders work for peaceful reforms, revolutionary movements led by Cuba and Nicaragua call for more radical changes in Latin American societies.
7. In the 1960's a world of independent regional groups emerged in which the superpowers could no longer control events.
8. By the early 1980's, the strategically valuable and oil-rich Middle East had become the world's leading crisis area due to the continuing Arab-Israeli conflict and the growing political turmoil in the Persian Gulf region.
9. Twentieth-century culture reached a new high of technological power and scientific knowledge. In the arts, a variety of new forms and techniques flourished to express individual feelings, to protest social injustice, and to promote political ideology.
10. In the early 1980's, the world's nations faced the challenges of preventing another world war, ending poverty and social injustice, and effectively using natural resources.

Developing Understanding

1. What were the policies of the superpowers that resulted in the cold war?
2. Why did the containment policy work in Europe but not in Southeast Asia?
3. How did the rise of independent countries in Asia, Africa, and Latin America affect the postwar balance of power in the world?
4. What role has Japan played in the world economy since World War II?
5. Why are the intellectual and artistic achievements of the twentieth century often considered revolutionary?
6. What achievements have been made in human rights during the postwar era?

Developing Skills

When historians develop differing interpretations of events, it is often due to the fact that they have different frames of reference. That is, their viewpoints have been subject to many influences, including the time period in which they write.

One example of the way frame of reference can influence interpretation can be found in the history of the cold war. In the 1950's, the accepted view of this conflict (in the West, of course, not in the Soviet Union) was that it arose as a response of the free world to Communist aggression. By the mid-1960's, some historians (called revisionists) were taking a new look at the history of the cold war and raising questions about the responsibility of the United States.

The first of the following readings was published in 1955 and is an example of the traditional view. The second, published in 1970, is an example of the revisionist view. To understand the frame of reference of each, answer these questions:

1. How strong was the anti-Communist mood in the United States in the 1950's? Why?
2. What new developments in the cold war had taken place by 1970? How did these developments influence perceptions?
3. How do the readings reflect the moods and perceptions of the time periods in which they were written?

Reading 1

The Soviet Union, unique in its power position in two continents, had demonstrated beyond any doubt that it was aggressive and expanding, and that its immediate design for dominion included as much of Europe and Asia and North Africa as it could get away with short of war with its Western allies. As the Russians had rolled the Germans back westward from Stalingrad, they had consistently subordinated military objectives to long-range political goals, whereas the United States and Great Britain had usually done the opposite. The consequence was that the Red armies had "liberated" or occupied all of Central Europe westward to the Elbe and all of the Balkans except Greece. . . . Wherever Soviet control had been extended, it stayed and reinforced itself.

The wartime alliance was clearly dead, and remained only to be officially buried. The bad public manners of the Russians toward their al-

lies at the San Francisco Conference progressed in succeeding months to [accusation], slander, and thence to full-scale, official propaganda warfare against the West. Stalin himself, in a public speech on February 9, 1946, formally launched the cold war on capitalist countries.*

Reading 2

We may pause in our review to reflect upon the historical fact that both the United States decision to oppose radical governments in Eastern Europe and the policy of opposition to the Soviet Union itself can ultimately be explained only by reference to the older, persistent tradition of opposition to revolutions of the left. The mix of ideas which guided men in the mid-twentieth century were the product of a long and continuous historical evolution. They must be understood if we are to comprehend how millions of Americans came so easily after World War II to permit the enormous waste and irrationality of the Cold War. And this requires that we study the forces, economic interests, and strategies which propelled American policy, ultimately, into such dubious posture around the globe. How, over the course of the century, did it come about that Americans—people of a rather insulated continent—came somehow to believe in the early postwar years their vital interests might depend on whether, for example, their government supported or opposed the bankrupt monarchy of R[o]mania—or, more recently, the military rulers of South Vietnam?

As we ponder such questions it is also important to remember that the purpose of reviewing the Cold War—and of focusing on American policies—is not to apportion credit and blame for the dreary history of the last twenty-five years, still less to condone the inhumanities and imperialism of Soviet policy. It is rather to understand how we got to where we now are—and to recall that the issues in dispute between the United States and the Soviet Union at the outset were very traditional ones.

(continued next page)

**The Fifteen Weeks,* Joseph M. Jones, © 1955 by Viking Press, pp. 40-41.

*They did not involve a general threat of Moscow-directed expansion to achieve global revolution. (The Russians were incredibly docile on that issue, as their acceptance of Chiang Kai-shek in China, reaction in Greece, and even the monarchy in Italy revealed.) At issue were very specific and very old questions in Eastern Europe—and the primary policy initiative came from the United States.**

Cold War Essays, Gar Alperovitz, © 1970 by Anchor Books, Doubleday, Inc., pp. 101-102

Suggested Activities

1. Imagine that you were the Soviet representative to the UN at the time of one of the following invasions: (a) Hungary, 1956 (b) Czechoslovakia, 1968 (c) Afghanistan, 1979. How would you have answered criticism of your country's action?

2. Debate either of the following questions: (a) "Is Israel justified in establishing settlements on the West Bank?" (b) "Do the Palestinian Arabs have a right to their own state?"

3. Prepare a time line for the significant events that have affected relations among the Soviet Union, the People's Republic of China, and the United States since World War II.

4. Develop a visual presentation illustrating the globalization of culture.

5. Write and give a report that compares and contrasts the origin, development, and practice of nonviolent social protest philosophies of Mohandas Gandhi and Martin Luther King, Jr.

6. Participate in a panel discussion on the toxic waste dump problem in the United States. Be sure to represent the Environmental Protection Agency, a major chemical company, and a national environmental group. Discuss the historical roots of the problem, its current status, and possible remedies.

Suggested Readings

Botting, Douglas. *The Aftermath*. New York: Time-Life Books, Inc., 1983. Discusses developments in postwar Europe from 1945 to 1950.

Collins, Larry and La Pierre, Dominique. *Freedom at Midnight*. New York: Simon and Schuster, 1975. Presents the Indian subcontinent at the time of independence.

Morton, W. Scott. *The Japanese: How They Live and Work*. New York: Praeger, 1973. Presents modern Japan.

Goodsell, James N. *Fidel Castro's Personal Revolution in Cuba*. New York: Knopf, 1975. Relates the impact of Castro's revolution on Cuba and the rest of Latin America.

Helitzer, Morrie. *The Cold War*. New York: Watts, 1977. Discusses Soviet-American relations from 1945 to the late 1970's.

MacDonald, Malcolm. *Inside China*. Boston: Little, Brown, and Company, 1980. Focuses on daily life in contemporary China.

APPENDIX

Atlas

Glossary

Index

ARCTIC OCEAN

ALASKA
(UNITED STATES)

C A N A D A

NORTH

AMERICA

UNITED STATES

Ottawa

New York

Washington, D.C.

Los Angeles

M
E
X
I
C
O

HAWAII
(U.S.)

Mexico City

BAHAMAS

CUBA
DOMINICAN
REPUBLIC

HAITI
JAMAICA

BELIZE
HONDURAS
GUATEMALA
EL SALVADOR
NICARAGUA

COSTA RICA
PANAMA

Caracas

VENEZUELA

TRINIDAD
AND
TOBAGO

GUYANA
SURINAME
FR. GUIANA

Bogotá
COLOMBIA

ECUADOR

PERU

Lima

SOUTH

BRAZIL

AMERICA

Brasilia

BOLIVIA

PARAGUAY

Santiago

A
R
G
E
N
T
I
N
A

C
H
I
L
E

URUGUAY

Buenos Aires

PACIFIC

OCEAN

EQUATOR

ATLANTIC

OCEAN

ICELAND

UNITED
KINGDOM
IRELAND

London

NET
BE
P
FRAN

DE

PORTUGAL
SPAIN

Madrid

MOROCCO

ALGER

MAURITANIA

MALI

A F

SENEGAL
CAPE
VERDE
GUINEA-BISSAU
SIERRA LEONE
LIBERIA

GAMBIA
GUINEA

U
VOLTA
IVORY
COAST
GHANA

BE
TO

CAM
EQUAT. G
G

CA
(AN

TU

INTERNATIONAL DATE LINE

PRIME MERIDIAN

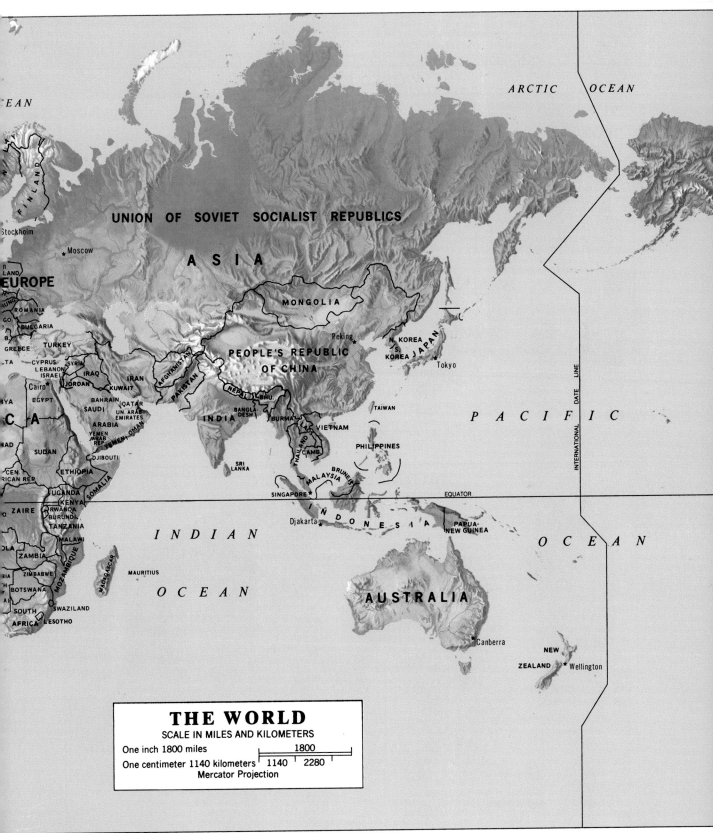

THE WORLD
SCALE IN MILES AND KILOMETERS

One inch 1800 miles

One centimeter 1140 kilometers

Mercator Projection

WORLD CLIMATES

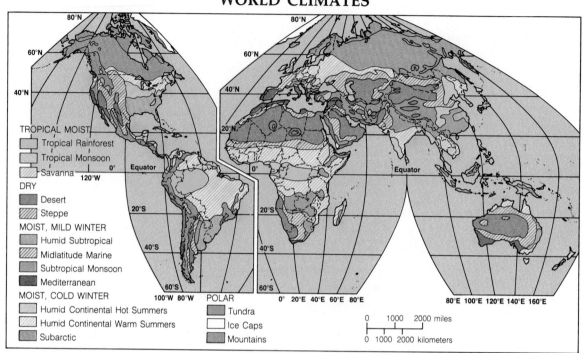

TROPICAL MOIST
- Tropical Rainforest
- Tropical Monsoon
- Savanna

DRY
- Desert
- Steppe

MOIST, MILD WINTER
- Humid Subtropical
- Midlatitude Marine
- Subtropical Monsoon
- Mediterranean

MOIST, COLD WINTER
- Humid Continental Hot Summers
- Humid Continental Warm Summers
- Subarctic

POLAR
- Tundra
- Ice Caps
- Mountains

NATURAL VEGETATION

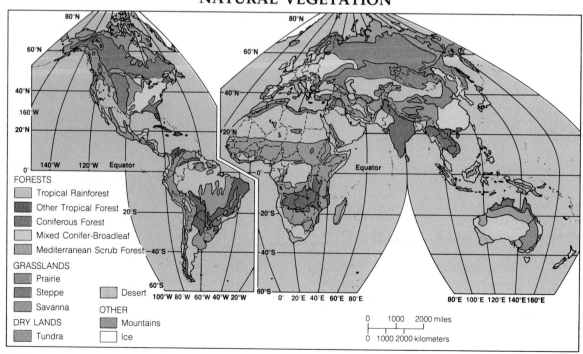

FORESTS
- Tropical Rainforest
- Other Tropical Forest
- Coniferous Forest
- Mixed Conifer-Broadleaf
- Mediterranean Scrub Forest

GRASSLANDS
- Prairie
- Steppe
- Savanna

DRY LANDS
- Tundra
- Desert

OTHER
- Mountains
- Ice

WORLD LAND USE

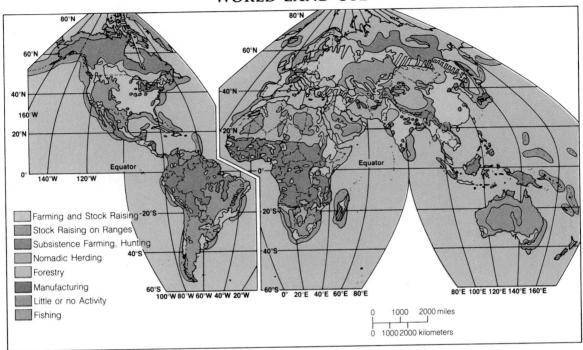

Farming and Stock Raising
Stock Raising on Ranges
Subsistence Farming, Hunting
Nomadic Herding
Forestry
Manufacturing
Little or no Activity
Fishing

0   1000   2000 miles
0   1000 2000 kilometers

MAJOR NATURAL RESOURCES

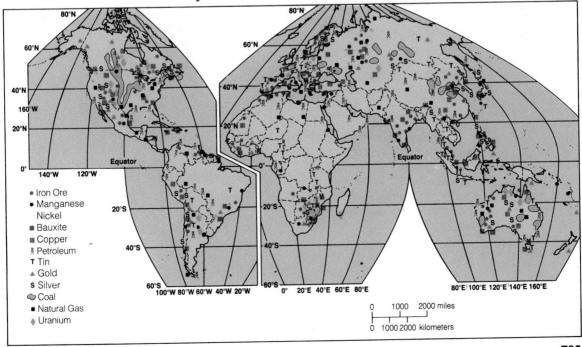

• Iron Ore
• Manganese
  Nickel
■ Bauxite
■ Copper
⚒ Petroleum
т Tin
▲ Gold
s Silver
⬡ Coal
■ Natural Gas
⬧ Uranium

0   1000   2000 miles
0   1000 2000 kilometers

WORLD POPULATION DENSITY

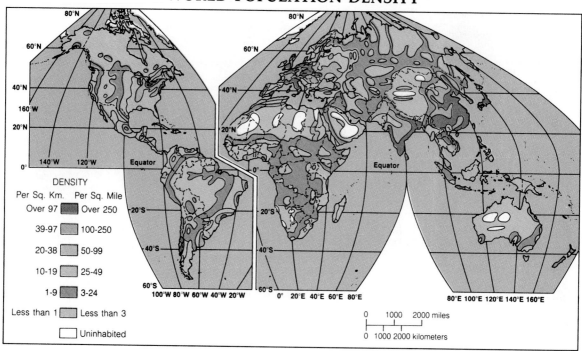

DENSITY

Per Sq. Km.		Per Sq. Mile
Over 97		Over 250
39-97		100-250
20-38		50-99
10-19		25-49
1-9		3-24
Less than 1		Less than 3
		Uninhabited

0   1000   2000 miles

0 1000 2000 kilometers

WORLD DISTRIBUTION OF WEALTH

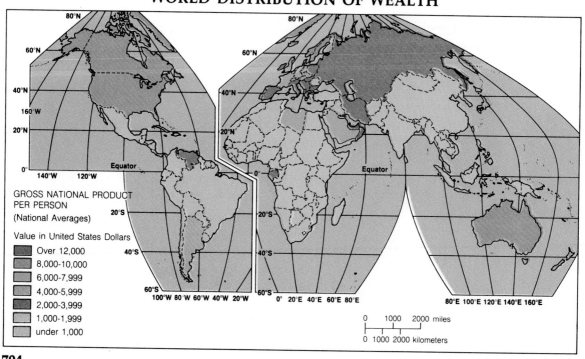

GROSS NATIONAL PRODUCT
PER PERSON
(National Averages)

Value in United States Dollars

	Over 12,000
	8,000-10,000
	6,000-7,999
	4,000-5,999
	2,000-3,999
	1,000-1,999
	under 1,000

0   1000   2000 miles

0 1000 2000 kilometers

MAJOR RELIGIONS

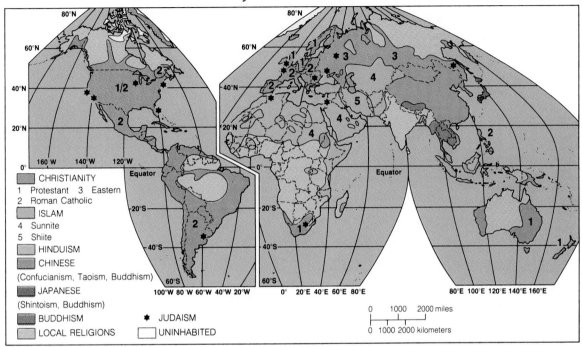

CHRISTIANITY
1 Protestant 3 Eastern
2 Roman Catholic

ISLAM
4 Sunnite
5 Shiite

HINDUISM

CHINESE
(Confucianism, Taoism, Buddhism)

JAPANESE
(Shintoism, Buddhism)

BUDDHISM ✱ JUDAISM

LOCAL RELIGIONS UNINHABITED

0   1000   2000 miles
0 1000 2000 kilometers

MAJOR LANGUAGES

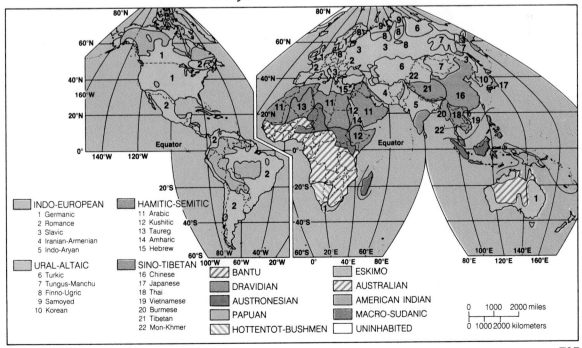

INDO-EUROPEAN
1 Germanic
2 Romance
3 Slavic
4 Iranian-Armenian
5 Indo-Aryan

URAL-ALTAIC
6 Turkic
7 Tungus-Manchu
8 Finno-Ugric
9 Samoyed
10 Korean

HAMITIC-SEMITIC
11 Arabic
12 Kushitic
13 Taureg
14 Amharic
15 Hebrew

SINO-TIBETAN
16 Chinese
17 Japanese
18 Thai
19 Vietnamese
20 Burmese
21 Tibetan
22 Mon-Khmer

BANTU
DRAVIDIAN
AUSTRONESIAN
PAPUAN
HOTTENTOT-BUSHMEN

ESKIMO
AUSTRALIAN
AMERICAN INDIAN
MACRO-SUDANIC
UNINHABITED

0   1000   2000 miles
0 1000 2000 kilometers

N

Laptev Sea

EURASIA
SCALE IN MILES AND KILOMETERS
One inch 600 miles
One centimeter 380 kilometers

600

380 | 760

Parabolic Equal Area Projection

70°

Lena

Verkhoyansk

S I B E R I A

River

KOLYMA MOUNTAINS

60°

KAMCHATKA PENINSULA

STANOVOY MOUNTAINS

Sea of Okhotsk

Krasnoyarsk

sibirsk

SOCIALIST   REPUBLICS

Lake Baikal

Irkutsk

SAYAN MOUNTAINS

Amur

River

Khabarovsk

50°

KURIL
ISLANDS

Ulan Bator

Pinkiang
(Harbin)

Vladivostok

HOKKAIDO

ke
hash

a-Ata

MONGOLIA

*GOBI
DESERT*

M A N C H U R I A

Shenyang
(Mukden)

NORTH
KOREA

*Sea
of Japan*

J
A
P
A
N

40°

Beijing
(Peking)

Luda
(Dairen)

Pyongyang

HONSHU

PAMIRS

TAKLA
MAKAN

NAN SHAN

Huang

Tianjin
(Tientsin)

*Yellow
Sea*

Seoul

SOUTH
KOREA

Pusan

Kyoto

Tokyo

Kobe Osaka

KUNLUN MOUNTAINS

C H I N A

He

TSINLING SHAN

Xi'an
(Sian)

Qingdao
(Tsingtao)

Nanjing
(Nanking)

KYUSHU

SHIKOKU

Islamabad

PLATEAU OF TIBET

Mekong River

Chang Jiang

Wuhan
(Wuhan)

Shanghai
(Shanghai)

30°

Lahore

Lhasa

Mt. Everest
29,141'

SZECHWAN

BASIN

*Tungting
Hu*

*East
China
Sea*

ISTAN

HIMA

NEPAL

BHUTAN

Brahmaputra R.

Chongqing
(Chunking)

OKINAWA

Delhi

New Delhi

Ganges

Lucknow

Katmandu

River

NAGA HILLS

Xi Jiang

Guangzhou
(Canton)

Taipei

THAR
DESERT

Kanpur

BANGLA-
DESH

Dacca

Red River

Hanoi

Victoria
(Hong Kong)

TAIWAN

Formosa Strait

TROPIC OF CANCER

Ahmadabad

Nagpur

Calcutta

Mandalay

*Gulf of
Tonkin*

20°

Jaipur

I N D I A

BURMA

S O U T H

REPUBLIC
OF THE
PHILIPPINES

Bombay

Pune

Bay of Bengal

Irrawaddy R.

Vientiane

L
A
O
S

VIETNAM

C H I N A

N

WESTERN

Hyderabad

Rangoon

THAILAND

S E A

Manila

GHATS

Bangalore

Madras

EASTERN

GHATS

Bangkok

CAMBODIA

Phnom Penh

*Tonle Sap
Gulf of
Siam*

Ho Chi Minh City
(Saigon)

10°

SRI LANKA

Colombo

*MALAY
PENINSULA*

MALDIVES

M A L A Y S I A

BRUNEI

Kuala
Lumpur

797

N D I A N   O C E A N

SINGAPORE

Singapore

0°

REPUBLIC OF INDONESIA

70°   80°   90°   100°   110°   120°   130°

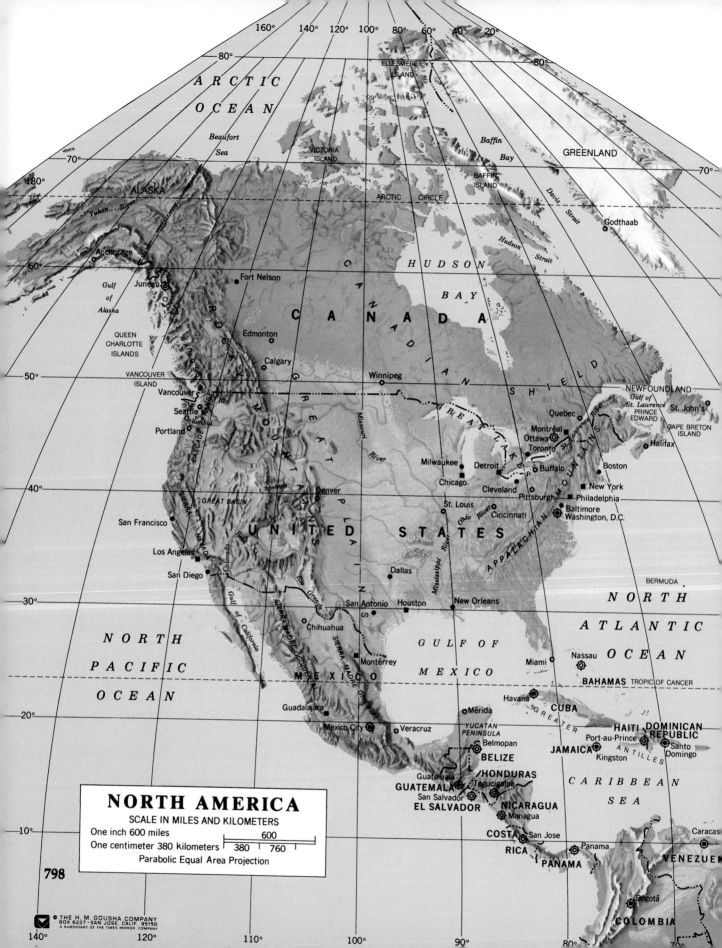

NORTH AMERICA

SCALE IN MILES AND KILOMETERS

One inch 600 miles

One centimeter 380 kilometers

600

380   760

Parabolic Equal Area Projection

798

THE H. M. GOUSHA COMPANY
BOX 6227 · SAN JOSE, CALIF. 95150
A SUBSIDIARY OF THE TIMES MIRROR COMPANY

SOUTH AMERICA

SCALE IN MILES AND KILOMETERS

One inch 600 miles

One centimeter 380 kilometers

600

380 | 760

Parabolic Equal Area Projection

799

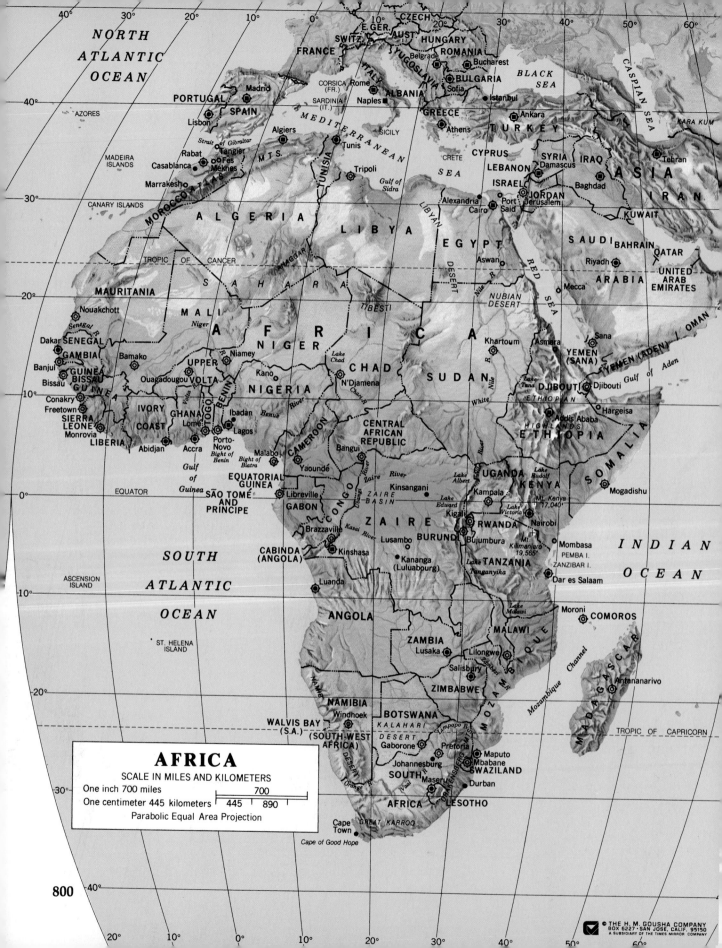

AFRICA

SCALE IN MILES AND KILOMETERS

One inch 700 miles

One centimeter 445 kilometers | 445 | 890 | 700

Parabolic Equal Area Projection

Glossary

A

abbot (ab′ uht)   monastery head

abdicated (ab′ duh kā tuhd)   gave up right to govern

aboriginals (ab uh rij′ uh nuhlz)   original natives of Australia

absolutism (ab′ suh lū tiz uhm)   political theory that states that monarchs hold supreme power and are responsible for their actions to God alone

acid rain   rainwater containing poisonous industrial wastes

acropolis (uh krop′ uh lis)   fortified hill

acupuncture (ak′ yū pungk chuhr)   method of treating pain by piercing the skin with needles at vital points

adobe (uh dō′ bē)   sun-dried brick

agora (ag′ uh ruh)   public square

aids   vassal's obligations to a lord

alliance (uh lī′ uhns) **systems**   international combinations of states

alphabet (al′ fuh bet)   series of symbols that represent sounds

amnesty (am′ nuh stē)   general pardon

anarchy (an′ uhr kē)   no government or institutions

apartheid (uh part′ hīt)   strict social policy separating the races

apostles (uh pos′ uhlz)   Christian missionaries

appeasement (uh pēz′ muhnt)   granting concessions to maintain peace

apprentices (uh pren′ tis uhz)   young workers learning a trade

arabesque (ār uh besk′)   type of decoration used to decorate books, rugs, swords, and entire walls

arbitration (ar buh trā′ shuhn)   settlement by a third party that is agreeable to both sides

archeologists (ar kē ol′ uh jists)   scientists who search for sites that contain the remains of past cultures

archbishops (arch′ bish′ uhps)   leading bishops in the Christian Church

archipelago (ar kuh pel′ uh gō)   chain of islands

archives (ar′ kīvz)   public records

archon (ar′ kon)   Greek official who supervised government administration

armistice (ar′ muh stis)   temporary halt of hostilities by mutual consent

arms control   limiting the use of weapons in certain locations and under certain conditions

arms race   competition to strengthen armed forces and weapons systems

arraigned (uh rānd′)   brought to court to answer charges

artifacts (ar′ tuh faktz)   objects made by humans

aristocrats (uh ris′ tuh kratz)   nobles who owned land

assimilate (uh sim′ uh lāt)   absorb

astrolabe (as′ truh lāb)   navigational tool used to determine latitude

attrition (uh trish′ uhn)   wearing down

authoritarian (uh thor uh tār′ ē uhn)   government of strict authority

autocracy (o tok′ ruh sē)   absolute rule

automation (o tuh mā′ shuhn)   use of machines

autonomy (o ton′ uh mē)   self-government

autos da fe (o′ duhz duh fā′)   public rituals of sentencing usually followed by executions during the Spanish Inquisition

avant-garde (o vont-gard′)   people who create new ideas and techniques

B

bailiffs (bā′ lifs)   royal agents that presided over local courts, collected taxes, and commanded military forces

balance of power   nations have equal power

balance of trade   nation's exports versus its imports

bards (bardz)   storytellers

baroque (buh rōk′)   "bizarre"; style of art in reaction to mannerism

basilicas (buh sil′ uh kuhz)   Roman assembly halls; models for early Christian churches

bazaar (buh zar′)   marketplace

beatniks (bēt′ niks)   nonconformists who felt alienated by American prosperity and material values

bedouins (bed′ ū uhnz)   Arab peoples who roamed the desert in search of pasture and water

belligerent (buh lij′ uh ruhnt)   fighting

bicameral (bī kam′ uh ruhl)   two-house legislature

billet (bil′ uht)   to board and lodge

bipolarism (bī pō′ luh riz uhm)   domination of world affairs by two superpowers

bishop (bish' uhp)   head of a diocese

blitz (blits)   series of air raids

blitzkrieg (blit' skrēg)   German strategy aimed at taking the enemy by surprise

blood feuds (fyūdz)   quarrels in which an injured tribe seeks revenge against an opponent

booty (bū' tē)   war prizes

bourgeois (būr zhwo')   members of the bourgeoisie

bourgeoisie (būr zhwo zē')   middle class

boyars (bō yarz')   councils of wealthy merchants and landed nobles

brahmans (bra' muhnz)   Aryan priests

buffer (buf' uhr)   neutral

bullion (būl' yuhn)   gold and silver; money

bunker (bung' kuhr)   fortified underground chamber or rooms

bureaucracy (byū rok' ruh sē)   branch of government that administers public policy

bureaucrats (byūr' uh kratz)   government officials

burgesses (ber' juh suhz)   important townspeople

burghers (ber' guhrz)   townspeople

bushido (bū shē' dō)   samurai code of honor

buying on the margin   buying stocks on credit

C

cabinet   small group of advisers

caliph (kā' lif)   Muslim leader

caliphate (kal' uh fāt)   office of caliph

calligraphy (kuh lig' ruh fē)   the art of elegant handwriting

cantons (kan' tuhnz)   districts

capital (kap' uh tuhl)   money to invest in labor, machines, and raw materials to produce goods and services

capitalism (kap' uh tuh liz uhm)   economic system in which the means of production are privately owned

capitalists (kap' uh tuh lists)   investors

cardinals (kard'n uhlz)   clergy of Rome

cash and carry   when foreign country pays cash for goods and transports them in their own ships

categorical imperative (kat uh gor' uh kuhl im per' uh tiv)   Kant's moral principle

caudillos (kou thē' yōz)   military dictators

ceilings   limits

censors (sen' suhrz)   keepers of tax and population records

centuries (sen' chuhr ēz)   military units of 100 men each

chancellor (chan' suh luhr)   chief minister

chansons de geste (sho sōnz' duh zhest)   French epic poems celebrating courage of feudal warriors

charters (char' tuhrz)   documents giving burghers control of their own affairs

chateaux (sha tōz')   French castles

chinampas (chuh nam' puhz)   artificial islands

chivalry (shiv' uhl rē)   code of behavior for knights

choreographer (kor ē og' ruh fuhr)   dance arranger

chronicles (kron' uh kuhlz)   lists of events arranged by year

churches   Christian communities formed for worship, fellowship, and instruction

citadel (sit' uh duhl)   fortress

civil disobedience   refusal to obey laws that are considered unjust

civil service (siv' uhl ser' vis)   bureaucracy in which officials are hired on the basis of examinations

clans   groups based on family ties

classical (klas' uh kuhl)   Greek or Roman

clergy (kler' jē)   church officials

coalition (kō uh lish' uhn)   alliance

cold war   attempt by opposing powers to gain world influence by means short of total war

collective bargaining   negotiations between employers and employees about wages and working conditions

collective security   what is needed to defend a group's common interests against enemy attack

collectivization (kuh lek' ti viz ā shuhn)   joint ownership of land

collegia (kuh lē' jē uh)   groups of Roman artisans that provided social and business services to members

colonae (kol' uh nī)   Roman fortified camps

colonies (kol' uh nēz)   permanent settlements

colons (kō' lonz)   settlers

comedian (kuh mē' dē uhn)   writer of comedies

comedy (kom' uh dē)   play with a humorous theme and a happy ending

commoners (kom' uh nuhrz)   non-nobles

common law   same legal rules for all parts of England

commons   public land

communes (kom' yūnz)   1. political groups that ended the power of feudal lords in twelfth-century Italy; made Italian towns independent city-states 2. rural cooperative farms

communism (kom' yuh niz uhm)   political ideology based on the ideas of Marx and Lenin

compass (kum' puhs)   navigational tool used to determine geographical direction

compensation (kohm puhn sā' shuhn)   payment

concentration camps   large prison camps in Nazi Germany

condottieri (kon do tye rē')   mercenary soldiers of Italian city-states

confederation (kuhn fed uh rā′ shuhn) league of independent states

congress system (kong′ gris sis′ tuhm) Concert of Europe or the Metternich system

conquistadores (kon kē′ stuh dor′ ēz) Spanish conquerors

consciousness-raising (kon′ shuhs nis rāz′ ing) self-awareness

conscripted (kuhn skrip′tuhd) drafted

constitutional monarchy (kon stuh tū′ shuh nuhl mon′ uhr kē) monarchy limited in its powers by a constitution

consul (kon′ suhl) diplomatic official

consuls (kon′ suhlz) two Roman executive officials elected for one-year terms

containment (kuhn tān′ muhnt) foreign policy designed to hold back the spread of communism

contraband (kon′ truh band) prohibited goods

contras (kahn′ truhz) Nicaraguan rebels

convoy technique (kon′ voi tek nēk′) group of ships surrounded by warships to protect them during wartime

copra (kō′ pruh) coconut products

cordon sanitaire (kor don′ san uh tār′) quarantine line

corporate (kor′ puhr it) **state** government of representation by industry instead of by political party or geographical area

corregidores (kuh re guh dōr′ ez) officials of Castile and Aragon

counter-revolutionaries (koun′ tuhr-rev uh lū′ shuh ner ēz) enemies of a revolution

cortes (kor tez′) representative assemblies in Castile and Aragon

counts local officials

coup d'etat (kū dā to′) sudden use of force by a small group to overthrow a government

covenant (kuv′ uh nuhnt) agreement

creoles (krē′ ōlz) in Spanish colonial America, Spaniards born in the colonies

crucified (krū′ suh fīd) Roman form of execution

cubism (kyū′ biz uhm) abstract art form that uses intersecting cubes and cones

cultural diffusion (kul′ chuhr uhl di fyū′ zhuhn) exchange of ideas and customs among different regions

culture (kul′ chuhr) human ways of living

culture area region that contains tribes with similar cultures

culture system use of forced labor to run an economy

cuneiform (kyū nē′ uh form) Sumerian system of writing

D

daimyo (di′ myō) group of powerful samurai

dasyus (dos′ yūs) enslaved people who performed manual labor for the Aryans

decipher (di sī′ fuhr) decode

de facto (di fak′ tō) actual

defected (di fekt′ uhd) escaped

deism (dē′ iz uhm) religion based on reason and natural law

delta (del′ tuh) fan-shaped area of swampy land

demographic (dem uh graf′ ik) population

depression (di presh′ uhn) economic decline

détente (dā tont′) period of mutual understanding and relaxation of tensions

deter (di ter′) discourage

deterrence (di ter′ uhns) prevention of war

developed nations nations that are highly industrialized and have well-developed economies

developing nations nations that are economically poor and primarily agricultural

devolution (dev uh lū′ shuhn) the granting of self-government

dharma (duhr′ muh) Hindu set of rules that determines moral conduct

dictator (dik′ tā tuhr) absolute ruler

dictatorship of the proletariat control by workers under the leadership of the Communist party

dictatorships (dik′ tā tuhr ships) governments controlled by one person or group

diet (dī′ uht) assembly

diocese (dī′ uh sēz) unit of church government made up of several parishes and headed by a bishop

direct democracy voters make decisions without having representatives act for them

disarmament (dis ar′ muh muhnt) reduction of military weapons

disciples (duh sī′ puhlz) followers

disfranchised (dis fran′ chīzd) without voting rights

dissidents (dis′ uh duhnts) opponents of government policies

dissonant (dis′n uhnt) lacking in harmony

divination (div uh nā′ shuhn) foretelling of future

divine right of kings power of monarchs comes from God and is absolute

doctrine (dok′ truhn) official church teaching

domestic system rural manufacturing

dominion (duh min′ yuhn) self-governing territory that owes allegiance to the British monarch

dowry (dou′ rē) wealth a woman brought with her when she married

dual monarchy (dū' uhl mon' uhr kē)   two kingdoms governed by one ruler

duma (dū' muh)   Russian national legislature

dvorianie (dvor ē on' ē uh)   Russian nobles

dynamo (dī' nuh mō)   generator

dynasty (dī' nuh stē)   line of rulers from one family

E

economy (i kon' uh mē)   ways in which people use their environment to meet their basic material needs

edubbas (ed' uh buhz)   Sumerian schools

elder   family leader

elect   God's chosen people

ellipses (i lip' sēz)   ovals

emancipation (i man suh pā' shuhn)   freeing

embalming (im bom' ing)   process used to preserve a dead body

émigrés (em' uh grāz)   emigrants

emperor (em' puhr uhr)   monarch with absolute power over a large territory

empires (em' pīrs)   groups of territories under one government

enclosure (en klō' zhuhr) **movement**   trend from open field system to private ownership

enlightened despotism (en līt' nd des puh tiz' uhm)   monarchies in which rulers have absolute powers and use those powers to reform society

entrepreneurs (on truh pruh nerz')   individuals that combine money, ideas, raw materials, and labor to make goods

ephors (ef' uhrz)   Spartan officials who managed public affairs

epistles (i pis' uhlz)   letters

equites (ek' wuh tās)   Roman business people

ersatz (er' zots)   replacement

estates (e stātz')   orders of society in France

ethics (eth' iks)   study of moral principles

ethical monotheism (eth' uh kuhl mon' uh thē iz uhm)   worship of one god, who is good and all-powerful and expects people to deal justly with each other

ethnic group (eth' nik grūp)   large group of people having common traits and customs

eucharist (yū' kuhr ist)   holy communion

existentialism (eg zis ten' shuhl iz uhm)   philosophy that states that human beings are forced to create their own values and ethics

exodus (ek' suh duhs)   escape

exploitation (ek sploi tā' shuhn)   unfair use

extraterritoriality (ek struh ter' uh tor ē al uh tē)   foreigners are removed from jurisdiction of law

F

factory system   organized method of production that brought together workers and machines under the control of managers

fascism (fash' iz uhm)   political creed that supports unity of all social groups under the control of the nation-state

federal (fed' uhr uhl) **system**   government in which power is divided between a central and regional governments

feminism (fem' uh niz uhm)   movement supporting women's rights

feudalism (fyū' dl iz uhm)   social organization characterized by ties of loyalty and duty among nobles, landholding, and rule by local officials

fez (fez)   Turkish brimless hat

fiefs (fēfs)   feudal estates with peasants

fission (fish' uhn)   separation of nuclear particles

foundries (foun' drēz)   buildings in which molten metals are cast into products

franchise (fran' chīz)   right to vote

freeholders (frē' hōl duhrz)   peasants on a manor who paid rent and provided the lord with a portion of their harvest

friars (frī' uhrz)   wandering preachers

fueros (fwe' rōs)   special royal charters for towns in Castile and Aragon

fusion (fyū' zhuhn)   combination of nuclear particles

futurologists (fyū chuhr ol' uh jists)   forecasters of the future

G

gauchos (gou' chōz)   cowboys of mixed Spanish and Indian ancestry

geishas (gā' shuhz)   Japanese women who are professional entertainers

general strike   strike in which all or a large number of workers participate in order to bring pressure on the government

gentry (jen' trē)   lower nobility

ghettos (get' ōz)   special areas where European Jews were forced to live

gospels (gos' puhlz)   stories about Jesus found in the New Testament

grand jury   group of 12 people that submitted the names of people in the area suspected of crimes

grand vizier (vi zir')   prime minister of the Ottoman Empire

Greek fire   chemical mixture that ignited when it came into contact with fire

grid (grid)   uniform network

gross (grōs) **national product** total value of goods and services produced in a year

guerrilla (guh ril' uh) **fighting** method of warfare using hit-and-run tactics

guilds (gildz) business associations

gurus (gū' rūz) wandering religious teachers of India

H

hajj (haj) pilgrimage

hanifs (ha nēfs') righteous men who denounced the worship of idols, lived simple lives, and believed in one god

hegemony (hi jem' uh nē) dominance

helots (hel' uhtz) Spartan slaves

hereditary (huh red' uh tār ē) passed down from parent to child

heresy (her' uh sē) false doctrine

hierarchy (hī' uhr ar kē) society of ranked order of social groups

hieratic (hī uh rat' ik) Egyptian writing system having cursive, or flowing, script

hieroglyphics (hī uhr uh glif' iks) Egyptian writing system of picture symbols

hippodrome (hip' uh drōm) racetrack

homage (hom' ij) feudal ceremony during which a noble becomes a vassal to a lord

home rule self-government

homogeneous (hō muh jē' nē uhs) uniform

humanism (hyū' muh niz uhm) interest in classical writings

humanists (hyū' muh nists) Italian scholars who promoted humanism

hydrogen (hī' druh juhn) **bombs** nuclear weapons many times more powerful than atomic bombs

hypothesis (hī poth' uh sis) possible explanation; step in the scientific method developed by Thales of Miletus

I

iconoclasts (ī kon' uh klastz) image breakers

iconography (ī kuh nog' ruh fē) making of icons

icons (ī' konz) sacred pictures or images used in church worship

iconostasis (ī kuh nos' tuh suhs) high thin wall covered with icons

ideology (ī dē ol' uh jē) political philosophy

ikebana (i kā bon uh) Japanese flower arrangement

illuminated (i lū' muh nā tid) decorated manuscript pages with elaborate designs and miniature pictures in brilliant colors

imam (i mam') prayer leader

imperialism (im pir' ē uhl iz uhm) national policies for establishing authority over other areas of the world

impresario (im pruh sor' ē ō) sponsor of a performing group

impressionism (im presh' uh niz uhm) art that presents the artists' immediate impression of their senses

incentive (in sen' tiv) motive

incidents (in' suh duhnts) certain rights that a lord could demand from a vassal

indemnity (in dem' nuh tē) payment for war damages

indulgences (in dul' juhn suhz) documents issued by the Church that freed their owners from time in purgatory

infallible (in fal' uh buhl) free from error

infidels (in' fuh duhls) unbelievers

inflation (in flā' shuhn) steady rise in prices

initiative (i nish' ē uh tiv) allows citizens to propose legislation to be considered by their country's national legislature

intendants (in ten' duhnts) agents of the French Crown who handled local government affairs

intercontinental ballistic missiles (in tuhr kon tuh nen' tl buh lis' tik mis' uhlz) long-range rockets

internal-combustion (in ter'nl kuhm bus' chuhn) **engine** device that uses a gas explosion behind a piston to transfer energy directly into mechanical power

isolationism (ī suh lā' shuh niz uhm) avoidance of ties with other countries

izbas (iz' buhz) log cabins

J

jati (jo' tē) subdivision of the four main Aryan social groups, or varnas; later, it became known as "caste"

jihad (juh had') holy war

jingoism (jing' gō iz uhm) patriotism provoked by foreign threat

joint stock companies business organizations formed for the purpose of selling shares

journeymen (jer' nē muhn) experienced workers who received daily wages; worked for masters

joust (joust) tournament event during which two knights in armor attempted to knock each other to the ground with long wooden lances

junks (jungks) Chinese ships

junta (hūn' tuh) council

justices of the peace local officials who enforced the law in England

K

kabuki (ka bū' kē)   Japanese form of theater

kaiser (kī' zuhr)   German emperor

kami (ko mē)   sacred objects in Japan's Shinto religion

kamikazes (kom i koz' ēz)   Japanese pilots who volunteered for suicide missions

kaolin (kā' uh luhn)   fine white clay used by the Chinese to make pottery

karma (kar' muh)   every action of a person in one life influences how he or she will be born in the next life

khan (kon)   absolute ruler; Mongol leader

kibbutzim (ki bū tsēm')   Israeli collective farm settlements in which the land is held in common

knights (nīts)   feudal mounted warriors

kowtow (kou' tou)   kneeling and touching head to floor

kshatriyas (kuh sha' trē yuhz)   Aryan group made up of warriors

kulaks (kū laks')   peasants who had become productive farmers in the U.S.S.R.

L

labor intensive (lā' buhr in ten' siv)   type of agriculture that relies on labor more than capital

labor theory of value   value of goods measured by the amount of labor it took to produce them

labyrinth (lab' uh rinth)   maze

lacquer (lak' uhr)   varnished

laissez faire (les ā fār')   policy of government non-intervention

laity (lā' uh tē)   church members who are not clergy

lateen (la tēn') **sail**   triangular-shaped sail

latifundias (lat uh fuhn' dē as)   large Roman estates

law of inertia (in er' shuh)   an object remains at rest or in straight-line motion unless acted upon by an external force

lay investiture (lā in ves' tuh chūr)   when secular rulers give symbols of office to bishops they appoint

lebensraum (lā' buhnz roum)   "living space"

legations (li gā' shuhnz)   diplomatic residences

legions (lē' juhnz)   units of the Roman army

legionaries (lē' juh ner ēz)   soldiers in Roman legion

legitimate (luh jit' uh mit)   legal

lend-lease   enabled United States to lend war equipment to any country whose defense was deemed vital to the defense of the United States

levée en masse (le vē' on mas)   mass mobilization

liberalism (lib' uhr uh liz uhm)   desire to change governments on the basis of democratic ideals

line of demarcation (dē mar kā' shuhn)   imaginary line dividing land

linguists (ling' gwists)   scientists who study the world's languages

locomotive (lō kuh mō' tiv)   movable steam engine

loess (lō' is)   rich yellow soil found in northern China

logic (loj' ik)   science of reasoning

lycées (lē sāz')   French secondary schools

M

madrasas (mad' ruhs ez)   theological schools

maize (māz)   corn

mandarins (man' duhr uhns)   class of scholarly civil servants in China

mandates (man' dāts)   territories administered by other countries

mannerists (man' uh rists)   artists that subjectively portray people and scenes

manorialism (muh nor' ē uhl iz uhm)   agricultural system of the Middle Ages

manors (man' uhrz)   large estates

margin call   payment in full for stock bought on the margin

mass   church's worship service

masters   guild members who owned their own shops and tools

mawali (muh wol' ē)   adopted members of an Arab tribe

mayors of the palace   government officials in eighth century Frankish kingdom

mendicants (men'duh kuhnts)   religious beggars

mercantilism (mer' kuhn tuh li zuhm)   theory of national economic policy in which wealth means power

messiah (muh sī' uh)   Jewish savior

mestizos (me stē' zōz)   people of mixed Spanish and Indian ancestry

metaphysics (met' uh fiz' iks)   aspects of philosophy that deal with universal, eternal questions

metics (met' iks)   resident aliens in Athens

metsuke (mé tsū kē)   intelligence-gathering officials for the Tokugawa rulers

mihrab (mer' uhb)   small arch

militarism (mil' uh tuh riz uhm)   policy of aggressive military preparedness

millet (mil' it)   Ottoman religious community

minarets (min uh retz')   towers from which people were called to prayer

minbar (min' bar)   wood or stone pulpit

ministers (min' uh stuhrz)   religious leaders of Protestant groups

mirs (mirz)   village communes

missi dominici (mē' sē dō mi nē' sē)   royal envoys of Charlemagne

mixed economy   some businesses are privately owned, while others are under the control of government

mobilization (mō buh luh zā' shuhn)   war readiness

moksha (mōk' shuh)   state of complete oneness with Brahman

monarchy (mon' uhr kē)   rule by a king or queen

monotheism (mon' uh thē iz uhm)   worship of one god

monsoon (mon sūn')   seasonal winds

mosaic (mō zā' ik)   Byzantine art form made by fitting small flat pieces of stone or colored glass to form a picture or design

moshavim (mō shoh vēm')   Israeli cooperative settlements in which farms are individually owned

most-favored-nation status   foreign country that receives all special privileges that are extended to all other foreign countries

muezzin (myū ez' n)   prayer crier

mulattos (muh lat' ōz)   people of mixed European and black ancestry

multinational corporations (mul ti nash' uh nuhl kor puh rā' shuhnz)   western-based businesses that produce or market in more than one country

multinational empire   empire that contains varied ethnic and religious groups who speak different languages and dialects

mummy (mum' ē)   wrapped body

mutiny (myūt' n ē)   to overthrow a ship's officers and take over the ship

mystery plays   religious dramas

mystery religions   religions in the Roman Empire that believed in mythical heroes, staged elaborate rituals, and promised followers a life after death

N

nationalism (nash' uh nuh liz uhm)   demand by national groups for independent states of their own

nationalized (nash' uh nuh līzd)   government takeover of some or all aspects of economy

nation-state   political organization containing one nationality

natural law   universal moral law knowable by reason

naturalism (nach' uhr uh liz uhm)   form of literature that describes everything with objective precision

neoclassicism (nē ō klas' i siz uhm)   new classicism; art style of the late 1700's

nihilists (nī' uhl istz)   people who reject all traditions

nirvana (nir vo' nuh)   state of complete oneness with the universe

nomadic (nō mad' ik)   wandering groups of Arabs who lived in the Arabian Peninsula

nomes (nōmz)   Egyptian provinces

nonaligned (non uh līnd')   neutral

nonbelligerency (non' buh lij uhr uhn sē)   when a country does not actively enter a war but extends material aid to other countries fighting

nuclear (nū' klē uhr) **freeze**   agreement not to increase weapons

nuclear proliferation (prō lif uh rā' shuhn)   spread of nuclear weapons to previously non-nuclear countries and areas

nuclear reactors (rē ak' tuhrz)   devices for generating power through the release of atomic energy by a controlled chain reaction

O

olympiad (ō lim' pē ad)   four-year interval between Olympic games

open hearth process   method of producing inexpensive steel

opium (ō' pē uhm)   drug made from poppies

oprichnina (ō prich nē' nuh)   land seized by the Russian tsar from boyars

oral traditions   legends and history passed by word of mouth from one generation to another

orders   church-approved groups

ostracism (os' truh siz uhm)   Greek practice by which the people voted to exile an undesirable politician for ten years

overkill   to destroy several times over

P

pacifist (pas' uh fist)   person opposed to war or violent conflict

page   assistant in the castle of a lord; first stage of training for knighthood

pagoda (puh gō' duh)   Chinese tower-like temple

papacy (pā' puh sē)   office of Pope

papyrus (puh pī' ruhs)   reed from the Nile used to make paper of the same name

pariahs (puh rī' uhz)   descendants of non-Aryans who were outside the varna system and worked at the dirtiest jobs

parish (par' ish)   local church

parity (par' uh tē)   equality

parliamentary (par luh men' tuhr ē) **government**   chief executive is prime minister, who is the head of the party that wins a majority in the parliament

parliaments (par' luh muhnts)   meetings of the Great Council

partitioned (par tish' uhnd) divided

patesi (puh tā' zē) Sumerian ruler-high priest

patriarchs (pā' trē arks) five leading archbishops

patricians (pu trish' uhnz) Roman aristocrats

patrons (pā' truhns) sponsors

peaceful coexistence (kō ig zis' tuhns) competition without war

peers (pirz) equals

penal colony (pē' nl kol' uh nē) settlement for criminals

peninsulares (puh nin suh lar' ez) in Spanish colonial America, Spaniards born in Spain

perioeci (per ē ē' sī) Spartan group made up of merchants, artisans, and farmers from conquered communities

permanent revolution Trotsky's belief that socialist revolution had to be spread all over the world before it could succeed in the U.S.S.R.

perspective (puhr spek' tiv) painting technique used to create depth

petty juries determine guilt or innocence of accused

phalansteries (fuh lan' stuh rēz) model communities

phalanx (fā' langks) infantry unit armed with spears and swords that fought in close formation, 16 rows deep

pharoah (fer' ō) Egyptian ruler

pictograms (pik' tuh gramz) picture symbols

playwrights (plā' rīts) writers of plays

plebians (pli bē' uhnz) non-aristocratic Romans

plebiscite (pleb' uh sīt) national vote

philosophes (fē luh zōfs') French word for "philosophers"; specifically Enlightenment thinkers

pluralistic (plur uh lis' tik) population made up of many different groups

pogroms (pō gromz') massacres

polemarch (pōl' march) Greek executive official who led the army

polis (pōl' uhs) Greek city-state

polygamy (puh lig' uh mē) when a person has more than one spouse

polytheists (pol ē thē' ists) Aryans who worshiped many gods and goddesses

popular referendum (ref uh ren' duhm) vote on a bill passed by a legislature

porteños (por tā' nyōs) middle and upper classes in Argentina

potlatch (pot' latch) special feast of the Indians of the Northwest

praetor (prē' tuhr) Roman judges

predestination (prē des tuh nā' shuhn) belief that God determines the fate of every human being

pragmatic (prag mat' ik) practical

prehistory period of human existence before writing

presbyter (prez' buh tuhr) Christian priest

prime minister (prīm min' uh stuhr) chief executive of a parliamentary government

principalities (prin suh pal' uh tēz) territories ruled by princes

proconsuls (prō kon' suhlz) governors in Roman provinces

proletariat (prō luh ter' ē uht) class of factory workers whose main asset is their labor

propaganda (prop uh gan' duh) ideas, facts, and rumors used to help or harm a cause

prophets (prof' itz) religious reformers, claiming to be Yahweh's messengers

protectorate (pruh tek' tuhr it) country that relinquishes foreign policy to an imperial authority

proven reserves known resources that are profitable to obtain

provisional (pruh vizh' uh nuhl) temporary

psychiatrist (sī kī' uh trist) doctor who studies the mind

psychoanalysis (sī kō uh nal' uh sis) Freud's technique of studying and treating the mind

publicans (pub' luh kuhns) Roman officials who collected taxes

purgatory (per' guh tor ē) place of suffering in the life to come

purge (perj) remove

Q

quipu (kē' pū) rope with knotted cords of different lengths and colors

R

racial segregation (rā' shuhl seg ruh gā' shuhn) separation of the races

rajah (ra' juh) Indian chief

ratified (rat' uh fīd) approved

realism (rē' uh liz uhm) art form that portrays life in a realistic and scientific manner

realpolitik (rā ol' pō li tēk) politics based on practical rather than theoretical goals

recession (ri sesh' uhn) period of decline in economic activity

reconnaissance (ri kon' uh suhns) surveying

refine (ri fīn') remove impurities from

reformation (ref uhr mā' shuhn) change in the ways the Church taught and practiced Christianity

regents (rē' juhnts) women who governed the empire as temporary rulers

reincarnation (rē in kar nā' shuhn) belief that the soul has to live in many bodies in many lifetimes

relativism (rel' uh tuh viz uhm) there are no absolutes in any field of knowledge or in moral values

relic (rel' ik) statue or holy object of a deity

reliefs (ri lēfz') raised carvings

reparations (rep uh rā' shuhnz) payment for damages caused

republic (ri pub' lik) government in which the people elect their leaders

resistance groups underground organizations that engage in secret operations and sabotage against an enemy

revelation (rev uh lā' shuhn) vision

revolution of rising expectations desire for economic improvement by developing countries

rhetoric (ret' uhr ik) public speaking

rococo (rō kō' kō) elaborate and delicate art style of the 1700's

romances (rō' man suhz) love stories about knights and ladies

romanticism (rō man' tuh siz uhm) emphasis of the senses and emotion over the intellect and reason

royalist (roi' uh list) pro-monarchy

rudder (rud' uhr) device used to steer a ship

S

sabbath (sab' uhth) Jewish holy day of rest

sacraments (sak' ruh muhnts) church rituals

salon (suh lon') meetings of writers, artists, and educated people during the Enlightenment in Paris

samurai (sam' ū rī) Japanese warrior landlords

sanctions (sangk' shuhnz) measures designed to inflict economic losses

sanctuary (sangk' chū er ē) altar area

sangha (suhng' uh) Buddhist community of monks and nuns

sankin-kotai (son kin-kō' tī) attendance by turn

satellites (sat' l līts) nations controlled by another power

satrap (sa trap') governor of a Persian province

satrapies (sa' truh pēz) Persian provinces

satyagraha (suh' tyuh gruh huh) Gandhi's doctrine of moral nonviolent protest

savannas (suh van' uhz) elevated dry grasslands

schism (siz' uhm) separation of the Church into the Roman Catholic Church in the west and the Eastern Orthodox Church in the east

scholasticism (skuh las' ti siz uhm) reconciles classical philosophy with church teachings

scorched-earth policy destroying everything during a retreat that could be of use to invaders

scribes (skrībz) ancient writers

scurvy (sker' vē) disease caused by lack of vitamin C

sea dogs sea captains turned pirates

seceded (si sēd' uhd) withdrew

sects (sekts) religious groups

secular (sek' yuh luhr) non-religious

self-determination right of national groups to set up independent nations

seminary (sem' uh ner ē) school to train priests

senators (sen' uh tuhrz) 300 representatives in the Roman Senate

seppuku (se pū' kū) Japanese ritual form of suicide

sepoys (sē' poiz) Indian soldiers who served in the British army in India

serfs (serfs) peasants who were bound to the soil and could not leave their manor without their lord's permission

service gentry (jen' trē) officials who worked for the state in the Ottoman Empire

shadoof (shuh dūf') Egyptian machine that lifts water from the river

shah (sha) Persian king

shari'a (shuh rē' uh) Islamic moral rules organized in a code of law

sheikh (shēk) chief (head of tribe); based on leadership abilities and consent of the tribe

shogun (shō' guhn) Japanese commander-in-chief

shogunate (shō' guhn uht) military government of Japan with shogun as head

shudras (shū' druhz) lowest Aryan group made up of unskilled laborers and servants

shuttle diplomacy (shut'l duh plō' muh sē) an official traveling back and forth between countries to mediate a dispute

signori (sē nyor' ē) powerful leaders of Italian city-states

simony (sī' muh nē) selling of church positions

sitzkrieg (sit' skrēg) "sitting war" or "phony war"

smelting (smel' ting) melting ore

socialism (sō' shuh liz uhm) government that represents society as a whole rather than the special interests of private individuals

socialist realism (sō' shuh list rē' uh liz uhm) art form that presents reality from the standpoint of Communist ideology

social realists American artists who painted to draw attention to the injustice, corruption, and human suffering caused by the depression

social revolution attempt to change structure of society

Socratic (sō krat' ik) **method**   teaching technique developed by Socrates

soma (sō'muh)   powerful Aryan drink

sonnets (son' its)   short poems

soothsayers (sūth' sā uhrs)   priests of Rome who foretold the future

sophists (sof' ists)   Greek tutors

sovereignty (sov' ruhn tē)   power to rule

soviets (sō' vē ets)   workers' councils

sphere of influence   territory whose trade is controlled by a foreign power

squire (skwīr)   second stage of knighthood training

stagflation (stag flā' shuhn)   combination of rising prices and high unemployment

status quo (stat' uhs kwō)   maintaining existing state of affairs

steam turbine (stēm ter' bīn)   rotary motor in which a current of steam, air, or water directly rotates the shaft in its bearings

steel (stēl)   iron mixed with carbon to remove impurities

steppe (step)   territory in Europe that begins in Europe and extends eastward into Asia

strategos (struh' tē gōz)   Athenian general

stupas (stū' puhz)   large stone mounds built over the bones of Buddhist saints

subcontinent (sub kon' tuh nuhnt)   large land mass like a continent, only smaller

sultan (sult'n)   ruler

sultanate (sult'n āt)   kingdom

summit conferences (sum' it kon' fuhr uhns uhz)   high-level meetings of political leaders

sumo (sū mō)   Japanese form of wrestling

suras (sūr' uhz)   chapters in Koran arranged with longer verses appearing first and shorter verses appearing last

surplus (ser' pluhs) **value**   the difference between what workers are paid and the real worth of their labor

surrealism (suh rē' uh liz uhm)   art form that uses dreamlike images and unnatural combinations of objects to explore the unconscious mind

suttee (suh tē')   practice of widows burning themselves to death at their husbands' funerals

swaraj (swuh roj')   Indian independence

symbolism (sim' buh liz uhm)   art that conveys impressions by suggestion rather than by direct statement

synagogue (sin' uh gog)   local community of Jews who meet to study and practice their religion

syndicates (sin' duh kits)   corporations of workers, employers, and government officials

T

taille (tā' uhl)   tax on land

technology (tek nol' uh jē)   combination of skills and tools that make economic activity possible

terra-cotta (ter' uh-kot' uh)   baked clay

terrorism (ter' uh riz uhm)   use of violence to achieve political aims

theocracies (thē ok' ruh sēz)   governments in which religious and political leadership is held by the same person

theology (thē ol' uh jē)   religious teachings

theory of relativity (rel uh tiv' uh tē)   there are no absolutes in measuring time and space

theses (thē' sēz)   statements

tithe (tīth)   10 percent of a believer's income, paid to the Church

totalitarianism (tō tal uh ter' ē uh niz uhm)   government that has total control over almost every aspect of people's lives

totem (tō' tuhm) **poles**   wooden carvings of people, animals, and mythical beings that represent tribal history and values

tournaments (ter' nuh muhnts)   special contests among knights

tragedian (truh jē' dē uhn)   writer of tragedies

tragedies (traj' uh dēz)   stories about human suffering that often have unhappy endings

transportation   eighteenth-century British practice of setting criminals free on the condition that they move to Australia

travois (tra' voi)   net or platform attached to two poles and usually pulled by dogs

trenches   ditches

tribes   groups having a common language and culture

tribunes (trib' yūnz)   ten plebian representatives in the Roman Republic

tribute (trib' yūt)   taxes

trilogy (tril' uh jē)   set of three plays

triumvirate (trī um' vuhr it)   group of three persons with equal power

troubadours (trū' buh dorz)   musician-singers

tsar (zar)   Russian ruler

typhoons (tī fūnz')   hurricanes

tyrants (tī' ruhnts)   Greek leaders who championed the common people and promised to give them better government

U

ultimatum (ul tuh mā' tuhm)   statement of terms that must be accepted

ultraroyalists (ul truh roi' uh lists) extremely conservative French aristocrats in the nineteenth century

unicameral (yū nuh kam' uhr uhl) one-house legislature

universal manhood suffrage (yū nuh ver' suhl man' hūd suf' rij) right of all males to vote

urbanization (er buh nuh zā' shuhn) growth of cities

utilitarianism (yū til uh ter' ē uhn iz uhm) rightness of any action, law, or political institution should be measured by its usefulness

utopias (yū tō' pē uhz) ideal societies

V

vaishyas (vīsh' yuhz) Aryan group made up of merchants, artisans, and farmers

varnas (vuhr' nuhz) four main Aryan social groups

vassal (vas' uhl) feudal noble who served a lord of the next higher rank

veches (ve' chuhz) assemblies that represented all free, adult male citizens

vernacular (vuhr nak' yuh luhr) everyday speech of the common people

veto (vē' tō) refuse to approve

viceroy (vīs' roi) representative of the Spanish monarch in the New World

viceroyalties (vīs roi' uhl tēz) administrative regions ruled by a viceroy

vizier (vi zir') Egyptian prime minister; chief advisor to the Abbasid caliphs during the Islamic empire

vocations (vō kā' shuhnz) callings in which people could serve God and their neighbors

W

war communism government take-over of all aspects of economy during wartime

warlords local military officials in China

"wars of liberation" (lib uh rā' shuhn) revolutionary movements against western political and economic influence

weltpolitik (velt' pō li tēk) "world policy"

westernization (wes ter nuh zā' shuhn) spread of European culture

wolf packs German clusters of submarines that shadowed convoys during the day and attacked them at night

woof (wūf) threads that run crosswise in woven cloth

writs of habeas corpus (rits uhv hā' bē uhs kor puhs) written orders to bring a person before a judge and show cause for imprisonment

Y

yang (yang) Chinese principle representing fury, light, and heat

yasa (yo' suh) code of Mongol laws

yeomen (yō' men) farmers with small landholdings in England

yeshivas (yuh shē' vuhz) special academies in which Jewish scholars studied the *Torah*

yin (yin) force representing serenity, darkness, and coldness

yoga (yō' guh) Hindu physical exercise to discipline mind and body

yurts (yertz) movable tents of the Mongols

Z

zaibatsu (zī bo tzū) large factory and banking combinations in Japan

zambos (zom' bōz) people of mixed Indian and black ancestry

zakat (zuh kot') income tax collected by the state used for schools or to help the poor

zemstvos (zem' svōz) local councils

ziggurat (zig' uh rat) Sumerian temple

INDEX

Arms race, 573, 667, 770-771
Armstrong, Louis, 749
Armstrong, Neil A., 677
Arouet, Francois Marie; *See* Voltaire
Arpads, 240
Art; *See also* specific styles; abstract, 627, 747; African. *See* African art; Buddhist, 39, 40, 41; Byzantine, 114, 124, 125; in China, 44; Enlightenment, 339-341; Etruscan, 81-82; in Greece, 72; under Guptas, 42; Hellenistic, 77; in India, 39, 40, 41, 42; and Industrial Revolution, 422ff; Italian Renaissance, 248-250; of Mayans, 197; of Minoans, 58; modern, 432-433, 627; primitivism in, 627; realism in, 248; Renaissance, 339-341
Articles of Confederation, 357
Arts, 746; *See also* specific fields; and Aztecs, 200; in China under T'ang dynasty, 218-220; in Egypt, 18-19; and government, 751-752; and Industrial Revolution, 427ff; Islamic, 150-151; in Japan, 226-227; in modern era, 751-752; in Nazi Germany, 751-752; in Sumer, 10; and technology, 763; in United States, 752; in U.S.S.R., 751, 754-755; in Venice, 245
Aryans, 27, 35-36
Ashikaga shogunate, 226-227
Ashikaga Takauji, 226
Ashkenazim, 702
Asia, 193, 727ff; *See also* specific countries; empires of, 209ff; France in, 557; imperialism in, 553ff; Russia in, 556-557
Asia Minor, 20, 27, 59, 65, 70, 87, 93, 116, 171, 209, 213, 622
Askia, Mohammed, 190, 191
Asoka, 39-40
Aspasia, 76-77
Aspects of the Rise of Economic Individualism, 301
Assembly of Athens, 63
Assembly of Centuries, 83
Assembly of Tribes, 83-84, 89
Assyrians, 22, 24, 25-26, 184
Astaire, Fred, 750
Astrolabe, 278
Astrology, 27
Astronomy, 27, 49, 77, 96, 329-330, 332; under Islamic empire, 150; Mayan, 197
Aswan High Dam, 702
Atahualpa, 288-289
Athena, 70, 72
Athens, 63-64, 65-66, 69, 70, 72; democracy in, 68; Golden Age of, 67-68; government of, 63; laws of, 63; philosophy in, 114
Atlantic Charter, 643, 647
Atlantic Ocean, 285, 520
Atomic bomb, 655
Atomic energy, 667
Atomic theory, 424
Aton, 14-16
Attila, 103
Attlee, Clement, 680
Augsburg, 271, 280; Peace of, 271, 316, 317
Augustine, 100
Augustus, Caesar, 91-92, 96, 98, 101
Aurangzeb, 217
Aurelian, 93
Auschwitz, 655

Ausgleich, 486
Australia, 395, 558-560, 690, 699
Austria, 486-488; and Bismarck, 468-470; and Catherine the Great, 325; and Congress of Vienna, 371, 460; and Enlightenment, 337; and France, 364, 372; and Germany, 271, 465, 572, 637; and Hapsburgs, 239, 316, 317; and Napoleon, 365; nationalism in, 487-488; vs. Prussia, 319-320; revolt in, 377-378, 461; and Treaty of Paris, 383; and U.S.S.R., 382
Austria-Hungary, 500, 579; *See also* Austria, Hungary; economy of, 486; nationalism in, 572; in WWI, 574
Austrian Empire, 361, 377, 459, 483ff; bureaucracy in, 483; government in, 483-485; nationalism in, 484
Austrian Netherlands, 367, 372, 375, 454; *See also* Belgium
Autobiography of Benvenuto Cellini, 247
Automation, 762
Automobiles, 708, 745
Avars, 114
Aviation, 408
Avignon, 231, 235-236
Axum, 185; *See also* Ethiopia
Azikiwe, B. N., 628
Azov Sea, 325
Aztecs, 198-200, 288, 291

B

Babur, 215
Babylon, 10, 25, 26, 27, 28, 70
Babylonia, 10-11
Babylonian Captivity, 235
Babylonians, 26; New (Chaldeans), 24, 26, 27, 28
Bach, Alexander, 483
Bach, Johann Sebastian, 341
Bacon, Francis, 330, 334
Badoglio, Pietro, 650
Bagehot, Walter, 437
Baghdad, 145, 147, 148, 210
Baghdad-Berlin railway, 571
Baghdad Pact, 702, 705
Bahamas, 294
Bahrain, 704
Baird, John Logie, 610
Bakunin, Michael, 493
Balaklava, Battle of, 382
Balance of power, 243, 310, 318, 372
Balanchine, George, 748
Balboa, Vasco Nunez de, 286
Baldwin, Count, 205
Balfour, Arthur, 624
Balfour Declaration, 624
Balkan League, 501
Balkan Peninsula, 57, 103, 114, 117, 127, 211, 318
Balkans, 92, 118, 499-500
Balkan Wars, 501-502
Ballets Russes, 748
Baltic Sea, 127, 131, 239, 241, 322
Baltimore, Maryland, 469
Balzac, Honore de, 427
Bangladesh, 33, 553, 729
Bank of Amsterdam, 281

Banking, 146, 246, 280, 292, 397; British, 403; and feudalism, 172; investment, 449; in medieval Europe, 172
Bantus, 553; kingdoms of, 192; languages of, 192; migrations of, 186; villages of, 187
Barbados, 294
Barbarossa, Frederick (Frederick I), Holy Roman Emperor, 171, 179
Barbary Coast, 545
Barca, Hamilcar, 85
Baroque, 339-341
Bartered Bride, The, 492
Baruch, Bernard, 667
Baryshnikov, Mikhail, 755
Bashkirs, 488
Basil II, 116
Basil, Bishop, 123
Basilian Rule, 123
Bastille, 360
Batavia (Jakarta), 295
Batista, Fulgencio, 712, 713
Battuta, Ibn, 182, 212
Batu, 210
Bauhaus architecture, 748
Bavaria, 341, 471
Bay of Pigs, 685
Beatles, 759
Beatniks, 753
Beckett, Samuel, 754
Bedouins, 135-136
Bee Gees, 759
Beer Hall Putsch, 604
Beethoven, Ludwig van, 343, 362, 423
Begin, Menachem, 719
Beijing (Peking, formerly Cambuluc), 223, 525
Belgian Congo, 709, 722
Belgium, 375, 433, 454; *See also* Austrian Netherlands; democracy in, 454; Hitler's attack on, 642; Industrial Revolution in, 403-404; post-WWII, 682; retreat of from Africa, 709-710; and WWI, 574
Belisarius, 113
Bella, Ahmed Ben, 706
Bell, Alexander Graham, 405
Belorussians, 127
Benedict, 158
Benedictine Rule, 158, 168
Benelux, 682
Bengal, 554, 555
Ben-Gurion, David, 700
Bentham, Jeremy, 417
Beowulf, 175
Berbers, 188, 189, 191
Berchtold, Leopold, 574
Berg, Alban, 749
Beria, Lavrenti, 672
Bering Strait, 193
Berlin, 378; blockade of, 670; Congress of, 500
Berlin-Baghdad railway, 571
Berlin Decree, 366
Berlioz, Hector, 423
Bernard of Clairvaux, 171
Bessemer, Henry, 400
Bhagavad Gita, 32, 37
Bible, 6, 22, 28, 99, 123, 130, 159, 174, 251, 256, 257, 260, 262, 264, 265, 270, 425
Bill of Rights; of Britain, 352; of United States, 357

Castelfidardo, 465
Caste system, 36, 38, 40, 42, 215, 554
Castiglione, Baldassare, 247
Castile, 237, 238, 305
Castlereagh, Viscount, 371
Castro, Fidel, 685, 712, 713
Categorical imperative, 339
Cathedral architecture, 167
Catherine II (the Great) of Russia, 325-326, 337
Catherine of Aragon, 266
Catholicism, 100, 115, 131, 251, 330, 337, 357, 361, 363, 365, 380, 451, 474-473, 484; in medieval Europe, 166ff; vs. Protestantism, 267, 293, 310, 315, 316-317, 347-348, 350, 351, 352, 445, 473; reform in, 168, 255ff, 265, 269-271; schism of Christian Church into Eastern Orthodox Church and, 117, 130
Caudillos, 512ff
Cavalier Parliament, 351
Cavalier, Robert (Sieur de La Salle), 296
Cavaliers, 349
Cave paintings; at Ajanta, 41; in Paleolithic Age, 3
Cavour, Camillo di, Count of Piedmont, 380, 462-463, 464, 465
Ceausescu, Nicolae, 675
Cellini, Benvenuto, 247
Cell theory, 425
Celts, 89, 92
Censorship, 48, 83, 269-270
Census, 92, 177
Central Africa, 186, 707-709; See also specific countries
Central America, 193, 196, 197, 507-508, 727; See also specific countries; geography of, 511
Central Asia, 49; See also specific countries
Central Intelligence Agency (CIA), 711, 724
Central Powers, 575
Cervantes Saavedra, Miguel de, 334, 342
Cetywayo, King of Zulus, 553
Ceylon (Sri Lanka), 283
Cezanne, Paul, 432
Chaeronea, Battle of, 70
Chaldean Empire, 28
Chaldeans (New Babylonians), 24, 26, 27
Chamberlain, Neville, 637, 639, 642
Chamoun, Camille, 703
Champollion, Jean Francois, 18
Chandragupta I, 40
Chandragupta II, 42
Ch'angan, 49, 218
Chang Jiang River (Yangtze River), 43, 221
Chansons de geste, 175
Chappe, Claude, 469
"Charge of the Light Brigade, The," 382
Charlemagne, 159, 179
Charles I, King of England, 347, 348-350
Charles II, King of England, 331, 350, 351
Charles II, King of Spain, 307, 315
Charles IV, Holy Roman Emperor, 239
Charles V, Holy Roman Emperor, 239, 259, 266, 271, 272
Charles VI, Holy Roman Emperor, 318
Charles VII, King of France, 234, 236
Charles IX, King of France, 273
Charles X, King of France, 376

Charles Albert, King of Piedmont, 461, 462
Charles the Bald, 160
Charles the Bold, Duke of Burgundy, 236
Charter of Liberties, 375, 378
Charters; See also specific types; of towns, 173, 177; of United Nations, 657
Chartists, 439, 441, 442
Chateaubriand, Francois de, 423
Chaucer, Geoffrey, 175
Cheka, 596
Chemistry, 149, 424
Chernenko, Konstantin, 738
Chiang Kai-shek, 619, 620, 644, 691
Ch'ien Lung, Chinese emperor, 527
Children and Industrial Revolution, 410
Chile, 200, 509, 724
China, 217ff, 691-693, 730, 731-732; ancient, 43ff; architecture of, 222; art of, 44; arts in under T'ang dynasty, 218-220; Buddhism in, 38; civil service in, 49, 217, 221; climate and geography of, 43; communism in, 619-620, 691ff; Cultural Revolution in, 693-694, 731; drama in, 221; dynasties of, 44-46; economy of, 217, 525-527; family in, 46-47; foreign influence on, 557-558; and Japan, 227, 530, 541; literature in, 218-220, 221; Mongols in, 210, 221; revolutionary movements in, 529, 533-534; split between U.S.S.R. and, 693; under T'ang dynasty, 217, 218-220; war between Japan and, 530, 541; writing in, 44
Ch'ing (Shih Huang Ti), 48
Chivalry, 164, 176
Chopin, Frederic, 423
Choson, 51, 227
Chosroes I, 113
Chou (Zhou), 44, 46
Chou En-lai, 691, 694, 732
Ch'in (Qin), 48
Christian IX, King of Denmark, 468
Christian Church, 99-100, 104; See also Catholicism, Christianity; schism of into Roman Catholic and Eastern Orthodox, 117, 130
Christian humanism, 251
Christianity, 109, 363; See also Christian Church; in Axum, 185; Byzantine, 117; and Constantine, 102; conversion of Europe to, 157-158; in Japan, 536; vs. Muslims, 169-171, 237-238; in New World, 289; in Ottoman Empire, 211, 214; and persecution, 99; rise of, 98-100; tension between western and Byzantine, 117
Ch'ung-chen, Chinese emperor, 525
Chung-kuo (Middle Kingdom), 43
Church of England; See Anglican Church
Church Fathers, 99, 159, 174
Churchill, Winston, 579-580, 642, 643, 647, 648, 649, 653, 664, 665, 666, 667, 680
Church of Scotland, 265, 349
Chu Teh, 620
CIA; See Central Intelligence Agency
Cicero, 88, 96
Cid, The, 334
Cities, 231; See also specific cities; growth of and Industrial Revolution, 408-410; under Islamic empire, 148; migration to in Roman Republic, 88-89

City-states; Greek, 61-63, 84, 87; Italian, 118, 243, 244-245; Mayan, 197; in Phoenicia, 20; in Sumer, 8
Civil rights laws, U.S., 678
Clans, 51, 52, 209-210
Clarendon Code, 351
Clark, Joshua Reuben, 631
Classical architecture, 248
Claudius, 92, 101
Clemenceau, Georges, 587
Clement V, Pope, 235
Cleopatra, 71, 90, 93
Clermont, 401
Clive, Robert, 554
Clouds, The, 74
Clovis, 158
Cluny, 168
Coal, 397, 398, 402, 475; mining of, 394
Cockerill, William, 403
Coinage, 62, 177, 281
Colbert, Jean Baptiste, 313, 314
Cold war, 665, 671, 677, 684, 711, 771
Coleridge, Samuel Taylor, 427
Colet, John, 251
Collective farms, 599, 702
Collective security, 635, 637
College of Cardinals, 235, 247
Colley, Richard (Lord Wellesley), 554
Colombia, 200, 509, 520; Gran (Great), 509
Colonies, 281, 284, 289, 294; British, 397; Greek, 61; in North America, 353ff; of Phoenicia, 21-22
Colorado, 194
Colosseum, 95
Columbus, Christopher, 284, 285-286
COMECON; See Council of Mutual Economic Assistance
Comedy, 74
Comintern (Communist International), 599, 637
Commercial Revolution, 280
Committee of Public Safety, 363
Commodus, 100
Common Market (European Economic Community), 679, 732
Common Sense, 355
Communications, 405-407, 610, 758
Communism, 596; in China, 619-620; 691ff; in Czechoslovakia, 671; in Soviet Union, 596ff; Vietnamese (Vietcong), 697
Communist International (Comintern), 599, 637
Communist Manifesto, The, 421, 422
Compass, 220-221, 278
Compromise of 1867, 486
Computers, 756, 762, 764
Concentration camps, 604, 655, 656
Concert of Europe (Congress system or Metternich system), 374-375, 380, 384
Concordat of 1801, 365
Concordat of Worms, 168
Condition of the Working Class in England in 1844, The, 420
Condor Legion, 638
Condottieri, 243
Confederation of the Rhine, 365, 466
Confessions, 100
Confucianism, 47, 48, 49, 50, 52, 53, 218, 228, 530
Confucius (Kung-fu-tzu), 46, 47, 49, 50

815

Detroit, 408
De Verrazano, Giovanni, 296
De Vlaminck, Maurice, 627
Diaghilev, Sergei, 748
Dias, Bartholomeu, 283
Diaz, Porfirio, 515
Dickens, Charles, 428
Dickinson, John, 362
Dictatorship, 83, 243, 350, 363, 365, 448, 512, 601-602; *See also* specific dictators
Diderot, Denis, 335
Diesel, Rudolf, 407
Diet of Worms, 259-260
Diggers, 350
Dilemma of a Ghost, The, 757
Diocletian, 101, 102
Dionysus, 73
Diplomacy, 243, 379-380, 718
Directory, 364
Disarmament, 612
Discourse Concerning Science and the Arts, 338
Discourse on Method, 330
Disease, 382; germ theory of, 424; in New World from Europe, 292
Disraeli, Benjamin, first earl of Beaconsfield, 441-442, 546
Divine Comedy, 175-176
Divine right of kings, 312, 347
DNA, 756
Dnieper River, 127, 128, 129
Dniester River, 127
Doctor Zhivago, 755
Doll's House, A, 430
Domesday Book, 177
Domestic system, 393-394, 401
Dominic, 169
Dominican Republic, 505, 521
Dominicans, 169, 246
Donatello, 248
Don Quixote, 334, 342
Dorians, 60, 64
Dos Passos, John, 747, 752
Dostoevsky, Feodor, 429
Draco, 63
Drake, Francis, 294
Drama; Chinese, 221; English, 252; Greek, 72-74; during Industrial Revolution, 430; Japanese, 227; in modern era, 754
Dravidians, 36
Dreiser, Theodore, 429, 430
Dresden, 404
Dreyfus, Alfred, 453-454
Druses, 498
Duarte, Jose Napoleon, 727
Dubcek, Alexander, 735
Dulles, John Foster, 690
Duma, 497, 593, 594
Dumas, Alexander, 426
Duncan, Isadora, 748
Dunkirk, 577
Dupin, Aurore (George Sand), 423f
Durham, Lord, 562
Dutch, 306; *See also* Netherlands; during age of European expansion, 294-296; vs. Spanish, 307
Dutch East India Company, 295
Dutch East Indies, 553, 648
Dutch language, 251
Dutch Netherlands; *See* Netherlands
Dutch West India Company, 295
"Duties of Man, The," 460

Dvorak, Anton, 492
Dyer, Reginald, 617

E

East Asia, 33ff, 525ff, 689ff; *See also* specific countries; nationalism in, 617ff
Eastern Europe, 735-736; *See also* specific countries; post-WWII, 665-667
Eastern Front, 576
Eastern Orthodox Church, 100, 118, 123, 129-130, 320, 380, 383, 498; and schism of Christian Church into Roman Catholic Church, 117, 130
Eastern Question, 380
Easter Rebellion, 607
East Germany (German Democratic Republic), 671, 674
East Indies, 278-279, 283, 294, 295
Ebla, 19
Economy, 415ff; of Austria-Hungary, 486; of Brazil, 517; of Britain, 309, 391, 442; of Byzantine Empire, 117-118, 122; of China under T'ang dynasty, 217; and European expansion, 278-279; of Europe during Late Middle Ages, 232, 241-242; of France, 311, 313-315, 448-449, 451; of Germany, 467; of Greek city-states, 61; of Imperial China, 525-527; and Industrial Revolution, 411; of Japan, 227, 536-537; laissez-faire, 415-417; of Mayans, 197; of medieval Europe, 172-173; and Reformation, 264; of Roman Empire, 94, 100, 102; of Roman Republic, 88-89; of Russian Empire, 496; of Spain, 292, 306; of U.S.S.R., 129, 324, 598, 599; of pre-industrial villages, 393; and WWI, 571; under Zhou dynasty, 47
Ecuador, 200, 509
Eden, Anthony, 680, 684
Edict of Milan, 102
Edict of Nantes, 310, 311, 315
Edison, Thomas Alva, 405
Education, 139, 338, 365, 451, 491; in Byzantine Empire, 123-124; and clergy, 173; in Greece, 74; in India, 555; during Italian Renaissance, 247; in medieval Europe, 173-174; in Meiji Japan, 538-539; in Roman Empire, 95
Edward I, King of England, 178
Edward III, King of England, 233, 426
Edward IV, King of England, Duke of York, 237
Edward VI, King of England, 268, 307
EEC; *See* European Economic Community
EFTA; *See* European Free Trade Association
Egypt; ancient, 11ff, 27, 70, 71, 87, 184, 185; arts and sciences in, 18-19; and Britain, 545-546, 553; geography of, 12; and Islam, 141, 147; and Israel, 700, 702, 703; literature in, 18; medicine in, 19; Middle Kingdom of, 14; nationalism in, 626; New Kingdom of, 14-16, 17; Old Kingdom of, 13-14; religion in, 14-16, 17; and Rome, 90, 91, 92, 93; women in, 17, 18; writing in, 17-18
Ehrenburg, Ilya, 754-755

Eightfold Path, 38
Einstein, Albert, 424, 749, 752
Eire, 607; *See also* Ireland, Northern Ireland, Ulster, Irish Free State
Eisenhower, Dwight D., 649, 650, 651, 678, 684, 685, 703
Eisenstein, Sergei, 751
Ekologa, 124
Elamites, 27
Elba, 367
Eleanor of Aquitaine, 176
Electoral reforms in Britain, 438-440
Electricity, 405-407, 469
Electronics, 764
Elements of Euclid, 77
El Escorial, 305
El Greco (Domenikos Theotokopoulos), 339
Eliot, George (Mary Ann Evans), 428
Eliot, T. S., 746
Elizabeth I, Queen of England, 267, 268, 294, 306, 308-310, 347
Elizabeth II, Queen of England, 444, 680
Elizabeth, wife of Henry VII, 237
El-Kassem, Karim, 704
Ellice Islands, 561
El-Sadat, Anwar, 718, 719
El Salvador, 508, 727
Emile, 338
Empress Augusta Bay, Battle of, 653
Ems Telegram, 471
Enclosure movement, 396
Encyclopedie, 335
Energy, 398-399, 424; atomic, 667; natural, 779; sources of, 779
Engels, Friedrich, 419ff
Engine; gasoline, 407-408; internal-combustion, 407-408; steam, 401
Engineering; of Inca, 201; of Roman Empire, 96-98
England; *See* Britain
England, Church of; *See* Anglican Church
English Channel, 306, 310, 469
English language, 256
Enlightened despotism, 336-337
Enlightenment, 38, 329, 333ff, 422, 505, 507; architecture during, 341, 342; art during, 339-341; literature during, 341-343; music during, 341; painting during, 341
Enquiry Concerning Human Understanding, An, 339
Entente Cordiale, 573
Epics, 175; of Greece, 60; of India, 37; of Roman Empire, 96
Epicureanism, 77
Epicurus, 77
Equal Rights Amendment (ERA), 738
ERA; *See* Equal Rights Amendment
Erasmus, 251
Eratosthenes, 77
Erhard, Ludwig, 681
Eridu, 8
Eritrea, 550
Eroica (Third Symphony of Beethoven), 362
Ershad, Hussein Mohammed, 729
Essay on the Principle of Population, 395-396
Essays of Michel de Montaigne, 251
Essays of Sir Francis Bacon, 334

Latin America, 289ff, 505ff, 724ff; See also specific countries; class structure in, 511; under colonial system, 511; Good Neighbor policy toward, 631; government in, 511, 712-713; nationalism in, 629-631; post-WWII, 710ff; railroads in, 403; and United States, 518ff, 631
Latin language, 112, 115, 159, 166, 256
Latins, 8
Latium, 81
Latvia, 589, 639
Latvians, 488
Laud, William, 348, 349
Lausanne Treaty, 622-623
La Venta, 197
Lavoisier, Antoine, 424
Law, 8, 10-11, 20, 140, 178, 417; and Age of Reason, 333; in Athens, 63; in Britain, 177, 354-355, 445; Byzantine, 113-114, 124, 130; common, 178; in France, 365; of Hebrews, 23; international, 333; Mongol, 210; natural, 331, 333, 355, 416; Roman, 84, 95-96, 174; in Russian Empire, 490; in U.S.S.R., 130
Lawrence, T. E., 585
League of the Iroquois, 195-196
League of Nations, 587, 593, 608, 609, 625, 636
League of the Three Emperors, 572
Lebanon, 590, 700, 703-704, 719-720
Lech, Battle of, 161
Leeuwenhoek, Anton van, 332
Legitimists, 447
Legnano, Battle of, 179
Leibniz, Gottfried Wilhelm von, 331
Leipzig, 367, 404
Lend-lease, 643
Leningrad, 323; See also Saint Petersburg
Lenin, Vladimir I., 495, 582, 594-595, 596, 597, 598
Leo III, Byzantine emperor, 115
Leo III, Pope, 159
Leo X, Pope, 247, 258, 259
Leo XIII, Pope, 473
Leonidas, 66
Leopold I, King of Belgium, 454
Leopold II, King of Austria, 337
Leopold II, King of Belgium, 548, 550
Leopold, Prince of Hohenzollern, 471
Lepanto, Battle of, 213
Lepidus, Marcus, 90
Les Demoiselles d'Avignon, 747
Les Miserables, 426
L'Esprit de Rivarol, 334
Les Rougon Macquart, The Natural and Social History of a Family Under the Second Empire, 429
La Tellier, François Michel (Marquis de Louvois), 313
Levelers, 350
Leviathan, 331
Lexington, 355, 362
Leyte Gulf, Battle of, 654
Liang Ch'i-ch'ao, 533
Liaotung (Liaodong) Peninsula, 530, 557
Liaqat Ali Khan, 695
Liberalism, 371, 374-375, 378
Liberals, 440, 441, 442-443, 446, 467, 474, 511, 514, 720; See also Whigs
Liberia, 706

"Liberty Song, The," 362
Libya, 548, 733
Lima, 510
Lincoln, Abraham, 518
Lin Piao, 693
Li Po, 208, 218
Lisbon, 511
Lister, Joseph, 424
Literature; See also specific books; in Africa, 629; in Babylonia, 11; in Byzantine Empire, 124; in China under Mongols, 221; in China under T'ang dynasty, 218-220; in Egypt, 18; during Enlightenment, 341-343; in France, 251; in Greece, 60; under Guptas, 42; of Hellenistic era, 77; and Industrial Revolution, 422ff; Islamic, 151; during Italian Renaissance, 247; in medieval Europe, 174-175; in modern era, 746, 757; realism in, 427-428; during Renaissance, 341-342; of Roman Empire, 96; in Third World, 757
Lithuania, 239, 320, 321, 589, 639
Lithuanians, 488
Liu Shao-ch'i, 691, 693
Liverpool, England, 408
Livingston, Robert, 355
Livingstone, David, 548
Livonia, 321
Livy, 96
Locarno treaties, 603, 608
Locke, John, 331-333, 334, 335, 355
Lollards, 256
Lombard League, 179
Lombards, 114, 117, 159, 244
Lombardy, 372, 378, 459, 460, 461, 463, 485
London, 178, 391, 428, 469
Long March, 620
Long Parliament, 349, 350, 351
Lorraine, 317, 449, 571, 576, 587
Lothair, 160
Louis I, King of Hungary, 240
Louis II, King of Hungary, 240
Louis VI, King of France, 175-177
Louis VII, King of France, 171, 176
Louis IX, King of France, 177
Louis XI, King of France, 236
Louis XIII, King of France, 311-312, 348
Louis XIV, King of France (Sun King), 296, 312ff
Louis XV, King of France, 316, 331, 358
Louis XVI, King of France, 360, 361; execution of, 361
Louis XVIII, King of France, 367, 372, 375, 376
Louis the German, 160
Louisiana, 296, 518
Louis Napoleon; See Napoleon III
Louis Philippe, King of France, 376-377
Louvois, Marquis de (François Michel Le Tellier), 313, 314
Low Countries, 236, 239, 251, 454; See also specific countries
Loyalists (Spanish republicans), 638
Loyang, 46
Lucca, 459
Lucretius, 96
Lui Pang, 48
Lulu, 749
Lumumba, Patrice, 709, 710
Lusitania, 581

Lutherans, 260-261, 271
Luther, Martin, 257ff, 264
Luxemburg, 671, 682
Lydia, 27, 62
Lyrical Ballads, 427

M

Macao, 283
MacArthur, Douglas, 652, 689, 690, 694
Macartney, George, 527
Maccabeus, Judas, 98
Macdonald, John A., 562
MacDonald, Ramsay, 606, 607
Macedonia, 69-71, 87
Macedonians, 116
Machiavelli, Niccolo, 247
MacMahon, Marshal, 451
Macmillan, Harold, 680
Madagascar, 706
Madame Bovary, 427-428
Madras, India, 294
Madrid, 305
Magadha, 38-39, 40
Magellan, Ferdinand, 287
Magellan Straits, 287
Maginot Line, 608, 642
Magna Carta, 178, 351
Magyar language, 487
Magyars, 160, 240, 378, 484, 486, 487
Mahabharata, 37
Mahavira, 37
Mahayana Buddhism, 38; in China, 50; in Japan, 53
Mahmud II, sultan of Ottoman Empire, 373
Maimonides, Moses, 152
Maine, 520
Makarova, Natalia, 755
Malacca, 283
Malaria, 520
Malawi, 708
Malaya, 283, 294, 553
Malaysia, 699
Maldive Islands, 212
Malenkov, Georgi, 672
Mali, 187, 189
Mali Empire, 182, 191
Mallarme, Stephane, 430
Malthus, Thomas, 395-396, 417
Malvinas (Falkland Islands), 724-726
Mamluks, 210
Mamun, 148-150
Manchester, England, 408, 409, 420, 438
Manchuria, 49, 496, 525, 541, 557, 635, 636
Manchus, 224, 525-527
Manet, Edouard, 431
Manhattan, 295
Manitoba, 562
Mannerism, 339
Manorialism, 165-166
Mantua, 248
Manuel, King of Spain, 456
Manufacturing, 393-394, 400ff, 406
Manzikert, Battle of, 116, 209
Maori, 559, 560
Maori Wars, 560
Mao Tse-tung, 620, 691, 692, 694, 732
Maratha chiefs, 554
Marathon, 65-66

Marc Antony, 90
Marches, The, 465
Marconi, Guglielmo, 407
Marcos, Ferdinand E., 731
Marcus Aurelius, 94, 100, 101
Marduk, 28
Margrethe I, Queen of Denmark, Norway and Sweden, 241
Marianas, 561
Maria Theresa, Queen of Austria, 318, 319, 320, 337
Marie, daughter of Eleanor of Aquitaine, 176
Marie Antoinette, Queen of France, 338, 360, 361, 363
Marius, Gaius, 89
Marlowe, Christopher, 252
Marmara, Sea of, 120
Marne, Battle of, 576
Marquesas, 561
Marquette, Jacques, 296
Marquez, Gabriel Garcia, 757
Marranos, 306
"Marseillaise, The," 362, 377
Marseilles, 362
Marshall, George, 668
Marshall Plan, 669-670
Martel, Charles, 158-159, 162
Martin V, Pope, 236, 256
Martin, Emile and Pierre, 400
Martinique, 297
Marxism, 495
Marx, Karl, 419ff, 495, 596
Mary I, Queen of England (Bloody Mary), 268, 308
Mary of Burgundy, wife of Maximilian I, 239
Mary, daughter of Charles the Bold, 236
Mary, daughter of Henry VIII and Catherine of Aragon, 266
Mary, daughter of King James II and wife of King William III of England, 351
Mary, mother of Jesus, 250
Mary Queen of Scots, 267, 310, 347
Masaccio, 248
Massachusetts, 294, 295, 355
Mathematical Principles of Natural Philosophy, 331
Mathematics, 331; of Hellenistic era, 77; under Islamic empire, 150; Mayan, 197
Matisse, Henri, 627
Mau Mau, 707, 708
Mauritania, 706
Maurya, Chandragupta, 39
Mauryan Empire, 39-40
Mawalis, 144
Maximian, 102
Maximilian I, Holy Roman Emperor, 239
Maximilian, Archduke of Austria, 449
Maximilian (of Austria), Emperor of Mexico, 515
Maya, 197, 198
Mayan language, 197
May Laws, 473
Mayors of the palace, 158
Mazarin, Cardinal, 312, 314
Mazzini, Giuseppe, 460, 461, 464
McCormick, Cyrus, 405
McKay, Claude, 747
Mecca, 136, 137, 138, 139, 140, 151; pilgrimage to, 136, 138, 140-141
Medes, 26, 27

Medici, Catherine de, 273
Medici, Cosimo de, 246
Medici, Lorenzo (the Magnificent) de, 246
Medici, Marie de, 311
Medicine, 76, 96, 124, 424; in Egypt, 19; under Guptas, 42; of Inca, 202; under Islamic empire, 149, 152; in modern era, 763
Medicis, 246
Medieval Europe, 157ff; *See also* specific countries; amusements in, 164; architecture in, 167; banking in, 172; economy of, 172-173; education in, 173-174; literature in, 174-175; migrations in, 172; religion in, 166ff; Roman Catholic Church in, 166ff; towns in, 172; trade in, 172; women in, 164, 176
Medina (Yathrib or Madinat al-Nabi), 138, 141
Meditations of Marcus Aurelius, 94
Mediterranean Sea, 20, 61, 85, 87, 244
Meerut, 555
Mehmet II, 118, 213
Meiji Japan, 538ff
Mein Kampf (My Struggle), 604, 637, 639
Meitner, Lise, 749
Memphis, 13
Menander, 77
Mendel, Gregor, 756
Menelik II, Ethiopian emperor, 550
Menes (Narmer), 13
Menlo Park, New Jersey, 405
Mensheviks, 495
Mercantilism, 281-282, 336, 353, 415-416
Meroë, 185
Mesolithic (Middle Stone) Age, 2, 3
Mesopotamia, 7ff, 25, 27, 34, 70, 92, 209
Mestizos, 292, 507, 511, 512, 515
Metals, 3, 186, 188, 189, 241-242; *See also* specific metals
Metamorphoses of Ovid, 96
Methodism, 339, 340
Methodius, 123
Metternich, Clemens Prince von, 371ff
Metternich system (Concert of Europe or Congress system), 374-375, 380, 384
Mexican Revolution, 515
Mexican War, 514
Mexico, 193, 194, 196, 197, 198, 288, 289-290, 291, 449, 507-508, 512ff, 629, 713
Mexico City, 291, 512, 514
Michael VIII, Byzantine emperor, 118
Michelanglo, 249-250
Microbiology, 425
Microchips, 764
Microscopes, 332
Middle Ages, 108ff, 452; Britain during, 177-178; France during, 175-177; High, 172; Late, 231ff
Middle class, 62, 411, 444, 460
Middle East, 14, 77, 92, 115, 116, 135, 210, 380, 699ff; *See also* specific countries; ancient, 7ff; nation building in, 622ff
Middle Stone Age (Mesolithic Age), 2, 3
Midway, Battle of, 648
Migration; of Anabaptists, 264; of the Bantu, 186; from Germany, 476; of Huguenots from France, 315; and Industrial Revolution, 408-410; in

medieval Europe, 172; to Americas, 193; to Argentina, 517; to Brazil, 517; to cities in Roman Republic, 88-89
Milan, 179, 378, 459
Miletus, 65
Militarism; and alliances, 572-573; in Japan, 621-622
Military; *See also* Armies, Navy; in Roman Republic, 88, 89-90; in Sparta, 64-65; under Umayyads, 144; of U.S.S.R., 770
Millet, Jean Francois, 427
Mill, John Stuart, 417-418
Milner, Alfred, 626
Milton, John, 341
Minamoto, 224-225
Minamoto Yoritomo, 225
Ming dynasty, 222-224, 525
Minoans, 57-59
Minos, 57
Miranda, Francisco de, 504, 508
Miro, Joan, 747
Miser, The, 334
Mishne Torah, 152
Missi dominici, 160
Missionaries, 123, 158, 263, 270, 290, 340; Jesuit, 296; Muslim, 215; in New World, 289, 296
Mississippi River, 289
Mississippi River Valley, 195, 296
Missouri, 655
Mistral, Gabriela, 757
Mithras cult, 99
Mitre, Bartolome, 516
Mitterand, Francois, 734
Mobutu, Joseph D. (later Mobutu Sese Seko), 722
Model Parliament, 178
Modena, 378, 459, 463
Modern art, 432-433, 627
Modern era, 745ff; amusements in, 750-751; architecture in, 748; arts in, 751-752; classical music in, 748-749; dance in, 748; drama in, 754; economics in, 751; ethics in, 763; family in, 757-758; literature in, 746, 757; medicine in, 763; music in, 759; population growth in, 775-777; religion in, 759-761; science in, 749-750; urban growth in, 775-776
Mogul Empire, 554
Moguls, 215-217, 555
Mohacs, Battle of, 240
Mohammed, 137
Mohammed V, Ottoman Sultan, 500
Mohammed Ahmad, 549
Mohenjo-Daro, 34
Moldau, The, 492
Moldavia, 380, 383, 485
Moliere (Jean Baptiste Poquelin), 334, 342
Molotov, Vyacheslav, 672
Moluccas (Spice Islands), 283, 295
Mona Lisa, 249
Monarchy, 163, 232, 335, 347, 372, 511; *See also* specific monarchs; absolute, 310ff, 331; in Britain, 444; constitutional, 351, 360, 375, 376, 437; dual, 486; in Egypt, 13; of Hebrews, 23; medieval, 175-179; vs. papacy, 236; revival of, 236ff
Monasteries, 131, 157-158, 159, 168; in Byzantine Empire, 123

North Atlantic Treaty Organization (NATO), 671, 678, 681, 705, 735
Northern Europe; See also specific countries
Northern Ireland, 607, 733
Northern Rhodesia (now Zambia), 708
North German Confederation, 471
North Korea, 694
North Vietnam, 697
Northwest Passage, 293, 296
Northwest Territory, 562
Norway, 240, 241, 580; democracy in, 454-455; Hitler's attack on, 642; post-WWII, 682
Nova Scotia, 293, 316, 562
November Revolution (Bolshevik Revolution), 595
Novgorod, 128, 131, 320
Novotny, Antonin, 675
Nubia, 14
Nuclear arms, 684, 769-771
Nuclear freeze, 771
Nuclear power, 779
Nuclear proliferation, 771
Nuclear reactors, 772
Nuclear war, 770
Number system, 10, 42, 150; Arabic, 42; Mayan, 197, 198
Nuremberg trials, 656-657
Nuremburg Laws, 604
Nureyev, Rudolf, 755
Nyasaland, 553, 708
Nyerere, Julius, 708

O

OAS; See Organization of American States
Obote, Milton, 722
Ocean floor, 779-780
Oceania, 558ff
Octavian, 90; See also Augustus, Caesar
October Manifesto (Freedom Manifesto), 497
October Revolution (Bolshevik Revolution), 595
Odaenthus, 93
Oda Nobunaga, 534
"Ode on a Grecian Urn," 427
Odoacer, 104
Odyssey, 60
Oedipus, 72
Oedipus Rex, 72
Of the Conduct of Understanding, 334
Ogadai Khan, 210
O'Higgins, Bernardo, 509
Ohio River Valley, 195, 297
Oil, 407, 408, 778; embargo on, 718
Okinawa, 654
Old Stone Age (Paleolithic Age), 2-3
Old Testament, 22
Oleg, 128
Olga, 129
Olmecs, 196-197
Olympiad, 74
Olympic Games, 66, 74, 740, 741
Omdurman, Battle of, 549
Oneida, 195
On Liberty, 418
Onondaga, 195
On the Nature of Things, 96

On the Revolutions of Heavenly Orbs, 329
Opera, 341, 492
Opium War, 528, 557
Optics, 149
Orange, William Prince of, 273
Oregon Territory, 518
Oresteia, 72
Organization of American States (OAS), 711
Orlando, Vittorio, 587
Orleanists, 447, 449
Orleans, 234
Orwell, George, 753
Osiris, 17
Osman, 211
Ostrogoths, 103, 113, 157
Otto I, 161
Ottoman Empire, 118, 121, 271, 318, 375, 378, 380, 383, 498ff, 579, 585, 622
Ovid, 96
Owen, Robert, 419

P

Pachacuti, 200
Pacific Ocean, 287, 520
Pacifists, 617, 635
Paekche, 51
Pahlavi, Mohammed Reza, Shah of Iran, 705, 720
Paine, Thomas, 355
Painting, 219; during Enlightenment, 341, 343; Flemish, 251; in Greece, 72; and Industrial Revolution, 426, 430ff; during Italian Renaissance, 248; in northern Europe, 251; in oils, 251; realism in, 427
Pakistan, 33, 553, 695, 696, 697, 729
Palaeologi dynasty, 118, 123
Paleolithic (Old Stone) Age, 2-3
Palestine, 27, 98-99, 114, 116, 141, 170-171, 176, 209, 380, 590, 622; Arab-Jewish rivalry in, 624-625; partition of, 700
Palestine Liberation Organization (PLO), 700, 703, 717, 720
Palladio, 245
Palmerston, Lord, 380
Palmyra, 93
Pamela, 343
Panama, 286, 509, 520
Panama Canal, 453, 520-521
Panama Company, 453
Panama scandal, 453
Pan-Arabism, 702
Panchatantra, 42
Pan-Islamism, 553
Pankhurst, Christabel, 443
Pankhurst, Emmeline, 443
Pankhurst, Sylvia, 443
P'an-ku, 44
Pan-Slavism, 499, 572
Pantagruel, 251
Papacy; See Pope
Papal States, 213, 246, 378, 459, 461, 463, 465
Papandreou, Andreas, 734
Papandreou, George, 684
Papua, 561
Paradise Lost, 341

Paris, 177, 310, 333, 360, 377, 383, 404, 433, 449, 450, 452; Commune of, 361, 449-450; Congress of, 463; Peace of, 586; Treaty of, 297, 320, 356, 383
Parliament Act of 1911, 447
Parma, 378, 459, 463
Parnell, Charles Stewart, 445
Parsons, Charles, 407
Parthenon, 72
Parthians, 94
Partido Revolucionario Institucional (PRI), 515
Pasternak, Boris, 755
Pasteur, Louis, 424, 425
Pataliputra, 39
Patriarch of Constantinople, 117, 123
Patricians, 82-83; vs. plebians, 83-84
Patton, George, 651
Paul, 99
Paul I, King of Greece, 683
Paul II, Pope, 269
Paul III, Pope, 270
Pavlov, Ivan, 424
Pax Romana, 94, 95
Pax Sinica, 49-50
Peace of Augsburg, 271, 316, 317
Peace Corps, 685
Peaceful coexistence, 684-686
Peace of Paris, 586
Pearl Harbor, 645-646
Peasants, 163, 164-166, 171, 232, 337, 358, 484, 490, 491-493; in Japan, 535; revolt of in Germany, 261; uprisings of, 232-233, 325; in U.S.S.R., 322, 324
Pedro I, Emperor of Brazil, 511, 517
Pedro II, Emperor of Brazil, 517
Peel Commission, 625
Peel, William, 625
Peisistratus, 64
Peking (Beijing), 223, 719
Peking man, 2
Peloponnesian League, 69
Peloponnesian Wars, 68-69, 72, 76
Peloponnesus, 64
Pena, Roque Saenz, 517
Pennsylvania, 297, 405
Penn, William, 333
People's Budget, 446-447
People's Charter, 439
People's Republic of China; See China
Pepin, 159
Pereire brothers, 449
Pergamum, 77, 87
Pericles, 67-68, 72
Peron, Eva, 712
Peron, Isabel, 724
Peron, Juan, 712, 724
Perry, Matthew, 537
Persecution; of Anabaptists, 264; of Calvinists, 272; of Catholics, 262; religious, 262, 264, 272, 273
Persepolis, 30, 70
Persia, 25, 70, 141, 143, 144, 147, 209, 211, 556, 623; See also Iran; influence of on India, 216-217; influence of on Islamic empire, 148-149; Sassanian empire of, 113
Persian Empire, 27-29, 65, 94, 141
Persian Gulf, 7, 8, 283, 720
Persian language, 151, 554
Persian Wars, 65-67, 75
Peru, 200, 288-289, 290, 507, 510

Transvaal, 552
Transylvania, 378
Travels of Ibn Battuta, 212
Trent, Council of, 270
Trevithick, Richard, 402
Tribonian, 113
Tribute Money, 248
Triennial Act, 349
Trieste, 579
Tripartite Pact, 645, 646
Triple Alliance, 572
Triple Entente, 573
Tripoli, 501, 545, 548, 649
Triumph and the Will, 752
Triumvirate, 88, 89
Troeltsch, Ernst, 301
Trojan War, 59-60, 74
Trojan Women, The, 74
Troppau, 375
Troppau Protocol, 375
Trotsky, Leon, 496-497, 596, 598, 599
Troy, 59, 74
Truman Doctrine, 668-669
Truman, Harry, 655, 666, 668, 691
Tshombe, Moise, 709, 710
Tuamotu Archipelago, 561
Tudor, Henry (Henry VII), 237, 251, 307
Tudors, 266, 307ff
Tu Fu, 218, 220
Tula, 198
Tunisia (formerly Tunis), 545, 626, 628, 649, 706
Tunis (now Tunisia), 545
Turgenev, Ivan, 429
Turgot, Robert, 358
Turin, 460
Turkestan, 556
Turkey, 20, 121, 500, 580, 639, 704-706;
  nationalism in, 622; post-WWII, 667; vs.
  U.S.S.R., 322; in WWI, 585
Turkish language, 213, 500
Tuscany, 378, 459, 461, 463
Tutenkhamon, 15, 16
Tver, 320
Twelve Tables, 84, 95
Twenty-one Demands, 621
Two Treatises of Government, 333
Tyndale, William, 265
Tyre, 20, 70
Tz'u-hsi (Dowager Empress), 531, 532

U

Uganda, 553, 708, 722
Ukraine, 322
Ukrainians, 123, 127
Ulema, 213
Ulpian, 95
Ulster, 607
Ultraroyalists, 375
Ulyanov, Vladimir Ilyich; *See* Lenin
Ulysses, 747
Umayyads, 143, 153; culture of, 144;
  military under, 144
Umbria, 465
Unconscious mind, 424, 746ff; collective,
  746
Union of Death (Black Hand), 574
Unions, 415, 416, 442

Union of South Africa; *See* South Africa
Union of Soviet Socialist Republics; *See*
  U.S.S.R.
United Arab Republic, 703, 704
United Empire Loyalists, 562
United Kingdom, 352; *See also* specific
  countries
United Nations, 653, 657, 667, 717, 718,
  722, 732
United States, 356, 366, 406, 408, 449,
  492, 699, 736, 738; anti-communism in,
  676; and arts, 752; Civil War in, 464,
  518; Constitution of, 335, 357, 512;
  consul of in Japan, 537; domestic unrest
  in, 678; goals of, 665; government of,
  356; industrialization in, 518; Industrial
  Revolution in, 403, 405; and Latin
  America, 518ff, 631; vs. Mexico, 514; in
  NATO alliance, 671; naturalism in, 429;
  occupation of Japan by, 689; post-WWI,
  608; post-WWII, 676-678; realism in,
  429; vs. Spain, 520; telegraphy in, 469;
  in WWI, 582
Universal manhood suffrage, 350, 447-448
Universities, 173-174
Upanishads, 36-37, 42
Ur, 8, 10
Urban II, Pope, 116, 169, 170
Urban VI, Pope (Bartolomeo Prignano),
  235
Urbanization, 408-410; in Bohemia and
  Moravia, 486; in Germany, 476; in
  modern era, 775-776
Urdu language, 216
Urquiza, Justo, 516
Uruguay, 516
Uruk, 8
Ushas, 36
U.S.S.R., 320ff, 496, 594; advances by in
  WWII, 652; architecture in, 323; arts in,
  751, 754-755; and Austria, 485; and
  Bismarck, 470; Civil War in, 595-596;
  and Congress of Vienna, 371, 372; and
  Crimean War, 383; de-Stalinization of,
  672-673, 693; economy of, 324, 598, 599;
  German invasion of, 643-644; and
  Japan, 541; Mongols in, 210, 211; and
  Napoleon, 365, 366, 367; nationalities
  in, 597; vs. Ottoman Empire, 499-500;
  post-WWII, 671ff; and Prussia, 319;
  Russian Revolution, 593ff; satellite
  countries of, 666; under Stalin, 599-600;
  vs. Turkey, 322; and United States, 736;
  war between Japan and, 495-496, 541,
  572; war between Turkey and, 499-500;
  in WWI, 574, 575-576; in WWII, 648
Utah, 194
Utilitarianism, 417
Utopian socialists, 418-419

V

Vancouver Island, 562
Vandals, 103, 113, 157
Van Eyck, Hubert, 251
Van Eyck, Jan, 251
Van Gogh, Vincent, 432, 433
Varangians, 127, 128
Vargas, Getulio, 629-630

Vassals, 162, 163
Vatican, 249-250, 466
V-E Day, 653
Vedas, 36
Velazquez, Diego, 341
Venetia, 372, 378, 459, 460, 461, 463,
  465-466, 470, 486
Venezuela, 508, 509, 629, 630; vs. Britain,
  520
Venice, 116, 117, 118, 125, 172, 213,
  244-245, 278-279, 378
Veracruz, 288, 514, 515
Verdun; Battle of, 579; Treaty of, 160
Vereeniging, Treaty of, 552
Verlaine, Paul, 430
Vermeer, Jan, 342
Versailles, 313, 314, 341, 360-361, 449,
  452; Treaty of, 587, 593, 609, 637
Vespasian, 101
Vespucci, Amerigo, 286
Victor Emmanuel II, King of Piedmont,
  462, 463, 464, 465, 466, 470
Victor Emmanuel III, King of Italy, 601,
  650
Victoria, Queen of England, 444, 474, 555
Vienna, 213, 318, 371, 377, 486
Vietcong, 697, 698, 730, 731
Vietminh (Vietnamese Nationalists), 697
Vietnam, 525, 697, 729-731; division of,
  697; North, 697; Socialist Republic of,
  730; South, 697-698
Vietnam War, 738
Vikings, 160-161, 162, 240-241
Villafranca, 463
Villages, 391; Bantu, 187; economy of
  pre-Industrial Revolution, 393; in
  medieval Europe, 165; rise of, 3
Virgil, 80, 96
Virginia, 294, 295
Virginia Company of London, 294
Vishnu, 42
Visigoths, 103, 113, 153, 157
Vision post-the Sermon, The, 433
Vittorio Veneto Battle, 585
Viziers, 13, 145-146; grand, 213
V-J Day, 655
Vladimir I, 129, 130
Vladimir-Suzdal, 131
Vladivostok, 556
Volga River, 127
Voltaire (Francois Marie Arouet), 328,
  335, 336, 357, 360
Von Clausewitz, Karl, 334
Von Goethe, Johann Wolfgang, 370, 423
Von Hardenberg, Karl, Prince of Prussia,
  371
Von Moltke, Helmuth, 576
Von Schiller, Friedrich, 423
Von Zinzendorf, Count, 339, 340
Voting rights, 376-377, 438, 440, 443-445,
  447-448, 454, 455, 517; universal
  manhood, 350, 447-448; women's, 443,
  455
Voznesensky, Andrei, 755
Vulgate Bible, 270

W

Wafd, 626
Wages, 416-417; controls on in Roman
  empire, 102; Iron Law of, 416